Beginning Visual Basic SQL Server 7.0

Theron Willis

Wrox Press Ltd. ®

Beginning Visual Basic SQL Server 7.0

First Reprint April 2000

Published by Wrox Press Ltd,
Arden House, 1102 Warwick Road, Acocks Green, Birmingham B27 6BH, UK.
Printed in Canada
2 3 4 5 TRI 04 03 02 01 00

ISBN 1-861003-0-64

Trademark Acknowledgements

Credits

Author
Theiron Willis

Technical Reviewers
James Beidleman
Matt Bortniker
Reed Call
Greg Clark
Louis Davidson
Robin Dewson
Mike Erickson
Mike Hanson
Hope Hatfield
Chris Madrid
Gary Vartanoff
Richard Ward

Development Editor
Dominic Lowe

Technical Editors
Catherine Alexander
Dianne Parker

Managing Editors
Joanna Mason
Dominic Lowe

Project Manager
Tony Berry

Design/Layout
Mark Burdett
Jonathan Jones
John McNulty
William Fallon

Figures
William Fallon

Index
Alessandro Ansa
Martin Brooks
Andrew Criddle

Cover
Chris Morris

About the Author

Thearon began his career in computers in 1980 as a computer operator. During the fall of 1980 he took a course in BASIC programming using the Radio Shack TSR-80 computer and has been hooked on programming ever since.

After learning the BASIC language Thearon moved on to learn COBOL, and began writing programs to help automate some of his daily tasks as a computer operator. Advancing his career, Thearon became an Operations Analyst and learned several other languages to assist in his job.

In 1989 Thearon moved into Systems Programming and started programming in S370 Assembler language. He coded batch programs in Assembler language and then moved on to code CICS programs. The Help Desk and Network Operations used these batch and on-line programs to perform some of their daily tasks, such as monitoring CICS printers and polling sales. During this time he started working with relational databases on the mainframe and immediately saw the benefits that relational databases provided.

Between the years of 1988 and 1993 Thearon learned several more programming languages, which include QBASIC, PASCAL and C++. Thearon decided that he enjoyed programming so much that he switched his career path and became a developer full time.

The first application that Thearon worked on was written in Assembler language and included over 70 Assembler programs. To help automate some of the tasks that were performed by the department that used this application, he wrote several programs in Visual Basic. One of these programs read and processed data from message queues that were populated from the mainframe and performed automated balancing.

Thearon first began working with Visual Basic in version 3.0. After version 4 was released he switched his career from the mainframe to client-server development. He still enjoys working with relational databases and uses SQL Server as the back end to all of his applications that store and retrieve data.

Thearon currently works as a senior consultant and develops intranet and Internet applications. He lives with his wife Margie and daughter Stephanie in Charlotte, North Carolina.

Author Acknowledgements

I would like to thank some of the folks at Wrox Press for making this book possible. First I would like to thank Dominic Lowe for giving me the opportunity to start writing for Wrox Press in the spring of 1999 and for working with me to get this project off the ground.

I would also like to thank the editorial staff: Tony Berry, Dianne Parker, Catherine Alexander and Joanna Mason, for all of their hard work in getting this book to print.

Last but not least I want to thank my wife Margie for her faith in me and her patience while I worked long hours writing this book.

WROX AUTO WORKS RACING

Table of Contents

WROX AUTO WORKS RACING

Introduction

Just about every major client-server application uses a relational database, and this book will help you get up to speed using SQL Server in your Visual Basic applications. SQL Server version 7.0 brought about some major changes, both in the database engine and the user interface, and this is an exciting time to begin working with SQL Server.

Whether you need to implement data access in your front-end programs or in business server components (ActiveX DLLs) this book is for you. You will learn how to use and access SQL Server from your Visual Basic programs using ActiveX Data Objects (ADO), in-line SQL statements, dynamic SQL statements, and stored procedures. The exercises in this book walk you through building both front-end programs and business server components that access SQL Server.

As an added bonus, the data access skills that you learn here working with SQL Server and Visual Basic can be carried forward to Web programming using SQL Server and Visual Basic Script.

What Is This Book About

This book will introduce you to SQL Server 7.0, starting with the basic components of a SQL Server database. This includes such topics as database and log files, tables, primary and foreign keys, indexes, and stored procedures. The first chapter also covers the theory of relational database design and normalization, helping to ensure that you get off on the right foot when designing relational databases. We also lead you through the steps required to install the Desktop version of SQL Server. We'll then move on to explore the user interface, to get you acquainted with the available features of SQL Server, and then we'll start to explore SQL Server from a developer's standpoint, by creating a development database and tables. This will acquaint you with the relationship between tables and the actual database. Moving on to look at primary and foreign keys and indexes, you will become familiar with the intricacies of these relationships. Stored procedures are covered in depth, and we will explore why we should use them and how to create and debug them.

Each chapter builds upon the previous chapter's content, both in SQL Server and VB. By the time you reach Chapter 13 and build the VB front-end program you will have built the majority of the stored procedures required for the application. You will be able to reuse most of the code from previous chapters, because classes are used to encapsulate the functions that execute the stored procedures.

Chapter 14 walks you through the steps to create a business server component using the classes from the previous chapters, and also modifying the front-end program built in the previous chapter to use the business server component that you build in this chapter. To help you document your business server component for other developers, we walk you through the steps of building a help file for use with your new business server component.

An application is not complete until we get it moved into the production environment, and Chapter 16 focuses on what needs to be done to prepare your application for both the test and production environments. This chapter uses the SQL Server Profiler and SQL Server Index Tuning Wizard to help ensure that your database is optimized and ready to be implemented in the test and production environments. In order to implement your database into these environments, we go through the process of generating SQL scripts that can be used by a Database Administrator to build your database in test and production. We also examine what changes are required to your business server component and front-end program.

To round off your learning experience and to give you plenty of chances to practice your newfound skills with hands on examples, three case studies have been provided. The first two case studies build upon your final application by modifying the database and application. This gives you a chance to learn more new skills and builds upon what you have already learned. With the addition of new tables, you will be creating new stored procedures and adding new functionality into your application. You will also be creating an on-line report using the Data Report Designer.

The last case study in this book focuses on English Query. This is a new feature to SQL Server 7.0 and this case study walks you through the steps required to build an English Query application. There are multiple deployment methods for an English Query application, including the Web and VB. We take a look at deploying your English Query application using VB, but sample programs are provided during the install of English Query that also allow you to also deploy your application over the Web.

How Is This Book Organized?

This section provides a summary of the contents of each chapter, showing how we start with the basics but lead up to developing complete applications combining SQL Server databases with Visual Basic front-ends.

Chapter 1 – Introduction to SQL Server

This chapter introduces the basics of SQL Server including version history, database structure, data and transaction log files, tables, primary and foreign keys, indexes, defaults, relational databases and normalization, stored procedures, triggers, and views. We also look at how VB and SQL Server communicate, using technologies such as OLE DB, ODBC, and ADO.

Chapter 2 – Installing the Desktop Edition of SQL Server

Here we discuss SQL Server editions, target platforms, and prerequisites, before stepping through the installation procedure. We follow this with a tour of the Enterprise Manager and Query Analyzer, and introduce the SQL Server Profiler, Wizards, Full Text Search, English Query, and OLAP tools.

Chapter 3 – Creating the Development Database

In this chapter we introduce suggested naming conventions, and we design and create the Wrox Auto Works development database. We also look at database views, and create tables, keys, and indexes.

Chapter 4 – SQL Server Security

This chapter covers all aspects of SQL Server security including authentication, object level access, users, and roles.

Chapter 5 – SQL Server Query Analyzer

This provides an introduction and tour of the Query Analyzer menus, and we learn how to create, execute, and save our insert, update, and delete queries. Also covered is how to debug queries.

Chapter 6 – Database Connections

Chapter 6 summarizes the ADO object model, and teaches us how to use DSN connections, DSN-less connections, and the Data Designer Environment to create connections to the database from VB applications.

Chapter 7 – Introduction to Stored Procedures

Here we define stored procedures, why and how we use them, and how to grant permissions. Also covered are owner prefixes, parameters and return values, and calling stored procedures from VB forms. The examples work through select, insert, update, and delete stored procedures, showing how to call them from VB programs.

Chapter 8 – Executing Stored Procedures vs Transact-SQL Statements

This chapter provides side-by-side comparisons of insert, update, and delete stored procedures versus in-line SQL, and shows how to optimize SQL statements using `Command.Prepared` and `Command.Parameters`. It also shows how to deal with multiple recordsets using `Recordset.NextRecordset`.

Chapter 9 – Selecting Data

This chapter covers `SELECT` stored procedures in detail. Joins, column aliases, and correlation names are introduced. `JOINS` in general are covered and the stored procedures created in this chapter take advantage of a simple `JOIN` to retrieve data from multiple tables. `LEFT OUTER JOINS` are used to retrieve data from the tables that may or may not contain data, and are also used to join the same table twice in the same stored procedure.

Chapter 10 – Inserting Data

This chapter covers `INSERT` stored procedures in detail and introduces using logic in your stored procedures through the use of the `If… Else` statements. These statements are used to control the processing flow of your stored procedures. Along with this is the introduction of error checking and error handling in your stored procedures. We show you how to raise your own errors and exit your stored procedure at the point of failure. Transactions are introduced to help maintain and ensure data integrity.

Chapter 11 – Updating Data

This chapter covers UPDATE stored procedures in detail and introduces two types of stored procedures. The first type of stored procedure simply updates all columns in a table. The second type of stored procedure can be called a dynamic stored procedure, because it checks the input parameters for data and dynamically builds the SQL string to execute, updating only the columns in a table for which the input parameters have been supplied. Dynamic in-line SQL is also introduced in VB to allow your VB program to dynamically build a SQL string to be executed.

Chapter 12 – Deleting Data

In this chapter we examine deleting data in two ways. First we examine deleting data by using triggers, and then move on to cover deleting data using a DELETE stored procedure. Using both triggers and a DELETE stored procedure we see how we can delete data from multiple tables by performing a cascading delete.

Chapter 13 – Creating a Front-End Program

In this chapter you will learn how to incorporate stored procedures that select and update data in your VB programs. The chapter covers data validation in the user interface, and the presentation and separation of data.

Chapter 14 – Creating a Business Server Component

Chapter 14 looks at MTS versus SQL Server transactions, and creates a business server component. We also create a help file for our business server component, and modify the front-end to use the new component.

Chapter 15 – Working With Text Data

Here we take a look at how SQL Server stores and manages text data. We examine text pointers, inserting and selecting text data, string functions that can be used with text data, and reading, writing, and updating text data. The AppendChunk method of the ADO Command object is introduced as well as the GetChunk method of the ADO Recordset object.

Chapter 16 – Preparing For the Test and Production Environments

After defining each environment, we capture a workload with SQL Server Profiler, use the Index Tuning wizard, learn about backups, generate database scripts, and prepare our VB programs for deployment.

Case Study 1 – Wrox Auto Works Customer Application

This case study brings together much of what we have learned, and we also see how to use SQL statements to create and modify tables. With the addition of new tables comes the addition of new stored procedures. You learn how to add new functionality to your business server component by implementing new functions to execute these stored procedures, as well as modifying the front-end program to incorporate the new functionality.

Case Study 2 – Wrox Auto Works Sales Staff Application

The second case study expands on the other examples in the book, and we learn how to use SQL statements that modify the database structure, and SQL Server aggregate functions. Also covered is creating and using temporary tables in a stored procedure. Finally we use the Data Environment Designer and the Data Report Designer to create a report from the database.

Case Study 3 – English Query Application

The final case study covers the installation of English Query, and gives an overview of English Query and its tools. We build the Customer English Query application, defining the entities and relationships required that allow us to ask natural English questions. Finally, we examine the deployment of our English Query application using VB.

There are also four reference Appendices:

Appendix A – T-SQL and VB Data Types

Appendix B - ADO 2.5 Object Model and Constants

Appendix C – SQL Server Functions

Appendix D - Support and Errata

Who Is This Book For

Since this is a Wrox 'Beginning' Series book, it is our goal to teach you everything you need to know to get up to speed using SQL Server from the ground up. This book is aimed at experienced Visual Basic developers who want to increase their knowledge and skill set by using an enterprise relational database.

Although experienced VB developers with little or no knowledge of databases should be able to learn all of the basics needed, there are two types of VB developers for whom this book is ideal:

- Experienced developers who are making the transistion from Access to SQL Server.
- Experienced developers who are making the transistion from some other type of enterprise relational database such as Oracle or Sybase.

This book assumes you are an experienced Visual Basic developer and as such will not teach you how to code Visual Basic, but instead will teach you how to create SQL Server stored procedures and call them from your Visual Basic front-end programs and business server components.

A basic understanding of relational database concepts will be helpful but is not assumed, as this topic is covered in the first chapter of this book. It is also not assumed that you have any experience working with **Microsoft ActiveX Data Objects** (**ADO**), but again it will be an advantage if you have.

What You Need To Use This Book

You will need a copy of SQL Server 7.0 to install the Desktop edition on your workstation. Your workstation can be Windows 9x, Windows NT 4.0, or Windows 2000 Professional. If you cannot get a copy of SQL Server 7.0 to install on your workstation, you can use an edition of SQL Server 7.0 (Standard or Enterprise) installed on your network. If you will be using a network-installed edition of SQL Server 7.0, consult with your database administrator about creating the sample database for you, and have them grant you database administrator rights to that database.

Since this book is about learning how to use SQL Server 7.0, we will step you through installing the Desktop edition on your workstation.

You will need a version of Microsoft ADO installed, preferably version 2.5.

You will also need to have Visual Basic 6.0 installed in order to develop and try the examples in this book.

Finally, the Help Workshop component of Visual Studio is also required if you want to create a help file for your business server component.

Where You Can Find The Sample Code

We provide the source code and associated files for all the code examples in this book for download from our web site. All the code for the book is contained in one zip file. When you extract the code on your machine, the zip file will create a folder for each chapter containing the relevant code.

To download the code navigate to `http://www.wrox.com` and click on the Download link on the menu bar at the top of the page. This will take you to a page where you should select Beginning Visual Basic SQL Server 7.0 from the dropdown list available, and click the Download Source Code button. You can then select to download from our US or our UK site.

The code samples are completely free; you just need to register on the Wrox site. If you have already registered, you will be prompted for your password, otherwise you will be asked to register during the download process – we've tried to make registration as quick and simple as possible.

Conventions

We have used a number of different styles of text and layout in the book to help differentiate between each kind of information. Here are examples of the styles we use and an explanation of what they mean:

> *Advice, hints, and background information comes indented and italicized, like this.*

> **Important information comes in boxes like this.**

Bullets are also indented, and appear with a little box marking each new bullet point, like this:

- ❑

Important Words are in a bold type font.

Words that appear on the screen, for example in menus like File or Window are in a similar font to the one that you see on screen.

Keys that you press on the keyboard, like *Ctrl* and *Return*, are in italics.

Code has several fonts. If it's a word that we're talking about in the text, for example when discussing the `For...Next` loop, it's in a fixed width font. If it's a block of code that you can type in as a program and run, then it's also in a gray box:

```
Set oCars = CreateObject("WCCCars.Cars")
Set recCars = oCars.GetAll(RegistryRestore("Showroom", "Not Set"))
```

Sometimes you'll see code in a mixture of styles, like this:

```
If IsMissing(ConnectionString) Then
    varConn = RegistryRestore("Showroom", "Not Set")
Else
    varConn = ConnectionString
End If
```

The code with a white background is code we've already looked at and that we don't wish to examine further.

Sometimes you will see an underscore character at the end of a line of code:

```
Window.Alert("An unforseen error occurred in this application. Error number: " _
             & Err.Number & "Details: " & Err.Description)
```

This indicates that the line was too long for the width of the book and has been continued on the next line. When typing in this code, if you wish you can ignore the underscore, line break and indentation - just type the whole line as one continuous line of code. Otherwise leave it in and VB will recognize it as a continuation character.

Try It Out

How It Works

The chapters in this book are sprinkled with mini-exercises called *Try It Outs*. Each one states an objective and then follows that, where appropriate, with the answer in code and a screen shot. Often, immediately following it is a *How It Works* section that dissects the code line-by line and explains the syntax, choice of techniques, purpose of variables, etc.

These formats are designed to make sure that you know what it is you're looking at. We hope they make life easier.

Tell Us What You Think

We've worked hard on this book to make it useful. We've tried to understand what you're willing to exchange your hard-earned money for, and we've tried to make the book live up to your expectations.

Please let us know what you think about this book. Tell us what we did wrong, and what we did right. This isn't just marketing flannel; we really do huddle around the e-mail to find out what you think. If you don't believe it, then send us a note. We'll answer, and we'll take whatever you say on board for future editions. The easiest way is to use e-mail:

`feedback@wrox.com`

You can also find more details about Wrox Press on our web site. There, you'll find the code for all of our books, sneak previews of forthcoming titles, and information about the authors and editors. You can order Wrox titles directly from the site, or find out the location of your nearest local bookstore which stocks Wrox titles.

Customer Support

If you find a mistake, please have a look at the errata page for this book on our web site first. Instructions for this are included as Appendix D. If you can't find an answer there, tell us about the problem and we'll do everything we can to answer promptly! Just send us an e-mail (with the title and ISBN of the book, and the page number you're referring to) to:

`support@wrox.com`

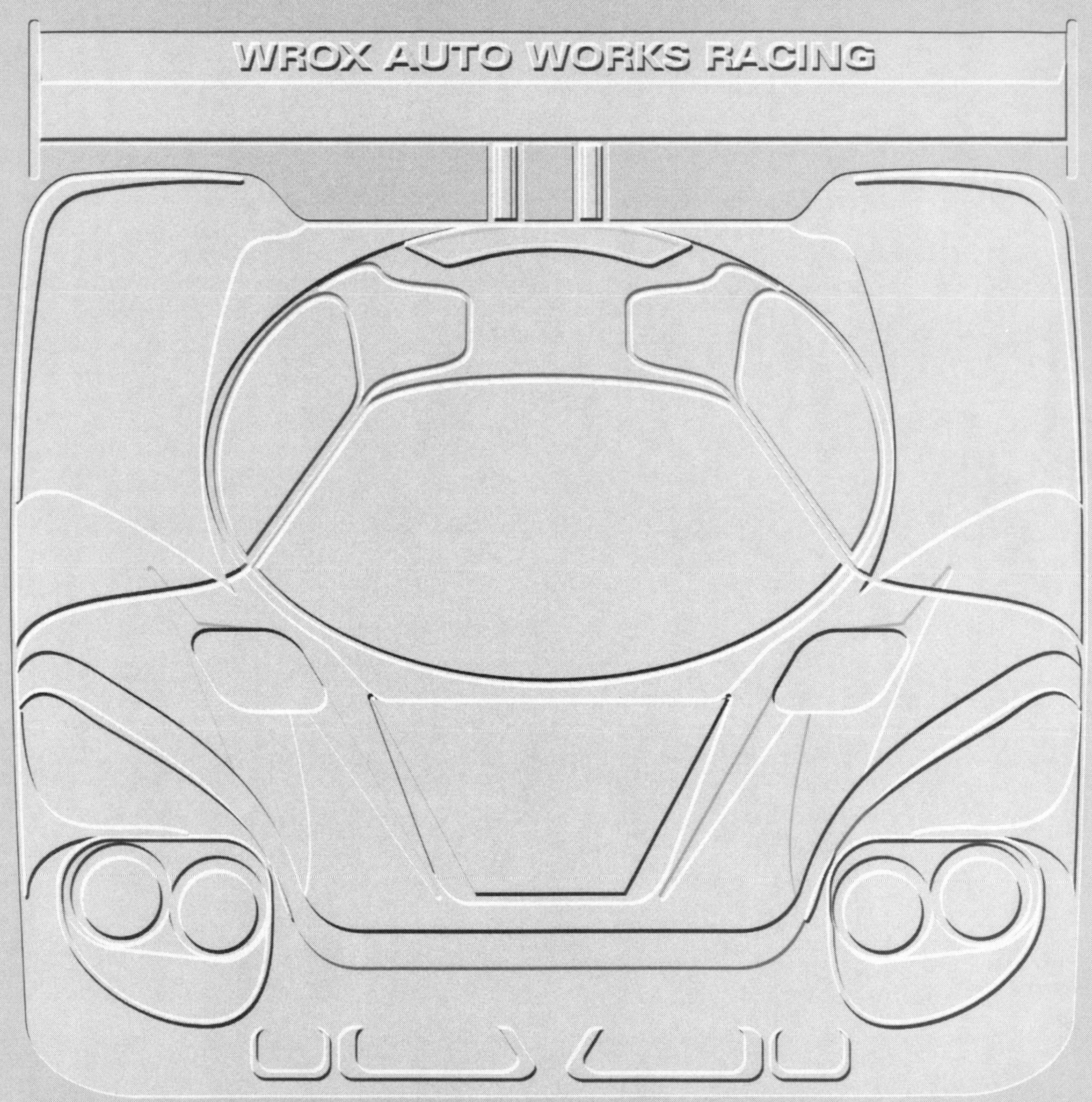
WROX AUTO WORKS RACING

Introduction to SQL Server

In the book's introduction we mentioned that this is an exciting time to begin working with SQL Server. This is true for many reasons, and just one of them is the provision of SQL Server's wizards, which offer invaluable assistance in performing complex administrative tasks. However, before we start to explore and use such wizards we need to begin with an introduction to SQL Server and some of the essential concepts of basic database theory.

This chapter covers some of the core concepts of SQL Server, such as databases, tables, indexes, and stored procedures. Our discussion of these topics includes how SQL Server implements these objects as part of the database.

We will also study some basic concepts of relational databases, including database design and normalization. Both of these topics are very important to designing and creating a relational database that performs optimally in SQL Server. Even if you already know about these topics, it is worth glancing over them, just as a refresher.

To complete our introduction to the core concepts of SQL Server, we will look at how SQL Server fits into the Visual Basic architecture. This will include a quick introduction to data access technologies such as OLE DB, ODBC, and ADO, and how they relate to SQL Server.

This chapter will introduce you to the following topics:

- SQL Server databases
- Data files and transaction logs
- Tables, indexes, keys, and defaults
- Relational database design and normalization
- Stored procedures, triggers, and views
- OLE DB, ODBC, and ADO

SQL Server History

Believe it or not, SQL Server has been around since version 1, but it only started gaining real popularity with version 4.21. This version ran on Windows NT 3.5 and started integrating the database with many of the features of the Windows NT operating system, such as **asynchronous I/O** and **threading**.

> ***Asynchronous input/output (I/O)*** *allows an application to send a request to a component and then continue processing other work. It communicates with the component later to see if the work has been completed. Using asynchronous I/O, SQL Server can maximize the work done by individual threads.*
>
> *A* ***thread*** *is an individual task that runs independently of the rest of the program, and which gets its own CPU time. A thread belongs to the process that created it, and an application can create multiple threads. Suppose you have an application that displays a clock, with hours, minutes, and seconds. You can create a thread to execute the code that displays the time. This way you can display dialogs and wait for user input while the clock keeps on getting updated, because it is running on its own thread and is getting CPU time of its own.*

The next major versions after 4.2 were 6.0 and 6.5. These releases of SQL Server introduced many new features that are found in SQL Server today, such as tighter integration with the Windows NT operating system, and support for multiple processors. Support for mail was also introduced, by allowing queries to send mail using the **Mail Application Programming Interface** (**MAPI**).

This latest version of SQL Server, 7.0, has gained widespread popularity as the release of SQL Server that competes head to head with Oracle, Sybase, and DB2. Many analyses have been performed which suggest that SQL Server provides a total lower cost of ownership than Oracle.

SQL Server provides scalability, which means you can scale up from a small database running on a laptop computer to large databases running on multiprocessor clusters. Along with this scalability is the fact that SQL Server is easily integrated with Microsoft Office 2000 running the new **Microsoft Data Engine** (**MSDE**). For example, if you create a database using Access 2000 and the new Microsoft Data Engine, your database is fully compatible with SQL Server.

SQL Server Databases

The purpose of a **database** is, as you are probably already aware, to store data. A database in SQL Server consists of multiple **objects (and is in fact an object itself).** These other objects include tables, keys, constraints, indexes, views, stored procedures, triggers, defaults, rules, and user-defined data types. We'll discuss these objects as we come across them throughout this chapter and the rest of the book.

A **SQL Server installation** consists of many databases, not all of which are user-defined. SQL Server itself uses databases to manage different objects, user-created databases, and SQL Server configuration options. When we install SQL Server in Chapter 2 we'll look at some of the databases that are automatically included.

All databases defined in SQL Server can be managed from one window within the **Enterprise Manager**, SQL Server's user interface. The `Enterprise Manager` will also be covered in detail in the next chapter, after we have installed SQL Server. From here you can view each database and its objects, and perform maintenance on the databases. You can also connect to other SQL Servers on your network and view the databases installed on them, as long as you have the necessary authorization.

The user who *creates* a database is considered the **owner** of that database. Only that user and the database administrator initially have access to that database. The owner of the database must grant **permissions** on the database to other **users** before they can access it. Then other users can create objects in the database, such as tables, stored procedures, and views, if they have been granted the appropriate permissions. We'll be looking at this more closely in Chapter 4 when we set up new users and grant them permissions to various objects.

Any application that accesses SQL Server does so through the use of **T-SQL** statements. These statements perform such actions as selecting, inserting, updating, and deleting data, and creating and modifying the structure of your database. When a set of SQL statements is run against the database this is known as a **query**. In Chapter 5 we'll be creating and running queries, and will learn more about the SQL language too.

SQL is an acronym for **Structured Query Language** and **T-SQL** is an acronym for **Transact Structured Query Language**. SQL complies with the **American National Standards Institute** (**ANSI**) SQL standards, while T-SQL is Microsoft's version of SQL based on ANSI SQL. The latest version of ANSI SQL is referred to as SQL-92. We'll be using T-SQL extensively throughout this book and will explain more about how it is used as we come across it.

Database Files

A database in SQL Server is physically implemented as two or more files. The actual data of the database makes up one file called a **data file**, while the **transaction log file** for a database makes up the other file. Transaction logs will be covered in the next section, and basically contain a record of every transaction performed against the database. As your database grows, you can allocate other data files that can be used to cater for the expansion of your database. These files can reside on different volumes and are automatically managed by SQL Server.

When creating a data or log file for SQL Server, these files can be created on either FAT or NTFS file systems.

> *FAT stands for File Allocation Table and is a file system that has been around since DOS. NTFS stands for NT File System and is more robust than FAT but is only available on Windows NT and Windows 2000. NTFS also provides security and recovery features that are not available in FAT.*

SQL Server can work with and manage the database files in both file systems. **Primary data files** are the files created when you initially create your database. If you have to manually expand the space your database needs, you create **secondary data files**. A database can have only one primary data file but can contain many secondary data files. Primary data files for a database are assigned an `.mdf` extension, while secondary data files for a database are assigned an `.ndf` extension. Log files are assigned an extension of `.ldf`. You can use other extensions when creating databases, but use of these extensions helps to maintain consistency in your SQL Server installation, and enables quick identification of the database files.

Consider the following diagram. Database A contains a primary data file that has been populated to capacity, meaning that there is no more space available in this file. Therefore a second data file was created for this database and it has a file extension of `.ndf`, indicating that it is a secondary database file. Each database in the diagram has its own transaction log file, which is used to record the transactions that occur in the database. Database B in the diagram only contains a primary data file and a transaction log file.

Notice how SQL Server sits on top of the database files as the **database management system** (**DBMS**). You as a developer really aren't concerned with the database at the lower level but it helps to understand how SQL Server works. All you really are concerned with are the objects that make up the database at the upper level, for example the tables and stored procedures. For clarity, the objects listed at the upper level are only a partial list of the objects that make up a database.

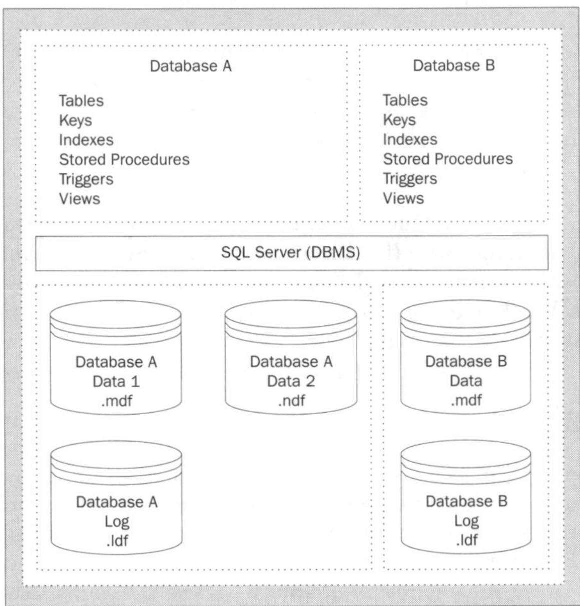

SQL Server sits in the middle and manages both the upper and lower level objects. It manages and displays (in the Enterprise Manager) the individual objects that represent the database. It also manages the lower level objects of the database, in other words the data and log files.

Chapter 3 will help you to better understand how databases are implemented in SQL Server, as we step through creating our own development database.

Transaction Logs

Each database defined has at least one **transaction log**. A **transaction** is the execution of a group of SQL statements as one logical unit of work, and a transaction log contains a record of all changes that have occurred in your database. This log will record the data before it was changed and the data after it was changed. The transaction log can be used to recover your database, either forwards or backwards, and is most effectively used as part of a sound **backup** strategy. Backups will be discussed in Chapter 16 when we look at preparing our database for the move from development to production.

- **A forward recovery** means that if you have a hardware failure, you can restore your database from the last backup, and then apply the transaction logs to recover the transactions from the point of the last backup.
- A **backward recovery** means that if your stored procedure or business component implements transactions, and somewhere in your processing your code decides that it needs to back out of the transactions, the transaction log will be used to recover the data to a state before it was changed.

Transaction logging is automatic; there is nothing that you need to do to make it happen. What you do need to do is to *backup* the transaction log frequently. This serves two purposes: first, it creates an incremental backup that can be used to recover transactions since your last database backup. Second, it clears the transaction log file, making room for new transactions and keeping the transaction log from becoming too large. If your transaction log fills up, the database will stop and you will be unable to use it until you back up the transaction log.

Truncating the transaction log is the process of removing old log records that are no longer needed to recover the database or back out transactions. Automatic log truncation occurs when the log has been backed up, or if a checkpoint is processed when the database has the Truncate Log On Checkpoint option turned on.

Checkpoints minimize the amount of data on the transaction log that must be used to recover the database. When a checkpoint of the log is taken, it writes unsaved changes in the log to disk, making them a permanent part of the database. When this process is complete, the pages of the transaction log are free to be used by new transactions. SQL Server automatically performs checkpoints of the log and uses the blocks that have been freed up by the checkpoint. A checkpoint is automatically performed, based on the *number of records* in the log and not based on *time.*

Tables

Tables are objects that store **rows** of data. Each row of data contains one or more **columns**, very similar to what you might find in a Microsoft Excel spreadsheet. (However, although the data in a table *looks* like a spreadsheet, you cannot *manipulate* the data in a table as you might in a spreadsheet.) Each row in a table represents a **record**, and each column in a row represents an individual piece of information in the record, as shown in the table below:

	Column 1 Employee ID	Column 2 First Name	Column 3 Last Name	Column 4 Employee Phone Number
Row 1	1	John	Smith	4312321
Row 2	2	Sandy	McBride	4907310
Row 3	3	Mike	Morris	5041163

Each database in SQL Server, whether system-defined or user-defined, contains a collection of tables. These tables contain data that is related in some way. This is part of what makes up a **relational database** – the relationship of objects. We'll be discussing in more detail the concept of relational database design later in this chapter.

A table can contain up to 1,024 columns but it is highly unlikely that we would actually have that many columns. We would usually follow the rules of **normalization** when designing our database. This will also be described later, but basically it results in us having *more* tables with *fewer* columns.

Each column in a table must contain a *unique* name, but you can have the same column name in multiple tables. Along these same rules, each table in a database must contain a unique name, but you can have the same table name in different databases. In Chapter 3 we'll see an example of a typical naming convention that can be used for tables and columns.

Like a database, you must grant *permission* to other users before they can access your tables. There are different levels of permissions that can be granted on a table to each user or **role**. (A role is a group of users who have the same permissions, and the role has a unique name.) You can, for example, allow one user/role to *select* data and another user/role to *select* and *insert* data. Object level permissions and roles will be discussed in detail in Chapter 4 when we study SQL Server security.

Each table in a database can contain one or more objects, such as constraints, triggers, and defaults. As we'll see later ,these objects help to preserve and enforce **data integrity** in your tables. Data integrity ensures that each column in a table contains the correct data value. These topics will be covered in more depth later in this chapter.

Like a Microsoft Access table, a SQL Server table can contain a column that automatically increments a numeric number to identify each row with a unique value. In Access this is called an AutoNumber field and in SQL Server it is called an **Identity column**. `Identity` columns are typically used in SQL Server to assign a unique number to each row in a table, which will ensure the uniqueness of the row's data. This column is also typically used as the primary key column and can be used in the index. We will be discussing indexes and primary keys next.

Indexes

Every table in your database usually has one or more **indexes**. **Indexes** are special objects, related to tables. They contain **keys** that are made up of one or more columns of data in a table. An index on a table is like the index in a book. The entries in the index point to specific rows of data in the table, just like the index of a book points to specific pages in the book. The index stores information for each key and its location in the table, and this information allows fast retrieval of the data in the table.

There are two different types of indexes in SQL Server – **clustered** and non-clustered.

Clustered indexes *sort* the data in the table rows by key. This provides a very efficient means to access data in the table. However, since a clustered index sorts the data in the table, there can be only one clustered index for a table. You can think of a clustered index as being like a phone book. The columns that define the index (for example, the phone owner's last name then their initial) are used to sort the table rows.

A clustered index actually stores the data rows of the table in the bottom leaf of the index. This means that the index consists of the index entries pointing to each row of data, and then the data rows are stored at the end of the index.

Non-clustered indexes store the keys of the table in the index and contain **pointers** to where the data actually resides in the table. The pointer in a non-clustered index is called a **row locator** because it actually locates the row of data in the table. If the table does not have a clustered indexed defined, then the row locator in a non-clustered index contains a pointer to the row of data in the table. If a clustered index is defined on a table, then the row pointer contains the clustered index key, which in turn leads to the row of data in the table, stored at the bottom of the index.

Indexes can either be **unique** or not. Indexes that are **unique** do not allow **duplicate keys** (keys that contain the same data value), and indexes that are not defined as unique can contain duplicate keys. Index keys should not be confused with primary keys in a table, which we'll cover soon. An index key can be generated for any column in a table that is used to access the data in that table.

Regardless of the type of index you choose, simply placing an index on your tables for columns that are used to access the data will speed up access to that data. This is true whether the access is a SQL SELECT, UPDATE, or DELETE statement. When you define an index on a table, SQL Server must maintain the entries in the index and this requires extra overhead. The extra overhead of using an index is usually offset by the increased efficiency that the index provides. Each INSERT, UPDATE, and DELETE statement performed against a table must also be used to update the index. SQL Server automatically takes care of keeping the index in sync with the table.

When designing indexes for your tables, you should consider what types of SQL statements are going to be used to select, insert, update, and delete data in your tables. You usually want to define indexes on columns that are specified in the WHERE, ORDER BY and GROUP BY clauses of such statements. An example of a SELECT statement that uses a WHERE clause and an ORDER BY clause is shown below:

```
SELECT First_Name_VC, Last_Name_VC
     FROM Customer_T
     WHERE Customer_ID = 4
        ORDER BY Last_Name_VC
```

This SQL statement selects the data in the First_Name_VC and Last_Name_VC columns of the Customer_T table, only where the value in the Customer_ID column is equal to 4. It presents the results in alphabetical order based on the Last_Name_VC column data.

We will be working with indexes in Chapter 3 when we design and build our example database. Actually creating the indexes will help you to gain a better understanding of how to design and use them.

Primary and Foreign Keys

Both primary and foreign keys are considered **constraints** and automatically enforce the integrity of your data. A **constraint** defines the rules regarding the values allowed in a column and is used to enforce the integrity of the data in that column. A single table can contain only one primary key but can contain multiple foreign keys.

A **primary key** identifies the column or columns whose values uniquely identify a row of data in the table. No two rows in a table can contain the same primary key. This is why primary key columns are often defined using an Identity data type; a unique value is automatically generated for each row of data. Also, primary key columns cannot contain **null values**, i.e. a value that is missing/does not exist.

An example of primary keys can be seen in the figure on the next page. The Employee_ID column is being used as the primary key and the value in this column must be unique for each row. In other words, there can only be one row containing an employee ID of 1.

When a primary key is created on a table, SQL Server automatically creates a unique index for the primary key on the table. Creating a unique index also ensures that no two primary keys can contain the same value. Using the index on the primary key column provides fast, efficient access to the data in a table.

If a primary key consists of data from multiple columns, then one column can contain duplicate values, but the columns that define the primary key as a whole can not contain duplicate values. In other words, if a primary key consists of data from column A and column B, then column B can contain duplicate values *or* column A can contain duplicate values. However, the *combination* of columns A and B must be *unique* within each row of the table.

Foreign keys are keys that point to a primary key in another table. A foreign key in one table points to an exact row of data in another table. The figure below shows how foreign keys in one table point to primary keys in another table:

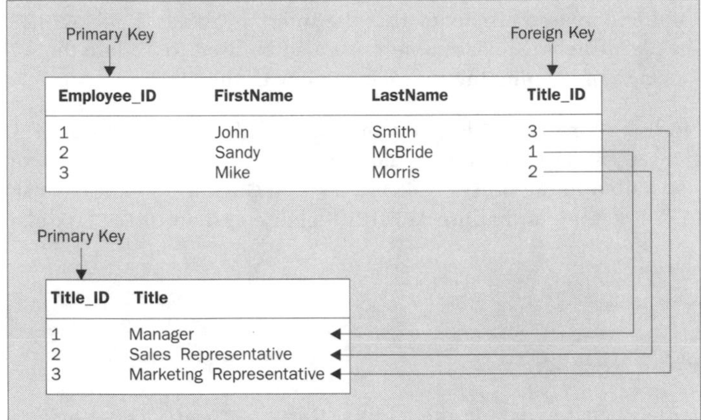

A foreign key value (unless it is null) cannot be inserted into a table if the row of data that it is pointing to in another table does not exist. This is just one of the constraints that are placed on foreign keys which help to ensure **referential integrity**. For example, we could not assign any of the employees a title ID of 4, because there isn't an entry for a title ID of 4 in the Title table.

Referential integrity enforces the defined relationship of data between tables, and is automatically applied to foreign keys. Just as we cannot insert a foreign key value for a row of data that does not exist in another table, referential integrity prevents us from deleting a row of data that is referenced by a foreign key. In order to delete a row of data that is referenced by a foreign key, we must first delete the row of data containing the foreign key, or update the column using a null value. Then we are able to delete the row containing the primary key.

For example, in the figure above, if we wanted to remove the first row of data from the Title table, we would first have to change the title ID for Sandy McBride to 2, 3 or null, or remove the entire row for employee ID number 2.

Referential integrity is based on the relationship between foreign and primary keys and it ensures that key values are consistent across all tables. Referential integrity is automatically enforced by SQL Server, and prevents a user from updating a primary or foreign key that would break the integrity of the data. In other words, you cannot update a primary key if a foreign key in another table is referencing it. As we mentioned above, SQL Server prevents you from inserting a foreign key that does not reference a valid primary key, and also prevents you from deleting a primary key that is being referenced by a foreign key.

Defaults

When you insert a new row into a table each column *must* contain data. In the case where columns allow null values, a null value is inserted. You can, however, create a **default** definition for a column, or groups of columns, in one or more tables. When a row of data is inserted and the value for a column is not specified, SQL Server will apply the default definition for that column. Default definitions are commonly used to specify a zero for numeric columns, instead of having a null value inserted into them, as this prevents problems when carrying out sorting operations, comparisons, or calculations.

When a column in a table does not allow null values and no default has been defined for that column, you *must* specify a value for that column when inserting data into that table.

Each column in a table can contain only one default. `Identity` columns or columns that contain the `Timestamp` data type cannot have defaults applied to them. A `Timestamp` data type is a database-wide unique number. A default can be any constant or expression that evaluates to a constant, such as a mathematical expression, or a SQL Server function such as `GetDate()`, which returns the current date and time.

A default can be created in one of three ways. You can specify a default value for a column when a table is created, or you can alter the table and add a default for a column. However, if you apply a default to an existing table, the default is only applied to *new* rows that are added – the *existing* rows are unaffected. Thirdly, a default can be created in the database as an object and shared with many tables. When created this way you can bind the default to multiple columns in multiple tables.

Relational Database Design

Before we look at relational database design we should define the term **relational database**. A relational database is a database that has been organized into related tables, rows, and columns. This type of database normally uses more tables that are narrow versus a few tables that are wide. This means that you have more tables that contain fewer columns. A normalized relational database actually improves performance even though there are physically more tables. We will be discussing normalization in the next section.

A relational database relates all tables in the database, hence the term relational. Each table in the database organizes related objects, and each column in a table represents an attribute of the object that the table represents. A row in the table represents a unique entry for the object that the table defines.

To design a relational database you must first identify all of the objects that will make up your database. We use the term object to represent a group of information. Let's assume that you want to design a database that contains the employees in your organization and their addresses. We first identify what objects make up the employees and their addresses. This example is really straightforward, as we have already described the objects that are required – *employees* and *addresses.*

Next, we want to identify what **attributes** make up employees and addresses. The following table illustrates the attributes that have been identified for employees and addresses:

Attribute	Description
First Name	Employee's first name
Last Name	Employee's last name
Employee ID Number	A number that uniquely identifies each employee
Title	A title that identifies what job function the employee performs
Work Phone Number	Work phone number of the employee
Street Address	Address where the employee lives
City	City in which the employee lives
State/Province	State/Province in which the employee lives
Postal Code	Postal code for the employee's address
Home Phone Number	Home phone number of the employee

Now that we have identified all of the attributes for employees and addresses, we must identify the tables that these attributes will be assigned to. Looking at the logical relationship of these attributes we can assign them to two tables as shown below. We use two tables to separate the two objects – employees and addresses. This allows us to expand these tables at a later date if needed and also allows for object reuse. In other words we can use the same address table to contain the addresses of our customers if we want.

Employee Table	**Address Table**
First Name	Street Address
Last Name	City
Employee ID Number	State/Province
Title	Postal Code
Work Phone Number	Home Phone Number

These two tables contain *related* information; the address is related to an employee. Thus these related tables are the tables of our relational database.

This is the start of a good relational design that lays the groundwork for optimal database performance. At this point our database design is relational because the tables relate to one another, however our design is not yet complete. To complete our database design we must normalize our database.

Normalization

Normalization is the process of eliminating duplicate data and providing a fast, efficient search path to the data. A normalized database will have improved performance over a database that is not normalized and one that has been over normalized, which we'll define in a moment. Normalization will also help to make your tables easier to maintain.

As normalization increases so will the number of **joins** required to access the data. Joins are a logical relationship between two tables that allow you to access data in both tables in the same query. Joins are usually defined in the form of foreign key relationships.

For example, using our tables from earlier in the chapter, we could have a join such as:

```
....
JOIN Employee ON Title
   WHERE Employee.Title_ID = Title.Title_ID
```

This would join the Employee and Title tables, matching records based on the foreign key of the Employee table (Title_ID), which relates to the primary key of the Title table (also called Title_ID).

The increase in the number of joins is outweighed by the benefits of normalization, as SQL Server is optimized to work with joins.

Normalizing a logical database design involves using formal methods to separate the data into multiple, related tables. Each method is usually referred to as a **normal form**. There are three normal forms to a normalized database: first normal form, second normal form, and third normal form. Over normalized databases will be normalized to the fourth and fifth forms, and they are rarely considered in practical relational database design.

- **First normal form** eliminates repeating groups of data in a table. We also create a separate table for each set of related data and identify each table with a primary key.
- **Second normal form** creates separate tables for sets of values that apply to multiple records, and relates these tables with foreign keys.
- **Third normal form** eliminates columns that do not depend on the primary key.

Using our example from above, let's walk through each normal form.

First Normal Form

The first rule of first normal form would be to eliminate repeating groups of data. Our tables do not contain any repeating groups of data. An example of repeating groups of data would be if we had a table containing managers, and a manager had a block of columns for each employee. We would then move employees into a separate but related table.

The second rule of first normal form is to create a table for each set of related data. We have already done that by creating the Employee and Address tables.

The third rule of first normal form is to assign a primary key to each table, as shown in the first column of our tables below. The primary key in each of these tables is suffixed with ID, indicating that it is the ID or key for each row of data. (Here we chose to use an Identity column for the primary key for both tables, but the Employee table could equally well have used the employee ID number for the key, as long as each number is unique.)

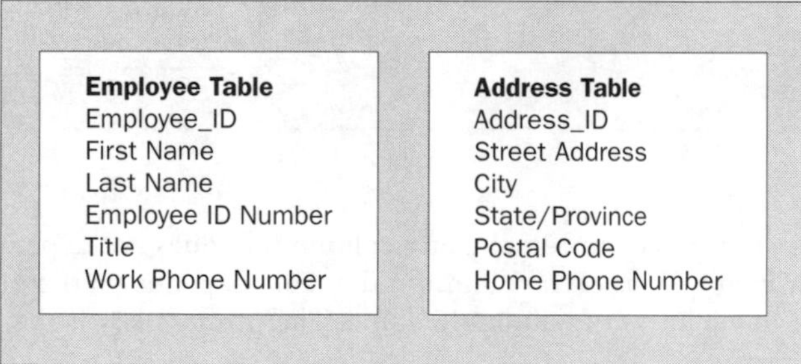

Second Normal Form

In the second normal form we want to create a separate table for sets of values that apply to multiple records, and relate these tables with foreign keys.

Since it is highly likely that more than one employee lives in the same city and state/province, and could also have the same postal code, we need to separate these columns into separate tables, as shown in the following figure. Otherwise we could have a value in the City, State/Province, and Postal Code columns that would apply to multiple records, thus ending up with duplicate values. Likewise with phone numbers. Also, since phone number is contained in both tables, we want to create just one table for both phone numbers.

The second rule of second normal form is to relate these tables with foreign keys, as we have also done in the tables shown below. The lines show how each of these tables relates, with the foreign key entry in one table pointing to the primary key in the related table. For example, the work phone number that was in the employee table now points to the work phone number in the phone number table, and home phone number that was in the address table now points to the home phone number in the phone number table.

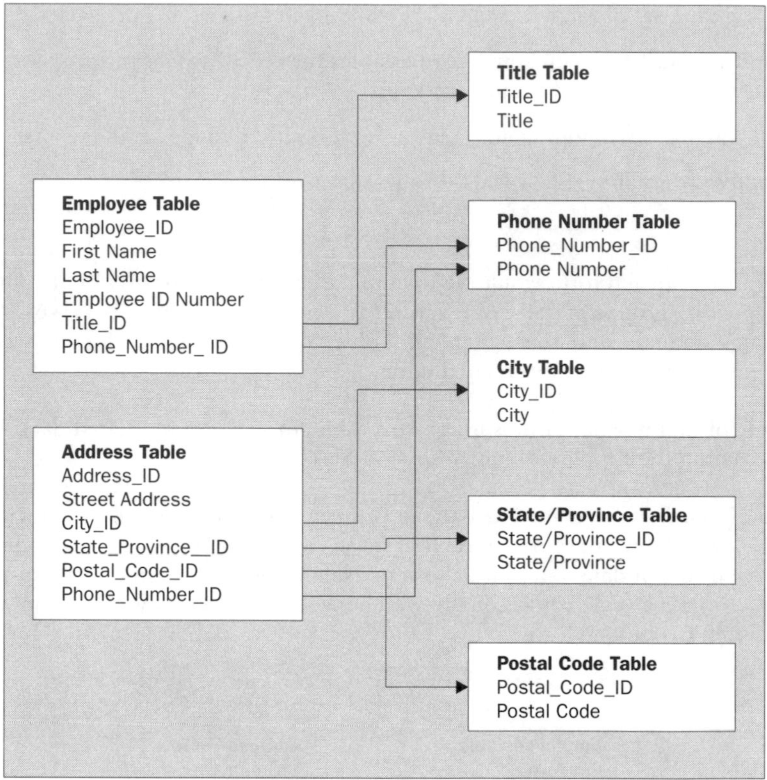

Third Normal Form

In the third normal form we need to remove any column that does not depend on the primary key. This does not apply in our example, as each column in the table depends on the primary key to uniquely identify each column in each row of data in the table. The primary key is the first column in each table.

As you can see from our example above, normalization of the database has yielded more narrow tables than the two wide tables that we started with. This normalization provides two key features. First we have eliminated duplicate data, by separating the columns that could contain values that apply to multiple rows into separate tables, and we've joined these tables using foreign keys. Second, the database will perform optimally in SQL Server because we now have a normalized relational database.

Once we have a database set up and filled with data, we will usually want to manipulate the data somehow, either from within SQL Server itself or from an external application. We already know that we use SQL statements to do this, and that we can build and run queries based on such SQL statements. But there is an alternative to running queries from within SQL Server – we can use stored procedures.

Stored Procedures

Stored procedures contain a group of SQL statements that are compiled and accessed by a unique name. (For those users who are migrating from Microsoft Access, you can relate stored procedures to Access queries.) SQL Server does a lot to optimize stored procedures, and using them has many performance advantages over **in-line SQL statements**. In-line SQL statements are SQL statements that are coded directly in your program as a string and then sent to SQL Server for execution.

Stored procedures increase application performance in two ways. First, there are less SQL statements to be transmitted across the network as we now only need to send the name of the stored procedure and any parameters it may require. Secondly, stored procedures are *parsed* and *optimized* when they are created. Stored procedures are compiled in the database when created and remain a part of your database until you drop (delete) them.

SQL Server **caches** stored procedures in memory when a stored procedure is executed. Cache is an area of memory that SQL Server uses to temporarily keep objects. Subsequent executions of the stored procedure are executed using the copy in cache, thus optimizing the performance of your application and SQL Server.

Stored procedures are similar to any programming procedure. They can contain both input and output parameters and can return values. They use logic to control the flow of processing, and there are numerous functions and SQL statements that can be used in stored procedures.

You can use stored procedures to execute routine data functions such as selecting, inserting, updating, and deleting data. Stored procedures can also be used to perform database functions, such as backing up your database and transaction log. A simple stored procedure is listed below:

```
CREATE PROCEDURE up_parmsel_comments (@comment_id Int) AS

SELECT Comments_TX
     FROM Customer_Comment_T
     WHERE Customer_Comment_ID = @comment_id
```

Each stored procedure to be created contains the `CREATE PROCEDURE` keywords. This instructs SQL Server to create the stored procedure. Then a name is assigned to the stored procedure, and any parameters the stored procedure expects are declared. The example listed above shows an input parameter called `@comment_id`, which is an `Integer` data type. Next come the SQL statements and functions that are to be performed by the stored procedure.

Stored procedures can be used to shield the complexities of the database from users. All they need to know is what stored procedure to execute and what parameters, if any, it expects, in order to get the results that they need. They do not need to know the relationship of the tables or even what tables exist in the database.

Chapter 7 will introduce stored procedures in more detail, and Chapter 8 explores the performance benefits of using stored procedures over in-line SQL statements. We will learn how to create stored procedures in SQL Server and then call them from our Visual Basic programs.

Triggers

Triggers are like stored procedures in that they contain SQL statements. A trigger is a special kind of stored procedure that is associated with a specific action on a table. Triggers are executed when the specified action is performed against a table. This can be when data is inserted into a table, updated in a table, or deleted from a table.

Triggers are most often used to enforce the business rules and to perform **cascading deletes** required by referential integrity. This is where related data exists in multiple tables and the data deleted from the top table requires the related data in other tables to also be deleted. When a `DELETE` statement is executed for data in the top table, a trigger is fired, and it will perform the deletes in all the related tables that are defined in the trigger.

Let's look at the following code fragment for a moment. Using our Employee and Phone Number tables from the examples earlier, let's assume you want to define a trigger on the Employee table that automatically deletes the phone number in the Phone Number table when an employee is deleted from the Employee table. The following code defines the trigger to perform this action:

```
CREATE TRIGGER delete_phone_number ON Employee
       FOR DELETE AS

DELETE FROM Phone_Number
       WHERE Phone_Number_ID = SELECT Phone_Number_ID FROM Deleted
```

Notice that in order to define a trigger, you must specify the `CREATE TRIGGER` keywords and assign the trigger a name. You must also specify what table the trigger should be defined on, and what action in the table fires the trigger. In this case the trigger is created on the `Employee` table and is fired when a `DELETE` statement is executed against this table. The rest of the code in a trigger resembles a stored procedure in that we use regular SQL statements to perform various actions. In this case we delete the row in the Phone Number table where the phone number ID matches that of the record just deleted from the Employee table. (The `Deleted` table is a temporary table used to store the deleted employee data.) Chapter 12 will be exploring triggers and temporary tables in depth.

You can have multiple triggers for one table as long as each trigger has a unique name. Triggers can also cause other triggers to be fired when an action is performed on another table that has a defined trigger, thereby increasing their effectiveness. You can nest up to 32 levels of triggers, having one trigger perform an action that causes another trigger to be executed. Because triggers can contain complex processing logic using SQL statements and functions, they are often used to help enforce data integrity. This is especially true when one trigger calls another to delete related data.

Views

A **view** is like a virtual table containing data from one or more tables. Views are generally used to let users see data from multiple tables in one view, thereby giving the illusion that the data exists as one table or group of data. This provides a couple of benefits. First, it provides the perception to the user that all of their data is in one table. They don't know that we have followed the rules of normalization and that their data actually exists in multiple tables. Secondly, it provides a security mechanism in that we can grant the user access to the view but not to the actual tables that the view is derived from.

There is a distinct overhead associated with views. First, the view is stored in the database as the actual SQL statements that make up the view, just like a stored procedure. When a user selects the view, the SQL statements are executed, a virtual table is built, and the data is populated in the virtual table and displayed for the user. This sequence of events happens *every* time the user executes the view.

Views can also be defined as updateable. That is, they can actually update data in multiple tables. There are some strict guidelines that must be adhered to in order for a view to update data in the underlying tables. The view cannot use any **aggregate functions** in the `SELECT` list. Aggregate functions are functions provided by SQL Server that perform calculations on the values in a column from multiple rows, and return a single result. Also views cannot contain the `TOP`, `GROUP BY`, `UNION`, or `DISTINCT` clauses.

Views are flexible in that they allow you to execute other views and stored procedures to achieve the end results. However, this flexibility only goes so far and there are some restrictions that are imposed on views. For example, you cannot use the `ORDER BY`, `COMPUTE`, or `COMPUTE BY` clauses, or the `INTO` keyword. These clauses will be defined in later chapters. Given the fact that you cannot use the `INTO` keyword, you also cannot use **temporary tables**. Temporary tables are very similar to permanent tables except they are stored in the TempDB database and are automatically deleted by SQL Server when your session ends. Populating a temporary table is usually done using the `INTO` keyword in a `SELECT` statement, hence the reason why we can't use temporary tables with views. We will cover temporary tables later in this book.

Visual Basic and SQL Server

Visual Basic provides several tools to work with SQL Server directly from within the VB environment. The first of these tools is the **Data View**. The Data View window allows you to create and work with database diagrams, tables, views, and stored procedures. A sample of the Data View is shown below. The Data View relies on an active connection to the database, using either a **Data Link**, which can be added directly from the Data View window, or the **Data Environment Designer** that also can be added from the Data View window. We'll be seeing how to add these in Chapter 6 when we look at database connections.

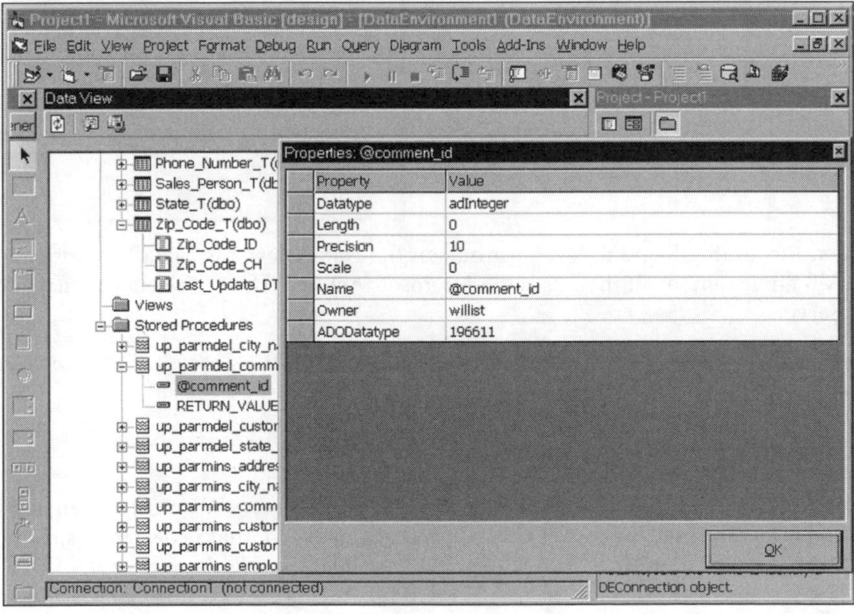

Another tool is the **Database Designer**, which allows you to graphically manage your SQL Server database from within the VB environment. You can create, update, and delete database objects such as tables, indexes, and primary and foreign key constraints. No changes are actually made to the underlying SQL Server database until you save your changes. You can also opt to create a database **script**, to submit to the database administrator, to implement the database changes you have made graphically.

A third tool is the **Query Designer**. This allows you to work with SQL Server queries in a number of different ways. You have the option to create queries graphically using drag and drop operations. You can drag the tables needed for the query and, using visual tools, connect the tables and select the fields that are to be included in the query. You also have the option of using the SQL window to code your queries without using the graphical environment.

So how does VB communicate with SQL Server? It uses the **Microsoft ActiveX Data Objects Library** (**ADO**) as the underlying data source to interact with SQL Server. This will become evident when we start to use the Data Environment Designer in Chapter 6. After adding the Data Environment Designer to your project, you can check the references in your project, and see that a reference has been added to **ADO**.

The adjacent diagram shows this interaction between Visual Basic and SQL Server:

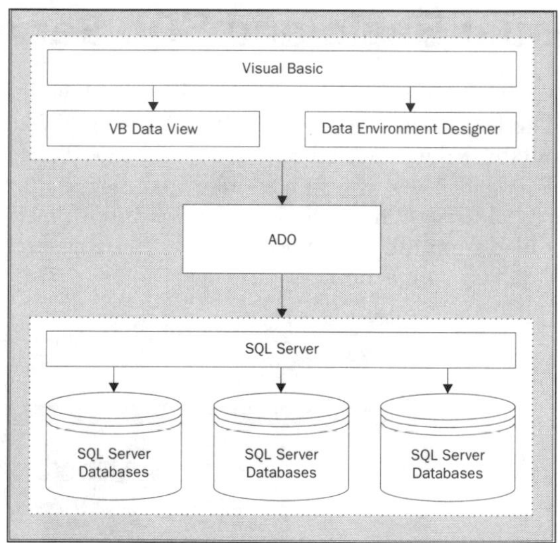

As you can see from the diagram, VB encapsulates the Data View and Data Environment Designer within the VB environment. It then uses the Microsoft ActiveX Data Objects Library to communicate with SQL Server.

The next section explores ADO in a little more depth, and explains how it is able to communicate with SQL Server.

OLE DB, ODBC, and ADO

Our VB applications do not communicate *directly* with SQL Server. We must use an **application programming interface** (**API**) such as OLE DB, ODBC, or ADO, that is designed specifically to access and expose the features of various data stores. For example, we might use an 'ODBC for SQL Server' driver, or if using Access we could use an 'OLE DB for Access' driver. Let's take a look at each of these types of API in turn.

Open Database Connectivity (**ODBC**) is an API that allows lower level languages, such as Visual C++, to access various databases. ODBC is a high performance API that tools, utilities, and system level applications use. ODBC is an older technology that has been built upon by many database vendors and third party suppliers of ODBC drivers.

ODBC is a complex API, and it is even hard for VC++ developers to master using it directly. Given this, Microsoft built several objects that reside on top of ODBC to make using ODBC easier. These include the **Microsoft Foundation Classes** (**MFC**), **Data Access Objects** (**DAO**) and **Remote Data Objects** (**RDO**). These objects provide an easier-to-use interface compared with using ODBC directly, and most of us have used one or more of these objects at one time or another.

As time progresses, so does technology, and so **OLE DB** (**Object Linking Embedding Database**) entered the scene. OLE DB is a low-level **COM** (**Component Object Model**) API that is used to access data from just about any type of data store, not just databases. SQL Server ships with Microsoft's version of the OLE DB API. This API provides high performance access to SQL Server, and supports the SQL-92 syntax to be compliant with the OLE DB 2.0 specification. Tools, utilities, and system level development also use this API when high performance is needed.

While OLE DB does provide an API that is easier to use than ODBC, it still isn't meant for every developer, because of its complex API interface. So ADO entered the scene as a COM object that provides an interface to OLE DB. ADO provides an easy to use, lightweight COM object that is used by general business applications. ADO is considered lightweight because of the relatively small size of the **DLL** (**Dynamic Link Library**) when compared with DAO and RDO. The DLL comprises the code necessary to make use of the ADO interface.

The following diagram illustrates how these technologies fit in with SQL Server:

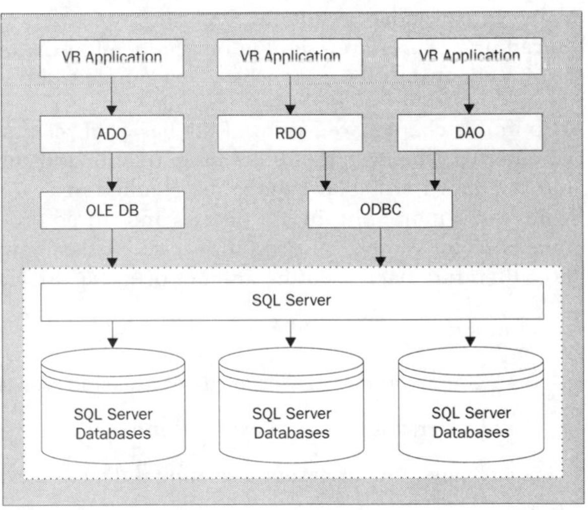

ADO evolved from DAO and RDO, providing an interface that is easier to learn and use. ADO also provides a feature set that most applications need to access data, whether the data resides in a flat file, database, or on the Internet. Because ADO is a COM object, it can be used by any programming language and technology that supports COM, such as Visual Basic, Visual C++, and ASP.

Chapter 6 provides a general overview of the ADO object model, and a more detailed introduction to ADO and how it can be used to enable interaction between VB front end applications and a SQL Server back end database.

Summary

This chapter has taken a look at some of the core concepts of SQL Server. In particular we have taken a look at the objects that make up a database in SQL Server. We have seen how SQL Server manages the database files, and shields the complexities of the database management system from us by only showing us the objects that make up the database.

From our discussion of the transaction log we now know what a vital part this object plays in managing the transactions that are applied against our database, and we have begun to understand the importance of backing up our database frequently.

Looking at tables and primary and foreign keys, we've seen what kind of constraints can be added to our tables to help enforce referential integrity. We have seen how we can reference data in other tables, and how SQL Server maintains the integrity of our data by not allowing us to create foreign keys for entries that do not exist. We have also seen how SQL Server prevents us from deleting data in a table that is being referenced by another table.

Another important part of managing our data in tables is through the use of indexes. These objects play an important role in helping us to maximize the performance of our database in general. They help to speed access to the data in our tables and increase the overall efficiency of our database. We know that, depending on the types of access that we will be performing against a table, we can create one or more indexes.

Looking at some of the other objects in our database, we have learned how stored procedures and views can provide access to our data and shield the end users from the complexities of our database structure. Views in particular are often useful for power users who need only the lower level control of the data. Stored procedures are useful in our code, and provide data access to our program so that we may display the results for users who like a simple front-end.

Also in this chapter we explored the basics of relational database design by following a simple example. To complete the design of this simple relational database we walked through the steps of normalization, and saw how normalizing the tables resulted in a more efficient database design. This completed design will require more joins in our queries and stored procedures, but SQL Server is optimized to handle joins efficiently. Also, as a result of this new design we have eliminated duplicate data in our tables, and have therefore decreased the amount of storage space that our database will consume.

To summarize, you should now:

- Understand SQL Server databases and transaction logs at a high level
- Understand tables, keys, and indexes
- Know how to design a relational database and perform the steps of normalization
- Understand how stored procedures and views provide a means to access and present data
- Be aware of how triggers are used to help enforce data integrity
- Have an understanding of how VB applications can communicate with SQL Server databases

Now that you understand the basic concepts, we can move on to the installation of SQL Server and begin to explore its features more closely.

WROX AUTO WORKS RACING

Installing the Desktop Edition of SQL Server

Now that we have had a brief introduction to the core concepts of SQL Server, it's time to move on to actually installing it. In the last chapter, we covered the objects that make up a database in SQL Server. This chapter focuses on the installation of SQL Server and the tools and wizards provided.

We will discuss the various platforms onto which we can install the Desktop edition of SQL Server, and things you should know before installation. After installing SQL Server, we will cover the various tools that come with SQL Server, such as the Enterprise Manager, which is SQL Server's user interface, and the Query Analyzer, which is used to execute queries and build stored procedures, triggers, and views.

We also need to examine some of the performance tools and wizards that come with SQL Server. The wizards are particularly useful whilst you are learning SQL Server – they shield a lot of the background detail involved in performing the more complex tasks. As you become more familiar with SQL Server you may come to rely on these wizards less and less.

By the end of this chapter you will have had a thorough introduction to SQL Server and its tools and wizards. You will then be ready to move on and create a database and begin working with SQL Server.

This chapter will cover:

- SQL Server editions and target platforms
- SQL Server prerequisites
- Installation overview
- Enterprise Manager
- Query Analyzer
- SQL Server Profiler
- Wizards
- Full-Text Search
- English Query
- Online Analytical Processing (OLAP)

SQL Server Editions

SQL Server comes in three editions – Enterprise, Standard, and Small Business Server. Each of these editions contains the **Desktop** edition. Users covered by a per-seat license can install SQL Server Desktop for development or production purposes.

The Desktop edition was really intended for mobile users who are not always connected to SQL Server on the network. But, as we will demonstrate, it is also great for development. By keeping the database local, we do not run the risk of affecting other users if things should go astray, such as running a query that deletes all the data by mistake.

While the Desktop edition runs on Windows 9x, Windows NT 4.0, and Windows 2000 Professional operating systems, and has no size limit to the database that it can support (other than the limit imposed by the available hardware), there are still some limitations. While these limitations are not likely to affect you, they are still worth mentioning so that you are aware of them. The Desktop edition will not support OLAP (Online Analytical Processing) and Full-Text Search, but will support English Query. We'll discuss these tools later in the chapter.

Likewise, when running the Desktop edition on a Windows 9x platform, there are some significant features not supported that *are* available when running on Windows NT 4.0 and Windows 2000 Professional. These include, but are not limited to, Windows NT authentication, asynchronous I/O, advanced memory management, and SQL Server Performance Monitor. If you will be running the Desktop edition on a Windows 9x platform, then after installation you can consult the SQL Server 7.0 on Windows 95/98 topic in the SQL Server Books Online for a complete list of features not supported.

The **Enterprise** edition of SQL Server can only run on Windows NT Server Enterprise Edition and Windows 2000 Advanced Server, and will support extended memory usage. It also has an unlimited database size, can support up to 32 symmetric multiprocessors, and provides SQL Server **Failover support**. Failover support allows SQL Server to run on two servers and automatically switch to the other server should the first server have a hardware failure. This switching is transparent to the user.

SQL Server **Standard** edition can run on Windows NT Server, Windows NT Server Enterprise Edition, Small Business Server, Windows 2000 Server, or Windows 2000 Advanced Server. It also has an unlimited database size and can support up to four symmetric multiprocessors. However, the Standard edition does not support extended memory, nor does it support SQL Server Failover.

The **Small Business Server** edition of SQL Server can only run on Windows NT – Microsoft BackOffice Small Business Server. It has a 10 GB database and 50 concurrent users limit. As you might expect, this edition will not support extended memory or SQL Server Failover but will, surprisingly enough, support up to four symmetric multiprocessors.

Target Platform

When choosing a Windows 9x (95 or 98) platform there are some limitations applied. The limitations that we are concerned with will be discussed in this section.

The first concern that we have is that Windows 9x does not support computer browsing in SQL Server. All dialogs that would normally show other SQL Server installations on the network are displayed empty. In order to connect to other SQL Servers on the network you must know the domain and the name of the Windows NT server running SQL Server. While this is not a concern for the exercises involved in this book, it is something you should be aware of.

Another feature that is not available on the Windows 9x platforms is NT authentication, for obvious reasons. This feature will be discussed in detail in Chapter 4, when we deal with security issues and setting up new users.

Memory management is implemented differently on a Windows 9x platform than it is on Windows NT and, while this will not be a great concern for us during development, it is still worth mentioning. On Windows 9x, SQL Server manages its memory requests based on the amount of database work being done. SQL Server on Windows NT maintains virtual memory at a point that minimizes swapping. Along with this, if you are installing the Desktop edition on a Windows 9x platform, you will be unable to run the SQL Server Performance Monitor.

All of the examples in this book will be run on a Windows NT 4.0 workstation with a minimum of Service Pack 4 installed. Any examples that will not work on a Windows 9x platform will be pointed out when the time comes.

SQL Server Prerequisites

Before installing SQL Server Desktop edition, there are some prerequisites that must be met:

- **Windows 95** requires DCOM 95, if you do not have Internet Explorer 4.01 with Service Pack 1 installed. The SQL Server installation CD can install DCOM 95 for you. If you are not using Internet Explorer 4.01 with Service Pack 1 and wish to install it, the installation CD will launch the Internet Explorer Setup Wizard. You will then be able to choose the components of Internet Explorer that you want to install. Doing so negates having to install DCOM 95.
- **Windows 98** ships with Internet Explorer 4.01 with Service Pack 1. This is installed with the operating system and SQL Server requires no further prerequisites for this version of Windows. Windows 98 Second Edition ships with Internet Explorer version 5, which is installed as part of the operating system and therefore requires no prerequisites.
- **Windows NT 4.0** requires a minimum of Service Pack 4 to be installed. This service pack is not included on the installation CD, but is available from Microsoft in CD format or as a download from their web site at `http://www.microsoft.com`. Internet Explorer 4.01 with Service Pack 1 is also required for certain types of installations. Internet Explorer is not required if you are running a minimum, connectivity, or a Server Only installation.
- **Windows 2000 Professional** edition installs Internet Explorer version 5 when the operating system is installed, and therefore has no prerequisites.

Installation Overview

After all prerequisites have been met, then you are ready to install SQL Server Desktop edition. The installation is the same for Windows 9x, Windows NT 4.0, and Windows 2000 Professional.

SQL Server will require approximately 170 MB of disk space for a typical installation and 180 MB of space for a full installation. The space for data files will grow, so ensure that you place them on a drive that has room for expansion. Remember though, one of the great features of SQL Server is the ability to span a database across partitions, disks, and even servers (although this is not necessarily advisable). Also, many database administrators prefer to separate partitions – one smaller partition for SQL Server installation files, and a large partition for databases.

Net-Libraries are DLLs that SQL Server uses to communicate with certain network protocols. They can be thought of as acting like an insulator between your client application and the network protocol – they serve a similar function at the server end too. The ones supplied with SQL Server 7.0 include Named Pipes, TCP/IP, Multiprotocol, NWLink IPX/SPX, AppleTalk, Banyan VINES, and Shared Memory. TCP/IP is the de-facto standard networking protocol, but if you plan on using additional net-libraries such as NWLink IPX/SPX, AppleTalk ADSP, or Banyan VINES, you will need to know the service name or object names of these net-libraries before beginning the installation. See your network administrator for assistance with the service name or object names.

When installing on a Windows NT 4.0 or Windows 2000 Professional platform, you have the option of selecting either the local system account or a domain user account to be used by the SQL Server and SQL Server Agent services. If you plan on using features such as Replication and SQL Mail you will need to use a domain user account that has access to the network. These types of features can not be used if using the local system account. In this case, it might be worthwhile to have a special domain account set up that has a permanent password, for use by SQL Server.

At this point, install SQL Server Desktop edition.

SQL Server Installation

The installation procedures covered here are for Windows 9x, Windows NT 4.0 and Windows 2000 Professional.

Insert the SQL Server installation CD. If after a few moments you do not see the following screen, execute the AutoRun.exe program in the root directory of the CD:

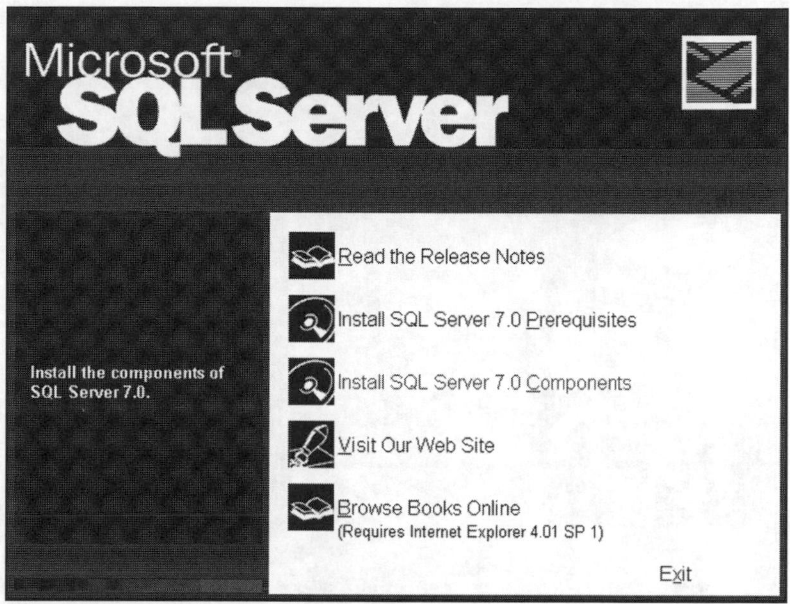

Click on Install SQL Server 7.0 Components to begin the installation process:

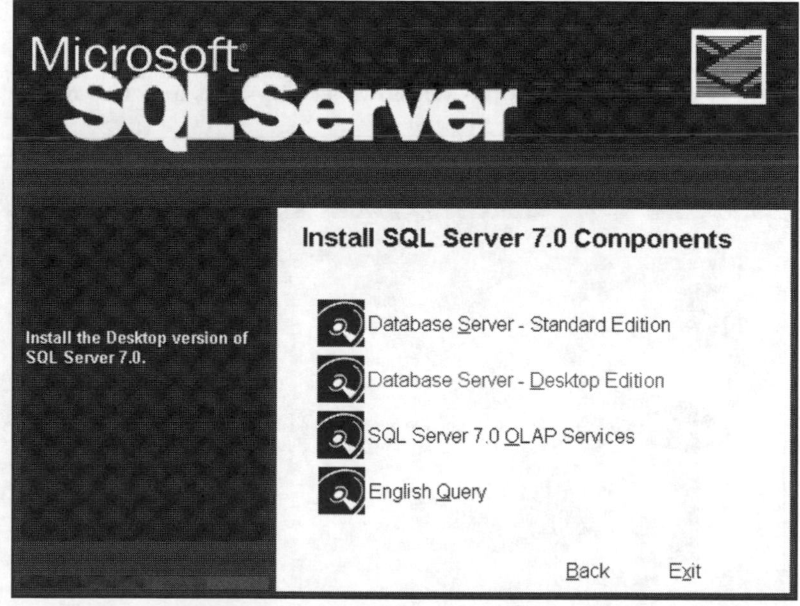

We want to install the Desktop Edition of SQL Server, so click on it to progress to the next step:

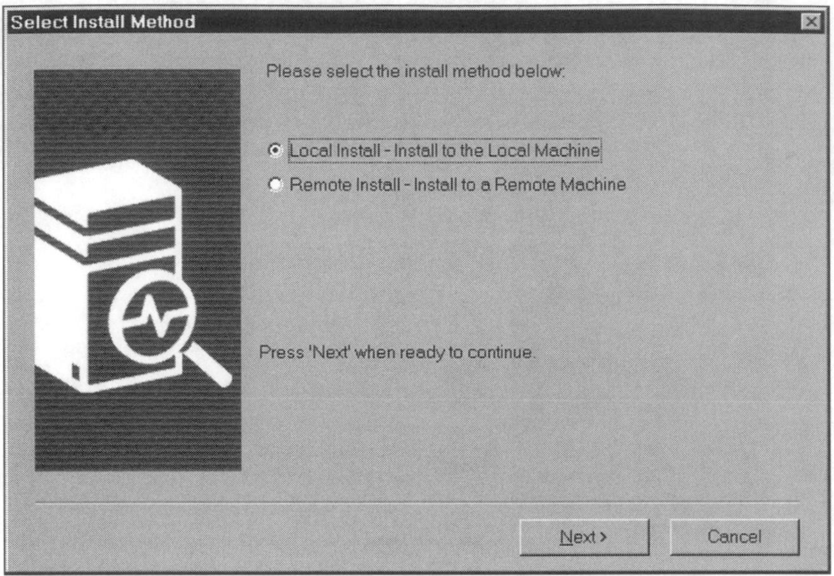

Since the purpose of this installation is to develop and test locally, we want to choose a Local Install as shown above. Click Next to continue:

> **This option is not available on the Windows 9x platforms and will not be displayed.**

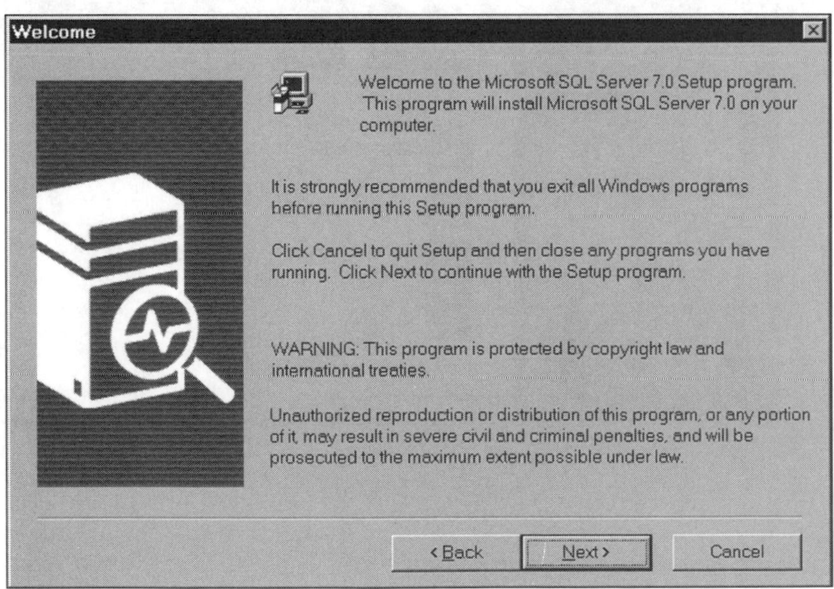

If you have any programs that are running, you should shut them down at this point. When SQL Server has finished installing you will have to restart your computer. You can access any open programs by pressing and holding the *Alt* key. While holding down the *Alt* key, press the *Tab* key until you see the program that you need to shut down. Once the program is highlighted, let go of the *Alt* and *Tab* keys and that program will have the focus so you can shut it down.

Repeat this process until all programs have been closed and then click Next to continue. Read the license agreement and then click Yes to continue:

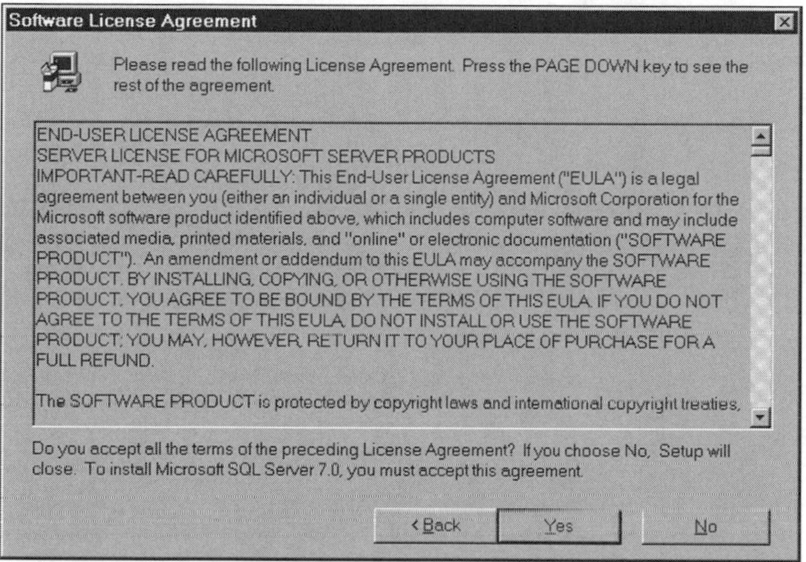

Your Name and Company Name should already be filled in with values read from the registry. If this is not the case, then enter your Name and Company Name and then click Next to continue:

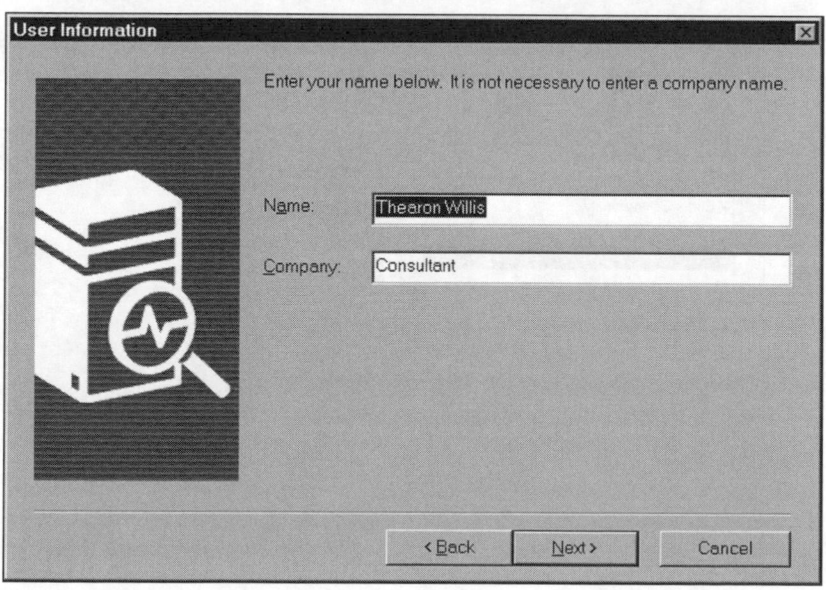

Note that if you already have SQL Server 6x installed on your machine, you will be asked if you want to run the SQL Server Upgrade Wizard to convert SQL Server 6x databases to the SQL Server 7.0 data for mats. To do this, check the **Yes, run the SQL Server Upgrade Wizard** *checkbox.*

We want to perform a Custom installation, so you need to click on the Custom option button. To change the directories that the program and data files get installed to, click on the Browse button for the appropriate option and chose a suitable drive and folder. When you are ready, click Next to continue:

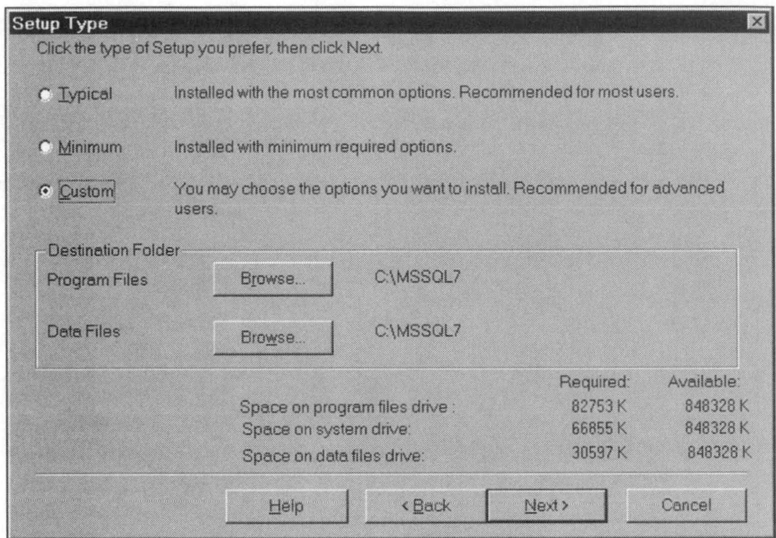

By default, no development components are installed. We want to go ahead and install the development components by clicking on the checkbox next to Development Tools in the Components list. This will check all Sub-Components and we can click Next to continue:

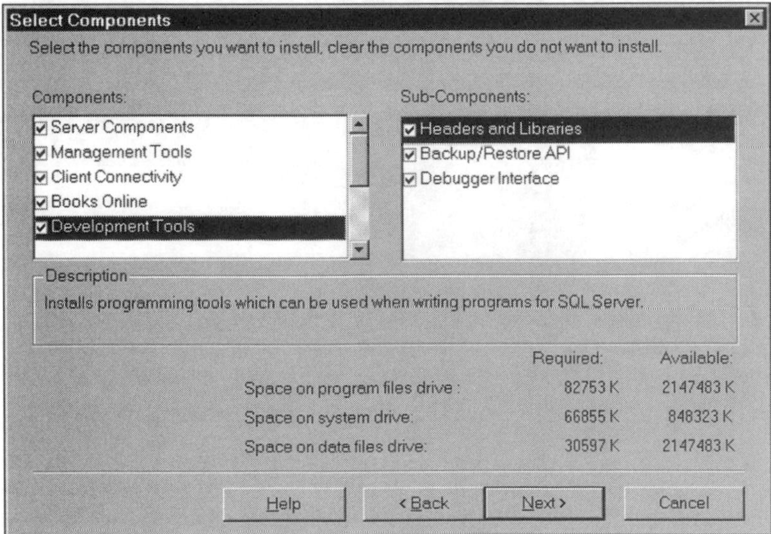

All of the fields are self-explanatory, but if you need further information, Help is just one click away and will go into the details of each of these fields. The Width-insensitive and Kana-insensitive options are only relevant to characters found in certain East Asian languages. We will take the defaults for all of these fields. When you are ready, click Next to continue:

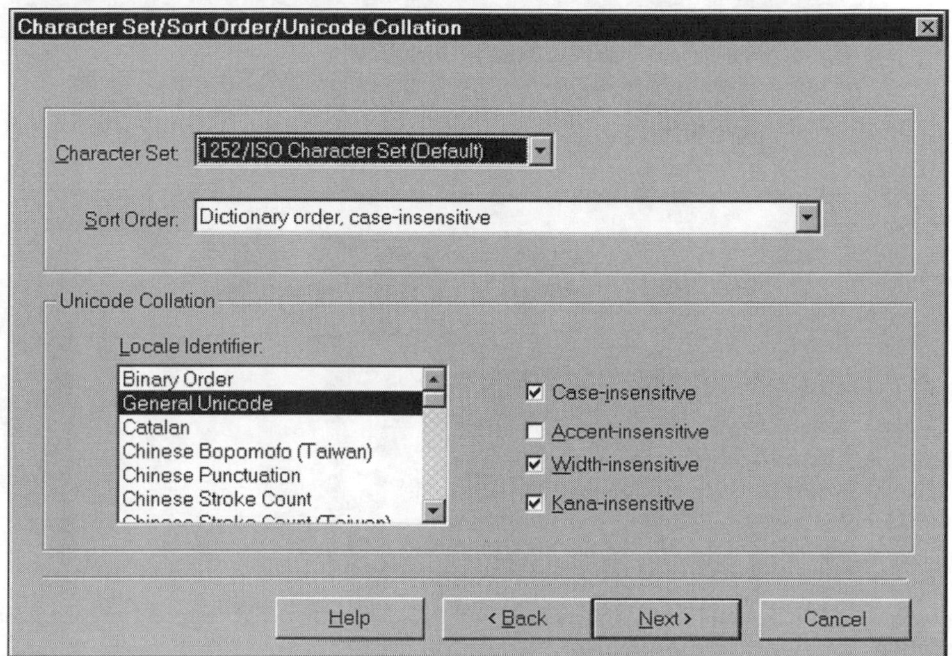

SQL Server uses network libraries to pass network packets between SQL Server and its clients. SQL Server can listen for packets from clients using multiple protocols. By default, SQL Server is set to listen for these packets on the Named Pipe shown in the dialog.

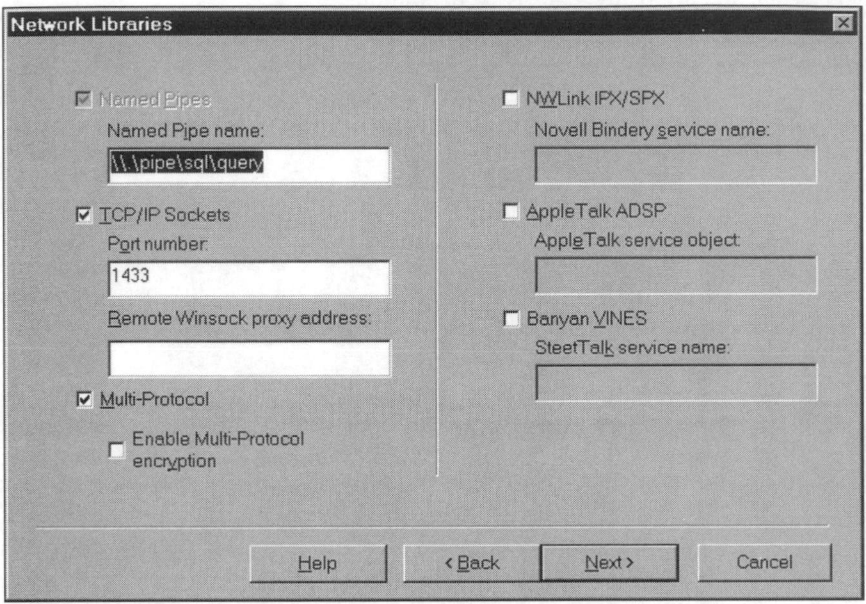

This option is only available on Windows NT and Windows 2000. This can be changed after installation.

Named Pipes is not supported on the Windows 9x platforms.

The TCP/IP network library allows SQL Server to communicate using standard Windows sockets. Windows 9x platforms use this protocol by default. The Port number of 1433 is the default port number for SQL Server. If you choose to have SQL Server listen for client packets on Microsoft Proxy Server, then you need to enter the server address in the Remote Winsock proxy address box.

The Multi-Protocol option uses the Windows remote procedure call facility and is checked by default. You can choose to encrypt data and passwords if you check the Enable Multi-Protocol encryption checkbox.

The Enable Multi-Protocol encryption option is not supported on the Windows 9x platforms, thus we can not perform encryption on these platforms.

If you choose to use the IPX/SPX network library you can check the NWLink IPX/SPX checkbox and supply the Novell Bindery service name.

If you choose to use the AppleTalk ADSP network library, check the checkbox and enter the AppleTalk server object name.

AppleTalk ADSP is not supported on the Windows 9x platforms.

Check the checkbox for Banyan VINES if this network library is to be used and supply the StreetTalk service name.

Banyan VINES is not supported on the Windows 9x platforms.

Once you have chosen the appropriate parameters for your platform and network, click the Next button:

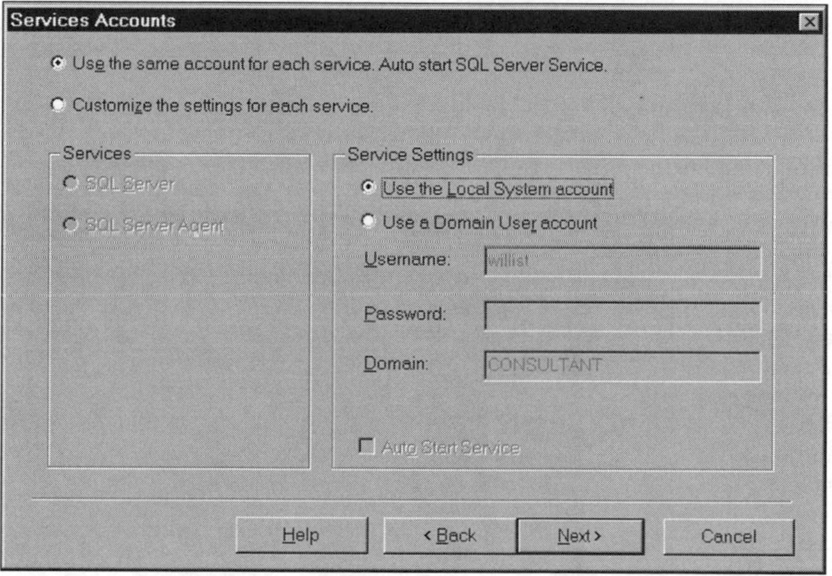

SQL Server and SQL Server Agent run as NT services and need a Windows NT account. You can choose to assign the same account to both of these services and this option is recommended. By default, the Use Domain User Account option is chosen. I chose the Use the Local System account option, but you are free to use whichever option you wish.

Click on the Help button for a full explanation and implications of these options.

Windows 9x platforms do not support NT services and SQL Server and SQL Server Agent run as executable programs. Therefore this dialog will not be shown for Windows 9x installations.

When you have chosen the appropriate options, click the Next button to continue:

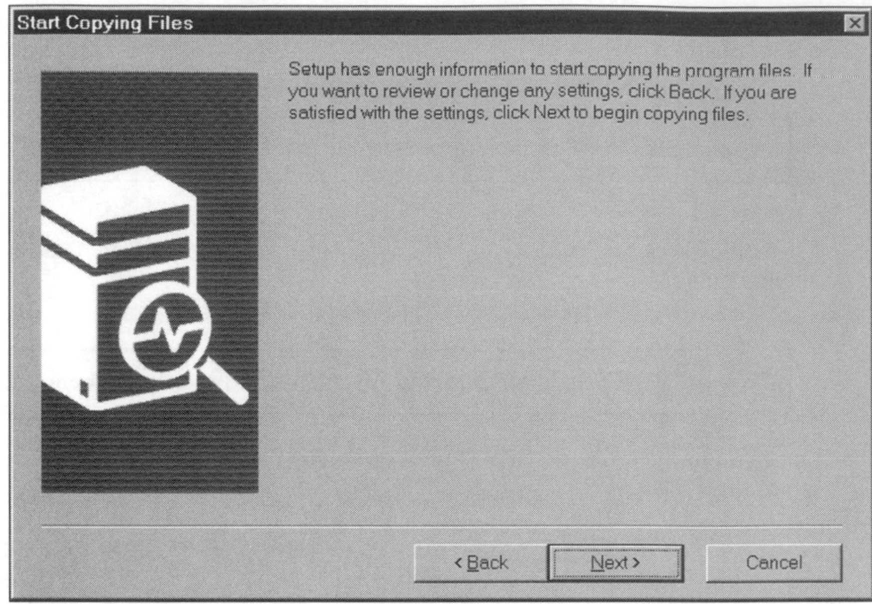

At this point, you have supplied all the required information and, after clicking the Next button, the setup program will start copying files. Once all files have been copied, the setup program will perform some steps to complete the installation.

This involves installing the Microsoft Management Console and HTML Help. The setup program configures the SQL Server services and starts and stops the SQL Server service multiple times. The setup program also configures SQL Server, registers ActiveX components and updates your system registry.

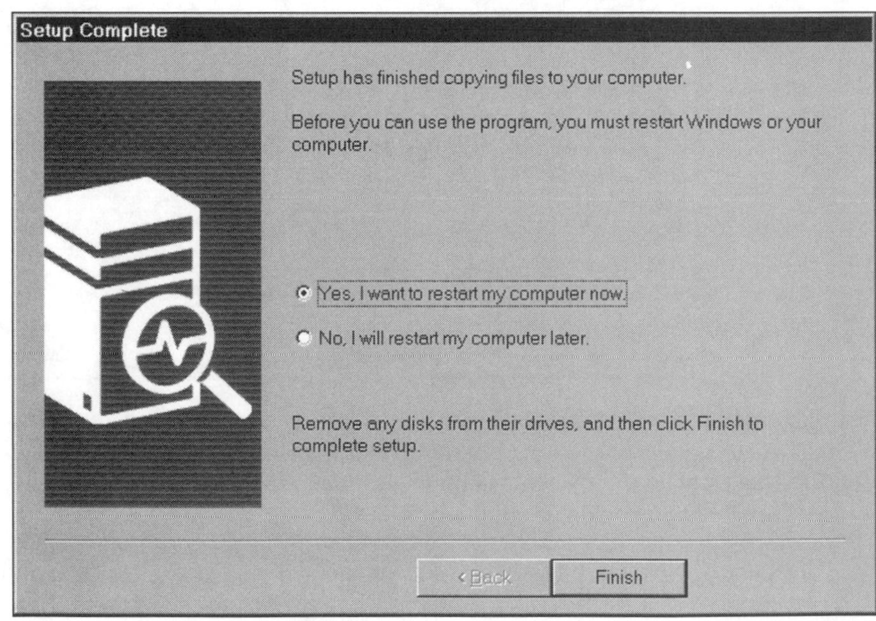

The last step of the installation will prompt you to restart your computer. Click the Finish button to have the setup program restart your computer.

> **Windows 9x platforms do not require a restart because no actual services are installed.**
>
> **Windows 2000 Professional also does not require a restart, even though services are supported and installed.**

Tour of SQL Server

After installing SQL Server, the program group for SQL Server contains many tools, as shown in the figure opposite:

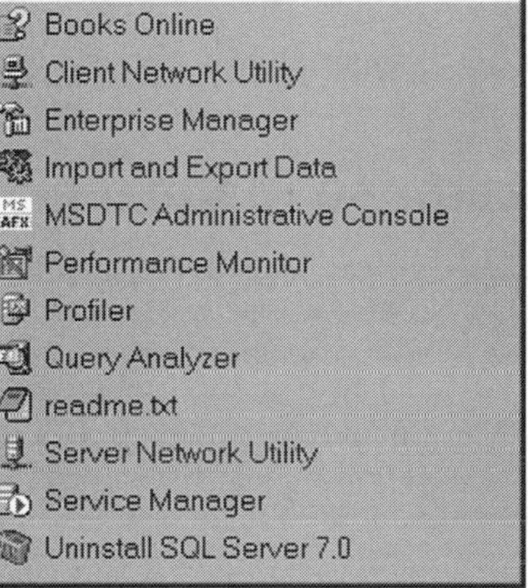

- The first entry in this program group is **Books Online**, which is SQL Server's online documentation. This documentation contains a wealth of information and is provided in HTML help file format.
- The **Client Network Utility** is a utility program that allows you to reconfigure how SQL Server communicates with clients. Both this and the Server Network Utility described below will be used most by the people setting up clients connecting to the server hosting your database, but it is still important to understand their function.
- The **Enterprise Manager** is the user interface for SQL Server, and we will be covering this tool in depth very shortly. It will be used throughout the rest of this book.
- **Import and Export Data** is the data transformation wizard that helps you import and export data.
- The **MSDTC Administrative Console** is the Distributed Transaction Coordinator (DTC) Administrative Console. The DTC manages transactions to make sure that all the statements either execute together or roll back together. This Administrative Console is really a monitoring application that lets you observe what transactions are going through the DTC. You can also start and stop the DTC service and view traces and statistics, as well as the transactions themselves.

- **Performance Monitor** is a graphical tool that allows you to monitor how your current settings are affecting the performance of SQL Server. For example, you can compare the percentage of reads coming from the cache as opposed to hard disk (hard disk reads are much slower).
- **Profiler** is a graphical tool that allows you to monitor and collect SQL Server events. The SQL Server Profiler will be discussed later in this chapter, and will be used in Chapter 16.
- **Query Analyzer** is used for developing queries and stored procedures. This tool will be discussed later in this chapter and will be used throughout the rest of this book.
- **Readme.txt** contains the latest information available for SQL Server that was not published in Books Online.
- The **Server Network Utility** program allows you to view and change the network utilities that SQL Server uses.
- **Service Manager** allows you to start, stop, or pause SQL Server and its related services, such as MSDTC and SQL Server Agent.
- **Uninstall SQL Server 7.0** will uninstall SQL Server.

Enterprise Manager

Before we can jump in and start working with SQL Server we need to familiarize ourselves with the SQL Server **Enterprise Manager**. Start the Enterprise Manager, which is located in the Microsoft SQL Server 7.0 program group.

If you expand the Microsoft SQL Servers group in the left hand pane, you will see the SQL Server that was installed on your workstation. The name of the SQL Server will be the name of your workstation.

*Enterprise Manager is built as a snap-in to the **Microsoft Management Console (MMC)**. Any developer that has used Microsoft Transaction Server or Internet Information Server is already familiar with the MMC. The MMC is the user interface and framework for Microsoft BackOffice server management and is a host that contains management snap-ins (such as Enterprise Manager). The MMC does not have any management properties of its own. Note that the MMC will be exclusively used for administration tools with Windows 2000.*

This user interface is very similar to Windows Explorer, as it provides a **Tree** pane on the left side of the console and the **Details** pane on the right side. Expanding your SQL Server gives you the different folders shown in the screen shot:

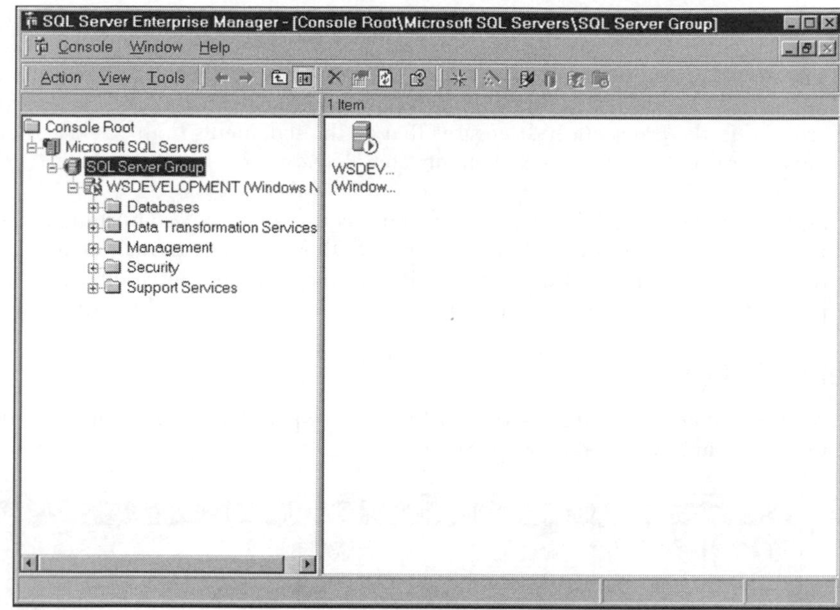

When you hover your mouse over an icon, a tooltip will be displayed describing what function the icons perform – feel free to explore these before we continue. Also notice that right clicking on any of the items in either pane provides us with a drop down menu of further options. We will cover some of these in this chapter and later in the book.

Support Services Folder

Let's take a quick look at the different folders in the Enterprise Manager. We will start at the bottom and work our way up. Start by expanding the Support Services folder:

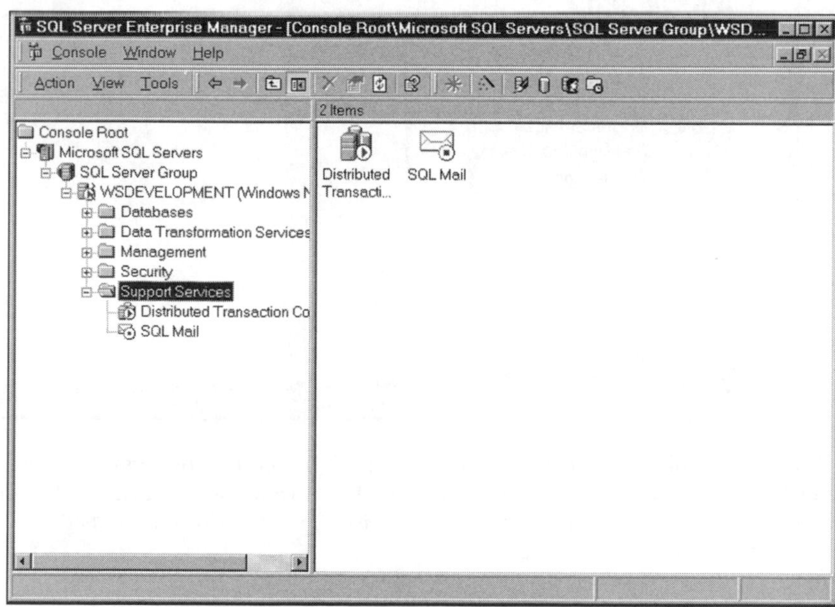

Here we find the Distributed Transaction Coordinator (DTC) and SQL Mail.

The **DTC** is a transaction manager that allows you to include more than one data source (even non-SQL Server data sources) in a transaction. It coordinates committing the transaction across all the servers enlisted in the transaction. It ensures that all the statements in the transaction complete as a whole unit of work or that none of the statements complete.

SQL Mail allows SQL Server to send and receive e-mail by establishing a client connection to Microsoft Exchange Server or a POP3 Server. Using SQL Mail, you can mail-enable your stored procedures and triggers. This is also useful when scheduling jobs, tasks, or alerts (discussed later in this chapter) to provide notification of errors by e-mail, although this can be a little difficult to configure.

Security Folder

Now let's take a look at the Security folder by expanding it. This folder contains the various security items that are managed by SQL Server:

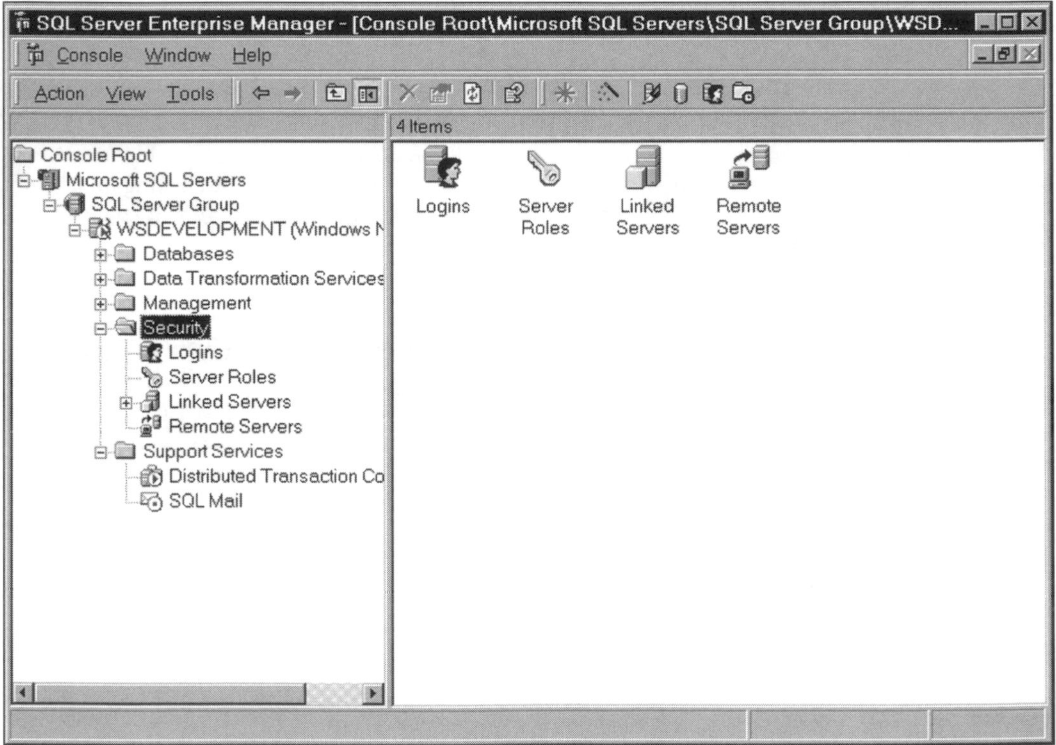

Logins lists all login IDs that have access to SQL Server. Here you can add, delete, and update logins. We will show you how to add logins later when we discuss security. SQL Server requires that you supply a login before allowing you access to SQL Server or any of its databases. Each login can be a user of one or more databases.

Server Roles contains several pre-defined roles with permissions that cannot be granted to user accounts. A role is a security group that a user login is assigned to. You then assign the role permissions to the various objects in your database. If a user requires the permissions that a server role has, you must add their login to the server role in question. This will be covered in detail in Chapter 4.

Linked Servers allows SQL Server to execute commands against other OLE DB data sources on another individual server. You could, for example, link to an Oracle database on another server (although sometimes this can incur problems) and execute a query to select or update data on that database.

Remote Servers allows a user connected to one SQL Server to execute a stored procedure on another SQL Server without establishing another connection. This feature is provided for backward compatibility and has been superceded by the Linked Servers option.

Management Folder

Moving on to the next folder in the tree view, we need to expand the Management folder. The figure below shows the details of the Management folder:

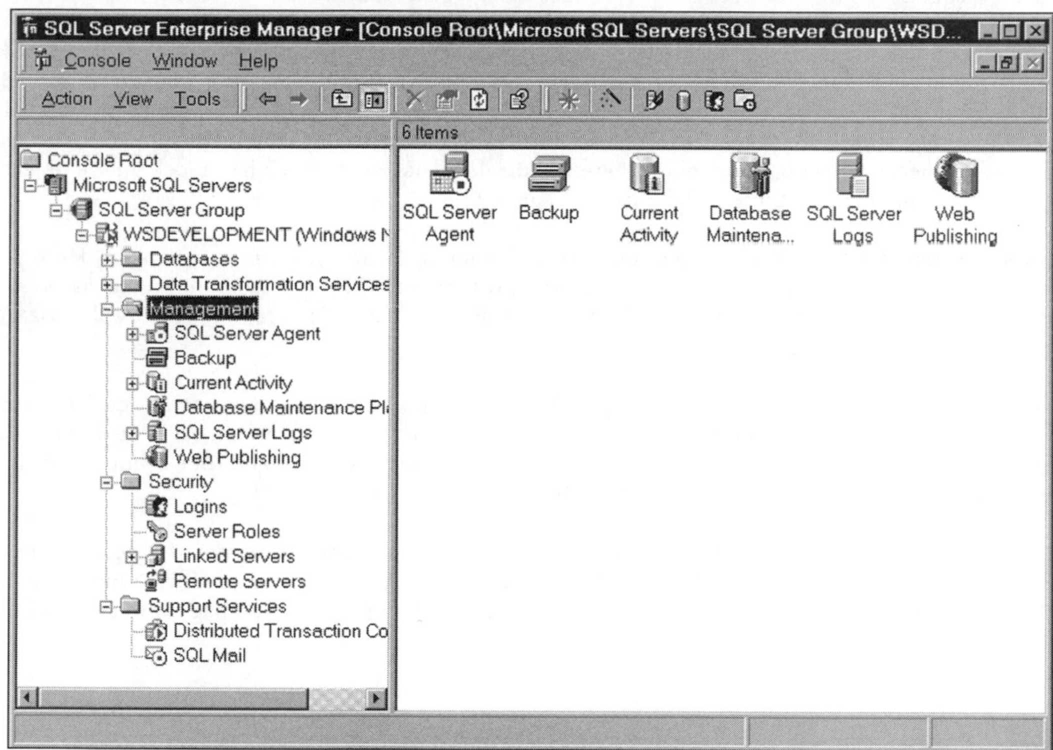

SQL Server Agent provides features that allow you to schedule activities and to provide notification events to problems that occur in SQL Server. Using **alerts**, you can define actions to be taken when a specific error or event occurs. Alerts can send mail or run jobs to correct the error. **Operators** are people identified as someone who can respond to alerts to fix the errors. Operators can be notified through e-mail, pager, or a net send network command. **Jobs** can define objects that contain one or more steps to be performed. These jobs can be scheduled to execute at specific times and perform such actions as automatically backing up your database and transaction logs.

The Backup option allows you to create new backup devices and perform database and transaction log backups. You can even schedule a one-off backup or a recurring backup here.

Current Activity allows you to view the volume and general types of activity being performed against SQL Server, for example, currently blocked and blocking transactions, currently connected users and the last statement executed, and locks that are currently in effect. A lock is a mechanism for preventing an action being performed on an object that conflicts with something already being done to that object. Locking prevents users from reading data being changed by other users, and stops multiple users from altering the same data at the same time. This ensures consistency of the data in the database and makes sure that queries to the database do not produce unexpected results.

Process Info displays what processes are running, who the owner is and what database the process is being run against. You can kill long running processes in this window or send a message to it. The Locks/Process ID option shows what processes have locks applied. Clicking on a specific lock will show general information about the lock. The Locks/Objects option displays the locks applied to the different database objects. Clicking on an object here will display what Process ID has a lock on the object, general information and the specific lock type applied.

Database Maintenance Plans displays information about the current maintenance plans. Here you view the history of a plan (right click for the dropdown menu) or even set up a new database maintenance plan using the Database Maintenance Plan Wizard. To access this use Tools/Wizards, then expand Management.

SQL Server Logs resemble the Event Log in NT, and are not related to transaction logs. Here you can view the current log or any archived logs. Detailed information is contained in each log about what processes SQL Server has performed. Along with each message is a date and time stamp indicating when the event happened and the source of the event.

Web Publishing allows you to generate HTML files by running queries and stored procedures to extract SQL data. Here you can use the Web Assistant Wizard to extract SQL data, publish reports from SQL data or server reports, and to schedule a task to automatically update a Web page with current SQL data.

Data Transformation Services Folder

When we expand the Data Transformation Services folder we find three items:

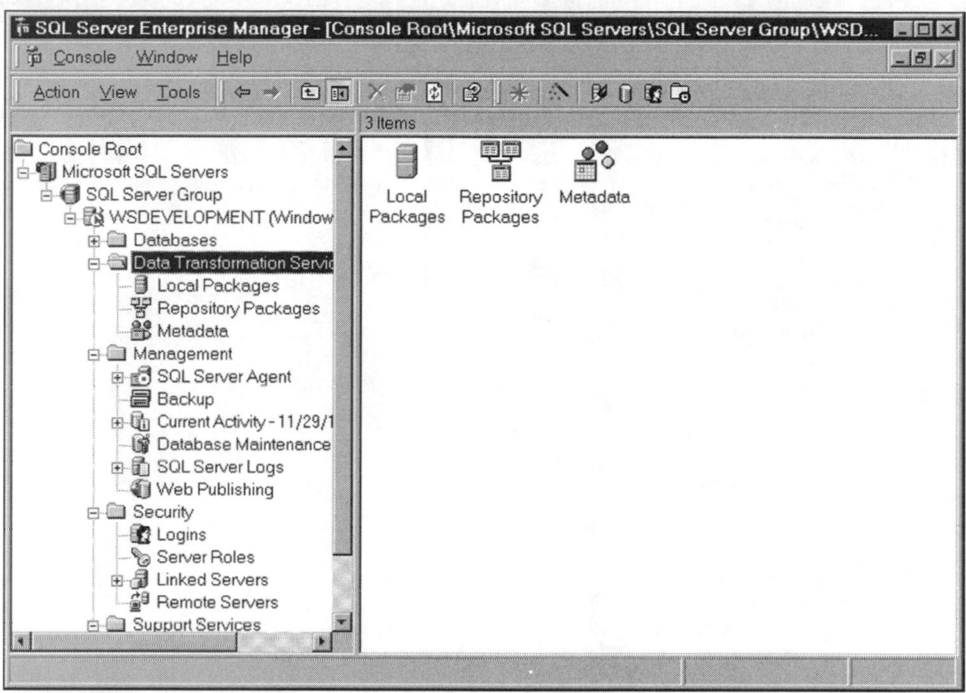

Data Transformation Services (DTS) provides a means to import and export data between heterogeneous data sources using an OLE DB provider. DTS also allows you to transfer database objects between SQL Server running on different machines across the network.

Local Packages allow you to set up tasks and packages to transform data between heterogeneous data sources and other SQL Servers on the network.

Repository Packages contain ActiveX control interfaces and information models that are used to define database schema and data transformations as specified by the **Data Warehousing Framework**. A data warehouse is a data store that holds the data collected during the company's conduction of business over a long period of time. The Data Warehousing Framework is a set of components and APIs that implement the data warehousing features of SQL Server; they provide a common interface to be used by various components seeking to build and use such a warehouse.

The Metadata option allows you to view the metadata stored in the **Repository**. Metadata is essentially data about data. It describes the way storage of the data is structured, it does not actually contain data itself. The Repository consists of a set of ActiveX interfaces and information modules used to define information about databases, schemas, tables, columns, and DTS packages. The Repository is installed by default in the `msdb` database. A SQL Server installation can contain multiple repositories. However, DTS supports only a single repository database per server in the SQL Server Enterprise Manager MMC console tree, and this must reside in the `msdb` database.

Databases Folder

The last folder that we want to expand and look at is the Databases folder:

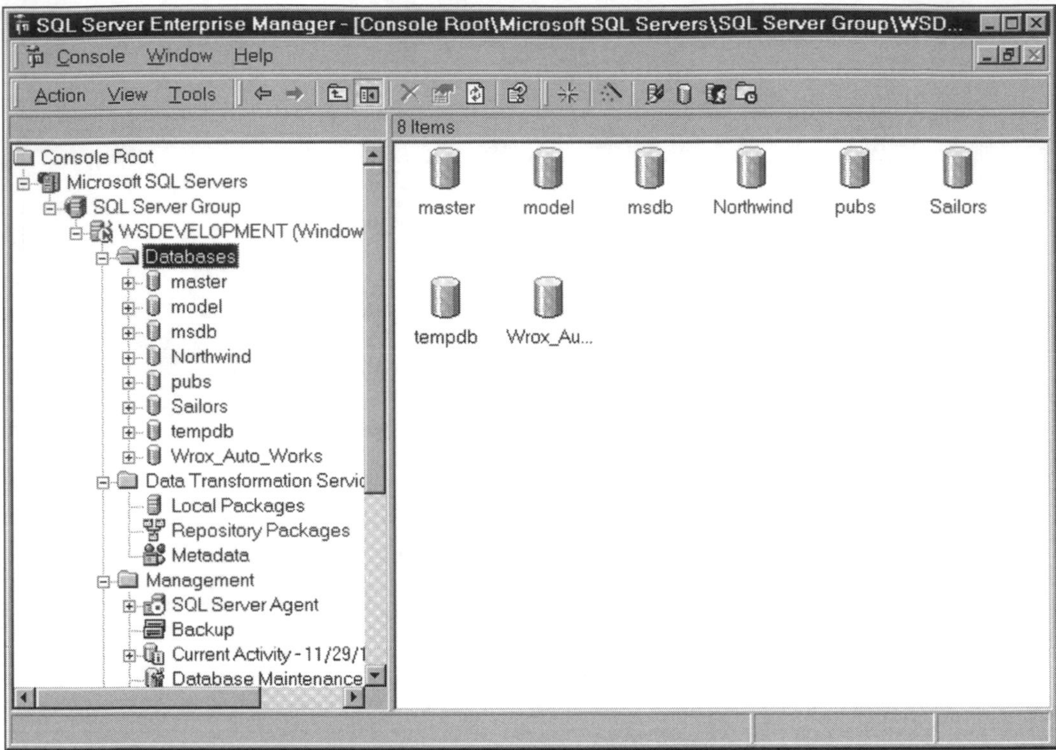

We will be spending most of our time in this folder throughout the book. Here we can manage the objects that make up our database. SQL Server installs two user databases, Northwind and pubs, that are used for demonstration and training purposes. There are four system databases that SQL Server uses to manage the SQL Server environment. They are master, model, msdb and tempdb.

The other databases you see in the above screen shot are user created within this server; including the Wrox_Auto_Works database that we will create in the next chapter and use throughout this book.

The master database contains system tables that are used to record all system level information for SQL Server. It contains all login accounts and system configuration settings, and also contains information about all user-defined databases. Since almost everything that describes your system is stored in here, this database is critical to your system and can not be deleted.

> **This database can be extremely useful – it can allow you to determine whether certain objects exist before you perform operations on them. However, use these system tables with great caution, especially when performing updates on objects in the master database. Microsoft recommends that you don't use them, and if you do, and SQL Server no longer functions, then I told you so!**

The model database is used as a template when you create a new database, although this database you create has to be at least as large as the model database. When a new database is created, the template is used to populate the new database with default tables, views, stored procedures, and roles. We will see this in the next chapter when we create our own database.

> **Again, this database can't be deleted, or your system will fail.**

The SQL Server Agent uses the msdb database for scheduling alerts and jobs, and recording operators.

The tempdb database holds all temporary objects in SQL Server, such as temporary tables and temporary stored procedures. The tempdb database is re-created every time SQL Server starts, and uses the model database as a template.

When you expand a database such as the pubs database, you will see all of the objects that make up a database, as described in Chapter 1. These objects are shown in the tree view. We will expand on this more in the next chapter.

SQL Server Query Analyzer

This is probably going to be one of your most frequently used tools for developing queries and stored procedures. You can code your T-SQL statements, run and debug your SQL statements, and analyze the **execution plan**. Execution plans are discussed in more detail in Chapter 5. Once you optimize your query, you can then create your stored procedure.

Here we see, in the top **query pane**, a simple query on the `authors` table, and the results in the bottom **results pane**:

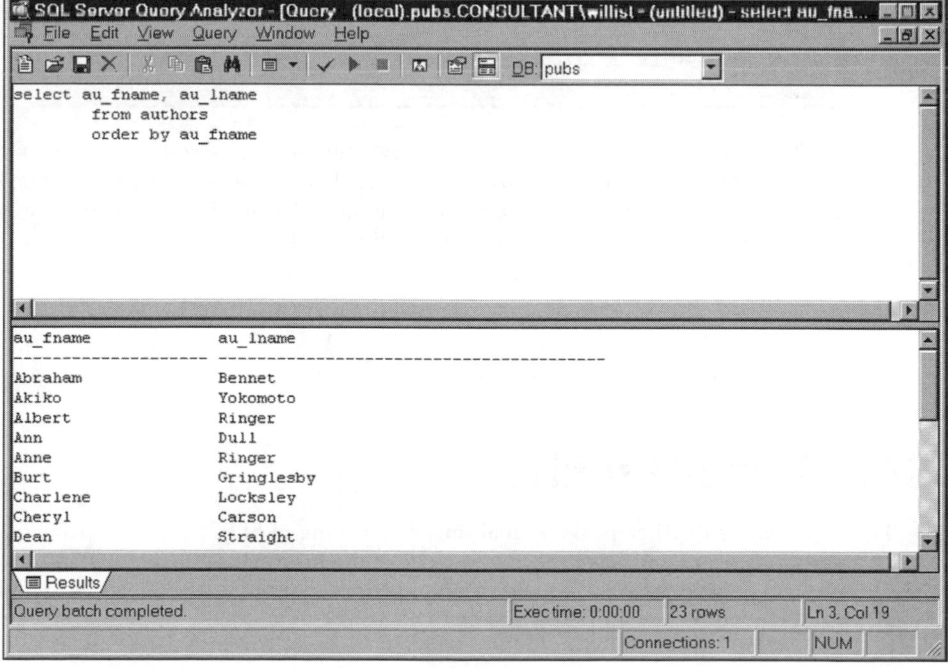

This powerful tool can show you the *estimated* plan of execution before executing your query or stored procedure. You can also perform an index analysis to see what indexes might need to be built. After execution of your query or stored procedure you can view the *actual* execution plan used to help optimize your query or stored procedure, as shown in the figure below:

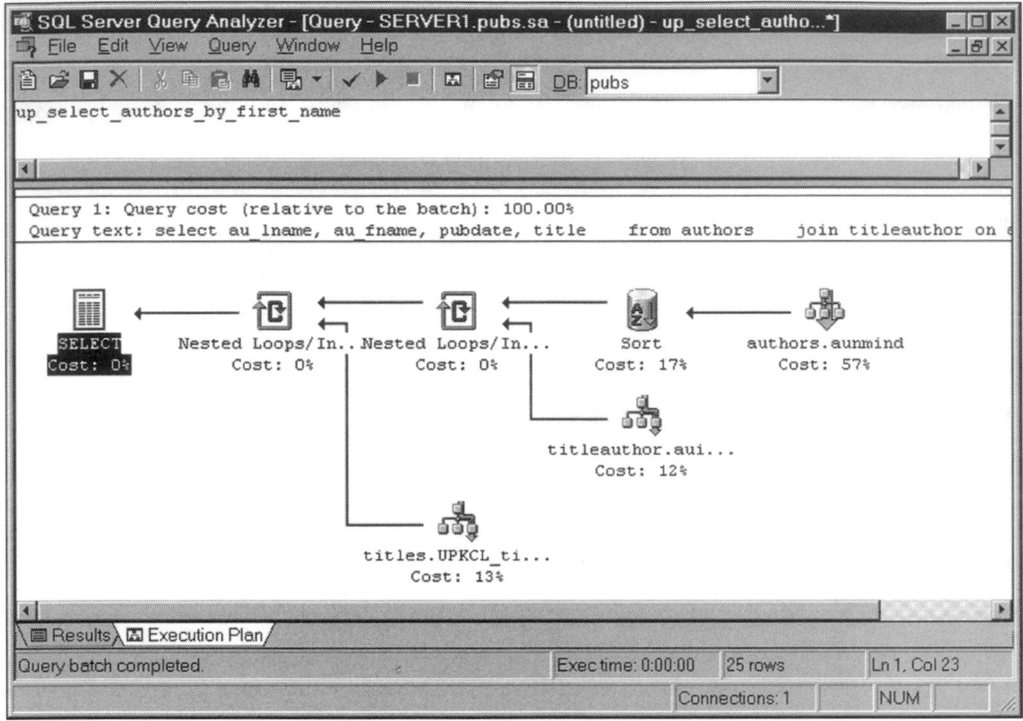

This might seem a little overwhelming right now, but we will be covering the features of this tool in detail in Chapter 5, and will also show you how to debug your queries. We will be using this valuable tool again in Chapter 7 and in all subsequent chapters. By the time you reach the end of the book, you should be very familiar and comfortable with using the Query Analyzer.

Before you can start to work with the Query Analyzer, you need to start your database using the Service Manager, if it is not already running. You will also need to log on using either SQL Server or NT authentication. This will be discussed in Chapters 4 and 5.

SQL Server Profiler

The **SQL Server Profiler** provides real-time monitoring of SQL Server events. You can set up the events you want to capture and have the choice to have the information displayed online, written to a text file, or written to a table. This tool is very useful in troubleshooting stored procedure bottlenecks as it displays the stored procedure being executed and the user executing the stored procedure. Information is also displayed about how much CPU time the stored procedure used, how many read and writes the stored procedure performed, and how long it took for the stored procedure to execute.

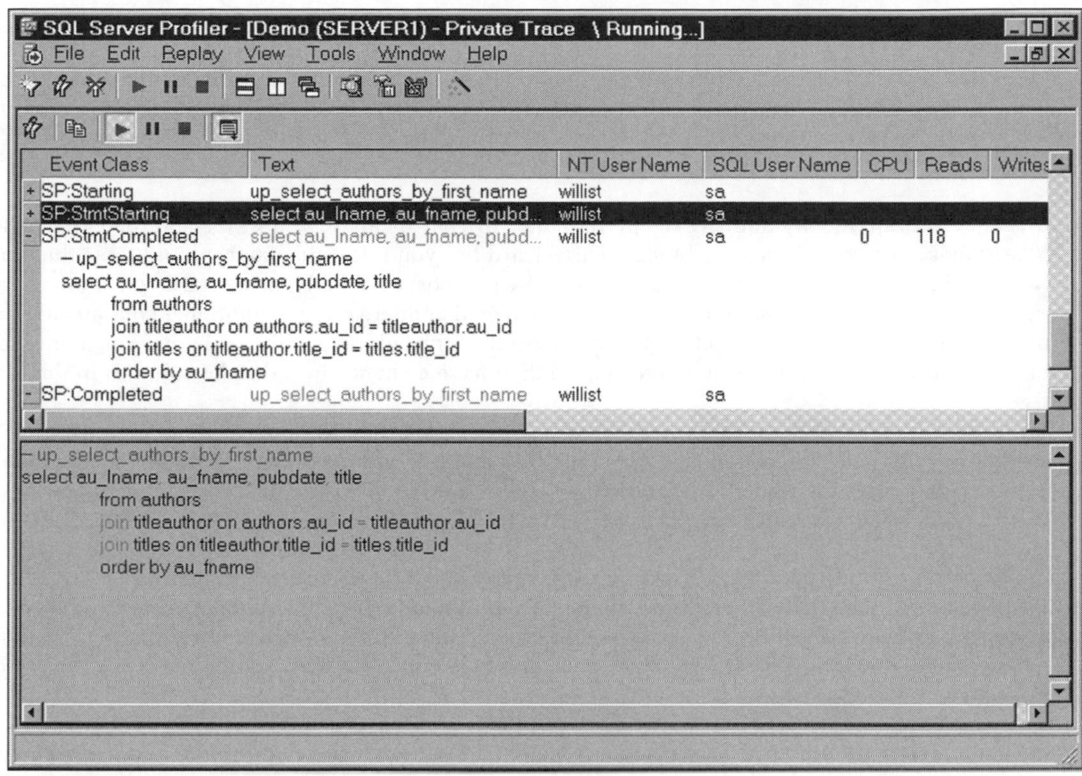

As you can see from the screen shot above, the stored procedure being executed is shown in the preview pane at the bottom and the event pane is displayed at the top. Notice that all of the events in the event pane can be expanded for further information and details about the event.

Wizards

SQL Server comes with dozens of **wizards** to assist you in managing your SQL Server environment. These wizards help you perform complex administrative tasks as well as tasks related to the development of your stored procedures.

This section will highlight just some of the available wizards in SQL Server. The wizards covered here will most likely be the wizards that you use the most. Remember that these wizards can be accessed by choosing Tools | Wizards and then selecting the wizard you want to use.

When you install the Desktop edition of SQL Server and start the Enterprise Manager, the server that you installed is automatically registered. You can, however, register other SQL Servers and access them through the Enterprise Manager. The Register Server Wizard provides assistance in this area by listing the available SQL Servers on your network in the domain that you are logged onto. You can then select the SQL Servers that you want registered in Enterprise Manager. Once registered, you can access these servers through the Enterprise Manager as if they were installed locally.

The Create Database Wizard steps you through the process of creating a database. This wizard prompts you for the name and location of the database files, and then moves on to let you specify the initial size of the database. You have the option to let SQL Server automatically manage the size of your database by increasing the size of your database files as needed. This is one of the great features of SQL Server and can prevent costly downtimes to resize your database. We will be using this wizard in the next chapter to build our development database.

Indexes can dramatically improve the performance of your database as a whole and the Create Index Wizard makes creating indexes a breeze. This wizard lets you select the database and table that you want to add an index to. If an index or indexes already exist on a table, this wizard will show you the current columns that are listed in the index you selected and let you add additional columns to the index. If no index exists, you will be prompted to select the columns in the table that you want indexed, select the type of index you want to create, and then have a chance to order the columns in the index.

The Create Login Wizard allows you to select the mode of authentication of a user, Windows NT account or SQL Server account, and select the roles the user will be allowed to participate in. You then select the databases the user will be allowed to access. We will be using this wizard in Chapter 4 when we add users to our development database.

The Create Stored Procedure Wizard can help you create a stored procedure that will `INSERT`, `UPDATE`, or `DELETE` data (or any combination of these) in a table. This wizard will step you through the process by letting you select the database, table, and action to be performed. Once the SQL statements are generated, you can edit the SQL statements and then complete the wizard by creating the stored procedure.

Backing up your programs and data is an everyday part of life for developers, and backing up your development database should be too. The Backup Wizard steps you through the process of creating a backup of your database. You can choose to create full or incremental backups, and can choose to create a new backup file or append the backup to an existing backup file. You can also schedule the backup to recur at specified intervals.

Full-Text Search

The **Full-Text Search** feature of SQL Server provides searching capabilities that allow you to search for keywords in columns and tables. The keywords contained in the data of a column are added to the Full-Text index. The information about the keyword and its location within the column is stored in the index. This facilitates the full-text search for a word or words in rows of data.

The Full-Text Search features searching for words or phrases that match exactly, words that are in close proximity to each other, and inflectional forms of verbs and nouns. Using this powerful feature of SQL Server, you can build robust applications that require search capabilities, such as a help desk application. The help desk operator could use your application to search for keywords of a problem and then have the answer displayed.

The Full-Text Search feature is not available in the Desktop edition of SQL Server. It runs as an NT service and is only available on SQL Server running on Windows NT Server. The Full-Text Search feature is also not available in SQL Server running in a Windows NT Enterprise Edition clustering environment.

Full-Text indexes are not automatically updated like regular table indexes. Tables that contain the Full-Text Search feature must have their indexes rebuilt at regular intervals. This is a resource intensive operation that should be scheduled during off-hours of operation. A wizard is provided to assist in the initial creation of Full-Text indexes.

English Query

English Query allows users to query the database using questions in natural English instead of trying to write queries that contain SQL statements. Suppose a user wanted to know how many authors there are in the Authors table in the pubs database. Normally they would be required to submit a query such as:

```
SELECT COUNT(Au_ID) FROM Authors
```

Now the user can pose a question using English Query such as:

```
How many authors exist?
```

English Query applications can be created in Visual Basic, and in Active Server Pages to be run on the Web. You provide information about your database, tables, and columns to the English Query domain editor. The English Query domain editor is used to create your English Query project in SQL Server. You define the **entities**, which consist of nouns (e.g. person, place, or thing) and what they refer to in your tables or columns. Then you define the **relationship** between entities.

SQL Server Books Online provides a good tutorial that steps you through the creation of an English Query application using the sample pubs database. Other topics include building and testing your English Query application and deploying your application.

A case study is provided in this book that walks you through the process of creating an English Query application using the database that we will be creating in the next chapter. By the time you reach this case study and start working through it, you will be amazed by what can be accomplished using English Query and the benefits it can provide to your end users.

Online Analytical Processing (OLAP)

SQL Server provides a system call **OLAP Services** (but remember that the Desktop edition does not support OLAP).

The OLAP services were built as a technology that enables client applications to efficiently access data in data warehouses. OLAP services provide a multidimensional model that makes it easy to select and navigate the data from your data warehouse. You can also use the OLAP services to create views of data using ad hoc calculation functions and to view complex business data relationships.

OLAP services allow you to process data from various data warehouse databases, such as SQL Server and Oracle, using either OLE DB or ODBC. Any database that supports OLE DB or ODBC can be used as a data source for OLAP services.

With this system, we do not need our database to conform to the principles of relational databases. This is because the data is rarely edited, it is there for query purposes only. Therefore we now have a dimensional database – this can be used to build **data cubes**, which are multidimensional representations of the data retrieved from data warehouses. The central table of this dimensional database is called the **fact table**, and it has **dimension tables** linked to it. Each of the dimension tables represents a dimension and forms the dimensions of the data cube. Each data cube can have up to 64 dimensions.

The multidimensional cube contains dimension and summary data in cells; each addressed by a set of coordinates that specify a position in the structure's dimensions. This data is used for analysis and can be viewed from Microsoft Excel using the PivotTable service. If you don't want to use Excel, you can use the **ADO Multidimensional extensions** to access the data in multidimensional cubes. You can even write-enable cubes of data so that users can perform different scenarios on the data.

Because of the complexities of OLAP, SQL Server provides a number of wizards to help you work with and build data using the OLAP services. There are wizards to help you build cubes of data and to help you create shared dimensions for use by other cubes. This is an advanced topic that is outside of the scope of this book, but it is covered in *Professional Data Warehousing with SQL Server 7.0 and OLAP Services* (ISBN 1-861002-81-5).

Summary

This chapter has taken a look at the various editions of SQL Server and we have focused our attention on the Desktop edition. We have covered the various platforms that the Desktop edition can be run on and covered the prerequisites that are required before installing it. The installation overview covered some important items that need to be considered before installation and we presented the actual step by step instructions for installing SQL Server.

The Enterprise Manager was introduced and we briefly covered the various services available. After walking through each of the folders in the tree view, you can see that SQL Server has a lot to offer in the way of services and functionality. While it is impossible to thoroughly cover each of these services in detail in a single book, we will cover as many of these as possible.

Our main focus in the rest of this book will be on the Databases and Security folders, as we create and manage our database, and set up logins that will be granted permissions to our database.

We covered the Query Analyzer with a brief overview of its functionality and purpose in the arsenal of tools provided by SQL Server. The use of this tool will become second nature to you by the end of this book. The other tool that we briefly covered was the SQL Server Profiler and we will also have a chance to use this tool in the last chapter of this book. We know that we can use this tool to provide real-time monitoring of SQL Server events that will aid us in troubleshooting performance bottlenecks.

There are so many wizards provided in SQL Server that we did not have time to cover them all. We highlighted some of the more important wizards that will be used throughout this book. As you will soon discover, these wizards will assist you in some of the more complex administrative tasks and relieve you of the details of what is going on behind the scenes. Once you have become more accustomed to SQL Server and your knowledge has increased, it is possible that you will want to perform these administrative tasks without the aid of a wizard.

We also covered three advanced features of SQL Server – Full-Text Search, English Query, and OLAP. These features and services provide enhanced functionality to SQL Server and help to make it the great database management system that it is.

To summarize, you should:

- Know how to install SQL Server Desktop edition
- Be familiar with the Enterprise Manager and know its vast capabilities
- Have been acquainted with the Query Analyzer and know what it is used for
- Know some of the more important wizards and what tasks they can assist you with
- Be familiar with some of the advanced features of SQL Server

WROX AUTO WORKS RACING

Creating the Development Database

Standards are vital to any organization and help to ensure consistency in the code that is written. In fact, standards do not just apply to code. If you look around, you will probably find standards in just about everything in your organization, from the format of corporate e-mails to user documentation. Code written to your company's standards helps to ensure that any developer can pick up a program and work with it efficiently; they don't have to spend time trying to figure out what naming conventions some other developer used.

Database standards are no different, and in this chapter we will cover some suggested naming conventions that could be used. Using standards in your database design and throughout your coding of stored procedures, views, and triggers, helps to ensure that any developer can pick up your code and know exactly what is going on. The code that we will use throughout the rest of this book will be written to the database standards presented in this chapter.

In the last chapter we installed SQL Server and took a look at the features provided in the Enterprise Manager. By now you are probably ready to get down to work and start using the Enterprise Manager to learn more about SQL Server. This chapter takes you through the contents of the `Databases` folder of the Enterprise Manager, and also exposes you to some of the wizards provided by SQL Server that help you perform some database administrative tasks. Here we will use them to help us create the database and a diagram of it. The wizards perform a lot of the more complex tasks and allow us to concentrate on getting the job done, without thinking what is going on behind the scenes. We also will cover setting up the development database that will be used throughout the rest of this book, and will create the tables, indexes, and primary and foreign keys.

This chapter will cover:

- Suggested naming conventions
- Viewing the database structure with the Enterprise Manager
- Creating the development database

Suggested Naming Conventions

As we mentioned above, standards are an important part of any organization and help to control the look and feel of applications, as well as the maintenance of those applications. The **database naming standards** suggested here are just that – *suggested*. If your organization already has database standards in place, then feel free to use them instead. If your organization has none, then this section can be used as a guideline in developing some. All of the examples in this book adhere to these standards, so you need to be aware of them, even if you don't plan to adopt them when developing your own databases.

The naming standards suggested here use suffixes. This is just a personal preference, as prefixes could be used just as well.

Identifying Objects

In Chapter 1 we discussed the various objects that make up a database, including tables, views, and stored procedures. When assigning names, each object should be suffixed with the first letter of the object (or, where more than one object shares the same first letter, a suitable alternative). An example for a customer address table would be `Customer_Address_T`.

Suffixing each object will help to quickly identify what the object is. This is especially useful when dealing with stored procedures, as distinguishing between data retrieved from a *table* named `Customer_Address` and a *view* named `Customer_Addresses` can be confusing and time-consuming for someone who did not write the stored procedure. Without a suffix appended to the object, you have to go through the list of tables and views in the database to determine what the object is.

Let's now look at the naming conventions for specific objects.

Tables

Table names can be up to 128 characters in length and should be as descriptive as possible. The first letter in each word in a table name should be capitalized, and an underscore character should separate each word. Abbreviations should be avoided wherever possible. Using upper and lower case letters, as well as underscore characters, helps to make object names easier to read. An example of a table name for customer financial information could be `Customer_Financial_Information_T`.

Columns

Column names can also be up to 128 characters in length and should follow the same naming conventions as a table. All column names should be suffixed with the *data type* of the column, according to the following table. An example of a column containing the last update date and time of a table would be `Last_Update_DT`. Appendix A details the Transact-SQL data types as well as the relationship of Transact-SQL to Visual Basic data types.

Suffix	Data Type
BN	Binary
BT	Bit
CH	Char
DT	DateTime
DC	Decimal
FL	Float
IM	Image
IN	Integer
MN	Money
NC	NChar
NT	NText
NV	NVarchar
RL	Real
SD	SmallDateTime
SI	SmallInteger
SM	SmallMoney
TX	Text
TS	TimeStamp
TI	TinyInt
VB	VarBinary
VC	VarChar

Using a suffix on each column will help other developers working with these columns in a stored procedure. They will know at a quick glance what type of data they are dealing with, according to the suffix of the column name.

Primary and Foreign Keys

All columns that are primary keys should end with a suffix of `_ID` and should have the same name as the table. This will help anyone looking at stored procedures and views to know what the keys are and to what tables they belong. If you are using more than one column to make up the primary key you could suffix the column names with `_PK`. All primary and foreign keys are usually `Integer` data types.

Indexes

When you create a table that contains a primary key, SQL Server will automatically place an index on that column using a name of `PK_table_name`, where `table_name` is the name of a table. An index on the primary key column for the `Customer_T` table created by SQL Server would look like this: `PK_Customer_T`.

In keeping with this, when we create *additional* indexes on a table, they should be prefixed with `IX_` followed by the table name. Thus if we wanted to create an additional index on the `Customer_T` table, our index name would look like this: `IX_Customer_T`.

If you create more than one index on a table you can suffix each index with `_n`, where `n` would represent the number of indexes added by you.

Views

View names can be up to 128 characters in length and should follow the same naming conventions as a table name. All views should be suffixed with `_V`.

Triggers

Trigger names can also be up to 128 characters in length, and should follow the same naming conventions as tables. All triggers should be suffixed with `_G`.

Stored Procedures

Stored procedures are at the heart of our development efforts and therefore naming standards are even more important here. The database administrator can create stored procedures that can be used enterprise-wide and which can be placed in your database. Developers also create stored procedures in the database. So a naming standard here is especially important, and takes a different twist to what we have observed thus far. The stored procedure naming standard that follows is one that I personally find useful, and I'll explain why after we review the standard:

All stored procedures created by the *database administrator* should be *prefixed* with `SP_`.

All stored procedures created by *developers* should be *prefixed* according to the table below:

Prefix	Description
`UP_PARMDEL_`	`UP_` indicates a user stored procedure, in other words one created by a developer. This stored procedure accepts parameters and will `DELETE` data.
`UP_PARMINS_`	This stored procedure accepts parameters and will `INSERT` data.
`UP_PARMSEL_`	This stored procedure accepts parameters and will `SELECT` data.
`UP_PARMUPD_`	This stored procedure accepts parameters and will `UPDATE` data.
`UP_SELECT_`	This stored procedure will `SELECT` data but does not have parameters.

We will be covering each of these types of stored procedures in the upcoming chapters. A medium to large database can have hundreds of stored procedures. If no naming standard has been implemented, a new developer will not know what each stored procedures does. Likewise, even the developers who wrote the stored procedures will have a difficult time finding the correct stored procedure to modify.

Using the suggested naming standard above serves three purposes. First, it lets you know at a quick glance what the purpose of each stored procedure is. Secondly, all of the stored procedures are grouped together, which makes finding a stored procedure that, for example, accepts parameters and updates data, easier to find in the list of hundreds of stored procedures. Last, the stored procedures that are prefixed with `SP_` indicate those created by the database administrator, DBA, which are used enterprise wide. (Note that the `SP_` prefix is also used for system stored procedures, for example `sp_dboption`, `sp_indexes`, that come with SQL Server.) This gives a clear differentiation between stored procedures created by the DBA and the developer.

Now that we have described the naming convention that we'll be using for our development database, we can go ahead and begin creating the database itself.

The Development Database

We need to create the database that will be used to develop the examples in this book. First we need to determine what it is that our database should store. Let's start by assuming that we have a company called Wrox Auto Works and that this company sells new cars. We want to provide our sales staff with a tool that will help make our customers feel valued.

We do this by storing all of the customer information in our database. When a customer comes in, we can look up their information in our database. If the customer has bought a vehicle from us before, we only need to update the information that is out of date. New customers will be required to supply all information so that we can store it in our database. Returning customers feel valued because a sales person can quickly evaluate the customer's needs when they look up the client's information. The database design allows for future expansion and will be amplified in our case studies. The data in our database can be used for several other purposes, such as marketing and, as we will show in a case study, for sales analysis.

Database Design

To that end, we have a database design that stores general customer information and addresses. The diagram below shows the tables required and the relationship between the tables:

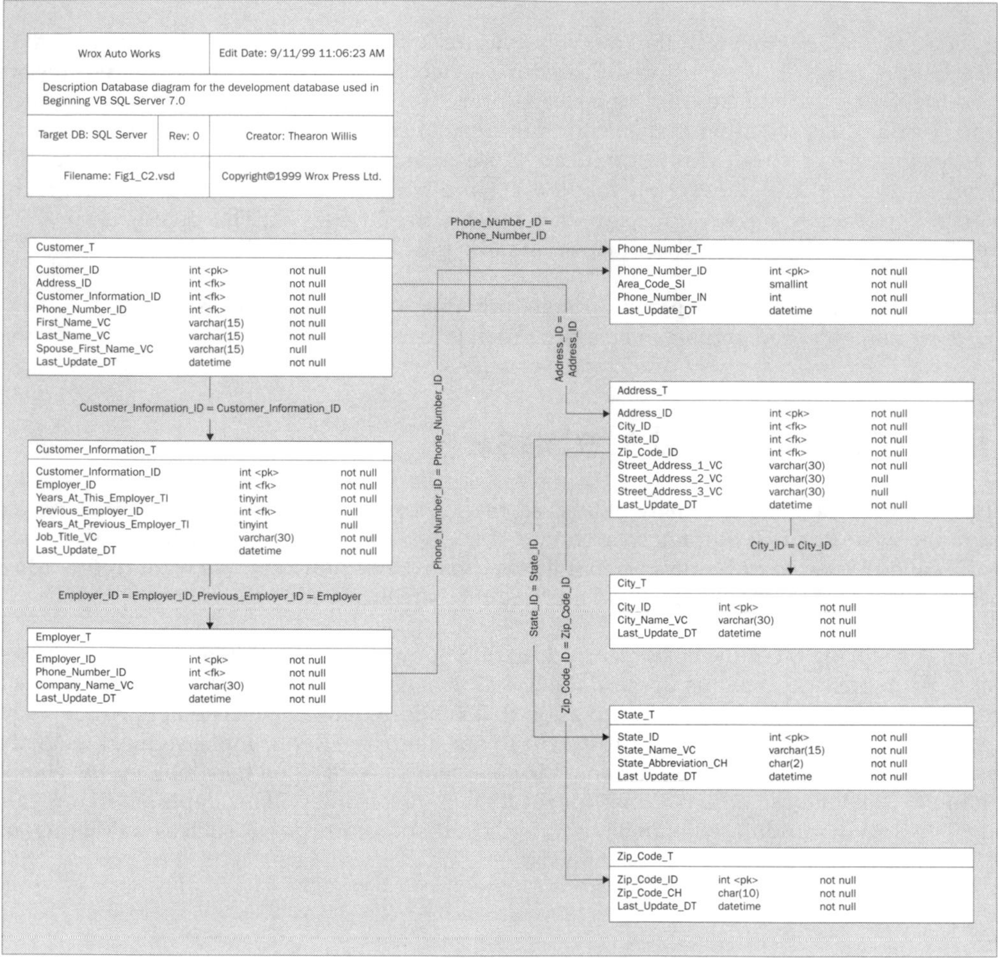

Let's take a moment to study the details of the figure above. Each box in the diagram represents a table. Within each table there are three columns. The first column represents the column name of the data in the table. The second column represent the data type; along with the data types are the symbols <pk>, which represents a primary key column, and <fk>, which represents a column that contains a foreign key. The third column represents whether or not the column of data can contain null values. Each table that contains a foreign key has a line that links it to the table that the foreign key references.

The overall design of our database might seem extreme to the new user of SQL Server. You might be tempted to combine the city, state, and zip code information into the table with the addresses. However, because we have followed the rules of normalization and relational database design, as outlined in Chapter 1, we have each of these data elements in separate but related tables. Normalized database designs will help SQL Server and your applications to perform optimally.

Tables, Keys, and Data Types

Now let's take a moment to look at each of these tables and talk about design choices regarding the column data types. The `Customer_T` table contains the first and last names of our customers, as well as their spouse's first name. We have foreign key references to the `Address_T`, `Phone_Number_T`, and `Customer_Information_T` tables. Information in these tables is related to the information in the `Customer_T` table by these foreign keys.

Notice that all of the columns, with the exception of `Spouse_First_Name_VC`, require data. This is indicated by the specification of not null. Also, all of our tables contain a `Last_Update_DT` field. This field can be used to determine the last date and time a row of information was updated.

We chose to keep the `Customer_T` table as narrow as possible by containing just the basic customer data. More specific customer information is contained in the `Customer_Information_T` table, which we will look at next.

The `Customer_Information_T` table contains *detailed* customer information. This table only contains employment information at this time, but can be expanded at a later date. The `Years_At_This_Employer_TI` and the `Years_At_Previous_Employer_TI` columns are `TinyInt` data types. `TinyInt` data types were chosen because they can contain a value of 0 – 255 and, most likely, the maximum value that we will have in this field is around 50.

There are two different foreign keys in this table referencing the same column in the `Employer_T` table. This is because the `Employer_T` table contains *all* of our employer information, and a customer could conceivably have a *previous* employer in addition to their *current* one. This allows us to point to two different entries in the `Employer_T` table.

Taking a look at the address tables, one might be tempted to prefix each of these tables with `Customer_` because the data really relates to the customer. But what if we add another table, for example to contain sales staff or supplier details, that needs to use addresses? Keeping the table names generic really helps us to be able to reuse these tables, not only within our own database, but also within other databases in SQL Server.

The last thing we need to point out is the `Zip_Code_T` table. This table contains a column for zip codes, named `Zip_Code_CH`. One might be tempted to make this an `Integer` data type, especially in light of the fact that all zip codes in the United States are numeric. BEWARE of this thinking. Zip codes can begin with a zero and as such will not be correctly displayed in your column. If you inserted a zip code of 01234 into the table, it is stored as 1234. This gets carried forward to your application as well; when you read this zip code and display it in your application, it is displayed as 1234. You would have to format this field in your application and in your edit checks. In addition, if you plan to use the `Zip_Code_CH` column to store foreign zip codes then you will definitely need to use the `Char` or `VarChar` data types, as foreign zip codes contain numbers as well as characters.

The performance trade-off of storage versus editing and formatting are argumentative. The storage for a `Char(10)` data type will be 10 bytes. If we chose to use a `VarChar(10)` data type, the storage would be the number of characters in that column. For our purposes we have chosen to go with a `Char` data type. The length of the zip code will always be 10 characters. If less than 10 characters are entered then SQL Server will pad the column to the right with spaces. This allows for a standard US zip code plus four digits. Whether or not you include the dash in the zip code is up to you.

Some DBAs will argue about when you will take a performance hit if using `VarChar` data types. Some say that columns containing less than 10 characters should be made a `Char` data type to avoid the extra overhead associated with using `VarChar` data types. Others argue that the number is around 15 characters. We will go with 10, so any character data that is going to be 10 characters or less will be made a `Char` data type. The overhead that is associated with a `VarChar` data type refers to the extra processing that SQL Server must go through to determine the storage needs for a `VarChar` data type. The storage needs for this data type depend on the number of characters contained in the column. For example, if we have a column defined as `VarChar(15)` and the data value stored in that column is only 10 characters in length, then SQL Server will use 10 bytes of storage to store that value. Likewise if the column contained a data value that was 15 characters in length, then SQL Server would use 15 bytes to store that value.

Having designed our database, we now need to actually create it in SQL Server. The following example will take us through the steps required.

Try It Out – Creating the Development Database

1. To complete the steps listed in this section, you will first need to start the Enterprise Manager. (Start | Programs | Microsoft SQL Server 7.0 | Enterprise Manager) and expand the Databases folder under the SQL Server Group:

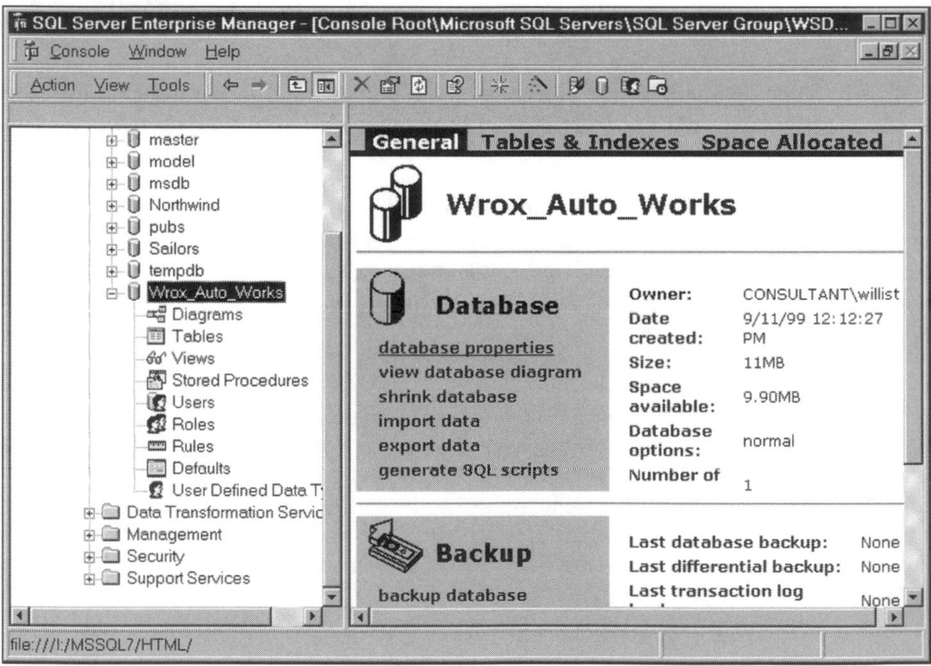

2. There are two ways to create our database. First, we can click on Databases, then from the Action menu select New Database, (or we can right click on the Databases group and choose New Database from the popup menu). The second method, which we are going to demonstrate here, is to use the Create Database Wizard.

   First, click on the Databases group, then click on the Tools menu and choose Wizards. A list of available wizards appears and we want to choose the Create Database Wizard from the Database group. Click OK to open the wizard:

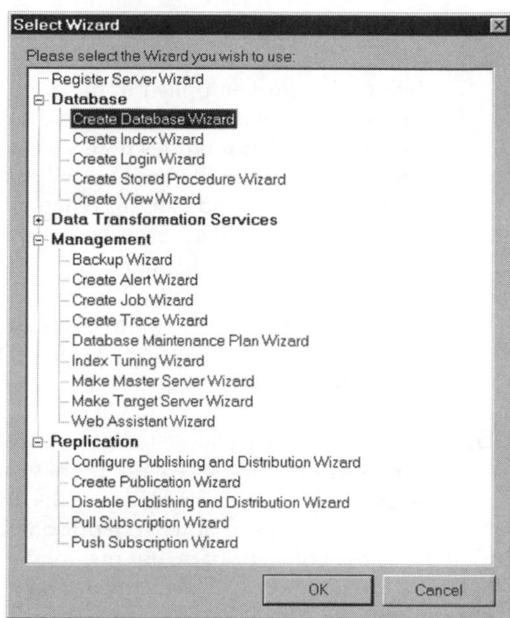

3. The first step of the wizard contains a welcome screen that details what the wizard can do for you. Click Next to proceed to the next step:

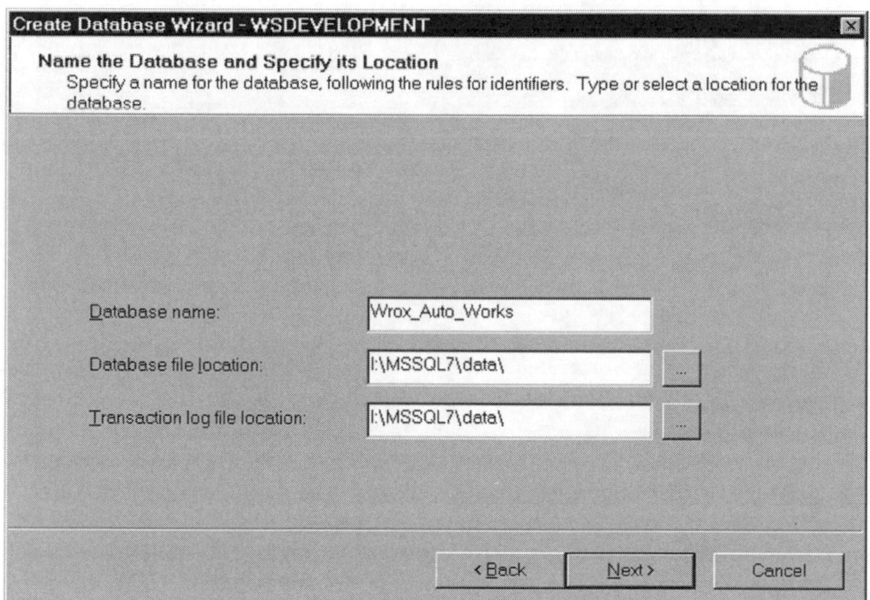

4. Enter the Database name as shown in the previous screenshot, and choose a directory that will contain the Database file and the Transaction log file. It is suggested that you use the default directory supplied in the dialog. SQL Server maintains all database and transaction log files in the same directory. As discussed in Chapter 1, every action performed against the database that modifies it gets logged in a file called a transaction log. The log information in this file can be used to recover the database in the event of a hardware failure or a corrupt database. When you have chosen the appropriate file locations, click Next to continue. SQL Server will append `_Data` on your database filename and `_Log` on your transaction log filename.

5. The next step prompts you to enter an initial size for the database. By default this value is set to 1 and can be overridden now or later. Enter a value of 10 and click the Next button to progress to the next step.

6. This is where we choose to automatically expand the database when needed. This is a wonderful feature, as we do not have to worry about running out of space in our database, or the complex administrative tasks involved in expanding a database. By default there is no restriction as to how large our database can be. This may be a concern if you do not have a lot of free space, but our total database shouldn't be more than 25 MB by the time we are finished. Click Next to accept the defaults and to continue:

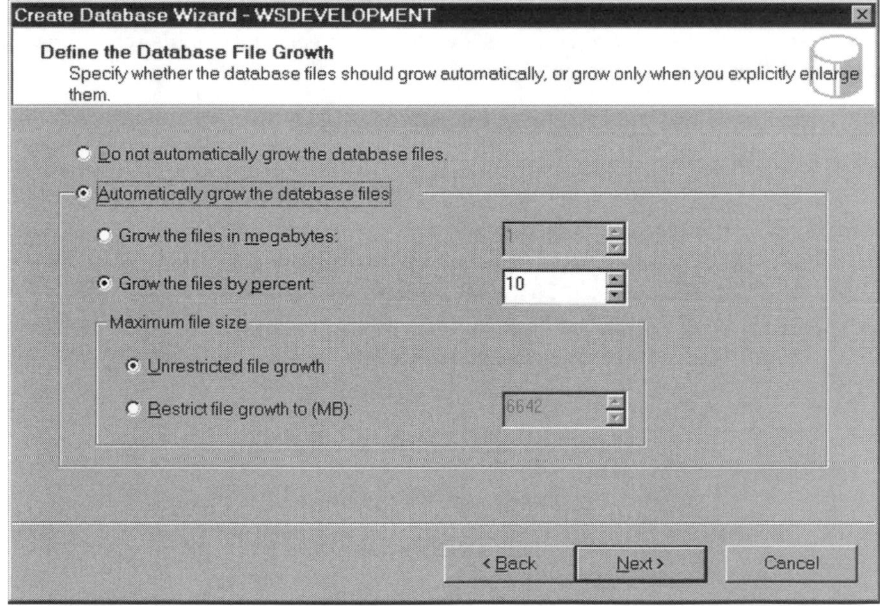

7. The next step specifies the initial size for our transaction log. We will accept the default size of 1 MB, so click the Next button to continue to the next step.

8. The next step defines how the transaction log will grow and is similar to the figure above. We will also accept the defaults on this screen, so click the Next button to continue on to the next step.

9. The last step summarizes the options you have chosen. If, after reviewing these options, you are not satisfied, you can click the Back button and change the appropriate option. Clicking the Finish button will create the database:

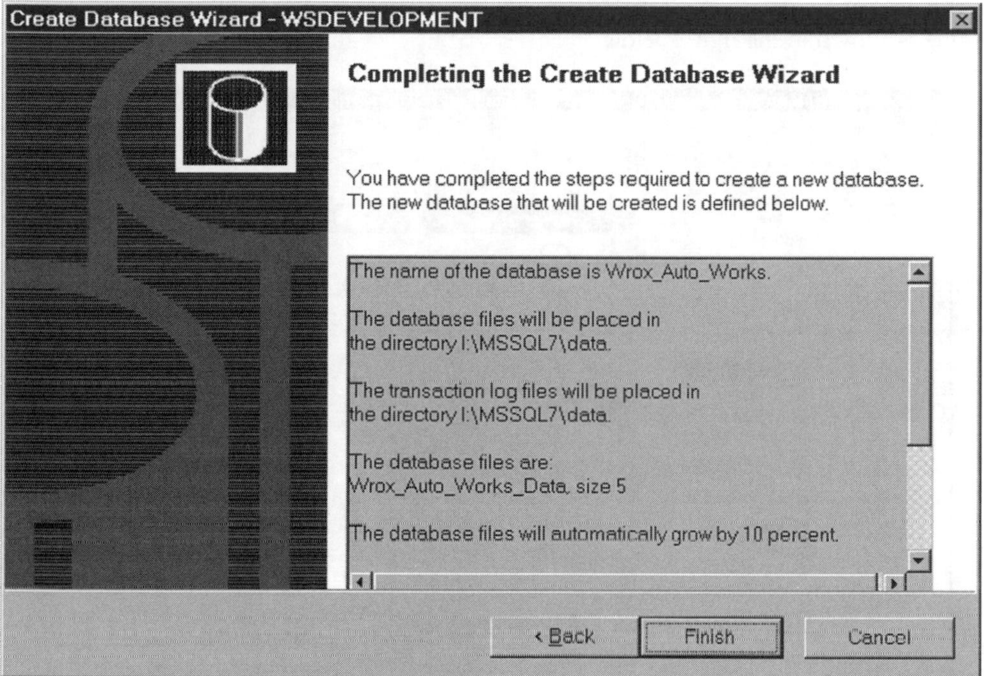

10. A message box is displayed, informing you that the database has been created. Click OK to accept the message.

11. A second message box appears asking if you want to create a database maintenance plan. We do not want to create a database maintenance plan at this time so click No. A database maintenance plan will be run on a regular basis and performs database integrity checks, updates statistics, and backs up your database.

The new database, Wrox_Auto_Works, now appears in the Enterprise Manager.

Wrox Auto Works Database View

Let's take a quick look at the different views in the database that we have just created. Start by clicking on the `Wrox_Auto_Works` database that we have just created, in the tree view, and then expand the database. You will see information about the database as a whole in the details pane on the right, as shown in the figure below:

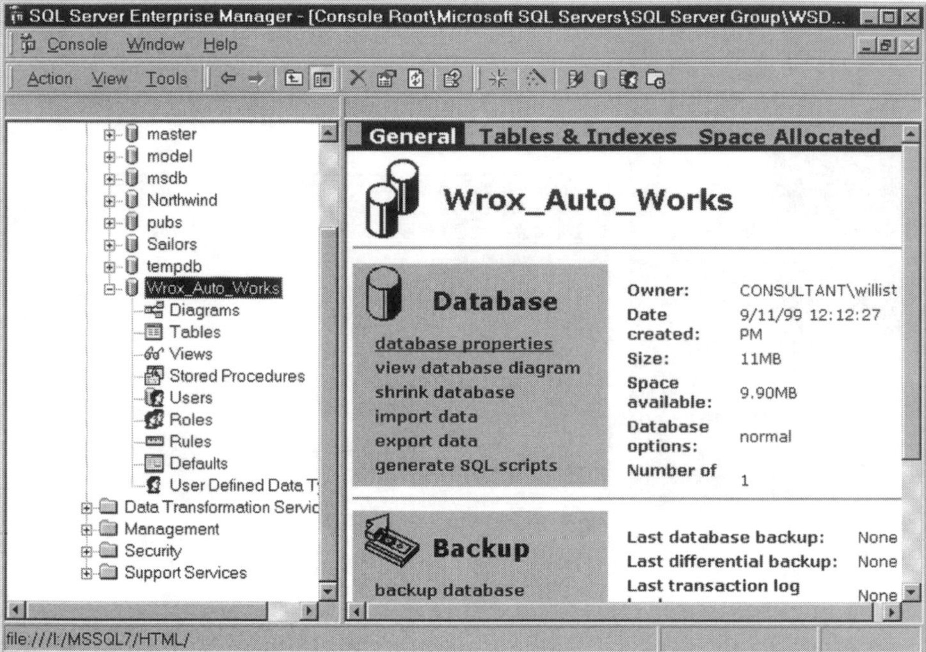

Notice that the information is contained as hyperlinks, and further information can be obtained by clicking on one of the hyperlinks.

Clicking on Diagrams in the tree pane does not show anything yet. We must build our complete database and then come back and generate a database diagram. A database diagram, similar to the diagram we used above to plan out our database, allows us to view, understand, and modify our database objects in a graphical view.

We will skip the Tables view for just a moment and will come back to it when we start creating our tables.

Clicking on Views will display a list of views that were generated when the database was built. Likewise, a list of stored procedures was also built when the database was created, and is shown when you click on Stored Procedures in the tree pane. We will be covering stored procedures starting in Chapter 7.

You can continue investigating, moving down the list of objects in our database. You can also right click on each object to see a menu list of options that can be performed on each one. We will be covering Users and Roles in the next chapter.

Creating the Tables

If you click on Tables, you will see that there are several tables already created. These are **system tables** that maintain information about your database. Taking a closer look at the table names, you can see how these tables relate to the information in your database. An example is the sysindexes table, which contains information about the indexes in your database.

Using Enterprise Manager you can quickly view data in a table, as shown below. Right clicking on a table pops up a menu giving you the options that you can perform on the highlighted table. To view data in the table, choose Open Table, and either choose Return all rows or Return Top. The first choice is obvious, as it returns all rows of data in the table. The Return Top menu option prompts you for how many rows it should display:

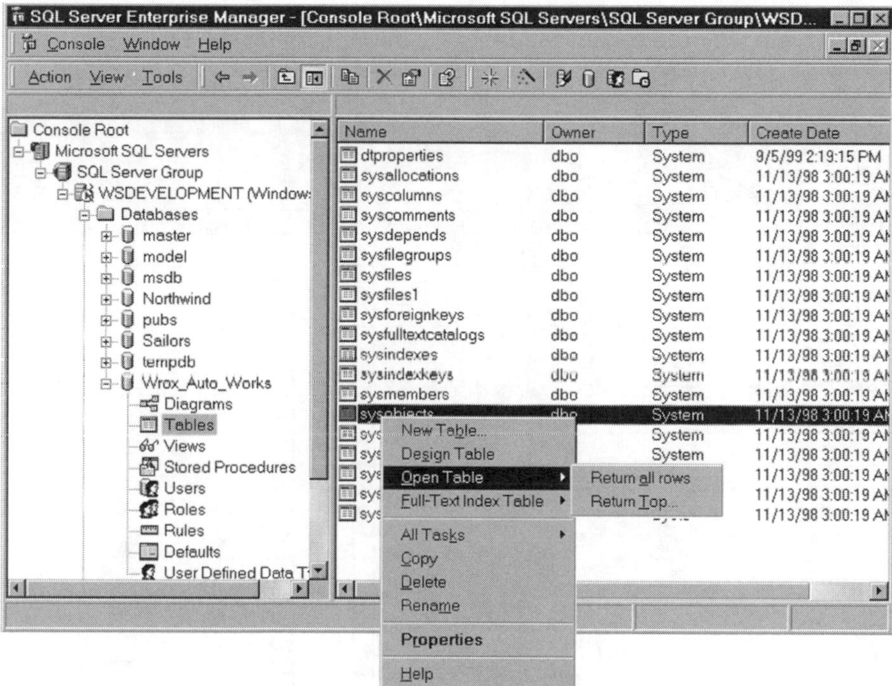

At the moment we only have system tables, but now we're going to start to create our own.

Try It Out – Creating a Table, Defining the Primary Key and Index

1. To start creating our tables, right click on Tables in the tree pane in the `Wrox_Auto_Works` database and choose New Table on the popup menu.

2. Enter `Customer_T` in the dialog that prompts you for a table name, then click OK. Table names are case sensitive in the way they are displayed, but not in the way they are accessed. In order words `Customer_T` is the same as `customer_t` when it comes to accessing this table.

3. The first column we want to add is `Customer_ID`, so type this in as the **Column Name**. This column is an `Integer` data type, so select **int** from the **Datatype** drop down list. The column should not allow null values so uncheck the **Allow Nulls** column. This will be an identity column so check the **Identity** checkbox. The **Identity Seed** should start at one and be incremented by one. An identity column is like a primary key, in that it uniquely identifies a row. SQL Server will automatically insert the next value in the identity column based on the seed and increment properties defined in the column. The **Length** column is the amount of storage that SQL Server will use to store the data value in a specific column. The columns for **Precision** and **Scale** are used for numeric data types such as `Integer` and `Decimal`. The **Precision** specifies the maximum number of digits in a number, while **Scale** specifies the number of digits to the right of the decimal point.

4. Since this is going to be our primary key, click on the **set primary key** icon on the toolbar.

5. Advance to the next column and complete the table using the details shown in the figure below:

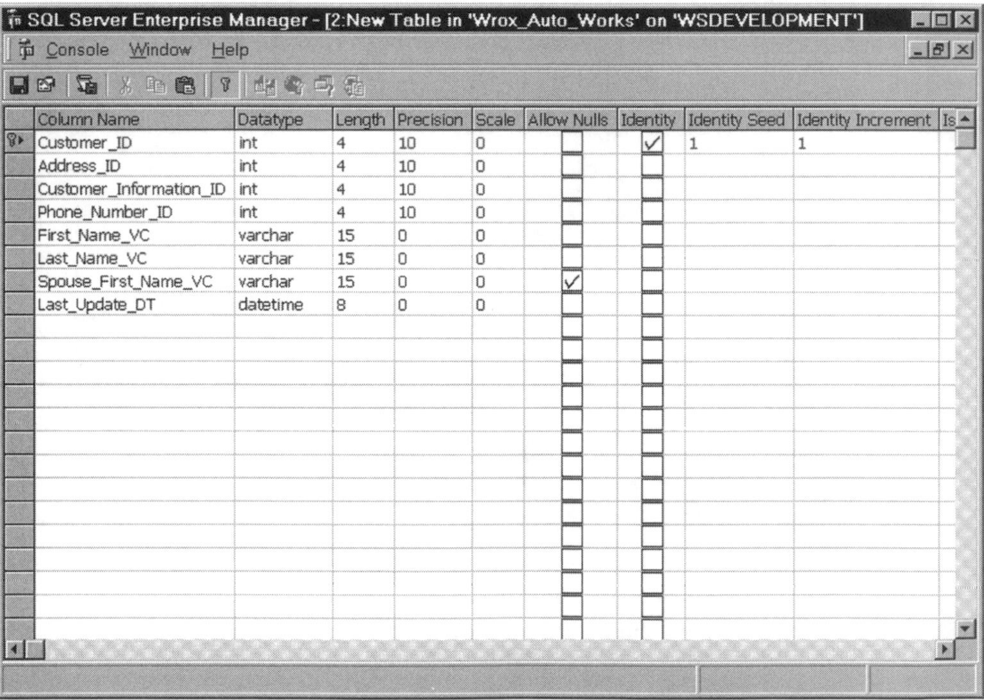

Column Name	Datatype	Length	Precision	Scale	Allow Nulls	Identity	Identity Seed	Identity Increment	Is
Customer_ID	int	4	10	0		✓	1	1	
Address_ID	int	4	10	0					
Customer_Information_ID	int	4	10	0					
Phone_Number_ID	int	4	10	0					
First_Name_VC	varchar	15	0	0					
Last_Name_VC	varchar	15	0	0					
Spouse_First_Name_VC	varchar	15	0	0	✓				
Last_Update_DT	datetime	8	0	0					

6. If you click on the **Table and Index Properties** icon on the toolbar and select the **Indexes/Keys** tab, you will see that SQL Server has already created an index for us using the primary key. We also want an index on the last name column in our table, to facilitate looking up customers by last name.

Click on the **New** button to start creating a new index. Most of the fields have already been filled in for us. Select **Last_Name_VC** in the **Column name** grid, and then check the **Create as CLUSTERED** checkbox at the bottom of the dialog. We do not want to create a unique index, as there could be duplicate last names. A clustered index is like a phone book, where all entries are ordered by last name. As we stated in Chapter 1, this enables us to quickly locate an entry in the database. Your new index should look like the one shown:

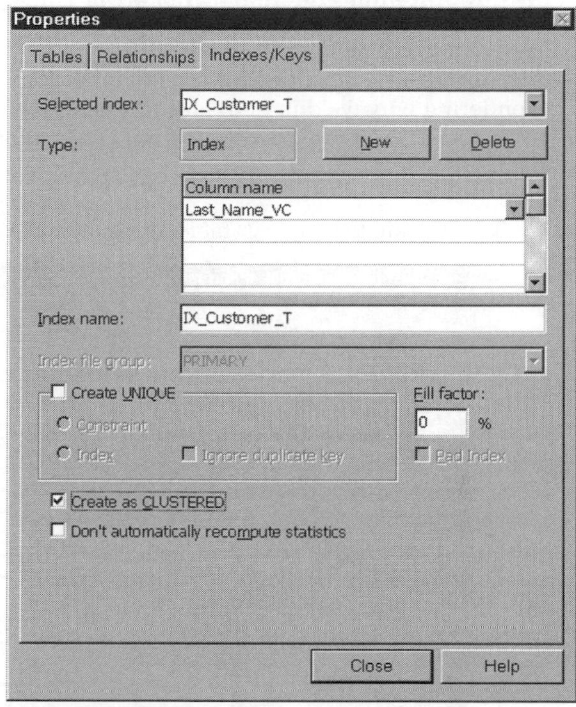

7. Click on the **Close** button in the dialog and then click on the **Save** icon on the toolbar. You will be prompted with a dialog asking if you want to save the script to a file – this is entirely up to you. Before you dismiss the dialog, scroll through the script and look at what has been generated, particularly the two indexes that were created. Script files can be used to create this table in another database. If you do not want to see this dialog in the future, uncheck the **Automatically generate change script on every save** checkbox.

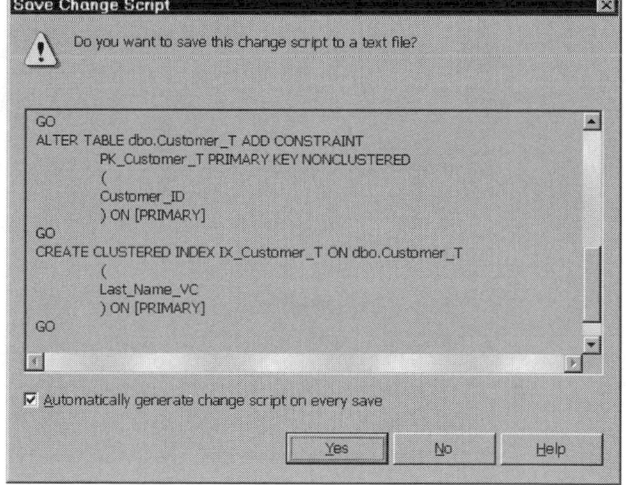

8. You can now close the table.

That's the first table done, but we still have seven more tables to set up. Now that you have done one, you can use the same process that you have just learned as you work through the following example.

Try It Out – Creating Additional Tables and Indexes

We want to create the rest of our tables and add additional indexes on two more tables: `City_T` and `Zip_Code_T`. This will help to facilitate the look ups of city names and zip codes. You might be wondering why we don't put an additional index on the `State_T` table also. Since there are only fifty states, this limited amount of data does not require an additional index to speed access to the data.

1. Create the `City_T` table using the table diagram shown below:

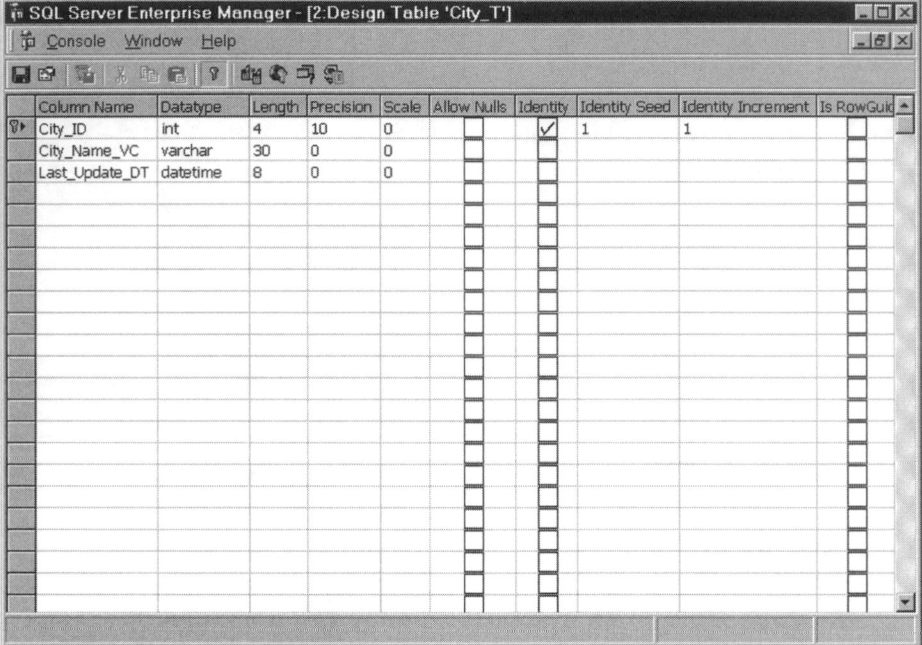

2. To create the additional index on `City_T`, right click on the `City_T` table and choose Design Table from the popup menu.

3. Click on the Table and Index Properties icon on the toolbar and click on the Indexes/Keys tab, if it is not already highlighted.

4. Click the New button to create a new index and select City_Name_VC in the Column name grid. We want this index to be *unique* and *clustered*, so check both of these options. Close the dialog, and save and close the table.

5. Create the `Zip_Code_T` table using the table diagram shown below:

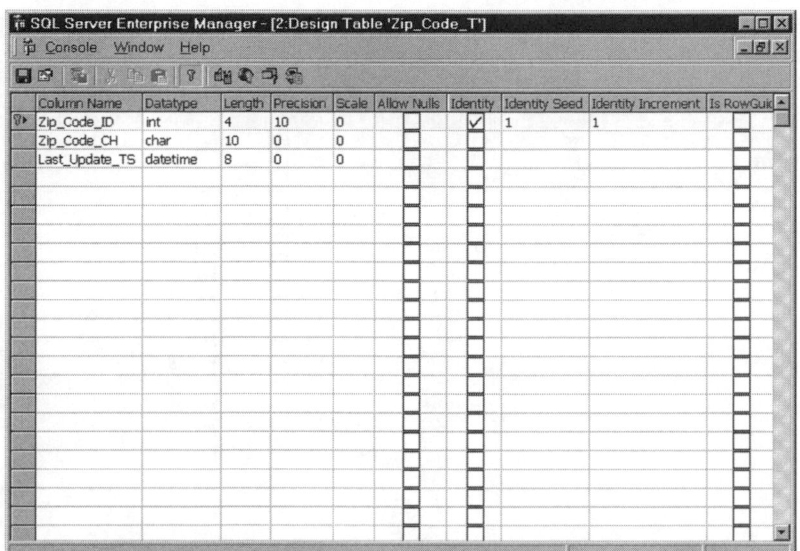

Column Name	Datatype	Length	Precision	Scale	Allow Nulls	Identity	Identity Seed	Identity Increment	Is RowGuid
Zip_Code_ID	int	4	10	0		✓	1	1	
Zip_Code_CH	char	10	0	0					
Last_Update_TS	datetime	8	0	0					

6. To create the additional index on `Zip_Code_T` follow the same steps as above. Select Zip_Code_CH in the Column name grid and choose a *unique* and *clustered* index. Close the dialog, and save and close the table.

7. Create the `Address_T` table using the table diagram shown below:

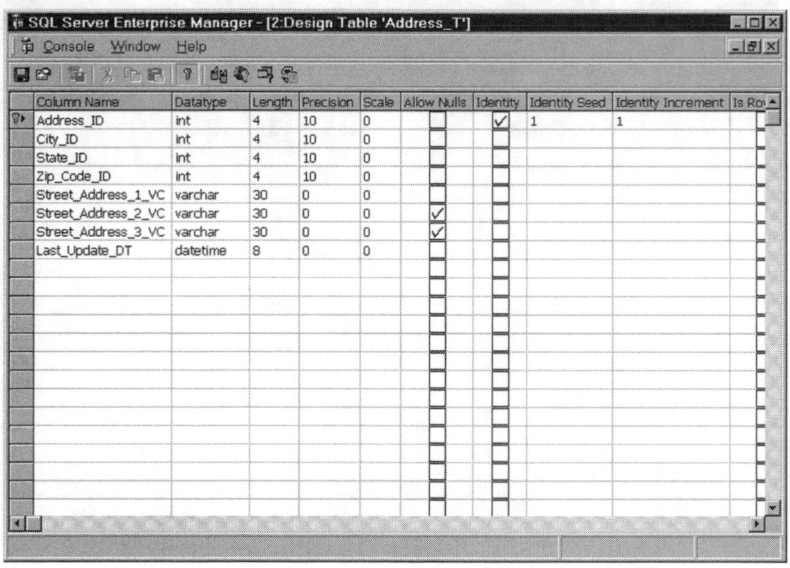

Column Name	Datatype	Length	Precision	Scale	Allow Nulls	Identity	Identity Seed	Identity Increment	Is Ro
Address_ID	int	4	10	0		✓	1	1	
City_ID	int	4	10	0					
State_ID	int	4	10	0					
Zip_Code_ID	int	4	10	0					
Street_Address_1_VC	varchar	30	0	0					
Street_Address_2_VC	varchar	30	0	0	✓				
Street_Address_3_VC	varchar	30	0	0	✓				
Last_Update_DT	datetime	8	0	0					

8. Now create the `Customer_Information_T` table using the table diagram shown below:

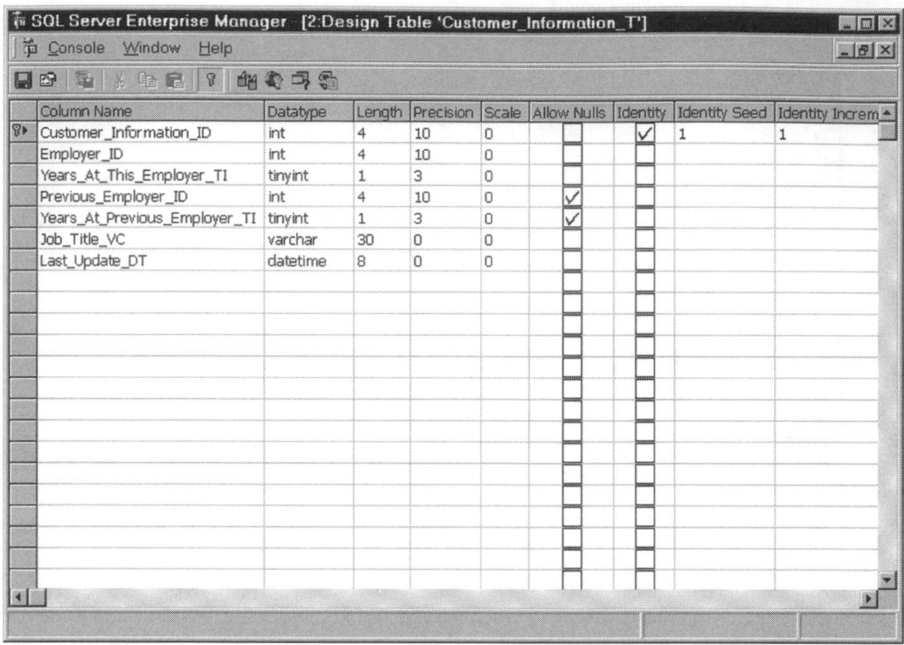

Column Name	Datatype	Length	Precision	Scale	Allow Nulls	Identity	Identity Seed	Identity Increm
Customer_Information_ID	int	4	10	0		✓	1	1
Employer_ID	int	4	10	0				
Years_At_This_Employer_TI	tinyint	1	3	0				
Previous_Employer_ID	int	4	10	0	✓			
Years_At_Previous_Employer_TI	tinyint	1	3	0	✓			
Job_Title_VC	varchar	30	0	0				
Last_Update_DT	datetime	8	0	0				

9. Then create the `Employer_T` table using the table diagram shown below:

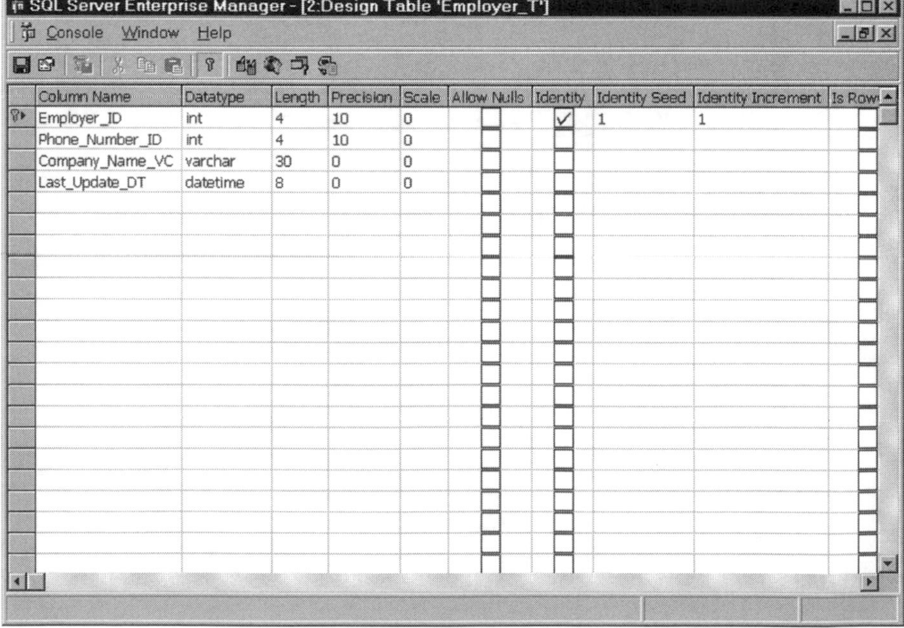

Column Name	Datatype	Length	Precision	Scale	Allow Nulls	Identity	Identity Seed	Identity Increment	Is Row
Employer_ID	int	4	10	0		✓	1	1	
Phone_Number_ID	int	4	10	0					
Company_Name_VC	varchar	30	0	0					
Last_Update_DT	datetime	8	0	0					

10. Create the `Phone_Number_T` table using the table diagram shown below:

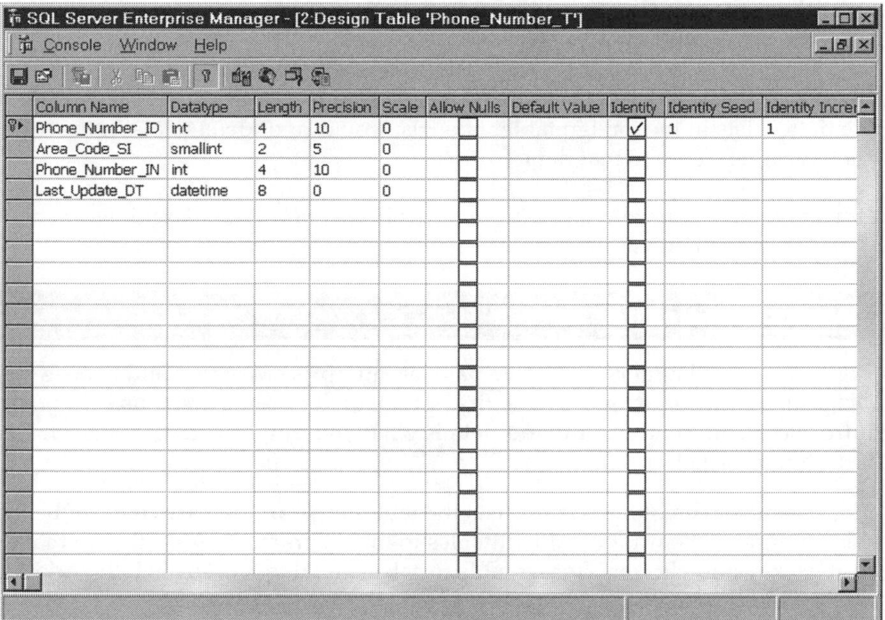

Column Name	Datatype	Length	Precision	Scale	Allow Nulls	Default Value	Identity	Identity Seed	Identity Incre
Phone_Number_ID	int	4	10	0	☐		✓	1	1
Area_Code_SI	smallint	2	5	0	☐		☐		
Phone_Number_IN	int	4	10	0	☐		☐		
Last_Update_DT	datetime	8	0	0	☐		☐		

11. Finally, create the `State_T` table using the table diagram shown below:

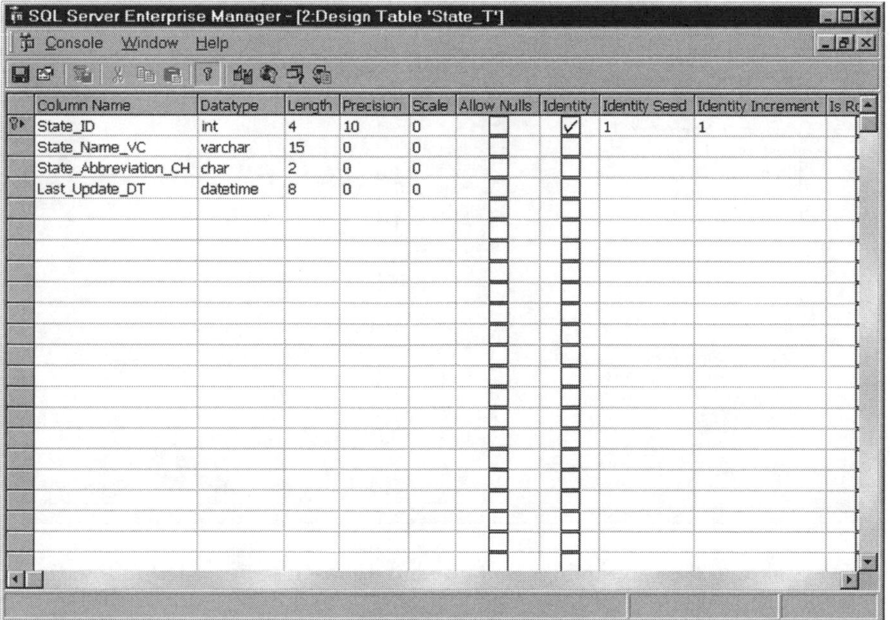

Column Name	Datatype	Length	Precision	Scale	Allow Nulls	Identity	Identity Seed	Identity Increment	Is R
State_ID	int	4	10	0	☐	✓	1	1	
State_Name_VC	varchar	15	0	0	☐	☐			
State_Abbreviation_CH	char	2	0	0	☐	☐			
Last_Update_DT	datetime	8	0	0	☐	☐			

Foreign Keys

While we were creating our tables, we defined the primary keys for each table. However, we also have foreign keys in these tables that refer to primary keys in other tables. This section will cover how to create those foreign keys.

A foreign key establishes a link between two tables and enforces that link by ensuring that the appropriate data exists in the foreign table. Likewise you cannot delete data in the foreign table as long as you have a reference to that data.

The easiest way to create our foreign key references is to create a database diagram and drag and drop our keys from one table to another.

Try It Out – Defining the Foreign Keys

1. Right click on Diagrams in the tree pane of Enterprise Manager and choose New Database Diagram on the popup menu. The first screen of the Create Database Diagram Wizard introduces you to the wizard and details what you can do with the wizard. Click the Next button to proceed.

2. The second screen of the wizard lists the tables in your database that can be included in your diagram. We want to add all tables to the diagram. Click on the first table, hold down the *Shift* key and click on the last table to select all tables. Then click the Add button. Click the Next button to proceed to the next step:

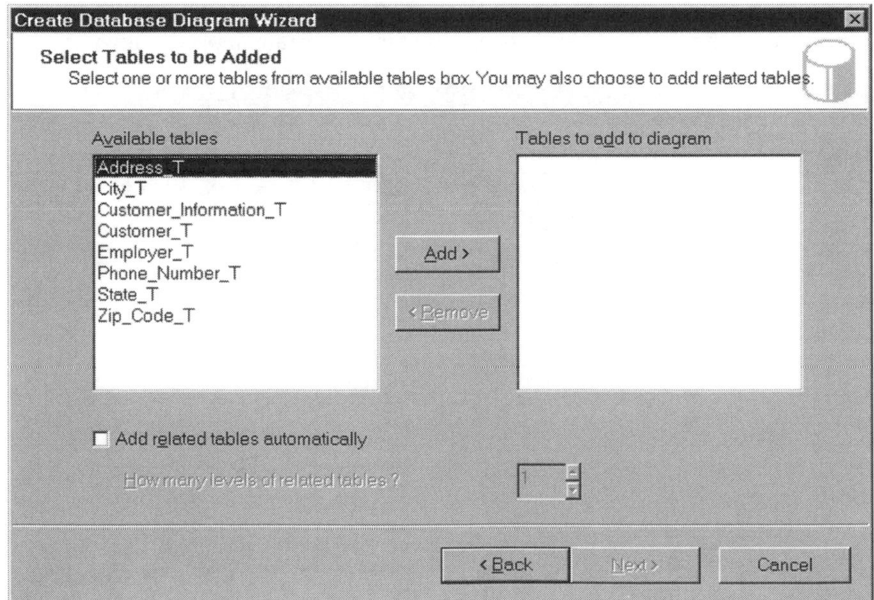

3. You are shown the list of tables that you have chosen to be added to the diagram. Click the Finish button to create the database diagram. Click the OK button on the dialog that informs you that the diagram has been created.

4. At this point the diagram looks small as all the tables are aligned in one row. If you cannot read the table names, zoom in a little until you can, using the Zoom icon on the toolbar. Arrange the tables in any fashion that you want. The layout shown below is only a suggestion:

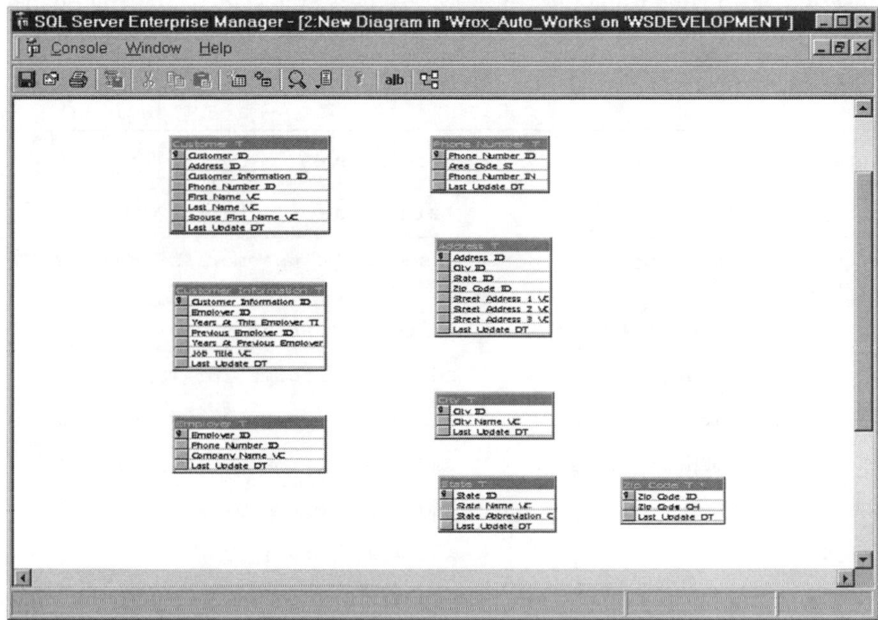

5. To create a foreign key reference, click to the left of the Address_ID column in the Customer_T table and drag it onto the Address_T table. Once the line connects to the Address_T table and you release the mouse, the Create Relationship dialog appears, as shown in the figure below:

Create Relationship

Relationship name:

FK_Customer_T_Address_T

Primary key table	Foreign key table
Address_T	Customer_T
Address_ID	Address_ID

Check existing data on creation

Enable relationship for INSERT and UPDATE

Enable relationship for replication

OK Cancel Help

6. The primary key table is listed on the left and the foreign key table is listed on the right. Ensure that the column names match and then click the OK button to dismiss the dialog. The Check existing data on creation checkbox applies the constraint to existing data. It will display an error message if any data violates the foreign key constraint. The Enable relationship for INSERT and UPDATE checkbox applies this constraint to data that is inserted or updated using the `INSERT` or `UPDATE` SQL statements. The Enable relationship for replication checkbox copies the constraint when the table is copied to another database.

7. Using the table below, create the rest of the foreign key references:

Primary Key Table_Name.Column_Name	Foreign Key Table_Name.Column-Name
Customer_Information_T.Customer_Information_ID	Customer_T.Customer_Information_ID
Phone_Number_T.Phone_Number_ID	Customer_T.Phone_Number_ID
Employer_T.Employer_ID	Customer_Information_T.Employer_ID
Employer_T.Employer_ID	Customer_Information_T.Previous_Employer_ID
Phone_Number_T.Phone_Number_ID	Employer_T.Phone_Number_ID
City_T.City_ID	Address_T.City_ID
State_T.State_ID	Address_T.State_ID
Zip_Code_T.Zip_Code_ID	Address_T.Zip_Code_ID

8. When you have completed making all of the foreign key references, save the diagram by clicking the Save icon on the toolbar. You will be prompted to enter a name for your diagram, so enter any name you wish, such as Wrox Diagram 1, and click OK. The next step will prompt you that the tables will be saved to your database; click the Yes button to finish the process.

Your completed diagram should look similar to the one opposite:

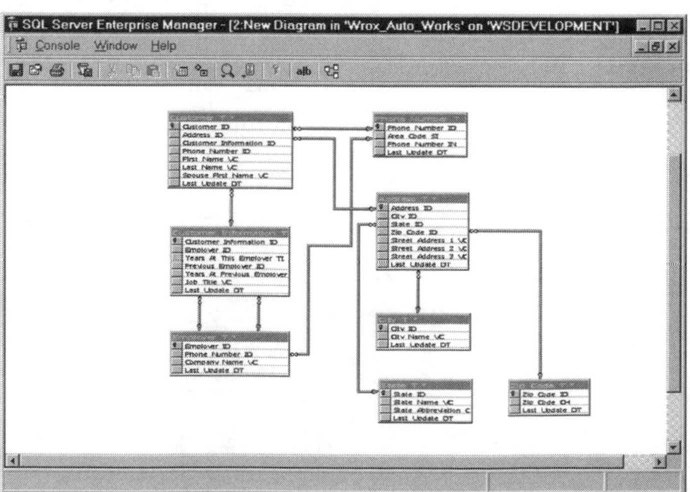

You can close the diagram and Enterprise Manager. That completes the initial setting up of the Wrox_Auto_Works database, although it doesn't have any data in it just yet.

Summary

This chapter has covered the benefits of using naming standards for the various database objects. We looked at a suggested standard, which we'll be using throughout the examples in this book. Having created some tables, columns, primary keys and foreign keys, you can see how important the standards can be. This will become more evident as we progress through the book and start writing stored procedures. You will be able to tell at a quick glance what action a stored procedure is performing just by its name, because of the use of a naming standard and descriptive name.

We have covered just about every major aspect of the SQL Server Enterprise Manager and you should now feel comfortable working with this user interface. Some of the wizards were used to create the database and diagram, and you should have a feel for how the wizards work. As you can see, the wizards perform a lot of the more complex tasks for you and allow you to concentrate on getting the job done without the worry of what is going on behind the scenes.

In summary, you should:

- Understand the importance of naming standards
- Understand the difference between primary and foreign keys
- Know how to create a database and tables
- Know how to create additional indexes
- Know how to define the foreign key relationships

At this point all of our tables, indexes, and primary and foreign keys have been created. The next logical step would be to set up security on our database so developers can access it. The next chapter discusses the issues regarding security, and steps you through creating a user and the permissions that the user should have.

WROX AUTO WORKS RACING

SQL Server Security

You can't pick up a newspaper or technical magazine these days without reading something about **security** and hackers. Security is on everyone's mind, from the developer to senior management. Keeping your data secure and out of the wrong hands helps to keep your business competitive.

This chapter focuses on another feature of SQL Server – security. We will discuss the types of users that you can set up in SQL Server and the roles they play in accessing your database. We will also discuss the various levels of security you can set for your database objects.

Our development database is currently secure in the fact that only the database administrator (that is you) has access to it. We will step through some practical exercises in adding new users to our database. These users will have various levels of authority.

In this chapter we will:

- Discuss general security issues
- Add new logins to SQL Server
- Add new users to our database
- Define roles and assign them to users
- Discuss database object security
- Apply different security levels to our objects

General Security Overview

Security is not just meant to protect your data from hackers or unauthorized personnel. It is also used to protect your data from *authorized* users. For example, you may have a user who you want to be able to read your data but not update it. Perhaps they are not knowledgeable enough to insert and update the data, but need to read the data to perform their job. Granting a user read-only access prevents them from accidentally deleting important data, or corrupting the data by using an `UPDATE` statement that updates the wrong row of data.

SQL Server provides two levels of security. First there is **authentication**, which simply means you have been assigned a user ID and password which allows you to log on. This first level allows *viewing* of available objects and data; but you cannot *create* objects or *edit* data. You cannot actually do anything until the second level of security has been provided.

This second level of security grants you various levels of **access** to one or more databases and their objects. Database administrators or the user who has permission to create databases will always have full access to these schema objects.

Authentication

Let's look at authentication first. SQL Server provides two modes of authentication. First, SQL Server can be configured to only provide **Windows NT authentication (Trusted Security)**, where SQL Server will use your Windows NT user account information to allow you access to SQL Server. SQL Server has to be running on a Windows NT or Windows 2000 machine for this feature to be enabled.

The second mode of authentication is called a **Mixed Mode**. This is where SQL Server will allow either Windows NT authentication (as above) or **SQL Server authentication** to be used. SQL Server authentication performs the verification itself, by checking to see that a SQL Server login account has been set up, and that the user ID and password you are supplying match those assigned by the database administrator. SQL Server authentication is not part of Windows NT/2000 security, thus it does not use Windows NT/2000 user accounts or groups. This process is summarized in the following diagram:

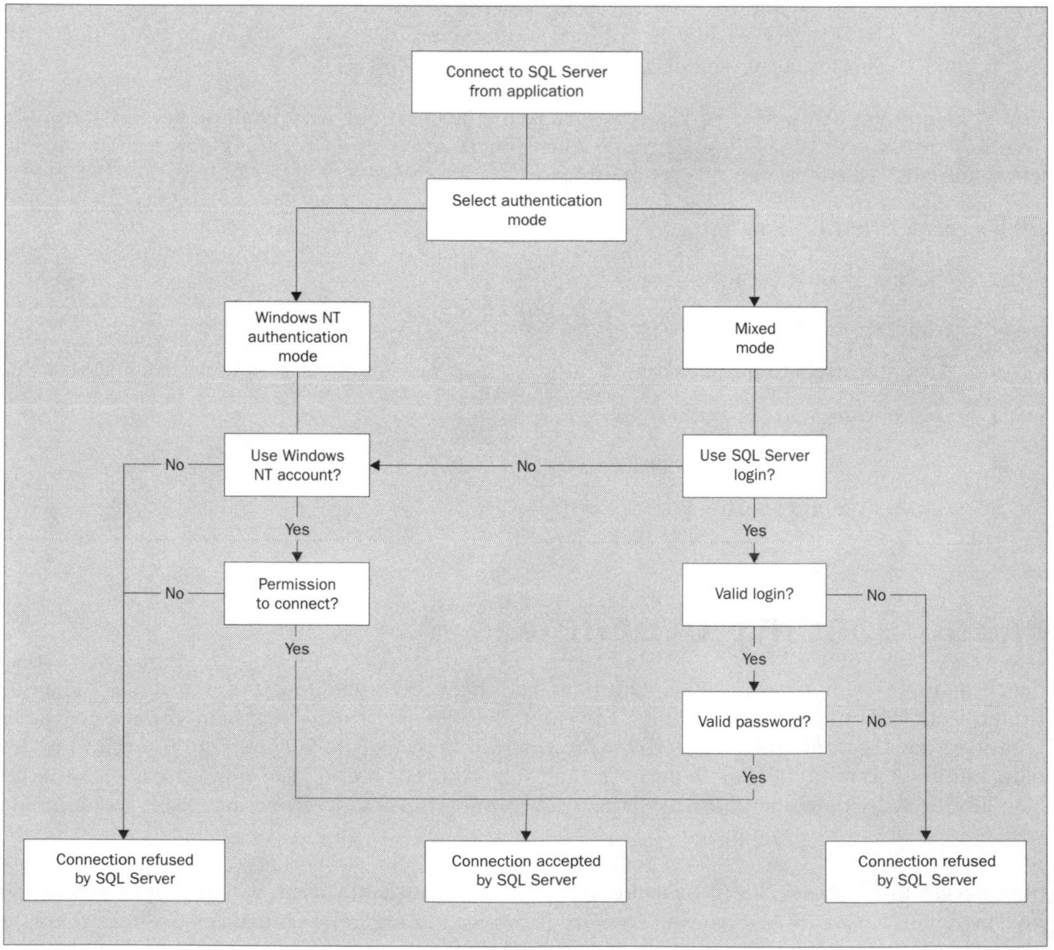

Before SQL Server 7.0 there was another security option, Standard Security, which used only SQL Server authentication. SQL Server authentication is needed for backwards compatibility with applications written for earlier versions of SQL Server and for SQL Server running on Windows 95/98. If you want to run things as you did with Standard Security there is still the Mixed Mode option – it's just that you also have to leave NT security as an option.

SQL Server installed on Windows 9x platforms will not support Windows NT authentication so you must use SQL Server authentication.

SQL Server Authentication Versus NT Authentication

As we mentioned above, SQL Server provides two modes of authentication – SQL Server and Windows NT. This section will explore the differences between these two modes and it will be up to you to decide which is best for your situation.

SQL Server Authentication

SQL Server authentication utilizes user accounts defined in SQL Server itself. The database administrator defines users and the databases they can access. The user can be assigned to a **role** that has the appropriate permissions for the job that the user is expected to perform. Roles reduce the maintenance of object permissions because there are usually more users than there are roles. Also, another user can be temporarily assigned to a role to perform the duties of a user who has taken a leave of absence.

User IDs and passwords defined in SQL Server operate independently to those of the operating system. The user logs onto the operating system using one user ID and password, and then to gain access to SQL Server they must enter another user ID and password – one that is defined in SQL Server.

SQL Server authentication also allows one user ID and password to be defined for a group of users. All users of that group can then use the same user ID and password to gain access to SQL Server. This is not recommended, but can be a time saver for small non-mission critical applications. Note also that this is not valid for distributed applications using MTS/COM, as they use Database Connection Pooling. This is, however, beyond the scope of this discussion.

Windows NT Authentication

Using Windows NT authentication, SQL Server validates that the Windows NT user account and password are valid and that the user has already logged onto the network; there is no need for a separate login ID and password to gain access to SQL Server.

There are some major benefits gained by using Windows NT authentication over SQL Server authentication. First, passwords are **secure** and are **encrypted.** Passwords are unreadable using both NT authentication and SQL Server authentication. The passwords are displayed in a field as asterisks and cannot be read by the administrator. Encrypted passwords are stored as an encrypted key and not the actual password itself. Both Windows NT/2000 and SQL Server encrypt passwords.

Password **expiration** is another feature of Windows NT/2000, and is where your password can be set to automatically expire after x number of days. Passwords are normally expired automatically after 30 days and you are prompted to enter a new password at that time. Different security measures can be set in Windows NT/2000 so that a history of x number of passwords is kept to prevent a user from using the same password over and over.

Windows NT/2000 also provides **account lockout** after x number of unsuccessful attempts to sign on, and accounts can be **audited**. When auditing is turned on in Windows NT/2000, user accounts can be audited to see what actions the user account has performed. Auditing can also expose potential security threats from a user account that repeatedly tries to access data or resources for which they do not have authorization. However, if a user leaves their machine unlocked, another employee could still access critical data. When auditing is turned on for user accounts, you can select the types of audit actions that are to be logged, such as failed logon attempts and attempts to access sensitive data.

These benefits are possible because SQL Server is tightly integrated with the Windows NT/2000 operating systems and uses the security services of Windows NT/2000.

Access to Database Objects

The second level of security allows access to the various database objects. In Chapter 1 we said that a database consists of multiple objects, such as tables, views, triggers, stored procedures and the like. Each of these objects implements security, which can be at the user level or the role level.

User level security is where we specify which objects an *individual user* can access. For example, if we granted a user permission to select data from the `Customer_T` table, it wouldn't automatically give them access to the `Customer_Information_T` table. We would need to set up that security separately.

Role level security can be thought of as a collection of permissions that can be assigned to a user or a group of users en masse. The user who created the database grants the role access to one or more database objects, such as tables or stored procedures. When a user is added to the role, they automatically have the appropriate permissions that have been granted to that role.

Suppose you have a very large financial database that contains your payroll tables and tables containing your retirement data. You could grant access to the payroll tables to one role, so that users assigned to that role could enter data into those tables, but not grant that role access to the retirement tables.

We have taken a general look at the security features provided by SQL Server. The following sections in this chapter should help to tie all of this information together. By the time you reach the end of this chapter you should fully understand how SQL Server implements security.

Adding New Users to SQL Server

The time has come to add new users to our database. Although this can be done at any stage, and does not have to be completed before we start adding data, we need to think about security before we design the database. This is because we might need to put some data into a separate table if it contains sensitive material.

If you are running on a Windows NT 4.0 or Windows 2000 Professional workstation you can add your user ID to SQL Server using Windows NT authentication. If you are running on a Windows 9x platform you *must* use SQL Server authentication. We will demonstrate both methods here to cover all readers.

Users are added to SQL Server as **logins** and then are added to the database as **users**. Therefore you must first create a login ID in SQL Server. We do this by navigating to the Security group in the Enterprise Manager and expanding that group. From here you add new logins to SQL Server using either Windows NT authentication or SQL Server authentication. At this point we are adding users to SQL Server, but the user will not have access to the database or any permissions, as we will be adding those rights later.

Try It Out – Add a New Login

You are going to add yourself as a new login to SQL Server. If you are running SQL Server on a Windows 9x platform you must use SQL Server authentication, otherwise use Windows NT authentication. After we have finished, you will see an entry in the Logins folder, similar to that shown below:

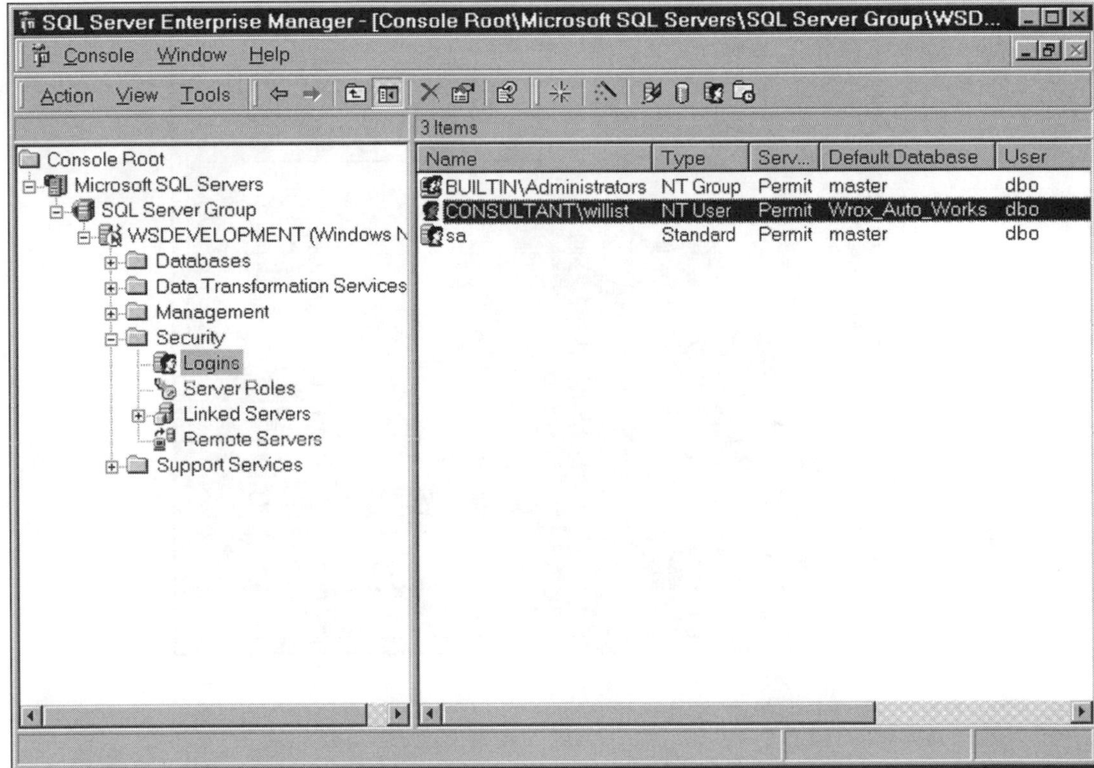

1. Open the SQL Server Enterprise Manager and expand the Security node under the SQL Server you wish to use. There are two methods for creating a new login. Firstly, we can right click on Logins in the tree view and choose New Login from the popup menu. The alternative is to click on Logins in the tree pane, then right click on Logins in the details pane on the right, and choose New Login from the popup menu there. The New Login window will appear, and we want to use the General tab.

2. This is where we split, depending on the Windows platform being used. Windows NT/2000 users will fill in their details as shown below, to use Windows NT authentication.

   The first step is to supply your user ID in the Name field and then select your Domain. The default Database that we want to use is Wrox_Auto_Works and we want to use the Default Language. A login can have access to more than one database, but there must be one default database assigned to a login. We are not going to assign any server roles or database access at this point, so once you have entered all the details, click OK to dismiss the dialog and have your user ID added to SQL Server:

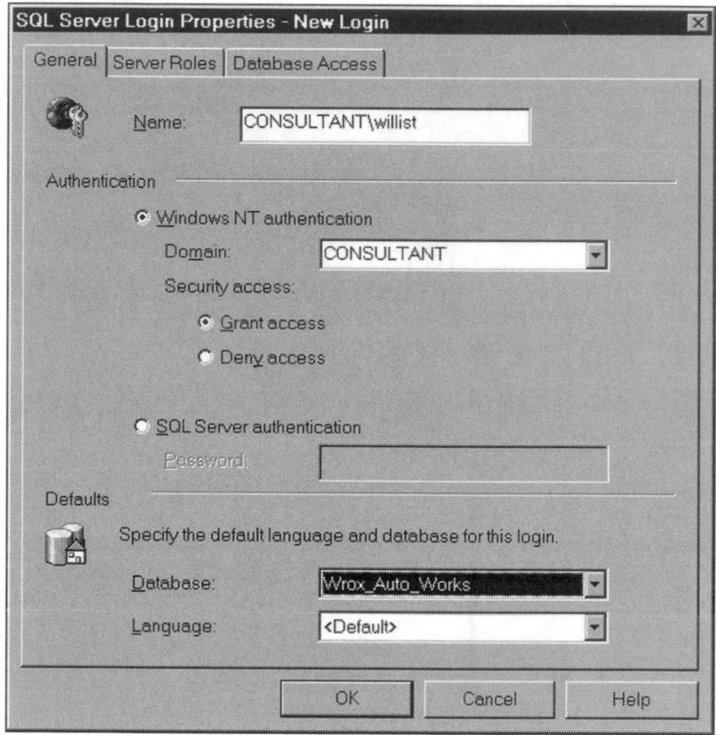

The Grant access and Deny access option buttons are used to control access for users who are defined with Windows NT authentication. This allows us to change their access at any time. Suppose you have a person who is out on leave; you can deny permission on their Login and no one can use their Login while they are out.

3. The next dialog just informs you that you have selected a specific database and the login will have access to that database, so click OK:

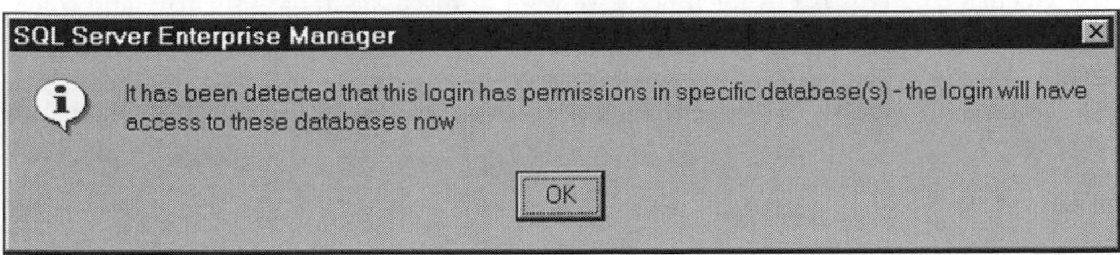

4. Windows 9x users will fill in their details in the dialog as shown below (replacing the name and password with your own details).

   We need to supply a login Name which can be the same as the one that you use to login to Windows, or you can choose a totally different login name. We also need to supply a Password. The default Database that we want to use is Wrox_Auto_Works and we want to use the Default Language. We are not going to assign any server roles or database access at this point, so click OK to dismiss the dialog and have your user ID added to SQL Server.

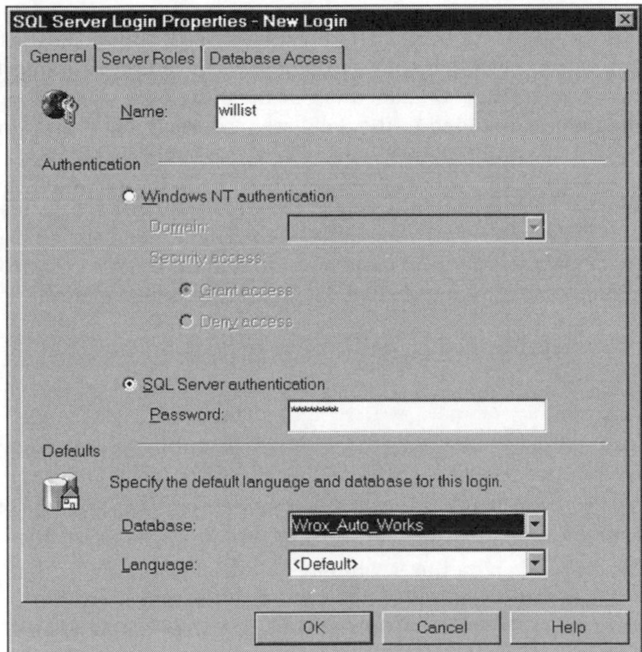

5. The next dialog that you will see asks you to confirm the password that you have entered, so type it in again and click OK. Passwords are case sensitive in SQL Server, just as they are in Windows. SQL Server allows passwords to be from 1 to 128 characters including letters, symbols, and digits.

6. For both Windows 9x and NT/2000 Professional the following warning is displayed, since we did not grant this user access to the Wrox_Auto_Works database in the Database Access tab. This is OK for now as we want to discuss database security and roles before we grant users access to our database. Click Yes to accept the warning:

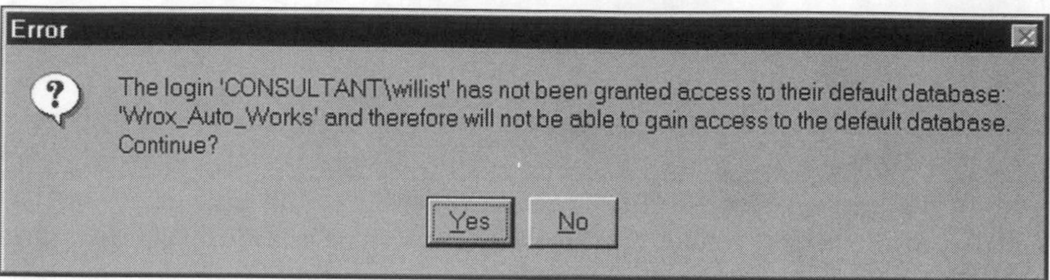

We will forego adding the rest of our users until we have defined the user roles in our database, which will be discussed shortly.

Database Security

Remember that, just because we have added a new user to SQL Server and set their default database to Wrox_Auto_Works, doesn't mean that they automatically have access to our database, as is evident from the message above. Users must be added to our database once their login has been added to SQL Server. Similarly, when a user is added to the database, it doesn't necessarily mean that they will be able to access any data.

SQL Server implements security at the *object level.* That is, SQL Server controls the security level for each individual object. This means that each table, view, trigger, and stored procedure that we define is secure. We can grant a user access to one table but not to another. We can also grant a user SELECT permissions to one table while granting them INSERT permissions to another.

Roles are one of the features provided by SQL Server to help us manage our database security, and we will be discussing them next.

Roles

Before we add new users to our database, we should first define the **roles** that the users will perform. You can think of a role as a job function. You, as a developer, have certain access rights to the database to perform your job. Likewise, an end-user will have a subset of the rights that you have to perform their jobs, and management will have a subset of the rights that the end-user has to perform their jobs. This section will cover the SQL Server **system-defined roles** and **user-defined roles**. We will take you through the steps to create user-defined roles in our development database, after we have determined what rights each group of users should have.

System Defined Roles

Before we jump into user defined roles, let's take a look at what roles SQL Server has provided. In the Enterprise Manager window, expand your SQL Server and then expand the Security group. Click on Server Roles and look at the information provided on the right side of the window.

Each system-defined role has a **full name**, a **short name**, and a **description**. Take a quick look at the descriptions and you can see how these roles could be used to assign different tasks to different users:

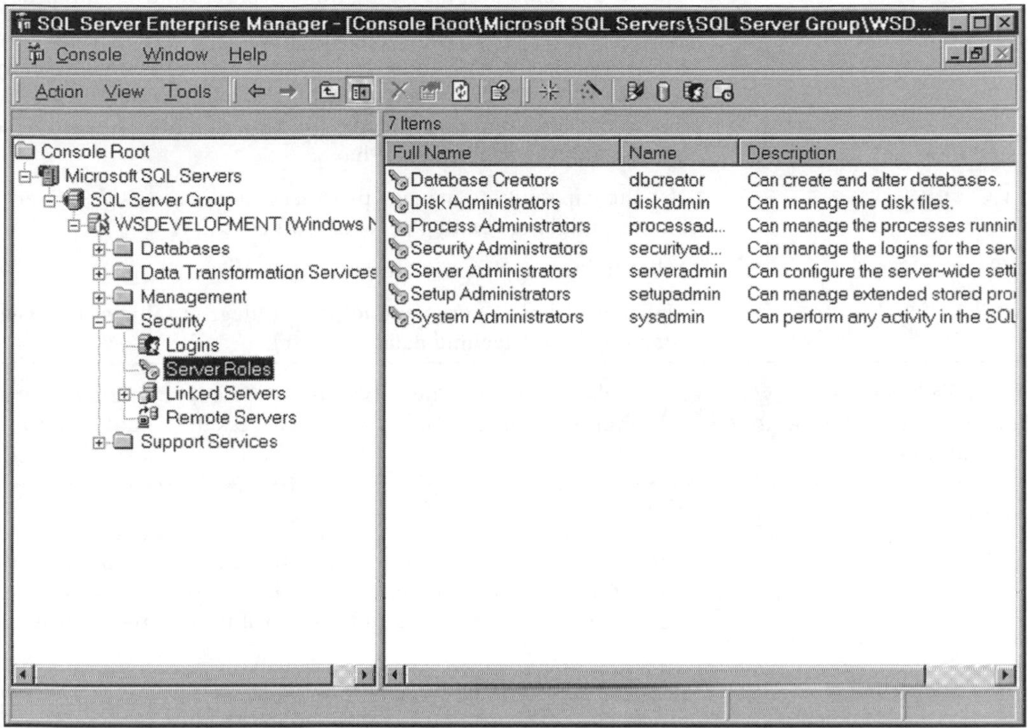

Let's look at these in more detail:

Role	Nature
`sysadmin`	This role can perform any activity on your SQL Server. Anyone with this role is essentially a system administrator (`sa`) for that server. The creation of this server role provides Microsoft with the capability to one day eliminate the `sa` login – indeed, the Books Online refers to `sa` as being legacy in nature. It's worth noting that the NT `Administrators` group on the SQL Server is automatically mapped into the `sysadmin` role. This means that anyone who is a member of your server's administrators group also has `sa`-level access to your SQL Server data. You can, if you need to, remove the NT administrators group from the `sysadmin` role to tighten that security loophole.
`serveradmin`	This one can set server-wide configuration options or shut down the server. It's rather limited in scope, yet the functions controlled by members of this role can have a very significant impact on the performance of your server.

Role	Nature
setupadmin	This one is limited to managing linked servers and startup procedures.
securityadmin	This one is very handy for logins that you create specifically to manage logins, read error logs, and create database permissions. In many ways, this one is the classic system operator role – it can handle most of the day-to-day stuff, but doesn't have the kind of global access that a true omnipotent super-user would have.
processadmin	Has the capability to manage processes running in SQL Server – this one can kill long running processes if necessary.
dbcreator	Is limited to creating and altering databases.
diskadmin	Manages disk files (for example, which filegroup things are assigned to, attaching and detaching databases, etc).

Just as we have fixed server roles, each database has its own fixed roles. By expanding the relevant database (under the Databases group) and clicking on Roles, we can access these. Let us now examine these in detail:

Role	Nature
db_owner	This role performs as if it were a member of all the other database roles. Using this role, you can create a situation where multiple users can perform the same functions and tasks as if they were the database owner.
db_accessadmin	Performs a portion of the functions similar to the securityadmin server role, except this role is limited to the individual database where it is assigned and the creation of users (not individual rights). It cannot create new SQL Server logins, but members of this role can add NT users and groups, as well as existing SQL Server logins, into the database.
db_datareader	Can issue a SELECT statement on all user tables in the database.
db_datawriter	Can issue INSERT, UPDATE, and DELETE statements on all user tables in the database.
db_ddladmin	Can add, modify, or drop objects in the database.
db_securityadmin	The other part of the database-level equivalent of the securityadmin server role. This database role cannot create new users in the database, but does manage roles and members of database roles as well as managing statement and object permissions in the database.
db_backupoperator	Backs up the database.
db_denydatareader	Provides the equivalent of a DENY SELECT on every table and view in the database.
db_denydatawriter	Similar to db_denydatareader, only it affects INSERT, UPDATE, and DELETE statements.

However, since these roles are for administrative tasks only, we need to bypass using them for now and create our own user-defined roles.

User-Defined Roles

User-defined roles can be broken down into two types. First there is the **standard** role in which we can add users, which is what we have discussed thus far. Note that all of these are limited in scope to the specific database defined for them; all of the server roles are fixed, and cannot therefore be user-defined.

The second type of user-defined role is an **application** role. This is where users can only access the database through an application, and the application must provide a password that we have chosen. This prevents direct user interaction, and the only information they can retrieve or update is what has been specified in the code of the application. As you can see, this is a secure method of controlling the integrity of the data, as long as you have a well-written application. You do not specify users in an application role, because any user that has access to the application will have access to the database. Security with your application becomes really important at this point if your application accesses sensitive information or updates information to the database.

We will not look at application roles in this book; the standard roles into which we will add users provide all the functionality we need. If you need to create and use application roles, a more in depth discussion can be found in *Professional SQL Server 7.0 Programming* (ISBN 1-861002-31-9) from Wrox Press.

In the last chapter we introduced our fictitious car company, Wrox Auto Works, and designed and built our database based on that. Now we want to add users and roles based on the various levels of this company.

The first group of users is the *Developers*. This group of users should have complete access to the database, as they are the ones who will be maintaining the database objects.

The second group of users we want to add is the *Sales Staff*. They will be the users who are responsible for inserting, updating, and deleting data in our database, as they deal with the customers. This group of users will need the appropriate permissions to perform their jobs.

The last group of users we want to add is *Management*. Managers are not familiar with the details of the job that the sales staff perform, and really only want data that can produce reports and graphs to tell them how well their business is performing. We will need to give this type of user read only access, by granting them `SELECT` permissions.

Now that we have identified the various roles of the users, we can add these roles to our database. Expand the `Wrox_Auto_Works` database in the Databases group within Enterprise Manager. If you click on Roles in the tree view you will notice that a set of default roles has already been defined for us. While we could use some of these roles in our car company, it would negate the purpose of this section. We have discussed the details of these roles earlier in this chapter.

Try It Out – Adding a New Role

We want to add three roles based on our discussion above. We will not set any permissions for these roles until we have had a chance to discuss security on the various database objects. We will create three roles named Developers, Sales Staff, and Management, as shown:

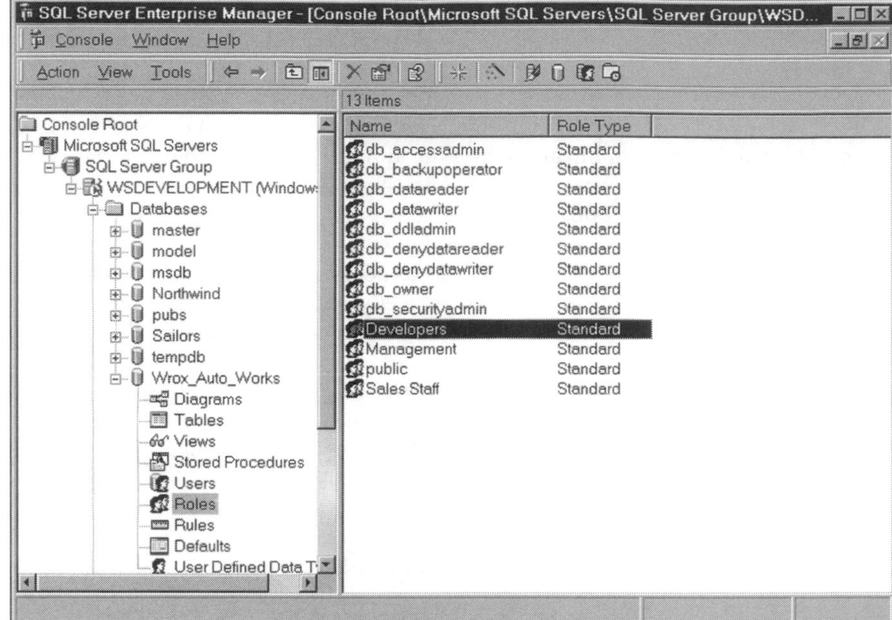

1. To create a role, either right click on Roles in the tree view and choose New Database Role in the popup menu, or select Roles and then right click in the detail view and choose the same option in the popup menu. The New Role window will appear:

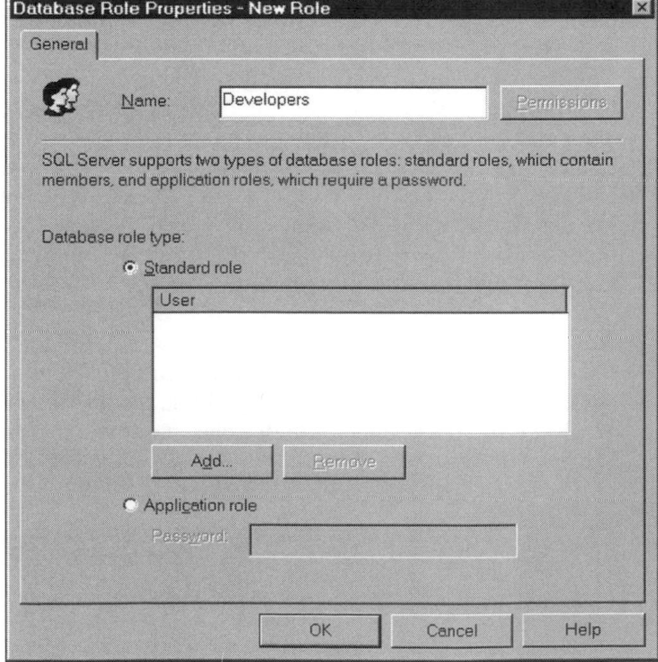

2. Notice that at this point you can select which type of role you want to create. The Standard role is checked by default. We can also add users at this point but will forego that for a moment. Enter the Name of the role (Developers) and click OK to dismiss the dialog.

3. Repeat this process and add the Sales Staff and Management roles.

Adding New Users to a Database

Now that we have a login defined in SQL Server and have the roles defined in our database, we are ready to add a user to our database. Remember that just because we added a login to SQL Server, it doesn't automatically add them to our database. We want to eventually add a test user for each of the roles that we have defined. We as developers have already defined our login, and we will soon define a login for both the Sales Staff and the Management roles. First we will show how to add a user to a database.

Try It Out – Adding New Users to a Database

You will be adding your login to the `Wrox_Auto_Works` database and placing yourself in the Developers role. The outcome of this will be something like the screen below:

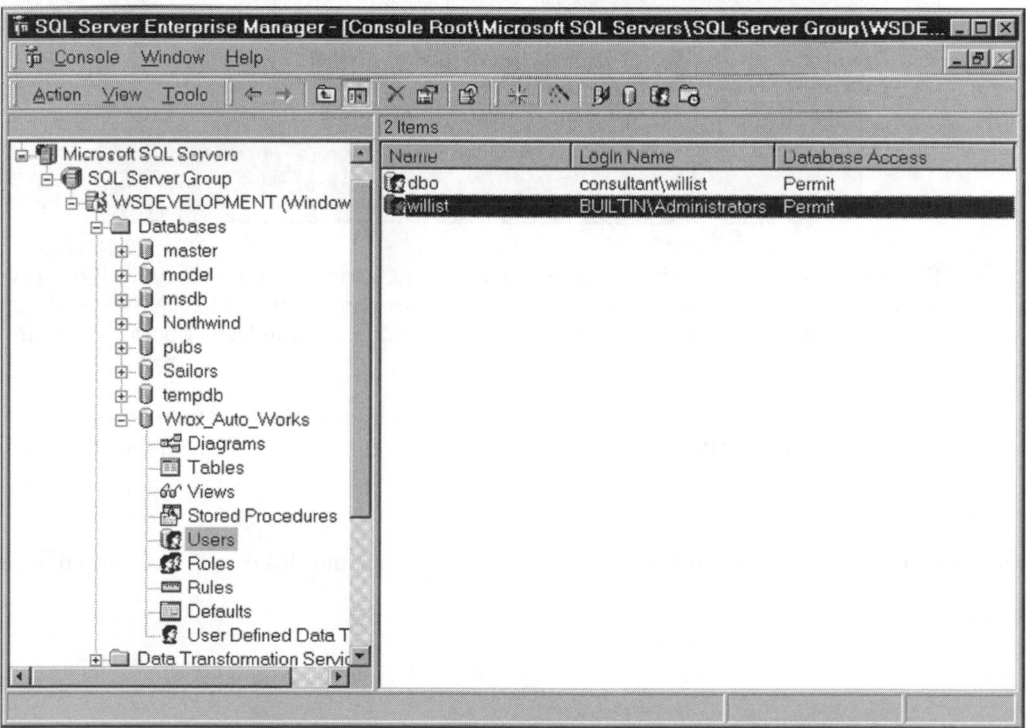

1. To add your login as a new user to the `Wrox_Auto_Works` database, either right click on Users in the tree view and choose New Database User from the popup menu, or select Users and then right click in the details pane and choose New Database User from the popup menu. Whichever way you do it, the following window appears:

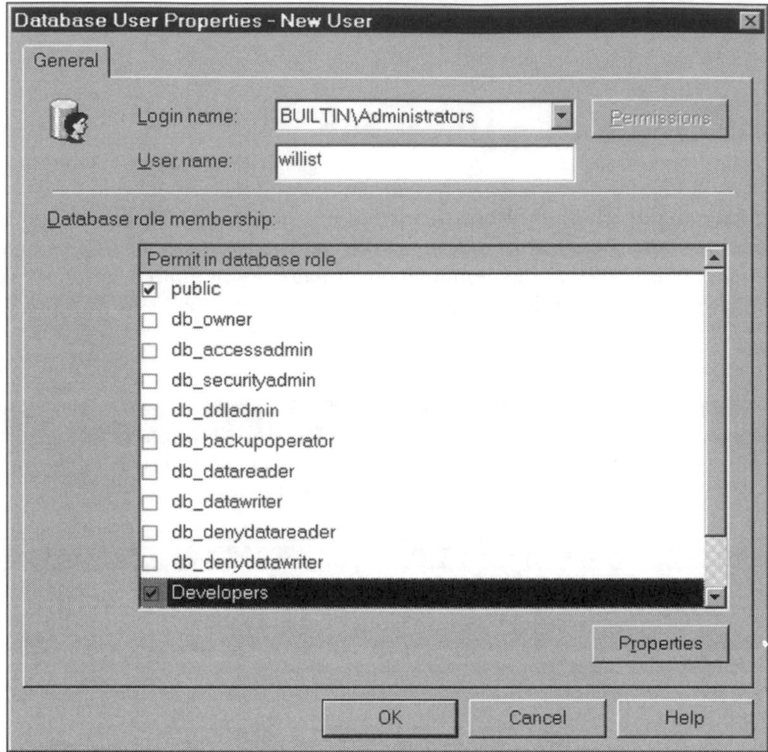

2. Since you are the one who installed the database, assuming you installed SQL Server while logged on with your Windows NT account, you are the BUILTIN\Administrators. Enter your login name in the User name field and check the Developers role in the membership list.

   If you did not install SQL Server, or you are running on a Windows 9x platform, select BUILTIN\Administrators as the Login name and enter your user name in the User name field.

3. Click OK to close the dialog.

Note that the Properties button lists the properties for the role, but this is not relevant to this discussion.

Adding Other Users

Since we have taken the appropriate steps to define our initial login and add ourselves to our database, let's take a look at setting up other users. First, we want to add two more logins to SQL Server. This time we are going to use the **Create Login Wizard** to create the new logins, and we are going to use SQL Server authentication.

Try It Out – Add New Logins Using the Create Login Wizard

We will be adding two new logins to SQL Server who will have access to the `Wrox_Auto_Works` database. The user names you will enter here do not have to be real users, as this step is only demonstrating adding users who will fill the Sales Staff and Management roles in our database. (For example, we have used the names Stephanie and Margie.) After adding the logins, your Logins folder in the Enterprise Manager will look something like the following:

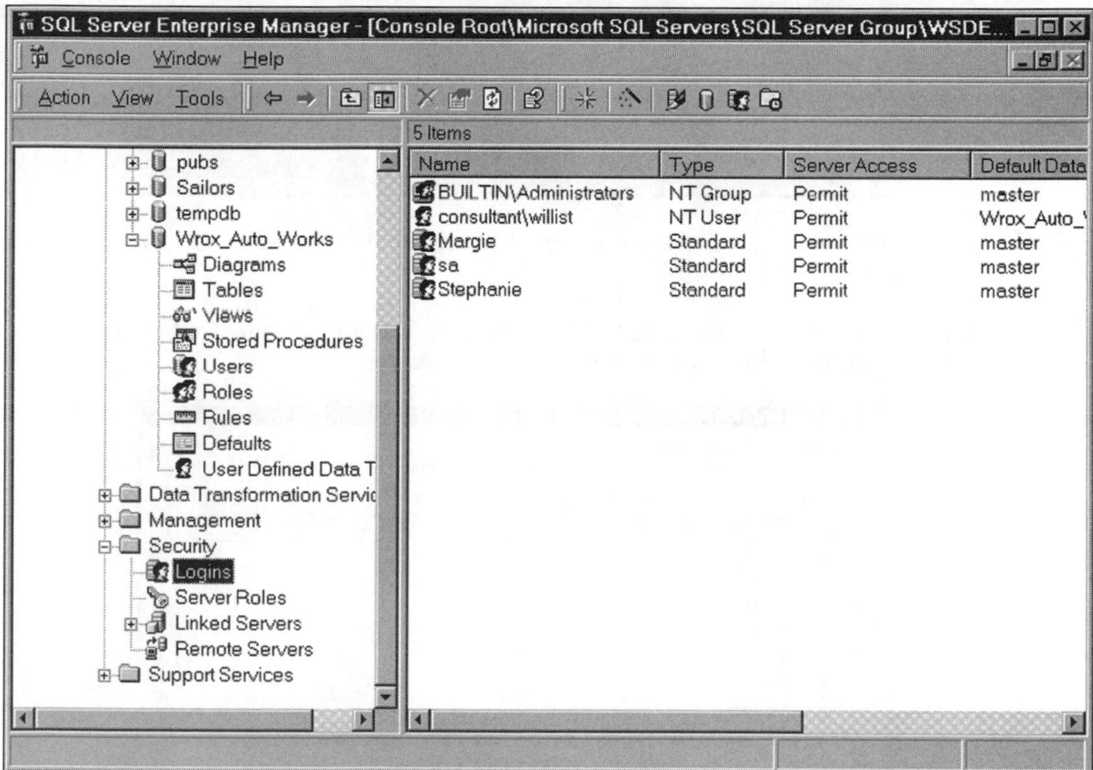

1. Start by choosing Wizards from the Tools menu and expand the Database group in the initial wizard dialog. Click on Create Login Wizard and click the OK button to proceed.

2. The first step of the wizard explains what the wizard can help you do. Click Next to progress to the next dialog screen, where you select the authentication mode that you want to use. Select SQL Server as the authentication mode and click Next to proceed.

3. Enter the Login ID and the Password of the new user and confirm the password. Remember that passwords are case sensitive. (In this case we have used the users' name, in lowercase, as their password.) Click Next to proceed:

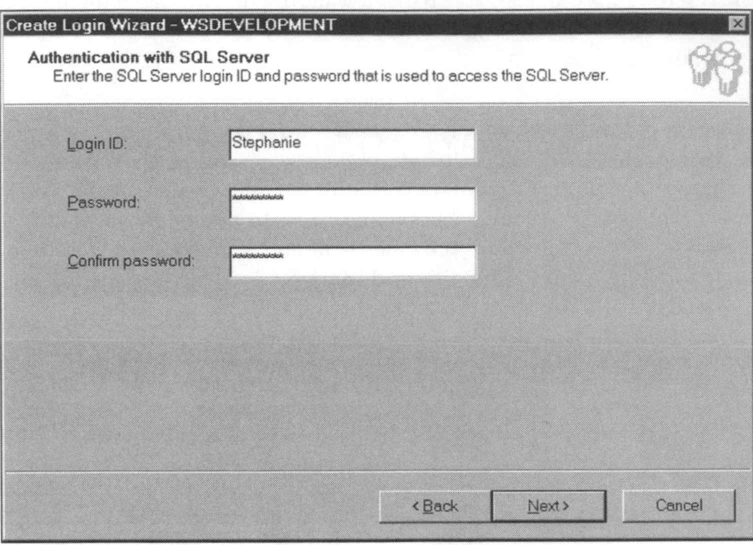

4. We do not want to grant these users any Security Roles just yet, so click Next to advance to the next step.

5. We want to select the Wrox_Auto_Works database since this is the database for which these logins are being added:

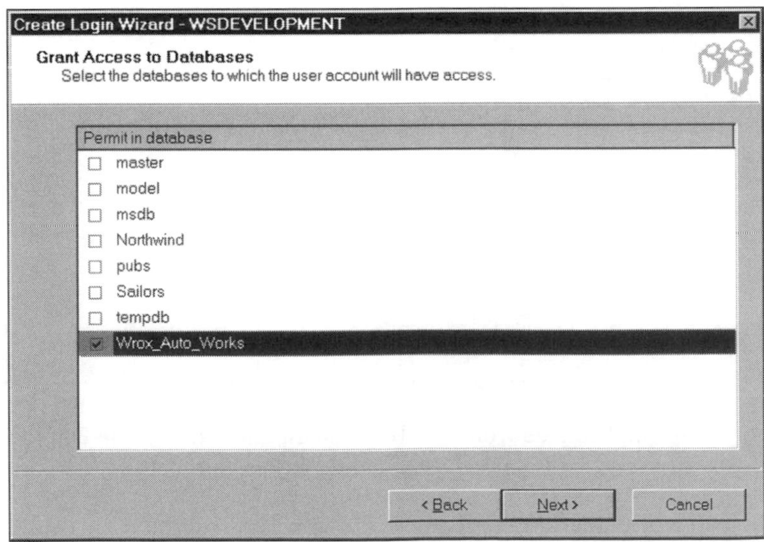

6. Click Next to proceed to the last step and click Finish to have the login added.

7. Click OK to accept the message which tells you the process was completed successfully.

8. Repeat the above steps to add another login.

9. In Enterprise Manager, expand the `Wrox_Auto_Works` database and click on Users. If you do not see the two new users, right click on Users and choose Refresh from the popup menu.

 Using the Create Login Wizard to create the new logins automatically added the new logins to our database, since we selected our database name in the Grant Access to Databases step in the wizard.

10. Remember that even though the new users are added to our database, they do not have the authority to do anything. We want to add these new users to the roles we have set up. Right click on one of the new users and choose Properties from the popup menu. The following dialog is displayed:

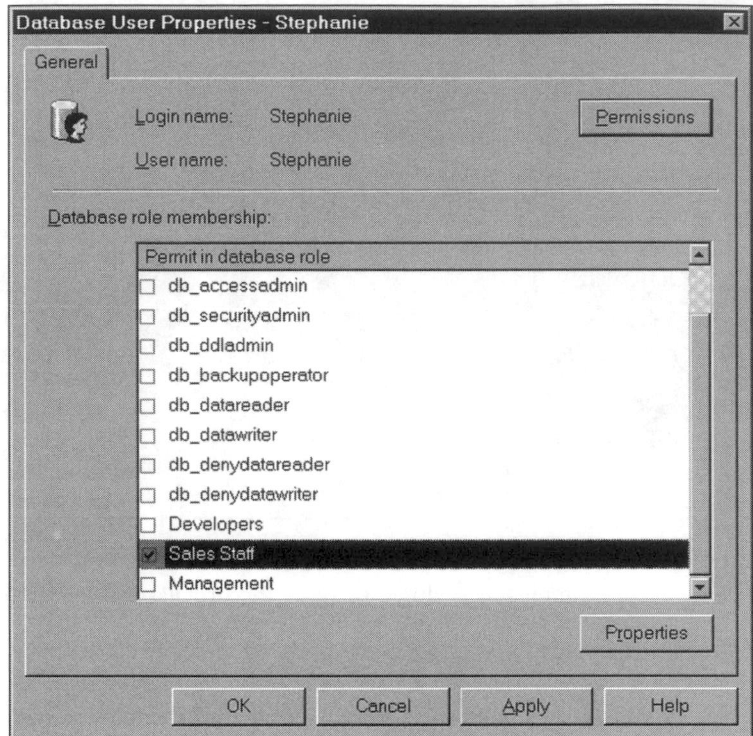

11. We do not want to manage the permissions for this user, as permissions operate at the object level. We only want to check the box to add this user to the Sales Staff role. Click OK to dismiss this dialog and then repeat the procedure to assign the other new user to the Management role.

We will come back and assign the appropriate permissions to the roles after we have discussed object security.

Object Security

Chapter 1 mentioned that a database contains many objects, such as tables, indexes, views, and stored procedures. Security in SQL Server is implemented at the object level. Each object has different security levels that can be set. For example, tables have security permissions that can be set for `SELECT`, `INSERT`, `UPDATE`, and `DELETE` operations, while stored procedures implement security permissions that allow a user to `EXECUTE` the stored procedure.

The next few sections will discuss the various objects and the security permissions that can and will be set for use in the rest of this book.

Table Security

Security can be implemented on table objects at various levels and can be implemented for users and/or roles. Object security applies to individual table objects – each table has permissions that must be set before other users can access data in that table. You can implement security on a table object at the column level or at the table level. We will be implementing security at the table level in our exercises.

The various permissions that we can grant users are `SELECT`, `INSERT`, `UPDATE`, and `DELETE`; as well as `DRI`, which is outside the scope of this book. Briefly, DRI (Declarative Referential Integrity) is a constraint that checks the data integrity for a specific table.

If we grant a user `SELECT` permissions to a table, they have the appropriate authority to select data, for read-only purposes, from all rows in our table. `INSERT` permissions allow users to insert new data into our tables, and `UPDATE` permissions allow users to update the existing data in our tables. When we grant a user `DELETE` permissions, they can delete rows of data from our table.

View Security

View security is implemented in the same manner as security for tables. Each view represents an object in the database and can have the same permissions granted as for a table. If you recall our discussion from Chapter 1, a view is a virtual representation of data from one or more columns from one or more tables. The code for a view is stored like a stored procedure, in that the actual SQL statements that get executed to open the view are stored in the database. The virtual table is built when the view is executed.

Stored Procedure Security

A stored procedure is a group of Transact-SQL statements that are stored in the database. Stored procedures can be coded to select data, insert data, update data, and delete data, or can provide a combination of the services. Since stored procedures return rows of data and do not actually contain data themselves, security is implemented on stored procedures a little differently from how it is on tables and views.

Security is still implemented at the object level and each stored procedure is considered an object. However, since stored procedures do not actually contain data, the only permissions that can be granted are `EXECUTE` permissions. This allows a user to execute the stored procedure and retrieve the data returned.

Statement Level Security

If you want a user to be able to create objects, whether from stored procedures, a query, or using the Enterprise Manager, you must grant that user statement level permissions. These types of permissions allow a user to create objects in a database, such as stored procedures and tables. Granting these permissions will allow a user or role to be able to create objects through the use of stored procedures or any other means.

Granting Access Rights by Assigning Role Permissions

Now that we have covered the basics of security for tables, views, and stored procedures, let's set the permissions for each of the three roles that we created. Since we have only created tables at this point, this is the only permission that we can assign to our roles. Once we create some stored procedures, in Chapter 7, we will then have to add those to the roles.

Each new object that gets added to the database will have to have its permissions set in the roles that we have created. That is, whenever we create a new table or stored procedure, we have to modify the roles and add the appropriate permissions to the new object. While this may seem time consuming, consider this. We have three roles defined and only three users at this point. What if we added 30 more users tomorrow? Setting the permissions for new objects on three roles beats setting permissions for 30 different users.

Try It Out – Assigning Role Permissions

We are going to modify the three roles we created, and apply the appropriate permissions for all the table objects we have created thus far.

The Developers role will have permissions for everything and will control the deleting of data. The Sales Staff role should be able to select, insert, and update data only, and the Management role should only be able to select data. The permissions for the Developers role will look something like this when we have finished:

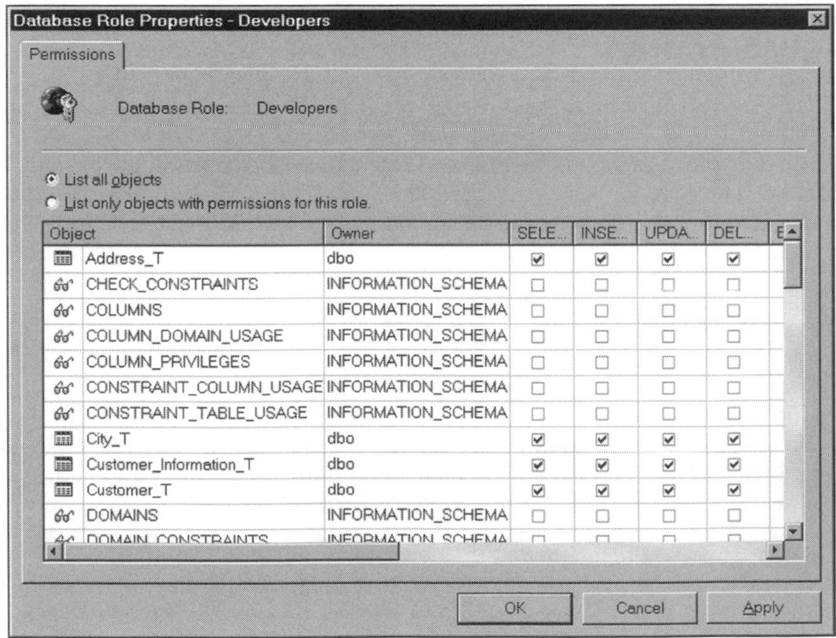

1. To apply the permissions to our roles, expand the `Wrox_Auto_Works` database, and select Roles. Right click on the Developers role and choose Properties on the popup menu. Click on the Permissions button and apply all permissions for all of the tables that we have created, as shown for four of the tables in the figure above. Click OK to close the Permissions dialog and then click OK to close the Properties dialog.

2. Apply the permissions for the Sales Staff role as shown in the figure below, applying the same permissions to all eight of our tables:

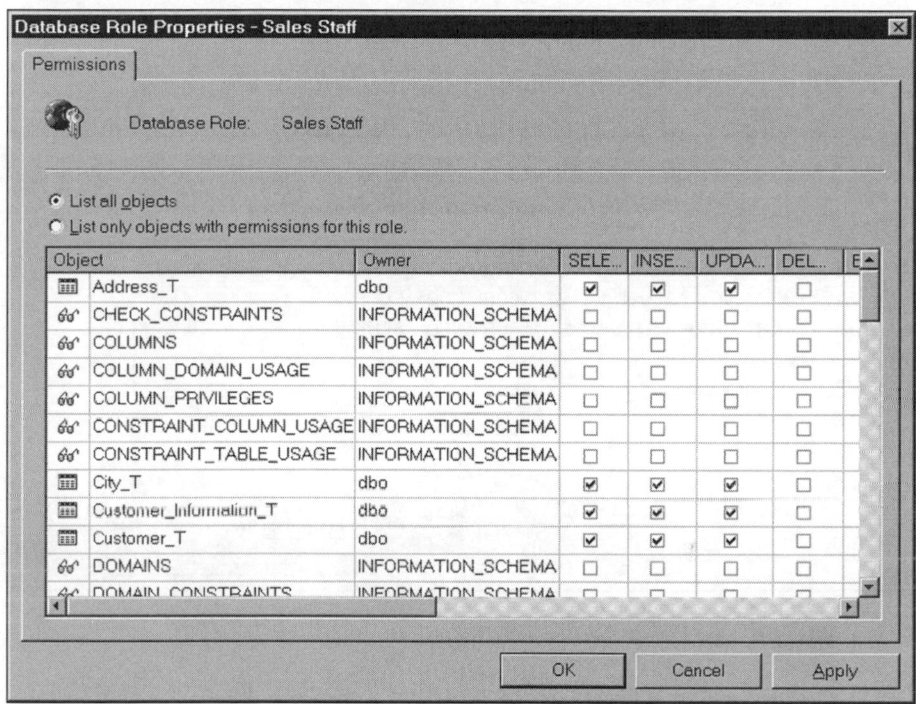

3. Set the permissions for the Management role as shown in the figure below, again applying the same permissions to all eight tables:

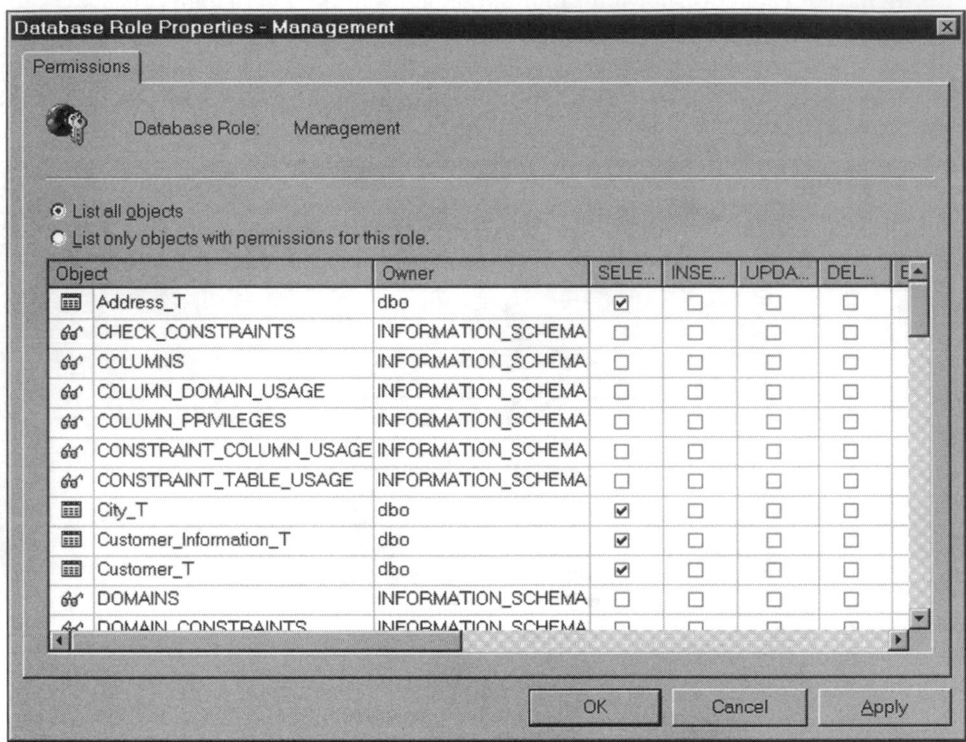

You can now close the Enterprise Manager.

Now that we have assigned the appropriate permissions to each of the roles that we have defined, setting up new users is just a matter of adding their logins, adding them to our database, and assigning them to a pre-existing role. As you can see, using roles simplifies the administrative tasks of maintaining users and their permissions.

Summary

This chapter has taken a detailed look at how SQL Server implements security. We have discussed SQL Server versus Windows NT authentication, and have learned what benefits Windows NT authentication provides over SQL Server authentication. Windows NT authentication provides:

- Authentication of the user, and ensures that they are logged on to the network
- Secure, encrypted passwords
- Automatic password expiration
- Account lockout after x number of unsuccessful attempts
- Account auditing

We have added new logins and users, both manually and using the Create Login Wizard. At this point you should feel comfortable adding new logins and users.

We have covered object security and learned the various permissions that can be granted to the various objects.

Roles played an important part in this chapter and we have seen how roles can be set up, users assigned, and object permissions set in each of the roles. Using roles can save you time administering object security, by applying permissions to each of the roles, rather than assigning permissions to each user.

In summary, this chapter has:

- Discussed Windows NT versus SQL Server authentication
- Examined roles
- Examined object security
- Demonstrated two ways to add new logins and users

We now have a secure database, albeit an empty one, and should be familiar with the features of the Enterprise Manager. We are now ready to learn how we can manipulate data in our database using another useful SQL Server tool – the Query Analyzer.

WROX AUTO WORKS RACING

SQL Server Query Analyzer

In Chapter 2 we took a look at the SQL Server user interface, specifically the Enterprise Manager. Chapters 3 and 4 expanded on this by using the Enterprise Manager to create new tables and users, and to set security permissions on our database objects. After working with the Enterprise Manager in the last three chapters, you can see why you will be spending a lot of time using it to manage your databases and tables. You also saw that it was useful for executing the various wizards that help you perform administrative tasks to manage your databases.

This chapter will focus on another useful tool that you will be spending a lot of time with – the Query Analyzer. We will cover some of the basic features of this tool and show how it can help you to debug your queries. We will also touch on execution plans so that you are familiar with all of the main features available in this tool.

In this chapter we will focus on:

- Creating and executing queries
- Selecting different databases to query
- Saving and opening query files
- Displaying and saving data
- Debugging your queries
- Execution plans

Introducing the Query Analyzer

A **query** is a way of interrogating and manipulating data in the database. Queries can be as basic or as complex as you want them to be. For example, we could simply insert a new customer into the `Wrox_Auto_Works` database. Or we could find out how many of our customers live in the town where our car showroom is located. We could then have the results returned to us as a list of customer names and telephone numbers, sorted by the date order of their latest car purchase. We could even exclude customers who bought a new car within the last six months.

Queries can be built and run to `SELECT`, `INSERT`, `UPDATE`, or `DELETE` data. We'll be taking a much closer look at each of these later. SQL Server provides a useful tool to help in building, debugging, and executing queries. It's called the **Query Analyzer**, and we'll be taking a look at its features, before we begin to build and execute our own queries.

The way we communicate with the database to perform these queries is by using a language called **Transact-SQL** or **T-SQL**. (SQL stands for **Structured Query Language**, and comes in many different flavors, of which T-SQL is the one used by SQL Server.) We'll be covering the syntax of this language as we come across it throughout this chapter and the rest of the book, and further information is given in the Transact-SQL Help feature available from within the Query Analyzer.

Quick Tour of the Query Analyzer

There are two recommended ways to start the **Query Analyzer**. Firstly, you can navigate to the Microsoft SQL Server 7.0 program group from the Windows Start menu, and click on Query Analyzer. Alternatively, you can start Enterprise Manager and start the Query Analyzer by clicking on the Tools menu and then clicking on SQL Server Query Analyzer.

Let's use the first method for now to start the Query Analyzer, so that we can look at some of the features it offers. Whichever method you use to start the Query Analyzer, the first screen you will be presented with is shown below:

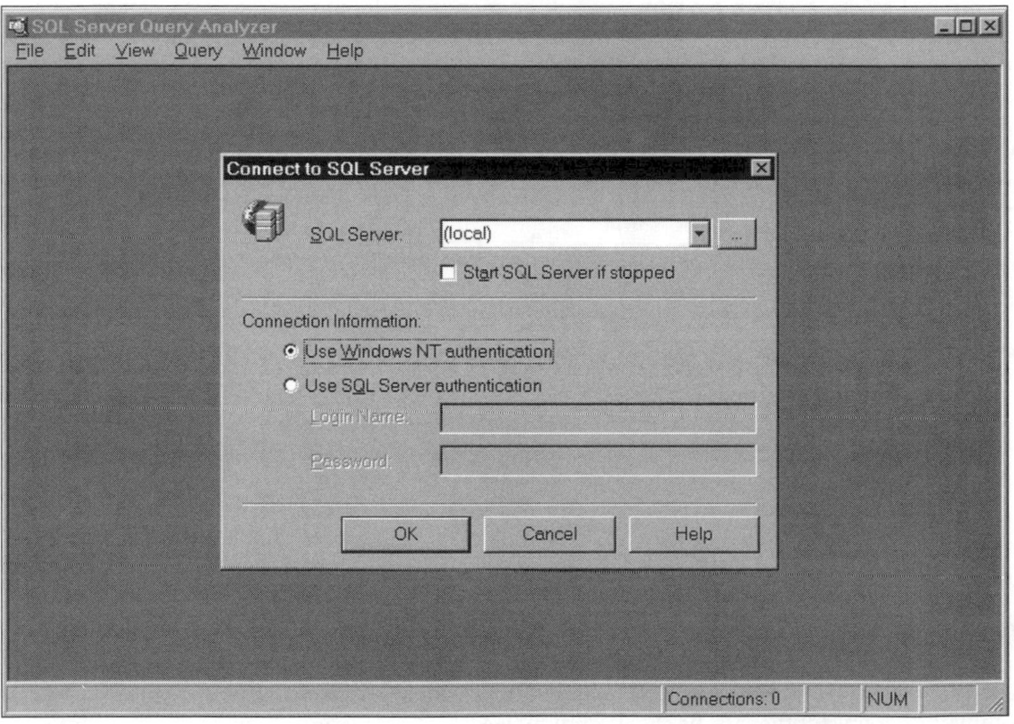

As you can see from the screen above, you are prompted to enter your login details. If you choose to use Windows NT authentication to log on with, you do not have to enter your ID and password, as SQL Server will gather this information automatically. If you are running on a Windows 9x platform, this option is not available to you and you must use SQL Server authentication. Enter your user ID and password, as discussed in the previous chapter, and then click on the OK button to log on. Query Analyzer starts with a blank screen, and the `master` database is selected by default:

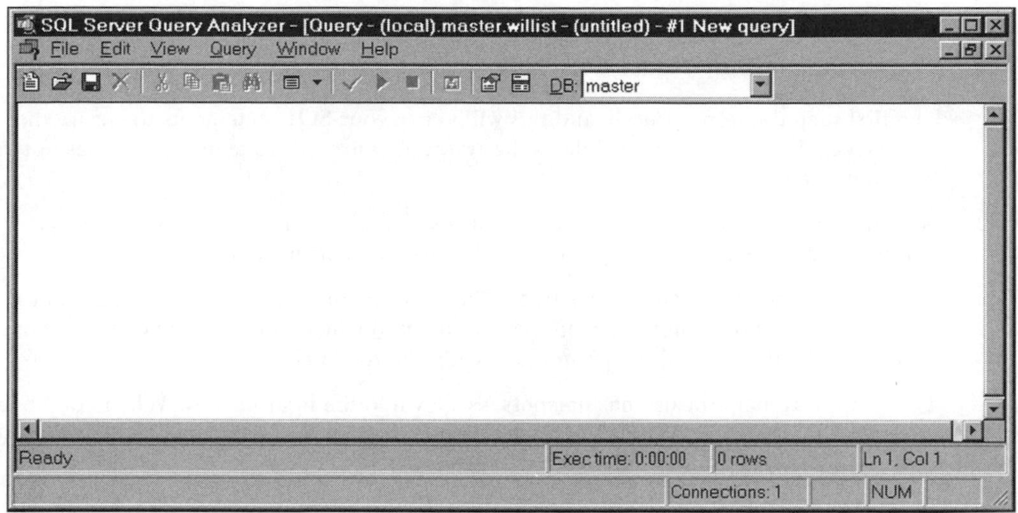

The view above shows the **query pane**. This is where you type in the SQL statements that make up your query. Once you have built and run a query, another pane also appears beneath the first, containing the results – and is surprisingly called the **results pane**. We'll be seeing more of this very soon.

Selecting a Database

If you look at the previous screen shot you will notice that there is a combo box, named DB, on the toolbar. This combo box provides a drop down list of all available databases in SQL Server. Let's start by selecting the pubs database in the list. All queries or stored procedures that we execute from now on will be performed against the pubs database, until we select a different database.

Before we get ahead of ourselves, let's take a quick look at the menus available in the Query Analyzer.

File Menu

The File menu provides a method for disconnecting from the local SQL Server installation and connecting to a networked version of SQL Server. We can also Open, Save, and Print our queries and query results. The File menu also contains a Configure option that will display a configuration dialog. This allows you to customize the Query Analyzer.

Edit Menu

The Edit menu contains the standard features you would expect to find, such as Cut, Copy, Paste, Undo, and Find, plus one that you would not expect. This is the Advanced option at the bottom of the drop down menu. Using this menu option you can change the case of selected text in the query pane to Upper Case or Lower Case.

View Menu

The View menu provides a means to customize the text in the Query Analyzer environment. Query Analyzer provides color-coded text for keywords and comments, just like the development environments in Visual Studio. Like all of these tools, Query Analyzer provides an option to let you customize the text font and colors to your own tastes.

Query Menu

The Query menu is quite busy and has a lot of features that are useful:

- The first menu option is Parse, and this will verify your SQL statements to ensure that they are correct. This parser only validates the *syntax* of your SQL statements – it does not validate the column and table names.
- Next on the Query menu is Execute, which is self-explanatory – it executes your query. Below that is Cancel Executing Query, which will cancel the currently running query.
- Next up is Display Estimated Execution Plan. This menu option will show a graphical representation of the estimated plan that will be used when you execute your query or stored procedure. Notice that this diagram is shown in the *results pane.*

  This graphical diagram also has **hotspots**, as shown in the figure below. When you hover your mouse over a picture (hotspot), a popup information window appears with some statistics.

  The graphical display in the results pane shows the data retrieval methods chosen by the SQL Server **Query Optimizer**, in order to carry out the query entered in the query pane. For example, if you are selecting first and last names from the `Customer_T` table, SQL Server will choose to use a clustered index scan; and if you are selecting the customer ID from the `Customer_T` table, SQL Server will choose to use the primary key index. These have been deemed to be the optimum methods for executing the query to balance fast results with minimum impact to other users.

  The popup window shown below displays the information that is being estimated to be used by an index scan of the `aunmind` index on the `authors` table of the `pubs` database:

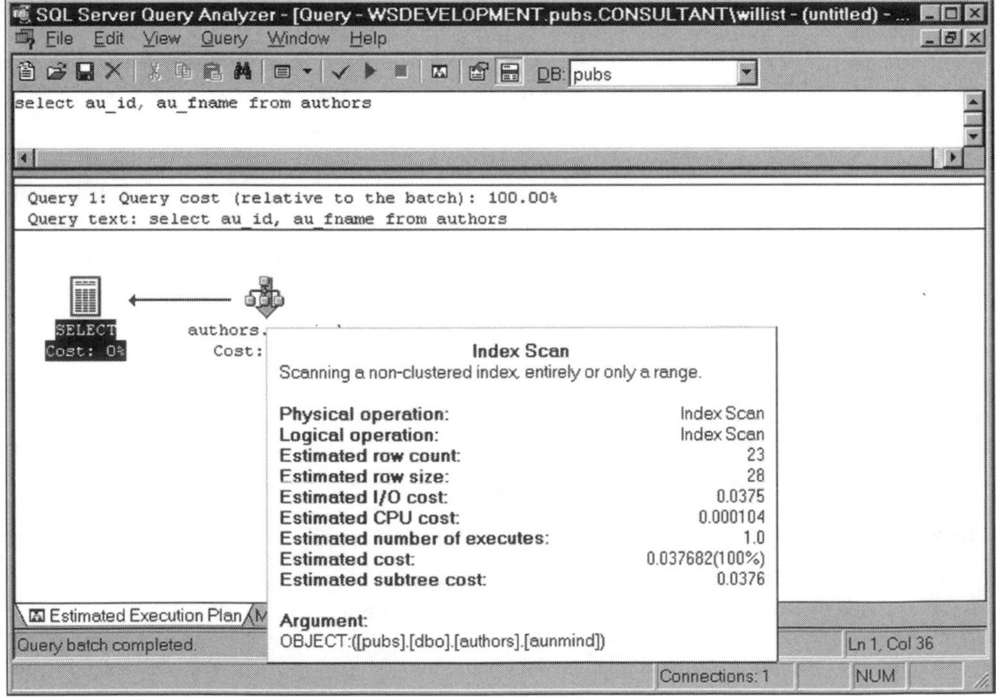

- Perform Index Analysis is the next menu option on the Query menu. This option will analyze the query statements and recommend the appropriate indexes if needed. In order to perform this analysis you must be a member of the `Sysadmin` role. An example of the analysis performed is shown in the next figure. Since this table already contains the appropriate indexes, no new ones were recommended:

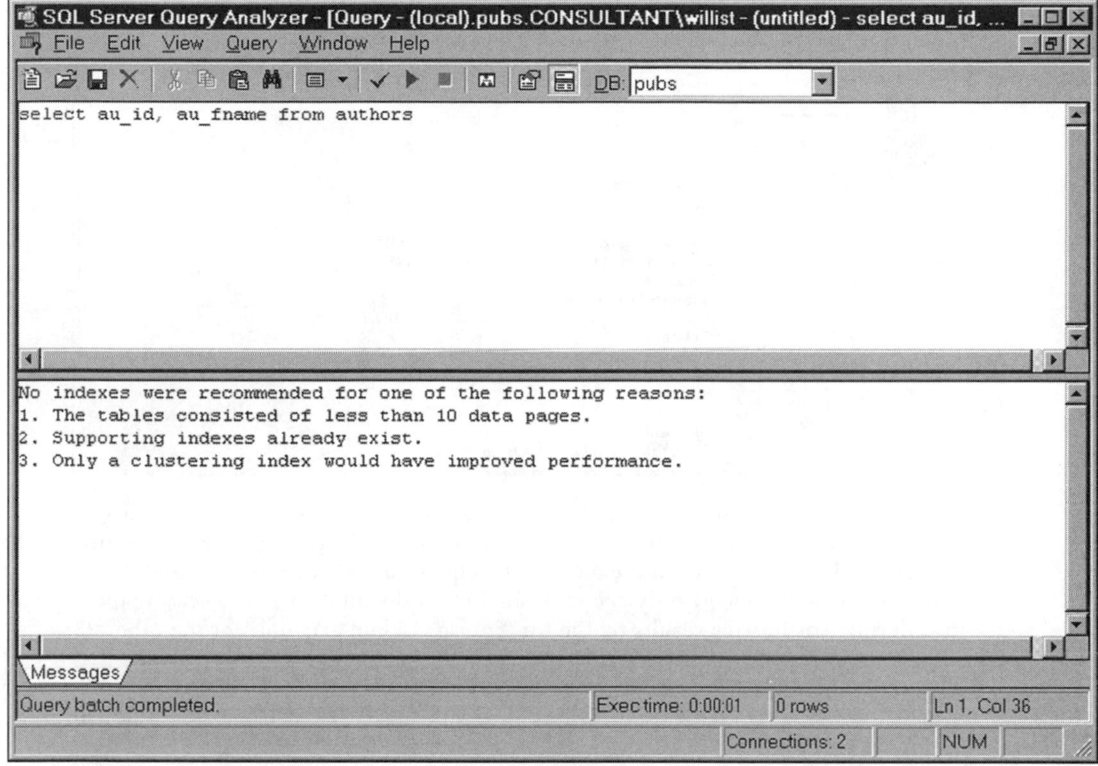

- The next two menu options, Results in Text and Results in Grid, will place the output of your query or stored procedure in, respectively, regular text format or a grid, the next time you run your query.

- Show Execution Plan is similar to the Display Estimated Execution Plan menu option, except this option displays the plan that *was* executed, as opposed to the one that was *estimated* to be executed. If you want to use this feature you must select this option *before* running your query or stored procedure. Then, after your query or stored procedure has executed, select the Execution Plan tab in the results window to view the execution plan. As with the Display Estimated Execution Plan option, this plan also contains hotspots that pop up additional information.

  Here we see the actual plan that was executed. This hotspot in the figure shows us the actual statistics of the operation that was performed to execute our query. The SQL Server Query Optimizer used an index scan on the `aunmind` index, and the hotspot shows the actual cost of executing this query in terms of I/O and CPU time. The total cost of executing this query is in the index scan of the `aunmind` index:

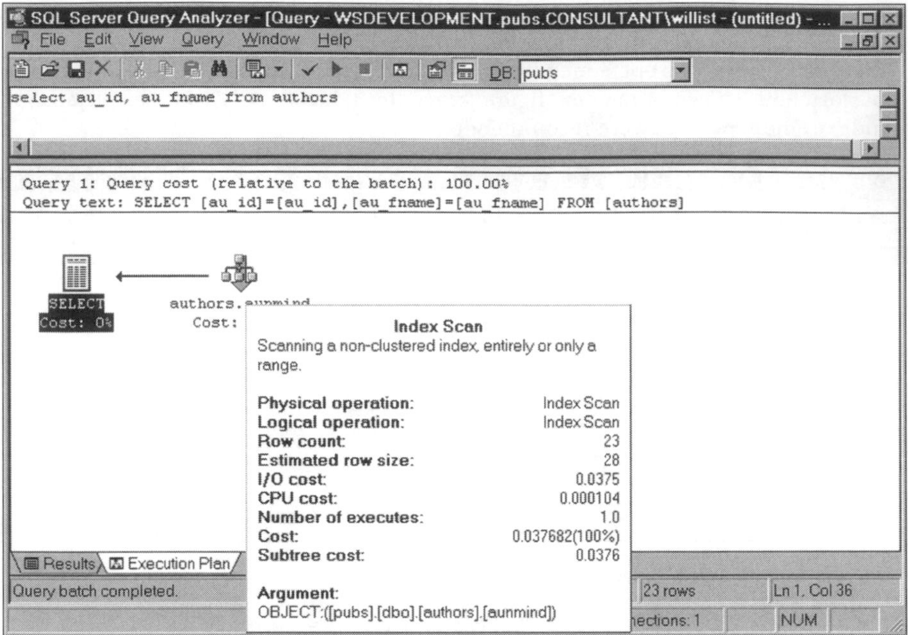

If we change the query slightly and order the results on a column that is not indexed, for example the `au_fname` column, the actual execution of this query changes, as shown in the next figure. Here the total cost of executing this query has changed because of the `ORDER BY` clause. The index scan now only accounts for 77% of the total cost of executing this query, and ordering (sorting) the results by the `au_fname` column accounts for the other 23%:

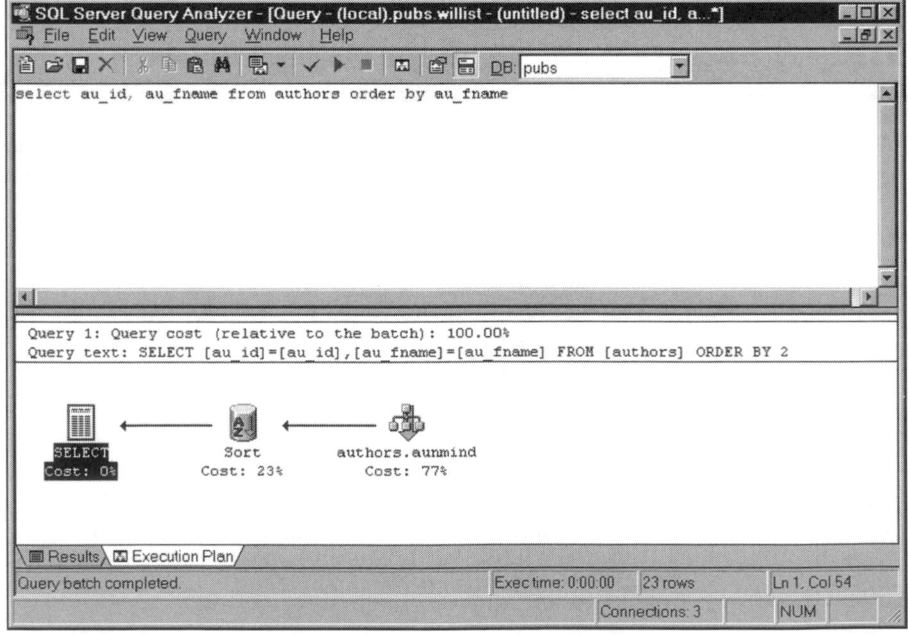

If you change the query once more and order the results by a column that is indexed, you get a totally different result. This next figure shows that we have executed the query and ordered the results by the au_id column, which is an indexed column and the primary key to the table. The index used this time is UPKCL_auidind, which is the index on the primary key aui_id. Since this is a clustered index, the rows are already sorted in the index by the primary key column. Therefore the SQL Server Query Optimizer does not have to perform a sort on the results, as it did in the last example.

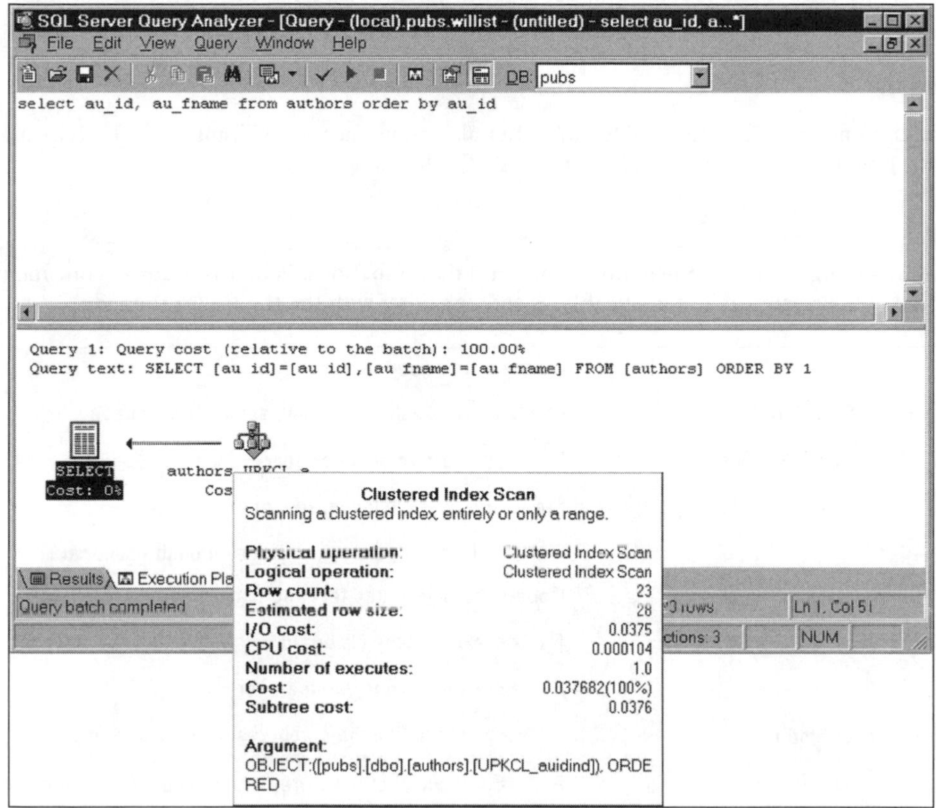

There's one last thing we want to mention here. If you look at these examples, you will notice that the index names do not make a lot of sense at first glance. If you start to study them closely you can see some similarities in the names. However, index names, like table names, can be up to 128 characters. There is no reason why, once we start applying our own indexes, we can't implement index names that are completely descriptive and conform to a standard such as the one suggested in Chapter 3.

- The New Query option opens a new query window, leaving the current query window intact. The Clear Window option clears the existing query in the current query window.
- The last menu option on the Query menu is Current Connection Options. This menu option displays a dialog containing various information about the current connection. Here you can set various options for your query and connection, and define how the results of your query should be displayed.

Window Menu

The Window menu options should be familiar to everyone. The Switch Pane menu option switches the focus from one pane to the next for the current query. The Move Splitter option sets the focus to the splitter so you can resize the query and results windows. The Hide Results Pane option hides the results pane for the current query window, and the menu option is replaced with the Show Results Pane option which will show the results pane again. We also have options to Cascade or Tile the query windows, and to Arrange Icons. As is usual for any Window menu, the open query windows are listed, with the current one checked for identification.

Help Menu

The Help menu contains the usual features, but also allows access to Transact-SQL Help, a useful resource giving syntax and examples for the T-SQL language.

Toolbar

The following figure shows the toolbar icons and their functions. When you hover your mouse over an icon the keyboard shortcut, if applicable, is shown, along with the tooltip for the icon.

Icon	Function
New Query	Opens a new query window
Load SQL Script	Loads a previously saved SQL script for execution
Save Query/Results	Saves the current query or query results
Clear Query Window	Clears the query in the current query window
Cut	Cuts the highlighted text and places it on the clipboard
Copy	Copies the highlighted text and places it on the clipboard
Paste	Pastes text from the clipboard
Find	Finds the specified text in the query
Execute Mode	Allows you to define the output results (text or grid) and whether or not to show the execution plan
Parse Query	Parses the syntax of the current query and displays any errors it finds
Execute Query	Executes the current query
Cancel Executing Query	Cancels the currently executing query
Display Estimated Execution Plan	Displays the estimated execution plan
Current Connection Options	Displays the **Current Connection Options** dialog
Hide Results Pane	Hides and shows the results pane

Creating, Executing, and Saving Queries

The examples that we will be running use the SELECT statement. The SELECT statement allows us to select columns and rows of data from one or more tables. The SELECT statement has a diverse syntax, and that presented below shows the basic elements:

```
SELECT Select_List
FROM Table_Name
[WHERE Search_Condition]
[GROUP BY Group_By_Expression]
[HAVING Restrictive_Condition_On_Group By_Results]
[ORDER BY Order_By_Expression]
```

The Select_List is a combination of columns from one or more tables. An asterisk can be used to specify that all columns are to be selected from the table or tables.

The Table_Name specifies the table or tables that data should be selected from. A comma should separate multiple tables.

The WHERE clause is optional and restricts the number of rows returned. If it is not specified, all rows are returned. The Search_Condition expression evaluates to a Boolean expression that returns True or False.

The GROUP BY clause is also optional, and the Group_By_Expression specifies how the rows of data that are returned are grouped.

The HAVING clause is only ever used if there is also a GROUP BY clause in your query, and again it is optional. It applies a restrictive condition to the results of the GROUP BY clause.

The ORDER BY clause is optional, and the Order_By_Expression specifies column names that determine in what order the rows of data are returned.

Try It Out – Executing a Query

Let's start by executing a simple query to select all columns and all rows in the authors table in the pubs database.

1. We start by opening the Query Analyzer and selecting the pubs database from the dropdown list.

2. Next we enter our SQL statement in the query window. Our SQL statement is listed below. Specifying an asterisk in the SELECT statement and no WHERE clause selects all columns and rows in the table.

```
SELECT * FROM authors
```

3. We then click on the Execute Query icon on the toolbar.

After execution, you will see the results listed in the results pane, listing each column in the `authors` table and each row of data, in text format:

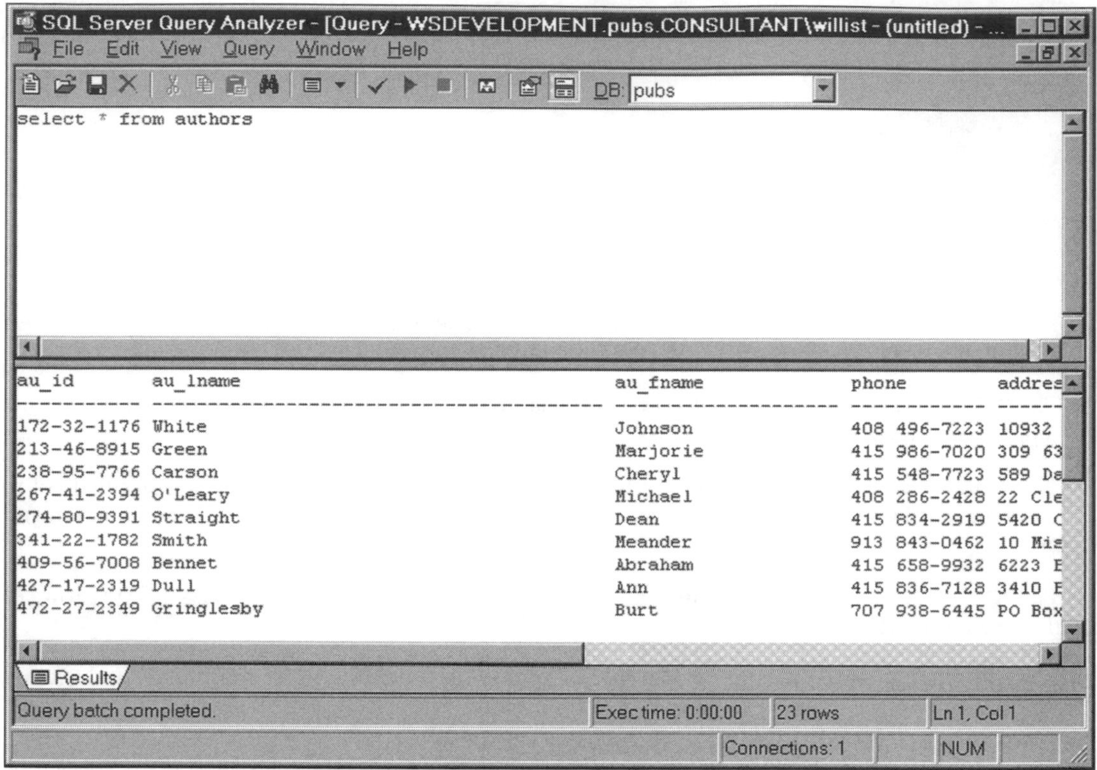

Try It Out – New Query

This example starts a new query in a different database. We want to select all columns and rows from the `State_T` table in the `Wrox_Auto_Works` database.

1. We start a new query by clicking on the New Query icon on the toolbar.

2. Next, we select the `Wrox_Auto_Works` database in the DB combo box on the toolbar.

3. We then enter and execute the following query:

```
SELECT * FROM State_T
```

Of course nothing will be displayed as we have not inserted any data yet, but you will see the column names of the table listed in the results pane, as shown:

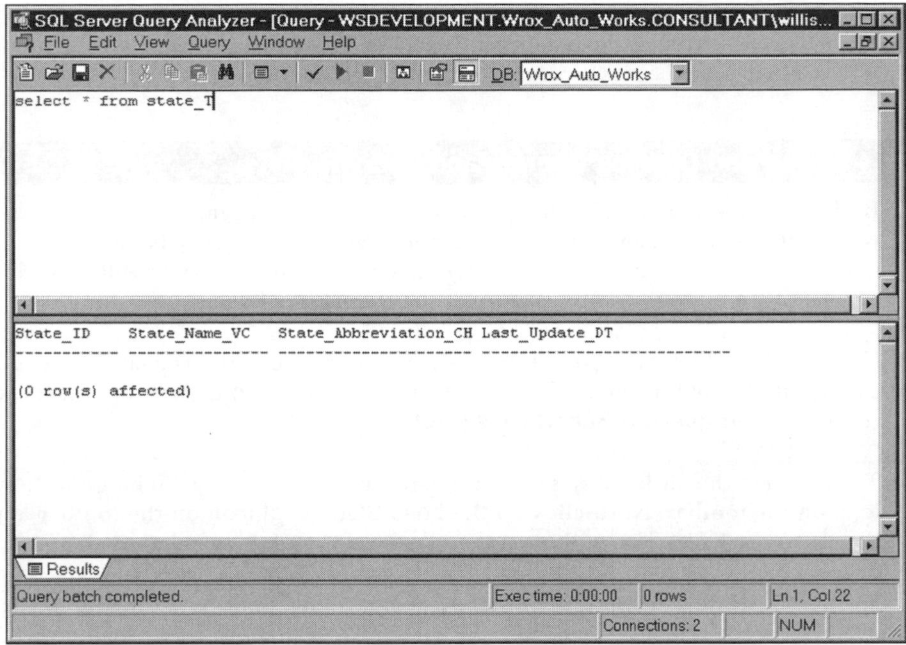

4. To switch back to the first query window, click on the Window menu and select the first query that you executed. The figure below shows the various queries listed in the Window menu option. (The query window that you are in is always checked to indicate that it is the *current* query window.)

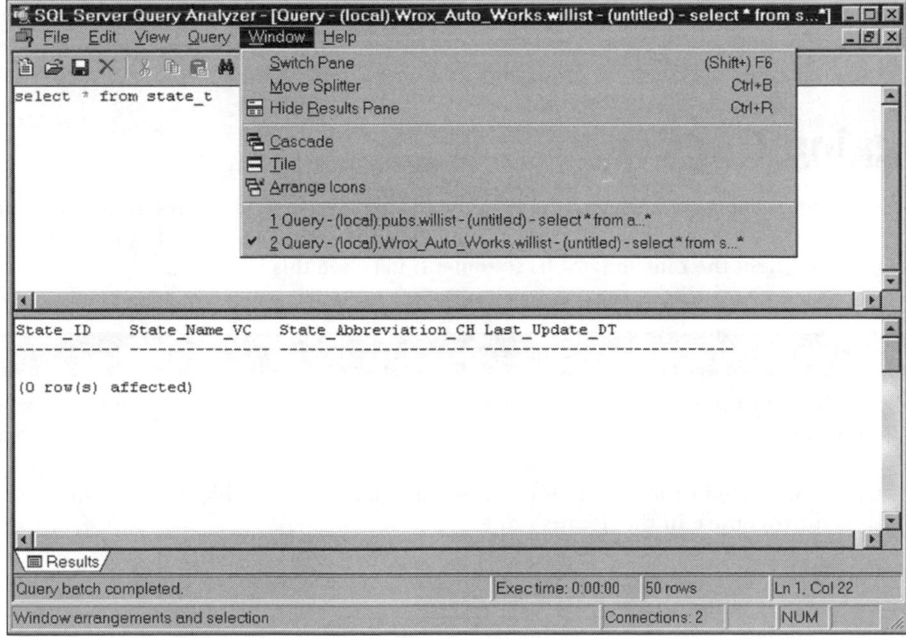

As you can see, we can select different databases, execute queries and stored procedures, and alternate between them using the Window menu option. What if we want to keep our query or results for re-use later? It is possible to save them as separate files, as we will now demonstrate.

Try It Out – Saving and Opening Queries and Query Results

1. In the Window menu, select the query that you executed against the `pubs` database. Ensure that your cursor is in the top window where your query is, then click on the Save icon on the toolbar. In the Save Query dialog, save your query as Authors. Notice that the Save as type option is set to save your query as Query Files (*.sql).

2. Next, click in the results pane to place your cursor there and repeat the steps above. You can use the same file name. Notice that this time the Save as type option is set to save the results of your query as Report Files (*.rpt).

3. To complete this little exercise, open a new query window by clicking the New Query icon on the toolbar. Next, click on the Load SQL Script icon on the toolbar and open the `Authors.sql` file. This will open the query that you just saved above.

4. We do not need either of these queries, so close both query windows, ignoring any prompts to save them.

As you can see, this is great for queries that you want to run without creating a stored procedure and storing it in the database. This is also a great method to use when developing very large queries. You can code several SQL statements, test them, and then save the file. You can add more SQL statements, test them, and then save as a new file. You can repeat this process until your complete query has been built. If you want to discard the last SQL statements and modifications that you just added, instead of saving them, simply close the query window and open a new one, and then open the previous version of the query file that you saved.

Debugging Queries

Debugging in SQL Server has come a long way with this release. It provides an intuitive debugger very similar to Visual C++. Error messages are displayed in the results pane, and double clicking on an error message will highlight the offending SQL statement. Let's see this in action.

Try It Out – Debugging a Query

1. If you don't have Enterprise Manager running, open it, and navigate to the `pubs` database.

2. Click on Stored Procedures in the tree pane and then double click on the `byroyalty` stored procedure in the details pane.

3. We want to copy (by selecting the text then pressing *Ctrl + C*) the following two lines of SQL statements from this stored procedure:

```
SELECT au_id FROM titleauthor
WHERE titleauthor.royaltyper = @percentage
```

4. Now close the `byroyalty` stored procedure, switch to the Query Analyzer, and start a new query by clicking on the New Query icon.

5. Paste the SQL statements into the new query, and select the `pubs` database in the database combo box on the toolbar.

6. Click the Execute Query icon on the toolbar to execute the query that you pasted in the query window. Notice that right off you get the following error message:

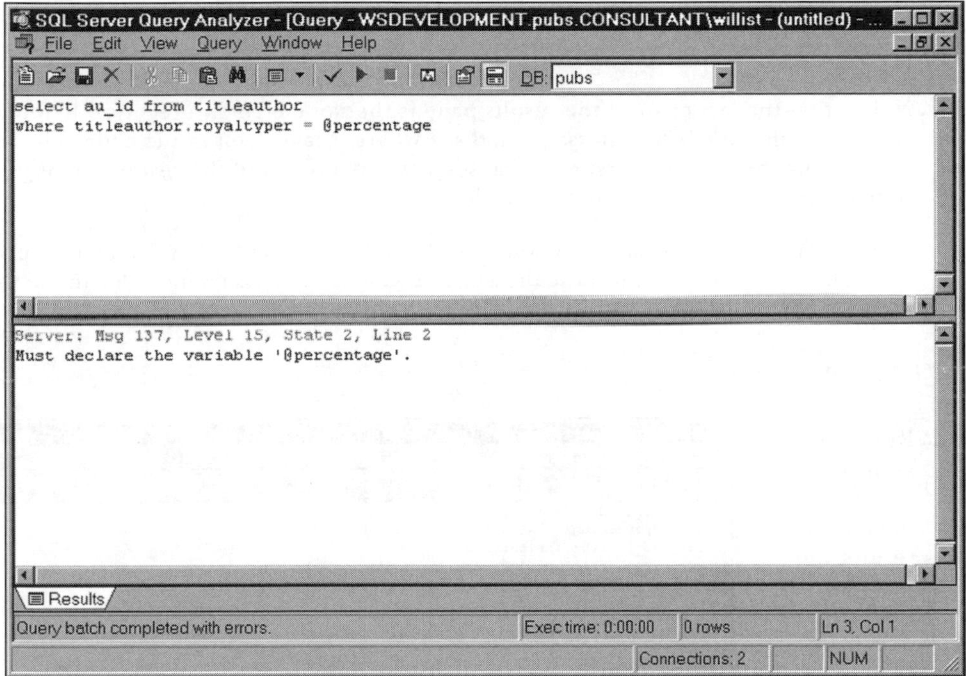

7. If you double click on the error message, the code that has caused the error is highlighted and your cursor is placed at the beginning of that line of code.

   To correct this problem, we must declare the `@percentage` variable. Add the following line of code to the beginning of this query:

```
DECLARE @percentage Int
```

   Local variables in Transact-SQL always begin with a single at sign (@) followed by the variable name. You must also specify the data type that this variable represents. In our code above, the variable represents an `Integer` data type.

8. Now run the query and see what happens. The query runs but does not return any rows. That brings us to another problem that we have to debug. Why didn't we get any data? Well, the `WHERE` clause of the `SELECT` statement is looking for rows of data where the `royaltyper` column matches the value in `@percentage`. We declared the `@percentage` variable but did not assign it a value.

   Add the following SQL statement to your query after the `DECLARE` statement:

```
DECLARE @percentage Int
@percentage = 30
```

9. Running the query now produces two errors, as shown below:

```
Server: Msg 170, Level 15, State 1, Line 2
Line 2: Incorrect syntax near '@percentage'.
Server: Msg 137, Level 15, State 1, Line 4
Must declare the variable '@percentage'.
```

10. Notice that the last error in the results pane is the same error we received before. Double click on each of the error messages and see where it takes you in the code. The second error occurs because the first error causes a syntax error and the rest of the SQL statements cannot be validated correctly.

    The first error is the one and only true error here. In Transact-SQL we cannot simply say `variable = value`, we must use the `SELECT` statement to assign the value to the variable, as shown below. Add the `SELECT` statement into your existing line of code, as shown:

```
SELECT @percentage = 30
```

11. Running your query now yields the correct results and lists two rows of data, as shown:

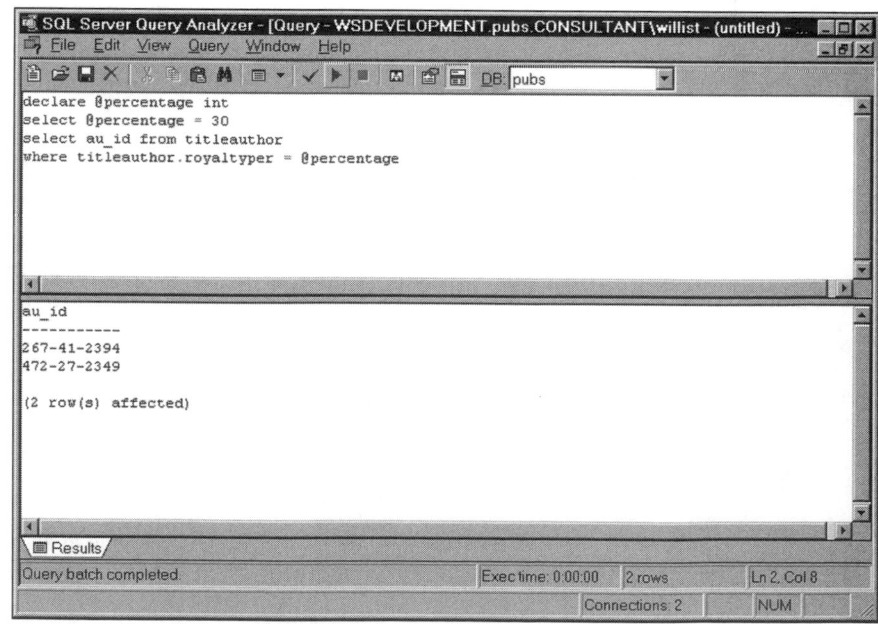

12. There is no need to keep this query, so close the query window and select No when prompted to save.

While this may have seemed liked a simplistic exercise, it has served two purposes. First, it has introduced you to debugging queries in the Query Analyzer. Secondly, it has introduced you to variables and demonstrated how to assign their values.

We will be covering more on debugging in the next section, and in Chapter 9 when we start looking in detail at stored procedures.

INSERT, UPDATE, and DELETE Statements

Since we have started working with the `SELECT` statement it only seems appropriate that we go ahead and introduce the `INSERT`, `UPDATE`, and `DELETE` statements as well. Most readers probably have a basic understanding of these statements and we are going to cover these statements as they relate to SQL Server. Since SQL is an acronym for Structured Query Language, it would seem that SQL statements in SQL Server would be the same as SQL statements in Access or Oracle or Sybase. While this is true for the most part, there are some minor differences, and we'll be concentrating on the particular version of SQL used by SQL Server – T-SQL.

This section will cover the basics of the `INSERT`, `UPDATE`, and `DELETE` SQL statements, and we will also look some more at debugging as we go along.

INSERT Statement

Without data the database would be useless, and the `INSERT` statement provides us a means of getting data into our tables. The `INSERT` statement allows us to insert one or more rows of data into our tables. The basic syntax of the `INSERT` statement is shown below:

```
INSERT [INTO] Table_Name
[(Column_List)]
VALUES(Value_List)
```

The `INTO` keyword, as well as the `Column_List` values, are optional as indicated by the square brackets. The `Table_Name` value specifies the name of the table that we want to insert data into. The `Column_List` value specifies a list of column names that we will be inserting data into, and the `Value_List` contains the values we want to insert. The `City_Name_VC` column specifies the name of the city and the `Last_Update_DT` column specifies the last date and time that this row of data was updated:

Let's take a quick look at a couple of different examples of inserting values into the `City_T` table:

```
INSERT INTO City_T (City_Name_VC, Last_Update_DT) VALUES('Charlotte',GetDate ())

INSERT INTO City_T (Last_Update_DT, City_Name_VC) VALUES(GetDate(),'Charlotte')
```

There are a few things that we need to mention here. First, there is a column called City_ID that we have not specified in the INSERT statement. This is because the City_ID column was set up as an identity column and a unique value will be inserted into it automatically for us, so we do not specify the value. Second, notice that the city name is enclosed in single quote marks. All string values must be enclosed by single quotes. Last, we are using the GetDate() function to get the current system date and time to be inserted into the Last_Update_DT column.

Both of these INSERT statements specify the column names that we will be inserting data into. The first example lists City_Name_VC first and the second example lists it second. By specifying the column names in the INSERT statement, you only have to supply data values for the columns that you want to insert data into. When specifying the column names, they can be in any order. Just ensure that the data values fall in the same order as the column names. However, to be consistent, all column names should be listed in the order in which they are defined in the table, as it makes the code easier to understand and to debug.

You do not have to specify the column names at all. This is great if you have columns in your table that provide default values, and the user has entered no values for those columns. However, specifying the column names is always a good idea. The reason behind this statement is, and it is especially true in stored procedures, that columns can be *added* to your table. By specifying the column names in your INSERT statement, you ensure that your query or stored procedure will not fail if additional columns have been added to the tables.

Let's expand on this for just a moment. Examining the following INSERT statement, we notice that the column names for the data values have not been supplied. While this INSERT statement will work today, there is no guarantee that it will work tomorrow:

```
INSERT INTO City_T VALUES('Charlotte',GetDate())
```

Let's say we add another column to the table tomorrow morning that has no default value. If you try to execute this SQL statement tomorrow, it will fail because not all values will have been supplied and you will receive the following error message:

```
Insert Error: Column name or number of supplied values does not match table
definition.
```

Specifying the column list in your queries and stored procedures is a good practice to follow, and makes good sense in the light of what we have just learned.

Try It Out – Insert Query

This example allows you to insert your city name into the City_T table.

1. You will need to start a new query by clicking on the **New Query** icon on the toolbar, and changing the database to Wrox_Auto_Works in the database combo box.

2. Enter and run the query as shown in the query pane below. You can substitute a different city name if you want. As we mentioned above, it is good practice to specify the column names in your query and we have done that here. Also notice that the City_ID column, which is an identity column, is not specified in the column list. The results pane shows that one row was affected, which indicates that the data was inserted into the table:

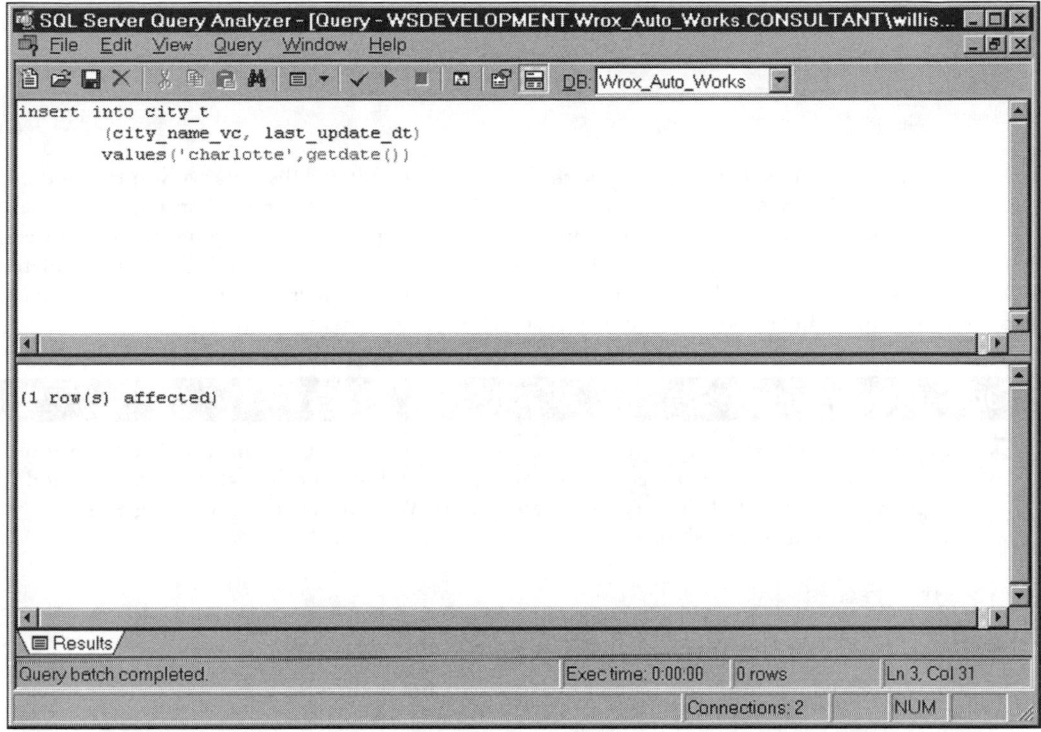

3. Now let's enter our state information into the `State_T` table. You can either start a new query, or delete the SQL statements in your current query and enter the new SQL statements to insert your state.

Enter and run the following query, substituting your state name and abbreviation if you chose a different city name in step 2. Key your state name and state abbreviation in lower case. Notice that the SQL statements have also been coded in upper case, but that Transact-SQL statements are not case sensitive, this just makes the code easier to read.

```
INSERT INTO State_T
   (State_Name_VC, State_Abbreviation_CH, Last_Update_DT)
   VALUES('North Carolina', 'NC', GetDate())
```

We have covered the basic `INSERT` statement in this section and have explained why it's best to always use the column name list in your `INSERT` statements. Chapters 7 and 10 will be going into much greater detail on using the `INSERT` statement.

UPDATE Statement

Over time, data in our database becomes out of date, and it would serve no useful purpose if we couldn't update it. This is where the `UPDATE` statement comes in. It allows us to keep our data up to date, thereby providing our business with valuable information. This section will cover the `UPDATE` statement and the various ways we can use it.

We want to start by taking a quick look at the basic syntax of the UPDATE statement:

```
UPDATE Table_Name
SET Column_Name = Expression
WHERE Column_Name = Search_Expression
```

The Table_Name value specifies the name of the table that contains the data we want to update. The SET keyword specifies a comma-separated list of Column_Name = Expression pairs. Column_Name specifies the column name that we want to update and the Expression specifies the data or expression that we want to update the column with. The WHERE clause specifies the condition of the update, and looks for rows of data where the Column_Name value specified equals the Search_Expression or data value specified. Let's take a look at the basic UPDATE statement in action.

Try It Out – Update Query

1. Either open a new query window or clear the existing query window. We want to update the city name that you inserted into the City_T table. The first thing that we need to do is get the City_ID of the city that we inserted. We will use the following SELECT statement to accomplish this:

```
SELECT * FROM City_T
```

2. Run this query and make a note of the City_ID value. Then code your UPDATE SQL statement using your city ID and city name. This is shown below:

```
UPDATE City_T
   SET City_Name_VC = 'Charlotte'
   WHERE City_ID =1
```

3. Run your query to execute it:

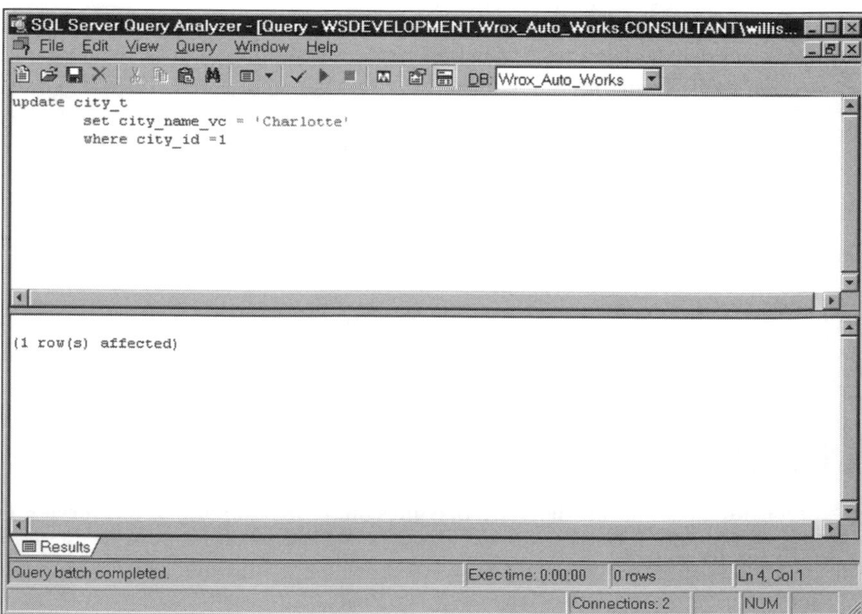

After running your query you should receive a message listed in the results pane, as shown in the figure above, which indicates that your update was successful. We have just demonstrated a very simple UPDATE statement, where we only updated one column.

The UPDATE statement specifies the table we want to update, and we use the SET keyword to set the column name equal to the value we specify. Because we are specifying a string value, we must enclose the string in single quotes. The WHERE clause evaluates to just a row of data in our table where the City_ID = 1.

4. Now let's move on to our next UPDATE statement, where we are going to update two columns using the data that you inserted into the State_T table. First we need to start a new query or delete the existing SQL statements in the current query. Then run a query to select the data from the State_T table:

```
SELECT * FROM State_T
```

5. Code your new UPDATE query as shown below, substituting your state name, state abbreviation, and the State_ID returned from your SELECT query. Notice that we have specified the string values in single quotes again, and have separated our Column_Name = Expression pairs using a comma:

```
UPDATE State_T
   SET State_Name_VC = 'North Carolina',
       State_Abbreviation_CH = 'NC'
   WHERE State_ID = 1
```

6. Now execute your query.

This section has covered the basics of the UPDATE statement, showing you how to update one and two columns. When we get to Chapters 7 and 11 we will be using parameters in our UPDATE statements, and our UPDATE statements will become more sophisticated as we progress through those chapters.

DELETE Statement

No matter how much we update our data, there comes a time when the data no longer serves a purpose or provides value to our business. This could simply be because the data is no longer needed by the application, the data has no relevance to the business, or it could be that some type of information that has become obsolete, such as an inventory item that we no longer carry. The DELETE statement will delete unwanted rows from our tables. This section will take a brief look at the syntax of the DELETE statement and how it is used.

The basic syntax of the DELETE statement is as follows:

```
DELETE [FROM] Table_Name
WHERE Expression
```

In the `DELETE` statement the `FROM` keyword is optional, but it helps to make the `DELETE` statement more readable. The `Table_Name` parameter specifies the name of the table from which we will be deleting rows of data. `Expression` represents a column name and value, or a Boolean expression that evaluates to `True`. Any rows matching the `Expression` will be deleted.

> **WARNING: If you do not specify a WHERE clause then *all* rows will be deleted.**

Try It Out – Delete Query

Let's use a simple example of the `DELETE` statement by deleting the city name that we inserted and updated in the `City_T` table.

1. Start a new query or delete the existing SQL statements in your current query, and enter a `DELETE` statement to delete your city, as shown in the figure below:

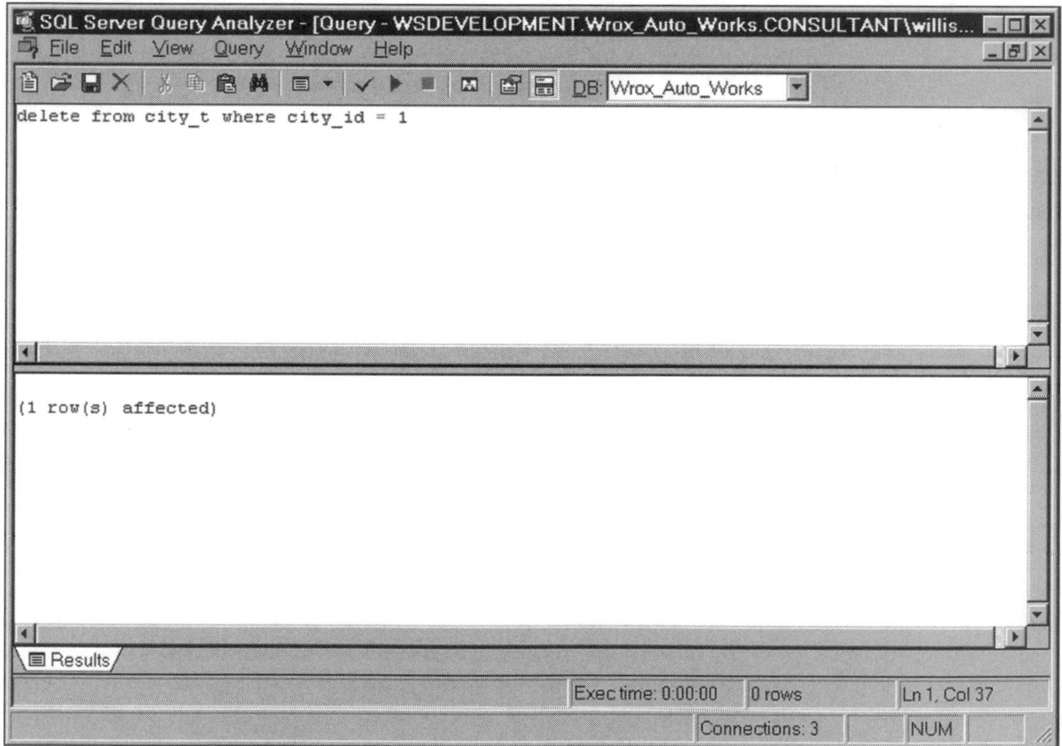

2. After running this example you should receive the message shown in the figure above, which indicates that your delete has been successful.

This example deletes one row of data in the City_T table because we have specified the City_ID in the WHERE clause. Instead of specifying this, we could have used the city name, as shown in the code below. However, using this type of statement deletes *all* rows that match the WHERE clause. This would not be a problem in this particular table because we have a unique index on the city name. This index does not allow duplicate values, so there would only be one city name that matches our WHERE clause below:

```
DELETE FROM City_T
WHERE City_Name_VC = 'Charlotte'
```

However, you should be very careful when using the DELETE statement and think carefully about the clauses you use. Otherwise you may end up deleting data that you did not intend to remove.

If you want to experiment with the DELETE statement, insert two new rows into the City_T table and then execute the DELETE statement without the WHERE clause specified. You will notice that all rows in the City_T table will be deleted.

This section has briefly covered the DELETE statement, but Chapters 7 and 12 will be getting into it in more detail.

Summary

This chapter has introduced you to the SQL Server Query Analyzer. We have acquainted ourselves with this new tool by using it to create and save queries, debug queries, and code and execute queries that insert, update, and delete data. We have seen how we can execute a query against one database, start a new query, and change to another database to execute another query.

You should now feel comfortable using this new tool, and can expect to use it extensively throughout the rest of this book. Most of the work we have done in this chapter is pretty basic, but we will be expanding on this in the coming chapters.

To summarize, you should know how to:

- Start the Query Analyzer and log on if needed
- Select different databases against which to execute queries
- Create and save a new query
- Open existing queries
- Debug your queries
- Code basic SELECT, INSERT, UPDATE, and DELETE statements

We've now set up a database, and learned how we can query the data contained in it from within SQL Server itself. But this book is about manipulating data from VB programs, so in the next chapter we'll be learning how to connect to the database from our VB applications.

WROX AUTO WORKS RACING

Database Connections

The last five chapters have focused on SQL Server and getting you familiar with the environment. We have installed the Desktop edition of SQL Server, created our database and logins, and have explored the Query Analyzer. We are now ready to get back to familiar territory by writing some Visual Basic code.

This chapter explores the various methods available to establish a connection from your VB client program to a SQL Server database. Once you have a connection to the database you can start working with the data it contains. There are several methods to connect to SQL Server and we will explore just some of the more popular methods here.

Before we can jump into writing some code we need to have a quick look at the ActiveX Data Objects (ADO) object model. The release of ADO that we will be working with in this book is version 2.5. This latest release has introduced some new objects and we just want to make you aware of them.

So, in this chapter we will:

- Look at the new ADO object model
- Discuss DSN connections
- Discuss DSN-less connections
- Discuss the Microsoft Data Environment Designer

Overview of the ADO 2.5 Object Model

As we briefly discussed in Chapter 1, **ActiveX Data Objects** (**ADO**) is part of the **Microsoft Data Access Components** (**MDAC**), which also include Remote Data Services (RDS), OLE DB, and Open Database Connectivity (ODBC). These components together make up Microsoft's **Universal Data Access** (**UDA**) strategy that allows access to relational and non-relational data across the enterprise.

ADO provides a lightweight object with high-performance access to data. Designed to provide access to any type of data store, ADO has replaced Data Access Objects (DAO) and Remote Data Objects (RDO) as the preferred data access method. ADO was designed to be easy to learn and use, as is evident from its programming model. It can be used throughout your n-tier and client-server applications, and in your Web applications.

As we mentioned above, this release of ADO has introduced some new objects into the ADO object model. At the time of writing, ADO 2.5 is still in beta but should be released very soon. The object model has also been restructured, so let's take a look at the *new* model:

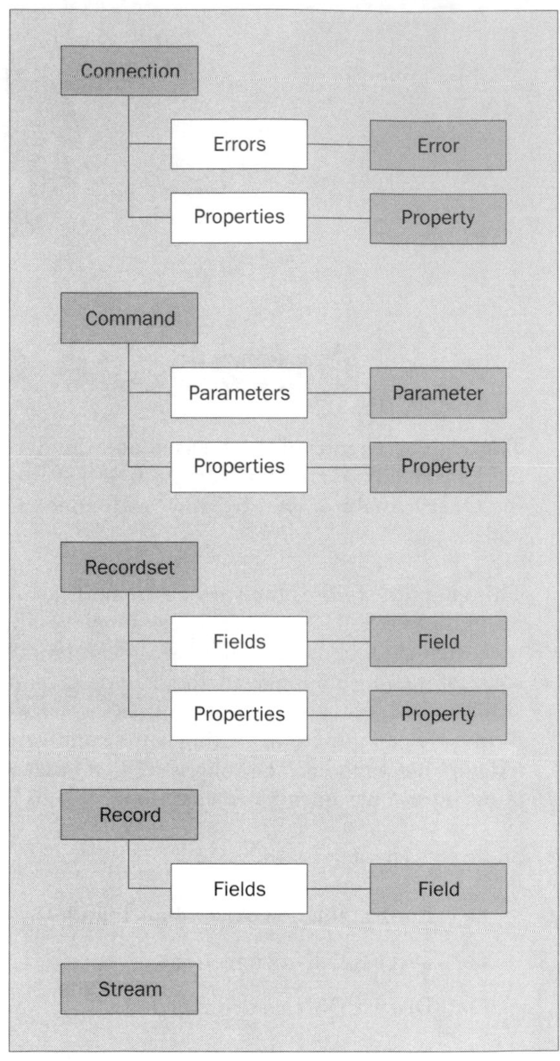

ADO Objects and Collections

If you are already familiar with the ADO object model, at first glance you might think that the `Properties` collection is new. But it has always existed – it was just never shown as part of the object model before.

The `Properties` collection is a collection that is applied to all ADO objects. Each object has a `Properties` collection, which is made up of `Property` objects. Each `Property` object represents a characteristic of an ADO object that is defined by the provider.

What are new are the `Record` and `Stream` objects. Let's take a look at each of the major objects in turn.

Connection Object

The Connection object is at the very heart of the model and allows you to connect to the data store. We'll be studying this object in greater detail in this chapter. All other objects in this model are derived from the Connection object. Once a connection is made, it is used to execute commands and transactions.

The Errors collection is derived from the Connection object, as all errors are returned from the underlying data store or from OLE DB to ADO. This collection contains any errors returned as a result of executing a method or setting a property of any of the ADO objects.

Command Object

The Command object executes stored procedures and in-line SQL statements. We'll see much more of this in Chapter 8. The Command object is an optional object in the model as not all data sources support command execution. The Command object can execute stored procedures and in-line SQL statements that return records and those that do not. Associated with the Command object is the Parameters collection, which allows you to add parameters that are required for a stored procedure or in-line SQL statements.

Recordset Object

The Recordset object should be familiar to everyone who has done any database programming with ADO before. While the Recordset object represents the entire collection of records from a table, or the results of executing a stored procedure or SQL statement, you can only access one row of data in the Recordset object at a time.

The Recordset object now supports the new Record object, which makes programming with the Recordset object easier. The Record object is covered next but basically represents a row of data in the Recordset object.

The Fields collection contains all the information about each field in the recordset, such as the field name in the database, the data type, attributes, and the actual value of the field. A field in the Recordset object corresponds to a column in the database.

Record Object

The Record object can represent a row of data in a Recordset object, a file, or a directory in a file system, or folders and messages in an e-mail system. Using the Record object, you can represent each directory on your computer as a parent Record and each file within the directories as a child Record. You can manage files on your computer that are represented by a Record object by using the CopyRecord, MoveRecord, and DeleteRecord methods. As one might imagine, this can be a powerful tool when working with the VB TreeView control, which provides parent and child nodes.

Stream Object

The Stream object represents a stream of text or binary data. When used in conjunction with the Record object, the Stream object can be used to open a file, read and write data to and from the file, and close the file represented by the Record object.

The complete ADO object model is listed in Appendix B, along with the methods and properties of each object.

Connection Object

Now that we have had a quick look at the objects in the ADO object model, let's turn our attention to the one that is the focus of this chapter – the `Connection` object. The `Connection` object establishes a connection to the database so that we can access and manipulate data using the other objects in ADO.

We use the `Open` method of the `Connection` object to actually establish and open the connection to SQL Server. The `Open` method has the following syntax:

```
objConn.Open (ConnectString, UserID, Password, Options)
```

The `objConn` in the syntax represents a valid `Connection` object defined by you, using this code:

```
Dim objConn as New ADODB.Connection
```

The `ConnectString` parameter contains the information that is used to establish a connection with the database. It can contain information such as the ODBC driver, OLE DB provider, or the Data Source Name being used (which will be covered shortly). `UserID` and `Password` are self-explanatory and contain your logon to SQL Server and your password. `Options` specifies whether the `Connection` should be returned asynchronously or synchronously.

A synchronous connection is when the method being executed must complete before the next method can be executed. Asynchronous connections allow your code to perform other tasks while a method is executing. When this parameter is not specified, a synchronous connection is established by default.

Once all processing has been completed, we close the database connection using the `Close` method of the `Connection` object:

```
objConn.Close
```

Setting Up a Data Source Name

A **Data Source Name** (**DSN**) provides all the information needed for the `Connection` object to establish a connection with the database. The DSN provides information such as what type of ODBC driver should be used, what the name of the database is, where the database resides, and various other information which will be covered shortly.

A DSN can be set up to be either a **User** type, **System** type, or **File** type. A User DSN is specific to the user who created it and cannot be shared. The System DSN can be created on a machine and all users can access it. A File DSN is similar to the System DSN, except that it is stored by default as a text file in the `$\Program Files\Common Files\ODBC\Data Sources` directory, whereas the User and System DSNs are stored in the registry. A File DSN is easier to port to other machines; thus it can be created and moved with your programs that use the DSN.

Try It Out – Create a DSN

We will create a System DSN called Wrox Auto Works that will allow us to access our database. We will be using a login that was created in Chapter 4 that uses SQL Server authentication.

1. We start by opening the Control Panel (from the Settings sub-menu in the Windows Start menu), and double clicking on the ODBC Data Sources (32bit) icon to invoke the ODBC Data Source Administrator, as shown in the figure below.

   Click on the System DSN tab, as this is the type of DSN that we want to create. Click the Add button to start the series of dialogs that walks you through setting up a DSN:

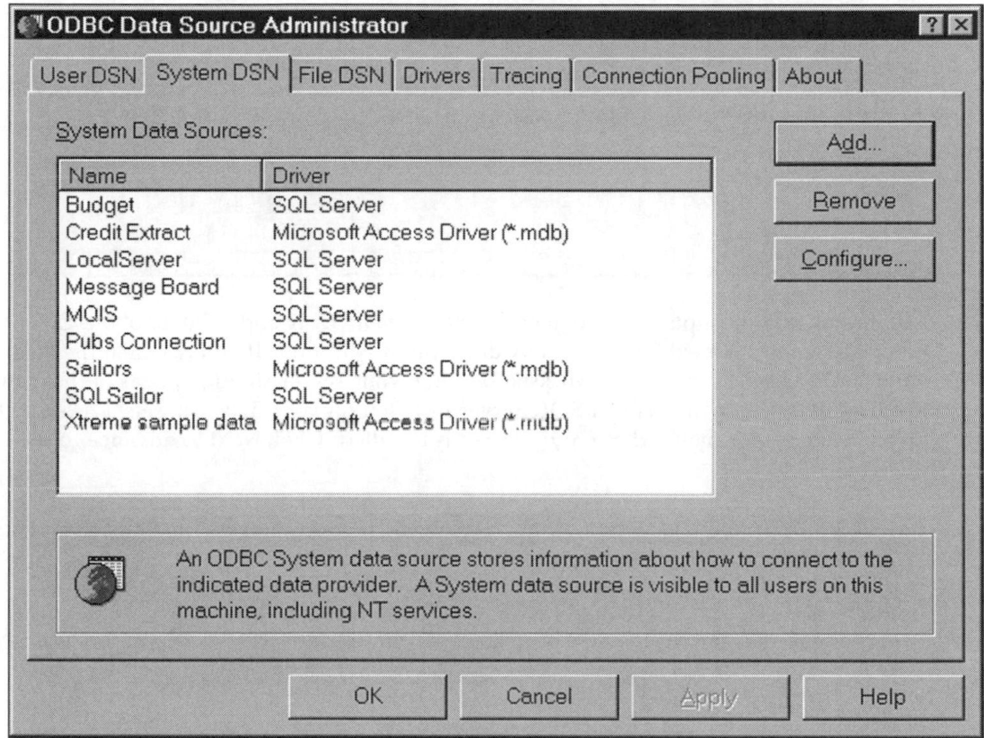

2. The first dialog you see prompts you to select the ODBC driver you want to use to access your database. Since we are dealing with SQL Server, our driver is going to be SQL Server. Select this and then click the Finish button to start the wizard for setting up a SQL Server DSN:

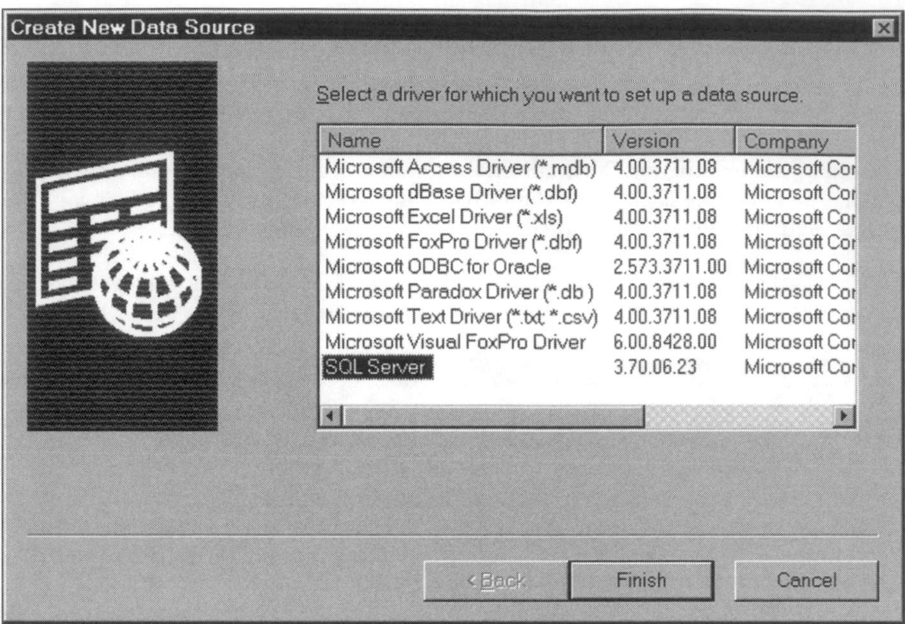

3. The first dialog prompts you to enter a Name for your DSN and a Description. Enter the name shown in the next figure and any description you want. If you installed the Desktop edition of SQL Server on your workstation, then your server should appear in the drop down list as (local). If you are using a SQL Server installed on your network, select or enter the appropriate server name where SQL Server is installed. Click Next to advance to the next dialog:

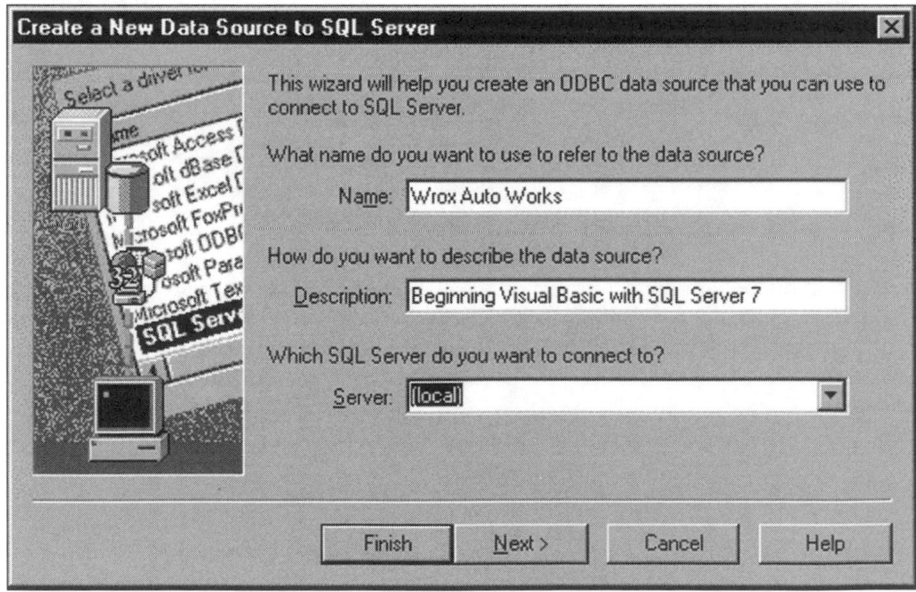

4. Experience has shown that the best method to use for authentication is SQL Server authentication. This provides the most secure DSN connections. If you use NT authentication and your login ID is set up for NT authentication in SQL Server, then anyone using your machine while you are logged on can access SQL Server with your permissions. Even if the user specifies another login ID and password, NT authentication will override it. For this reason and to provide a more secure DSN, use SQL Server authentication.

   You will need to select the With SQL Server authentication radio button and then enter a Login ID and Password that uses SQL Server authentication. If you used NT authentication to setup your own login ID, then enter one of the two users that were set up for the Sales Staff and Management roles in Chapter 4. Clicking on the Client Configuration button lets you define the connection protocol, although this is outside the realms of this book. Click Next to continue on to the next step:

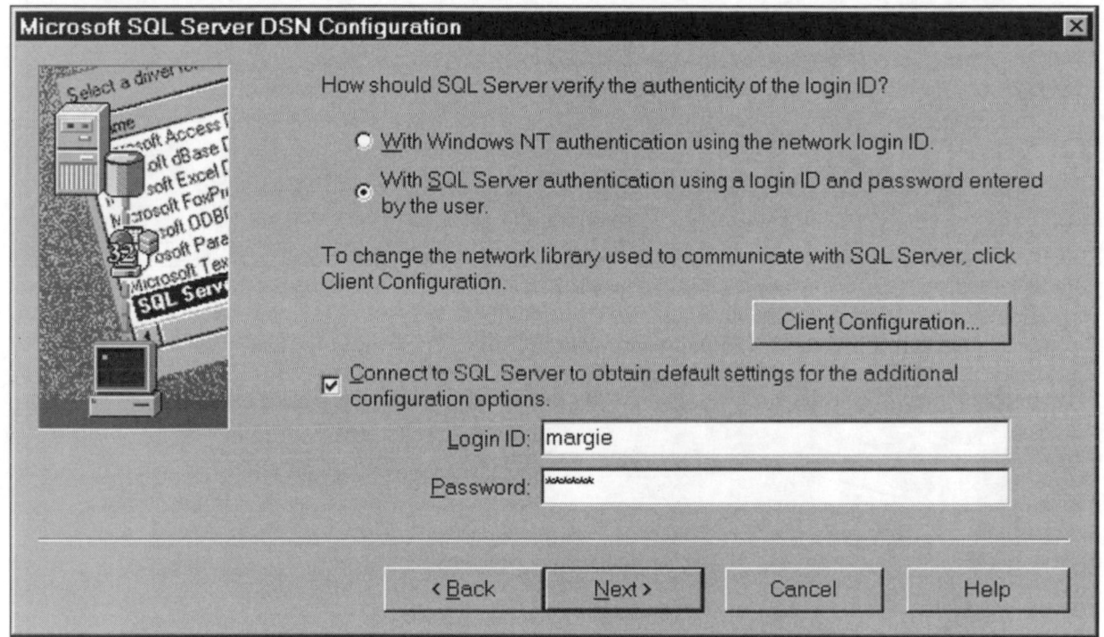

5. Check the Change the default database to: checkbox and select the Wrox_Auto_Works database. Accept all other defaults on this dialog, as shown below, and click Next to proceed:

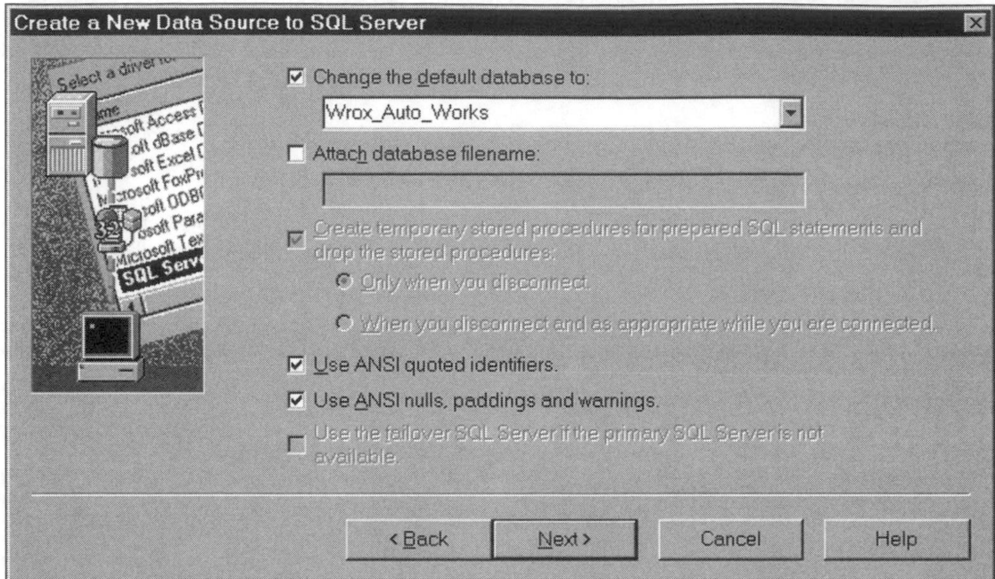

6. Unless you want to change your default language or turn on logging, click the Finish button to proceed to the next dialog:

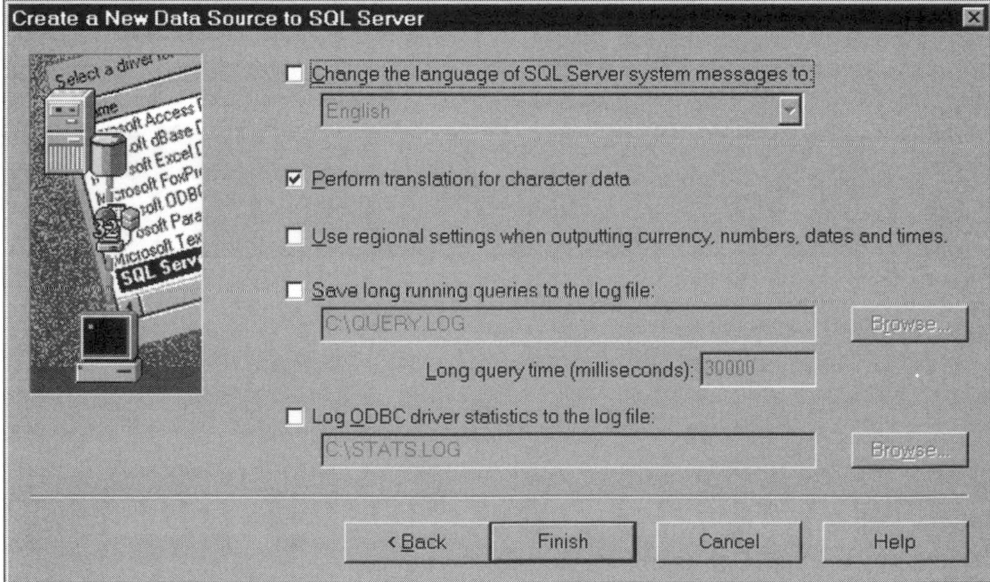

7. It is always a good idea to test your DSN at this point and you can do so by clicking on the Test Data Source button:

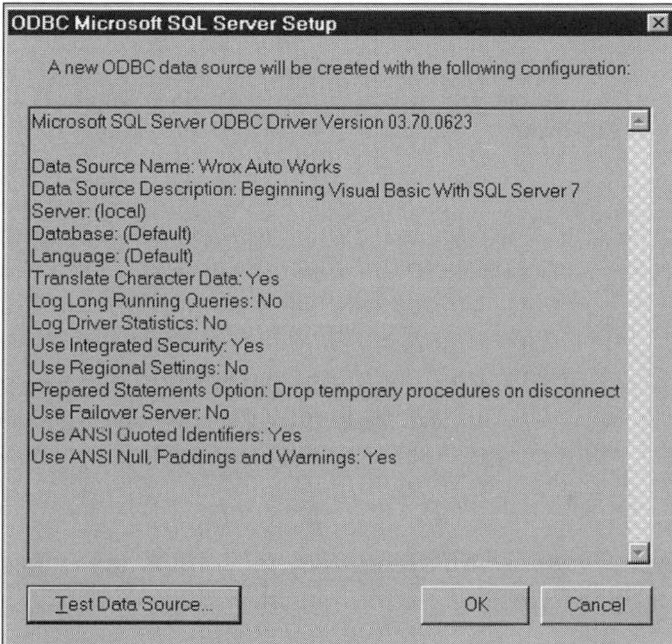

8. If your tests were successful you will see the next dialog:

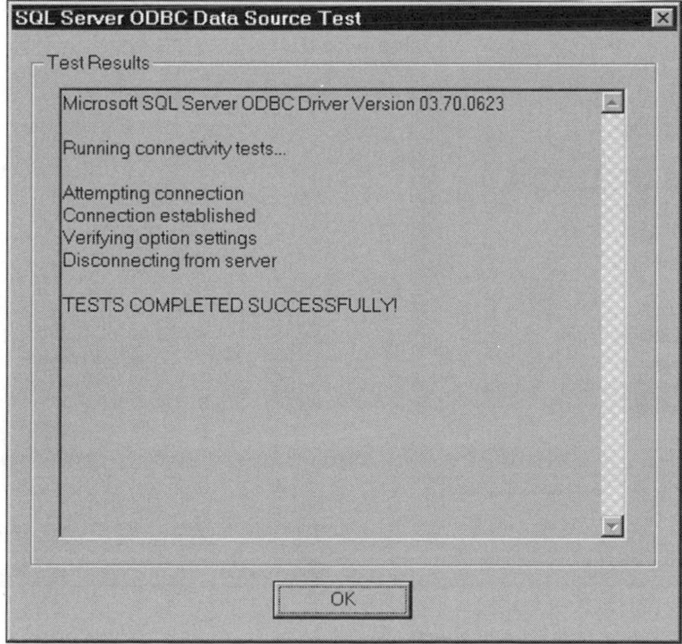

If they were not, go back and repeat the steps above, verifying that the information you have entered is correct. Click the OK button to dismiss the dialog and you will be returned back to the previous dialog.

9. This is the last step in creating your DSN, and clicking the OK button will finalize the DSN and write it to the registry. You will be returned to the original screen seen at the beginning of this example, but this time the Wrox Auto Works DSN will appear. You can now close the Data Source Administrator dialog.

At this point our DSN is ready for use. For those of you who are security conscious, don't worry. As we stated earlier, anyone who can log on to this machine can access and use this DSN, however there is one small catch – they will need a valid login ID and password in SQL Server before they can use it. While creating the DSN, you supplied a login ID and password, but only so that the dialog could establish a connection with SQL Server to gather some information and to validate the DSN. Your password is not stored as part of the DSN.

The registry entries defining this DSN are shown in the next figure. If you want to view the information for the DSN that you have just set up, start the Registry Editor by clicking on the Start button and choosing Run. Enter RegEdit and click OK. Once the Registry Editor is open, expand the HKEY_LOCAL_MACHINE hive and then expand the Software folder. Find ODBC and expand that, then expand odbc.ini. Click on the Wrox Auto Works folder to display the information:

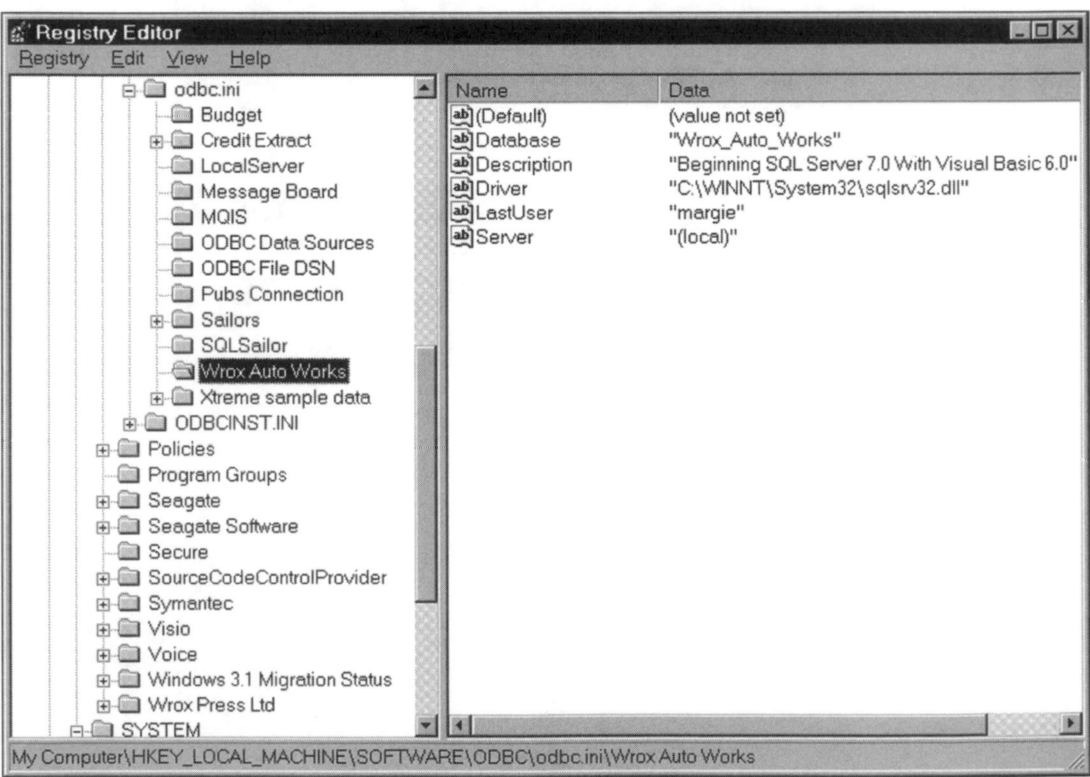

Should you ever want to remove the DSN that you have just created from your system, you need to click on the ODBC Data Sources (32bit) icon in the Control Panel to invoke the ODBC Data Source Administrator. Then highlight the DSN to be deleted and click on the Remove button:

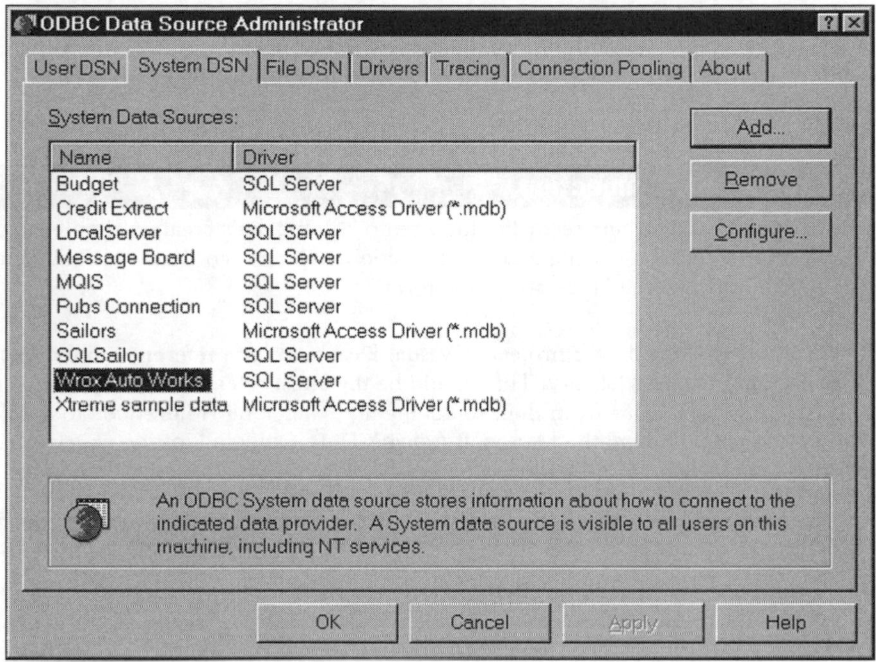

Should you ever need to reconfigure the DSN to point it to a SQL Server on another machine, you would click the Configure button in the dialog above. This would take you to the dialog shown earlier in step 3, and you would repeat the same steps described above to reconfigure the DSN.

DSN Connections

As we mentioned at the beginning of this chapter, there are several ways to establish a connection from your Visual Basic program to SQL Server. This section explores the DSN connection. That is, we use a DSN to connect to SQL Server. Using a DSN in Visual Basic server components is probably the most common use of DSNs. A server component is an ActiveX DLL that implements business rules and performs specific business tasks. We are going to be using a DSN in a front-end program within this chapter for demonstration purposes. Chapter 14 will explore server components in more depth and we will also be using a DSN with our components in that chapter.

We are going to use the `Open` method syntax of the `Connection` object that was described earlier in this chapter, so your connection statement will look similar to the code fragment below. You, of course, will have to substitute the user ID and password for one of the test users you set up, or any user ID that uses SQL Server authentication.

```
objConn.Open "DSN=Wrox Auto Works;UserID=margie;PWD=margie"
```

Of course, the ConnectString does not have to be hard coded and really shouldn't be. There are many reasons for not hard coding your ConnectString and the main reason is security of your user ID and password. This ConnectString could be passed in as a string variable that has been read from the registry or supplied as information when a user logs on.

After you have opened a connection, you should verify the state of the connection using the State property of the Connection object. This property will tell you if the Connection object is open, closed, connecting, executing or fetching. More on this in a moment.

Try It Out – Using a DSN Connection

Since we have entered at least one record in the State_T table, let's create a simple front-end program that will connect to the database using a DSN connection, open a recordset returning data from the State_T table, and display the first state on the form.

1. Open a new Standard EXE project in Visual Basic and set a reference to the Microsoft ActiveX Data Objects Library. This should be the latest release you have installed, preferably release 2.5. This is done from the Project menu, by clicking References to invoke the References dialog. Find the Microsoft ActiveX Data Objects Library, check the checkbox, and then click OK to dismiss the dialog:

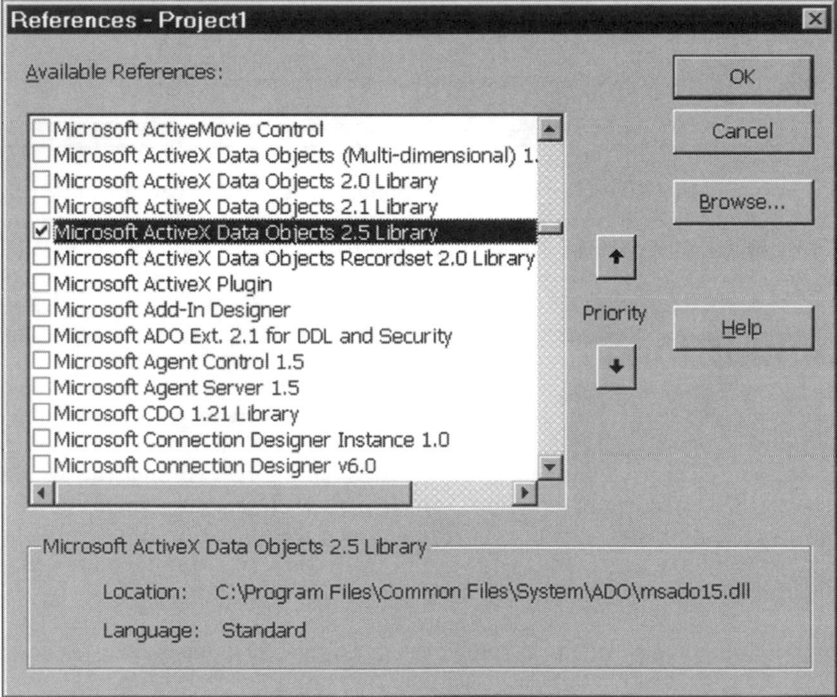

2. Change the name of the form to frmTryItOut2 and change the form caption to Try It Out #2 - DSN Connection, if you wish.

3. On the form, place a label control and use the default name of Label1. Enter the following code, which is available as `frmTryItOut2.frm`, changing the `UID` and `PWD` if necessary. Then run your project.

```
Private Sub Form_Load()
   'Use the standard Windows icon
   Me.Icon = Nothing

   'Declare database objects
   Dim objConn As New ADODB.Connection
   Dim objRS As New ADODB.Recordset
   Dim objErr As ADODB.Error

   'Establish a database connection using SQL Server Authentication
   objConn.Open "DSN=Wrox Auto Works;UID=margie;PWD=margie"

   'Check the state of the connection to ensure we are connected
   If objConn.State = adStateOpen Then

      'Open a recordset
      objRS.Open "State_T", objConn, adOpenForwardOnly, adLockReadOnly, adCmdTable
      If Not objRS.EOF And Not objRS.BOF Then
         Label1.Caption = objRS!State_Name_VC
      End If
      objRS.Close

   Else

      'Display all errors
      For Each objErr In objConn.Errors
         Debug.Print objErr.Description
      Next

   End If

   'De-reference the database objects
   Set objRS = Nothing
   objConn.Close
   Set objConn = Nothing
End Sub
```

You will see the following:

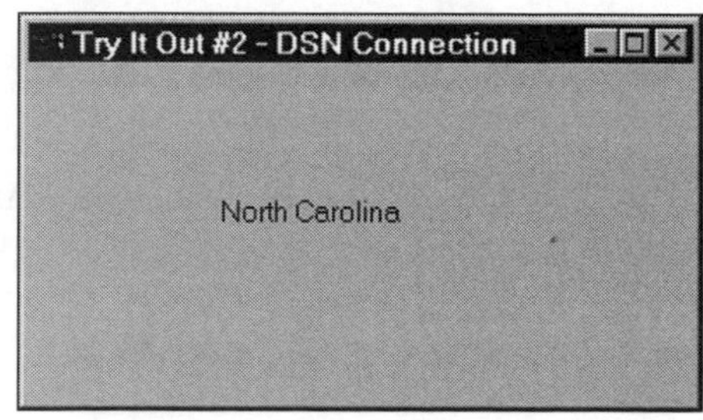

How It Works - Using A DSN Connection

This example is pretty straightforward, but we will step through the code just to make sure everyone is comfortable with what we are doing. All of this code was placed in the `Form_Load` event to keep this example simple.

If you take a look at the form in design view, you will notice that the icon on the form is the default form icon provided by VB. Instead of replacing it with some other icon, we enter the first line of code to set the current form icon to `Nothing`, which then gets replaced with the Windows default icon when the program is run. We can use the `Me` keyword to represent the current object, in this case `frmTryItOut2`. This provides an easier means to reference the properties and methods of the form without trying to type a long form name:

```
Private Sub Form_Load()
   'Use the standard Windows icon
   Me.Icon = Nothing
```

Then we declare the database objects that we need, in this case a `Connection` object to establish a connection to the database, a `Recordset` object to hold the returned records, and an `Error` object – just in case we encounter any errors:

```
   'Declare database objects
   Dim objConn As New ADODB.Connection
   Dim objRS As New ADODB.Recordset
   Dim objErr As ADODB.Error
```

Next, we establish a connection with the database, specifying our DSN in the `ConnectString`. But wait, the user ID and password are part of the `ConnectString` and are not specified separately. According to the syntax of the `Open` method that we explored above, we need to specify the user ID and password separately from the `ConnectString`. Well, this is not quite true. All parameters of the `Open` method are optional, and since our DSN requires a user ID and password, we can pass them as parameters of the `ConnectString` as we have done in the code fragment below:

```
'Establish a database connection using SQL Server Authentication
   objConn.Open "DSN=Wrox Auto Works;UID=margie;PWD=margie"
```

The `UID` and `PWD` parameters in the `ConnectString` can be passed as parameters of the connection string, or can be passed separately as parameters of the `Connection` object's `Open` method. Just to prove our point, substitute the following line of code, using your user ID and password, and run your project. Notice that this also works. The user ID and password, although specified separately, are passed to the DSN so a connection can be established:

```
'Establish a database connection using SQL Server Authentication
   objConn.Open "DSN=Wrox Auto Works", "margie", "margie"
```

This section of code applies to those readers who have set up their login ID in SQL Server using NT authentication. Since you are running on Windows NT, you don't have to specify a user ID and password at all, as is demonstrated in the next code fragment:

```
'Establish a database connection using NT Authentication
   objConn.Open "DSN=Wrox Auto Works"
```

In fact, if you try to pass a user ID and password that use NT authentication in SQL Server, you will get the error shown below. This is because SQL Server will think that the user ID and password you are passing are using SQL Server authentication.

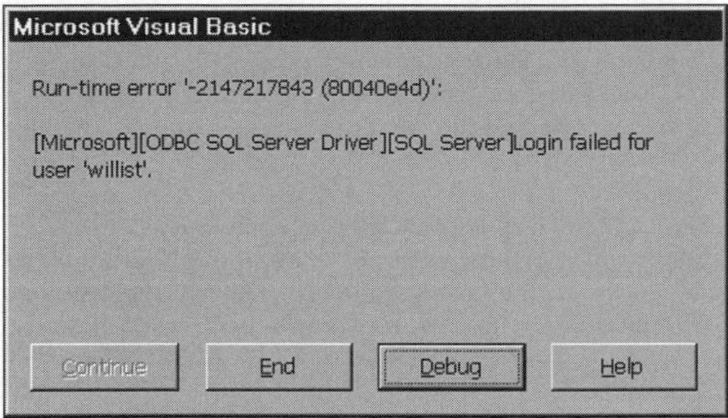

Moving on, we next check the state of the connection using the `Connection` object's `State` property. Remember earlier we said that the `State` property indicates the current state of the `Connection` object. We are using the `adStateOpen` constant from the `ObjectStateEnum` enumeration to compare to the current state of the `Connection` object:

```
'Check the state of the connection to ensure we are connected
If objConn.State = adStateOpen Then
```

If the `State` of the `Connection` object is open then we execute the next few lines of code. But before we examine them, let's take a quick look at the parameters of the `Open` method of the `Recordset` object:

- The first parameter is the `Source` parameter and specifies a table name to be opened, in-line SQL statements, or the stored procedure to be executed.
- The `ActiveConnection` parameter lets the `Open` method know how it should access the database. This parameter can be in the form of a `Connection` object or a connection string.
- The `CursorType` parameter specifies what type of cursor the database should use when opening the recordset. A cursor controls how the recordset is navigated and how the data is updated in the recordset.
- `LockType` specifies what type of locking the database should use on the recordset when editing of records occurs.
- The last parameter of the `Open` method is the `Options` parameter. It tells the database how it should interpret the `Source` parameter. This is an optional parameter, but by specifying it, we can improve the performance of our code, because the processor doesn't need to work out for itself what type of `Source` parameter we are supplying.

The `Recordset.Open` parameters must be specified in order. If you leave out a parameter to use the default that is provided by ADO, then you must insert a comma in its place before specifying the next parameter, as shown below:

```
objRS.Open "State_T", objConn, , , adCmdTable
```

Getting back to our code, first we open the Recordset object, passing it the following parameters. The Source parameter is set to the State_T table and the ActiveConnection parameter is set to the Connection object. We have specified adOpenForwardOnly as the CursorType parameter because we only want to read the recordset in one direction. This constant is listed in the CursorTypeEnum enumeration. The LockType parameter uses the adLockReadOnly constant from the LockTypeEnum enumeration. Since we are only reading this data, there is less overhead associated with this lock type. And finally, the adCmdTable constant from the CommandTypeEnum enumeration has been specified for the Options parameter. All of these enumerations are viewable in the Object Browser in VB.

After opening the Recordset object, we check for an end of file (EOF) and a beginning of file (BOF) condition. If both the BOF and EOF properties are True, it would indicate that our recordset is empty. If it is not empty, then we execute the next line of code. This sets the caption of the label control to the state name contained in the State_Name_VC field of the first record of our recordset:

```
      'Open a recordset
      objRS.Open "State_T", objConn, adOpenForwardOnly, adLockReadOnly, adCmdTable
      If Not objRS.EOF And Not objRS.BOF Then
         Label1.Caption = objRS!State_Name_VC
      End If
      objRS.Close
```

If the State of the Connection object is not equal to open, then we display each error in the debug window. We do this by using a For Each loop, enumerating through each of the errors in the Errors collection of the Connection object. We are only displaying the error description, but you could display more error information if you wanted to. See the Error object in Appendix B, the ADO help file, or MSDN Library for all the available properties that can be displayed.

```
   Else

      'Display all errors
      For Each objErr In objConn.Errors
         Debug.Print objErr.Description
      Next

   End If
```

Last, we close and de-reference all of our database objects:

```
   'De-reference the database objects
   Set objRS = Nothing
   objConn.Close
   Set objConn = Nothing
End Sub
```

This section has covered the DSN connection and has shown you various ways to connect using a DSN and SQL Server authentication. We have also covered using a DSN connection with NT authentication. We have explained why you should use SQL Server authentication when setting up your DSN, and explained why you set your DSN up as a System DSN as opposed to a User or File DSN.

DSN-Less Connections

Using a DSN connection in your code requires that a DSN be set up on the server or computer that your program or server component is running on. SQL Server can be on the same computer or on some other computer on the network. This scenario, while good in some circumstances, restricts where your code can run. Because a DSN-less connection specifies all of the parameters necessary to connect to SQL Server, using a DSN-less connection allows your program to be run on different machines without having to set up a new DSN.

This section explores the **DSN-less connection**. A DSN-less connection, as its names implies, uses no DSN. What it does use is the required parameters that will let the `Connection` object know how to establish a connection to SQL Server. Using a DSN-less connection in your server components helps to make your applications n-tier scalable, because your server components are not restricted to running on one server. As your components use a DSN-less connection, they can be moved from a server running with your database, or from the computer running your program, to a server that runs just the components. This spreads the workload among different servers and your application has scaled from 2-tier to n-tier.

Let's take a look at some of the required parameters for a DSN-less connection. If you remember, in the first step of setting up a DSN we specified what type of ODBC driver we wanted to use. A DSN-less connection is no different and we must specify the ODBC driver to be used, in our case SQL Server. This is specified as `Driver = SQL Server`.

The next step when we set up our DSN was to select the server where SQL Server was running – in our case it was `Local`. `Local` will not work here, so we need to specify the actual name of our computer. For our DSN-less connection we specify `Server = WSDevelopment`, where `WSDevelopment` is my computer's name.

Once we have specified the server where SQL Server is running, we need to let our DSN-less connection know which database in SQL Server we want to access, and we do so by specifying `Database = Wrox_Auto_Works`.

The following code fragment is what our `Connection` object looks like at this point:

```
objConn.Open "Driver=SQL Server;Server=WSDevelopment;Database=Wrox_Auto_Works"
```

If you are using a Windows NT authentication login in SQL Server, then this is all the information you need. You would be able to establish a connection at this point. For those readers who are using a SQL Server authentication login you must also specify a user ID and password, as shown in the next code fragment:

```
objConn.Open "Driver=SQL Server;Server=WSDevelopment;Database=Wrox_Auto_Works;" & _
    UID=margie;PWD=margie"
```

Now that we know how to create a DSN-less connection, let's put this information to use in a hands-on example.

Try It Out – Using a DSN-Less Connection

We will create a program similar to the last one, using a simple form to display the state name. This program should use a DSN-less connection and select all data from the `State_T` table. We will display only the first state on the form.

1. You will need to open a new **Standard EXE** project and set a reference to the **Microsoft ActiveX Data Objects Library**, as described in the previous example.

2. Change the name of the form to `frmTryItOut3` and change the form caption to `Try It Out #3 - DSN-less Connection` if you want to.

3. Place a label control on the form and use the default name of **Label1**. The Caption property of the label can be left as it is, or you can remove the text in the Caption property.

4. Enter the following code, which can be found in `frmTryItOut3.frm`. (Note that if you are using SQL Server authentication you will need to add your user ID and password details to the connection string – refer to the *How It Works* section below for more help with this.)

```
Private Sub Form_Load()
   'Use the standard Windows icon
   Me.Icon = Nothing

   'Declare database objects
   Dim objConn As New ADODB.Connection
   Dim objRS As New ADODB.Recordset
   Dim objErr As ADODB.Error

   'Establish a database connection using NT Authentication
   objConn.Open "Driver=SQL Server;Server=WSDevelopment;Database=Wrox_Auto_Works"

   'Check the state of the connection to ensure we are connected
   If objConn.State = adStateOpen Then

      'Open a recordset
      objRS.Open "SELECT * FROM State_T", objConn, adOpenForwardOnly, _
                 adLockReadOnly, adCmdText
      If Not objRS.EOF And Not objRS.BOF Then
         Label1.Caption = objRS!State_Name_VC
      End If
      objRS.Close

   Else

      'Display all errors
      For Each objErr In objConn.Errors
         Debug.Print objErr.Description
      Next
```

```
    End If

    'De-reference the database objects
    Set objRS = Nothing
    objConn.Close
    Set objConn = Nothing
End Sub
```

5. Run the program and you should see something like the following:

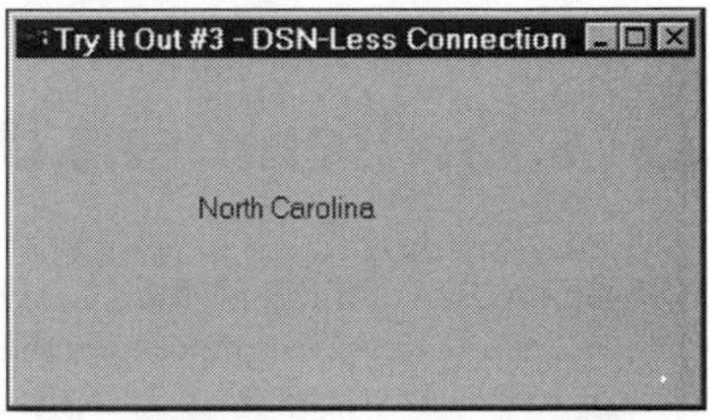

How It Works – Using a DSN-Less Connection

The first part of the code in this example is the same as the last one. The difference comes when we open our database connection using the `Connection` object. Here we are using a DSN-less connection as we discussed above, and are using a SQL Server login that uses NT authentication:

```
'Establish a database connection using NT Authentication
objConn.Open "Driver=SQL Server;Server=WSDevelopment;Database=Wrox_Auto_Works"
```

For those readers whose SQL Server login uses SQL Server authentication, substitute one of the following code fragments to connect. Don't forget to substitute your server name, login ID and password. The first code fragment uses one `ConnectString` that specifies the user ID and password. The second code fragment is an alternative that uses a `ConnectString`, with the user ID and password specified as separate parameters:

```
'Establish a database connection using SQL Server Authentication
objConn.Open "Driver=SQL Server;Server=WSDevelopment;" & _
   "Database=Wrox_Auto_Works;UID=margie;PWD=margie"
```

```
'Establish a database connection using SQL Server Authentication
objConn.Open "Driver=SQL Server;Server=WSDevelopment;" & _
   "Database=Wrox_Auto_Works", "margie", "margie"
```

This next part of code is a little different from our last example, and shows an alternative way to select data from the `State_T` table. While this change is not necessary in your code, it does demonstrate another method of selecting the same data. We are using an actual SQL statement instead of the table name to select the state names. The rest of the parameters of the `Open` method are the same, except the last parameter. Since we are using a SQL statement, we must specify the `adCmdText` constant from the `CommandTypeEnum` enumeration for the `Options` parameter:

```
    'Open a recordset
    objRS.Open "SELECT * FROM State_T", objConn, adOpenForwardOnly, _
               adLockReadOnly, adCmdText
    If Not objRS.EOF And Not objRS.BOF Then
       Label1.Caption = objRS!State_Name_VC
    End If
    objRS.Close
```

As you can see, using a DSN or DSN-less connection is very easy and very straightforward. These types of connections are usually reserved for server components, but are often found in front-end programs also.

Either way, these types of connections are quick to set up, and you can prompt the user for their user ID and password before establishing a connection to the database, instead of including them as part of the `ConnectString`.

Data Environment Designer Connections

The last method of connecting to a database that we are going to cover is the **Data Environment Designer**. This built-in ActiveX control provides a quick code-less method of adding a database connection. This designer uses either a DSN or a DSN-less connection. All of the connection information is stored for you in the ActiveX control as properties of the control. You simply provide all of the information for the connection and the Data Environment Designer will take care of the rest of the work for you.

You can also add a `Command` object that will execute SQL statements, stored procedures, tables, and views. All of this is set up through dialogs that step you through the process. Best of all is that you don't have to write any code to provide this functionality, as this is all handled within the Data Environment Designer.

The objects created for you behind the scenes by the Data Environment Designer can be used by **data aware controls** on your forms. A data aware control is one that can be bound to a data source, such as an ActiveX data control or recordset. You can also access these objects through code. When using the Data Environment Designer's `Command` object you can drag and drop the fields from the `Command` object onto your form, as will be demonstrated shortly.

Try It Out – Using the Data Environment Designer

In this example, we will be creating a Standard EXE project that contains a form with no controls. The controls shown in the screen shot below will be added from the Data Environment Designer. We will add the Data Environment Designer and set the connection using the DSN that we have used previously. We will then add a `Command` object to the Data Environment Designer to open the `State_T` table. Finally, we will add the `State_Name_VC` field to the form. Our completed form will look something like this:

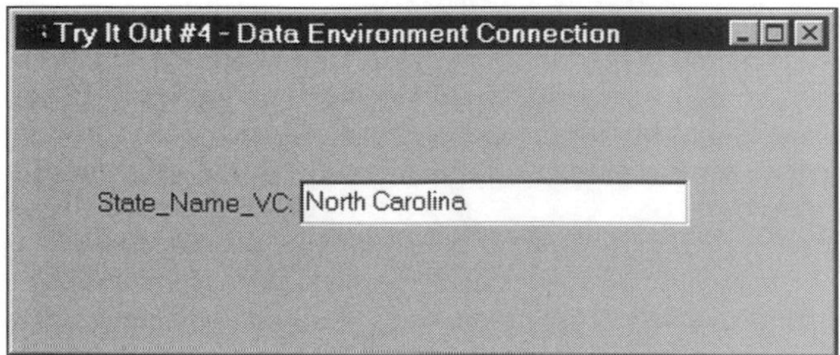

1. We start by opening a new **Standard EXE** project in VB, and renaming/captioning the form if required.

2. Add the following code to the `Form_Load` event. This code can be found in `frmTryItOut4.frm`:

```
Private Sub Form_Load()
   'Use the standard Windows icon
   Me.Icon = Nothing
End Sub
```

3. This is the only code that we are adding and the only code that will be in our project. Next, add the Data Environment Designer by selecting the **Project** menu and then selecting **Add Data Environment**. If **Add Data Environment** isn't listed here, you should select **More ActiveX Designers** in the **Project** menu and then choose **Data Environment** from the sub menu. The location of **Data Environment** in the **Project** menu is related to the number of third-party ActiveX controls that have been installed for VB. If you still do not see the Data Environment Designer then click on the **Project** menu and choose **Components**. On the **Designers** tab, check the checkbox next to **Data Environment** and then click **OK** on this dialog. You should now see **Data Environment** in the **Project** menu.

   At this point your project should look like the screen shot shown below:

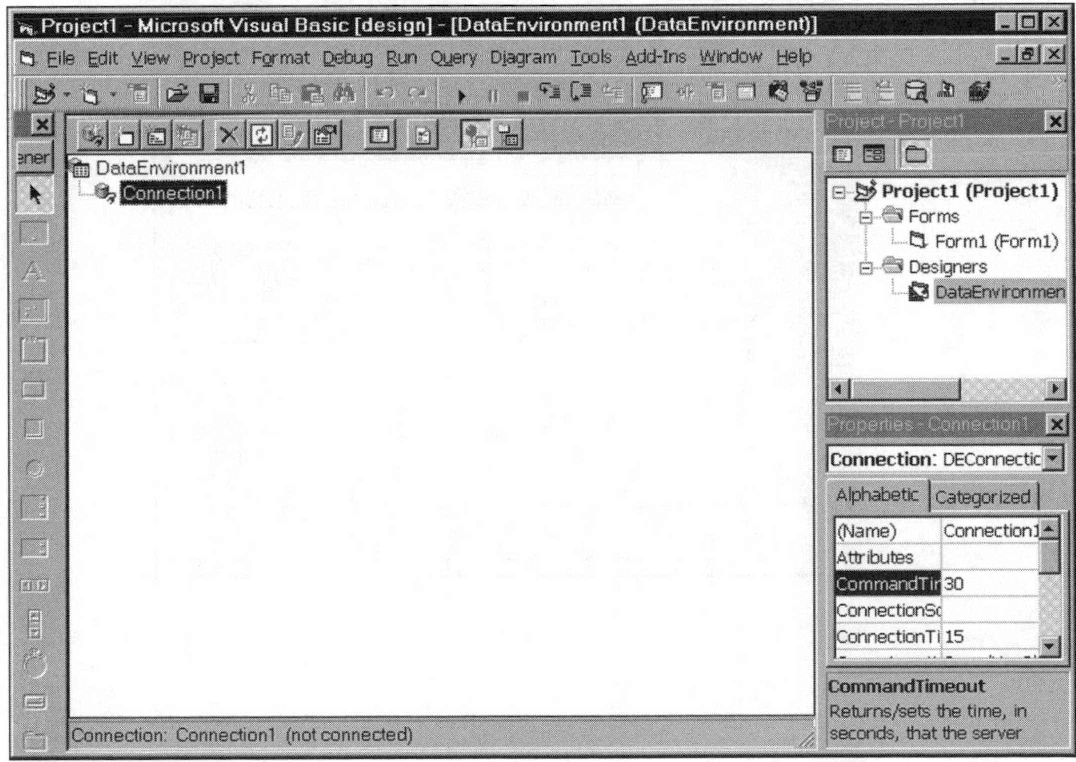

4. Right click on Connection1 and choose Properties from the popup menu, or click on the Properties icon on the Data Designer Environment toolbar. Click on the Connection tab in the Data Link Properties dialog. Select the Wrox Auto Works DSN in the Use data source name combo box.

5. If you are using NT authentication you do not need to specify any more information. If you are using SQL Server authentication for your login ID then enter your User name and Password in the appropriate boxes. Check the Allow saving password checkbox so you are not prompted for your password anymore.

6. All readers should test their connection at this point by clicking on the Test Connection button. Once your connection has been verified, close this dialog by clicking on the OK button:

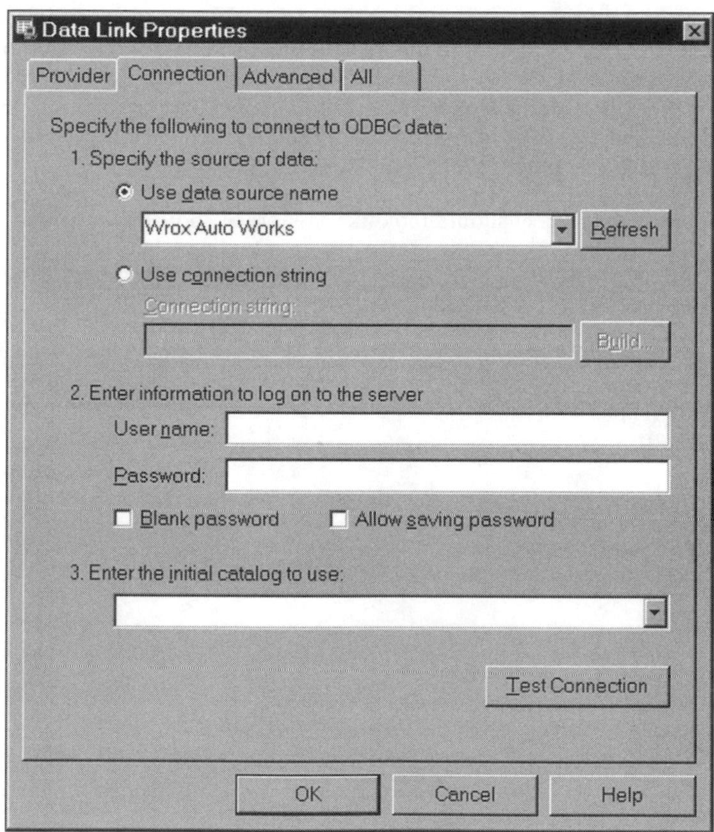

7. The next step we want to perform is to add a `Command` object to the Data Environment Designer by clicking on the **Add Command** icon on the **Data Environment Designer** toolbar, or by right clicking in the white space and choosing **Add Command** from the popup menu. The `Command` object will provide a method to retrieve the state names from the `State_T` table in the database.

8. To access the `Command` object **Properties** dialog, right click on the **Command1** object and choose **Properties** in the popup menu, or click the **Properties** icon on the Data Environment Designer toolbar. The source of data for this example will be the `State_T` table as in the first example. We need to select **Table** from the **Database Object** combo box and in the **Object Name** combo box choose **State_T** from the list of tables in our database. That's all we need for this example, but feel free to poke around in this dialog and look at the various options in the different tabs. When you are done, click the **OK** button to dismiss this dialog:

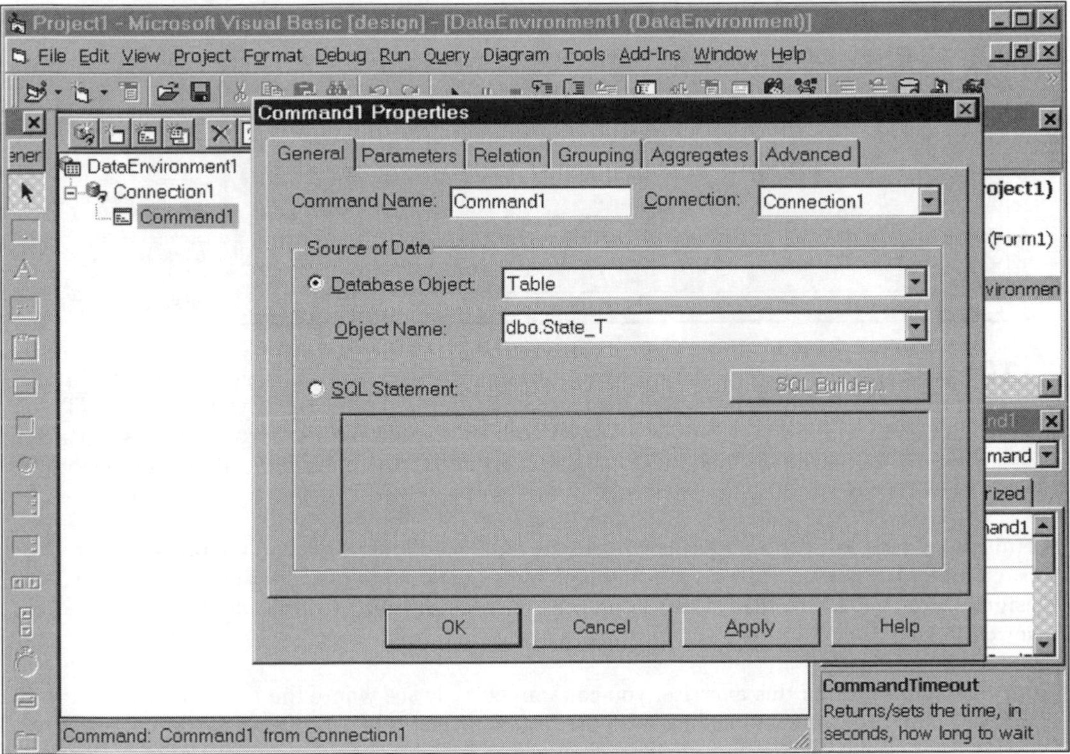

9. Now that we have the `Command` object set with the data that it should retrieve, expand the `Command` object and it will display all of the columns in the `State_T` table. At this point, tile your windows in VB so that the Data Environment Designer and form are both displayed. Click on the **State_Name_VC** column in the Data Environment Designer and drag it onto the form:

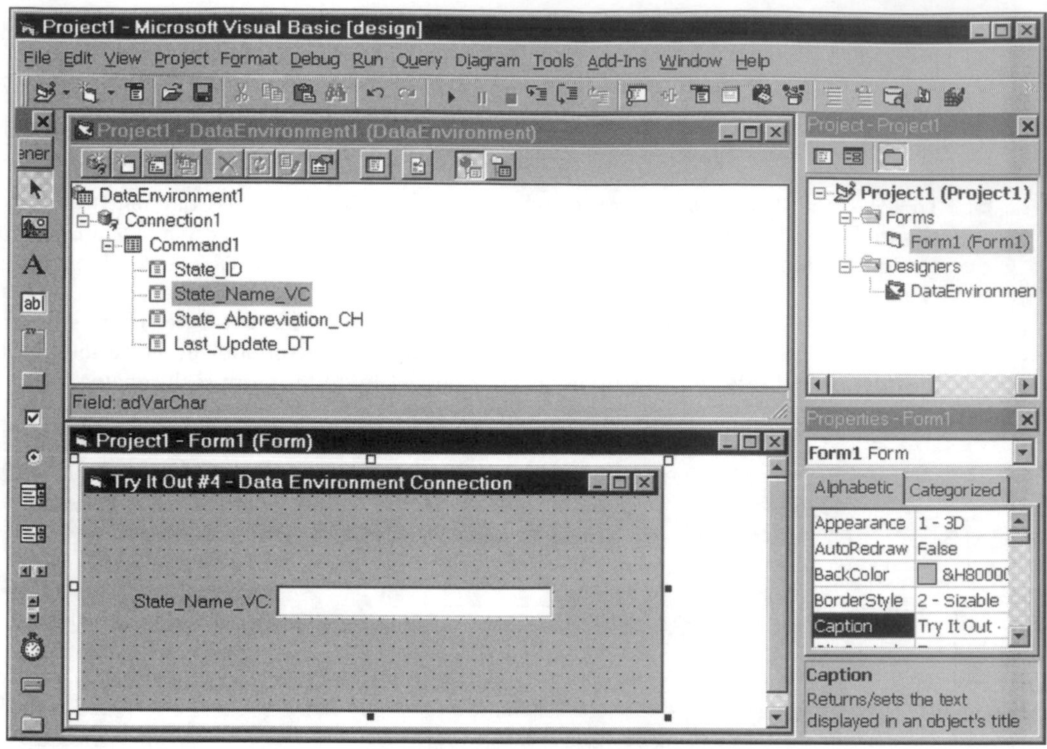

10. At this point, believe it or not, we are ready to run our project, so go ahead and start your project. You will be prompted with a SQL Server Login dialog. If you are using NT authentication in SQL Server, ensure that the Login ID and Password fields are blank and then click on the OK button. If you are using SQL Server authentication, enter your Login ID and Password and then click on OK.

At this point your form should display your state name and look similar to the one shown at the start of this example. If you stop your project and look at the code in the form and Data Environment Designer, you will notice that the only code that is listed in your project is the few lines of code that we inserted in step 2.

After having performed this exercise, you can immediately see where the Data Environment Designer can save you lots of time and coding to implement data access in your front-end programs. There is only one thing that you should be aware of. By default, the Data Environment Designer sets a reference to Microsoft ActiveX Data Objects Library version *2.0*. In order to take advantage of the latest fixes and advancements in ADO, you should remove this reference and set a reference to version 2.5, or the latest version that you have available.

If you want to, you can experiment on your own with the Data Environment Designer, using code to control the connection and displaying of the `Command` object data.

Summary

This chapter has taken a look at the steps required to set up a DSN. You should now be familiar with setting up a DSN, know what types are available, and which type to use for your own particular situation. You should also understand the difference between NT authentication and SQL Server authentication, which method to use in your DSN, and why.

We have covered three methods of establishing a connection with the database to provide data access in our programs. Each has its own merits and its own method of use; the choice of method depends on what functions your program or server component needs to perform. You should be comfortable using all three methods, as the examples we have provided demonstrate establishing a basic connection by each method in turn. Once you have experimented with these examples on your own, you will discover the power of these connections, and how you can pass the parameters as variables that you retrieve from the user or registry settings, to control who is able to log on.

In summary, we have:

- Highlighted the objects of the ADO object model
- Walked through the steps of setting up a DSN
- Explored the DSN connection
- Explored the DSN-less connection
- Explored using the Data Designer Environment to add a connection
- Taken a look at the different authentication methods that can be used with the different connections that we have demonstrated

So far we have covered all of the necessary steps to set up a database, grant users access to its objects, and connect to the database from VB. We are now going to look at how we can communicate with the database, to make use of the data contained within it.

WROX AUTO WORKS RACING

Introduction to Stored Procedures

In Chapter 5 we used SQL statements to insert, select, update, and delete data, and in the last chapter we used SQL statements to select data from the `State_T` table. While the use of in-line SQL statements is great for ad-hoc queries, they are not generally used in production applications. They do, however, have their place in production applications where *dynamic* SQL statements are to be built and executed. Dynamic SQL statements are SQL statements that are built in your VB code, thus they are generated dynamically at run-time. You typically use `If.. Else.. End If` statements to build the SQL statements needed to retrieve the data that the user has requested. For the most part stored procedures are used, and provide many benefits over in-line Transact-SQL statements.

This chapter explores stored procedures and demonstrates some of the basic tasks that can be accomplished with them. We will take a look at stored procedure parameters and see how they can be used to build robust stored procedures. All of the stored procedures created in this chapter will be executed in a VB front-end program that we will create.

In this chapter we will examine:

- Stored procedure performance
- Input and output parameters and the return value
- Stored procedures that select, insert, update, and delete data

Stored Procedure vs Transact-SQL Performance

Before we begin talking about performance issues, we first need to define what a **stored procedure** is. A stored procedure consists of one or more SQL statements that perform a unit of work, that are compiled into an **execution plan** when executed. An execution plan contains two parts; one part that contains the code to be executed, and one part that contains the variables and parameters that are to be used by the code.

Stored procedures provide a way to share code, in much the same way that a server component can be shared among multiple programs and applications. Multiple users and programs can execute the same stored procedures, thus providing code reuse. Stored procedure maintenance becomes easier because we can change one stored procedure and it immediately becomes effective for all users and programs.

Stored procedures are more efficient than SQL statements, when executed from a program. The reason why this is true is that when the stored procedure is created and saved it is *compiled*. During the compilation process, SQL Server creates and *optimizes* an execution plan for the stored procedure. Also, once a stored procedure is executed, it is placed in SQL Server *cache*. This means that subsequent executions are executed from cache, which also provides improved performance.

SQL statements executed from your programs, however, are not as efficient. Each time the SQL statements are executed by your program, SQL Server must compile and optimize them before they actually get executed. While this performance decrease is not that noticeable with small numbers of SQL statements, or on your personal computer running the Desktop edition of SQL Server, it becomes more evident on large scale SQL Server systems with multiple databases and hundreds of concurrent clients.

If you must execute SQL statements from your program, and you are executing the same SQL statements in a loop, then ADO can help. The ADO `Command` object provides a property called `Prepared` which, when set to `True`, will instruct SQL Server to compile and save a copy of your SQL statements in cache. After you execute the SQL statements the first time, subsequent executions are executed from the SQL Server cache. While this will help *subsequent* executions of your SQL statements, you still take a performance hit on the *first* execution.

As you can see from this scenario, you can gain some benefits if you use ADO to help you to optimize your SQL statements. Using stored procedures, however, will provide the greatest performance benefit overall. We'll be covering this subject of performance comparisons in much more depth in the next chapter – for now let's take a look at how we actually create stored procedures.

Permissions on Stored Procedures

Before we can create stored procedures, we first need to have the appropriate access to create objects. Remember our discussion on database objects from Chapter 1? We learned that stored procedures are considered objects, just as tables and views are. If we want to create stored procedures, we first need to grant the Developers role the appropriate permission to do so.

Try It Out – Granting Permission to Create Stored Procedures

1. In Enterprise Manager, expand the `Wrox_Auto_Works` database and then click on Roles in the tree view.

2. Right click on the db_ddladmin role and choose Properties from the popup menu.

3. Click on Add. We want to select the Developers role to add to the db_ddladmin role as a User, and then click the OK button to close the dialog. Click OK again.

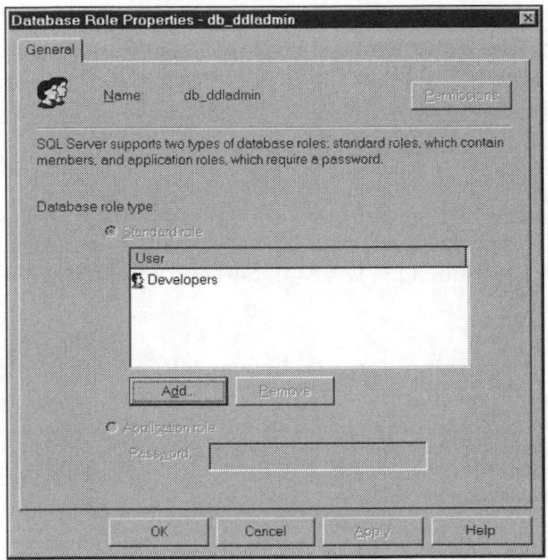

Your login now has the rights to create stored procedures. The db_ddladmin role will permit you to create, modify, and drop objects in the `Wrox_Auto_Works` database.

Stored Procedure Owner Prefixes

When you create a stored procedure you become the **owner** of that stored procedure. Your login becomes the stored procedure **prefix** that must be used when executing your stored procedure from VB or SQL Server by other users. You and the database administrator are the only ones who can change your stored procedure – no other users have the authority to drop or modify your stored procedure. The figure below shows a user-created stored procedure with the login (in this case willist) as the owner of that stored procedure. Notice that User is the type listed in the Type column of the details pane:

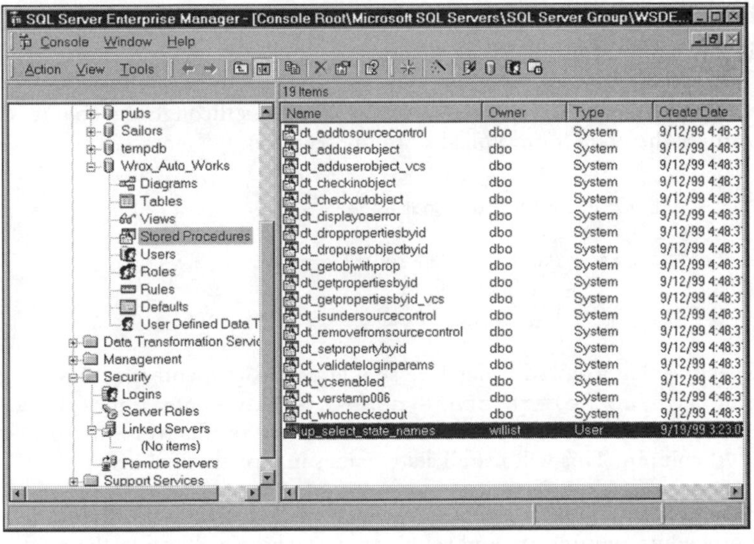

As we explained above, when another user wants to execute a stored procedure created by us they must specify the appropriate prefix, as shown in the following code fragment:

```
objRS.Open "willist.up_SELECT_state_names", objConn, adOpenForwardOnly, _
    adLockReadOnly, adCmdStoredProc
```

Notice that we have prefixed our stored procedure with the owner prefix. Also notice that the `Options` parameter of the `Open` method specifies the `adCmdStoredProc` constant from the `CommandTypeEnum` enumeration. This lets SQL Server know that we want to execute a stored procedure.

If you are executing stored procedures created by yourself, you do not have to specify the owner prefix. Likewise, you do not have to specify the `dbo` prefix for stored procedures created by the database administrator. However, it is a good idea to prefix *all* stored procedures with the owner prefix. This allows you to share your code during development, and quickly identify who wrote the stored procedure in case changes are needed.

Let's look at the basic syntax of a stored procedure, which is shown below:

```
CREATE PROCEDURE procedure_name [@parameter_name data_type [OUTPUT] [,…n]] AS

sql statements to go here
```

- `procedure_name` represents the name of the stored procedure and can be up to 128 characters in length.
- `@parameter_name` is the name of the parameter. All parameters names must be prefixed with the at (`@`) sign, which signifies that this is a local variable.
- `data_type` specifies the data type of the parameter.
- The optional `OUTPUT` keyword specifies that this parameter is an output parameter that will be returned to the caller.
- `n` is a place holder for other parameters.

We will be covering this syntax in more detail as we progress through the chapters. Before we go much further let's examine the code for a typical stored procedure:

```
CREATE PROCEDURE up_SELECT_state_names AS

SELECT State_ID, State_Name_VC, State_Abbreviation_CH
   FROM State_T
   ORDER BY State_Name_VC
```

The first line specifies that a stored procedure should be created, and specifies the name that the stored procedure should have (`up_select_state_names`). Next, we enter our SQL statements to `SELECT` certain columns from the `State_T` table. We also order the results from the `SELECT` statement by the `State_Name_VC` column. This will list all state names in alphabetical order.

We will cover the details of creating stored procedures in just a little bit. Before we do that we need to discuss stored procedure parameters and return values, which we'll do in the next section.

Parameters and Return Values

In order for any server component to be useful to multiple applications, it must accept and return **parameters** (values). Stored procedures are no different, and both accept and return parameters and values. Using parameters allows us to limit the amount of data that the stored procedure must select from tables and work with. Stored procedures can contain input and output parameters and return values.

Input parameters are the default and we do not have to specify anything specific when creating input parameters in our stored procedures. All we need to do is specify the data type that the parameter represents. Let's look at the following code fragment. This specifies a stored procedure name that is to be created and specifies one input parameter. The at sign prefixing the parameter name, `@state_name`, is *required* and signifies a local variable. Notice that we have specified the data type for this parameter – this is also required. The parameters are always enclosed in parentheses:

```
CREATE PROCEDURE up_parmsel_state_abbreviation (@state_name VarChar(15),
    @state_code Char(2) OUTPUT) AS
```

Output parameters have the same required syntax as input parameters, plus they require the `OUTPUT` keyword. In the code fragment above, the `@state_code` parameter is an output parameter, as is evident by the `OUTPUT` keyword.

Return values indicate a return code from the stored procedure. The return value does not have to be specified as the parameters do. We simply use the `RETURN` SQL statement to return a value. This value has to be an `Integer` data type and can return any value you need. For example, this value can be a return code, the number of rows affected by a SQL statement, or the number of rows in a table. Basically any integer data that you want to return can be specified in a return value in your stored procedure.

The following code fragment shows a stored procedure returning a return code that has been set in the local variable `@rc`:

```
Return @rc
```

Let's apply our knowledge gained thus far about stored procedure parameters and return values by trying a hands-on example.

Try It Out – Stored Procedure Parameters and Return Value

We will create a stored procedure named `up_parmsel_state_abbreviation` that will accept the state name as an input parameter and return the state abbreviation as an output parameter. This stored procedure will return a return code of zero if the stored procedure was successful, and a return code of one if the stored procedure was not successful.

1. Open the Query Analyzer as described in Chapter 5. Ensure you select the `Wrox_Auto_Works` database in the database name combo box.

2. The code for the stored procedure is shown below, and is also available for download as `up_parmsel_state_abbreviation`. Enter this code into the query pane and run it. This will create this stored procedure:

```
CREATE PROCEDURE up_parmsel_state_abbreviation (@state_name VarChar(15),
   @state_code Char(2) OUTPUT) AS

-- Declare variables
DECLARE @rc Int

SELECT @state_code = State_Abbreviation_CH
   FROM State_T
   WHERE State_Name_VC = @state_name

IF @@RowCount > 0
   BEGIN
   SELECT @rc = 0
   RETURN @rc
   END

ELSE

   BEGIN
   SELECT @rc = 1
   RETURN @rc
   END
```

3. When you create an object in SQL Server, you are the owner of that object. No one else except the database administrator has access to that object. Therefore, you must grant permission for other users to access your object, as was discussed earlier in this chapter and also in Chapter 4.

In Enterprise Manager, expand the `Wrox_Auto_Works` database and click on Stored Procedures in the tree view:

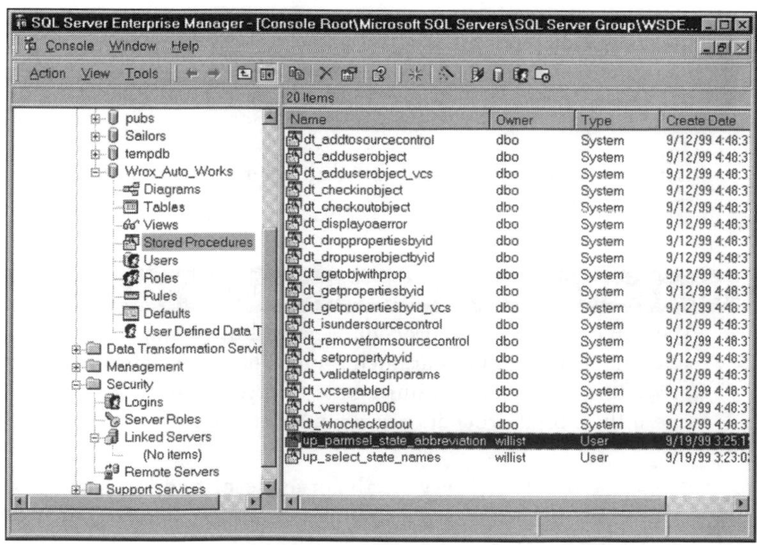

4. Find your stored procedure in the list in the details pane and right click on it. Choose All Tasks from the popup menu. On the sub menu, choose Manage Permissions.

5. Notice that all Roles and all Users are listed. In keeping our administrative tasks simple, we only want to grant *execute* permissions to our stored procedure to the Developers, Management, and Sales Staff roles, and we do this by checking the checkbox next to each role. Click on the OK button to close the dialog. Now all three roles have permission to execute the stored procedure we have created.

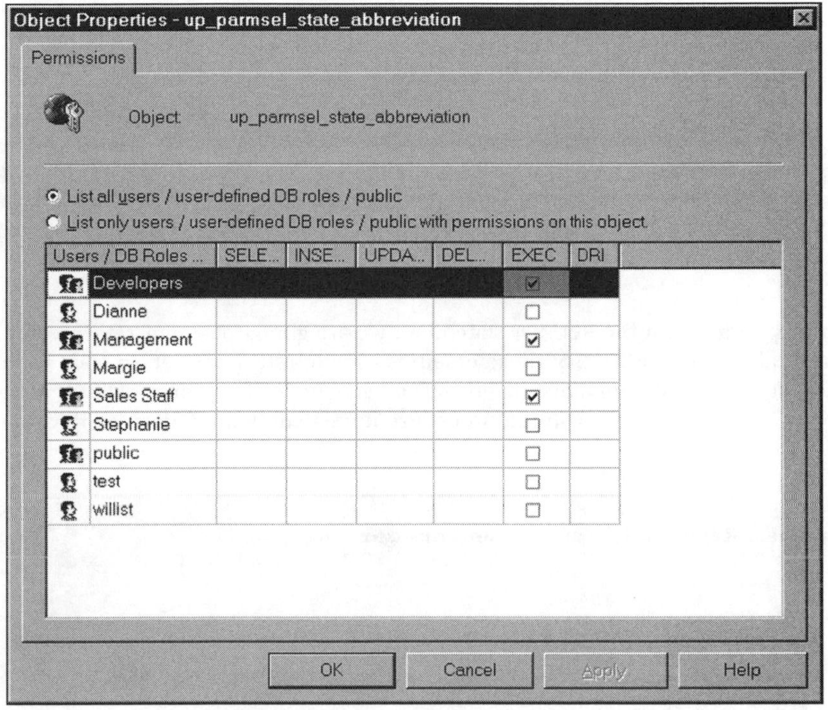

How It Works – Stored Procedure Parameters and Return Value

The first line of code specifies that a stored procedure is to be created, and that it has an input parameter called `@state_name`, which is a `VarChar` field that can contain up to 15 characters. The second parameter, `@state_code`, is an output parameter, as specified by the `OUTPUT` keyword, and is a `Char` field that contains two characters:

```
CREATE PROCEDURE up_parmsel_state_abbreviation (@state_name VarChar(15),
    @state_code Char(2) OUTPUT) AS
```

Unlike VB, we must declare all variables that we are going to use, and this next line of code declares a variable for our return code. Notice that we must also specify the data type, which in this case is an integer as all return values must be `Integer` data types:

```
-- Declare variables
DECLARE @rc Int
```

Next we are selecting the State_Abbreviation_CH column into our output parameter, @state_code, from the State_T table, but only if the State_Name_VC column equals the state name passed in the input parameter @state_name:

```
SELECT @state_code = State_Abbreviation_CH
   FROM State_T
   WHERE State_Name_VC = @state_name
```

We use the built-in function @@RowCount to determine the number of rows affected by the last SQL statement. If a row was found then @@RowCount will return 1 indicating that one row was found, otherwise it will return 0, which indicates that no rows were found. We are using an IF ELSE condition to set our return code and end our stored procedure.

In SQL Server, an IF ELSE condition is not terminated with an END IF like in VB. Instead it ends with the last statement in the ELSE condition. If you want to process more than one SQL statement in an IF ELSE condition, you must specify a BEGIN and END block. This ensures that all SQL statements within the BEGIN END block are executed. We'll be using BEGIN END blocks more later in the book.

If a match was found from the SELECT statement, we are going to set our return value, @rc, to zero and return to the caller. The RETURN SQL statement is used to return the return code to the caller. This SQL statement halts execution immediately and no statements following RETURN get executed. Thus you can use RETURN to exit your stored procedure immediately upon determining an error.

Reminder: Return values must be an `Integer` data type.

```
IF @@RowCount > 0
   BEGIN
   SELECT @rc = 0
   RETURN @rc
   END
```

If we did not find a match, we are going to return with a return code of 1:

```
ELSE

   BEGIN
   SELECT @rc = 1
   RETURN @rc
   END
```

This stored procedure does not have to use a variable to return the return code; we could simply specify RETURN 0 or RETURN 1. We used the @rc variable in this exercise to introduce you to local variables. We will be working more with local variables as we move on.

Try It Out – Creating a VB Form to Call the Stored Procedure

Now that we have our stored procedure coded and permissions set so other users can access it, it's time to code the VB front-end program to execute our stored procedure.

1. Create a Standard EXE VB program to call the stored procedure just created. On the form, place two labels and two textboxes with the following properties:

Control	Name	Caption or Text
Label	`Label1`	State Abbreviation
Label	`Label2`	Return Code
TextBox	`txtAbbreviation`	
TextBox	`txtReturnCode`	

2. Change the caption of the form if you wish. Your form should now look similar to this, but without the data values in the textboxes:

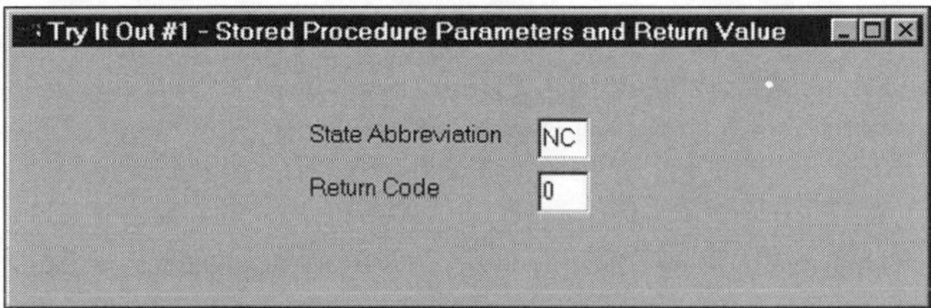

3. Set a reference to Microsoft ActiveX Data Objects Library version 2.5, or the latest version you have. We saw how to do this in Chapter 6.

4. The code which you need to enter into your VB form is presented step by step in the *How It Works* section below, and is available as `frmTryItOut1.frm`.

How It Works – Creating a VB Form to Call the Stored Procedure

This section presents and explains the code that makes up the VB form. As with the previous examples we have coded, we are using the `Form_Load` event to keep things simple. We start by setting the form icon to nothing and declaring our database objects. Notice that this time, instead of the `Recordset` object, we are using the `Command` object:

```
Private Sub Form_Load()
   'Use the standard Windows icon
   Me.Icon = Nothing

   'Declare database objects
   Dim objConn As New ADODB.Connection
   Dim objCmd As New ADODB.Command
   Dim objErr As ADODB.Error
```

We establish a connection to the database using our DSN that was set up in Chapter 6 and then we check the State of the Connection object. For those readers who are using SQL Server authentication, you will need to specify the UID and PWD parameters specifying your SQL Server login and password respectively.

```
'Establish a database connection using NT Authentication
objConn.Open "DSN=Wrox Auto Works"

'Check the state of the connection to ensure we are connected
If objConn.State = adStateOpen Then
```

If the State of our connection is open, then we proceed with our code by setting the various properties of the Command object. Here we are setting the ActiveConnection property to our Connection object and the CommandText property to our stored procedure name. The CommandType property gets set to the adCmdStoredProc constant from the CommandTypeEnum enumeration, which specifies that a stored procedure is to be executed.

Once again notice that we have specified the user prefix of the stored procedure that we want to execute, and the prefix will need to be changed to the prefix of the stored procedure that you created. This is not entirely necessary for any stored procedures that we create, or stored procedures that have the dbo prefix. But this is a good habit to get into because it will help when we make the transition from development to test and production, as we will demonstrate in Chapter 16.

```
'Set the Command object properties
Set objCmd.ActiveConnection = objConn
objCmd.CommandText = "willist.up_parmsel_state_abbreviation"
objCmd.CommandType = adCmdStoredProc
```

Since we have two parameters and a return value in our stored procedure, we must append three parameters to the Command object's Parameters collection. A return value is also considered a parameter from an ADO perspective. The first parameter we need to append to the Parameters collection is the return value. If a return value is coded in your stored procedure, it must *always* be the first parameter in the collection, because of the syntax of a stored procedure call.

> *You can think of a call to a stored procedure in much the same way as you would a call to an API function that returns a return code. The return code is always set to a value equal to the call of the function.*

All other parameters must be appended to the Parameters collection in the order in which they are listed in the stored procedure.

We are using the CreateParameter method of the Command object to create and append our parameters to the Parameters collection. For the return value, we specify a Name for the parameter in the Parameters collection, and then specify the DataType of the parameter. We specify the direction of the parameter, and in this case we have specified the adParamReturnValue constant from the ParameterDirectionEnum enumeration, which indicates that this is a return value:

```
'Set the Command object parameters
objCmd.Parameters.Append _
    objCmd.CreateParameter("RC", adInteger, adParamReturnValue)
```

The second parameter that we want to append to the Parameters collection is the input parameter. This time we have given the parameter a Name of StateName, and specified the DataType adVarChar constant from the DataTypeEnum enumeration. We specify the Direction of the parameter, and in this case it is an input parameter. Since this is a VarChar data type, we must specify the Size of the parameter and here we have specified a size of 15. Last, we specify the Value that we want to pass to the parameter, and for this we have specified our state name:

```
objCmd.Parameters.Append _
   objCmd.CreateParameter("StateName", adVarChar, adParamInput, _
      15, "North Carolina")
```

The last parameter that we must append to the Parameters collection is the output parameter. We give it a Name of Abbreviation, a DataType of adChar, and specify that this is an output parameter by using the adParamOutput constant. Last, we specify the Size of the data type and in this case we have specified 2. Since this is an output parameter, we do not specify a Value:

```
objCmd.Parameters.Append _
   objCmd.CreateParameter("Abbreviation", adChar, adParamOutput, 2)
```

Now that we have set the Command object's properties and appended the parameters to the Parameters collection, it's time to execute the Command object, as shown in the next line of code:

```
'Execute the Command object
objCmd.Execute
```

After executing the Command object, we need to check the return value from the stored procedure. We set the return value in a parameter called RC and we are checking it in the next line of code. If the return value from the stored procedure is not equal to zero then we know that our stored procedure did not find a match and the output parameter is going to be Null.

If a match was not found for the state name that we passed, then we set the text in the txtAbbreviation textbox to an empty string by specifying two double quotes. We also set the txtReturnCode textbox to the return value returned by the stored procedure.

If a match was found then we set the txtAbbreviation textbox to the value of the Abbreviation parameter. Notice that we are accessing the parameter from the Parameters collection in this statement by specifying a parameter Item in the Parameters collection, which is part of the Command object. We then set the txtReturnCode textbox to the return value returned by the stored procedure using a different syntax. Since the Parameters collection is the default collection of the Command object, we can access the parameters directly from the Command object by just specifying their names.

We could also access the parameters in the Command object by ordinal reference instead of their names. The RC parameter would have an ordinal reference of 0 and the Abbreviation parameter would have an ordinal reference of 2.

```
If objCmd("RC") <> 0 Then
   txtAbbreviation.Text = ""
   txtReturnCode.Text = objCmd("RC")
Else
   txtAbbreviation.Text = objCmd.Parameters.Item("Abbreviation")
   txtReturnCode.Text = objCmd.Parameters.Item("RC")
End If
```

If the State of the Connection object is not opened, then we enumerate through the Errors collection as we did in the last chapter:

```
    Else

       'Display all errors
       For Each objErr In objConn.Errors
          Debug.Print objErr.Description
       Next

    End If
```

The last part of our code de-references all of our database objects and then our form is displayed:

```
    'Dereference the database objects
    Set objCmd = Nothing
    objConn.Close
    Set objConn = Nothing
End Sub
```

After having run your project and obtaining successful results, try misspelling the state name you are passing in the code and see what results you get then, in particular note the Return Code.

Select Stored Procedures

In our last example we took a look at input and output parameters and return values. The stored procedure we created was a SELECT stored procedure as it was selecting a certain column from a row, based on the parameter passed. The first stored procedure that was shown at the beginning of this chapter selected *all* rows from the State_T table. At this point, if you have not created that stored procedure to select the state names, then do so now. The code for that stored procedure is listed below:

```
CREATE PROCEDURE up_select_state_names AS

SELECT State_ID, State_Name_VC, State_Abbreviation_CH
   FROM State_T
   ORDER BY State_Name_VC
```

After creating the stored procedure, don't forget to set the permissions for the Developers, Sales Staff, and Management roles so they will be able to execute this stored procedure. You may need to choose Refresh in the Action menu to refresh the Stored Procedure view, before you see the new one that you just added.

As you can see from the two stored procedures that we have created thus far in this chapter, SELECT stored procedures can select all data from all rows, or certain data from certain rows, and can either accept parameters or not. In Chapter 9 we will begin to create complex stored procedures that select data from multiple tables and use **cursors**. Cursors are database elements that control how we are able to navigate the Recordset object, and how we can perform updates to the fields in the Recordset object.

Try It Out – Select Stored Procedure

This example will display all state names and state abbreviations using the `up_select_state_names` stored procedure you just created, and will be the building block for our next three examples. Once you reach the end of the chapter, this program will be a fully functional data entry program for states.

With this in mind, we must give some thought to the design of our front-end program. To enable us to reuse some of this code in other front-end programs and server components, we will place all of the stored procedures (only one for now) in a class that will manage the states in our `State_T` table. This will allow us to reuse this class in other programs that need to manage state names and abbreviations.

This program should use a DSN-less connection, and the connection will be open throughout the execution of the program. The state name and abbreviation should be displayed on the form, and you should have navigation buttons that allow you to navigate throughout the recordset.

1. Start a new Standard EXE VB project. This table lists the modules that make up our project:

Module	Name
Form	`frmTryItOut2`
Class	`clsStates`

2. Change the caption of the form if you wish. The following table details the controls that should be placed on the form:

Control	Name	Caption/Notes
Label	`Label1`	State Name
Label	`Label2`	State Abbreviation
TextBox	`txtStateName`	Set the Text property to nothing
TextBox	`txtStateAbbreviation`	Set the Text property to nothing
Label	`lblMsg`	Place this label below `Label2`, set its Caption property to nothing, and set the AutoSize property to True
CommandButton	`cmdMoveFirst`	First
CommandButton	`cmdMovePrevious`	Previous
CommandButton	`cmdMoveNext`	Next
CommandButton	`cmdMoveLast`	Last
CommandButton	`cmdExit`	Exit

The form should look something like this:

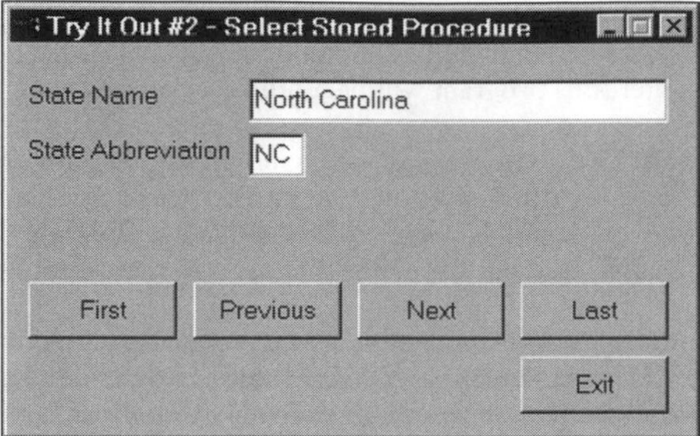

3. Don't forget to set a reference to the Microsoft ActiveX Data Objects Library in your project.

4. Add a class module, change its name to `clsStates`, and add the following code in the `clsStates` class. Change the owner prefix as necessary:

```
Option Explicit

Public Function GetAllStates(ByRef objConn As ADODB.Connection) As Recordset
   'Declare local objects
   Dim objRS As New ADODB.Recordset

   'Setup error handling
   On Error GoTo GetAllStates_EH

   'Set recordset cursor location and open recordset
   objRS.CursorLocation = adUseClient
   objRS.Open "willist.up_select_state_names", objConn, _
         adOpenStatic, adLockReadOnly, adCmdStoredProc

   'Disconnect recordset
   Set objRS.ActiveConnection = Nothing

   'Return with the recordset
   Set GetAllStates = objRS
   Set objRS = Nothing

   'All was successful, exit function
   On Error GoTo 0
   Exit Function

GetAllStates_EH:
   Set GetAllStates = Nothing
   Set objRS = Nothing
   On Error GoTo 0
End Function
```

5. Since this is a public method in our class, we should set the description in the procedure attributes. On the Tools menu choose Procedure Attributes and enter a description for this method.

6. The code which needs to be added to the form is presented step by step in the *How It Works – The Form* section. You should work through and add this code to the frmTryItOut2 form.

How It Works – The States Class

The GetAllStates function in the clsStates class accepts the Connection object that is set in the Form_Load event, and is passed by reference in case any properties are set as a result of the execution of the recordset. This function returns a Recordset object containing a list of all state names and abbreviations.

The first thing we do is to declare a Recordset object and set up error handling:

```
Public Function GetAllStates(ByRef objConn As ADODB.Connection) As Recordset
    'Declare local objects
    Dim objRS As New ADODB.Recordset

    'Setup error handling
    On Error GoTo GetAllStates_EH
```

Since we are going to be passing the recordset back to the caller, we need to use a client-side cursor, which allows us to disconnect the recordset from the Connection object. Next we open the Recordset object, specifying the stored procedure (with the owner prefix) as the Source parameter of the Open method. We specify the Connection object that was passed by reference as the ActiveConnection parameter, and the adOpenStatic constant from the CursorTypeEnum enumeration as the CursorType parameter. Since we are only going to be reading the data, we specify the adLockReadOnly constant from the LockTypeEnum for the LockType parameter. Last, we specify the adCmdStoredProc constant from the CommandTypeEnum as the Options parameter, since we are executing a stored procedure.

We use a static cursor so that we can navigate through our recordset in both directions and use bookmarks. This type of cursor does not reflect changes by other users, which really does not matter since we are using a disconnected recordset anyway:

```
    'Set recordset cursor location and open recordset
    objRS.CursorLocation = adUseClient
    objRS.Open "willist.up_select_state_names", objConn, _
          adOpenStatic, adLockReadOnly, adCmdStoredProc
```

We then disconnect our recordset by setting its ActiveConnection property to Nothing:

```
    'Disconnect recordset
    Set objRS.ActiveConnection = Nothing
```

After we have successfully opened and disconnected our recordset, we need to have the function return the recordset. We do this by setting the function name equal to the Recordset object, and then set the Recordset object to Nothing, thereby releasing its resources. You may be tempted to close the recordset before setting it to Nothing. Avoid this temptation, as closing the Recordset object, even after setting the function to the recordset, will return a closed recordset.

```
'Return with the recordset
   Set GetAllStates = objRS
   Set objRS = Nothing
```

Last, we exit the function if everything was normal. If an error occurred, we set the function to Nothing and de-reference our Recordset object:

```
   'All was successful, exit function
   On Error GoTo 0
   Exit Function

GetAllStates_EH:
   Set GetAllStates = Nothing
   Set objRS = Nothing
   On Error GoTo 0
End Function
```

How It Works – The Form

While this is a lot of code and most of it is pretty straightforward, we will step through it all because you will need to enter each section of it into your form.

The first part of code that we want to look at in the form is the code in the general declarations section. We want to ensure that our project includes the Option Explicit statement so that all of our variables must be declared, and any keying errors of the variable names will be caught. Then we define our database objects that will be common to all procedures in our form. Here we are declaring a Connection and a Recordset object:

```
Option Explicit

'Declare database objects
Private m_objConn As ADODB.Connection
Private m_objRS As ADODB.Recordset
```

Whenever a database error occurs we will disable all navigation buttons, and have placed that function into a separate procedure listed here. We set the Enabled property of all of the navigation buttons to False:

```
Private Sub DisableButtons()
   'Disable navigation buttons
   cmdMoveFirst.Enabled = False
   cmdMovePrevious.Enabled = False
   cmdMoveNext.Enabled = False
   cmdMoveLast.Enabled = False
End Sub
```

Since we will be executing the stored procedure to get the state names and abbreviations more than once in subsequent revisions of this program, it makes sense to place this function into a separate procedure as we have done here.

The first thing we want to do is to check the Recordset object to see if it has been set to a recordset. If it has and it is currently open then we want to close it. We do this by checking to see if the Recordset object is equal to Nothing. If it is not then we check to see if the State of the object is open using the adStateOpen constant from the ObjectStateEnum, just like we did for the Connection object in the Form_Load event:

```
Private Sub GetStates()
   'If the recordset has been set and is open, then close it
   If Not m_objRS Is Nothing Then
      If m_objRS.State = adStateOpen Then
         m_objRS.Close
      End If
   End If
```

We need to instantiate the clsStates class, which contains the code to get the state names, and then we call the method in that class that will return the state names in a recordset. Notice that we are passing the Connection object to the GetAllStates function in our call:

```
   'Instantiate an instance of the clsStates class
   Dim objSelect As New clsStates

   'Call the method to return a recordset of states
   Set m_objRS = objSelect.GetAllStates(m_objConn)
```

After the function completes, we need to check the Recordset object to ensure that it is not equal to Nothing which would indicate that an error occurred in getting the state names. If it is equal to Nothing then we set an error message and disable the navigation buttons, otherwise we call the cmdMoveFirst_Click method which will move to the first record and display it:

```
   If m_objRS Is Nothing Then
      'Error occured getting recordset, display message
      Call SetMsg("Error occured getting recordset", vbRed)
      Call DisableButtons
   Else
      'Move to the first record
      Call cmdMoveFirst_Click
   End If
```

The last line of code will de-reference our class and set it to Nothing to free the resources that it used:

```
   'Dereference the class
   Set objSelect = Nothing
End Sub
```

This next procedure uses the parameters passed to load the state name and state abbreviation textboxes:

```
Private Sub LoadFields(strStateName As String, _
                       strStateAbbreviation As String)

   'Load fields
   txtStateName.Text = strStateName
   txtStateAbbreviation.Text = strStateAbbreviation
End Sub
```

The next procedure will display the error message that we pass, and set the color of the font. Notice that the font color is an optional parameter that has a default color assigned. We are using the built-in `ColorConstants` enumeration for our font color parameter:

```
Private Sub SetMsg(strMessage As String, _
               Optional lngFontColor As ColorConstants = vbBlack)
```

The first thing we do in the procedure is to set the `Caption` property of our message label to the message that was passed as a parameter. Then we set the `ForeColor` property to the font color passed. If no font color was passed, this procedure uses a default font color of black, which sets the font color back to normal:

```
   'Set the message
   lblMsg.Caption = strMessage

   'Set the message font color
   lblMsg.ForeColor = lngFontColor
End Sub
```

In the `Form_Load` event we want to set the form icon to nothing and set up error handling for this procedure. Since we are going to be keeping a connection to the database open during the entire execution of our program, it makes sense to place the code here – we do not need to place it into a separate procedure.

We set the `m_objConn` variable to an ADO `Connection` object, and then open the connection using NT authentication with a DSN-less connection. You can use SQL Server authentication instead of NT authentication if that was how your login was defined to SQL Server. If using SQL Server authentication you will need to specify the `UID` and `PWD` parameters as you did in the last chapter. Also remember to change the server name.

```
Private Sub Form_Load()
   'Use the standard Windows icon
   Me.Icon = Nothing

   'Set up error handling
   On Error GoTo Form_Load_EH

   'Set a reference to the ADO conection object
   Set m_objConn = New ADODB.Connection

   'Establish a database connection using NT Authentication
   m_objConn.Open "Driver=SQL Server;Server=WSDevelopment;" & _
      "Database=Wrox_Auto_Works"
```

After we open our connection we need to check the `State` of the connection to ensure that it is open, which we do in the next statement. If the `State` of the connection is not open, we call the procedures to display our error message and to disable the navigation buttons:

```
    'Check connection state
    If Not m_objConn.State = adStateOpen Then
       Call SetMsg("Connection Failed", vbRed)
       Call DisableButtons
       Exit Sub
    End If
```

If all goes well, we find ourselves here and we execute the procedure to get the state names. We then turn off error handling for this procedure and exit the procedure, bypassing the error handling routine:

```
    'Get a recordset of the states
    Call GetStates

    On Error GoTo 0
    Exit Sub
```

The error handling routine merely calls the procedure to display a message that the connection failed and set the font color to red. Then we call the procedure to disable the navigation buttons:

```
 Form_Load_EH:
    Call SetMsg("Connection Failed", vbRed)
    Call DisableButtons
 End Sub
```

The `cmdMoveFirst_Click` procedure clears any existing error messages by passing the `Empty` keyword to the `SetMsg` procedure:

```
 Private Sub cmdMoveFirst_Click()
    'Clear any previous messages
    Call SetMsg(Empty)
```

Then we move to the first record in our recordset and call the `LoadFields` procedure, passing it the recordset fields to be used to load the form fields:

```
    'Move to the first record
    m_objRS.MoveFirst

    'Load the form fields
    Call LoadFields(m_objRS!State_Name_VC, _
       m_objRS!State_Abbreviation_CH)
 End Sub
```

The `cmdMovePrevious_Click` and `cmdMoveNext_Click` procedures clear any existing error messages and then move in the appropriate direction.

Let's take a look at the cmdMovePrevious_Click procedure first. The first thing we do is to clear any existing error messages, and then move to the previous record using the MovePrevious method of the Recordset object:

```
Private Sub cmdMovePrevious_Click()
    'Clear any previous messages
    Call SetMsg(Empty)

    'Move to the previous record
    m_objRS.MovePrevious
```

After we reposition the recordset we must verify that a beginning of file condition has not occurred by checking the BOF property of the Recordset object. If this property is set to True, we display a message that we were already on the first record and then call the MoveNext method to move back to the first record:

```
    'Check for an BOF condition and correct if necessary
    If m_objRS.BOF Then
        Call SetMsg("Already at first record", vbBlue)
        m_objRS.MoveNext
    End If
```

Regardless of whether a beginning of file condition exists, we call the procedure to load the fields on the form:

```
    'Load the form fields
    Call LoadFields(m_objRS!State_Name_VC, _
        m_objRS!State_Abbreviation_CH)
End Sub
```

The cmdMoveNext_Click procedure performs the exact opposite of the cmdMovePrevious_Click procedure. Again we clear any existing error messages and this time we move forward one record position in the recordset:

```
Private Sub cmdMoveNext_Click ()
    'Clear any previous messages
    Call SetMsg(Empty)

    'Move to the next record
    m_objRS.MoveNext
```

This time we check to see if we have moved past the last record in the recordset by checking the EOF property. If it is set to True this indicates that an end of file condition has occurred. If an end of file condition has been reached, we display an error message and move back to the last record:

```
    'Check for an EOF condition and correct if necessary
    If m_objRS.EOF Then
        Call SetMsg("Already at last record", vbBlue)
        m_objRS.MovePrevious
    End If
```

Then we call the procedure to load the fields on the form:

```
    'Load the form fields
    Call LoadFields(m_objRS!State_Name_VC, _
       m_objRS!State_Abbreviation_CH)
End Sub
```

The `cmdMoveLast_Click` procedure performs the same function as the `cmdMoveFirst_Click` procedure, except it moves to the *last* record in the recordset:

```
Private Sub cmdMoveLast_Click()
    'Clear any previous messages
    Call SetMsg(Empty)

    'Move to the last record
    m_objRS.MoveLast

    'Load the form fields
    Call LoadFields(m_objRS!State_Name_VC, _
       m_objRS!State_Abbreviation_CH)
End Sub
```

The `cmdExit_Click` procedure is executed when we click on the Exit button, and it unloads the form, which in turn fires the `Form_Unload` event:

```
Private Sub cmdExit_Click()
    Unload Me
End Sub
```

The `Form_Unload` event contains all of the code to close and de-reference our database objects. We first ensure that the objects are set by checking to see if they are not equal to `Nothing`, and then check the `State` of the objects to see if they are open. We `Close` and set the objects to `Nothing`, thereby freeing all resources:

```
Private Sub Form_Unload(Cancel As Integer)
    'Close and dereference database objects
    If Not m_objRS Is Nothing Then
       If m_objRS.State Then
          m_objRS.Close
       End If
       Set m_objRS = Nothing
    End If

If Not m_objConn Is Nothing Then
       If m_objConn.State Then
          m_objConn.Close
       End If
       Set m_objConn = Nothing
    End If
End Sub
```

You can run this example program and, if you entered more than one state name and abbreviation, you will be able to navigate forwards and backwards in the recordset. If you have entered only one state then be patient – the next example you will code will allow you to insert more state names and abbreviations.

Insert Stored Procedures

Now that we have covered stored procedure parameters, it's time to see how we can apply them to an INSERT stored procedure. If we couldn't provide parameters to an INSERT stored procedure, the stored procedure really wouldn't do us any good and we would have to use in-line SQL statements instead. This section covers simple INSERT stored procedures and how we use parameters to maximize their usefulness.

Let's start by looking at what is required to build an INSERT stored procedure to insert the state names and state abbreviations. Our table design has four columns in the State_T table: State_ID, State_Name_VC, State_Abbreviation_CH, and Last_Update_DT. The first column, State_ID, is an Identity column. We do not have to specify any values for that column, as SQL Server will automatically populate that column for us with the next available number. The last column, Last_Update_DT, contains the last date and time the row of data was inserted or updated. SQL Server provides a built-in function called GetDate() that we can call to populate that column, so we do not need to pass the stored procedure data for that column. That leaves us with two columns for which we need to pass data to the stored procedure.

If you recall our discussion on parameters at the beginning of this chapter, we need to prefix our parameter names with the @ sign, and specify the data types.

Looking at the following stored procedure code fragment, we see that we have specified two input parameters that the stored procedure will require. The first parameter is a VarChar data type and can contain up to 15 characters. The second parameter is a Char data type and requires two characters. If you only pass one character, SQL Server will pad that parameter with an extra character, because a Char data type requires the *exact* number of characters that are specified.

```
CREATE PROCEDURE up_parmins_state_name (@state_name VarChar(15),
   @state_abbreviation Char(2)) AS
```

The parameters that are specified are considered local variables because they are required to be prefixed with the @ sign. We can use these variables in our stored procedure just like we could in VB. We can change the values of these variables, and we could use them in an expression that tests their values to ensure that they are equal to something.

The actual heart of the INSERT stored procedure is to insert values into a table. This can be coded in one of two ways, as we discussed in Chapter 5. We could use the following short method:

```
INSERT [Into] TableName VALUES(ValueList)
```

Or we could use the proper method, shown below, which will cause us less headaches in the long run. This also makes the stored procedure easier to build and debug, as well as maintain.

```
INSERT [Into] TableName [(ColumnList)] VALUES(ValueList)
```

We will be using the last method in our stored procedures, and our parameters will get populated in the ValueList. So let's move on and build our INSERT stored procedure and VB program to execute the stored procedure.

Try It Out – Insert Stored Procedure

1. The first thing we need to do is to build the `INSERT` stored procedure to insert state names and state abbreviations, as shown in the figure below.

2. Execute the SQL statements to create the stored procedure.

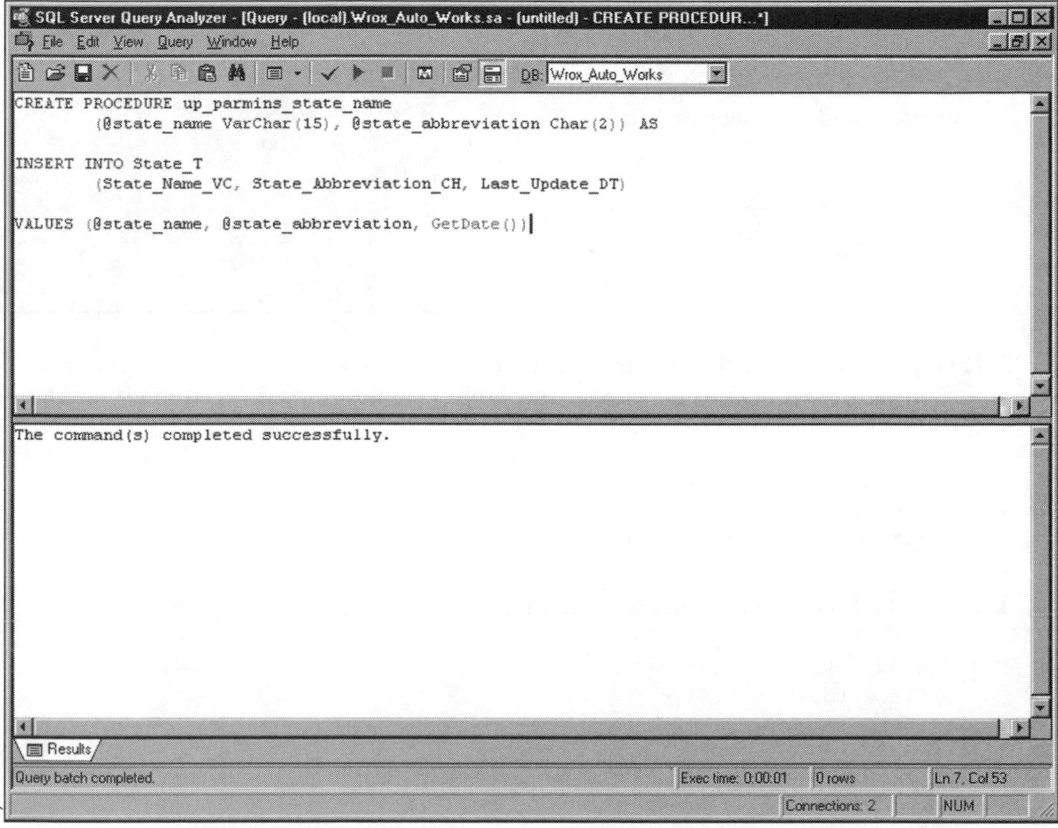

3. Next you need to use Enterprise Manager to set the permissions for this stored procedure, to allow the Developers and Sales Staff roles to execute this stored procedure.

4. To build the VB project, start by copying the `frmTryItOut2.frm` form from the last example (for example by using Windows Explorer) and name it `frmTryItOut3.frm`.

5. Start a new Standard EXE VB project and set a reference to the Microsoft ActiveX Data Objects Library.

6. Remove the current form and add the existing form that you just copied. You will need to change the form name once it is loaded in your project, and change the form caption.

7. Now add the `clsStates` class from your last project to this project – we do not want to change the name of the class or copy it to another file.

8. Last, change the start up object for your project in the **Project Properties** dialog to start with the form `frmTryItOut3`. At this point the project should run and behave as in the last example.

9. We want to add a command button to execute our `INSERT` stored procedure, as shown opposite, giving it a **Name** of **cmdAdd** and a **Caption** of **Add**:

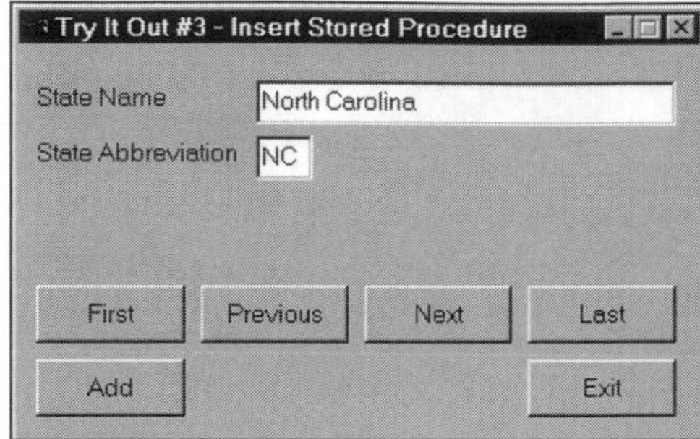

10. To provide the functionality to execute the `INSERT` stored procedure we have just created, add the following code to your project. In the general declarations of the form add:

```
'Declare module level variables
Private m_varBookMark As Variant
Private m_strLastState As String
```

11. Add the following code to the `cmdAdd_Click` procedure:

```
Private Sub cmdAdd_Click()
   'Declare local variables
   Dim lngRC As Long
   Dim strError As String

   'Save the current record
   m_varBookMark = m_objRS.Bookmark
   m_strLastState = m_objRS!State_Name_VC

   'Instantiate an instance of the clsStates class
   Dim objAdd As New clsStates

   'Call the method to add the state
   lngRC = objAdd.AddState(m_objConn, _
      txtStateName.Text, txtStateAbbreviation.Text, strError)

   'Check for errors
   If lngRC = 0 Then
      'No error, get a new listing of state names
      Call GetStates
   Else
```

```
        'An error occurred, display the error
        Call SetMsg(strError, vbRed)
    End If

    'Dereference the class
    Set objAdd = Nothing
End Sub
```

12. Modify the `GetStates` procedure by adding the following code:

```
Private Sub GetStates()
    'If the recordset has been set and is open, then close it
    If Not m_objRS Is Nothing Then
        If m_objRS.State = adStateOpen Then
            m_objRS.Close
        End If
    End If

    'Instantiate an instance of the clsStates class
    Dim objSelect As New clsStates

    'Call the method to return a recordset of states
    Set m_objRS = objSelect.GetAllStates(m_objConn)

    If m_objRS Is Nothing Then
        'Error occurred getting recordset, display message
        Call SetMsg("Error occurred getting recordset", vbRed)
        Call DisableButtons
    Else
        If Not IsEmpty(m_varBookMark) Then
            'Move to the appropriate record and load the fields
            m_objRS.Bookmark = m_varBookMark
            If m_objRS!State_Name_VC < m_strLastState Then
                Call cmdMoveNext_Click
            Else
                Call LoadFields(m_objRS!State_Name_VC, _
                    m_objRS!State_Abbreviation_CH)
            End If
        Else
            'Move to the first record
            Call cmdMoveFirst_Click
        End If
    End If

    'Dereference the class
    Set objSelect = Nothing
End Sub
```

13. The code which needs to be added to the end of the `clsStates` class is listed in the *How It Works – The States Class Module* section. Don't forget to add a description for this method in the Procedure Attributes, as described in the last example.

How It Works – The Stored Procedure

Let's take a look at the INSERT stored procedure. As we mentioned in Chapter 5, we specify each column name that we are inserting data into to avoid confusion and problems later. Next we insert the values using the parameters that were specified in the first line of our stored procedure. SQL Server provides a built-in function called GetDate() to get the current date and time in the required format for a DateTime data type. We use this function to insert the current date and time into the Last_Update_DT column:

```
CREATE PROCEDURE up_parmins_state_name (@state_name VarChar(15),
   @state_abbreviation Char(2)) AS

INSERT INTO State_T
   (State_Name_VC, State_Abbreviation_CH, Last_Update_DT)
   VALUES(@state_name, @state_abbreviation, GetDate())
```

The States Class Module

We want to take a look at the code in our class module next. All of the code presented step by step in this section needs to be entered into the class module. Before we add a new state to the database we need to validate that some data exists and that the state name passed is not greater than 15 characters. We do this in a validation routine that accepts the state name as a parameter and returns a Boolean value indicating success or failure of the validation:

```
Private Function ValidateStateAbbreviation( _
                  ByVal strStateAbbreviation As String) As Boolean
```

The first thing we do in this function is to set up the return value, which by default is set to True:

```
   'Set default return value
   ValidateStateAbbreviation = True
```

Next we validate that the parameter passed in, state abbreviation, contains some data, by checking to ensure that the length of the parameter is not equal to zero. If it is then we set the function return value to False:

```
   'Validate data exists
   If Len(Trim(strStateAbbreviation)) = 0 Then
      ValidateStateAbbreviation = False
   End If
```

Next we ensure that the state abbreviation is exactly two characters. If it is any more or any less than two characters we set the function to return a value of False:

```
   'Validate state name is equal to 2 characters
   If Len(Trim(strStateAbbreviation)) <> 2 Then
      ValidateStateAbbreviation = False
   End If
End Function
```

We provide similar functionality for the state name:

```
Private Function ValidateStateName(ByVal strStateName As String) As Boolean

   'Set default return value
   ValidateStateName = True

   'Validate data exists
   If Len(Trim(strStateName)) = 0 Then
      ValidateStateName = False
   End If

   'Validate state name is not greater than 15 characters
   If Len(Trim(strStateName)) > 15 Then
      ValidateStateName = False
   End If
End Function
```

The method in our class to add a new state accepts the `Connection` object by reference, and the state name and state abbreviation by value. We need a means to know what error message was encountered, if any, so we pass a string variable by reference. This method will set the `strError` variable to the error description it encountered. We will return a long return code of zero if everything was successful:

```
Public Function AddState(ByRef objConn As ADODB.Connection, _
                           ByVal strStateName As String, _
                           ByVal strStateAbbreviation As String, _
                           ByRef strError As String) As Long
```

The first thing we do in our function is to declare the database objects and local variables that we need. Then we set up our error handling to force us to our error handler if we encounter any errors:

```
   'Declare database objects and local variables
   Dim objErr As ADODB.Error
   Dim strSQL As String

   'Setup error handling
   On Error GoTo AddState_EH
```

We call our validation routines to validate the data passed. If validation failed, we raise an error using the VB `Error` object's `Raise` method. We really aren't concerned with the error number so we use the same error number in both routines. What we are concerned with is the error *message*, which is unique for each error. After an error is raised, we are forced to the error handler at the bottom of our procedure:

```
   'Validate data
   If Not ValidateStateName(strStateName) Then
      'Raise an error
      Err.Raise vbObjectError + 513, "clsStates.AddState", _
         "State Name is either empty or exceeds 15 characters"
   End If
```

```
    If Not ValidateStateAbbreviation(strStateAbbreviation) Then
        'Raise an error
        Err.Raise vbObjectError + 513, "clsStates.AddState", _
            "State Abbreviation is either empty or not equal to 2 characters"
    End If
```

If the data has passed validation then we build our SQL string next. Since we are not expecting any return parameters or a return value from the stored procedure, we will not use the `Command` object to execute our stored procedure. Instead we are going to use the `Connection` object and we need only pass it a SQL string to execute.

Here we specify the stored procedure to execute, prefixed with the owner ID, which you must remember to change. The parameters that are passed to the stored procedure need to be enclosed in parentheses and all string parameters need to be enclosed in single quotes. A comma separates each parameter passed to the stored procedure. Notice that we are forcing the state abbreviation to uppercase using the built-in VB `UCase` function:

```
    'Build the SQL string
    strSQL = "willist.up_parmins_state_name ('" & _
        strStateName & "','" & UCase(strStateAbbreviation) & "')"
```

We execute our SQL string using the `Connection` object. If an error occurs we are forced to the error handler:

```
    'Insert the state data
    objConn.Execute strSQL
```

If all goes well, we find ourselves here and set a good return code, de-reference our database objects and exit the function:

```
    'Return with a good return code
    AddState = 0

    'Dereference the database objects
    Set objErr = Nothing

    'All was successful, exit function
    On Error GoTo 0
    Exit Function
```

Our error handler code is a bit more complex than the last method that we coded in this class. Here we could receive either a database error or an error that we raised from the validation of data. First we check to see if the `Errors` collection contains any errors, by querying the `Count` property. If it is greater than zero we know that the error that forced us here came from ADO or SQL Server. Since we are only interested in the first error message, we set the `objErr` object to the first error message in the `Errors` collection, and then set the `strError` variable to the error description:

```
AddState_EH:
    'Ensure the error came from ADO
    If objConn.Errors.Count > 0 Then
        'Get the first error in the errors collection
        Set objErr = objConn.Errors(0)
        'Set the error message
        strError = objErr.Description
```

If the error came from the VB `Error` object we set the `strError` variable to the description of the VB `Error` object:

```
    Else
       'Set the error message
       strError = Err.Description
    End If
```

Last we de-reference our database objects and set the return code for this function:

```
    'Dereference the database objects
    Set objErr = Nothing
    'Return with a bad return code
    AddState = 1
    On Error GoTo 0
 End Function
```

The Form

Switching to our VB code in the form, we added a variant variable to the general declarations section of our form to hold a bookmark. When we add a new state we need to have that state added to our recordset. Since we are using a disconnected recordset, we must call the `GetStates` procedure to get a new copy of the recordset. Providing a good UI, we reposition the user to the record they were on when they added the new state. We also add a variable to hold the last state name, which we will explain shortly:

```
'Declare module level variables
Private m_varBookMark As Variant
Private m_strLastState As String
```

When a user clicks on the Add button on the form we want to execute the code below. This will call the method above to add the state name and abbreviation. First we declare the local variables that we need in this procedure:

```
Private Sub cmdAdd_Click()
   'Declare local variables
   Dim lngRC As Long
   Dim strError As String
```

Just in case the user has navigated through the recordset, we save the current position. We do this by setting the bookmark variable, so we can return them to this point in the recordset once we have added the new record. We also save the current state name that will be used shortly:

```
   'Save the current record
   m_varBookMark = m_objRS.Bookmark
   m_strLastState = m_objRS!State_Name_VC
```

We instantiate an instance of the `clsStates` class and execute the method to add the new state, passing it the required parameters. The `strError` variable that we have declared locally is being passed by reference. If an error occurs, this variable will contain the error description set by the `AddState` method:

```
    'Instantiate an instance of the clsStates class
    Dim objAdd As New clsStates

    'Call the method to add the state
    lngRC = objAdd.AddState(m_objConn, _
       txtStateName.Text, txtStateAbbreviation.Text, strError)
```

After executing the `AddState` method we need to check the return code. If it equals zero then everything was successful. We then need to get a new copy of the recordset that contains the state just added, by calling the `GetStates` procedure.

If an error occurred then we call the `SetMsg` procedure, passing it the `strError` variable that contains the error that was set in the `AddState` method:

```
    'Check for errors
    If lngRC = 0 Then
       'No error, get a new listing of state names
       Call GetStates
    Else
       'An error occurred, display the error
       Call SetMsg(strError, vbRed)
    End If
```

Last, we de-reference the instance of the `clsStates` class by setting it to `Nothing`:

```
    'Dereference the class
    Set objAdd = Nothing
End Sub
```

In the `GetStates` procedure we need to modify the code to reposition the recordset to the current record that was displayed when the user added a new state. We do this by checking to see if the `m_varBookMark` variable is empty. If it is not then we want to reposition the user to the record they were on before the add was carried out. We do this by setting the `Bookmark` property of the `Recordset` object to the bookmark that we saved.

While the bookmark method is efficient at repositioning us to the current record we were on, there is one little drawback. First, we have got a new recordset that contains one more row than before. Second, the state names are returned in our recordset alphabetically. If you add a state that comes before the state you were on, you are positioned to the state you were on minus one. In other words, if the state displayed is North Carolina and you add Arizona, then Arizona becomes the current record. This is assuming of course that there is only one state listed in the recordset. Using the `m_strLastState` variable we can compare the current state name in the recordset with the saved state name. If the recordset contains a state name less than what was saved, then we know that we need to advance one record position forward to return the user to the exact record they were on.

If we move forward one record, the `cmdMoveNext_Click` procedure will take care of loading the fields with the correct data. If the bookmark was accurate then we need to call the procedure `LoadFields` to load the current data:

```
If Not IsEmpty(m_varBookMark) Then
      'Move to the appropriate record and load the fields
      m_objRS.Bookmark = m_varBookMark
      If m_objRS!state_name_vc < m_strLastState Then
         Call cmdMoveNext_Click
      Else
         Call LoadFields(m_objRS!State_Name_VC, _
            m_objRS!State_Abbreviation_CH)
      End If
   Else
      'Move to the first record
      Call cmdMoveFirst_Click
   End If
End If
```

At this point you should be able to run your program and add a new state. After entering a new state name, tab to the state abbreviation field. What you will notice is that you have to highlight the text before entering a new abbreviation. After you enter a couple of states and abbreviations you can see what a nuisance this is.

Try It Out – Inserting State Data

1. To help make our UI more user-friendly we need to automatically highlight the text when the user tabs to a textbox, and we achieve this using the following code, which you should add to the form:

```
Private Sub txtStateAbbreviation_GotFocus()
   txtStateAbbreviation.SelLength = Len(txtStateAbbreviation.Text)
End Sub

Private Sub txtStateName_GotFocus()
   txtStateName.SelLength = Len(txtStateName.Text)
End Sub
```

2. Enter the state names and abbreviations listed in the table below:

State Name	Abbreviation	State Name	Abbreviation
Alabama	AL	Montana	MT
Alaska	AK	Nebraska	NE
Arizona	AZ	Nevada	NV
Arkansas	AR	New Hampshire	NH
California	CA	New Jersey	NJ
Colorado	CO	New Mexico	NM
Connecticut	CT	New York	NY
Delaware	DE	North Carolina	NC
Florida	FL	North Dakota	ND
Georgia	GA	Ohio	OH
Hawaii	HI	Oklahoma	OK
Idaho	ID	Oregon	OR
Illinois	IL	Pennsylvania	PA
Indiana	IN	Rhode Island	RI
Iowa	IA	South Carolina	SC
Kansas	KS	South Dakota	SD
Kentucky	KY	Tennessee	TN
Louisiana	LA	Texas	TX
Maine	ME	Utah	UT
Maryland	MD	Vermont	VT
Massachusetts	MA	Virginia	VA
Michigan	MI	Washington	WA
Minnesota	MN	West Virginia	WV
Mississippi	MS	Wisconsin	WI
Missouri	MO	Wyoming	WY

Update Stored Procedures

People make mistakes, that's just human nature. While entering the state names and abbreviations, you might have made one or two spelling mistakes yourself. `UPDATE` stored procedures come to our rescue by providing a means to correct our mistakes. They also help us to keep our data from becoming obsolete, such as data in a rate table. This section focuses on `UPDATE` stored procedures.

In Chapter 5 we discussed the syntax of the `UPDATE` statement but, to refresh our memory, let's just take a quick look at it again:

```
UPDATE TableName SET ColumnName = Expression WHERE ColumnName = Expression
```

It should all be coming back to you now, and all we need to do is to create a stored procedure that accepts parameters and updates our columns using the parameters passed. Let's take a look at the following stored procedure code fragment. This stored procedure will be used to update the state names, as indicated by the stored procedure name. Because we are using the naming standard discussed in Chapter 3 we can quickly identify what function this stored procedure is performing.

```
CREATE PROCEDURE up_parmupd_state_names (@state_id Int,
   @state_name VarChar(15), @state_abbreviation Char(2)) AS
```

If you compare this code fragment to the `INSERT` stored procedure you created earlier, you will notice the addition of the `@state_id` input parameter. This is because the `WHERE` clause in the `UPDATE` SQL statement needs to know what row of data it should update. This parameter will be used to limit the update to one row – the row whose `State_ID` column matches the `@state_id` parameter passed.

The `WHERE` clause does not have to match just *one* row. It can be used to make a generic update against *many* rows of data. This all depends on the data in the table you are updating and the expression in the `WHERE` clause.

Try It Out – Update Stored Procedure

1. We want to build our `UPDATE` stored procedure using the code shown in the figure below. After executing the query to create your stored procedure, you need to grant execute authority to the Developers and Sales Staff roles.

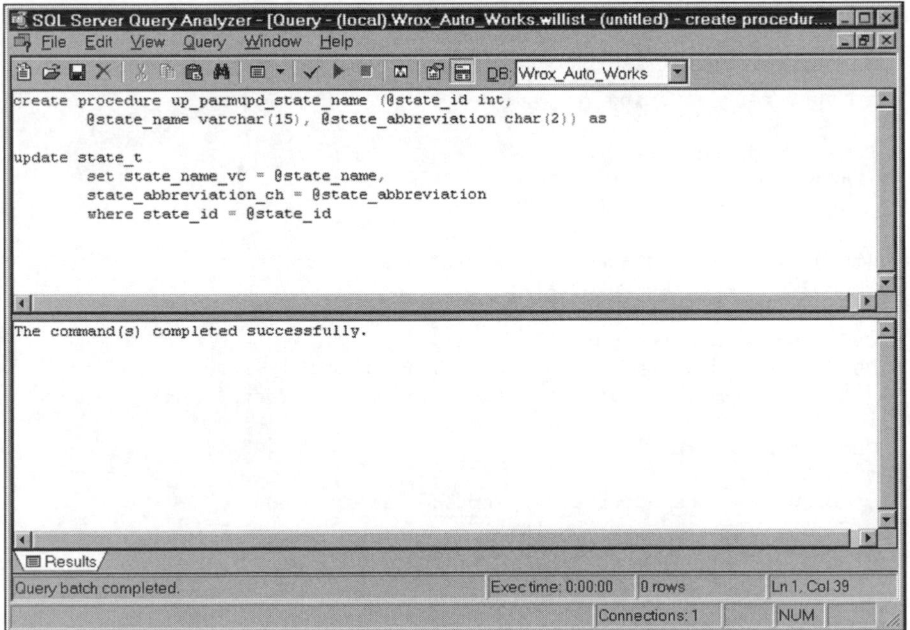

2. To build this example we want to follow the same steps as we did in the last example. We start by copying the form from the last example and naming it `frmTryItOut4.frm`.

3. Then start a new Standard EXE VB project and set a reference to the Microsoft ActiveX Data Objects Library.

4. Remove the current form and add the existing form that you just copied. Change the form name once it is loaded in your project, and change the form caption.

5. Add the `clsStates` class from the last example to your project, and change the start up object for your project in the Project Properties dialog to start with the form `frmTryItOut4`. At this point the project should run and behave as in the last example, with select and insert functionality.

6. This time we want to add a command button to execute our `UPDATE` stored procedure as shown below, giving it a Name of cmdUpdate and a Caption of Update:

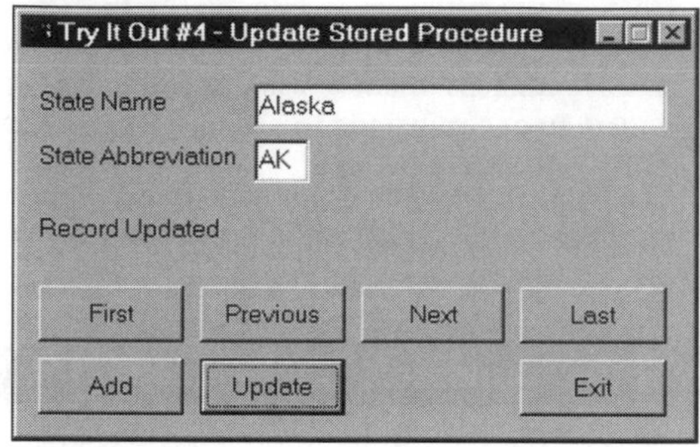

7. Add the following code to the `cmdUpdate_Click` procedure:

```
Private Sub cmdUpdate_Click()
   'Declare local variables
   Dim lngRC As Long
   Dim strError As String

   'Save the current record
   m_varBookMark = m_objRS.Bookmark
   m_strLastState = m_objRS!State_Name_VC

   'Instantiate an instance of the clsStates class
   Dim objUpdate As New clsStates

   'Call the method to update the state
   lngRC = objUpdate.UpdateState(m_objConn, m_objRS!State_ID, _
      txtStateName.Text, txtStateAbbreviation.Text, strError)

   'Check for errors
   If lngRC = 0 Then
      'Display a message that the update was applied
      Call SetMsg("Record Updated")
      'No error, get a new listing of state names
      Call GetStates
   Else
```

```
        'An error occurred, display the error
        Call SetMsg(strError, vbRed)
    End If

    'Dereference the class
    Set objUpdate = Nothing
End Sub
```

8. Add the following code to the `clsStates` class, changing the owner prefix of the stored procedure:

```
Public Function UpdateState(ByRef objConn As ADODB.Connection, _
                            ByVal lngStateID As Long, _
                            ByVal strStateName As String, _
                            ByVal strStateAbbreviation As String, _
                            ByRef strError As String) As Long

    'Declare database objects and local variables
    Dim objErr As ADODB.Error
    Dim strSQL As String

    'Setup error handling
    On Error GoTo UpdateState_EH

    'Validate data
    If Not ValidateStateName(strStateName) Then
        'Raise an error
        Err.Raise vbObjectError + 513, "clsStates.UpdateState", _
            "State Name is either empty or exceeds 15 characters"
    End If

    If Not ValidateStateAbbreviation(strStateAbbreviation) Then
        'Raise an error
        Err.Raise vbObjectError + 513, "clsStates.UpdateState", _
            "State Abbreviation is either empty or not equal to 2 characters"
    End If

    'Build the SQL string
    strSQL = "willist.up_parmupd_state_name (" & _
        lngStateID & ",'" & strStateName & "','" & _
        UCase(strStateAbbreviation) & "')"

    'Update the state data
    objConn.Execute strSQL

    'Return with a good return code
    UpdateState = 0

    'Dereference the database objects
    Set objErr = Nothing

    'All was successful, exit function
    On Error GoTo 0
    Exit Function
```

```
UpdateState_EH:
    'Ensure the error came FROM ADO
    If objConn.Errors.Count > 0 Then
        'Get the first error in the errors collection
        Set objErr = objConn.Errors(0)
        'Set the error message
        strError = objErr.Description
    Else
        'Set the error message
        strError = Err.Description
    End If
    'Dereference the database objects
    Set objErr = Nothing
    'Return with a bad return code
    UpdateState = 1
    On Error GoTo 0
End Function
```

How It Works – The Stored Procedure

The first line of this stored procedure contains the input parameters that are required to be passed by the calling program. Since this stored procedure is using the `UPDATE` SQL statement, we use the `SET` keyword to set the column values equal to the local variables (input parameters). The `WHERE` clause specifies the condition of the update, and only updates rows of data that satisfy the `WHERE` condition:

```
CREATE PROCEDURE up_parmupd_state_name (@state_id Int,
    @state_name VarChar(15), @state_abbreviation Char(2)) AS

UPDATE State_T
    SET State_Name_VC = @state_name,
    State_Abbreviation_CH = @state_abbreviation
    WHERE State_ID = @state_id
```

The VB Program

The code that we need in order to incorporate update functionality in our VB program is minimal, and is contained in two procedures. Let's start with the `UpdateState` method in our class. This method is essentially the same as the `AddState` method, except that it contains one extra parameter – the ID of the state that should be updated:

```
Public Function UpdateState(ByRef objConn As ADODB.Connection, _
                            ByVal lngStateID As Long, _
                            ByVal strStateName As String, _
                            ByVal strStateAbbreviation As String, _
                            ByRef strError As String) As Long
```

The next difference comes when we build the SQL string. The first parameter that our stored procedure expects is the state ID and we have specified it first in this string, followed by the state name and abbreviation:

```
    'Build the SQL string
    strSQL = "willist.up_parmupd_state_name (" & _
        lngStateID & ",'" & strStateName & "','" & _
        UCase(strStateAbbreviation) & "')"
```

The rest of the code is the same as the AddState method. We still validate the state name and abbreviation to ensure that we do not allow empty fields to be inserted, or that the data is not longer than what the database can handle. Some may wonder why we do not validate the state ID. There are a couple of reasons, the first of which is that a valid Long data type must be passed in order for this method to be executed. Secondly, if the value passed does not exist on the database, no updates will be performed.

The cmdUpdate_Click procedure is basically the same as the cmdAdd_Click procedure. When we execute the UpdateState method we pass the state ID contained in the current record:

```
'Call the method to update the state
lngRC = objUpdate.UpdateState(m_objConn, m_objRS!State_ID, _
   txtStateName.Text, txtStateAbbreviation.Text, strError)
```

If the call to the UpdateState method was successful, we display a message indicating that the record was updated, and get a new copy of the recordset to reflect the changes made:

```
'Check for errors
If lngRC = 0 Then
   'Display a message that the update was applied
   Call SetMsg("Record Updated")
   'No error, get a new listing of state names
   Call GetStates
```

At this point our little data entry program can execute a stored procedure to select records, execute a stored procedure to add new data to our table, and execute a stored procedure to update records. Let's move on and complete our program.

Delete Stored Procedures

No matter how much we update the data in our database there will come a time when some data just becomes obsolete and we need to delete it from our tables. There could also be an instance where data was entered into multiple columns in our table, or the data could be totally inaccurate. Instead of trying to go through and update all of the fields, it would be easier to delete the row of data and insert a new one. This is where our DELETE stored procedure comes into play.

We can delete rows of data based on the criteria passed to the DELETE statement. To refresh our memory, take a look at the syntax of the DELETE statement that we covered in Chapter 5.

```
DELETE [From] TableName WHERE Expression
```

We need only specify the table name and the expression to delete data. If the expression evaluates to a Boolean value that matches multiple rows, then multiple rows of data will be deleted. If we use the primary key of the table, then only one row of data will be deleted.

DELETE stored procedures, like INSERT and UPDATE stored procedures, usually need to accept parameters to be of any use. Normally you will use just one parameter that specifies a primary key of the row to be deleted. However, there will come a time when you need to pass multiple parameters and use logic in your stored procedures to selectively delete rows of data. The DELETE stored procedure that we will be working with accepts only one parameter and the value in this parameter represents a primary key value in the table:

```
CREATE PROCEDURE up_parmdel_state_name (@state_id Int) AS
```

As you can see from the stored procedure code fragment above, the syntax is the same as the previous two stored procedures that we created. This time, however, we are only specifying one input parameter.

Try It Out – Delete Stored Procedure

1. We start this example by building the DELETE stored procedure using the code listed in the figure below:

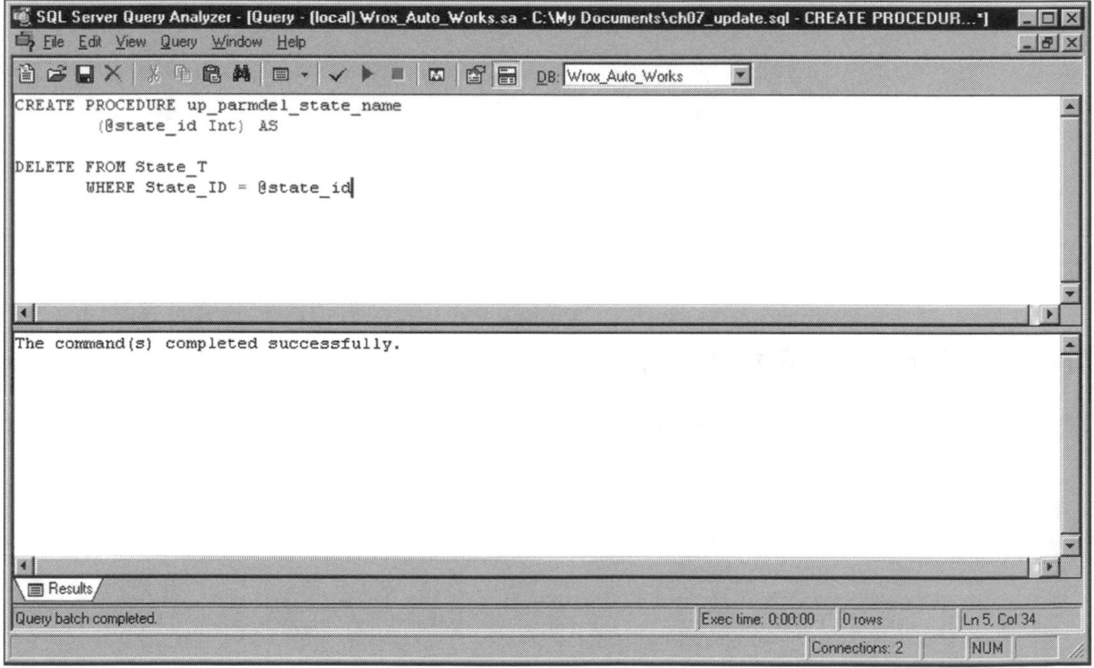

2. Once you have executed the query to create the stored procedure, you need to grant execute authority to the Developers and Sales Staff roles.

3. We start this project as we did the last, by copying the form from the last example and naming it frmTryItOut5.frm.

4. Start a new Standard EXE VB project and set a reference to the Microsoft ActiveX Data Objects Library.

5. Then remove the current form and add the new form that you just copied. You will need to change the form name once it is loaded in your project, and change the form caption.

6. Next we need to add the `clsStates` class from our last example to this project, and change the start up object for your project in the Project Properties dialog to start with the form `frmTryItOut5`.

7. We want to add a command button to execute our `DELETE` stored procedure, as shown below, giving it a Name of cmdDelete and a Caption of Delete:

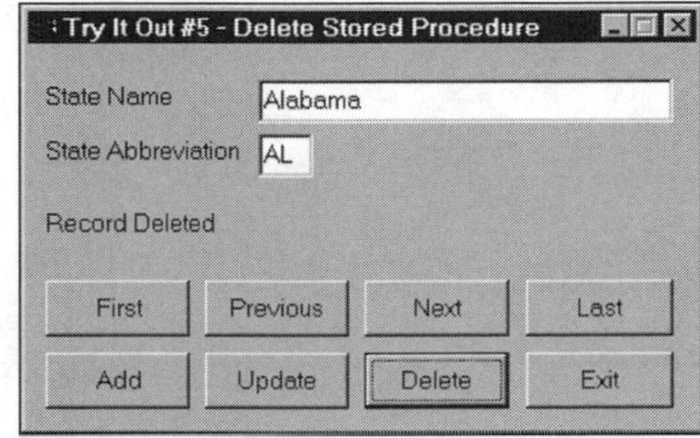

8. Add the following code to the `cmdDelete_Click` procedure:

```
Private Sub cmdDelete_Click()
   'Declare local variables
   Dim lngRC As Long
   Dim strError As String

   'Save the current record
   m_varBookMark = m_objRS.Bookmark
   m_strLastState = m_objRS!State_Name_VC

   'Instantiate an instance of the clsStates class
   Dim objDelete As New clsStates

   'Call the method to delete the state
   lngRC = objDelete.DeleteState(m_objConn, m_objRS!State_ID, _
      strError)

   'Check for errors
   If lngRC = 0 Then
      'Display a message that the record was deleted
      Call SetMsg("Record Deleted")
      'No error, get a new listing of state names
      Call GetStates
   Else
      'An error occurred, display the error
      Call SetMsg(strError, vbRed)
   End If

   'Dereference the class
   Set objDelete = Nothing
End Sub
```

9. Add the following code to the `clsStates` class, again changing the owner prefix of the stored procedure:

```
Public Function DeleteState(ByRef objConn As ADODB.Connection, _
                            ByVal lngStateID As Long, _
                            ByVal strError As String) As Long

   'Declare database objects and local variables
   Dim objErr As ADODB.Error
   Dim strSQL As String

   'Setup error handling
   On Error GoTo DeleteState_EH

   'Build the SQL string
   strSQL = "willist.up_parmdel_state_name (" & lngStateID & ")"

   'Delete the state data
   objConn.Execute strSQL

   'Return with a good return code
   DeleteState = 0

   'Dereference the database objects
   Set objErr = Nothing

   'All was successful, exit function
   On Error GoTo 0
   Exit Function

DeleteState_EH:
   'Ensure the error came from ADO
   If objConn.Errors.Count > 0 Then
      'Get the first error in the errors collection
      Set objErr = objConn.Errors(0)
      'Set the error message
      strError = objErr.Description
   Else
      'Set the error message
      strError = Err.Description
   End If
   'Dereference the database objects
   Set objErr = Nothing
   'Return with a bad return code
   DeleteState = 1
   On Error GoTo 0
End Function
```

10. Modify the `GetStates` procedure in the form as follows:

```
Private Sub GetStates()
   'Setup error handling
   On Error GoTo GetStates_EH
```

```
    'If the recordset has been set and is open, then close it
    If Not m_objRS Is Nothing Then
       If m_objRS.State = adStateOpen Then
          m_objRS.Close
       End If
    End If

    'Instantiate an instance of the clsStates class
    Dim objSelect As New clsStates

    'Call the method to return a recordset of states
    Set m_objRS = objSelect.GetAllStates(m_objConn)

    If m_objRS Is Nothing Then
       'Error occured getting recordset, display message
       Call SetMsg("Error occured getting recordset", vbRed)
       Call DisableButtons
    Else
       If Not IsEmpty(m_varBookMark) Then
          'Move to the appropriate record and load the fields
          m_objRS.Bookmark = m_varBookMark
          If m_objRS!State_Name_VC < m_strLastState Then
             Call cmdMoveNext_Click
          Else
             Call LoadFields(m_objRS!State_Name_VC, _
                m_objRS!State_Abbreviation_CH)
          End If
       Else
          'Move to the first record
          Call cmdMoveFirst_Click
       End If
    End If

    'Dereference the class
    Set objSelect = Nothing

    'Exit the procedure
    On Error GoTo 0
    Exit Sub

 GetStates_EH:
    Select Case Err.Number
       Case -2147217906       'Invalid bookmark
          m_objRS.MoveFirst
          m_strLastState = "##"
          Resume Next
    End Select
 End Sub
```

11. Don't forget to modify the description in the procedure attributes.

How It Works – The Stored Procedure

The stored procedure is straightforward as it only accepts one parameter, the ID of the state to delete:

```
    'Build the SQL string
    strSQL = "willist.up_parmdel_state_name (" & lngStateID & ")"
```

The Class Module

The `DeleteState` method in our class accepts three parameters, the `Connection` object, the state ID, and the error string:

```
Public Function DeleteState(ByRef objConn As ADODB.Connection, _
                            ByVal lngStateID As Long, _
                            ByVal strError As String) As Long
```

There is no validation in this function as we are deleting a row of data. The rest of this function is the same as the `UpdateState` function and as such has not been covered again.

The `cmdDelete_Click` procedure is the same as the `cmdUpdate_Click` procedure, except for this line of code where we execute the method to delete a state. We also need to change the message that is displayed, to state that a record was deleted:

```
    'Call the method to delete the state
    lngRC = objDelete.DeleteState(m_objConn, m_objRS!State_ID, strError)
```

Because we are deleting a record from the `State_T` table, it is possible that the bookmark will no longer be valid. To handle this we add error handling to the `GetStates` procedure, as shown below. The first line of code sets up the error handling for this procedure:

```
Private Sub GetStates()
    'Setup error handling
    On Error GoTo GetStates_EH
```

The error handler uses a `Select Case` statement to determine which error was received. At this point we are only trapping the error for an invalid bookmark. We want to move to the first record in the recordset, and set the `m_strLastState` variable to a low value. We do this so the comparison of the state will fail and we will stay on the first record. We then resume at the next line of code after the line that caused the error:

```
GetStates_EH:
    Select Case Err.Number
        Case -2147217906        'Invalid bookmark
            m_objRS.MoveFirst
            m_strLastState = "##"
            Resume Next
    End Select
End Sub
```

At this point you are ready to run your program and test this new functionality. This wraps up this program and we now have a fully functional data entry program that uses stored procedures.

Summary

As we wrap things up in this chapter you should feel pretty good about your data entry program. Not only have you coded a program that uses stored procedures and performs all types of data entry, but you have also encapsulated all of the basic functionality into one class. This class can be used by other programs and server components, or can even be made into a server component by itself. We will be using this class in other examples later in the book.

We have taken a look at stored procedure performance and user prefixes. We now know why we should use stored procedures versus in-line SQL statements, and why we should always prefix our stored procedures with the user prefix.

We have also explored the basic `SELECT`, `INSERT`, `UPDATE`, and `DELETE` stored procedures and have used them in our program. You should feel comfortable using stored procedures and passing parameters to them. You should also understand the difference between stored procedure input and output parameters and return values.

In summary, you should know:

- The different parameters of a stored procedure
- How to process the data in an output parameter returned from a stored procedure
- How to process a return value returned from a stored procedure
- How to create stored procedures and code stored procedure parameters
- How to execute stored procedures in your VB programs
- Why and how to set permissions on your stored procedures

In the next chapter we will take a closer look at the benefits of stored procedures over in-line SQL statements, and consider some ways to optimize both.

WROX AUTO WORKS RACING

Stored Procedures vs T-SQL Statements

In the last chapter we touched briefly on the performance of stored procedures versus Transact-SQL statements. We know that stored procedures will execute faster than SQL statements called from your program, and that they provide many more benefits other than performance alone. This chapter will provide a side-by-side comparison of executing SQL statements from your VB programs, and executing the same SQL statements in a stored procedure called from your VB programs. Stored procedures are the best choice in most circumstances. This chapter details where in-line SQL has its advantages and also Chapter 11 uses dynamic in-line SQL.

We will also cover the `Command` object in more depth, using the various methods of creating and appending parameters to the `Parameters` collection. The `Command` object can be used to optimize your in-line SQL statements by using the `Command` object's `Prepared` property, which we will also examine.

We will also take a look at a couple of ways of working with multiple results sets, firstly using stored procedures, and secondly using the `Recordset` object.

In this chapter we will cover:

- Side-by-side comparisons of stored procedure and SQL statement executions
- Passing parameters to a stored procedure using the `Command` object
- Retrieving parameters returned from stored procedures
- Optimizing your SQL statements using the `Command` object's `Prepared` property
- Using stored procedures to return multiple results sets
- Obtaining multiple recordsets in a single execution of a `Recordset` object

Comparison – Stored Procedures vs In-line SQL

In the last chapter we built simple stored procedures and executed them from our VB program. Once again we will be doing the same. We will also be using the same SQL statements from those stored procedures, but this time running them as **in-line SQL statements** in our VB programs. As we stated in Chapter 1, in-line SQL statements are SQL statements that are coded directly in your program as a string and then sent to SQL Server for execution.

The purpose of these exercises is twofold. First and foremost, you will get a good understanding of how to execute in-line SQL statements from your VB programs. Secondly, you will gain an understanding of how this compares to executing the same SQL statements as a stored procedure, and any differences will be pointed out as we go along.

These examples are not as elaborate as our data entry program in the last chapter, but do provide a side-by-side comparison of executing stored procedures and in-line SQL statements. After completing these exercises, you should be able to determine which method best suits your needs, and be able to code either with ease.

INSERT Stored Procedure

We start our comparisons with an `INSERT` stored procedure. This stored procedure will insert a city name into the `City_T` table, and return the `City_ID` of the entry just inserted, as a return value. Because this stored procedure *returns a value*, you must use the `Command` object to retrieve the value returned.

Try It Out – INSERT Stored Procedure

1. After having created stored procedures in the last chapter, you should be able to create this stored procedure in the Query Analyzer and execute it with no problems. The stored procedure is listed in the figure below:

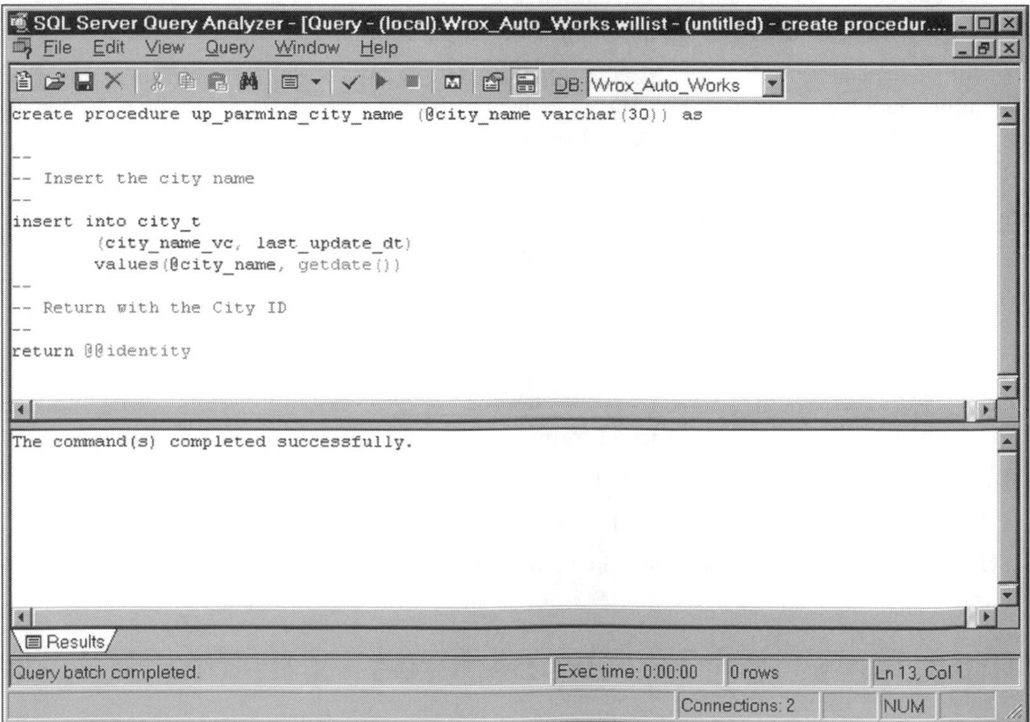

2. After you execute the query to create the stored procedure, don't forget to set the permissions so that the Developers and Sales Staff roles have access to it (we learned how to do this in Chapter 4).

How It Works – INSERT Stored Procedure

The code for this stored procedure should look familiar to you except for the last line, which we will explain in just a few moments. This is a basic stored procedure that accepts a parameter, and uses that parameter to insert the city name.

Let's take a look at the last part of this stored procedure. We discussed stored procedure parameters and return values in the last chapter, and used a return code in our stored procedure to return a value. This time we are using the `@@Identity` function to provide a return value.

SQL Server provides this built-in function, `@@Identity`, which returns the last identity value inserted into a row. We can then use this function to return the key of the identity column for the entry that we have just inserted into our table. Remember that the `RETURN` statement accepts only integer data types to return. The identity column must be a numeric data type (unless the identity value has exceeded the upper limit of integer values – however, an integer's upper limit is 2,147,483,648, so this is not something we need to be concerned with at this point). Thus the `@@Identity` function provides a good match for the `RETURN` statement.

After our `INSERT` statement to insert a new city name, we return with the value that was automatically inserted into the `City_ID` column by SQL Server:

```
INSERT INTO City_T
        (City_Name_VC, Last Update_DT)
        Values(@City_Name, GetDate())
--
-- Return with the City ID
--
RETURN @@Identity
```

Now that you have built your stored procedure, it's time to move on and create the VB program that will be used to execute this stored procedure.

Try It Out – INSERT Program Using Stored Procedure

The program we want to build will provide dual functionality. Firstly, it will allow us to enter a city name and click a button to execute the stored procedure to insert the new city name. Secondly, it will provide another button that will allow us to execute in-line SQL statements to perform the same function, using another city name. The functionality for the in-line SQL will come later, but we can go ahead and add the button at this point. The result will look something like the following:

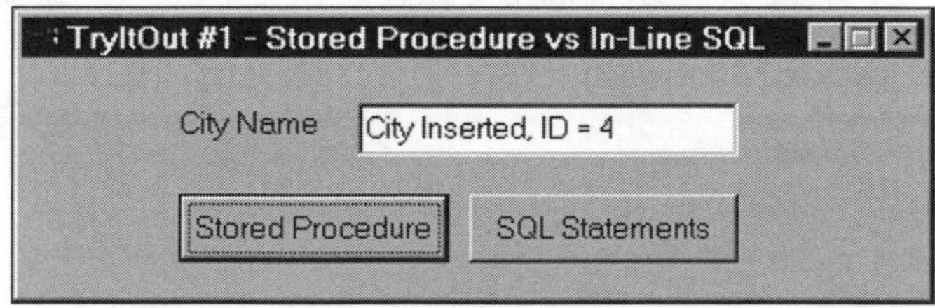

1. Start a new Standard EXE project in Visual Basic and set a reference to the Microsoft ActiveX Data Objects Library (as stated previously, use the latest version you have). Then place the controls listed in the following table onto the form:

Control	Name	Caption/Notes
Label	label1	City Name
TextBox	txtCityName	The Text property should be set to nothing
Command Button	cmdStoredProcedure	Stored Procedure
Command Button	cmdSQLStatements	SQL Statements

2. Rename and caption the form if you wish.

3. Enter the code below, which can be found in the file `frmTryItOut1.frm`, changing the stored procedure owner prefix as necessary:

```
Option Explicit

'Declare database objects
Private m_objConn As ADODB.Connection
Private m_objCmd As ADODB.Command


Private Sub cmdSQLStatements_Click()
  'In-line statements will go in here later
End Sub


Private Sub cmdStoredProcedure_Click()
   'Set a reference to the ADO Command object
   Set m_objCmd = New ADODB.Command

   'Set the Command object properties
   Set m_objCmd.ActiveConnection = m_objConn
   m_objCmd.CommandText = "willist.up_parmins_city_name"
   m_objCmd.CommandType = adCmdStoredProc

   'Set the parameters
   m_objCmd.Parameters.Append m_objCmd.CreateParameter( _
      "CityID", adInteger, adParamReturnValue)
   m_objCmd.Parameters.Append m_objCmd.CreateParameter( _
      "CityName", adVarChar, adParamInput, 30, txtCityName.Text)

   'Execute the Command object
   m_objCmd.Execute

   'Display message
   txtCityName.Text = "City Inserted, ID = " & m_objCmd("CityID")
```

```
   'De-reference Command object
   Set m_objCmd = Nothing
End Sub

Private Sub Form_Load()
   'Use the standard Windows icon
   Me.Icon = Nothing

   'Set a reference to the ADO Connection object
   Set m_objConn = New ADODB.Connection

   'Establish a database connection using NT authentication
   m_objConn.Open "DSN=Wrox Auto Works"

   'Check connection state
   If m_objConn.State <> adStateOpen Then
      txtCityName.Text = "Connection Failed"
   End If
End Sub

Private Sub Form_Unload(Cancel As Integer)
   'Close and de-reference database objects
   If Not m_objConn Is Nothing Then
      If m_objConn.State Then
         m_objConn.Close
      End If
      Set m_objConn = Nothing
   End If
End Sub
```

How It Works – INSERT Program Using Stored Procedure

We start by declaring our database objects in the general declarations section of the form:

```
Option Explicit

'Declare database objects
Private m_objConn As ADODB.Connection
Private m_objCmd As ADODB.Command
```

Note that the `Command` object is declared here as this object is used by multiple procedures in this form, and therefore has been declared global to the form.

Next we move on to the `Form_Load` event, set our form icon to nothing, and set our `Connection` object:

```
Private Sub Form_Load()
   'Use the standard Windows icon
   Me.Icon = Nothing

   'Set a reference to the ADO Connection object
   Set m_objConn = New ADODB.Connection
```

We open our database connection using the DSN we set up in Chapter 6. We are using NT authentication in this example, but if your SQL Server logon uses SQL Server authentication you should by now know what modifications you need to make (this was also discussed in Chapter 6). After we open our connection, we check the `State` of the connection, and if the connection failed we display a short message in the `txtCityName` textbox:

```
   'Establish a database connection using NT authentication
   m_objConn.Open "DSN=Wrox Auto Works"

   'Check connection state
   If m_objConn.State <> adStateOpen Then
      txtCityName.Text = "Connection Failed"
   End If
End Sub
```

The `cmdStoredProcedure_Click` procedure executes the stored procedure, passing it the text from the `txtCityName` textbox. The first thing we need to do in this procedure is to set a reference to the `Command` object and then set the `Command` object's properties. We set the `ActiveConnection` property to our `Connection` object and set the `CommandText` property to our stored procedure name. Notice once again that we have prefixed our stored procedure with the user prefix. You will need to replace the stored procedure prefix with the prefix of your login. Since we are executing a stored procedure, we set the `CommandType` property to the `adCmdStoredProc` constant from the `CommandTypeEnum` enumeration:

```
Private Sub cmdStoredProcedure_Click()
   'Set a reference to the ADO Command object
   Set m_objCmd = New ADODB.Command

   'Set the Command object properties
   Set m_objCmd.ActiveConnection = m_objConn
   m_objCmd.CommandText = "willist.up_parmins_city_name"
   m_objCmd.CommandType = adCmdStoredProc
```

Once again we are using the `Parameters` collection to pass parameters to the stored procedure.

> **The first parameter that we must pass is for the return value. This must always be the first parameter when a return value is being returned.**

The other parameters are added in the same order that the stored procedure expects them. In our case there is only one input parameter, which contains the city name.

Since the first parameter is a return value, we know that it is an `Integer` data type, we do not have to specify the `Size`, nor do we have to specify a `Value`. The second parameter is a `VarChar` data type and we must specify the `Size` of the field, in this case the database will accept up to 30 characters in this field, so this is what we have specified. The `Value` for this parameter is being passed from the `txtCityName` textbox:

```
   'Set the parameters
   m_objCmd.Parameters.Append m_objCmd.CreateParameter( _
      "CityID", adInteger, adParamReturnValue)
   m_objCmd.Parameters.Append m_objCmd.CreateParameter( _
      "CityName", adVarChar, adParamInput, 30, txtCityName.Text)
```

Once our parameters have been created and appended to the `Parameters` collection, we execute the `Command` object. We then display the city ID that was returned from the stored procedure to the `Command` object. We access the parameter in the `Parameters` collection via the `Command` object, using the name that we gave it in the parameter, in this case `CityID`.

Last, we de-reference our `Command` object and end the procedure:

```
   'Execute the Command object
   m_objCmd.Execute

   'Display message
   txtCityName.Text = "City Inserted, ID = " & m_objCmd("CityID")

   'De-reference Command object
   Set m_objCmd = Nothing
End Sub
```

The `Form_Unload` event fires when we end our program, and we close and de-reference our database objects here:

```
Private Sub Form_Unload(Cancel As Integer)
   'Close and de-reference database objects
   If Not m_objConn Is Nothing Then
      If m_objConn.State Then
         m_objConn.Close
      End If
      Set m_objConn = Nothing
   End If
End Sub
```

At this point you should be able to run your program and insert city names. You need to click on the Stored Procedure button to run this example. The SQL Statement button doesn't have any code and will not do anything if you click on it. Go ahead and insert one or two city names to see how this program functions. Notice that you get the city ID returned from the stored procedure.

Note that we do not have any error handling at the moment, this will be discussed later.

To view the city names you have just inserted, run the following query in the Query Analyzer. This query will select all columns and all rows in the `City_T` table:

```
SELECT * FROM City_T
```

INSERT SQL Statement

We know from Chapter 7 that we can execute SQL statements from within our VB programs. But how do they relate to the SQL statements in a stored procedure? Actually they are the same, although there are some limitations applied to in-line SQL statements, as we will see in just a moment.

Let's take as an example the stored procedure that we just created. The SQL is shown below:

```
INSERT INTO City_T
       (City_Name_VC, Last_Update_DT)
       Values(@City_Name, GetDate())

RETURN @@Identity
```

If you were to take the exact SQL statements shown above and try to execute them in your VB program, you would receive the error shown below:

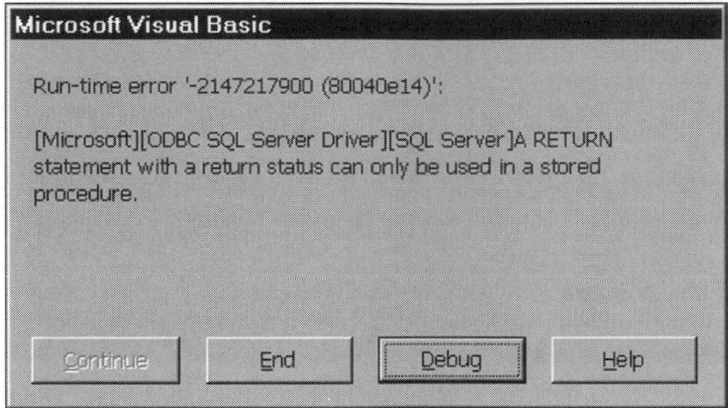

In-line SQL statements can not perform all of the functions that our stored procedures can. In this case the in-line SQL statements can not return a return value. This is just one of the limitations of in-line SQL statements. In-line SQL statements also do not allow us to declare and use variables or use logic to control the flow of processing as stored procedures do. They are also not compiled so they are not as efficient as stored procedures. While in-line SQL statements do have their place, they are not as robust as stored procedures, as was demonstrated by this example.

So how do we code the same in-line SQL statements that are contained in our stored procedure? Actually we can't – we can code the same `INSERT` statement, but we can't code the return value. So what ends up happening here is that our in-line SQL statements cannot provide the same robust functionality that was provided by our stored procedure using the same SQL statements. We can still insert city names but we have to code a separate `SELECT` statement to retrieve the city ID of the row that we just inserted.

So let's take a look at what code is required to implement the second part of our program:

Try It Out – INSERT Program Using In-line SQL

1. The code listed below implements the functionality for the `cmdSQLStatements` button, and should be entered in your `frmTryItOut1.frm`:

```
Private Sub cmdSQLStatements_Click()
   'Set a reference to the ADO Command object
   Set m_objCmd = New ADODB.Command

   'Set the Command object properties
   Set m_objCmd.ActiveConnection = m_objConn
   m_objCmd.CommandText = "Insert Into City_T " & _
      "(City_Name_VC, Last_Update_DT) " & _
      "Values('" & txtCityName.Text & "', GetDate())"
   m_objCmd.CommandType = adCmdText

   'Execute the Command object
   m_objCmd.Execute

   'Declare a Recordset object
   Dim objRS As New ADODB.Recordset

   'Open the Recordset object to get the City_ID just inserted
   objRS.Open "SELECT City_ID FROM City_T WHERE City_Name_VC = '" & _
      txtCityName.Text & "'", m_objConn, adOpenForwardOnly, adLockReadOnly, _
      adCmdText

   'Display message
   txtCityName.Text = "City Inserted, ID = " & objRS!City_ID

   'De-reference database objects
   objRS.Close
   Set objRS = Nothing
   Set m_objCmd = Nothing
End Sub
```

How It Works – INSERT Program Using In-line SQL

Looking at what's different from the same functionality provided by the stored procedure, we notice that the `CommandText` property of the `Command` object is set to the actual SQL string that we will be executing. This SQL string uses the `txtCityName` textbox as input, instead of a parameter as our stored procedure did. Also, we cannot return a value from our SQL string, so we have to code a separate statement to retrieve the `City_ID` that was just inserted, using a `Recordset` object.

The `CommandType` property is set to the `adCmdText` constant from the `CommandTypeEnum` enumeration because we are executing a textual string:

```
'Set the Command object properties
   Set m_objCmd.ActiveConnection = m_objConn
   m_objCmd.CommandText = "INSERT INTO City_T " & _
      "(City_Name_VC, Last_Update_DT) " & _
      "Values('" & txtCityName.Text & "', GetDate())"
   m_objCmd.CommandType = adCmdText
```

After executing our SQL string to insert the city name, we declare a `Recordset` object that will be used to execute a SQL string to retrieve the `City_ID` that has just been inserted:

```
'Execute the Command object
m_objCmd.Execute

'Declare a Recordset object
Dim objRS As New ADODB.Recordset
```

Using a `SELECT` statement with in-line SQL statements, we open a `Recordset` object to retrieve the `City_ID` that was just inserted. The `WHERE` clause in this `SELECT` statement uses the city name that was entered into the textbox to limit the selection of data to the one row that was just inserted:

```
'Open the Recordset object to get the City_ID just inserted
objRS.Open "SELECT City_ID FROM City_T WHERE City_Name_VC = '" & _
   txtCityName.Text & "'", m_objConn, adOpenForwardOnly, adLockReadOnly, _
   adCmdText
```

After we have opened the recordset, we display the same message as in the last example. This time however, the `City_ID` is coming from our `Recordset` object instead of the `Command` object:

```
'Display message
txtCityName.Text = "City Inserted, ID = " & objRS!City_ID
```

Last, we close and de-reference our database objects:

```
'De-reference database objects
objRS.Close
Set objRS = Nothing
Set m_objCmd = Nothing
```

You can now run your program and insert a new city name, using either the stored procedure or the in-line SQL statement.

This side-by-side comparison has shown that although the stored procedure and SQL statements are basically the same, we lose some functionality by using in-line SQL statements, as we cannot execute all of the SQL statements that are available to stored procedures. We must rely on additional SQL statements to provide the same functionality as stored procedures. In the example above we must declare another database object (in this case a Recordset object) and open a recordset to get the `City_ID` that was inserted. This requires extra processing by our program to perform the same task that the stored procedure performed, and the in-line SQL also takes longer to perform because of the extra object that must be used.

The reason this happens is because stored procedures use T-SQL statements. If you remember our discussion from Chapter 1, T-SQL statements are Microsoft's version of SQL statements used exclusively with SQL Server. We cannot always use these T-SQL statements as in-line SQL statements in our programs.

UPDATE Stored Procedure

The `UPDATE` stored procedure we are going to be building is very straightforward. It simply updates the city name for the city ID that you pass. There are no return values or output parameters in this stored procedure. So let's take a look at this stored procedure:

Try It Out – UPDATE Stored Procedure

1. Create the stored procedure which is listed in the figure below:

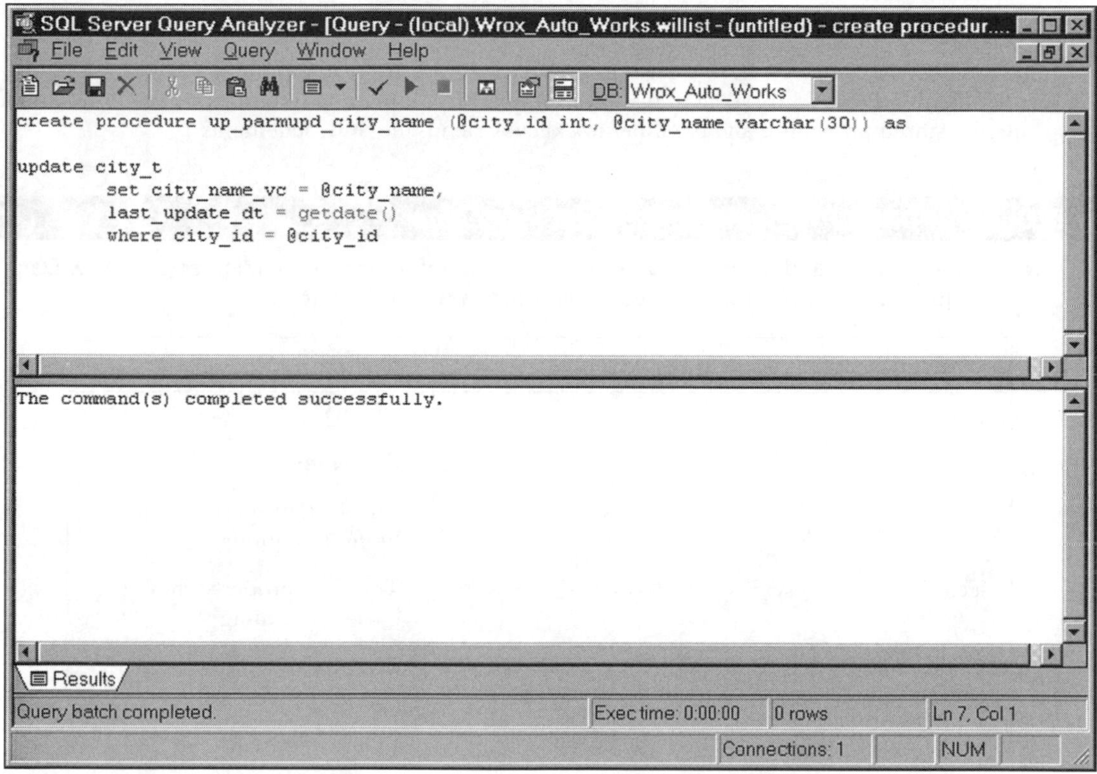

2. After you have built this stored procedure, don't forget to set the permissions so that the Developers and Sales Staff roles can execute it.

How It Works – UPDATE Stored Procedure

Breaking down this stored procedure, we see that the first line specifies that an `UPDATE` stored procedure is to be created, as is evident by the naming standards that we are using. We also see that this stored procedure will accept two input parameters, the first being the city ID, which is specified as an `Integer` data type. The second parameter contains the city name and it is a `VarChar` data type with a maximum length of 30 characters:

```
CREATE PROCEDURE up_parmupd_city_name (@City_ID Int, @City_Name VarChar(30)) AS
```

The UPDATE SQL statement used in this stored procedure is very straightforward. We are updating two columns in the City_T table: City_Name_VC and Last_Update_DT. The City_Name_VC column gets its value from the @City_Name parameter that we pass, and the Last_Update_DT column gets a value from the SQL Server built-in function GetDate() which we have covered before in Chapter 7. The WHERE clause of the UPDATE statement uses the @City_ID parameter to restrict the update to the row whose value in the City_ID column matches the @City_ID parameter:

```
UPDATE City_T
        SET City_Name_VC = @City_Name,
        Last_Update_DT = GetDate()
        WHERE City_ID = @City_ID
```

At this point we have our UPDATE stored procedure built and are ready to build a VB program to execute this stored procedure. Like in the last example we will place two buttons on the form, one to execute the stored procedure and the other to execute the in-line SQL statements.

Try It Out – UPDATE Program Using Stored Procedure

1. Start a new Standard EXE VB project and set a reference to the Microsoft ActiveX Data Objects Library. Next add the controls listed in the table below:

Control	Name	Caption/Notes
Label	label1	City ID
Label	label2	City Name
TextBox	txtCityID	The Text property should be set to nothing
TextBox	txtCityName	The Text property should be set to nothing
Command Button	cmdStoredProcedure	Stored Procedure
Command Button	cmdSQLStatements	SQL Statements

2. Rename and caption the form if required.

3. Add the following code, available as frmTryItOut2.frm, to your project, changing the owner prefix and connection string if necessary:

```
Option Explicit

'Declare database objects
Private m_objConn As ADODB.Connection
Private m_objCmd As ADODB.Command

Private Sub cmdStoredProcedure_Click()
   'Set a reference to the ADO Command object
   Set m_objCmd = New ADODB.Command

   'Set the Command object properties
   Set m_objCmd.ActiveConnection = m_objConn
   m_objCmd.CommandText = "willist.up_parmupd_city_name (" & _
      CLng(txtCityID.Text) & ",'" & txtCityName.Text & "')"
   m_objCmd.CommandType = adCmdStoredProc

   'Execute the Command object
   m_objCmd.Execute

   'Display message
   txtCityName.Text = "City Name Updated"

   'De-reference Command object
   Set m_objCmd = Nothing
End Sub


Private Sub Form_Load()
   'Use the standard Windows icon
   Me.Icon = Nothing

   'Set a reference to the ADO Connection object
   Set m_objConn = New ADODB.Connection

   'Establish a database connection using NT authentication
   m_objConn.Open "DSN=Wrox Auto Works"

   'Check connection state
   If m_objConn.State <> adStateOpen Then
      txtCityName.Text = "Connection Failed"
   End If
End Sub


Private Sub Form_Unload(Cancel As Integer)
   'Close and de-reference database objects
   If Not m_objConn Is Nothing Then
      If m_objConn.State Then
         m_objConn.Close
      End If
      Set m_objConn = Nothing
   End If
End Sub
```

The figure below shows the program after a city has been updated using the Stored Procedure button:

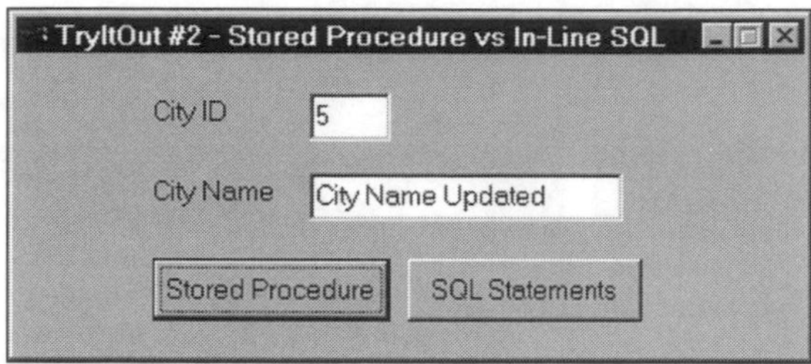

How It Works – UPDATE Program Using Stored Procedure

Like the last program that we coded, the `Form_Load` event is used to establish a connection with the database using a DSN and NT authentication. Change the authentication mode if necessary to match your SQL Server logon. Also the `Form_Unload` event contains the code to de-reference our database objects. Our database objects are declared in the general declarations section of the form, as in the last example, and we are using the same objects.

The code that is different is contained in the `cmdStoredProcedure_Click` procedure. Here we are using a different stored procedure and different syntax. This time, instead of passing the parameters in the `Parameters` collection, we are passing them as part of the stored procedure in the `CommandText` property. This gives you the opportunity to explore the various methods of using the `Command` object to pass parameters to stored procedures.

Notice that we have enclosed the parameters in a set of parentheses and our string parameter is enclosed in single quotes (apostrophes).

> *Note here that if your city name contains a single quote, then your call will fail because you have enclosed the city name parameter in single quotes, and you will receive an error about an un-terminated quote. We will address this issue in Chapter 11. If you added a city name that contained single quotes in the last example, that worked because we used the* `Parameters` *collection. The* `Parameters` *collection automatically took care of this for us.*

Since the `@City_ID` parameter in our stored procedure expects a SQL Server `Integer` data type, we must convert the value from the `txtCityID` textbox to a VB `Long` data type. A `Long` data type in VB is equal to an `Integer` data type in SQL Server, as shown in Appendix A.

```
Private Sub cmdStoredProcedure_Click()
   'Set a reference to the ADO Command object
   Set m_objCmd = New ADODB.Command

   'Set the Command object properties
   Set m_objCmd.ActiveConnection = m_objConn
   m_objCmd.CommandText = "willist.up_parmupd_city_name (" & _
      CLng(txtCityID.Text) & ",'" & txtCityName.Text & "')"
   m_objCmd.CommandType = adCmdStoredProc

   'Execute the Command object
   m_objCmd.Execute
```

At this point you should be able to run your program (remember that only the Stored Procedure button is functional at this time). You will need to know the city ID of the city name that you want to update. You can find this information in one of two ways. First, you can run a query in the Query Analyzer using the SQL statement below:

```
SELECT * FROM City_T
```

The other method you can use to find the City ID is to use the Enterprise Manager. Expand the Wrox_Auto_Works database and click on Tables in the tree view. Right click on the City_T table and choose Open Table from the popup menu. Then choose Return All Rows from the sub menu. All of the information that is displayed in the Query Analyzer is displayed here. The difference is that the table is opened in edit mode; you can directly edit all of the columns and rows in the table.

UPDATE SQL Statements

The UPDATE SQL statement that we are going to be using in this example comes straight from our stored procedure, with a few minor modifications for the parameters of course.

Try It Out – UPDATE Program Using In-line SQL

1. The code for the cmdSQLStatements_Click procedure is listed below. At this point enter the code in your frmTryItOut2.frm program, but before running it, we'll take a look at the UPDATE statement.

Note that the SQL statements for this UPDATE statement were taken directly from our stored procedure. The only modifications required are to substitute the parameters with the values from the txtCityName and txtCityID textboxes.

```
Private Sub cmdSQLStatements_Click()
   'Set a reference to the ADO Command object
   Set m_objCmd = New ADODB.Command

   'Set the Command object properties
   Set m_objCmd.ActiveConnection = m_objConn
   m_objCmd.CommandText = "UPDATE City_T " & _
      "SET City_Name_VC = '" & txtCityName.Text & "'," & _
      "Last_Update_DT = GetDate() " & _
      "WHERE City_ID = " & CLng(txtCityID.Text)
   m_objCmd.CommandType = adCmdText

   'Execute the Command object
   m_objCmd.Execute

   'Display message
   txtCityName.Text = "City Name Updated"

   'De-reference command object
   Set m_objCmd = Nothing
End Sub
```

How It Works – UPDATE Program Using In-line SQL

Notice that we have enclosed our string value in single quotes and we are once again using the SQL Server GetDate() function to update the current date and time in our row. Again we convert our value from the txtCityID textbox to a VB Long data type, since the City_ID in the City_T table is a SQL Server Integer data type.

Also notice that we are once again using the adCmdText constant for the CommandType parameter, as we are executing SQL statements instead of a stored procedure.

```
'Set the Command object properties
m_objCmd.CommandText = "UPDATE City_T " & _
    "SET City_Name_VC = '" & txtCityName.Text & "'," & _
    "Last_Update_DT = GetDate() " & _
    "WHERE City_ID = " & CLng(txtCityID.Text)
m_objCmd.CommandType = adCmdText
```

At this point you are ready to run your modified program and update a city name, using either the UPDATE stored procedure or the UPDATE SQL statements.

This example has provided a side-by-side comparison of a stored procedure and an in-line SQL statement in which we did not lose any functionality by using SQL statements.

DELETE Stored Procedure

To round off our side-by-side comparison of stored procedures versus SQL statements, we are going to look at a stored procedure that will delete a city from the City_T table. As you might have guessed, this stored procedure will only accept one parameter, the City_ID, which is the primary key in the City_T table.

Try It Out – DELETE Stored Procedure

1. The figure below lists the up_parmdel_city_name stored procedure. At this point go ahead and create this stored procedure:

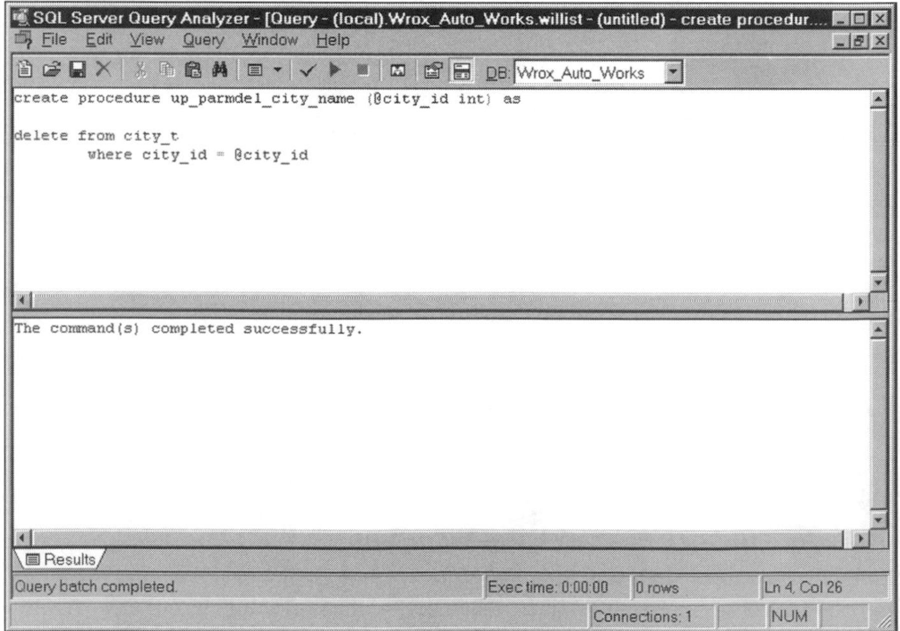

2. After creating it, set the permissions so that the Developers and Sales Staff roles have access to execute this stored procedure.

How It Works – DELETE Stored Procedure

This stored procedure is simple and straightforward. The first line of the stored procedure creates the stored procedure and accepts one parameter, `@City_ID`, which is an `Integer` data type. The `DELETE` SQL statement in our stored procedure will delete the row in the `City_T` table `WHERE` the `City_ID` matches our parameter `@City_ID`.

Now that our `DELETE` stored procedure has been built and the permissions set, we need to build a VB program to execute this stored procedure and ultimately the `DELETE` SQL statements.

Try It Out – DELETE Program Using Stored Procedure

1. Start a new Standard EXE VB project and set a reference to the Microsoft ActiveX Data Objects Library. Then, using the table below, add the following controls onto your form:

Control	Name	Caption/Notes
Label	`label1`	City ID
TextBox	`txtCityID`	The Text property should be set to nothing
Command Button	`cmdStoredProcedure`	Stored Procedure
Command Button	`cmdSQLStatements`	SQL Statements

2. Rename the form and give it a caption if you want to.

3. The code listed below, from file `frmTryItOut3.frm`, should be added to your project – it is basically the same code from the last two examples. The part that is different is contained in the `cmdStoredProcedure_Click` procedure. Don't forget to change the owner prefix and connection string if applicable.

```
Option Explicit

'Declare database objects
Private m_objConn As ADODB.Connection
Private m_objCmd As ADODB.Command


Private Sub cmdStoredProcedure_Click()
   'Set a reference to the ADO Command object
   Set m_objCmd = New ADODB.Command

   'Set the Command object properties
   Set m_objCmd.ActiveConnection = m_objConn
   m_objCmd.CommandText = "willist.up_parmdel_city_name (" & _
      CLng(txtCityID.Text) & ")"
   m_objCmd.CommandType = adCmdStoredProc
```

```
   'Execute the Command object
   m_objCmd.Execute

   'Display message
   txtCityID.Text = "City Deleted"

   'De-reference Command object
   Set m_objCmd = Nothing
End Sub

Private Sub Form_Load()
   'Use the standard Windows icon
   Me.Icon = Nothing

   'Set a reference to the ADO Connection object
   Set m_objConn = New ADODB.Connection

   'Establish a database connection using NT authentication
   m_objConn.Open "DSN=Wrox Auto Works"

   'Check connection state
   If m_objConn.State <> adStateOpen Then
      MsgBox "Connection Failed"
   End If
End Sub

Private Sub Form_Unload(Cancel As Integer)
   'Close and de-reference database objects
   If Not m_objConn Is Nothing Then
      If m_objConn.State Then
         m_objConn.Close
      End If
      Set m_objConn = Nothing
   End If
End Sub
```

The finished program will appear as shown:

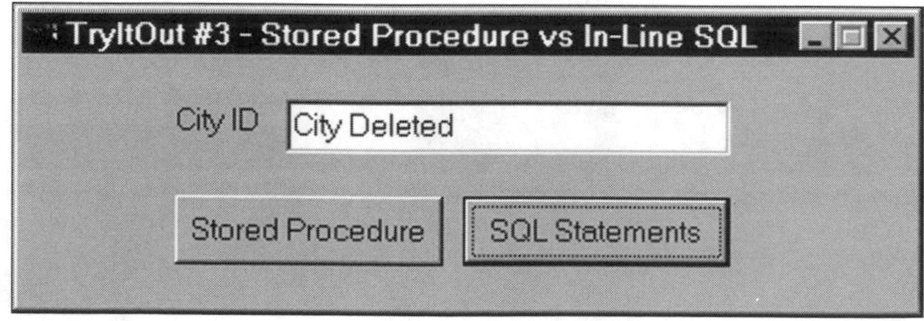

How It Works – DELETE Program Using Stored Procedure

As we mentioned above this is basically the same code as the previous two examples. The code that is different is contained in the `cmdStoredProcedure_Click` procedure. Our stored procedure this time will delete a city name from the `City_T` table, and accepts the `City_ID` that we have entered in the `txtCityID` textbox.

Notice that once again we have enclosed our parameter in parentheses and, since this parameter is an `Integer` data type, we do not have to use the single quote marks. We do, however, have to convert the value to a `Long` data type.

After execution of the stored procedure we display a very simple message stating that the city has been deleted:

```
Private Sub cmdStoredProcedure_Click()
   'Set a reference to the ADO Command object
   Set m_objCmd = New ADODB.Command

   'Set the Command object properties
   Set m_objCmd.ActiveConnection - m_objConn
   m_objCmd.CommandText = "willist.up_parmdel_city_name (" & _
      CLng(txtCityID.Text) & ")"
   m_objCmd.CommandType = adCmdStoredProc

   'Execute the Command object
   m_objCmd.Execute

   'Display message
   txtCityID.Text = "City Deleted"
```

Go ahead and test your program and enter the city ID of an existing entry. Use the Query Analyzer or the Enterprise Manager to look at the rows that exist in the `City_T` table.

If, after running your program, you do not have any rows left in the `City_T` table, use the program that we created in the first example and insert a couple more city names, as we'll need to have some data in the table for use later on.

DELETE SQL Statement

The `DELETE` SQL statement that we are using comes directly from the stored procedure. We need only modify the parameter, substituting the value from the `txtCityID` textbox and converting it to a VB `Long` data type.

Try It Out – DELETE Program Using In-line SQL

1. The entire code listing for the `cmdSQLStatements_Click` procedure is given below, and you should enter it into your `frmTryItOut3.frm` program:

```
Private Sub cmdSQLStatements_Click()
   'Set a reference to the ADO Command object
   Set m_objCmd = New ADODB.Command
```

```
    'Set the Command object properties
    Set m_objCmd.ActiveConnection = m_objConn
    m_objCmd.CommandText = "DELETE FROM City_T " & _
       "WHERE City_ID = " & CLng(txtCityID.Text)

    m_objCmd.CommandType = adCmdText

    'Execute the Command object
    m_objCmd.Execute

    'Display message
    txtCityID.Text = " City Deleted"

    'De-reference Command object
    Set m_objCmd = Nothing
End Sub
```

Run your program and delete a city name using the SQL statement. After you are done testing your program, ensure that you have at least one city name left in the `City_T` table for use in later examples. Preferably you will have three or four entries left in your table.

Comparison Summary

In the previous sections we have taken a look at side-by-side comparisons of stored procedures and their equivalent in-line SQL statements. As we discovered in the first example, in-line SQL statements cannot always provide the same robust functionality that stored procedures can. However, when limited functionality or extra SQL statements are acceptable, in-line SQL statements can be used and they do have their place, as we will demonstrate later when we update data in Chapter 11.

We have seen that we must often code extra in-line SQL statements and use extra ADO objects in order to get the same results produced by a stored procedure. The extra in-line SQL statements and objects do hinder performance because we must execute extra VB code to create the objects and execute the in-line SQL statements. Stored procedures are optimized and can take advantage of the features of SQL Server to efficiently produce the desired results.

While the purpose of the comparison we performed here was to point out the similarities in the SQL statements that were used in the stored procedures and the in-line SQL statements, we did not discuss *performance.* As we mentioned in the last chapter, stored procedures are considered compiled and thus will run faster than in-line SQL statements. The next section takes a look at what can be done to improve the performance of your in-line SQL statements.

Security plays another important part in using stored procedures, as well as the fact that the code from a stored procedure can easily be shared among applications such as a VB program for the front end and an ASP page for a Web application. Using stored procedures also allows us to change the code in a stored procedure without having to recompile the programs that use it. For example, we could add more columns to the SELECT statement in a stored procedure, thus providing the new functionality required by a new program, while not impacting the functionality provided to the older programs.

Optimizing SQL Statements

While the performance of stored procedures versus in-line SQL statements can be hard to measure on your workstation, more accurate performance benchmark tests can be performed on a SQL Server installed on your network, with hundreds of concurrent users. Since most of you reading this book will not have access to create the `Wrox_Auto_Works` database on your network, we will demonstrate a simple example running on your workstation. While we do show some benchmark testing, the real intent of this section is to show you how to optimize your in-line SQL statements using the `Command` object.

The `Command` object provides a property called `Prepared`. When this property is set to `True`, ADO will have the database compile, and will save a version of, your SQL statements before it executes them. This slows down the first execution of your in-line SQL statements, but subsequent executions are faster because they are executed using the compiled version that the database has stored in memory. Be careful not to use `Prepared` on *every* statement that is executed, or the memory gets filled up, and this defeats the purpose of using this property.

Try It Out – Command Object Prepared Property

We want to create a simple program that will execute a SQL statement to select the state name and abbreviation from the `State_T` table. We will execute this SQL statement in a loop 25 times. Then we will use the `Command` object's `Prepared` property to have the database save a compiled version, and execute the SQL statement 25 more times. We will compare the time it takes each loop to complete. Our program will display the results as follows:

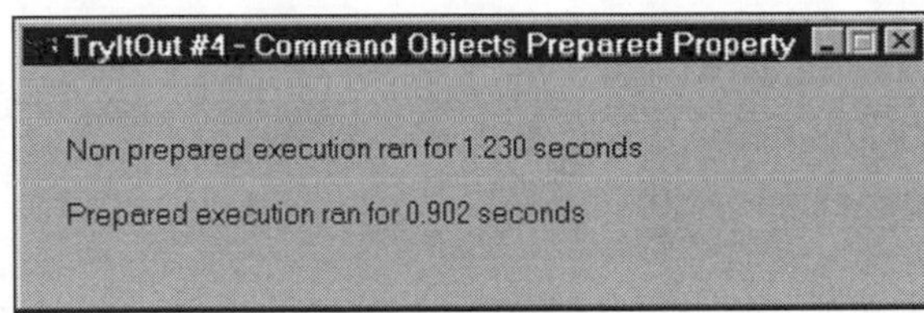

1. You will need to start a new Standard EXE project in Visual Basic and set a reference to the Microsoft ActiveX Data Objects Library.

2. Give the form a new name and caption if you wish.

3. Add two labels to the form using the default names of `Label1` and `Label2`, and enter the following code, which can be found in `frmTryItOut4.frm`, changing the connection string depending on the authentication method you are using:

```
Private Sub Form_Load()
   'Use the standard Windows icon
   Me.Icon = Nothing

   'Declare Connection object
   Dim objConn As New ADODB.Connection
   'Declare Command object for unprepared execution
   Dim objCmd1 As New ADODB.Command
```

```
'Declare Command object for prepared execution
Dim objCmd2 As New ADODB.Command
'Declare variables to hold the start and end times
Dim sngStart As Single
Dim sngEnd As Single
'Declare variable for loop counter
Dim intLoop As Integer

'Establish a database connection using NT authentication
objConn.Open "DSN=Wrox Auto Works"

'Check connection state
If objConn.State <> adStateOpen Then
   Label1.Caption = "Connection Failed"
   Exit Sub
End If

'Set the properties of the first Command object
Set objCmd1.ActiveConnection = objConn
objCmd1.CommandText = "SELECT State_Name_VC, " & _
   "State_Abbreviation_CH FROM State_T ORDER BY State_Name_VC"
objCmd1.CommandType = adCmdText

'Save the start time
sngStart = Timer

'Execute the loop
For intLoop = 1 To 25
   objCmd1.Execute
Next intLoop

'Save the end time
sngEnd = Timer

'Display the results
Label1.Caption = "Non prepared execution ran for " & _
   Format(sngEnd - sngStart, "#0.000") & " seconds"

'Set the properties of the second Command object
Set objCmd2.ActiveConnection = objConn
objCmd2.CommandText = "SELECT State_Name_VC, " & _
   "State_Abbreviation_CH FROM State_T ORDER BY State_Name_VC"
objCmd2.CommandType = adCmdText
objCmd2.Prepared = True

'Save the start time
sngStart = Timer

'Execute the loop
For intLoop = 1 To 25
   objCmd2.Execute
Next intLoop
```

```
    'Save the end time
    sngEnd = Timer

    'Display the results
    Label2.Caption = "Prepared execution ran for " & _
       Format(sngEnd - sngStart, "#0.000") & " seconds"

    'Close and de-reference database objects
    Set objCmd1 = Nothing
    Set objCmd2 = Nothing
    objConn.Close
    Set objConn = Nothing
End Sub
```

How It Works - Command Object Prepared Property

All the code in this example gets executed in the `Form_Load` event of your program. The first thing that we must do is to declare the variables that we are going to be using. Along with our database objects we have declared a couple of variables to keep track of time:

```
Private Sub Form_Load()
    'Use the standard Windows icon
    Me.Icon = Nothing

    'Declare database objects and local variables
    Dim objConn As New ADODB.Connection
    Dim objCmd1 As New ADODB.Command
    Dim objCmd2 As New ADODB.Command
    Dim sngStart As Single
    Dim sngEnd As Single
    Dim intLoop As Integer
```

After establishing a connection to the database, we check the state of the database to ensure it is open, and then continue on:

```
    'Establish a database connection using NT authentication
    objConn.Open "DSN=Wrox Auto Works"

    'Check connection state
    If objConn.State <> adStateOpen Then
       Label1.Caption = "Connection Failed"
       Exit Sub
    End If
```

The SQL statements that we are using for our example `SELECT` the `State_Name_VC` and `State_Abbreviation_CH` columns from the `State_T` table, and then order the results by the `State_Name_VC` column. Since we are executing in-line SQL statements, we must set the `CommandType` property to the `adCmdText` constant:

```
    'Set the properties of the first Command object
    Set objCmd1.ActiveConnection = objConn
    objCmd1.CommandText = "SELECT State_Name_VC, " & _
       "State_Abbreviation_CH FROM State_T ORDER BY State_Name_VC"
    objCmd1.CommandType = adCmdText
```

We use the VB built-in function `Timer`, which returns the number of seconds that have elapsed since midnight, to set our start variable. After executing the `Command` object 25 times in a loop we capture the end time, and then display the results in the label named `Label1`:

```
'Start the timer
sngStart = Timer

'Execute the loop
For intLoop = 1 To 25
   objCmd1.Execute
Next intLoop

'Stop the timer
sngEnd = Timer

'Display the results
Label1.Caption = "Non prepared execution ran for " & _
   Format(sngEnd - sngStart, "#0.000") & " seconds"
```

To try to keep things as even as possible, we use a separate `Command` object to execute the second execution of our SQL statement. Once again we set the same SQL statement in the `CommandText` property, but this time we also set the `Prepared` property to `True`:

```
'Set the properties of the second Command object
Set objCmd2.ActiveConnection = objConn
objCmd2.CommandText = "SELECT State_Name_VC, " & _
   "State_Abbreviation_CH FROM State_T OREDR BY State_Name_VC"
objCmd2.CommandType = adCmdText
objCmd2.Prepared = True
```

We set the start time, then execute a loop 25 times, capture the end time and display the results, this time in the label named `Label2`:

```
'Start the timer
sngStart = Timer

'Execute the loop
For intLoop = 1 To 25
   objCmd2.Execute
Next intLoop

'Stop the timer
sngEnd = Timer

'Display the results
Label2.Caption = "Prepared execution ran for " & _
   Format(sngEnd - sngStart, "#0.000") & " seconds"
```

To wrap things up we close and de-reference our database objects:

```
    'Close and de-reference database objects
    Set objCmd1 = Nothing
    Set objCmd2 = Nothing
    objConn.Close
    Set objConn = Nothing
End Sub
```

To get the best results you may need to run this example several times. Jot down the results, reboot your workstation, run the test again and see what results you then get. The reason that you need to reboot after each execution is because SQL Server will cache the SQL statements and rebooting will clear all memory. Also the order of running could be reversed, in other words run the `Prepared` loop before the non-`Prepared` loop, such that even if the first `Prepared` iteration has to bring the data pages into cache, the loop still runs faster.

As you can see, most of the time the SQL statements that have the `Prepared` property set to `True` runs faster. Of course, as we mentioned, this really isn't an accurate test as this program is the only client running against SQL Server. We really need hundreds of concurrent clients to perform an accurate test and to get true benchmark results.

Using Command Object Parameters

The `Command` object provides a lot of flexibility when it comes to passing parameters to our stored procedures. There are several methods by which you can pass parameters and we have already examined a couple of these in this chapter.

The first program we coded in this chapter used the `Parameters` collection, and we appended the parameters to the `Parameters` collection using the `CreateParameter` method of the `Command` object, as shown in the code fragment below:

```
    'Set the parameters
    m_objCmd.Parameters.Append m_objCmd.CreateParameter( _
        "CityID", adInteger, adParamReturnValue)
    m_objCmd.Parameters.Append m_objCmd.CreateParameter( _
        "CityName", adVarChar, adParamInput, 30, txtCityName.Text)
```

This is the easiest way to append parameters to the `Parameters` collection when you are using simple parameters that are `VarChar`, `Char`, and `Integer` data types. This method is one of two methods that must also be used when your stored procedure returns an output parameter or return value. In the code fragment above we were expecting a return value from our stored procedure.

What if we are not expecting output parameters or a return value? Then we simply bypass appending parameters to the `Parameters` collection and pass our parameters directly as part of the stored procedure text, as we did in the second and third examples, as shown in the next code fragment:

```
m_objCmd.CommandText = "willist.up_parmupd_city_name (" & _
    CLng(txtCityID.Text) & ",'" & txtCityName.Text & "')"
```

In this code fragment we are not expecting any output parameters or return values and we can simply include the parameters as part of the stored procedure call. This is the most common method used when you are only passing input parameters. Of course, when this method is used the `Connection` object is typically used to execute the stored procedure, instead of the `Command` object.

What if we are expecting output parameters, or our input parameters are of `Money` data type? The answer to the first part of this question is simple – use the `Parameters` collection. The second part is not so simple as there is an alternative to using the `Parameters` collection. If there are no output parameters in your stored procedure you could use the built-in VB function `CCur` to convert your data to a VB `Currency` data type, which gets translated into a SQL Server `Money` data type. This is done in much the same way that we converted our values from the textbox to VB `Long` data types, in order to have them translated into SQL Server `Integer` data types. Converting these values in VB to their appropriate SQL data types helps to catch errors in your VB code before you waste a network trip and resources on a server.

The next method of creating parameters and appending them to the `Parameters` collection uses the `Parameter` object, as shown in the next code fragment. Using this method, we must first declare a `Parameter` object and then we are able to set some or all of the `Parameter`'s properties. When we used the `CreateParameter` method in our first program we were limited to just the `Name`, `Type`, `Direction`, `Size`, and `Value` properties. This method here is ideal for data types that also specify a numeric scale and precision, such as SQL Server `Money` and `Decimal` data types.

```
'Set the input parameter properties and append it to the
'parameters collection
objParm.Name = "TotalHours"
objParm.Type = adDecimal
objParm.Direction = adParamInput
objParm.Precision = 8
objParm.NumericScale = 2
objParm.Value = 180.25
objCmd.Parameters.Append objParm
```

After we have set all of the `Parameter`'s properties, we append the parameter to the `Parameters` collection and move on to the next parameter.

To get a true feel for how this method works and to really understand it, let's examine this method in a hands-on exercise.

Try It Out – Command Object Output Parameter

The first program in this chapter retrieved a return value from a stored procedure, and it only seems fitting that we complete our discussion on parameters with another output parameter exercise.

The stored procedure that we want to create for this example should insert a zip code into the `Zip_Code_T` table, and return the ID of the zip code just inserted as a return parameter. This is very similar to the stored procedure that we created for our first program, except that stored procedure returned the city ID as a return value. This is what the program should display when we are finished:

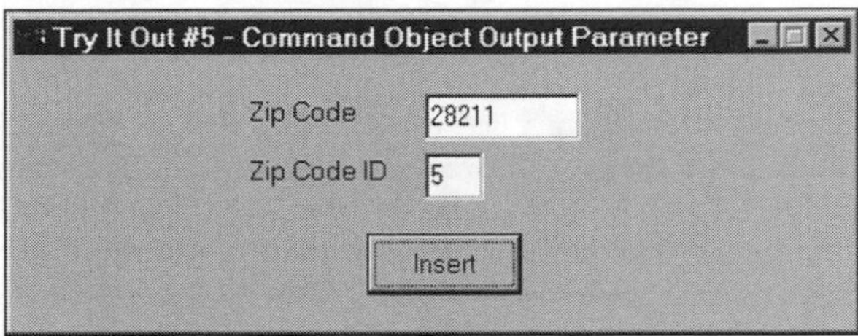

1. The following figure lists the stored procedure that needs to be created for this exercise:

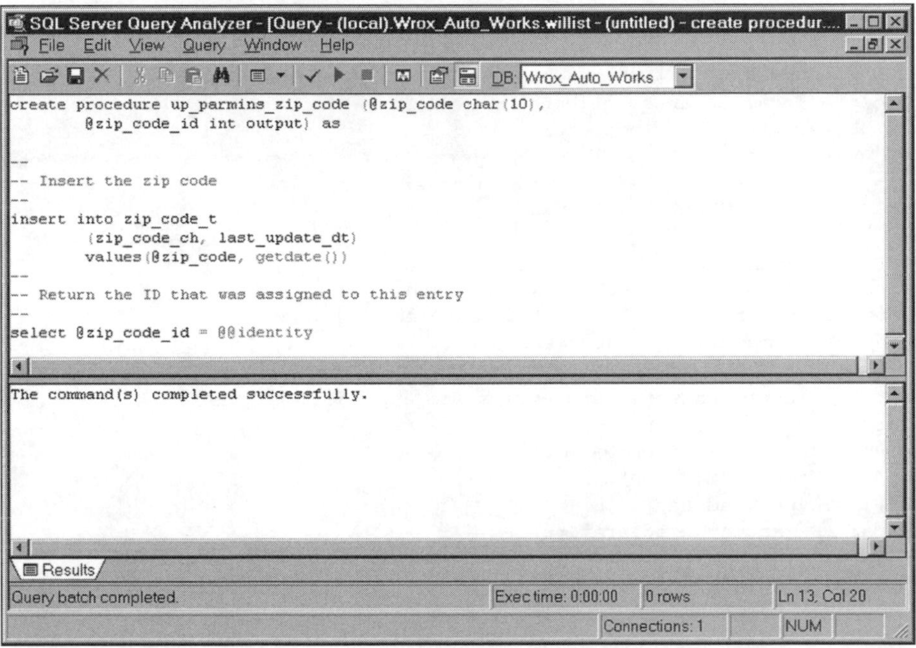

2. After having created the stored procedure, don't forget to set the permissions to allow the Developers and Sales Staff roles to execute it.

3. To start your VB project, open a Standard EXE project, set a reference to Microsoft ActiveX Data Objects Library, and use the table below to add your controls to the form:

Control	Name	Caption/Notes
Label	`Label1`	Zip Code
TextBox	`txtZipCode`	The Text property should be set to nothing
Label	`Label2`	Zip Code ID
TextBox	`txtZipCodeID`	The Text property should be set to nothing
Command Button	`cmdInsert`	Insert

4. Again, you can rename and caption the form if you want to.

5. Enter the following code, from `frmTryItOut5.frm`, which makes up our VB program. Make sure you change the stored procedure owner prefix and the connection string as appropriate:

```
Option Explicit

'Declare database objects
Private m_objConn As ADODB.Connection
Private m_objCmd As ADODB.Command


Private Sub cmdInsert_Click()
   'Declare local database objects
   Dim objParm As ADODB.Parameter

   'Set a reference to the ADO Command object
   Set m_objCmd = New ADODB.Command

   'Set the Command object properties
   Set m_objCmd.ActiveConnection = m_objConn
   m_objCmd.CommandText = "willist.up_parmins_zip_code"
   m_objCmd.CommandType = adCmdStoredProc

   'Set the input parameter properties and append it to the
   'Parameters collection
   Set objParm = New ADODB.Parameter
   objParm.Name = "ZipCode"
   objParm.Type = adChar
   objParm.Direction = adParamInput
   objParm.Size = 10
   objParm.Value = txtZipCode.Text
   m_objCmd.Parameters.Append objParm

   'Set the output parameter properties and append it to the
   'Parameters collection
   Set objParm = New ADODB.Parameter
   objParm.Name = "ZipCodeID"
   objParm.Type = adInteger
   objParm.Direction = adParamOutput
   m_objCmd.Parameters.Append objParm

   'Execute the Command object
   m_objCmd.Execute

   'Display Zip Code ID that was returned as an
   'ouput parameter
   txtZipCodeID.Text = m_objCmd("ZipCodeID")
```

```
   'De-reference database objects
   Set objParm = Nothing
   Set m_objCmd = Nothing
End Sub

Private Sub Form_Load()
   'Use the standard Windows icon
   Me.Icon = Nothing

   'Set a reference to the ADO Connection object
   Set m_objConn = New ADODB.Connection

   'Establish a database connection using NT authentication
   m_objConn.Open "DSN=Wrox Auto Works"

   'Check connection state
   If m_objConn.State <> adStateOpen Then
      MsgBox "Connection Failed"
   End If
End Sub

Private Sub Form_Unload(Cancel As Integer)
   'Close and de-reference database objects
   If Not m_objConn Is Nothing Then
      If m_objConn.State Then
         m_objConn.Close
      End If
      Set m_objConn = Nothing
   End If
End Sub
```

How It Works – Command Object Output Parameter

We start our stored procedure by instructing SQL Server to create a stored procedure with the name that we have given it. The first parameter of our stored procedure is an input parameter, of `Char` data type, and will contain the zip code to be inserted. The second parameter is an output parameter, as specified by the `OUTPUT` keyword, and is an `Integer` data type:

```
CREATE PROCEDURE up_parmins_zip_code (@Zip_Code Char(10),
        @Zip_Code_ID Int OUTPUT) AS
```

You might have noticed that we are using more and more comments in our stored procedures. Being good developers, we place comments in our code wherever possible to help document our code for ourselves and for others. Stored procedures are no different from VB in that the logic and code in a stored procedure can become pretty complex, as we will start to demonstrate in the next chapter. Therefore, comments become ever increasingly important and, the more we comment now, the easier it will be later when we come back and revisit them.

Stored procedure comments can be coded in one of two ways. Firstly, simply start the comment with two dashes followed by any text. This type of comment can be on a separate line or on a line with SQL statements. This type of comment must be preceded with the comment character (two dashes `--`) on each line for a comment that spans multiple lines. The second type of comment follows the same rules as a Visual C ++ comment. You start the comment with a slash asterisk pair and continue the comment for as many lines as you wish. To end the comment code an asterisk slash pair (e.g. `/* this is a comment */`).

The INSERT statement inserts the zip code that we passed and uses the SQL Server GetDate() function to insert the current date and time:

```
--
-- Insert the zip code
--
INSERT INTO Zip_Code_T
        (Zip_Code_CH, Last_Update_DT)
        Values(@Zip_Code, GetDate())
```

We explained earlier that the @@Identity function (also called a global variable) returns the last identity number that was inserted into a row. Here we are assigning that number to our output parameter, @Zip_Code_ID. In order to assign values to our local variables we will use the SELECT statement (we could also have used the SET statement) as we have done here. We cannot assign values to our variables like we do in VB. Once the output parameter has been assigned a value, the stored procedure will end and we can then retrieve this value from the Command object's Parameters collection:

```
--
-- Return the ID that was assigned to this entry
--
SELECT @Zip_Code_ID = @@Identity
```

We start our VB code by declaring the database objects that will be global to our form, in the general declarations section of the form:

```
Option Explicit

'Declare database objects
Private m_objConn As ADODB.Connection
Private m_objCmd As ADODB.Command
```

The Form_Load event contains the code to establish a connection to the database and check the State of our database connection, and does not need to be explained further.

The cmdInsert_Click procedure contains the code to insert a new zip code in the Zip_Code_T table. The first thing that we do in this procedure is to declare our Parameter object and set a reference to the Command object:

```
Private Sub cmdInsert_Click()
   'Declare local database objects
   Dim objParm As ADODB.Parameter

   'Set a reference to the ADO Command object
   Set m_objCmd = New ADODB.Command
```

Next, we set the Command object's properties. Notice how we have coded only the stored procedure prefix and stored procedure name for the CommandText property this time:

```
   'Set the Command object properties
   Set m_objCmd.ActiveConnection = m_objConn
   m_objCmd.CommandText = "willist.up_parmins_zip_code"
   m_objCmd.CommandType = adCmdStoredProc
```

As we mentioned earlier, we can set some or all of the Parameter properties using this method. Here we only set the properties that we need. Notice that the first parameter is an input parameter, as indicated by the Direction property, and the second parameter is an output parameter. After we have set all of the properties for the parameter, we then append it to the Parameters collection:

```
    'Set the input parameter properties and append it to the
    'Parameters collection
    Set objParm = New ADODB.Parameter
    objParm.Name = "ZipCode"
    objParm.Type = adChar
    objParm.Direction = adParamInput
    objParm.Size = 10
    objParm.Value = txtZipCode.Text
    m_objCmd.Parameters.Append objParm

    'Set the output parameter properties and append it to the
    'Parameters collection
    Set objParm = New ADODB.Parameter
    objParm.Name = "ZipCodeID"
    objParm.Type = adInteger
    objParm.Direction = adParamOutput
    m_objCmd.Parameters.Append objParm
```

Next we want to execute the Command object to insert the zip code. After execution, we retrieve the output parameter from the Parameters collection by using the name of the output parameter that we assigned above, in this case ZipCodeID, and display it in the txtZipCodeID textbox:

```
    'Execute the Command object
    m_objCmd.Execute

    'Display Zip Code ID that was returned as an
    'ouput parameter
    txtZipCodeID.Text = m_objCmd("ZipCodeID")
```

Lastly we de-reference the database objects that we used in this procedure:

```
    'De-reference database objects
    Set objParm = Nothing
    Set m_objCmd = Nothing
End Sub
```

When we end our program the Form_Unload event fires, and we close and de-reference our Connection object.

You are now ready to run your program and insert zip codes into the Zip_Code_T table. Notice that every time you insert a zip code, the ID of the zip code inserted is returned in the txtZipCodeID textbox.

This stored procedure is another example where we would lose functionality if we were to execute it as in-line SQL statements, because we cannot return output parameters using in-line SQL statements.

Multiple Recordsets

When dealing with data that is related, it would make sense if we could retrieve all of the related data at one time instead of having to open multiple recordsets, or opening the same recordset multiple times with different stored procedures to retrieve the related data. SQL Server and ADO can both help solve this dilemma.

SQL Server provides this functionality in stored procedures. We can have one stored procedure execute one or more other stored procedures, and return all of the results in one stored procedure as separate results sets.

ADO provides this functionality in the `Recordset` object and provides a method called `NextRecordset`, which allows us to navigate to the next recordset within the current `Recordset` object. The two methods together make a powerful combination that enables us to write feature-rich applications. We'll take a look at both methods in the following examples.

Using Stored Procedures to Return Multiple Results Sets

When we deal with zip code data, we are usually dealing with city and state data also. Together they provide the individual elements that make up part of an address. We want to select the data from all of the tables at one time, using a single stored procedure.

Let's take a look at how a stored procedure can implement this functionality. The figure below shows three `SELECT` statements being executed and three results sets being returned:

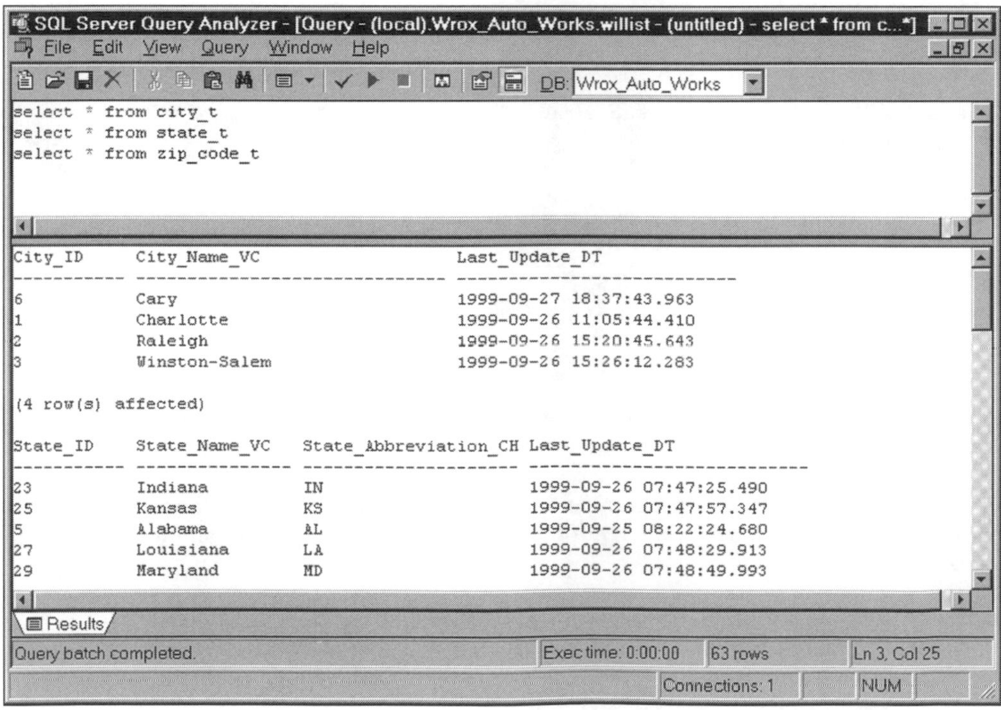

This is a great feature that can be handy when developing, as you can look at data from multiple tables at one time. Stored procedures can implement this same functionality by using these SQL statements or by calling other stored procedures.

Try It Out – Return Multiple Results Sets Using Stored Procedure

We want our stored procedure to execute other stored procedures, and before we can implement this functionality in a stored procedure we must build a couple more stored procedures to select the city names and zip codes.

1. The code listed below will build a stored procedure to select all city IDs and city names from the `City_T` table and order the results by city name. Go ahead and create this stored procedure:

```
CREATE PROCEDURE up_select_city_names AS

SELECT City_ID, City_Name_VC
      FROM City_T
      ORDER BY City_Name_VC
```

2. In order to create a stored procedure to select zip codes, enter and run the following code. This code selects the zip code IDs and zip codes from the `Zip_Code_T` table and orders the results by zip code:

```
CREATE PROCEDURE up_select_zip_codes AS

SELECT Zip_Code_ID, Zip_Code_CH
      FROM Zip_Code_T
      ORDER BY Zip_Code_CH
```

3. Set permissions for all three roles to execute these stored procedures.

4. We already have a stored procedure to select all state names, which we built in the last chapter. In order to combine all three of these together, we use the code that is shown in the figure below:

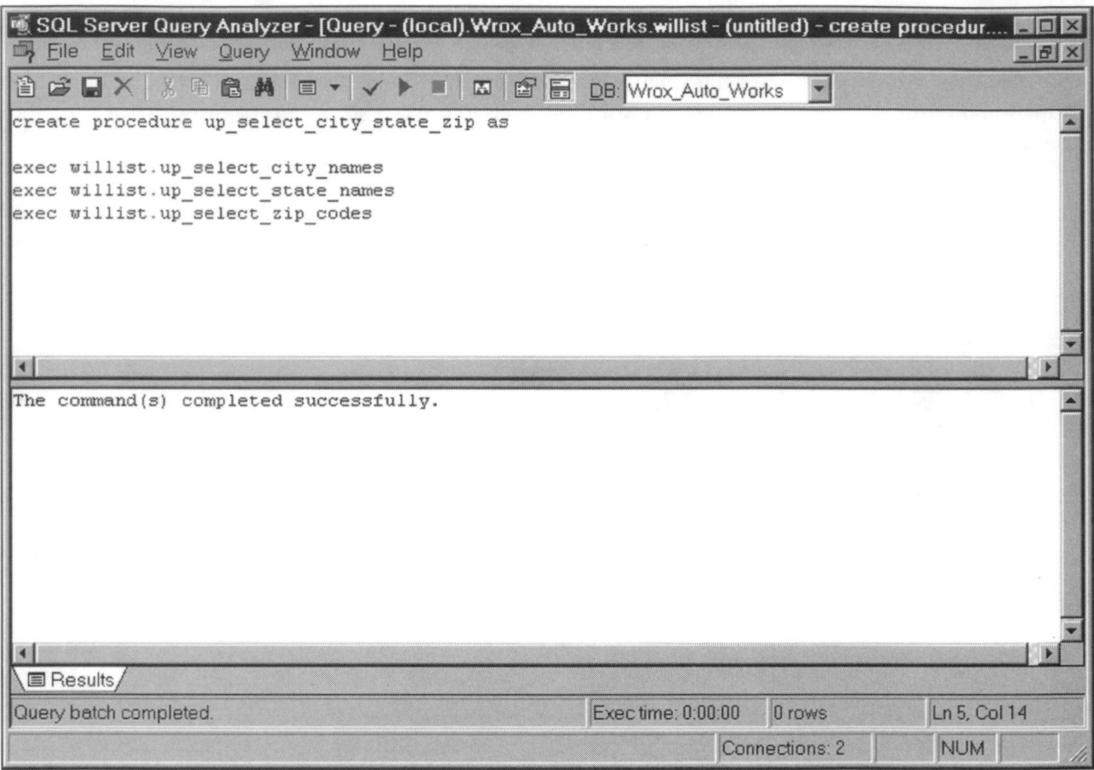

Notice that we prefix each stored procedure with the `EXEC` statement. We must use the `EXEC` statement so that SQL Server knows that we are executing *multiple* stored procedures, otherwise it tries to use the second stored procedure as a parameter for the first one and we receive an error.

Also notice that we have prefixed each of our stored procedure names with the user prefix. This is so that other users can execute this stored procedure, and SQL Server will know what stored procedures to execute. This may be a little confusing, so let's explain further.

We know that when we create a stored procedure, our logon is used as the prefix for that stored procedure. Another user can create a stored procedure with the same name and their logon will be used as the prefix for their stored procedure. The prefix combined with the stored procedure name is how SQL Server keeps track of stored procedures. Together these make a *unique object* in SQL Server (remember that stored procedures are objects).

With all that being said; create this stored procedure, changing the user prefixes as appropriate.

5. Now execute the newly created stored procedure in the Query Analyzer, using just the stored procedure name as shown in the code below:

```
up_select_city_state_zip
```

   Notice that you get three separate results sets returned, just as when the three separate SQL statements above were executed.

6. Before we move on, don't forget to set the permissions on this stored procedure so that the Developers, Sales Staff and Management roles have the authority to execute this stored procedure.

Now that we know how a stored procedure can return multiple results sets, let's take a look at how the `Recordset` object can achieve the same.

Using a Recordset Object to Return Multiple Results Sets

Using the `Recordset` object, we can execute a stored procedure that returns multiple results sets, or we can execute multiple SQL statements that perform the same tasks, as shown in the code fragments below:

```
'Open the Recordset
objRS.Open "willist.up_select_city_state_zip", objConn, _
   adOpenForwardOnly, adLockReadOnly, adCmdStoredProc
```

```
'Open the Recordset
objRS.Open "SELECT City_Name_VC FROM City_T;" & _
   "SELECT State_Name_VC FROM State_T;" & _
   "SELECT Zip_Code_CH FROM Zip_Code_T", _
   objConn, adOpenForwardOnly, adLockReadOnly, adCmdText
```

The first code fragment uses a stored procedure to return multiple results sets, which translate into multiple recordsets within one `Recordset` object. The second code fragment uses multiple SQL statements to perform the same tasks. Notice that we have placed a semi colon after each SQL statement so that the database will know where one SQL statement ends and the next one begins. As you can see, this is another example where stored procedures and in-line SQL statements provide the same functionality.

Once an end of file condition (`EOF`) has been reached on the first recordset in the `Recordset` object, you execute the `NextRecordset` method of the `Recordset` object to clear the current recordset and return the next recordset, as shown in the following code fragment:

```
'Get the next recordset
 Set objRS = objRS.NextRecordset
```

Normally you will know how many recordsets are expected in a `Recordset` object. The example above demonstrates retrieving three recordsets in one `Recordset` object. However, a sure-fire way to test this is to check the `State` of the `Recordset` object before trying to get the next recordset, as shown in the next code fragment. We are using the `State` property here to see if the recordset is in an open state.

```
If objRS.State = adStateOpen Then

    'Get the next Recordset
    Set objRS = objRS.NextRecordset
```

There is one little catch with using multiple recordsets in one `Recordset` object. You can't use this feature if you are using **client-side cursors** or **disconnected recordsets**.

A cursor is a database element that controls how records in a recordset are navigated, updated, and seen by the user. A client-side cursor is processed on the client side without direct interaction with the database. Once all processing has been performed on the client side, the program can call a method of the `Recordset` object to update the changes made in the recordset.

A disconnected recordset is a `Recordset` object that has been physically disconnected from the active database connection.

Client side cursors and disconnected recordsets are typically used in conjunction with one another as this allows the user to make all the necessary changes to the recordset without holding an active connection to the database. Once the user has made all of the changes, the `Recordset` object can be reconnected to the database and the updates in the `Recordset` object can be applied to the database.

Let's put this newfound knowledge to use in a practical exercise.

Try It Out – Multiple Recordsets

We want to create a program that will execute the `up_select_city_state_zip` stored procedure. The results will be used to populate three listboxes with the city names, state names, and zip codes, as shown:

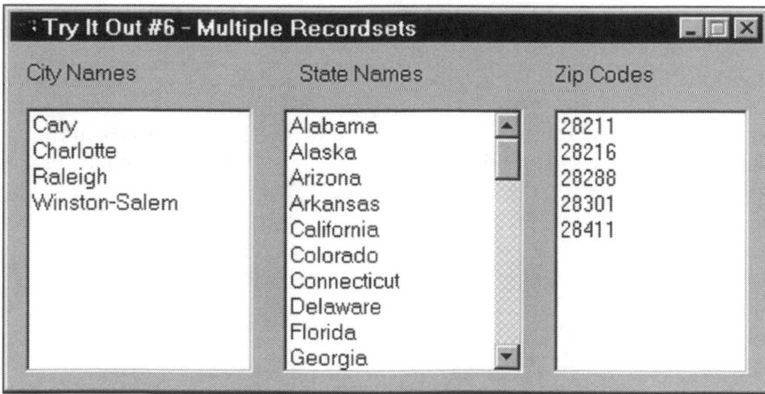

1. Create a new Standard EXE VB project and set a reference to the Microsoft ActiveX Data Object Library. Using the table below, add the following controls to your form:

Control	Name	Caption
Label	label1	City Names
Label	label2	State Names
Label	label3	Zip Codes
ListBox	lstCities	
ListBox	lstStates	
ListBox	lstZipCodes	

2. Change the form's name and caption if you so desire.

3. Add the following code, taken from `frmTryItOut6.frm`, to your project, changing the owner prefix and connection string as appropriate:

```
Private Sub Form_Load()
   'Use the standard Windows icon
   Me.Icon = Nothing

   'Declare database objects
   Dim objConn As New ADODB.Connection
   Dim objRS As New ADODB.Recordset

   'Establish a database connection using NT authentication
   objConn.Open "DSN=Wrox Auto Works"

   'Check connection state
   If objConn.State = adStateOpen Then

      'Open the Recordset
      objRS.Open "willist.up_select_city_state_zip", objConn, _
         adOpenForwardOnly, adLockReadOnly, adCmdStoredProc

      'Process the first Recordset loading city names
      Do While Not objRS.EOF
         lstCities.AddItem objRS!City_Name_VC
         objRS.MoveNext
      Loop

      'Get the next Recordset
      Set objRS = objRS.NextRecordset

      'Process the second Recordset loading state names
      Do While Not objRS.EOF
         lstStates.AddItem objRS!State_Name_VC
         objRS.MoveNext
      Loop
```

```
      'Get the next Recordset
      Set objRS = objRS.NextRecordset

      'Process the third Recordset loading zip codes
      Do While Not objRS.EOF
         lstZipCodes.AddItem objRS!Zip_Code_CH
         objRS.MoveNext
      Loop

   Else

      MsgBox "Connection Failed"

   End If

   'Close and de-reference database objects
   If Not objRS Is Nothing Then
      If objRS.State Then
         objRS.Close
      End If
      Set objRS = Nothing
   End If

   If Not objConn Is Nothing Then
      If objConn.State Then
         objConn.Close
      End If
      Set objConn = Nothing
   End If
End Sub
```

How It Works – Multiple Recordsets

All of the code in this example is executed in the `Form_Load` event, and the first thing that we do is to declare our database objects, and open and check the connection. If the `State` of our connection is open, then we continue and open our `Recordset` object, specifying the stored procedure to execute.

Since we will only be reading from the recordset, and only moving in a forward direction in the recordset, we have specified the `adOpenForwardOnly` constant for the `CursorType` parameter and the `adLockReadOnly` constant for the `LockType` parameter.

```
'Check connection state
   If objConn.State = adStateOpen Then

      'Open the recordset
      objRS.Open "willist.up_select_city_state_zip", objConn, _
         adOpenForwardOnly, adLockReadOnly, adCmdStoredProc
```

After our recordset is opened, we process all rows from our `Recordset` object, loading the `lstCities` listbox until we reach an `EOF` condition:

```
      'Process the first Recordset loading city names
      Do While Not objRS.EOF
         lstCities.AddItem objRS!City_Name_VC
         objRS.MoveNext
      Loop
```

After the EOF condition has been reached, we get the next recordset in our Recordset object by using the NextRecordset method, and then we start the process over, loading the next listbox:

```
'Get the next Recordset
Set objRS = objRS.NextRecordset

'Process the second Recordset loading state names
Do While Not objRS.EOF
   lstStates.AddItem objRS!State_Name_VC
   objRS.MoveNext
Loop
```

Once we are done, we close and de-reference our database objects and the form is displayed.

By now I'm sure you have already thought of a couple of applications for this newfound method. It is especially great when you need to load several combo or listboxes with data, where they contain related data, and you don't need to hold an open recordset.

Summary

This chapter has taken a broad look at the comparisons between stored procedures versus in-line SQL statements. For the most part, in-line SQL statements can be used to perform the same functions as stored procedures when the stored procedure is used to perform relatively simple tasks. We have seen where in-line SQL statements fall short:

- Can not use T-SQL statements such as RETURN to return a value
- Require extra SQL statements and ADO objects to obtain the same results produced by a stored procedure
- Not optimized and take longer to execute

The following chapters will demonstrate this further as our stored procedures become more complex.

During our comparisons, we have taken a more in-depth look at the Parameters collection and have discovered several ways to pass parameters to a stored procedure. Which method is best is really determined by the type of parameter being passed, and whether or not a return value or return parameters are expected.

We have also taken a look at a Recordset method that will allow us to retrieve multiple recordsets at one time. This little known feature of the Recordset object can really come in handy when related data needs to be retrieved, and can cut down on the amount of coding that must be done.

In summary, you should know:

- That in-line SQL statements can not be used to return a value using the `RETURN` keyword
- That in-line SQL statements can not be used to return output parameters
- Which SQL statements in a stored procedure can be used as in-line SQL statements
- How stored procedures and in-line SQL statements compare
- How to optimize in-line SQL statements using the `Command` object's `Prepared` property
- The different methods of passing parameters to a stored procedure using the `Parameters` collection
- How to retrieve multiple recordsets in one `Recordset` object

Now that we know how and when to use stored procedures, we're going to start looking at each of the four types – `SELECT`, `INSERT`, `UPDATE`, and `DELETE`, in more detail.

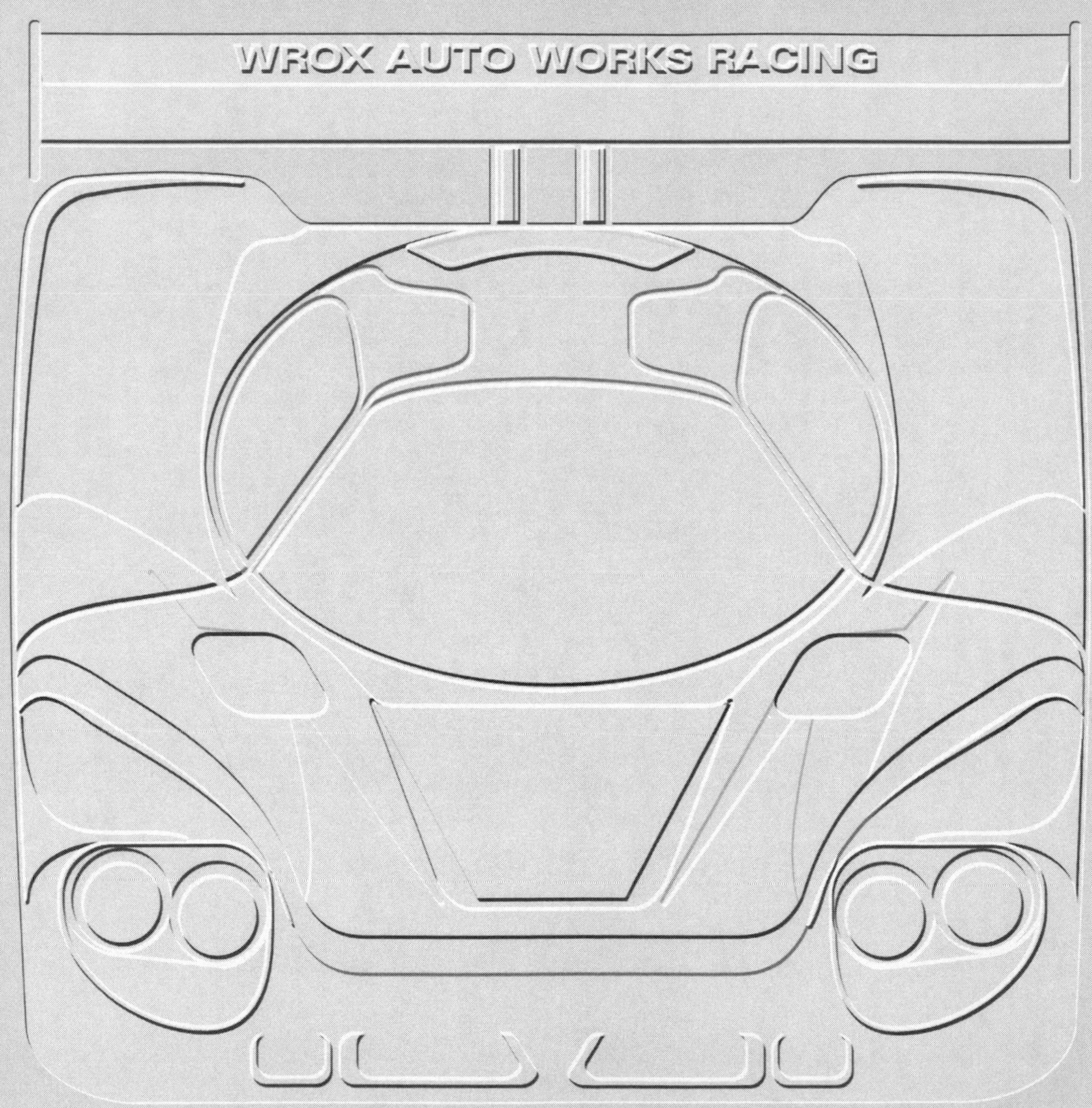
WROX AUTO WORKS RACING

Selecting Data

The last two chapters have introduced you to stored procedures, and you have had hands on experience of creating and executing stored procedures. While these stored procedures have been elementary, they have given you the skills to create stored procedures and to execute them from VB, and some basic skills to build upon. We have taken a look at stored procedures that select, insert, update, and delete data, as well as stored procedures that return values and contain output parameters. All of these stored procedures have dealt with data from just one table.

This chapter picks up the pace as we start dealing with data from multiple tables and using terms like `JOIN`, column aliases, and correlation names. We will concentrate our efforts in this chapter on creating stored procedures that `SELECT` data. While the stored procedures in this chapter will not contain processing logic, they can be complicated enough by the use of correlation names and `JOIN`s. These terms will be defined shortly.

In this chapter we will use:

- `JOIN`s to select data from multiple tables
- Column aliases to assign unique names to columns
- Correlation names to join the same table twice in a stored procedure
- Multiple stored procedures in a VB program

Preparing Our Tables

Before we can build stored procedures to select data, we need to insert data into a couple of tables that we haven't dealt with yet. If you remember our database design from Chapter 3, we have yet to insert data into the `Address_T`, `Phone_Number_T`, `Employer_T`, `Customer_Information_T`, and `Customer_T` tables. In order to expedite things without complicating them too much, we will insert data into these tables manually.

Try It Out – Manually Inserting Data

1. To begin, we need to run a simple query in the Query Analyzer to SELECT all city names, as shown in the code below. (Don't forget to change the database to Wrox_Auto_Works.) Select a city name that you want to use for your address, and write down the City_ID for future use:

```
SELECT * FROM City_T
```

2. Next, run another query to SELECT all state names, and chose a state name that you want to use for your address. Write down the corresponding State_ID. Perform the same process to select a zip code and its corresponding Zip_Code_ID.

3. We want to insert three phone numbers in the Phone_Number_T table. The first phone number will be used as our personal phone number and the second two will be used as business phone numbers. Before we insert these phone numbers, let's take a quick look at the syntax of the INSERT statement again, which is listed below. We specify the table name that we want to insert data into, and also specify the column names and the values that are being inserted into the columns:

```
INSERT [INTO] TableName [(ColumnList)] VALUES(ValueList)
```

Use the following code as a guide for creating a query to insert your phone numbers:

```
-- Insert a personal phone number
--
INSERT INTO Phone_Number_T
     (Area_Code_SI, Phone_Number_IN, Last_Update_DT)
     VALUES(555,1234567,GetDate())
--
-- Insert a business phone number
--
INSERT INTO Phone_Number_T
     (Area_Code_SI, Phone_Number_IN, Last_Update_DT)
     VALUES(555,9876543,GetDate())
--
-- Insert a second business phone number
--
INSERT INTO Phone_Number_T
     (Area_Code_SI, Phone_Number_IN, Last_Update_DT)
     VALUES(555,1036417,GetDate())
```

You should verify that the Phone_Number_ID column contains values 1, 2, and 3 by selecting all data from the Phone Number table.

4. Next, we want to insert two employers that we will use as our current and previous employer. Using the code below as a guide, insert the employer information. Notice that we are using the Phone_Number_ID that was generated by SQL Server in the previous step. If the Phone_Number_ID values are different from the ones used below, substitute the values that you have for the ones listed in the code below. Verify that the Employer_ID values are 1 and 2 after you have run the INSERT statements:

```
--
-- Insert an employer
--
INSERT INTO Employer_T
     (Phone_Number_ID, Company_Name_VC, Last_Update_DT)
     VALUES(2,'Wrox Consultants',GetDate())
--
-- Insert a second employer
--
INSERT INTO Employer_T
     (Phone_Number_ID, Company_Name_VC, Last_Update_DT)
     VALUES(3,'Greystone Technology',GetDate())
```

5. Next up is our customer information. We need to insert the appropriate values for our current employer and previous employer, as well as our job title, as shown below:

```
--
-- Insert customer information
--
INSERT INTO Customer_Information_T
     (Employer_ID, Years_At_This_Employer_TI, Job_Title_VC, Previous_Employer_ID,
          Years_At_Previous_Employer_TI, Last_Update_DT)
     VALUES(1,5,'Consultant',2,9,GetDate())
```

6. To insert our address, we will use the values that you wrote down a few minutes ago for the city, state, and zip code. We also want to insert at least one street address. You can insert more than one street address, but don't forget to add the extra column name for the second and/or third streets in the column list. Verify the `Address_ID` that was inserted into your table:

```
--
-- Insert address
--
INSERT INTO Address_T
     (City_ID, State_ID, Zip_Code_ID, Street_Address_1_VC, Last_Update_DT)
     VALUES(1,42,1,'202 S. College Street',GetDate())
```

7. Last comes the `Customer_T` table, which ties all of the pieces of information together. Use the code below as a guide to insert your customer data. Verify the values for `Address_ID`, `Customer_Information_ID`, and `Phone_Number_ID` before running your `INSERT` query:

```
--
-- Insert customer
--
INSERT INTO Customer_T
     (Address_ID, Customer_Information_ID, Phone_Number_ID, First_Name_VC,
          Last_Name_VC, Spouse_First_Name_VC, Last_Update_DT)
     VALUES(1,1,1,'Thearon','Willis','Margie',GetDate())
```

At this point we have some basic data to use for our `SELECT` stored procedures. If you feel ambitious, insert another set of data for another customer, but only assign them a current employer. Let the previous employer information default to null values in the `Customer_Information_T` table.

Simple SELECT Stored Procedure

Once again we start things off pretty simply. The stored procedure we want to create for our first example simply selects certain columns from the `Customer_T` table, giving us the customer's name and their spouse's name, along with a couple of other columns. We want to arrange the data in alphabetical order using the last name and then the first name, and we do this using the `ORDER BY` clause.

We don't need to go into the details of the `SELECT` statement again because you have seen it enough to build this simple stored procedure. So let's move on to our example to create the stored procedure and program. This first example sets the stage for the two examples that follow, and will be the base that we will build upon.

Try It Out – Simple SELECT Stored Procedure

We need to create a stored procedure to select all customers from the `Customer_T` table. In addition to the customer's name, we want to select the `Customer_ID` and the `Last_Update_DT` columns. The results should be ordered by the customer's last name to begin with and then by their first name.

1. The following code shows the stored procedure to be created:

```
CREATE PROCEDURE up_select_customer_names AS

SELECT Customer_ID, First_Name_VC, Last_Name_VC, Spouse_First_Name_VC,
Last_Update_DT
     FROM Customer_T
     ORDER BY Last_Name_VC, First_Name_VC
```

   As you can see, this stored procedure is straightforward in that it does not accept any parameters and selects certain columns from the `Customer_T` table. The results of the `SELECT` statement are sorted by last name and then by first name.

2. After the stored procedure has been created, set the permissions on this object so that the Developers, Management, and Sales Staff roles can execute it.

Having created the stored procedure, let's now create the VB front-end to call it.

Try It Out – VB Code to Implement SELECT Stored Procedure – Class Module

1. Start a new VB project and set a reference to the Microsoft ActiveX Data Objects Library. Use the latest version that you have installed, which should be 2.1 or later.

2. Add a class module to your project and give it a name of `clsCustomer`. Add the following code to your class, changing the owner prefixes as necessary:

```
Option Explicit

Public Function GetCustomerNames(ByRef objConn As ADODB.Connection, _
                            ByRef objRS As ADODB.Recordset) As Long

   'Set a reference to the Recordset object
   Set objRS = New ADODB.Recordset
```

```
    'Setup error handling
    On Error GoTo GetCustomerNames_EH

    'Open the Recordset
    objRS.Open "willist.up_select_customer_names", objConn, _
       adOpenKeyset, adLockReadOnly, adCmdStoredProc

    'Return with a good return code
    GetCustomerNames = 0

    'All was successful, exit function
    On Error GoTo 0
    Exit Function

GetCustomerNames_EH:
    'Display error messages
    Dim objErr As ADODB.Error
    For Each objErr In objConn.Errors
       Debug.Print objErr.Description
    Next
    Set objErr = Nothing
    GetCustomerNames = 1
    On Error GoTo 0
End Function
```

How It Works – VB Code to Implement SELECT Stored Procedure – Class Module

Before we add code to our form, we need to build the class that supports the customer data. The `clsCustomer` class only has one function in it now, but we will be expanding this class in the next three chapters. This class will end up providing all of the logic for selecting, validating, inserting, updating, and deleting customer data.

The function that we are adding now is the `GetCustomerNames` function, which will accept an ADO `Connection` object and a `Recordset` object. It will populate the recordset with customer names and return a `Long` value indicating success or failure.

Notice that the objects being passed are being passed by reference. This is so that we can modify the properties of the objects and return a populated recordset. In a previous example, we demonstrated how to return a disconnected `Recordset` object, and in this example we are demonstrating how to populate a `Recordset` object passed in by reference:

```
Public Function GetCustomerNames(ByRef objConn As ADODB.Connection, _
                                 ByRef objRS As ADODB.Recordset) As Long
```

The first thing we need to do is set a reference to the ADO `Recordset` object using the `Recordset` object passed in. Then we set up our error handling to catch any error that may occur:

```
    'Set a reference to the Recordset object
    Set objRS = New ADODB.Recordset

    'Setup error handling
    On Error GoTo GetCustomerNames_EH
```

Next we open the `Recordset` object, executing the stored procedure that we created earlier. Since it is our intention to be able to navigate the recordset, we are using the `adOpenKeyset` constant as the `CursorType` parameter of the `Recordset` object. We will not be modifying the data so we can use the `adLockReadOnly` constant for the `LockType` parameter. Since this is a stored procedure that we are executing, we need to specify the `adCmdStoredProc` constant for the `Options` parameter:

```
    'Open the Recordset
    objRS.Open "willist.up_select_customer_names", objConn, _
       adOpenKeyset, adLockReadOnly, adCmdStoredProc
```

After our recordset is opened, we set the function to return a zero return code, because at this point our recordset is open and we have not encountered any errors. Then we turn off error handling for this function and exit the function:

```
    'Return with a good return code
    GetCustomerNames = 0

    'All was successful, exit function
    On Error GoTo 0
    Exit Function
```

The error handling routine is pretty simple. You will need to apply the appropriate error handling that meets your standards and best practices in a real world application. This applies to all examples in this book that deal with error handling.

We declare an ADO `Error` object and enumerate through the `Errors` collection displaying each error message in the debug window. After all errors have been enumerated, we de-reference our `Error` object, set the function to return a bad return code and turn off error handling:

```
GetCustomerNames_EH:
    'Display error messages
    Dim objErr As ADODB.Error
    For Each objErr In objConn.Errors
       Debug.Print objErr.Description
    Next
    Set objErr = Nothing
    GetCustomerNames = 1
    On Error GoTo 0
End Function
```

That completes the class module, but before we can run our program we need to create a user interface.

Try It Out – VB Code to Implement SELECT Stored Procedure – Form

The form for this VB program is simple, with only three fields to display the customer's names and spouse's name.

1. The following table should be used as a guide for the controls to be placed on the form, which you should rename and caption appropriately:

Control	Name	Properties
Label	`Label1`	`Caption` = Last Name
Label	`Label2`	`Caption` = First Name
Label	`Label3`	`Caption` = Spouse Name
ComboBox	`cboLastName`	Style = 2 – Drop Down List
TextBox	`txtFirstName`	The `Text` property should be set to nothing
TextBox	`txtSpouseName`	The `Text` property should be set to nothing

Once completed, your form will look something like this:

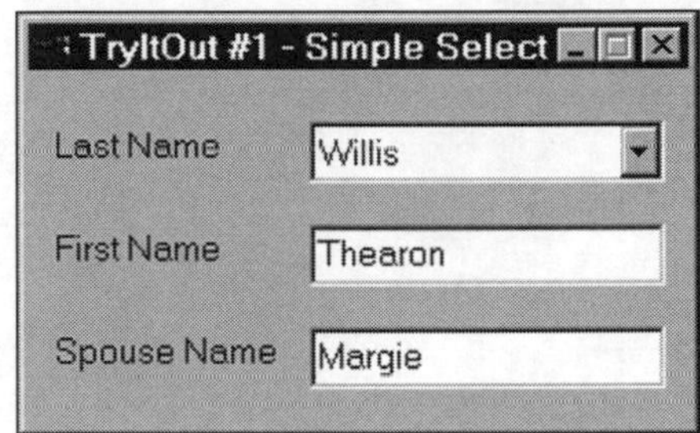

2. Add the following code, available as `frmTryItOut1.frm`, to your form, changing the connection string as appropriate:

```
Option Explicit

'Declare database objects
Dim m_objConn As ADODB.Connection
Dim m_objRS As ADODB.Recordset
Dim m_objErr As ADODB.Error

'Declare class objects
Dim m_objCustomer As clsCustomer


Private Sub cboLastName_Click()
   'Navigate to the correct record based on the index
   m_objRS.MoveFirst
   m_objRS.Move cboLastName.ListIndex

   'Load the text boxes with the correct data
   txtFirstName.Text = m_objRS!First_Name_VC
   txtSpouseName.Text = _
      IIf(IsNull(m_objRS!Spouse_First_Name_VC), "", _
         m_objRS!Spouse_First_Name_VC)
End Sub
```

```
Private Sub Form_Load()
    'Use the standard Windows icon
    Me.Icon = Nothing

    'Set up error handling
    On Error GoTo Form_Load_EH

    'Set a reference to the Database objects
    Set m_objConn = New ADODB.Connection

    'Declare local variables
    Dim lngRC As Long

    'Establish a Database connection using NT authentication
    m_objConn.Open "Driver=SQL Server;Server=WSDevelopment;" & _
       "Database=Wrox_Auto_Works"

    'Check connection state
    If m_objConn.State <> adStateOpen Then
       MsgBox "Connection Failed"
       Exit Sub
    End If

    'Instantiate the class
    Set m_objCustomer = New clsCustomer

    'Get a list of customer names
    lngRC = m_objCustomer.GetCustomerNames(m_objConn, m_objRS)

    'If the return code is not zero, raise an error
    If lngRC <> 0 Then
       Err.Raise vbObjectError + 513, "frmTryItOut1.Form_Load", _
          "Call to clsCustomer.GetCustomerNames failed"
    End If

    'Load the combo box
    Do While Not m_objRS.EOF
       cboLastName.AddItem m_objRS!Last_Name_VC
       m_objRS.MoveNext
    Loop

    'All done, exit procedure
    On Error GoTo 0
    Exit Sub

Form_Load_EH:
    'Ensure the error came from ADO
    If m_objConn.Errors.Count > 0 Then
       For Each m_objErr In m_objConn.Errors
          Debug.Print m_objErr.Description
       Next
    Else
       Debug.Print Err.Description
    End If
End Sub
```

```
Private Sub Form_Unload(Cancel As Integer)
    'Close and de-reference database objects
    If Not m_objRS Is Nothing Then
        If m_objRS.State Then
            m_objRS.Close
        End If
        Set m_objRS = Nothing
    End If

    Set m_objErr = Nothing

    If Not m_objConn Is Nothing Then
        If m_objConn.State Then
            m_objConn.Close
        End If
        Set m_objConn = Nothing
    End If

    'De-reference class objects
    Set m_objCustomer = Nothing
End Sub
```

How It Works – VB Code to Implement SELECT Stored Procedure – Form

We start the code in our form by declaring some form level objects that will be used throughout our form. We have declared the standard ADO `Connection`, `Recordset`, and `Error` objects. Then we declare an object for our customer class:

```
Option Explicit

'Declare Database objects
Dim m_objConn As ADODB.Connection
Dim m_objRS As ADODB.Recordset
Dim m_objErr As ADODB.Error

'Declare class objects
Dim m_objCustomer As clsCustomer
```

The `Form_Load` event is typically used for startup code that is used to initialize your program, and our example program is no different. We have once again set the standard form icon to `Nothing` so we can use the Windows default icon, and then we set up error handling:

```
Private Sub Form_Load()
    'Use the standard Windows icon
    Me.Icon = Nothing

    'Set up error handling
    On Error GoTo Form_Load_EH
```

We set a reference to the `Connection` object and declare our local variables. Then we open the database connection using the DSN-Less connection that we explored in Chapters 6 and 7. We are using NT authentication here, but if your logon uses SQL Server authentication, you need to add the `UID` and `PWD` parameters and specify your login and password.

Also, you will need to change the `Server` parameter in the code below to point to the name of the computer where you installed SQL Server:

```
'Set a reference to the Database objects
Set m_objConn = New ADODB.Connection

'Declare local variables
Dim lngRC As Long

'Establish a database connection using NT Authentication
m_objConn.Open "Driver=SQL Server;Server=WSDevelopment;" & _
   "Database=Wrox_Auto_Works"
```

After we have connected to the database, we want to check the `State` of the connection to ensure that it is indeed open. If not, then we display a message box and exit the procedure. Next we instantiate an instance of our customer class:

```
'Check connection state
If m_objConn.State <> adStateOpen Then
   MsgBox "Connection Failed"
   Exit Sub
End If

'Instantiate the class
Set m_objCustomer = New clsCustomer
```

We execute the `GetCustomerNames` method of our class, passing it the `Connection` and `Recordset` objects. After the execution has completed we check the return code, and raise an error if the return code is not zero.

We are using a standard error number of 513 throughout our project, as we really aren't concerned with the error number, just the error message. When we raise an error in VB, we have a range of numbers from 513 - 65535 that we can use for our own errors. We must add our number to the `vbObjectError` constant as shown in our code below, and give it a source and description. Raising an error will throw us to our error handler:

```
'Get a list of customer names
lngRC = m_objCustomer.GetCustomerNames(m_objConn, m_objRS)

'If the return code is not zero, raise an error
If lngRC <> 0 Then
   Err.Raise vbObjectError + 513, "frmTryItOut1.Form_Load", _
      "Call to clsCustomer.GetCustomerNames failed"
End If
```

All is successful at this point, so we load the combo box with the last names from the recordset. Once we have loaded the combo box, we turn off error handling for this procedure and exit:

```
    'Load the combo box
    Do While Not m_objRS.EOF
       cboLastName.AddItem m_objRS!Last_Name_VC
       m_objRS.MoveNext
    Loop

    'All done, exit procedure
    On Error GoTo 0
    Exit Sub
```

Our error handler will display messages from SQL Server or ADO and from the VB `Error` object. If the error came from SQL Server or ADO, we loop through the `Errors` collection and display each error. Otherwise we display the error message from the VB `Error` object:

```
Form_Load_EH:
    'Ensure the error came from ADO
    If m_objConn.Errors.Count > 0 Then
       For Each m_objErr In m_objConn.Errors
          Debug.Print m_objErr.Description
       Next
    Else
       Debug.Print Err.Description
    End If
End Sub
```

When we click on an item in the combo box, we re-position the recordset to the correct record by using the `ListIndex` of the item selected in the combo box. Both the recordset and the combo box use a zero-based index, so there is a one-to-one match between the two. We move to the first record using the `MoveFirst` method, and then move to the correct record using the `Move` method and the `ListIndex` as the number of records to move:

```
Private Sub cboLastName_Click()
    'Navigate to the correct record based on the index
    m_objRS.MoveFirst
    m_objRS.Move cboLastName.ListIndex
```

After we have re-positioned the recordset to the appropriate record, we display the first name and spouse name from the recordset. We must check the spouse name to ensure it is not null, and we do this in an `Immediate If` function. The `IIF` function accepts the expression to be evaluated, along with the value or expression to be returned. This value or expression will depend on whether the expression being evaluated is true or false. Both of these (true and false) values or expressions are evaluated by the `IIF` function, so if expressions are used, they must be coded such that they can always be evaluated without causing an error:

```
    'Load the text boxes with the correct data
    txtFirstName.Text = m_objRS!First_Name_VC
    txtSpouseName.Text = _
       IIf(IsNull(m_objRS!Spouse_First_Name_VC), "", _
          m_objRS!Spouse_First_Name_VC)
End Sub
```

When we end our program, we need to close and de-reference our database objects and de-reference our class. This code has been placed in the `Form_Unload` event of our form:

```
Private Sub Form_Unload(Cancel As Integer)
   'Close and de-reference database objects
   If Not m_objRS Is Nothing Then
      If m_objRS.State Then
         m_objRS.Close
      End If
      Set m_objRS = Nothing
   End If

   Set m_objErr = Nothing

   If Not m_objConn Is Nothing Then
      If m_objConn.State Then
         m_objConn.Close
      End If
      Set m_objConn = Nothing
   End If

   'De-reference class objects
   Set m_objCustomer = Nothing
End Sub
```

When you run your program, focus is set to the combo box. You can either navigate the list of items using your up and down arrows or the mouse. Notice that each time you select a new name in the list, the appropriate fields on the form are populated with the associated data.

Joins and Column Aliases

`JOIN`s are used to select data from two or more tables. One table is joined to another based on a logical relationship between the two tables. That is, there is a common element in both tables that is used to join them together. This usually takes the form of primary and foreign key relationships, but can be any column in both tables that contains the same information. When specifying the columns from each table to join you specify an operator such as equal (=), less than (<), and greater than (>). This operator is used to filter the rows in the joined table based on values in the primary table.

`JOIN`s can be broken down into five different categories: `CROSS JOIN`, `INNER`, `LEFT OUTER`, `RIGHT OUTER`, and `FULL OUTER`. Let's take a quick look at the different `JOIN`s:

Refer to the SQL Server Books Online for a full explanation of `JOIN`s and how to use them.

A `CROSS JOIN` returns each row from both tables as one results set, in what is known as a **Cartesian Product**. So if you have five rows in table 1 and five rows in table 2, the results you will see are 25 rows of data (the rows in table 1 multiplied by the rows in table 2). A `CROSS JOIN` does not use a logical relationship between the tables as all rows from both tables are returned. Each row in table 2 is returned for each row in table 1. This is useful for the quick generation of test data. The following code shows how a `CROSS JOIN` works:

```
SELECT First_Name_VC, Last_Name_VC, Street_Address_1_VC
      FROM Customer_T
      CROSS JOIN Address_T
      ORDER BY Last_Name_VC
```

An `INNER JOIN`, which is the default for `JOIN`, returns rows from the joined table whose column or columns match the table to which it is joined. It differs from the other types of `JOIN` in that it is an *exclusive* join – it excludes all records that don't have a value in both tables, and thus is comparable to a `WHERE` clause. This is the type of join we will be using, so we will be getting into the details of this in just a few minutes.

The next two code fragments show how an `INNER JOIN` is coded. Notice that using the keyword `INNER` is optional when coding this type of `JOIN`. All of our examples that use this type of join will be coded without the `INNER` keyword:

```
SELECT First_Name_VC, Last_Name_VC, Street_Address_1_VC
      FROM Customer_T
      INNER JOIN Address_T
            ON Customer_T.Address_ID = Address_T.Address_ID
      ORDER BY Last_Name_VC
```

```
SELECT First_Name_VC, Last_Name_VC, Street_Address_1_VC
      FROM Customer_T
      JOIN Address_T
            ON Customer_T.Address_ID = Address_T.Address_ID
      ORDER BY Last_Name_VC
```

Before we look at `OUTER JOIN`s, we need to consider `LEFT` and `RIGHT` tables. Basically the table that comes before the `JOIN` keyword is considered to be the `LEFT` table, and the table after the `JOIN` keyword is the `RIGHT` table.

A `LEFT OUTER JOIN` is used to return all left outer rows even where there is no matching data in the joined (`RIGHT`) table. Remember that left outer rows are the rows in the table on the left side of the `JOIN` statement. When a row in the `LEFT` table has no matching rows in the `RIGHT` table, a `NULL` value is returned for the `RIGHT` table. We will be exploring the `LEFT OUTER JOIN` later in this chapter and an example is shown below:

```
SELECT Customer_Information_ID, Customer_Information_T.Previous_Employer_ID,
Company_Name_VC
      FROM Customer_Information_T
      LEFT OUTER JOIN Employer_T
      ON Customer_Information_T.Previous_Employer_ID =Employer_T.Employer_ID
```

A `RIGHT OUTER JOIN` is similar to a `LEFT OUTER JOIN` except it returns all right outer rows even if there is no match, and returns `NULL` values in those cases. A `RIGHT OUTER JOIN` returns all rows in the second (`RIGHT`) table regardless of whether there is matching data in the first (`LEFT`) table. An example of a `RIGHT OUTER JOIN` is shown in the code below:

```
SELECT Customer_Information_ID, Customer_Information_T.Previous_Employer_ID,
Company_Name_VC
      FROM Customer_Information_T
      RIGHT OUTER JOIN Employer_T
      ON Customer_Information_T.Previous_Employer_ID =Employer_T.Employer_ID
```

A FULL OUTER JOIN is similar to a CROSS JOIN, except that is uses a logical relationship to join the tables, uses the ON operator, and does not produce a Cartesian Product. All rows from both tables are returned. Any time a row has no match in the other table, a NULL value is returned. An example of this type of join is shown below:

```
SELECT First_Name_VC, Last_Name_VC, Street_Address_1_VC
     FROM Customer_T
     FULL OUTER JOIN Address_T
          ON Customer_T.Address_ID = Address_T.Address_ID
     ORDER BY Last_Name_VC
```

When we join tables, there usually exists a column with the same name in both tables. If we want to return the results of both columns, we can do so by specifying the table name as a prefix for the column, as shown in the first line of the code fragment below which uses an INNER JOIN. We do this to prevent an ambiguous column name, which causes an error:

```
SELECT Customer_T.Address_ID, Address_T.Address_ID, Street_Address_1_VC
     FROM Customer_T
     JOIN Address_T
     ON Customer_T.Address_ID = Address_T.Address_ID
```

Enter and run this query to see the results set that is returned. You can also leave off the table prefix to see what type of error message that you get.

After a successful results set is returned, you will notice that, apart from the table name prefix, we have two columns with the same name. This could still be confusing – this is where the **Column Alias** comes to the rescue.

We can assign the column name an alias in one of two ways. The first method we can use is to assign the column to a column alias as shown in the next code fragment:

```
SELECT Customer_T.Address_ID, 'Address_Table_Address_ID'=Address_T.Address_ID
```

The second method that we can use is to specify the AS clause to assign a column alias as shown below:

```
SELECT Customer_T.Address_ID, Address_T.Address_ID AS 'Address_Table_Address_ID'
```

Trying both of these methods, you will notice that you get the same results and which method you use is entirely up to you. We will be demonstrating the first method in the next stored procedure we create; and use the second method in the stored procedure after that. This will give you a working example of both methods to refer to later.

Try It Out – Joins and Column Aliases – Stored Procedure

In this example we will create a stored procedure to select address and phone number information for a specific customer. This stored procedure includes five joined tables to get all of the information we need. The code for the stored procedure is listed below. Don't let the size of the code fool you, as it really is pretty simple and we will step through each line of it. After creating this stored procedure, don't forget to grant EXECUTE permission to all of the roles that we have defined:

```
CREATE PROCEDURE up_parmsel_customer_address (@Customer_ID int) AS

SELECT Address_T.Address_ID, Street_Address_1_VC, Street_Address_2_VC,
Street_Address_3_VC,
     Address_T.Last_Update_DT,
     City_T.City_ID, City_Name_VC,
     State_T.State_ID, State_Name_VC,
     Zip_Code_T.Zip_Code_ID, Zip_Code_CH,
     Phone_Number_T.Phone_Number_ID, Area_Code_SI, Phone_Number_IN,
     'Phone_Number_Last_Update_DT' = Phone_Number_T.Last_Update_DT

     FROM Customer_T

     JOIN Address_T ON Customer_T.Address_ID = Address_T.Address_ID
     JOIN City_T ON Address_T.City_ID = City_T.City_ID
     JOIN State_T ON Address_T.State_ID = State_T.State_ID
     JOIN Zip_Code_T ON Address_T.Zip_Code_ID = Zip_Code_T.Zip_Code_ID
     JOIN Phone_Number_T ON Customer_T.Phone_Number_ID =
             Phone_Number_T.Phone_Number_ID

     WHERE Customer_ID = @Customer_ID
```

How It Works – Joins and Column Aliases – Stored Procedure

As you can see from the first line, we are creating a stored procedure to select data and this stored procedure only accepts one input parameter, the Customer_ID:

```
CREATE PROCEDURE up_parmsel_customer_address (@Customer_ID int) AS
```

The next line of our stored procedure is selecting data from the Address_T table, and we have specified the table name as a prefix for the non-unique columns that are contained in other tables that we are joining:

```
SELECT Address_T.Address_ID, Street_Address_1_VC, Street_Address_2_VC,
Street_Address_3_VC,
     Address_T.Last_Update_DT,
```

This line selects data from the City_T table, and the next line selects data from the State_T table. Once again we have specified the table name as a prefix for those columns that are not unique:

```
     City_T.City_ID, City_Name_VC,
     State_T.State_ID, State_Name_VC,
```

Next, we select data from the Zip_Code_T table and the Phone_Number_T table. Notice that we have assigned a column alias for the Last_Update_DT column in the Phone_Number_T table, to demonstrate column aliases:

```
     Zip_Code_T.Zip_Code_ID, Zip_Code_CH,
     Phone_Number_T.Phone_Number_ID, Area_Code_SI, Phone_Number_IN,
     'Phone_Number_Last_Update_DT' = Phone_Number_T.Last_Update_DT
```

The primary table that the data originates from is the `Customer_T` table and this table is specified in the `FROM` clause. This table contains the data in our `WHERE` clause, as well as the primary keys for the address and phone number data:

```
FROM Customer_T
```

Since we know that the address is required in the `Customer_T` table, we can use a simple `JOIN (INNER JOIN)` to join the Address table. The `Address_T` table is joined to the `Customer_T` table, where data in the `Address_ID` column in the `Address_T` table equals the data in the `Address_ID` column in the `Customer_T` table:

```
JOIN Address_T ON Customer_T.Address_ID = Address_T.Address_ID
```

The same principle that we just discussed holds true for the rest of the tables that we are joining. The `City_T`, `State_T`, and `Zip_Code_T` tables are joined to the `Address_T` table because the `Address_T` table holds the foreign key reference to the entries in those tables:

```
JOIN City_T ON Address_T.City_ID = City_T.City_ID
JOIN State_T ON Address_T.State_ID = State_T.State_ID
JOIN Zip_Code_T ON Address_T.Zip_Code_ID = Zip_Code_T.Zip_Code_ID
```

The last table that we want to `JOIN` contains the phone number information, and the `Customer_T` table holds the foreign key reference to the phone number data.

The `WHERE` clause limits the selection of data to just one customer, as we are using the `Customer_ID`, which is the primary key in our `Customer_T` table:

```
JOIN Phone_Number_T ON Customer_T.Phone_Number_ID =
          Phone_Number_T.Phone_Number_ID

WHERE Customer_ID = @Customer_ID
```

Try It Out – Joins and Column Aliases – VB Code for the Class Module

Start a new Standard EXE VB Project. Create a new class named `clsAddress` that will be used to manage our address data, and add the following code, changing the stored procedure owner prefixes:

```
Option Explicit

Public Enum AddressType
    Customer = 1
    SalesPerson = 2
End Enum

Public Function GetAddress(ByRef objConn As ADODB.Connection, _
                           ByVal lngParentID As Long, _
                           ByVal lngAddressType As AddressType) _
                           As Recordset

   'Declare local objects
   Dim objRS As New ADODB.Recordset
```

```
    'Setup error handling
    On Error GoTo GetAddress_EH

    'Set recordset cursor location
    objRS.CursorLocation = adUseClient

    If lngAddressType = Customer Then

        'Open the recordset
        objRS.Open "willist.up_parmsel_customer_address (" & _
            lngParentID & ")", objConn, adOpenForwardOnly, _
            adLockReadOnly, adCmdStoredProc

    End If

    'Disconnect recordset
    Set objRS.ActiveConnection = Nothing

    'Return with the recordset
    Set GetAddress = objRS
    Set objRS = Nothing

    'All was successful, exit function
    On Error GoTo 0
    Exit Function

GetAddress_EH:
    'Display error messages
    Dim objErr As ADODB.Error
    For Each objErr In objConn.Errors
        Debug.Print objErr.Description
    Next
    Set GetAddress = Nothing
    Set objRS = Nothing
    Set objErr = Nothing
    On Error GoTo 0
End Function

Public Function GetCityStateZip(ByRef objConn As ADODB.Connection, _
                               ByRef objRS As ADODB.Recordset) As Long

    'Set a reference to the Recordset object
    Set objRS = New ADODB.Recordset

    'Setup error handling
    On Error GoTo GetCityStateZip_EH

    'Open the recordset
    objRS.Open "willist.up_select_city_state_zip", objConn, _
            adOpenStatic, adLockReadOnly, adCmdStoredProc

    'Return with a good return code
    GetCityStateZip = 0
```

```
    'All was successful, exit function
    On Error GoTo 0
    Exit Function

GetCityStateZip_EH:
    'Display error messages
    Dim objErr As ADODB.Error
    For Each objErr In objConn.Errors
       Debug.Print objErr.Description
    Next
    Set objErr = Nothing
    GetCityStateZip = 1
    On Error GoTo 0
End Function
```

How It Works – Joins and Column Aliases – VB Code for the Class Module

Before we jump into coding our form, we must first build the business class that will provide the address information to our project. This business class will manage all address and phone data in our database. Since we want this class to handle every possible address, we want to add an enumeration to select address information for customers and sales staff. Since this address information is the same for both, it would only make sense to encapsulate both processes in the same function, with a way to differentiate between the two. We will be building a table to hold sales staff information in Case Study 2.

This is where the enumeration listed below comes into play. This enumeration will differentiate the different requests for an address, whether it's for a customer or a salesperson. We will be using this enumeration in the function call to get addresses next:

```
Option Explicit

Public Enum AddressType
    Customer = 1
    SalesPerson = 2
End Enum
```

The `GetAddress` function accepts three parameters. The `Connection` object is passed by reference and is used by the `Recordset` object to retrieve the address information. The parent ID is the key to the `Customer_T` table that will be used to retrieve the address information. Later it will also be used to retrieve the address for a salesperson. The address type is specified as the enumeration we just talked about. When you are coding a call to this function in your form, the enumeration list will drop down and let you choose the appropriate option.

This function returns a disconnected `Recordset` object containing the address information:

```
Public Function GetAddress(ByRef objConn As ADODB.Connection, _
                           ByVal lngParentID As Long, _
                           ByVal lngAddressType As AddressType) _
                           As Recordset
```

The first thing we want to do in our function is to declare our `Recordset` object and set up error handling:

```
    'Declare local objects
    Dim objRS As New ADODB.Recordset

    'Setup error handling
    On Error GoTo GetAddress_EH
```

Next, we set the cursor location of the recordset to use a client side cursor, and then open the recordset, executing the stored procedure to select customer address information. Once again we have enclosed our stored procedure parameters in parentheses. Since this recordset will only contain one record, we will open the recordset as forward-only and read-only:

```
    'Set recordset cursor location
    objRS.CursorLocation = adUseClient

    If lngAddressType = Customer Then

        'Open the recordset
        objRS.Open "willist.up_parmsel_customer_address (" & _
            lngParentID & ")", objConn, adOpenForwardOnly, _
            adLockReadOnly, adCmdStoredProc

    End If
```

After our recordset has been opened, we disconnect the recordset, and set the function to return the recordset. We then set our `Recordset` object to `Nothing`, turn off error handling, and return to the caller:

```
    'Disconnect recordset
    Set objRS.ActiveConnection = Nothing

    'Return with the recordset
    Set GetAddress = objRS
    Set objRS = Nothing

    'All was successful, exit function
    On Error GoTo 0
    Exit Function
```

If for some unexpected reason things don't go well, we find ourselves here. We declare an ADO `Error` object and enumerate the `Errors` collection, displaying all error messages that have occurred. We then set the function to return `Nothing` and then de-reference our `database` objects:

```
GetAddress_EH:
    'Display error messages
    Dim objErr As ADODB.Error
    For Each objErr In objConn.Errors
        Debug.Print objErr.Description
```

```
    Next
    Set GetAddress = Nothing
    Set objRS = Nothing
    Set objErr = Nothing
    On Error GoTo 0
End Function
```

Since we are dealing with address information in this class, it only makes sense to use our stored procedure to select city names, state names, and zip codes that we created in the last chapter. There is one little catch here though, since this stored procedure returns multiple results sets, we cannot use a disconnected client-side cursor.

To get around this limitation, this function accepts the `Connection` object and `Recordset` object as parameters and both are passed by reference so we can modify them. A `Long` value is returned from this function and will indicate success or failure:

```
Public Function GetCityStateZip(ByRef objConn As ADODB.Connection, _
                        ByRef objRS As ADODB.Recordset) As Long
```

The first thing we do in this function is to set a reference to the ADO `Recordset` object. Then we set up error handling to handle any errors that might occur:

```
    'Set a reference to the Recordset object
    Set objRS = New ADODB.Recordset

    'Setup error handling
    On Error GoTo GetCityStateZip_EH
```

Next we open the recordset, executing the stored procedure to return city names, state names, and zip codes. We are using a static cursor in case the caller wants to navigate the recordset. A static cursor allows us to navigate the recordset backwards and forwards and also lets us use the `Find` method of the `Recordset` object. After execution, we set the return code for the function, turn off error handling and exit the function:

```
    'Open the recordset
    objRS.Open "willist.up_select_city_state_zip", objConn, _
          adOpenStatic, adLockReadOnly, adCmdStoredProc

    'Return with a good return code
    GetCityStateZip = 0

    'All was successful, exit function
    On Error GoTo 0
    Exit Function
```

If an error occurs, we find ourselves here, and perform the same steps as we did in the last function to display all errors. We set the function to return a return code of 1 here and turn off error handling:

```
GetCityStateZip_EH:
   'Display error messages
   Dim objErr As ADODB.Error
   For Each objErr In objConn.Errors
      Debug.Print objErr.Description
   Next
   Set objErr = Nothing
   GetCityStateZip = 1
   On Error GoTo 0
End Function
```

Try It Out – Joins and Column Aliases – VB Code for the Form

Using our last program as a starting point, we will expand the functionality of that program to display address information for the customer that we select in the combo box.

1. Start by copying `frmTryItOut1.frm` as `frmTryItOut2.frm`. Then remove `Form1` and add the new form you just copied. Make this the start up form.

2. Also add the `clsCustomer` class, we do not need to make a copy of that class.

3. Set a reference to the Microsoft ActiveX Data Objects Library and then, using the table below, add the extra controls to the form. The labels on your form can either be individual labels or a control array of labels:

Control	Name	Properties
Label	`Label1(3)`	Caption = Address Line 1
Label	`Label1(4)`	Caption = Address Line 2
Label	`Label1(5)`	Caption = Address Line 3
Label	`Label1(6)`	Caption = City
Label	`Label1(7)`	Caption = State
Label	`Label1(8)`	Caption = Zip Code
Label	`Label1(9)`	Caption = Area Code
Label	`Label1(10)`	Caption = Phone Number
TextBox	`txtAddress1`	Set the Text property to nothing
TextBox	`txtAddress2`	Set the Text property to nothing
TextBox	`txtAddress3`	Set the Text property to nothing
ComboBox	`cboCity`	Style = 0 – Dropdown Combo
ComboBox	`cboState`	Style = 2 – Dropdown List
ComboBox	`cboZipCode`	Style = 0 – Dropdown Combo
TextBox	`txtAreaCode`	Set the Text property to nothing
TextBox	`txtPhoneNumber`	Set the Text property to nothing

Your form should look similar to the following:

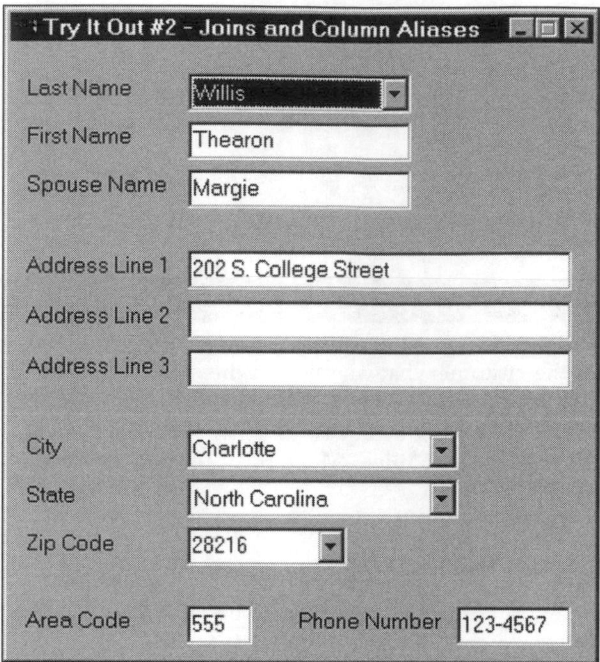

4. Add the following new code to your general declarations section of the form:

```
'Declare database objects
Dim m_objConn As ADODB.Connection
Dim m_objRS As ADODB.Recordset
Dim m_objRSAddress As ADODB.Recordset
Dim m_objErr As ADODB.Error

'Declare class objects
Dim m_objAddress As clsAddress
Dim m_objCustomer As clsCustomer

'Declare module level variables
Dim arrCity() As Long
Dim arrState() As Long
Dim arrZipCode() As Long
```

5. Add the following new code to the `Form_Load` event:

```
Private Sub Form_Load()
   'Use the standard Windows icon
   Me.Icon = Nothing

   'Set up error handling
   On Error GoTo Form_Load_EH
```

```
'Set a reference to the Database objects
Set m_objConn = New ADODB.Connection
Set m_objRS = New ADODB.Recordset

'Declare local variables
Dim lngIndex As Long, lngLastValue As Long, lngRC As Long

'Establish a Database connection using NT Authentication
m_objConn.Open "Driver=SQL Server;Server=WSDevelopment;" & _
   "Database=Wrox_Auto_Works"

'Check connection state
If m_objConn.State <> adStateOpen Then
   MsgBox "Connection Failed"
   Exit Sub
End If

'Instantiate the class
Set m_objCustomer = New clsCustomer

'Get a list of customer names
lngRC = m_objCustomer.GetCustomerNames(m_objConn, m_objRS)

'If the return code is not zero, raise an error
If lngRC <> 0 Then
   Err.Raise vbObjectError + 513, "frmTryItOut2.Form_Load", _
      "Call to clsCustomer.GetCustomerNames failed"
End If

'Load the combo box
lngIndex = -1
Do While Not m_objRS.EOF
   'Add the last name
   cboLastName.AddItem m_objRS!Last_Name_VC
   lngIndex = lngIndex + 1
   'Add the customer id
   cboLastName.ItemData(lngIndex) = m_objRS!Customer_ID
   m_objRS.MoveNext
Loop

'Show the form to give the impression all processing
'is complete
Me.Show
cboLastName.SetFocus
DoEvents

'Instantiate the class
Set m_objAddress = New clsAddress

'Get a list of cities, states and zip codes
lngRC = m_objAddress.GetCityStateZip(m_objConn, m_objRSAddress)
```

```
'If the return code is not zero, raise an error
If lngRC <> 0 Then
   Err.Raise vbObjectError + 513, "frmTryItOut2.Form_Load", _
      "Call to clsAddress.GetCityStateZip failed"
End If

'Load the city combo box and array
lngIndex = -1
lngLastValue = -1
Do While Not m_objRSAddress.EOF
   'Add the city name
   cboCity.AddItem m_objRSAddress!City_Name_VC
   lngIndex = lngIndex + 1
   'Add the city id
   cboCity.ItemData(lngIndex) = m_objRSAddress!City_ID
   If lngLastValue < m_objRSAddress!City_ID Then
      'Redim the array
      ReDim Preserve arrCity(m_objRSAddress!City_ID)
      lngLastValue = m_objRSAddress!City_ID
   End If
   'Add the current position of the city to the array
   arrCity(m_objRSAddress!City_ID) = lngIndex
   'Advance the recordset
   m_objRSAddress.MoveNext
Loop

'Load the state combo box and array
lngIndex = -1
lngLastValue = -1
Set m_objRSAddress = m_objRSAddress.NextRecordset
Do While Not m_objRSAddress.EOF
   'Add the state name
   cboState.AddItem m_objRSAddress!State_Name_VC
   lngIndex = lngIndex + 1
   'Add the state id
   cboState.ItemData(lngIndex) = m_objRSAddress!State_ID
   If lngLastValue < m_objRSAddress!State_ID Then
      'Redim the array
      ReDim Preserve arrState(m_objRSAddress!State_ID)
      lngLastValue = m_objRSAddress!State_ID
   End If
   'Add the current position of the state to the array
   arrState(m_objRSAddress!state_id) = lngIndex
   'Advance the recordset
   m_objRSAddress.MoveNext
Loop

'Load the zip code combo box and array
lngIndex = -1
lngLastValue = -1
Set m_objRSAddress = m_objRSAddress.NextRecordset
Do While Not m_objRSAddress.EOF
   'Add the zip code
```

```
        cboZipCode.AddItem m_objRSAddress!Zip_Code_CH
        lngIndex = lngIndex + 1
        'Add the zip code id
        cboZipCode.ItemData(lngIndex) = m_objRSAddress!Zip_Code_ID
        If lngLastValue < m_objRSAddress!Zip_Code_ID Then
            'Redim the array
            ReDim Preserve arrZipCode(m_objRSAddress!Zip_Code_ID)
            lngLastValue = m_objRSAddress!Zip_Code_ID
        End If
        'Add the current position of the zip code to the array
        arrZipCode(m_objRSAddress!Zip_Code_ID) = lngIndex
        'Advance the recordset
        m_objRSAddress.MoveNext
    Loop

    'Close and de-reference recordset and class object
    m_objRSAddress.Close
    Set m_objRSAddress = Nothing
    Set m_objAddress = Nothing

    'All done, exit procedure
    On Error GoTo 0
    Exit Sub

Form_Load_EH:
    'Ensure the error came from ADO
    If m_objConn.Errors.Count > 0 Then
        For Each m_objErr In m_objConn.Errors
            Debug.Print m_objErr.Description
        Next
    Else
        Debug.Print Err.Description
    End If
End Sub
```

6. Add the following new code to the `cboLastName_Click` procedure:

```
Private Sub cboLastName_Click()
    'Set up error handling
    On Error GoTo cboLastName_Click_EH

    'Navigate to the correct record based on the index
    m_objRS.MoveFirst
    m_objRS.Move cboLastName.ListIndex

    'Load the text boxes with the correct data
    txtFirstName.Text = m_objRS!First_Name_VC
    txtSpouseName.Text = _
        IIf(IsNull(m_objRS!Spouse_First_Name_VC), "", _
            m_objRS!Spouse_First_Name_VC)

    'Instantiate the class
    Set m_objAddress = New clsAddress
```

```
    'Get the customers address
    Set m_objRSAddress = m_objAddress.GetAddress(m_objConn, _
       cboLastName.ItemData(cboLastName.ListIndex), Customer)

    'Ensure the function returned a recordset
    If m_objRSAddress Is Nothing Then
       Err.Raise vbObjectError + 513, _
          "frmTryItOut2.cboLastName_Click", _
          "Call to clsAddress.GetAddress failed"
    End If

    'Load the address fields
    txtAddress1.Text = m_objRSAddress!Street_Address_1_VC
    txtAddress2.Text = IIf(IsNull(m_objRSAddress!Street_Address_2_VC), _
       "", m_objRSAddress!Street_Address_2_VC)
    txtAddress3.Text = IIf(IsNull(m_objRSAddress!Street_Address_3_VC), _
       "", m_objRSAddress!Street_Address_3_VC)

    'Load the city, state, zip fields
    cboCity.ListIndex = arrCity(m_objRSAddress!City_ID)
    cboState.ListIndex = arrState(m_objRSAddress!State_ID)
    cboZipCode.ListIndex = arrZipCode(m_objRSAddress!Zip_Code_ID)

    'Load phone number fields
    txtAreaCode.Text = m_objRSAddress!Area_Code_SI
    txtPhoneNumber.Text = _
       Format(m_objRSAddress!Phone_Number_IN, "###-####")

    'Close and dereference Recordset object
    m_objRSAddress.Close
    Set m_objRSAddress = Nothing

    'Exit procedure
    On Error GoTo 0
    Exit Sub

 cboLastName_Click_EH:
    'Display all errors
    For Each m_objErr In m_objConn.Errors
       Debug.Print m_objErr.Description
    Next
    Debug.Print Err.Description
 End Sub
```

How It Works – Joins and Column Aliases – VB Code for the Form

In the form, we need to add some new module level objects and variables. We have added a new `Recordset` object to hold our address information and a new object to reference our new Address class. We are also setting up three arrays to keep track of the positions of the data in our combo boxes. We'll explain more on this in just a few minutes:

```
Dim m_objRSAddress As ADODB.Recordset

Dim m_objAddress As clsAddress

'Declare module level variables
Dim arrCity() As Long
Dim arrState() As Long
Dim arrZipCode() As Long
```

The `Form_Load` event contains some new local variables that we have defined here:

```
   'Declare local variables
   Dim lngIndex As Long, lngLastValue As Long, lngRC As Long
```

This time when we load our list of customer names in the `cboLastName` combo box, we need to also load the `Customer_ID` of each customer. This information will be used to select the customer's address information. We are using the `ItemData` property of the combo box to keep track of this information. The `ItemData` property works well for this as it stores `Long` values and our `Customer_ID` is also a `Long` value:

```
   'Load the combo box
   lngIndex = -1
   Do While Not m_objRS.EOF
      'Add the last name
      cboLastName.AddItem m_objRS!Last_Name_VC
      lngIndex = lngIndex + 1
      'Add the customer id
      cboLastName.ItemData(lngIndex) = m_objRS!Customer_ID
      m_objRS.MoveNext
   Loop
```

After our combo box has been loaded, we display the form and set focus to the combo box, to give the impression that all processing has been completed and the application is ready for the user to use:

```
   'Show the form to give the impression all processing
   'is complete
   Me.Show
   cboLastName.SetFocus
   DoEvents
```

Now we instantiate an instance of our Address class and get a recordset containing the city, state, and zip code data. After execution of the `GetCityStateZip` function, we check the return code and raise an error if we do not have a zero return code:

```
   'Instantiate the class
   Set m_objAddress = New clsAddress

   'Get a list of cities, states and zip codes
   lngRC = m_objAddress.GetCityStateZip(m_objConn, m_objRSAddress)

   'If the return code is not zero, raise an error
   If lngRC <> 0 Then
      Err.Raise vbObjectError + 513, "frmTryItOut2.Form_Load", _
         "Call to clsAddress.GetCityStateZip failed"
   End If
```

Since we will be loading the combo boxes with city names, state names, and zip code, and then closing our recordset, we have no way to know which entry in the combo box matches the customer's city, state, and zip code data without looping through the combo every time. This would be an inefficient method to use and while the impact may be small now, it could quickly grow and become more noticeable.

What we will do is use the `City_ID` to navigate to the appropriate record in the combo box. Since the city names are in order, this means that the `City_IDs` are not, and so we must rely on an array to help us to keep track of which city name is in which position in the combo box.

We load the `City_ID` in the `ItemData` property and load the current index position of this entry in an array. The key to the array will be the `City_ID`, thus we need only to access the array using the `City_ID` that is returned from the address recordset, and we instantly know the correct index to reposition the combo box to. This will become more evident a little later.

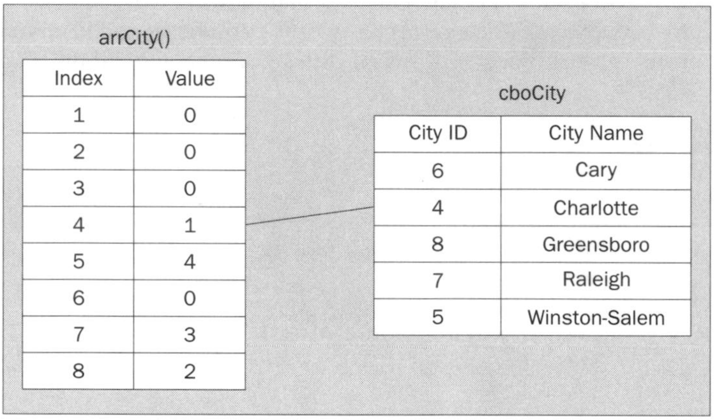

arrCity()

Index	Value
1	0
2	0
3	0
4	1
5	4
6	0
7	3
8	2

cboCity

City ID	City Name
6	Cary
4	Charlotte
8	Greensboro
7	Raleigh
5	Winston-Salem

The illustration above shows what will happen when the `City_ID` returned in the address recordset equals 4. We retrieve the value contained in the array at position 4, which contains the index of the city combo box, and we then set the `ListIndex` property to the value in the array.

We know that entries have been deleted from the `City_T` table, and this will leave gaps in our array that do not contain data. This is a small price to pay for the efficient method that the array provides, and we will only be accessing the array directly based on the `City_ID` of an entry in the combo box.

Looking at the code, we set an index to be used to load the `ItemData` property and also to load the array. The `lngLastValue` variable is used to keep track of the highest `City_ID`. We only want to `ReDim` our array when we need more room, and since the next `City_ID` could be less than the one we are currently processing, we don't want to `ReDim` the array every time:

```
'Load the city combo box and array
lngIndex = -1
lngLastValue = -1
Do While Not m_objRSAddress.EOF
```

Then we add the city name to the combo box and increment the index variable. Next, we set the `ItemData` property using the `City_ID` and then check to see if the last value variable is less than the current `City_ID`. If it is, then we re-dimension the array using the `City_ID` and set the last value variable to the current `City_ID`:

```
      'Add the city name
      cboCity.AddItem m_objRSAddress!City_Name_VC
      lngIndex = lngIndex + 1
      'Add the city id
      cboCity.ItemData(lngIndex) = m_objRSAddress!City_ID
      If lngLastValue < m_objRSAddress!City_ID Then
         'Redim the array
         ReDim Preserve arrCity(m_objRSAddress!City_ID)
         lngLastValue = m_objRSAddress!City_ID
      End If
```

Now we can add the `lngIndex` variable as a value to the array, using the `City_ID` as the index to the array. Then we loop and start all over:

```
      'Add the current position of the city to the array
      arrCity(m_objRSAddress!City_ID) = lngIndex
      'Advance the recordset
      m_objRSAddress.MoveNext
   Loop
```

The same process is performed for the combo boxes for the states and zip codes. Notice that we are setting the `Recordset` object to the next recordset to get the recordset that contains the states:

```
   'Load the state combo box and array
   lngIndex = -1
   lngLastValue = -1
   Set m_objRSAddress = m_objRSAddress.NextRecordset
   Do While Not m_objRSAddress.EOF
      'Add the state name
      cboState.AddItem m_objRSAddress!State_Name_VC
      lngIndex = lngIndex + 1
      'Add the state id
      cboState.ItemData(lngIndex) = m_objRSAddress!State_ID
      If lngLastValue < m_objRSAddress!State_ID Then
         'Redim the array
         ReDim Preserve arrState(m_objRSAddress!State_ID)
         lngLastValue = m_objRSAddress!State_ID
      End If
      'Add the current position of the state to the array
      arrState(m_objRSAddress!State_ID) = lngIndex
      'Advance the recordset
      m_objRSAddress.MoveNext
   Loop

   'Load the zip code combo box and array
   lngIndex = -1
   lngLastValue = -1
   Set m_objRSAddress = m_objRSAddress.NextRecordset
   Do While Not m_objRSAddress.EOF
      'Add the zip code
      cboZipCode.AddItem m_objRSAddress!Zip_Code_CH
      lngIndex = lngIndex + 1
      'Add the zip code id
      cboZipCode.ItemData(lngIndex) = m_objRSAddress!Zip_Code_ID
```

```
        If lngLastValue < m_objRSAddress!Zip_Code_ID Then
            'Redim the array
            ReDim Preserve arrZipCode(m_objRSAddress!Zip_Code_ID)
            lngLastValue = m_objRSAddress!Zip_Code_ID
        End If
        'Add the current position of the zip code to the array
        arrZipCode(m_objRSAddress!Zip_Code_ID) = lngIndex
        'Advance the recordset
        m_objRSAddress.MoveNext
    Loop
```

Once all of the combo boxes have been loaded, we close and de-reference our `Recordset` and `Class` objects:

```
    'Close and de-reference recordset and class object
    m_objRSAddress.Close
    Set m_objRSAddress = Nothing
    Set m_objAddress = Nothing
```

In the `cboLastName_Click` procedure we have added some error handling code at the beginning of our procedure:

```
Private Sub cboLastName_Click()
    'Set up error handling
    On Error GoTo cboLastName_Click_EH
```

After we have loaded the name fields, we want to instantiate the Address class and get the address information for this customer. We execute the `GetAddress` procedure, passing it the `Connection` object and the `Customer_ID` that is contained in the `cboLastName` combo box. We have also specified the `Customer` constant from the `AddressType` enumeration:

```
    'Instantiate the class
    Set m_objAddress = New clsAddress

    'Get the customers address
    Set m_objRSAddress = m_objAddress.GetAddress(m_objConn, _
        cboLastName.ItemData(cboLastName.ListIndex), Customer)
```

To ensure that a recordset has been returned, we check the `Recordset` object for `Nothing` and raise an error if it is:

```
    'Ensure the function returned a recordset
    If m_objRSAddress Is Nothing Then
        Err.Raise vbObjectError + 513, _
            "frmTryItOut2.cboLastName_Click", _
            "Call to clsAddress.GetAddress failed"
    End If
```

We load the address fields using data returned in our recordset:

```
    'Load the address fields
    txtAddress1.Text = m_objRSAddress!Street_Address_1_VC
    txtAddress2.Text = IIf(IsNull(m_objRSAddress!Street_Address_2_VC), _
       "", m_objRSAddress!Street_Address_2_VC)
    txtAddress3.Text = IIf(IsNull(m_objRSAddress!Street_Address_3_VC), _
       "", m_objRSAddress!Street_Address_3_VC)
```

To position the city, state, and zip code combo boxes to the correct entries, we simply use the `City_ID`, `State_ID`, and `Zip_Code_ID` as the index for the array, and use the value in the array as the value to set the `ListIndex` property:

```
    'Load the city, state, zip fields
    cboCity.ListIndex = arrCity(m_objRSAddress!City_ID)
    cboState.ListIndex = arrState(m_objRSAddress!State_ID)
    cboZipCode.ListIndex = arrZipCode(m_objRSAddress!Zip_Code_ID)
```

We need to format the phone number before displaying it, as it is stored in the database as a SQL Server `Integer` data type. After we have completed loading all of the fields on the form, we close and de-reference our objects, then turn off error handling and exit the procedure:

```
    'Load phone number fields
    txtAreaCode.Text = m_objRSAddress!Area_Code_SI
    txtPhoneNumber.Text = _
       Format(m_objRSAddress!Phone_Number_IN, "###-####")

    'Close and dereference Recordset object
    m_objRSAddress.Close
    Set m_objRSAddress = Nothing

    'Exit procedure
    On Error GoTo 0
    Exit Sub
```

The error handling routine simply enumerates through the `Errors` collection, displaying each error message in the debug window:

```
cboLastName_Click_EH:
    'Display all errors
    For Each m_objErr In m_objConn.Errors
       Debug.Print m_objErr.Description
    Next
    Debug.Print Err.Description
End Sub
```

If you entered more than one name in the Customer_T table, you should now be able to click on the different names, see how the address information is loaded, and watch the city, state, and zip code data change in their respective combo boxes.

Now that we have a method and stored procedures to retrieve and display customer names and their addresses, it's time to move on and get their employment information, so we can also display it too.

Left Outer Joins and Correlation Names

In the last section we briefly discussed LEFT OUTER JOINs. To refresh your memory a LEFT OUTER JOIN is used to return all left outer rows even where there is no matching data. This type of join is perfect for our next example. If you take a look back at the table design for the Customer_Information_T table, you will notice that there are two columns that are foreign keys to the Employer_T table.

The first column, Employer_ID, is required so we know that we will always get data when joining the Employer_T table in a SELECT query. However, the second column, Previous_Employer_ID may or may not contain data, and thus a simple JOIN would return no results at all if this column contains a NULL value. Let's take a look at the pair of queries listed below.

The data in the Customer_Information_T table contains only a current employer; it does not contain any data for a previous employer. If you have inserted data into this table and have left the previous employer information NULL, then you will be able to run the following queries and see the results that we are discussing here.

The first query selects the employer name for the current employer. Notice that we have joined the Employer_T table on the Customer_Information_T.Employer_ID column. This query will return data in the results window of the Query Analyzer:

```
SELECT Job_Title_VC, Company_Name_VC
      FROM Customer_Information_T
      JOIN Employer_T
      ON Customer_Information_T.Employer_ID = Employer_T.Employer_ID
      WHERE Customer_Information_ID = 2
```

This second query joins the Employer_T table on the Customer_Information_T.Previous_Employer_ID column. After running this query you will notice that you get no data back whatsoever. Now change the JOIN statement to a LEFT OUTER JOIN (by changing the word JOIN to LEFT OUTER JOIN) and run the query. Notice that you get a NULL in the Company_Name_VC field in the results. This is because the LEFT OUTER JOIN will return the columns in the left table even if it has to return NULLs.

```
SELECT Job_Title_VC, Company_Name_VC
      FROM Customer_Information_T
      JOIN Employer_T
      ON Customer_Information_T.Previous_Employer_ID = Employer_T.Employer_ID
      WHERE Customer_Information_ID = 2
```

This is a good join to use when data in the left table may or may not contain data. This prevents the entire query from failing and will return nulls where the right table does not have any matching records for data in the left table.

As you can see from the previous two queries, we need to select the data from the `Employer_T` table for both the current employer and the previous employer. This can be a problem because we do not want to run two separate queries to get the results we need. Trying to join the same table twice will cause an error because the same table name would be used twice, and this is illegal in SQL Server.

Correlation names are used to assign distinct names to the tables that we want to join. Correlation names are also known as and referred to as **table aliases** and can be assigned by one of two methods, with or without the `AS` keyword. The following example shows the two methods that we can use. To use a correlation name, you specify the actual table followed by the correlation name:

```
LEFT OUTER JOIN Employer_T Previous_Employer
     ON Customer_Information_T.Previous_Employer_ID = Employer_T.Employer_ID
```

```
LEFT OUTER JOIN Employer_T AS Previous_Employer
     ON Customer_Information_T.Previous_Employer_ID = Employer_T.Employer_ID
```

Once a correlation name has been assigned to a table, all references to this table must be made using the correlation name. This means that if you use the table name prefix on a column in the `SELECT` list, you must use the correlation name as the table name prefix. In other words, if you assign a correlation name of `Table_X` to the `Employer_T` table, then you must use `Table_X.Company_Name_VC` in the `SELECT` list when selecting the `Company_Name_VC` column from the `Table_X` table.

After we have chosen a method to use, we can then complete our query, joining the `Employer_T` table twice in one query to get the desired results. Notice that we have used a correlation name of `Previous_Employer` for the second joining of the `Employer_T` table. We have also prefixed the column name in the `SELECT` statement with this new name, as well as assigning the column a column alias, so that the column name is unique:

```
SELECT Job_Title_VC, Employer_T.Company_Name_VC,
     Previous_Employer.Company_Name_VC AS Previous_Company_Name_VC
     FROM Customer_Information_T
     JOIN Employer_T
           ON Customer_Information_T.Employer_ID = Employer_T.Employer_ID
     LEFT OUTER JOIN Employer_T AS Previous_Employer
           ON Customer_Information_T.Previous_Employer_ID =
              Previous_Employer.Employer_ID
     WHERE Customer_Information_ID = 2
```

Running this query now will give you the desired results as well as unique column names. Now that we have a better understanding of `LEFT OUTER JOIN`s, let's put this knowledge to use in a practical example.

Try It Out – Left Outer Joins and Correlation Names – Stored Procedure

The stored procedure that we want to build will select all of the employer information for a customer. This includes their current and previous employer information. As we discussed above, we will need to use `LEFT OUTER JOIN`s and correlation names, as well as column aliases, in our stored procedure.

1. Below is the code for the stored procedure and we will discuss it thoroughly in the *How It Works* section.

2. After you create your stored procedure, set the permission on this stored procedure so all of the roles have access to execute it.

```
CREATE PROCEDURE up_parmsel_customer_employers (@Customer_ID int) AS
--
-- Select data from Customer_Information_T
--
SELECT Customer_Information_T.Customer_Information_ID, Years_At_This_Employer_TI,
     Years_At_Previous_Employer_TI, Job_Title_VC,
        Customer_Information_T.Last_Update_DT,
--
-- Select current employer data from Employer_T
--
     Current_Employer.Employer_ID, Current_Employer.Company_Name_VC,
     Current_Employer.Last_Update_DT AS 'Current_Employer_Last_Update_DT',
--
-- Select current employer phone data from Phone_Number_T
--
     Current_Employer_Phone.Phone_Number_ID, Current_Employer_Phone.Area_Code_SI,
     Current_Employer_Phone.Phone_Number_IN,
     Current_Employer_Phone.Last_Update_DT AS
        'Current_Employer_Phone_Last_Update_DT',
--
-- Select previous employer data from Employer_T
--
     Previous_Employer.Employer_ID AS 'Previous_Employer_ID',
     Previous_Employer.Company_Name_VC AS 'Previous_Employer_Company_Name_VC',
     Previous_Employer.Last_Update_DT AS 'Previous_Employer_Last_Update_DT',
--
-- Select previous employer phone data from Phone_Number_T
--
     Previous_Employer_Phone.Phone_Number_ID AS
        'Previous_Employer_Phone_Number_ID',
     Previous_Employer_Phone.Area_Code_SI AS 'Previous_Employer_Area_Code_SI',
     Previous_Employer_Phone.Phone_Number_IN AS
        'Previous_Employer_Phone_Number_IN',
     Previous_Employer_Phone.Last_Update_DT AS
        'Previous_Employer_Phone_Last_Update_DT'
--
-- From the Customer_T table
--
     FROM Customer_T
--
-- Join the Customer_Information_T table
--
     JOIN Customer_Information_T ON
     Customer_T.Customer_Information_ID
        =Customer_Information_T.Customer_Information_ID
-- Join the Employer_T table to get current employer data
--
     JOIN Employer_T AS Current_Employer ON
           Customer_Information_T.Employer_ID = Current_Employer.Employer_ID
```

```
--
-- Join the Phone_Number_T table to get current employer phone data
--
     JOIN Phone_Number_T AS Current_Employer_Phone ON
           Current_Employer.Phone_Number_ID =
              Current_Employer_Phone.Phone_Number_ID
--
-- left Outer Join the Employer_T table to get previous employer data
-- If no data exists, then null values are returned
--
     LEFT OUTER JOIN Employer_T AS Previous_Employer ON
           Customer_Information_T.Previous_Employer_ID =
              Previous_Employer.Employer_ID
--
-- Left Outer Join the Phone_Number_T table to get previous employer phone data
-- If no data exists, then null values are returned
--
     LEFT OUTER JOIN Phone_Number_T AS Previous_Employer_Phone ON
           Previous_Employer.Phone_Number_ID =
              Previous_Employer_Phone.Phone_Number_ID
--
-- Perform all of this where the Customer_ID in Customer_T equals our input parameter
--
     WHERE Customer_ID = @Customer_ID
```

How It Works – Left Outer Joins and Correlation Names – Stored Procedure

Since this stored procedure is fairly complex, we have broken it down into sections and added comments. This serves two functions. First it makes the stored procedure easier to build and debug. It also makes it easier to manage later.

When you are building a stored procedure of this size and complexity, it helps to build it in stages as a query first. You can add the columns from one table in the `SELECT` list and then add the table. You hard code the value in the `WHERE` clause and run the query. Once you debug your query and get the desired results, add the columns for another table and join the second table, then run the query again.

Keep performing this process until the query is built and you are getting the desired results. Then convert it to a stored procedure, replacing the hard coded values with parameters. Using this method makes debugging your query easier, as you are less prone to making errors, and the errors that you do encounter are easy to fix.

The first line of our stored procedure creates a `SELECT` stored procedure, as is evident by the stored procedure name, and accepts one input parameter:

```
CREATE PROCEDURE up_parmsel_customer_employers (@Customer_ID int) AS
```

The first line of our `SELECT` statement is selecting data from the `Customer_Information_T` table. We have prefixed the non-unique column names with the table name, as we will have duplicate column names in our stored procedure. It is arguable whether or not to add the table prefix to all column names in the `SELECT` list. I prefer to only use the table prefix when necessary, but this is a judgement call on your part.

```
--
-- Select data from Customer_Information_T
--
SELECT Customer_Information_T.Customer_Information_ID, Years_At_This_Employer_TI,
      Years_At_Previous_Employer_TI, Job_Title_VC,
         Customer_Information_T.Last_Update_DT,
```

The second part of our SELECT statement is selecting data from the Employer_T table, as shown by our comments. Since we are joining the Employer_T table twice in this stored procedure, we must use a correlation name for the table, and we have chosen to use Current_Employer as the correlation name. Notice also that since there are duplicate columns in the SELECT list, we have assigned column aliases that are made up of the correlation name and the original column name:

```
--
-- Select current employer data from Employer_T
--
      Current_Employer.Employer_ID, Current_Employer.Company_Name_VC,
      Current_Employer.Last_Update_DT AS 'Current_Employer_Last_Update_DT',
```

We continue the SELECT statement by selecting data from the various tables that make up a complete customer information record. We have joined the Employer_T and Phone_Number_T tables twice in this stored procedure and have used correlation names for all of these tables:

```
--
-- Select current employer phone data from Phone_Number_T
--
      Current_Employer_Phone.Phone_Number_ID, Current_Employer_Phone.Area_Code_SI,
      Current_Employer_Phone.Phone_Number_IN,
      Current_Employer_Phone.Last_Update_DT AS
         'Current_Employer_Phone_Last_Update_DT',
--
-- Select previous employer data from Employer_T
--
      Previous_Employer.Employer_ID AS 'Previous_Employer_ID',
      Previous_Employer.Company_Name_VC AS 'Previous_Employer_Company_Name_VC',
      Previous_Employer.Last_Update_DT AS 'Previous_Employer_Last_Update_DT',
--
-- Select previous employer phone data from Phone_Number_T
--
      Previous_Employer_Phone.Phone_Number_ID AS
         'Previous_Employer_Phone_Number_ID',
      Previous_Employer_Phone.Area_Code_SI AS 'Previous_Employer_Area_Code_SI',
      Previous_Employer_Phone.Phone_Number_IN AS
         'Previous_Employer_Phone_Number_IN',
      Previous_Employer_Phone.Last_Update_DT AS
         'Previous_Employer_Phone_Last_Update_DT'
```

The parent table from which all data is derived is the Customer_T table so this is naturally the table in the FROM clause:

```
--
-- From the Customer_T table
--
      FROM Customer_T
```

The first table that we are joining is the Customer_Information_T table. Since this table is only joined once, we do not have to specify a correlation name for this table. We also are using a simple JOIN, as we know that data exists in this table, because the foreign key to this table in the Customer_T table is a required column:

```
--
-- Join the Customer_Information_T table
--
      JOIN Customer_Information_T ON
      Customer_T.Customer_Information_ID
         =Customer_Information_T.Customer_Information_ID
```

The second table that we are joining is the Employer_T table. We are joining this table on the Employer_ID column in the Customer_Information_T table to get the current employer information. This foreign key in the Customer_Information_T table is also a required column, so we know data will exist for this join:

```
--
-- Join the Employer_T table to get current employer data
--
      JOIN Employer_T AS Current_Employer ON
            Customer_Information_T.Employer_ID = Current_Employer.Employer_ID
```

The next table that we want to join is the Phone_Number_T table. We are joining this table twice in this stored procedure, so we use a correlation name to assign a unique table name. This table is joined to the Employer_T table, as we want the phone number for this employer:

```
--
-- Join the Phone_Number_T table to get current employer phone data
--
      JOIN Phone_Number_T AS Current_Employer_Phone ON
            Current_Employer.Phone_Number_ID =
               Current_Employer_Phone.Phone_Number_ID
```

This next join is the second join for the Employer_T table and this time data may or may not exist. We use a LEFT OUTER JOIN so that the columns contained in the SELECT list will be returned with NULL values if data does not exist. We are using the Previous_Employer_ID column in the Customer_Information_T table to join this table. This join will return the previous employer information for this customer if it exists. Notice that we have used a correlation name of Previous_Employer for this table:

```
--
-- Left Outer Join the Employer_T table to get previous employer data
-- If no data exists, then null values are returned
--
      LEFT OUTER JOIN Employer_T AS Previous_Employer ON
            Customer_Information_T.Previous_Employer_ID =
               Previous_Employer.Employer_ID
```

We once again join the Phone_Number_T table using a correlation name of Previous_Employer_Phone, and use a LEFT OUTER JOIN to join this table to the Previous_Employer (Employer_T) table. Because data may or may not exist in the Previous_Employer table, we must use a LEFT OUTER JOIN:

```
--
-- Left Outer Join the Phone_Number_T table to get previous employer phone data
-- If no data exists, then null values are returned
--
      LEFT OUTER JOIN Phone_Number_T AS Previous_Employer_Phone ON
            Previous_Employer.Phone_Number_ID =
               Previous_Employer_Phone.Phone_Number_ID
```

The WHERE clause in our stored procedure is based on the primary key in the Customer_T table, and only selects data from the underlying tables where the Customer_ID is equal to the parameter that we have passed in:

```
--
-- Perform all of this where the Customer_ID in Customer_T equals our input parameter
--
      WHERE Customer_ID = @Customer_ID
```

After you have created your stored procedure and before you close the Query Analyzer, remove all the comments from this stored procedure. This will demonstrate how useful comments are. As you can see, removing the comments just leaves a bunch of code that can be quite confusing especially if you come back some months later and need to modify this stored procedure to add new columns. Comments do make a difference and help the maintainability of your stored procedures.

Try It Out – Left Outer Joins and Correlation Names – VB Code

1. For our VB project, we will use the last example as a starting point for this project. Copy the form frmTryItOut2.frm as frmTryItOut3.frm.

2. Then start a new VB project, remove the current form and add the new form you just copied. Make this the start up form.

3. You will also need to add the Address and Customer classes to this project, and set a reference to the Microsoft ActiveX Data Objects Library.

4. Modify frmTryItOut3.frm as shown in the figure by adding a button to access the employer information, and set the Name property to cmdEmployer and the Caption property to Employer:

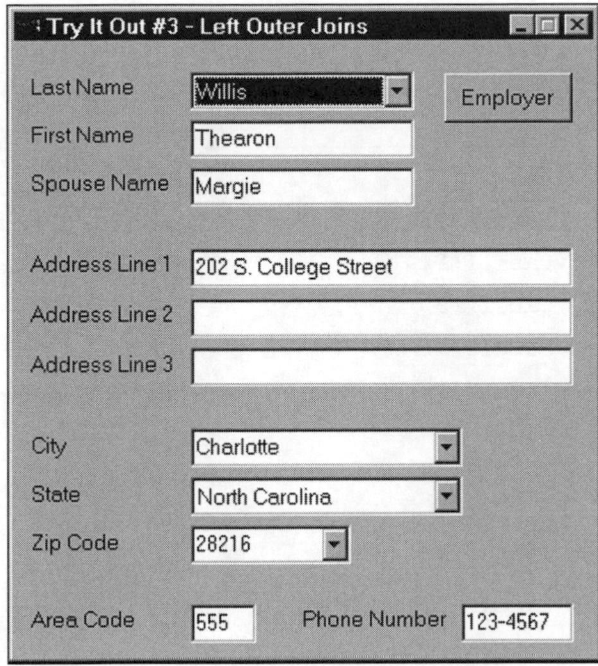

5. Add the following code to the `cmdEmployer_Click` procedure:

```
Private Sub cmdEmployer_Click()
   Me.Hide
   'Call the employer form to process and display employer info
   Call frmTI03Employer.Process(m_objConn, _
      cboLastName.ItemData(cboLastName.ListIndex), Me)
   Me.Show
   'We are back, set focus to the combo box
   cboLastName.SetFocus
End Sub
```

6. Add the following new code in the `cboLastName_Click` procedure:

```
'Close and dereference Recordset object
m_objRSAddress.Close
Set m_objRSAddress = Nothing


   'Enable Employer button and exit procedure
   On Error GoTo 0
   cmdEmployer.Enabled = True
   Exit Sub
```

7. Change the references to `frmTryItOut2.frm` to `frmTryItOut2.frm`.

8. We want to add a new form to our project to display the employer information. Using the table and figure below, add the following controls to your form. Give the form a name of `frmTIO3Employer.frm`. I added all my labels in a control array but you are free to add individual labels:

Control	Name	Properties
Label	`Label1(0)`	Caption = Current Employer
Label	`Label1(1)`	Caption = Area Code
Label	`Label1(2)`	Caption = Phone Number
Label	`Label1(3)`	Caption = Job Title
Label	`Label1(4)`	Caption = Years Employed
Label	`Label1(5)`	Caption = Previous Employer
Label	`Label1(6)`	Caption = Area Code
Label	`Label1(7)`	Caption = Phone Number
Label1	`Label1(8)`	Caption = Years Employed
TextBox	`txtCurrentEmployer`	Set the Text property to nothing
TextBox	`txtCEAreaCode`	Set the Text property to nothing
TextBox	`txtCEPhoneNumber`	Set the Text property to nothing
TextBox	`txtJobTitle`	Set the Text property to nothing
TextBox	`txtCEYearsEmployed`	Set the Text property to nothing
TextBox	`txtPreviousEmployer`	Set the Text property to nothing
TextBox	`txtPEAreaCode`	Set the Text property to nothing
TextBox	`txtPEPhoneNumber`	Set the Text property to nothing
TextBox	`txtPEYearsEmployed`	Set the Text property to nothing
CommandButton	`cmdClose`	Caption = Close

The form should look similar to this:

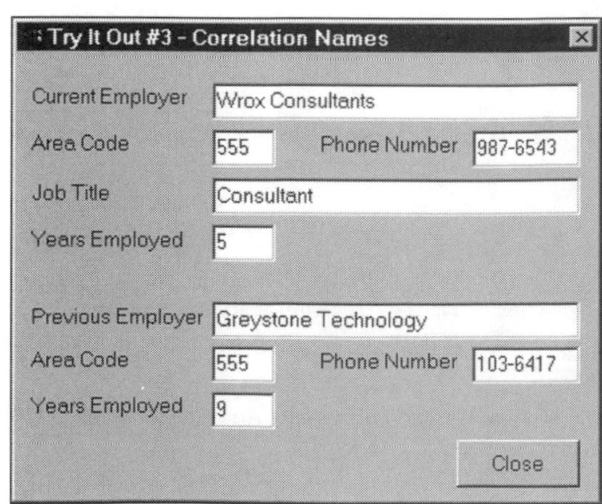

9. Add the following code to this new form:

```
Option Explicit

Public Sub Process(ByRef objConn As ADODB.Connection, _
                   ByVal lngCustomerID As Long, ByVal frmParent As Form)

   'Set up error handling
   On Error GoTo Process_EH

   'Declare Recordset object
   Dim objRS As New ADODB.Recordset

   'Instantiate the class
   Dim objEmployer As New clsEmployer

   'Get the employer information for this customer
   Set objRS = objEmployer.GetEmployers(objConn, lngCustomerID)

   'Ensure the function returned a recordset
   If objRS Is Nothing Then
      Err.Raise vbObjectError + 513, _
         "frmTIOEmployer.Process", _
         "Call to clsEmployer.GetEmployers failed"
   End If

   'Load the current employer fields
   txtCurrentEmployer.Text = objRS!Company_Name_VC
   txtCEAreaCode.Text = objRS!Area_Code_SI
   txtCEPhoneNumber.Text = Format(objRS!Phone_Number_IN, "###-####")
   txtJobTitle.Text = objRS!Job_Title_VC
   txtCEYearsEmployed.Text = objRS!Years_At_This_Employer_TI

   If Not IsNull(objRS!Previous_Employer_Company_Name_VC) Then
      'Load the previous employer fields
      txtPreviousEmployer.Text = _
         objRS!Previous_Employer_Company_Name_VC
      txtPEAreaCode.Text = _
         objRS!Previous_Employer_Area_Code_SI
      txtPEPhoneNumber.Text = _
         Format(objRS!Previous_Employer_Phone_Number_IN, "###-####")
      txtPEYearsEmployed.Text = _
         objRS!Years_At_Previous_Employer_TI
   End If

   'Close and de-reference objects
   objRS.Close
   Set objRS = Nothing
   Set objEmployer = Nothing

   On Error GoTo 0
```

```
    'Show the form
    Show vbModal, frmParent
    Exit Sub

Process_EH:
    Dim objErr As ADODB.Error
    For Each objErr In objConn.Errors
       Debug.Print objErr.Description
    Next
    Set objRS = Nothing
    Set objErr = Nothing
    Set objEmployer = Nothing
    On Error GoTo 0
End Sub


Private Sub cmdClose_Click()
   Unload Me
End Sub


Private Sub Form_Load()
   'Use the standard Windows icon
   Me.Icon = Nothing
End Sub
```

10. In order for this form to function, we need to add a class to manage the employer information. Create a new class, name it `clsEmployer.cls`, and add the following code to this class:

```
Option Explicit


Public Function GetEmployers(ByRef objConn As ADODB.Connection, _
                             ByVal lngCustomerID As Long) _
                             As Recordset

   'Declare local objects
   Dim objRS As New ADODB.Recordset

   'Setup error handling
   On Error GoTo GetEmployers_EH

   'Set recordset cursor location and open recordset
   objRS.CursorLocation = adUseClient
   objRS.Open "willist.up_parmsel_customer_employers (" & _
      lngCustomerID & ")", objConn, adOpenForwardOnly, _
      adLockReadOnly, adCmdStoredProc

   'Disconnect recordset
   Set objRS.ActiveConnection = Nothing
   'Return with the recordset
   Set GetEmployers = objRS
   Set objRS = Nothing
```

```
    'All was successful, exit function
    On Error GoTo 0
    Exit Function

GetEmployers_EH:
    'Display error messages
    Dim objErr As ADODB.Error
    For Each objErr In objConn.Errors
        Debug.Print objErr.Description
    Next
    Set GetEmployers = Nothing
    Set objRS = Nothing
    Set objErr = Nothing
    On Error GoTo 0
End Function
```

How It Works – Left Outer Joins and Correlation Names – VB Code

We want to look at the `GetEmployers` procedure in the `clsEmployer` class first. This procedure will return a recordset of the employer information for the customer ID that was passed. We start by defining all of the input parameters to this procedure. We are passing the `Connection` object by reference and passing the customer ID by value. The procedure returns a `Recordset` object on successful completion.

We then declare a `Recordset` object and set up our error handling:

```
Public Function GetEmployers(ByRef objConn As ADODB.Connection, _
                            ByVal lngCustomerID As Long) _
                            As Recordset

    'Declare local objects
    Dim objRS As New ADODB.Recordset

    'Setup error handling
    On Error GoTo GetEmployers_EH
```

Since we are returning a recordset, we will return a disconnected recordset, so we set the `CursorLocation` property to use a client-side cursor. We then open our recordset by executing the stored procedure, passing it the customer ID. Notice that once again we have enclosed our parameter in parentheses.

After our recordset is open, we disconnect our `Recordset` object by setting the `ActiveConnection` property to `Nothing`:

```
    'Set recordset cursor location and open recordset
    objRS.CursorLocation = adUseClient
    objRS.Open "willist.up_parmsel_customer_employers (" & _
        lngCustomerID & ")", objConn, adOpenForwardOnly, _
        adLockReadOnly, adCmdStoredProc

    'Disconnect recordset
    Set objRS.ActiveConnection = Nothing
```

We then set up the procedure to return the recordset and set the Recordset object to nothing. Next, we turn off error handling and exit the function:

```
    'Return with the recordset
    Set GetEmployers = objRS
    Set objRS = Nothing

    'All was successful, exit function
    On Error GoTo 0
    Exit Function
```

Our error handler is the same as in previous examples, and only displays the error messages in the debug window and sets up the procedure to return Nothing:

```
GetEmployers_EH:
    'Display error messages
    Dim objErr As ADODB.Error
    For Each objErr In objConn.Errors
       Debug.Print objErr.Description
    Next
    Set GetEmployers = Nothing
    Set objRS = Nothing
    Set objErr = Nothing
    On Error GoTo 0
End Function
```

Moving on to the code in our new form, we start with the Process procedure. This is the initial entry point into this form and the procedure that we will be calling from the frmTryItOut3 form. We are passing the procedure three parameters, the first of which is the Connection object, which is passed by reference. The second parameter is the customer ID and is passed by value. The third is the parent form, which is also passed by value:

```
Public Sub Process(ByRef objConn As ADODB.Connection, _
                     ByVal lngCustomerID As Long, ByVal frmParent As Form)
```

We set up our error handler and declare our Recordset and class objects:

```
    'Set up error handling
    On Error GoTo Process_EH

    'Declare Recordset object
    Dim objRS As New ADODB.Recordset

    'Instantiate the class
    Dim objEmployer As New clsEmployer
```

We execute the `GetEmployers` procedure in the `clsEmployer` class to get the employer information for this customer, and then check to ensure that the execution was successful:

```
'Get the employer information for this customer
Set objRS = objEmployer.GetEmployers(objConn, lngCustomerID)

'Ensure the function returned a recordset
If objRS Is Nothing Then
   Err.Raise vbObjectError + 513, _
      "frmTIOEmployer.Process", _
      "Call to clsEmployer.GetEmployers failed"
End If
```

We then load the fields for the current employer and format the phone number field. If the first field of the previous employer information contains a `NULL` value, then we know that all of the fields for the previous employer information are `NULL`, and we do not need to load those text fields on the form. If the first field is not a `NULL` value, then we load the text fields for the previous employer information:

```
'Load the current employer fields
txtCurrentEmployer.Text = objRS!Company_Name_VC
txtCEAreaCode.Text = objRS!Area_Code_SI
txtCEPhoneNumber.Text = Format(objRS!Phone_Number_IN, "###-####")
txtJobTitle.Text = objRS!Job_Title_VC
txtCEYearsEmployed.Text = objRS!Years_At_This_Employer_TI

If Not IsNull(objRS!Previous_Employer_Company_Name_VC) Then
   'Load the previous employer fields
   txtPreviousEmployer.Text = _
      objRS!Previous_Employer_Company_Name_VC
   txtPEAreaCode.Text = _
      objRS!Previous_Employer_Area_Code_SI
   txtPEPhoneNumber.Text = _
      Format(objRS!Previous_Employer_Phone_Number_IN, "###-####")
   txtPEYearsEmployed.Text = _
      objRS!Years_At_Previous_Employer_TI
End If
```

After all fields have been loaded, we close and de-reference our `Recordset` and class objects. We then show the form modally using the parent form that was passed as a parameter. Our error handler does not need further explanation, as it is the same error handler that has been used throughout this chapter:

```
'Close and de-reference objects
objRS.Close
Set objRS = Nothing
Set objEmployer = Nothing

On Error GoTo 0

'Show the form
Show vbModal, frmParent
Exit Sub
```

The Form_Load event simply sets the form icon to nothing, so that the default Windows icon is displayed. The cmdClose_Click procedure unloads the form and returns control back to the parent form:

```
Private Sub Form_Load()
   'Use the standard Windows icon
   Me.Icon = Nothing
End Sub


Private Sub cmdClose_Click()
   Unload Me
End Sub
```

In order to show this new form, we use the code in the cmdEmployer_Click procedure in the frmTryItOut3 form. The first thing we do here is to hide the parent form. This is my own personal preference and is not a necessary step.

Then we call the Process procedure in the frmTIO3Employer form, passing it the required parameters. Notice that we are getting the customer ID from the ItemData property of the cboLastName combo box for the currently selected item:

```
Private Sub cmdEmployer_Click()
   Me.Hide
   'Call the employer form to process and display employer info
   Call frmTIO3Employer.Process(m_objConn, _
      cboLastName.ItemData(cboLastName.ListIndex), Me)
```

After control has been returned to the parent form, we show the form again and then set focus to the cboLastName combo box:

```
   Me.Show
   'We are back, set focus to the combo box
   cboLastName.SetFocus
End Sub
```

We are now ready to run our program and test it. After you select a customer, the **Employer** button becomes enabled and you can click on it to see the customer's employer information. When you close the Employer form, control is returned to the parent form.

Using two forms keeps our UI very simple for the user to use. We don't end up cluttering the first form with too much data.

Summary

In this chapter we have once again taken a look at and created a simple stored procedure. We then moved on to create a stored procedure that used a simple `JOIN` (`INNER JOIN`) to join multiple tables. This stored procedure also introduced you to column aliases, and showed you two different techniques to use to create column aliases. We learned why we must sometimes use the table name as a prefix to column names – columns from different tables can contain the same name and we need a method to distinguish between the two. We also used column aliases in these circumstances to ensure that a unique column name was returned in our results set.

We moved on to create a more complex stored procedure that used simple `JOINs` and `LEFT OUTER JOINs` to join the same table multiple times using different criteria. This caused us to use correlation names, by which we assigned the joined table an alias in order to keep the table names unique. This stored procedure also used column aliases to keep the column names unique, and the correlation names were used as the table prefixes for the duplicate column names. This stored procedure was heavily commented to help keep the stored procedure understandable and easier to maintain in the future.

Early in the chapter we touched briefly on the other types of joins and you should have a basic understanding of them now that we have used simple `JOINs` and a `LEFT OUTER JOIN`.

In summary, you should know and understand:

- How to use a simple `JOIN`
- How to use a `LEFT OUTER JOIN`
- How to create and use column aliases and correlation names (table aliases)
- The importance of commenting your stored procedures

In the next chapter we'll take a look at `INSERT` stored procedures.

WROX AUTO WORKS RACING

Inserting Data

In the last chapter we saw how our stored procedures grew in size as they became more and more complex. It quickly became apparent that comments were needed in our stored procedures, to help us document our SQL statements as we coded, and for maintainability. The stored procedures that we created were SELECT stored procedures and they did not contain any logic.

This chapter changes all of that as we introduce processing logic into our stored procedures. Our stored procedures will become even more complex, and commenting our SQL statements helps us to document our processing logic. It will also help us later should we need to perform any maintenance on these stored procedures.

The logic that we will be introducing into our stored procedures is very similar to VB logic. We will use variables to keep track of numbers and string data, and use processing flow logic with the aid of IF ELSE statements. We will also use error handling to check and raise errors that return user defined messages. SQL Server also provides some built-in functions that help us to control the processing flow of our stored procedures, and we will introduce them as they come up.

In this chapter we will:

- Use IF ELSE statements to control processing of SQL statements
- Use SQL Server functions, such as DATALENGTH and CAST to check variable lengths and to convert variables
- Use error functions to check for errors, and to raise errors that return messages
- Use transactions to help maintain data integrity
- Use output parameters to return table keys and custom messages

Stored Procedures that Use Logic

Continuing with the project from the last chapter, we now need a method to *insert* data into the various tables that make up our database. We built three SELECT stored procedures to select customer data, address data, and employment data. In keeping with that we start this chapter by building a stored procedure to insert *address* data, and later we will build stored procedures to insert the other data.

Because of the relationship of the tables that make up a complete customer record, we will build three separate stored procedures and only one VB project. We need to complete all three stored procedures and run them one after another to insert a complete customer record. The last stored procedure that we will build depends on the data returned from the first two stored procedures, and thus they must all run together to form a complete unit of work.

The stored procedure that we will code first introduces a number of new functions, some of which are specific to SQL Server, and others that are universal to the SQL language as a whole.

Controlling the Flow

Before we begin creating the stored procedure, let's take a look at some of the functions we'll be using. The first thing we want to examine is *controlling the flow* of logic in our stored procedures. This is accomplished with `IF ELSE` statements. The `IF ELSE` statements evaluate an expression or expressions and control the execution, limiting it to a specific block of SQL statements. Unlike the `IF ELSE` statements in VB, there is no `THEN` statement, nor is there an `END IF` statement. What SQL Server provides are `BEGIN` and `END` blocks. All code that lies between the `BEGIN` and `END` blocks is executed.

Take a look at the following code fragment. If the variable `@Key` is equal to zero then the first set of SQL statements contained within the `BEGIN` and `END` blocks is executed. If the expression evaluates to a false condition, then the second set of SQL statements is executed. The `IF ELSE` block ends after the last `END` keyword, and the next statement is then executed, in this case a `SELECT` statement:

```
IF @Key = 0
   BEGIN
   ...
   END
ELSE
   BEGIN
   ...
   END
SELECT * FROM Customer_T
```

Evaluating Data

There are numerous functions that can be used to *evaluate data* and we will touch on just a few here. The first function that we want to explore is the string function `LTRIM`. This function works just like its named counterpart in VB, by *trimming* or removing all leading spaces from the left side of a variable. This function should be familiar to everyone and needs no further explanation. SQL Server only provides the `LTRIM` and `RTRIM` functions for trimming leading and trailing spaces; it does not provide a `Trim` function to trim *all* spaces.

The second function we want to look at is the `DATALENGTH` function. This function performs like its VB counterpart, the `Len` function, by returning the number of characters in a string variable. The following code fragment shows how we can use the `DATALENGTH` and the `LTRIM` functions together. Here we are checking the length of a string variable to see if it is equal to zero after all leading spaces have been removed:

```
IF DATALENGTH(LTRIM(@Variable1)) = 0
   BEGIN
   ...
```

Sometimes it's necessary to *convert* one data type to another, similar to how we do in VB when using CStr to convert a Numeric data type to a String data type. SQL Server provides a similar function called CAST. We can CAST one data type to another and it works as shown in the following code fragment. Here we are converting the Integer data type to a VarChar data type using the CAST function. Remember our discussion about assigning values to variables, from the previous chapter? We use the SELECT statement to assign values to our variables.

```
DECLARE @Variable1 VarChar(10), @Variable2 Int
SELECT @Variable1 = CAST(@Variable2 as VarChar(10))
```

Another method that can be used to assign values to our variables is to use the SET clause, as shown below. Both methods accomplish the same task of assigning a value to our variable.

```
DECLARE @Variable1 VarChar(10), @Variable2 Int
SET @Variable1 = CAST(@Variable2 AS VarChar(10))
```

We are now armed with enough information to create our first INSERT stored procedure for this chapter. Remember that we will create this stored procedure now and call it from a VB program later in this chapter.

Try It Out – Stored Procedure that Uses Logic

The stored procedure we want to create will accept all address information, including city, state, zip code, and phone number, as input parameters. We will perform data validation on these fields and place any error messages in the message output parameter. There are two other output parameters that will be used in this stored procedure: one that contains the phone number ID that was inserted, and one that contains the address ID that was inserted. The stored procedure will return a 1 if processing cannot proceed due to errors, and a 0 upon successful completion.

1. Create the up_parmins_address stored procedure, using the code which is presented throughout the *How It Works* section below. The entire code is also available in the download files.

2. Don't forget to set the permissions on this stored procedure so that only the Developers and Sales Staff roles can execute it.

How It Works – Stored Procedure that Uses Logic

While this is a lot of code for a stored procedure, most of the code is used for data validation to ensure data integrity. We will step through all the major facets of this stored procedure and skim over the repeated steps.

We start by coding the statements to create a stored procedure and list all of the input and output parameters. The output parameters that we are using are `@Address_ID`, `@Phone_Number_ID`, and `@Message`. The first two parameters will return the ID numbers that were inserted into the address and phone number tables. The `@Message` parameter is used to return error messages that are recorded as a result of failed data validation.

```
CREATE PROCEDURE up_parmins_address (@Street_Address1 VarChar(30),
    @Street_Address2 VarChar(30), @Street_Address3 VarChar(30), @City_ID Int,
    @City_Name VarChar(30), @State_ID Int, @Zip_Code_ID Int, @Zip_Code Char(10),
    @Area_Code SmallInt, @Phone_Number Int, @Address_ID Int OUTPUT,
    @Phone_Number_ID Int OUTPUT, @Message VarChar(300) OUTPUT) AS
```

The next thing we want to do is to declare any variables that we may need during the processing of this stored procedure. Unfortunately, SQL Server does not provide a Boolean function like VB does. So we must rely on a `Bit` data type that we will set to 1 for true and 0 for false. We declare the two variables that we are going to use, and set the first variable to a default value of 1. The second variable will be explained shortly.

```
--
***************************************************************************
-- Declare variables
--
***************************************************************************
DECLARE @Continue    Bit,
     @Name_Required    Bit
--
-- Turn on default value to continue
--
SELECT @Continue = 1
```

The `@Address_ID`, `@Phone_Number_ID`, and `@Message` variables are output parameters that we defined above. It is possible that these variables may never be set because of errors during the process. To prevent VB from having to deal with null values in the return parameters, we set these variables to zero. The `@Message` variable gets set to an empty string by using two single quotes, as this variable is a `VarChar` data type:

```
--
-- Set default values
--
SELECT @Address_ID = 0
SELECT @Phone_Number_ID = 0
SELECT @Message = ''
```

The first validation that we perform is to check whether the first line of the street address is present. This is a *required* column in the table and we must ensure we have data in the parameter. We perform two checks, the first of which is to ensure that a null value was not passed for the address. This is accomplished through the use of the `IS NULL` function. The second validation that we perform is to check for a zero length string. A zero length string is a string variable that contains no data but is not set to `Null`.

Notice that we are using an `IF ELSE` statement without the `ELSE` keyword. Also notice that all SQL statements for this `IF` statement are enclosed in the `BEGIN` and `END` blocks.

If the validation fails, we insert a message into the `@Message` variable by using the `SELECT` statement. We also set our variable to zero to let us know whether to continue processing. We still perform the rest of the data validations but we do not insert any data into the tables.

Notice the heavy use of comments thus far. It helps to make the code easier to read and understand, and will definitely help later on should we have to come back and revisit this stored procedure.

```
--
*****************************************************************************
-- Validate street address 1 exists
--
*****************************************************************************
--
-- Ensure address is not null or empty
--
IF @Street_Address1 IS NULL OR DATALENGTH(LTRIM(@Street_Address1)) = 0
   BEGIN
   SELECT @Message = 'Street address line 1 is required. '
   SELECT @Continue = 0
   END
```

When a user chooses to insert data into the Address table, we have no way of knowing ahead of time whether they are inserting a *new* city name or using the primary key of an *existing* city. To handle this, our stored procedure accepts both, and validates the `@City_ID` first. If the `@City_ID` parameter is null or contains a zero then we know that the primary key of a city is not being used and we will be inserting a new city name.

We are using an `IF ELSE` statement to validate whether or not the `@City_ID` parameter will be used. To control the flow of logic to determine whether or not we should validate the city name, we are using a variable named `@Name_Required`:

```
--
*****************************************************************************
-- Validate city id or city name exists
--
*****************************************************************************
--
-- Check city id first
--
IF @City_ID IS NULL OR @City_ID = 0
   BEGIN
   --
   -- City name is required
   --
   SELECT @Name_Required = 1
   END
```

```
ELSE
   BEGIN
   --
   -- City name is not required
   --
   SELECT @Name_Required = 0
   END
```

If the `@Name_Required` variable is true, indicated by a value of 1, then we validate the city name to ensure that it is present and that it does not contain a null value or a zero length string.

In order to return all messages from the validation portion of our stored procedure code, we need to concatenate the messages in the `@Message` output parameter. In VB we have the option of using the ampersand (&) character or the plus sign (+) character. In SQL Server we can only use the plus sign (+) character to concatenate data. This works well as long as you are not using variables that are numeric data types. In those cases you need to use the `CAST` function to change the data type when you concatenate. If you concatenate two numeric variables, for example 5 + 3, SQL Server will actually add the values (giving the result of 8) instead of concatenating one to the other (which would result in 53).

In this example we are simply concatenating `VarChar` data types.

```
--
-- If @Name_Required = 1 then the city name is required
--
IF @Name_Required = 1
   BEGIN
   --
   -- Ensure city name is not null or empty
   --
   IF @City_Name IS NULL OR DATALENGTH(LTRIM(@City_Name)) = 0
      BEGIN
      SELECT @Message = @Message + 'City name or city id is required. '
      SELECT @Continue = 0
      END
   END
```

Since we have loaded our State table, we will not allow new state names to be added, because the `State_T` table already contains all of the states. For this validation we need only validate the `@State_ID` parameter to ensure that it is not null or equal to zero:

```
--
***********************************************************************************
-- Validate state id exists
--
***********************************************************************************
IF @State_ID IS NULL OR @State_ID = 0
   BEGIN
   SELECT @Message = @Message + 'State id is required. '
   SELECT @Continue = 0
   END
```

The zip code validation is performed in the same manner as the city validation and will not be explained further:

```
--
***********************************************************************************
-- Validate zip code id or zip code exists
--
***********************************************************************************
--
-- Check zip code id first
--
IF @Zip_Code_ID IS NULL OR @Zip_Code_ID = 0
   BEGIN
   --
   -- Zip code is required
   --
   SELECT @Name_Required = 1
   END
ELSE
   BEGIN
   --
   -- Zip code is not required
   --
   SELECT @Name_Required = 0
   END

--
-- If @Name_Required = 1 then the zip code is required
--
IF @Name_Required = 1
   BEGIN
   --
   -- Ensure zip code is not null or empty
   --
   IF @Zip_Code IS NULL OR DATALENGTH(LTRIM(@Zip_Code)) = 0
      BEGIN
      SELECT @Message = @Message + 'Zip code or zip code id is required. '
      SELECT @Continue = 0
      END
   END
```

There are two validations that we need to perform on the area code and phone number. First we validate the `@Area_Code` parameter to ensure that it is not null and that it does not contain a zero:

```
--
***********************************************************************************
-- Validate area code and phone number
***********************************************************************************
```

```
--
-- Validate area code is not null or zero
--
IF @Area_Code IS NULL OR @Area_Code = 0
   BEGIN
   SELECT @Message = @Message + 'Area code is a required field. '
   SELECT @Continue = 0
   END
```

Second, we validate the length of the `@Area_Code` parameter, using the `DATALENGTH` function, to ensure that it contains only three digits. In order to perform this test, we must first `CAST` the parameter from a `SmallInt` data type to a `VarChar` data type. Since a `SmallInt` data type can contain up to five digits we are using a `VarChar(5)` data type in our `CAST` function. We then check to see if the parameter contains just three digits. If not, we add a message to the `@Message` output parameter and set our `@Continue` variable to zero, which indicates that, after the validations have been completed, we will return to the caller without inserting any data:

```
--
-- Validate area code is three digits
--
IF DATALENGTH(CAST(@Area_Code AS VarChar(5))) <> 3
   BEGIN
   SELECT @Message = @Message + 'Area code is not valid. '
   SELECT @Continue = 0
   END
```

The same validations that we performed for the area code apply for the phone number. The difference here is that the `@Phone_Number` parameter is an `Integer` data type which can contain up to 10 digits, so we use a `Varchar(10)` data type in our `CAST` function:

```
--
-- Validate phone number is not null or zero
--
IF @Phone_Number IS NULL OR @Phone_Number = 0
   BEGIN
   SELECT @Message = @Message + 'Phone number is a required field. '
   SELECT @Continue = 0
   END
--
-- Validate phone number is seven digits
--
IF DATALENGTH(CAST(@Phone_Number AS VarChar(10))) <> 7
   BEGIN
   SELECT @Message = @Message + 'Phone number is not valid. '
   SELECT @Continue = 0
   END
```

After all data has been validated we check to see if our `@Continue` variable is set to zero, which would indicate that there were validation errors and we cannot proceed with the inserts. In this case we simply end by returning to the caller with a return code of 1. In a previous discussion about the `RETURN` function, we mentioned that `RETURN` is immediate. That is, no SQL statements are executed after a `RETURN` statement is executed.

```
--
***********************************************************************************
-- All data has been validated, we either continue processing or return to the
-- caller with a bad return code and the messages
--
***********************************************************************************
IF @Continue = 0
   BEGIN
   --
   -- Return to the caller with a bad return code
   -- The messages are in the @message output parameter
   --
   RETURN 1
   END
```

If all validation tests passed we find ourselves here – ready to determine whether or not to insert a new city name, or if the key to an existing city was passed. We determine this by checking the `@City_ID` parameter that was passed to see if it is null or equal to zero. If it is then we know that we need to insert a city name:

```
ELSE
   BEGIN
   --
   -- Continue processing
   --
   --
*********************************************************************************
   -- Insert the city name if city id is null or zero
   --
*********************************************************************************
   IF @City_ID IS NULL OR @City_ID = 0
```

We go ahead and insert the new city name into the `City_T` table using the `INSERT` statement, which you are already familiar with. We need to save the `identity` value that was just inserted, so we use the `@@Identity` function and place the value in the `@City_ID` parameter for use later when we insert our address:

```
      BEGIN
      --
      -- Insert the city
      --
      INSERT INTO City_T
         (City_Name_VC, Last_Update_DT)
         VALUES(@City_Name, GETDATE())
      --
      -- Get the city id that was just inserted
      --
      SELECT @City_ID = @@Identity
      END
```

We perform the same test for the zip code that we performed for the city, and insert a new zip code if necessary. We then save the identity value for later use:

```
--
***************************************************************************************
-- Insert the zip code if zip code id is null or zero
--
***************************************************************************************
IF @Zip_Code_ID IS NULL OR @Zip_Code_ID = 0
   BEGIN
   --
   -- Insert the zip code
   --
   INSERT INTO Zip_Code_T
      (Zip_Code_CH, Last_Update_DT)
      VALUES(@Zip_Code, GETDATE())
   --
   -- Get the zip code id that was just inserted
   --
   SELECT @Zip_Code_ID = @@Identity
   END
```

We then insert the area code and phone number and save the identity value in the output parameter `@Phone_Number_ID`:

```
--
***************************************************************************************
-- Insert the area code and phone number
--
***************************************************************************************
INSERT INTO Phone_Number_T
   (Area_Code_SI, Phone_Number_IN, Last_Update_DT)
   VALUES(@Area_Code, @Phone_Number, GETDATE())
--
-- Get the phone number id that was just inserted
--
SELECT @Phone_Number_ID = @@Identity
```

If the second and third lines of the address contain no data, we want to convert them to null values. Otherwise when we insert them they will be inserted with a blank space, and will just end up wasting space in our database. We do this by checking to see if the lengths of the address parameters are zero. If they are, we simply `SELECT` a null value into the parameters:

```
--
***************************************************************************************
-- Before inserting the address convert the second and third street address
-- lines to null if they contain no data
--
***************************************************************************************
```

```
    IF DATALENGTH(LTRIM(@Street_Address2)) = 0
       BEGIN
       --
       -- Convert it to null
       --
       SELECT @Street_Address2 = NULL
       END
    IF DATALENGTH(LTRIM(@Street_Address3)) = 0
       BEGIN
       --
       -- Convert it to null
       --
       SELECT @Street_Address3 = NULL
       END
```

As we come to the end of our stored procedure, we are using values that were passed as parameters and values from the `INSERT` statements that preceded this one. Here we insert the address information into the `Address_T` table, which partly consists of the primary keys to the City, State, and Zip Code tables, which are foreign keys in the `Address_T` table.

After we insert the data into the Address table, we get the `identity` value that was inserted and place it into the `@Address_ID` output parameter. We then return to the caller with a zero return code:

```
   --
********************************************************************************
   -- Now insert the address
   --
********************************************************************************
   INSERT INTO Address_t
      (City_ID, State_ID, Zip_Code_ID, Street_Address_1_VC, Street_Address_2_VC,
         Street_Address_3_VC, Last_Update_DT)
      VALUES(@City_ID, @State_ID, @Zip_Code_ID, @Street_Address1,
         @Street_Address2, @Street_Address3, GETDATE())
   --
   -- Get the address id just inserted
   --
   Select @Address_ID = @@Identity

   --
********************************************************************************
   -- Return to the caller with a successful return code
   --
********************************************************************************
   RETURN 0
   END
```

When you try to execute your query to create this stored procedure for the first time, you may encounter some errors due to typing mistakes. The figure below shows an error that I encountered:

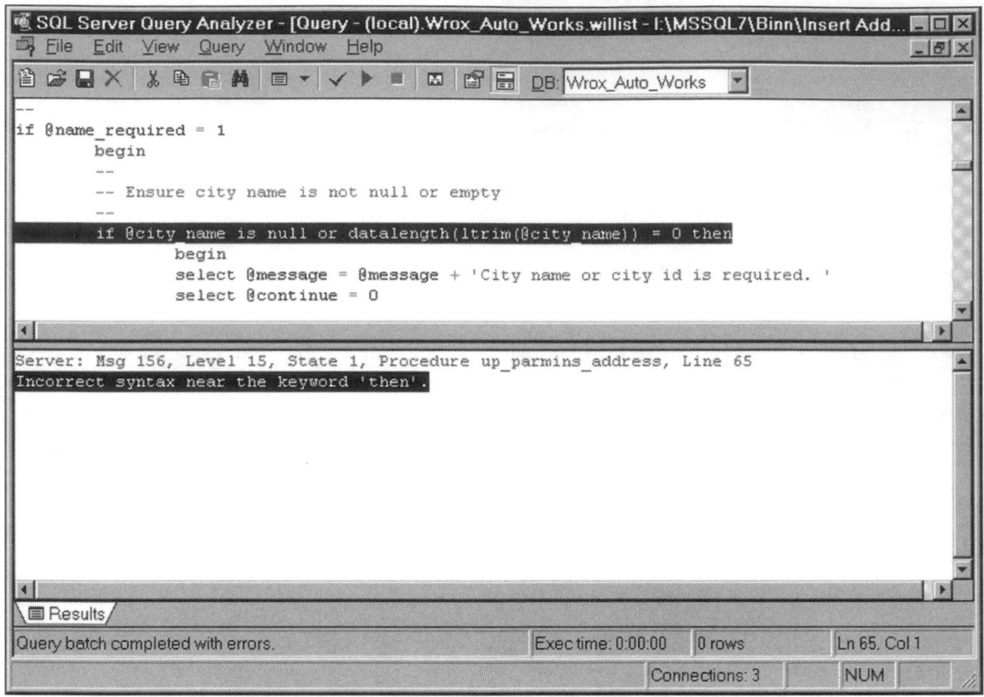

Even as someone who is experienced at writing stored procedures I sometimes make mistakes. I had just finished writing some VB code when I started writing this stored procedure. I got so wrapped up in coding this stored procedure that I coded the `THEN` keyword after my `IF` statement. Of course this is fine in VB but does not work in SQL Server, as we mentioned earlier.

Remember our discussion on debugging from Chapter 5? Well that knowledge will definitely come in handy in this chapter and the subsequent chapters as we write more complex stored procedures. All you need to do is double click on the error message and the offending code will be highlighted, as shown above. Correct the error and then try to execute the query again.

Notes of Interest

It is up to the calling program to retrieve the return code and output parameters returned by this stored procedure. You can use the VB `Split` function to separate the individual messages in the `@Message` output parameter, because all messages end with a period. The VB `Split` function accepts a string expression and the delimiter, and splits the string into a one-dimensional array. We see how to retrieve the output parameters later in this chapter, when we code our VB program that calls this stored procedure and the other ones that we are going to create.

There is great controversy over whether or not to place the business logic in a stored procedure or in some n-tier component. This mostly depends of the type of processing being performed and your application's requirements, as well as your shop's standards.

One thing we do know, now that we have created this stored procedure, is that if some component or front-end program fails to validate data before calling this stored procedure, we won't end up corrupting our database with bad data. We can't validate the *validity* of the data but we can validate that the data meets our standards, such as area code and phone number lengths. In other words we can not determine if the data being passed is valid for a specific column, such as phone number, but we can validate that the phone number meets the correct length and data type specifications.

Coding this stored procedure, you have gained the knowledge of how to control the flow of logic within stored procedures, and how to use some of the functions in SQL Server to validate data. We have also made extensive use of output parameters to pass data back to the calling program, and we will see how this works on the VB side later in this chapter.

We are now ready to move on and learn about other functions that SQL Server provides to help make our stored procedures more robust.

Stored Procedures that Use Transactions

SQL Server provides **concurrency**, which means that it does not allow a user to update or delete the same data that another user is working on. Nothing needs to be done to reap the benefits of concurrency – SQL Server provides this automatically. This works well when the data we are working on only exists in one table, but what if we need to work with data in multiple tables? Then we must use SQL Server **transactions**.

A transaction is considered a single logical unit of work and contains many SQL statements that perform operations against multiple tables. A logical unit of work must exhibit four properties known as **ACID** (**Atomicity**, **Consistency, Isolation**, and **Durability**).

Atomicity is a term used to ensure that all transactions are complete as a *group*. That is, if you insert, update, or delete data in one table and move on to insert, update, or delete data in another table, and that function fails, then the entire transaction is backed out. In other words, the changes to the first table are not committed to the database. This helps to ensure the integrity of your data. SQL Server and **Microsoft Transaction Server** (**MTS**) both provide transactional support that provides atomicity. For now we will discuss the transactional support provided by SQL Server and will discuss MTS in Chapter 14.

> ***Consistency** is when a transaction completes and leaves the data in a consistent state. **Isolation** is when a transaction isolates the modifications made from other transactions. **Durability** is when the changes made by a transaction are made a permanent part of the system when the transaction completes.*

In order to use transactions you must explicitly start and end a transaction. If anything goes wrong in your processing you must decide whether or not you want to **commit** the work done thus far or **rollback** the work. To start a transaction you specify the keywords `BEGIN TRANSACTION` and can specify a transaction name. A transaction name can be up to 255 characters in length, but only the first 32 characters are actually used. This should be kept in mind if you are coding a stored procedure that contains multiple transactions – make sure that each transaction is named uniquely within the first 32 characters. The following code fragment shows a transaction being started:

```
BEGIN TRANSACTION Update_Customer_Data
```

After a transaction has begun, we perform all of our inserts, updates, and deletes to as many tables as we need. If we encounter an error, we usually want to abort all processing, in which case we need to ROLLBACK all work performed up to this point. A ROLLBACK will undo all data modifications back to when the transaction was started. If we want to ROLLBACK a transaction we use the code shown below:

```
ROLLBACK TRANSACTION Update_Customer_Data
```

The ROLLBACK will release any resources and **locks** held by the transaction. SQL Server uses locks automatically with transactions to ensure transactional integrity. A lock is an object used by SQL Server to secure resources held by one user, and does not allow other users to perform operations on the resource that would affect the user owning the lock. Locks are managed automatically by SQL Server and are acquired and released based on what action a user is performing.

After all processing has been performed we want to COMMIT the transaction, to have all changes permanently applied to the database. In this case we use the code below to COMMIT the transaction, and SQL Server will apply all changes to the database, releasing all resources and locks held by the transaction.

```
COMMIT TRANSACTION Update_Customer_Data
```

There are a lot more options for using transactions in SQL Server, but we have covered only the basics here to help get you started using transactions. Once you are familiar with how transactions work and are comfortable using them, you should read about transactions in the SQL Server Books Online to explore their full power. Wrox Press offers a book titled 'Professional SQL Server 7 Programming' (ISBN 1-861002-31-9) which covers transactions in depth.

Checking for Errors

In VB we can check the Error object to determine what was the last error number recorded by VB. SQL Server provides similar functionality in the @@ERROR function. The @@ERROR function gets set to the error number after every SQL statement executes. If no error occurred then the @@ERROR function gets set to zero. This will happen for *every* SQL statement executed. Therefore, if you want to check for an error you must do so immediately after the SQL statement, or else save the value of the @@ERROR function to a variable and check it later. Let's see how this function works by examining the code fragment below:

```
INSERT INTO City_T
   (City_Name_VC, Last_Update_DT)
   VALUES(0, GETDATE())
IF @@ERROR <> 0
   . . .
```

The code above would cause an error because we are trying to insert a numeric value into a VarChar data type column. We are checking the @@ERROR function to see if the last SQL statement returned anything other than a zero. As you can see, we can use the @@ERROR function to help us to determine whether or not a transaction should be aborted and rolled back, or if we should continue processing.

Another function provided by SQL Server is the `RAISERROR` function. This function lets us raise our own custom errors and pass back custom error messages to the calling program. The `RAISERROR` function has many parameters but we are going to use just a subset so as not to complicate things too much. We are going to be using a message string that will be passed back to the caller, as well as a user-defined severity level, and the state of the error. The severity level indicates how severe an error is. SQL Server passes the error message to ADO and you can see this error message in the `Description` property of the `Errors` collection. Let's take a look at the following code fragment:

```
RAISERROR('Insert for current employer phone number failed.',18,1)
```

As you can see, the first parameter that we have passed to the `RAISERROR` method is the error **message** itself. The second parameter is the user-defined **severity level**, which can be from 0 to 18. We have chosen to use `18` as the severity level of this message. The last parameter that we have specified is the **state** of the error and we have set this value to `1`. The available range for this parameter is 1 to 127. A unique state code is assigned in each place an error is raised. Microsoft support engineers can use the state code from an error to find the location in the source code where that error code is being raised.

As with transactions, the `RAISERROR` method is pretty robust and we are using just the basics of this function here. Once you are comfortable using this function, you should explore the SQL Server Books Online to get a full understanding of the `RAISERROR` function, and learn how to increase the effectiveness of your own stored procedures by using its full potential.

Once again we are armed with enough information about these new functions to move on and create a stored procedure that implements them.

Try It Out – Stored Procedure that Uses Transactions

The stored procedure that we want to create should insert new employer information into the `Employer_T` table, and their associated phone number into the `Phone_Number_T` table. Once all employer information has been inserted, the primary keys for the employers, along with their related data, will be inserted into the `Customer_Information_T` table.

We will once again be returning an output parameter containing any error messages, and also an output parameter containing the identity value that was inserted into the `Customer_Information_T` table.

Like the last stored procedure, this stored procedure should also validate all data before attempting to insert any data. We are also going to use a transaction in this stored procedure so that if any part of this stored procedure fails, all changes will be rolled back.

1. Create the `up_parmins_employer_information` stored procedure using the code listed in the following *How It Works* section. This code is also available in the download files.

2. Again, don't forget to set the permissions on this stored procedure so that only the Developers and Sales Staff roles can execute it.

How It Works – Stored Procedure that Uses Transactions

As with the last stored procedure that we created, we list all of the input and output parameters first. Notice the various data types that we are using here:

```
CREATE PROCEDURE up_parmins_employer_information (@Current_Employer_ID Int,
   @Current_Employer_Name VarChar(30), @Current_Employer_Area_Code SmallInt,
   @Current_Employer_Phone_Number Int, @Years_At_Current_Employer TinyInt,
   @Job_Title VarChar(30), @Previous_Employer_ID Int,
   @Previous_Employer_Name VarChar(30), @Previous_Employer_Area_Code SmallInt,
   @Previous_Employer_Phone_Number Int, @Years_At_Previous_Employer TinyInt,
   @Customer_Information_ID Int OUTPUT, @Message VarChar(300) OUTPUT) AS
```

We declare the variables that we will be using in this stored procedure, and also set the default values for the ones that will be used to control the flow of logic within our stored procedure:

```
--
*******************************************************************************************
-- Declare variables
--
*******************************************************************************************
DECLARE @Continue                                    Bit,
   @Name_Required                                    Bit,
   @Current_Employer_Phone_Number_ID      Int,
   @Previous_Employer_Phone_Number_ID          Int

--
-- Turn on default value to continue
--
SELECT @Continue = 1

--
-- Set default values
--
SELECT @Customer_Information_ID = 0
SELECT @Message = ''
```

The validation routines in this stored procedure are very similar to the ones used in the previous stored procedure and we do not need to cover them again:

```
--
*******************************************************************************************
-- Validate current employer id or current employer name exists
--
*******************************************************************************************
--
-- Check current employer id first
--
```

```
IF @Current_Employer_ID IS NULL OR @Current_Employer_ID = 0
   BEGIN
   --
   -- Current employer name is required
   --
   SELECT @Name_Required = 1
   END
ELSE
   BEGIN
   --
   -- Current employer name is not required
   --
   SELECT @Name_Required = 0
   END

--
-- If @Name_Required = 1 then the current employer name is required
--
IF @Name_Required = 1
   Begin
   --
   -- Ensure current employer name is not null or empty
   --
   IF @Current_Employer_Name IS NULL OR DATALENGTH(LTRIM(@Current_Employer_Name))
= 0
      BEGIN
      SELECT @Message = 'Current employer name or id is required. '
      SELECT @Continue = 0
      END
   END

--
*********************************************************************************
-- Validate current employer area code and phone number
--
*********************************************************************************
--
-- Validate area code is not null or zero
--
IF @Current_Employer_Area_Code IS NULL OR @Current_Employer_Area_Code = 0
   BEGIN
   SELECT @Message = @Message + 'Current employer area code is a required field. '
   SELECT @Continue = 0
   END
--
-- Validate area code is three digits (as US area codes are always 3 digits)
--
IF DATALENGTH(CAST(@Current_Employer_Area_Code AS VarChar(5))) <> 3
   BEGIN
   SELECT @Message = @Message + 'Current employer area code is not valid. '
   SELECT @CONTINUE = 0
   END
--
-- Validate phone number is not null or zero
--
```

```
IF @Current_Employer_Phone_Number IS NULL OR @Current_Employer_Phone_Number = 0
   Begin
   SELECT @Message = @Message + 'Current employer phone number is a required
field. '
   SELECT @Continue = 0
   END
--
-- Validate phone number is seven digits
--
IF DATALENGTH(CAST(@Current_Employer_Phone_Number AS VarChar(10))) <> 7
   BEGIN
   SELECT @Message = @Message + 'Current employer phone number is not valid. '
   SELECT @Continue = 0
   END

--
*********************************************************************************
-- Validate current employer years of employment
--
*********************************************************************************
--
-- Validate years is not null or zero
--
IF @Years_At_Current_Employer IS NULL OR @Years_At_Current_Employer = 0
   BEGIN
   SELECT @Message = @Message + 'Years at current employer is required. '
   SELECT @Continue = 0
   END
--
-- Validate years is within an acceptable range
--
IF @Years_At_Current_Employer > 50
   BEGIN
   SELECT @Message = @Message + 'Years at current employer is invalid. '
   SELECT @Continue = 0
   END

--
*********************************************************************************
-- Validate job title
--
*********************************************************************************
IF @Job_Title IS NULL OR DATALENGTH(LTRIM(@job_title)) = 0
   BEGIN
   SELECT @Message = @Message + 'Job title is required. '
   SELECT @Continue = 0
   END
```

The validations for the previous employer are very similar to those for the existing employer:

```
--
*******************************************************************************
-- Validate previous employer id or previous employer name exists
--
*******************************************************************************
--
-- If either previous employer id or name exists, perform the validations
--
IF @Previous_Employer_ID  > 0 OR DATALENGTH(LTRIM(@Previous_Employer_Name)) > 0

   BEGIN
   --
   -- Check previous employer id first
   --
   IF @Previous_Employer_ID IS NULL OR @Previous_Employer_ID = 0
      BEGIN
      --
      -- Previous employer name is required
      --
      SELECT @Name_Required = 1
      END
   ELSE
      BEGIN
      --
      -- Previous employer name is not required
      --
      SELECT @Name_Required = 0
      END

   --
   -- If @Name_Required = 1 then the previous employer name is required
   --
   IF @Name_Required = 1
      BEGIN
      --
      -- Ensure previous employer name is not null or empty
      --
      IF @Previous_Employer_Name IS NULL OR
         DATALENGTH(LTRIM(@Previous_Employer_Name)) = 0
         BEGIN
         SELECT @Message = @Message +
            'Previous employer name or id has been specified but ' +
            'is not valid. '
         SELECT @Continue = 0
         END
      END

   --
*******************************************************************************
   -- Validate previous employer area code and phone number
   --
*******************************************************************************
```

```
   --
   -- Validate area code is not null or zero
   --
   IF @Previous_Employer_Area_Code IS NULL OR @Previous_Employer_Area_Code = 0
      BEGIN
      SELECT @Message = @Message + 'Previous employer area code is a required ' +
         'field when a previous employer has been specified. '
      SELECT @Continue = 0
      END
   --
   -- Validate area code is three digits
   --
   IF DATALENGTH(CAST(@Previous_Employer_Area_Code AS VarChar(5))) <> 3
      BEGIN
      SELECT @Message = @Message + 'Previous employer area code is not valid. '
      SELECT @Continue = 0
      END
   --
   -- Validate phone number is not null or zero
   --
   IF @Previous_Employer_Phone_Number IS NULL OR @Previous_Employer_Phone_Number =
0
      BEGIN
      SELECT @Message = @Message + 'Previous employer phone number is a ' +
         'required field when a previous employer has been specified. '
      SELECT @Continue = 0
      End
   --
   -- Validate phone number is seven digits
   --
   IF DATALENGTH(CAST(@Previous_Employer_Phone_Number AS VarChar(10))) <> 7
      BEGIN
      SELECT @Message = @Message + 'Previous employer phone number is not valid. '
      SELECT @Continue = 0
      END
   --
********************************************************************************
   -- Validate previous employer years of employment
   --
********************************************************************************
   --
   -- Validate years is not null or zero
   --
   IF @Years_At_Previous_Employer IS NULL OR @Years_At_Previous_Employer = 0
      BEGIN
      SELECT @Message = @Message + 'Years at previous employer is required ' +
         'when a previous employer has been specified. '
      SELECT @Continue = 0
      END
   --
   -- Validate years is within an acceptable range
   --
   IF @Years_At_Previous_Employer > 50
      BEGIN
      SELECT @Message = @Message + 'Years at previous employer is invalid. '
      SELECT @Continue = 0
      END
   END
```

We want to take a detailed look at this stored procedure after all validations have been processed. If the validations failed, then we return to the caller with a return code of 1, and the caller can retrieve the messages in the `@Message` output parameter:

```
--
*****************************************************************************
-- All data has been validated, either return to the caller with a bad return code
-- and messages or continue on and insert the values
--
*****************************************************************************
IF @Continue = 0
   BEGIN
   --
   -- Return to the caller with a bad return code
   -- The messages are in the @message output parameter
   --
   RETURN 1
   END
```

If data validations have been successful we start a transaction so that, if any insert fails, all inserts will be rolled back. In this way we maintain data integrity on our database:

```
ELSE
   BEGIN
   --
*****************************************************************************
   -- Start a transaction, if any code fails then we back out everything
   --
*****************************************************************************
   BEGIN TRANSACTION Employer_Information
```

We first determine if we are using an existing employer or inserting a new one. This is the same type of check that we performed for the city and zip code in the last stored procedure. If we are inserting a new employer, we insert their phone number first, as the phone number is required as a foreign key for the employer information.

```
   --
*****************************************************************************
   -- Determine if we are using an existing employer or inserting a new one
   --
*****************************************************************************
   IF @Current_Employer_ID IS NULL OR @Current_Employer_ID = 0
      BEGIN
      --
      -- We are inserting a new current employer
      --
      -- **********************************************************************
      -- Insert the current employer phone number
      -- **********************************************************************
```

```
INSERT INTO Phone_Number_T
   (Area_Code_SI, Phone_Number_IN, Last_Update_DT)
   VALUES(@Current_Employer_Area_Code,
      @Current_Employer_Phone_Number, GETDATE())
```

After we insert the phone number we check for errors by using the `@@ERROR` function. Here we are checking to see if an error number other than zero was returned, which would indicate that an error occurred.

If an error occurred, we rollback the transaction using the `ROLLBACK TRANSACTION` function, and then raise a user-defined error message and return to the caller with an arbitrary return code of 99. The error message that we raise here will be placed in the ADO `Errors` collection, which will be available to the calling program.

```
--
-- Check for errors
--
IF @@ERROR <> 0
   BEGIN
   --
   -- ROLLBACK the transaction and return to the caller
   --
   ROLLBACK TRANSACTION Employer_Information
   RAISERROR('Insert for current employer phone number failed.',18,1)
   RETURN 99
   END
```

If no errors occurred then we save the identity value that was inserted into the `Phone_Number_T` table for use in the next `INSERT` statement:

```
--
-- Get the phone number id just inserted
--
SELECT @Current_Employer_Phone_Number_ID = @@Identity
```

The next insert that we perform is to insert the data for the current employer into the `Employer_T` table. We are using the input parameters passed to the stored procedure, and also the identity value that we saved in the previous statement:

```
-- ************************************************************************
-- Insert the current employer
-- ************************************************************************
INSERT INTO Employer_T
   (Phone_Number_ID, Company_Name_VC, Last_Update_DT)
   VALUES(@Current_Employer_Phone_Number_ID, @Current_Employer_Name,
      GETDATE())
```

We again check for errors and, if an error occurred, the previous INSERT statement that inserted the phone number will be rolled back when we execute the ROLLBACK TRANSACTION function:

```
   --
   -- Check for errors
   --
   IF @@ERROR <> 0
      BEGIN
      --
      -- ROLLBACK the transaction and return to the caller
      --
      ROLLBACK TRANSACTION Employer_Information
      RAISERROR('Insert for current employer failed.',18,1)
      RETURN 99
      END
```

Once again we save the identity value that was inserted, for use later:

```
   --
   -- Get the employer id just inserted
   --
   SELECT @Current_Employer_ID = @@Identity
   END
```

We perform the same steps for the previous employer that we performed for the current employer. First we check to see if a previous employer was passed, as this information is optional. We do this by first checking to see if the @Previous_Employer_ID is null or zero and then checking the length of the @Previous_Employer_Name parameter. If the @Previous_Employer_Name parameter contains data then we insert the new previous employer:

```
   --
***************************************************************************
   -- Determine if previous employer information exists
   --
***************************************************************************
   --
   -- If previous employer id is null or zero check the previous employer name
   --
   IF @Previous_Employer_ID IS NULL OR @Previous_Employer_ID = 0

      BEGIN
      -- ************************************************************************
      -- Determine if data exists to insert a new employer
      -- ************************************************************************
      IF DATALENGTH(LTRIM(@Previous_Employer_Name)) > 0
         BEGIN
         -- ***************************************************************
         -- Insert the previous employer phone number
         -- ***************************************************************
```

```
INSERT INTO Phone_Number_T
   (Area_Code_SI, Phone_Number_IN, Last_Update_DT)
   VALUES(@Previous_Employer_Area_Code,
      @Previous_Employer_Phone_Number, GETDATE())

--
-- Check for errors
--
IF @@ERROR <> 0
   BEGIN
   --
   -- ROLLBACK the transaction and return to the caller
   --
   ROLLBACK TRANSACTION Employer_Information
   RAISERROR('Insert for previous employer phone number failed.',
      18,1)
   RETURN 99
   END

--
-- Get the phone number id just inserted
--
SELECT @Previous_Employer_Phone_Number_ID = @@Identity

-- ***************************************************************
-- Insert the previous employer
-- ***************************************************************
INSERT INTO Employer_T
   (Phone_Number_ID, Company_Name_VC, Last_Update_DT)
   VALUES(@Previous_Employer_Phone_Number_ID,
      @Previous_Employer_Name, GETDATE())

--
-- Check for errors
--
IF @@ERROR <> 0
   BEGIN
   --
   -- ROLLBACK the transaction and return to the caller
   --
   ROLLBACK TRANSACTION Employer_Information
   RAISERROR('Insert for previous employer failed.',18,1)
   RETURN 99
   END

--
-- Get the employer id just inserted
--
SELECT @Previous_Employer_ID = @@Identity
END
```

If no previous employer exists then we set those parameters to null, so we don't encounter any errors when we insert those values into the `Customer_Information_T` table. If they were set to zero then we would get a foreign key constraint error, because an employer with a primary key of zero does not exist in the `Employer_T` table.

```
        Else

            BEGIN
            --
            -- No previous employment exists, ensure all values are null
            --
            SELECT @Previous_Employer_ID = NULL
            SELECT @Years_At_Previous_Employer = NULL
            END
        END
```

The last `INSERT` statement in our stored procedure inserts data into the `Customer_Information_T` table. The input parameters, as well as the `identity` values from the other inserts, are used as input values to this `INSERT` statement. After the insert we once again check for errors and rollback all other inserts if this one failed:

```
    --
******************************************************************************
    -- Now insert the all employment data into the customer information table
    --
******************************************************************************
    INSERT INTO Customer_Information_T
        (Employer_ID, Years_At_This_Employer_TI, Previous_Employer_ID,
            Years_At_Previous_Employer_TI, Job_Title_VC, Last_Update_DT)
        VALUES(@Current_Employer_ID, @Years_At_Current_Employer,
            @Previous_Employer_ID, @Years_At_Previous_Employer, @Job_Title,
            GETDATE())

    --
    -- Check for errors
    --
    IF @@ERROR <> 0
        BEGIN
        --
        -- ROLLBACK the transaction and return to the caller
        --
        ROLLBACK TRANSACTION Employer_Information
        RAISERROR('Insert of all employment information failed.',18,1)
        RETURN 99
        END
```

If the insert was successful, we save the identity value in the output parameter @Customer_Information_ID. We then commit our transaction, making all inserts a permanent part of the data in our database, by using the COMMIT TRANSACTION function. After that we return to the caller with a zero return code, indicating a successful transaction:

```
    --
    -- Get the employer id just inserted
    --
    SELECT @Customer_Information_ID = @@Identity

    --
*****************************************************************************
    -- We made it to the end so commit the transaction
    --
*****************************************************************************
    COMMIT TRANSACTION Employer_Information

    --
    -- End if statement block
    --
    END

  --
  -- Return to the caller with a successful return code
  --
  RETURN 0
```

Once again you may encounter errors when trying to execute your query to create this stored procedure, because of typing errors. Use the debugging techniques that you have learned to debug your query.

The Customer_T table requires three foreign keys, the first of which is for the customer's phone number. This foreign key was returned as an output parameter from the first stored procedure. The second foreign key is for the customer's address. This foreign key was also returned as an output parameter from the first stored procedure. The last foreign key that is required is for the customer information, which is returned as an output parameter from the stored procedure that we just created.

The combination of this stored procedure and the last one gives us all of the foreign key data that we need in order to insert a customer into the Customer_T table. All that is left to do is to code a stored procedure to insert the customer data.

At this point you have learned in this chapter all of the necessary skills to code this last stored procedure. While this next stored procedure is relatively small and simple, it should not be taken lightly. This last stored procedure completes the data needed to create a complete customer record. If the stored procedure that we create next fails to insert a customer record into the Customer_T table using the foreign keys from the Phone_Number_T, Address_T, and Customer_Information_T tables then you will have **orphan data** in the database. Orphaned data is when you have data in some tables that does not relate to any other table, and provides no use on its own.

Try It Out – Simple Insert Stored Procedure

As we mentioned above, this stored procedure will insert the foreign keys to the data in the other tables to complete the customer record. It also inserts the customer's name and spouse's name into the `Customer_T` table. Validation needs to be performed to ensure that the foreign keys and customer's name are present and valid.

1. Create the `up_parmins_customer` stored procedure using the code listed in the *How It Works* section below, and which is available in the download files.

2. Once again, don't forget to set the permissions on this stored procedure so that only the Developers and Sales Staff roles can execute it.

How It Works – Simple Insert Stored Procedure

As always, the first line of our stored procedure defines the stored procedure name, all of the parameters the stored procedure expects as input, and those it expects to return as output. We then declare our variables and there is only one this time. We then set the default value for our variable and start our processing:

```
CREATE PROCEDURE up_parmins_customer (@Address_ID Int, @Phone_Number_ID Int,
   @Customer_Information_ID Int, @First_Name VarChar(15), @Last_Name VarChar(15),
   @Spouse_Name VarChar(15), @Message VarChar(100) OUTPUT) AS

--
**********************************************************************************
-- Declare variables
--
**********************************************************************************
DECLARE @Continue   Bit

--
-- Turn on default value to continue
--
SELECT @Continue = 1
```

We need to validate that all three foreign keys were passed and that they are not null, or do not contain zeros:

```
--
**********************************************************************************
-- Validate required id parameters are present
--
**********************************************************************************
```

```
IF @Address_ID IS NULL OR @Address_ID = 0
   BEGIN
   SELECT @Message = 'Address id is required. '
   SELECT @Continue = 0
   END

IF @Phone_Number_ID IS NULL OR @Phone_Number_ID = 0
   BEGIN
   SELECT @Message = @message + 'Phone number id is required. '
   SELECT @Continue = 0
   END

IF @Customer_Information_ID IS NULL OR @Customer_Information_ID = 0
   BEGIN
   SELECT @Message = @Message + 'Customer information id is required. '
   SELECT @Continue = 0
   END
```

Since only the customer's first and last names are required, this is all we need to validate. We do not validate the spouse's name, as this column can contain null values:

```
--
*********************************************************************************
-- Validate required customer names are present
--
*********************************************************************************
IF @First_Name IS NULL OR DATALENGTH(LTRIM(@First_Name)) = 0
   BEGIN
   SELECT @Message = @Message + 'First name is required. '
   SELECT @Continue = 0
   END

IF @Last_Name IS NULL OR DATALENGTH(LTRIM(@Last_Name)) = 0
   BEGIN
   SELECT @Message = @Message + 'Last name is required. '
   SELECT @Continue = 0
   END
```

If any of the validations have failed, we return to the caller with a return code of 1. The messages are in the `@Message` output parameter:

```
--
*********************************************************************************
-- All data has been validated, either return to the caller with a bad return code
-- and messages or continue on and insert the values
--
*********************************************************************************
```

```
IF @Continue = 0
   BEGIN
   --
   -- Return to the caller with a bad return code
   -- The messages are in the @message output parameter
   --
   RETURN 1
   END
```

We check the spouse's name to see if it contains any data. If it does not then we set it to null to prevent it from taking up any space in our database:

```
ELSE
   BEGIN
   --
*******************************************************************************
   -- If spouse name is empty then convert it to null
   --
*******************************************************************************
   IF DATALENGTH(LTRIM(@Spouse_Name)) = 0
      BEGIN
      SELECT @Spouse_Name = NULL
      END
```

There is only one `INSERT` statement in this stored procedure, but it binds together all of the tables that make up the complete customer record, through the use of foreign keys. Here we are inserting all of the data in the `Customer_T` table. After the insert, we return to the caller with a zero return code:

```
   --
*******************************************************************************
   -- Insert the data into the customer table
   --
*******************************************************************************
   INSERT INTO Customer_T
      (Address_ID, Phone_Number_ID, Customer_Information_ID, First_Name_VC,
         Last_Name_VC, Spouse_First_Name_VC, Last_Update_DT)
      VALUES(@Address_ID, @Phone_Number_ID, @Customer_Information_ID,
         @First_Name, @Last_Name, @Spouse_Name, GETDATE())

   --
*******************************************************************************
   -- Return to the caller with a good return code
   --
*******************************************************************************
   RETURN 0
   END
```

As you can see, this stored procedure is very simple yet very important. Now that we have our stored procedures built, it's time to move on and complete this chapter by building the VB program that implements these stored procedures.

Try It Out – VB Program to use Insert Stored Procedures – Classes

1. The VB program that we want to build to execute all of the stored procedures will use the VB program from the last chapter as a base. Copy `frmTryItOut3.frm` and `frmTIO3Employer.frm` from the last chapter and name them `frmTryItOut4.frm` and `frmTIO4Employer.frm` respectively.

2. We also want to copy the three classes from the last chapter and use their current names (`clsAddress.cls`, `clsEmployer.cls` and `clsCustomer.cls`).

3. Then start a new Standard EXE project and set a reference to the Microsoft ActiveX Data Objects Library.

4. Remove `Form1.frm` from the project and add the new forms and three classes that you just copied. Set the `frmTryItOut4.frm` as the start up form in the Project Properties dialog.

5. Next we need to modify the classes. Add the new procedures, which are presented in the *How It Works* section, to each class (`clsAddress.cls, clsEmployer.cls, clsCustomer.cls`) changing the owner prefix as necessary.

How It Works – VB Program to Use Insert Stored Procedures – Address Class

We want to start by explaining the code that we must add to the Address class. This function accepts a lot of parameters, not all of which are input parameters to the stored procedure. All of the input parameters to the stored procedure are passed by *value* to this function. The output parameters in the stored procedure are passed to this function by *reference.* Just as a refresher, by value means that a copy of the actual data for a variable is passed to the function, and by reference means that a pointer to the variable is passed to the function. That is so we can modify the value of those parameters directly. We have also passed the `Connection` and `Command` objects by reference. This function returns a `Long` value indicating success or failure.

```
Public Function InsertAddress(ByVal strAddress1 As String, _
      ByVal strAddress2 As String, _
      ByVal strAddress3 As String, _
      ByVal lngCityID As Long, _
      ByVal strCityName As String, _
      ByVal lngStateID As Long, _
      ByVal lngZipCodeID As Long, _
      ByVal strZipCode As String, _
      ByVal intAreaCode As Integer, _
      ByVal lngPhoneNumber As Long, _
      ByRef lngAddressID As Long, _
      ByRef lngPhoneNumberID As Long, _
      ByRef strMessage() As String, _
      ByRef objConn As ADODB.Connection, _
      ByRef objCmd As ADODB.Command) As Long
```

The first thing we want to do is to set up our error handling and declare our local variables:

```
'Setup error handling
On Error GoTo InsertAddress_EH

'Declare local variables
Dim intIndex As Integer
```

Next we set the `Command` object properties by specifying the `ActiveConnection`, `CommandText`, and `CommandType`. You should be familiar with these by now. At this point you should be looking at the stored procedure name and wondering if you set the permissions on all of your stored procedures. If you didn't you will get an error when you try to execute it. You will also need to change the user prefix of your stored procedures to match *your* user prefix.

```
'Set the command object properties
Set objCmd.ActiveConnection = objConn
objCmd.CommandText = "willist.up_parmins_address"
objCmd.CommandType = adCmdStoredProc
```

Because our stored procedure returns a return value as well as output parameters, we must use the `Command` object and append the various parameters to the `Parameters` collection. Using the `Command` object addresses the issue of inserting names that contain single quotes. We don't have to worry about that because the `Command` object will take care of it for us.

When a return value is being returned from a stored procedure it must always be the first parameter in the `Parameters` collection. We have mentioned this before, but it is very important and worth mentioning again. Notice that the return value parameter and the output parameters do not have values assigned to them. We will retrieve this data from the `Parameters` collection after the stored procedure has executed.

```
'Append the parameters
objCmd.Parameters.Append objCmd.CreateParameter("RC", adInteger, _
        adParamReturnValue)
objCmd.Parameters.Append objCmd.CreateParameter("Address1", adVarChar, _
        adParamInput, 30, strAddress1)
objCmd.Parameters.Append objCmd.CreateParameter("Address2", adVarChar, _
        adParamInput, 30, strAddress2)
objCmd.Parameters.Append objCmd.CreateParameter("Address3", adVarChar, _
        adParamInput, 30, strAddress3)
objCmd.Parameters.Append objCmd.CreateParameter("CityID", adInteger, _
        adParamInput, , lngCityID)
objCmd.Parameters.Append objCmd.CreateParameter("CityName", adVarChar, _
        adParamInput, 30, strCityName)
objCmd.Parameters.Append objCmd.CreateParameter("StateID", adInteger, _
        adParamInput, , lngStateID)
objCmd.Parameters.Append objCmd.CreateParameter("ZipCodeID", adInteger, _
        adParamInput, , lngZipCodeID)
objCmd.Parameters.Append objCmd.CreateParameter("ZipCode", adChar, _
        adParamInput, 10, strZipCode)
```

```
objCmd.Parameters.Append objCmd.CreateParameter("AreaCode", adSmallInt, _
        adParamInput, , intAreaCode)
objCmd.Parameters.Append objCmd.CreateParameter("PhoneNumber", adInteger, _
        adParamInput, , lngPhoneNumber)
objCmd.Parameters.Append objCmd.CreateParameter("AddressID", _
        adInteger, adParamOutput)
objCmd.Parameters.Append objCmd.CreateParameter("PhoneNumberID", _
        adInteger, adParamOutput)
objCmd.Parameters.Append objCmd.CreateParameter("Message", adVarChar, _
        adParamOutput, 300)
```

After all parameters have been appended, we execute the `Command` object. We then check the return code from the stored procedure by querying the `RC` parameter in the `Parameters` collection, using the `Command` object. If it is not zero, then we re-dimension our message string and add the `@Message` output parameter to the message string:

```
'Execute the command object
objCmd.Execute

'If the return code is greater than zero
If objCmd("RC") <> 0 Then
   'Add the message to the message string
   ReDim Preserve strMessage(0)
   strMessage(0) = objCmd("Message")
End If
```

We retrieve the `AddressID` and `PhoneNumberID` output parameters from the `Parameters` collection and assign them to the variables that we passed by reference to this function. Then we return to the caller of this function with the return code from the stored procedure, and exit the function:

```
'Set the return parameters
lngAddressID = objCmd("AddressID")
lngPhoneNumberID = objCmd("PhoneNumberID")

'Return to the caller with the return code from the
'stored procedure
InsertAddress = objCmd("RC")
On Error GoTo 0
Exit Function
```

The error handling that we are using this time is a little different to what we have used in the past. This function accepts a string array by reference that will be used to write all messages to. Here we are looping through the `Errors` collection and writing each message to the string array. In order to do this we must re-dimension the string array each time we want to add a message.

Just in case there is an associated error message in the VB `Error` object, we add that error message also, and then we return to the caller with an arbitrary return code of 99 which indicates that errors have occurred:

```
InsertAddress_EH:
   Dim objErr As ADODB.Error
   intIndex = -1
   'Add each ADO error to the message string
   For Each objErr In objConn.Errors
      intIndex = intIndex + 1
      ReDim Preserve strMessage(intIndex)
      strMessage(intIndex) = objErr.Description
   Next
   'Add any VB error message to the message string
   intIndex = intIndex + 1
   ReDim Preserve strMessage(intIndex)
   strMessage(intIndex) = Err.Description
   'Return to the caller
   InsertAddress = 99
   On Error GoTo 0
End Function
```

Employer Class

The function to insert employer information in the Employer class also accepts a lot of parameters. Like the function in the Address class, this function accepts all parameters that are input to the stored procedure by value. The stored procedure output parameters are passed by reference to this class. Take notice of the various data types that we are using here.

If you need to, refer to Appendix A to refresh your memory about the differences between VB and SQL Server data types.

```
Public Function InsertEmployer(ByVal lngCurrentEmployerID As Long, _
      ByVal strCurrentEmployerName As String, _
      ByVal intCurrentEmployerAreaCode As Integer, _
      ByVal lngCurrentEmployerPhoneNumber As Long, _
      ByVal bytYearsAtCurrentEmployer As Byte, _
      ByVal strJobTitle As String, _
      ByVal lngPreviousEmployerID As Long, _
      ByVal strPreviousEmployerName As String, _
      ByVal intPreviousEmployerAreaCode As Integer, _
      ByVal lngPreviousEmployerPhoneNumber As Long, _
      ByVal bytYearsAtPreviousEmployer As Byte, _
      ByRef lngCustomerInformationID As Long, _
      ByRef strMessage() As String, _
      ByRef objConn As ADODB.Connection, _
      ByRef objCmd As ADODB.Command) As Long
```

The first thing that we do in our function is to set up our error handling and declare our local variables. Then we set the properties for the `Command` object:

```
    'Setup error handling
    On Error GoTo InsertEmployer_EH

    'Declare local variables
    Dim intIndex As Integer

    'Set the command object properties
    Set objCmd.ActiveConnection = objConn
    objCmd.CommandText = "willist.up_parmins_employer_information"
    objCmd.CommandType = adCmdStoredProc
```

Then we append all of the parameters to the `Parameters` collection as we did in the last function. Take note of the various data types that we are using. If you get an error about a wrong data type being passed, you probably specified the wrong data type in the parameter, and this should be the first thing you check.

```
    'Append the parameters
    objCmd.Parameters.Append objCmd.CreateParameter("RC", adInteger, _
            adParamReturnValue)
    objCmd.Parameters.Append objCmd.CreateParameter("CurrentEmployerID", adInteger, _
            adParamInput, , lngCurrentEmployerID)
    objCmd.Parameters.Append objCmd.CreateParameter("CurrentEmployerName", adVarChar, _
            adParamInput, 30, strCurrentEmployerName)
    objCmd.Parameters.Append objCmd.CreateParameter("CurrentEmployerAreaCode", _
            adSmallInt, adParamInput, , intCurrentEmployerAreaCode)
    objCmd.Parameters.Append objCmd.CreateParameter("CurrentEmployerPhoneNumber", _
            adInteger, adParamInput, , lngCurrentEmployerPhoneNumber)
    objCmd.Parameters.Append objCmd.CreateParameter("YearsAtCurrentEmployer", _
            adTinyInt, adParamInput, , bytYearsAtCurrentEmployer)
    objCmd.Parameters.Append objCmd.CreateParameter("JobTitle", adVarChar, _
            adParamInput, 30, strJobTitle)
    objCmd.Parameters.Append objCmd.CreateParameter("PreviousEmployerID", adInteger, _
            adParamInput, , lngPreviousEmployerID)
    objCmd.Parameters.Append objCmd.CreateParameter("PreviousEmployerName", _
            adVarChar, adParamInput, 30, strPreviousEmployerName)
    objCmd.Parameters.Append objCmd.CreateParameter("PreviousEmployerAreaCode", _
            adSmallInt, adParamInput, , intPreviousEmployerAreaCode)
    objCmd.Parameters.Append objCmd.CreateParameter("PreviousEmployerPhoneNumber", _
            adInteger, adParamInput, , lngPreviousEmployerPhoneNumber)
    objCmd.Parameters.Append objCmd.CreateParameter("YearsAtPreviousEmployer", _
            adTinyInt, adParamInput, , bytYearsAtPreviousEmployer)
    objCmd.Parameters.Append objCmd.CreateParameter("CustomerInformationID", _
            adInteger, adParamOutput)
    objCmd.Parameters.Append objCmd.CreateParameter("Message", adVarChar, _
            adParamOutput, 300)
```

After all of the parameters have been appended to the `Parameters` collection, we execute the `Command` object and then check the return code from the stored procedure, using the `RC` parameter that was set up as a return value parameter. If an error was encountered in the stored procedure, we assign the `@Message` output parameter to the `strMessage` string array variable:

```
      'Execute the command object
      objCmd.Execute

      'If the return code is greater than zero
      If objCmd("RC") <> 0 Then
         'Add the message to the message string
         ReDim Preserve strMessage(0)
         strMessage(0) = objCmd("Message")
      End If
```

The only primary key that this stored procedure returns is the customer information ID. We assign this value to the variable `lngCustomerInformationID`, which was passed by reference. We then set the function to return the return code from the stored procedure:

```
      'Set the return parameters
      lngCustomerInformationID = objCmd("CustomerInformationID")

      'Return to the caller with the return code from the
      'stored procedure
      InsertEmployer = objCmd("RC")
      On Error GoTo 0
      Exit Function
```

Our error handling is the same as the last function and does not need to be explained again:

```
   InsertEmployer_EH:
      Dim objErr As ADODB.Error
      intIndex = -1
      'Add each ADO error to the message string
      For Each objErr In objConn.Errors
         intIndex = intIndex + 1
         ReDim Preserve strMessage(intIndex)
         strMessage(intIndex) = objErr.Description
      Next
      'Add any VB error message to the message string
      intIndex = intIndex + 1
      ReDim Preserve strMessage(intIndex)
      strMessage(intIndex) = Err.Description
      'Return to the caller
      InsertEmployer = 99
      On Error GoTo 0
   End Function
```

Customer Class

The last function that we need to set up is the function to insert a customer. This function is set up in the Customer class and accepts the three variables that were passed to the other two functions by reference. Since they have already been set they are passed to this function by value, as we do not need to modify them. The only variable that we may need to modify is the message string array, which is passed by reference along with the `Connection` and `Command` objects:

```
Public Function InsertCustomer(ByVal lngAddressID As Long, _
      ByVal lngPhoneNumberID As Long, _
      ByVal lngCustomerInformationID As Long, _
      ByVal strFirstName As String, _
      ByVal strLastName As String, _
      ByVal strSpouseName As String, _
      ByRef strMessage() As String, _
      ByRef objConn As ADODB.Connection, _
      ByRef objCmd As ADODB.Command) As Long
```

Once again we set up our error handling and declare our local variables. Then we set the `Command` object properties and append the parameters to the `Parameters` collection:

```
   'Setup error handling
   On Error GoTo InsertCustomer_EH

   'Declare local variables
   Dim intIndex As Integer

   'Set the command object properties
   Set objCmd.ActiveConnection = objConn
   objCmd.CommandText = "willist.up_parmins_customer"
   objCmd.CommandType = adCmdStoredProc

   'Append the parameters
   objCmd.Parameters.Append objCmd.CreateParameter("RC", adInteger, _
         adParamReturnValue)
   objCmd.Parameters.Append objCmd.CreateParameter("AddressID", adInteger, _
         adParamInput, , lngAddressID)
   objCmd.Parameters.Append objCmd.CreateParameter("PhoneNumberID", adInteger, _
         adParamInput, , lngPhoneNumberID)
   objCmd.Parameters.Append objCmd.CreateParameter("CustomerInformationID", _
         adInteger, adParamInput, , lngCustomerInformationID)
   objCmd.Parameters.Append objCmd.CreateParameter("FirstName", adVarChar, _
         adParamInput, 15, strFirstName)
   objCmd.Parameters.Append objCmd.CreateParameter("LastName", adVarChar, _
         adParamInput, 15, strLastName)
   objCmd.Parameters.Append objCmd.CreateParameter("SpouseName", adVarChar, _
         adParamInput, 15, strSpouseName)
   objCmd.Parameters.Append objCmd.CreateParameter("Message", adVarChar, _
         adParamOutput, 100)
```

Finally we execute the `Command` object and check the return code from the stored procedure, just as we did in the last two functions. We add the message to the message string array if the return code was not zero. Then we return to the caller with the return code from the stored procedure:

```
    'Execute the command object
    objCmd.Execute

    'If the return code is greater than zero
    If objCmd("RC") <> 0 Then
       'Add the message to the message string
       ReDim Preserve strMessage(0)
       strMessage(0) = objCmd("Message")
    End If

    'Return to the caller with the return code from the
    'stored procedure
    InsertCustomer = objCmd("RC")
    On Error GoTo 0
    Exit Function
```

The error handling is also the same as for the last two functions:

```
InsertCustomer_EH:
    Dim objErr As ADODB.Error
    intIndex = -1
    'Add each ADO error to the message string
    For Each objErr In objConn.Errors
       intIndex = intIndex + 1
       ReDim Preserve strMessage(intIndex)
       strMessage(intIndex) = objErr.Description
    Next
    'Add any VB error message to the message string
    intIndex = intIndex + 1
    ReDim Preserve strMessage(intIndex)
    strMessage(intIndex) = Err.Description
    'Return to the caller
    InsertCustomer = 99
    On Error GoTo 0
End Function
```

Try It Out – VB Program to Use Insert Stored Procedures – Employer Form

1. We now move on to our Employer form. Add a new command button to the `frmTIO4Employer.frm`, from the last chapter, setting its Name property to cmdInsert and the Caption property to Insert. The form should then look like the figure overleaf:

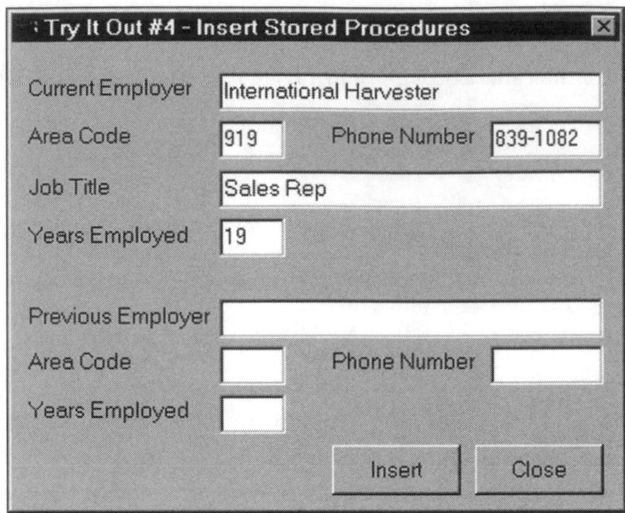

2. Add the following module level variable to the general declarations section of this form:

```
'Declare form level variables
Private m_blnLoaded As Boolean
```

3. Add the following new properties to the form:

```
Public Property Let Loaded(ByVal blnLoaded As Boolean)
   m_blnLoaded = blnLoaded
End Property

Public Property Get Loaded() As Boolean
   Loaded = m_blnLoaded
End Property
```

4. Modify the `Form_Load` event by adding the new code listed below:

```
'Use the standard Windows icon
   Me.Icon = Nothing

   'Set the form's loaded property to true
   Loaded = True
```

5. Add the following new code to the `Form_UnLoad` event:

```
Private Sub Form_Unload(Cancel As Integer)
   'Set the form's loaded property to false
   Loaded = False
End Sub
```

6. Add the new code listed below to the `cmdInsert_Click` procedure:

```
Private Sub cmdInsert_Click()
   'Validate current employer information

   'Validate current employer
   If Len(Trim(txtCurrentEmployer.Text)) = 0 Then
      MsgBox "Current Employer is a required field", vbOKOnly, _
         "Try It Out #4"
      txtCurrentEmployer.SetFocus
      Exit Sub
   End If

   'Validate area code is present
   If Len(Trim(txtCEAreaCode.Text)) = 0 Then
      MsgBox "Current Employer Area Code is a required field", _
         vbOKOnly, "Try It Out #4"
      txtCEAreaCode.SetFocus
      Exit Sub
   'Validate area code is numeric
   ElseIf Not IsNumeric(txtCEAreaCode.Text) Then
      MsgBox "Current Employer Area Code must be numeric", _
         vbOKOnly, "Try It Out #4"
      txtCEAreaCode.SetFocus
      Exit Sub
   End If

   'Validate phone number is present
   If Len(Trim(txtCEPhoneNumber.Text)) = 0 Then
      MsgBox "Current Employer Phone Number is a required field", _
         vbOKOnly, "Try It Out #4"
      txtCEPhoneNumber.SetFocus
      Exit Sub
   'Validate phone number is numeric
   ElseIf Not IsNumeric(txtCEPhoneNumber.Text) Then
      MsgBox "Current Employer Phone Number must be numeric", _
         vbOKOnly, "Try It Out #4"
      txtCEPhoneNumber.SetFocus
      Exit Sub
   End If

   'Validate job title is present
   If Len(Trim(txtJobTitle.Text)) = 0 Then
      MsgBox "Current Employer Job Title is a required field", _
         vbOKOnly, "Try It Out #4"
      txtJobTitle.SetFocus
      Exit Sub
   End If

   'Validate years employed is present
```

```
        If Len(Trim(txtCEYearsEmployed.Text)) = 0 Then
           MsgBox "Current Employer Years Employed is a required field", _
              vbOKOnly, "Try It Out #4"
           txtCEYearsEmployed.SetFocus
           Exit Sub
        'Validate years employed is numeric
        ElseIf Not IsNumeric(txtCEYearsEmployed.Text) Then
           MsgBox "Current Employer Years Employed must be numeric", _
              vbOKOnly, "Try It Out #4"
           txtCEYearsEmployed.SetFocus
           Exit Sub
        End If

        'Validate previous employer information if the employer name
        'is present
        If Len(Trim(txtPreviousEmployer.Text)) > 0 Then

           'Validate area code is present
           If Len(Trim(txtPEAreaCode.Text)) = 0 Then
              MsgBox "Previous Employer Area Code is a required field", _
                 vbOKOnly, "Try It Out #4"
              txtPEAreaCode.SetFocus
              Exit Sub
           'Validate area code is numeric
           ElseIf Not IsNumeric(txtPEAreaCode.Text) Then
              MsgBox "Previous Employer Area Code must be numeric", _
                 vbOKOnly, "Try It Out #4"
              txtPEAreaCode.SetFocus
              Exit Sub
           End If

           'Validate phone number is present
           If Len(Trim(txtPEPhoneNumber.Text)) = 0 Then
              MsgBox "Previous Employer Phone Number is a required field", _
                 vbOKOnly, "Try It Out #4"
              txtPEPhoneNumber.SetFocus
              Exit Sub
           'Validate phone number is numeric
           ElseIf Not IsNumeric(txtPEPhoneNumber.Text) Then
              MsgBox "Previous Employer Phone Number must be numeric", _
                 vbOKOnly, "Try It Out #4"
              txtPEPhoneNumber.SetFocus
              Exit Sub
           End If

           'Validate years employed is present
           If Len(Trim(txtPEYearsEmployed.Text)) = 0 Then
              MsgBox "Previous Employer Years Employed is a required field", _
                 vbOKOnly, "Try It Out #4"
              txtPEYearsEmployed.SetFocus
              Exit Sub
           'Validate years employed is numeric
```

```
        ElseIf Not IsNumeric(txtPEYearsEmployed.Text) Then
            MsgBox "Previous Employer Years Employed must be numeric", _
                vbOKOnly, "Try It Out #4"
            txtPEYearsEmployed.SetFocus
            Exit Sub
        End If

    End If

    'Hide the form so fields are accessible from parent form
    Me.Hide
End Sub
```

How It Works – Employer Form

We have added two public properties to the form that let us set a Boolean value in the form to indicate if it is loaded, and query whether the value is set.

We do this so that we know if the form is loaded or not. The reason for this is twofold. First, it allows us to quickly check to see if the form is loaded, which indicates that data exists to be inserted. And second, in the `Form_UnLoad` event in the `frmTryItOut4` form, which we'll be modifying next, we need to unload the `frmTIO4Employer` form if it is still loaded. This was not a problem before as we displayed the employer information for a customer, and when we clicked on the **Close** button we unloaded the form. However, we have added another button to allow us to insert the employer information. The insert does not take place in this form, but in the `frmTryItOut4` form. For this reason we just hide the `frmTIO4Employer` form and the form remains in memory. This is so that we can access the fields on this form from the `frmTryItOut4` form.

```
Public Property Let Loaded(ByVal blnLoaded As Boolean)
   m_blnLoaded = blnLoaded
End Property

Public Property Get Loaded() As Boolean
   Loaded = m_blnLoaded
End Property
```

When the `Form_Load` event is fired, we call the `Let` method to set the `Loaded` property to `True`. Likewise in the `Form_UnLoad` event, we call the `Let` method again to set the `Loaded` property to `False`.

```
   'Use the standard Windows icon
   Me.Icon = Nothing

   'Set the form's loaded property to true
   Loaded = True

Private Sub Form_Unload(Cancel As Integer)
   'Set the form's loaded property to false
   Loaded = False
End Sub
```

When a user clicks on the Insert button, we validate the fields on the form to ensure that the required data is present and to validate the data types. This is elementary data validation and we will explore a more proper method of data validation in Chapter 13.

We validate that the current employer textbox contains data, and display a message box if the data is not present. We then set the focus to that field and exit the validations:

```
Private Sub cmdInsert_Click()
    'Validate current employer information

    'Validate current employer
    If Len(Trim(txtCurrentEmployer.Text)) = 0 Then
       MsgBox "Current Employer is a required field", vbOKOnly, _
          "Try It Out #4"
       txtCurrentEmployer.SetFocus
       Exit Sub
    End If
```

The validation for the area code is the same as for the current employer. However, we also need to carry this validation one step further to ensure that the area code is a numeric value:

```
    'Validate area code is present
    If Len(Trim(txtCEAreaCode.Text)) = 0 Then
       MsgBox "Current Employer Area Code is a required field", _
          vbOKOnly, "Try It Out #4"
       txtCEAreaCode.SetFocus
       Exit Sub
    'Validate area code is numeric
    ElseIf Not IsNumeric(txtCEAreaCode.Text) Then
       MsgBox "Current Employer Area Code must be numeric", _
          vbOKOnly, "Try It Out #4"
       txtCEAreaCode.SetFocus
       Exit Sub
    End If
```

The rest of the validations are the same and don't need to be explained further. After all validations have been performed, we hide the form so we are able to access the fields from the `frmTryItOut4` form. Hiding this form returns control back to the parent form.

```
    'Hide the form so fields are accessible from parent form
    Me.Hide
End Sub
```

Try It Out – VB Program to use Insert Stored Procedures – Start Up Form

1. We need to add one new control to the `frmTryItOut4.frm`, which is a command button. Set the Name property to cmdInsert and set the Caption property to Insert. We also need to set the Enabled property of the cmdEmployer button to True. The finished `frmTryItOut4` form will look something like this:

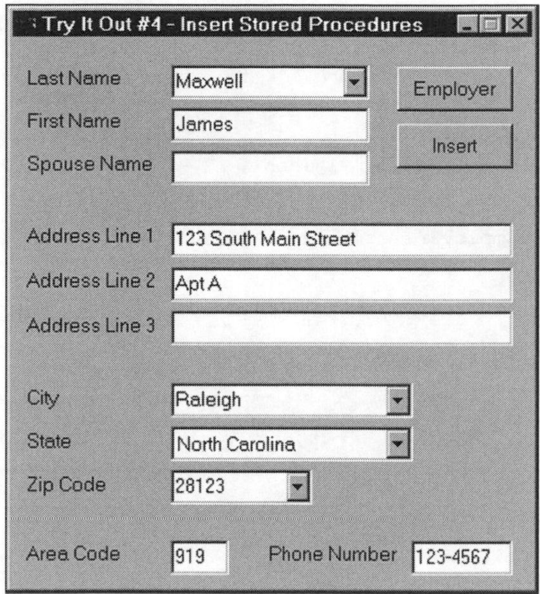

2. Add the following new objects to the general declarations section of the form:

```
'Declare database objects
Dim m_objConn As ADODB.Connection
Dim m_objCmd As ADODB.Command
Dim m_objRS As ADODB.Recordset
Dim m_objRSAddress As ADODB.Recordset
Dim m_objErr As ADODB.Error

'Declare class objects
Dim m_objAddress As clsAddress
Dim m_objCustomer As clsCustomer
Dim m_objEmployer As clsEmployer
```

3. Add the following new code to the `Form_Unload` event:

```
'Dereference class objects
   Set m_objAddress = Nothing
   Set m_objCustomer = Nothing

   'Unload employer form if is still loaded
   If frmTIO4Employer.Loaded Then
      Unload frmTIO4Employer
   End If
```

4. Change the style property of the `cboLastName` combo box to 0 - Dropdown Combo.

5. Modify the `cmdEmployer_Click` procedure with the new code shown below:

```
Private Sub cmdEmployer_Click()
   Me.Hide

   'Determine if employer form should be shown with or without data
   If cboLastName.ListIndex <> -1 Then

      'Call the employer form to process and display employer info
      Call frmTIO4Employer.Process(m_objConn, _
         cboLastName.ItemData(cboLastName.ListIndex), Me)

   Else

      'Display employer form with no data
      frmTIO4Employer.Show vbModal

   End If

   Me.Show
   'We are back, set focus to the combo box
   cboLastName.SetFocus
End Sub
```

6. Add the code listed in the *Insert Functionality* section of the *How It Works* description to the new `cmdInsert_Click` procedure.

How It Works – Start Up Form

On the `frmTryItOut4` form we need to modify the `cmdEmployer_Click` procedure. We need to know if the user wants to display employer information for an existing customer or to display the Employer form for data entry. We achieve this by checking the `ListIndex` property of the `cboLastName` combo box. If the `ListIndex` property does not point to a valid entry then we display the Employer form for data entry. If the combo box contains a customer, then we display the employer information for that customer:

```
Private Sub cmdEmployer_Click()
   Me.Hide

   'Determine if employer form should be shown with or without data
   If cboLastName.ListIndex <> -1 Then

      'Call the employer form to process and display employer info
      Call frmTIO4Employer.Process(m_objConn, _
         cboLastName.ItemData(cboLastName.ListIndex), Me)

   Else

      'Display employer form with no data
      frmTIO4Employer.Show vbModal

   End If

   Me.Show
   'We are back, set focus to the combo box
   cboLastName.SetFocus
End Sub
```

Insert Functionality

The `cmdInsert_Click` procedure is a new procedure that was added when we added the **Insert** button. This is where we validate the fields on the current form and call our functions to insert the data.

First, we validate that the employer information has been entered and do this by querying the `Loaded` property of the `frmTIO4Employer` form. If the form is loaded, then we know that the **Insert** button was clicked and the data has already been validated.

```
Private Sub cmdInsert_Click()
   'Validate employer information has been entered
   If Not frmTIO4Employer.Loaded Then
      MsgBox "Employer information is required", vbOKOnly, _
         "Try It Out #4"
      Exit Sub
   End If
```

We perform validations of the fields on the current form in much the same manner as we did in the `frmTIO4Employer` form. As we have already covered the basic validations we won't go into that again.

```
   'Validate last name is present
   If Len(Trim(cboLastName.Text)) = 0 Or _
      cboLastName.Text = "cboLastName" Then
      MsgBox "Last Name is required", vbOKOnly, "Try It Out #4"
      cboLastName.SetFocus
      Exit Sub
   End If

   'Validate first name is present
   If Len(Trim(txtFirstName.Text)) = 0 Then
      MsgBox "First Name is required", vbOKOnly, "Try It Out #4"
      txtFirstName.SetFocus
      Exit Sub
   End If

   'Validate address line 1 is present
   If Len(Trim(txtAddress1.Text)) = 0 Then
      MsgBox "Address line 1 is required", vbOKOnly, "Try It Out #4"
      txtAddress1.SetFocus
      Exit Sub
   End If
```

What we need to point out is the validation of data in the combo boxes. First there is no validation for a state name as this combo box has its `Style` property set to `2 - Dropdown List`. We can only *select* data in this combo box; we cannot *enter* any.

The city and zip code combo boxes are checked to see if their `ListIndex` property is set to a valid entry, in other words anything greater than `-1`. If they are not, then we validate the `Text` property to ensure that it contains data:

```
 'Validate city name is present
   If cboCity.ListIndex = -1 Then
      If Len(Trim(cboCity.Text)) = 0 Then
         MsgBox "City name is required", vbOKOnly, "Try It Out #4"
         cboCity.SetFocus
         Exit Sub
      End If
   End If

   'Validate zip code is present
   If cboZipCode.ListIndex = -1 Then
      If Len(Trim(cboZipCode.Text)) = 0 Then
         MsgBox "Zip Code is required", vbOKOnly, "Try It Out #4"
         cboZipCode.SetFocus
         Exit Sub
      'Validate zip code is not greater than 10 characters
      ElseIf Len(cboZipCode.Text) > 10 Then
         MsgBox "Zip Code can not be greater than 10 characters", _
            vbOKOnly, "Try It Out #4"
         cboZipCode.SetFocus
         Exit Sub
      End If
   End If
```

We also need to validate the phone number data:

```
   'Validate area code is present
   If Len(Trim(txtAreaCode.Text)) = 0 Then
      MsgBox "Area code is required", vbOKOnly, "Try It Out #4"
      txtAreaCode.SetFocus
      Exit Sub
   'Validate area code is numeric
   ElseIf Not IsNumeric(txtAreaCode.Text) Then
      MsgBox "Area code must be numeric", vbOKOnly, "Try It Out #4"
      txtAreaCode.SetFocus
      Exit Sub
   End If

   'Validate phone number is present
   If Len(Trim(txtPhoneNumber.Text)) = 0 Then
      MsgBox "Phone number is required", vbOKOnly, "Try It Out #4"
      txtPhoneNumber.SetFocus
      Exit Sub
   'Validate phone number is numeric
   ElseIf Not IsNumeric(txtPhoneNumber.Text) Then
      MsgBox "Phone Number must be numeric", vbOKOnly, "Try It Out #4"
      txtPhoneNumber.SetFocus
      Exit Sub
   End If
```

After all data validation has been completed, we declare the local variables that will be used in the rest of this procedure:

```
'Declare local variables
Dim strMsg() As String, lngAddressID As Long, _
   lngPhoneNumberID As Long, lngRC As Long, lngCityID As Long, _
   lngZipCodeID As Long, lngCustomerInformationID As Long, _
   intAreaCode As Integer, lngPhoneNumber As Long, _
   bytYearsEmployed As Byte
```

If no city or state was selected then we set the variables for these to 0, otherwise we set the values to the `ItemData` property for the current selection. If you remember from the last chapter, the `ItemData` property was loaded with the primary key of the city, state, and zip codes.

```
'Set city and zip code ids
If cboCity.ListIndex = -1 Then
   lngCityID = 0
Else
   lngCityID = cboCity.ItemData(cboCity.ListIndex)
End If
If cboZipCode.ListIndex = -1 Then
   lngZipCodeID = 0
Else
   lngZipCodeID = cboZipCode.ItemData(cboZipCode.ListIndex)
End If
```

Next we instantiate the `Address` class and set a reference to the `Command` object:

```
'Instantiate the class and set a reference to the command object
Set m_objAddress = New clsAddress
Set m_objCmd = New ADODB.Command
```

We execute the method to insert an address, passing it the required parameters. We use the `Text` properties for the address fields and the variable for the city ID. The city name comes from the `Text` property of the `cboCity` combo box, and the state ID comes from the `ItemData` property of the `cboState` combo box. The zip code ID is passed using the variable that we defined and set a few moments ago, and the zip code data comes from the `Text` property of the `cboZipCode` combo box. Notice that we are converting the area code and phone number data that we are retrieving, from their respective `Text` properties to their correct data types. The variables `lngAddressID`, `lngPhoneNumberID`, and `strMsg()` are being passed by reference and currently contain no data. They will be set after the stored procedure is executed.

```
'Insert the address
lngRC = m_objAddress.InsertAddress(txtAddress1.Text, _
   txtAddress2.Text, _
   txtAddress3.Text, _
   lngCityID, _
   cboCity.Text, _
   cboState.ItemData(cboState.ListIndex), _
   lngZipCodeID, _
   cboZipCode.Text, _
```

```
        CInt(txtAreaCode.Text), _
        CLng(txtPhoneNumber.Text), _
        lngAddressID, _
        lngPhoneNumberID, _
        strMsg(), _
        m_objConn, _
        m_objCmd)
```

After execution, we check the return code from the function, which received its return code from the stored procedure. If it is not zero, then we display the first message in the string array. We will provide a better method to display error messages in Chapter 13.

```
   'Display messages
   If lngRC <> 0 Then
      MsgBox strMsg(0), vbCritical + vbOKOnly, "Try It Out #4"
      Exit Sub
   End If
```

After our address has been inserted, we de-reference our objects and re-dimension our message string array:

```
   'Dereference objects and clear message
   Set m_objCmd = Nothing
   Set m_objAddress = Nothing
   ReDim strMsg(0)
```

To prepare for the insertion of our employer information, we check the previous employer information to see if it exists. This is optional data that does not have to exist, and if it does not we set the default values for them to zeroes:

```
   'Set previous employer numeric values
   If Len(frmTIO4Employer.txtPEAreaCode.Text) = 0 Then
      intAreaCode = 0
   Else
      intAreaCode = CInt(frmTIO4Employer.txtPEAreaCode.Text)
   End If

   If Len(frmTIO4Employer.txtPEPhoneNumber.Text) = 0 Then
      lngPhoneNumber = 0
   Else
      lngPhoneNumber = CLng(frmTIO4Employer.txtPEPhoneNumber.Text)
   End If

   If Len(frmTIO4Employer.txtPEYearsEmployed.Text) = 0 Then
      bytYearsEmployed = 0
   Else
      bytYearsEmployed = CByte(frmTIO4Employer.txtPEYearsEmployed.Text)
   End If
```

Once again we instantiate and set a reference to our objects:

```
'Instantiate the class and set a reference to the command object
Set m_objEmployer = New clsEmployer
Set m_objCmd = New ADODB.Command
```

The method to insert employer information contains various data types, and we specifically convert the numeric values to their appropriate data types. The `lngCustomerInformationID` variable is an output parameter from the stored procedure and thus contains no data at this point. Notice that we are passing a zero for the current and previous employer IDs. Later we will be using a combo box to display employer data and will be using the `ItemData` property for these parameters.

After we execute the method to insert employer information we check for and display any errors that may have occurred:

```
'Insert the employer information
lngRC = m_objEmployer.InsertEmployer(0, _
   frmTI04Employer.txtCurrentEmployer.Text, _
   CInt(frmTI04Employer.txtCEAreaCode.Text), _
   CLng(frmTI04Employer.txtCEPhoneNumber.Text), _
   CByte(frmTI04Employer.txtCEYearsEmployed.Text), _
   frmTI04Employer.txtJobTitle.Text, _
   0, _
   frmTI04Employer.txtPreviousEmployer.Text, _
   intAreaCode, _
   lngPhoneNumber, _
   bytYearsEmployed, _
   lngCustomerInformationID, _
   strMsg(), _
   m_objConn, _
   m_objCmd)

'Display messages
If lngRC <> 0 Then
   MsgBox strMsg(0), vbCritical + vbOKOnly, "Try It Out #4"
   Exit Sub
End If
```

Once again we de-reference our objects and re-dimension our message string array. Next, we instantiate and set a reference to the objects in preparation for the next call:

```
'Dereference objects and clear message
Set m_objCmd = Nothing
Set m_objEmployer = Nothing
ReDim strMsg(0)

'Instantiate the class and set a reference to the command object
Set m_objCustomer = New clsCustomer
Set m_objCmd = New ADODB.Command
```

This is the last method we need to call to complete the insertion of information that makes a complete customer record. The first three variables that we are passing to this method were set in the previous two methods as output parameters.

```
    'Insert the customer information
    lngRC = m_objCustomer.InsertCustomer(lngAddressID, _
       lngPhoneNumberID, _
       lngCustomerInformationID, _
       txtFirstName.Text, _
       cboLastName.Text, _
       txtSpouseName.Text, _
       strMsg(), _
       m_objConn, _
       m_objCmd)
```

After execution of our method we check for errors and display the error message if appropriate. Then we de-reference our objects and we are done:

```
    'Display messages
    If lngRC <> 0 Then
       MsgBox strMsg(0), vbCritical + vbOKOnly, "Try It Out #4"
    End If

    'Dereference objects
    Set m_objCmd = Nothing
    Set m_objEmployer = Nothing
 End Sub
```

To test your program you need to display the Employer form, enter some employment data, and then click on the Insert button. Then enter some customer data on the Customer (start up) form and click on the Insert button. When entering phone number data enter a seven-digit phone number without a dash (e.g. 1234567).

If, while testing the program, the procedure we have just covered fails, you will have **orphan** data. You will need to use the Query Analyzer to display and optionally delete the orphan data. The only data that might be orphaned is data from the first stored procedure (`up_parmins_address`) that we executed. The second stored procedure used transactions and will have taken care of rolling back the transaction. Chapter 13 will take a closer look at how we can control the integrity of data when using multiple stored procedures.

Summary

This chapter has taken a good look at using logic in your stored procedures to control the flow of processing. We have walked you through the steps to create complex stored procedures. You have used many new functions and have learned how you can manipulate string variables using SQL Server's string functions. The stored procedures created in this chapter also make extensive use of output parameters, and you should feel very comfortable using them in your own stored procedures and in VB.

We created a stored procedure that uses transactions, and have learned how this can benefit you and how it can help to preserve data integrity in your database. Along with transactions, you learned how to check for errors in your stored procedures, and how you can raise your own user-defined errors that get returned through ADO to your VB program. As this chapter has demonstrated, SQL Server provides its own language when it comes to writing stored procedures and you have seen how powerful it can be.

This chapter has also demonstrated some pretty complex stored procedures and once again we stressed the importance of comments in your stored procedures. This is especially true for beginners to SQL Server, as comments will help you to better understand these stored procedures now, and will help you in the future when performing maintenance.

In summary, you should know how to:

- Use logic to control the flow of execution
- Use output parameters in your stored procedures and how to retrieve output parameters in your VB programs
- Use the string functions provided by SQL Server
- Use transactions to maintain data integrity
- Check for and raise errors

In the next chapter we'll be looking at a different type of stored procedure – to *update* data.

WROX AUTO WORKS RACING

Updating Data

Now that we have had an introduction to and have created complex stored procedures that use logic, it's time to expand on that knowledge. We have learned many new functions to help us to validate data and control the flow of logic in our stored procedures. Through the use of transactions, we ensured that our stored procedures either process completely or roll back any partial work, thereby ensuring data integrity in our database.

When we insert data into a table, we must follow the rules that are defined for the columns in that table. Certain columns must contain data and certain columns can contain NULL values. Some columns contain constraints, in that data must exist in another table before we can insert a value into that column.

Updating data is very different to inserting data. When we update data there is no way for the typical stored procedure to know which column should be updated, short of selecting data from the row to be updated and comparing it against the input parameters. This would be a very inefficient method and is one that shouldn't be used. Also we don't always want to update every column of data in the row, but how do we determine which columns should be updated? There are multiple ways to update existing data in our database, and this chapter will demonstrate the three most popular methods.

In this chapter, we will:

- Use a stored procedure to update all columns in a row of data
- Create a stored procedure that uses logic to determine which columns should be updated
- Build a dynamic SQL string to update data, and execute it from VB

Stored Procedure that Uses Transactions and Logic

In the last chapter we learned how to create a stored procedure that validated data and used transactions to help ensure data integrity. The stored procedure that we will create in this section will be no different. Because of the relationship between the tables for employer information, we want to update several tables in one stored procedure. This stored procedure becomes an ideal candidate for transactions. This ensures that either all of the UPDATEs are applied or none of them are applied.

Because we do not know which of the fields on the form the user has updated, we must pass all data to the stored procedure so that all columns in each table can be updated. This is very much the same way we coded the INSERT stored procedure to perform the same task. The difference here is that we will be using transactions and we already know the keys to the tables.

If you think back to Chapters 7 and 8, we created and executed UPDATE queries and stored procedures. In the UPDATE statement, we set the column value equal to something, and limit the number of rows that are updated by specifying the WHERE clause. We want to perform the same basic tasks in this stored procedure, but on more than just one table.

We have already covered the logic that can be used to control the flow of execution in our stored procedures as we validate data and then decide on whether or not to continue processing. The logic that we will use in our next stored procedure will be very similar, as we also want to validate data before applying the UPDATEs.

We have covered transactions and know how they can be used to help ensure data integrity, and we will again use transactions in this next stored procedure.

We have used the output parameters to return data to the user, and have used return values to supply a return code. This next stored procedure will also use these to communicate the status of the execution of the stored procedure back to the caller.

It seems that we have all the necessary skills to go ahead and create a stored procedure that updates data, so let's move on.

Try It Out - UPDATE Stored Procedure

The stored procedure that we want to create for this example is very similar to the up_parmins_employer_information stored procedure that we created in the last chapter, which can be used as a starting point if so desired. The tables that we want to update are the Employer_T table and the Phone_Number_T table for the current employer, and the Employer_T and Phone_Number_T tables for a previous employer, if one exists. Then we want to update the Customer_Information_T table, which ties all of the information together.

If a previous employer did not exist before, and data for the previous employer has now been supplied to the stored procedure, then we want to insert it. This causes a little more processing logic, because we need to determine if a previous employer already exists, or whether a new one should be added. All of this is determined based on the parameters passed to the stored procedure.

1. The code for the UPDATE stored procedure, up_parmupd_employer_information, is listed in the *How It Works* section below. After entering your code in the Query Analyzer, execute your code to create the stored procedure. If you did not get a successful execution, use the debugging techniques that we have discussed in the previous chapters to debug your stored procedure code.

2. After you have successfully created your stored procedure, set the permissions for it so the Developers and Sales Staff roles have permission to execute it.

How It Works - UPDATE Stored Procedure

Since the majority of this stored procedure is the same as its counterpart that we built in the last chapter, there's no reason to rehash every detail. Instead we will present it all here but only explain the *new* code in this stored procedure.

Most of the parameters are the same as in the INSERT counterpart, with the exception of the @Customer_Information_ID parameter. This parameter is an *input* parameter this time, instead of an *output* parameter. We have also added phone number parameters for the current and previous employer:

```
CREATE PROCEDURE up_parmupd_employer_information (@Current_Employer_ID INT,
   @Current_Employer_Name VARCHAR(30), @Current_Employer_Phone_Number_ID INT,
   @Current_Employer_Area_Code SMALLINT, @Current_Employer_Phone_Number INT,
   @Years_At_Current_Employer TINYINT, @Job_Title VARCHAR(30),
   @Previous_Employer_ID INT, @Previous_Employer_Name VARCHAR(30),
   @Previous_Employer_Phone_Number_ID INT, @Previous_Employer_Area_Code SMALLINT,
   @Previous_Employer_Phone_Number INT, @Years_At_Previous_Employer TINYINT,
   @Customer_Information_ID INT, @Message VARCHAR(300) OUTPUT) AS

--
*********************************************************************************
-- Declare variables
--
*********************************************************************************
DECLARE @Continue   BIT,
   @Last_Update   DATETIME

--
-- Turn on default value to continue
--
SELECT @Continue = 1

--
-- Set default values
--
SELECT @Message = ''
```

Validations for the current employer are pretty much the same as for the INSERT stored procedure, with only a few minor differences, which are easy to understand. The difference in this stored procedure versus its INSERT counterpart is that *all* employer information must be present:

```
--
*********************************************************************************
-- Validate current employer ID and current employer name exists
--
*********************************************************************************
--
-- Validate current employer ID is not null or zero
--
IF @Current_Employer_ID IS NULL OR @Current_Employer_ID = 0
   BEGIN
   SELECT @Message = 'Current employer ID is required. '
   SELECT @Continue = 0
   END
```

```
--
-- Validate current employer name is not null or empty
--
IF @Current_Employer_Name IS NULL OR DATALENGTH(LTRIM(@Current_Employer_Name)) = 0
   Begin
   SELECT @Message = 'Current employer name is required. '
   SELECT @Continue = 0
   END

--
*******************************************************************************
-- Validate current employer phone number ID, area code and phone number exists
--
*******************************************************************************
--
-- Validate phone number ID is not null or zero
--
IF @Current_Employer_Phone_Number_ID IS NULL OR @Current_Employer_Phone_Number_ID =
0
   BEGIN
   SELECT @Message = @Message + 'Current employer phone number ID is required. '
   SELECT @Continue = 0
   END
--
-- Validate area code is not null or zero
--
IF @Current_Employer_Area_Code IS NULL OR @Current_Employer_Area_Code = 0
   BEGIN
   SELECT @Message = @Message + 'Current employer area code is required. '
   SELECT @Continue = 0
   END
--
-- Validate area code is three digits (we use VARCHAR(5) as 5 is the
-- number of digits in a small integer)
--
IF DATALENGTH(CAST(@Current_Employer_Area_Code AS VARCHAR(5))) <> 3
   BEGIN
   SELECT @Message = @Message + 'Current employer area code is not valid. '
   SELECT @Continue = 0
   END
--
-- Validate phone number is not null or zero
--
IF @Current_Employer_Phone_Number IS NULL OR @Current_Employer_Phone_Number = 0
   BEGIN
   SELECT @Message = @Message + 'Current employer phone number is required. '
   SELECT @Continue = 0
   END
--
-- Validate phone number is seven digits (we use VARCHAR(10) as 10 is the
-- number of digits in an integer)
--
```

```
IF DATALENGTH(CAST(@Current_Employer_Phone_Number AS VARCHAR(10))) <> 7
   BEGIN
   SELECT @Message = @Message + 'Current employer phone number is not valid. '
   SELECT @Continue = 0
   END

--
***************************************************************************
-- Validate current employer years of employment
--
***************************************************************************
--
-- Validate years Is Not Null Or zero
--
IF @Years_At_Current_Employer IS NULL OR @Years_At_Current_Employer = 0
   BEGIN
   SELECT @Message = @Message + 'Years at current employer is required. '
   SELECT @Continue = 0
   END
--
-- Validate years is within an acceptable range
--
IF @Years_At_Current_Employer > 50
   BEGIN
   SELECT @Message = @Message + 'Years at current employer is invalid. '
   SELECT @Continue = 0
   END

--
***************************************************************************
-- Validate job title
--
***************************************************************************
IF @Job_Title IS NULL OR DATALENGTH(LTRIM(@Job_Title)) = 0
   BEGIN
   SELECT @Message = @Message + 'Job title is required. '
   SELECT @Continue = 0
   END
```

Validations for the previous employer are slightly different also. If information exists for a previous employer, which is optional, then we want to validate that *all* information for the previous employer exists:

```
--
***************************************************************************
-- Check if previous employer ID or name is present, if so validate previous
-- employer
***************************************************************************
--
-- If previous employer ID exists, perform the validations
--
```

```
IF @Previous_Employer_ID > 0 OR (@Previous_Employer_ID = 0 AND
   DATALENGTH(LTRIM(@Previous_Employer_Name)) > 0)

   BEGIN
   --
   -- Validate previous employer name is not null or empty
   --
   IF @Previous_Employer_Name IS NULL OR
      DATALENGTH(LTRIM(@Previous_Employer_Name)) = 0
      BEGIN
      SELECT @Message = @Message + 'Previous employer name is required. '
      SELECT @Continue = 0
      END

   -- ************************************************************************
   -- Validate previous employer phone number ID, area code & phone number exists
   -- ************************************************************************
   --
   -- Validate phone number ID is not null or zero
   --
   IF (@Previous_Employer_Phone_Number_ID IS NULL OR
      @Previous_Employer_Phone_Number_ID = 0) And
      DATALENGTH(LTRIM(@Previous_Employer_Area_Code)) = 0
      BEGIN
      SELECT @Message = @Message + 'Previous employer phone number id is required.
'
      SELECT @Continue = 0
      END
   --
   -- Validate area code is not null or zero
   --
   IF @Previous_Employer_Area_Code IS NULL OR @Previous_Employer_Area_Code = 0
      Begin
      SELECT @Message = @Message + 'Previous employer area code is required. '
      SELECT @Continue = 0
      END
   --
   -- Validate area code is three digits
   --
   IF DATALENGTH(CAST(@Previous_Employer_Area_Code AS VARCHAR(5))) <> 3
      BEGIN
      SELECT @Message = @Message + 'Previous employer area code is not valid. '
      SELECT @Continue = 0
      END
   --
   -- Validate phone number is not null or zero
   --
   IF @Previous_Employer_Phone_Number IS NULL OR @Previous_Employer_Phone_Number =
0
      BEGIN
      SELECT @Message = @Message + 'Previous employer phone number is required. '
      SELECT @Continue = 0
      END
```

```
    --
    -- Validate phone number is seven digits
    --
    IF DATALENGTH(CAST(@Previous_Employer_Phone_Number AS Varchar(10))) <> 7
       BEGIN
       SELECT @Message = @Message + 'Previous employer phone number is not valid. '
       SELECT @Continue = 0
       END

    -- ***************************************************************************
    -- Validate previous employer years of employment
    -- ***************************************************************************
    --
    -- Validate years is not null or zero
    --
    IF @Years_At_Previous_Employer IS NULL OR @Years_At_Previous_Employer = 0
       Begin
       SELECT @Message = @Message + 'Years at previous employer is required. '
       SELECT @Continue = 0
       END
    --
    -- Validate years is within an acceptable range
    --
    IF @Years_At_Previous_Employer > 50
       BEGIN
       SELECT @Message = @Message + 'Years at previous employer is invalid. '
       SELECT @Continue = 0
       END
    END
```

As before, if the validations failed, we return to the caller with a return code of 1:

```
  --
  *******************************************************************************
  -- All data has been validated, either return to the caller with a bad return code
  -- and messages or continue on and insert the values
  --
  *******************************************************************************
  IF @Continue = 0
     BEGIN
     --
     -- Return to the caller with a bad return code
     -- The messages are in the @Message output parameter
     --
     RETURN 1
     END
```

When we start processing the UPDATEs, we start a transaction and update the phone number for the current employer. In an UPDATE statement we SET the column values equal to the parameters, and separate each column value/parameter pair by commas, as shown in our code below:

```
ELSE
   BEGIN
   -- ************************************************************************
   -- Start a transaction, if any code fails then we back out everything
   -- ************************************************************************
   BEGIN TRANSACTION Employer_Information

   -- ************************************************************************
   -- Update the current employer phone number
   -- ************************************************************************
   UPDATE Phone_Number_T
      SET Area_Code_SI = @Current_Employer_Area_Code,
      Phone_Number_IN = @Current_Employer_Phone_Number,
      Last_Update_DT = GetDate()
      WHERE Phone_Number_ID = @Current_Employer_Phone_Number_ID
```

After the UPDATE statement has been executed, we check for errors and roll back the transaction if necessary. Once again we are raising user-defined errors when we encounter an error and roll back the transaction:

```
   --
   -- Check for errors
   --
   IF @@ERROR <> 0
      BEGIN
      --
      -- Roll back the transaction and return to the caller
      --
      ROLLBACK TRANSACTION Employer_Information
      RAISERROR('Update for current employer phone number failed.',18,1)
      RETURN 99
      END
```

After we have updated the phone number for the current employer, we then proceed to update the other details for the current employer. After the update has been performed, we once again check for errors:

```
   -- ************************************************************************
   -- Update the current employer
   -- ************************************************************************
   UPDATE Employer_T
      SET Company_Name_VC = @Current_Employer_Name,
      Last_Update_DT = GetDate()
      WHERE Employer_ID = @Current_Employer_ID

   --
   -- Check for errors
   --
```

```
      IF @@ERROR <> 0
         BEGIN
         --
         -- Roll back the transaction and return to the caller
         --
         ROLLBACK TRANSACTION Employer_Information
         RAISERROR('Update for current employer failed.',18,1)
         RETURN 99
         END
```

To check whether or not a previous employer exists, we check the `@Previous_Employer_ID` parameter for `NULL` or zero. If the parameter is any one of these values, then we move on to check to see if a previous employer name has been specified. If it has, then we know that we need to insert a *new* previous employer (we will discuss what happens if a previous employer name hasn't been specified in a few minutes):

```
      -- ***********************************************************************
      -- Determine if previous employer information exists
      -- ***********************************************************************
      --
      -- If previous employer ID is null or zero check the previous employer name
      --
      IF @Previous_Employer_ID IS NULL OR @Previous_Employer_ID = 0

         BEGIN
         -- ***********************************************************************
         -- Determine if data exists to insert a new employer
         -- ***********************************************************************
         IF DATALENGTH(LTRIM(@Previous_Employer_Name)) > 0
```

The first step of inserting a new previous employer is to insert the phone number for the previous employer. Once the `INSERT` has been performed, we check for errors:

```
            BEGIN
            -- ************************************************************
            -- Insert the previous employer phone number
            -- ************************************************************
            INSERT INTO Phone_Number_T
               (Area_Code_SI, Phone_Number_IN, Last_Update_DT)
               VALUES(@Previous_Employer_Area_Code,
                  @Previous_Employer_Phone_Number, GetDate())

            --
            -- Check for errors
            --
            IF @@ERROR <> 0
               BEGIN
               --
               -- Roll back the transaction and return to the caller
               --
```

```
    ROLLBACK TRANSACTION Employer_Information
    RAISERROR('Insert for previous employer phone number failed.',18,1)
    RETURN 99
    END
```

We need to retrieve the identity value that was inserted into the primary key of the Phone_Number_T table, so we can use that value when inserting the previous employer. We retrieve the value using the @@Identity function:

```
--
-- Get the phone number ID just inserted
--
SELECT @Previous_Employer_Phone_Number_ID = @@IDENTITY
```

Now that the phone number for the previous employer has been inserted and we have retrieved the identity value, we are ready to insert the previous employer. After inserting the previous employer, we check for errors and roll back the transaction if necessary:

```
-- ******************************************************************
-- Insert the previous employer
-- ******************************************************************
INSERT INTO Employer_T
   (Phone_Number_ID, Company_Name_VC, Last_Update_DT)
   VALUES(@Previous_Employer_Phone_Number_ID,
      @Previous_Employer_Name, GetDate())

--
-- Check for errors
--
IF @@ERROR <> 0
   BEGIN
   --
   -- Roll back the transaction and return to the caller
   --
   ROLLBACK TRANSACTION Employer_Information
   RAISERROR('Insert for previous employer failed.',18,1)
   RETURN 99
   END

--
-- Get the employer ID just inserted
--
SELECT @Previous_Employer_ID = @@IDENTITY
END
```

If the @Previous_Employer_ID parameter is NULL or zero and no previous employer name exists, then we have no previous employer, and we want to ensure all values for the previous employer are NULL. This next set of statements sets the previous employer parameters to NULL. These two parameters will be used to update the Customer_Information_T table, and we don't want to insert empty data if no data exists, so we will be inserting NULL values into those columns:

```
    ELSE

       BEGIN
       --
       -- No previous employment exists, ensure all values are null
       --
       SELECT @Previous_Employer_ID = NULL
       SELECT @Years_At_Previous_Employer = NULL
       END

    END
```

If the @Previous_Employer_ID parameter is greater than zero, a previous employer already exists and we want to update the values for that employer. We do so by updating the phone number for that employer first, and then checking for errors:

```
-- *************************************************************************
-- If previous employer ID > 0, update existing previous employer
-- *************************************************************************
ELSE IF @Previous_Employer_ID > 0

   BEGIN
   -- *********************************************************************
   -- Update the previous employer phone number
   -- *********************************************************************
   UPDATE Phone_Number_T
      SET Area_Code_SI = @Previous_Employer_Area_Code,
      Phone_Number_IN = @Previous_Employer_Phone_Number,
      Last_Update_DT = GetDate()
      WHERE Phone_Number_ID = @Previous_Employer_Phone_Number_ID

   --
   -- Check for errors
   --
   IF @@ERROR <> 0
      BEGIN
      --
      -- Roll back the transaction and return to the caller
      --
      ROLLBACK TRANSACTION Employer_Information
      RAISERROR('Update for previous employer phone number failed.',18,1)
      RETURN 99
      END
```

We then update the previous employer details and again check for errors:

```
   -- *********************************************************************
   -- Update the previous employer
   -- *********************************************************************
   UPDATE Employer_T
      SET Company_Name_VC = @Previous_Employer_Name,
      Last_Update_DT = GetDate()
```

```
      WHERE Employer_ID = @Previous_Employer_ID

   --
   -- Check for errors
   --
   IF @@ERROR <> 0
      BEGIN
      --
      -- Roll back the transaction and return to the caller
      --
      ROLLBACK TRANSACTION Employer_Information
      RAISERROR('Update for current employer failed.',18,1)
      RETURN 99
      END
   END
```

At this point all information for the employer and previous employer has been updated and inserted if necessary, and it's time to update the `Customer_Information_T` table. After we update this table, we once again check for errors, and roll back the transaction if necessary:

```
-- ***************************************************************************
-- Now update all employment data in the customer information table
-- ***************************************************************************
UPDATE Customer_Information_T
   SET Employer_ID = @Current_Employer_ID,
   Years_At_This_Employer_TI = @Years_At_Current_Employer,
   Previous_Employer_ID = @Previous_Employer_ID,
   Years_At_Previous_Employer_TI = @Years_At_Previous_Employer,
   Job_Title_VC = @Job_Title,
   Last_Update_DT = GetDate()
   WHERE Customer_Information_ID = @Customer_Information_ID

--
-- Check for errors
--
IF @@ERROR <> 0
   BEGIN
   --
   -- Roll back the transaction and return to the caller
   --
   ROLLBACK TRANSACTION Employer_Information
   RAISERROR('Update of customer information failed.',18,1)
   RETURN 99
   END
```

After this last update, we have made it to the end of our stored procedure and want to COMMIT all changes made as shown in the code below. We then return to the caller with a good return code:

```
    -- ************************************************************************
    -- We made it to the end so commit the transaction
    -- ************************************************************************
    COMMIT TRANSACTION Employer_Information

    --
    -- End if statement block
    --
    END

--
-- Return to the caller with a successful return code
--
RETURN 0
```

Now that we have created the stored procedure, we need to write a VB program to call it.

Try It Out – VB Program to Execute UPDATE Stored Procedure

1. The VB program that we want to create to execute this stored procedure will be built using the example from the last chapter as a base. You need to copy the forms, frmTryItOut4.frm and frmTIO4Employer.frm as frmTryItOut1.frm and frmTIO1Employer.frm respectively. Also copy the classes, clsAddress.cls, clsCustomer.cls and clsEmployer.cls without renaming them (we are expanding the functionality of the classes which will be used in later chapters).

2. Then start a new VB project, remove the current form, and add the two new forms to your project. Add the three classes that you just copied to your project also.

3. Set a reference to the latest version of the Microsoft ActiveX Data Objects Library and change the startup form in the project properties to frmTryItOut1.frm.

4. Perform a global change in your project, changing all frmTIO4Employer to frmTIO1Employer. Also change #4 to #1 in your project, which changes the title that is displayed in the message boxes.

5. On the Employer form, frmTIO1Employer.frm, we want to add an Update button to allow us to execute the stored procedure we just created to update the employer information. Set the Name property of this button to cmdUpdate and set its Caption property to Update. The figure opposite shows where the button should be placed on the form:

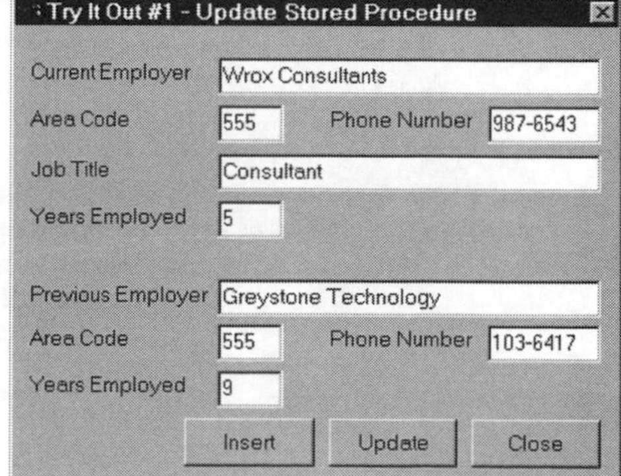

6. Add the following code to the `cmdUpdate_Click` procedure:

```
Private Sub cmdUpdate_Click()
   'Validate current employer
   If Len(Trim(txtCurrentEmployer.Text)) = 0 Then
      MsgBox "Current Employer is a required field", vbOKOnly, "Try It Out #1"
      txtCurrentEmployer.SetFocus
      Exit Sub
   End If

   'Validate area code is present
   If Len(Trim(txtCEAreaCode.Text)) = 0 Then
      MsgBox "Current Employer Area Code is a required field", vbOKOnly, _
               "Try It Out #1"
      txtCEAreaCode.SetFocus
      Exit Sub
   'Validate area code is numeric
   ElseIf Not IsNumeric(txtCEAreaCode.Text) Then
      MsgBox "Current Employer Area Code must be numeric", vbOKOnly, _
               "Try It Out #1"
      txtCEAreaCode.SetFocus
      Exit Sub
   End If

   'Validate phone number is present
   If Len(Trim(txtCEPhoneNumber.Text)) = 0 Then
      MsgBox "Current Employer Phone Number is a required field", vbOKOnly, _
               "Try It Out #1"
      txtCEPhoneNumber.SetFocus
      Exit Sub
   'Validate phone number is numeric
   ElseIf Not IsNumeric(EditPhoneNumber(txtCEPhoneNumber.Text)) Then
      MsgBox "Current Employer Phone Number must be numeric", vbOKOnly, _
               "Try It Out #1"
      txtCEPhoneNumber.SetFocus
      Exit Sub
   End If

   'Validate job title is present
   If Len(Trim(txtJobTitle.Text)) = 0 Then
      MsgBox "Current Employer Job Title is a required field", vbOKOnly, _
               "Try It Out #1"
      txtJobTitle.SetFocus
      Exit Sub
   End If

   'Validate years employed is present
   If Len(Trim(txtCEYearsEmployed.Text)) = 0 Then
      MsgBox "Current Employer Years Employed is a required field", vbOKOnly, _
               "Try It Out #1"
      txtCEYearsEmployed.SetFocus
      Exit Sub
```

```
'Validate years employed is numeric
ElseIf Not IsNumeric(txtCEYearsEmployed.Text) Then
   MsgBox "Current Employer Years Employed must be numeric", vbOKOnly, _
             "Try It Out #1"
   txtCEYearsEmployed.SetFocus
   Exit Sub
End If

'Declare local variables
Dim lngRC As Long, intAreaCode As Integer, lngPhoneNumber As Long, _
   bytYearsEmployed As Byte, strMsg() As String

'Set previous employer numeric values
If Len(txtPEAreaCode.Text) = 0 Then
   intAreaCode = 0
Else
   intAreaCode = CInt(txtPEAreaCode.Text)
End If

If Len(txtPEPhoneNumber.Text) = 0 Then
   lngPhoneNumber = 0
Else
   lngPhoneNumber = EditPhoneNumber(txtPEPhoneNumber.Text)
End If

If Len(txtPEYearsEmployed.Text) = 0 Then
   bytYearsEmployed = 0
Else
   bytYearsEmployed = CByte(txtPEYearsEmployed.Text)
End If

'Instantiate the class and set a reference to the Command object
Dim objEmployer As New clsEmployer
Dim objCmd As New ADODB.Command

'Update the employer information
lngRC = objEmployer.UpdateEmployer(m_lngCurrentEmployerID, _
   txtCurrentEmployer.Text, _
   m_lngCEPhoneNumberID, _
   CInt(txtCEAreaCode.Text), _
   EditPhoneNumber(txtCEPhoneNumber.Text), _
   CByte(txtCEYearsEmployed.Text), _
   txtJobTitle.Text, _
   m_lngPreviousEmployerID, _
   txtPreviousEmployer.Text, _
   m_lngPEPhoneNumberID, _
   intAreaCode, _
   lngPhoneNumber, _
   bytYearsEmployed, _
   m_lngCustomerInformationID, _
   strMsg(), _
   frmTryItOut1.m_objConn, _
   objCmd)
```

```
    'Display messages
    If lngRC <> 0 Then
        MsgBox strMsg(0), vbCritical + vbOKOnly, "Try It Out #1"
    End If

    'De-reference objects and clear message
    Set objCmd = Nothing
    Set objEmployer = Nothing
End Sub
```

7. Add the following variables to the general declarations section of the `frmTI01Employer` form:

```
'Declare form level variables
Private m_blnLoaded As Boolean

'Primary keys
Private m_lngCustomerInformationID As Long
Private m_lngCurrentEmployerID As Long
Private m_lngCEPhoneNumberID As Long
Private m_lngPreviousEmployerID As Long
Private m_lngPEPhoneNumberID As Long
```

8. Add the following code to the `Process` procedure:

```
    'Save all primary keys
    m_lngCustomerInformationID = objRS!Customer_Information_ID
    m_lngCurrentEmployerID = objRS!Employer_ID
    m_lngCEPhoneNumberID = objRS!Phone_Number_ID
    m_lngPreviousEmployerID = IIf(IsNull(objRS!Previous_Employer_ID), 0, _
                 objRS!Previous_Employer_ID)
    m_lngPEPhoneNumberID = IIf(IsNull(objRS!Previous_Employer_Phone_Number_ID), 0, _
                 objRS!Previous_Employer_Phone_Number_ID)

    'Close and de-reference objects
    objRS.Close
    Set objRS = Nothing
    Set objEmployer = Nothing
```

9. In the Employer class, add the following function to perform the update of employer information. Don't forget to change the stored procedure user prefix to match your user prefix:

```
Public Function UpdateEmployer(ByVal lngCurrentEmployerID As Long, _
      ByVal strCurrentEmployerName As String, _
      ByVal lngCurrentEmployerPhoneNumberID As Long, _
      ByVal intCurrentEmployerAreaCode As Integer, _
      ByVal lngCurrentEmployerPhoneNumber As Long, _
      ByVal bytYearsAtCurrentEmployer As Byte, _
      ByVal strJobTitle As String, _
      ByVal lngPreviousEmployerID As Long, _
```

```
    ByVal strPreviousEmployerName As String, _
    ByVal lngPreviousEmployerPhoneNumberID As Long, _
    ByVal intPreviousEmployerAreaCode As Integer, _
    ByVal lngPreviousEmployerPhoneNumber As Long, _
    ByVal bytYearsAtPreviousEmployer As Byte, _
    ByVal lngCustomerInformationID As Long, _
    ByRef strMessage() As String, _
    ByRef objConn As ADODB.Connection, _
    ByRef objCmd As ADODB.Command) As Long

'Setup error handling
On Error GoTo UpdateEmployer_EH

'Declare local variables
Dim intIndex As Integer

'Set the Command object properties
Set objCmd.ActiveConnection = objConn
objCmd.CommandText = "willist.up_parmupd_employer_information"
objCmd.CommandType = adCmdStoredProc

'Append the parameters
objCmd.Parameters.Append objCmd.CreateParameter("RC", adInteger, _
              adParamReturnValue)
objCmd.Parameters.Append objCmd.CreateParameter("CurrentEmployerID", _
              adInteger, adParamInput, , lngCurrentEmployerID)
objCmd.Parameters.Append objCmd.CreateParameter("CurrentEmployerName", _
              adVarChar, adParamInput, 30, strCurrentEmployerName)
objCmd.Parameters.Append objCmd.CreateParameter("CurrentEmployerPhoneNumberID", _
              adInteger, adParamInput, , lngCurrentEmployerPhoneNumberID)
objCmd.Parameters.Append objCmd.CreateParameter("CurrentEmployerAreaCode", _
              adSmallInt, adParamInput, , intCurrentEmployerAreaCode)
objCmd.Parameters.Append objCmd.CreateParameter("CurrentEmployerPhoneNumber", _
              adInteger, adParamInput, , lngCurrentEmployerPhoneNumber)
objCmd.Parameters.Append objCmd.CreateParameter("YearsAtCurrentEmployer", _
              adTinyInt, adParamInput, , bytYearsAtCurrentEmployer)
objCmd.Parameters.Append objCmd.CreateParameter("JobTitle", adVarChar, _
              adParamInput, 30, strJobTitle)
objCmd.Parameters.Append objCmd.CreateParameter("PreviousEmployerID", _
              adInteger, adParamInput, , lngPreviousEmployerID)
objCmd.Parameters.Append objCmd.CreateParameter("PreviousEmployerName", _
              adVarChar, adParamInput, 30, strPreviousEmployerName)
objCmd.Parameters.Append objCmd.CreateParameter("PreviousEmployerPhoneNumberID", _
              adInteger, adParamInput, , lngPreviousEmployerPhoneNumberID)
objCmd.Parameters.Append objCmd.CreateParameter("PreviousEmployerAreaCode", _
              adSmallInt, adParamInput, , intPreviousEmployerAreaCode)
```

```
    objCmd.Parameters.Append objCmd.CreateParameter("PreviousEmployerPhoneNumber", _
                  adInteger, adParamInput, , lngPreviousEmployerPhoneNumber)
    objCmd.Parameters.Append objCmd.CreateParameter("YearsAtPreviousEmployer", _
                  adTinyInt, adParamInput, , bytYearsAtPreviousEmployer)
    objCmd.Parameters.Append objCmd.CreateParameter("CustomerInformationID", _
                  adInteger, adParamInput, , lngCustomerInformationID)
    objCmd.Parameters.Append objCmd.CreateParameter("Message", adVarChar, _
                  adParamOutput, 300)

    'Execute the Command object
    objCmd.Execute

    'If the return code is greater than zero
    If objCmd("RC") <> 0 Then
       'Add the message to the message string
       ReDim Preserve strMessage(0)
       strMessage(0) = objCmd("Message")
    End If

 'Return to the caller with the return code from the stored procedure
    UpdateEmployer = objCmd("RC")
    On Error GoTo 0
    Exit Function

UpdateEmployer_EH:
    Dim objErr As ADODB.Error
    intIndex = -1
    'Add each ADO error to the message string
    For Each objErr In objConn.Errors
       intIndex = intIndex + 1
       ReDim Preserve strMessage(intIndex)
       strMessage(intIndex) = objErr.Description
    Next
    'Add any VB error message to the message string
    intIndex = intIndex + 1
    ReDim Preserve strMessage(intIndex)
    strMessage(intIndex) = Err.Description
    'Return to the caller
    UpdateEmployer = 99
    On Error GoTo 0
End Function
```

10. Add a module to your project, set its Name property to modUtility, and then add the following procedure to it:

```
Public Function EditPhoneNumber(ByVal strPhoneNumber As String) As Long
    'Declare local variables
    Dim intPos As Integer
```

```
    'Remove all occurrences of a hyphen
    Do
       intPos = InStr(1, strPhoneNumber, "-", vbTextCompare)
       If intPos > 0 Then
          strPhoneNumber = Left$(strPhoneNumber, intPos - 1) & _
             Right$(strPhoneNumber, Len(strPhoneNumber) - intPos)
       End If
    Loop While intPos > 0
    EditPhoneNumber = CLng(strPhoneNumber)
End Function
```

11. Finally, we need to modify the `Connection` object defined in the `frmTryItOut1.frm` to be public, so that we can access it from other forms:

```
'Declare database objects
Public m_objConn As ADODB.Connection
Dim m_objCmd As ADODB.Command
Dim m_objRS As ADODB.Recordset
Dim m_objRSAddress As ADODB.Recordset
Dim m_objErr As ADODB.Error
```

How It Works – VB Program to Execute UPDATE Stored Procedure – Utility Module

We need a function to remove the hyphen from the phone number before validating it and passing it as a parameter to the `Update` function. In the `Utility` module that we added to our project in step 10 above, we have a public function that can be called from any class or form. This function accepts the phone number by value as a string, removes all hyphens from the phone number, and then returns the phone number as a `Long` data type. The `InStr` function returns the position of one string within another. In the example below, the `strPhoneNumber` variable is the string being searched, and the string we want to find is a hyphen. The `Left` function returns a specified number of characters from the left side of a string and the `Right` function returns a specified number of characters from the right side of a string. With the three functions combined, we can find the position of the hyphen. We can then build a new string, containing all of the characters on the left side of the hyphen and all of the characters on the right side of the hyphen, thereby excluding the hyphen from the new string:

```
Public Function EditPhoneNumber(ByVal strPhoneNumber As String) As Long
    'Declare local variables
    Dim intPos As Integer

    'Remove all occurrences of a hyphen
    Do
       intPos = InStr(1, strPhoneNumber, "-", vbTextCompare)
       If intPos > 0 Then
          strPhoneNumber = Left$(strPhoneNumber, intPos - 1) & _
             Right$(strPhoneNumber, Len(strPhoneNumber) - intPos)
       End If
    Loop While intPos > 0
    EditPhoneNumber = CLng(strPhoneNumber)
End Function
```

The UpdateEmployer Function

The UpdateEmployer function that we added in step 9 above is very similar to the InsertEmployer function, and does not need to be reproduced here. Most of the parameters this time are passed by value, except for the message string and the database objects. As with this function's counterpart, the UpdateEmployer function also returns a long value indicating success or failure. The return code comes from the stored procedure, unless a critical database error occurs, and we fall through to our error handling code.

After setting up error handling for this function and declaring our local variables, we then set the Command object's properties and append all parameters to the Parameters collection, just as we did in the InsertEmployer function.

We execute the Command object and then check the return code returned from the stored procedure. If it is not zero, then we retrieve the messages from the @Message output parameter and set them to our string variable that was passed by reference. We then return to the caller using the return code returned from the stored procedure.

Our error handling routine is the same as previous examples and does not need to be explained further.

The Process Procedure

In our Process procedure in the frmTI01Employer.frm, we save all the primary keys for the current and previous employers and their phone number. We also save the primary key for the Customer_Information_T table. This allows us to pass these keys to the stored procedure so it knows which entries to update. If the previous employer's primary key is NULL, then we set it to zero. The same holds true for the previous employer's phone number primary key:

```
'Save all primary keys
   m_lngCustomerInformationID = objRS!Customer_Information_ID
   m_lngCurrentEmployerID = objRS!Employer_ID
   m_lngCEPhoneNumberID = objRS!Phone_Number_ID
   m_lngPreviousEmployerID = _
      IIf(IsNull(objRS!Previous_Employer_ID), 0, _
      objRS!Previous_Employer_ID)
   m_lngPEPhoneNumberID = _
      IIf(IsNull(objRS!Previous_Employer_Phone_Number_ID), 0, _
      objRS!Previous_Employer_Phone_Number_ID)
```

The cmdUpdate_Click Procedure

The cmdUpdate_Click procedure validates all data just like the cmdInsert_Click procedure. The only difference in the validations is for the phone number. When we populate that field with data from the recordset, we format the phone number for display by placing a hyphen in it. The hyphen must be removed before validating the phone number, and it is run through the EditPhoneNumber function to remove the hyphen:

```
'Validate phone number is numeric
   ElseIf Not IsNumeric(EditPhoneNumber(txtCEPhoneNumber.Text)) Then
      MsgBox "Current Employer Phone Number must be numeric", _
         vbOKOnly, "Try It Out #1"
      txtCEPhoneNumber.SetFocus
      Exit Sub
   End If
```

The rest of the validations are the same as the cmdInsert_Click procedure and do not need to be explained again.

Instead of *hiding* the form after the data has been validated, we are actually going to *update* the data. This is because the Employer data can be updated independently of the Customer or Address data, as the data already exists, and one update does not depend on the other.

We instantiate and set references to our class and database objects. Then we call the UpdateEmployer method in the Employer class, passing it all of the required parameters. Notice that we have once again converted the text fields to their appropriate data types as required by the UpdateEmployer method.

We are using the Connection object from the frmTryItOut1.frm. Since the object was made public we are able to access it from this form:

```
'Instantiate the class and set a reference to the Command object
Dim objEmployer As New clsEmployer
Dim objCmd As New ADODB.Command

'Update the employer information
lngRC = objEmployer.UpdateEmployer(m_lngCurrentEmployerID, _
   txtCurrentEmployer.Text, _
   m_lngCEPhoneNumberID, _
   CInt(txtCEAreaCode.Text), _
   EditPhoneNumber(txtCEPhoneNumber.Text), _
   CByte(txtCEYearsEmployed.Text), _
   txtJobTitle.Text, _
   m_lngPreviousEmployerID, _
   txtPreviousEmployer.Text, _
   m_lngPEPhoneNumberID, _
   intAreaCode, _
   lngPhoneNumber, _
   bytYearsEmployed, _
   m_lngCustomerInformationID, _
   strMsg(), _
   frmTryItOut1.m_objConn, _
   objCmd)
```

After the update has been performed, we check for errors and display the message returned from the stored procedure in a message box, if an error occurred. Then we de-reference our objects and we are done.

You are now ready to test your program. When you run your project you should be able to update a customer who has one or two employers, and also add a previous employer to a customer who only has a current employer.

While this may seem like a lot of code, we are updating more than just one table. In all, we could be updating as many as five tables. Because we are concerned with data integrity, we are not relying on the front-end program to perform data validations. We perform the validations in our stored procedure to ensure that all required data is present before updating our tables.

Stored Procedure that Builds and Executes a Dynamic SQL String

When we need to update data, we usually want to update only one or two columns in a row of data. Because of the extra processing required to determine which columns should be updated, many developers create a stored procedure that will update *all* columns, as we demonstrated in the previous example. This is fine for tables that contain a small number of columns, as the amount of data that must be sent across the network is relatively small, but what about a table that contains hundreds of columns? An alternative must be found to reduce the volume of data that must be sent across the network, and to increase the efficiency of our application.

Since we have learned how to control the flow of processing in our stored procedure using logic, it stands to reason that we could also control which columns are updated. We know the necessary SQL Server functions to validate whether or not data exists, so we could build a better stored procedure – one that only updates the columns that contain data in the parameters passed.

One solution would be to build several `UPDATE` statements in our stored procedure and execute the appropriate one, based on which parameters contain data. This would be OK for a table that contains only a few columns, but if a table contained hundreds of columns that would mean we would have hundreds of combinations of `UPDATE` statements to consider. This does not seem like a reasonable approach after all.

What if we could build a dynamic SQL statement that only contains the columns for which data exists in the parameters passed? This would make sense and would drastically cut down on the amount of code that would be required in our stored procedure. This is more than just a possibility – it is a reality, and we are going to demonstrate how to accomplish this task in this section.

Since we know that we want to build a *dynamic SQL string*, we must declare a variable in our stored procedure to hold the string to be executed. This string should be a `VarChar` data type that is large enough to hold the string that we will build. SQL Server allows us to declare a `VarChar` variable that can contain up to 8,000 characters, which will be more than large enough to hold the SQL string that we are going to build for this project. But what if 8,000 characters are not enough room to hold our dynamic SQL string? Then we declare more than one string variable and concatenate the two when we execute them.

This is demonstrated below. The following code fragment shows the end of the first string being built and the second string being built. When we execute the strings, we simply concatenate the two strings together:

```
SELECT @SQL1 = @SQL1 + 'Column100 = ''' + @Parameter100 + ''''
SELECT @SQL2 = 'WHERE PrimaryKeyID = ' + CAST(@ParameterID AS VARCHAR(10))
EXECUTE (@SQL1 + @SQL2)
```

The code fragment above brings up two new points to discuss - string concatenation and the EXECUTE SQL statement. String concatenation is accomplished with the **string concatenation operator**, which is a plus sign (+). This works well to concatenate one string to another. But what if we want to concatenate a numeric data type to a string, as shown in the code fragment above? If we try this without the CAST function we would get an error because SQL Server would try to add the numeric value to the string. We must CAST the numeric value to a string value when we concatenate it to our string, as shown in the second line of the code fragment above.

In order to have the string parameter concatenated in the SQL string and for it to be enclosed in single quotes, we must add extra single quotes, as shown in the first line of the first code fragment above. We will see more of this in the stored procedure that we create.

Here we will be executing a string that contains the SQL statements to be carried out. We can execute one or more strings that contain SQL statements and do so by concatenating the strings together, as shown in the code fragment above.

Armed with this new information we are ready to create a stored procedure that builds and executes a dynamic SQL statement.

Try It Out - Dynamic UPDATE Stored Procedure

The table that we have chosen to use for this example is the Address_T table. Like the last stored procedure that we created, we could also have *new* data that would need to be inserted. The city name and the zip code could change, and we might end up having to insert new data into these two tables as well. If the state changes, we simply have a new ID to update in the Address_T table.

Because this stored procedure will be building a dynamic SQL string to be executed, we do not know ahead of time which parameters will be passed. Because of this we must provide all parameters in the stored procedure, so that the caller can pass data for the fields that contain UPDATEs, and empty strings for the fields that do not.

The code listed in the *How It Works* section below represents the stored procedure that we want to create. After you have created this stored procedure, set the appropriate permissions on the various roles.

How It Works - Dynamic UPDATE Stored Procedure

Our stored procedure accepts all the parameters required to insert a new city and zip code and also to update the City_T, Zip_Code_T, and Address_T tables. Since we do not know which parameters will contain data and which will not, we do not perform data validations to ensure that all fields contain data. Also, due to the length of this stored procedure, data validations for the parameters that do contain data have been omitted. You should add such data validations yourself in your stored procedures, using the knowledge you've learned so far.

We start the procedure in the usual way:

```
CREATE PROCEDURE up_parmupd_address (@Address_ID INT, @Street_Address1 VARCHAR(30),
   @Street_Address2 VARCHAR(30), @Street_Address3 VARCHAR(30), @City_ID INT,
   @City_Name VARCHAR(30), @State_ID INT, @Zip_Code_ID INT, @Zip_Code CHAR(10),
   @Phone_Number_ID INT, @Area_Code SMALLINT, @Phone_Number INT,
   @Message Varchar(300) OUTPUT) AS
```

We declare our string variable that will be used to build our SQL statement to update the `Address_T` table. This variable has been defined as a `VarChar` data type with 500 characters, which will be more than large enough to contain our `UPDATE` statement.

To help ensure data integrity we start a transaction, because multiple tables could be modified by this stored procedure:

```
--
**********************************************************************************
-- Declare variables
--
**********************************************************************************
DECLARE @Sql   VARCHAR(500)

--
**********************************************************************************
-- Begin a transaction
--
**********************************************************************************
BEGIN TRANSACTION Address_Information
```

If the `@City_ID` parameter contains a zero and the length of the `@City_Name` parameter contains data, we know we need to insert a new city name. After inserting a new city name, we check for errors and roll back the transaction if necessary. If no errors occurred, we get the identity value that was inserted into the `City_ID` column by SQL Server:

```
--
**********************************************************************************
-- Insert a new city name if city ID is zero and city name contains data
--
**********************************************************************************
IF @City_ID = 0 AND DATALENGTH(LTRIM(@City_Name)) > 0

   BEGIN
   --
   -- Insert the city
   --
   INSERT INTO City_T
      (City_Name_VC, Last_Update_DT)
      VALUES(@City_Name, GetDate())

   --
   -- Check for errors
   --
   IF @@ERROR <> 0
      BEGIN
      --
      -- Roll back the transaction and return to the caller
      --
```

```
        ROLLBACK TRANSACTION Address_Information
        RAISERROR('Insert of city name failed.',18,1)
        RETURN 99
        END

    --
    -- Get the city ID that was just inserted
    --
    SELECT @City_ID = @@IDENTITY
    END
```

We perform the same check and processing for the zip code as we just performed for the city:

```
--
*********************************************************************************
-- Insert a new zip code if zip code ID is zero and zip code contains data
--
*********************************************************************************
IF @Zip_Code_ID = 0 AND DATALENGTH(LTRIM(@Zip_Code)) > 0

   BEGIN
   --
   -- Insert the zip code
   --
  INSERT INTO Zip_Code_T
      (Zip_Code_CH, Last_Update_DT)
      VALUES(@Zip_Code, GetDate())

   --
   -- Check for errors
   --
   IF @@ERROR <> 0
      BEGIN
      --
      -- Roll back the transaction and return to the caller
      --
      ROLLBACK TRANSACTION Address_Information
      RAISERROR('Insert of zip code failed.',18,1)
      RETURN 99
      END

   --
   -- Get the zip code ID that was just inserted
   --
   SELECT @Zip_Code_ID = @@IDENTITY
   END
```

If the `@Phone_Number_ID` parameter is greater than zero, it indicates that the primary key to the `Phone_Number_T` table has been passed. We also check to see if either the `@Area_Code` or `@Phone_Number` parameters contain data, which would indicate that the Phone Number table should be updated.

We begin by building the first part of our UPDATE statement in the SQL string that will be executed:

```
--
*****************************************************************************
-- If phone number data is present then update the phone number
--
*****************************************************************************
IF @Phone_Number_ID > 0 AND (@Area_Code > 0 OR @Phone_Number > 0)
   BEGIN
   --
   -- Build the SQL string
   --
   SELECT @Sql = 'UPDATE Phone_Number_T SET '
```

We then check to see if the @Area_Code parameter contains data. If it does, we concatenate the code to update the Area_Code_SI column to the SQL string. Notice that we have to cast the @Area_Code parameter to a VarChar data type. A SmallInt data type can contain up to five digits, but since we restrict an area code to only three digits that is all we will allow:

```
   --
   -- if area code is present add it to the SQL string
   --
   IF @Area_Code > 0
      BEGIN
      SELECT @Sql = @Sql + 'Area_Code_SI = ' + CAST(@Area_Code AS VARCHAR(3)) +
','
      END
```

If data exists for the @Phone_Number parameter, we want to concatenate the code to update the Phone_Number_IN column to the SQL string. This time we cast the @Phone_Number parameter to a VarChar data type that contains seven characters, as this is all we allow for a phone number.

Notice that since we are using numeric values to update the numeric columns, we do not enclose the values in single quote marks in our SQL string:

```
   --
   -- if phone number is present add it to the SQL string
   --
   IF @Phone_Number > 0
      BEGIN
      SELECT @Sql = @Sql + 'Phone_Number_IN = ' + CAST(@Phone_Number AS
                     VARCHAR(7)) + ','
      END
```

The last column that gets updated in our table is the Last_Update_DT column and we have included it here in the code for our UPDATE statement. We have also specified the WHERE clause in our SQL string and CAST the @Phone_Number_ID parameter to a VarChar data type that contains 10 characters. This is because an Integer data type, represented by the @Phone_Number_ID parameter, can contain up to 10 digits:

```
--
-- Complete the SQL string
--
SELECT @Sql = @Sql + 'Last_Update_DT = GetDate() WHERE Phone_Number_ID = ' +
   CAST(@Phone_Number_ID AS VARCHAR(10))
```

After the string has been completed, we execute it as shown below. After executing the SQL string we check for errors and roll back the transaction if necessary:

```
--
-- Execute the SQL string
--
EXECUTE(@Sql)

--
-- Check for errors
--
IF @@ERROR <> 0
   BEGIN
   --
   -- Roll back the transaction and return to the caller
   --
   ROLLBACK TRANSACTION Address_Information
   RAISERROR('Update of phone number failed.',18,1)
   RETURN 99
   END
END
```

Next we check to see if the `@Address_ID` parameter is greater than zero, indicating a primary key was passed, and if any of the parameters that are contained in the `Address_T` table contain data. If any of them do, then we step through each parameter, checking it to see which ones contain data, and we append the appropriate code to the SQL string to update the `Address_T` table:

```
--
******************************************************************************
-- If address data is present then update the address
--
******************************************************************************
IF @Address_ID > 0 AND (@City_ID > 0 OR @State_ID > 0 OR @Zip_Code_ID > 0 OR
   @Phone_Number_ID > 0 OR DATALENGTH(LTRIM(@Street_Address1)) > 0 OR
   DATALENGTH(LTRIM(@Street_Address2)) > 0 OR DATALENGTH(LTRIM(@Street_Address3))
> 0)
```

We start our SQL string by indicating the table that we want to `update` and specifying the `SET` keyword:

```
BEGIN
--
-- Build the SQL string
--
SELECT @Sql = 'UPDATE Address_T SET '
```

Then we check each parameter for data and append it to the string to be updated:

```
--
-- If city ID is present add it to the SQL string
--
IF @City_ID > 0
   BEGIN
   SELECT @Sql = @Sql + 'City_ID = ' + CAST(@City_ID AS VARCHAR(10)) + ','
   END

--
-- If state ID is present add it to the SQL string
--
IF @State_ID > 0
   BEGIN
   SELECT @Sql = @Sql + 'State_ID = ' + CAST(@State_ID As VARCHAR(10)) + ','
   END

--
-- If zip code ID is present add it to the SQL string
--
IF @Zip_Code_ID > 0
   BEGIN
   SELECT @Sql = @Sql + 'Zip_Code_ID = ' +
      CAST(@Zip_Code_ID AS VARCHAR(10)) + ','
   END
```

Since an address line contains string data and is a `VarChar` data type, we do not need to `CAST` it to another data type. We simply need to enclose the string parameter in single quotes. After we specify the `Street_Address_1_VC` column, we use three single quotes to terminate the string and to have the string contain a single quote. Then we concatenate the `@Street_Address1` parameter to the string, and use three single quotes to begin the next part of the string which, when concatenated, will contain one single quote in the SQL string to be executed. This ensures that all string values are enclosed in single quotes, which is a requirement of SQL Server:

```
--
-- If address line 1 is present add it to the SQL string
--
IF DATALENGTH(LTRIM(@Street_Address1)) > 0
   BEGIN
   SELECT @Sql = @Sql + 'Street_Address_1_VC = ''' + @Street_Address1 + ''','
   END

--
-- If address line 2 is present add it to the SQL string
--
IF DATALENGTH(LTRIM(@Street_Address2)) > 0
   BEGIN
   SELECT @Sql = @Sql + 'Street_Address_2_VC = ''' + @Street_Address2 + ''','
   END
```

```
--
-- If address line 3 is present add it to the SQL string
--
IF DATALENGTH(LTRIM(@Street_Address3)) > 0
   BEGIN
   SELECT @Sql = @Sql + 'Street_Address_3_VC = ''' + @Street_Address3 + ''','
   END
```

To complete our SQL string, we concatenate the code to update the `Last_Update_DT` column with the current date and time, and specify the `WHERE` clause.

After we execute the SQL string, we check for errors and roll back the transaction if necessary:

```
--
-- Finish building the SQL string
--
SELECT @Sql = @Sql + 'Last_Update_Dt = GetDate() '
SELECT @Sql = @Sql + 'WHERE Address_ID = ' + CAST(@Address_ID AS VARCHAR(10))
--
-- Execute the SQL string
--
EXECUTE(@Sql)

--
-- Check for errors
--
IF @@ERROR <> 0
   BEGIN
   --
   -- Roll back the transaction and return to the caller
   --
   ROLLBACK TRANSACTION Address_Information
   RAISERROR('Update of address failed.',18,1)
   RETURN 99
   END
END
```

If all has gone well we find ourselves here, and are ready to commit the transaction, to make all changes to the tables a permanent part of the database. We then return a zero return code to the caller and our stored procedure ends:

```
--
***************************************************************************
-- Commit the transaction and return to the caller with a successful return code
--
***************************************************************************
COMMIT TRANSACTION Address_Information
RETURN 0
```

When building a stored procedure like this it is sometimes tricky to get all of the single quotes coded correctly. A method that I find helpful is to code the stored procedure as a query first and replace the `EXECUTE` statements with `PRINT` statements. This way you print the SQL string instead of executing it and you can see what the final SQL string will look like if executed. You can then tweak your code as necessary.

Now that we have our stored procedure, it's time to create a front end for it.

Try It Out – VB Program to Execute Dynamic UPDATE Stored Procedure

As in previous examples, we will be using the previous program as a base upon which we build our next program.

1. Copy the two forms from the first example and name them `frmTryItOut2.frm` and `frmTIO2Employer.frm`. We will also need to include the classes and the new Utility module that was built earlier in this chapter. Add a new button to the `frmTryItOut2.frm` as shown in the figure below and set its **Name** property to **cmdUpdate**. Change the MsgBox titles in this project to reflect `Try It Out #2` and also change the code that calls the `frmTIO1Employer` to `frmTIO2Employer`.

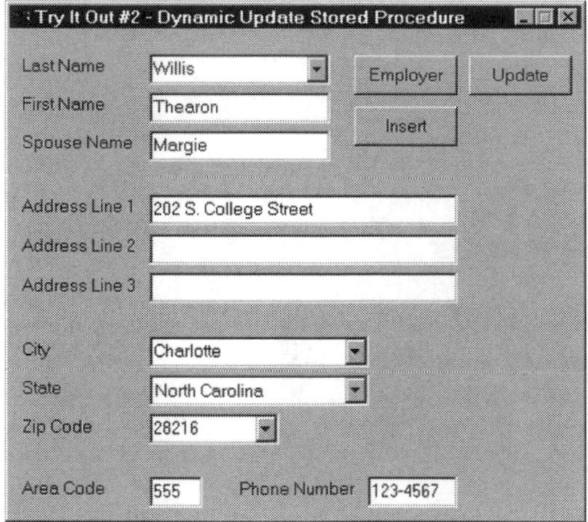

2. Add the following code to the `cmdUpdate_Click` procedure in the `frmTryItOut2` form:

```
Private Sub cmdUpdate_Click()
   'Validate address line 1 is present
   If Len(Trim(txtAddress1.Text)) = 0 Then
      MsgBox "Address line 1 is required", vbOKOnly, "Try It Out #2"
      txtAddress1.SetFocus
      Exit Sub
   End If

   'Validate city name is present
   If cboCity.ListIndex = -1 Then
```

```
      If Len(Trim(cboCity.Text)) = 0 Then
         MsgBox "City name is required", vbOKOnly, "Try It Out #2"
         cboCity.SetFocus
         Exit Sub
      End If
   End If

   'Validate zip code is present
   If cboZipCode.ListIndex = -1 Then
      If Len(Trim(cboZipCode.Text)) = 0 Then
         MsgBox "Zip Code is required", vbOKOnly, "Try It Out #2"
         cboZipCode.SetFocus
         Exit Sub
      'Validate zip code is not greater than 10 characters
      ElseIf Len(cboZipCode.Text) > 10 Then
         MsgBox "Zip Code can not be greater than 10 characters", _
            vbOKOnly, "Try It Out #2"
         cboZipCode.SetFocus
         Exit Sub
      End If
   End If

   'Validate area code is present
   If Len(Trim(txtAreaCode.Text)) = 0 Then
      MsgBox "Area code is required", vbOKOnly, "Try It Out #2"
      txtAreaCode.SetFocus
      Exit Sub
   'Validate area code is numeric
   ElseIf Not IsNumeric(txtAreaCode.Text) Then
      MsgBox "Area code must be numeric", vbOKOnly, "Try It Out #2"
      txtAreaCode.SetFocus
      Exit Sub
   End If

   'Validate phone number is present
   If Len(Trim(txtPhoneNumber.Text)) = 0 Then
      MsgBox "Phone number is required", vbOKOnly, "Try It Out #2"
      txtPhoneNumber.SetFocus
      Exit Sub
   'Validate phone number is numeric
   ElseIf Not IsNumeric(EditPhoneNumber(txtPhoneNumber.Text)) Then
      MsgBox "Phone Number must be numeric", vbOKOnly, "Try It Out #2"
      txtPhoneNumber.SetFocus
      Exit Sub
   End If

   'Declare local variables
   Dim strMsg() As String, lngRC As Long, lngCityID As Long, _
      lngZipCodeID As Long
```

```
    'Set city and zip code IDs
    If cboCity.ListIndex = -1 Then
       lngCityID = 0
    Else
       lngCityID = cboCity.ItemData(cboCity.ListIndex)
    End If
    If cboZipCode.ListIndex = -1 Then
       lngZipCodeID = 0
    Else
       lngZipCodeID = cboZipCode.ItemData(cboZipCode.ListIndex)
    End If

    'Instantiate the class and set a reference to the Command object
    Set m_objAddress = New clsAddress
    Set m_objCmd = New ADODB.Command

    'Update the address
    lngRC = m_objAddress.UpdateAddress(m_lngAddressID, _
       IIf(m_blnAddress1Dirty, txtAddress1.Text, ""), _
       IIf(m_blnAddress2Dirty, txtAddress2.Text, ""), _
       IIf(m_blnAddress3Dirty, txtAddress3.Text, ""), _
       lngCityID, _
       IIf(m_blnCityDirty, cboCity.Text, ""), _
       IIf(m_blnStateDirty, cboState.ItemData(cboState.ListIndex), 0), _
       lngZipCodeID, _
       IIf(m_blnZipCodeDirty, cboZipCode.Text, ""), _
       m_lngPhoneNumberID, _
       IIf(m_blnAreaCodeDirty, CInt(txtAreaCode.Text), 0), _
       IIf(m_blnPhoneNumberDirty, EditPhoneNumber(txtPhoneNumber.Text), 0), _
       strMsg(), _
       m_objConn, _
       m_objCmd)

    'Display messages
    If lngRC <> 0 Then
       MsgBox strMsg(0), vbCritical + vbOKOnly, "Try It Out #2"
    End If

    'De-reference objects and clear message
    Set m_objCmd = Nothing
    Set m_objAddress = Nothing

    'ReLoad City, State and Zip Code combo boxes
    Call LoadCityStateZip

    'Reload address fields from new recordset
    Call cboLastName_Click
End Sub
```

3. Add the following variables to the general declarations section of the `frmTryItOut2.frm`:

```
'Declare primary key variables
Dim m_lngAddressID As Long
Dim m_lngPhoneNumberID As Long

'Declare dirty flags
Dim m_blnAddress1Dirty As Boolean
Dim m_blnAddress2Dirty As Boolean
Dim m_blnAddress3Dirty As Boolean
Dim m_blnCityDirty As Boolean
Dim m_blnStateDirty As Boolean
Dim m_blnZipCodeDirty As Boolean
Dim m_blnAreaCodeDirty As Boolean
Dim m_blnPhoneNumberDirty As Boolean
```

4. Add the following procedure to the `frmTryItOut2.frm`:

```
Private Sub LoadCityStateZip()
   'Declare local variables
   Dim lngRC As Long, lngLastValue As Long, lngIndex As Long

   'Clear any existing entries
   cboCity.Clear
   cboState.Clear
   cboZipCode.Clear

   'Instantiate the class
   Set m_objAddress = New clsAddress

   'Get a list of cities, states and zip codes
   lngRC = m_objAddress.GetCityStateZip(m_objConn, m_objRSAddress)

   'If the return code is not zero, raise an error
   If lngRC <> 0 Then
      Err.Raise vbObjectError + 513, "frmTryItOut3.Form_Load", _
         "Call to clsAddress.GetCityStateZip failed"
   End If

   'Load the city combo box and array
   lngIndex = -1
   lngLastValue = -1
   Do While Not m_objRSAddress.EOF
      'Add the city name
      cboCity.AddItem m_objRSAddress!City_Name_VC
      lngIndex = lngIndex + 1
      'Add the city ID
      cboCity.ItemData(lngIndex) = m_objRSAddress!City_ID
      If lngLastValue < m_objRSAddress!City_ID Then
         'Redim the array
         ReDim Preserve arrCity(m_objRSAddress!City_ID)
         lngLastValue = m_objRSAddress!City_ID
      End If
```

```
        'Add the current position of the city to the array
        arrCity(m_objRSAddress!City_ID) = lngIndex
        'Advance the recordset
        m_objRSAddress.MoveNext
    Loop

    'Load the state combo box and array
    lngIndex = -1
    lngLastValue = -1
    Set m_objRSAddress = m_objRSAddress.NextRecordset
    Do While Not m_objRSAddress.EOF
        'Add the state name
        cboState.AddItem m_objRSAddress!State_Name_VC
        lngIndex = lngIndex + 1
        'Add the state id
        cboState.ItemData(lngIndex) = m_objRSAddress!State_ID
        If lngLastValue < m_objRSAddress!State_ID Then
            'Redim the array
            ReDim Preserve arrState(m_objRSAddress!State_ID)
            lngLastValue = m_objRSAddress!State_ID
        End If
        'Add the current position of the state to the array
        arrState(m_objRSAddress!State_ID) = lngIndex
        'Advance the recordset
        m_objRSAddress.MoveNext
    Loop

    'Load the zip code combo box and array
    lngIndex = -1
    lngLastValue = -1
    Set m_objRSAddress = m_objRSAddress.NextRecordset
    Do While Not m_objRSAddress.EOF
        'Add the zip code
        cboZipCode.AddItem m_objRSAddress!Zip_Code_CH
        lngIndex = lngIndex + 1
        'Add the zip code id
        cboZipCode.ItemData(lngIndex) = m_objRSAddress!Zip_Code_ID
        If lngLastValue < m_objRSAddress!Zip_Code_ID Then
            'Redim the array
            ReDim Preserve arrZipCode(m_objRSAddress!Zip_Code_ID)
            lngLastValue = m_objRSAddress!Zip_Code_ID
        End If
        'Add the current position of the zip code to the array
        arrZipCode(m_objRSAddress!Zip_Code_ID) = lngIndex
        'Advance the recordset
        m_objRSAddress.MoveNext
    Loop

    'Close and de-reference Recordset and class objects
    m_objRSAddress.Close
    Set m_objRSAddress = Nothing
    Set m_objAddress = Nothing
End Sub
```

5. Modify the `Form_Load` event, removing the code that was added to the `LoadCityStateZip` procedure and replacing it with the following call to this new procedure:

```
'Show the form to give the impression all processing
'is complete
Me.Show
cboLastName.SetFocus
DoEvents

'Load City, State and Zip Code combo boxes
Call LoadCityStateZip

'All done, exit procedure
On Error GoTo 0
Exit Sub
```

6. Modify the `cboLastName_Click` procedure adding the following code:

```
'Save the primary keys for later use
m_lngAddressID = m_objRSAddress!Address_ID
m_lngPhoneNumberID = m_objRSAddress!Phone_Number_ID

'Load the address fields
txtAddress1.Text = m_objRSAddress!Street_Address_1_VC
txtAddress2.Text = IIf(IsNull(m_objRSAddress!Street_Address_2_VC), _
   "", m_objRSAddress!Street_Address_2_VC)
txtAddress3.Text = IIf(IsNull(m_objRSAddress!Street_Address_3_VC), _
   "", m_objRSAddress!Street_Address_3_VC)


'Close and de-reference Recordset and class objects
m_objRSAddress.Close
Set m_objRSAddress = Nothing
Set m_objAddress = Nothing

'All fields are dirty because of the load, reset all flags
m_blnAddress1Dirty = False
m_blnAddress2Dirty = False
m_blnAddress3Dirty = False
m_blnCityDirty = False
m_blnStateDirty = False
m_blnZipCodeDirty = False
m_blnAreaCodeDirty = False
m_blnPhoneNumberDirty = False
```

7. Add the following code to the following procedures to indicate that a field was changed:

```
Private Sub cboCity_Change()
   m_blnCityDirty = True
End Sub

Private Sub cboState_Click()
   m_blnStateDirty = True
End Sub

Private Sub cboZipCode_Change()
   m_blnZipCodeDirty = True
End Sub

Private Sub txtAddress1_Change()
   m_blnAddress1Dirty = True
End Sub

Private Sub txtAddress2_Change()
   m_blnAddress2Dirty = True
End Sub

Private Sub txtAddress3_Change()
   m_blnAddress3Dirty = True
End Sub

Private Sub txtAreaCode_Change()
   m_blnAreaCodeDirty = True
End Sub

Private Sub txtPhoneNumber_Change()
   m_blnPhoneNumberDirty = True
End Sub
```

8. Add the following procedure to the Address class:

```
Public Function UpdateAddress(ByVal lngAddressID As Long, _
      ByVal strAddress1 As String, _
      ByVal strAddress2 As String, _
      ByVal strAddress3 As String, _
      ByVal lngCityID As Long, _
      ByVal strCityName As String, _
      ByVal lngStateID As Long, _
      ByVal lngZipCodeID As Long, _
      ByVal strZipCode As String, _
      ByVal lngPhoneNumberID As Long, _
      ByVal intAreaCode As Integer, _
      ByVal lngPhoneNumber As Long, _
      ByRef strMessage() As String, _
      ByRef objConn As ADODB.Connection, _
      ByRef objCmd As ADODB.Command) As Long
```

```
'Setup error handling
On Error GoTo UpdateAddress_EH

'Declare local variables
Dim intIndex As Integer

'Set the Command object properties
Set objCmd.ActiveConnection = objConn
objCmd.CommandText = "willist.up_parmupd_address"
objCmd.CommandType = adCmdStoredProc

'Append the parameters
objCmd.Parameters.Append objCmd.CreateParameter("RC", adInteger, _
                 adParamReturnValue)
objCmd.Parameters.Append objCmd.CreateParameter("AddressID", adInteger, _
                 adParamInput, , lngAddressID)
objCmd.Parameters.Append objCmd.CreateParameter("Address1", adVarChar, _
                 adParamInput, 30, strAddress1)
objCmd.Parameters.Append objCmd.CreateParameter("Address2", adVarChar, _
                 adParamInput, 30, strAddress2)
objCmd.Parameters.Append objCmd.CreateParameter("Address3", adVarChar, _
                 adParamInput, 30, strAddress3)
objCmd.Parameters.Append objCmd.CreateParameter("CityID", adInteger, _
                 adParamInput, , lngCityID)
objCmd.Parameters.Append objCmd.CreateParameter("CityName", adVarChar, _
                 adParamInput, 30, strCityName)
objCmd.Parameters.Append objCmd.CreateParameter("StateID", adInteger, _
                 adParamInput, , lngStateID)
objCmd.Parameters.Append objCmd.CreateParameter("ZipCodeID", adInteger, _
                 adParamInput, , lngZipCodeID)
objCmd.Parameters.Append objCmd.CreateParameter("ZipCode", adChar, _
                 adParamInput, 10, strZipCode)
objCmd.Parameters.Append objCmd.CreateParameter("PhoneNumberID", _
                 adInteger, adParamInput, , lngPhoneNumberID)
objCmd.Parameters.Append objCmd.CreateParameter("AreaCode", adSmallInt, _
                 adParamInput, , intAreaCode)
objCmd.Parameters.Append objCmd.CreateParameter("PhoneNumber", adInteger, _
                 adParamInput, , lngPhoneNumber)
objCmd.Parameters.Append objCmd.CreateParameter("Message", adVarChar, _
                 adParamOutput, 300)

'Execute the Command object
objCmd.Execute

'If the return code is greater than zero
If objCmd("RC") <> 0 Then
   'Add the message to the message string
   ReDim Preserve strMessage(0)
   strMessage(0) = objCmd("Message")
End If
```

```
    'Set the return parameters
    lngAddressID = objCmd("AddressID")
    lngPhoneNumberID = objCmd("PhoneNumberID")

    'Return to the caller with the return code from the
    'stored procedure
    UpdateAddress = objCmd("RC")
    On Error GoTo 0
    Exit Function

UpdateAddress_EH:
    Dim objErr As ADODB.Error
    intIndex = -1
    'Add each ADO error to the message string
    For Each objErr In objConn.Errors
       intIndex = intIndex + 1
       ReDim Preserve strMessage(intIndex)
       strMessage(intIndex) = objErr.Description
    Next
    'Add any VB error message to the message string
    intIndex = intIndex + 1
    ReDim Preserve strMessage(intIndex)
    strMessage(intIndex) = Err.Description
    'Return to the caller
    UpdateAddress = 99
    On Error GoTo 0
End Function
```

How It Works – VB Program to Execute Dynamic UPDATE Stored Procedure

We first need to code the `UpdateAddress` procedure in the Address class. This procedure is almost identical to the `InsertAddress` procedure and does not need to be discussed further.

Declarations

In the general declarations section of our form we have declared some Boolean variables that are global to our form. These variables are used to keep track of which fields on the form have changed. The variables contain the word `Dirty`, which indicates the data has changed. In the `Change` event for each field, we set the Boolean variable to `True` to indicate that the data in the form field has changed, as shown below:

```
Private Sub cboCity_Change()
   m_blnCityDirty = True
End Sub
```

Form_Load Event

In the `Form_Load` event, we have removed the code that loaded the city, state, and zip code combo boxes, and have placed it into a procedure in the form. We then replaced the code with a call to the procedure, as shown below. (Note that the `Call` keyword is optional, but helps to document your code so that you know a procedure is being called.) The reason this was done is because, when we update the address, we could be inserting a new city or zip code. After the update we will call this procedure to reload the combo boxes:

```
'Load City, State and Zip Code combo boxes
Call LoadCityStateZip
```

cboLastName_Click Procedure

In the cboLastName_Click procedure we added some code to save the primary keys that are related to the address, as shown here:

```
'Save the primary keys for later use
m_lngAddressID = m_objRSAddress!Address_ID
m_lngPhoneNumberID = m_objRSAddress!Phone_Number_ID
```

We also reset the Boolean variables after we loaded an address, because the loading of the fields causes the Change event to fire:

```
'All fields are dirty because of the load, reset all flags
m_blnAddress1Dirty = False
m_blnAddress2Dirty = False
m_blnAddress3Dirty = False
m_blnCityDirty = False
m_blnStateDirty = False
m_blnZipCodeDirty = False
m_blnAreaCodeDirty = False
m_blnPhoneNumberDirty = False
```

cmdUpdate_Click Procedure

The cmdUpdate_Click procedure validates that the required fields are present before calling the UPDATE procedure. These are the same validations that were performed for an INSERT, and we don't need to cover them again.

After the validations have been performed, we declare our local variables and then check to see if the city and zip code combo boxes have had data added to them. If the ListIndex property is –1 then we know that no entry is selected and that data has been keyed in. In this case we set the variables that we are using for these combo boxes to zero:

```
'Declare local variables
Dim strMsg() As String, lngRC As Long, lngCityID As Long, _
   lngZipCodeID As Long

'Set city and zip code ids
If cboCity.ListIndex = -1 Then
   lngCityID = 0
Else
   lngCityID = cboCity.ItemData(cboCity.ListIndex)
End If
If cboZipCode.ListIndex = -1 Then
   lngZipCodeID = 0
Else
   lngZipCodeID = cboZipCode.ItemData(cboZipCode.ListIndex)
End If
```

We are now ready to execute the UpdateAddress procedure. We instantiate and set a reference to our class and database objects and then call the UpdateAddress procedure. As part of passing the parameters, we use the immediate if (IIF) statement to determine if the fields are dirty, that is, have they been changed. If they have not, then we pass an empty string for the string variables and pass a zero for the numeric variables. If the fields have changed then we pass the data in the fields:

```
    'Instantiate the class and set a reference to the Command object
    Set m_objAddress = New clsAddress
    Set m_objCmd = New ADODB.Command

    'Update the address
    lngRC = m_objAddress.UpdateAddress(m_lngAddressID, _
       IIf(m_blnAddress1Dirty, txtAddress1.Text, ""), _
       IIf(m_blnAddress2Dirty, txtAddress2.Text, ""), _
       IIf(m_blnAddress3Dirty, txtAddress3.Text, ""), lngCityID, _
       IIf(m_blnCityDirty, cboCity.Text, ""), _
       IIf(m_blnStateDirty, cboState.ItemData(cboState.ListIndex), 0), _
       lngZipCodeID, _
       IIf(m_blnZipCodeDirty, cboZipCode.Text, ""), m_lngPhoneNumberID, _
       IIf(m_blnAreaCodeDirty, CInt(txtAreaCode.Text), 0), _
       IIf(m_blnPhoneNumberDirty, EditPhoneNumber(txtPhoneNumber.Text), 0), _
       strMsg(), m_objConn, m_objCmd)
```

After the UpdateAddress procedure has been executed, we check the return code that was returned. If it is not equal to zero, then we display any messages returned from that procedure:

```
    'Display messages
    If lngRC <> 0 Then
       MsgBox strMsg(0), vbCritical + vbOKOnly, "Try It Out #2"
 End If
```

We de-reference our objects and then reload the city, state, and zip code combo boxes just in case a new city or zip code was added. Then we call the cboLastName_Click procedure, which will reload the current address using values retrieved from the database:

```
    'De-reference objects and clear message
    Set m_objCmd = Nothing
    Set m_objAddress = Nothing

    'ReLoad City, State and Zip Code combo boxes
    Call LoadCityStateZip

    'Reload address fields from new recordset
    Call cboLastName_Click
 End Sub
```

You are now ready to test your code. You can update just one or two fields on the form and trace the code through the update process. As you can see, this would be a great method to use if the update consisted of more than a handful of fields.

The last two examples have shown two stored procedures that updated data in two very different ways. As you can imagine, there are benefits to using each method, which will be discussed in the summary. Before we end this chapter we want to demonstrate yet a third method to update data.

Building and Executing a Dynamic SQL String in VB

Sometimes a stored procedure just doesn't fit the bill and you need to use in-line SQL statements. That's where this section comes in. We are going to build a dynamic SQL string to update the `Customer_T` table. The method that we will be using to build our dynamic in-line SQL statement is very similar to the method we used in our last stored procedure to build a dynamic SQL statement. However, instead of using a *stored procedure* to build and execute the SQL string, we will be using *VB* to build and execute the SQL string.

Because we are building a dynamic SQL string to be executed, we will not be using the `Command` object. This is because we are not executing a stored procedure but rather a SQL string. We could execute this SQL string with the `Command` object, but we have already demonstrated that. Instead, we are going to be using the `Connection` object to execute our dynamic SQL string.

Try It Out - Dynamic SQL String

There are three columns in the `Customer_T` table that we can update: `First_Name_VC`, `Last_Name_VC` and `Spouse_First_Name_VC`. Using the same principle as in the last program that we built, we will only update the fields that have changed.

1. To that end, we want to start our next program by copying the `frmTryItOut2.frm` and `frmTIO2Employer.frm` forms as `frmTryItOut3.frm` and `frmTIO3Employer.frm` respectively. Start a new VB project, remove the current form, and add the two new forms you just copied.

2. Set the `frmTryItOut3.frm` as the startup form and set a reference to the Microsoft ActiveX Data Objects Library. Add the three classes and module from the last example to this project. Change the title of all MsgBox functions to `Try It Out #3` and change the calls to `frmTIO2Employer` to `frmTIO3Employer`.

3. Modify the general declarations section of the `frmTryItOut3.frm` form to include the following new variables:

```
'Declare primary key variables
Dim m_lngAddressID As Long
Dim m_lngPhoneNumberID As Long
Dim m_lngCustomerID As Long

Dim m_blnAreaCodeDirty As Boolean
Dim m_blnPhoneNumberDirty As Boolean
Dim m_blnFirstNameDirty As Boolean
Dim m_blnLastNameDirty As Boolean
Dim m_blnSpouseNameDirty As Boolean
```

4. Add the following code to set the Boolean flags to `True` when the data in the field has changed:

```
Private Sub cboLastName_Change()
   m_blnLastNameDirty = True
End Sub

Private Sub txtFirstName_Change()
   m_blnFirstNameDirty = True
End Sub

Private Sub txtSpouseName_Change()
   m_blnSpouseNameDirty = True
End Sub
```

5. Add the following code to the `cboLastName_Click` procedure:

```
   'Load the text boxes with the correct data
   txtFirstName.Text = m_objRS!First_Name_VC
   txtSpouseName.Text = _
      IIf(IsNull(m_objRS!Spouse_First_Name_VC), "", _
         m_objRS!Spouse_First_Name_VC)

   'Save the primary key and reset Boolean flags
   m_lngCustomerID = m_objRS!Customer_ID
   m_blnFirstNameDirty = False
   m_blnLastNameDirty = False
   m_blnSpouseNameDirty = False
```

6. Add the following code to the `cmdUpdate_Click` procedure:

```
   'Display messages
   If lngRC <> 0 Then
      MsgBox strMsg(0), vbCritical + vbOKOnly, "Try It Out #3"
      Exit Sub
   End If

   'De-reference objects and clear message
   Set m_objCmd = Nothing
   Set m_objAddress = Nothing
   ReDim strMsg(0)

   'Instantiate the class
   Set m_objCustomer = New clsCustomer

   'Update the customer record
   lngRC = m_objCustomer.UpdateCustomer(m_lngCustomerID, _
      strMsg(), _
      m_objConn, _
```

```
      IIf(m_blnFirstNameDirty, txtFirstName.Text, Empty), _
      IIf(m_blnLastNameDirty, cboLastName.Text, Empty), _
      IIf(m_blnSpouseNameDirty, txtSpouseName.Text, Empty))

   'Display messages
   If lngRC <> 0 Then
      MsgBox strMsg(0), vbCritical + vbOKOnly, "Try It Out #3"
      Exit Sub
   End If

   'De-reference objects and clear message
   Set m_objCustomer = Nothing

   'ReLoad City, State and Zip Code combo boxes
   Call LoadCityStateZip

   'Reload address fields from new recordset
   Call cboLastName_Click
End Sub
```

7. Add the following procedure to the `Customer` class:

```
Public Function UpdateCustomer(ByVal lngCustomerID As Long, _
      ByRef strMessage() As String, _
      ByRef objConn As ADODB.Connection, _
      Optional ByVal strFirstName As Variant, _
      Optional ByVal strLastName As Variant, _
      Optional ByVal strSpouseName As Variant) As Long

   'Setup error handling
   On Error GoTo UpdateCustomer_EH

   'Declare local variables
   Dim intIndex As Integer, strSQL As String, blnExecute As Boolean

   'Build update sql string
   strSQL = "UPDATE Customer_T SET "

   'Add first name if present
   If Not IsEmpty(strFirstName) Then
      strSQL = strSQL & "First_Name_VC = '" & _
      Replace(strFirstName, "'", "''") & "',"
      blnExecute = True
   End If

   'Add last name if present
   If Not IsEmpty(strLastName) Then
      strSQL = strSQL & "Last_Name_VC = '" & _
      Replace(strLastName, "'", "''") & "',"
      blnExecute = True
   End If

   'Add spouse's name if present
   If Not IsEmpty(strSpouseName) Then
```

```
        strSQL = strSQL & "Spouse_First_Name_VC = '" & _
         Replace(strSpouseName, "'", "''") & "',"
        blnExecute = True
     End If

     'If any of the optional fields are present, complete the SQL string
     'and execute it
     If blnExecute Then
        strSQL = strSQL & "Last_Update_DT = GetDate() "
        strSQL = strSQL & "WHERE Customer_ID = " & lngCustomerID
        objConn.Execute strSQL
     End If

     'Return to the caller
     UpdateCustomer = 0
     On Error GoTo 0
     Exit Function

  UpdateCustomer_EH:
     Dim objErr As ADODB.Error
     intIndex = -1
     'Add each ADO error to the message string
     For Each objErr In objConn.Errors
        intIndex = intIndex + 1
        ReDim Preserve strMessage(intIndex)
        strMessage(intIndex) = objErr.Description
     Next
     'Add any VB error message to the message string
     intIndex = intIndex + 1
     ReDim Preserve strMessage(intIndex)
     strMessage(intIndex) = Err.Description
     'Return to the caller
     UpdateCustomer = 99
     On Error GoTo 0
  End Function
```

How It Works – Dynamic SQL String

Since there is no stored procedure associated with this example, we want to start looking at our VB code in the Customer class.

Customer Class

The `UpdateCustomer` procedure in the `Customer` class is the procedure that we will call to build the dynamic SQL string to update the `Customer_T` table. We start our procedure by defining the customer ID as the first parameter, which is the primary key to the `Customer_T` table. Then we define the message parameter, which is passed by reference, so we can add any error message to the string. Next we define the `Connection` object by reference as we have done in the past examples. The last parameters that we define are for the names. Notice that these parameters are defined as optional parameters. This is because any one of these parameters may or may not exist:

```
Public Function UpdateCustomer(ByVal lngCustomerID As Long, _
      ByRef strMessage() As String, _
      ByRef objConn As ADODB.Connection, _
      Optional ByVal strFirstName As Variant, _
      Optional ByVal strLastName As Variant, _
      Optional ByVal strSpouseName As Variant) As Long
```

We set up error handling for our procedure and declare our local variables:

```
   'Setup error handling
   On Error GoTo UpdateCustomer_EH

   'Declare local variables
   Dim intIndex As Integer, strSQL As String, blnExecute As Boolean
```

We start building our SQL string before checking any parameters, just like we did in our last stored procedure. Then we check the first optional parameter to see if any data was passed. On a normal optional parameter, defined as a variant, we would normally use the `IsMissing` keyword to check to see if an optional parameter was passed. However, since our code that calls this procedure is static, we must use the `IsEmpty` keyword to check for a missing parameter. This will become clear very shortly.

If the first parameter, first name, is not empty then we concatenate the code to update the first name to our SQL string. Notice that the name parameter is converted as it is added to the string. This is because we have enclosed our string variable in single quotes, as required by SQL Server. If the first name contains a single quote in it, we would get an error about an un-terminated string, if we did not double the occurrence of the single quote in the name. We are using the VB `Replace` function, which replaces all occurrences of one string with another. We have passed this function the string to be converted, the string to look for, in this case a single quote, and the string to be used as a replacement string: two consecutive single quotes. If we have executed the statements in this `If Then - End If` block, then we set a Boolean variable to `True`:

```
   'Build update SQL string
   strSQL = "UPDATE Customer_T SET "

   'Add first name if present
   If Not IsEmpty(strFirstName) Then
      strSQL = strSQL & "First_Name_VC = '" & _
      Replace(strFirstName, "'", "''") & "',"
      blnExecute = True
   End If
```

Following the same steps as above we check to see if the last name and the spouse's name have been passed. If they have, we also concatenate the code to update these columns to our SQL string:

```
   'Add last name if present
   If Not IsEmpty(strLastName) Then
      strSQL = strSQL & "Last_Name_VC = '" & _
      Replace(strLastName, "'", "''") & "',"
      blnExecute = True
   End If
```

```
    'Add spouse's name if present
    If Not IsEmpty(strSpouseName) Then
       strSQL = strSQL & "Spouse_First_Name_VC = '" & _
        Replace(strSpouseName, "'", "''") & "',"
       blnExecute = True
    End If
```

The `blnExecute` variable is used to determine if any of the optional parameters were passed. If they were, we complete our dynamic SQL string and execute it. Once again we are updating the date and time in the `Last_Update_DT` column in our table:

```
    'If any of the optional fields are present, complete the SQL string
    'and execute it
    If blnExecute Then
       strSQL = strSQL & "Last_Update_DT = GetDate() "
       strSQL = strSQL & "WHERE Customer_ID = " & lngCustomerID
       objConn.Execute strSQL
    End If
```

Regardless of whether or not we execute a SQL string, we return to the caller with a zero return code. If we executed the SQL string and encountered an error, we would be thrown into our error handling code below:

```
    'Return to the caller
    UpdateCustomer = 0
    On Error GoTo 0
    Exit Function

 UpdateCustomer_EH:
    Dim objErr As ADODB.Error
    intIndex = -1
    'Add each ADO error to the message string
    For Each objErr In objConn.Errors
       intIndex = intIndex + 1
       ReDim Preserve strMessage(intIndex)
       strMessage(intIndex) = objErr.Description
    Next
    'Add any VB error message to the message string
    intIndex = intIndex + 1
    ReDim Preserve strMessage(intIndex)
    strMessage(intIndex) = Err.Description
    'Return to the caller
    UpdateCustomer = 99
    On Error GoTo 0
 End Function
```

Form Level Declarations

To prepare for our call to our procedure to perform the update of the Customer table, we must declare some more form level variables, and have those variables set to `True` if any data in the name fields changes:

```
'Declare primary key variables
Dim m_lngAddressID As Long
Dim m_lngPhoneNumberID As Long
Dim m_lngCustomerID As Long

Dim m_blnAreaCodeDirty As Boolean
Dim m_blnPhoneNumberDirty As Boolean
Dim m_blnFirstNameDirty As Boolean
Dim m_blnLastNameDirty As Boolean
Dim m_blnSpouseNameDirty As Boolean

Private Sub cboLastName_Change()
   m_blnLastNameDirty = True
End Sub

Private Sub txtFirstName_Change()
   m_blnFirstNameDirty = True
End Sub

Private Sub txtSpouseName_Change()
   m_blnSpouseNameDirty = True
End Sub
```

cmdUpdate_Click Procedure

After executing the procedure to update the `Address_T` table, we execute the code to update the names in the Customer table. We start by re-dimensioning our message variable and instantiating our Customer class:

```
   'Display messages
   If lngRC <> 0 Then
      MsgBox strMsg(0), vbCritical + vbOKOnly, "Try It Out #3"
      Exit Sub
   End If

   'De-reference objects and clear message
   Set m_objCmd = Nothing
   Set m_objAddress = Nothing
   ReDim strMsg(0)

   'Instantiate the class
   Set m_objCustomer = New clsCustomer
```

In our call to the `UpdateCustomer` procedure, we once again use the `IIf` statement to check if the data in the form field has changed. Instead of passing an empty string using double quotes, we pass the value `Empty`. This allows us to check the optional parameter, using the `IsEmpty` function in our `UpdateCustomer` function:

```
    'Update the customer record
    lngRC = m_objCustomer.UpdateCustomer(m_lngCustomerID, strMsg(), _
       m_objConn, IIf(m_blnFirstNameDirty, txtFirstName.Text, Empty), _
       IIf(m_blnLastNameDirty, cboLastName.Text, Empty), _
       IIf(m_blnSpouseNameDirty, txtSpouseName.Text, Empty))
```

After we execute our procedure, we check for a non-zero return code and display any error messages:

```
    'Display messages
    If lngRC <> 0 Then
       MsgBox strMsg(0), vbCritical + vbOKOnly, "Try It Out #3"
       Exit Sub
    End If
```

If everything has gone well, we de-reference our class object, reload the city, state, and zip code combo boxes, and then refresh the data by calling the `cboLastName_Click` procedure:

```
    'De-reference objects and clear message
    Set m_objCustomer = Nothing

    'ReLoad City, State and Zip Code combo boxes
    Call LoadCityStateZip

    'Reload address fields from new recordset
    Call cboLastName_Click
End Sub
```

Once again you are ready to test your code. If you set a breakpoint in your project you can walk through the code and watch the dynamic SQL string being built and executed. As you can see, this is also an efficient method that can be used to update data. Although this method is not commonly used, it does have its place in some applications. Only you can determine when the situation is right to use it.

Summary

This chapter has taken a look at three different methods of updating data in our tables. The first method that we used was to build a stored procedure that validated and updated all columns in the table, regardless of whether the data had changed or not. The second method also used a stored procedure, but introduced you to a new concept in stored procedures – building and executing a dynamic SQL string in a stored procedure. This stored procedure only updated the columns in the table that data was passed for. And finally, the third method that we introduced was to build and execute a dynamic SQL string in VB. Each of these methods has their advantages and disadvantages and it is up to you to decide when to use each method.

Sometimes you will need to create a stored procedure that accepts multiple optional parameters and you will need to build the stored procedure dynamically as was shown in the second example. And sometimes you will choose to forgo building a stored procedure and build a dynamic SQL string in your VB code to perform the same function. These methods could be useful when creating SQL statements that provide data for ad-hoc reports. In this case you would never know what data the user wants until they submit the parameters that specify the report data.

Some of the disadvantages of using dynamic in-line SQL statements are that you must hard code column names in your logic. If a column name changes or an extra column has been added to a table, you must make the appropriate changes to the program and recompile. A disadvantage to using dynamic stored procedures is that they are not as efficient as static stored procedures because the SQL string is being built dynamically. SQL Server does not know how to optimize the stored procedure until it is executed.

We have taken a detailed look at two SQL Server functions. The first is the string concatenation operator, which is used to concatenate one string to another. We took a look at this function in the last chapter to concatenate messages, but this chapter has really expanded on this function. We have seen how this works, with first hand experience of using it in our stored procedures. The second function is the `EXECUTE` function that was used in this chapter to execute SQL strings instead of stored procedures.

We now know of alternative ways to build a stored procedure using dynamic SQL statements, and there will come a time when you will use this method, not so much to selectively update data, but as an alternative way of executing code in a stored procedure.

To summarize, you should know:

- How to create a stored procedure that builds and executes dynamic SQL statements
- How to build and execute a dynamic SQL statement from VB
- That there are alternatives to the standard approach to updating data
- How to concatenate strings, numeric parameters, and variables to a string

We've almost come to the end of our in depth look at stored procedures – we have just one more type to look at. This is covered in the next chapter when we study deleting data.

WROX AUTO WORKS RACING

Deleting Data

The last three chapters have used stored procedures to SELECT, INSERT, and UPDATE data in our tables. This chapter completes our discussion on stored procedures and covers *deleting* data. In Chapter 5 we covered simple DELETE queries and deleted data from just one table. However, our knowledge and use of our database has grown, and we now know that data exists in multiple tables that are related. For example, a single entry in the Customer_T table has related data in other tables.

Realizing this, we know that we must not only delete data from the Customer_T table for a single customer, but we must also delete the data in all of the associated tables that are related to that customer. While this chapter does complete our discussion on stored procedures, and we will cover deleting data from more than one table in a single stored procedure, there is an alternative approach that must also be explored – the use of triggers.

Triggers can be defined for a table and can cause cascading deletes that will delete data in all associated tables. Using triggers is an alternative approach to complex stored procedures and helps to ensure referential integrity of our data. This chapter will cover triggers as they relate to deleting data, and how they can be used in combination with stored procedures to delete data from multiple related tables.

In this chapter we will cover:

- Referential integrity
- Triggers that delete data from multiple tables
- Stored procedures that delete data from multiple tables

Referential Integrity

Referential integrity is based on the relationship of data between two tables, using columns that are defined as primary and foreign keys. This ensures that the entries in each table are *unique* and that they *relate* to one another. The table that contains the foreign key cannot reference an entry in the table that contains the primary key unless that entry exists. Likewise, the table that contains the primary key entry cannot be deleted until the table that holds the foreign key reference is also deleted.

The referential integrity between the two tables that contain the primary and foreign keys is maintained by the primary and foreign key constraints, which were discussed in Chapter 1. When deleting data from tables that contain primary and foreign keys, we must be aware of the relationship between all the tables involved.

When data was inserted into the Customer_T table, there were inserts into other tables that had to *precede* the insert of the customer record in the Customer_T table. When we delete the data from the Customer_T table, we must follow the reverse order of the insert. This is because we cannot delete an entry in a table that contains a primary key while another table holds a foreign key reference to it. An example of this would be the Address_T table. (Refer back to the database diagram in Chapter 3 if you need to be reminded of the relationship of these tables.) The customer to be deleted has an entry in the Address_T table and the Customer_T table has a foreign key reference (Address_ID) to that address entry. We cannot delete the customer until the address record has been deleted first.

SQL Server automatically provides referential integrity up to a point. It will not allow us to add a foreign key to a non-existent entry. Likewise, it will not allow us to delete a primary key entry while a foreign key in another table is referencing it. What *we* must provide is atomicity. When we delete the customer record from the Customer_T table, we must ensure that all related customer records are also deleted. Atomicity, as we saw in Chapter 10, is used to ensure that a transaction either completes successfully or fails. Any item in the transaction that fails causes the entire transaction to fail.

We can provide atomicity in one of two ways. First, we can use a stored procedure that uses transactions and ROLLBACKs. This ensures that if a delete from any of the tables fails, the entire transaction will be rolled back. The second method that we can use is triggers; which brings us on to our next topic of discussion.

Triggers

Foreign key constraints are great for ensuring and enforcing referential integrity when inserting data into multiple related tables. However, they lack the ability to provide **cascading deletes**. This is where **triggers** come in. If you remember back to our definition of triggers in Chapter 1, we said that they are a special kind of stored procedure that are fired as the result of some specified action on a table. Because of this, they provide a mechanism to perform cascading deletes. Cascading deletes are where you initiate a DELETE on one table, and that DELETE triggers a DELETE on another table, and that table triggers a DELETE on another table, and so on.

Since triggers cannot return data, use of the SELECT statement is highly discouraged, except to assign values to variables that are used for processing. Triggers contain SQL statements and processing logic just like a stored procedure, and can contain transactions that will roll back all work should anything fail.

Triggers get fired automatically by SQL Server when a specific action is taken against a table. Triggers can be defined to fire when data is inserted, updated, deleted, or any combination of the three and are fired automatically when these events occur. A trigger can cause the firing of other triggers by taking action on other tables that also have triggers defined. In addition, a single table can contain more than one trigger, provided that the trigger *name* is *unique*. A table can contain as many triggers as necessary, as long as the number of objects defined in the database does not exceed 2,147,483,647.

When a delete is performed against a table, SQL Server deletes the data and places it into a special temporary table called Deleted. After the data has been deleted the trigger is fired and it has access to the data in the Deleted table. You can query the data in the Deleted table and use it to perform logical processing in your trigger.

Let's take a look at how a trigger can examine data from a row that has been deleted. The following code fragment could be from a trigger defined on the Address_T table. When a row of data is deleted from the Address_T table the trigger is fired and executes the following code. Variables are defined in the first line of this code fragment, and then the trigger selects the ID values of the foreign keys of the row of data that was deleted. These variables can then be used in a DELETE statement to delete the appropriate rows in the City_T, State_T, and Zip_Code_T tables. We will be taking a detailed look at this type of processing in our example very shortly.

```
DECLARE @City_ID    INT,
   @State_ID    INT,
   @Zip_Code_ID    INT

--
*************************************************************************************
-- Get the foreign keys from the row just deleted
--
*************************************************************************************
SELECT @City_ID = City_ID,
   @State_ID = State_ID,
   @Zip_Code_ID = Zip_Code_ID
   FROM Deleted
```

As you can see from the code fragment above, we have selected data from the temporary Deleted table, which contains the row of data that was deleted. We could then use the values of the foreign key columns to cascade the delete to the related entries in the City_T, State_T, and Zip_Code_T tables. Let's see this in action in an example.

Try It Out – Creating a Trigger

If you recall from the database diagram presented in Chapter 3, there are several tables that contain data that make up a complete customer record. These tables include the Address_T, Phone_Number_T, and Customer_Information_T tables. When a customer record is deleted from the Customer_T table we want a trigger to delete the related customer data from these other tables as well.

> *You may be wondering why we don't also delete the data from the City_T, Zip_Code_T, and State_T tables. The reason is that entries in these tables may be referenced by another address. Likewise, the data in the Employer_T table may be referenced by another customer and should not be deleted.*

1. To this end, we want to create a trigger on the Customer_T table that will delete the related data in the Address_T, Phone_Number_T, and Customer_Information_T tables. We create this trigger just like we would create a stored procedure, by using the Query Analyzer. However, there is an alternative, which is to use the Enterprise Manager.

Using the Enterprise Manager, right click on the Customer_T table, choose All Tasks from the popup menu and then choose Manage Triggers from the sub-menu. The Trigger Properties dialog appears and you can enter the code below. The major drawback here is that there is no interactive debugging. There is a Check Syntax button, but it does not highlight the offensive code. Instead it merely checks the syntax and notifies you that you have an error.

2. The tool of choice is yours to make (Enterprise Manager or Query Analyzer) and either one can be used to create this trigger. Enter the code and then click on the Execute Query button to have the trigger created on the `Customer_T` table. If you encounter errors, double click the error message to have the line of code in error highlighted.

The code listed below contains the trigger to be created, and is available in the download files:

```
CREATE TRIGGER delete_customer_record_trigger ON Customer_T
   FOR DELETE AS

--
*********************************************************************************
-- Declare variables
--
*********************************************************************************
DECLARE @Address_ID          INT,
   @Phone_Number_ID          INT,
   @Customer_Information_ID    INT

--
*********************************************************************************
-- Get the foreign keys from the row just deleted
--
*********************************************************************************
SELECT @Address_ID = Address_ID,
   @Phone_Number_ID = Phone_Number_ID,
   @Customer_Information_ID = Customer_Information_ID
   FROM Deleted

--
*********************************************************************************
-- Delete the foreign key entries related to this customer
--
*********************************************************************************
DELETE FROM Address_T
   WHERE Address_ID = @Address_ID
DELETE FROM Phone_Number_T
   WHERE Phone_Number_ID = @Phone_Number_ID
DELETE FROM Customer_Information_T
   WHERE Customer_Information_ID = @Customer_Information_ID
```

How It Works – Creating a Trigger

The first line in our trigger defines it as a trigger, specifies the name of the trigger, and the table on which it should be created. The second line specifies the actions that will cause this trigger to be executed, in our case a `DELETE` statement:

```
CREATE TRIGGER delete_customer_record_trigger ON Customer_T
   FOR DELETE AS
```

In the next part of our trigger we declare the variables that we will be using, just like we do in a stored procedure:

```
--
**********************************************************************************
-- Declare variables
--
**********************************************************************************
DECLARE @Address_ID          INT,
   @Phone_Number_ID          INT,
   @Customer_Information_ID    INT
```

Next we select the foreign keys contained in the deleted row and assign them to our variables. Notice that we are selecting the data from the `Deleted` table, which contains the row of data that was deleted:

```
--
**********************************************************************************
-- Get the foreign keys from the row just deleted
--
**********************************************************************************
SELECT @Address_ID = Address_ID,
   @Phone_Number_ID = Phone_Number_ID,
   @Customer_Information_ID = Customer_Information_ID
   FROM Deleted
```

Now that we have the foreign keys for the customer who was deleted, we can delete the related data. Here we are executing three separate `DELETE` statements, using the variables that were set in the previous `SELECT` statement:

```
--
**********************************************************************************
-- Delete the foreign key entries related to this customer
--
**********************************************************************************
DELETE FROM Address_T
   WHERE Address_ID = @Address_ID
DELETE FROM Phone_Number_T
   WHERE Phone_Number_ID = @Phone_Number_ID
DELETE FROM Customer_Information_T
   WHERE Customer_Information_ID = @Customer_Information_ID
```

This trigger will be fired on any type of delete on the Customer_T table. This can be a DELETE query run from the Query Analyzer, deleting a record while editing the table in the Enterprise Manager, or a delete from a stored procedure, called from our VB program for example.

Testing the Trigger

To put this trigger to the test, let's execute a DELETE query in the Query Analyzer to delete a customer record.

Try It Out – Testing the Trigger

1. The first thing we want to do is select all records in the Customer_T table.

2. Now make a note of the Customer_ID that you want to delete and then open a new query window.

3. Enter the following DELETE statement, substituting the x in the query with the ID of the customer that you want to delete:

```
DELETE FROM Customer_T
   WHERE Customer_ID = x
```

4. After executing the query, switch back to the first query window, and make a note of the Address_ID, Phone_Number_ID, and the Customer_Information_ID.

5. Open a new query window, and select all data from these tables. Notice that the entries for the deleted customer have also been deleted from these tables.

As you can see, using a trigger to delete related data is very handy and easy to set up. It also helps to maintain referential integrity of our data.

Managing Triggers

As we mentioned above, you can have more than one trigger on a table. This could be in the form of a trigger for an INSERT, a trigger for an UPDATE, and a trigger for a DELETE. You could also have multiple triggers for INSERT, UPDATE, and DELETE actions against the table.

The SQL Server Books Online provides some excellent examples of using triggers to send e-mail when a table has been altered, as well as logging the changes made on a table to an audit log. This can be very useful for sensitive data, such as payroll information, when you need to know who modified it and what modifications were made.

To manage triggers for a table, use the Enterprise Manager and right click on the appropriate table. Choose All Tasks from the popup menu, and then choose Manage Triggers from the sub-menu. The Trigger Properties dialog appears and you can enter code for a new trigger or can manage the existing triggers listed in the Name listbox at the top of the dialog. When you select an existing trigger in the listbox, you then have the option of modifying the trigger or deleting it.

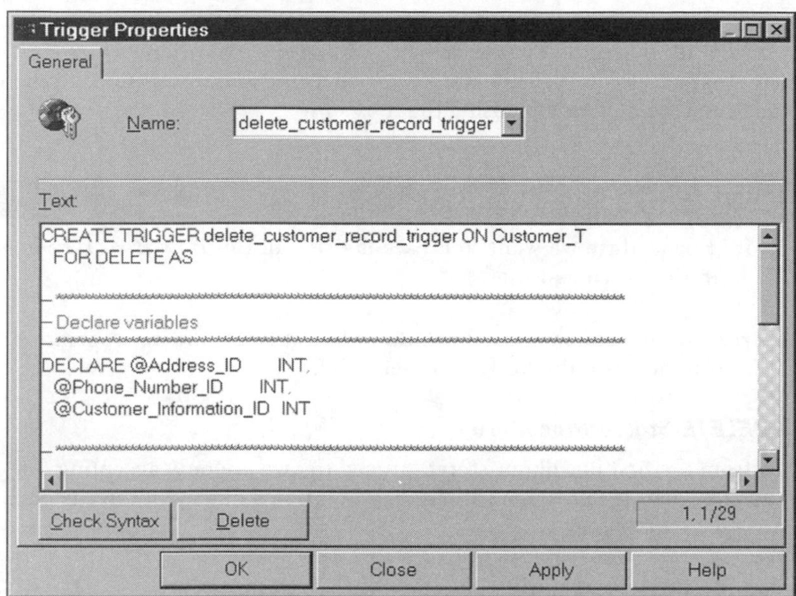

Using the Enterprise Manager is the quickest way to manage the triggers on a table. You can, however, use the Query Analyzer to manage triggers on tables, but this requires more coding skill with triggers and the SQL statements to create, alter, and drop triggers. SQL Server provides a built-in stored procedure named `sp_helptrigger` that will accept parameters and list the triggers for a table. This list provides the trigger name, the owner of the trigger, and what type of trigger it is – `INSERT`, `UPDATE`, or `DELETE`.

At this point we want to delete the trigger created on the `Customer_T` table, as we are going to use a stored procedure to perform the deleting of customers. In the Trigger Properties dialog shown above, click the Delete button.

DELETE Stored Procedure

The trigger we used above deleted customer data from multiple related tables. The stored procedure we want to create will have to perform the same tasks. In order to do this we must create a stored procedure that will use the `Customer_ID` as an input parameter and select the foreign keys from the `Customer_T` table for the row of data to be deleted. This will be performed in the same manner as was done in the trigger, except we will be selecting the data from the `Customer_T` table instead of the `Deleted` table.

When using a stored procedure, we must first select the foreign keys, delete the row from the `Customer_T` table, and finally delete the rows from the `Address_ID`, `Phone_Number_ID`, and the `Customer_Information_ID` tables. Why perform the delete in this order? We must first delete the row of data that contains the foreign keys because of the foreign key constraint. SQL Server will not let us delete a row of data in a table that contains a primary key while it is being referenced as a foreign key in another table. In other words we cannot delete the row of data from the `Address_T` table while it is being referenced in the `Customer_T` table as a foreign key.

In order to ensure data integrity, it is critical that this stored procedure uses *transactions.* If any of the deletes fail, we want to roll back all of the deletes. To this end, we will be using *error checking* to ensure that each delete was successful. We have used error checking and transactions in the last two chapters, and you should feel quite comfortable using them by now.

Try It Out – DELETE Stored Procedure

1. The stored procedure we want to create is listed in the *How It Works* section below, and is available in the download files.

2. After creating this stored procedure, don't forget to set the appropriate permissions on it, which in this case is only the Developers role.

How It Works – DELETE Stored Procedure

As you can see from the first line of our stored procedure, we are only accepting one input parameter. The `@Customer_ID` parameter is the primary key of the row of data in the customer table for the customer that we want to delete.

We then declare the variables that will be used in our stored procedure. We have declared three variables to hold the foreign keys from the `Customer_T` table:

```
CREATE PROCEDURE up_parmdel_customer (@Customer_ID INT) AS

--
*********************************************************************************
-- Declare variables
--
*********************************************************************************
DECLARE @Address_ID          INT,
   @Phone_Number_ID          INT,
   @Customer_Information_ID   INT
```

Next, we begin our transaction. If any errors occur during the deleting of data from any of the tables, we will roll back the entire transaction, thus undoing all of the deletes that were performed:

```
--
*********************************************************************************
-- Begin Transaction
--
*********************************************************************************
BEGIN TRANSACTION Delete_Customer
```

We assign our variables the foreign keys from the Customer_T table by selecting the values from the appropriate columns into our variables. We limit the selection of data by specifying that only the row of data containing the Customer_ID that matches our input parameter should be selected:

```
--
**********************************************************************************
-- Get the foreign keys to the associated tables
--
**********************************************************************************
SELECT @Address_ID = Address_ID, @Phone_Number_ID = Phone_Number_ID,
   @Customer_Information_ID = Customer_Information_ID
   FROM Customer_T
   WHERE Customer_ID = @Customer_ID
```

Now that our variables contain the foreign keys from the row of data to be deleted, we can proceed by deleting the row of data from the Customer_T table. Once again we are limiting the delete to the row of data where the Customer_ID matches the input parameter @Customer_ID:

```
--
**********************************************************************************
-- Delete the customer from the primary table
--
**********************************************************************************
DELETE FROM Customer_T
   WHERE Customer_ID = @Customer_ID
```

We check for errors by checking the @@Error function to see what error number it contains. If it is not equal to zero then we roll back the transaction and raise an error. We then return to the caller with a bad return code:

```
--
-- Check for errors
--
If @@ERROR <> 0
   BEGIN
   --
   -- Rollback the transaction and return to the caller
   --
   ROLLBACK TRANSACTION Delete_Customer
   RAISERROR('Delete from Customer_T failed.',18,1)
   RETURN 99
   END
```

If everything was successful on the last delete then we perform a delete on the Customer_Information_T table, deleting the row of data that was related to the customer record that was just deleted. Here we are using the @Customer_Information_ID variable that contains the primary key of the row to be deleted:

```
--
******************************************************************************************
-- Delete the customer information from the customer information table
--
******************************************************************************************
DELETE FROM Customer_Information_T
   WHERE Customer_Information_ID = @Customer_Information_ID
```

We once again check for errors and roll back the transaction if any errors occurred:

```
--
-- Check for errors
--
If @@ERROR <> 0
   BEGIN
   --
   -- Rollback the transaction and return to the caller
   --
   ROLLBACK TRANSACTION Delete_Customer
   RAISERROR('Delete from Customer_Information_T failed.',18,1)
   RETURN 99
   END
```

The next delete that we want to perform is on the `Phone_Number_T` table, which contains the phone number of the customer who we have deleted. Once again we are using our variable that contains the primary key of the row to be deleted to limit which rows of data are deleted.

After the delete we check for errors, and roll back the transaction if necessary:

```
--
******************************************************************************************
-- Delete the customer phone number from the phone number table
--
******************************************************************************************
DELETE FROM Phone_Number_T
   WHERE Phone_Number_ID = @Phone_Number_ID

--
-- Check for errors
--
If @@ERROR <> 0
   BEGIN
   --
   -- Rollback the transaction and return to the caller
   --
   ROLLBACK TRANSACTION Delete_Customer
   RAISERROR('Delete from Phone_Number_T failed.',18,1)
   RETURN 99
   END
```

The last table that we want to delete data from is the `Address_T` table, which contains the customer's address. Using the `@Address_ID` variable, we limit the deletion of data to the exact row of data that matches this variable.

We again check for errors and roll back the transaction if necessary:

```
--
**********************************************************************************
-- Delete the customer address from the address table
--
**********************************************************************************
DELETE FROM Address_T
   WHERE Address_ID = @Address_ID

--
-- Check for errors
--
If @@ERROR <> 0
   BEGIN
   --
   -- Rollback the transaction and return to the caller
   --
   ROLLBACK TRANSACTION Delete_Customer
   RAISERROR('Delete from Address_T failed.',18,1)
   RETURN 99
   END
```

At this point all deletes have been performed and, if we find ourselves at this point in the stored procedure, everything was successful. Given this, we commit the transaction to make all deletes a permanent change on the database. We then return to the caller with a good return code:

```
--
**********************************************************************************
-- Commit Transaction
--
**********************************************************************************
COMMIT TRANSACTION Delete_Customer

--
-- Return to the caller
--
RETURN 0
```

Once again, we need to point out the importance of using comments in our stored procedures. You can quickly tell what this stored procedure is doing every step of the way by just reading the comments. The comments make the stored procedure much more readable and manageable.

Try It Out – VB Program to Implement DELETE Stored Procedure

1. Using the last project from Chapter 11 as a base, copy the `frmTryItOut3.frm` and `frmTIO3Employer.frm` forms as `frmTryItOut2.frm` and `frmTIO2Employer.frm` respectively.

2. Start a new project, remove the current form, and add these two forms that you have just copied. Copy the `modUtility.bas` module from the last chapter and add it to the project. Copy the `clsAddress.cls`, `clsCustomer.cls` and `clsEmployer.cls` classes from the previous chapter and also add them to the new project.

3. Set a reference to the latest version of the Microsoft ActiveX Data Objects Library and save your new project. Set the startup form to `frmTryItOut2`.

4. Add a command button to the `frmTryItOut2` form, set its Name property to cmdDelete and its Caption property to Delete. Place it on the form as shown in the figure below:

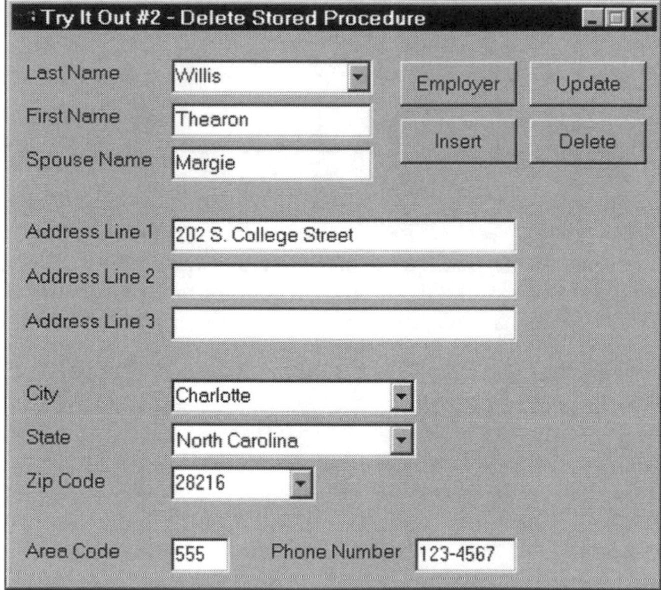

5. Add the following code to the `cmdDelete_Click` procedure:

```
Private Sub cmdDelete_Click()
    'Declare local variables
    Dim strMsg() As String, lngRC As Long

    'Instantiate the class and set a reference to the Command object
    Set m_objCustomer = New clsCustomer
    Set m_objCmd = New ADODB.Command
```

```
    'Insert the employer information
    lngRC = m_objCustomer.DeleteCustomer(m_lngCustomerID, _
       strMsg(), _
       m_objConn, _
       m_objCmd)

    'Display messages
    If lngRC <> 0 Then
       MsgBox strMsg(0), vbCritical + vbOKOnly, "Try It Out #2"
    End If

    'De-reference objects
    Set m_objCmd = Nothing
    Set m_objEmployer = Nothing
End Sub
```

6. Add the following function to the `clsCustomer` class, changing the database owner prefix if necessary:

```
Public Function DeleteCustomer(ByVal lngCustomerID As Long, _
       ByRef strMessage() As String, _
       ByRef objConn As ADODB.Connection, _
       ByRef objCmd As ADODB.Command) As Long

    'Setup error handling
    On Error GoTo DeleteCustomer_EH

    'Declare local variables
    Dim intIndex As Integer

    'Set the Command object properties
    Set objCmd.ActiveConnection = objConn
    objCmd.CommandText = "willist.up_parmdel_customer"
    objCmd.CommandType = adCmdStoredProc

    'Append the parameters
    objCmd.Parameters.Append objCmd.CreateParameter("RC", adInteger, _
          adParamReturnValue)
    objCmd.Parameters.Append objCmd.CreateParameter("CustomerID", adInteger, _
          adParamInput, , lngCustomerID)

    'Execute the Command object
    objCmd.Execute

    'If the return code is greater than zero
    If objCmd("RC") <> 0 Then
       'Add the message to the message string
       ReDim Preserve strMessage(0)
       strMessage(0) = "Delete of Customer Failed"
```

```
    End If

    'Return to the caller with the return code from the stored procedure
    DeleteCustomer = objCmd("RC")
    On Error GoTo 0
    Exit Function

DeleteCustomer_EH:
    Dim objErr As ADODB.Error
    intIndex = -1
    'Add each ADO error to the message string
    For Each objErr In objConn.Errors
        intIndex = intIndex + 1
        ReDim Preserve strMessage(intIndex)
        strMessage(intIndex) = objErr.Description
    Next
    'Add any VB error message to the message string
    intIndex = intIndex + 1
    ReDim Preserve strMessage(intIndex)
    strMessage(intIndex) = Err.Description
    'Return to the caller
    DeleteCustomer = 99
    On Error GoTo 0
End Function
```

How It Works – VB Program to Implement DELETE Stored Procedure

In our VB code, we need to add a new function in our customer class. This function, `DeleteCustomer`, will execute the stored procedure we just created. We start the function by declaring the parameters that it expects. The first parameter is the customer ID that is passed by value. The last three parameters are passed by reference, as we will be modifying some or all of them:

```
Public Function DeleteCustomer(ByVal lngCustomerID As Long, _
        ByRef strMessage() As String, _
        ByRef objConn As ADODB.Connection, _
        ByRef objCmd As ADODB.Command) As Long
```

We then set up our error handling and declare our local variables:

```
    'Setup error handling
    On Error GoTo DeleteCustomer_EH

    'Declare local variables
    Dim intIndex As Integer
```

We set the `Command` object's properties using the `Connection` object that was passed by reference and the stored procedure to delete the customer record.

Next, we append the parameters to the `Parameters` collection. Since this stored procedure will return a return value, we must append that parameter to the `Parameters` collection first. We append the customer ID input parameter next:

```
    'Set the Command object properties
    Set objCmd.ActiveConnection = objConn
    objCmd.CommandText = "willist.up_parmdel_customer"
    objCmd.CommandType = adCmdStoredProc

    'Append the parameters
    objCmd.Parameters.Append objCmd.CreateParameter("RC", adInteger, _
            adParamReturnValue)
    objCmd.Parameters.Append objCmd.CreateParameter("CustomerID", adInteger, _
            adParamInput, , lngCustomerID)
```

After executing the `Command` object we check the return value from the stored procedure. If it is not equal to zero then we add a message to the message parameter that was passed in by reference:

```
    'Execute the command object
    objCmd.Execute

    'If the return code is greater than zero
    If objCmd("RC") <> 0 Then
       'Add the message to the message string
       ReDim Preserve strMessage(0)
       strMessage(0) = "Delete of Customer Failed"
    End If
```

Regardless of any errors, we return to the caller with the return code from the stored procedure, and then we exit the function:

```
    'Return to the caller with the return code FROM the
    'stored procedure
    DeleteCustomer = objCmd("RC")
    On Error GoTo 0
    Exit Function
```

Our error handling is the same error handling routine as the other functions that we have added to this class. Briefly, it loops through the ADO `Errors` collection and appends any and all errors to the message parameter passed to this function. Then, if there is any associated VB error message, we append that error message to the parameter also, and return with a return code indicating there was an error in this function:

```
 DeleteCustomer_EH:
    Dim objErr As ADODB.Error
    intIndex = -1
    'Add each ADO error to the message string
    For Each objErr In objConn.Errors
       intIndex = intIndex + 1
       ReDim Preserve strMessage(intIndex)
       strMessage(intIndex) = objErr.Description
```

```
    Next
    'Add any VB error message to the message string
    intIndex = intIndex + 1
    ReDim Preserve strMessage(intIndex)
    strMessage(intIndex) = Err.Description
    'Return to the caller
    DeleteCustomer = 99
    On Error GoTo 0
End Function
```

The `cmdDelete_Click` procedure in our form contains the code to execute the delete function that we have just set up. The first thing that we do is to declare our local variables and set a reference to our objects:

```
Private Sub cmdDelete_Click()
    'Declare local variables
    Dim strMsg() As String, lngRC As Long

    'Instantiate the class and set a reference to the command object
    Set m_objCustomer = New clsCustomer
    Set m_objCmd = New ADODB.Command
```

Using the module level variable that contains the primary key of the currently displayed customer, we call the `DeleteCustomer` function to perform the delete. Notice that we are passing the `strMsg()` variable that will contain the error messages, if any, after the call completes. We also pass the `Connection` and `Command` objects to the function:

```
    'Insert the employer information
    lngRC = m_objCustomer.DeleteCustomer(m_lngCustomerID, _
       strMsg(), _
       m_objConn, _
       m_objCmd)
```

After our call completes, we check for errors, and display the errors in a message box if an error occurred.

The last thing we do in this procedure is to de-reference our objects:

```
    'Display messages
    If lngRC <> 0 Then
       MsgBox strMsg(0), vbCritical + vbOKOnly, "Try It Out #2"
    End If

    'Dereference objects
    Set m_objCmd = Nothing
    Set m_objEmployer = Nothing
End Sub
```

You are now ready to test your modified program. Before running your program and deleting a customer, run a query in the Query Analyzer to select all rows from the `Customer_T` table. Now run your program and pick a customer to delete from your VB program. If you set a break point in your program you can step through the function that will delete the customer. After deleting a customer, go back to the Query Analyzer and take note of the foreign keys for the customer that you deleted. You can now run a query against the `Address_T`, `Phone_Number_T` and `Customer_Information_T` tables and notice that the related data in those tables has also been deleted.

Summary

This chapter has covered two very important methods of deleting data from multiple tables at one time. Each of these methods has its own merits and both are easy to code and set up.

Triggers can be a very powerful tool in helping to maintain referential integrity and data integrity. We have also discovered that triggers are fired no matter what method was used to delete the data, and this can be a good thing, especially in tables that contain sensitive data. This is also good because we can create triggers that perform audit trails on tables and, no matter how the data gets deleted, we can maintain an audit trail on it. We can set up our triggers to write the deleted data to an audit log, which can then be examined by the appropriate parties. We can define multiple triggers on a single table, and one trigger can fire another by performing the appropriate actions (`INSERT`, `UPDATE`, or `DELETE`).

We have also examined using a stored procedure that performed the same function as the trigger, and included transactional processing. This also helps to ensure referential integrity (in other words that primary and foreign key constraints aren't violated) and data integrity (preventing orphan data) among our tables. The stored procedure approach does offer one advantage over a trigger. The trigger is fired *after* the data has been deleted. The stored procedure can delete the data when the time is appropriate. In other words, we can perform any number of processes against other tables in this stored procedure before actually deleting the data. This can be a benefit, especially when another table has a foreign key reference to the table that we want to delete from. The stored procedure could delete all of the foreign key references to this table and then delete the row of data in this table. A trigger does not offer that flexibility.

In summary you should know:

- How to create a trigger
- How to delete a trigger
- How to create a stored procedure that deletes data and uses transactions
- The advantages of using triggers and stored procedures to delete data

Now that we've covered the four different types of stored procedure in detail, we're ready to move on and create a front end to provide our users with a friendly interface to the database.

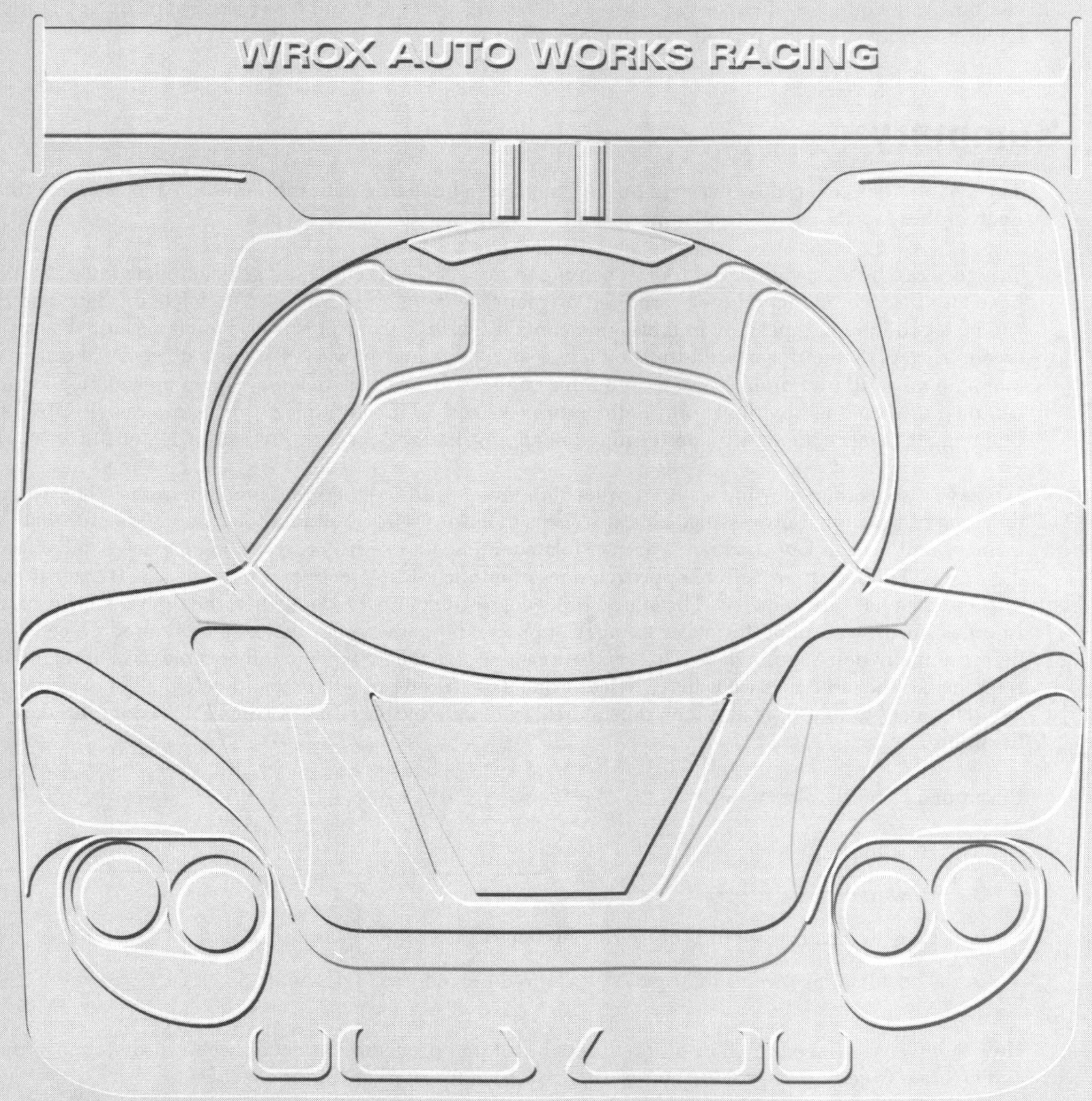
WROX AUTO WORKS RACING

Creating a Front-End Program

Up to this point, we have created a number of stored procedures that do everything from selecting data to deleting data. The functions that execute these stored procedures start with simple functions and progress to more complex ones. Along the way, we have used these stored procedures in VB programs and have introduced some techniques that help us to reuse our code and stored procedures, such as using functions in classes to execute our stored procedures. We have also introduced some techniques useful in a User Interface (UI), such as reloading the combo boxes when data has been changed.

This chapter expands on all of this information by building a VB front-end program that implements most of the techniques that we have explored so far. What we will attempt to do in this chapter is to focus most of our attention on building the UI that implements calls to most of the stored procedures that we have built. We will focus on what can be done in the UI to validate data before passing it to our stored procedures. We will also explore some techniques that can be employed to ensure the data fields have data before allowing the user to insert them into the database.

In order to build a friendlier UI, we will need to create a few more stored procedures. While these stored procedures are simple in nature, they go a long way in helping to provide a better UI and will be used to populate combo boxes with data that gives the user a selection of items to choose from.

While the UI will be far from a complete and functional UI, we will implement some of the controls that help to make a UI more user friendly, such as a toolbar and status bar. The status bar will be fully functional, but only one icon on the toolbar will be functional. The rest of the icons are for appearance at this point and can be completed by you at a later date if you so choose.

In this chapter, we will cover:

- Stored procedures that select and update data
- Form design for the UI
- Data validation in the UI
- Presentation and separation of data

Stored Procedures

Up to this point we have been entering employer information without regard to any data that already existed in the Employer_T table. The UI that we build in this chapter will present the user with a selection of employers to choose from in a combo box. If the employer they need does not exist, then they will be able to enter a new employer in the combo box. To that end, we need to create a stored procedure to return all employers listed in the Employer_T table.

The following code lists the up_select_employers stored procedure. Go ahead and create this stored procedure and set the appropriate permissions on it:

```
CREATE PROCEDURE up_select_employers AS

SELECT Employer_ID, Company_Name_VC
     FROM Employer_T
     ORDER By Company_Name_VC
```

On our previous Employment forms we also entered and displayed the phone number for the employer. This UI is no different and we need to create a stored procedure to select the phone number for the employer the user chooses. The following code lists the stored procedure that needs to be created to select the employer phone number:

```
CREATE PROCEDURE up_parmsel_employer_phone_number (@Employer_ID INT) AS

SELECT Phone_Number_T.Phone_Number_ID, Area_Code_SI, Phone_Number_IN
     FROM Employer_T
     JOIN Phone_Number_T
          ON Employer_T.Phone_Number_ID = Phone_Number_T.Phone_Number_ID
     WHERE Employer_ID = @Employer_ID
```

There is one last stored procedure that we want to create. In Chapter 10, we created dynamic in-line SQL to update the customer information. The UI that we will be building in this chapter will execute a function in the Customer class to update the customer's name and spouse's name. The function will in turn execute the following stored procedure. After creating this stored procedure don't forget to set the appropriate permissions on it:

```
CREATE PROCEDURE up_parmupd_customer (@Customer_ID INT, @First_Name VARCHAR(30),
     @Last_Name VARCHAR(30), @Spouse_Name VARCHAR(30)) AS

--
*****************************************************************************************
-- Update the customer names
--
*****************************************************************************************
UPDATE Customer_T
     SET First_Name_VC = @First_Name,
     Last_Name_VC = @Last_Name,
     Spouse_First_Name_VC = @Spouse_Name,
     Last_Update_DT = GETDATE()
     WHERE Customer_ID = @Customer_ID
```

This completes the new stored procedures needed for the UI. The rest of the stored procedures have already been built and tested, and the functions to execute them reside in the classes that we have been building in the last four chapters.

Wrox Auto Works Customer Application

Our customer application will allow the sales staff of the fictitious company, Wrox Auto Works, to look up and display customer information. Having the customer's information at hand allows the sales staff to treat returning customers with respect for their time and help make them feel valued. New customers will be asked to provide this information so we can enter it, and our valued customers will just verify the information we already have.

There are several controls that are commonplace in every application we use today. These include such items as a menu, toolbar and status bar. Our application will be no different and will include all of these, so let's take a look at each of these in turn.

The menu that is displayed in your application is really dependent on the functionality implemented by your application. However, regardless of the menu options provided, the menu should provide a look and feel that is consistent with the Windows interface. All menus should be accessible through the use of keyboard shortcut keys such as *Alt+F* to open the File menu.

There are certain menus that are common and consistent in the Windows interface such as the File menu, which contains items to Open, Close and Save files, as well as to Print and Exit the application. Other common menus include the Edit, View and Help menus that provide basic usability for your application. While these menus are not required, they should be used where appropriate to avoid losing some of the functionality of your application.

All of these menus have been included in our application, but have not had all of their functionality implemented. If you choose to complete this application at a later date, you can implement the functionality in these menus.

The toolbar and status bar are also common controls that are found in all applications that conform to Windows Interface Guidelines. This guideline provides general information about what features a user interface should contain. You can find this guide in the Platform SDK in the MSDN Library that came with Visual Studio or it can be accessed online at http://msdn.microsoft.com/library/default.htm. The toolbar contains buttons that provide shortcuts to commonly used menu items, while the status bar provides an informational display about the status of your application, and can also be used to provide feedback about the controls and what their purposes are.

Visual Elements

Let's start building our customer application by placing the required controls on our form. Once we have the Main form (`frmMain`) complete, we will move on to the Employment form (`frmEmployment`) and build a splash screen. We start building our Main form (`frmMain`) by placing the common controls on the form.

Start a new project and set the project's Name property to WAWCustomerApplication. Set the form's Name property to frmMain and its Caption property to Wrox Auto Works Customer Application. The form's Height property should be set to 6708, its Width property to 7800, and set the MaxButton property to False.

In order to add the toolbar and status bar you will need to add the Microsoft Windows Common Controls 6.0 component to your toolbox.

To add a menu to your form, click on the Menu Editor from the Tools menu, to invoke the Menu Editor dialog. The Menu controls in the table below are the top-level menus listed in your form, such as File and Edit. The Menu Items are the items under the top-level menus. Use the right arrow key in the Menu Editor dialog to indent menu items.

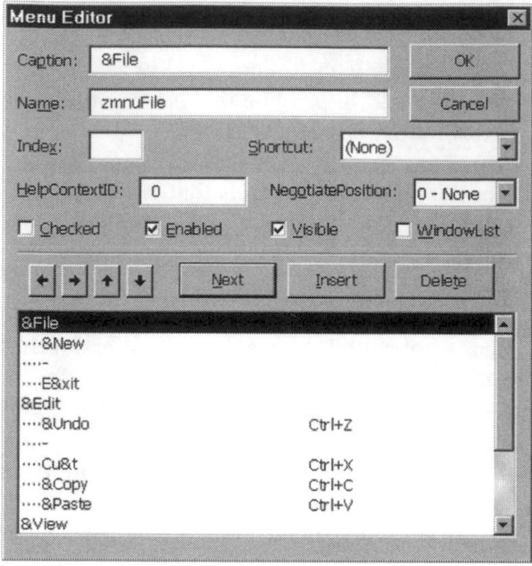

Using the table and figure below, add the following controls to the Main form. Menu names that begin with the letter z are named as such so they are at the bottom of the Object combo box in VB, since we will not be adding code to these objects.

Control	Name	Properties
Menu	`zmnuFile`	Caption = &File
Menu Item	`mnuFileNew`	Caption = &New
Menu Item	`zmnuSep1`	Caption = -
Menu Item	`mnuFileExit`	Caption = E&xit
Menu	`zmnuEdit`	Caption = &Edit
Menu Item	`mnuEditUndo`	Caption = &Undo, ShortCut = Ctrl+Z
Menu Item	`zmnuSep2`	Caption = -
Menu Item	`mnuEditCut`	Caption = Cu&t, ShortCut = Ctrl+X
Menu Item	`mnuEditCopy`	Caption = &Copy, ShortCut = Ctrl+C
Menu Item	`mnuEditPaste`	Caption = &Paste, ShortCut = Ctrl+V
Menu	`zmnuView`	Caption = &View
Menu Item	`mnuViewEmployment`	Caption = &Employment

Control	Name	Properties
Menu	`zmnuHelp`	Caption = &Help
Menu Item	`mnuHelpContents`	Caption = &Contents and Index
Menu Item	`zmnuSep3`	Caption = -
Menu Item	`mnuHelpAbout`	Caption = &About Customer Application
Image List	`ImlToolbarIcons`	ImageHeight = 16, ImageWidth = 16, add the images shown on the toolbar in the screen shot overleaf. These images are typically found in the following directory: C:\Program Files\Microsoft Visual Studio\Common\Graphics\Bitmaps\TlBr_W95
ToolBar	`Toolbar1`	ImageList = ImlToolbarIcons Button 1: Style = 3 – tbrSeparator Button 2: Style = 0 – tbrDefault, Key = New, ToolTipText = New Button 3: Style = 3 – tbrSeparator Button 4: Style = 0 – tbrDefault, Key = Cut, ToolTipText = Cut Button 5: Style = 0 – tbrDefault, Key = Copy, ToolTipText = Copy Button 6: Style = 0 – tbrDefault, Key = Paste, ToolTipText = Paste Button 7: Style = 3 – tbrSeparator Button 8: Style = 0 – tbrDefault, Key = Undo, ToolTipText = Undo Button 9: Style = 0 – tbrSeparator Button 10: Style = 0 – tbrDefault, Key = Help What's This, ToolTipText = Help What's This Button 11: Style = 0 – tbrDefault, Key = Help, ToolTipText = Help Contents and Index
Line	`Line1(0)`	Make this control and all controls that have a number in parentheses a control array. BorderColor = &H00808080&, X1 = 0, X2 = 8160, Y1 = 360, Y2 = 360

Control	Name	Properties
Line	`Line1(1)`	BorderColor = &H00FFFFFF&, X1 = 0, X2 = 8160, Y1 = 366, Y2 = 366
Status Bar	`StatusBar1`	Panel 1: Key = Msg, Minimum Width = 1440.00, Alignment = 0 – sbrLeft, Style = 0 – sbrText, AutoSize = 1 – sbrSpring Panel 2: Minimum Width = 1000.06, Alignment = 1 – sbrCenter, Style = 6 – sbrDate, AutoSize = 0 - sbrNoAutoSize

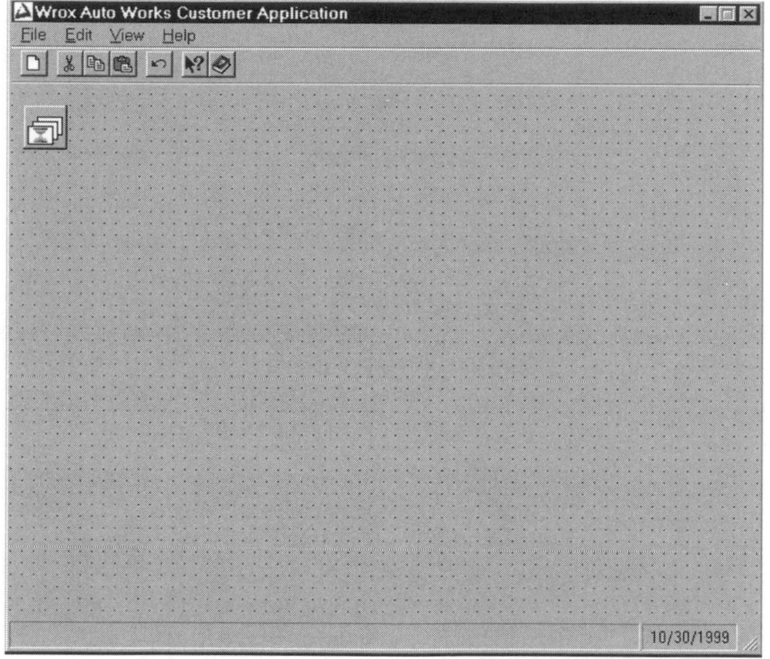

Data Presentation

In order to create an application that will be useful to the user and one that the user will use, we must give careful consideration to the presentation of data. The form that we design can not be too complicated to use nor can it be too cluttered. Looking back at the example programs that we have built in the last four chapters, we know what data must be displayed on the main form and we also know how the data is separated in the database. We know that the address and phone number are separate from the customer's name, and we should convey that these are two separate, but related, pieces of data.

The next figure shows how the data is separated. Notice that we use frames not only to separate the controls from each other, but also to group the related controls. We also use captions to give a one-word explanation of what each frame does. Notice that the Customer frame displays customer names and that the Address frame displays customer address information. The Actions frame contains the controls that let us perform some type of action on the data and the Views frame lets us know that we can view other data. The Checklist frame contains a checklist.

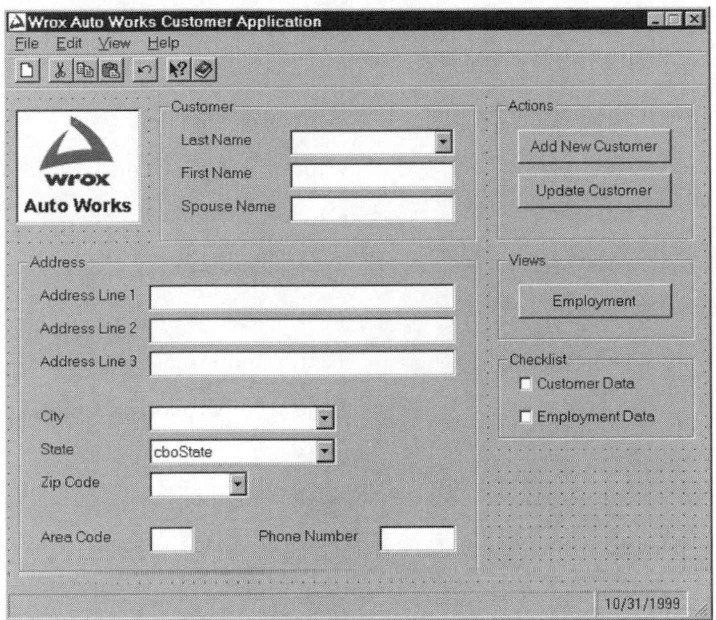

Using the table below and figure above, add the following controls to the Main form (`frmMain`):

Control	Name	Properties
Image	`Image1`	
Frame	`Frame1`	Caption = Customer
Label	`Label1(0)`	Caption = Last Name
Label	`Label1(1)`	Caption = First Name
Label	`Label1(2)`	Caption = Spouse Name
ComboBox	`cboLastName`	Style = 0 – Dropdown Combo, Text = nothing
TextBox	`txtFirstName`	Text = nothing
TextBox	`txtSpouseName`	Text = nothing
Frame	`Frame2`	Caption = Address

Control	Name	Properties
Label	Label1(3)	Caption = Address Line 1
Label	Label1(4)	Caption = Address Line 2
Label	Label1(5)	Caption = Address Line 3
Label	Label1(6)	Caption = City
Label	Label1(7)	Caption = State
Label	Label1(8)	Caption = Zip Code
Label	Label1(9)	Caption = Area Code
Label	Label1(10)	Caption = Phone Number
TextBox	txtAddress1	Text = nothing
TextBox	txtAddress2	Text = nothing
TextBox	txtAddress3	Text = nothing
ComboBox	cboCity	Style = 0 – Dropdown Combo, Text = nothing
ComboBox	cboState	Style = 2 – Dropdown List
ComboBox	cboZipCode	Style = 0 – Dropdown Combo, Text = nothing
TextBox	txtAreaCode	Text = nothing
TextBox	txtPhoneNumber	Text = nothing
Frame	Frame3	Caption = Actions
Command Button	cmdAdd	Caption = Add New Customer, Enabled = False
Command Button	cmdUpdate	Caption = Update Customer
Frame	Frame4	Caption = Views
Command Button	cmdEmployment	Caption = Employment, CauseValidation = False
Frame	Frame5	Caption = Checklist
CheckBox	chkCustomerData	Caption = Customer Data, TabStop = False
CheckBox	chkEmploymentData	Caption = Employment Data, TabStop = False

This wraps up the design and controls for the Main form. We will move on to design the Employment form (frmEmployment) next, and come back and add the code later.

Employment Form

This section discusses the elements of the Employment form (`frmEmployment`). This form is quite different from the Main form in that it is shown modally over the Main form. When a form is shown modally, no other form in the project can receive focus until the form that is being shown is unloaded or hidden. This form can not be minimized and has no menus or toolbars. Our application is so small that it does not warrant the complexities of a Multiple Document Interface (MDI) application, hence the absence of the menu and toolbar. It does however have a status bar, in which it can display any error and informational messages.

The design of the Employment form (`frmEmployment`) is very similar to what we have been using in the previous chapters. All of the information is the same; just the presentation is different. In keeping with the Main form, we want to provide a separation of data. Therefore the current employer information is separated from the previous employer information. While both employers are stored in one table, one piece of information is required, while the second piece of information is optional.

In order to give the user the option of choosing an employer that already exists or entering a new employer, we will be using combo boxes to display the current and previous employer data. When a user clicks on an employer in the combo box, the program will execute a function to retrieve the currently displayed employer's phone number and display it in the phone number fields.

To start, let's add a new form to our project and set the following properties for this form:

Property	**Value**
`Name`	`frmEmployment`
`Caption`	Customer Employment Information
`BorderStyle`	3 – Fixed Dialog
`Icon`	None (Use the delete key to delete the current icon)
`Height`	4440
`Width`	7380

Add a status bar to this form and set its properties as follows:

Property	**Value**
`Name`	Statusbar1
`Key`	Msg
`Alignment`	0 – sbrLeft
`Style`	0 – sbrText
`AutoSize`	1 - sbrSpring

To complete the Employment form (`frmEmployment`), add the controls listed in the table below. Use the following figure as a guideline for the placement of these controls on the form:

Control	Name	Properties
Frame	`Frame1`	`Caption` = Current Employer
Label	`Label1(0)`	`Caption` = Current Employer
Label	`Label1(1)`	`Caption` = Area Code
Label	`Label1(2)`	`Caption` = Phone Number
Label	`Label1(3)`	`Caption` = Job Title
Label	`Label1(4)`	`Caption` = Years Employed
ComboBox	`cboCurrentEmployer`	`Style` = 0 – Dropdown Combo
TextBox	`txtCEAreaCode`	`Text` = nothing
TextBox	`txtCEPhoneNumber`	`Text` = nothing
TextBox	`txtJobTitle`	`Text` = nothing
TextBox	`txtCEYearsEmployed`	`Text` = nothing
Frame	`Frame2`	`Caption` = Previous Employer
Label	`Label1(5)`	`Caption` = Previous Employer
Label	`Label1(6)`	`Caption` = Area Code
Label	`Label1(7)`	`Caption` = Phone Number
Label	`Label1(8)`	`Caption` = Years Employed
ComboBox	`cboPreviousEmployer`	`Style` = 0 – Dropdown Combo
TextBox	`txtPEAreaCode`	`Text` = nothing
TextBox	`txtPEPhoneNumber`	`Text` = nothing
Textbox	`txtPEYearsEmployed`	`Text` = nothing
Frame	`Frame3`	`Caption` = Actions
Command Button	`cmdAdd`	`Caption` = Add Employers
Command Button	`cmdUpdate`	`Caption` = Update Employer
Command Button	`cmdClose`	`Caption` = Close

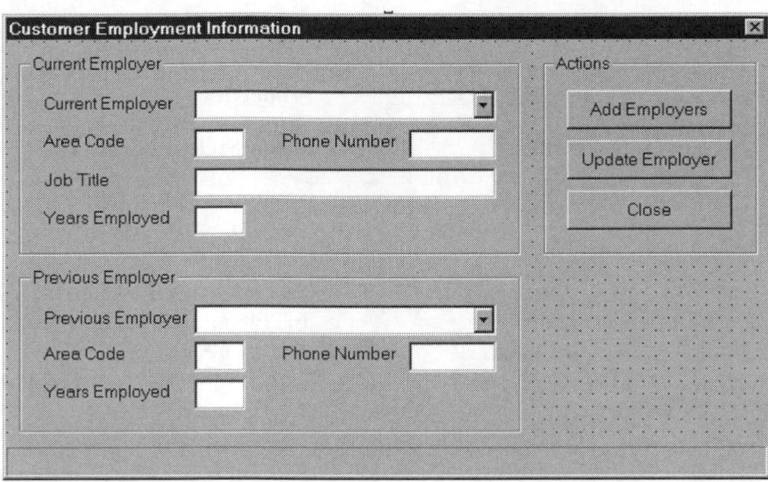

This wraps up the Employment form (`frmEmployment`) and the controls needed to implement displaying and editing the employment information.

About/Splash Form

Because the initial connection to the database takes a few seconds, we want to display a splash screen for our users. The About form that is displayed for most applications resembles the splash screen in a lot of ways. We are going to use a form that combines both the Splash screen and the About form in one. This form is provided by Microsoft who allow us to use, modify and distribute this form freely as long as we agree that Microsoft has no warranty, obligations or liability whatsoever.

We are going to modify this form and code slightly but the full-unmodified version can be downloaded from the Wrox Web site at `http://www.wrox.com`.

Add a new form to your project and set the form's properties as follows:

Property	Value
`Name`	AbSplash
`Caption`	application title
`BorderStyle`	3 – Fixed Dialog
`Icon`	None
`Height`	5256
`Width`	6432

Using the table and figure below, add the following controls to the form:

Control	Name	Properties
Image	`imgIcon`	BorderStyle = 0 – None
Label	`lblTitle`	Caption = application title
Timer	`Timer1`	Enabled = False
Label	`lblComanyName`	Caption = nothing (this label is between lblTitle and lblVersion)
Label	`lblVersion`	Caption = version information
Line	`linDivide(0)`	X1 = 120, X2 = 6240, Y1 = 1440, Y2 = 1440
Label	`lblCopyright`	Caption = copyright information
Label	`lblTrademark`	Caption = trademark information
Label	`lblFileDescription`	Caption = file description
Label	`lblMisc`	Caption = This product is licensed to:
PictureBox	`Picture1`	
Label	`lblUserName`	Caption = user name
Label	`lblUserInfo`	Caption = user information
Label	`lblPathEXE`	Caption = path and exe information, Alignment = 1 – Right Justify
Line	`linDivide(1)`	X1 = 120, X2 = 6240, Y1 = 3600, Y2 = 3600
Label	`lblWarning`	Caption = generic warning
Command Button	`cmdOK`	Caption = OK
Command Button	`cmdSysInfo`	Caption = &System Info

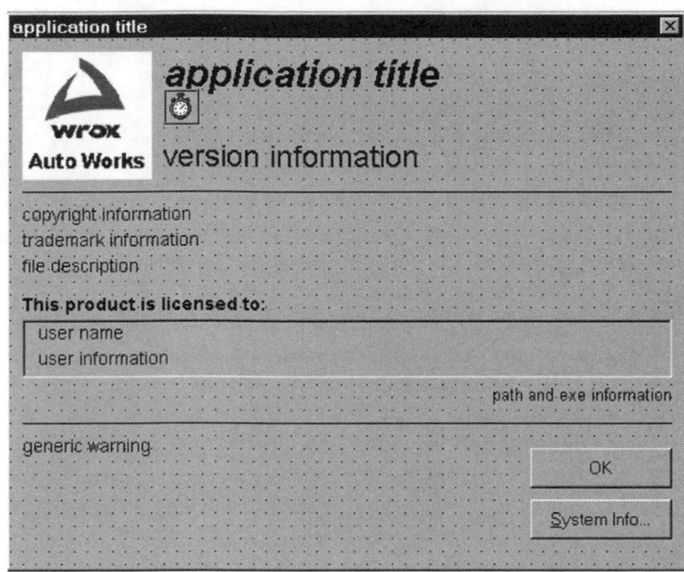

This completes the forms required in our project. We will move on to add the classes that will provide the functionality to execute our stored procedure and implement the code in these forms.

Classes

The whole idea behind placing all of our functions that executed our stored procedures in classes was that we would be able to reuse them. Given this we can reuse the classes that we have been building in the past several chapters. Copy the Address, Customer and Employer classes to the project directory and add them to this project. Also copy and add the Utility module.

Because we built several new stored procedures, we need to implement the functions to execute them in our classes. These functions are very simple and resemble the functions that you have built in the previous chapters. We start with the Employer class to add a function to select all employers. This function will be called from the Employment form (`frmEmployment`) and be used to load the employer combo boxes. The code for this function is listed below:

```
Public Function GetAllEmployers(ByRef objConn As ADODB.Connection, _
      ByRef objRS As ADODB.Recordset) As Long

   'Setup error handling
   On Error GoTo GetAllEmployers_EH

   'Set a reference to the Recordset object
   Set objRS = New ADODB.Recordset

   'Open the recordset
   objRS.Open "willist.up_select_employers", objConn, _
      adOpenForwardOnly, adLockReadOnly, adCmdStoredProc
```

```
    'Return with a good return code
    GetAllEmployers = 0

    'All was successful, exit function
    On Error GoTo 0
    Exit Function

GetAllEmployers_EH:
    GetAllEmployers = 1
    On Error GoTo 0
End Function
```

The next function will also be called from the Employment form (`frmEmployment`) and will execute this function in the Address class. When a user selects an employer in the Employer combo box, we need to get the employer's phone number. Since we consider a phone number part of the address, this next function should be implemented in the `Address` class:

```
Public Function GetPhoneNumber(ByRef objConn As ADODB.Connection, _
      ByRef objRS As ADODB.Recordset, _
      ByVal lngParentID As Long, _
      ByVal lngPhoneType As PhoneType) As Long

   'Setup error handling
   On Error GoTo GetPhoneNumber_EH

   'Set a reference to the Recordset object
   Set objRS = New ADODB.Recordset

   'Retreive the correct phone number
   Select Case lngPhoneType
      Case ptSalesPerson

      Case ptEmployer

         'Open the recordset
         objRS.Open "willist.up_parmsel_employer_phone_number (" & _
               lngParentID & ")", objConn, _
               adOpenStatic, adLockReadOnly, adCmdStoredProc

   End Select

   'Return with a good return code
   GetPhoneNumber = 0

   'All was successful, exit function
   On Error GoTo 0
   Exit Function

GetPhoneNumber_EH:
   GetPhoneNumber = 1
   On Error GoTo 0
End Function
```

Notice that we are using an enumeration for the phone number type. This is because we have plans to expand the phone numbers that are used and have set up the following enumeration in the general declarations section of the Address class:

```
Public Enum PhoneType
   ptSalesPerson = 1
   ptEmployer = 2
End Enum
```

The last stored procedure that we created replaced the dynamic in-line SQL to update a customer. Because of this we need to update the `UpdateCustomer` function in the Customer class. The code listed next shows the updates to this function:

```
Public Function UpdateCustomer(ByVal lngCustomerID As Long, _
      ByVal strFirstName As String, _
      ByVal strLastName As String, _
      ByVal strSpouseName As String, _
      ByRef objConn As ADODB.Connection, _
      ByRef objCmd As ADODB.Command) As Long

   'Setup error handling
   On Error GoTo UpdateCustomer_EH

   'Set the command object properties
   Set objCmd.ActiveConnection = objConn
   objCmd.CommandText = "willist.up_parmupd_customer"
   objCmd.CommandType = adCmdStoredProc

   'Append the parameters
   objCmd.Parameters.Append objCmd.CreateParameter("CustomerID", adInteger, _
         adParamInput, , lngCustomerID)
   objCmd.Parameters.Append objCmd.CreateParameter("FirstName", adVarChar, _
         adParamInput, 30, strFirstName)
   objCmd.Parameters.Append objCmd.CreateParameter("LastName", adVarChar, _
         adParamInput, 30, strLastName)
   objCmd.Parameters.Append objCmd.CreateParameter("SpouseName", adVarChar, _
         adParamInput, 30, strSpouseName)

   'Execute the Command object
   objCmd.Execute

   'Return with a good return code
   UpdateCustomer = 0
   On Error GoTo 0
   Exit Function

UpdateCustomer_EH:
   'Return to the caller
   UpdateCustomer = 99
   On Error GoTo 0
End Function
```

AbSplash Form Code

We start entering the code in the forms in the reverse order in which we have built them. This is because this form will be the first form called and displayed from the Main form (`frmMain`). Also the Employment form (`frmEmployment`) is called from the Main form, and the procedure that is called from the Main form must be built first.

Try It Out – AbSplash Form Code

This form contains the functionality to perform as both a Splash form and an About form. Add the code that exposes this functionality to the Main form. This form contains quite a lot of code, some of which might be advanced for some readers. Therefore, we will present and explain it all in the *How It Works* section.

How It Works – AbSplash Form Code – General Declarations

Let's examine the code in this form in detail starting with the code in the general declarations section. This form makes heavy use of reading values from the registry to retrieve information about the user logged on, thus there must be some APIs declared for this purpose. The first two APIs listed below are used to show and hide the title bar of the form. The last three APIs are used to open, read and close a registry key. You access registry keys just like a file. You must first open the key before you can read it and close the key after you have finished reading it:

```
' -------------------------------------------------------------------------
'      Copyright © 1997 Microsoft Corporation.  All rights reserved.
'
' You have a royalty-free right to use, modify, reproduce and distribute
' the Sample Application Files (and/or any modified version) in any way
' you find useful, provided that you agree that Microsoft has no warranty,
' obligations or liability for any Sample Application Files.
' -------------------------------------------------------------------------

Option Explicit

' API declarations
Private Declare Function GetWindowLong Lib "user32" Alias "GetWindowLongA" _
        (ByVal hWnd As Long, ByVal nIndex As Long) As Long
Private Declare Function SetWindowLong Lib "user32" Alias "SetWindowLongA" _
        (ByVal hWnd As Long, ByVal nIndex As Long, ByVal dwNewLong As Long) _
         As Long
Private Declare Function RegOpenKeyEx Lib "advapi32" Alias "RegOpenKeyExA" _
        (ByVal hKey As Long, ByVal lpSubKey As String, ByVal ulOptions As Long, _
         ByVal _
          samDesired As Long, ByRef phkResult As Long) As Long
Private Declare Function RegQueryValueEx Lib "advapi32" Alias "RegQueryValueExA" _
        (ByVal hKey As Long, ByVal lpValueName As String, ByVal lpReserved _
         As Long, ByRef _
          lpType As Long, ByVal lpData As String, ByRef lpcbData As Long) As Long
Private Declare Function RegCloseKey Lib "advapi32" (ByVal hKey As Long) As Long
```

When dealing with the registry there are security settings that can be applied to the various keys in the various hives of the registry when running on Windows NT. Windows 9x platforms do not support these security settings. A hive is a discrete body of keys, subkeys, and values rooted at the top of the Registry hierarchy and which are permanent components of the Registry. Microsoft has defined some of the more common security constants here:

```
' Reg Key Security Options...
Const READ_CONTROL = &H20000
Const KEY_QUERY_VALUE = &H1
Const KEY_SET_VALUE = &H2
Const KEY_CREATE_SUB_KEY = &H4
Const KEY_ENUMERATE_SUB_KEYS = &H8
Const KEY_NOTIFY = &H10
Const KEY_CREATE_LINK = &H20
Const KEY_ALL_ACCESS = KEY_QUERY_VALUE + KEY_SET_VALUE + _
                       KEY_CREATE_SUB_KEY + KEY_ENUMERATE_SUB_KEYS + _
                       KEY_NOTIFY + KEY_CREATE_LINK + READ_CONTROL
```

As we just mentioned, there are several hives in the registry and the APIs expect the hive where the registry key is located as one of their parameters. The constants defining the various registry hives are listed next with their associated hexadecimal values. Along with this are the constants defining two of the most common types of registry keys that can be used to. The registry actually supports three types of key values to: string, binary and DWORD. A key that contains a string value is just like strings in VB, while keys that contain a binary value are stored in binary (1s and 0s). A key that contains a DWORD value is stored in hexadecimal but also shows the decimal equivalent value:

```
' Reg Key ROOT Types...
Const HKEY_CLASSES_ROOT = &H80000000
Const HKEY_CURRENT_USER = &H80000001
Const HKEY_LOCAL_MACHINE = &H80000002
Const ERROR_SUCCESS = 0
Const REG_SZ = 1                           ' Unicode nul terminated string
Const REG_DWORD = 4                        ' 32-bit number
```

Next are the constants that are used to turn the title bar on and off:

```
' API Constants
Private Const GWL_STYLE          As Long = (-16)
Private Const WS_CAPTION         As Long = &HC00000
Private Const WS_CAPTION_NOT     As Long = &HFFFFFFFF - WS_CAPTION
```

There's a lot to be learned by reading other programmers' code and reading code from Microsoft is no different. Here we discover some of the locations in the registry for various information about the software that runs on the different operating systems, as defined in these constants:

```
Private Const gREGKEYSYSINFOLOC As String = "SOFTWARE\Microsoft\Shared Tools
Location"
Private Const gREGKEYSYSINFO    As String = "SOFTWARE\Microsoft\Shared
Tools\MSINFO"

Private Const gREGVALSYSINFOLOC As String = "MSINFO"
```

```
Private Const gREGVALSYSINFO     As String = "PATH"

' NT location of user name and company
Private Const gNTREGKEYINFO      As String = "SOFTWARE\Microsoft\Windows
NT\CurrentVersion"
Private Const gNTREGVALUSER      As String = "RegisteredOwner"
Private Const gNTREGVALCOMPANY   As String = "RegisteredOrganization"

' Win95 locataion of user name and company
Private Const g95REGKEYINFO      As String = "Software\Microsoft\MS Setup
(ACME)\User Info"
Private Const g95REGVALUSER      As String = "DefName"
Private Const g95REGVALCOMPANY   As String = "DefCompany"
```

The following three constants are to be used by you if you want to change the default values that are displayed. These constants are used to display information on the form such as the user name and information when the values can not be read from the registry. At the very least here is where you would change the default warning message that gets displayed on the About form:

```
' Change these to what you want the default name and user info to be
Private Const DEFAULT_USER_NAME As String = "USER INFORMATION NOT AVAILABLE"
Private Const DEFAULT_USER_INFO As String = vbNullString

' Information for warning information at bottom of form
Private Const gWarningInfo       As String = "generic warning information"
```

The last part of the declarations declares some variables that are used throughout the form, which are self-explanatory:

```
Private mBoxHeight               As Integer
Private mStyle                   As StyleType
Private mTitleBarHidden          As Boolean

' Type declarations
Private Type StyleType
    OldStyle As Long
    NewStyle As Long
End Type 'StyleType
```

SplashOn Procedure

The `SplashOn` procedure gets called from the Main form when the Main form starts to load. This procedure provides the Splash screen that gives the user something to read and an indication that our program is loading. There is one required parameter and that is the parent form (the name of the form that called this procedure). The next three parameters are optional and are used to control how long the splash screen is displayed for, and optional user information to override reading the values from the registry:

```
Public Sub SplashOn(frmParent As Form, Optional MinDisplay As Long, _
                    Optional lUserName As String, Optional lUserInfo As String)
```

Once this form is displayed either through the `SplashOn` procedure or through the `About` procedure, the form is hidden and not unloaded. Therefore subsequent requests to display the form are much faster. Given this, the first line of code checks to see if the form is already loaded in memory and is hidden. If it is not, then it goes through the process of reading the registry and building the form. As part of this check, the `Form_Load` event is fired and the code there is executed. We will examine this event very shortly. The first thing this procedure does is to disable the command buttons.

We have commented out the loading of the parent form's icon and have placed our own bitmap in the image control as was seen in the form design:

```
    If Not Visible Then
        Dim lHeight As Integer

'        imgIcon.Picture = frmParent.Icon
        cmdOK.Enabled = False
        cmdSysInfo.Enabled = False
```

If the form is requested to be displayed for a specified amount of time, then the timer is set and enabled:

```
'       If a delay is specified, set up the Timer
        If MinDisplay > 0 Then
            Timer1.Interval = MinDisplay
            Timer1.Enabled = True
        End If
```

If the optional parameters for the user information contain data, then they supersede reading the values from the registry and are used on the form instead:

```
'       Add user information to form
        If lUserName <> "" Then
            lblUserName.Caption = lUserName
            lblUserInfo.Caption = lUserInfo
        Else
            lblUserName.Caption = GetUserName
            lblUserInfo.Caption = GetUserCompany
        End If
```

Because a Splash screen does not contain a title bar, the `HideTitleBar` procedure is called to do what its name implies. We will be covering this procedure shortly. After the title bar is hidden, the form is resized to get the correct height without the title bar. Notice that as part of resizing the form, the code uses the second line (`linDivide(1)`) on the `AbSplash` form as a point from which to gauge the bottom of the form:

```
'       Modify the form style to hide the title bar
        HideTitleBar

'       Need to cause a form resize in order to get updated ScaleHeight value
        lHeight = Height
        Height = 0
        Height = lHeight

'       Set height to hide the "About Box Only" information
        Height = linDivide(1).Y1 + (Height - ScaleHeight)
```

At this point, the form is shown modeless and a `Refresh` is performed:

```
'        Show the form
         Show vbModeless, frmParent

'        For some reason, need a Refresh to make sure Splash Screen gets painted
         Refresh
     End If
End Sub
```

Form_Load Event

When the `Form_Load` event is fired, the labels on the form are set using the information gathered here. As you can see from the first line of code, the warning constant is used to set the warning message on the form. Then the built-in VB `App` object is used to gather some more basic information such as title and company name, and the appropriate labels on the form are loaded with the information gathered from it:

```
Private Sub Form_Load()
    lblWarning.Caption = gWarningInfo

'   Fill in all of the information that comes from the App object
    With App
        Caption = "About " & .Title
        lblTitle.Caption = .Title

        If .CompanyName <> "" Then
            lblCompanyName.Caption = "A product of " & .CompanyName
        Else
            lblCompanyName.Caption = ""
        End If

        lblVersion.Caption = "Version " & .Major & "." & .Minor & "." & _
                             .Revision & " (32-bit)"
        lblCopyright.Caption = .LegalCopyright
        lblTrademark.Caption = .LegalTrademarks
        lblPathEXE.Caption = .Path & "\" & .EXEName & " "
        lblFileDescription.Caption = .FileDescription
    End With 'App

'   Get "default" height of About Box
    mBoxHeight = Height
End Sub
```

GetUserName Procedure

The `GetUserName` procedure uses the registry APIs to read the user information from the registry. The first query of the registry is for Windows NT in the `HKEY_LOCAL_MACHINE` hive of the registry. If the user name was not found there, it is assumed that you are running on a Windows 95/98 machine and a query is performed in the `HKEY_CURRENT_USER` hive of the registry. If that query fails then the default constant from the general declarations section is used:

```
Private Function GetUserName() As String
    Dim KeyVal As String

'   For WindowsNT
   If (GetKeyValue(HKEY_LOCAL_MACHINE, gNTREGKEYINFO, gNTREGVALUSER, KeyVal)) Then
        GetUserName = KeyVal
'   For Windows95
   ElseIf (GetKeyValue(HKEY_CURRENT_USER, g95REGKEYINFO, g95REGVALUSER, KeyVal)) _
        Then
        GetUserName = KeyVal
'   None of the above
    Else
        GetUserName = DEFAULT_USER_NAME
    End If
End Function
```

GetUserCompany Procedure

The same procedure as above is used for the `GetUserCompany` procedure:

```
Private Function GetUserCompany() As String
    Dim KeyVal As String

'   For WindowsNT
If (GetKeyValue(HKEY_LOCAL_MACHINE, gNTREGKEYINFO, gNTREGVALCOMPANY, KeyVal)) Then
        GetUserCompany = KeyVal
'   For Windows95
    ElseIf (GetKeyValue(HKEY_CURRENT_USER, g95REGKEYINFO, g95REGVALCOMPANY, _
            KeyVal)) Then
        GetUserCompany = KeyVal
'   None of the above
    Else
        GetUserCompany = DEFAULT_USER_INFO
    End If
End Function
```

GetKeyValue Procedure

The `GetKeyValue` procedure is at the heart of reading the registry in this form. This procedure performs all of the necessary steps to open, read and close a registry key:

```
Private Function GetKeyValue(KeyRoot As Long, KeyName As String, SubKeyRef As _
        String, ByRef KeyVal As String) As Boolean
    Dim I As Long                       ' Loop Counter
    Dim rc As Long                      ' Return Code
    Dim hKey As Long                    ' Handle To An Open Registry Key
    Dim hDepth As Long                                    '
    Dim KeyValType As Long              'Data Type Of A Registry Key
    Dim tmpVal As String                ' Temporary Storage For A Registry Key Value
    Dim KeyValSize As Long              ' Size Of Registry Key Variable
```

The first thing that is done after declaring the local variables is to open the registry key. Reading the registry is like reading a file, first we open it, then read from it and then close it. After the registry key is opened the code checks for errors, and then allocates an estimated amount of space in the variable to hold the key value being read:

```
    '------------------------------------------------------------
    ' Open RegKey Under KeyRoot {HKEY_LOCAL_MACHINE...}
    '------------------------------------------------------------
    rc = RegOpenKeyEx(KeyRoot, KeyName, 0, KEY_ALL_ACCESS, hKey)
    ' Open Registry Key

    If (rc <> ERROR_SUCCESS) Then GoTo GetKeyError     ' Handle Error...

    tmpVal = String$(1024, 0)                         ' Allocate Variable Space
    KeyValSize = 1024                                 ' Mark Variable Size
```

To read a registry key we must use the `RegQueryValueEx` API function. After reading the registry key, the code checks for errors and then trims any null values it finds. Then, using the `KeyValSize` variable that is set with the length of the key read with the code removes all excess spaces from the temp variable that contains the key read:

```
    '------------------------------------------------------------
    ' Retrieve Registry Key Value...
    '------------------------------------------------------------
    rc = RegQueryValueEx(hKey, SubKeyRef, 0, _
                     KeyValType, tmpVal, KeyValSize)    ' Get/Create Key Value

    If (rc <> ERROR_SUCCESS) Then GoTo GetKeyError          ' Handle Errors
```

```
    If (Asc(Mid(tmpVal, KeyValSize, 1)) = 0) Then
  ' Win95 Adds Null Terminated String...
        tmpVal = Left(tmpVal, KeyValSize - 1)
  ' Null Found, Extract From String
    Else
  ' WinNT Does NOT Null Terminate String...
        tmpVal = Left(tmpVal, KeyValSize)
  ' Null Not Found, Extract String Only
    End If
```

Using a `Select Case` statement the code determines what type of key was read using the `KeyValType` enumeration. A string value requires no conversion - however, a double word value requires conversion and is performed here. If you recall a double word stores a value in the registry as a hexadecimal value:

```
    '------------------------------------------------------------
    ' Determine Key Value Type For Conversion...
    '------------------------------------------------------------
    Select Case KeyValType                              ' Search Data Types
    Case REG_SZ                                  ' String Registry Key Data Type
        KeyVal = tmpVal                                 ' Copy String Value
    Case REG_DWORD                          ' Double Word Registry Key Data Type
        For I = Len(tmpVal) To 1 Step -1                ' Convert Each Bit
            KeyVal = KeyVal + Hex(Asc(Mid(tmpVal, I, 1)))
  ' Build Value Char. By Char.
        Next
        KeyVal = Format$("&h" + KeyVal)     ' Convert Double Word To String
    End Select
```

After the key value read has been converted or not, the registry key is closed and the code exits the function.

The error handling routine in this function sets the `KeyVal` variable to a zero length string and returns `False`:

```
    GetKeyValue = True                                  ' Return Success
    rc = RegCloseKey(hKey)                              ' Close Registry Key
    Exit Function                                       ' Exit

GetKeyError:      ' Cleanup After An Error Has Occurred...
    KeyVal = ""                              ' Set Return Val To Empty String
    GetKeyValue = False                                 ' Return Failure
    rc = RegCloseKey(hKey)                              ' Close Registry Key
End Function
```

HideTitleBar Procedure

The HideTitleBar procedure checks to see if the title bar is already hidden, and exits the procedure if it is. If not, then it sets the form level variable, mTitleBarHidden, to True and executes the API functions to hide the title bar:

```
Private Sub HideTitleBar()
'   Change the style of the form to not show a title bar
    If mTitleBarHidden Then Exit Sub

    mTitleBarHidden = True

    With mStyle
        .OldStyle = GetWindowLong(hWnd, GWL_STYLE)
        .NewStyle = .OldStyle And WS_CAPTION_NOT
        SetWindowLong hWnd, GWL_STYLE, .NewStyle
    End With 'mStyle
End Sub
```

SplashOff Procedure

We call the SplashOff procedure to turn the splash form off. This procedure will wait until the elapsed time has expired before turning the splash form off, if one was specified when we called the SplashOn procedure. It then hides the form and calls the ShowTitleBar procedure to show the title bar on its next execution:

```
Public Sub SplashOff()
    If Visible Then
'       Wait until any minimum display time elapses
        Do While Timer1.Enabled
            DoEvents
        Loop

        Hide ' If you want to unload the form, change this to Unload Me

'       Modify the form style to show the title bar
        ShowTitleBar

'       Set height of About Box to "default" height
        Height = mBoxHeight
    End If
End Sub
```

ShowTitleBar Procedure

The ShowTitleBar procedure ensures the title bar is indeed hidden and then sets the form level variable, mTitleBarHidden, to False, to indicate that the title bar is not hidden. Then a call to the SetWindowLong API brings the title bar back:

```
Private Sub ShowTitleBar()
'   Change the style of the form to show a title bar
    If Not mTitleBarHidden Then Exit Sub
    mTitleBarHidden = False
    SetWindowLong hWnd, GWL_STYLE, mStyle.OldStyle
End Sub
```

About Procedure

When we execute the `About` procedure to display the About part of this form, the command buttons are enabled and the optional user information parameters are checked. If they are present, they take precedence over the values in the registry and they are used to display the user information on the form. If they are not present, then a call to the `GetUserName` and `GetUserCompany` procedures takes place and the values are read from the registry:

```
Public Sub About(frmParent As Form, Optional lUserName As String, _
                 Optional lUserInfo As String)
'    imgIcon.Picture = frmParent.Icon
    cmdOK.Enabled = True
    cmdSysInfo.Enabled = True

'   Add user information to form
    If lUserName <> "" Then
        lblUserName.Caption = lUserName
        lblUserInfo.Caption = lUserInfo
    Else
        lblUserName.Caption = GetUserName
        lblUserInfo.Caption = GetUserCompany
    End If
```

To ensure the title bar is displayed, a call to the `ShowTitleBar` procedure is made. Then the height of the form is adjusted to ensure the title bar is once again displayed; the form is then shown modally:

```
'   Modify the form style to show the title bar
    ShowTitleBar

'   A resize event is needed in order to apply the changes to the form style.
'   Setting the height to 0 should do it.
    If Height = mBoxHeight Then
        Height = 0
    End If

'   Set height of About Box to "default" height
    Height = mBoxHeight

    Show vbModal, frmParent
End Sub
```

cmdOK_Click Procedure

This code gets executed when you click on the OK button:

```
Private Sub cmdOK_Click()
    Hide ' If you want to unload the form, change this to Unload Me
End Sub
```

cmdSysInfo_Click Procedure

This calls the `StartSysInfo` procedure:

```
Private Sub cmdSysInfo_Click()
    Call StartSysInfo
End Sub
```

StartSysInfo Procedure

The `StartSysInfo` procedure makes a call to the `GetKeyValue` procedure to get the System Info Program Path and name from the registry. If it can't find the path and name, it then attempts to find the path only. The validation of the path and program name is performed after execution of the `ElseIf` statement:

```
Private Sub StartSysInfo()
    On Error GoTo SysInfoErr

    Dim rc As Long
    Dim SysInfoPath As String

    ' Try To Get System Info Program Path\Name From Registry...
    If GetKeyValue(HKEY_LOCAL_MACHINE, gREGKEYSYSINFO, gREGVALSYSINFO, _
                   SysInfoPath) Then
    ' Try To Get System Info Program Path Only From Registry...
    ElseIf GetKeyValue(HKEY_LOCAL_MACHINE, gREGKEYSYSINFOLOC, gREGVALSYSINFOLOC, _
                   SysInfoPath) Then
        ' Validate Existence Of Known 32 Bit File Version
        If (Dir(SysInfoPath & "\MSINFO32.EXE") <> "") Then
            SysInfoPath = SysInfoPath & "\MSINFO32.EXE"
```

If both of these procedures fail, the code then goes to the error handling routine and a message box is displayed:

```
        ' Error - File Can Not Be Found...
        Else
            GoTo SysInfoErr
        End If
    ' Error - Registry Entry Can Not Be Found...
    Else
        GoTo SysInfoErr
    End If
```

If everything succeeded, then a call is made to the built-in VB `Shell` function, passing it the program path and name, and how the window should be displayed. The `Shell` function runs a program independently of the program that executed the `Shell` function. The first parameter of the `Shell` function accepts the path and program name to execute and the second parameter accepts the style of window to use while running the program, in this case a normal window which has the focus:

```
    Call Shell(SysInfoPath, vbNormalFocus)

    Exit Sub
SysInfoErr:
    MsgBox "System Information Is Unavailable At This Time", vbOKOnly
End Sub
```

This wraps up our code for the AbSplash form. As you can see from the form design to the code that this form implements, this form helps to provide a professional appearance to our UI in the Splash screen and About dialog. We now have the controls on all of our forms and have added the code to make the AbSplash form functional.

Employment Form Code

The Employment form (frmEmployment) can be displayed for a current customer or for no customer at all. If we are displaying the Employment form for a current customer we will call the Process procedure. If we display the Employment form for no customer, then we simply show the form modally.

The examples in the last few chapters that used this form implemented most of the functionality that this form has, and the code will not be explained again. The code that has been carried forward from the previous examples is listed below. Take note that there are a few minor differences and they will be pointed out along the way.

This code is contained in the general declarations section is listed below:

```
Option Explicit

'Declare module level variables
Private m_blnLoaded As Boolean
Private arrEmployers() As Long

'Declare Primary keys
Private m_lngCustomerInformationID As Long
Private m_lngCEPhoneNumberID As Long
Private m_lngPEPhoneNumberID As Long
```

The Process procedure is listed next. Notice that we are loading a combo box, which requires a call to the Form_Load event, which in turn calls the LoadEmployers procedure. You have seen this type of code before and it needs no further explanation:

```
Public Sub Process(ByRef objConn As ADODB.Connection, _
      ByVal lngCustomerID As Long, ByVal frmParent As Form)

   'Set up error handling
   On Error GoTo Process_EH

   'Load the form which will load the employer combo boxes
   Call Form_Load
```

```
    'Set a reference to the objects
    Dim objRS As New ADODB.Recordset
    Dim objEmployer As New clsEmployer

    'Get the employer information for this customer
    Set objRS = objEmployer.GetEmployers(objConn, lngCustomerID)

    'Ensure the function returned a recordset
    If objRS Is Nothing Then
       Err.Raise vbObjectError + 513, "frmEmployment.Process", _
          "Call to clsEmployer.GetEmployers failed"
    End If

    'Load the current employer fields
    cboCurrentEmployer.ListIndex = arrEmployers(objRS!Employer_ID)
    txtCEAreaCode.Text = objRS!area_code_si
    txtCEPhoneNumber.Text = Format(objRS!Phone_Number_IN, "###-####")
    txtJobTitle.Text = objRS!Job_Title_VC
    txtCEYearsEmployed.Text = objRS!Years_At_This_Employer_TI

    If Not IsNull(objRS!Previous_Employer_Company_Name_VC) Then
       'Load the previous employer fields
       cboPreviousEmployer.ListIndex = arrEmployers(objRS!Previous_Employer_ID)
       txtPEAreaCode.Text = objRS!Previous_Employer_Area_Code_SI
       txtPEPhoneNumber.Text = Format(objRS!Previous_Employer_Phone_Number_IN, _
                "###-####")
       txtPEYearsEmployed.Text = objRS!Years_At_Previous_Employer_TI
    End If

    'Save all primary keys
    m_lngCustomerInformationID = objRS!Customer_Information_ID
    m_lngCEPhoneNumberID = objRS!Phone_Number_ID
    m_lngPEPhoneNumberID = IIf(IsNull(objRS!Previous_Employer_Phone_Number_ID), _
       0, objRS!Previous_Employer_Phone_Number_ID)

    'Close and de-reference objects
    objRS.Close
    Set objRS = Nothing
    Set objEmployer = Nothing

    On Error GoTo 0

    'Show the form
    Show vbModal, frmParent
    Exit Sub

Process_EH:
    Dim objErr As ADODB.Error
    'Ensure the error came from ADO
    If objConn.Errors.Count > 0 Then
       Dim strMsg As String
       For Each objErr In objConn.Errors
          strMsg = strMsg & " " & objErr.Description
       Next
```

```
        StatusBar1.Panels("Msg") = strMsg
    Else
        StatusBar1.Panels("Msg") = Err.Description
    End If
End Sub
```

The LoadEmployers procedure loads the current and previous employer combo boxes and is new to this form:

```
Public Sub LoadEmployers(ByRef objConn As ADODB.Connection)
    'Set up error handling
    On Error GoTo LoadEmployers_EH

    'Declare local variables
    Dim lngLastValue As Long, lngIndex As Long, lngRC As Long

    'Clear any existing entries
    cboCurrentEmployer.Clear
    cboPreviousEmployer.Clear

    'Set a reference to the objects
    Dim objRS As New ADODB.Recordset
    Dim objEmployer As New clsEmployer

    'Get the employer information for this customer
    lngRC = objEmployer.GetAllEmployers(objConn, objRS)

    'If the return code is not zero, raise an error
    If lngRC <> 0 Then
        Err.Raise vbObjectError + 513, "frmHistory.Process", _
            "Call to clsVehicle.GetPurchaseHistory failed"
    End If

    'Load the employer (current and previous) combo boxes and array
    lngIndex = -1
    lngLastValue = -1
    Do While Not objRS.EOF
        'Add the employer name
        cboCurrentEmployer.AddItem objRS!Company_Name_VC
        cboPreviousEmployer.AddItem objRS!Company_Name_VC
        lngIndex = lngIndex + 1
        'Add the employer id
        cboCurrentEmployer.ItemData(lngIndex) = objRS!Employer_ID
        cboPreviousEmployer.ItemData(lngIndex) = objRS!Employer_ID
        If lngLastValue < objRS!Employer_ID Then
            'Redim the array
            ReDim Preserve arrEmployers(objRS!Employer_ID)
            lngLastValue = objRS!Employer_ID
        End If
        'Add the current position of the employer to the array
        arrEmployers(objRS!Employer_ID) = lngIndex
        'Advance the recordset
```

```
        objRS.MoveNext
    Loop

    'Close and de-reference objects
    objRS.Close
    Set objRS = Nothing
    Set objEmployer = Nothing

    'Exit sub
    On Error GoTo 0
    Exit Sub

LoadEmployers_EH:
    Dim objErr As ADODB.Error
    'Ensure the error came from ADO
    If objConn.Errors.Count > 0 Then
        Dim strMsg As String
        For Each objErr In objConn.Errors
            strMsg = strMsg & " " & objErr.Description
        Next
        StatusBar1.Panels("Msg") = strMsg
    Else
        StatusBar1.Panels("Msg") = Err.Description
    End If
End Sub
```

The code for the `Loaded` property is listed below:

```
Public Property Let Loaded(ByVal blnLoaded As Boolean)
    m_blnLoaded = blnLoaded
End Property

Public Property Get Loaded() As Boolean
    Loaded = m_blnLoaded
End Property
```

The `cboCurrentEmployer_Click` procedure is new to the Employment form, but you have seen this type of code in the Main form in previous examples in the past chapters. Essentially, this procedure loads the current employer and phone number; when a user clicks on an employer, a call to the `GetPhoneNumber` function is performed, and the data returned from that function is loaded into the current employer phone number fields:

```
Private Sub cboCurrentEmployer_Click()
    'Set up error handling
    On Error GoTo cboCurrentEmployer_EH

    'Declare local variables
    Dim lngRC As Long

    'Set a reference to the objects
    Dim objRS As New ADODB.Recordset
    Dim objAddress As New clsAddress
```

```
    'Get the phone number for this employer
    lngRC = objAddress.GetPhoneNumber(frmMain.m_objConn, _
       objRS, _
       cboCurrentEmployer.ItemData(cboCurrentEmployer.ListIndex), _
       ptEmployer)

    'If the return code is not zero, raise an error
    If lngRC <> 0 Then
       Err.Raise vbObjectError + 513, "frmEmployment.cboCurrentEmployer", _
          "Call to clsAddress.GetPhoneNumber failed"
    End If

    'Load the current employer phone number fields
    m_lngCEPhoneNumberID = objRS!Phone_Number_ID
    txtCEAreaCode.Text = objRS!Area_Code_SI
    txtCEPhoneNumber.Text = Format(objRS!Phone_Number_IN, "###-####")

    'Close and de-reference objects
    objRS.Close
    Set objRS = Nothing
    Set objAddress = Nothing

    On Error GoTo 0
    Exit Sub

cboCurrentEmployer_EH:
    Dim objErr As ADODB.Error
    'Ensure the error came from ADO
    If frmMain.m_objConn.Errors.Count > 0 Then
       Dim strMsg As String
       For Each objErr In frmMain.m_objConn.Errors
          strMsg = strMsg & " " & objErr.Description
       Next
       StatusBar1.Panels("Msg") = strMsg
    Else
       StatusBar1.Panels("Msg") = Err.Description
    End If
End Sub
```

The `cboPreviousEmployer_Click` procedure performs the same steps as the `cboCurrentEmployer_Click` procedure, only for the previous employer:

```
Private Sub cboPreviousEmployer_Click()
    'Set up error handling
    On Error GoTo cboPreviousEmployer_EH

    'Declare local variables
    Dim lngRC As Long

    'Set a reference to the objects
    Dim objRS As New ADODB.Recordset
    Dim objAddress As New clsAddress
```

```
    'Get the phone number for the previous employer
    lngRC = objAddress.GetPhoneNumber(frmMain.m_objConn, _
       objRS, _
       cboPreviousEmployer.ItemData(cboPreviousEmployer.ListIndex), _
       ptEmployer)

    'If the return code is not zero, raise an error
    If lngRC <> 0 Then
       Err.Raise vbObjectError + 513, "frmEmployment.cboPreviousEmployer", _
          "Call to clsAddress.GetPhoneNumber failed"
    End If

    'Load the previous employer fields
    m_lngPEPhoneNumberID = objRS!Phone_Number_ID
    txtPEAreaCode.Text = objRS!Area_Code_SI
    txtPEPhoneNumber.Text = Format(objRS!Phone_Number_IN, "###-####")

    'Close and de-reference objects
    objRS.Close
    Set objRS = Nothing
    Set objAddress = Nothing

    On Error GoTo 0
    Exit Sub

 cboPreviousEmployer_EH:
    Dim objErr As ADODB.Error
    'Ensure the error came from ADO
    If frmMain.m_objConn.Errors.Count > 0 Then
       Dim strMsg As String
       For Each objErr In frmMain.m_objConn.Errors
          strMsg = strMsg & " " & objErr.Description
       Next
       StatusBar1.Panels("Msg") = strMsg
    Else
       StatusBar1.Panels("Msg") = Err.Description
    End If
 End Sub
```

The cmdAdd_Click and cmdClose_Click procedures have not changed and are listed below:

```
 Private Sub cmdAdd_Click()
    'Hide the form so fields are accessible from parent form
    Me.Hide
 End Sub
```

```
 Private Sub cmdClose_Click()
    Unload Me
 End Sub
```

The `cmdUpdate_Click` procedure has changed in the fact that we must now determine if an employer was chosen in the combo box, or if a new employer has been added. The same holds true for the previous employer:

```
Private Sub cmdUpdate_Click()
   'Set up error handling
   On Error GoTo cmdUpdate_EH

   'Declare local variables
   Dim lngRC As Long, lngCurrentEmployerID As Long, _
      lngPreviousEmployerID As Long, intAreaCode As Integer, _
      lngPhoneNumber As Long, bytYearsEmployed As Byte, _
      strMsg() As String, varText As Variant

   'Set current employer numeric values
   If cboCurrentEmployer.ListIndex = -1 Then
      lngCurrentEmployerID = 0
   Else
      lngCurrentEmployerID = _
                cboCurrentEmployer.ItemData(cboCurrentEmployer.ListIndex)
   End If

   'Set previous employer numeric values
   If cboPreviousEmployer.ListIndex = -1 Then
      lngPreviousEmployerID = 0
   Else
      lngPreviousEmployerID = _
                cboPreviousEmployer.ItemData(cboPreviousEmployer.ListIndex)
   End If
   If Len(txtPEAreaCode.Text) = 0 Then
      intAreaCode = 0
   Else
      intAreaCode = CInt(txtPEAreaCode.Text)
   End If

   If Len(txtPEPhoneNumber.Text) = 0 Then
      lngPhoneNumber = 0
   Else
      lngPhoneNumber = EditPhoneNumber(txtPEPhoneNumber.Text)
   End If

   If Len(txtPEYearsEmployed.Text) = 0 Then
      bytYearsEmployed = 0
   Else
      bytYearsEmployed = CByte(txtPEYearsEmployed.Text)
   End If

   'Set a reference to the objects
   Dim objEmployer As New clsEmployer
   Dim objCmd As New ADODB.Command
```

```
    'Update the employer information
    lngRC = objEmployer.UpdateEmployer(lngCurrentEmployerID, _
       cboCurrentEmployer.Text, _
       m_lngCEPhoneNumberID, _
       CInt(txtCEAreaCode.Text), _
       EditPhoneNumber(txtCEPhoneNumber.Text), _
       CByte(txtCEYearsEmployed.Text), _
       txtJobTitle.Text, _
       lngPreviousEmployerID, _
       cboPreviousEmployer.Text, _
       m_lngPEPhoneNumberID, _
       intAreaCode, _
       lngPhoneNumber, _
       bytYearsEmployed, _
       m_lngCustomerInformationID, _
       strMsg(), _
       frmMain.m_objConn, _
       objCmd)

    'Display any error messages
    If lngRC <> 0 Then
       For Each varText In strMsg
          StatusBar1.Panels("Msg").Text = StatusBar1.Panels("Msg").Text & _
             varText
       Next
    End If

    'Dereference objects
    Set objCmd = Nothing
    Set objEmployer = Nothing

    'Display message
    StatusBar1.Panels("Msg") = "Customer's Employment Information Updated"
    Exit Sub

 cmdUpdate_EH:
    Dim objErr As ADODB.Error
    'Ensure the error came from ADO
    If frmMain.m_objConn.Errors.Count > 0 Then
       For Each objErr In frmMain.m_objConn.Errors
          StatusBar1.Panels("Msg") = StatusBar1.Panels("Msg") & " " & _
                      objErr.Description
       Next
    Else
       StatusBar1.Panels("Msg") = Err.Description
    End If
 End Sub
```

The `Form_Load` event makes the call to the `LoadEmployers` procedure to load the employer combo boxes. The reason this call has been placed here is because, if we call the `Process` procedure, the `Form_Load` event gets fired upon the first access to any control on the form. If we show the form modally when no employment information is displayed for a customer, the `Form_Load` event is fired. Either way, the employer combo boxes get loaded.

Nothing has changed in the `Form_Unload` event listed below:

```
Private Sub Form_Load()
   'Load Employers
   Call LoadEmployers(frmMain.m_objConn)

   'Set the forms loaded property to true
   Loaded = True
End Sub

Private Sub Form_Unload(Cancel As Integer)
   'Set the forms loaded property to false
   Loaded = False
End Sub
```

Try It Out – Data Validation

There are two new UI features that we want to implement into our project. The first is to automatically highlight any existing text in a textbox when it gets focus. This method is straightforward and we have already covered it in a previous chapter.

The second method that we want to implement is to use the new `Validate` event. Before version 6.0 of VB, we used to place our data validation code in the `LostFocus` event and then if the validation failed, had to shift focus back to the control. The new `Validate` event performs all validations before the control loses focus; and you can prevent the control from ever losing focus until all validations have been passed. Each control has a `CausesValidation` property, which by default is set to `True`, which fires the `Validate` event for the control trying to lose focus. This prevents the user from trying to click on another control to bypass the validation. The `Validate` event also has a parameter, which when set to `True`, prevents the control from losing focus.

1. Add data validation to the Current Employer combo box to ensure either an employer was selected or an employer has been entered. The code for this is listed below:

```
Private Sub cboCurrentEmployer_Validate(Cancel As Boolean)
   'If no item is selected...
   If cboCurrentEmployer.ListIndex = -1 Then
      'Ensure some text was entered
      If Len(cboCurrentEmployer.Text) = 0 Then
         StatusBar1.Panels("Msg").Text = "Current Employer is required"
         Label1(0).ForeColor = vbRed
         Beep
         Cancel = True
      Else
         'Validation was passed
         StatusBar1.Panels("Msg").Text = Empty
         Label1(0).ForeColor = vbWindowText
         Cancel = False
      End If
   End If
End Sub
```

2. Add code to the Current Employer Area Code text box to highlight any existing text when the control gets focus. The code is listed below:

```
Private Sub txtCEAreaCode_GotFocus()
   'Select text
   txtCEAreaCode.SelStart = 0
   txtCEAreaCode.SelLength = Len(txtCEAreaCode.Text)
End Sub
```

3. Add validation code to this control to ensure the area code is exactly three digits:

```
Private Sub txtCEAreaCode_Validate(Cancel As Boolean)
   'Display an error if area code is not 3 digits
   If Len(txtCEAreaCode.Text) <> 3 Then
      StatusBar1.Panels("Msg").Text = _
         "Current Employer Area Code is required in the format of nnn"
      Label1(1).ForeColor = vbRed
      Beep
      Cancel = True
   Else
      'Validation passed
      StatusBar1.Panels("Msg").Text = Empty
      Label1(1).ForeColor = vbWindowText
      Cancel = False
   End If
End Sub
```

4. The code for the rest of the `GotFocus` and `Validate` events is listed below:

```
Private Sub txtCEPhoneNumber_GotFocus()
   'Select text
   txtCEPhoneNumber.SelStart = 0
   txtCEPhoneNumber.SelLength = Len(txtCEPhoneNumber.Text)
End Sub
```

```
Private Sub txtCEPhoneNumber_Validate(Cancel As Boolean)
   'Display an error message if phone number is not 8 digits
   If Len(txtCEPhoneNumber.Text) <> 8 Then
      StatusBar1.Panels("Msg").Text = _
         "Current Employer Phone Number is required in the format of nnn-nnnn"
      Label1(2).ForeColor = vbRed
      Beep
      Cancel = True
   Else
      'Validation passed
      StatusBar1.Panels("Msg").Text = Empty
      Label1(2).ForeColor = vbWindowText
      Cancel = False
```

```
    End If
End Sub
```

```
Private Sub txtCEYearsEmployed_GotFocus()
    'Select text
    txtCEYearsEmployed.SelStart = 0
    txtCEYearsEmployed.SelLength = Len(txtCEYearsEmployed.Text)
End Sub
```

```
Private Sub txtCEYearsEmployed_Validate(Cancel As Boolean)
    'Display an error if nothing was entered
    If Len(txtCEYearsEmployed.Text) = 0 Then
        StatusBar1.Panels("Msg").Text = "Current Employer Years Employed is
                    required"
        Label1(4).ForeColor = vbRed
        Beep
        Cancel = True
    'Display an error if value is greater than 50
    ElseIf CInt(txtCEYearsEmployed.Text) > 50 Then
        StatusBar1.Panels("Msg").Text = _
            "Current Employer Years Employed must be between 1 and 50"
        Label1(4).ForeColor = vbRed
        Beep
        Cancel = True
    Else
        'Validation passed
        StatusBar1.Panels("Msg").Text = Empty
        Label1(4).ForeColor = vbWindowText
        Cancel = False
    End If
End Sub
```

```
Private Sub txtJobTitle_GotFocus()
    'Select text
    txtJobTitle.SelStart = 0
    txtJobTitle.SelLength = Len(txtJobTitle.Text)
End Sub
```

```
Private Sub txtJobTitle_Validate(Cancel As Boolean)
    'Display an error if nothing was entered
    If Len(txtJobTitle.Text) = 0 Then
        StatusBar1.Panels("Msg").Text = "Job Title is required"
        Label1(3).ForeColor = vbRed
        Beep
        Cancel = True
    Else
        'Validation passed
        StatusBar1.Panels("Msg").Text = Empty
        Label1(3).ForeColor = vbWindowText
        Cancel = False
    End If
End Sub
```

```
Private Sub txtPEAreaCode_GotFocus()
   'Select text
   txtPEAreaCode.SelStart = 0
   txtPEAreaCode.SelLength = Len(txtPEAreaCode.Text)
End Sub
```

```
Private Sub txtPEAreaCode_Validate(Cancel As Boolean)
   'If anything is entered, then validate
   If Len(txtPEAreaCode.Text) > 0 Then
      'Display an error if area code is not 3 digits
      If Len(txtPEAreaCode.Text) <> 3 Then
         StatusBar1.Panels("Msg").Text = "Previous Employer Area Code nust be in
                    the format of nnn"
         Label1(6).ForeColor = vbRed
         Beep
         Cancel = True
      Else
         'Validation passed
         StatusBar1.Panels("Msg").Text = Empty
         Label1(6).ForeColor = vbWindowText
         Cancel = False
      End If
   End If
End Sub
```

```
Private Sub txtPEPhoneNumber_GotFocus()
   'Select text
   txtPEPhoneNumber.SelStart = 0
   txtPEPhoneNumber.SelLength = Len(txtPEPhoneNumber.Text)
End Sub
```

```
Private Sub txtPEPhoneNumber_Validate(Cancel As Boolean)
   'If anything is entered then validate
   If Len(txtPEPhoneNumber.Text) > 0 Then
      'Display an error if phone number is not 8 digits
      If Len(txtPEPhoneNumber.Text) <> 8 Then
         StatusBar1.Panels("Msg").Text = _
            "Previous Employer Phone Number is required in the format of nnn-nnnn"
         Label1(7).ForeColor = vbRed
         Beep
         Cancel = True
      Else
         'Validation passed
         StatusBar1.Panels("Msg").Text = Empty
         Label1(7).ForeColor = vbWindowText
         Cancel = False
      End If
   End If
End Sub
```

```
Private Sub txtPEYearsEmployed_GotFocus()
   'Select text
   txtPEYearsEmployed.SelStart = 0
   txtPEYearsEmployed.SelLength = Len(txtPEYearsEmployed.Text)
End Sub
```

```
Private Sub txtPEYearsEmployed_Validate(Cancel As Boolean)
   'If anything is entered then validate
   If Len(txtPEYearsEmployed.Text) > 0 Then
      'Display an error if greater than 50
      If CInt(txtPEYearsEmployed.Text) > 50 Then
         StatusBar1.Panels("Msg").Text = _
            "Previous Employer Years Employed must be between 1 and 50"
         Label1(8).ForeColor = vbRed
         Beep
         Cancel = True
      Else
         'Validation passed
         StatusBar1.Panels("Msg").Text = Empty
         Label1(8).ForeColor = vbWindowText
         Cancel = False
      End If
   End If
End Sub
```

How It Works- Data Validation

The first validation that we want to take a look at is for the Current Employer combo box. When a user tabs to this field, they must have either selected an entry in the combo box or entered some data before they can tab out or click another control on the form.

The exception to this is the Close button. This button had its `CausesValidation` property set to `False`, which allows the user to close the form without making any changes.

We check the `ListIndex` property of the `cboCurrentEmployer` combo box and if it is equal to `-1` then we know that no item has been selected:

```
Private Sub cboCurrentEmployer_Validate(Cancel As Boolean)
   'If no item is selected...
   If cboCurrentEmployer.ListIndex = -1 Then
```

We then move on to check the length of the `Text` property. If it is equal to zero, we display a message in the status bar and set the caption of this field to red, beep to warn the user and set the `Cancel` parameter to `True`. Setting the `Cancel` parameter to `True` prevents this control from losing focus, except when the user clicks on the Close button, in which case the validation code is not executed:

```
      'Ensure some text was entered
      If Len(cboCurrentEmployer.Text) = 0 Then
         StatusBar1.Panels("Msg").Text = "Current Employer is required"
         Label1(0).ForeColor = vbRed
         Beep
         Cancel = True
```

If the user has entered some text, we clear any existing messages in the status bar, set the caption text back to normal, and set the `Cancel` parameter to `False`, which lets the user tab from this field:

```
        Else
            'Validation was passed
            StatusBar1.Panels("Msg").Text = Empty
            Label1(0).ForeColor = vbWindowText
            Cancel = False
        End If
    End If
End Sub
```

The rest of the validations are pretty straightforward and use the same type of logic.

The validation for the years employed, however, does deserve a little explanation. The first validation that is performed here is to ensure that something exists in the textbox, by checking the length of the textbox for a zero length. The second validation ensures the years employed is not greater than 50. If you recall, our stored procedures that insert and update employer information perform this same check. This method shows you how you could implement data validation in your form versus in your stored procedures:

> *The stored procedure is designed to be called from many clients so it must enforce the rule. While we are writing this client application, we test for the condition and can save a trip across the network for something we know will fail in the stored procedure.*

```
Private Sub txtCEYearsEmployed_Validate(Cancel As Boolean)
    'Display an error if nothing was entered
    If Len(txtCEYearsEmployed.Text) = 0 Then
        StatusBar1.Panels("Msg").Text = "Current Employer Years Employed is
                    required"
        Label1(4).ForeColor = vbRed
        Beep
        Cancel = True
    'Display an error if value is greater than 50
    ElseIf CInt(txtCEYearsEmployed.Text) > 50 Then
        StatusBar1.Panels("Msg").Text = _
            "Current Employer Years Employed must be between 1 and 50"
        Label1(4).ForeColor = vbRed
        Beep
        Cancel = True
    Else
        'Validation passed
        StatusBar1.Panels("Msg").Text = Empty
        Label1(4).ForeColor = vbWindowText
        Cancel = False
    End If
End Sub
```

The validations for the previous employer information are slightly different. Since the previous employer information is optional, we only perform the validations if something already exists. This way, if the user enters something in the previous employer fields, we will force validation on that data, otherwise we skip validation:

```
Private Sub txtPEAreaCode_Validate(Cancel As Boolean)
    'If anything is entered, then validate
    If Len(txtPEAreaCode.Text) > 0 Then
        'Display an error if area code is not 3 digits
        If Len(txtPEAreaCode.Text) <> 3 Then
            StatusBar1.Panels("Msg").Text = "Previous Employer Area Code nust be in
                           the format of nnn"
            Label1(6).ForeColor = vbRed
            Beep
            Cancel = True
        Else
            'Validation passed
            StatusBar1.Panels("Msg").Text = Empty
            Label1(6).ForeColor = vbWindowText
            Cancel = False
        End If
    End If
End Sub
```

This wraps up the code for the Employment form (`frmEmployment`). We will see the `Validate` event in action when we complete the project and run it. At this point we have added the necessary code to the Employment form to make this form fully functional. Once we add the code to the Main form (`frmMain`) we will be able to call the Employment form and display employment information.

Main Form Code

The code for the Main form (`frmMain`) is pretty much the same code that we have been using in our examples in the past several chapters. There are a few minor differences and they will be pointed out along the way.

Basically, all required fields on the form must be validated before the Customer Data checkbox will be checked. The Employment field must be loaded before the Employment checkbox will be checked. In order for the Employment form (`frmEmployment`) to be loaded, it will go through validations on the data in its fields. Once both checkboxes have been checked, the Add New Customer button will become enabled and allow the user to add a new customer.

Once a new customer has been added, the checkboxes will be cleared and the Add New Customer button will once again become disabled.

Try It Out – Main Form Code

The entire code listing for the Main form is listed next. After the code listing, we will point out the differences in the procedures, where they exist, in the *How it Works* section. There is one thing to take note of here; we are not checking to see if the various fields have been changed as we did in Chapter 10. We will pass all data to the stored procedures, not just the fields that have changed.

1. Enter the following code for the general declarations:

```
Option Explicit

'Declare database objects
Public m_objConn As ADODB.Connection
Private m_objCmd As ADODB.Command
Private m_objRS As ADODB.Recordset
Private m_objRSAddress As ADODB.Recordset
Private m_objErr As ADODB.Error

'Declare class objects
Private m_objAddress As clsAddress
Private m_objCustomer As clsCustomer
Private m_objEmployer As clsEmployer

'Declare module level variables
Private arrCity() As Long
Private arrState() As Long
Private arrZipCode() As Long
Private lngRecordPosition As Long

'Declare primary keys
Private m_lngAddressID As Long
Private m_lngPhoneNumberID As Long
Private m_lngCustomerID As Long

'Declare validation variables
Private blnLastName As Boolean
Private blnFirstName As Boolean
Private blnAddress As Boolean
Private blnCity As Boolean
Private blnZipCode As Boolean
Private blnAreaCode As Boolean
Private blnPhoneNumber As Boolean
```

2. Enter the following code for the `LoadCityStateZip` procedure:

```
Private Sub LoadCityStateZip()
   'Set up error handling
   On Error GoTo LoadCityStateZip_EH

   'Declare local variables
   Dim lngRC As Long, lngLastValue As Long, lngIndex As Long
```

```
'Clear any existing entries
cboCity.Clear
cboState.Clear
cboZipCode.Clear

'Instantiate the class
Set m_objAddress = New clsAddress

'Get a list of cities, states and zip codes
lngRC = m_objAddress.GetCityStateZip(m_objConn, m_objRSAddress)

'If the return code is not zero, raise an error
If lngRC <> 0 Then
   Err.Raise vbObjectError + 513, "frmMain.LoadCityStateZip", _
      "Call to clsAddress.GetCityStateZip failed"
End If

'Load the city combo box and array
lngIndex = -1
lngLastValue = -1
Do While Not m_objRSAddress.EOF
   'Add the city name
   cboCity.AddItem m_objRSAddress!City_Name_VC
   lngIndex = lngIndex + 1
   'Add the city id
   cboCity.ItemData(lngIndex) = m_objRSAddress!City_ID
   If lngLastValue < m_objRSAddress!City_ID Then
      'Redim the array
      ReDim Preserve arrCity(m_objRSAddress!City_ID)
      lngLastValue = m_objRSAddress!City_ID
   End If
   'Add the current position of the city to the array
   arrCity(m_objRSAddress!City_ID) = lngIndex
   'Advance the recordset
   m_objRSAddress.MoveNext
Loop

'Load the state combo box and array
lngIndex = -1
lngLastValue = -1
Set m_objRSAddress = m_objRSAddress.NextRecordset
Do While Not m_objRSAddress.EOF
   'Add the state name
   cboState.AddItem m_objRSAddress!State_Name_VC
   lngIndex = lngIndex + 1
   'Add the state id
   cboState.ItemData(lngIndex) = m_objRSAddress!State_ID
   If lngLastValue < m_objRSAddress!State_ID Then
      'Redim the array
      ReDim Preserve arrState(m_objRSAddress!State_ID)
      lngLastValue = m_objRSAddress!State_ID
   End If
```

```
      'Add the current position of the state to the array
      arrState(m_objRSAddress!State_ID) = lngIndex
      'Advance the recordset
      m_objRSAddress.MoveNext
   Loop

   'Load the zip code combo box and array
   lngIndex = -1
   lngLastValue = -1
   Set m_objRSAddress = m_objRSAddress.NextRecordset
   Do While Not m_objRSAddress.EOF
      'Add the zip code
      cboZipCode.AddItem m_objRSAddress!Zip_Code_CH
      lngIndex = lngIndex + 1
      'Add the zip code id
      cboZipCode.ItemData(lngIndex) = m_objRSAddress!Zip_Code_ID
      If lngLastValue < m_objRSAddress!Zip_Code_ID Then
         'Redim the array
         ReDim Preserve arrZipCode(m_objRSAddress!Zip_Code_ID)
         lngLastValue = m_objRSAddress!Zip_Code_ID
      End If
      'Add the current position of the zip code to the array
      arrZipCode(m_objRSAddress!Zip_Code_ID) = lngIndex
      'Advance the recordset
      m_objRSAddress.MoveNext
   Loop

   'Close and de-reference objects
   m_objRSAddress.Close
   Set m_objRSAddress = Nothing
   Set m_objAddress = Nothing
   On Error GoTo 0
   Exit Sub

LoadCityStateZip_EH:
   'Ensure the error came from ADO
   If m_objConn.Errors.Count > 0 Then
      For Each m_objErr In m_objConn.Errors
         StatusBar1.Panels("Msg") = StatusBar1.Panels("Msg") & " " & _
         m_objErr.Description
      Next
   Else
      StatusBar1.Panels("Msg") = Err.Description
   End If
End Sub
```

3. Enter the following code for the `LoadCustomerNames` procedure:

```
Private Sub LoadCustomerNames()
   'Set up error handling
   On Error GoTo LoadCustomerNames_EH

   'Declare local variables
   Dim lngIndex As Long, lngRC As Long

   'Clear any existing entries
   cboLastName.Clear

   'If the recordset has been set and is open, then close it
   If Not m_objRS Is Nothing Then
      If m_objRS.State = adStateOpen Then
         m_objRS.Close
      End If
   End If

   'Instantiate the class
   Set m_objCustomer = New clsCustomer

   'Get a list of customer names
   lngRC = m_objCustomer.GetCustomerNames(m_objConn, m_objRS)

   'If the return code is not zero, raise an error
   If lngRC <> 0 Then
      Err.Raise vbObjectError + 513, "frmMain.LoadCustomerNames", _
         "Call to clsCustomer.GetCustomerNames failed"
   End If

   'Load the combo box
   lngIndex = -1
   Do While Not m_objRS.EOF
      'Add the last name
      cboLastName.AddItem m_objRS!Last_Name_VC
      lngIndex = lngIndex + 1
      'Add the customer id
      cboLastName.ItemData(lngIndex) = m_objRS!Customer_ID
      m_objRS.MoveNext
   Loop

   'Set the index to the first entry and exit sub
   cboLastName.ListIndex = 0
   cboLastName.SetFocus
   On Error GoTo 0
   Exit Sub
```

```
LoadCustomerNames_EH:
   'Ensure the error came from ADO
   If m_objConn.Errors.Count > 0 Then
      For Each m_objErr In m_objConn.Errors
         StatusBar1.Panels("Msg") = StatusBar1.Panels("Msg") & " " & _
         m_objErr.Description
      Next
   Else
      StatusBar1.Panels("Msg") = Err.Description
   End If
End Sub
```

4. Enter the following code for the `ValidateData` procedure:

```
Private Sub ValidateData()
   'Validate all fields and check customer data check box if necessary
   If blnLastName And blnFirstName And blnAddress And blnCity And _
      blnZipCode And blnAreaCode And blnPhoneNumber Then
      chkCustomerData.Value = vbChecked
   End If

   'Validate check boxes and enable add button
   If chkCustomerData.Value = vbChecked And _
      chkEmploymentData.Value = vbChecked Then
      cmdAdd.Enabled = True
   End If
End Sub
```

5. Enter the following code for the `cboCity_Validate` procedure:

```
Private Sub cboCity_Validate(Cancel As Boolean)
   'If no entry was selected...
   If cboCity.ListIndex = -1 Then
      'Display an error if no text was entered
      If Len(cboCity.Text) = 0 Then
         StatusBar1.Panels("Msg").Text = "City Name is required"
         Label1(6).ForeColor = vbRed
         Beep
         Cancel = True
      Else
         'Validation passed
         StatusBar1.Panels("Msg").Text = Empty
         Label1(6).ForeColor = vbWindowText
         Cancel = False
         blnCity = True
      End If
   Else
      'If an item was selected turn on validation flag
      blnCity = True
   End If
   Call ValidateData
End Sub
```

6. Enter the following code for the cboLastName_Click procedure:

```
Private Sub cboLastName_Click()
   'Set up error handling
   On Error GoTo cboLastName_Click_EH

   'Navigate to the correct record based on the index
   m_objRS.MoveFirst
   m_objRS.Move cboLastName.ListIndex

   'Load the text boxes with the correct data
   txtFirstName.Text = m_objRS!First_Name_VC
   txtSpouseName.Text = _
      IIf(IsNull(m_objRS!Spouse_First_Name_VC), "", _
         m_objRS!Spouse_First_Name_VC)

   'Save the primary key
   m_lngCustomerID = m_objRS!Customer_ID

   'Instantiate the class
   Set m_objAddress = New clsAddress

   'Get the customers address
   Set m_objRSAddress = m_objAddress.GetAddress(m_objConn, _
      cboLastName.ItemData(cboLastName.ListIndex), Customer)

   'Ensure the function returned a recordset
   If m_objRSAddress Is Nothing Then
      Err.Raise vbObjectError + 513, "frmMain.cboLastName_Click", _
         "Call to clsAddress.GetAddress failed"
   End If

   'Save the primary keys for later use
   m_lngAddressID = m_objRSAddress!Address_ID
   m_lngPhoneNumberID = m_objRSAddress!Phone_Number_ID

   'Load the address fields
   txtAddress1.Text = m_objRSAddress!Street_Address_1_VC
   txtAddress2.Text = IIf(IsNull(m_objRSAddress!Street_Address_2_VC), _
      "", m_objRSAddress!street_address_2_vc)
   txtAddress3.Text = IIf(IsNull(m_objRSAddress!Street_Address_3_VC), _
      "", m_objRSAddress!Street_Address_3_VC)

   'Load the city, state, zip fields
   cboCity.ListIndex = arrCity(m_objRSAddress!City_ID)
   cboState.ListIndex = arrState(m_objRSAddress!State_ID)
   cboZipCode.ListIndex = arrZipCode(m_objRSAddress!Zip_Code_ID)

   'Load phone number fields
   txtAreaCode.Text = m_objRSAddress!Area_Code_SI
   txtPhoneNumber.Text = _
      Format(m_objRSAddress!Phone_Number_IN, "###-####")
```

```
    'Close and de-reference objects
    m_objRSAddress.Close
    Set m_objRSAddress = Nothing
    Set m_objAddress = Nothing

    On Error GoTo 0
    Exit Sub

cboLastName_Click_EH:
    'Ensure the error came from ADO
    If m_objConn.Errors.Count > 0 Then
        For Each m_objErr In m_objConn.Errors
            StatusBar1.Panels("Msg") = StatusBar1.Panels("Msg") & " " & _
                m_objErr.Description
        Next
    Else
        StatusBar1.Panels("Msg") = Err.Description
    End If
End Sub
```

7. Enter the following code for the `cboLastName_Validate` procedure:

```
Private Sub cboLastName_Validate(Cancel As Boolean)
    'If no entry was selected...
    If cboLastName.ListIndex = -1 Then
        'Display an error if no text was entered
        If Len(cboLastName.Text) = 0 Then
            StatusBar1.Panels("Msg").Text = "Last Name is required"
            Label1(0).ForeColor = vbRed
            Beep
            Cancel = True
        Else
            'Validation passed
            StatusBar1.Panels("Msg").Text = Empty
            Label1(0).ForeColor = vbWindowText
            Cancel = False
            blnLastName = True
        End If
    Else
        'If an item was selected turn on validation flag
        blnLastName = True
    End If
    Call ValidateData
End Sub
```

8. Enter the following code for the `cboZipCode_Validate` procedure:

```
Private Sub cboZipCode_Validate(Cancel As Boolean)
   'If no entry was selected...
   If cboZipCode.ListIndex = -1 Then
      'Display an error if no text was entered
      If Len(cboZipCode.Text) = 0 Then
         StatusBar1.Panels("Msg").Text = "Zip Code is required"
         Label1(8).ForeColor = vbRed
         Beep
         Cancel = True
      Else
         'Validation passed
         StatusBar1.Panels("Msg").Text = Empty
         Label1(8).ForeColor = vbWindowText
         Cancel = False
         blnZipCode = True
      End If
   Else
      'If an item was selected turn on validation flag
      blnZipCode = True
   End If
   Call ValidateData
End Sub
```

9. Enter the following code for the `chkCustomerData_GotFocus` procedure:

```
Private Sub chkCustomerData_GotFocus()
   'Don't let the user check the check box
   cboLastName.SetFocus
End Sub
```

10. Enter the following code for the `chkEmploymentData_GotFocus` procedure:

```
Private Sub chkEmploymentData_GotFocus()
   'Don't let the user check the check box
   cboLastName.SetFocus
End Sub
```

11. Enter the following code for the `cmdAdd_Click` procedure:

```
Private Sub cmdAdd_Click()
   'Set up error handling
   On Error GoTo cmdAdd_EH

   'Declare local variables
   Dim strMsg() As String, lngRC As Long, lngAddressID As Long, _
      lngPhoneNumberID As Long, lngCityID As Long, _
      lngZipCodeID As Long, lngCustomerInformationID As Long, _
```

```
   lngCurrentEmployerID As Long, lngPreviousEmployerID As Long, _
   intAreaCode As Integer, lngPhoneNumber As Long, _
   bytYearsEmployed As Byte, varText As Variant

'Set city and zip code IDs
If cboCity.ListIndex = -1 Then
   lngCityID = 0
Else
   lngCityID = cboCity.ItemData(cboCity.ListIndex)
End If

If cboZipCode.ListIndex = -1 Then
   lngZipCodeID = 0
Else
   lngZipCodeID = cboZipCode.ItemData(cboZipCode.ListIndex)
End If

'Set a reference to the objects
Set m_objCmd = New ADODB.Command
Set m_objAddress = New clsAddress

'Insert the address
lngRC = m_objAddress.InsertAddress(txtAddress1.Text, _
   txtAddress2.Text, _
   txtAddress3.Text, _
   lngCityID, _
   cboCity.Text, _
   cboState.ItemData(cboState.ListIndex), _
   lngZipCodeID, _
   cboZipCode.Text, _
   CInt(txtAreaCode.Text), _
   EditPhoneNumber(txtPhoneNumber.Text), _
   lngAddressID, _
   lngPhoneNumberID, _
   strMsg(), _
   m_objConn, _
   m_objCmd)

'Display any error messages
If lngRC <> 0 Then
   For Each varText In strMsg
      StatusBar1.Panels("Msg").Text = StatusBar1.Panels("Msg").Text & _
         varText
   Next
   Exit Sub
End If

'De-reference objects and clear message variable
Set m_objCmd = Nothing
Set m_objAddress = Nothing
ReDim strMsg(0)
```

```
'Set current employer numeric values
If frmEmployment.cboCurrentEmployer.ListIndex = -1 Then
   lngCurrentEmployerID = 0
Else
   lngCurrentEmployerID = frmEmployment.cboCurrentEmployer.ItemData( _
      frmEmployment.cboCurrentEmployer.ListIndex)
End If

'Set previous employer numeric values
If frmEmployment.cboPreviousEmployer.ListIndex = -1 Then
   lngPreviousEmployerID = 0
Else
   lngPreviousEmployerID = frmEmployment.cboPreviousEmployer.ItemData( _
      frmEmployment.cboPreviousEmployer.ListIndex)
End If

If Len(frmEmployment.txtPEAreaCode.Text) = 0 Then
   intAreaCode = 0
Else
   intAreaCode = CInt(frmEmployment.txtPEAreaCode.Text)
End If

If Len(frmEmployment.txtPEPhoneNumber.Text) = 0 Then
   lngPhoneNumber = 0
Else
   lngPhoneNumber = EditPhoneNumber(frmEmployment.txtPEPhoneNumber.Text)
End If

If Len(frmEmployment.txtPEYearsEmployed.Text) = 0 Then
   bytYearsEmployed = 0
Else
   bytYearsEmployed = CByte(frmEmployment.txtPEYearsEmployed.Text)
End If

'Set a reference to the objects
Set m_objCmd = New ADODB.Command
Set m_objEmployer = New clsEmployer

'Insert the employer information
lngRC = m_objEmployer.InsertEmployer(lngCurrentEmployerID, _
   frmEmployment.cboCurrentEmployer.Text, _
   CInt(frmEmployment.txtCEAreaCode.Text), _
   EditPhoneNumber(frmEmployment.txtCEPhoneNumber.Text), _
   CByte(frmEmployment.txtCEYearsEmployed.Text), _
   frmEmployment.txtJobTitle.Text, _
   lngPreviousEmployerID, _
   frmEmployment.cboPreviousEmployer.Text, _
   intAreaCode, _
   lngPhoneNumber, _
   bytYearsEmployed, _
```

```
        lngCustomerInformationID, _
        strMsg(), _
        m_objConn, _
        m_objCmd)

    'Display any error messages
    If lngRC <> 0 Then
        For Each varText In strMsg
            StatusBar1.Panels("Msg").Text = StatusBar1.Panels("Msg").Text & _
                varText
        Next
        Exit Sub
    End If

    'De-reference objects and clear message variable
    Set m_objCmd = Nothing
    Set m_objEmployer = Nothing
    ReDim strMsg(0)

    'Set a reference to the objects
    Set m_objCmd = New ADODB.Command
    Set m_objCustomer = New clsCustomer

    'Insert the customer information
    lngRC = m_objCustomer.InsertCustomer(lngAddressID, _
        lngPhoneNumberID, _
        lngCustomerInformationID, _
        txtFirstName.Text, _
        cboLastName.Text, _
        txtSpouseName.Text, _
        strMsg(), _
        m_objConn, _
        m_objCmd)

    'Display any error messages
    If lngRC <> 0 Then
        For Each varText In strMsg
            StatusBar1.Panels("Msg").Text = StatusBar1.Panels("Msg").Text & _
                varText
        Next
        Exit Sub
    End If

    'De-reference objects
    Set m_objCmd = Nothing
    Set m_objCustomer = Nothing

    'Disable add button
    cmdAdd.Enabled = False

    'Turn off checklist
    chkCustomerData.Value = vbUnchecked
```

```
    chkEmploymentData.Value = vbUnchecked

    'ReLoad City, State and Zip Code combo boxes
    Call LoadCityStateZip

    'Reload data from new recordset
    Call LoadCustomerNames

    'Set focus to the combo box
    cboLastName.SetFocus

    'Display message
    StatusBar1.Panels("Msg").Text = "Customer Added"
    Exit Sub

cmdAdd_EH:
    Dim objErr As ADODB.Error
    'Ensure the error came from ADO
    If m_objConn.Errors.Count > 0 Then
       For Each objErr In m_objConn.Errors
          StatusBar1.Panels("Msg") = StatusBar1.Panels("Msg") & " " & _
             objErr.Description
       Next
    Else
       StatusBar1.Panels("Msg") = Err.Description
    End If
End Sub
```

12. Enter the following code for the `cmdEmployment_Click` procedure:

```
Private Sub cmdEmployment_Click()
    'Determine if employer form should be shown with or without data
    If cboLastName.ListIndex <> -1 Then

       'Call the employer form to process and display employer info
       Call frmEmployment.Process(m_objConn, _
          cboLastName.ItemData(cboLastName.ListIndex), Me)

    Else

       'Display employer form with no data
       frmEmployment.Show vbModal

    End If

    'We are back, set focus to the combo box
    cboLastName.SetFocus
```

```
    'Check status of employment form
    If frmEmployment.Loaded Then
        chkEmploymentData.Value = vbChecked
    End If

    Call ValidateData
End Sub
```

13. Enter the following code for the `cmdUpdate_Click` procedure:

```
Private Sub cmdUpdate_Click()
    'Set up error handling
    On Error GoTo cmdUpdate_EH

    'Declare local variables
    Dim strMsg() As String, lngRC As Long, lngCityID As Long, _
        lngZipCodeID As Long, varText As Variant

    'Set city and zip code IDs
    If cboCity.ListIndex = -1 Then
        lngCityID = 0
    Else
        lngCityID = cboCity.ItemData(cboCity.ListIndex)
    End If

    If cboZipCode.ListIndex = -1 Then
        lngZipCodeID = 0
    Else
        lngZipCodeID = cboZipCode.ItemData(cboZipCode.ListIndex)
    End If

    'Set a reference to the objects
    Set m_objCmd = New ADODB.Command
    Set m_objAddress = New clsAddress

    'Update the address
    lngRC = m_objAddress.UpdateAddress(m_lngAddressID, _
        txtAddress1.Text, _
        txtAddress2.Text, _
        txtAddress3.Text, _
        lngCityID, _
        cboCity.Text, _
        cboState.ItemData(cboState.ListIndex), _
        lngZipCodeID, _
        cboZipCode.Text, _
        m_lngPhoneNumberID, _
        CInt(txtAreaCode.Text), _
        EditPhoneNumber(txtPhoneNumber.Text), _
        strMsg(), _
        m_objConn, _
        m_objCmd)
```

```
'Display any error messages
If lngRC <> 0 Then
   For Each varText In strMsg
      StatusBar1.Panels("Msg").Text = StatusBar1.Panels("Msg").Text & _
         varText
   Next
   Exit Sub
End If

'De-reference objects and clear message variable
Set m_objCmd = Nothing
Set m_objAddress = Nothing
ReDim strMsg(0)

'Set a reference to the objects
Set m_objCmd = New ADODB.Command
Set m_objCustomer = New clsCustomer

'Update the customer record
lngRC = m_objCustomer.UpdateCustomer(m_lngCustomerID, _
   txtFirstName.Text, _
   cboLastName.Text, _
   txtSpouseName.Text, _
   m_objConn, _
   m_objCmd)

'Display any error messages
If lngRC <> 0 Then
   StatusBar1.Panels("Msg").Text = "Update of customer failed"
   Exit Sub
End If

'De-reference objects
Set m_objCmd = Nothing
Set m_objCustomer = Nothing

'Save the current record position
lngRecordPosition = cboLastName.ListIndex

'ReLoad City, State and Zip Code combo boxes
Call LoadCityStateZip

'Reload data from new recordset
Call LoadCustomerNames

'Reload from the address fields
cboLastName.ListIndex = lngRecordPosition
Call cboLastName_Click

'Set focus to the combo box
cboLastName.SetFocus
```

```
    'Display message
    StatusBar1.Panels("Msg").Text = "Customer Updated"
    Exit Sub

cmdUpdate_EH:
    Dim objErr As ADODB.Error
    'Ensure the error came from ADO
    If m_objConn.Errors.Count > 0 Then
        For Each objErr In m_objConn.Errors
            StatusBar1.Panels("Msg") = StatusBar1.Panels("Msg") & " " & _
                objErr.Description
        Next
    Else
        StatusBar1.Panels("Msg") = Err.Description
    End If
End Sub
```

14. Enter the following code for the `Form_Unload` procedure:

```
Private Sub Form_Unload(Cancel As Integer)
    'Unload all loaded forms
    Dim frmForm As Form
    For Each frmForm In Forms
        Unload frmForm
    Next
End Sub
```

15. Enter the following code for the `mnuFileExit_Click` procedure:

```
Private Sub mnuFileExit_Click()
    Unload Me
End Sub
```

16. Enter the following code for the `mnuFileNew_Click` procedure:

```
Private Sub mnuFileNew_Click()
    'Clear all fields on the form
    cboLastName.ListIndex = -1
    txtFirstName.Text = Empty
    txtSpouseName.Text = Empty
    txtAddress1.Text = Empty
    txtAddress2.Text = Empty
    txtAddress3.Text = Empty
    cboCity.ListIndex = -1
    cboState.ListIndex = -1
    cboZipCode.ListIndex = -1
    txtAreaCode.Text = Empty
    txtPhoneNumber.Text = Empty
```

```
    'Clear checklist
    chkCustomerData.Value = vbUnchecked
    chkEmploymentData.Value = vbUnchecked

    'Reset Boolean values
    blnLastName = False
    blnFirstName = False
    blnAddress = False
    blnCity = False
    blnZipCode = False
    blnAreaCode = False
    blnPhoneNumber = False

    'Clear messages
    StatusBar1.Panels("Msg").Text = Empty
End Sub
```

17. Enter the following code for the `mnuHelpAbout_Click` procedure:

```
Private Sub mnuHelpAbout_Click()
   Call AbSplash.About(Me)
End Sub
```

18. Enter the following code for the `mnuViewEmployment_Click` and `Toolbar_Buttonclick` procedures:

```
Private Sub mnuViewEmployment_Click()
   Call cmdEmployment_Click
End Sub

Private Sub Toolbar1_ButtonClick(ByVal Button As MSComctlLib.Button)
   On Error Resume Next
   Select Case Button.Key
      Case "New"
         mnuFileNew_Click
      Case "Cut"
      Case "Copy"
      Case "Paste"
      Case "Undo"
      Case "Help What's This"
      Case "Help"
   End Select
End Sub
```

19. Enter the following code for the `Form_Load` procedure:

```
Private Sub Form_Load()
   'Load the splash form
   Call AbSplash.SplashOn(Me)

   'Set up error handling
   On Error GoTo Form_Load_EH
```

```
    'Set a reference to the database objects
    Set m_objConn = New ADODB.Connection
    Set m_objRS = New ADODB.Recordset

    'Establish a database connection using NT authentication
    m_objConn.Open "Driver=SQL Server;Server=WSDevelopment;" & _
       "Database=Wrox_Auto_Works"

    'Check connection state
    If m_objConn.State <> adStateOpen Then
       StatusBar1.Panels("Msg") = "Database Connection Failed"
       Exit Sub
    Else
       m_objConn.Errors.Clear
    End If

    'Show the form to give the impression all processing is complete
    Me.Show
    DoEvents

    'Load City, State and Zip Code combo boxes
    Call LoadCityStateZip

    'Load customer names
    Call LoadCustomerNames
    cboLastName.SetFocus

    'Unload the splash form
    Call AbSplash.SplashOff

    'All done, exit procedure
    On Error GoTo 0
    Exit Sub

Form_Load_EH:
    'Unload the splash form
    Call AbSplash.SplashOff

    'Ensure the error came from ADO
    If m_objConn.Errors.Count > 0 Then
       For Each m_objErr In m_objConn.Errors
          StatusBar1.Panels("Msg") = StatusBar1.Panels("Msg") & " " & _
             m_objErr.Description
       Next
    Else
       StatusBar1.Panels("Msg") = Err.Description
    End If
End Sub
```

20. Enter the following code for the txtAddress1_GotFocus procedure:

```
Private Sub txtAddress1_GotFocus()
   'Select text
   txtAddress1.SelStart = 0
   txtAddress1.SelLength = Len(txtAddress1.Text)
End Sub
```

21. Enter the following code for the txtAddress1_Validate procedure:

```
Private Sub txtAddress1_Validate(Cancel As Boolean)
   'Display an error if no text was entered
   If Len(txtAddress1.Text) = 0 Then
      StatusBar1.Panels("Msg").Text = "Address Line 1 is required"
      Label1(3).ForeColor = vbRed
      Beep
      Cancel = True
   Else
      'Validation passed
      StatusBar1.Panels("Msg").Text = Empty
      Label1(3).ForeColor = vbWindowText
      Cancel = False
      blnAddress = True
   End If
   Call ValidateData
End Sub
```

22. Enter the following code for the txtAddress2_GotFocus procedure:

```
Private Sub txtAddress2_GotFocus()
   'Select text
   txtAddress2.SelStart = 0
   txtAddress2.SelLength = Len(txtAddress2.Text)
End Sub
```

23. Enter the following code for the txtAddress3_GotFocus procedure:

```
Private Sub txtAddress3_GotFocus()
   'Select text
   txtAddress3.SelStart = 0
   txtAddress3.SelLength = Len(txtAddress3.Text)
End Sub
```

24. Enter the following code for the txtAreaCode_GotFocus procedure:

```
Private Sub txtAreaCode_GotFocus()
   'Select text
   txtAreaCode.SelStart = 0
   txtAreaCode.SelLength = Len(txtAreaCode.Text)
End Sub
```

25. Enter the following code for the `txtAreaCode_Validate` procedure:

```
Private Sub txtAreaCode_Validate(Cancel As Boolean)
   'Display an error if area code is not 3 digits
   If Len(txtAreaCode.Text) <> 3 Then
      StatusBar1.Panels("Msg").Text = "Area Code is required in the format of nnn"
      Label1(9).ForeColor = vbRed
      Beep
      Cancel = True
   Else
      'Validation passed
      StatusBar1.Panels("Msg").Text = Empty
      Label1(9).ForeColor = vbWindowText
      Cancel = False
      blnAreaCode = True
   End If
   Call ValidateData
End Sub
```

26. Enter the following code for the `txtFirstName_GotFocus` procedure:

```
Private Sub txtFirstName_GotFocus()
   'Select text
   txtFirstName.SelStart = 0
   txtFirstName.SelLength = Len(txtFirstName.Text)
End Sub
```

27. Enter the following code for the `txtFirstName_Validate` procedure:

```
Private Sub txtFirstName_Validate(Cancel As Boolean)
   'Display an error if no text was entered
   If Len(txtFirstName.Text) = 0 Then
      StatusBar1.Panels("Msg").Text = "First Name is required"
      Label1(1).ForeColor = vbRed
      Beep
      Cancel = True
   Else
      'Validation passed
      StatusBar1.Panels("Msg").Text = Empty
      Label1(1).ForeColor = vbWindowText
      Cancel = False
      blnFirstName = True
   End If
   Call ValidateData
End Sub
```

28. Enter the following code for the `txtPhoneNumber_GotFocus` procedure:

```
Private Sub txtPhoneNumber_GotFocus()
   'Select text
   txtPhoneNumber.SelStart = 0
   txtPhoneNumber.SelLength = Len(txtPhoneNumber.Text)
End Sub
```

29. Enter the following code for the `txtPhoneNumber_Validate` procedure:

```
Private Sub txtPhoneNumber_Validate(Cancel As Boolean)
   'Display an error if phone number is not 8 digits
   If Len(txtPhoneNumber.Text) <> 8 Then
      StatusBar1.Panels("Msg").Text = "Phone Number is required in the format of
                 nnn-nnnn"
      Label1(10).ForeColor = vbRed
      Beep
      Cancel = True
   Else
      'Validation passed
      StatusBar1.Panels("Msg").Text = Empty
      Label1(10).ForeColor = vbWindowText
      Cancel = False
      blnPhoneNumber = True
   End If
   Call ValidateData
End Sub
```

30. Enter the following code for the `txtSpouseName_GotFocus` procedure:

```
Private Sub txtSpouseName_GotFocus()
   'Select text
   txtSpouseName.SelStart = 0
   txtSpouseName.SelLength = Len(txtSpouseName.Text)
End Sub
```

How It Works - Main Form Code

As we mentioned above, most of the code in this form is the same code that we have been working with over the past several chapters. Only the code that is new or different will be discussed.

All procedures that implement an error handling routine now display the error messages in the status bar versus using a debug window or message box.

General Declarations

The dirty flags in the general declarations section have been replaced with flags for each of the fields. When a field has been successfully validated, the flag for that field will be turned on. When all flags have been turned on, the Customer Data checkbox will be checked:

```
'Declare validation variables
Private blnLastName As Boolean
Private blnFirstName As Boolean
Private blnAddress As Boolean
Private blnCity As Boolean
Private blnZipCode As Boolean
Private blnAreaCode As Boolean
Private blnPhoneNumber As Boolean
```

Form_Load Procedure

The `Form_Load` event has changed slightly. The first change that you will see is that we are now displaying the Splash screen by calling the `SplashOn` procedure in the `AbSplash` form. We are passing the parent form as the first parameter:

```
Private Sub Form_Load()
   'Load the splash form
   Call AbSplash.SplashOn(Me)

   'Set up error handling
   On Error GoTo Form_Load_EH

   'Set a reference to the database objects
   Set m_objConn = New ADODB.Connection
   Set m_objRS = New ADODB.Recordset

   'Establish a database connection using NT Authentication
   m_objConn.Open "Driver=SQL Server;Server=WSDevelopment;" & _
      "Database=Wrox_Auto_Works"

   'Check connection state
   If m_objConn.State <> adStateOpen Then
      StatusBar1.Panels("Msg") = "Database Connection Failed"
      Exit Sub
   Else
      m_objConn.Errors.Clear
   End If

   'Show the form to give the impression all processing is complete
   Me.Show
   DoEvents

   'Load City, State and Zip Code combo boxes
   Call LoadCityStateZip
```

The second change that you will notice is that instead of loading the customer names in the `Form_Load` event, we have set up a procedure to handle this and are calling it here:

```
      'Load customer names
      Call LoadCustomerNames
      cboLastName.SetFocus
```

After all processing has completed we call the `SplashOff` procedure in the `AbSplash` form to turn off the Splash screen. The first time you run your project you will see the Splash screen for a few seconds while the database connection is established. As part of the process of establishing a database connection, certain DLLs get loaded into memory and this takes a while. After you end your program, the DLLs are moved from main memory to what is called a Standby List. On subsequent executions, the DLLs are loaded from the Standby List, which is much faster than loading them from disk. Thus you will barely get to see the Splash screen at all on subsequent executions of your program:

```
      'Unload the splash form
      Call AbSplash.SplashOff

      'All done, exit procedure
      On Error GoTo 0
      Exit Sub
```

As we mentioned above, the error handling routines have changed. The first change here is specific to the error handling routine in the `Form_Load` event. If some type of error occurred, we want to turn off the Splash screen and do so in the same manner as above.

Then we check the ADO `Errors` collection and if it contains any errors, we loop through the `Errors` collection and display each message in the status bar. If the error came from VB, we display the error from the `Error` object in the status bar:

```
   Form_Load_EH:
      'Unload the splash form
      Call AbSplash.SplashOff

      'Ensure the error came from ADO
      If m_objConn.Errors.Count > 0 Then
         For Each m_objErr In m_objConn.Errors
            StatusBar1.Panels("Msg") = StatusBar1.Panels("Msg") & " " & _
               m_objErr.Description
         Next
      Else
         StatusBar1.Panels("Msg") = Err.Description
      End If
   End Sub
```

LoadCustomerNames Procedure

The `LoadCustomerNames` procedure is totally new, but contains code that is very familiar. Briefly, we set up error handling for this procedure, declare our local variables, and clear any existing entries in the combo box:

```
Private Sub LoadCustomerNames()
   'Set up error handling
   On Error GoTo LoadCustomerNames_EH

   'Declare local variables
   Dim lngIndex As Long, lngRC As Long

   'Clear any existing entries
   cboLastName.Clear
```

If the `Recordset` object is not `Nothing`, then we check the `State` property to see if it is open. If it is, we close it and then move on to instantiate the Customer class. Then we execute the function to get a list of all customer names and then check for errors:

```
   'If the recordset has been set and is open, then close it
   If Not m_objRS Is Nothing Then
      If m_objRS.State = adStateOpen Then
         m_objRS.Close
      End If
   End If

   'Instantiate the class
   Set m_objCustomer = New clsCustomer

   'Get a list of customer names
   lngRC = m_objCustomer.GetCustomerNames(m_objConn, m_objRS)

   'If the return code is not zero, raise an error
   If lngRC <> 0 Then
      Err.Raise vbObjectError + 513, "frmMain.LoadCustomerNames", _
         "Call to clsCustomer.GetCustomerNames failed"
   End If
```

We loop through the recordset, adding the last name for each customer to the combo box. The `ItemData` property gets set to the `Customer_ID` for each customer:

```
   'Load the combo box
   lngIndex = -1
   Do While Not m_objRS.EOF
      'Add the last name
      cboLastName.AddItem m_objRS!Last_Name_VC
      lngIndex = lngIndex + 1
      'Add the customer id
      cboLastName.ItemData(lngIndex) = m_objRS!Customer_ID
      m_objRS.MoveNext
   Loop
```

After the combo box is loaded, we set the `ListIndex` property to the first entry in the combo box and set focus to it.

The error handling displays all error messages in the status bar:

```
    'Set the index to the first entry and exit sub
    cboLastName.ListIndex = 0
    cboLastName.SetFocus
    On Error GoTo 0
    Exit Sub

LoadCustomerNames_EH:
    'Ensure the error came from ADO
    If m_objConn.Errors.Count > 0 Then
        For Each m_objErr In m_objConn.Errors
            StatusBar1.Panels("Msg") = StatusBar1.Panels("Msg") & " " & _
            m_objErr.Description
        Next
    Else
        StatusBar1.Panels("Msg") = Err.Description
    End If
End Sub
```

cmdAdd_Click Procedure

The procedure to add a new customer has changed slightly from the previous examples, so let's run through the new code fairly quickly. The first thing we do in this procedure is to set up error handling and declare our local variables:

```
Private Sub cmdAdd_Click()
    'Set up error handling
    On Error GoTo cmdAdd_EH

    'Declare local variables
    Dim strMsg() As String, lngRC As Long, lngAddressID As Long, _
        lngPhoneNumberID As Long, lngCityID As Long, _
        lngZipCodeID As Long, lngCustomerInformationID As Long, _
        lngCurrentEmployerID As Long, lngPreviousEmployerID As Long, _
        intAreaCode As Integer, lngPhoneNumber As Long, _
        bytYearsEmployed As Byte, varText As Variant
```

Then we check the `ListIndex` property of the `cboCity` and `cboZipCode` combo boxes to determine if an existing entry was selected or a new entry inputted. We set the local variable either to the `ItemData` property of the entry selected or to zero if a new entry was entered:

```
    'Set city and zip code IDs
    If cboCity.ListIndex = -1 Then
        lngCityID = 0
    Else
        lngCityID = cboCity.ItemData(cboCity.ListIndex)
    End If
```

```
If cboZipCode.ListIndex = -1 Then
   lngZipCodeID = 0
Else
   lngZipCodeID = cboZipCode.ItemData(cboZipCode.ListIndex)
End If
```

We set a reference to our objects and then execute the function to insert a new address. Remember that the `lngAddressID` and `lngPhoneNumberID` variables are being passed by reference, and when control returns from this function, these variables will contain the primary key of the new entries added, if no errors occurred:

```
'Set a reference to the objects
Set m_objCmd = New ADODB.Command
Set m_objAddress = New clsAddress

'Insert the address
lngRC = m_objAddress.InsertAddress(txtAddress1.Text, _
   txtAddress2.Text, _
   txtAddress3.Text, _
   lngCityID, _
   cboCity.Text, _
   cboState.ItemData(cboState.ListIndex), _
   lngZipCodeID, _
   cboZipCode.Text, _
   CInt(txtAreaCode.Text), _
   EditPhoneNumber(txtPhoneNumber.Text), _
   lngAddressID, _
   lngPhoneNumberID, _
   strMsg(), _
   m_objConn, _
   m_objCmd)
```

We check for errors and then de-reference our objects and re-dimension our message string variable:

```
'Display any error messages
If lngRC <> 0 Then
   For Each varText In strMsg
      StatusBar1.Panels("Msg").Text = StatusBar1.Panels("Msg").Text & _
         varText
   Next
   Exit Sub
End If

'De-reference objects and clear message variable
Set m_objCmd = Nothing
Set m_objAddress = Nothing
ReDim strMsg(0)
```

We perform the same checks on the combo boxes in the Employment form as we did above. Since the previous employer information is optional, we check to see if the numeric fields contain data. If they do not, we set our local variables to zero, in preparation for our call to the function to add employment information for a customer:

```
'Set current employer numeric values
If frmEmployment.cboCurrentEmployer.ListIndex = -1 Then
   lngCurrentEmployerID = 0
Else
   lngCurrentEmployerID = frmEmployment.cboCurrentEmployer.ItemData( _
      frmEmployment.cboCurrentEmployer.ListIndex)
End If

'Set previous employer numeric values
If frmEmployment.cboPreviousEmployer.ListIndex = -1 Then
   lngPreviousEmployerID = 0
Else
   lngPreviousEmployerID = frmEmployment.cboPreviousEmployer.ItemData( _
      frmEmployment.cboPreviousEmployer.ListIndex)
End If

If Len(frmEmployment.txtPEAreaCode.Text) = 0 Then
   intAreaCode = 0
Else
   intAreaCode = CInt(frmEmployment.txtPEAreaCode.Text)
End If

If Len(frmEmployment.txtPEPhoneNumber.Text) = 0 Then
   lngPhoneNumber = 0
Else
   lngPhoneNumber = EditPhoneNumber(frmEmployment.txtPEPhoneNumber.Text)
End If

If Len(frmEmployment.txtPEYearsEmployed.Text) = 0 Then
   bytYearsEmployed = 0
Else
   bytYearsEmployed = CByte(frmEmployment.txtPEYearsEmployed.Text)
End If
```

We set a reference to our objects and execute the function to insert employment information. The `lngCustomerInformationID` local variable is being passed by reference, and will contain the primary key of the employment information for this customer after the function returns:

```
'Set a reference to the objects
Set m_objCmd = New ADODB.Command
Set m_objEmployer = New clsEmployer

'Insert the employer information
lngRC = m_objEmployer.InsertEmployer(lngCurrentEmployerID, _
   frmEmployment.cboCurrentEmployer.Text, _
   CInt(frmEmployment.txtCEAreaCode.Text), _
```

```
      EditPhoneNumber(frmEmployment.txtCEPhoneNumber.Text), _
      CByte(frmEmployment.txtCEYearsEmployed.Text), _
      frmEmployment.txtJobTitle.Text, _
      lngPreviousEmployerID, _
      frmEmployment.cboPreviousEmployer.Text, _
      intAreaCode, _
      lngPhoneNumber, _
      bytYearsEmployed, _
      lngCustomerInformationID, _
      strMsg(), _
      m_objConn, _
      m_objCmd)
```

We again check for errors and de-reference our objects:

```
   'Display any error messages
   If lngRC <> 0 Then
      For Each varText In strMsg
         StatusBar1.Panels("Msg").Text = StatusBar1.Panels("Msg").Text & _
            varText
      Next
      Exit Sub
   End If

   'De-reference objects and clear message variable
   Set m_objCmd = Nothing
   Set m_objEmployer = Nothing
   ReDim strMsg(0)
```

We set a reference to the objects required to insert the main customer record and execute that function. Notice that we are passing the local variables that were set in the previous two functions as parameters to this function. The primary keys of the Address, Phone Number and Customer Information tables are inserted into the `Customer_T` tables:

```
   'Set a reference to the objects
   Set m_objCmd = New ADODB.Command
   Set m_objCustomer = New clsCustomer

   'Insert the customer information
   lngRC = m_objCustomer.InsertCustomer(lngAddressID, _
      lngPhoneNumberID, _
      lngCustomerInformationID, _
      txtFirstName.Text, _
      cboLastName.Text, _
      txtSpouseName.Text, _
      strMsg(), _
      m_objConn, _
      m_objCmd)
```

After the function executes, we check for and display any errors that might have occurred. Then we de-reference our objects.

```
    'Display any error messages
    If lngRC <> 0 Then
       For Each varText In strMsg
          StatusBar1.Panels("Msg").Text = StatusBar1.Panels("Msg").Text & _
             varText
       Next
       Exit Sub
    End If

    'De-reference objects
    Set m_objCmd = Nothing
    Set m_objCustomer = Nothing
```

This part of this procedure is new and did appear in previous examples. Here we disable the **Add** button and turn off the checklists. Then we reload the City, State and Zip Code combo boxes, as well as the Last Name combo box. Reloading these combo boxes will pick up any additions that may have been inserted into the tables:

```
    'Disable add button
    cmdAdd.Enabled = False

    'Turn off checklist
    chkCustomerData.Value = vbUnchecked
    chkEmploymentData.Value = vbUnchecked

    'ReLoad City, State and Zip Code combo boxes
    Call LoadCityStateZip

    'Reload data from new recordset
    Call LoadCustomerNames
```

Next, we set focus back to the Last Name combo box and then display a message that the customer was added. Our error handling routine has already been covered:

```
    'Set focus to the combo box
    cboLastName.SetFocus

    'Display message
    StatusBar1.Panels("Msg").Text = "Customer Added"
    Exit Sub

 cmdAdd_EH:
    Dim objErr As ADODB.Error
    'Ensure the error came from ADO
    If m_objConn.Errors.Count > 0 Then
       For Each objErr In m_objConn.Errors
          StatusBar1.Panels("Msg") = StatusBar1.Panels("Msg") & " " & _
             objErr.Description
       Next
```

```
    Else
       StatusBar1.Panels("Msg") = Err.Description
    End If
End Sub
```

cmdUpdate_Click Procedure

The `cmdUpdate_Click` procedure functions in a similar manner to the `cmdAdd_Click` procedure. The difference comes when we update the Customer record shown below. In the past examples, we updated the Customer record using a dynamic SQL statement. Here we are using the stored procedure that we built at the beginning of this chapter:

```
    'Update the customer record
    lngRC = m_objCustomer.UpdateCustomer(m_lngCustomerID, _
       txtFirstName.Text, _
       cboLastName.Text, _
       txtSpouseName.Text, _
       m_objConn, _
       m_objCmd)
```

After the Customer record has been updated, we check for errors and de-reference our objects:

```
    'Display any error messages
    If lngRC <> 0 Then
       StatusBar1.Panels("Msg").Text = "Update of customer failed"
       Exit Sub
    End If

    'De-reference objects
    Set m_objCmd = Nothing
    Set m_objCustomer = Nothing
```

To ensure we pick up any changes in our combo boxes, we save the current record position using the `ListIndex` property of the `cboLastName` combo box, and then reload all combo boxes on the form:

```
    'Save the current record position
    lngRecordPosition = cboLastName.ListIndex

    'ReLoad City, State and Zip Code combo boxes
    Call LoadCityStateZip

    'Reload data from new recordset
    Call LoadCustomerNames
```

After the combo boxes have been reloaded, we reposition the cboLastName combo box to the record we just updated and call the cboLastName_Click procedure to reload the address information. Then we set focus back to the cboLastName combo box and display a message that the customer was updated:

```
'Reload from the address fields
cboLastName.ListIndex = lngRecordPosition
Call cboLastName_Click

'Set focus to the combo box
cboLastName.SetFocus

'Display message
StatusBar1.Panels("Msg").Text = "Customer Updated"
Exit Sub
```

This wraps up the code in our Main form as well as the code for our entire project. We have built three separate forms in this project and have added all of the necessary code to make this a functional application. We first built each form and added the necessary controls; then added the code to make each form functional. The Main form provides the code necessary to show the other forms.

Testing

To start the testing set a break point in the cboLastName_Validate event and the txtFirstName_Validate event in the Main form (frmMain) as shown below:

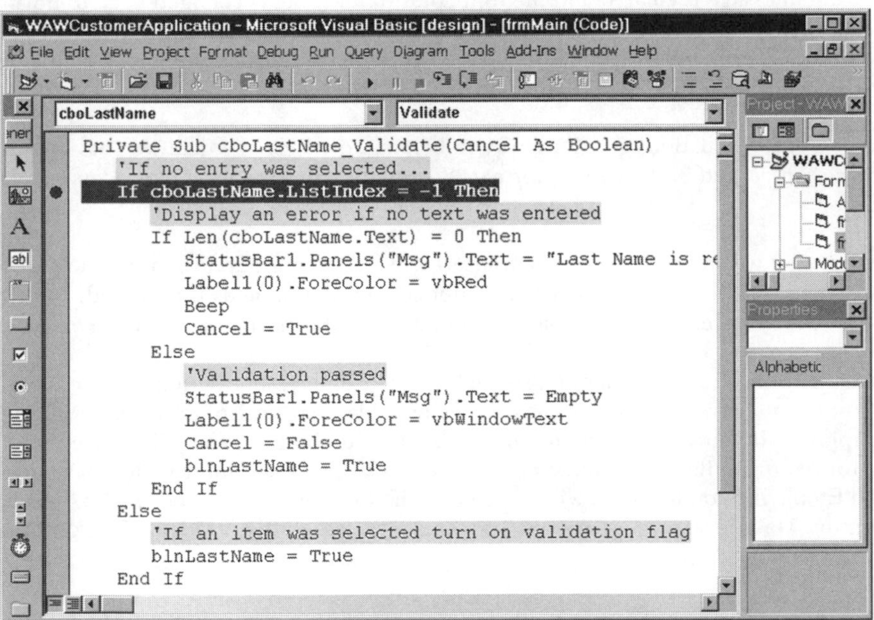

Start your project and delete the text in the cboLastName combo box. Try to tab to the next field and then step through the code in the cboLastName_Validate event:

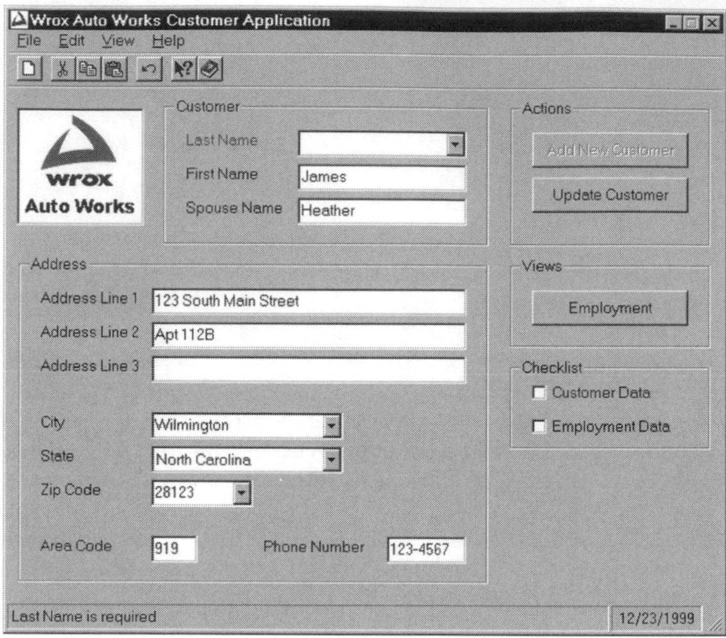

Now enter some text in this combo box, and then tab to the next field and step through the code again. Notice how the message is cleared and the font color of the label is changed back to normal.

Perform the same steps above for the First Name textbox. The validation code is a little different but demonstrates how the validation is performed.

As you can see, the validations go a long way in helping to ensure the data we pass to our stored procedure is correct, and in the correct format. We will be implementing more data validations later in this book.

The other test that we want to perform is to insert a new customer. Start by removing all break points, then click on the New icon on the toolbar and notice how all the fields are cleared. At this point it does not matter in which order we insert data, entering data for the customer or for the employment.

We will start with the employment data, so click on the Employment button. Notice that the Employment form (frmEmployment) has all of the fields cleared also. Enter some information for the current employer. If you selected an employer from the combo box, you will notice that the phone number information is filled in automatically. Once all employment information has been entered, click on the Add Employers button. You will notice that the Employment Data checkbox has become checked on the Main form and we are one step closer to having the Add New Customer button become enabled.

Enter data in the various customer fields and stop when you get to the Phone Number field. Once you enter data in the Phone Number field and tab off, you will notice that the Customer Data checkbox will become checked and the Add New Customer button will become enabled.

Add the new customer and notice that the Add New Customer button becomes disabled and the check boxes cleared. The check boxes are good visual indicators for the user that the required information has been completed. Enabling and disabling the Add New Customer button prevents the user from accidentally trying to add a customer without all of the required information or adding a duplicate customer.

Summary

While this has been a fairly long chapter, we have covered some important techniques to help ensure data integrity in our database. We have learned how to use the `Validate` event to help validate the data in a field before the field loses focus. We have applied the validation of data to both text and combo boxes; and know how the validation of data differs between the two.

There were a couple more stored procedures required for this chapter and they were straightforward. These stored procedures were used to help present the data in the Employment form in a user-friendly manner. Through the reuse of our classes, we have taken advantage of the functions and stored procedures that we have already written up to this point.

The common elements of the UI were covered and although our menu, toolbar and status bar are simple, they are highly effective. They allow the user to navigate through the various forms in our application and they also provide invaluable feedback to the user when things go wrong and when things go right.

We used the `AbSplash` form to display both a splash screen when our application starts and for an about dialog for our application. The `frmEmployment` form displayed both current and previous employer information for a given customer and the `frmMain` form displayed a customer and their address information. After having covered the layout of controls in these forms, you should realize the importance of data separation and presentation. Through the use of visual indicators, the user knows what pieces of information are missing and what pieces of information have been completed.

In a real application you would want to implement full functionality of the toolbar and menus to include such standard features as cut, copy and paste. Depending on the number of customers in your database you may even want to include a search feature to make it easier to find a customer, instead of having to scroll through the list of customers in the Customer Last Name combo box. An intuitive help file with context sensitive help would also go a long way to make this a more user-friendly interface.

In summary, you should know:

- How to use the `Validate` event to validate data
- How to create and use the common elements of an application
- How to present data that is clear and grouped together
- How to use visual indicators to aid the user

WROX AUTO WORKS RACING

Creating a Business Server Component

Over the past five chapters we have written dozens of stored procedures and have created functions that call these stored procedures in reusable classes. Because we have used classes we have made our user interface (UI) easier to manage by keeping the calls to the stored procedures in one place. We have also thoroughly tested the functions and classes.

Now comes the time when we want to share these functions with other applications. In order to do this we could simply share these classes as stand-alone code, but that wouldn't be very secure and other developers would be able to modify the functions. This wouldn't be a step in the right direction to ensuring data integrity. Instead, we are going to encapsulate these classes into an ActiveX business server component. When we talk about encapsulation we are referring to placing our code in an ActiveX component to isolate the code from the rest of the application. This chapter focuses on the steps required to create a business server component that will allow us to share our functions in a secure manner.

In this chapter we will:

- Look at MTS versus SQL Server transactions
- Create a business server component
- Create a help file for our business server component
- Modify the front-end to use the new component

What is a Business Server Component

When we talk about **business server components**, we are referring to **ActiveX DLLs** that implement business rules and perform specific business tasks. An ActiveX DLL is a dynamic link library that has a COM interface, in other words it is a compiled component that can be linked to your application at run-time.

Business server components allow us to encapsulate business rules and data, and provide services to many types of clients simultaneously. They also help us to build component-based applications that can be distributed across the enterprise in an n-tier application.

When we talk about **business rules** most people traditionally think about data retrieval and storage. However, business rules go far beyond data access, in that they describe a business's preferred method of handling and manipulating data. Business rules also define how a business performs various functions and operations, such as calculations.

Business server components expose **interfaces** to other applications and objects. These interfaces normally accept a standard set of parameters, do the required processing based on the business rules, and return a return code to the requesting application or object. These components can be shared with other applications in the enterprise that need to expose similar functionality. Other programs don't need to know the details of a component, only the required interface to get the desired results.

Using a business server component provides two major benefits. First, it allows us to share our functions in a secure manner by exposing an *interface* and not code. Second, it cuts down on the maintenance and total cost of ownership for the component through *reuse*. If the implementation of a function changes, we simply make the change to our component and it is immediately available for everyone to use.

When we talk about **n-tier applications** we are referring to an application that divides its processing into layers or tiers. N-tier applications are normally divided into three parts: the user services, the business services, and the data services. The **user service layer** is responsible for gathering data from the user and displaying data for the user, and is located in the first tier of an n-tier application. The **business service layer** provides the data access and implements business rules. This layer is usually located in the middle tier of an n-tier application, however the business services can be expanded to operate on multiple layers, for example providing messaging and transactional support. The **data service layer**, which usually resides at the top tier, manages the actual data.

MTS versus SQL Server Transactions

For those readers not familiar with **Microsoft Transaction Server** (**MTS**), it is a component-based transaction server that processes transactions for compiled and interpreted components. MTS provides security and transactional processing of your components while ensuring data integrity on your backend data stores. MTS provides the middle tier in an n-tier programming model, as shown in the following figure:

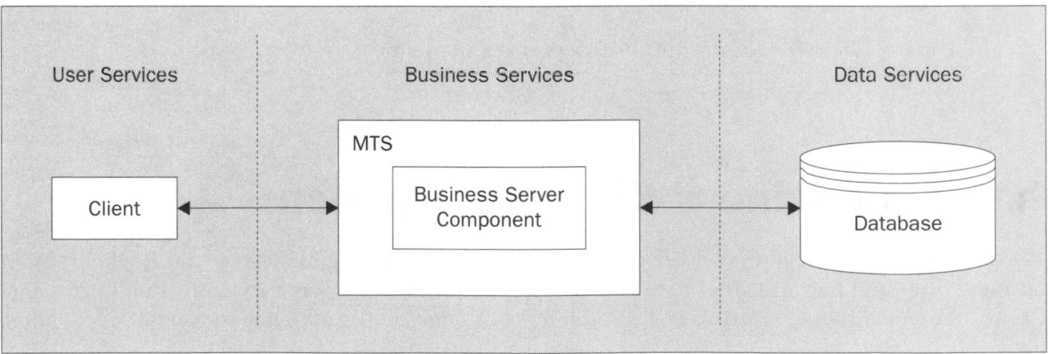

The following list summarizes just some of the benefits that MTS provides:

- MTS is part of the Windows NT operating system, and can be leveraged without any additional cost when deploying your server components on Windows NT Server.
- MTS provides object management which instantiates objects more efficiently.
- It provides security for our components so that unauthorized users cannot use them.
- MTS components can be packaged and added to other servers, thus providing scalability.
- It provides automatic transaction support in that you do not specifically have to code transaction support in your components, thus allowing two-tier applications to take advantage of three-tier architecture.
- MTS supports COM components that do not specifically implement MTS within their code.
- It provides integration with SQL Server, Microsoft Message Queue (MSMQ), and Internet Information Server (IIS).
- MTS uses DCOM, which supports component-to-component communications across the network, helping you to build n-tier systems that are scalable.

Looking at the above list, we can see that MTS has many benefits to offer. MTS achieves everything that using SQL Server transactions can, and then some. However, to take full advantage of MTS a more detailed understanding of it is required, and you should read a dedicated book, such as *Professional MTS MSMQ with VB and ASP* by Wrox Press (ISBN 1-861001-46-0).

MTS should also be implemented in our code so that we can control when a transaction begins and when it is either committed or aborted. VB supports MTS through the `MTSTransactionMode` property in each class. In addition, you can set a reference to the **Microsoft Transaction Server Type Library**, and include specific transactional support in each of your functions by starting, committing, and aborting transactions.

One of the greatest benefits of MTS, from a developer's standpoint, is that we can code our stored procedures and components as if only one user will be using them. MTS handles all the complex details of concurrency, database connection pooling, and security. Database connection pooling is where a pool of database connections is maintained, which are then shared amongst multiple clients as required.

As we discussed in previous chapters, SQL Server itself provides concurrency and transactional support. It also does an excellent job of providing security. Where MTS wins over SQL Server is that it is a component-based transaction server that allows us to implement *transactions* in our *components.* This allows us to efficiently call other components located on the same machine or across the network and have them take advantage of the benefits that MTS provides.

SQL Server and MTS both have their place, and when you use one over the other depends on your requirements and the project you are working on. MTS is great in managing transactions for components that must access two different data stores in one transaction, as it will back out changes to both databases if the transaction fails. For our purposes we will use SQL Server transactions, as this is the focus of this book. You should, however, read up and experiment with MTS as it has a lot to offer, especially when dealing with business server components.

Creating A Business Server Component

Because we have used classes to implement the functions that execute our stored procedures, converting them to a business server component will be easy. We have implemented limited business rules in our classes, as most of the business rules have been implemented in our stored procedures. Creating a business server component will allow us to implement more of the business rules in our component should we so desire, thus creating smaller stored procedures.

Where you place your business rules depends greatly on the type of business rules that are being implemented, and your shop's standards. We could move the data validations, which validate the types and format of data, from the stored procedures to our business component. This would allow us to avoid a server trip, by validating that the data is present and in the correct format before executing our stored procedures. However, we are going to leave the stored procedures as they are for now. What we are going to do is to create a component that will replace the functionality that was previously provided by our classes.

Try It Out – Creating a Business Server Component

1. To create our business server component, we first need to copy the classes and Utility module from the last chapter into a new directory. You can name this directory whatever you like and can place it anywhere you choose.

2. Next, start a new ActiveX DLL project and remove the current class. Add the Utility module and then add the Address, Customer, and Employer classes. On each of these classes, change the `Instancing` property to `5 - MultiUse`. This changes our classes to public so that other applications can instantiate our DLL and access the functions in our classes.

Notice that the Properties window has expanded and the `MTSTransactionMode` and `Persistable` properties are now available. The `Persistable` property determines if this object can save and restore data across instances. If you were going to add MTS support to your component, this is where you would set the `MTSTransactionMode` property.

3. The next thing we need to do is to set a reference to the Microsoft ActiveX Data Objects Library.

4. In order to set up our component for context sensitive help, we need to assign help context IDs to each of our procedures. Starting with the Address class, click on the first function, `GetAddress`. On the Tools menu choose Procedure Attributes and then enter the number 1 in the Help Context ID textbox:

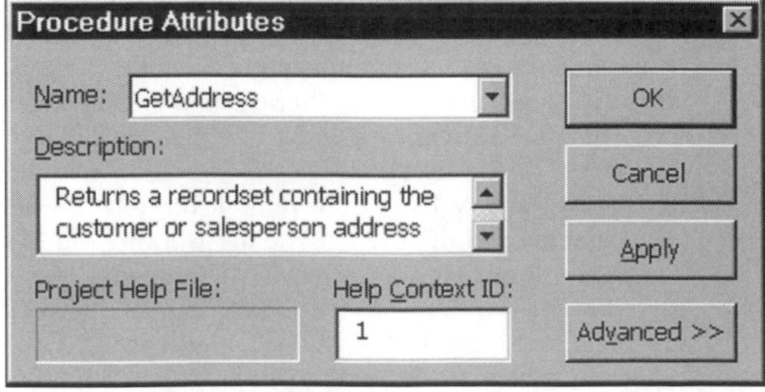

5. Going through all the functions in this class, enter an incremental number in the Help Context ID textbox. The last number that should be used in this class is the number 5 as we have five functions.

6. Moving on to the Customer class and starting with the number 6, enter an incremental number in the Help Context ID textbox for all the functions. Then perform the same steps for the Employer class using the next incremental number where the Customer class left off. The modifications that we have just made to our classes are all that is required. The Utility module requires no modifications whatsoever.

7. The last change we need to make to our component is to set the various project properties. Open the Project Properties dialog and change the Project Name to AutoWorks on the General tab.

   The Project Description property is the text that will be displayed in the References dialog once our component is compiled. Choosing a meaningful description here is important. Let's set this property to Wrox Auto Works ActiveX Business Object.

8. The next thing we want to change on this tab is to check the checkbox for Unattended Execution. This will ensure that any unexpected errors will not be displayed in a dialog, but instead will be written to the NT Event Log when running on Windows NT, or the `VBEvents.log` file on Windows 9x platforms.

9. Even though we do not have a help file yet we can enter just the name for the help file. When we create our help file in the next example we will call it `AutoWorks.hlp`, so let's enter this for the Help File Name property.

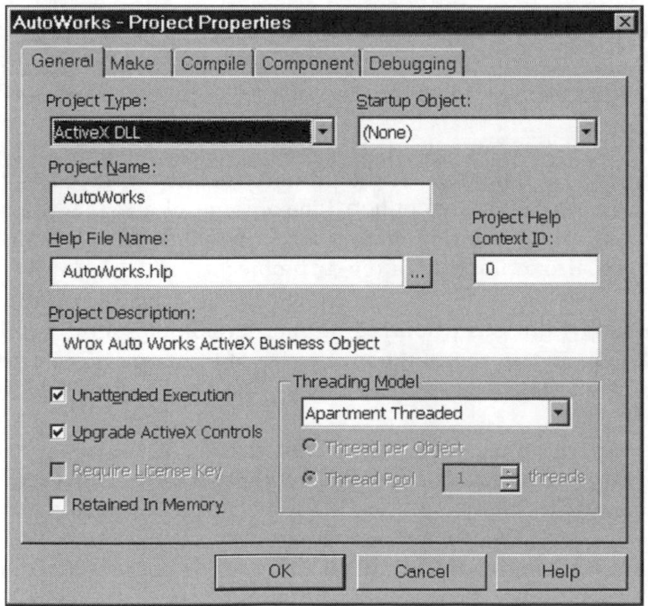

10. Switching to the Make tab, we want to start by checking the Auto Increment checkbox. This will automatically increment the revision number each time we compile our component, and will help us to maintain version control. These numbers get displayed on the Version tab of the Properties dialog for our compiled DLL. They are also properties of the `App` object. The `App` object is a global object in all VB programs. This object provides general information about the application, such as title, version information, program name, and paths for the executable and help files.

    The Application Title is set to the project name by default and can be changed. The name that is currently populating this field is fine for our purposes. The Application Title is also a property of the `App` object, and is used in the Setup wizard as the name that gets displayed in the Add/Remove Programs dialog once your component is installed.

    Since this is an ActiveX DLL and there are no forms associated with this project, there is no icon to choose from and the system will assign a default icon to our DLL. Normally, every form associated with your project will be listed in the Icon combo box and you can choose which form's icon would be assigned to the executable.

11. The next thing we want to look at on this tab is the Version Information. For the Comments, enter something appropriate for this component. I chose to enter the following description:

    ActiveX DLL that exposes classes containing business rules for managing data on the Wrox Auto Works database.

    The comments also get displayed in the Version tab of the Properties dialog for our compiled DLL, and are also a property of the `App` object.

12. The Company Name property is set to the company name registered on your computer by default. You can change this as needed, and this is also a property of the `App` object. The Company Name gets displayed on the Version tab of the Properties dialog for our compiled DLL.

13. The File Description property is the property that is displayed on the Version tab of the Properties dialog as the Description. The amount of text that is displayed is very limited and you should use a one liner here to describe the DLL at a high level. The File Description is also a property of the `App` object.

14. The Legal Copyright gets displayed on the Version tab of the Properties dialog as the Copyright. This is also one of the properties of the `App` object. Even if you set no other properties on the Make tab, at least set the File Description and Legal Copyright.

15. The next property in the list is Legal Trademarks. This property affects both the `App` object and the Properties dialog for our compiled DLL. However, if we do not place anything here, it will not be displayed in the Properties dialog for our compiled DLL.

16. The Product Name also affects both the `App` object and the Properties dialog. However, if you do not enter any text here, the Product Name gets assigned the name that you entered for the Application Title.

We will accept the defaults for the last three properties on this tab:

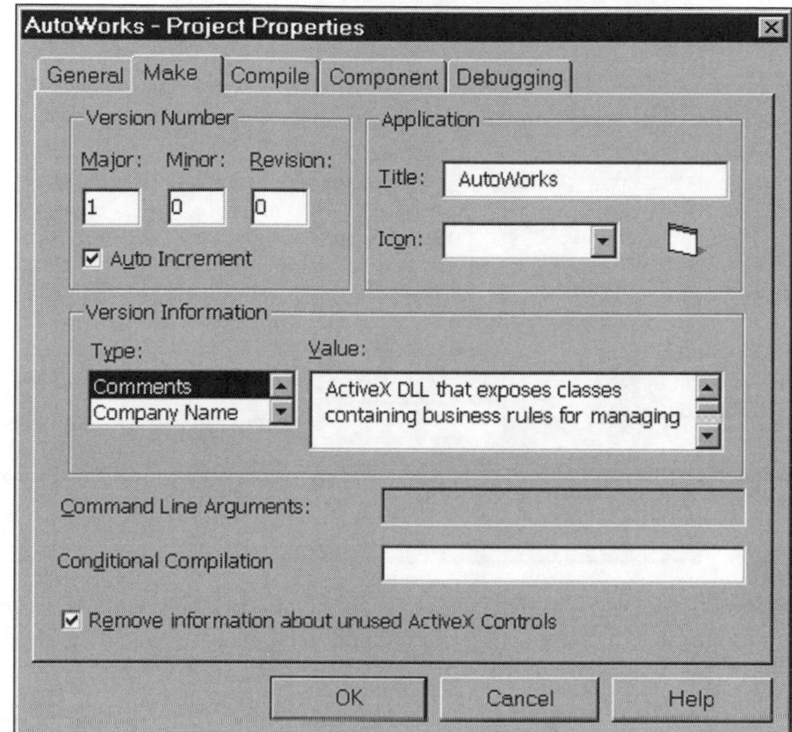

17. Moving on to the Compile tab, shown overleaf, we want to accept the defaults for the compile options. What we do want to change on this tab is the DLL Base Address. When the operating system loads a DLL, it tries to load it in memory as its base address, in other words the address specified in the DLL. If the memory address already contains another component, the system must go through what is called a fix-up process, whereby it finds another free address space in memory where it can place your DLL, and then performs the necessary steps to place it there. This process slows down the loading of your component.

To avoid this, we want to assign a unique base address to our component. In order to do this you must keep track of the addresses of all your components. The range of addresses available for VB components (ActiveX DLLs and OCXs) is from `&H11000000` to `&H80000000`. These addresses are on 64K boundaries and, even if your component is less than 64K in size, the entire address space is reserved for your component. Likewise, if your component is 65K then your component will reserve two consecutive address spaces.

With this is mind we want to change the address for the DLL Base Address property to &H1a6e0000. This is a random hexadecimal number that I chose that falls on a 64K-address boundary.

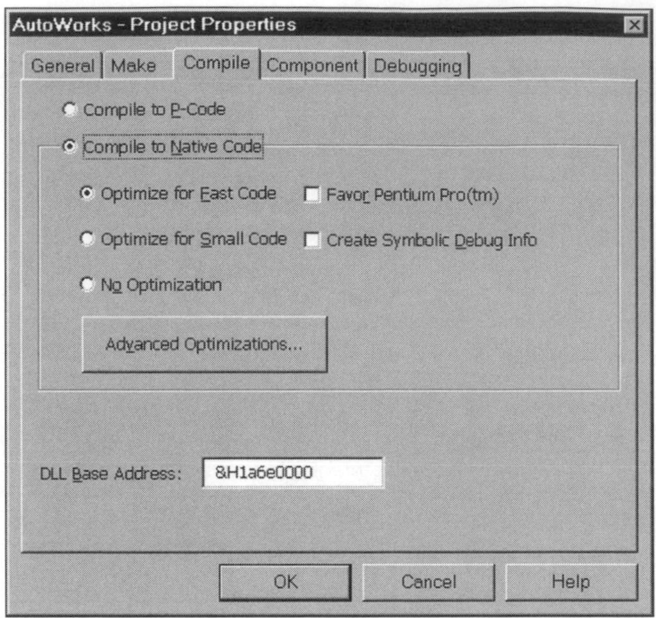

18. The next and last tab that we want to take a look at in the Project Properties dialog is the Component tab. The only thing we are concerned with on this tab is the Version Compatibility. There are three levels of compatibility and the first is No Compatibility. As its name implies, this option provides no compatibility whatsoever. Each time you compile your project new **class IDs** and **interface IDs** are generated. A class ID is a unique number assigned by VB to each class in your component, and an interface ID is a unique number assigned to each public function that you have defined in your class.

Project Compatibility maintains the type library identifier and class IDs from previous versions when you recompile your project. Interface IDs are only changed for classes that are no longer binary compatible with the previous version. Classes stop being binary compatible when their public interface is changed.

Binary Compatibility is a bit more complicated but overall is probably the best choice. Binary compatibility maintains the same class IDs and interface IDs when you recompile your component. This does, however, impose several restrictions on the changes you can make. You cannot *change* the public method interfaces (function parameters) of your component in any way without breaking binary compatibility, but you can *add new* interfaces to your project. If you break binary compatibility, Visual Basic will warn you when you recompile your project – heed this warning. The major benefit that binary compatibility provides is the ability to add new or enhanced functionality to your component without having to recompile the programs or other ActiveX DLLs that use this component. This functionality cannot be achieved if you select No Compatibility or Project Compatibility.

For our first compile we will use Project Compatibility, which is already set as the default. At this point click OK to save the changes we have made in the Project Properties dialog and to close it.

19. We want to create a sub directory in our project folder called `Compatibility`, in which we will compile the compatibility version of our component.

20. Then make your component in the `Compatibility` folder by choosing Make Autoworks.DLL from the File menu.

21. Now open the Project Properties dialog, go to the Component tab, and change the Version Compatibility to Binary Compatibility. Notice that our component is already listed in the Binary Compatibility box. We make a version of our DLL in the `Compatibility` folder so that when we make changes to our component and make a new version, the original DLL is used as the binary component to which the functions are compared in order to ensure that they have not changed. If you do change the functions you will be presented with a dialog informing you that you have broken binary compatibility.

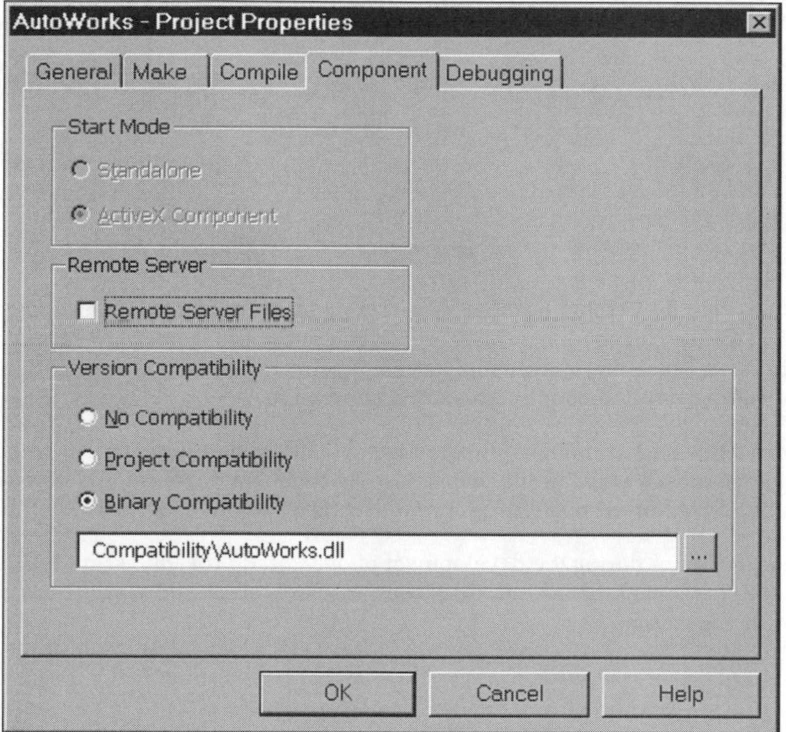

22. While we are here, click on the Make tab and notice that the Revision number is now 1. This number will be incremented with every compile of your component.

23. Compile your component again, but this time compile it in the project folder. Save your project and close it.

24. At this point we want to examine the DLL. Right click on `AutoWorks.dll` in your project folder and choose Properties from the popup menu. Click on the Version tab and notice the various properties that were set in the Project Properties dialog of your project:

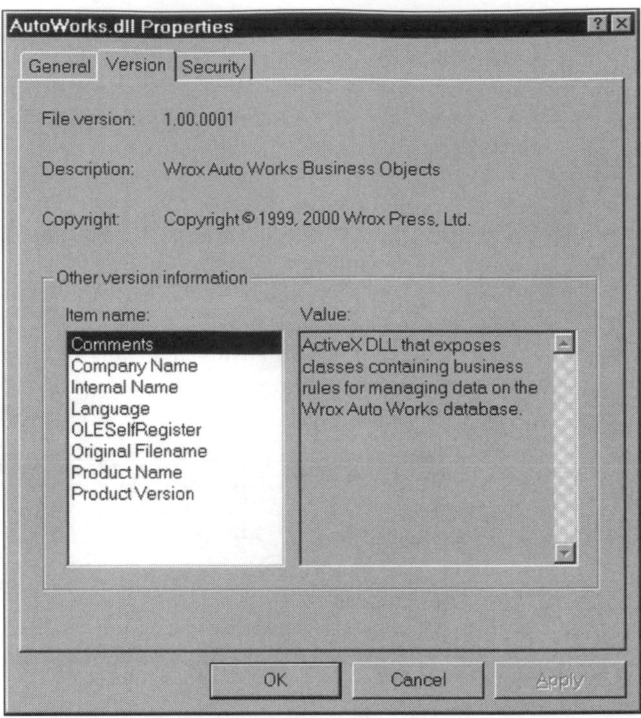

25. Notice the File version number. Now take a look at the component that you compiled for compatibility purposes in your `Compatibility` folder. Notice that there is no revision number because this component does not get compiled. This is the original component that the recompiled components are compared to.

Every time you recompile your component, the Revision number will be incremented by one. When you make a significant change in your component, you should manually change the Major and Minor version numbers to reflect the changes made.

Because we used classes during the development of our stored procedures and functions, creating this business server component that uses those classes was fairly quick and easy. There is a lot to be said for using classes in your projects.

Help File

Because we have wrapped up the functionality to insert, update, and delete data in our database into a business server component, we need to write a **help file** for our component so that other developers can pick up and use our component with little to no help at all.

The help file that we will create should include the details about the call to each function, listing and explaining each parameter that the function expects. In addition we should provide a list of related functions; for example an *insert* function would have a related *update* function. Just to avoid possible confusion about the calls to our functions, we should also provide an example call to each function.

Creating a help file that contains this information makes it very clear to other developers what each function expects and how to use the function. Creating an **index** and **table of contents** for this type of help file is optional, but can go a long way to providing a complete and comprehensive help file for our component.

Given the space limitations in this chapter, we will create an *abridged* version of the help file. This will get you started and will show you the basics of creating a help file. You can then come back at a later date and complete your help file, or complete it before moving on to the next chapter.

We will be using the **Help Workshop** that comes with Visual Studio, or which can be downloaded from the Microsoft web site. This will allow us to compile a **WinHelp** help file for our component.

Let's take a look at the different elements that make up our completed help file. First we have the compiled **help file** with an `.hlp` extension, and along with this is the **contents file** having a `.cnt` extension. The only file that we access directly is the help file. When we double click on a help file the contents associated with that help file are displayed, as shown in the figure below:

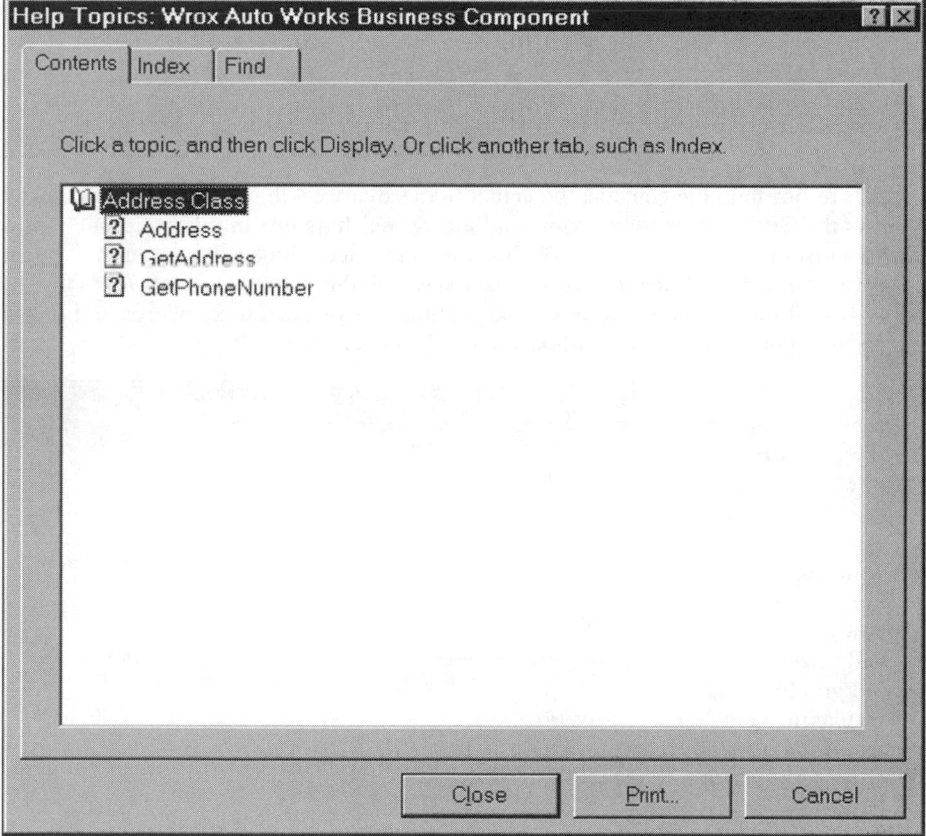

During our project to build a help file we will be building a contents file that will contain the information shown in the figure above.

If we want to display the index for this help file we click on the Index tab and the index is displayed, as shown in this figure:

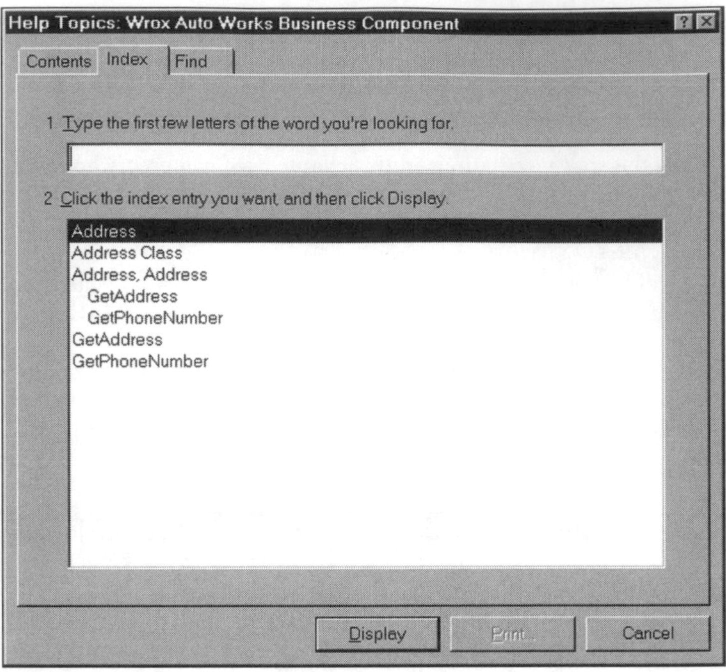

The last part of our help file contains the actual **topics** that we will be defining very shortly. This next figure shows the GetPhoneNumber topic and the various **hotspots** in this topic, such as **jumps** and **popups**. As most of you are aware, words that are underlined with a solid green line are either a jump to another topic or a **KLink** macro. KLink macros search the help file for keywords that have been defined by **K footnotes**. A K footnote is a special footnote assigned to keywords and topics that allows the help file to identify them in the index. We will be covering this shortly.

Words underlined with a dashed green line contain popups. Popups are special topics that are not listed in the index and are typically used to *define* words in your topic. Popups pop up in their own window and are automatically sized to fit the text and graphics that they are displaying. The figure opposite shows a popup for the acronym of ADO:

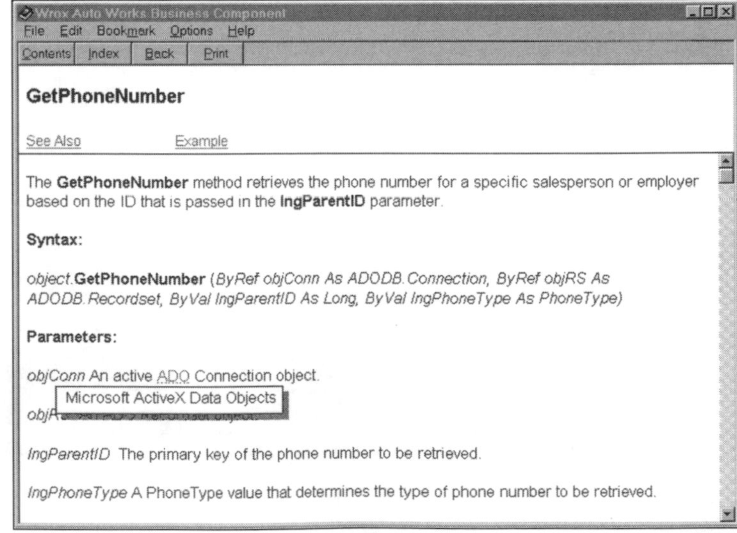

So basically our compiled help file consists of topics defined with jumps, KLink macros, popups, and an index. The contents are contained in a separate file that is merged when the help file is displayed.

The next three *Try It Out* examples will step you through creating a topics file, table of contents, and a complete help project.

Try It Out – Creating a Help Topic File

The file that we will create in this section contains the help topics that we will write, and is saved in a **rich text format** (**RTF**) file. You use a word processor such as Microsoft Word to create this rich text file. Each topic should describe a specific function in your business server component. The topics give a brief overview of the function and show the parameters the function expects. You then list each parameter and describe what each parameter is for. If there are any special notes they should be listed at the end of the topic.

Each topic title should have the Heading1 style applied. The Heading1 style in Word automatically contains a table with six columns, of which we need to use five. Each column in the table contains categories that will eventually contain jumps to related topics and examples. After the last line of each topic, we must insert a hard page break. We can do this in Word by holding down the *Ctrl* key and pressing the *Enter* key. Then we start our next topic.

Each topic we define in our help file must contain a **topic ID footnote mark**. All other footnote marks are optional and are only used to implement the required functionality that they provide. The following table details the custom footnote marks that we will use to identify topics, popup topics, and jumps:

Help Parameter	Footnote Mark	Description
Topic ID	#	Defines a topic
Title	$	Specifies the title of the topic as it appears in the Topics Found dialog
Keyword	K	Specifies keywords that are found in the index and in KLink macros
A-Keyword	A	Specifies words that identify the topic to the ALink macros

The easiest way to complete the help documentation is to start with a class module in your component and document each method within that module. During documentation apply the appropriate formatting for the headers and any other special formatting you see fit. Once the documentation is complete, you can then come back and add all the footnotes to tie the topics together.

The following section shows the entire help file (three topics only due to limited space, plus two examples and one popup topic) and the appropriate formatting. Since it is hard to tell what formatting has been applied we will discuss the formatting at a general level now and discuss the details when we walk through each topic.

1. At this point open your favorite word processing package and enter the text shown below, applying the Heading1 style to format the text. The first topic gives a general overview of the Address class in the business server component:

```
Address
 See Also       Example       Properties       Methods       Events
```

2. Next add the text to describe the topic just defined, and insert a hard page break at the end:

```
The Address class provides the necessary functionality to select, insert and update
address information. This information relates to phone number information and address
information, which includes city, state and zip code data.

Individual methods have been provided to retrieve this information for customers,
sales persons and employers.
. . . . . . . . . . . . . . . . . . . . . Page Break . . . . . . . . . . . . . . . . . . . . .
```

3. The next two topics describe the `GetAddress` and `GetPhoneNumber` functions. Following these topics are examples on how to call the `GetAddress` and `GetPhoneNumber` functions. The last topic will be used as a popup topic defining ADO. Enter the text below, applying the Heading1 style to each of the topic titles, and inserting a hard page break before each new topic.

```
GetAddress
 See Also     Example

The GetAddress method retrieves the address for a specific customer or salesperson
based on the ID that is passed in the lngParentID parameter.

Syntax:

object.GetAddress (ByRef objConn As ADODB.Connection, ByVal lngParentID As Long, ByVal
lngAddressType As AddressType)

Parameters:

objConn An active ADO Connection object.

lngParentID  The primary key of the address to be retrieved.

lngAddressType An AddressType value that determines the type of address to be
retrieved.

Remarks:
```

The GetAddress method returns the address in an ADO Recordset object. If the call to this function is successful, a populated Recordset is returned. If a failure occurs, the Recordset object is set to Nothing.

. . . . Page Break . . . .

GetPhoneNumber

See Also	Example

The **GetPhoneNumber** method retrieves the phone number for a specific salesperson or employer based on the ID that is passed in the **lngParentID** parameter.

Syntax:

object.**GetPhoneNumber** (ByRef objConn As ADODB.Connection, ByRef objRS As ADODB.Recordset, ByVal lngParentID As Long, ByVal lngPhoneType As PhoneType)

Parameters:

objConn An active ADO Connection object.

objRS An ADO Recordset object.

lngParentID The primary key of the phone number to be retrieved.

lngPhoneType A PhoneType value that determines the type of phone number to be retrieved.

Remarks:

The GetPhoneNumber method returns a long value indicating success. The phone number retrieved is returned in the Recordset object. The Recordset object is opened using a static cursor and read only lock.

. . . . Page Break . . . .

GetAddress Example

The following code demonstrates how to set a reference to the **AutoWorks** DLL and call the **GetAddress** method. The Recordset object used has been defined as an ADO Recordset object. The **lngParentID** parameter is being passed from the *ItemData* property of a combo box for the selected entry.

```
'Set a reference to the business object
Set m_objWroxAddress = New AutoWorks.clsAddress

'Get the customer's address
Set m_objRSAddress = m_objWroxAddress.GetAddress(m_objConn, _
     cboLastName.ItemData(cboLastName.ListIndex), Customer)
```

. . . . Page Break . . . .

GetPhoneNumber Example

The following code demonstrates how to set a reference to the **AutoWorks** DLL and call the **GetAddress** method. The ADO Recordset object used is local to the procedure in which this method is called. The **lngParentID** parameter is being passed from the *ItemData* property of a combo box for the selected entry.

```
        'Set a reference to the objects
        Dim objRS As New ADODB.Recordset
        Dim objAddress As New AutoWorks.clsAddress

        'Get the phone number for this employer
        lngRC = objAddress.GetPhoneNumber(frmMain.m_objConn, _
              objRS, _
              cboCurrentEmployer.ItemData(cboCurrentEmployer.ListIndex), _
              ptEmployer)
. . . . . . . . . . . . . . . . . . . . Page Break . . . . . . . . . . . . . . . . . . . .
Microsoft ActiveX Data Objects
. . . . . . . . . . . . . . . . . . . . Page Break . . . . . . . . . . . . . . . . . . . .
```

4. Save your file in a rich text format and give the file a name of `AutoWorks.rtf`.

5. Before we begin explaining how to insert all the special formatting required by the help compiler, there are two buttons that should be added to your toolbar. It is assumed that you are using Microsoft Word to create your rich text format help file. If you are using another word processor, consult its help file for instructions on how to customize your toolbar.

   In Word, right click on a blank area of the toolbar and choose Customize from the popup menu. Click on the Commands tab and then click on Format in the Categories list box. Find the Double Underline command and drag it onto the toolbar in any spot you like. Now find the Hidden command and drag it onto the toolbar. Click the Close button to dismiss the dialog. The three buttons that we will be using the most to apply the special formatting required by the help compiler are the Single Underline, Double Underline, and Hidden buttons.

6. To start, place your cursor in front of the first topic, Address, and then on the Insert menu choose Footnote. The Footnote and Endnote dialog appears and we want to enter the pound sign (#) in the Custom mark textbox. Then click OK to dismiss the dialog:

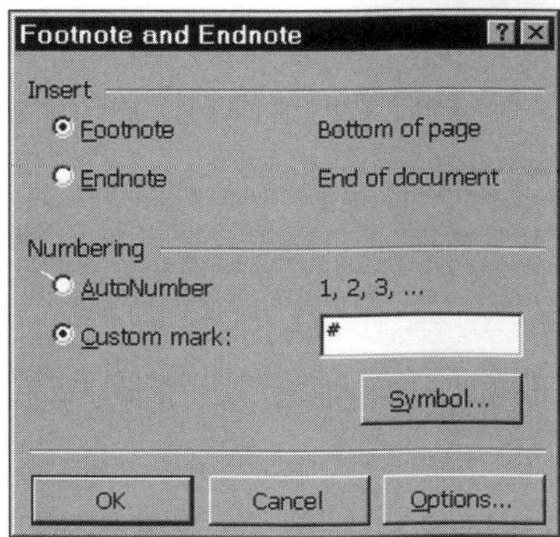

7. The Footnote section of `Word` appears and you need to enter the topic ID for the topic, in this case Address. Topic IDs can contain spaces and can be up to 255 characters. You can not use the reserved characters #, =, +, @, *, % and !. At this point your topic title should look like the one shown below:

```
#Address
  See Also      Example      Properties      Methods      Events
```

8. We want to assign a title to this topic so that it will appear in the Topics Found dialog. To do this, once again place your cursor in front of the topic Address and, following the procedure in steps 6 and 7, insert a footnote mark of $. The title that we are going to use is Address so enter this in the Footnote section. Your topic title should now look like this:

```
#$Address
  See Also      Example      Properties      Methods      Events
```

9. This topic should be listed in the index of our help file and we need to use the keyword parameter to have this topic listed in the index. Again, place your cursor in front of the topic Address and insert a footnote mark of K. The keyword that we want to assign to this topic in the index is Address Class so type this in the Footnote section of the `Word document`. At this point we have inserted three footnote marks for the topic title Address:

```
#$KAddress
  See Also      Example      Properties      Methods      Events
```

10. In order to provide an indented section of topics in the index for Address we must use another keyword parameter, which is specified a little differently. We still use the keyword parameter so insert another footnote mark of K in front of the topic Address. The text that we enter for this keyword is shown in the following code fragment:

```
Address;Address, Address;
```

We specify the first level index entry followed by a semicolon. Immediately following the semicolon, with no space, we specify the first level index again, followed by a comma. Then we insert a space and specify the second level index, in this case Address, followed by a semicolon. At this point, we have entered all of the footnote marks for this topic title and your topic title should look like the one shown below:

```
#$KKAddress
  See Also      Example      Properties      Methods      Events
```

This topic contains a popup Topics Found dialog when a developer clicks on Methods. However, before adding jumps and popup topics to our topic, we must first define all topics in our rich text document, so we will come back to this later.

11. The second topic lists the GetAddress method and the parameters, and then briefly explains the parameters. This topic will display the Topics Found dialog when the developer clicks on the See Also hotspot. When they click on the Example hotspot, the help file will jump to the GetAddress Example topic. However, before we explain how those tasks are accomplished, we must complete the definition of topics.

    As before, we must define the topic ID and title for this topic. Using the method name GetAddress for both of these, go ahead and define the Topic ID and Title. Again we must insert a # and $ footnote mark for the Topic ID and Title. After you insert the Topic ID and Title for the GetAddress topic, it should look like the code shown below:

```
#$GetAddress
 See Also        Example
```

12. We want this topic defined in the index as GetAddress. Before the word GetAddress, insert a footnote mark of K and in the Footnote section of Word enter GetAddress. After inserting this footnote mark your topic title should look like this:

```
#$KGetAddress
 See Also        Example
```

13. We also want this method listed in the index as an indented topic under Address. Using the code fragment below as a guide, we want to insert another keyword (K) footnote mark for this topic:

```
Address;Address, GetAddress;
```

    As before, we specify the first level index entry followed by a semicolon. Immediately following the semicolon, with no space, we specify the first level index again, followed by a comma. Then we insert a space and specify the second level index, in this case GetAddress, followed by a semicolon. Your topic title should now look like the one below:

```
#$KKGetAddress
 See Also        Example
```

14. We need to specify a way to get to this topic from other topics – the **ALink macro** provides such a method. When we specify the ALink macro in our document, `WinHelp` will search the help file for all topics defined with the ALink macro name and display them in a Topics Found dialog. `WinHelp` is smart enough to not display the current topic if it is also defined with the same ALink macro name. This provides the functionality to display a list of related topics.

    To define an ALink macro, insert a footnote mark of A before the topic GetAddress. Enter Address Methods for the macro name in the Footnote section of Word. Finally, your topic title should look like the one shown below:

```
#$KKAGetAddress
 See Also        Example
```

15. Moving on to the GetPhoneNumber method, we need to define the topic ID and title as in the previous two examples and your topic should end up looking like this:

```
#$GetPhoneNumber
 See Also       Example
```

16. The two keywords and ALink macro are shown in the code fragment below. Insert the appropriate footnote marks (K, K, and A) and use the text below to define these parameters:

```
KGetPhoneNumber
KAddress;Address, GetPhoneNumber;
AAddress Methods
```

Your finished topic title should look like this:

```
#$KKAGetPhoneNumber
 See Also       Example
```

17. The example for the GetAddress method is only defined with a topic ID, title, and an ALink macro. This example will not be listed in the index of our help file. We only want the developer to get to this example after they have read the description of the GetAddress method.

The definition of the topic ID, title, and an ALink macro are listed in the following code fragment:

```
#GetAddress Example
$GetAddress Example
AGetAddress Example
```

Your finished topic title should look like the one shown below:

```
#$AGetAddress Example
```

18. The example for the GetPhoneNumber method is defined as the last example using only a topic ID, title, and an ALink macro. The definition of the topic ID, title, and an ALink macro are listed in the following code fragment:

```
#GetPhoneNumber Example
$GetPhoneNumber Example
AGetPhoneNumber Example
```

The finished topic title should look like this:

```
#$AGetPhoneNumber Example
```

You can apply special formatting to the text in this topic if you want. I chose to format the text for this example using an Arial font and the code in a Courier New font. This helps the code stand out from the text explaining it.

19. The last item that we have defined in our help file is the popup topic defining ADO. Notice that this topic only has a topic ID assigned which is named ADO. Since this is a popup topic, we do not assign it a title nor do we list it in the index. Popup topics are normally used to define terms used in your help documentation, such as we are doing here. Insert a footnote mark of # and enter ADO as the Topic ID. The topic should now look like this:

```
#Microsoft ActiveX Data Objects
```

20. Now that we have defined all of our topics and have specified the ALink macros for them, we can go through our help documentation and add the appropriate jumps and popup topics.

    Starting with the Address topic, we want to add an ALink macro for the Address Methods. When the developer clicks on the Methods hotspot, the Topics Found dialog will appear listing all topics that have the Address Methods ALink macro defined.

    To define an ALink macro hotspot, we place our cursor immediately following the word Methods and enter an exclamation mark (!) followed by the ALink macro identifier ALink. Then in parentheses, we enter the name of the ALink macro. The following code fragment shows what this looks like:

```
Methods!ALink(Address Methods)
```

21. Now highlight everything you just entered except the word Methods and then click on the Hidden button on the toolbar. This hides the ALink macro definition and applies the first part of our hotspot. Then we need to highlight the word Methods and click on the Double Underline button on the toolbar. This completes the hotspot for this word and your hotspot code should look like this (after you hide the ALink macro definition).

```
#$KKAddress
```

See Also	Example	Properties	Methods	Events

22. At this point you should highlight the table row and then select Borders and Shading from the Format menu. On the Borders tab of the Borders and Shading dialog, remove all borders of the table. This will give your topic a more professional appearance in your compiled help file.

23. When a developer clicks on the Methods hotspot, the Topics Found dialog will appear and list both the GetAddress and GetPhoneNumber methods. The GetAddress topic has two hotspots, one for See Also and one for Example.

    The hotspot for See Also is defined in exactly the same way as the hotspot we just defined, and is listed in the following code fragment:

```
See Also!ALink(Address Methods)
```

    The hotspot that is defined for Example is just a little different. When a developer clicks on this hotspot, we want them to go directly to the GetAddress Example. To perform this feat, we define this hotspot exactly as we have done before, and add the Jump keyword to the definition. The following code fragment shows what this should look like:

```
Example!ALink(GetAddress Example,Jump)
```

If we wanted this topic listed in the index, we would have defined this topic with a Keyword footnote mark instead of an A-Keyword footnote mark. We would then use a KLink macro to define the hotspot for Example.

The final code for this, after the macros are hidden, looks like the example shown below. Again you want to remove the table borders to present a more professional appearance.

```
#$KKAGetAddress
See Also                                   Example
```

24. In each topic except for Address, we mention ADO one or more times. We want to define a popup topic for the first mention of ADO in each topic. A popup topic is normally used as a definition of terms and contains a brief description of the term.

To define a hotspot for a popup topic we simply specify the topic ID (ADO) immediately following the word or words to be used as the hotspot. We then highlight the topic ID and click on the Hidden button on the toolbar to hide the Topic ID. Then we highlight the word or words that define the hotspot, and then click on the Single Underline button on the toolbar. The following code fragment shows what this hotspot should look like before the Topic ID is hidden. Notice that there is no space between the word ADO and the topic ID ADO:

```
Parameters:

objConn An active ADO Connection object.

lngParentID  The primary key of the address to be retrieved.
```

25. The hotspots for the `GetPhoneNumber` method are defined in the same manner as we performed above. The following two code fragments show the definitions that should be used to define the ALink macros:

```
See Also!ALink(Address Methods)
```

```
Example!ALink(GetPhoneNumber Example,Jump)
```

The final results after you hide the macros should be as shown below. Again, remove the borders from the table.

```
#$KKAGetPhoneNumber
See Also                                 Example
```

26. This covers all of the formatting that needs to be applied to our rich text format help documentation. At this point save this file again.

Try It Out – Creating a Table of Contents

Now that we have created the topics file in a rich text format document, we need to move on and create a table of contents. The file that we create here will be used by the final compiled help file to display the table of contents. The complete table of contents as defined in the Help Workshop is shown in the figure below:

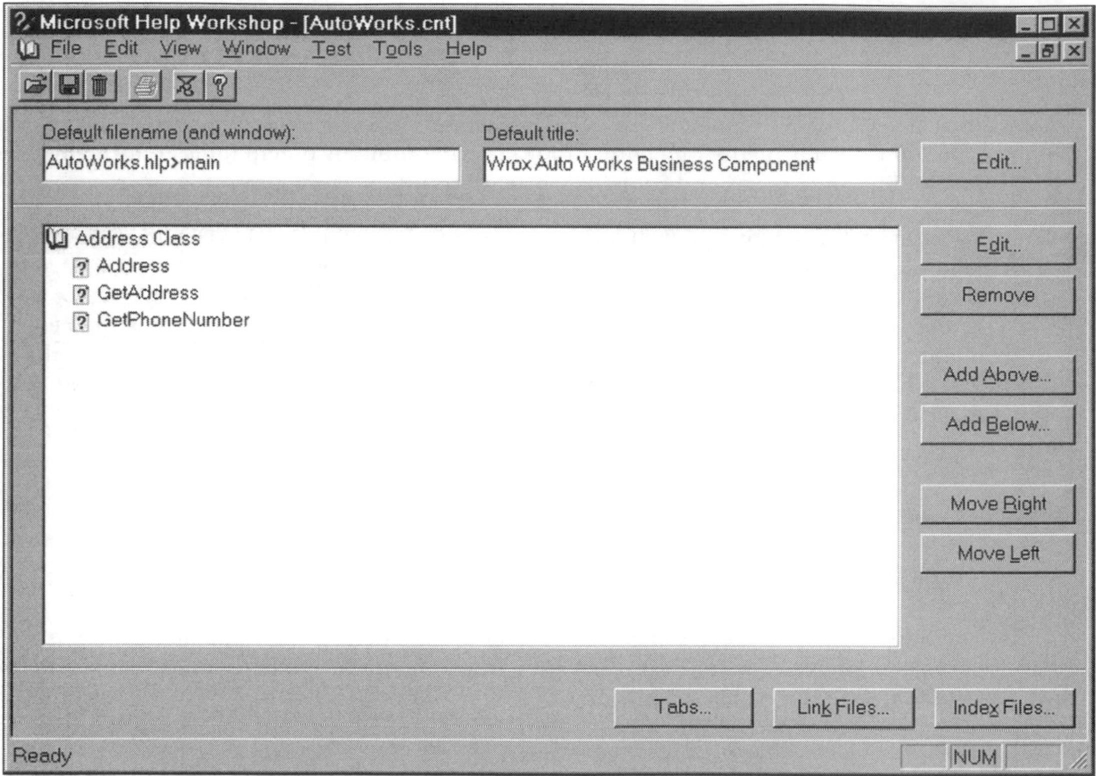

1. Start the Help Workshop, which is located in the Microsoft Visual Studio 6.0 Tools program group. On the File menu choose New, and then choose Help Contents in the New dialog.

2. In the Default filename (and window) textbox, enter AutoWorks.hlp>main. This lists the final help file name and the window that it should be displayed in. We will cover the window later when we discuss the help project. In the Default title textbox enter Wrox Auto Works Business Component. This will become our dialog title when the contents and index are displayed.

3. To add a heading or topic, click the Add Above or Add Below buttons to the right of the screen. This displays the Edit Contents Tab Entry dialog shown below. The first thing we want to add is a heading, so we must select the Heading radio button as shown. In the Title textbox, enter Address Class and click OK:

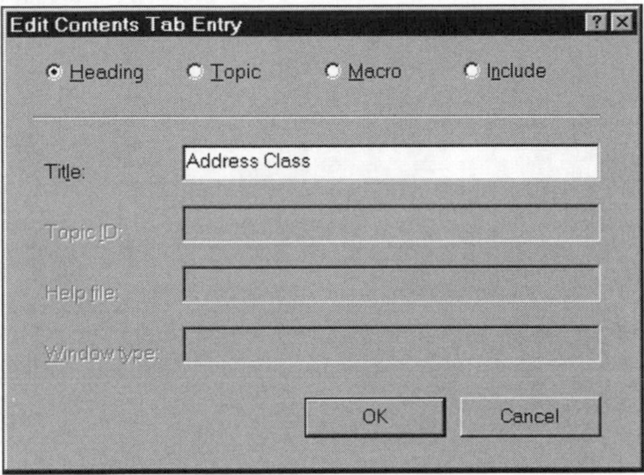

4. To add the individual topics under this heading, click on the Add Below button, click the Topic radio button, and enter the Title of the topic and the Topic ID that was assigned in the `Word` rich text document. The figure below shows the Address topic being added. The Title can be different from the Topic ID; however, the Topic ID must match the defined topic ID that was entered in your RTF file.

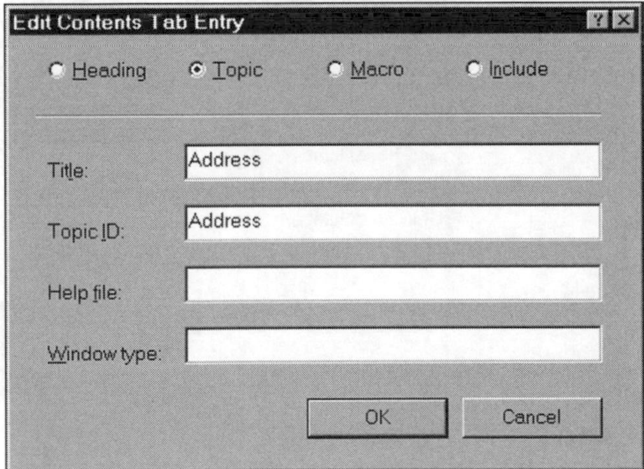

5. The next topic we need to define is the GetAddress topic. Click on the Add Below button, select the Topic radio button, and enter the Title of GetAddress and the Topic ID of GetAddress. Again the Title can be different from the Topic ID. However, since we are writing a help file for our business server component, the topic IDs that we are using match the function names in our class. The figure below shows how this topic is added:

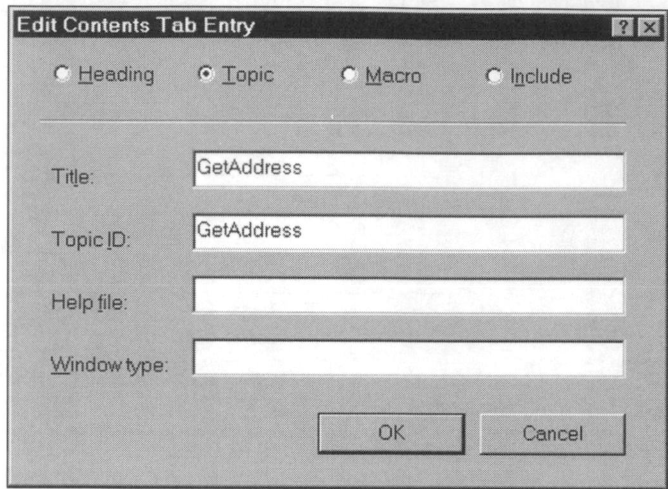

6. The last topic that we are going to add is GetPhoneNumber. This topic is shown in the next figure, and you should add it using the same procedure just used for the Address and GetAddress topics:

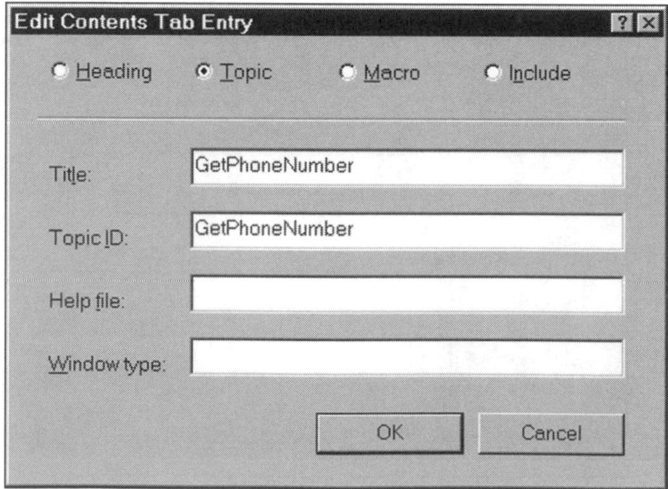

7. This is all of the topics that we are going to add to our help file. You can come back later and add to this example once you have written a complete help file for the business server component. Save the help contents file as `AutoWorks.cnt`.

Try It Out – Creating a Help Project

This section ties together all the work we have done in the last two sections. The help project that we will be creating will use the topics file and contents file when it compiles the final help file. The help project file defines how our compiled help file will look, how it will be displayed, and the functionality that it will provide.

We can specify what type of full text search will be included in our help file as well as the window size and the color of the window. We also can specify whether or not the window will default to staying on top, and if it should automatically adjust to the resolution size of the screen of the user.

Let's get started by creating our help project file.

1. To create a new help project, in the Help Workshop click on the File menu and choose New. In the New dialog choose Help Project. You will be prompted for a file name to save the help project as, so enter AutoWorks.

2. Click on the Options button so that we can set the various options for our help project. Enter Address for the Default topic and Wrox Auto Works Business Component for the Help title. This is the help title that will be displayed on all of the help topics. You can display your own copyright information in the Version Information dialog by entering your Copyright information on the General tab:

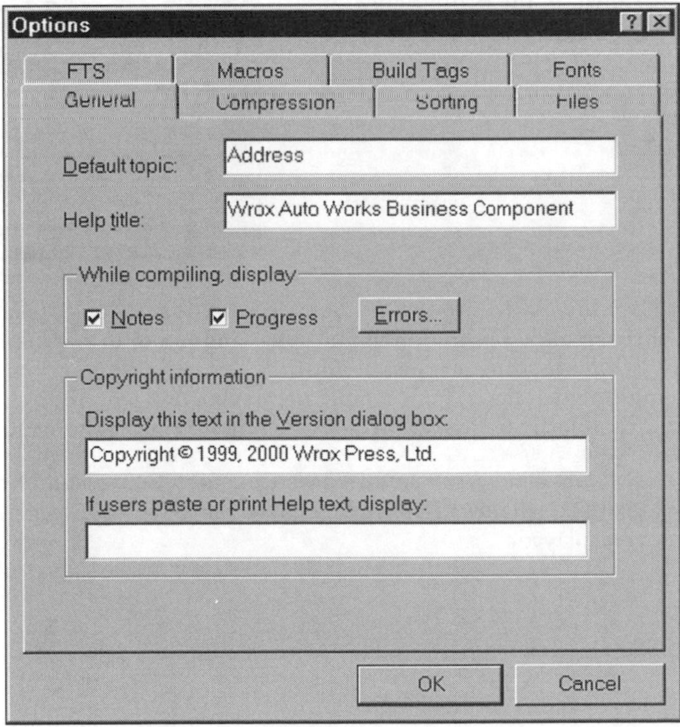

3. On the Compression tab, check the Maximum (recommended) radio button. This applies maximum compression to your help file, keeping it as small as possible.

4. The Files tab is where we specify all of the files that make up our help project. Enter AutoWorks.hlp as the Help File, AutoWorks.rtf for the Rich Text Format (RTF) files, and AutoWorks.cnt for the Contents File.

5. The FTS tab contains the options for the full text search capabilities of your compiled help file. Check the Generate full text search index checkbox and the Enter search for similar topics (max. functionality) radio button. This will provide your help file with the maximum search capabilities. At this point click the OK button to save your changes and to dismiss this dialog.

6. Click the Windows button to define a help window in which to display your help topics. The Create a window dialog appears and the window name that we will be using is main. Remember, when we created our contents file we specified the window name. This is the window that we were referring to. This window should be based on the Procedure window, as shown in the figure below:

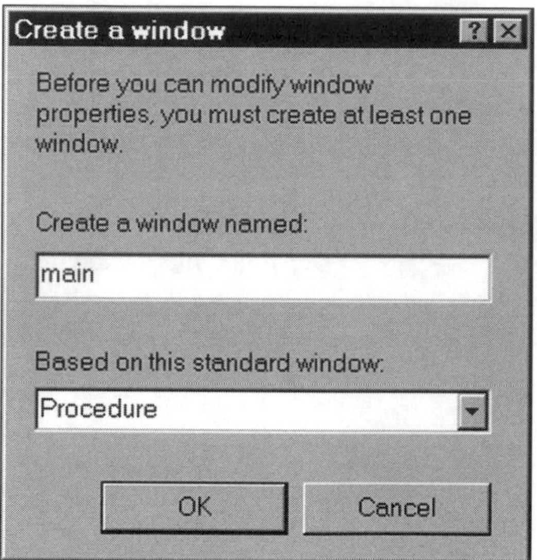

7. Once you click the OK button the Windows Properties dialog appears. The Windows Properties dialog allows us to define multiple windows to display our help topics in. For our purposes, we are using just one window. If our help file was more sophisticated we could use multiple windows, for example displaying our help topics in one window and our popup examples in a different window, while leaving the topic displayed.

   On the General tab, enter Wrox Auto Works Business Component for the Title bar text and check Maximize window. This will maximize the help window to fill the full screen when a help topic is displayed.

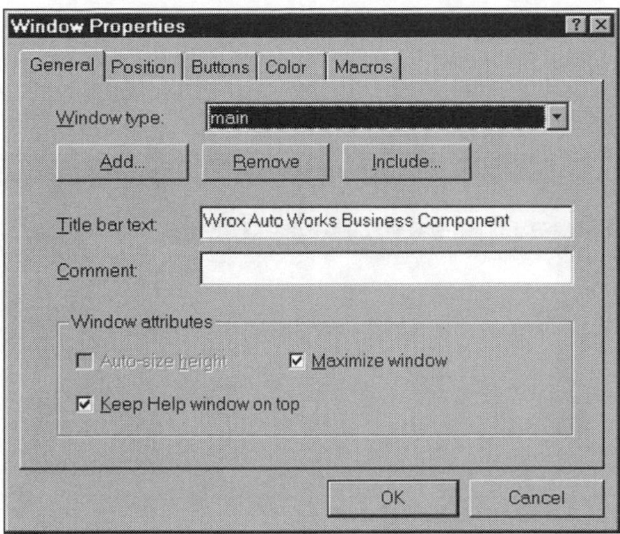

8. If you don't want the help topic to be maximized you can set the help window size and position on the Position tab.

9. The next tab that we are concerned with in this dialog is the Color tab. This tab allows you to change the color of the Nonscrolling area of the help topic and the color of the Topic area. I chose white for both of these, but you can choose any color combination that you like. After you have made your color choices click OK to dismiss this dialog.

10. The last thing we need to do in our help project is to map the Context ID numbers from our component to the Help Topics in our help file. This will provide our component with context sensitive help and the help file will know which topic to display when the user presses the *F1* key for help. Click on the Map button to display the Map dialog. On the Map dialog click the Add button to map a topic. The first topic that we want to map is the GetAddress topic. This topic gets mapped to the number that you entered in the Context ID box in the Procedure Attributes dialog in your component, in this case the number one. Fill in the details then click the OK button to map this topic.

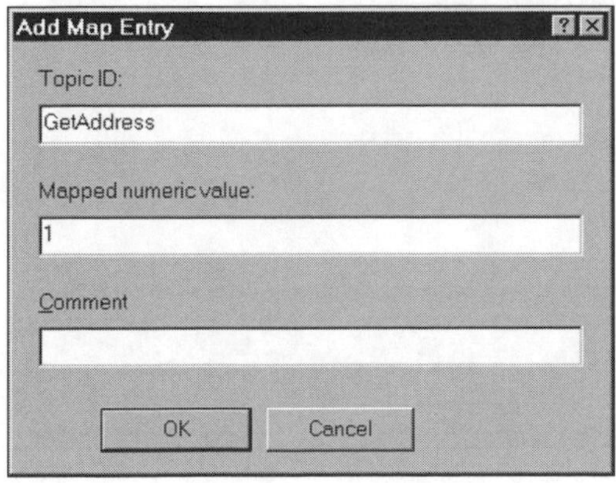

11. Add another Map Entry for GetPhoneNumber. Once completed you should see the dialog shown in the figure below. Of course we have only defined two topics in our help file that relate to specific functions in our component, but you can come back later and complete the help file with all of the topics.

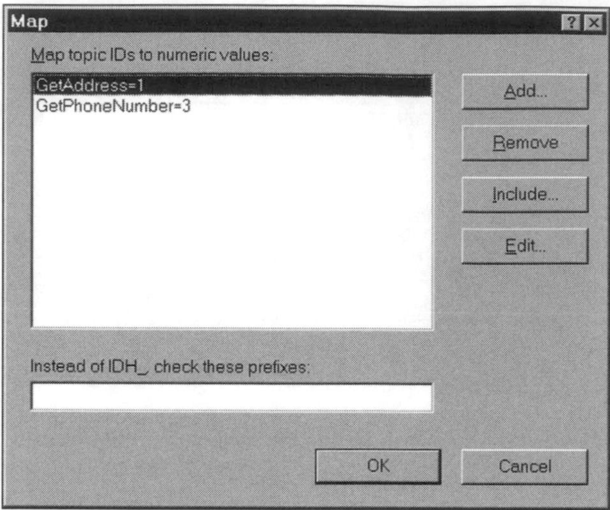

12. At this point your completed help project should like the one shown in the next figure:

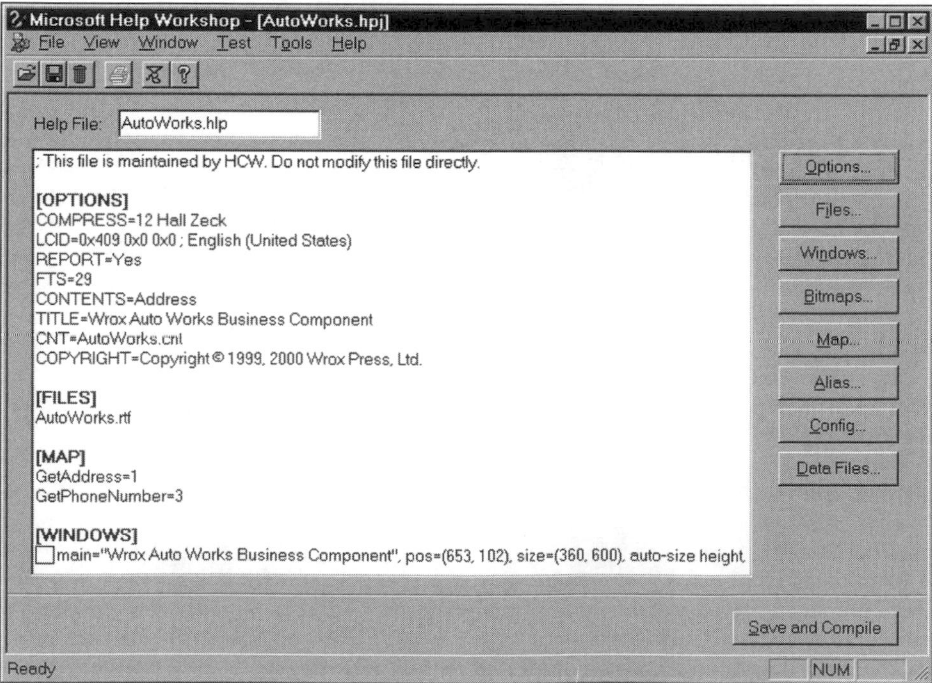

13. At this point click the Save and Compile button at the bottom of the Help Workshop window. This will save your help project and compile the completed help file. For some unknown reason the Help Workshop will write the name of your compiled help file in all upper case. You can rename your help file using both upper and lower case letters. Subsequent compiles will then leave the help file in both upper and lower case letters.

You can now test your help file by double clicking on it and navigating through the Contents, Index and Find tabs. After selecting a topic, you can navigate through the help file using the hotspots, and can test the popup topics.

Modifying the UI

Now that we have a compiled business server component and associated help file, we need to modify our user interface (UI) to use the new business server component. The business server component that we have created has implemented all of the functionality of our classes. We need to change the references in our UI project to access the `AutoWorks` DLL instead of the classes. All of the function calls are the same except that we are calling the methods in our server component instead of the classes in our project.

Try It Out – Modify the UI to Use the AutoWorks DLL

1. Start by copying the UI project (`WAWCustomerApplication.vbp`) that we created in the last chapter to a new directory of your choice. Open the project and remove the classes. We want to keep the Utility module in this project.

2. Next, set a reference to the Wrox Auto Works ActiveX Business Object as shown in the following figure. When we compiled our business server component earlier, VB took care of some details for us. First, it registered the component in the system registry. Secondly, it added the component as an available reference that can be included in any of our projects.

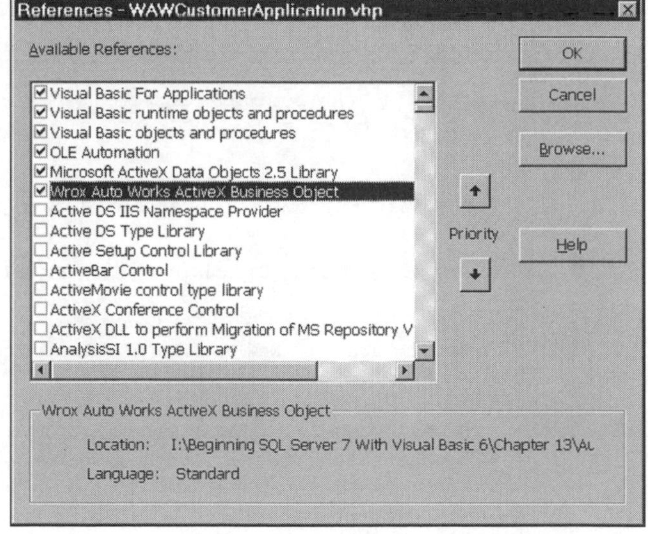

3. Modify the following code in the main form (`frmMain`). In the general declarations section of the form, modify the existing declarations as follows:

```
'Declare database objects
Public m_objConn As ADODB.Connection
Private m_objCmd As ADODB.Command
Private m_objRS As ADODB.Recordset
Private m_objRSAddress As ADODB.Recordset
Private m_objErr As ADODB.Error

'Declare business objects
Private m_objWroxAddress As AutoWorks.clsAddress
Private m_objWroxCustomer As AutoWorks.clsCustomer
Private m_objWroxEmployer As AutoWorks.clsEmployer
```

4. Make the following modifications to the `LoadCityStateZip` procedure:

```
'Set a reference to the business object
   Set m_objWroxAddress = New AutoWorks.clsAddress

   'Get a list of cities, states and zip codes
   lngRC = m_objWroxAddress.GetCityStateZip(m_objConn, m_objRSAddress)

'Close and dereference objects
   m_objRSAddress.Close
   Set m_objRSAddress = Nothing
   Set m_objWroxAddress = Nothing
   On Error GoTo 0
   Exit Sub
```

5. The `LoadCustomerNames` procedure needs to be modified with the following code:

```
'Set a reference to the business object
   Set m_objWroxCustomer = New AutoWorks.clsCustomer

   'Get a list of customer names
   lngRC = m_objWroxCustomer.GetCustomerNames(m_objConn, m_objRS)
```

6. In the `cboLastName_Click` procedure modify the following code:

```
'Set a reference to the business object
   Set m_objWroxAddress = New AutoWorks.clsAddress

   'Get the customer's address
   Set m_objRSAddress = m_objWroxAddress.GetAddress(m_objConn, _
            cboLastName.ItemData(cboLastName.ListIndex), Customer)

   'Close and dereference objects
   m_objRSAddress.Close
   Set m_objRSAddress = Nothing
   Set m_objWroxAddress = Nothing
```

7. The `cmdAdd_Click` procedure needs to be modified as follows:

```
'Set a reference to the objects
   Set m_objCmd = New ADODB.Command
   Set m_objWroxAddress = New AutoWorks.clsAddress

   'Insert the address
   lngRC = m_objWroxAddress.InsertAddress(txtAddress1.Text, _
      txtAddress2.Text, _
      txtAddress3.Text, _
      lngCityID, _
      cboCity.Text, _
      cboState.ItemData(cboState.ListIndex), _
      lngZipCodeID, _
      cboZipCode.Text, _
      CInt(txtAreaCode.Text), _
      EditPhoneNumber(txtPhoneNumber.Text), _
      lngAddressID, _
      lngPhoneNumberID, _
      strMsg(), _
      m_objConn, _
      m_objCmd)

   'Dereference objects and clear message variable
   Set m_objCmd = Nothing
   Set m_objWroxAddress = Nothing
   ReDim strMsg(0)

   'Set a reference to the objects
   Set m_objCmd = New ADODB.Command
   Set m_objWroxEmployer = New AutoWorks.clsEmployer

   'Insert the employer information
   lngRC = m_objWroxEmployer.InsertEmployer(lngCurrentEmployerID, _
      frmEmployment.cboCurrentEmployer.Text, _
      CInt(frmEmployment.txtCEAreaCode.Text), _
      EditPhoneNumber(frmEmployment.txtCEPhoneNumber.Text), _
      CByte(frmEmployment.txtCEYearsEmployed.Text), _
      frmEmployment.txtJobTitle.Text, _
      lngPreviousEmployerID, _
      frmEmployment.cboPreviousEmployer.Text, _
      intAreaCode, _
      lngPhoneNumber, _
      bytYearsEmployed, _
      lngCustomerInformationID, _
      strMsg(), _
      m_objConn, _
      m_objCmd)

   'Dereference objects and clear message variable
   Set m_objCmd = Nothing
   Set m_objWroxEmployer = Nothing
   ReDim strMsg(0)
```

```
    'Set a reference to the objects
    Set m_objCmd = New ADODB.Command
    Set m_objWroxCustomer = New AutoWorks.clsCustomer

    'Insert the customer information
    lngRC = m_objWroxCustomer.InsertCustomer(lngAddressID, _
       lngPhoneNumberID, _
       lngCustomerInformationID, _
       txtFirstName.Text, _
       cboLastName.Text, _
       txtSpouseName.Text, _
       strMsg(), _
       m_objConn, _
       m_objCmd)

    'Dereference objects
    Set m_objCmd = Nothing
    Set m_objWroxCustomer = Nothing
```

8. Next, we need to modify the cmdUpdate_Click procedure with the following code:

```
'Set a reference to the objects
    Set m_objCmd = New ADODB.Command
    Set m_objWroxAddress = New AutoWorks.clsAddress

    'Update the address
    lngRC = m_objWroxAddress.UpdateAddress(m_lngAddressID, _
       txtAddress1.Text, _
       txtAddress2.Text, _
       txtAddress3.Text, _
       lngCityID, _
       cboCity.Text, _
       cboState.ItemData(cboState.ListIndex), _
       lngZipCodeID, _
       cboZipCode.Text, _
       m_lngPhoneNumberID, _
       CInt(txtAreaCode.Text), _
       EditPhoneNumber(txtPhoneNumber.Text), _
       strMsg(), _
       m_objConn, _
       m_objCmd)

    'Dereference objects and clear message variable
    Set m_objCmd = Nothing
    Set m_objWroxAddress = Nothing
    ReDim strMsg(0)

    'Set a reference to the objects
    Set m_objCmd = New ADODB.Command
    Set m_objWroxCustomer = New AutoWorks.clsCustomer
```

```
'Update the customer record
lngRC = m_objWroxCustomer.UpdateCustomer(m_lngCustomerID, _
   txtFirstName.Text, _
   cboLastName.Text, _
   txtSpouseName.Text, _
   m_objConn, _
   m_objCmd)

'Dereference objects
Set m_objCmd = Nothing
Set m_objWroxCustomer = Nothing
```

9. We also need to make some code modifications in the Employment form (`frmEmployment`). In the `LoadEmployers` procedure make the following modification:

```
'Set a reference to the objects
   Dim objRS As New ADODB.Recordset
   Dim objEmployer As New AutoWorks.clsEmployer
```

10. Modify the `Process` procedure as follows:

```
'Set a reference to the objects
   Dim objRS As New ADODB.Recordset
   Dim objEmployer As New AutoWorks.clsEmployer
```

11. In the `cboCurrentEmployer_Click` procedure make the following modification:

```
'Set a reference to the objects
   Dim objRS As New ADODB.Recordset
   Dim objAddress As New AutoWorks.clsAddress
```

12. Make the following modification in the `cboPreviousEmployer_Click` procedure:

```
'Set a reference to the objects
   Dim objRS As New ADODB.Recordset
   Dim objAddress As New AutoWorks.clsAddress
```

13. Finally, modify the `cmdUpdate_Click` procedure as follows:

```
'Set a reference to the objects
   Dim objEmployer As New AutoWorks.clsEmployer
   Dim objCmd As New ADODB.Command
```

14. At this point we are ready to compile our UI. But before we do so, we need to increase the Minor Version Number and reset the Revision Number, as shown in the following figure. This reflects the minor changes made to our UI by removing the classes and replacing them with a reference to the `AutoWorks DLL`. There were no significant code additions or changes that would represent a *major* change in our UI.

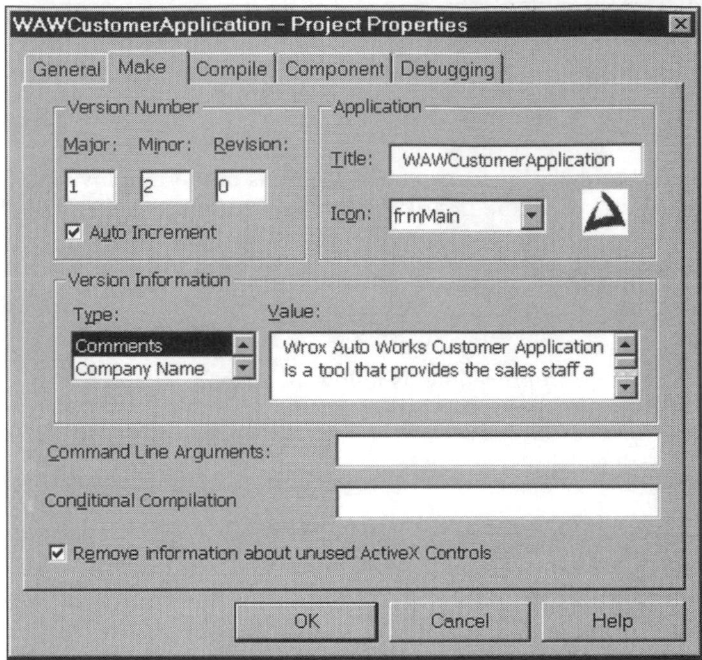

15. Once you have recompiled your UI, save all changes and you are done.

How It Works – Modify the UI to Use the AutoWorks DLL

Basically we have replaced all references to the individual classes with references to their respective classes in the `AutoWorks` DLL. We started in the general declarations section of the main form, replacing the old declarations for the objects that represented the classes with new declarations that represent the respective classes in the `AutoWorks` DLL. The following two code fragments show the before and after code declarations:

```
'Declare class objects
Private m_objAddress As clsAddress
Private m_objCustomer As clsCustomer
Private m_objEmployer As clsEmployer
```

```
'Declare business objects
Private m_objWroxAddress As AutoWorks.clsAddress
Private m_objWroxCustomer As AutoWorks.clsCustomer
Private m_objWroxEmployer As AutoWorks.clsEmployer
```

Next we replaced all the references to the classes with references to their respective classes in the `AutoWorks` DLL. The following two code fragments show the before and after declarations:

```
'Instantiate the class
Set m_objAddress = New clsAddress

'Get a list of cities, states and zip codes
lngRC = m_objAddress.GetCityStateZip(m_objConn, m_objRSAddress)
```

```
'Set a reference to the business object
Set m_objWroxAddress = New AutoWorks.clsAddress

'Get a list of cities, states and zip codes
lngRC = m_objWroxAddress.GetCityStateZip(m_objConn, m_objRSAddress)
```

We continued throughout the project replacing all references to the individual classes with references to their respective classes in the `AutoWorks` DLL. These changes are straightforward and the actual function that gets called does not change, nor does its parameters.

Try It Out – Testing the Help File

1. In order to test the help file for our component, go to the `cboLastName_Click` procedure and position your cursor on the `GetAddress` method shown in the following code fragment:

```
'Get the customer's address
  Set m_objRSAddress = m_objWroxAddress.GetAddress(m_objConn, _
     cboLastName.ItemData(cboLastName.ListIndex), Customer)
```

2. Then press the *F1* key, and help for the GetAddress topic should be displayed, as shown in the following figure:

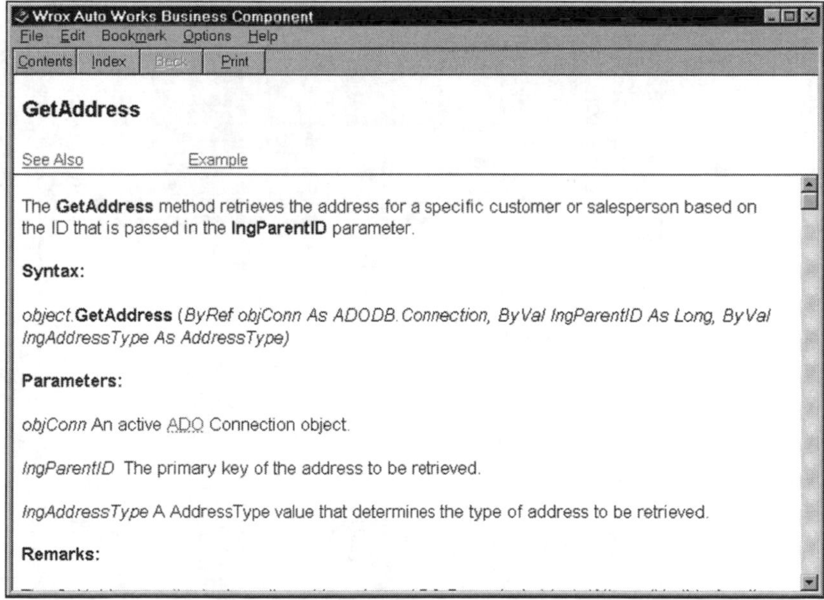

3. If you click the Example hotspot, the GetAddress Example is displayed as shown below:

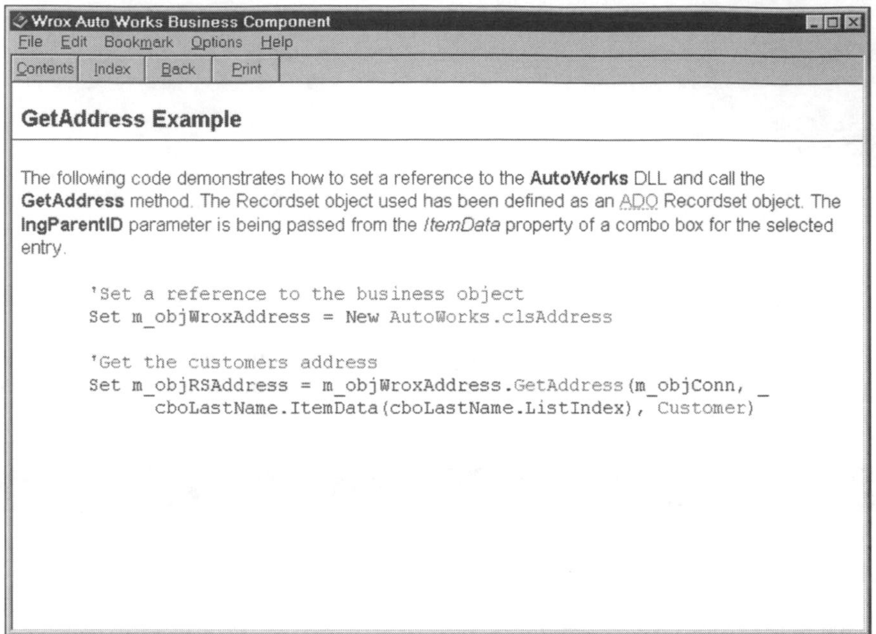

4. The same context sensitive help works in the Object Browser in VB. Open the Object Browser, select the AutoWorks library, and then click on the clsAddress class. Next click on the GetAddress method, press *F1* and the GetAddress help topic is displayed.

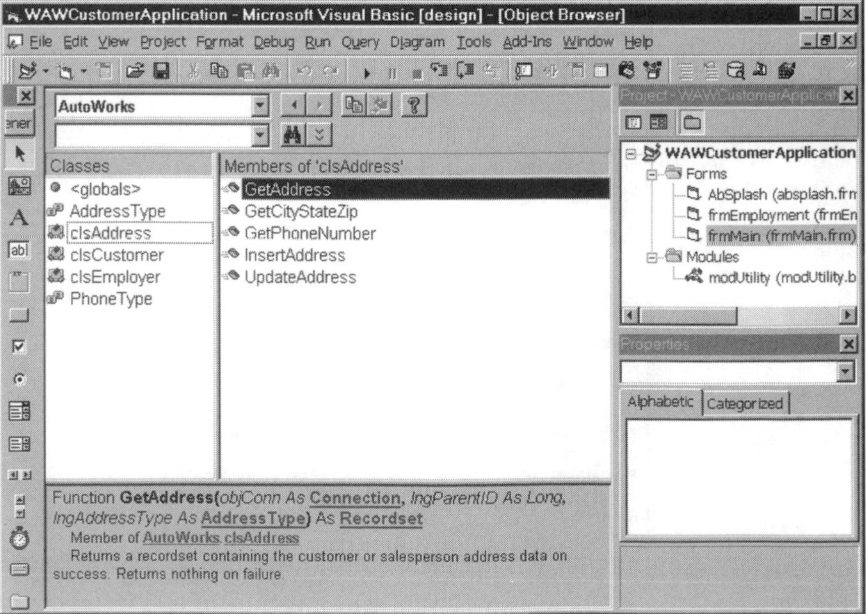

Summary

This chapter has covered a lot of material in a fairly short amount of space. We started off by exploring the benefits provided by MTS. Whether you choose to use MTS or SQL Server transactions to maintain data integrity is entirely dependent on your application and your requirements. Both provide numerous benefits, and it is arguable as to whether one is better than the other, as each has its own place.

We moved on to cover creating a business server component. Because we used classes in the previous chapters to encompass the functionality to execute our stored procedures, creating the server component was quick and easy. It required very little work and the majority of our time was spent on setting the project properties of our ActiveX DLL. We entered a context ID for each method in our server component, and you can come back and add the appropriate help topics to your help file without needing to make any modifications to the ActiveX DLL.

The help file that we created was without a doubt the most complex topic covered in this chapter. Creating the rich text format document containing the help documentation can be tricky at times. There were a lot of new concepts introduced to enable us to provide all the major functionality of a professional help file. But the effort should pay off, as creating this help file for our business server component will assist other developers in understanding how to use our component. This is especially important when writing a generic component that is shared among development teams. Having the appropriate help documentation, and examples showing the correct calls to the various methods in your component, is invaluable.

The modifications that were made to the UI were almost as painless as creating the server component. This did require a little more work, but the work was minimal and did not take a lot of time. Again, you can see the benefits of using classes to build the functionality to execute your stored procedures. The only changes required were to replace the definition of the classes to their respective classes in the `AutoWorks` DLL.

To summarize, you should know:

- The benefits of using both MTS and SQL Server transactions
- How to create a server component using classes from your UI
- How to set the various properties of your server component
- How to create a help file for your server component
- The benefits provided by documenting your server component in a help file
- How to modify your UI to use the new server component instead of classes in your UI project

In the next chapter we are going to change tack slightly and take a look at how SQL Server copes with manipulating text data.

WROX AUTO WORKS RACING

Working With Text Data

2,147,483,647 characters. That is the maximum number of characters that a `Text` data type in SQL Server can hold. Two billion characters doesn't sound like a lot of data, but consider this. You could place the text from this entire book in a single text field in SQL Server. In fact, you could place just over nine hundred copies of the text from this book in a single text field. Now it's beginning to sound like a lot of data! Actually, a text field can contain two gigabytes of data, which equates to 2,147,483,647 characters. Now it definitely sounds like a lot of data and it is!

Working with the `Text` data type is not as straightforward as the other data types that we have dealt with in the rest of this book. There are a lot of idiosyncrasies that we must deal with when working with text data in SQL Server. This chapter examines how SQL Server stores and manages text data, and how you can access and manage text data using stored procedures and ADO.

The concepts that we will be using in this chapter haven't been introduced as of yet. We will be exploring some new concepts in SQL statements that allow us to access and manage data in a text field, as well as new concepts in ADO that help us to select and insert data into text fields.

In this chapter we will:

- Look at how SQL Server stores and manages text data
- Examine text pointers
- Inserting and selecting text data
- String functions that can be used with text data
- Reading, writing and updating text data

Introduction to Text Data

SQL Server supports three forms of long data types, `Text`, `nText` and `Image`. Text data types contain variable length character data from 1 to 2,147,483,647 bytes. `nText` data types contain variable length Unicode data from 1 to 1,073,741,823 bytes. The reason the `nText` data type contains fewer characters is because a Unicode character is actually made up to two bytes. Unicode data contains characters from all of the various character sets includes letters, numbers, and symbols used in languages. `Image` data types contain variable length binary data from 1 to 2,147,483,647 bytes.

The focus of this chapter is `Text` data types, but the principles discussed here apply equally as well to both `nText` and `Image` data types.

Working with text data can be good and bad. Good, because SQL Server provides a means to manage large amounts of data in one field. We could store entire articles, books or even large text reports in a text field. Unlike a `Char` or `VarChar` data type, we can selectively update portions of a text field.

Bad, because we must use special SQL statements and techniques to work with data fields. We must also incorporate special code in our VB program to handle the large amount of data. This is primarily due to memory constraints on some systems that our programs could be running on.

If a text field contains 8,000 characters or less (the maximum size of a `VarChar` data type) we can manipulate the data through stored procedures and programs just like `Char` and `VarChar` data types. When our text exceeds that limit in a text field, we must use the special functions provided by SQL Server to read, write and update the data. We will discuss this in length later in the chapter.

How SQL Server Manages The Data

As we mentioned earlier, SQL Server manages data in a text column in a different way compared to any other data type. From a VB standpoint, all we see is a single field of very large data. However, SQL Server does not store text data in a data row, but stores it in a collection of 8K pages called **text pages**. The data row for a text field contains a 16-byte binary pointer, which is a pointer to the address in the root of a B-tree structure, which manages text pages.

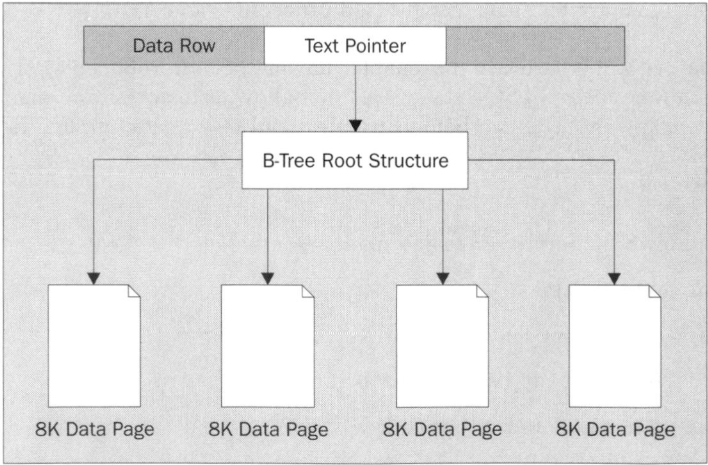

Text pages can contain text data from multiple rows in your table, and the text pages from one row of data may not necessary reside next to each other physically. They are, however, arranged logically in the B-tree structure. SQL Server manages the text pages so that a complete text page is filled with data even if it comes from more than one row in your table. Likewise, if your application only fills part of a page with 4K of data, and then comes back later to add another 8K of data, the first page is filled with data and the remaining 4K of data is written to another page.

This type of data management provides two major benefits. First, SQL Server can efficiently manage the entire text column. If you want to read data in the middle of the text column, SQL Server can quickly locate the text page that contains the data to be read. Secondly, this method of data storage is very efficient, as there is no wasted space in your database. SQL Server fills an entire 8K page before creating another, even if this means combining data from several rows in your table.

So how do we access this data in these text pages? Actually we don't access them directly; SQL Server provides a text pointer to the B-tree structure, and we use a pointer to access this data. SQL Server takes care of all of this behind the scenes. We only need to use text pointers when we want to work with specific portions of the data. SQL Server provides three functions that allow us to work with specific portions of data in a text column. They are `READTEXT`, `WRITETEXT` and `UPDATETEXT`. All three of these functions require us to use a text pointer to access specific portions of the data. We will be covering these functions later in the chapter.

When we use an `INSERT` statement to insert data into a text column, we do not need to use a text pointer. Likewise, when we select data from a text column, we are selecting the entire amount of data in the column, and we also do not need to use a text pointer in this case. However, given the large amount of data that a text field can contain, it is highly unlikely that you will want to select all data at one time and try to manage that from a VB program. This is where the functions mentioned above come into play.

Customer_Comment_T Table

In order to help you follow along with the discussion on `text` data types, we need to create a new table in our database. Since we don't plan to actually use this table in our application, we will forego creating a foreign key reference to the `Customer_T` table. Instead, we will just say that a customer could go up to the computer in the show room of our fictitious car company and enter their comments anonymously.

To that end, we need to create a new table named `Customer_Comment_T`. To start, bring up the `Enterprise Manager` and expand the `Wrox_Auto_Works` database. Right click on Tables in the tree view and choose New Table from the popup menu. Enter the table name `Customer_Comment_T` in the Choose Name dialog and click OK.

Following good database design, we need to create a primary key column that will uniquely identify each row in our table. Enter a column name of `Customer_Comment_ID` and choose `Int` for the data type. Since this is the primary key column, we do not want to allow `NULL` values, so uncheck the Allow Nulls checkbox. We do want this column to be an identity column, so check the Identity check box. The default value of one is fine for Identity Seed and Identity Increment. We also want this column to be the primary key, so click on the Set Primary Key icon on the toolbar.

The second column that we want to add is the `Comments_TX` column. This column will have a data type of `Text` and we do want to allow `NULL` values for this column.

At this point your table should look like this. Click the Save icon on the toolbar and close the table:

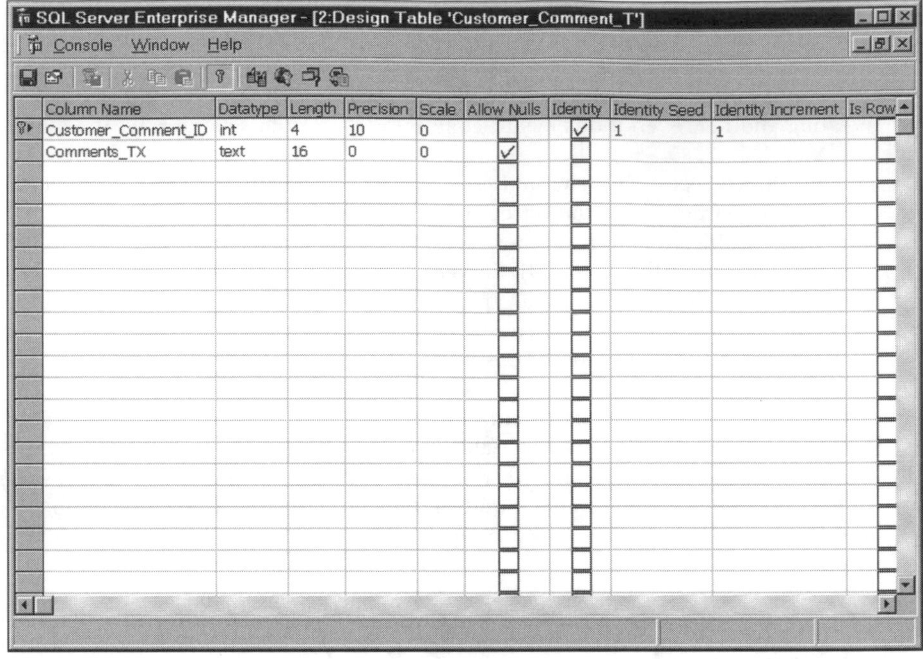

At this point we need to set the permissions on this table so the various Roles have the appropriate permissions. Right click on the table and choose Properties from the popup menu. On the Table Properties dialog, click the Permissions button to display the Object Properties dialog.

The Developers Role should have `SELECT`, `INSERT`, `UPDATE` and `DELETE` permissions. The Sales Staff Role should have `SELECT`, `INSERT` and `UPDATE` permissions; and the Management Role should have only `SELECT` permissions.

Click OK to close this dialog, and then click OK to close the Table Properties dialog.

Now that our new table has been created, we want to take a look populating this table with data.

Inserting Text Data

When dealing with text data, more likely than not, we are going to be managing this data from a program. While it is not impossible to manage this amount of data from the `Query Analyzer`, it is quite cumbersome to do so. Using a VB program and ADO, we are able to manage the large amounts of data in a text column quite easily.

Let's start by looking at what is required to insert data into a text column. We can use the `INSERT` SQL statement to insert data into a text column in SQL Server. However, the amount of text that we want to insert is usually larger than that which our program can handle at one time. From a SQL Server perspective there is no limit. From a VB perspective this is limited by the amount of available memory. This restriction is not placed upon us by VB, but by the OS that our program runs on. Two gigabytes of data in one variable is a lot of data, not to mention memory for an operating system to deal with at one time.

This is where ADO comes to the rescue. ADO provides the `GetChunk` and `AppendChunk` methods for the `Recordset Field` object, and the `AppendChunk` method for the `Parameter` object. We can insert data using either the `Recordset Field` object, or the `Parameter` object and executing the `Command` object. For our examples, we will be using the `Command` object and `Parameter` object to insert data.

Basically, the `AppendChunk` method allows us to append a large amount of data to the `Parameter` object in segments. This makes the data more manageable and does not consume as many system resources. We perform this manipulation of data in a loop, calling the `AppendChunk` method each time through the loop. The first call to the `AppendChunk` method writes the data to the `Parameter` object, overwriting any existing data that may have been there. Each subsequent call to the `AppendChunk` method appends the chunk of data (at the end of the current data) to the `Parameter` object.

The `INSERT` statement is a logged operation and can quickly fill up the transaction log, if it is not set to automatically grow or there is a size limit to the log. Therefore, after a large amount of text has been inserted, the transaction log should be backed up. This will be covered in the next chapter.

Try It Out #1 – Insert Text Using SQL Statements

The examples that we will be dealing with are very small, given the fact that we must key them in. You can substitute the data that we are inserting with a very large text file if you so desire.

We want to create a program that will use the `Command` object to execute a SQL string. The SQL string will insert data into the text column in the `Customer_Comment_T` table. We will be using the `AppendChunk` method of the `Parameter` object to append the data.

1. Start by creating a new VB project and change the project name to `TryItOut1` and the form name to `frmTryItOut1`. Set a reference to the Microsoft ActiveX Data Objects Library. Add a list box to the form as shown in the figure below and accept the default name of `List1`:

We use a list box rather than a text box so that we can display error messages, should they occur.

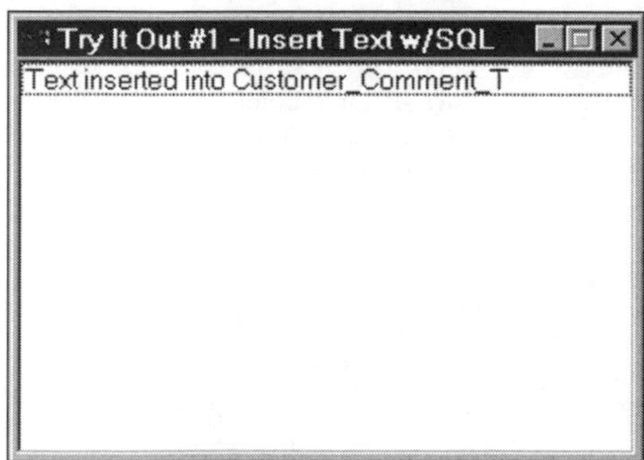

2. Add the following code to the `Form_Load` event:

```
Private Sub Form_Load()
   'Use the standard Windows icon
   Me.Icon = Nothing

   'Set up error handling
   On Error GoTo Form_Load_EH

   'Declare local variables
   Dim strText As String, intStart As Integer, intLength As Integer

   'Declare local database objects
   Dim objConn As New ADODB.Connection
   Dim objCmd As New ADODB.Command
   Dim objParm As New ADODB.Parameter
   Dim objErr As ADODB.Error

   'Establish a database connection using NT authentication
   objConn.Open "DSN=Wrox Auto Works"

   'Check connection state
   If objConn.State <> adStateOpen Then
      List1.AddItem "Connection Failed"
      Exit Sub
   End If

   'Set the string to be inserted
   strText = "This example uses the Command object and Parameters " & _
       "Collection to insert text into a SQL Server text field. We " & _
       "must use the AppendChunk method of the Parameter object to " & _
       "append the entire text string to the Parameter. This is usually " & _
       "done in chunks as the amount of data to be inserted is usually " & _
       "very large. However, this example is fairly small compared to " & _
       "the text that would normally be inserted in a real-world application."

   'Set the Command object properties
   Set objCmd.ActiveConnection = objConn
   objCmd.CommandText = "INSERT INTO Customer_Comment_T " & _
                        "(Comments_TX) " & _
                        "VALUES(?)"
   objCmd.CommandType = adCmdText

   'Set the Parameter object properties
   objParm.Attributes = adFldLong
   objParm.Name = "Comments"
   objParm.Type = adLongVarChar
   objParm.Direction = adParamInput
   objParm.Size = 500
```

```
    'Loop through the string appending chunks of data in
    '100 byte increments to the parameter object
    intStart = 1
    intLength = 100
    Do
       'If there are less than 100 bytes left
       If (intStart + intLength) > Len(strText) Then
          'Then change the length of data to be appended
          intLength = Len(strText) - intStart + 1
       End If
       'Append a chunk of data, normally 100 bytes
       objParm.AppendChunk Mid(strText, intStart, intLength)
       'Advance the starting position
       intStart = intStart + intLength
    Loop While intLength = 100

    'Append the Parameter object to the Parameters collection
    'and execute the Command object
    objCmd.Parameters.Append objParm
    objCmd.Execute

    'Close and de-reference objects
    Set objParm = Nothing
    Set objCmd = Nothing
    Set objErr = Nothing
    objConn.Close
    Set objConn = Nothing

    'All done, exit procedure
    List1.AddItem "Text inserted into Customer_Comment_T"
    Exit Sub

 Form_Load_EH:
    'Display all errors
    For Each objErr In objConn.Errors
       List1.AddItem objErr.Description
    Next
    List1.AddItem Err.Description
 End Sub
```

How It Works

As we have done in previous examples, we use the standard Windows icon by setting the form icon to nothing. Then we set up our error handling, which is critical in this example if we want to debug problems:

```
 Private Sub Form_Load()
    'Use the standard Windows icon
    Me.Icon = Nothing

    'Set up error handling
    On Error GoTo Form_Load_EH
```

Next we declare our local variables and our database objects. Notice the various database objects that we are using in this example:

```
'Declare local variables
Dim strText As String, intStart As Integer, intLength As Integer

'Declare local database objects
Dim objConn As New ADODB.Connection
Dim objCmd As New ADODB.Command
Dim objParm As New ADODB.Parameter
Dim objErr As ADODB.Error
```

Next, we establish a connection to the database using a DSN connection. After we open the connection, we check the state of the connection and if it is not open, we display a message in the list box:

```
'Establish a database connection using NT authentication
objConn.Open "DSN=Wrox Auto Works"

'Check connection state
If objConn.State <> adStateOpen Then
   List1.AddItem "Connection Failed"
   Exit Sub
End If
```

This is the string text that we will be using for this program. If you want to insert more data, either key in more data or open a large text file, read the data (an example of this is included later) and assign it to the variable `strText`:

```
'Set the string to be inserted
strText = "This example uses the Command object and Parameters " & _
   "Collection to insert text into a SQL Server text field. We " & _
   "must use the AppendChunk method of the Parameter object to " & _
   "append the entire text string to the Parameter. This is usually " & _
   "done in chunks as the amount of data to be inserted is usually " & _
   "very large. However, this example is fairly small compared to " & _
   "the text that would normally be inserted in a real-world application."
```

We are using the `Command` object to execute a SQL string. Notice that we have included a placeholder (?) for the parameter value that we will be supplying. Since this is a SQL string, we have specified the `adCmdText` constant from the `CommandTypeEnum` for the `CommandType` property:

```
'Set the Command object properties
Set objCmd.ActiveConnection = objConn
objCmd.CommandText = "INSERT INTO Customer_Comment_T " & _
                     "(Comments_TX) " & _
                     "VALUES(?)"
objCmd.CommandType = adCmdText
```

In order to use the `AppendChunk` method of the `Parameter` object, we must specify the `adFldLong` constant for the `Attributes` property. Along with that, we specify the `Parameter` `Name`, `Type` and `Direction` properties. The `Size` property needs to be set to the maximum amount of data that you will be inserting. For this example a `Size` of 500 characters is fine, unless you are using more data:

```
'Set the Parameter object properties
objParm.Attributes = adFldLong
objParm.Name = "Comments"
objParm.Type = adLongVarChar
objParm.Direction = adParamInput
objParm.Size = 500
```

We want to perform a loop and append the data to the `Parameter` object in 100 byte chunks. In reality this could be in 100,000 or even 500,000 byte chunks. This would largely be determined by the amount of memory available on your target client machines. Before we start our loop, we set the `intStart` variable to 1, so we start reading the string variable at position 1, and set the `intLength` variable to the amount of data that we will be appending:

```
'Loop through the string appending chunks of data in
'100 byte increments to the parameter object
intStart = 1
intLength = 100
```

Our loop is performed while the length of the `intLength` variable is equal to 100. The first thing we do in our loop is to check the `intStart` and `intLength` variables to see if they are greater than the length of the string variable. If they are, we know that we have less than 100 characters left to append, and set a new length to the `intLength` variable:

```
Do
   'If there are less than 100 bytes left
   If (intStart + intLength) > Len(strText) Then
      'Then change the length of data to be appended
      intLength = Len(strText) - intStart + 1
   End If
```

We append data to the `Parameter` object using the `AppendChunk` method, and use the VB `Mid` function to get a chunk of data from the string variable. Then we increment the starting position of the `intStart` variable by adding the length of the `intlength` variable to it.

We continue processing our loop until the `intLength` variable is no longer equal to 100, which indicates we have appended all of the data from our string variable to the `Parameter` object:

```
   'Append a chunk of data, normally 100 bytes
   objParm.AppendChunk Mid(strText, intStart, intLength)
   'Advance the starting position
   intStart = intStart + intLength
Loop While intLength = 100
```

Now that we have appended all of the data to the `Parameter` object, we need to append the `Parameter` object to the `Parameters` collection. Then we execute the `Command` object:

```
'Append the Parameter object to the Parameters collection
'and execute the Command object
objCmd.Parameters.Append objParm
objCmd.Execute
```

Now that our data has been inserted, we close and de-reference our objects:

```
    'Close and de-reference objects
    Set objParm = Nothing
    Set objCmd = Nothing
    Set objErr = Nothing
    objConn.Close
    Set objConn = Nothing
```

Last, we add a message to the list box indicating that the data was inserted and exit the procedure:

```
    'All done, exit procedure
    List1.AddItem "Text inserted into Customer_Comment_T"
    Exit Sub
```

Our error handling routine simply loops through the `Errors` collection and adds each error to the list box, hence the use of the list box in this example. It is critical to handle the errors for this example, and the list box provides a large enough area to handle multiple messages, should we encounter any errors:

```
Form_Load_EH:
    'Display all errors
    For Each objErr In objConn.Errors
        List1.AddItem objErr.Description
    Next
    List1.AddItem Err.Description
End Sub
```

At this point, execute your program, and you should receive the message that the text was inserted.

Selecting Text Data

In order to see the data that you have just inserted, open the Query Analyzer and run the following query:

```
SELECT * FROM Customer_Comment_T
```

If you scroll all the way to the right of the window, you will notice that part of the data is missing. Actually it is not missing; we just need to adjust a parameter in the Query Analyzer. On the Query menu, choose Current Connection Options to display the Current Connection Options dialog. The Advanced tab has an option for Maximum Characters per Column, which is probably set to 256. Change this option to 8,000 characters and click OK to close the dialog:

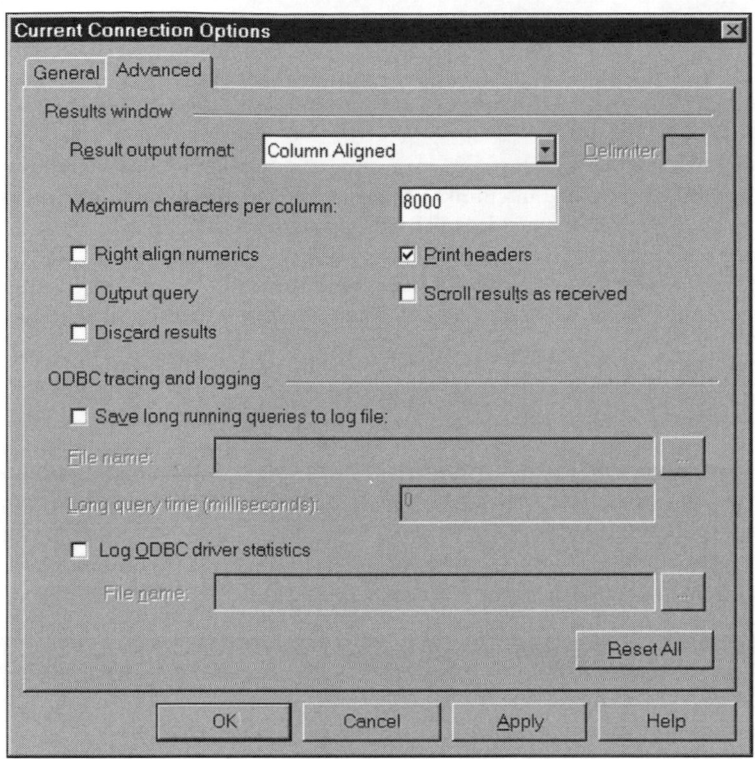

Re-run your query and you will be able to see all of your text this time. If, however, you chose to load a large text file, it is possible that you are still not seeing all of the text. There is a option in SQL Server called `TextSize` that limits the maximum length, in bytes, that a `SELECT` statement will return for a text column. The default value for `TextSize` is 4K, and you can query the value that is currently set by executing the following query. This query uses the SQL Server function `@@TextSize`, which returns the current value of the `TextSize` option:

```
SELECT @@TextSize
```

To change the value contained in the `TextSize` option, you can use the `SET TextSize` function. This function accepts a numeric value or variable containing the size in bytes that should be set. The maximum value that can be set is 2,147,483,647, which is the maximum size of a `Text` data type. To reset the `TextSize` option back to its original default value of 4K, supply a numeric value of zero.

The following two examples show the `TextSize` option being set to a higher value and then being reset to its original default value. After the `TextSize` option has been changed, the `@@TextSize` function is executed to display the new value. Run this query and see what results that you get:

```
SET TextSize 12288
SELECT @@TextSize
```

```
SET TextSize 0
SELECT @@TextSize
```

We do not need to be concerned with this limitation when selecting data from our VB program. This is because the Microsoft OLE DB Provider for SQL Server and the SQL Server ODBC driver automatically set the `TextSize` value to the maximum value of 2,147,483,647 when a connection is made.

To display the entire text in our VB programs, we need to open a recordset and use the `GetChunk` method to retrieve the entire text in chunks. After we get a chunk of data, we can assign it to a variable, write it to a file, or display it in a text box. The `GetChunk` method of the `Field` object works the opposite of the `AppendChunk` method of the `Parameter` object. The `Parameter` object does not contain a `GetChunk` method so we can not use it here. Instead of appending a chunk of data, we are getting a chunk of data from the `Field` object. The `GetChunk` method has the following format:

```
variable = field.GetChunk(size)
```

The size is a long value that determines the number of bytes to be returned from the `Field` object. The next code fragment shows the `GetChunk` method retrieving a determined number of bytes from the field `Comments_TX` and assigning it to the `strText` variable. The `lngChunk` variable contains the number of bytes to be retrieved:

```
strText = m_objRS!Comments_TX.GetChunk(lngChunk)
```

Try It Out #2 – Select Text

Before we code a VB program to select text, let's code a stored procedure that will be executed by the `Recordset` object in the `Open` method. This stored procedure will simply select the text comments for a specific row of data.

1. The code below lists the stored procedure that we need to create:

```
CREATE PROCEDURE up_parmsel_comments (@Comment_ID INT) AS

SELECT Comments_TX
      FROM Customer_Comment_T
      WHERE Customer_Comment_ID = @Comment_ID
```

After you create this stored procedure, don't forget to set the appropriate permissions on it.

The VB program that we will build in this section will be the basis for the rest of the examples in this chapter. This program will use the `GetChunk` method of the `Field` object that we discussed above to read the entire text of the `Comments_TX` column.

2. Start a new project and set a reference to the Microsoft ActiveX Data Objects Library. Change the project name to `TryItOut2` and the form name to `frmTryItOut2`. Set the forms `Height` property to `4236` and its `Width` property to `6732`. Using the table and figure below, add the controls to the form:

Control	Name	Properties
TextBox	`Text1`	`Height` = 3015, `Width` = 6612, `MultiLine` = True, `Text` = nothing, `ScrollBars` = 3 - Both
Textbox	`Text2`	`Text` = nothing
Label	`Label1`	`Caption` = ID
ComboBox	`cboID`	`Style` = 2 – Dropdown List
Command Button	`cmdSelect`	`Caption` = Select

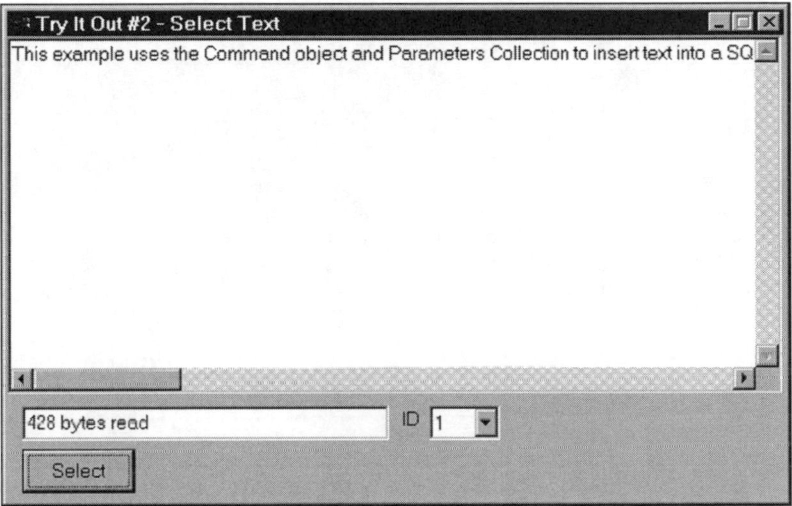

This screen shot shows what you will see once you have run the program, not what it should look like now.

3. Add the following code to the `General Declarations` section of the form:

```
Option Explicit

'Declare database objects
Private m_objConn As ADODB.Connection
Private m_objCmd As ADODB.Command
Private m_objParm As ADODB.Parameter
Private m_objRS As ADODB.Recordset
Private m_objErr As ADODB.Error
```

4. Create a procedure called `LoadIDs` and add the following code:

```
Private Sub LoadIDs()
   'Clear combo box
   cboID.Clear

   'Set a reference to the Recordset object
   Set m_objRS = New ADODB.Recordset

   'Open the recordset
   m_objRS.Open "SELECT Customer_Comment_ID FROM Customer_Comment_T", _
      m_objConn, adOpenForwardOnly, adLockReadOnly, adCmdText

   'Load the combo box
   Do While Not m_objRS.EOF
      cboID.AddItem m_objRS!Customer_Comment_ID
      m_objRS.MoveNext
   Loop

   'Set the index to the first item
   cboID.ListIndex = 0

   'Close and de-reference Recordset object
   m_objRS.Close
   Set m_objRS = Nothing
End Sub
```

5. Add the following code to the `Form_Load` event:

```
Private Sub Form_Load()
   'Use the standard Windows icon
   Me.Icon = Nothing

   'Set up error handling
   On Error GoTo Form_Load_EH

   'Set a reference to the Connection object
   Set m_objConn = New ADODB.Connection

   'Establish a database connection using NT authentication
   m_objConn.Open "DSN=Wrox Auto Works"

   'Check connection state
   If m_objConn.State <> adStateOpen Then
      Text1.Text = "Connection failed"
      Exit Sub
   Else
      m_objConn.Errors.Clear
   End If
```

```
    'Load combo box
    Call LoadIDs

    'Display the message
    Text2.Text = "Ready"

    Exit Sub

Form_Load_EH:
    For Each m_objErr In m_objConn.Errors
        Text1.Text = Text1.Text & m_objErr.Description & vbCrLf
    Next
End Sub
```

6. Add the following code to the `Form_UnLoad` event:

```
Private Sub Form_Unload(Cancel As Integer)
    If Not m_objRS Is Nothing Then
        If m_objRS.State = adStateOpen Then
            m_objRS.Close
        End If
    End If
    Set m_objRS = Nothing

    Set m_objCmd = Nothing
    Set m_objParm = Nothing
    Set m_objErr = Nothing

    m_objConn.Close
    Set m_objConn = Nothing
End Sub
```

7. Add the following code to the `cmdSelect_Click` procedure:

```
Private Sub cmdSelect_Click()
    'Set up error handling
    On Error GoTo cmdSelect_Click_EH

    'Declare local variables
    Dim strSQL As String, lngChunk As Long, lngSize As Long, lngOffset As Long

    'Set a reference to the Recordset object
    Dim m_objRS As New ADODB.Recordset

    'Clear text boxes
    Text1.Text = Empty
    Text2.Text = Empty

    'Set the SQL string
    strSQL = "willist.up_parmsel_comments (" & CLng(cboID.Text) & ")"
```

```
    'Open the recordset
    lngChunk = 100
    m_objRS.Open strSQL, m_objConn, adOpenStatic, adLockReadOnly, adCmdStoredProc
    lngSize = m_objRS!Comments_TX.ActualSize

    'Load the text box using GetChunk
    Do While lngOffset < lngSize
       Text1.Text = Text1.Text & m_objRS!Comments_TX.GetChunk(lngChunk)
       lngOffset = lngOffset + lngChunk
    Loop

    'Display the message
    Text2.Text = Format(m_objRS!Comments_TX.ActualSize, "#,###,###,##0") & " bytes
read"

    'Close and de-reference Recordset object
    m_objRS.Close
    Set m_objRS = Nothing

    Exit Sub

cmdSelect_Click_EH:
    Text1.Text = Empty
    For Each m_objErr In m_objConn.Errors
       Text1.Text = Text1.Text & m_objErr.Description & vbCrLf
    Next
End Sub
```

How It Works

The stored procedure itself is very simple and needs no explanation.

General Declarations

The `General Declarations` section of the form contains all of the database objects that we will be using in the rest of the examples in this chapter:

```
Option Explicit

'Declare database objects
Private m_objConn As ADODB.Connection
Private m_objCmd As ADODB.Command
Private m_objParm As ADODB.Parameter
Private m_objRS As ADODB.Recordset
Private m_objErr As ADODB.Error
```

We want to create a procedure to load the combo box on our form with all available IDs from the `Customer_Comment_T` table. This procedure will be called from several procedures in our form as our examples progress.

The first thing this procedure does is to clear any existing entries from the combo box. Then we set a reference to the Recordset object:

```
Private Sub LoadIDs()
    'Clear combo box
    cboID.Clear

    'Set a reference to the Recordset object
    Set m_objRS = New ADODB.Recordset
```

For this Recordset, we are using in-line SQL statements instead of coding a stored procedure. We have been working with stored procedures so much since Chapter 6, I thought it might be good to use another example with in-line SQL, just to refresh your memory. This SQL statement is selecting the Customer_Comment_ID column from the Customer_Comment_T table for all rows.

Notice that since we are using in-line SQL, we have specified the adCmdText constant from the CommandTypeEnum for the Options parameter. We only need to read the recordset once, so we have specified the adOpenForward and adLockReadOnly constants for the CursorType and LockType parameters:

```
    'Open the recordset
    m_objRS.Open "SELECT Customer_Comment_ID FROM Customer_Comment_T", _
        m_objConn, adOpenForwardOnly, adLockReadOnly, adCmdText
```

After our recordset has been opened, we loop through the recordset, loading the Customer_Comment_IDs into the combo box. Our examples will be using the Text property of the combo box to retrieve the Customer_Comment_ID, so we don't need to add it to the ItemData property of the combo box:

```
    'Load the combo box
    Do While Not m_objRS.EOF
        cboID.AddItem m_objRS!Customer_Comment_ID
        m_objRS.MoveNext
    Loop
```

After the combo box has been loaded, we set its ListIndex property to 0, which selects the first entry in the combo box. Then we close and de-reference our Recordset object:

```
    'Set the index to the first item
    cboID.ListIndex = 0

    'Close and de-reference Recordset object
    m_objRS.Close
    Set m_objRS = Nothing
End Sub
```

Form_Load Event

The `Form_Load` event starts by setting the form's icon to `Nothing`, so we can use the Windows default icon. Then we set up our error handling and set a reference to the `Connection` object:

```
Private Sub Form_Load()
   'Use the standard Windows icon
   Me.Icon = Nothing

   'Set up error handling
   On Error GoTo Form_Load_EH

   'Set a reference to the Connection object
   Set m_objConn = New ADODB.Connection
```

We open the database connection using our DSN that was set up earlier in the book. This example uses Windows NT authentication, but if your Logon uses SQL Server authentication, you need to provide the UID and PWD parameters and specify your SQL Server Logon and Password:

```
   'Establish a database connection using NT authentication
   m_objConn.Open "DSN=Wrox Auto Works"
```

After our connection is opened, we check the state of the connection to ensure that it is open. If the connection is not open, we display a message in the text box and exit the procedure. If the connection is open, we clear any warning messages in the `Errors` collection:

```
   'Check connection state
   If m_objConn.State <> adStateOpen Then
      Text1.Text = "Connection failed"
      Exit Sub
   Else
      m_objConn.Errors.Clear
   End If
```

Next we call the procedure to load all available IDs in the combo box. Then we display a message that we are ready and exit the procedure:

```
   'Load combo box
   Call LoadIDs

   'Display the message
   Text2.Text = "Ready"

   Exit Sub
```

Our error handling routine is very simple. We loop through the `Errors` collection and display each message in the text box. Since the text box has its `MultiLine` property set to `True`, we add a carriage return line feed character after each message, so each message is displayed on a separate line:

```
Form_Load_EH:
   For Each m_objErr In m_objConn.Errors
      Text1.Text = Text1.Text & m_objErr.Description & vbCrLf
   Next
End Sub
```

Form_Unload Event

The Form_UnLoad event contains all of the code to de-reference our objects. First we check to see if the Recordset object is being used, by checking to see if it is not equal to Nothing. Then we check to see if the Recordset object is currently open. If it is, we close it. Then we set the Recordset object to Nothing.

We don't need to check the State property for the Command, Parameter or Error objects; we can just set them to Nothing to de-reference them. The Connection object must be closed and then set to Nothing:

```
Private Sub Form_Unload(Cancel As Integer)
    If Not m_objRS Is Nothing Then
        If m_objRS.State = adStateOpen Then
            m_objRS.Close
        End If
    End If
    Set m_objRS = Nothing

    Set m_objCmd = Nothing
    Set m_objParm = Nothing
    Set m_objErr = Nothing

    m_objConn.Close
    Set m_objConn = Nothing
End Sub
```

CmdSelect_Click Procedure

When we click on the SELECT button, the cmdSelect_Click procedure is executed, which executes our stored procedure. The first thing we do in this procedure is to set up error handling and then declare all the local variables that we will need in this procedure:

```
Private Sub cmdSelect_Click()
    'Set up error handling
    On Error GoTo cmdSelect_Click_EH

    'Declare local variables
    Dim strSQL As String, lngChunk As Long, lngSize As Long, lngOffset As Long
```

We set a reference to the Recordset object, and then clear the text boxes by setting their Text property to empty:

```
    'Set a reference to the Recordset object
    Dim m_objRS As New ADODB.Recordset

    'Clear text boxes
    Text1.Text = Empty
    Text2.Text = Empty
```

We set our SQL string using the stored procedure we created earlier and the Text property from the combo box. Notice that since our stored procedure expects a long value, we are using the CLng function to convert the value in the Text property to a long value:

```
    'Set the SQL string
    strSQL = "willist.up_parmsel_comments (" & CLng(cboID.Text) & ")"
```

We are going to be reading the data in 100 byte increments, but as we discussed earlier, you would use a larger value in a real world application. After setting the lngChunk variable to 100, we open the recordset. Since we need to get the size of the Comments_TX field, we are using the adOpenStatic constant for the CursorType parameter. Then we set the lngSize variable to the size of the Comments_TX field, using the ActualSize property of the Field object:

```
    'Open the recordset
    lngChunk = 100
    m_objRS.Open strSQL, m_objConn, adOpenStatic, adLockReadOnly, adCmdStoredProc
    lngSize = m_objRS!Comments_TX.ActualSize
```

We can now perform a loop while the lngOffset variable is less than the size of the Field object. The first thing we do in the loop is to get a chunk of data from the Field object using the GetChunk method and add it to the text box. Then we increment the lngOffset variable with the length of the chunk of data that was retrieved. If the Field object contains less data than what has been specified in the lngChunk variable, the Field object returns the remaining data with no errors:

```
    'Load the text box using GetChunk
    Do While lngOffset < lngSize
       Text1.Text = Text1.Text & m_objRS!Comments_TX.GetChunk(lngChunk)
       lngOffset = lngOffset + lngChunk
    Loop
```

After we have read all of the data in the Field object, we display a message with the exact number of bytes read. Using the Format function, we format the number with commas:

```
    'Display the message
    Text2.Text = Format(m_objRS!Comments_TX.ActualSize, "#,###,###,##0") & " bytes
read"
```

We close and de-reference our Recordset object and exit the procedure. The error handling routine is the same as we just saw in the Form_Load event:

```
    'Close and dereference Recordset object
    m_objRS.Close
    Set m_objRS = Nothing

    Exit Sub

cmdSelect_Click_EH:
    Text1.Text = Empty
    For Each m_objErr In m_objConn.Errors
       Text1.Text = Text1.Text & m_objErr.Description & vbCrLf
    Next
End Sub
```

Since we only have one row in our table, the combo box will only display one entry. Later you will be able to select the entry that you want to display in the combo box, and then click on the Select button. For now run your project and select the only entry that does exist. The display should be similar to the screen shot at the beginning of this Try It Out. If you set a break point in the procedure above, you can step through the loop and see how the data is appended to the text box and how chunks of data are read.

Try It Out #3 – Insert Text

In the first example that we coded, we used the `Command` and `Parameter` objects to insert text using in-line SQL statements. This next example also uses the `Command` and `Parameter` objects, but will use a stored procedure to insert the text data. Also we will be reading the data from the text box (`text1`) on the form to retrieve the data to be inserted, so our loop to append data to the `Parameter` object will look a little different.

1. Let's start by creating the stored procedure that will insert the data into the `Customer_Comment_T` table. Don't forget to set the appropriate permissions on this stored procedure after it has been created:

```
CREATE PROCEDURE up_parmins_comments (@Text_Data TEXT) AS

INSERT INTO Customer_Comment_T
     (Comments_TX)
     VALUES(@Text_Data)
```

The project that you create here is optional, as we will be building upon the last example. You can create a new project or add to the existing project. However, for consistency you should copy the `frmTryItOut2` form as `frmTryItOut3`.

2. Start a new project and set a reference to the Microsoft ActiveX Data Objects Library and remove the form. Add the new form you just copied and set it as the default startup form in the Project Properties dialog. Give this new project a name of `TryItOut3`.

3. Using the figure below as a guide, add a new button and set its `Name` property to `cmdInsert` and its `Caption` property to `Insert`:

This screen shot shows what you will see once you have run the program, not what it should look like now.

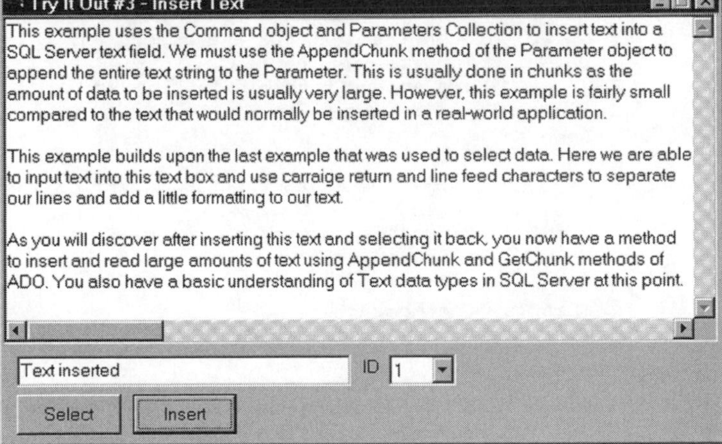

4. Add the following code to the `cmdInsert_Click` procedure:

```
Private Sub cmdInsert_Click()
   'Set up error handling
   On Error GoTo cmdInsert_Click_EH

   'Declare local variables
   Dim strSQL As String, lngChunk As Long, lngSize As Long, lngOffset As Long

   'Set a reference to the database objects
   Dim m_objCmd As New ADODB.Command
   Dim m_objParm As New ADODB.Parameter

   'Clear text boxes
   Text2.Text = Empty

   'Set the Command object properties
   Set m_objCmd.ActiveConnection = m_objConn
   m_objCmd.CommandText = "willist.up_parmins_comments"
   m_objCmd.CommandType = adCmdStoredProc

   'Set the Parameter object properties
   m_objParm.Attributes = adFldLong
   m_objParm.Name = "Comments"
   m_objParm.Type = adLongVarChar
   m_objParm.Direction = adParamInput
   m_objParm.Size = Len(Text1.Text)

   'Set default values
   lngChunk = 100
   lngOffset = 1
   lngSize = Len(Text1.Text)

   'Loop through the text box and append the text to the Parameter object
   Do While lngOffset < lngSize
      m_objParm.AppendChunk Mid(Text1.Text, lngOffset, lngChunk)
      lngOffset = lngOffset + lngChunk
   Loop

   'Append the parameter to the Parameters collection and execute the
   'Command object
   m_objCmd.Parameters.Append m_objParm
   m_objCmd.Execute

   'Display the message
   Text2.Text = "Text inserted"

   'De-reference database objects
   Set m_objParm = Nothing
   Set m_objCmd = Nothing

   'Reload combo box
   Call LoadIDs

   Exit Sub
```

```
cmdInsert_Click_EH:
   Text1.Text = Empty
   For Each m_objErr In m_objConn.Errors
      Text1.Text = Text1.Text & m_objErr.Description & vbCrLf
   Next
End Sub
```

How It Works

The stored procedure above is very straightforward and needs no explanation.

The only code that we have added in this example is to the `cmdInsert_Click` procedure. This procedure reads the text in the text box and appends chunks of data to the `Parameter` object to be inserted into the database.

We start this procedure by setting up our error handling and declaring our local variables. Then we set a reference to our database objects and clear the second text box, which is used to display basic messages:

```
Private Sub cmdInsert_Click()
   'Set up error handling
   On Error GoTo cmdInsert_Click_EH

   'Declare local variables
   Dim strSQL As String, lngChunk As Long, lngSize As Long, lngOffset As Long

   'Set a reference to the database objects
   Dim m_objCmd As New ADODB.Command
   Dim m_objParm As New ADODB.Parameter

   'Clear text boxes
   Text2.Text = Empty
```

We set the basic properties of the `Command` object and use a stored procedure, this time in the `CommandText` property. Because we have used a stored procedure, we must set the `CommandType` property using the `adCmdStoredProc` constant from the `CommandTypeEnum`:

```
   'Set the Command object properties
   Set m_objCmd.ActiveConnection = m_objConn
   m_objCmd.CommandText = "willist.up_parmins_comments"
   m_objCmd.CommandType = adCmdStoredProc
```

The Parameter object also has properties that must be set. The most important of them is the Attributes property. Unless we set this property using the adFldLong constant, we will be unable to use the AppendChunk method. Also, notice that this time we are using the VB Len function to determine the length of the text in the text box, so we can set the Size property accurately:

```
'Set the Parameter object properties
m_objParm.Attributes = adFldLong
m_objParm.Name = "Comments"
m_objParm.Type = adLongVarChar
m_objParm.Direction = adParamInput
m_objParm.Size = Len(Text1.Text)
```

We set the various local variables that we have declared. The first variable, lngChunk, is used as the parameter in the AppendChunk method to specify how much data to append. The lngOffset variable is used to specify the starting position for the VB Mid function and the lngSize variable is used as a reference to know how much data needs to be appended to the Parameter object:

```
'Set default values
lngChunk = 100
lngOffset = 1
lngSize = Len(Text1.Text)
```

If you look at the loop in this example and the loop in the first example, you will notice quite a difference. This loop is using the lngSize and lngOffset variables to control how long the loop is processed.

Using the VB Mid function as a source for the text, we append a chunk of text from the text box to the Parameter object using the AppendChunk method. Then we increment the lngOffset variable, which gives us a new starting position in the text box for the next Mid function:

```
'Loop through the text box and append the text to the parameter object
Do While lngOffset < lngSize
   m_objParm.AppendChunk Mid(Text1.Text, lngOffset, lngChunk)
   lngOffset = lngOffset + lngChunk
Loop
```

Once all the data has been appended to the Parameter object, we append the Parameter object to the Parameters collection and execute the Command object:

```
'Append the parameter to the Parameters collection and execute the
'Command object
m_objCmd.Parameters.Append m_objParm
m_objCmd.Execute
```

Then we display a message that the data has been inserted and de-reference our database objects. We call the LoadIDs procedure to reload the combo box to reflect the new row of data that has been inserted into the Customer_Comment_T table. Then we exit this procedure:

```
    'Display the message
    Text2.Text = "Text inserted"

    'De-reference database objects
    Set m_objParm = Nothing
    Set m_objCmd = Nothing

    'Reload combo box
    Call LoadIDs

    Exit Sub
```

The error handling routine is short and sweet. It simply loops through the `Errors` collection and adds each error message to the text box:

```
cmdInsert_Click_EH:
    Text1.Text = Empty
    For Each m_objErr In m_objConn.Errors
        Text1.Text = Text1.Text & m_objErr.Description & vbCrLf
    Next
End Sub
```

To test the new functionality that you have just added, run your project and select the one and only entry available in the combo box and click the Select button. When we inserted this entry, we had used a string variable that contained the text. This string variable did not contain any carriage return line feed characters and was added as one long string.

Because we are now using a text box with its `MultiLine` property set to `True`, we can add carriage return line feed characters to this string by pressing the `Enter` key to force a line break. This makes the text appear in the text box in a more pleasing manner versus one long string. Then we can add some more text and then click the Insert button.

After you have inserted your new text, select the text from the first entry by selecting the first ID in the combo box and clicking the Select button. Then select the second entry in the combo box and click the Select button. Using a text box to format the text makes a big difference in how the data is entered and displayed.

Text Pointers

As we mentioned earlier, SQL Server stores a 16-byte binary text pointer to our text data. This pointer is stored in the column in the data row of our table and points to the first 8K text page of our data. A column that contains a `NULL` value does not have a valid text pointer and is considered not initialized until data has been either inserted or updated.

The following figure shows what the text pointers look like and also shows a column that has not been initialized as indicated by the NULL value:

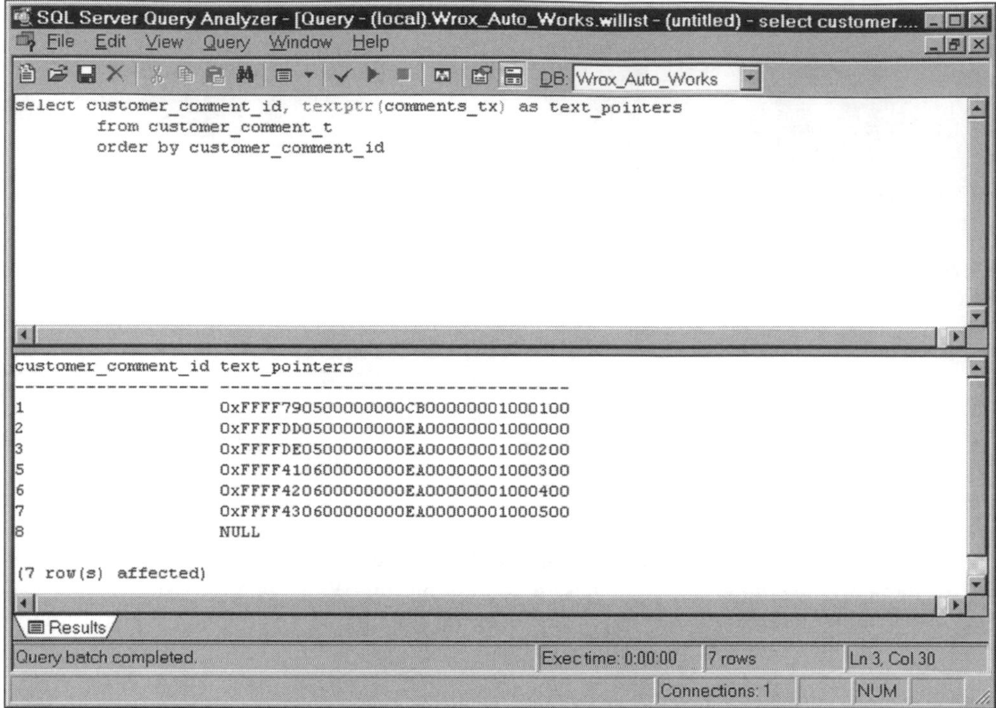

Let's take a moment and look at the query above. SQL Server provides a function called TEXTPTR that returns the text pointer for a column of text data. If the column of data has not been initialized, as shown in the last row of the results, there is no text pointer.

The TEXTPTR function returns a binary value that represents the address in the root of a B-tree structure of the first 8K text page of data. The B-Tree contains the actual address where the data is stored, so we just point at this address in the root. If a column has not been initialized, then the TEXTPTR function returns a null pointer. There is a companion function for the TEXTPTR function called TEXTVALID. This function verifies that a valid text pointer was returned and returns 1 if the TEXTPTR is valid and a 0 if it is not valid.

Let's look at the format of these two functions as shown below:

```
TEXTPTR(column_name)
```

```
TEXTVALID('table_name.column_name',text_pointer)
```

The format for the TEXTPTR function only requires the column_name of the column containing the text data. The TEXTVALID function requires the table_name, followed by the column_name, separated by a period and enclosed in single quote marks. The text_pointer parameter of this function is either a valid text pointer variable or the TEXTPTR function specified with a column name.

The following code shows a text pointer variable being declared in the first line of code. The second line of code shows the text pointer being retrieved using the `TEXTPTR` function. Here we have to specify the table name and the specific row of data that the text pointer should be retrieved for. The last line of code in this example shows the text pointer variable, `@textptr`, being validated using the `TEXTVALID` function:

```
--
-- Delcare text pointer variable
--
DECLARE @Textptr VARBINARY(16), @Valid INT
--
-- Initialize the text pointer
--
SELECT @Textptr = TEXTPTR(Comments_TX)
     FROM Customer_Comment_T
     WHERE Customer_Comment_ID = 1
--
-- Validate text pointer
--
SELECT TEXTVALID('Customer_Comment_T.Comments_TX',@Textptr) AS Valid_Text_Pointer
```

Let's look at an alternative approach to the above example. This next code fragment shows a text pointer being validated without actually retrieving the text pointer. This example simply validates the pointer, while the example above has actually retrieved the text pointer and can now perform read, write and update operations against the text data in the column referenced by the text pointer:

```
--
-- Validate text pointer
--
SELECT TEXTVALID('Customer_Comment_T.Comments_TX',TEXTPTR(Comments_TX)) AS
Valid_Text_Pointer
     FROM Customer_Comment_T
     WHERE Customer_Comment_ID = 1
```

The next three functions that we will explore require the use of the `TEXTPTR`. These functions allow us to work with small blocks of data in a text column. The `TEXTPTR` is used in conjunction with the offset value to determine the exact location of data to read or update.

Reading Text Data

You might look at the heading for this topic and the topic titled *Selecting Text Data* and may be thinking that isn't selecting data the same as reading data? In most cases this is true, but when it comes to dealing with the `Text` data type in SQL Server, this is not the case. When we talk about reading data from a text column in SQL Server, we are talking about reading only a specific portion of the data. Because a text column can contain such a large amount data, it might not always be feasible or necessary to read the entire amount of data. We need a way to work with just a portion of the data available in the text column.

This is where the READTEXT function of SQL Server comes in. This function provides a method of reading just a portion of the data in a text column. The READTEXT function has the following syntax (note the lack of commas).

```
READTEXT table_name.column.name text_pointer offset size
```

The READTEXT function expects the table name and column name from which it should read data. The text pointer parameter specifies a valid text pointer that has been initialized and is required. You can't use READTEXT (or UPDATETEXT and WRITETEXT) without a valid text pointer. The offset and size parameters specify at what point in the text column we should start reading data (how many bytes should be skipped) and how many bytes of data should be read.

We discussed the TEXTPTR function in the last topic and you should have a basic understanding of it at this point. From here on out, we will be using a text pointer to work with just a specific portion of the text, and when we have completed the chapter, you will have a solid understanding of how to use the text pointer.

If you recall our discussion on text pointers, the TEXTPTR function contains an address to the beginning of the page that contains our data. Used in conjunction with the READTEXT function, we can read just a portion of the data contained in the text column using the offset and length parameters.

If you are using the READTEXT function in a query in the Query Analyzer, you need to be aware of the TextSize option that we discussed earlier. The TextSize option will limit the amount of data that can be read. You may need to increase this option in your query using the SET TextSize function. We do not have to worry about this in our VB program because the Microsoft OLE DB Provider for SQL Server and the SQL Server ODBC driver automatically set the TextSize value to the maximum value.

Try It Out #4 – Read Text

We need to create a stored procedure to read just a portion of the data in the text column. However, before we can read the data, a TEXTPTR variable must be declared and initialized. Then, using the TEXTPTR variable in conjunction with the READTEXT function, we can read just a portion of the data.

1. The code for this stored procedure is listed below. Don't forget to set the appropriate permissions on this stored procedure after it has been created:

```
CREATE PROCEDURE up_parmsel_read_comments (@Comment_ID INT, @Offset INT, @Length
INT) AS

--
*****************************************************************************
******
-- Declare variable for the text pointer
--
*****************************************************************************
******
DECLARE @Text_Pointer VARBINARY(16)
--
*****************************************************************************
******
Initialize the text pointer
```

```
--
****************************************************************************************
******
SELECT @Text_pointer = TEXTPTR(Comments_TX)
     FROM Customer_Comment_T
     WHERE Customer_Comment_ID = @Comment_ID

--
****************************************************************************************
******
-- Read the text data
--
****************************************************************************************
******
READTEXT Customer_Comment_T.Comments_TX @Text_Pointer @Offset @Length
```

2. The code for our VB program is built using the last example as a base. Start by copying the `frmTryItOut3` form as `frmTryItOut4`. Then start a new project and set a reference to the Microsoft ActiveX Data Objects Library. Remove the current form and add the `frmTryItOut3` form you just created. Set the new form as the startup form in the Project Properties dialog.

3. Using the table and figure below, add the following controls to the form:

Control	Name	Properties
Label	`Label2`	`Caption` = Offset
TextBox	`txtOffset`	`Text` = nothing
Label	`Label3`	`Caption` = Length
Textbox	`txtLength`	`Text` = nothing
Command Button	`cmdRead`	`Caption` = Read

Again, this screen shot shows what you will see once you have run the program, not what it should look like now.

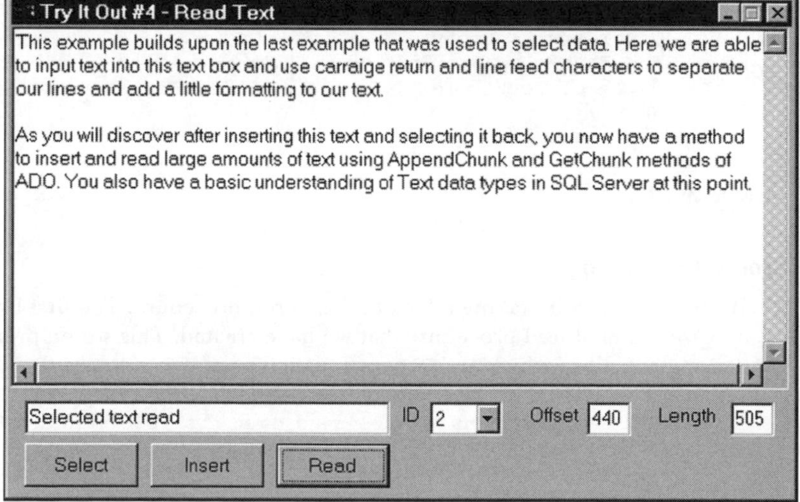

4. Add the following code to the `cmdRead_Click` procedure:

```
Private Sub cmdRead_Click()
   'Set up error handling
   On Error GoTo cmdRead_Click_EH

   'Declare local variables
   Dim strSQL As String

   'Check offset and length before proceeding
   If Len(txtoffset.Text) = 0 Or Len(txtLength.Text) = 0 Then
      Beep
      Text2.Text = "Offset and Length are required for read"
      Exit Sub
   End If

   'Set a reference to the Recordset object
   Dim m_objRS As New ADODB.Recordset

   'Clear text boxes
   Text1.Text = Empty
   Text2.Text = Empty

   'Set the SQL string
   strSQL = "willist.up_parmsel_read_comments (" & CLng(cboID.Text) & "," & _
      CLng(txtoffset.Text) & "," & CLng(txtLength.Text) & ")"

   'Open the recordset
   m_objRS.Open strSQL, m_objConn, adOpenForwardOnly, adLockReadOnly, _
      adCmdStoredProc

   'Display the text
   Text1.Text = m_objRS!Comments_TX
   Text2.Text = "Selected text read"

   'Close and de-reference Recordset object
   m_objRS.Close
   Set m_objRS = Nothing

   Exit Sub

cmdRead_Click_EH:
   Text1.Text = Empty
   For Each m_objErr In m_objConn.Errors
      Text1.Text = Text1.Text & m_objErr.Description & vbCrLf
   Next
End Sub
```

How It Works

Stored Procedure

We want to start by taking a look at the stored procedure. The first line of our stored procedure looks like any other stored procedure that we have created. This stored procedure accepts three input parameters, all of which are `Integer` data types:

```
CREATE PROCEDURE up_parmsel_read_comments (@Comment_ID INT, @Offset INT, @Length
INT) AS
```

The second line of our stored procedure declares a variable to be used as the text pointer. Since the data row for the `Comments_TX` column contains a 16-byte binary pointer to the actual text data, we must declare our variable as a `VarBinary` data type. Notice our use of comments to describe what each section of this stored procedure is doing:

```
--
**************************************************************************
******
-- Declare variable for the text pointer
--
**************************************************************************
******
DECLARE @Text_Pointer VARBINARY(16)
```

Before we can use our text pointer variable, we must initialize it by using the `TEXTPTR` function. We talked about this function earlier. A call to the `TEXTPTR` function returns the text pointer for the column that we specify. Here we are assigning the text pointer returned to our text pointer variable.

In order to get just one text pointer, we specify the exact row of data that we want the text pointer for:

```
--
**************************************************************************
******
-- Initialize the text pointer
--
**************************************************************************
******
SELECT @Text_Pointer = TEXTPTR(Comments_TX)
      FROM Customer_Comment_T
      WHERE Customer_Comment_ID = @Comment_ID
```

Now that we have a valid text pointer, we can read the specific block of text from our text column, using the `READTEXT` function. As we discussed above, the syntax for this function requires that we specify both the table name and column name as shown here. Then we specify a valid text pointer and the offset that we should start reading from, followed by the length of data that should be read:

```
--
**************************************************************************
******
-- Read the text data
--
**************************************************************************
******
READTEXT Customer_Comment_T.Comments_TX @Text_Pointer @Offset @Length
```

The results of the `READTEXT` function are returned using the column name of `Comments_TX`, because that is the column that the text pointer points to.

cmdRead_Click Procedure

Switching to our VB code, we want to take a look at the `cmdRead_Click` procedure. This procedure starts off like the rest of our procedures, by setting up our error handling and declaring our local variables for this procedure:

```
Private Sub cmdRead_Click()
    'Set up error handling
    On Error GoTo cmdRead_Click_EH

    'Declare local variables
    Dim strSQL As String
```

Because the `offset` and `length` are required parameters to the stored procedure, we want to ensure that the values for these two parameters have been supplied in the appropriate text boxes. Here we are performing a rudimentary check, by checking the length of the text boxes using the `Len` function.

If one or both of the text boxes have a zero length, we display a message that these parameters are required and exit the procedure:

```
    'Check offset and length before proceeding
    If Len(txtoffset.Text) = 0 Or Len(txtLength.Text) = 0 Then
        Beep
        Text2.Text = "Offset and Length are required for read"
        Exit Sub
    End If
```

Next, we set a reference to the `Recordset` object and clear both text boxes on our form:

```
    'Set a reference to the Recordset object
    Dim m_objRS As New ADODB.Recordset

    'Clear text boxes
    Text1.Text = Empty
    Text2.Text = Empty
```

We use a string variable to specify the stored procedure to be executed, along with the appropriate parameters. We are once again using the value in the `Text` property of the combo box, and again we convert it to a long value using the `CLng` function. The last two parameters are coming from the two text boxes that we added to our form, and these values must also be converted to long values:

```
    'Set the SQL string
    strSQL = "willist.up_parmsel_read_comments (" & CLng(cboID.Text) & "," & _
        CLng(txtoffset.Text) & "," & CLng(txtLength.Text) & ")"
```

Because we already know the length of data that is being returned and we aren't using the length for anything in the procedure, we open the `Recordset` object using a forward only cursor:

```
    'Open the recordset
    m_objRS.Open strSQL, m_objConn, adOpenForwardOnly, adLockReadOnly, _
        adCmdStoredProc
```

Since the amount of text that we are dealing with here is a specified amount, we do not need to use the `GetChunk` method to retrieve the data. That's the whole purpose behind the `READTEXT` SQL function, to allow us to read a manageable amount of text to work with.

We load the text box with the data in the `Comments_TX` field of the recordset and display a message that the selected text was read:

```
    'Display the text
    Text1.Text = m_objRS!Comments_TX
    Text2.Text = "Selected text read"
```

Then we close and de-reference our `Recordset` object and exit the procedure. The error handling routine needs no further explanation:

```
    'Close and de-reference Recordset object
    m_objRS.Close
    Set m_objRS = Nothing

    Exit Sub

cmdRead_Click_EH:
    Text1.Text = Empty
    For Each m_objErr In m_objConn.Errors
        Text1.Text = Text1.Text & m_objErr.Description & vbCrLf
    Next
End Sub
```

At this point we are ready to test this new functionality. The text that I chose to read in my program starts with the text that I added in the last example, as shown in the screen shot at the beginning of this Try It Out which is repeated below. You can experiment reading various portions of the text from any of the rows in the table, by specifying the `offset` and `length` values:

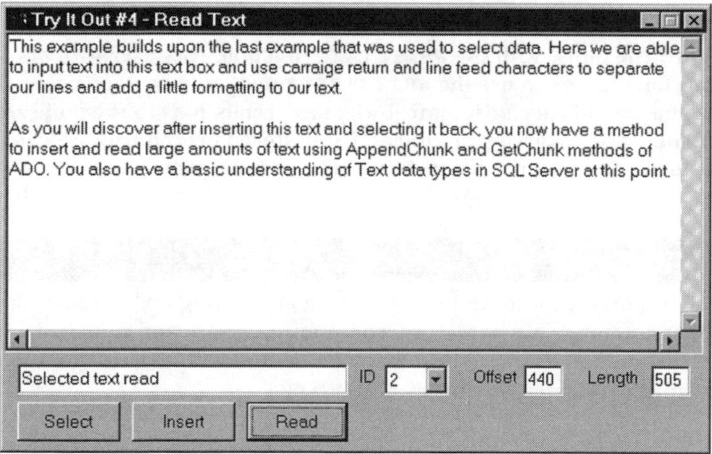

Writing Text Data

The WRITETEXT function in SQL Server provides a method to overwrite all existing text in a text column. This function replaces all text in the column, so use extreme caution. Up to this point we have used the INSERT statement to insert data into a text column, which was a logged transaction. The WRITETEXT function is typically a non-logged transaction and therefore can not be undone or recovered using the transaction log.

> *Note that there is an option to log the changes made by the WRITETEXT function, the WITH LOG argument seen in the syntax below. That is you must specifically turn logging on for this statement.*

After a WRITETEXT function has been performed a backup of the database should be done. The Backup Log SQL statement can not be used to back up the log after a non-logged operation has occurred; a full database backup must be performed. The next chapter will examine database and log backups in more detail.

The WRITETEXT function can only be used on a text column that has already been initialized. It can not be used to insert text into a column in a row that does not yet exist or contains a NULL value. We must use the INSERT statement to insert data into a text column before we can use the WRITETEXT function. The INSERT statement initializes the column with a valid text pointer to the text page.

The WRITETEXT function has the following format:

```
WRITETEXT table_name.column_name text_pointer [WITH LOG] data
```

The table name parameter specifies the table name that contains the text_column and the column_name parameter specifies the column that contains the text data. The text_pointer parameter evaluates to a valid text pointer or text pointer variable. The WITH LOG option logs this transaction and can quickly fill up your log. The data parameter is the data to be written.

> **There is one little quirk with the WRITETEXT function. Any user who has SELECT permissions on a table can use the WRITETEXT function to replace the existing data. Therefore you should carefully control who has permissions to the table and enforce the permissions using stored procedures. Using stored procedures, we can deny access to users who we don't want writing data to our text column.**

Try It Out #5 – Write Text

We need to create a stored procedure to write text in an existing text column, thereby replacing any existing text in that column. This stored procedure must declare and initialize a text pointer to be used by the WRITETEXT function. Because this stored procedure will be writing data to the text column, we must specify an input parameter with a Text data type.

1. The code below lists the stored procedure to be created. Because a user with SELECT permissions on a table has the authorization to the use the WRITETEXT function, we only want to grant permissions on this stored procedure to the Developers and Sales Staff Roles:

```
CREATE PROCEDURE up_parmupd_write_comments (@Comment_ID INT, @Text_Data TEXT) AS

--
*******************************************************************************
******
-- Declare variable for the text pointer
--
*******************************************************************************
******
DECLARE @Text_Pointer VARBINARY(16)

--
*******************************************************************************
******
-- Initialize the text pointer
--
*******************************************************************************
******
SELECT @Text_Pointer = TEXTPTR(Comments_TX)
     FROM Customer_Comment_T
     WHERE Customer_Comment_ID = @Comment_ID

--
*******************************************************************************
******
-- Write the text, replacing any existing text
--
*******************************************************************************
******
WRITETEXT Customer_Comment_T.Comments_TX @Text_Pointer @Text_Data
```

2. Start by copying the form from the last example as `frmTryItOut5`. Then start a new VB project and set a reference to the Microsoft ActiveX Data Objects Library. Remove the current form and add the `frmTryItOut5` form and set it as the default startup form in the Project Properties dialog.

3. Using the figure below, add a new button to the form and set its `Name` property to `cmdWrite` and its `Caption` property to `Write`:

   Again, this screen shot shows what you will see once you have run the program, not what it should look like now.

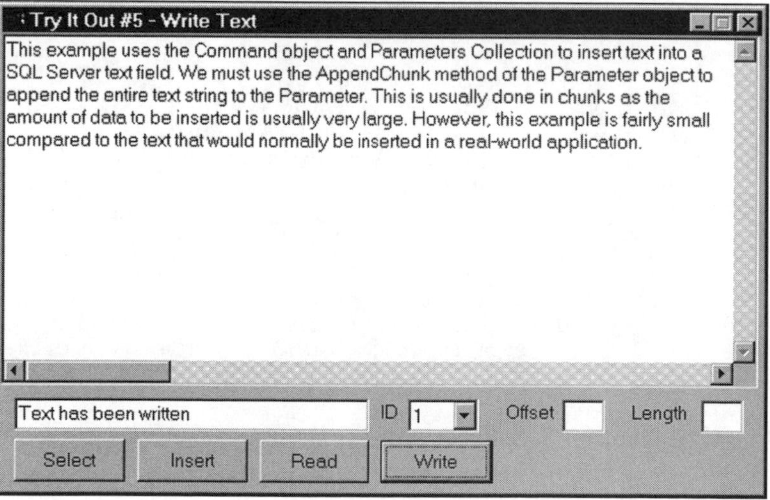

4. Add the following code to the `cmdWrite_Click` procedure:

```
Private Sub cmdWrite_Click()
   'Set up error handling
   On Error GoTo cmdWrite_Click_EH

   'Declare local variables
   Dim strSQL As String, lngChunk As Long, lngSize As Long, lngOffset As Long

   'Set a reference to the database objects
   Set m_objCmd = New ADODB.Command
   Set m_objParm = New ADODB.Parameter

   'Clear text boxes
   Text2.Text = Empty

   'Set the Command object properties
   Set m_objCmd.ActiveConnection = m_objConn
   m_objCmd.CommandText = "willist.up_parmupd_write_comments"
   m_objCmd.CommandType = adCmdStoredProc

   'Set the Parameter object properties
   m_objParm.Name = "Key"
   m_objParm.Type = adInteger
   m_objParm.Direction = adParamInput
   m_objParm.Value = CLng(cboID.Text)

   'Append the parameter to the Parameters collection
   'and reset Parameter object
   m_objCmd.Parameters.Append m_objParm
   Set m_objParm = Nothing
   Set m_objParm = New ADODB.Parameter

   'Set the Parameter object properties
   m_objParm.Attributes = adFldLong
   m_objParm.Name = "Comments"
   m_objParm.Type = adLongVarChar
   m_objParm.Direction = adParamInput
   m_objParm.Size = Len(Text1.Text)

   'Loop through the text box and append the text to the Parameter object
   lngChunk = 100
   lngOffset = 1
   lngSize = Len(Text1.Text)
   Do While lngOffset < lngSize
      m_objParm.AppendChunk Mid(Text1.Text, lngOffset, lngChunk)
      lngOffset = lngOffset + lngChunk
   Loop
```

```
    'Append the parameter to the Parameters collection and execute the
    'Command object
    m_objCmd.Parameters.Append m_objParm
    m_objCmd.Execute

    'Display the message
    Text2.Text = "Text has been written"

    'De-reference database objects
    Set m_objParm = Nothing
    Set m_objCmd = Nothing

    Exit Sub

cmdWrite_Click_EH:
    Text1.Text = Empty
    For Each m_objErr In m_objConn.Errors
       Text1.Text = Text1.Text & m_objErr.Description & vbCrLf
    Next
End Sub
```

How It Works

Stored Procedure

The stored procedure accepts two parameters, one for the row to update and one containing the data to write:

```
CREATE PROCEDURE up_parmupd_write_comments (@Comment_ID INT, @Text_Data TEXT) AS
```

Again we declare a variable that will be used as a text pointer and use the VarBinary data type:

```
--
***********************************************************************************
******
-- Declare variable for the text pointer
--
***********************************************************************************
******
DECLARE @Text_Pointer VARBINARY(16)
```

We initialize the text pointer using the row of data that we want to write our new text in:

```
--
***********************************************************************************
******
-- Initialize the text pointer
--
***********************************************************************************
******
SELECT @Text_Pointer = TEXTPTR(Comments_TX)
     FROM Customer_Comment_T
     Where Customer_Comment_ID = @Comment_ID
```

Using the WRITETEXT function we write the new text to the text column, replacing all existing data in that column. Here we have specified the table name and column name that should be used in the write operation and a valid text pointer:

```
--
******************************************************************************
******
-- Write the text, replacing any existing text
--
******************************************************************************
******
WRITETEXT Customer_Comment_T.Comments_TX @Text_Pointer @Text_Data
```

The code for the cmdWrite_Click procedure is very similar to the procedure to insert data. This procedure sets up the error handling and declares the local variables:

```
Private Sub cmdWrite_Click()
   'Set up error handling
   On Error GoTo cmdWrite_Click_EH

   'Declare local variables
   Dim strSQL As String, lngChunk As Long, lngSize As Long, lngOffset As Long
```

Then we set a reference to our database objects and clear the text box that we display our messages in:

```
   'Set a reference to the database objects
   Set m_objCmd = New ADODB.Command
   Set m_objParm = New ADODB.Parameter

   'Clear text boxes
   Text2.Text = Empty
```

Writing text in a text column is basically the same as inserting data. There could be a large amount of text, and we must use the AppendChunk method of the Parameter object. Therefore we use the Command object and set it to the stored procedure we want to execute:

```
   'Set the Command object properties
   Set m_objCmd.ActiveConnection = m_objConn
   m_objCmd.CommandText = "willist.up_parmupd_write_comments"
   m_objCmd.CommandType = adCmdStoredProc
```

Because this stored procedure accepts two input parameters, we set the properties of the first parameter, which contains the ID of the row that we will be writing data to. We are using the ID contained in the Text property of the combo box as the Value property of the Parameter object:

```
   'Set the Parameter object properties
   m_objParm.Name = "Key"
   m_objParm.Type = adInteger
   m_objParm.Direction = adParamInput
   m_objParm.Value = CLng(cboID.Text)
```

After all of the `Parameter` properties have been set, we append the `Parameter` object to the `Parameters` collection, and then reset the `Parameter` object for the next parameter:

```
'Append the parameter to the Parameters collection
'and reset Parameter object
m_objCmd.Parameters.Append m_objParm
Set m_objParm = Nothing
Set m_objParm = New ADODB.Parameter
```

The second parameter contains the actual text that is to be written, and we must set the `Attributes` property using the `adFldLong` constant. We once again set the `Size` property to the length of the text box using the `Len` function:

```
'Set the Parameter object properties
m_objParm.Attributes = adFldLong
m_objParm.Name = "Comments"
m_objParm.Type = adLongVarChar
m_objParm.Direction = adParamInput
m_objParm.Size = Len(Text1.Text)
```

As with the `INSERT` procedure, we perform a loop appending text to the `Parameter` object in 100 byte increments using the `AppendChunk` method:

```
'Loop through the text box and append the text to the Parameter object
lngChunk = 100
lngOffset = 1
lngSize = Len(Text1.Text)
Do While lngOffset < lngSize
   m_objParm.AppendChunk Mid(Text1.Text, lngOffset, lngChunk)
   lngOffset = lngOffset + lngChunk
Loop
```

After all the data has been appended to the `Parameter` object, we add the `Parameter` object to the `Parameters` collection and execute the `Command` object:

```
'Append the parameter to the Parameters collection and execute the
'Command object
m_objCmd.Parameters.Append m_objParm
m_objCmd.Execute
```

Then we display a message that the text has been written, and clean up by de-referencing our database objects. Then we exit the procedure:

```
'Display the message
Text2.Text = "Text has been written"

'De-reference database objects
Set m_objParm = Nothing
Set m_objCmd = Nothing

Exit Sub
```

Our error handling routine needs no further explanation:

```
cmdWrite_Click_EH:
   Text1.Text = Empty
   For Each m_objErr In m_objConn.Errors
      Text1.Text = Text1.Text & m_objErr.Description & vbCrLf
   Next
End Sub
```

To test this new function, I selected the text for the first row of data in the `Customer_Comment_T` table. I then added carriage return line feeds to the text by pressing the Enter key, so the text would fit in the text box without having to scroll horizontally. Then I used the procedure above, by clicking the `Write` button, to write the new text to the first row, replacing the existing text that was there. The results of this test are shown in the screen shot at the beginning of this Try It Out which is repeated below:

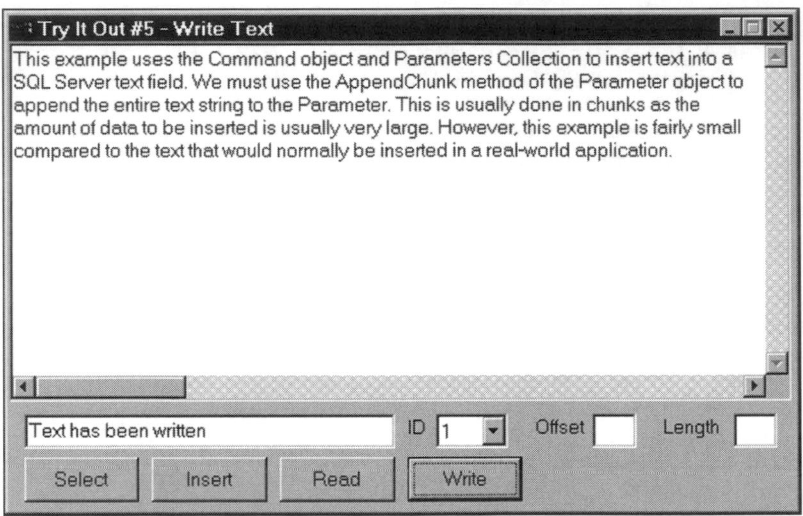

Updating Text Data

As you might have guessed, since we can read and write text data, there must be a function that allows us to update text data. The `UPDATETEXT` function allows us to do just that. This is a very powerful function because not only can we update a certain portion of the text, we can also delete it using this function.

The `UPDATETEXT` function has the following format:

```
UPDATETEXT table_name.column_name text_pointer
     NULL|offset
     NULL|length
     [WITH LOG]
     insert_data|source_table_name.source_column_name source_text_pointer
```

As you can see from the format of this function it is very powerful and versatile many options. We are going to explore just one of the many possible options of the `UPDATETEXT` function.

The `table_name` parameter specifies the table name to be updated and the `column_name` parameter specifies the column to be updated. The `text_pointer` parameter specifies a valid text pointer that must be initialized before use.

> **You can either use a `NULL` value for the `offset` or specify a value, which indicates the starting position for the update. A `NULL` value indicates that the text is to be appended at the end of the existing text.**
>
> **The `length` parameter can contain either a `NULL` value or the length of the data to be updated. If a `NULL` value is passed for this parameter, all data starting at the `offset` to the end of the text column is deleted. If you specify a zero for this parameter, then no data is deleted and just new data is appended. If a value other than zero is specified then that is the length of data that will be updated.**

The `WITH LOG` keywords specify that this operation should be logged in the transaction log, so that it may be recovered if necessary. This can quickly increase the size of the log file and should be used with caution. If this option is going to be used, you need to ensure your log file has the Automatically Grow File option checked and the Unrestricted File Growth option checked. These were discussed in Chapter 3.

The `insert_data` parameter can be used as the source of data for the update. If you choose not to supply a source parameter, you can update the existing text with data from another text column. The `source_table_name` and `source_column_name` parameters specify the table and column name that should be used as the source of text. Along with that is a `source_text_pointer`, which contains a valid text pointer to the source.

As you can see from all of the various parameters of the `UPDATETEXT` function, this function provides multiple uses and is very powerful. For our discussion here today, we are going to use this function to update a specific portion of text in our text column with a parameter that we supply.

You should keep in mind that you could use the `UPDATETEXT` function to delete a portion or all of the text in a text column. You can also use this function to append text to the end of the text column.

The source of the data to be used to update existing text or to be appended can come from either a parameter that you supply or from another text column in the same or a different table.

Try It Out #6 – Update Text

The stored procedure that we want to create will update a portion of text in the text column with new text. This stored procedure will require that both the `offset` and `length` parameters be passed along with the text to be used as the insert data parameter of the `UPDATETEXT` function.

1. The code for this stored procedure is listed below:

```
CREATE PROCEDURE up_parmupd_update_comments (@Comment_ID INT, @Offset INT, @Length
INT,
     @Text_Data TEXT) AS
```

```
--
***************************************************************************************
******
-- Declare variable for the text pointer
--
***************************************************************************************
******
DECLARE @Text_Pointer VARBINARY(16)

--
***************************************************************************************
******
-- Initialize the text pointer
--
***************************************************************************************
******
SELECT @Text_Pointer = TEXTPTR(Comments_TX)
     FROM Customer_Comment_T
     WHERE Customer_Comment_ID = @Comment_ID

--
***************************************************************************************
******
-- Update a specific portion of text data
--
***************************************************************************************
******
UPDATETEXT Customer_Comment_T.Comments_TX @Text_Pointer @Offset @Length @Text_Data
```

2. Start by copying the form from the last example as `frmTryItOut6`. Then start a new VB project and set a reference to the Microsoft ActiveX Data Objects Library. Remove the current form, add the new form and set it as the default startup form in the Project Properties dialog.

3. Using the figure below as a guide, add a command button to the form and set its `Name` property to `cmdUpdate` and its `Caption` property to `Update`:

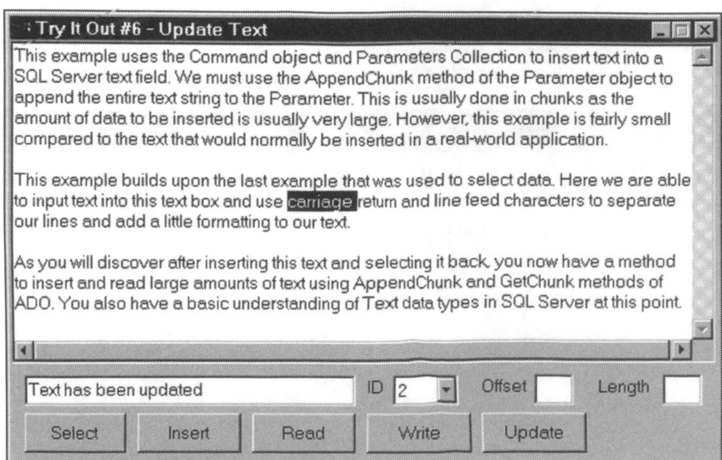

Again, this screen shot shows what you will see once you have run the program, not what it should look like now.

4. The code for the `cmdUpdate_Click` procedure is listed next:

```
Private Sub cmdUpdate_Click()
   'Set up error handling
   On Error GoTo cmdUpdate_Click_EH

   'Declare local variables
   Dim strSQL As String, lngSize As Long, lngOffset As Long

   'Set a reference to the database objects
   Set m_objCmd = New ADODB.Command

   'Clear text boxes
   Text2.Text = Empty

   'Determine offset and size to be updated
   lngOffset = InStr(1, Text1.Text, Text1.SelText, vbTextCompare) - 1
   lngSize = Len(Text1.SelText)

   'Set the Command object properties
   Set m_objCmd.ActiveConnection = m_objConn
   m_objCmd.CommandText = "willist.up_parmupd_update_comments"
   m_objCmd.CommandType = adCmdStoredProc

   'Append the parameters
   m_objCmd.Parameters.Append m_objCmd.CreateParameter("Key", adInteger, _
     adParamInput, CLng(cboID.Text))
   m_objCmd.Parameters.Append m_objCmd.CreateParameter("OffSet", adInteger, _
     adParamInput, lngOffset)
   m_objCmd.Parameters.Append m_objCmd.CreateParameter("Length", adInteger, _
     adParamInput, lngSize)
   m_objCmd.Parameters.Append m_objCmd.CreateParameter("Text", adLongVarChar, _
     adParamInput, lngSize, Text1.SelText)

   'Execute the Command object
   m_objCmd.Execute

   'Display the message
   Text2.Text = "Text has been updated"

   'De-reference database objects
   Set m_objCmd = Nothing

   Exit Sub
```

```
cmdUpdate_Click_EH:
   Text1.Text = Empty
   For Each m_objErr In m_objConn.Errors
      Text1.Text = Text1.Text & m_objErr.Description & vbCrLf
   Next
End Sub
```

How It Works

Stored Procedure

The stored procedure to update text requires four parameters. The first parameter is the `ID` of the row that we want to update. The second and third parameters contain the `offset` and `length` of text to be updated, and the last parameter contains the text that will be used to update the existing text with:

```
CREATE PROCEDURE up_parmupd_update_comments (@Comment_ID INT, @Offset INT, @Length
INT,
     @Text_Data TEXT) AS
```

Once again we must declare and initialize a text pointer to be used to access the text in the text column:

```
--
*********************************************************************************
******
-- Declare variable for the text pointer
--
*********************************************************************************
******
DECLARE @Text_Pointer VARBINARY(16)

--
*********************************************************************************
******
-- Initialize the text pointer
--
*********************************************************************************
******
SELECT @Text_Pointer = TEXTPTR(Comments_TX)
     FROM Customer_Comment_T
     WHERE Customer_Comment_ID = @Comment_ID
```

As we mentioned above, we are going to be using the `UPDATETEXT` function to update existing text with new text. Here we have specified the table name and column name that we want to update, along with the text pointer variable. We have also specified the `offset` and `length` variables that point to the specific text to be updated, and text data parameter contains the text that will be used to update the existing text:

```
--
*****************************************************************************
******
-- Update a specific portion of text data
--
*****************************************************************************
******
UPDATETEXT Customer_Comment_T.Comments_TX @Text_Pointer @Offset @Length @Text_Data
```

cmdUpdate_Click Procedure

Switching to the VB code, we start the `cmdUpdate_Click` procedure by setting up the error handling and declaring our local variables:

```
Private Sub cmdUpdate_Click()
   'Set up error handling
   On Error GoTo cmdUpdate_Click_EH

   'Declare local variables
   Dim strSQL As String, lngSize As Long, lngOffset As Long
```

Then we set a reference to the `Command` object and clear the text box that is used to display messages:

```
   'Set a reference to the database objects
   Set m_objCmd = New ADODB.Command

   'Clear text boxes
   Text2.Text = Empty
```

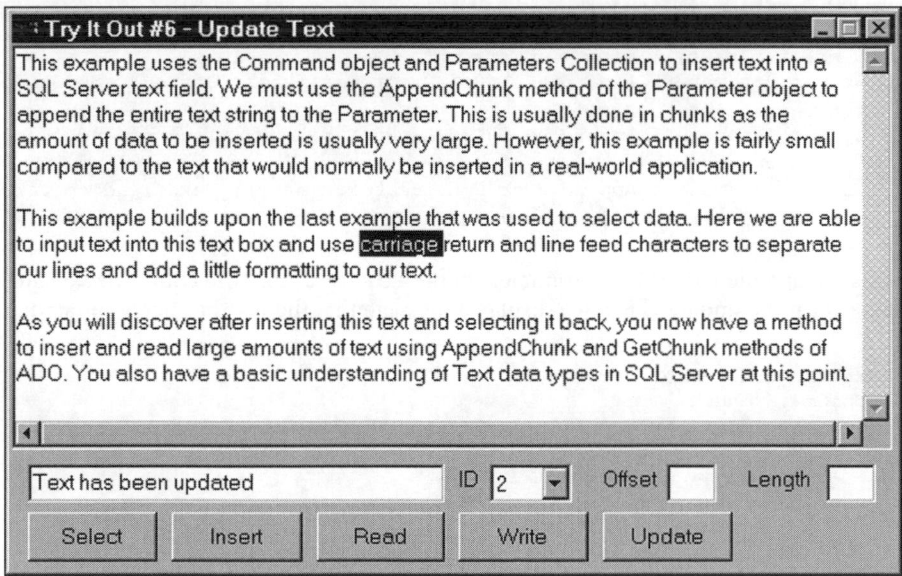

The text that is highlighted in the text box, as seen in the screen shot above, is the text that we want to update in the database. Based on that, we set the lngOffset variable to the starting position of the text using the value returned by the InStr function. The InStr function is used to find the text that is highlighted in the text box. Then, using the length of the highlighted text, we set the lngSize variable:

```
'Determine offset and size to be updated
lngOffset = InStr(1, Text1.Text, Text1.SelText, vbTextCompare) - 1
lngSize = Len(Text1.SelText)
```

Next, we set the Command object properties to execute the stored procedure:

```
'Set the Command object properties
Set m_objCmd.ActiveConnection = m_objConn
m_objCmd.CommandText = "willist.up_parmupd_update_comments"
m_objCmd.CommandType = adCmdStoredProc
```

Since all of the input parameters are simple, we can use the CreateParameter method of the Command object to create and append our parameters to the Parameters collection. The value for the first parameter, which is the ID of the row to be updated, is retrieved using the Text property of the combo box. Again we must convert the value to a long data type, and have done so using the CLng function.

The second and third parameters are using the variables that we set above for the offset and length.

The last parameter contains the text that will be used to update the text in the database. This text is retrieved from the highlighted text in the text box on the form:

```
'Append the parameters
m_objCmd.Parameters.Append m_objCmd.CreateParameter("Key", adInteger, _
    adParamInput, , CLng(cboID.Text))
m_objCmd.Parameters.Append m_objCmd.CreateParameter("OffSet", adInteger, _
    adParamInput, , lngOffset)
m_objCmd.Parameters.Append m_objCmd.CreateParameter("Length", adInteger, _
    adParamInput, , lngSize)
m_objCmd.Parameters.Append m_objCmd.CreateParameter("Text", adLongVarChar, _
    adParamInput, lngSize, Text1.SelText)
```

After we have appended all of our parameters to the Parameters collection, we execute the Command object to perform the update. Then we display a message that the text has been updated:

```
'Execute the Command object
m_objCmd.Execute

'Display the message
Text2.Text = "Text has been updated"
```

We close and de-reference the Command object and exit the procedure. The error handling routine needs no explanation:

```
    'De-reference database objects
    Set m_objCmd = Nothing

    Exit Sub

cmdUpdate_Click_EH:
    Text1.Text = Empty
    For Each m_objErr In m_objConn.Errors
        Text1.Text = Text1.Text & m_objErr.Description & vbCrLf
    Next
End Sub
```

To test this project I selected the text for the second row in the table, by choosing the entry number 2 in the combo box and then clicked on the Select button. I then changed the word carriage as I had misspelled it before. I corrected the word, then highlighted it and clicked on the Update button. The results of my test are shown in the screen shot at the beginning of this Try It Out (the previous screenshot is a repeat of this).

Deleting Text Data

Deleting text data can be performed in a couple of different ways. The first method that you could use is a method described above, using the UPDATETEXT function. The second method you could use is the traditional way, which is to delete the row of data. These two methods differ greatly in that the first method only deletes the data in the text column, leaving the row of data in the table, while the second method deletes the entire row of data. Depending on what other columns exist in a row of data, it might be better to just delete the data in the text column.

Let's take a look at the first method, using the UPDATETEXT function. When we delete all of the data in the text column, SQL Server leaves a valid text pointer in that column in the data row of our table. Therefore we can perform any operation on the text column using the READTEXT, WRITETEXT and UPDATETEXT functions. Of course the text page that the text pointer points to actually contains no data. The length of the text is zero.

Let's try a little experiment. Using the last program that you created above, insert a new row of text data. The amount of text that you insert is not important. Check the text that you inserted by selecting it using the Select button. The text that I inserted for my experiment was the third row of data in the Customer_Comment_T table.

Using the following code, enter and run this query in the Query Analyzer substituting the ID of the row of data that you inserted:

```
--
*******************************************************************************
******
-- Declare variable for the text pointer
```

```
--
*****************************************************************************
******
DECLARE @Text_Pointer VARBINARY(16)

--
*****************************************************************************
******
-- Initialize the text pointer
--
*****************************************************************************
******
SELECT @Text_Pointer = TEXTPTR(Comments_TX)
     FROM Customer_Comment_T
     WHERE Customer_Comment_ID = 3

--
*****************************************************************************
******
-- Update a specific portion of text data
--
*****************************************************************************
******
UPDATETEXT Customer_Comment_T.Comments_TX @Text_Pointer 0 NULL
```

Because we have specified an `offset` value of zero and a `length` of `NULL`, all data will be deleted, starting at `offset` zero. Notice that we did not supply a value or variable for the text to be inserted because we want to delete data, not update existing data.

To verify that a valid text pointer still exists for the deleted row, enter and run the following query. This query will list all text pointers for all rows in the table. You will notice that a valid text pointer still exists for the row of data that was deleted:

```
SELECT Customer_Comment_ID, TEXTPTR(Comments_TX) AS Text_Pointers
     FROM Customer_Comment_T
     ORDER BY Customer_Comment_ID
```

Now, to verify the length of the row of data that was deleted, compared to the other rows, enter and run this query:

```
SELECT DATALENGTH(Comments_TX) AS Length_Of_Text
     FROM Customer_Comment_T
     ORDER BY Customer_Comment_ID
```

As you can see, the length of the text column that was deleted using the `UPDATETEXT` function is now zero, but we still have a valid text pointer and can perform any operation on this column using any of the text functions that require a valid text pointer.

You can now use the WRITETEXT or UPDATETEXT functions to re-populate this column. If you are using the WRITETEXT function, you can use the last program that you built to first select the data for the column that was deleted. You will receive a message that 0 bytes were read. Then enter some text and then click on the Write button and the text will be written to the column.

If you want to use the UPDATETEXT function to repopulate this column you will need to use a query similar to the one shown below:

```
--
***********************************************************************************
******
-- Declare variable for the text pointer
--
***********************************************************************************
******
DECLARE @Text_Pointer VARBINARY(16)

--
***********************************************************************************
******
-- Initialize the text pointer
--
***********************************************************************************
******
SELECT @Text_Pointer = TEXTPTR(Comments_TX)
     FROM Customer_Comment_T
     WHERE Customer_Comment_ID = 3

--
***********************************************************************************
******
-- Update a specific portion of text data
--
***********************************************************************************
******
UPDATETEXT Customer_Comment_T.Comments_TX @Text_Pointer 0 0 'This is some data'
```

Notice that we have specified zero for the length of data to be deleted. This means no text will be deleted/updated and the inserted data that is specified will be appended to the end of the column, which in this case would be at the beginning.

As you can see, the UpdateText function can be used for more than just updating a specific portion of the text contained in a text column. We have shown that it can also be used to delete the entire text in the column, and then be used to repopulate the column with data.

The second method of deleting data is more permanent than the first method. This is the traditional method of deleting data, whereby we delete the entire row. This method uses the DELETE statement that we covered in Chapter 12. We specify the specific ID of the row of data that we want to delete and the row is deleted, gone forever. This is the method that we will use in the last example for our program.

Try It Out #7 – Delete Data

This example uses the traditional method to delete a row of data.

1. The stored procedure listed below is very simple and straightforward:

```
CREATE PROCEDURE up_parmdel_comments (@Comment_ID INT) AS

--
*******************************************************************************
******
-- Delete comments
--
*******************************************************************************
******
DELETE FROM Customer_Comment_T
       WHERE Customer_Comment_ID = @Comment_ID
```

2. To implement this functionality into your VB project, start a new VB project and set a reference to the Microsoft ActiveX Data Objects Library. Then copy the `frmTryItOut6` form as `frmTryItOut7`. Remove the current form from your project and add the new form. Set this form as the default start up form in the Project Properties dialog.

3. Using the figure below as a guide, add a new button and set its `Name` property to `cmdDelete` and its `Caption` property to `Delete`:

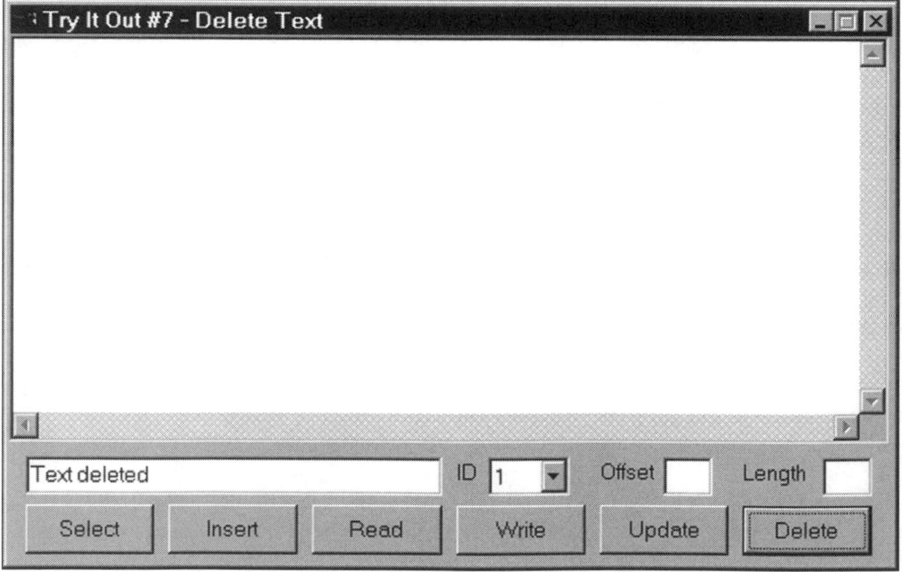

4. Add the following code the `cmdDelete_Click` procedure:

```
Private Sub cmdDelete_Click()
   'Set up error handling
   On Error GoTo cmdDelete_Click_EH

   'Set a reference to the database objects
   Dim m_objCmd As New ADODB.Command

   'Clear text boxes
   Text2.Text = Empty

   'Set the Command object properties
   Set m_objCmd.ActiveConnection = m_objConn
   m_objCmd.CommandText = "willist.up_parmdel_comments (" & CLng(cboID.Text) & ")"
   m_objCmd.CommandType = adCmdStoredProc

   'Execute the Command object
   m_objCmd.Execute

   'Display the message
   Text2.Text = "Text deleted"

   'De-reference database objects
   Set m_objCmd = Nothing

   'Reload combo box
   Call LoadIDs

   Exit Sub

cmdDelete_Click_EH:
   Text1.Text = Empty
   For Each m_objErr In m_objConn.Errors
      Text1.Text = Text1.Text & m_objErr.Description & vbCrLf
   Next
End Sub
```

How It Works

Stored Procedure

This stored procedure is very simple. We delete a row of data from the `Customer_Comment_T` table where the `Customer_Comment_ID` matches the value passed in by the parameter `@Comment_ID`:

```
CREATE PROCEDURE up_parmdel_comments (@Comment_ID INT) AS

--
*******************************************************************************
******
-- Delete comments
--
*******************************************************************************
******
DELETE FROM Customer_Comment_T
     WHERE Customer_Comment_ID = @Comment_ID
```

cmdDelete_Click Procedure

The `cmdDelete_Click` procedure sets up the error handling and sets a reference to the `Command` object. There are no local variables for this procedure. We then clear any message that may be in the text box that is used to display messages:

```
Private Sub cmdDelete_Click()
   'Set up error handling
   On Error GoTo cmdDelete_Click_EH

   'Set a reference to the database objects
   Dim m_objCmd As New ADODB.Command

   'Clear text boxes
   Text2.Text = Empty
```

We set the `Command` object properties to the stored procedure that we want to execute. We pass it the one and only parameter, which is the ID contained in the combo box. Again we need to convert the value in the combo box to a `long` value using the `CLng` function:

```
   'Set the Command object properties
   Set m_objCmd.ActiveConnection = m_objConn
   m_objCmd.CommandText = "willist.up_parmdel_comments (" & CLng(cboID.Text) & ")"
   m_objCmd.CommandType = adCmdStoredProc
```

We execute the `Command` object, and then display a message that the text was deleted:

```
   'Execute the Command object
   m_objCmd.Execute

   'Display the message
   Text2.Text = "Text deleted"
```

Then we de-reference our `Command` object, and call the procedure to reload the combo box to remove the entry that was deleted. Then we exit the procedure. The error handler needs no explanation:

```
   'De-reference database objects
   Set m_objCmd = Nothing

   'Reload combo box
   Call LoadIDs

   Exit Sub

cmdDelete_Click_EH:
   Text1.Text = Empty
   For Each m_objErr In m_objConn.Errors
      Text1.Text = Text1.Text & m_objErr.Description & vbCrLf
   Next
End Sub
```

You can test this code and delete a row of data from the `Customer_Comment_T` table. This row will be permanently deleted, so ensure it is one that you want to delete.

Summary

While the methods discussed in this chapter have dealt solely with the SQL Server Text data type, all of the methods apply equally to the nText and Image data types as well. If you recall from the discussion at the beginning of this chapter, the nText data type contains variable length Unicode data and the Image data type contains variable length binary data.

This chapter has explained how SQL Server manages the Text, nText and Image data types and how we obtain and use text pointers to this data. We have demonstrated through practical examples how to declare and initialize a text pointer and then use it to read, write and update data. We have also discussed and shown an example on how to verify the text pointer returned is valid.

We have walked through some examples that inserted and selected data from a text column; and have shown how ADO can be a useful tool to aid us in working with the large amounts of data contained in a text column. Using the GetChunk and AppendChunk methods, we now know how to read and write large amounts of data to and from the database using our VB program.

After going through the examples that use the READTEXT, WRITETEXT and UPDATETEXT functions, you can see how these functions allow you to manipulate and manage small blocks of data in a text column. These functions proved to be useful in allowing us to work with this data in an efficient manner.

Further exploration of the UPDATETEXT method has shown that not only can this method be used to update specific blocks of data, but it can also be used to delete all of the data in a text column. While this method deletes the data in a text column, it leaves a valid text pointer that can be used with the WRITETEXT, UPDATETEXT and READTEXT methods.

In summary, you should know how:

- To obtain and use a text pointer
- SQL Server stores data for a text column
- To insert and select data to and from a text column
- To read, write and update data in a text column
- To use the UPDATETEXT function to delete data in a text column

WROX AUTO WORKS RACING

Preparing for the Test and Production Environments

In the previous chapters we have used the fictitious car company *Wrox Auto Works* and have built for them a sample front-end program and a business server component. Along with these are the numerous stored procedures, roles, and tables that we have developed. All of these items must now be prepared for implementation in the test and production environments.

There are several issues that must be taken into consideration when preparing your application for the move to the test and production environments. First and foremost, we must consider the database. Have we done all we can do to optimize the tables by using the appropriate indexes? Have we used normalized tables in our database design? How about our stored procedures – are they efficiently designed? Then there are the programs to think about. Are they ready to be moved to test and production?

All of these questions will be answered in this chapter, as we take a look at what is required to prepare our database and programs for the move to the test and production environments.

We will be exploring how to design a backup strategy for our database and transaction log. We need to ensure that we have the appropriate indexes, and will take a look at the `Index Tuning Wizard`. Then there comes the question of how to get the database from development to test and production. We will take a look at generating the appropriate scripts to achieve this, and also what modifications need to be made to our programs.

In this chapter we will cover:

- Index tuning
- Database and transaction log backups
- Generating scripts
- Preparing our programs

Index Tuning

We have developed and tested all of our code in the development environment and are ready to prepare our application for the move to the production environment. Once in the production environment, real users will be accessing the application, and any problems which arise will have a real impact on the operation of the business. So before we deploy the application for real, we move it to the test environment. The test environment should be an exact duplicate of the production environment, and offers us the chance to thoroughly test all functionality before we move the application into production.

Now that we have written our last line of code and are ready to move our application to the test environment, we must first examine a few things. We want our application to perform optimally, and we need to ensure that we have done everything possible to optimize our database. Probably the single most important task that we can perform to ensure optimal efficiency of our database, outside of a good physical design, is to ensure that we have the appropriate *indexes.*

The appropriate indexes, and mix of indexes, can improve the performance of our database and increase the speed of our stored procedures. Our stored procedures and queries benefit from the use of indexes when we specify the `WHERE` and `ORDER BY` clauses. Any SQL statement that specifies how data is selected or ordered can benefit from an index. Designing the right index and especially the right mix of indexes can sometimes be difficult.

SQL Server provides a powerful tool to aid us in this area. The **Index Tuning Wizard** performs a complete analysis of our tables, current indexes, and stored procedures, and recommends the best possible mix of indexes based on a particular **workload**.

A workload is an event log of selected activities performed against the database. This log is created by capturing a sequence (**trace**) of events. SQL statements such as `SELECT`, `INSERT`, `UPDATE`, and `DELETE` can be captured. You can also capture information from stored procedures, such as when a stored procedure, or a statement within it, begins and ends. The workload is created using the **SQL Server Profiler** and the trace of events is saved to a file or table.

Before we can run the Index Tuning Wizard, we must first create a workload file. Thus we must use the SQL Server Profiler. This allows us to set up a filter of those events that we want captured. The SQL Server Profiler then runs in real time and captures the events that are performed against the database by our application.

After we have set up the events that we want captured, we start the SQL Server Profiler. We then run our application, going through all of the functions, and executing all of the stored procedures that we have written. After we have exercised the complete functionality of our application, we end our application, stop the SQL Server Profiler, and our trace file is saved with a complete workload. The Index Tuning Wizard then uses this workload file, examines the events, and recommends the best possible mix of indexes.

Now that we have a basic understanding of the steps involved in tuning our indexes, let's get started by creating a workload file for the Index Tuning Wizard.

Try It Out – Using the SQL Server Profiler to Capture a Workload

1. Start the Enterprise Manager, expand the Database group and select the Wrox_Auto_Works database. On the Tools menu, choose SQL Server Profiler. The SQL Server Profiler comes up with an empty window. We want to start a new trace, so click on the New Trace icon on the toolbar to invoke the Trace Properties dialog.

2. The first tab, General, contains general information about the trace that we want to set up. We need to enter a name for the trace and specify how we want the trace saved. I chose to enter a Trace Name of Wrox Trace and chose to capture the trace to a file. A private trace type only allows the user who created the trace file to access it while a shared trace type allows all users to share the trace file.

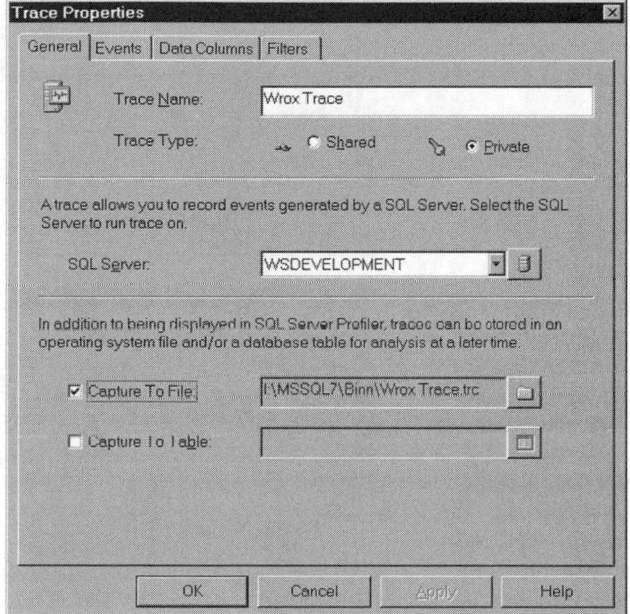

3. The second tab, Events, lists all the available events generated by SQL Server that can be captured by the SQL Server Profiler. The events that we are interested in are shown in the Available events list, in the SQL Operators category. We need to add the Delete, Insert, Select, and Update events to the list of Selected events that we want to trace, and we do so by selecting them in the Available events list and clicking on the Add button.

4. The next category that we want to look at is Stored Procedures. We want to add all events in this category to our list of Selected events.

5. The last category that we need to choose from is Transactions. We need only choose the SQL Transaction event as this event traces all BEGIN, COMMIT, SAVE, and ROLLBACK TRANSACTION statements. At this point the Trace Properties dialog should look like this:

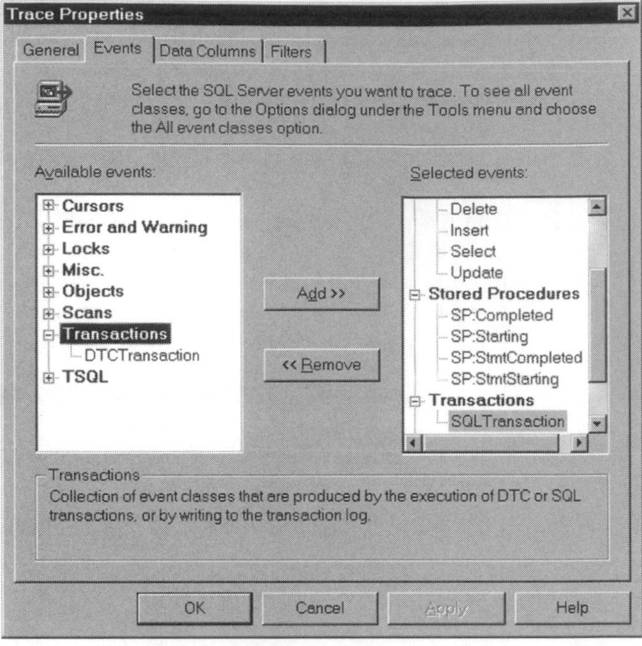

6. Switching to the Data Columns tab, we want to select data columns that are applicable to our database. This tab contains the data columns that can be captured for each **event class**. Event classes are the different events that can be captured, such as stored procedures or transactions starting and ending. Not all data columns are applicable for every event class. We want to select all data columns except the ones shown in the Unselected data list below:

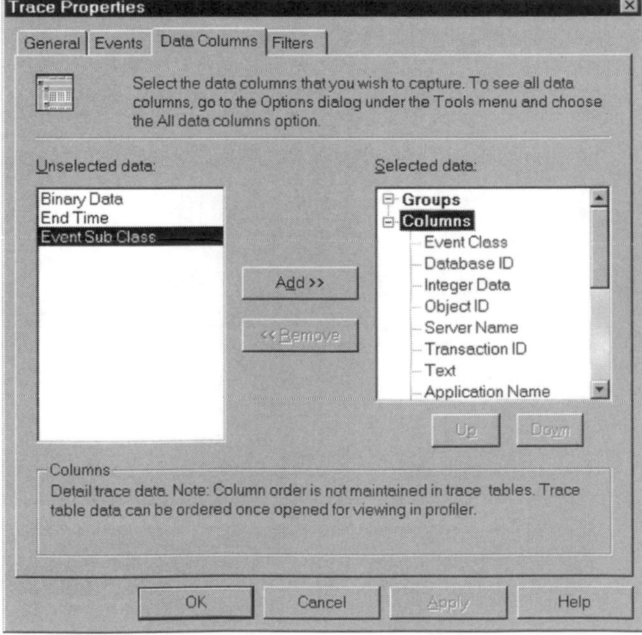

7. We will accept all the defaults on the Filters tab. This tab specifies the criteria for capturing events. You can specify values, and minimum and maximum values for certain events. You can also specify that certain events be included or excluded.

8. Click OK to save the properties that we have selected and to close the dialog. The trace starts running and is waiting to capture events generated by SQL Server.

9. To generate the appropriate events we need to run the final program (`WAWCustomerApplication`) that was compiled in Chapter 14. Exercise all of the options in the program by selecting, inserting, and updating data for different customers.

10. When you have exercised the program by going through all of the functions, end the program and switch back to the SQL Server Profiler. On the toolbar click the Stop Traces button to end the trace. Once the trace has been stopped, exit the SQL Server Profiler. The trace data has been written to the trace file and is now ready for use by the Index Tuning Wizard. The following screenshot shows a segment of the trace for the actions I carried out in step 9:

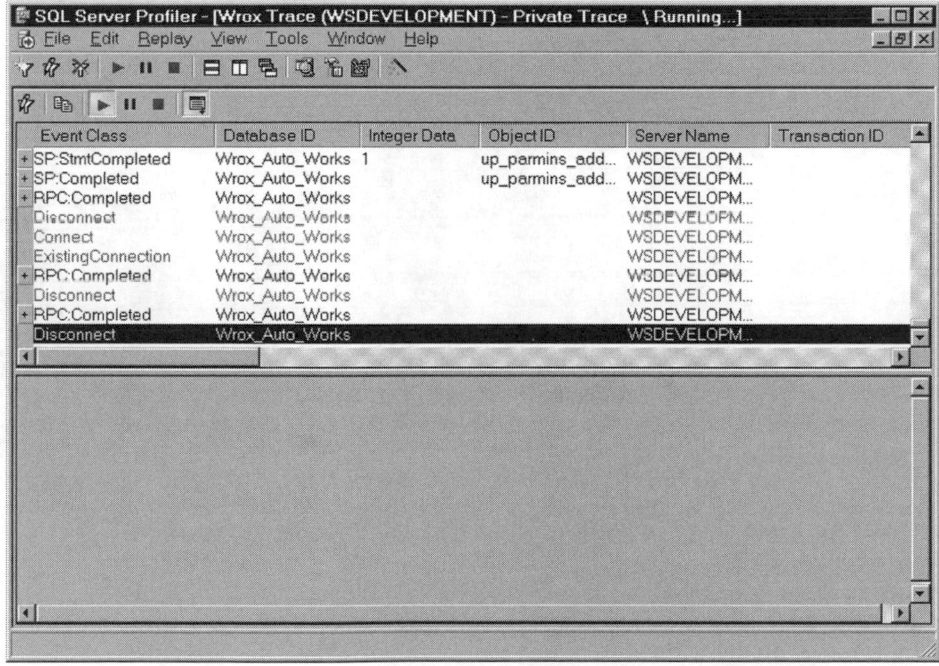

When you are through, you can close the SQL Server Profiler. We are now ready to use our workload with the Index Tuning Wizard. Not only does the Index Tuning Wizard recommend the best mix of indexes for our database, but it also analyzes the effects that the changes it proposes will have on the database. An Analysis button is provided after the analysis has been performed to show the various scenarios that the Index Tuning Wizard has come up with.

Try It Out – Using the Index Tuning Wizard

1. To start the Index Tuning Wizard, select the Tools menu in the Enterprise Manager and then select Wizards. In the Select Wizard dialog, expand the Management group and select Index Tuning Wizard.

2. The first step of the Index Tuning Wizard is an introductory screen that explains what the Index Tuning Wizard will do for you. Click the Next button to proceed to the next step.

3. The next screen of the Index Tuning Wizard, shown below, gathers some basic information about what database is to be tuned and what type of analysis it should perform. Select the correct server and the Wrox_Auto_Works database, and uncheck the Keep all existing indexes option. Then check the Perform thorough analysis checkbox. Selecting this checkbox will allow the Index Tuning Wizard to perform a thorough analysis on the workload file that we created with the SQL Server Profiler, and drop and replace indexes on our tables as it sees fit.

4. Click the Next button to proceed:

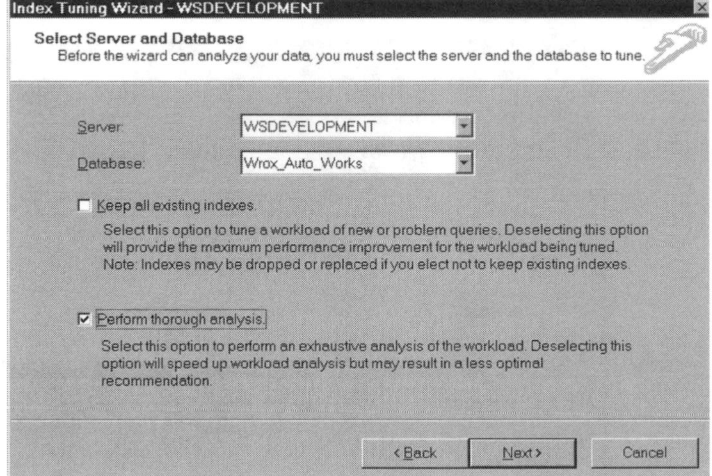

5. This next step of the Index Tuning Wizard identifies the workload. Check the I have a saved workload file option button and click Next to specify the name and location of the workload file.

6. In the Workload frame, check the My workload file option button, and then click on the button next to the textbox to open your saved workload file. The Advanced Options button near the bottom of this dialog provides some index tuning parameters. The options specified here are more than adequate for the size of our database. If we had a very large database that we expected to grow by gigabytes, we would need to adjust the Maximum space for the recommended indexes parameter. Click the Next button to proceed to the next step:

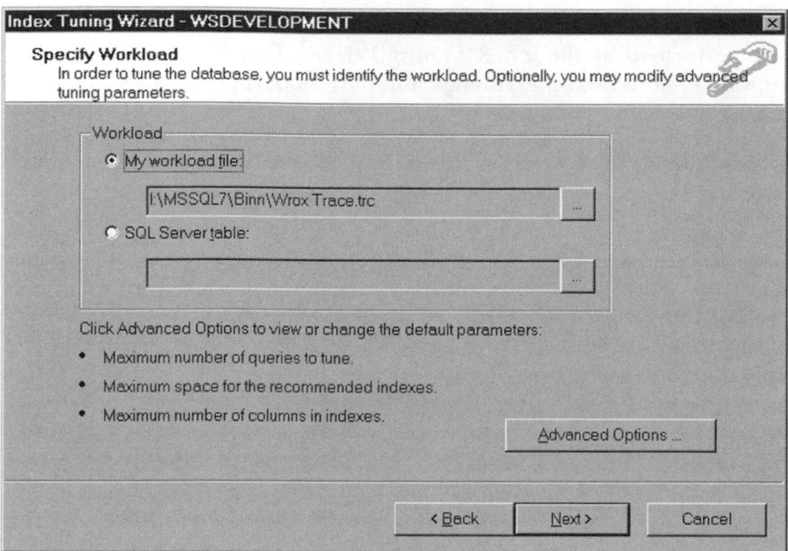

7. The next step lists the tables to tune and by default all tables are selected. You can, if needed, remove certain tables from the list of table to be tuned. However, for our purposes we want to tune *all* tables. Click the Next button to proceed.

8. The next step starts the analysis and tuning of your indexes. When the analysis is complete the screen below is shown. As you can see, we had already chosen the best possible mix of indexes for our database, and we will therefore see no improvement:

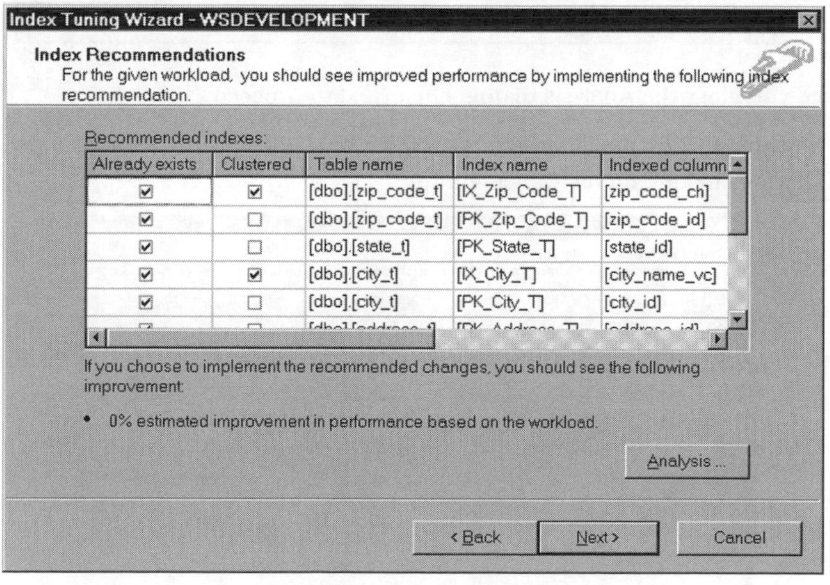

9. Before leaving this step of the wizard, click on the Analysis button to view a complete analysis performed by the Index Tuning Wizard. Of particular interest is the last report in the Reports combo box: the Tuning Summary Report. This report summarizes the operations of the Index Tuning Wizard.

10. The Index Tuning Wizard has recommended that no indexes be created and has not recommended dropping any of our existing indexes. You can save the various reports on this screen to a text file for later examination or documentation:

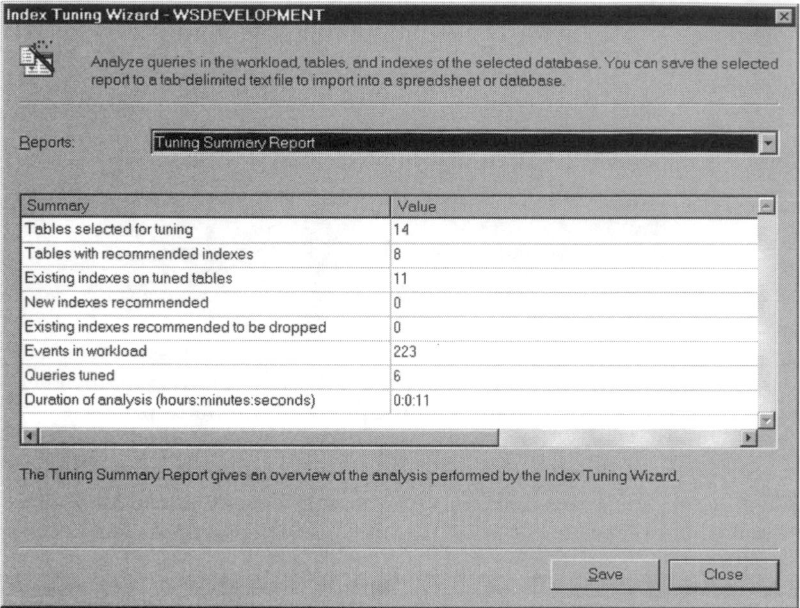

11. Once you close the Analysis dialog, click Next to proceed.

12. At this point we have no changes to apply, so we can cancel out of the Index Tuning Wizard by clicking on the Cancel button:

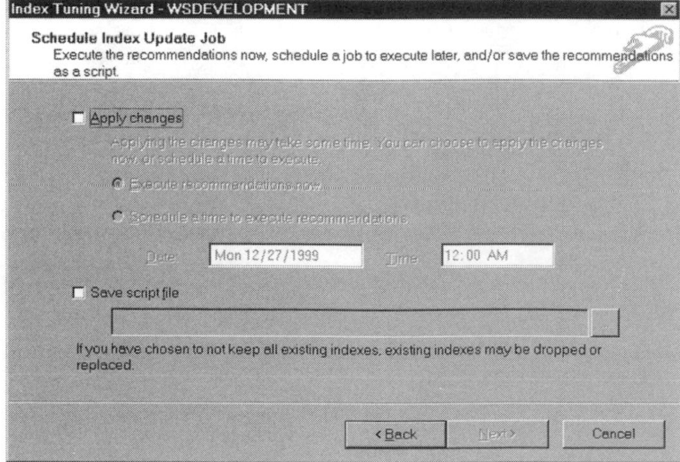

We have just used two very powerful tools in the SQL Server arsenal. While we briefly covered the SQL Server Profiler to create a workload file, it can be used for much more. The SQL Server Profiler can also be used to monitor server and database activities, and help troubleshoot performance bottlenecks such as transactions and stored procedures. By applying filters you can focus on just the events that you want to trace.

The Index Tuning Wizard, as we have just demonstrated, is a very powerful tool that can help improve the overall performance of your database by selecting the optimal mix of indexes. This is very useful when you are designing and using very large databases, when the number of tables and stored procedures is in the hundreds.

At this point, we have done enough to ensure that our database will perform optimally when moved to the test and production environments. Should we notice any performance problems in test or production, we can run the steps above again and capture a true workload. Then we can run the Index Tuning Wizard again to see any recommended index changes. We can also use the SQL Server Profiler to analyze any bottlenecks that we may have.

Backing Up Your Database

When you think about backing up the database you may be assuming that we just need to run the backup utility and we're done. Actually that's only part of it. You need to think on a grander scale; you need to think **backup** and **restore**. So what if you have a backup of the database? What happens three days from now or next week when your system crashes? Do you know how to recover? Can you afford to lose multiple days worth of work? Thinking about a backup strategy can save you countless hours and grief should it become necessary to recover your database.

A backup is not only used to recover your database in the event of a system crash or hardware failure, but can also be used to recover your database should you have data problems as the result of accidentally deleting the wrong data. Suppose you spent days building and populating a table and you wanted to delete a specific row. Suppose you forgot to specify a `WHERE` clause in the `DELETE` statement that you just executed. What then, when all the data is gone?

A sound backup strategy would consist of a **complete** database backup, for example once a week, with **incremental** backups of the transaction log throughout the week. Depending on the amount of work being performed on your development database, you may perform a transaction log backup one or more times a day, and in production it is typical to have the transaction log backed up every hour.

A *complete database backup* backs up the entire database and transaction log. A *transaction log backup* backs up all transactions on the log at the time the backup starts. The transaction log contains all modifications that have occurred in the database since the last database backup or transaction log backup.

Suppose you backed up your database last week on Friday before you left work. You have been backing up your transaction log once a day since the database backup. Today is Thursday and your system crashes. You can recover your database up to the point of your last transaction log backup, which let's say was yesterday. You would first restore the database using the database backup from last Friday, and then apply the transaction log backups in the order in which they were taken, up until yesterday's transaction log backup.

Try It Out – Backup the Wrox_Auto_Works Database

1. To backup your database, expand the Database group in the Enterprise Manager and click on the Wrox_Auto_Works database. In the detail view, click on the backup database hyperlink to invoke the SQL Server Backup dialog.

2. The first tab of the SQL Server Backup dialog contains general information about the backup. Here we specify the name of the backup as well as a description.

3. Since we want to make a complete backup we check the Database – Complete option and then we add a destination for the backup. The Destination section does not recognize mapped network drives on your computer, so if you backup to a local drive ensure that you copy your backup file to a secure location such as a network drive where you store your own backup files. Click the Add button to specify a drive and file name.

4. You can choose to *append to* or *overwrite* any existing media. Since we are performing a complete backup we can overwrite any existing media, which in our case is none at this point.

5. Given the size of our development database there is no reason why we can't perform the backup right away. However, you can schedule the backup to occur at another time if you wish, such as overnight. You can also schedule your backup to be performed on a recurring schedule. These options become visible when you check the Schedule checkbox and browse to see the options.

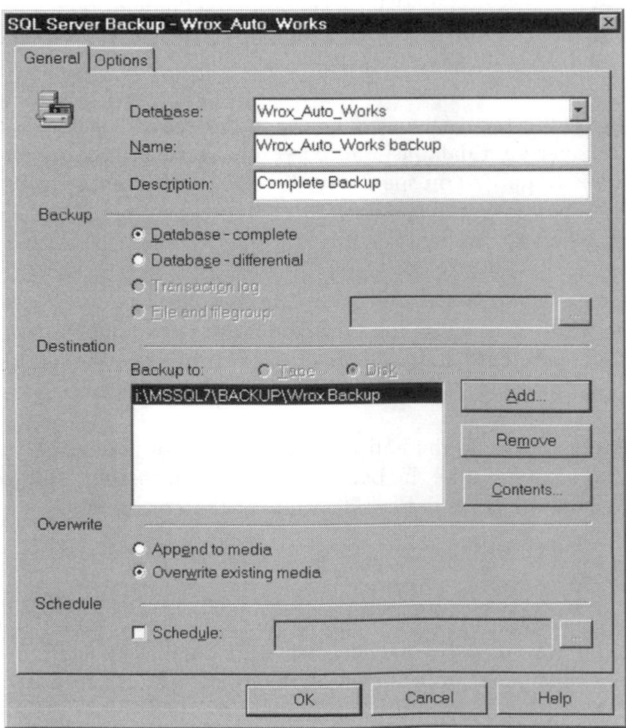

6. The Options tab allows us to verify the backup after it has been taken. This is probably a wise choice and doesn't take that much time. We can specify an expiration date for our backups and give our backups a **media name**, if we so choose. Media names are simply a name assigned to your backup. The expiration date lets SQL Server know that it can overwrite this file after the specified date:

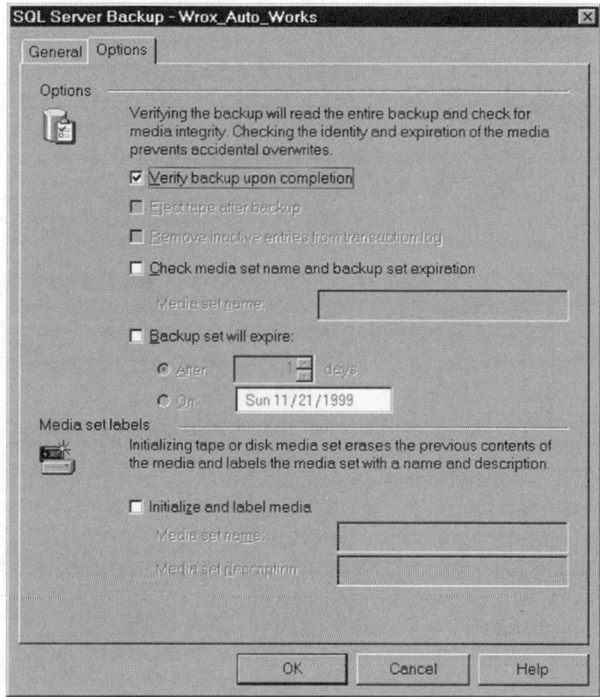

7. Click OK to begin the backup and verification process. This only takes a few minutes to complete. Once the process has completed, SQL Server will display an informational dialog specifying that the backup and verification have completed.

8. Before we can backup the transaction log, we need to ensure that the Truncate Log on Checkpoint option is turned off in the database.

When this option is checked SQL Server removes log entries that reference committed transactions. Also you can not backup the transaction log when this option is checked.

9. To uncheck this option, expand the Database group in the Enterprise Manager and click on the Wrox_Auto_Works database. In the detail view, click on the Database Properties hyperlink to invoke the Properties dialog for the database.

10. On the Options tab, ensure that the Truncate Log On Checkpoint option is not checked. If it is, uncheck it and then click OK to close the dialog.

11. To schedule a recurring backup of the transaction log, click on the Backup Database hyperlink to invoke the SQL Server Backup dialog. Enter a Description that represents the task at hand. I chose to enter the description shown in the figure below.

12. Select the Transaction log backup option and use the current backup destination that we created a few moments ago. We want to ensure we append this backup to the current media, so ensure that the Append to media option is checked.

13. We want the transaction log backed up a least a couple of times a day, so check the Schedule option button and then click on the button to add a new schedule:

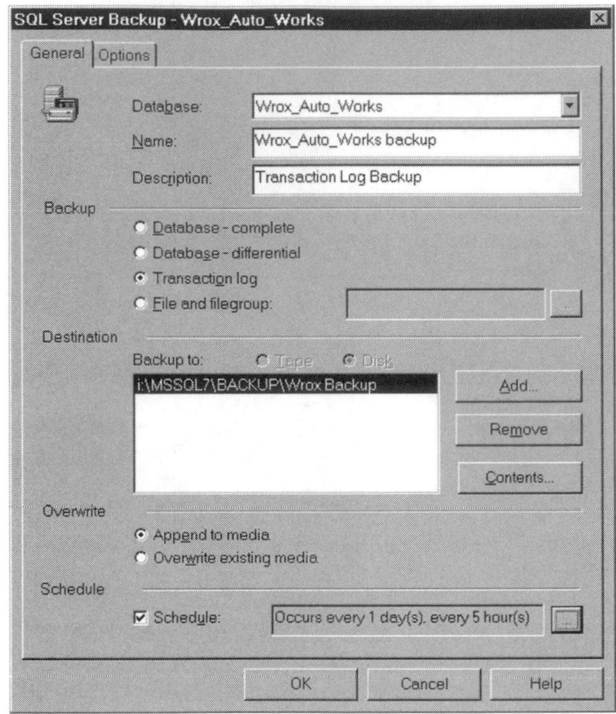

14. We need to give the schedule a name and specify that this should be a recurring schedule. After checking the Recurring option, click the Change button to change the schedule:

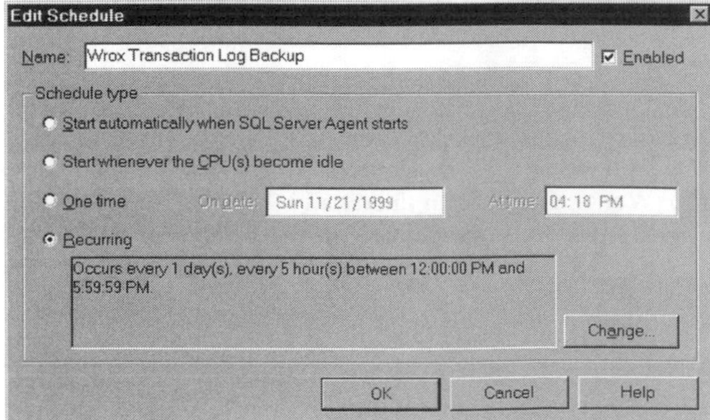

15. The Edit Recurring Job Schedule dialog allows you to schedule your backup in several different ways. I chose to run my backup on a daily basis every five hours starting at 12 noon and ending at 5:59 PM. This will backup all my changes that occur in the morning before lunch and all the changes made after lunch.

16. When you are satisfied with the schedule that you have set up, click the OK button to close the dialog. Click the OK button twice more to close the previous two dialogs and to save all changes:

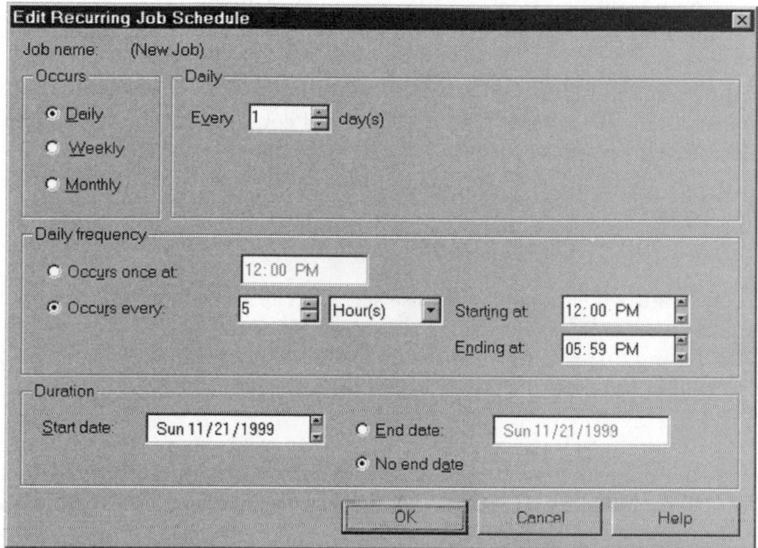

17. After a transaction log has been backed up, you can invoke the SQL Server Backup dialog and view the contents of the backup media by clicking on the Contents button. The figure below shows what is contained in the typical contents of a backup media file.

18. What you can't see in this figure is the other information, such as the date of the backup, the size of the backup file, and the description:

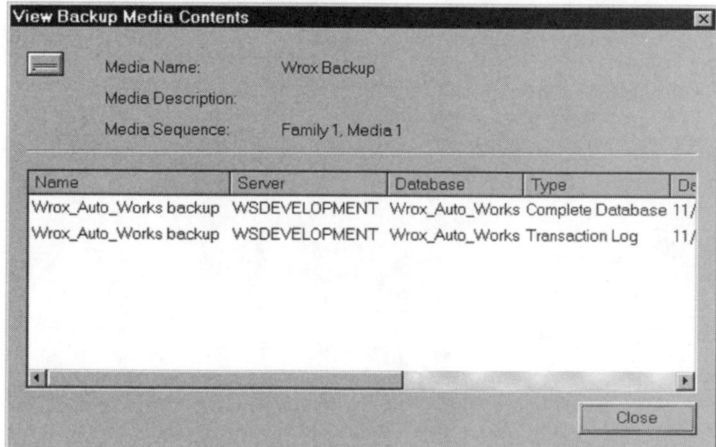

Now that we have a current backup of our database and have scheduled a recurring backup of our transaction log, it's time to move on to the other preparations for test and production.

Generating Scripts

Most companies don't allow developers to have database administration rights to the test and production databases. Why? Because the test environment should be an *exact duplicate* of the production environment in order to ensure a smooth transition from test to production. Although the test environment looks exactly like production architecturally, the test environment may not contain as much data.

To that end, we need to generate scripts of the changes that must be implemented to move the database into the test and production environments. These scripts will contain any object that is part of the implementation required. This includes such objects as tables, indexes, triggers, views, and stored procedures. The scripts will contain the SQL statements to create the database tables, indexes, stored procedures and other database objects. Once our script file has been generated, it will be turned over for implementation to the appropriate parties who have database administrative authority.

SQL Server provides a tool to generate our database scripts. The **Generate SQL Scripts** dialog contains numerous options that allow us to generate database scripts for certain or all objects. Likewise, we can choose the type of formatting that should be applied to each object scripted. We can also choose to include security information, such as database users and logins, as well as SQL Server and Windows NT logins.

Before we create our database scripts, we must decide how we want our scripts created. The Generate SQL Scripts dialog provides the option of creating one file that contains all of the scripts, or we can choose to have a file created for each object. The best method that I have found is to create one script file containing all the scripts to be implemented. You can then rename the file to include either a date or version number. This makes version control and future maintenance more manageable.

Try It Out – Generating a Script

1. For our example here we will be creating one script for all objects. To begin, expand the Database group in the Enterprise Manager and select the Wrox_Auto_Works database. Click on the Generate SQL Scripts hyperlink to invoke the Generate SQL Scripts dialog.

2. The General tab contains the various objects for which scripts can be generated. By default *all* objects are selected. Since we have not defined any Views, Defaults, Rules, or User-Defined Data Types, we can uncheck those objects.

3. The Preview button allows you to preview the generated script and then decide whether or not you want to save the script file:

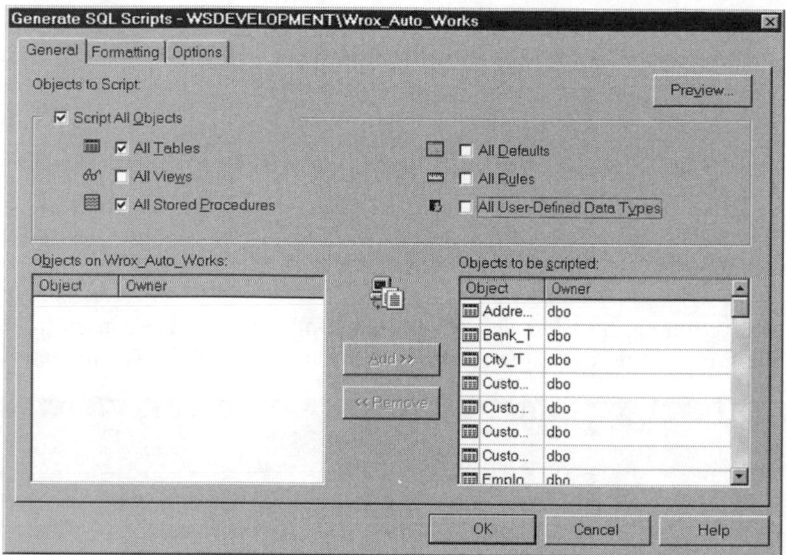

4. The Formatting tab provides some basic information about how the scripts should be formatted. We of course want to generate the CREATE <object> command for each object as well as the DROP <object> command. This facilitates removing any existing objects before we try to create a new one. Since we have not created any user-defined data types, we do not need to check the checkbox for dependent objects. We do, however, want to include a descriptive header for each object for which a script is generated:

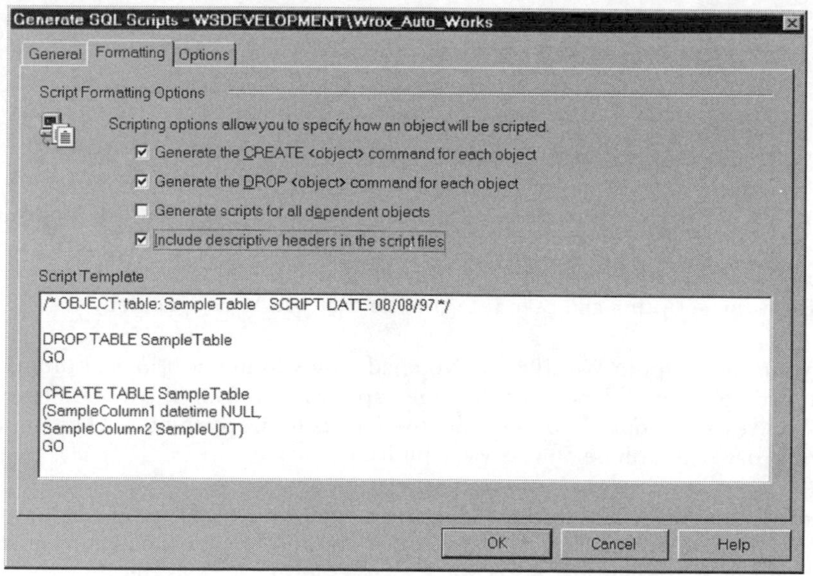

5. The Options tab contains all of the various options that did not fall into a specific category. For the Security options we want to check all checkboxes to have the Roles and Database Users added to our script, as well as all SQL Server and Windows NT Logins added. It is very important to have the permissions for all of our objects scripted so we also check the Object-Level Permissions checkbox.

6. For the Table Scripting Options section on this tab, we need only check the checkboxes to have the Indexes and Constraints added to our script. We have not created any Full Text Indexes nor have we created any Triggers.

7. The last section on this tab deals with the File Options. We have chosen to use a Windows Text file format and have chosen to have the script for all objects generated in one file:

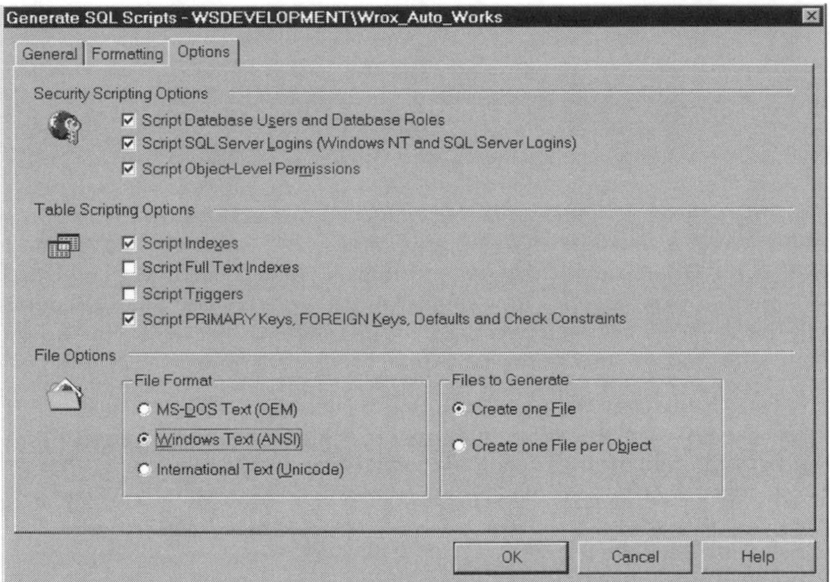

8. When you click the OK button at the bottom of this dialog, you will be prompted for a file name and location of where the script file should be saved. I chose a file name of Create Wrox Database. Once you click the Save button, the Generate SQL Scripts dialog will perform the scripting and save it to the file that you have specified.

9. Viewing the script in WordPad or Notepad, you will notice a logical order of the scripts that were generated. First, all constraints are dropped from the tables. Then all stored procedures are dropped, followed by the scripts to drop all tables. This represents the reverse order that these objects were built in.

10. All of the database users, logins, and roles are added next, and the appropriate permissions set. Then the tables are created, followed by the appropriate indexes and constraints. Next, the appropriate permissions are set on the tables for the various roles.

11. Last, the scripts for the stored procedures are created, along with the appropriate permissions for the various roles. Notice that the user prefix of the developer who created the stored procedure is included in the script.

12. It is common practice in most companies for the database administrator to control ownership of stored procedures and, in fact, all objects in the test and production environments for security reasons. This prevents other users and developers from modifying the database and causing problems. Given this, we need to change the user prefix for all stored procedures from the developer who created them to the database administrator (`dbo`).

13. The following two code fragments show the `up_select_zip_codes` stored procedure before the change and after the change. All references of `willist` were changed to `dbo` so that the database administrator will control ownership of these stored procedures:

```
/****** Object:  Stored Procedure willist.up_select_zip_codes
Script Date: 11/21/1999 8:57:40 PM ******/
setuser N'willist'
GO

CREATE PROCEDURE up_select_zip_codes AS

SELECT Zip_Code_ID, Zip_Code_CH
   FROM Zip_Code_T
   ORDER BY Zip_Code_CH

GO

setuser
GO

SET QUOTED_IDENTIFIER  OFF    SET ANSI_NULLS  ON
GO

GRANT  EXECUTE  ON [willist].[up_select_zip_codes]  TO [Developers]
GO

GRANT  EXECUTE  ON [willist].[up_select_zip_codes]  TO [Sales Staff]
GO

GRANT  EXECUTE  ON [willist].[up_select_zip_codes]  TO [Management]
GO
```

```
/****** Object:  Stored Procedure dbo.up_select_zip_codes
Script Date: 11/21/1999 8:57:40 PM ******/
setuser N'dbo'
GO

CREATE PROCEDURE up_select_zip_codes AS

SELECT Zip_Code_ID, Zip_Code_CH
   FROM Zip_Code_T
```

```
    ORDER BY Zip_Code_CH

GO

setuser
GO

SET QUOTED_IDENTIFIER  OFF    SET ANSI_NULLS  ON
GO

GRANT  EXECUTE  ON [dbo].[up_select_zip_codes]  TO [Developers]
GO

GRANT  EXECUTE  ON [dbo].[up_select_zip_codes]  TO [Sales Staff]
GO

GRANT  EXECUTE  ON [dbo].[up_select_zip_codes]  TO [Management]
GO
```

14. Along with this change, you must be cognizant of any stored procedures that execute other stored procedures, such as the `up_select_city_state_zip` stored procedure below. The change has already been made to this stored procedure, replacing the stored procedure user prefix of `willist` with `dbo`:

```
CREATE PROCEDURE up_select_city_state_zip AS

EXEC dbo.up_select_city_names
EXEC dbo.up_select_state_names
EXEC dbo.up_select_zip_codes
```

15. When making these changes in your script file, don't forget to change the script that drops the stored procedure as well.

16. There may be some tables that contain values that don't change that we need to generate a script for. A case in point would be the `State_T` table. We populated this table early in the book and have not changed the values. You could create a script that would load these values into this table in the test and production environments.

17. The sample query below shows both the query and the results of the query. As you can see, we have generated a file that can be saved and executed as a script, to insert new values into the `State_T` table in test and production:

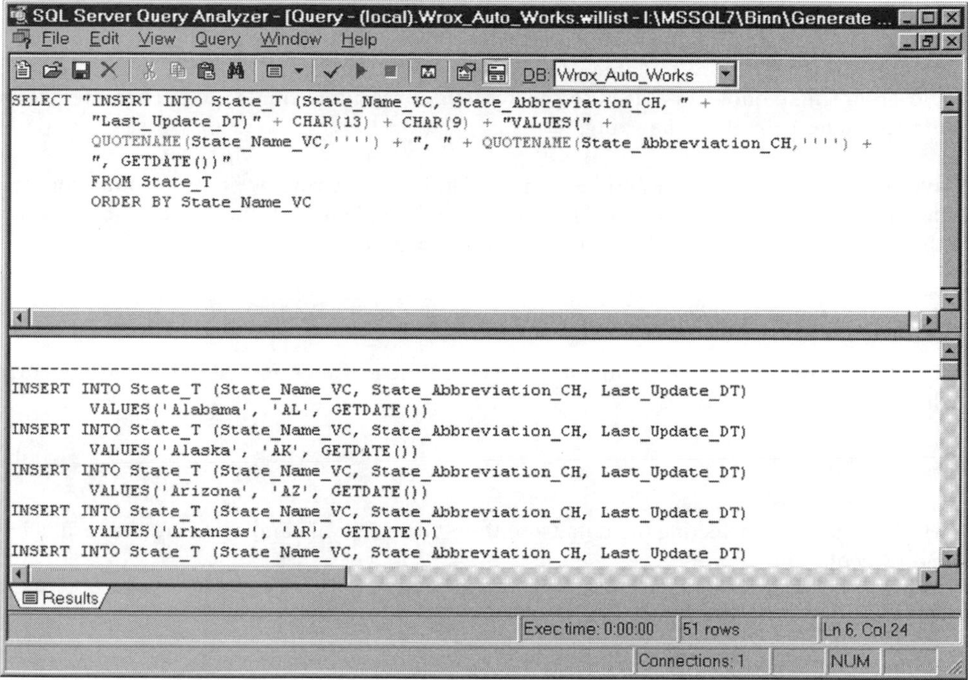

How It Works – Generating a Script

Let's take a quick look at this query. Basically, all this script does is to use string constants and append the data from the columns to the string constant. So what we end up with is one long string, containing the data to be inserted into the table, for each row selected.

The first line builds the first part of the SQL string, containing the `INSERT` statement and the columns that we want to insert data into:

```
SELECT "INSERT INTO State_T (State_Name_VC, State_Abbreviation_CH, " +
```

The second line finishes the column list, and adds a carriage return character so that our string will be broken into two separate lines. This was done so you could see the entire string that was built in the `SELECT` statement. Using the `Char` string function we have specified the carriage return character `Char(13)`. The `Char` string function is commonly used to insert control characters into strings, as we have done here.

Since we broke the string into two separate lines, we need to indent the second line for readability. This is accomplished using the `Char` string function `Char(9)` which represents a tab character. Then we append the string that specifies the beginning of the values to be inserted:

```
    "Last_Update_DT)" + Char(13) + Char(9) + "VALUES(" +
```

Next, using the QuoteName string function, we append the data from the State_Name_VC column to the string. The QuoteName string function returns a string with the delimiters added to make the input string a valid delimited identifier. The quote character that was used is a single quote. Since the quote character must be enclosed in single quotes, we need to specify four consecutive single quote characters to have just the one quote character printed in the string.

After we have selected the state name and have appended it to the string, we need to build the string that separates the values, in this case a comma. Then we append the data from the State_Abbreviation_CH column to the string, again using the QuoteName string function:

```
QuoteName(State_Name_VC,'''') + ", " + QuoteName(State_Abbreviation_CH,'''') +
```

The last part of our string contains a comma and the GetDate() function that will insert the current date and time when we run this script:

```
", GetDate())"
```

The last part of our query is selecting the data from the State_T table and ordering the results by the State_Name_VC column:

```
FROM State_T
ORDER BY State_Name_VC
```

Once you run the query you can save the results as a script by specifying a .sql extension. When you load the file into the Query Analyzer for execution you will notice that the first line of dashes were saved in the file. Not to worry as these are treated as comments.

As you can see, this is a very efficient way to extract data into a script file for execution on another SQL Server. Once the script file has been generated it would be turned over to the person(s) responsible for maintaining the test and production environments for execution.

Preparing Your Programs

Along with the changes to the stored procedures, you must also change the business server component (ActiveX DLL) that executes these stored procedures to include the correct user prefix. Once this component has been updated using the correct user prefix of dbo, you must recompile the component for the test environment. This brings up another good point. You need to manage the versions that are executed in development and the versions that are executed in test and production separately.

The same component that runs in testing should also run in production without any changes. The compatibility component should be placed on a machine that is accessible to every developer. This way, any developer can compile a new component for testing. The business server component can be recompiled with the changes to the stored procedures without breaking binary compatibility, thus this requires no recompile of the front-end program.

The business server component that we designed fits into the middle tier of the Windows DNA architecture by providing the business services to our front-end program. Our front-end program has no direct interaction with the stored procedures that are executed. It simply calls the methods in the business server component that execute the stored procedures and handle the presentation of data in the first tier of the Windows DNA architecture. In other words it is the presentation layer.

Thus with the separation of business and presentation services between the business server component and the front-end program, maintenance of these components becomes much more manageable, and changes to one do not necessarily affect the other. This is especially true when binary compatibility has not been broken.

There is one change that is required to the front-end program. In Chapter 14 we used a DSN-less connection to establish a connection to the database. You must now decide whether you use a DSN connection, a DSN-less connection with hard-coded values, or a DSN-less connection with values read from the registry. Only you can decide what method best suits your shop standards and best practices. Refer back to Chapter 6 for help with setting up each of these options.

Summary

This chapter has introduced some new but very important topics that will help to ensure a smooth and successful implementation of your application in the test and production environments. Probably the most important topic discussed was how to tune your indexes. Leading up to this discussion was the introduction to the SQL Server Profiler. This chapter has only scratched the surface of using this very powerful and important tool. We used the SQL Server Profiler to create a workload file for the Index Tuning Wizard. This tool should be explored in more depth as time permits, by reading the SQL Server Books Online and experimenting with the tool itself.

When we used the Index Tuning Wizard we had one thing in mind – performance. We wanted to squeeze out as much performance from our database as possible. We knew that we did everything possible to design a normalized database, and we built the indexes that we thought were the most logical choices. Our stored procedures were efficiently designed and took advantage of the indexes that we built. We used the Index Tuning Wizard to provide an analysis of the current mix of indexes to see if we had left anything out.

In this case the Index Tuning Wizard did not recommend any new indexes, but you can see how this tool can be used to ensure optimal performance of your database. This tool becomes ever increasingly important as the size of our database grows and multiple developers are working with it.

This chapter has also taken a look at backing up our database and transaction log. You should now realize the importance of a good backup strategy, and how backups of the transaction log can be used to help recover your database to any given point in time. A full backup once a week with incremental backups of your transaction log can help you to quickly recover your database in the event of a hardware failure or system crash.

We generated scripts to be run in test and production to build the database and populate some tables with data. Generating scripts was a fairly easy task to perform but there are a lot of options that were presented in the Generate SQL Scripts dialog. Choosing the right mix of options is important to ensuring the successful implementation of your application. The script file was not complete after generation; we had to change the user prefix for our stored procedures to use the database administrator prefix (`dbo`).

We also took at look at what changes were required to our programs. We know that the changes required to our business server component did not break binary compatibility and that these changes did not require a recompile of our front-end program. We must be particularly aware when multiple developers start working on a project, and they all create stored procedures. We need to ensure that all user prefixes for the stored procedures in our business server component are changed to `dbo`.

To summarize, you should know:

- How to use the SQL Server Profiler to create a workload file
- How to use the workload file in the Index Tuning Wizard to tune your indexes
- How to backup your database and transaction log
- The importance of a good backup strategy
- How to generate scripts for test and production to build the database, and what changes are required to the scripts
- What changes are required to your programs

So where do you go from here? There are three case studies in this book. These case studies were designed to allow you to practice the skills that you have learned throughout this book. At the same time these case studies also introduce some new topics to help you keep learning. After completing all three case studies you should feel comfortable striking out on your own, designing your own database, and creating stored procedures and programs to build a complete application.

WROX AUTO WORKS RACING

Case Study 1 – Wrox Auto Works Customer Application

Wrox Auto Works Customer Application – Part 1

By now you have covered all of the material in this book and are ready to apply your newfound knowledge in a real world application. The goal of this case study is to help you apply the skills and techniques that you have learned throughout this book, and at the same time still teach you something new. The new techniques will be kept to a minimum and will be covered first, so as to allow you to apply your skills and knowledge about SQL Server and stored procedures in the rest of this case study.

Due to the size of this case study, it will be broken into three parts. The first part concentrates on SQL Server. This case study implements some new tables that will allow you the opportunity to practice your skills by writing some new stored procedures. It also introduces you to altering tables and creating primary and foreign keys using SQL statements, instead of using the Enterprise Manager.

The second part of this case study builds upon the business server component that we created in Chapter 14. We need to add some new functions to the existing classes in that server component, as well as add some new classes to support the new tables. The business object implements the database calls to execute stored procedures, while sheltering the UI from the complexities of the database side of our application.

The third part of this case study creates the user interface (UI). We will build upon the UI that we created in Chapter 13, and will add new functionality to validate data before calling the methods to execute our stored procedures. While the UI that we will create is not a complete user interface, it does implement a lot of the functionality that a good UI should. Two new forms will be added to support the additional tables in our database.

Modified Database Design

We want to add some new functionality to our application, which requires that we modify our database design. In addition to keeping a record of employment, we also want to keep track of a customer's financial institution. This requires adding a new table for financial institutions, `Bank_T`, and modifying the Customer Information table. Like the Employer table, we want to associate a phone number with each financial institution, so we will need a foreign key reference from the Bank table to the Phone Number table.

In addition to this, we also want to keep a history of our customers' purchases. This requires adding three new tables; one for the history and one each for vehicle make and model. Like the Customer Information table, the Customer Purchase History table will have two foreign key references to the same table. The Customer Purchase History table will have a foreign key reference to the Make and Model tables for the vehicle purchased, as well as for the vehicle traded, if there was one.

The following diagram lists the new tables and shows how they relate to our existing tables:

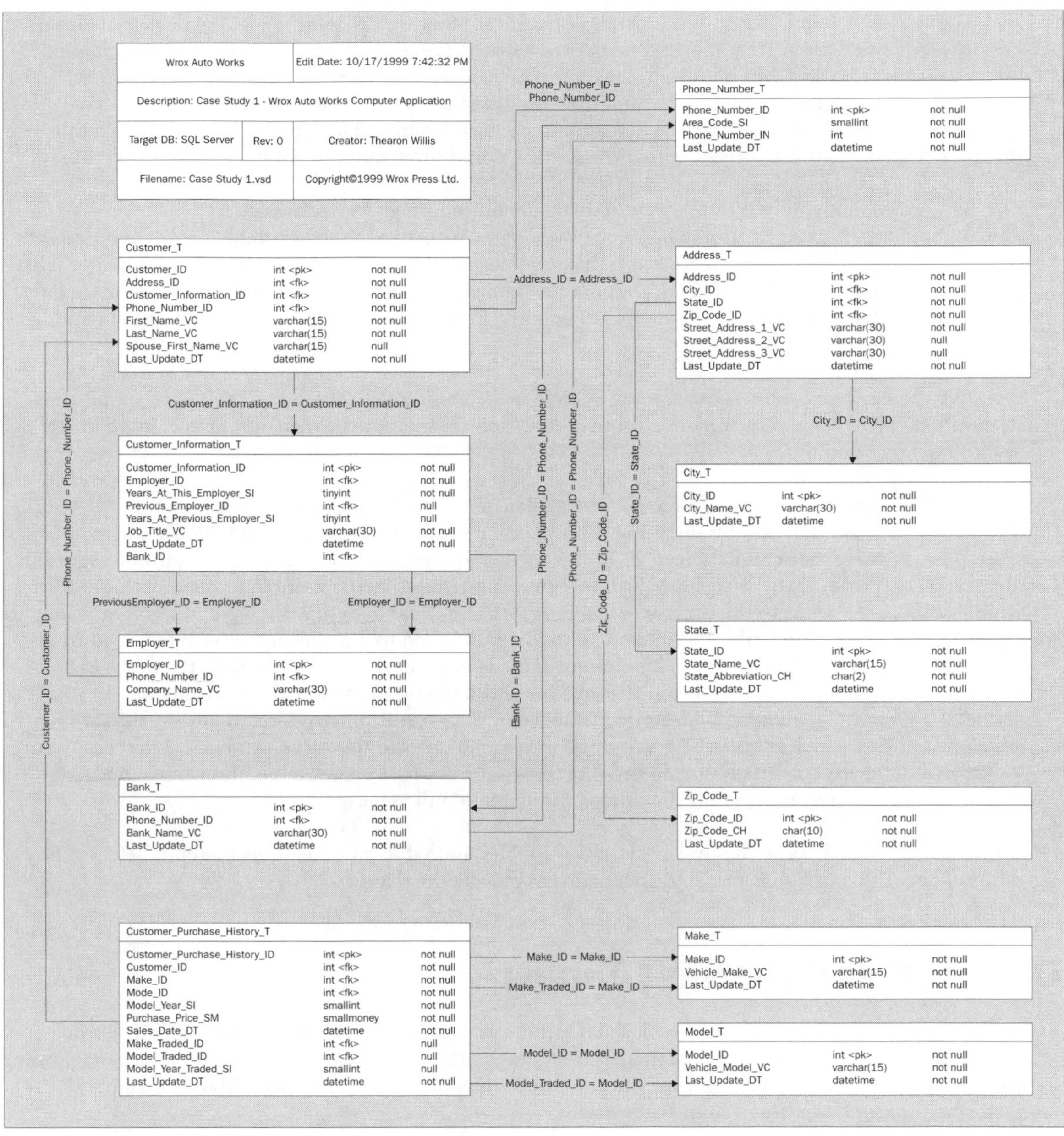

Notice that we have created a new table, named `Bank_T`, and that the `Customer_Information_T` table contains a foreign key reference to this table. Also notice that the foreign key is defined as accepting null values. This is not what we really want, but SQL Server applies this limitation upon us, and here's the reason why. We can modify an existing table and add a new column to it. This column could be defined as `Not Null`, but since the table already contains data, we would have to assign a default value to this column. This would be fine in any other circumstances, but since the column we are adding is a foreign key to another table which does not yet contain any data, we have no choice but to define this new column as `Null`.

We should therefore use our stored procedures to ensure that we do not allow null values to be inserted into this column. This is great if everyone uses our stored procedures or business server component to insert data in our tables, but this is not always the case. The other alternative would be to insert a dummy record into the `Bank_T` table, and then use that key as the default value for the `Customer_Information_T` table when adding the new column. The choice is yours, but for this case study we are going with the first approach – using a stored procedure to validate data for this column.

The `Bank_T` table, like the `Employer_T` table, contains a foreign key reference to the `Phone_Number_T` table. It should be clear to you by now that keeping your table names and designs generic allows you to use a table for more than one purpose. Had we prefixed the phone number table with '`Customer`' it would have indicated that the table contained phone numbers for customers only, and we would have needed to create another phone number table for the employers, and then another again for the financial institutions.

We have created two tables to contain the vehicle make and model. These two tables are simple and straightforward as they only contain a primary key, one column for the data, and one column for the last update date and time.

The new `Customer_Purchase_History_T` table contains a foreign key reference to the `Customer_T` table. This allows this table to contain a many-to-one relationship with the `Customer_T` table. That is, there can be many records in the `Customer_Purchase_History_T` for one record in the `Customer_T` table, because each customer may (hopefully!) make more than one purchase. This table is also very similar to the `Customer_Information_T` table in that we have two columns that are foreign keys to the same table. The make and model purchased by the customer are referenced in this table by the `Make_ID` and `Model_ID` columns. If a customer traded a vehicle, then the make and model of vehicle that they traded are referenced in this table by the `Make_Traded_ID` and `Model_Traded_ID` columns. Both `Make_ID` and `Make_Traded_ID` are foreign keys to the `Make_T` table, and `Model_ID` and `Model_Traded_ID` are foreign keys to the `Model_T` table. Like the `Previous_Employer_ID` column in the `Customer_Information_T` table, the vehicle make and model traded are optional and these columns can contain null values.

Now that we have covered the design of our new tables and table modifications in depth, let's see how we implement this design using SQL statements to modify the database.

Creating and Altering Tables

In Chapter 3 we created the initial tables and foreign keys using the Enterprise Manager. Then in Chapter 4 we used the Enterprise Manager to define the roles, and set security on our tables by granting the roles various levels of access. Every task we performed using the Enterprise Manager can be performed through the use of SQL statements.

This section will walk you through the SQL statements that will be used to create the new tables and modify existing ones. We will also use SQL statements to add primary and foreign keys to our tables and to set the permissions on our tables.

The CREATE TABLE SQL statement has a very complex syntax and we are only going to cover the basics here. The basic syntax is listed below:

```
CREATE TABLE table_name (column_name data_type [Identity(seed, increment)]
Null|Not Null)
```

We specify the table name to create and the column names, along with their data types, and whether or not the column will accept null values. If the column is an Identity column, then we specify the optional Identity keyword and the seed and increment values. In the Wrox Auto Works database all primary key columns that we define for our tables are Identity columns.

Like the CREATE TABLE SQL statement, the ALTER TABLE SQL statement also has a long and complicated syntax. Again, we are only going to cover the basic syntax here. Three basic syntaxes are listed below:

```
ALTER TABLE table_name ADD (column_name data_type Null|Not Null)

ALTER TABLE table_name ADD CONSTRAINT constraint_name PRIMARY KEY
Clustered|NonClustered
   (column_name)

ALTER TABLE table_name ADD CONSTRAINT constraint_name FOREIGN KEY (column_name)
REFERENCES
   table_name (column_name)
```

As you can see from the different syntaxes listed above, we use the ALTER TABLE SQL statement to add a number of features to our tables, such as primary and foreign keys. In the first syntax example, we are using the ALTER TABLE SQL statement to add a new column to a table. Each column to be added would be separated by a comma and the entire column listed would be enclosed in parentheses.

The second example shows how we use the ALTER TABLE SQL statement to add a primary key constraint to a table, and the third syntax shows how we add a foreign key constraint to a table.

In order for the different roles to be able to access the new tables that we create, we must grant the roles permissions. We do this using the GRANT SQL statement. Like the previous two SQL statements that we have looked at, the GRANT SQL statement also has a fairly complex syntax. You can grant object level permissions or column level permissions with the GRANT SQL statement. We are going to grant our roles object level permissions, as shown in the following syntax:

```
GRANT SELECT|INSERT|UPDATE|DELETE ON object_name TO security_account
```

The object name represents the SQL Server object on which we want to grant permissions, and the security account represents an individual logon or a role.

To learn more about these three SQL statements that we have just covered, check out the SQL Server Books Online. We now have enough information to proceed and create the SQL statements that will modify our database.

Try It Out – Using SQL Statements to Modify the Database

Using the database diagram shown previously, we want to create a script containing SQL statements to create the new tables and modify the `Customer_Information_T` table to add the extra column.

> *Modifying your database structure can be a very tricky business, and very dangerous if you are dropping and recreating tables. Fortunately our design does not call for any existing tables to be unloaded, dropped, recreated, and then reloaded. Every table we create can be dropped and recreated if necessary, because at this stage they contain no data.*

The code for this example is listed in the *How It Works* section. You should enter it in the Query Analyzer section by section.

After you have double-checked your typing and spelling, go ahead and execute this script in the Query Analyzer.

How It Works – Using SQL Statements to Modify the Database

We start by creating the new tables that are listed in our database diagram. Each `CREATE TABLE` SQL statement specifies the table name to be created, along with all columns and their data types, and whether the column can contain null values or not. Notice that each column is separated by a comma and that the entire column list is contained in parentheses.

After we have specified the table name to be created, along with all of the columns for that table, we specify the `GO` command. The `GO` command tells the Query Analyzer to execute a batch of SQL statements. The batch is comprised of all SQL statements since the last `GO` command or the start of a session. The thing to watch out for here is that if your third batch contains an error, the first two batches will have been executed before the Query Analyzer catches the error in the third batch. You need to ensure that each batch is error free before execution, or alternatively you can execute each batch separately.

```
--*******************************************************************************
-- Create Bank_T Table
--
*********************************************************************************
CREATE TABLE Bank_T
   (
   Bank_ID          Int          IDENTITY(1,1) Not Null,
   Phone_Number_ID          Int         Not Null,
   Bank_Name_VC          VarChar(30)      Not Null,
   Last_Update_DT           DateTime      Not Null
   )
GO
```

```
--
*********************************************************************************
-- Create Customer_Purchase_History_T Table
--
*********************************************************************************
CREATE TABLE Customer_Purchase_History_T
   (
   Customer_Purchase_History_ID Int        IDENTITY(1,1) Not Null,
   Customer_ID          Int          Not Null,
   Make_ID          Int          Not Null,
   Model_ID         Int          Not Null,
   Model_Year_SI         SmallInt      Not Null,
   Purchase_Price_SM         SmallMoney      Not Null,
   Sales_Date_DT         DateTime      Not Null,
   Make_Traded_ID         Int          Null,
   Model_Traded_ID         Int          Null,
   Model_Year_Traded_SI      SmallInt       Null,
   Last_Update_DT         DateTime       NOT  Null
   )
GO

--
*********************************************************************************
-- Create Make_T Table
--
*********************************************************************************
CREATE TABLE Make_T
   (
   Make_ID          Int          IDENTITY(1,1) Not Null,
   Vehicle_Make_VC         VarChar(15)       Not Null,
   Last_Update_DT         DateTime       Not Null
   )
GO

--
*********************************************************************************
-- Create Model_T Table
--
*********************************************************************************
CREATE TABLE Model_T
   (
   Model_ID          Int          IDENTITY(1,1) Not Null,
   Vehicle_Model_VC         VarChar(15)       Not Null,
   Last_Update_DT         DateTime       Not Null
   )
GO
```

After we have specified all of the different CREATE TABLE SQL statements and have executed them by issuing the GO command, we code the ALTER TABLE SQL statements to add the primary and foreign key constraints. This must be done in a specific order otherwise you will receive an error.

Let's step through this part for each table. The first table that we want to alter is the Bank_T table. We add the primary key constraint and then add the foreign key constraint to the Phone_Number_T table. We specify the GO command to have the Query Analyzer execute these SQL statements to perform the task:

```
--
*****************************************************************************************
-- Add Constraints (Primary and Foreign Keys) To Bank_T
--
*****************************************************************************************
ALTER TABLE Bank_T
   ADD
   CONSTRAINT PK_Bank_T PRIMARY KEY NonClustered (Bank_ID),
   CONSTRAINT FK_Bank_T_Phone_Number_T FOREIGN KEY (Phone_Number_ID)
      REFERENCES Phone_Number_T (Phone_Number_ID)
GO
```

Now that the Bank_T table has been created and the primary key constraint defined, we can alter the Customer_Information_T table to add the column that will be a foreign key to the Bank_T table. This is one of the primary reasons to use the GO command; we ensure that the Bank_T table is actually created and the primary key constraint defined *before* we alter the Customer_Information_T table.

```
--
*****************************************************************************************
-- Alter Table Customer_Information_T To Add A New Column
--
*****************************************************************************************
ALTER TABLE Customer_Information_T
   ADD
   Bank_ID          Int          Null
GO
```

After the column has been defined and executed by the Query Analyzer, we can alter the Customer_Information_T table to add the foreign key reference to the Bank_T table. As you can see, the preceding steps must be completed in order otherwise you will receive an error. The column must be added to the table before we attempt to use it as a foreign key reference.

```
--
****************************************************************************************
-- Add Constraints (Foreign Key) To Customer_Information_T
--
****************************************************************************************
ALTER TABLE Customer_Information_T
   Add
   CONSTRAINT FK_Customer_Information_T_Bank_T FOREIGN KEY (Bank_ID)
      REFERENCES Bank_T (Bank_ID)
GO
```

Next, we add the primary key constraints to the `Make_T` and `Model_T` tables. These constraints must be complete before moving on to the next `ALTER TABLE` SQL statement, and we ensure that this is complete by specifying the `GO` command:

```
--
****************************************************************************************
-- Add Constraints (Primary Key) To Make_T
--
****************************************************************************************
ALTER TABLE Make_T
   ADD
   CONSTRAINT PK_Make_T PRIMARY KEY NonClustered (Make_ID)
GO

--
****************************************************************************************
-- Add Constraints (Primary Key) To Model_T
--
****************************************************************************************
ALTER TABLE Model_T
   ADD
   CONSTRAINT PK_Model_T PRIMARY KEY NonClustered (Model_ID)
GO
```

The `Customer_Purchase_History_T` table contains one primary key constraint and five foreign key constraints. The first foreign key constraint is for the `Customer_ID`, which resides in the `Customer_T` table.

The next two foreign key constraints are for `Make_ID` and `Model_ID`, which reside in the `Make_T` and `Model_T` tables.

The last two foreign key constraints have different names in each table. In the Customer_Purchase_History_T table the foreign keys are named Make_Traded_ID and Model_Traded_ID, and they reference Make_ID in the Make_T table and Model_ID in the Model_T table respectively:

```
--
*********************************************************************************
-- Add Constraints (Primary and Foreign Keys) To Customer_Purchase_History_T
--
*********************************************************************************
ALTER TABLE Customer_Purchase_History_T
   ADD
   CONSTRAINT PK_Customer_Purchase_History_T PRIMARY KEY NonClustered
      (Customer_Purchase_History_ID),
   CONSTRAINT FK_Customer_Purchase_History_Customer_T FOREIGN KEY (Customer_ID)
      REFERENCES Customer_T (Customer_ID),
   CONSTRAINT FK_Customer_Purchase_History_Make_T FOREIGN KEY (Make_ID)
      REFERENCES Make_T (Make_ID),
   CONSTRAINT FK_Customer_Purchase_History_Model_T FOREIGN KEY (Model_ID)
      REFERENCES Model_T (Model_ID),
   CONSTRAINT FK_Customer_Purchase_History_Make_T1 FOREIGN KEY (Make_Traded_ID)
      REFERENCES Make_T (Make_ID),
   CONSTRAINT FK_Customer_Purchase_History_Model_T1 FOREIGN KEY (Model_Traded_ID)
      REFERENCES Model_T (Model_ID)
GO
```

Now that all of the tables have been created and the constraints added, we need to set the permissions of each of the new tables for each of the roles that were defined in Chapter 4. This is another classic example where using roles is better than using individual logons. We could have hundreds of logons but only a few roles. It involves much less typing and administrative management to maintain a few roles versus hundreds of logons.

If you recall our discussions from Chapter 4, we granted the Developers role full access to all objects, the Sales Staff role SELECT, INSERT, and UPDATE privileges, and the Management role SELECT privileges only. In keeping with that, we want to grant these roles those privileges on each of the new tables:

```
--
*********************************************************************************
-- Grant Permissions On Bank_T
--
*********************************************************************************
GRANT SELECT, INSERT, UPDATE, DELETE ON Bank_T TO Developers
GRANT SELECT, INSERT, UPDATE ON Bank_T TO [Sales Staff]
GRANT SELECT ON Bank_T TO Management
GO
```

```
--
**********************************************************************************
-- Grant Permissions On Customer_Purchase_History_T
--
**********************************************************************************
GRANT SELECT, INSERT, UPDATE, DELETE ON Customer_Purchase_History_T TO Developers
GRANT SELECT, INSERT, UPDATE ON Customer_Purchase_History_T TO [Sales Staff]
GRANT SELECT ON Customer_Purchase_History_T TO Management
GO

--
**********************************************************************************
-- Grant Permissions On Make_T
--
**********************************************************************************
GRANT SELECT, INSERT, UPDATE, DELETE ON Make_T TO Developers
GRANT SELECT, INSERT, UPDATE ON Make_T TO [Sales Staff]
GRANT SELECT ON Make_T TO Management
GO
--
**********************************************************************************
-- Grant Permissions On Model_T
--
**********************************************************************************
GRANT SELECT, INSERT, UPDATE, DELETE ON Model_T TO Developers
GRANT SELECT, INSERT, UPDATE ON Model_T TO [Sales Staff]
GRANT SELECT ON Model_T TO Management
GO
```

Once complete, if you want to see the tables that have been created, you can either execute a `SELECT *` from each of the tables or switch to the Enterprise Manager and look at the tables there.

We are now ready to move on and create the required stored procedures to support these new tables.

Stored Procedures

After having created these new tables, there are some stored procedures that we want to create. We need stored procedures to select all data from the `Make_T` and `Model_T` tables as well as the `Bank_T` table.

Try It Out – Creating SELECT Stored Procedures

1. The code below lists the stored procedures to be created. Since they are simple and straightforward they need no explanation, so go ahead and create them. Don't forget to set the appropriate permissions on these stored procedures, and all the others created in this case study.

2. The first stored procedure is `up_select_make`:

```
CREATE PROCEDURE up_select_make AS

SELECT Make_ID, Vehicle_Make_VC
   FROM Make_T
   ORDER BY Vehicle_Make_VC
```

3. The second stored procedure is up_select_model:

```
CREATE PROCEDURE up_select_model AS

SELECT Model_ID, Vehicle_Model_VC
   FROM Model_T
   ORDER BY Vehicle_Model_VC
```

4. The third stored procedure is up_select_banks:

```
CREATE PROCEDURE up_select_banks AS

SELECT Bank_ID, Bank_Name_VC, Phone_Number_T.Phone_Number_ID, Area_Code_SI,
       Phone_Number_IN
   FROM Bank_T
   JOIN Phone_Number_T ON Bank_T.Phone_Number_ID = Phone_Number_T.Phone_Number_ID
   ORDER BY Bank_Name_VC
```

Try It Out – Modify INSERT Stored Procedure

Since we modified the `Customer_Information_T` table by adding a new column, we need to update the stored procedure that inserts data into this table. We do not need to modify the `UPDATE` stored procedure, as the financial information can be updated independently from the rest of the data in this table, just like the employer information.

There are two ways that you can modify this stored procedure. The first method is by using the Enterprise Manager. Locate the stored procedure in the list and double click on it. The Stored Procedure Properties *dialog pops up listing the code for the stored procedure. As you can see you can modify the SQL statements in the stored procedure here and save it. There is one drawback and it is a* ***major*** *one. There is no interactive debugging in this window and if you have made a keying error it will be very hard to track down, especially in a large stored procedure such as this one. However, this is a great method to use when, for example, you simply need to add an extra column to the* `SELECT` *list.*

1. The best thing to do is to use the second method – the Query Analyzer. Copy the `up_parmins_employer_information` stored procedure code from the Stored Procedure Properties dialog window, paste it into the Query Analyzer and make your modifications.

2. When you are ready to execute your query to recreate this stored procedure, you will need to switch back to the Enterprise Manager and drop the current stored procedure. Do this by right clicking on the stored procedure, choose Delete from the popup menu, and then click on the Drop All button in the Drop Objects dialog.

3. The code below lists the new parameters and variables for the stored procedure:

```
CREATE PROCEDURE up_parmins_employer_information (@Current_Employer_ID Int,
   @Current_Employer_Name VarChar(30), @Current_Employer_Area_Code SmallInt,
   @Current_Employer_Phone_Number Int, @Years_At_Current_Employer TinyInt,
   @Job_Title VarChar(30), @Previous_Employer_ID Int,
   @Previous_Employer_Name VarChar(30), @Previous_Employer_Area_Code SmallInt,
   @Previous_Employer_Phone_Number Int, @Years_At_Previous_Employer TinyInt,
   @Bank_ID Int, @Bank_Name VarChar(30), @Bank_Area_Code SmallInt,
   @Bank_Phone_number Int,   @Customer_Information_ID Int OUTPUT,
   @Message VarChar(300) OUTPUT) AS

--
**********************************************************************************
-- Declare variables
--
**********************************************************************************
DECLARE @Continue              Bit,
   @Name_Required              Bit,
   @Current_Employer_Phone_Number_ID    Int,
   @Previous_Employer_Phone_Number_ID Int,
   @Bank_Phone_Number_ID          Int
```

4. After validation of the previous employer years of employment, add the new code as shown below:

```
--
**********************************************************************************
-- Validate bank ID or bank name exists
--
**********************************************************************************
--
-- Check bank ID first
--
IF @Bank_ID IS Null OR @Bank_ID = 0
```

```
   BEGIN
   --
   -- Current bank name is required
   --
   SELECT @Name_Required = 1
   END
ELSE
   BEGIN
   --
   -- Current bank name is not required
   --
   SELECT @Name_Required = 0
   End

--
-- If @name_required = 1 then the bank name is required
--
IF @Name_Required = 1
   BEGIN
   --
   -- Ensure bank name is Not Null or empty
   --
   IF @Bank_Name IS Null OR DataLength(LTrim(@Bank_Name)) = 0
      BEGIN
      SELECT @Message = @Message + 'Bank name or id is required. '
      SELECT @Continue = 0
      END
   END

--
*********************************************************************************
-- Validate bank area code and phone number
--
*********************************************************************************
--
-- Validate area code is Not Null or zero
--
IF @Bank_Area_Code IS Null OR @Bank_Area_Code = 0
   BEGIN
   SELECT @Message = @Message + 'Bank area code is a required field. '
   SELECT @Continue = 0
   END
--
-- Validate area code is three digits
--
IF DataLength(CAST(@Bank_Area_Code AS VarChar(5))) <> 3
   BEGIN
   SELECT @Message = @Message + 'bank area code is not valid. '
   SELECT @Continue = 0
   END
--
```

```
-- Validate phone number is Not Null or zero
--
IF @Bank_Phone_Number IS Null OR @Bank_Phone_Number = 0
   BEGIN
   SELECT @Message = @Message + 'Bank phone number is a required field. '
   SELECT @Continue = 0
   END
--
-- Validate phone number is seven digits
--
IF DataLength (CAST(@Bank_Phone_Number AS VarChar(10))) <> 7
   BEGIN
   SELECT @Message = @Message + 'Bank phone number is not valid. '
   SELECT @Continue = 0
   END
```

5. Insert the following code before the `INSERT` statement for the `Customer_Information_T` table:

```
   --
******************************************************************************
   -- Determine if we are using an existing bank or inserting a new one
   --
******************************************************************************
   IF @Bank_ID IS Null OR @Bank_ID = 0
      BEGIN
      --
      -- We are inserting a new bank
      --
         *********************************************************************
      -- Insert the bank phone number
      -- *********************************************************************
      INSERT INTO Phone_Number_T
         (Area_Code_SI, Phone_Number_IN, Last_Update_DT)
         VALUES(@Bank_Area_Code, @Bank_Phone_Number,
            GetDate())

      --
      -- Check for errors
      --
      IF @@ERROR <> 0
         BEGIN
         --
         -- Roll back the transaction and return to the caller
         --
         ROLLBACK TRANSACTION Employer_Information
         RAISERROR('Insert for bank phone number failed.',18,1)
         RETURN 99
         END
```

```
    --
    -- Get the phone number ID just inserted
    --
    SELECT @Bank_Phone_Number_ID = @@IDENTITY

    -- ******************************************************************
    -- Insert the bank
    -- ******************************************************************
    INSERT INTO Bank_T
       (Phone_Number_ID, Bank_Name_VC, Last_Update_DT)
       VALUES(@Bank_Phone_Number_ID, @Bank_Name,
          GetDate())

    --
    -- Check for errors
    --
    IF @@ERROR <> 0
       BEGIN
       --
       -- Rollback the transaction and return to the caller
       --
       ROLLBACK TRANSACTION Employer_Information
       RAISERROR('Insert for bank failed.',18,1)
       RETURN 99
       END

    --
    -- Get the bank ID just inserted
    --
    SELECT @Bank_ID = @@IDENTITY
    END
```

6. Modify the INSERT statement for the Customer_Information_T table, as shown in the code below:

```
  --
******************************************************************************
  -- Now insert all the employment data into the customer information table
  --
******************************************************************************
  INSERT INTO Customer_Information_T
     (Employer_ID, Years_At_This_Employer_TI, Previous_Employer_ID,
        Years_At_Previous_Employer_TI, Job_Title_VC, Last_Update_DT,
        Bank_ID)
     VALUES(@Current_Employer_ID, @Years_At_Current_Employer,
        @Previous_Employer_ID, @Years_At_Previous_Employer, @Job_Title,
        GetDate(), @Bank_ID)
```

How It Works – Modify INSERT Stored Procedure

We have added some new input parameters for this stored procedure, for the bank and the bank phone number.

The validations are the same as those performed for a current employer. We validate that either the `Bank_ID` contains a valid number or that the bank name is present. If a bank name is required, we then validate the phone number for the bank.

Inserting a bank follows the same guidelines as inserting a current employer. Either we have the primary key to an existing bank, or we insert the phone number for the new bank followed by the bank itself.

The final `INSERT` SQL statement contains the `Bank_ID` of the new bank inserted or the ID of the bank passed as input.

Financial Institute Stored Procedures

We will be displaying the financial information for a customer in a combo box on a separate form. To this end, we need to create a stored procedure to select the bank for a particular customer so that we can display the correct entry in the combo box. Along with this we will be displaying the phone number for the bank on the form.

Try It Out – Financial Institute Stored Procedures

1. The following stored procedure lists the code to perform this task. Go ahead and create this stored procedure and set the appropriate permissions on it:

```
CREATE PROCEDURE up_parmsel_customer_financial_information (@Customer_ID Int) AS

SELECT Bank_T.Bank_ID, Bank_Name_VC, Phone_Number_T.Phone_Number_ID,
   Area_Code_SI, Phone_Number_IN

   FROM Customer_T
   JOIN Customer_Information_T ON Customer_T.Customer_Information_ID =
      Customer_Information_T.Customer_Information_ID
   JOIN Bank_T ON Customer_Information_T.Bank_ID = Bank_T.Bank_ID
   JOIN Phone_Number_T ON Bank_T.Phone_Number_ID = Phone_Number_T.Phone_Number_ID

   WHERE Customer_T.Customer_ID = @Customer_ID
```

2. When we select an entry in the Financial Institute combo box, we need to get the phone number associated with that entry from the database and display that phone number on the form. This next stored procedure will select a phone number for a particular bank. Create this stored procedure and set the appropriate permissions:

```
CREATE PROCEDURE up_parmsel_bank_phone_number (@Bank_ID Int) AS

SELECT Phone_Number_T.Phone_Number_ID, Area_Code_SI, Phone_Number_IN
   FROM Bank_T
   JOIN Phone_Number_T ON Bank_T.Phone_Number_ID = Phone_Number_T.Phone_Number_ID
   WHERE Bank_ID = @Bank_ID
```

Once the financial information has been inserted into the `Customer_Information_T` table, we can update that information independently of the employer information. The `up_parmupd_customer_financial_information` stored procedure to be created is listed in the *How It Works* section below. It accepts the financial institute information to be updated along with the customer's primary key. Either a new financial institute has been selected for this customer or we are making updates to the current financial institute and phone number.

How It Works – Financial Institute Stored Procedures

The `up_parmupd_customer_financial_information` stored procedure accepts the primary key for the current customer and the financial institution information, along with the phone number. It also accepts an output parameter that will be used to return messages back to the caller:

```
CREATE PROCEDURE up_parmupd_customer_financial_information (@Customer_ID Int,
   @Bank_ID Int, @Bank_Name VarChar(30), @Bank_Area_Code SmallInt,
   @Bank_Phone_Number Int, @Message VarChar(300) OUTPUT) AS
```

We have declared four variables to be used in this stored procedure. The first two should look familiar to you as these two variables are used in the validation of data. The second two variables will be used to retrieve the primary key to the `Phone_Number_T` table and the `Customer_Information_T` tables. After our variables are declared, we set the default values for some of them:

```
--
*********************************************************************************
-- Declare variables
--
*********************************************************************************
DECLARE @Continue          Bit,
   @Name_Required          Bit,
   @Customer_Information_ID   Int,
   @Bank_Phone_Number_ID      Int

--
-- Turn on default value to continue
--
SELECT @Continue = 1

--
-- Set default values
--
SELECT @Message = ''
```

The validation of data is no different from that in the stored procedure that inserts the data, as listed in step 4 of the previous example, and thus will not listed again here.

After the validations have been performed, we either return to the caller or continue processing:

```
--
*********************************************************************************
-- All data has been validated, either return to the caller with a bad return code
-- and messages or continue on and insert the values
--
*********************************************************************************
IF @Continue = 0
   BEGIN
   --
   -- Return to the caller with a bad return code
   -- The messages are in the @message output parameter
   --
   RETURN 1
   END
```

When we continue processing, we begin a transaction. Since we are dealing with updates and inserts to multiple tables, we want to ensure that either the entire stored procedure finishes or we roll back any work performed up to the point of failure:

```
ELSE
   BEGIN
   --
*********************************************************************************
   -- Start a transaction, if any code fails then we back out everything
   --
*********************************************************************************
   BEGIN TRANSACTION Financial_Information
```

Next we determine if we are using an existing financial institute or inserting a new one. If we are inserting a new financial institute, we insert the phone number first so that we can use the `Phone_Number_ID` as the foreign key in the `Bank_T` table:

```
   --
*********************************************************************************
   -- Determine if we are using an existing bank or inserting a new one
   --
*********************************************************************************
   IF @Bank_ID IS Null OR @Bank_ID = 0
      BEGIN
      --
      -- We are inserting a new bank
      --
      -- *****************************************************************
      -- Insert the bank phone number
      -- *****************************************************************
      INSERT INTO Phone_Number_T
         (Area_Code_SI, Phone_Number_IN, Last_Update_DT)
         VALUES(@Bank_Area_Code, @Bank_Phone_Number, GetDate())
```

After inserting the phone number we check for errors and roll back the transaction if necessary. Otherwise we continue on and get the `Identity` value that was inserted into the `Phone_Number_T` table:

```
--
-- Check for errors
--
IF @@ERROR <> 0
   BEGIN
   --
   -- Roll back the transaction and return to the caller
   --
   ROLLBACK TRANSACTION Financial_Information
   RAISERORR('Insert for bank phone number failed.',18,1)
   RETURN 99
   END

--
-- Get the phone number ID just inserted
--
SELECT @Bank_Phone_Number_ID = @@IDENTITY
```

After the new phone number has been inserted, we insert the new financial institution name along with the `Phone_Number_ID` that was just inserted and saved to our variable, `@Bank_Phone_Number_ID`. We then check for errors and roll back the transaction if necessary. If no errors occurred, we save the `Identity` value in the `@Bank_ID` parameter:

```
-- ************************************************************************
-- Insert the bank
-- ************************************************************************
INSERT INTO Bank_T
   (Phone_Number_ID, Bank_Name_VC, Last_Update_DT)
   VALUES(@Bank_Phone_Number_ID, @Bank_Name, GetDate())

--
-- Check for errors
--
IF @@ERROR <> 0
   BEGIN
   --
   -- Roll back the transaction and return to the caller
   --
   ROLLBACK TRANSACTION Financial_Information
   RAISERROR('Insert for bank failed.',18,1)
   RETURN 99
   END

--
-- Get the bank ID just inserted
--
SELECT @Bank_ID = @@IDENTITY
END
```

Before we can update the Customer_Information_T table, we need to get the primary key to that table. We do this by selecting the primary key for this table into the @Customer_Information_ID variable. Since we have the primary key for the Customer_T table, we are selecting the foreign key reference to the Customer_Information_T table from the Customer_T table. Once again we check for errors and roll back the transaction if any errors occurred.

Notice how we SELECT the value of the data contained in a column and assign it to a variable. This is a very useful and efficient technique for selecting a primary or foreign key from a column and assigning it to a variable, as we have done here:

```
   --
*******************************************************************************
   -- Now get the customer information ID
   --
*******************************************************************************
   SELECT @Customer_Information_ID = Customer_Information_ID
      FROM Customer_T
      WHERE Customer_ID = @Customer_ID

   --
   -- Check for errors
   --
   IF @@ERROR <> 0
      BEGIN
      --
      -- Roll back the transaction and return to the caller
      --
      ROLLBACK TRANSACTION Financial_Information
      RAISERROR('Retreival of customer information ID failed.',18,1)
      RETURN 99
      END
```

Now that we have all the required information, we can update the Customer_Information_T table. After the update we check for errors and roll back the transaction if necessary:

```
   --
*******************************************************************************
   -- Update the financial information
   --
*******************************************************************************
   UPDATE Customer_Information_T
      SET Bank_ID = @Bank_ID
      WHERE Customer_Information_ID = @Customer_Information_ID

   --
   -- Check for errors
   --
   IF @@ERROR <> 0
      BEGIN
      --
      -- Roll back the transaction and return to the caller
      --
```

```
        ROLLBACK TRANSACTION Financial_Information
        RAISERROR('Update of customer financial information failed.',18,1)
        RETURN 99
        END
```

If all processing was successful, we commit the transaction and return to the caller with a return code of zero.

```
   --
*******************************************************************************
   -- Commit the transaction and return to the caller
   --
*******************************************************************************
   COMMIT TRANSACTION Financial_Information
   RETURN 0
   END
```

Customer Purchase History Stored Procedures

Like the financial information, the customer's purchase history is displayed on a separate form. This form will display every purchase the customer has ever made. The purchase history is a separate record from the customer record. When we create a customer record, the history information is not created with it. We must use a separate form to insert and update history information for a customer.

Try It Out – Customer Purchase History SELECT Stored Procedure

We need to create a stored procedure to insert the vehicle make, model, and model year that the customer has purchased, along with the sales date and purchase price. If the customer traded a vehicle, then we also want to insert the model year of the vehicle traded, along with the make and model of that vehicle.

The stored procedure to accomplish this is listed below:

```
CREATE PROCEDURE up_parmsel_customer_purchase_history (@Customer_ID Int) AS

SELECT Customer_Purchase_History_ID, Model_Year_SI, Purchase_Price_SM,
   Sales_Date_DT, Model_Year_Traded_SI,
--
-- Select make and model purchased
--
   Make_Purchased.Make_ID AS Vehicle_Make_Purchased_ID,
   Make_Purchased.Vehicle_Make_VC AS Vehicle_Make_Purchased,
   Model_Purchased.Model_ID AS Vehicle_Model_Purchased_ID,
   Model_Purchased.Vehicle_Model_VC AS Vehicle_Model_Purchased,
--
-- Select make and model traded
--
```

```
    Make_Traded.Make_ID AS Vehicle_Make_Traded_ID,
    Make_Traded.Vehicle_Make_VC AS Vehicle_Make_Traded,
    Model_Traded.Model_ID AS Vehicle_Model_Traded_ID,
    Model_Traded.Vehicle_Model_VC AS Vehicle_Model_Traded
--
-- From
--
    FROM Customer_Purchase_History_T
--
-- Join make_t to get vehicle make purchased
--
    JOIN Make_T AS Make_Purchased ON
       Customer_Purchase_History_T.Make_ID = Make_Purchased.Make_ID
--
-- Join model_t to get vehicle model purchased
--
    JOIN Model_T AS Model_Purchased ON
       Customer_Purchase_History_T.Model_ID = Model_Purchased.Model_ID
--
-- Left outer join make_t to get vehicle make traded if any
--
    LEFT OUTER JOIN Make_T AS Make_Traded ON
       Customer_Purchase_History_T.Make_Traded_ID = Make_Traded.Make_ID
--
-- Left outer join model_t to get vehicle model traded if any
--
    LEFT OUTER JOIN Model_T AS Model_Traded ON
       Customer_Purchase_History_T.Model_Traded_ID = Model_Traded.Model_ID
--
-- Where
--
    WHERE Customer_ID = @Customer_ID
--
-- Order results
--
    ORDER BY Sales_Date_dt DESC, Customer_Purchase_History_ID DESC
```

How It Works – Customer Purchase History SELECT Stored Procedure

This stored procedure is very similar to the one that selects customer employer information. We are joining the same table twice, and the second joined table may or may not contain data.

To start, our stored procedure only accepts one parameter, `Customer_ID`. The first line of the `SELECT` statement is selecting basic information that is contained solely in the `Customer_Purchase_History_T` table.

```
CREATE PROCEDURE up_parmsel_customer_purchase_history (@Customer_ID Int) AS

SELECT Customer_Purchase_History_ID, Model_Year_SI, Purchase_Price_SM,
   Sales_Date_DT, Model_Year_Traded_SI,
```

The next part of our SELECT statement is selecting make and model information for the vehicle purchased. The Make_T and Model_T tables are joined twice in this stored procedure, so we are using *correlation names* for the table and *column aliases* for the columns to keep the column names unique:

```
--
-- Select make and model purchased
--
   Make_Purchased.Make_ID AS Vehicle_Make_Purchased_ID,
   Make_Purchased.Vehicle_Make_VC AS Vehicle_Make_Purchased,
   Model_Purchased.Model_ID AS Vehicle_Model_Purchased_ID,
   Model_Purchased.Vehicle_Model_VC AS Vehicle_Model_Purchased,
```

The next part of our SELECT statement is selecting the make and model information for the vehicle traded, if such information exists. Again we are using correlation names for the joined tables, and column aliases:

```
--
-- Select make and model traded
--
   Make_Traded.Make_ID AS Vehicle_Make_Traded_ID,
   Make_Traded.Vehicle_Make_VC AS Vehicle_Make_Traded,
   Model_Traded.Model_ID AS Vehicle_Model_Traded_ID,
   Model_Traded.Vehicle_Model_VC AS Vehicle_Model_Traded
```

The main table we are selecting data from is the Customer_Purchase_History_T table and that is the table listed in the FROM clause:

```
--
-- From
--
   FROM Customer_Purchase_History_T
```

We know that the vehicle make and model purchased is required, so we can use a simple JOIN to join the Make_T and Model_T tables. Notice that we have specified the correlation names for these joined tables:

```
--
-- Join make_t to get vehicle make purchased
--
   JOIN Make_T AS Make_Purchased ON
      Customer_Purchase_History_T.Make_ID = Make_Purchased.Make_ID
--
-- Join model_t to get vehicle model purchased
--
   JOIN Model_T AS Model_Purchased ON
      Customer_Purchase_History_T.Model_ID = Model_Purchased.Model_ID
```

Since the vehicle traded information is optional, there may or may not be an entry in the `Make_T` and `Model_T` tables for the vehicle traded. To that end, we must use a `LEFT OUTER JOIN` to join these tables and to return nulls in the columns in the `SELECT` list in those instances. Once again notice that we have used correlation names for the joined tables:

```
--
-- Left outer join make_t to get vehicle make traded if any
--
   LEFT OUTER JOIN Make_T AS Make_Traded ON
      Customer_Purchase_History_T.Make_Traded_ID = Make_Traded.Make_ID
--
-- Left outer join model_t to get vehicle model traded if any
--
   LEFT OUTER JOIN Model_T AS Model_Traded ON
      Customer_Purchase_History_T.Model_Traded_ID = Model_Traded.Model_ID
```

Since we only want to select data for a particular customer, we limit the number of rows returned by specifying the `Customer_ID` in the `WHERE` clause. We want the results returned in the recordset with the most recent purchase first, so we use the `DESC` keyword to sort the results by sales date and then by the primary key of the `Customer_Purchase_History_T` table:

```
--
-- Where
--
   WHERE Customer_ID = @Customer_ID
--
-- Order results
--
   ORDER BY Sales_Date_DT DESC, Customer_Purchase_History_ID DESC
```

Try It Out – Customer Purchase History INSERT Stored Procedure

Now that we have a means by which we can *select* purchase history data, we need a method to *insert* purchase history data. Like most of the previous stored procedures that have foreign keys, this stored procedure will also insert a new value into the foreign key tables if necessary. This stored procedure also contains optional data – the make and model of the vehicle traded. Like the stored procedure to insert an employer, this stored procedure must test to see whether or not these parameters contain data.

The code for the stored procedure is presented in the *How It Works* section below.

How It Works – Customer Purchase History INSERT Stored Procedure

The code for this stored procedure is very similar to the stored procedure to insert an employer and does not require a lot of explanation, as the principle is the same. This stored procedure accepts all of the parameters required to insert a complete row of data into the `Customer_Purchase_History_T` table. It also contains the extra parameters to insert a new make and model into the `Make_T` and `Model_T` tables if necessary.

There are only two variables declared and they are used for the validation of data:

```
CREATE PROCEDURE up_parmins_customer_purchase (@Customer_ID Int,
   @Make_Purchased_ID Int, @Make_Purchased VarChar(15), @Model_Purchased_ID Int,
   @Model_Purchased VarChar(15), @Model_Year_Purchased SmallInt,
   @Purchase_Price SmallMoney, @Sales_Date DateTime, @Make_Traded_ID Int,
   @Make_Traded VarChar(15), @Model_Traded_ID Int, @Model_Traded VarChar(15),
   @Model_Year_Traded SmallInt, @Message VarChar(300) OUTPUT) AS

--
**********************************************************************************
-- Declare variables
--
**********************************************************************************
DECLARE @Continue   Bit,
   @Name_Required   Bit

--
-- Turn on default value to continue
--
SELECT @Continue = 1

--
-- Set default values
--
SELECT @Message = ''
```

The validation of data is the same as the other validations that we have been performing throughout this book, and does not need to be covered again. We have not listed all of the code here, just the list of validations to be performed; you should by now be able to code these yourself:

```
--
**********************************************************************************
-- Validate customer ID
--
**********************************************************************************
--
**********************************************************************************
-- Validate model year purchased
--
**********************************************************************************
--
**********************************************************************************
-- Validate purchase price
--
**********************************************************************************
```

```
--
**********************************************************************************
-- Validate sales date
--
**********************************************************************************
--
**********************************************************************************
-- Validate make purchased ID or make purchased exists
--
**********************************************************************************
--
**********************************************************************************
-- Validate model purchased ID or model purchased exists
--
**********************************************************************************
--
**********************************************************************************
-- Validate make and model traded if they exist
--
**********************************************************************************
```

At this point, we either return to the caller if the validations have failed or continue processing:

```
--
**********************************************************************************
-- All data has been validated, either return to the caller with a bad return code
-- and messages or continue on and insert the values
--
**********************************************************************************
IF @Continue = 0
   BEGIN
   --
   -- Return to the caller with a bad return code
   -- The messages are in the @message output parameter
   --
   RETURN 1
   END
```

If we continue processing, we begin a new transaction because we are dealing with multiple tables and want to either complete the unit of work as a whole or roll back all work performed up to the point of failure:

```
ELSE
   BEGIN
   --
*******************************************************************************
   -- Start a transaction, if any code fails then we back out everything
   --
*******************************************************************************
   BEGIN TRANSACTION Customer_Purchase
```

At this point we must determine if we are inserting a new vehicle make or if the primary key to an existing entry in this table was passed as a parameter. If we insert a new vehicle make, we check for errors after the insert, and roll back the transaction if any errors occur. We then save the `Identity` value that was inserted for use later in this stored procedure:

```
   --
*******************************************************************************
   -- Determine if we are using an existing make or inserting a new one
   --
*******************************************************************************
   IF @Make_Purchased_ID IS Null OR @Make_Purchased_ID = 0
      BEGIN
      --
      -- We are inserting a new make
      --
      -- ***************************************************************************
      -- Insert the make purchased
      -- ***************************************************************************
      INSERT INTO Make_T
         (Vehicle_Make_VC, Last_Update_DT)
         VALUES(@Make_Purchased, GetDate())

      --
      -- Check for errors
      --
      IF @@ERROR <> 0
         BEGIN
         --
         -- Rollback the transaction and return to the caller
         --
         ROLLBACK TRANSACTION Customer_Purchase
         RAISERROR('Insert for make purchased failed.',18,1)
         RETURN 99
         END

      --
      -- Get the make id just inserted
      --
      SELECT @Make_Purchased_ID = @@IDENTITY
      END
```

We perform the same process for the vehicle model:

```
-- ***************************************************************************
-- Determine if we are using an existing model or inserting a new one
-- ***************************************************************************
IF @Model_Purchased_ID IS Null OR @Model_Purchased_ID = 0
      BEGIN
      --
      -- We are inserting a new model
      --
      -- *********************************************************************
      -- Insert the model purchased
      -- *********************************************************************
      INSERT INTO Model_T
            (Vehicle_Model_VC, Last_Update_DT)
            VALUES(@Model_Purchased, GetDate())

      --
      -- Check for errors
      --
      IF @@ERROR <> 0
            BEGIN
            --
            -- Roll back the transaction and return to the caller
            --
            ROLLBACK TRANSACTION Customer_Purchase
            RAISERROR('Insert for model purchased failed.',18,1)
            RETURN 99
            END

      --
      -- Get the make ID just inserted
      --
      SELECT @Model_Purchased_ID = @@IDENTITY
      END
```

We must determine if a vehicle make and model was traded. If the `@Make_Traded_ID` parameter is either null or zero we check to see if the `@Make_Traded` contains data. If it does, we insert a new make in the `Make_T` table and save the `Identity` value for later use. If the `@Make_Traded` parameter contains no data then we set the `@Make_Traded_ID` to null, because no make and model traded exists.

```
   --
*****************************************************************************
   -- Determine if make and model traded exists
   --
*****************************************************************************
   --
   -- If either make traded id is null or zero check the make traded
   --
```

```
IF @Make_Traded_ID IS Null OR @Make_Traded_ID = 0
   BEGIN
   -- ***********************************************************************
   -- Determine if data exists to insert a new make
   -- ***********************************************************************
   IF DataLength(LTrim(@Make_Traded)) > 0
      BEGIN
      -- ***********************************************************
      -- Insert the make traded
      -- ***********************************************************
      INSERT INTO Make_T
         (Vehicle_Make_VC, Last_Update_DT)
         VALUES(@Make_Traded, GetDate())

      --
      -- Check for errors
      --
      IF @@ERROR <> 0
         BEGIN
         --
         -- Roll back the transaction and return to the caller
         --
         ROLLBACK TRANSACTION Customer_Purchase
         RAISERROR('Insert for make traded failed.',18,1)
         RETURN 99
         END

      --
      -- Get the make ID just inserted
      --
      SELECT @make_Traded_ID = @@IDENTITY
      END

   ELSE

      BEGIN
      --
      -- No make traded exists, ensure all values are null
      --
      SELECT @Make_Traded ID = Null
      END
   END
```

We perform the same check and processing steps for the model traded:

```
   --
   -- If either model traded ID is null or zero check the model traded
   --
   IF @Model_Traded_ID IS Null OR @Model_Traded_ID = 0
      BEGIN
      --
```

```
*******************************************************************
        -- Determine if data exists to insert a new model
        -- ****************************************************************
        IF DataLength(LTrim(@Model_Traded)) > 0
            BEGIN
            -- ****************************************************
            -- Insert the model traded
            -- ****************************************************
            INSERT INTO Model_T
                (Vehicle_Model_VC, Last_Update_DT)
                VALUES(@Model_Traded, GetDate())

            --
            -- Check for errors
            --
            IF @@ERROR <> 0
                BEGIN
                --
                -- Roll back the transaction and return to the caller
                --
                ROLLBACK TRANSACTION Customer_Purchase
                RAISERROR('Insert for model traded failed.',18,1)
                RETURN 99
                END

            --
            -- Get the model ID just inserted
            --
            SELECT @Model_Traded_ID = @@IDENTITY
            END

        ELSE

            BEGIN
            --
            -- No make traded exists, ensure all values are null
            --
            SELECT @Model_Traded_ID = Null
            END
        END

    --
    -- If model year traded is zero, set model year traded to null
    --
    IF @Model_Year_Traded = 0
        BEGIN
        SELECT @Model_Year_Traded = Null
        END
```

At this point in the stored procedure, we are ready to insert the values into the `Customer_Purchase_History_T` table. All parameters that contain ID values either contain a valid foreign key value or they contain null. We then insert the values into the table and check for errors. If an error occurred we roll back the transaction and return to the caller with a return code of 99. If there were no errors, we commit the transaction and return to the caller with a return code of zero.

```
   --
*********************************************************************************
   -- Finally, insert all purchase data in the customer purchase history table
   --
*********************************************************************************
   INSERT INTO Customer_Purchase_History_T
      (Customer_ID, Make_ID, Model_ID, Model_Year_SI, Purchase_Price_SM,
         Sales_Date_DT, Make_Traded_ID, Model_Traded_ID,
         Model_Year_Traded_SI, Last_Update_DT)
      VALUES(@Customer_ID, @Make_Purchased_ID, @Model_Purchased_ID,
         @Model_Year_Purchased, @Purchase_Price, @Sales_Date,
         @Make_Traded_ID, @Model_Traded_ID, @Model_Year_Traded, GetDate())

   --
   -- Check for errors
   --
   IF @@ERROR <> 0
      BEGIN
      --
      -- Roll back the transaction and return to the caller
      --
      ROLLBACK TRANSACTION Customer_Purchase
      RAISERROR('Insert of customer purchase history failed.',18,1)
      RETURN 99
      END

   --
*********************************************************************************
   -- Commit the transaction and return to the caller
   --
*********************************************************************************
   COMMIT TRANSACTION Customer_Purchase
   RETURN 0
   --
   -- End if statement block
   --
   END
```

Try It Out - Customer Purchase History Update Stored Procedure

Once a record has been *inserted* into the History table, we need a means to *update* it. Our SELECT stored procedure selects all history records for a customer. However, the most recent record is listed first in the results set and this provides us a means to know which record is the most current. This record will be displayed separately on the form from the other records so as to allow us to modify and update it if necessary.

1. This UPDATE stored procedure looks and performs essentially the same as its insert counterpart. The code for this stored procedure which is different to the INSERT stored procedure is presented below.

```
CREATE PROCEDURE up_parmupd_customer_purchase (@Customer_Purchase_History_ID Int,
   @Make_Purchased_ID Int, @Make_Purchased VarChar(15), @Model_Purchased_ID Int,
   @Model_Purchased VarChar(15), @Model_Year_Purchased SmallInt,
   @Purchase_Price SmallMoney, @Sales_Date DateTime, @Make_Traded_ID Int,
   @Make_Traded VarChar(15), @Model_Traded_ID Int, @Model_Traded VarChar(15),
   @Model_Year_Traded SmallInt, @Message VarChar(300) OUTPUT) AS
```

2. Instead of validating the customer ID, validate the customer purchase history ID.

3. This section replaces the insert section in the INSERT stored procedure:

```
   --
******************************************************************************
   -- Finally, update all purchase data in the customer purchase history table
   --
******************************************************************************
   UPDATE Customer_Purchase_History_T
      SET Make_ID = @Make_Purchased_ID,
      Model_ID = @Model_Purchased_ID,
      Model_Year_SI = @Model_Year_Purchased,
      Purchase_Price_SM = @Purchase_Price,
      Sales_Date_DT = @Sales_Date,
      Make_Traded_ID = @Make_Traded_ID,
      Model_Traded_ID = @Model_Traded_ID,
      Model_Year_Traded_SI = @Model_Year_Traded,
      Last_Update_DT = GetDate()
      WHERE Customer_Purchase_History_ID = @Customer_Purchase_History_ID

   --
   -- Check for errors
   --
   IF @@ERROR <> 0
      BEGIN
      --
      -- Rollback the transaction and return to the caller
      --
      ROLLBACK TRANSACTION Customer_Purchase
      RAISERROR('Insert of customer purchase history failed.',18,1)
      RETURN 99
      END
```

```
    --
****************************************************************************
    -- Commit the transaction and return to the caller
    --
****************************************************************************
    COMMIT TRANSACTION Customer_Purchase
    RETURN 0
    --
    -- End if statement block
    --
    END
```

How It Works – Customer Purchase History Update Stored Procedure

All the input and output parameters are the same except for the first one. In the `INSERT` stored procedure, the first parameter was the `@Customer_ID` and it has been replaced here with the `@Customer_Purchase_History_ID`, which is the key to the record that we want to update.

All of the validations are the same as the previous stored procedure, except instead of checking the customer ID we check the customer purchase history ID. Also the checks performed against the vehicle make and model. Again they are not listed here, as you should be able to code these using the validations previously covered.

If a new make or model has been specified, then the new entry will be inserted and the `Identity` value for that entry will be used in the `UPDATE` statement. The `UPDATE` statement updates all columns in the `Customer_Purchase_History_T` table with the exception of the `Customer_ID`. If an error occurs during the update, we roll back the transaction and return to the caller with a return code of 99. If everything was successful, we commit the transaction and return with a return code of zero.

Summary

This wraps up the database side of our case study. We have taken a look at how to add new tables to our database, as well as how to alter a table by adding a new column. Because the column that was added was a foreign key to another table which had yet to be populated with data, we could not set the properties of that column to `Not Null`. The issues surrounding this were discussed and an alternative was suggested, although not implemented in this case study.

During the process of creating and altering tables we found that we must also use the `ALTER TABLE` SQL statement to add primary and foreign keys. During this entire process, we learned how to perform all of these functions through a SQL script, instead of using the Enterprise Manager to perform these tasks. We also covered setting permissions on these new objects using SQL statements.

The benefits of using a SQL script to alter your database are twofold. First, it allows you to examine the entire alteration before actually performing it. Second, this script can be used to alter your test and production databases as you migrate your changes forward. This is a lot safer than manually altering your databases.

This part of the case study also covered the new stored procedures that are required, and there should have been no surprises there. The methods that were used in these stored procedures were the same methods that have been used throughout this book.

Wrox Auto Works Customer Application – Part 2

Part one of this case study concentrated on the database modifications and the stored procedures. This part of the case study concentrates on the business server component to implement the calls to the new stored procedures. We will be using the business server component that we built in Chapter 14 and will be enhancing the functionality of that ActiveX component.

Our component has been designed so that it can run on the client machine, under MTS control on an n-tier server or on the same server as the database. Since the component doesn't know about the database connection it can run anywhere we see fit. If you remember the calls to the functions in our component, we have to pass it an active connection so that it can access the database. This serves two purposes, the first of which is *security*. If our component is running on an n-tier system everyone has access to it. That is, anyone can access our component and use it in their programs if they use a little initiative. However, they cannot use it unless they have a logon to our database, because it will not retrieve any data unless you pass it an active database connection. Second, it allows the component to be moved from server to server without the worry of a DSN or recompiling the component because of some machine specific code such as a DSN-less connection.

Finance Class

Because of the database changes that have occurred, we must add some new classes to our component to support the new database design. The Finance class supports all data required for a customer's financial institution. Because the data in the `Bank_T` table is so closely related to the customer, the financial data is inserted along with the employer information in the function in the Employer class. We will cover this later. Updates to the financial data can be performed independently of the other customer information data.

The financial information for a customer will be displayed on a form separate from all other information. To this end, we will be displaying all financial institutes in a combo box for the user to choose from. The area code and phone number for each institute will also be displayed on the form.

Given this information, we need to create three functions in our Finance class, one to retrieve a list of all banks, one to retrieve the bank for a particular customer, and one to update the financial information for a customer.

Try It Out – Adding the Finance Class

1. Before we can add a new function, we must first add a new class to the AutoWorks business server component. Add a new class and set its Name property to clsFinance.

2. We need to add a function to retrieve all bank names, and the code for this new function is listed below. This function is very straightforward and needs no further explanation, so go ahead and enter this code. Don't forget to change the user prefix of the stored procedures to your own user prefix in this and all examples in this case study:

```
Public Function GetBanks(ByRef objConn As ADODB.Connection, _
      ByRef objRS As ADODB.Recordset) As Long

   'Setup error handling
   On Error GoTo GetBanks_EH

   'Set a reference to the Recordset object
   Set objRS = New ADODB.Recordset

   'Open the recordset
   objRS.Open "willist. up_select_banks", objConn, _
      adOpenDynamic, adLockReadOnly, adCmdStoredProc

   'Return with a good return code
   GetBanks = 0

   'All was successful, exit function
   On Error GoTo 0
   Exit Function

GetBanks_EH:
   GetBanks = 1
   On Error GoTo 0
End Function
```

3. The second function that we need to add to the Finance class is a function to retrieve the financial information for a particular customer. The code for that function is listed below and again this function needs no further explanation.

4. We do, however, want to point out the stored procedure call. Notice that we have enclosed the parameter that is passed to the stored procedure in parentheses and that the recordset is being opened as forward-only and read-only. This is because this recordset will only contain one record.

5. Proceed by entering this code:

```
Public Function GetFinancialInformation(ByRef objConn As ADODB.Connection, _
      ByRef objRS As ADODB.Recordset, _
      ByVal lngCustomerID As Long) As Long

   'Setup error handling
   On Error GoTo GetFinancialInformation_EH

   'Set a reference to the Recordset object
   Set objRS = New ADODB.Recordset

   'Open the recordset
   objRS.Open "willist.up_parmsel_customer_financial_information (" & _
      lngCustomerID & ")", objConn, adOpenForwardOnly, _
      adLockReadOnly, adCmdStoredProc

   'Return with a good return code
   GetFinancialInformation = 0

   'All was successful, exit function
   On Error GoTo 0
   Exit Function

GetFinancialInformation_EH:
   GetFinancialInformation = 1
   On Error GoTo 0
End Function
```

6. This next function updates the financial information for a customer and uses the Command object to pass and retrieve parameters to and from the stored procedure. We could be updating the customer's financial record with an existing financial institution or we could be passing data to have a new financial institution added.

7. The code in the *How It Works* section below lists the UpdateFinancialInformation function, which should also be added to the Finance class.

How It Works – Adding the Finance Class

The `UpdateFinancialInformation` function should look very familiar to you, as we have used this type of function before to update data. We pass the parameters that are input to the stored procedure by value, and the output parameters form the stored procedure are passed to the function by reference so they can be modified. This function returns a long value, which is set using the return code from the stored procedure.

```
Public Function UpdateFinancialInformation(ByVal lngCustomerID As Long, _
      ByVal lngBankID As Long, _
      ByVal strBankName As String, _
      ByVal intAreaCode As Integer, _
      ByVal lngPhoneNumber As Long, _
      ByRef strMessage() As String, _
      ByRef objConn As ADODB.Connection, _
      ByRef objCmd As ADODB.Command) As Long
```

After our error handling has been set up and our local variable declared, we set the `Command` object properties. Then we append the parameters to the `Parameters` collection. Once again it is important to point out that when a stored procedure returns a return value, the return value parameter must be the first parameter in the `Parameters` collection:

```
'Setup error handling
On Error GoTo UpdateFinancialInformation_EH

'Declare local variables
Dim intIndex As Integer

'Set the Command object properties
Set objCmd.ActiveConnection = objConn
objCmd.CommandText = "willist.up_parmupd_customer_financial_information"
objCmd.CommandType = adCmdStoredProc

'Append the parameters
objCmd.Parameters.Append objCmd.CreateParameter("RC", adInteger, _
          adParamReturnValue)
objCmd.Parameters.Append objCmd.CreateParameter("CustomerID", adInteger, _
          adParamInput, , lngCustomerID)
objCmd.Parameters.Append objCmd.CreateParameter("BankID", adInteger, _
          adParamInput, , lngBankID)
objCmd.Parameters.Append objCmd.CreateParameter("BankName", adVarChar, _
          adParamInput, 30, strBankName)
objCmd.Parameters.Append objCmd.CreateParameter("AreaCode", adSmallInt, _
          adParamInput, , intAreaCode)
objCmd.Parameters.Append objCmd.CreateParameter("PhoneNumber", adInteger, _
          adParamInput, , lngPhoneNumber)
objCmd.Parameters.Append objCmd.CreateParameter("Message", adVarChar, _
          adParamOutput, 300)
```

After we execute the `Command` object, we check the return code returned from the stored procedure in the `RC` parameter of the `Parameters` collection. If it is not equal to zero, then we add the data from the stored procedure output `Message` parameter to the `strMessage` parameter that was passed to this function by reference:

```
'Execute the Command object
objCmd.Execute

'If the return code is greater than zero
If objCmd("RC") <> 0 Then
   'Add the message to the message string
   ReDim Preserve strMessage(0)
   strMessage(0) = objCmd("Message")
End If
```

Next, we return to the caller with the return code from the stored procedure and exit the function:

```
    'Return to the caller with the return code from the
    'stored procedure
    UpdateFinancialInformation = objCmd("RC")
    On Error GoTo 0
    Exit Function
```

If any type of occurred, we add any error messages from the `Errors` collection to the `strMessage` variable and then add any VB error to that variable also. We return to the caller with a return code of 99, which is the number we arbitrarily chose to indicate that errors occurred:

```
UpdateFinancialInformation_EH:
    Dim objErr As ADODB.Error
    intIndex = -1
    'Add each ADO error to the message string
    For Each objErr In objConn.Errors
        intIndex = intIndex + 1
        ReDim Preserve strMessage(intIndex)
        strMessage(intIndex) = objErr.Description
    Next
    'Add any VB error message to the message string
    intIndex = intIndex + 1
    ReDim Preserve strMessage(intIndex)
    strMessage(intIndex) = Err.Description
    'Return to the caller
    UpdateFinancialInformation = 99
    On Error GoTo 0
End Function
```

This wraps up the code needed for the Finance class. There is one additional function that is related to the financial information – the function to retrieve the financial institute's phone number. Since we consider this information to also be address related, this function is in the Address class, which we will cover later.

Vehicle Class

The Vehicle class contains all of the functions that relate to the `Make_T`, `Model_T`, and `Customer_Purchase_History_T` tables. Because the customer's purchase history is a separate record from the customer record, all inserting and updating of customer purchases is contained in this class. There are five functions that we need to implement in this class. All of these functions will be covered in this section. First we need a function to retrieve the customer purchase record. We also need functions to insert and update customer purchases. The vehicle make and model will be displayed in a combo box that allows the user to select the appropriate make and model. To this end, we need a function to retrieve a list of vehicle makes and a function to retrieve a list of vehicle models. Both of these functions are straightforward and are listed below.

Try It Out – Modifying the Vehicle Class

1. At this point add a new class to your component, set its `Name` property to `clsVehicle`, and add the following two functions to this new class.

2. The first retrieves the vehicle *make*:

```
Public Function GetVehicleMake(ByRef objConn As ADODB.Connection, _
         ByRef objRS As ADODB.Recordset) As Long

   'Set a reference to the Recordset object
   Set objRS = New ADODB.Recordset

   'Setup error handling
   On Error GoTo GetVehicleMake_EH

   'Open the recordset
   objRS.Open "willist.up_select_make", objConn, _
      adOpenDynamic, adLockReadOnly, adCmdStoredProc

   'Return with a good return code
   GetVehicleMake = 0

   'All was successful, exit function
   On Error GoTo 0
   Exit Function

GetVehicleMake_EH:
   GetVehicleMake = 1
   On Error GoTo 0
End Function
```

3. The second retrieves the vehicle *model*:

```
Public Function GetVehicleModel(ByRef objConn As ADODB.Connection, _
         ByRef objRS As ADODB.Recordset) As Long

   'Set a reference to the Recordset object
   Set objRS = New ADODB.Recordset

   'Setup error handling
   On Error GoTo GetVehicleModel_EH

   'Open the recordset
   objRS.Open "willist.up_select_model", objConn, _
      adOpenDynamic, adLockReadOnly, adCmdStoredProc

   'Return with a good return code
   GetVehicleModel = 0

   'All was successful, exit function
   On Error GoTo 0
   Exit Function
```

```
GetVehicleModel_EH:
   GetVehicleModel = 1
   On Error GoTo 0
End Function
```

4. After the combo boxes have been populated with a list of vehicle makes and models, we need to retrieve the customer's purchase history. This next function is also straightforward and retrieves a recordset containing all purchases this customer has made. The code for this function is listed below and should be entered now:

```
Public Function GetPurchaseHistory(ByRef objConn As ADODB.Connection, _
      ByRef objRS As ADODB.Recordset, _
      ByVal lngCustomerID As Long) As Long

   'Set a reference to the Recordset object
   Set objRS = New ADODB.Recordset

   'Setup error handling
   On Error GoTo GetPurchaseHistory_EH

   'Open the recordset
   objRS.Open "willist.up_parmsel_customer_purchase_history (" & _
      lngCustomerID & ")", objConn, adOpenForwardOnly, _
      adLockReadOnly, adCmdStoredProc

   'Return with a good return code
   GetPurchaseHistory = 0

   'All was successful, exit function
   On Error GoTo 0
   Exit Function

GetPurchaseHistory_EH:
   GetPurchaseHistory = 1
   On Error GoTo 0
End Function
```

As one might expect, we need to pass a parameter to the stored procedure so that it knows for which customer it should retrieve the history. We pass this function the `Customer_ID` of the customer in question and pass this parameter to the stored procedure, enclosed in parentheses.

Try It Out – Customer Purchase History Functions

The last two functions for the `Vehicle` class are a little more complex. As you might imagine, having already created the stored procedures for these, these functions contain a number of parameters that make up the customer purchase record. If the vehicle make and model, purchased or traded, is not contained in the list, then the user is able to enter them in. This function will then execute the stored procedure that will insert the vehicle make and model into the `Make_T` and `Model_T` tables. The other function allows the data to be updated.

Given this, we need to accept the make and model ID as well as the make and model name. This applies to both vehicles, purchased and traded.

The code for the insert function is listed below in the *How It Works* section. At this point go ahead and enter this new function in the Vehicle class.

The update function is almost exactly identical – the differences are highlighted in the *How It Works* section.

How It Works – Customer Purchase History Functions

The insert function accepts all parameters that are input to the stored procedure by value. The `strMessage` parameter is passed by reference so that any messages returned from the stored procedure can be set in this parameter, and the caller has access to those messages.

```
Public Function InsertCustomerPurchase(ByVal lngCustomerID As Long, _
      ByVal lngMakePurchasedID As Long, _
      ByVal strMakePurchased As String, _
      ByVal lngModelPurchasedID As Long, _
      ByVal strModelPurchased As String, _
      ByVal intModelYearPurchased As Integer, _
      ByVal curPurchasePrice As Currency, _
      ByVal dteSalesDate As Date, _
      ByVal lngMakeTradedID As Long, _
      ByVal strMakeTraded As String, _
      ByVal lngModelTradedID As Long, _
      ByVal strModelTraded As String, _
      ByVal intModelYearTraded As Integer, _
      ByRef strMessage() As String, _
      ByRef objConn As ADODB.Connection, _
      ByRef objCmd As ADODB.Command) As Long
```

The first thing we do in this function is to set up error handling and declare our local variables:

```
   'Setup error handling
   On Error GoTo InsertCustomerPurchase_EH

   'Declare local variables
   Dim intIndex As Integer
```

Next, we set the `Command` object's properties and append the parameters to the `Parameters` collection. Once again, the stored procedure that we are executing returns a return value as well as an output parameter. As always, the return value parameter is specified as the first parameter in the `Parameters` collection:

```
'Set the Command object properties
Set objCmd.ActiveConnection = objConn
objCmd.CommandText = "willist.up_parmins_customer_purchase"
objCmd.CommandType = adCmdStoredProc

'Append the parameters
objCmd.Parameters.Append objCmd.CreateParameter("RC", adInteger, _
            adParamReturnValue)
objCmd.Parameters.Append objCmd.CreateParameter("CustomerID", adInteger, _
            adParamInput, , lngCustomerID)
objCmd.Parameters.Append objCmd.CreateParameter("MakePurchasedID", adInteger, _
            adParamInput, , lngMakePurchasedID)
objCmd.Parameters.Append objCmd.CreateParameter("MakePurchased", adVarChar, _
            adParamInput, 15, strMakePurchased)
objCmd.Parameters.Append objCmd.CreateParameter("ModelPurchasedID", adInteger, _
            adParamInput, , lngModelPurchasedID)
objCmd.Parameters.Append objCmd.CreateParameter("ModelPurchased", adVarChar, _
            adParamInput, 15, strModelPurchased)
objCmd.Parameters.Append objCmd.CreateParameter("ModelYearPurchased", adSmallInt, _
            adParamInput, , intModelYearPurchased)
objCmd.Parameters.Append objCmd.CreateParameter("PurchasePrice", adCurrency, _
            adParamInput, , curPurchasePrice)
objCmd.Parameters.Append objCmd.CreateParameter("SalesDate", adDBTimeStamp, _
            adParamInput, , dteSalesDate)
objCmd.Parameters.Append objCmd.CreateParameter("MakeTradedID", adInteger, _
            adParamInput, , lngMakeTradedID)
objCmd.Parameters.Append objCmd.CreateParameter("MakeTraded", adVarChar, _
            adParamInput, 15, strMakeTraded)
objCmd.Parameters.Append objCmd.CreateParameter("ModelTradedID", adInteger, _
            adParamInput, , lngModelTradedID)
objCmd.Parameters.Append objCmd.CreateParameter("ModelTraded", adVarChar, _
            adParamInput, 15, strModelTraded)
objCmd.Parameters.Append objCmd.CreateParameter("ModelYearTraded", adSmallInt, _
            adParamInput, , intModelYearTraded)
objCmd.Parameters.Append objCmd.CreateParameter("Message", adVarChar, _
            adParamOutput, 300)
```

After we have executed the `Command` object, we check for errors by checking the return value from the stored procedure. If the return value is not equal to zero, we set the `strMessage` parameter to the `Message` output parameter returned from the stored procedure:

```
'Execute the Command object
objCmd.Execute

'If the return code is greater than zero
If objCmd("RC") <> 0 Then
   'Add the message to the message string
   ReDim Preserve strMessage(0)
   strMessage(0) = objCmd("Message")
End If
```

We return to the caller using the return value from the stored procedure, accessed through the Command object:

```
    'Return to the caller with the return code from the
    'stored procedure
    InsertCustomerPurchase = objCmd("RC")
    On Error GoTo 0
    Exit Function
```

Our error handling routine is the same as the previous error handling routines and does not need to be covered again:

```
InsertCustomerPurchase_EH:
   Dim objErr As ADODB.Error
   intIndex = -1
   'Add each ADO error to the message string
   For Each objErr In objConn.Errors
      intIndex = intIndex + 1
      ReDim Preserve strMessage(intIndex)
      strMessage(intIndex) = objErr.Description
   Next
   'Add any VB error message to the message string
   intIndex = intIndex + 1
   ReDim Preserve strMessage(intIndex)
   strMessage(intIndex) = Err.Description
   'Return to the caller
   InsertCustomerPurchase = 99
   On Error GoTo 0
End Function
```

The function to update the customer's purchase record is the same as the insert function that we just covered. The differences are the stored procedure name and the first parameter in the function. When we inserted a customer purchase record we used the Customer_ID as the first parameter. When we update the customer purchase record, we use the Customer_Purchase_History_ID, which is the key of the record being updated:

```
Public Function UpdateCustomerPurchase(ByVal lngCustomerHistoryID As Long, _
```

The name of the error handling routine is also different, and needs changing in two places:

```
   'Setup error handling
   On Error GoTo UpdateCustomerPurchase_EH
```

```
UpdateCustomerPurchase_EH:
```

The stored procedure that we call has a different name:

```
'Set the Command object properties
Set objCmd.ActiveConnection = objConn
objCmd.CommandText = "willist.up_parmupd_customer_purchase"
objCmd.CommandType = adCmdStoredProc
```

As mentioned, we use the customer history ID instead of the customer ID:

```
'Append the parameters
objCmd.Parameters.Append objCmd.CreateParameter("RC", adInteger, _
             adParamReturnValue)
objCmd.Parameters.Append objCmd.CreateParameter("CustomerHistoryID", adInteger, _
             adParamInput, , lngCustomerHistoryID)
```

Finally, the error handling routine uses `UpdateCustomerPurchase` instead of `InsertCustomerPurchase`:

```
'Return to the caller with the return code from the
'stored procedure
UpdateCustomerPurchase = objCmd("RC")
On Error GoTo 0
Exit Function

'Return to the caller
UpdateCustomerPurchase = 99
On Error GoTo 0
```

Address Class

We need to make a few minor modifications to the Address class to support retrieving the bank phone number. The first modification we need to make is to the `PhoneType` enumeration, as shown in the code below:

```
Public Enum PhoneType
   ptSalesPerson = 1
   ptEmployer = 2
   ptBank = 3
End Enum
```

The next modification we need to make is to the `GetPhoneNumber` function. We need to modify this function to support retrieving the phone number for a financial institution. We built the stored procedure to select the phone number for a given financial institution in the first part of this case study, and this is the stored procedure we are executing here.

```
Public Function GetPhoneNumber(ByRef objConn As ADODB.Connection, _
      ByRef objRS As ADODB.Recordset, _
      ByVal lngParentID As Long, _
      ByVal lngPhoneType As PhoneType) As Long

   'Setup error handling
   On Error GoTo GetPhoneNumber_EH

   'Set a reference to the recordset object
   Set objRS = New ADODB.Recordset

   'Retrieve the correct phone number
   Select Case lngPhoneType
      Case ptSalesPerson


      Case ptEmployer

         'Open the recordset
         objRS.Open "willist.up_parmsel_employer_phone_number (" & _
               lngParentID & ")", objConn, _
               adOpenStatic, adLockReadOnly, adCmdStoredProc

      Case ptBank

         'Open the recordset
         objRS.Open "willist.up_parmsel_bank_phone_number (" & _
               lngParentID & ")", objConn, _
               adOpenStatic, adLockReadOnly, adCmdStoredProc

   End Select

   'Return with a good return code
   GetPhoneNumber = 0

   'All was successful, exit function
   On Error GoTo 0
   Exit Function

GetPhoneNumber_EH:
   GetPhoneNumber = 1
   On Error GoTo 0
End Function
```

Employer Class

In the first part of this case study, we altered the `Customer_InformationT` table by adding a foreign key reference to the `Bank_T` table. Because the reference to the `Bank_T` table exists in this table, we had to modify the stored procedure that inserted employers to also insert a financial institution for the customer that we were adding. Due to these changes in that stored procedure, the function to insert an employer must also be changed to support the additional parameters required by the stored procedure.

To that end, the code listed below shows the modifications to be made to the `InsertEmployer` function:

```
Public Function InsertEmployer(ByVal lngCurrentEmployerID As Long, _
      ByVal strCurrentEmployerName As String, _
      ByVal intCurrentEmployerAreaCode As Integer, _
      ByVal lngCurrentEmployerPhoneNumber As Long, _
      ByVal bytYearsAtCurrentEmployer As Byte, _
      ByVal strJobTitle As String, _
      ByVal lngPreviousEmployerID As Long, _
      ByVal strPreviousEmployerName As String, _
      ByVal intPreviousEmployerAreaCode As Integer, _
      ByVal lngPreviousEmployerPhoneNumber As Long, _
      ByVal bytYearsAtPreviousEmployer As Byte, _
      ByVal lngBankID As Long, _
      ByVal strBankName As String, _
      ByVal intBankAreaCode As Integer, _
      ByVal lngBankPhoneNumber As Long, _
      ByRef lngCustomerInformationID As Long, _
      ByRef strMessage() As String, _
      ByRef objConn As ADODB.Connection, _
      ByRef objCmd As ADODB.Command) As Long

   'Setup error handling
   On Error GoTo InsertEmployer_EH

   'Declare local variables
   Dim intIndex As Integer

   'Set the Command object properties
   Set objCmd.ActiveConnection = objConn
   objCmd.CommandText = "willist.up_parmins_employer_information"
   objCmd.CommandType = adCmdStoredProc

   'Append the parameters
   objCmd.Parameters.Append objCmd.CreateParameter("RC", adInteger, _
              adParamReturnValue)
   objCmd.Parameters.Append objCmd.CreateParameter("CurrentEmployerID", adInteger, _
              adParamInput, , lngCurrentEmployerID)
   objCmd.Parameters.Append objCmd.CreateParameter("CurrentEmployerName", adVarChar, _
              adParamInput, 30, strCurrentEmployerName)
   objCmd.Parameters.Append objCmd.CreateParameter("CurrentEmployerAreaCode", _
              adSmallInt, adParamInput, , intCurrentEmployerAreaCode)
   objCmd.Parameters.Append objCmd.CreateParameter("CurrentEmployerPhoneNumber", _
              adInteger, adParamInput, , lngCurrentEmployerPhoneNumber)
   objCmd.Parameters.Append objCmd.CreateParameter("YearsAtCurrentEmployer", _
              adTinyInt, adParamInput, , bytYearsAtCurrentEmployer)
   objCmd.Parameters.Append objCmd.CreateParameter("JobTitle", adVarChar, _
              adParamInput, 30, strJobTitle)
   objCmd.Parameters.Append objCmd.CreateParameter("PreviousEmployerID", adInteger, _
```

```
                adParamInput, , lngPreviousEmployerID)
    objCmd.Parameters.Append objCmd.CreateParameter("PreviousEmployerName", _
                adVarChar, adParamInput, 30, strPreviousEmployerName)
    objCmd.Parameters.Append objCmd.CreateParameter("PreviousEmployerAreaCode", _
                adSmallInt, adParamInput, , intPreviousEmployerAreaCode)
    objCmd.Parameters.Append objCmd.CreateParameter("PreviousEmployerPhoneNumber", _
                adInteger, adParamInput, , lngPreviousEmployerPhoneNumber)
    objCmd.Parameters.Append objCmd.CreateParameter("YearsAtPreviousEmployer", _
                adTinyInt, adParamInput, , bytYearsAtPreviousEmployer)
    objCmd.Parameters.Append objCmd.CreateParameter("BankID", adInteger, _
                adParamInput, , lngBankID)
    objCmd.Parameters.Append objCmd.CreateParameter("BankName", adVarChar, _
                adParamInput, 30, strBankName)
    objCmd.Parameters.Append objCmd.CreateParameter("BankAreaCode", adSmallInt, _
                adParamInput, , intBankAreaCode)
    objCmd.Parameters.Append objCmd.CreateParameter("BankPhoneNumber", adInteger, _
                adParamInput, , lngBankPhoneNumber)
    objCmd.Parameters.Append objCmd.CreateParameter("CustomerInformationID", _
                adInteger, adParamOutput)
    objCmd.Parameters.Append objCmd.CreateParameter("Message", adVarChar, _
                adParamOutput, 300)

    'Execute the Command object
    objCmd.Execute

    'If the return code is greater than zero
    If objCmd("RC") <> 0 Then
       'Add the message to the message string
       ReDim Preserve strMessage(0)
       strMessage(0) = objCmd("Message")
    End If

    'Set the return parameters
    lngCustomerInformationID = objCmd("CustomerInformationID")

    'Return to the caller with the return code from the
    'stored procedure
    InsertEmployer = objCmd("RC")
    On Error GoTo 0
    Exit Function

InsertEmployer_EH:
    Dim objErr As ADODB.Error
    intIndex = -1
    'Add each ADO error to the message string
    For Each objErr In objConn.Errors
       intIndex = intIndex + 1
       ReDim Preserve strMessage(intIndex)
       strMessage(intIndex) = objErr.Description
    Next
    'Add any VB error message to the message string
    intIndex = intIndex + 1
```

```
    ReDim Preserve strMessage(intIndex)
    strMessage(intIndex) = Err.Description
    'Return to the caller
    InsertEmployer = 99
    On Error GoTo 0
End Function
```

As you can see we have added the parameters that support either using an existing financial institute or inserting a new financial institute, along with its phone number.

Completing the AutoWorks Component

Because of the modifications to the `InsertEmployer` function, we will break binary compatibility of our component. In other words the changes to the functions will require a new interface ID to be generated which will break binary compatibility, because the interface ID will not be the same as the old one. To rectify this situation, we need to recompile a new binary version of our DLL for compatibility purposes.

Try It Out – Recompile the AutoWorks Component

1. In the Project Properties dialog, click on the Make tab, change the Major version number to a 2 and set the Minor and Revision version numbers to 0. This is done because we have made a major change to the component: we have added new functionality and changed some of the current functions, and want to reflect this in the version number:

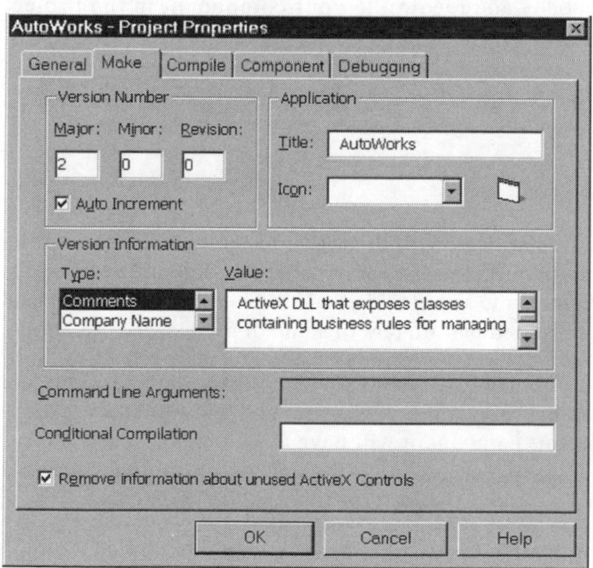

2. Next, click on the Component tab and set the Version Compatibility to Project Compatibility as shown in the figure below. Click OK to save your changes:

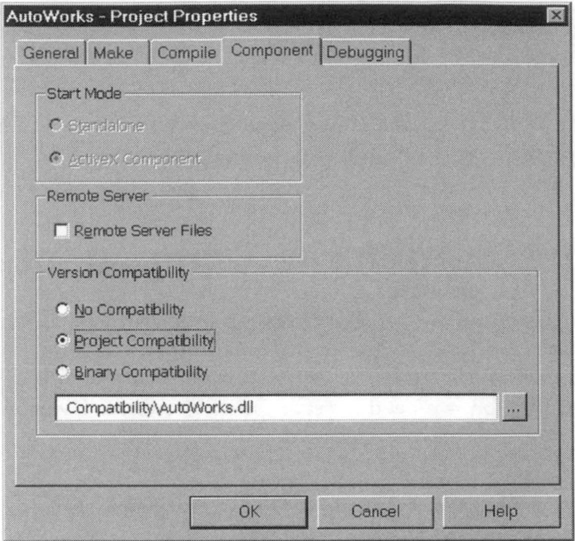

3. Recompile your component in the Compatibility folder, replacing the existing DLL that is there. This will give us a new component to be used as the binary compatible component.

4. Then come back to the Project Properties dialog and change the Version Compatibility to Binary Compatibility and recompile your component in the project directory. This will ensure that any future changes to our component will be compared against the binary component and a dialog will be displayed if we attempt to break binary compatibility again.

Summary

This part of the case study has dealt with the required modifications to our business server component. We have added a couple of new classes to support the new database design and stored procedures. We have also made enhancements to some of the existing functions, which caused us to break binary compatibility because we added parameters to some of the existing functions.

Because of this compatibility issue, we had to recompile our compatibility component. During this recompile process we have changed the version numbers to indicate a major change in our component. Any programs that used this component will have to be recompiled as a result of breaking compatibility. This isn't a problem for us, but it could be a problem in real world applications where more than one compiled program shares a business server component.

Because the database design has been enhanced, we would hope that all applications that access our database would want to take advantage of the new design and modify their programs as such. However, this can't be guaranteed and we must be cognizant of these other applications when we make changes in our business component that will break compatibility.

Wrox Auto Works Customer Application – Part 3

This is the third and final part of our Customer Application case study. The first part of our case study covered the modified database design that provided significant enhancements to the database. In that part of this case study we executed the SQL scripts to modify the database and created new stored procedures to support the new tables. In the second part of our case study we made the enhancements necessary to our business server component to support the new database design, by adding new classes and functions and modifying some existing functions.

To tie everything together, this part of the case study focuses on the user interface. In Chapter 13 we implemented code in the `Validate` event to perform data validation on the data that the user entered. We used this event to ensure that the data entered met certain criteria before we let the field lose focus. This part of the case study will take this data validation one step further by using objects defined with the `WithEvents` keyword to handle the events raised by our objects. Data validation is the key to ensuring integrity of data in our database and we want to do everything possible in our UI to help ensure this.

Controls Class

As we just mentioned, data validation on the front-end helps to ensure data integrity on the backend. While our stored procedures do perform data validation, it is important to perform them on the front-end also. We don't want the user to enter any type of data and submit it, only to receive an error message that some piece of information is missing or is of the wrong data type.

This new class that we will be implementing goes a long way to help ensure this data validation. We will be defining and setting up standard objects using the `WithEvents` keyword. This allows us to implement data validation code in this class that can be used by any of our controls on our forms. The best part of using this method is that we need only maintain the validation code in one place. The validations performed in this class are *specialized* and *generalized*. They are specialized in that they perform special data validations, such as validations for phone number fields, and generalized because they can be used on any textbox that needs to validate data, such as phone numbers. They do not *replace* the validations that we have already coded in our forms but instead *enhance* them.

The objects (e.g. textboxes, combo boxes) in our forms are considered the **event sources**. The objects defined in our Controls class handle the events raised by the objects in our form, and are considered the **event handlers**. In order to connect the two, we must declare a variable for the event handler in our form and set a reference to the event handler. We then assign our objects to the event handler variable defined in our form.

Try It Out – Controls Class Event Handlers

We want to create a Controls class and define four event handlers for textboxes. These event handlers will be used to control the entry of phone numbers, numeric data, dates, and currency data. Each of these event handlers will implement the appropriate code to disallow the entry of character data, and will only allow the entry of special characters as they apply and numeric data.

1. To start, copy the `WAWCustomerApplication` project to a new directory, add a new class to your project, and set the `Name` property to `clsControls`.

2. The code listed below is to be defined in the general declarations section of the `clsControls` class:

```
Option Explicit

Public WithEvents evtPhoneNumberField As TextBox
Public WithEvents evtNumericField As TextBox
Public WithEvents evtDateField As TextBox
Public WithEvents evtCurrencyField As TextBox
```

3. This section of code handles the entry of *currency* data:

```
Private Sub evtCurrencyField_GotFocus()
   evtCurrencyField.SelStart = 0
   evtCurrencyField.SelLength = Len(evtCurrencyField.Text)
End Sub

Private Sub evtCurrencyField_KeyPress(KeyAscii As Integer)
   Select Case KeyAscii
      Case 8                  '8 = backspace
         'Just let it happen
      Case 48 To 57           '48-57 = 0-9
         'Automatically place $ in field
         If Len(evtCurrencyField) = 0 Then
            evtCurrencyField.Text = Chr(36)
            evtCurrencyField.SelStart = Len(evtCurrencyField.Text)
         End If
      Case 36                 '36 = $
         'If position is not 1 don't accept the $ character
         If Len(evtCurrencyField) <> 1 Then
            KeyAscii = 0
         End If
      Case 44, 46             '44 = , and 46 = .
         'Just let it happen
      Case Else
         KeyAscii = 0
         Beep
   End Select
End Sub
```

4. This next section of code handles the entry of *date* data:

```
Private Sub evtDateField_GotFocus()
   evtDateField.SelStart = 0
   evtDateField.SelLength = Len(evtDateField.Text)
End Sub

Private Sub evtDateField_KeyPress(KeyAscii As Integer)
   Select Case KeyAscii
      Case 8                 '8 = backspace
         'Just let it happen
      Case 48 To 57          '48-57 = 0-9
         'Automatically place / in field
         If Len(evtDateField) = 2 Or Len(evtDateField) = 5 Then
            evtDateField.Text = evtDateField.Text & Chr(47)
            evtDateField.SelStart = Len(evtDateField.Text)
         End If
      Case 47                '47 = /
         'If position is not 3 or 6 don't accept the / character
         If Len(evtDateField) <> 2 And Len(evtDateField) <> 5 Then
            KeyAscii = 0
         End If
      Case Else
         KeyAscii = 0
         Beep
   End Select
End Sub
```

5. This section of code handles the entry of *numeric* data:

```
Private Sub evtNumericField_GotFocus()
   evtNumericField.SelStart = 0
   evtNumericField.SelLength = Len(evtNumericField.Text)
End Sub

Private Sub evtNumericField_KeyPress(KeyAscii As Integer)
   Select Case KeyAscii
      Case 8, 48 To 57       '8 = backspace, 48-57 = 0-9
      Case Else
         KeyAscii = 0
         Beep
   End Select
End Sub
```

6. This last section of code handles the entry of *phone number* data:

```
Private Sub evtPhoneNumberField_GotFocus()
   evtPhoneNumberField.SelStart = 0
   evtPhoneNumberField.SelLength = Len(evtPhoneNumberField.Text)
End Sub
```

```
Private Sub evtPhoneNumberField_KeyPress(KeyAscii As Integer)
   Select Case KeyAscii
      Case 8              '8 = backspace
         'Just let it happen
      Case 48 To 57  '48-57 = 0-9
         'Automatically place the dash in the field
         If Len(evtPhoneNumberField) = 3 Then
            evtPhoneNumberField.Text = evtPhoneNumberField.Text & Chr(45)
            evtPhoneNumberField.SelStart = Len(evtPhoneNumberField.Text)
         End If
      Case 45             '45 = dash
         'If position not equal 3 then don't accept the - character
         If Len(evtPhoneNumberField) <> 3 Then
            KeyAscii = 0
         End If
      Case Else
         KeyAscii = 0
         Beep
   End Select
End Sub
```

How It Works – Controls Class Event Handlers

We define the different events that we want to handle and specify the appropriate objects. In this case they are all textboxes:

```
Option Explicit

Public WithEvents evtPhoneNumberField As TextBox
Public WithEvents evtNumericField As TextBox
Public WithEvents evtDateField As TextBox
Public WithEvents evtCurrencyField As TextBox
```

Since we will be handling the different events raised by the form objects, it only makes sense to handle the `GotFocus` event and highlight whatever text exists in the textbox. These next lines of code should look familiar, and they highlight any text that exists:

```
Private Sub evtCurrencyField_GotFocus()
   evtCurrencyField.SelStart = 0
   evtCurrencyField.SelLength = Len(evtCurrencyField.Text)
End Sub
```

The `KeyPress` event handles an input field for currency values. We have defined the various special characters that could be entered in a currency field, such as a dollar sign, comma, and a period. We will accept these special characters and numeric values only.

We do this by trapping the ASCII value of the character entered in the `KeyPress` event. We are using a `Select Case` statement with the `KeyAscii` value that corresponds to the key pressed passed to this event by VB.

```
Private Sub evtCurrencyField_KeyPress(KeyAscii As Integer)
   Select Case KeyAscii
      Case 8                 '8 = backspace
         'Just let it happen
      Case 48 To 57          '48-57 = 0-9
```

If the user does not enter a dollar sign in the first position of the field, then this routine will automatically place it there for them. Likewise, we won't accept a dollar sign anywhere except in the first position:

```
         'Automatically place $ in field
         If Len(evtCurrencyField) = 0 Then
            evtCurrencyField.Text = Chr(36)
            evtCurrencyField.SelStart = Len(evtCurrencyField.Text)
         End If
      Case 36                '36 = $
         'If position is not 1 don't accept the $ character
         If Len(evtCurrencyField) <> 1 Then
            KeyAscii = 0
         End If
      Case 44, 46            '44 = , and 46 = .
         'Just let it happen
```

If the user tries to enter any character other than what we have defined here, we terminate the `KeyPress` event by setting the `KeyAscii` value to 0 and then sound a beep to let the user know that they have entered an invalid character. Terminating the `KeyPress` event prevents the character from being placed and displayed in the textbox.

```
      Case Else
         KeyAscii = 0
         Beep
   End Select
End Sub
```

The event to handle the date field performs a similar function. The `GotFocus` event highlights any text in the date field when the user tabs to this field:

In the `KeyPress` event for the date field, we will only accept numeric values and a forward slash. The forward slash must be in position 3 or 6; any position other than those will be rejected. If the user does not enter a forward slash at all in the date, then this routine will enter it for them:

```
      Case 48 To 57          '48-57 = 0-9
         'Automatically place / in field
         If Len(evtDateField) = 2 Or Len(evtDateField) = 5 Then
            evtDateField.Text = evtDateField.Text & Chr(47)
            evtDateField.SelStart = Len(evtDateField.Text)
         End If
      Case 47                '47 = /
         'If position is not 3 or 6 don't accept the / character
         If Len(evtDateField) <> 2 And Len(evtDateField) <> 5 Then
            KeyAscii = 0
         End If
```

The GotFocus event for a numeric field performs the same function as the other GotFocus events. The KeyPress event for a numeric field is very simple, we only accept numeric values and that's it.

```
        Case 8, 48 To 57        '8 = backspace, 48-57 = 0-9
        Case Else
           KeyAscii = 0
           Beep
```

The GotFocus event for a phone number field performs the same functions as the other GotFocus events by highlighting any text.

The KeyPress event for a phone number field functions in a very similar manner to the date field KeyPress event. We only accept numeric values in the phone number field and will accept a dash in position 4 only. If the user does not enter a dash then one will be entered for them. If they enter a dash in any other position then it is rejected.

Some readers may be wondering why go to all of this trouble, why not just use the Masked Edit control in VB. There are a couple of reasons actually. First and foremost is that you may have learned a new technique that you did not know before. The whole purpose of books is to share our knowledge and to learn. The second reason is that the Masked Edit control weighs in at 163 KB and this class is only 4 KB. Pretty simple math, right?

Financial Form

The Financial form is a new form that we must add to our UI to support the financial aspects of our customers. As part of the Customer Information record, we keep track of the customer's financial institution. To that end we must add a new form and the code to support this. If you recall from the first part of this case study, we had to modify the insert employer stored procedure to handling inserting the financial information. It therefore stands to reason that this form will be designed in a very similar fashion to the Employer form.

Try It Out – Financial Form

1. We want to add a new form to our project, set its Name property to frmFinancial and its BorderStyle property to 3 - Fixed Dialog. Since we are designing this form in a similar fashion to the Employer form, we need a method to call this form to display the current customer's financial information, and a method to display an empty form if there is no current customer displayed. This code will be shown very shortly.

2. Using the table and figure below, add the following controls to this form:

Control	Name	Properties
Frame	Frame1	Caption = Financial Institution
Label	Label1(0)	Caption = Institution Name
Label	Label1(1)	Caption = Area Code
Label	Label1(2)	Caption = Phone Number

Control	Name	Properties
ComboBox	cboInstitutionName	Style = 0 – Dropdown Combo, Text = nothing
TextBox	txtAreaCode	Text = nothing
TextBox	txtPhoneNumber	Text = nothing
Frame	Frame2	Caption = Actions
CommandButton	cmdAdd	Caption = Add Institute
CommandButton	cmdUpdate	Caption = Update Institute
CommandButton	cmdClose	Caption = Close, CausesValidation = False
StatusBar	StatusBar1	Panel Key = Msg, Panel AutoSize = 1 - sbrSpring

3. After adding the controls, your form should look something like this:

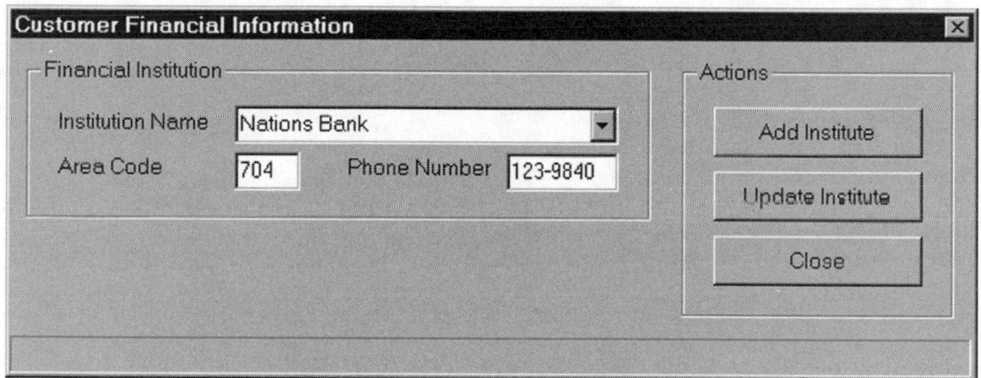

4. Add the following code to the general declarations section of the form:

```
'Declare object events
Private m_evtAreaCode As clsControls
Private m_evtPhoneNumber As clsControls

'Declare module level variables
Private m_blnLoaded As Boolean
Private arrBanks() As Long

'Declare Primary keys
Private m_lngBankID As Long
Private m_lngCustomerID As Long
```

5. Add the following properties to the form:

```
Public Property Let Loaded(ByVal blnLoaded As Boolean)
   m_blnLoaded = blnLoaded
End Property

Public Property Get Loaded() As Boolean
   Loaded = m_blnLoaded
End Property
```

6. Add the following procedure to the form:

```
Public Sub LoadBanks(ByRef objConn As ADODB.Connection)
   'Set up error handling
   On Error GoTo LoadBanks_EH

   'Declare local variables
   Dim lngLastValue As Long, lngIndex As Long, lngRC As Long

   'Clear any existing entries
   cboInstitutionName.Clear

   'Set a reference to the objects
   Dim objRS As New ADODB.Recordset
   Dim objFinance As New AutoWorks.clsFinance

   'Get a list of financial institutions
   lngRC = objFinance.GetBanks(objConn, objRS)

   'If the return code is not zero, raise an error
   If lngRC <> 0 Then
      Err.Raise vbObjectError + 513, "frmFinancial.LoadBanks", _
         "Call to clsFinance.GetBanks failed"
   End If

   'Load the financial institution combo box and array
   lngIndex = -1
   lngLastValue = -1
   Do While Not objRS.EOF
      'Add the institution name
      cboInstitutionName.AddItem objRS!Bank_Name_VC
      lngIndex = lngIndex + 1
      'Add the institution id
      cboInstitutionName.ItemData(lngIndex) = objRS!Bank_ID
      If lngLastValue < objRS!Bank_ID Then
         'Redim the array
         ReDim Preserve arrBanks(objRS!Bank_ID)
         lngLastValue = objRS!Bank_ID
      End If
```

```
        'Add the current position of the institution to the array
        arrBanks(objRS!Bank_ID) = lngIndex
        'Advance the recordset
        objRS.MoveNext
    Loop

    'Close and de-reference objects
    objRS.Close
    Set objRS = Nothing
    Set objFinance = Nothing

    'Exit sub
    On Error GoTo 0
    Exit Sub

LoadBanks_EH:
    Dim objErr As ADODB.Error
    'Ensure the error came from ADO
    If objConn.Errors.Count > 0 Then
        Dim strMsg As String
        For Each objErr In objConn.Errors
            strMsg = strMsg & " " & objErr.Description
        Next
        StatusBar1.Panels("Msg") = strMsg
    Else
        StatusBar1.Panels("Msg") = Err.Description
    End If
End Sub
```

7. Add this procedure too:

```
Public Sub Process(ByRef objConn As ADODB.Connection, _
        ByVal lngCustomerID As Long, _
        ByVal frmParent As Form)

    'Set up error handling
    On Error GoTo Process_EH

    'Save customer's primary key
    m_lngCustomerID = lngCustomerID

    'Load the form which will load the institution combo box
    Call Form_Load

    'Declare local variables
    Dim lngRC As Long

    'Set a reference to the objects
    Dim objRS As New ADODB.Recordset
    Dim objFinance As New AutoWorks.clsFinance
```

```
    'Get the financial information for this customer
    lngRC = objFinance.GetFinancialInformation(objConn, _
       objRS, _
       lngCustomerID)

    'If the return code is not zero, raise an error
    If lngRC <> 0 Then
       Err.Raise vbObjectError + 513, "frmFinancial.Process", _
          "Call to clsFinance.GetFinancialInformation failed"
    End If

    'Load the phone number for the institution
    cboInstitutionName.ListIndex = arrBanks(objRS!Bank_ID)
    txtAreaCode.Text = objRS!Area_Code_SI
    txtPhoneNumber.Text = Format(objRS!Phone_Number_IN, "###-####")

    'Save all primary keys
    m_lngBankID = objRS!Bank_ID

    'Close and dereference objects
    objRS.Close
    Set objRS = Nothing
    Set objFinance = Nothing

    On Error GoTo 0

    'Show the form
    Show vbModal, frmParent
    Exit Sub

Process_EH:
    Dim objErr As ADODB.Error
    'Ensure the error came from ADO
    If objConn.Errors.Count > 0 Then
       Dim strMsg As String
       For Each objErr In objConn.Errors
          strMsg = strMsg & " " & objErr.Description
       Next
       StatusBar1.Panels("Msg") = strMsg
    Else
       StatusBar1.Panels("Msg") = Err.Description
    End If

    'Show the form
    Show vbModal, frmParent
End Sub
```

8. Add the following code to the cboInstitutionName_Click procedure:

```
Private Sub cboInstitutionName_Click()
    'Set up error handling
    On Error GoTo cboInstitutionName_EH

    'Declare local variables
    Dim lngRC As Long

    'Set a reference to the objects
    Dim objRS As New ADODB.Recordset
    Dim objAddress As New AutoWorks.clsAddress

    'Get the phone number for this institution
    lngRC = objAddress.GetPhoneNumber(frmMain.m_objConn, _
       objRS, _
       cboInstitutionName.ItemData(cboInstitutionName.ListIndex), _
       ptBank)

    'If the return code is not zero, raise an error
    If lngRC <> 0 Then
       Err.Raise vbObjectError + 513, "frmFinancial.cboInstitutionName", _
          "Call to clsAddress.GetPhoneNumber failed"
    End If

    'Load the phone number fields
    txtAreaCode.Text = objRS!Area_Code_SI
    txtPhoneNumber.Text = Format(objRS!Phone_Number_IN, "###-####")

    'Close and de-reference objects
    objRS.Close
    Set objRS = Nothing
    Set objAddress = Nothing

    On Error GoTo 0
    Exit Sub

cboInstitutionName_EH:
    Dim objErr As ADODB.Error
    'Ensure the error came from ADO
    If frmMain.m_objConn.Errors.Count > 0 Then
       Dim strMsg As String
       For Each objErr In frmMain.m_objConn.Errors
          strMsg = strMsg & " " & objErr.Description
       Next
       StatusBar1.Panels("Msg") = strMsg
    Else
       StatusBar1.Panels("Msg") = Err.Description
    End If
End Sub
```

9. Add the following code to the `cboInstitutionName_Validate` procedure:

```
Private Sub cboInstitutionName_Validate(Cancel As Boolean)
   'If no item is selected...
   If cboInstitutionName.ListIndex = -1 Then
      'Display an error if no text was entered
      If Len(cboInstitutionName.Text) = 0 Then
         StatusBar1.Panels("Msg").Text = "Financial Institution Name is required"
         Label1(0).ForeColor = vbRed
         Beep
         Cancel = True
      Else
         'Validation passed
         StatusBar1.Panels("Msg").Text = Empty
         Label1(0).ForeColor = vbWindowText
         Cancel = False
      End If
   End If
End Sub
```

10. Add the following code to the `cmdAdd_Click` procedure:

```
Private Sub cmdAdd_Click()
   'Hide the form so fields are accessible from parent form
   Me.Hide
End Sub
```

11. Add the following code to the `cmdClose_Click` procedure:

```
Private Sub cmdClose_Click()
   Unload Me
End Sub
```

12. Add the following code to the `cmdUpdate_Click` procedure:

```
Private Sub cmdUpdate_Click()
   'Set up error handling
   On Error GoTo cmdUpdate_EH

   'Declare local variables
   Dim lngRC As Long, lngFinancialInstitutionID As Long, _
      strMsg() As String, varText As Variant

   'Set financial institution numeric values
   If cboInstitutionName.ListIndex = -1 Then
      lngFinancialInstitutionID = 0
   Else
      lngFinancialInstitutionID = _
                  cboInstitutionName.ItemData(cboInstitutionName.ListIndex)
   End If
```

```
   'Set a reference to the objects
   Dim objFinance As New AutoWorks.clsFinance
   Dim objCmd As New ADODB.Command

   'Update the financial information
   lngRC = objFinance.UpdateFinancialInformation(m_lngCustomerID, _
      lngFinancialInstitutionID, _
      cboInstitutionName.Text, _
      CInt(txtAreaCode.Text), _
      EditPhoneNumber(txtPhoneNumber.Text), _
      strMsg(), _
      frmMain.m_objConn, _
      objCmd)

   'Display any error messages
   If lngRC <> 0 Then
      For Each varText In strMsg
         StatusBar1.Panels("Msg").Text = StatusBar1.Panels("Msg").Text & _
            varText
      Next
   End If

   'De-reference objects
   Set objCmd = Nothing
   Set objFinance = Nothing

   'Display message and exit sub
   StatusBar1.Panels("Msg") = "Customer's Financial Institution Updated"
   Exit Sub

cmdUpdate_EH:
   Dim objErr As ADODB.Error
   'Ensure the error came from ADO
   If frmMain.m_objConn.Errors.Count > 0 Then
      For Each objErr In frmMain.m_objConn.Errors
         StatusBar1.Panels("Msg") = StatusBar1.Panels("Msg") & " " & _
            objErr.Description
      Next
   Else
      StatusBar1.Panels("Msg") = Err.Description
   End If
End Sub
```

13. Add the following code to the Form_Load event:

```
Private Sub Form_Load()
   'Setup textbox control events
   Set m_evtAreaCode = New clsControls
   Set m_evtAreaCode.evtNumericField = txtAreaCode
```

```
    Set m_evtPhoneNumber = New clsControls
    Set m_evtPhoneNumber.evtPhoneNumberField = txtPhoneNumber

    'Load institution names
    Call LoadBanks(frmMain.m_objConn)

    'Set the forms loaded property to true
    Loaded = True
End Sub
```

14. Add the following code to the Form_Unload event:

```
Private Sub Form_Unload(Cancel As Integer)
    'Set the forms loaded property to false
    Loaded = False

    'Remove references to control events
    Set m_evtAreaCode = Nothing
    Set m_evtPhoneNumber = Nothing
End Sub
```

15. Add the following code to the txtAreaCode_Validate procedure:

```
Private Sub txtAreaCode_Validate(Cancel As Boolean)
    'Display an error if area code is not 3 digits
    If Len(txtAreaCode.Text) <> 3 Then
        StatusBar1.Panels("Msg").Text = "Area Code is required in the format of nnn"
        Label1(1).ForeColor = vbRed
        Beep
        Cancel = True
    Else
        'Validation passed
        StatusBar1.Panels("Msg").Text = Empty
        Label1(1).ForeColor = vbWindowText
        Cancel = False
    End If
End Sub
```

16. Add the following code to the txtPhoneNumber_Validate procedure:

```
Private Sub txtPhoneNumber_Validate(Cancel As Boolean)
    'Display an error if phone number is not 8 digits
    If Len(txtPhoneNumber.Text) <> 8 Then
        StatusBar1.Panels("Msg").Text = _
            "Phone Number is required in the format of nnn-nnnn"
        Label1(2).ForeColor = vbRed
        Beep
        Cancel = True
    Else
```

```
        'Validation passed
        StatusBar1.Panels("Msg").Text = Empty
        Label1(2).ForeColor = vbWindowText
        Cancel = False
    End If
End Sub
```

How It Works – Financial Form

We have already covered the majority of this code when we built the Employer form in Chapter 13 and as such we will only cover the highlights and the new code.

We want to start with the variable declarations for our form. Notice that the first two variables are referencing the Controls class. These variables will get set in the `Form_Load` event. We have already seen the rest of the variables before and they require no further discussion:

```
'Declare object events
Private m_evtAreaCode As clsControls
Private m_evtPhoneNumber As clsControls
```

Process Procedure

The `Process` procedure gets called from the Main form when a customer is displayed and we click on the `Financial` button. As in the previous `Process` procedures, we pass the `Connection` object by reference and the Customer ID by value. We set up error handling for this procedure and save the Customer ID for later use.

```
Public Sub Process(ByRef objConn As ADODB.Connection, _
        ByVal lngCustomerID As Long, _
        ByVal frmParent As Form)

    'Set up error handling
    On Error GoTo Process_EH

    'Save customer's primary key
    m_lngCustomerID = lngCustomerID
```

We call the `Form_Load` event to have the Financial Institution combo loaded. The reason the call to load this combo box is in the `Form_Load` event is because we want the combo box loaded whether we are displaying financial information for a current customer or whether we are showing a blank form to add financial information for a new customer. If we are displaying a blank form, the current procedure is not executed.

We declare our local variables next and then set a reference to our objects:

```
'Load the form which will load the institution combo box
Call Form_Load

'Declare local variables
Dim lngRC As Long

'Set a reference to the objects
Dim objRS As New ADODB.Recordset
Dim objFinance As New AutoWorks.clsFinance
```

We get the financial information for the current customer that is displayed by calling the `GetFinancialInformation` function. We pass this function the `Connection` object and `Recordset` object by reference and the Customer ID by value. This function will return a zero on successful completion.

If we did not receive a zero return code from the function, we raise an error and fall through to our error handling routine:

```
'Get the financial information for this customer
lngRC = objFinance.GetFinancialInformation(objConn, objRS, lngCustomerID)

'If the return code is not zero, raise an error
If lngRC <> 0 Then
   Err.Raise vbObjectError + 513, "frmFinancial.Process", _
      "Call to clsFinance.GetFinancialInformation failed"
End If
```

If all was successful, we set the `ListIndex` property of the combo box to display the correct entry. We then display the area code and phone number for this institution. Notice that we are using an array to determine the correct index position of the combo box, just as we did in the Employer and Main forms.

We save the primary key for the current institution being displayed and close and de-reference our objects:

```
'Load the phone number for the institution
cboInstitutionName.ListIndex = arrBanks(objRS!bank_id)
txtAreaCode.Text = objRS!area_code_si
txtPhoneNumber.Text = Format(objRS!phone_number_in, "###-####")

'Save all primary keys
m_lngBankID = objRS!bank_id

'Close and de-reference objects
objRS.Close
Set objRS = Nothing
Set objFinance = Nothing
```

We turn off error handling and show the form modally. The error handling routine is the same as the previous error handling routines for the UI, and does not need to be discussed further so it is not shown:

```
    On Error GoTo 0

    'Show the form
    Show vbModal, frmParent
    Exit Sub
```

Form_Load Event

The `Form_Load` event contains the code to set our controls to the event variables that were defined in the general declarations section of our form. We set a reference to the Controls class and then set our objects to the appropriate event handler that will handle the events for our controls. Now when our controls raise events, the event handler in the Controls class handles them:

```
Private Sub Form_Load()
    'Setup textbox control events
    Set m_evtAreaCode = New clsControls
    Set m_evtAreaCode.evtNumericField = txtAreaCode

    Set m_evtPhoneNumber = New clsControls
    Set m_evtPhoneNumber.evtPhoneNumberField = txtPhoneNumber
```

We then call the `LoadBanks` procedure, passing it the `Connection` object by reference. The `LoadBanks` procedure will load the Institution combo box.

Next, we set the form's `Loaded` property to `True` and we are done:

```
    'Load institution names
    Call LoadBanks(frmMain.m_objConn)

    'Set the forms loaded property to true
    Loaded = True
End Sub
```

cmdUpdate_Click Procedure

As we discussed in the first and second part of this case study, the financial institution can be updated independently of the rest of the customer information. We therefore handle the updates in this form in the `cmdUpdate_Click` procedure.

The first thing we need to do in this procedure is set up error handling. Then we declare our local variables and determine if a financial institution name has been selected or if a new financial institution name is being added. We then set the `lngFinancialInstitutionID` variable to the `ItemData` of the entry selected or set it to zero:

```
Private Sub cmdUpdate_Click()
    'Set up error handling
    On Error GoTo cmdUpdate_EH
```

```
'Declare local variables
Dim lngRC As Long, lngFinancialInstitutionID As Long, _
   strMsg() As String, varText As Variant

'Set financial institution numeric values
If cboInstitutionName.ListIndex = -1 Then
   lngFinancialInstitutionID = 0
Else
   lngFinancialInstitutionID = _
          cboInstitutionName.ItemData(cboInstitutionName.ListIndex)
End If
```

Next, we set a reference to our objects and then call the `UpdateFinancialInformation` function to update the current financial institution for this customer. If you recall the stored procedure for this function from the first part of this case study, it will either update the customer's record, indicating an existing financial institution, or insert a new financial institution for this customer:

```
'Set a reference to the objects
Dim objFinance As New AutoWorks.clsFinance
Dim objCmd As New ADODB.Command

'Update the financial information
lngRC = objFinance.UpdateFinancialInformation(m_lngCustomerID, _
   lngFinancialInstitutionID, _
   cboInstitutionName.Text, _
   CInt(txtAreaCode.Text), _
   EditPhoneNumber(txtPhoneNumber.Text), _
   strMsg(), _
   frmMain.m_objConn, _
   objCmd)
```

If any errors were encountered, we display in the status bar the messages returned from the function. Next, we de-reference our objects and display a message that the financial institution was updated. The error handling is the same as previous error handling routines and does not need to be discussed again.

History Form

The History form is the second new form that we need to add to our project. This form displays the customer's purchase history and gives the user the opportunity to add a new purchase or update the most recent purchase. The only information required by this form is the Customer ID, which is used to retrieve the purchase history. The history information for a customer is independent of the customer record, and the code to add and update a purchase resides in this form.

Try It Out – History Form

This form uses a list view control to display history records. I personally find that the list view control is easier to use and requires less code when all we need to do is display data, especially when loading the control through code and not using a bound recordset. As you can see in the figure below, the list view control has properties that can be set to make it look like a grid control.

1. We need to start by adding a new form to this project and setting its `Name` property to `frmHistory`. Set the `BorderStyle` property to `3 - Fixed Dialog`. Using the table and figure below, add the controls to the form:

Control	Name	Properties
Frame	`Frame1`	Caption = Vehicle Purchased
Label	`Label1(0)`	Caption = Make
Label	`Label1(1)`	Caption = Model
Label	`Label1(2)`	Caption = Model Year
Label	`Label1(3)`	Caption = Purchase Price
Label	`Label1(4)`	Caption = Sales Date
ComboBox	`cboMakePurchased`	Style = 0 – DropDown Combo, Text = nothing
ComboBox	`cboModelPurchased`	Style = 0 – DropDown Combo, Text = nothing
TextBox	`txtYearPurchased`	Text = nothing
TextBox	`txtPurchasePrice`	Text = nothing
TextBox	`txtSalesDate`	Text = nothing
Frame	`Frame2`	Caption = Vehicle Traded
Label	`Label1(5)`	Caption = Make
Label	`Label1(6)`	Caption = Model
Label	`Label1(7)`	Caption = Model Year
ComboBox	`cboMakeTraded`	Style = 0 – DropDown Combo, Text = nothing
ComboBox	`cboModelTraded`	Style = 0 – DropDown Combo, Text = nothing
TextBox	`txtYearTraded`	Text = nothing
Frame	`Frame3`	Caption = Actions

Control	Name	Properties
CommandButton	cmdAdd	Caption = Add Purchase
CommandButton	cmdUpdate	Caption = Update Purchase
CommandButton	cmdClose	Caption = Close, CausesValidation = False
ListView	lvwHistory	FullRowSelect = True, Gridlines = True, HotTracking = True, HoverSelection = True, View = 3 - lvwReport
StatusBar	StatusBar1	Panel Key = Msg, AutoSize = 1 - sbrSpring

2. Once you've added all the controls, your form should look similar to this:

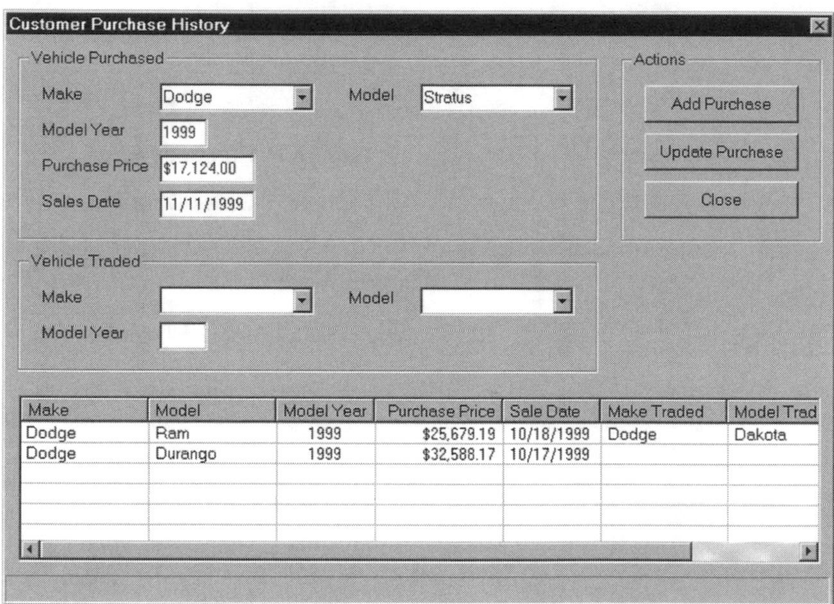

3. Add the following code to the general declarations section of the form:

```
'Declare object events
Private m_evtCurrentModelYear As clsControls
Private m_evtPurchasePrice As clsControls
Private m_evtSalesDate As clsControls
Private m_evtTradedModelYear As clsControls

'Declare module level variables
Private m_blnLoaded As Boolean
Private arrMake() As Long
Private arrModel() As Long
```

```
'Declare Primary keys
Private m_lngCustomerID As Long
Private m_lngCustomerHistoryID As Long
Private m_lngMakePurchasedID As Long
Private m_lngModelPurchasedID As Long
Private m_lngMakeTradedID As Long
Private m_lngModelTradedID As Long
```

4. Add the following properties to the form:

```
Public Property Let Loaded(ByVal blnLoaded As Boolean)
   m_blnLoaded = blnLoaded
End Property


Public Property Get Loaded() As Boolean
   Loaded = m_blnLoaded
End Property
```

5. Add the following procedure to the form:

```
Public Sub LoadMakeModel(ByRef objConn As ADODB.Connection)
   'Set up error handling
   On Error GoTo LoadMakeModel_EH

   'Declare local variables
   Dim lngLastValue As Long, lngIndex As Long, lngRC As Long

   'Clear any existing entries
   cboMakePurchased.Clear
   cboModelPurchased.Clear
   cboMakeTraded.Clear
   cboModelTraded.Clear

   'Set a reference to the objects
   Dim objRS As New ADODB.Recordset
   Dim objVehicle As New AutoWorks.clsVehicle

   'Get a list of all makes
   lngRC = objVehicle.GetVehicleMake(objConn, objRS)

   'If the return code is not zero, raise an error
   If lngRC <> 0 Then
      Err.Raise vbObjectError + 513, "frmHistory.LoadMakeModel", _
         "Call to clsVehicle.GetVehicleMake failed"
   End If

   'Load the purchased and traded make combo boxes and array
   lngIndex = -1
   lngLastValue = -1
   Do While Not objRS.EOF
```

```
        'Add the vehicle make
        cboMakePurchased.AddItem objRS!Vehicle_Make_VC
        cboMakeTraded.AddItem objRS!Vehicle_Make_VC
        lngIndex = lngIndex + 1
        'Add the vehicle make id
        cboMakePurchased.ItemData(lngIndex) = objRS!Make_ID
        cboMakeTraded.ItemData(lngIndex) = objRS!Make_ID
        If lngLastValue < objRS!Make_ID Then
            'Redim the array
            ReDim Preserve arrMake(objRS!Make_ID)
            lngLastValue = objRS!Make_ID
        End If
        'Add the current position of the vehicle make to the array
        arrMake(objRS!Make_ID) = lngIndex
        'Advance the recordset
        objRS.MoveNext
    Loop

    'Close recordset
    objRS.Close

    'Get a list of all models
    lngRC = objVehicle.GetVehicleModel(objConn, objRS)

    'If the return code is not zero, raise an error
    If lngRC <> 0 Then
        Err.Raise vbObjectError + 513, "frmHistory.LoadMakeModel", _
            "Call to clsVehicle.GetVehicleModel failed"
    End If

    'Load the pruchased and traded model combo boxes and array
    lngIndex = -1
    lngLastValue = -1
    Do While Not objRS.EOF
        'Add the vehicle model
        cboModelPurchased.AddItem objRS!Vehicle_Model_VC
        cboModelTraded.AddItem objRS!Vehicle_Model_VC
        lngIndex = lngIndex + 1
        'Add the vehicle model id
        cboModelPurchased.ItemData(lngIndex) = objRS!Model_ID
        cboModelTraded.ItemData(lngIndex) = objRS!Model_ID
        If lngLastValue < objRS!Model_ID Then
            'Redim the array
            ReDim Preserve arrModel(objRS!Model_ID)
            lngLastValue = objRS!Model_ID
        End If
        'Add the current position of the vehicle model to the array
        arrModel(objRS!Model_ID) = lngIndex
        'Advance the recordset
        objRS.MoveNext
    Loop
```

```
    'Close and de-reference objects
    objRS.Close
    Set objRS = Nothing
    Set objVehicle = Nothing

    'Exit sub
    On Error GoTo 0
    Exit Sub

LoadMakeModel_EH:
    Dim objErr As ADODB.Error
    'Ensure the error came from ADO
    If objConn.Errors.Count > 0 Then
        Dim strMsg As String
        For Each objErr In objConn.Errors
            strMsg = strMsg & " " & objErr.Description
        Next
        StatusBar1.Panels("Msg") = strMsg
    Else
        StatusBar1.Panels("Msg") = Err.Description
    End If
End Sub
```

6. Also add this procedure:

```
Public Sub Process(ByRef objConn As ADODB.Connection, _
        ByVal lngCustomerID As Long, _
        ByVal frmParent As Form)

    'Set up error handling
    On Error GoTo Process_EH

    'Load vehicle make and model combo boxes
    Call LoadMakeModel(objConn)

    'Declare local variables
    Dim lngRC As Long, lstItem As ListItem

    'Clear the list and define column headers
    lvwHistory.ListItems.Clear
    lvwHistory.ColumnHeaders.Clear
    lvwHistory.ColumnHeaders.Add , , "Make", 1300
    lvwHistory.ColumnHeaders.Add , , "Model", 1300
    lvwHistory.ColumnHeaders.Add , , "Model Year", 1000
    lvwHistory.ColumnHeaders.Add , , "Purchase Price", 1300
    lvwHistory.ColumnHeaders.Add , , "Sale Date", 1000
    lvwHistory.ColumnHeaders.Add , , "Make Traded", 1300
    lvwHistory.ColumnHeaders.Add , , "Model Traded", 1300
    lvwHistory.ColumnHeaders.Add , , "Model Year", 1000
```

```
'Set column data alignment
lvwHistory.ColumnHeaders.Item(3).Alignment = lvwColumnCenter
lvwHistory.ColumnHeaders.Item(4).Alignment = lvwColumnRight
lvwHistory.ColumnHeaders.Item(8).Alignment = lvwColumnCenter

'Save customer's primary key
m_lngCustomerID = lngCustomerID

'Set default dates
txtYearPurchased = Year(Now)
txtSalesDate = Format(Now, "mm/dd/yyyy")

'Set a reference to the objects
Dim objRS As New ADODB.Recordset
Dim objVehicle As New AutoWorks.clsVehicle

'Get the purchase history for this customer
lngRC = objVehicle.GetPurchaseHistory(objConn, objRS, lngCustomerID)

'If the return code is not zero, raise an error
If lngRC <> 0 Then
   Err.Raise vbObjectError + 513, "frmHistory.Process", _
      "Call to clsVehicle.GetPurchaseHistory failed"
End If

'Load the purchased fields
cboMakePurchased.ListIndex = arrMake(objRS!Vehicle_Make_Purchased_ID)
cboModelPurchased.ListIndex = arrModel(objRS!Vehicle_Make_Purchased_ID)
txtYearPurchased.Text = objRS!Model_Year_SI
txtPurchasePrice.Text = Format(objRS!Purchase_Price_SM, "$###,##0.00")
txtSalesDate.Text = Format(objRS!Sales_Date_DT, "mm/dd/yyyy")

If Not IsNull(objRS!Vehicle_Make_Traded_ID) Then
   'Load the traded fields
   cboMakeTraded.ListIndex = arrMake(objRS!Vehicle_Make_Traded_ID)
   cboModelTraded.ListIndex = arrModel(objRS!Vehicle_Make_Traded_ID)
   txtYearTraded.Text = objRS!Model_Year_Traded_SI
End If

'Save all primary keys
m_lngCustomerHistoryID = objRS!Customer_Purchase_History_ID
m_lngMakePurchasedID = objRS!Vehicle_Make_Purchased_ID
m_lngModelPurchasedID = objRS!Vehicle_Model_Purchased_ID
m_lngMakeTradedID = IIf(IsNull(objRS!Vehicle_Make_Traded_ID), 0, _
   objRS!Vehicle_Make_Traded_ID)
m_lngModelTradedID = IIf(IsNull(objRS!Vehicle_Model_Traded_ID), 0, _
   objRS!Vehicle_Model_Traded_ID)

'Move to the next record
objRS.MoveNext
```

```
    Do While Not objRS.EOF
        'Load the history list with all other data
        Set lstItem = lvwHistory.ListItems.Add(, , objRS!Vehicle_Make_Purchased)
        lstItem.SubItems(1) = objRS!Vehicle_Model_Purchased
        lstItem.SubItems(2) = objRS!Model_Year_SI
        lstItem.SubItems(3) = Format(objRS!Purchase_Price_SM, "$###,##0.00")
        lstItem.SubItems(4) = Format(objRS!Sales_Date_DT, "mm/dd/yyyy")
        lstItem.SubItems(5) = IIf(IsNull(objRS!Vehicle_Make_Traded), "", _
            objRS!Vehicle_Make_Traded)
        lstItem.SubItems(6) = IIf(IsNull(objRS!Vehicle_Model_Traded), "", _
            objRS!Vehicle_Model_Traded)
        lstItem.SubItems(7) = IIf(IsNull(objRS!Model_Year_Traded_SI), "", _
            objRS!Model_Year_Traded_SI)
        objRS.MoveNext
    Loop

    'Close and de-reference objects
    objRS.Close
    Set objRS = Nothing
    Set objVehicle = Nothing

    On Error GoTo 0

    'Show the form
    Show vbModal, frmParent
    Exit Sub

Process_EH:
    Dim objErr As ADODB.Error
    'Ensure the error came from ADO
    If objConn.Errors.Count > 0 Then
        For Each objErr In objConn.Errors
            StatusBar1.Panels("Msg") = StatusBar1.Panels("Msg") & " " & _
                    objErr.Description
        Next
    Else
        StatusBar1.Panels("Msg") = Err.Description
    End If
    'Show the form
    Show vbModal, frmParent
End Sub
```

7. Add the following code to the `cboMakePurchased_Validate` procedure:

```
Private Sub cboMakePurchased_Validate(Cancel As Boolean)
    'If no entry is selected...
    If cboMakePurchased.ListIndex = -1 Then
        'Display an error if no text was entered
        If Len(cboMakePurchased.Text) = 0 Then
            StatusBar1.Panels("Msg").Text = "Make Purchased is required"
            Label1(0).ForeColor = vbRed
            Beep
            Cancel = True
        Else
```

```
            'Validation passed
            StatusBar1.Panels("Msg").Text = Empty
            Label1(0).ForeColor = vbWindowText
            Cancel = False
        End If
    End If
End Sub
```

8. Add the following code to the `cboModelPurchased_Validate` procedure:

```
Private Sub cboModelPurchased_Validate(Cancel As Boolean)
    'If no entry was selected...
    If cboModelPurchased.ListIndex = -1 Then
        'display an error if no text was entered
        If Len(cboModelPurchased.Text) = 0 Then
            StatusBar1.Panels("Msg").Text = "Model Purchased is required"
            Label1(1).ForeColor = vbRed
            Beep
            Cancel = True
        Else
            'Validation passed
            StatusBar1.Panels("Msg").Text = Empty
            Label1(1).ForeColor = vbWindowText
            Cancel = False
        End If
    End If
End Sub
```

9. Add the following code to the `cmdAdd_Click` procedure:

```
Private Sub cmdAdd_Click()
    'Set up error handling
    On Error GoTo cmdAdd_EH

    'Declare local variables
    Dim strMsg() As String, lngRC As Long, varText As Variant, _
        lngMakePurchasedID As Long, lngModelPurchasedID As Long, _
        lngMakeTradedID As Long, lngModelTradedID As Long, _
        intYearTraded As Integer

    'Set default values for make and model purchased
    If cboMakePurchased.ListIndex = -1 Then
        lngMakePurchasedID = 0
    Else
        lngMakePurchasedID = cboMakePurchased.ItemData(cboMakePurchased.ListIndex)
    End If

    If cboModelPurchased.ListIndex = -1 Then
        lngModelPurchasedID = 0
    Else
        lngModelPurchasedID = _
                   cboModelPurchased.ItemData(cboModelPurchased.ListIndex)
    End If
```

```
'Set default values for make and model traded
If cboMakeTraded.ListIndex = -1 Then
   lngMakeTradedID = 0
Else
   lngMakeTradedID = cboMakeTraded.ItemData(cboMakeTraded.ListIndex)
End If

If cboModelTraded.ListIndex = -1 Then
   lngModelTradedID = 0
Else
   lngModelTradedID = cboModelTraded.ItemData(cboModelTraded.ListIndex)
End If

If Len(txtYearTraded.Text) = 0 Then
   intYearTraded = 0
Else
   intYearTraded = CInt(txtYearTraded.Text)
End If


'Set a reference to the objects
Dim objCmd As New ADODB.Command
Dim objVehicle As New AutoWorks.clsVehicle

'Insert the customer purchase
lngRC = objVehicle.InsertCustomerPurchase(m_lngCustomerID, _
   lngMakePurchasedID, _
   cboMakePurchased.Text, _
   lngModelPurchasedID, _
   cboModelPurchased.Text, _
   CInt(txtYearPurchased.Text), _
   CCur(txtPurchasePrice.Text), _
   txtSalesDate.Text, _
   lngMakeTradedID, _
   cboMakeTraded.Text, _
   lngModelTradedID, _
   cboModelTraded.Text, _
   intYearTraded, _
   strMsg(), _
   frmMain.m_objConn, _
   objCmd)

'Display any error messages
If lngRC <> 0 Then
   For Each varText In strMsg
      StatusBar1.Panels("Msg").Text = StatusBar1.Panels("Msg").Text & _
         varText
   Next
   Exit Sub
End If
```

```
    'De-reference objects
    Set objCmd = Nothing
    Set objVehicle = Nothing

    'Display message
    StatusBar1.Panels("Msg").Text = "Customer Purchase Added"
    Exit Sub

cmdAdd_EH:
    Dim objErr As ADODB.Error
    'Ensure the error came from ADO
    If frmMain.m_objConn.Errors.Count > 0 Then
        For Each objErr In frmMain.m_objConn.Errors
            StatusBar1.Panels("Msg") = StatusBar1.Panels("Msg") & " " & _
                objErr.Description
        Next
    Else
        StatusBar1.Panels("Msg") = Err.Description
    End If
End Sub
```

10. Add the following code to the `cmdClose_Click` procedure:

```
Private Sub cmdClose_Click()
    Unload Me
End Sub
```

11. Add the following code to the `cmdUpdate_Click` procedure:

```
Private Sub cmdUpdate_Click()
    'Set up error handling
    On Error GoTo cmdUpdate_EH

    'Declare local variables
    Dim strMsg() As String, lngRC As Long, varText As Variant, _
        lngMakePurchasedID As Long, lngModelPurchasedID As Long, _
        lngMakeTradedID As Long, lngModelTradedID As Long, _
        intYearTraded As Integer

    'Set default values for make and model purchased
    If cboMakePurchased.ListIndex = -1 Then
        lngMakePurchasedID = 0
    Else
        lngMakePurchasedID = cboMakePurchased.ItemData(cboMakePurchased.ListIndex)
    End If

    If cboModelPurchased.ListIndex = -1 Then
        lngModelPurchasedID = 0
    Else
        lngModelPurchasedID = _
                   cboModelPurchased.ItemData(cboModelPurchased.ListIndex)
    End If
```

```
'Set default values for make and model traded
If cboMakeTraded.ListIndex = -1 Then
   lngMakeTradedID = 0
Else
   lngMakeTradedID = cboMakeTraded.ItemData(cboMakeTraded.ListIndex)
End If

If cboModelTraded.ListIndex = -1 Then
   lngModelTradedID = 0
Else
   lngModelTradedID = cboModelTraded.ItemData(cboModelTraded.ListIndex)
End If

If Len(txtYearTraded.Text) = 0 Then
   intYearTraded = 0
Else
   intYearTraded = CInt(txtYearTraded.Text)
End If

'Set a reference to the objects
Dim objVehicle As New AutoWorks.clsVehicle
Dim objCmd As New ADODB.Command

'Update the customer's purchase
lngRC = objVehicle.UpdateCustomerPurchase(m_lngCustomerHistoryID, _
   lngMakePurchasedID, _
   cboMakePurchased.Text, _
   lngModelPurchasedID, _
   cboModelPurchased.Text, _
   CInt(txtYearPurchased.Text), _
   CCur(txtPurchasePrice.Text), _
   txtSalesDate.Text, _
   lngMakeTradedID, _
   cboMakeTraded.Text, _
   lngModelTradedID, _
   cboModelTraded.Text, _
   intYearTraded, _
   strMsg(), _
   frmMain.m_objConn, _
   objCmd)

'Display any error messages
If lngRC <> 0 Then
   For Each varText In strMsg
      StatusBar1.Panels("Msg").Text = StatusBar1.Panels("Msg").Text & _
         varText
   Next
   Exit Sub
End If
```

```
    'De-reference objects
    Set objCmd = Nothing
    Set objVehicle = Nothing

    'Display message
    StatusBar1.Panels("Msg").Text = "Customer Purchase Updated"
    Exit Sub

cmdUpdate_EH:
    Dim objErr As ADODB.Error
    'Ensure the error came from ADO
    If frmMain.m_objConn.Errors.Count > 0 Then
        For Each objErr In frmMain.m_objConn.Errors
            StatusBar1.Panels("Msg") = StatusBar1.Panels("Msg") & " " & _
                objErr.Description
        Next
    Else
        StatusBar1.Panels("Msg") = Err.Description
    End If
End Sub
```

12. Add the following code to the Form_Load event:

```
Private Sub Form_Load()
    'Setup textbox control events
    Set m_evtCurrentModelYear = New clsControls
    Set m_evtCurrentModelYear.evtNumericField = txtYearPurchased

    Set m_evtPurchasePrice = New clsControls
    Set m_evtPurchasePrice.evtCurrencyField = txtPurchasePrice

    Set m_evtSalesDate = New clsControls
    Set m_evtSalesDate.evtDateField = txtSalesDate

    Set m_evtTradedModelYear = New clsControls
    Set m_evtTradedModelYear.evtNumericField = txtYearTraded
End Sub
```

13. Add the following code to the Form_Unload event:

```
Private Sub Form_Unload(Cancel As Integer)
    'Set the forms loaded property to false
    Loaded = False

    'Remove references to control events
    Set m_evtCurrentModelYear = Nothing
    Set m_evtPurchasePrice = Nothing
    Set m_evtSalesDate = Nothing
    Set m_evtTradedModelYear = Nothing
End Sub
```

14. Add the following code to the `txtPurchasePrice_Validate` procedure:

```
Private Sub txtPurchasePrice_Validate(Cancel As Boolean)
    'Display an error if not text was entered
    If Len(txtPurchasePrice.Text) = 0 Then
        StatusBar1.Panels("Msg").Text = "Purchase price is required"
        Label1(3).ForeColor = vbRed
        Beep
        Cancel = True
    'Display an error if purchase price is less than 1
    ElseIf CCur(txtPurchasePrice.Text) < 1 Then
        StatusBar1.Panels("Msg").Text = "Purchase price must be 1 dollar or greater"
        Label1(3).ForeColor = vbRed
        Beep
        Cancel = True
    Else
        'Automatically append cents to price
        If Len(txtPurchasePrice.Text) = 2 Then
            txtPurchasePrice.Text = txtPurchasePrice.Text & ".00"
        Else
            'If the price does not contain the cents, add it
          If Mid$(txtPurchasePrice.Text, Len(txtPurchasePrice.Text) - 2, 1) <> "." Then
                txtPurchasePrice.Text = txtPurchasePrice.Text & ".00"
            End If
        End If
        'Validations passed
        StatusBar1.Panels("Msg").Text = Empty
        Label1(3).ForeColor = vbWindowText
        Cancel = False
    End If
End Sub
```

15. Add the following code to the `txtSalesDate_Validate` procedure:

```
Private Sub txtSalesDate_Validate(Cancel As Boolean)
    'Display an error if sales date is not 10 digits
    If Len(txtSalesDate.Text) <> 10 Then
        StatusBar1.Panels("Msg").Text = _
                "Sales Date is required in the format of mm/dd/yyyy"
        Label1(4).ForeColor = vbRed
        Beep
        Cancel = True
    Else
        'Validations passed
        StatusBar1.Panels("Msg").Text = Empty
        Label1(4).ForeColor = vbWindowText
        Cancel = False
    End If
End Sub
```

16. Add the following code to the txtYearPurchased_Validate procedure:

```
Private Sub txtYearPurchased_Validate(Cancel As Boolean)
   'Display an error if year is not 4 digits
   If Len(txtYearPurchased.Text) <> 4 Then
      StatusBar1.Panels("Msg").Text = _
            "Model Year Purchased is required in the format of yyyy"
      Label1(2).ForeColor = vbRed
      Beep
      Cancel = True
   Else
      'Validations passed
      StatusBar1.Panels("Msg").Text = Empty
      Label1(2).ForeColor = vbWindowText
      Cancel = False
   End If
End Sub
```

17. Add the following code to the txtYearTraded_Validate procedure:

```
Private Sub txtYearTraded_Validate(Cancel As Boolean)
   'If data exist...
   If Len(txtYearTraded.Text) > 0 Then
      'Display an error if year is not 4 digits
      If Len(txtYearTraded.Text) <> 4 Then
         StatusBar1.Panels("Msg").Text = _
               "Model Year Traded must be in the format of yyyy"
         Label1(7).ForeColor = vbRed
         Beep
         Cancel = True
      Else
         'Validation passed
         StatusBar1.Panels("Msg").Text = Empty
         Label1(7).ForeColor = vbWindowText
         Cancel = False
      End If
   End If
End Sub
```

How It Works – History Form

We start this form by declaring the event handler variables for our numeric, currency, and date fields. Then we declare our array variables and variables to hold the primary keys for the customer and vehicles:

```
'Declare object events
Private m_evtCurrentModelYear As clsControls
Private m_evtPurchasePrice As clsControls
Private m_evtSalesDate As clsControls
Private m_evtTradedModelYear As clsControls
```

```
'Declare module level variables
Private m_blnLoaded As Boolean
Private arrMake() As Long
Private arrModel() As Long

'Declare Primary keys
Private m_lngCustomerID As Long
Private m_lngCustomerHistoryID As Long
Private m_lngMakePurchasedID As Long
Private m_lngModelPurchasedID As Long
Private m_lngMakeTradedID As Long
Private m_lngModelTradedID As Long
```

Process Procedure

The only entry point into this form is through a call to the `Process` procedure. This procedure, like the other `Process` procedures, accepts the `Connection` object, customer ID, and the parent form as input parameters.

The first thing we do is set up our error handling and then call the procedure to load the Make and Model combo boxes. Then we declare our local variables that are required for this procedure. Notice that one of the variables is a `ListItem`. This variable will be needed to load the list view control:

```
Public Sub Process(ByRef objConn As ADODB.Connection, _
      ByVal lngCustomerID As Long, _
      ByVal frmParent As Form)

   'Set up error handling
   On Error GoTo Process_EH

   'Load vehicle make and model combo boxes
   Call LoadMakeModel(objConn)

   'Declare local variables
   Dim lngRC As Long, lstItem As ListItem
```

Just in case the form was still loaded when we entered the `Process` procedure, we clear any data and column headers from the list view control. Then we add the new headers, specifying their names and widths.

Next we align the column data for the Model Year and Purchase Price. Notice that the list view uses a 1-based index for the column headers:

```
   'Clear the list and define column headers
   lvwHistory.ListItems.Clear
   lvwHistory.ColumnHeaders.Clear
   lvwHistory.ColumnHeaders.Add , , "Make", 1300
   lvwHistory.ColumnHeaders.Add , , "Model", 1300
   lvwHistory.ColumnHeaders.Add , , "Model Year", 1000
   lvwHistory.ColumnHeaders.Add , , "Purchase Price", 1300
   lvwHistory.ColumnHeaders.Add , , "Sale Date", 1000
```

```
    lvwHistory.ColumnHeaders.Add , , "Make Traded", 1300
    lvwHistory.ColumnHeaders.Add , , "Model Traded", 1300
    lvwHistory.ColumnHeaders.Add , , "Model Year", 1000

    'Set column data alignment
    lvwHistory.ColumnHeaders.Item(3).Alignment = lvwColumnCenter
    lvwHistory.ColumnHeaders.Item(4).Alignment = lvwColumnRight
    lvwHistory.ColumnHeaders.Item(8).Alignment = lvwColumnCenter
```

We save the customer ID and set some default values for the Year Purchased and Sales Date fields:

```
    'Save customer's primary key
    m_lngCustomerID = lngCustomerID

    'Set default dates
    txtYearPurchased = Year(Now)
    txtSalesDate = Format(Now, "mm/dd/yyyy")
```

Next, we set a reference to our objects and then get the purchase history for this customer. We check the return code and if an error occurred, we raise an error, which will then throw us into our error handling routine:

```
    'Set a reference to the objects
    Dim objRS As New ADODB.Recordset
    Dim objVehicle As New AutoWorks.clsVehicle

    'Get the purchase history for this customer
    lngRC = objVehicle.GetPurchaseHistory(objConn, objRS, lngCustomerID)

    'If the return code is not zero, raise an error
    If lngRC <> 0 Then
       Err.Raise vbObjectError + 513, "frmHistory.Process", _
          "Call to clsVehicle.GetPurchaseHistory failed"
    End If
```

At this point, the Make and Model combo boxes have been loaded, the list view control for the history has had the column headers built, the Year Purchased and Sales Date fields have been set with default data, and the customer ID has been saved. If this customer has no purchase history, we will be thrown into our error handling routine with this next statement and receive a message that either beginning of file (BOF) or end of file (EOF) is True. This is the reason that the code above was executed first. It builds the form with the default data that we need.

If we have data, then we load the fields for the last vehicle purchased and, if a vehicle was traded, load those fields also:

```
    'Load the purchased fields
    cboMakePurchased.ListIndex = arrMake(objRS!Vehicle_Make_Purchased_ID)
    cboModelPurchased.ListIndex = arrModel(objRS!Vehicle_Model_Purchased_ID)
    txtYearPurchased.Text = objRS!Model_Year_SI
    txtPurchasePrice.Text = Format(objRS!Purchase_Price_SM, "$###,##0.00")
    txtSalesDate.Text = Format(objRS!Sales_Date_DT, "mm/dd/yyyy")
```

```
If Not IsNull(objRS!Vehicle_Make_Traded_ID) Then
   'Load the traded fields
   cboMakeTraded.ListIndex = arrMake(objRS!Vehicle_Make_Traded_ID)
   cboModelTraded.ListIndex = arrModel(objRS!Vehicle_Model_Traded_ID)
   txtYearTraded.Text = objRS!Model_Year_Traded_SI
End If
```

Then we save all of the primary keys for the current purchase history record and the vehicle purchased and traded. Once the primary keys have been saved, we move to the next record:

```
'Save all primary keys
m_lngCustomerHistoryID = objRS!Customer_Purchase_History_ID
m_lngMakePurchasedID = objRS!Vehicle_Make_Purchased_ID
m_lngModelPurchasedID = objRS!Vehicle_Model_Purchased_ID
m_lngMakeTradedID = IIf(IsNull(objRS!Vehicle_Make_Traded_ID), 0, _
   objRS!vehicle_make_traded_id)
m_lngModelTradedID = IIf(IsNull(objRS!Vehicle_Model_Traded_ID), 0, _
   objRS!Vehicle_Model_Traded_ID)

'Move to the next record
objRS.MoveNext
```

If the recordset contains any more records, we load them into the list view control. To do this, we add the first column of data to the list view control and set the `lstItem` variable to that row of data. Then, using the `lstItem` variable, we are able to set the data for the other columns in the current row.

While the column headers for the list view control use a 1-based index, the row data uses a 0-based index. We move to the next record in the recordset and continue loading the list view control until there are no more records:

```
Do While Not objRS.EOF
   'Load the history list with all other data
   Set lstItem = lvwHistory.ListItems.Add(, , objRS!Vehicle_Make_Purchased)
   lstItem.SubItems(1) = objRS!Vehicle_Model_Purchased
   lstItem.SubItems(2) = objRS!Model_Year_SI
   lstItem.SubItems(3) = Format(objRS!Purchase_Price_SM, "$###,##0.00")
   lstItem.SubItems(4) = Format(objRS!sales_date_dt, "mm/dd/yyyy")
   lstItem.SubItems(5) = IIf(IsNull(objRS!Vehicle_Make_Traded), "", _
      objRS!Vehicle_Make_Traded)
   lstItem.SubItems(6) = IIf(IsNull(objRS!Vehicle_Model_Traded), "", _
      objRS!Vehicle_Model_Traded)
   lstItem.SubItems(7) = IIf(IsNull(objRS!Model_Year_Traded_SI), "", _
      objRS!Model_Year_Traded_SI)
   objRS.MoveNext
Loop
```

After all data has been loaded, we close and de-reference our objects and show the form modally:

```
    'Close and de-reference objects
    objRS.Close
    Set objRS = Nothing
    Set objVehicle = Nothing

    On Error GoTo 0

    'Show the form
    Show vbModal, frmParent
    Exit Sub
```

If we fall through to our error handling routine, we display any messages in the status bar and show the form modally:

```
Process_EH:
    Dim objErr As ADODB.Error
    'Ensure the error came from ADO
    If objConn.Errors.Count > 0 Then
       For Each objErr In objConn.Errors
          StatusBar1.Panels("Msg") = StatusBar1.Panels("Msg") & " " & _
                 objErr.Description
       Next
    Else
       StatusBar1.Panels("Msg") = Err.Description
    End If
    'Show the form
    Show vbModal, frmParent
End Sub
```

LoadMakeModel Procedure

The `LoadMakeModel` procedure makes two calls to the Vehicle class in the `AutoWorks.dll`, one for the vehicle make and one for the vehicle model. The first thing we do in this procedure is to set up error handling and declare our local variables. Then we clear any existing entries in the combo boxes:

```
Public Sub LoadMakeModel(ByRef objConn As ADODB.Connection)
    'Set up error handling
    On Error GoTo LoadMakeModel_EH

    'Declare local variables
    Dim lngLastValue As Long, lngIndex As Long, lngRC As Long

    'Clear any existing entries
    cboMakePurchased.Clear
    cboModelPurchased.Clear
    cboMakeTraded.Clear
    cboModelTraded.Clear
```

After setting a reference to our objects, we call the `GetVehicleMake` function to get a list of vehicle makes. We pass the `Connection` and `Recordset` objects by reference to this procedure. If the function returned a non-zero return code we raise an error, which throws us into our error handling routine:

```
'Set a reference to the objects
Dim objRS As New ADODB.Recordset
Dim objVehicle As New AutoWorks.clsVehicle

'Get a list of all makes
lngRC = objVehicle.GetVehicleMake(objConn, objRS)

'If the return code is not zero, raise an error
If lngRC <> 0 Then
   Err.Raise vbObjectError + 513, "frmHistory.LoadMakeModel", _
      "Call to clsVehicle.GetVehicleMake failed"
End If
```

Using the `Vehicle_Make_VC` field in the recordset, we load the combo boxes for both vehicle make purchased and traded. During the load process, we load the position of the vehicle make in the combo box into an array for later use. This is the same procedure that we used when we loaded the City, State and Zip Code combo boxes:

```
'Load the purchased and traded make combo boxes and array
lngIndex = -1
lngLastValue = -1
Do While Not objRS.EOF
   'Add the vehicle make
   cboMakePurchased.AddItem objRS!Vehicle_Make_VC
   cboMakeTraded.AddItem objRS!Vehicle_Make_VC
   lngIndex = lngIndex + 1
   'Add the vehicle make id
   cboMakePurchased.ItemData(lngIndex) = objRS!Make_ID
   cboMakeTraded.ItemData(lngIndex) = objRS!Make_ID
   If lngLastValue < objRS!Make_ID Then
      'Redim the array
      ReDim Preserve arrMake(objRS!Make_ID)
      lngLastValue = objRS!Make_ID
   End If
   'Add the current position of the vehicle make to the array
   arrMake(objRS!Make_ID) = lngIndex
   'Advance the recordset
   objRS.MoveNext
Loop
```

After all records have been processed, we close the `Recordset` object and then get a list of all vehicle models:

```
'Close recordset
objRS.Close

'Get a list of all models
lngRC = objVehicle.GetVehicleModel(objConn, objRS)

'If the return code is not zero, raise an error
If lngRC <> 0 Then
   Err.Raise vbObjectError + 513, "frmHistory.LoadMakeModel", _
      "Call to clsVehicle.GetVehicleModel failed"
End If
```

Using the same procedure as above, we use the `Vehicle_Model_VC` field to load the vehicle model purchased and traded combo boxes.

```
'Load the pruchased and traded model combo boxes and array
lngIndex = -1
lngLastValue = -1
Do While Not objRS.EOF
   'Add the vehicle model
   cboModelPurchased.AddItem objRS!Vehicle_Model_VC
   cboModelTraded.AddItem objRS!Vehicle_Model_VC
   lngIndex = lngIndex + 1
   'Add the vehicle model id
   cboModelPurchased.ItemData(lngIndex) = objRS!Model_ID
   cboModelTraded.ItemData(lngIndex) = objRS!Model_ID
   If lngLastValue < objRS!Model_ID Then
      'Redim the array
      ReDim Preserve arrModel(objRS!Model_ID)
      lngLastValue = objRS!Model_ID
   End If
   'Add the current position of the vehicle model to the array
   arrModel(objRS!Model_ID) = lngIndex
   'Advance the recordset
   objRS.MoveNext
Loop
```

We close and de-reference our objects and exit the procedure. The error handling routine is the same as all other error handling routines in this application and as such has not been covered again.

```
'Close and de-reference objects
objRS.Close
Set objRS = Nothing
Set objVehicle = Nothing

'Exit sub
On Error GoTo 0
Exit Sub
```

cmdAdd_Click Procedure

We mentioned earlier that the customer purchase history record is separate and independent of the customer record and therefore the procedure to add a new customer purchase record is contained in this form. When the user clicks on the Add button, the `cmdAdd_Click` procedure is executed.

The first thing that we need to do is to set up our error handling routine and declare our local variables:

```
Private Sub cmdAdd_Click()
   'Set up error handling
   On Error GoTo cmdAdd_EH

   'Declare local variables
   Dim strMsg() As String, lngRC As Long, varText As Variant, _
      lngMakePurchasedID As Long, lngModelPurchasedID As Long, _
      lngMakeTradedID As Long, lngModelTradedID As Long, _
      intYearTraded As Integer
```

We determine if an existing entry for make and model purchased has been selected in the combo boxes or if a new make and model were entered. We set the variables that we have declared to either the `ItemData` property of the combo boxes, or set the variables to zero if a make and model were entered:

```
   'Set default values for make and model purchased
   If cboMakePurchased.ListIndex = -1 Then
      lngMakePurchasedID = 0
   Else
      lngMakePurchasedID = cboMakePurchased.ItemData(cboMakePurchased.ListIndex)
   End If

   If cboModelPurchased.ListIndex = -1 Then
      lngModelPurchasedID = 0
   Else
      lngModelPurchasedID = _
                 cboModelPurchased.ItemData(cboModelPurchased.ListIndex)
   End If
```

We perform the same check for the make and model traded:

```
   'Set default values for make and model traded
   If cboMakeTraded.ListIndex = -1 Then
      lngMakeTradedID = 0
   Else
      lngMakeTradedID = cboMakeTraded.ItemData(cboMakeTraded.ListIndex)
   End If

   If cboModelTraded.ListIndex = -1 Then
      lngModelTradedID = 0
   Else
      lngModelTradedID = cboModelTraded.ItemData(cboModelTraded.ListIndex)
   End If
```

```
    If Len(txtYearTraded.Text) = 0 Then
       intYearTraded = 0
    Else
       intYearTraded = CInt(txtYearTraded.Text)
    End If
```

Next, we set a reference to our objects and then execute the function to insert a new customer purchase history record. Like the other functions in our business server component, this function also accepts the ID as well as the name for the entries in our combo boxes. Either the existing entry will be used if the ID is greater than zero, or the name passed will be inserted as a new entry in our tables:

```
    'Set a reference to the objects
    Dim objCmd As New ADODB.Command
    Dim objVehicle As New AutoWorks.clsVehicle

    'Insert the customer purchase
    lngRC = objVehicle.InsertCustomerPurchase(m_lngCustomerID, _
       lngMakePurchasedID, _
       cboMakePurchased.Text, _
       lngModelPurchasedID, _
       cboModelPurchased.Text, _
       CInt(txtYearPurchased.Text), _
       CCur(txtPurchasePrice.Text), _
       txtSalesDate.Text, _
       lngMakeTradedID, _
       cboMakeTraded.Text, _
       lngModelTradedID, _
       cboModelTraded.Text, _
       intYearTraded, _
       strMsg(), _
       frmMain.m_objConn, _
       objCmd)
```

After we return from our function, we check for errors and display any error messages in the status bar. If no errors occurred, we de-reference our objects and display a message that the customer purchase history record was added. The error handling routine is not covered here as it is the same as the other error handling routines presented in this project.

cmdUpdate_Click Procedure

The cmdUpdate_Click procedure performs an update of the most recent customer purchase history record and is very similar to the cmdAdd_Click procedure. We set up our error handling and declare our local variables:

```
 Private Sub cmdUpdate_Click()
    'Set up error handling
    On Error GoTo cmdUpdate_EH

    'Declare local variables
    Dim strMsg() As String, lngRC As Long, varText As Variant, _
       lngMakePurchasedID As Long, lngModelPurchasedID As Long, _
```

```
    lngMakeTradedID As Long, lngModelTradedID As Long, _
    intYearTraded As Integer
```

Next, we set our variables to the `ItemData` value of the combo box if an entry was *selected*, or we set the variable to zero if an entry was *entered*. We perform the same check for both make and model purchased and make and model traded:

```
'Set default values for make and model purchased
If cboMakePurchased.ListIndex = -1 Then
   lngMakePurchasedID = 0
Else
   lngMakePurchasedID = cboMakePurchased.ItemData(cboMakePurchased.ListIndex)
End If

If cboModelPurchased.ListIndex = -1 Then
   lngModelPurchasedID = 0
Else
   lngModelPurchasedID = _
              cboModelPurchased.ItemData(cboModelPurchased.ListIndex)
End If

'Set default values for make and model traded
If cboMakeTraded.ListIndex = -1 Then
   lngMakeTradedID = 0
Else
   lngMakeTradedID = cboMakeTraded.ItemData(cboMakeTraded.ListIndex)
End If

If cboModelTraded.ListIndex = -1 Then
   lngModelTradedID = 0
Else
   lngModelTradedID = cboModelTraded.ItemData(cboModelTraded.ListIndex)
End If

If Len(txtYearTraded.Text) = 0 Then
   intYearTraded = 0
Else
   intYearTraded = CInt(txtYearTraded.Text)
End If
```

We set a reference to our objects next and then execute the function to update the customer purchase history record. This time however, instead of passing the customer ID as the first parameter, we pass the customer history ID, which is the primary key for the record being updated:

```
'Set a reference to the objects
Dim objVehicle As New AutoWorks.clsVehicle
Dim objCmd As New ADODB.Command

'Update the customer's purchase
lngRC = objVehicle.UpdateCustomerPurchase(m_lngCustomerHistoryID, _
   lngMakePurchasedID, _
   cboMakePurchased.Text, _
```

```
        lngModelPurchasedID, _
        cboModelPurchased.Text, _
        CInt(txtYearPurchased.Text), _
        CCur(txtPurchasePrice.Text), _
        txtSalesDate.Text, _
        lngMakeTradedID, _
        cboMakeTraded.Text, _
        lngModelTradedID, _
        cboModelTraded.Text, _
        intYearTraded, _
        strMsg(), _
        frmMain.m_objConn, _
        objCmd)
```

After execution of the update function, we check for and display any errors that might have occurred. Then we de-reference our objects and display a message that the customer purchase history record was updated. Since the error handling routine is the same as previous routines, it is not covered again here.

This wraps up the major code for the History form. All of the code listed above is fairly straightforward and covers some basic functions, such as validations, setting up our event handler, and de-referencing our event handler variables.

Existing Forms

We finally need to make some alterations to two of our existing forms – the Employment form and the Main form.

Try It Out – Modify Employment Form

We need to add some extra code to the Employment form (`frmEmployment.frm`) to help validate the data entered. The amount of code added is very minimal and goes a long way to help ensure data integrity.

1. The following variables are added to the general declarations section of the form and are used to set up our event handlers. These event handlers are used to perform extra validations, as we explained when we discussed the Financial form:

```
'Declare object events
Private m_evtCEAreaCode As clsControls
Private m_evtCEPhoneNumber As clsControls
Private m_evtCEYearsEmployed As clsControls
Private m_evtPEAreaCode As clsControls
Private m_evtPEPhoneNumber As clsControls
Private m_evtPEYearsEmployed As clsControls
```

2. The Form_Load event contains added code to set up the event handlers to recognize the events raised by our controls. Notice that we are handling events raised by the controls that contain numeric and phone number data:

```
Private Sub Form_Load()
   'Setup textbox control events
   Set m_evtCEAreaCode = New clsControls
   Set m_evtCEAreaCode.evtNumericField = txtCEAreaCode

   Set m_evtCEPhoneNumber = New clsControls
   Set m_evtCEPhoneNumber.evtPhoneNumberField = txtCEPhoneNumber

   Set m_evtCEYearsEmployed = New clsControls
   Set m_evtCEYearsEmployed.evtNumericField = txtCEYearsEmployed

   Set m_evtPEAreaCode = New clsControls
   Set m_evtPEAreaCode.evtNumericField = txtPEAreaCode

   Set m_evtPEPhoneNumber = New clsControls
   Set m_evtPEPhoneNumber.evtPhoneNumberField = txtPEPhoneNumber

   Set m_evtPEYearsEmployed = New clsControls
   Set m_evtPEYearsEmployed.evtNumericField = txtPEYearsEmployed

   'Load Employers
   Call LoadEmployers(frmMain.m_objConn)

   'Set the forms loaded property to true
   Loaded = True
End Sub
```

3. The following code that is to be added to the Form_Unload event de-references our event handlers:

```
Private Sub Form_Unload(Cancel As Integer)
   'Set the forms loaded property to false
   Loaded = False

   'Remove references to control events
   Set m_evtCEAreaCode = Nothing
   Set m_evtCEPhoneNumber = Nothing
   Set m_evtCEYearsEmployed = Nothing
   Set m_evtPEAreaCode = Nothing
   Set m_evtPEPhoneNumber = Nothing
   Set m_evtPEYearsEmployed = Nothing
End Sub
```

Try It Out – Modify the Main Form

The Main form (`frmMain.frm`) needs some new controls and code added to support the two new forms we have added to our project.

1. Using the table and figure below, add the following controls to the form:

Control	Name	Properties
CommandButton	`cmdFinancial`	Caption = Financial
CommandButton	`cmdHistory`	Caption = History
CheckBox	`chkFinancialData`	Caption = Financial Data, Value = 0 – UnChecked

2. Once completed, your form should look like the one shown:

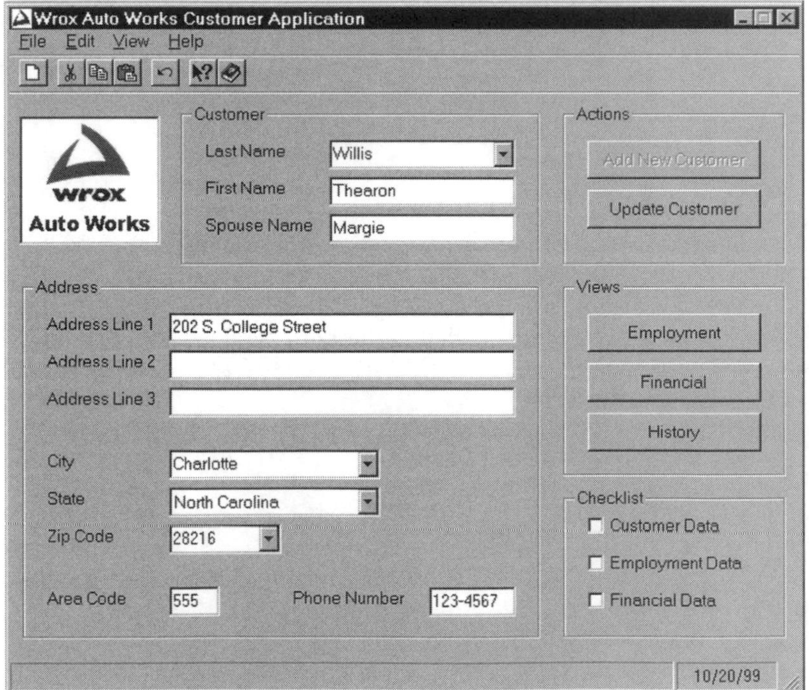

3. Add the following variables to the general declarations section of the form, to be used as our event handler variables:

```
'Declare object events
Private m_evtAreaCode As clsControls
Private m_evtPhoneNumber As clsControls
```

4. The ValidateData procedure now needs to also check the Financial checkbox, as shown in the following code:

```
   'Validate check boxes and enable add button
   If chkCustomerData.Value = vbChecked And _
      chkEmploymentData.Value = vbChecked And _
      chkFinancialData.Value = vbChecked Then
      cmdAdd.Enabled = True
   End If
End Sub
```

5. Add the following code to the chkFinancialData_GotFocus procedure, which forces the user back to the Last Name combo box:

```
Private Sub chkFinancialData_GotFocus()
   'Don't let the user check the check box
   cboLastName.SetFocus
End Sub
```

6. The cmdFinancial_Click procedure needs to determine if a current customer is being displayed, so as to display the Financial form with the customer's financial data, or if we are entering a new customer so it can display a blank form to be filled in. This procedure handles this, as well as checking the Financial checkbox if the Financial form is still loaded when control is returned to the Main form:

```
Private Sub cmdFinancial_Click()
   'Determine if financial form should be show with or without data
   If cboLastName.ListIndex <> -1 Then

   'Call the financial form to process and display financial info
   Call frmFinancial.Process(m_objConn, _
      cboLastName.ItemData(cboLastName.ListIndex), Me)

   Else

      'Display financial form with no data
      frmFinancial.Show vbModal

   End If

   'We are back, set focus to the combo box
   cboLastName.SetFocus

   'Check status of financial form
   If frmFinancial.Loaded Then
      chkFinancialData.Value = vbChecked
   End If

   Call ValidateData
End Sub
```

7. The cmdHistory_Click procedure needs only to display the History form, passing it the customer ID of the current customer, the Connection object, and the parent form:

```
Private Sub cmdHistory_Click()
   'Call the history form to process and display history info
   Call frmHistory.Process(m_objConn, _
      cboLastName.ItemData(cboLastName.ListIndex), Me)

   'We are back, set focus to the combo box
   cboLastName.SetFocus
End Sub
```

8. Modify the Form_Load event with the following code, to set up our controls as an event source to raise events:

```
   'Set up error handling
   On Error GoTo Form_Load_EH

   'Setup textbox control events
   Set m_evtAreaCode = New clsControls
   Set m_evtAreaCode.evtNumericField = txtAreaCode

   Set m_evtPhoneNumber = New clsControls
   Set m_evtPhoneNumber.evtPhoneNumberField = txtPhoneNumber

   'Set a reference to the database objects
   Set m_objConn = New ADODB.Connection
   Set m_objRS = New ADODB.Recordset
```

9. The Form_UnLoad event contains the code to de-reference our event controls:

```
Private Sub Form_Unload(Cancel As Integer)
   'Unload all loaded forms
   Dim frmForm As Form
   For Each frmForm In Forms
      Unload frmForm
   Next

   'Remove references to control events
   Set m_evtAreaCode = Nothing
   Set m_evtPhoneNumber = Nothing
End Sub
```

10. Add the following entries to the View menu to support viewing the new forms:

Caption	Name
&Financial	mnuViewFinancial
&History	mnuViewHistory

11. Add the following code to the mnuViewFinancial_Click procedure:

```
Private Sub mnuViewFinancial_Click()
   Call cmdFinancial_Click
End Sub
```

12. Add the following code to the mnuViewHistory_Click procedure:

```
Private Sub mnuViewHistory_Click()
   Call cmdHistory_Click
End Sub
```

13. Modify the mnuFileNew_Click procedure with the following code:

```
   'Clear checklist
   chkCustomerData.Value = vbUnchecked
   chkEmploymentData.Value = vbUnchecked
   chkFinancialData.Value = vbUnchecked
```

14. Since the financial data is added as part of the employment information, we need to modify the cmdAdd_Click procedure, modifying the code to add employment information:

```
   'Declare local variables
   Dim strMsg() As String, lngRC As Long, lngAddressID As Long, _
      lngPhoneNumberID As Long, lngCityID As Long, _
      lngZipCodeID As Long, lngCustomerInformationID As Long, _
      lngCurrentEmployerID As Long, lngPreviousEmployerID As Long, _
      intAreaCode As Integer, lngPhoneNumber As Long, _
      bytYearsEmployed As Byte, lngFinancialInstitutionID As Long, _
      varText As Variant

. . .

   If Len(frmEmployment.txtPEYearsEmployed.Text) = 0 Then
      bytYearsEmployed = 0
   Else
      bytYearsEmployed = CByte(frmEmployment.txtPEYearsEmployed.Text)
   End If

   'Set financial institution numeric values
   If frmFinancial.cboInstitutionName.ListIndex = -1 Then
      lngFinancialInstitutionID = 0
   Else
      lngFinancialInstitutionID = frmFinancial.cboInstitutionName.ItemData( _
         frmFinancial.cboInstitutionName.ListIndex)
   End If
```

```
'Set a reference to the objects
Set m_objCmd = New ADODB.Command
Set m_objWroxEmployer = New AutoWorks.clsEmployer

'Insert the employer information
lngRC = m_objWroxEmployer.InsertEmployer(lngCurrentEmployerID, _
   frmEmployment.cboCurrentEmployer.Text, _
   CInt(frmEmployment.txtCEAreaCode.Text), _
   EditPhoneNumber(frmEmployment.txtCEPhoneNumber.Text), _
   CByte(frmEmployment.txtCEYearsEmployed.Text), _
   frmEmployment.txtJobTitle.Text, _
   lngPreviousEmployerID, _
   frmEmployment.cboPreviousEmployer.Text, _
   intAreaCode, _
   lngPhoneNumber, _
   bytYearsEmployed, _
   lngFinancialInstitutionID, _
   frmFinancial.cboInstitutionName.Text, _
   CInt(frmFinancial.txtAreaCode.Text), _
   EditPhoneNumber(frmFinancial.txtPhoneNumber.Text), _
   lngCustomerInformationID, _
   strMsg(), _
   m_objConn, _
   m_objCmd)

. . .

'Disable add button
cmdAdd.Enabled = False

'Turn off checklist
chkCustomerData.Value = vbUnchecked
chkEmploymentData.Value = vbUnchecked
chkFinancialData.Value = vbUnchecked
```

Testing

At this point all modifications and new code have been added to our project and we are ready for testing. Before testing the Financial form, you can either add one or two entries to the `Financial_T` table using the Query Analyzer, or run your project and use the Financial form to add a financial institution for a current customer.

Using the Financial form or any of the other forms, enter data in the different textboxes. If the textbox is a phone number textbox, try entering a phone number without entering a dash and notice that the dash is automatically added for you. You can try this with the currency and date textboxes as well.

Once a couple of financial institutions have been added to the database, you will be able to see how the Financial form really works. Click on different entries in the financial institution combo box and watch the phone number change. Every click event fires the procedure to get the phone number for the Financial Institution being displayed.

Pick a customer and add three or four customer purchase history records using different sales dates. During the process of adding a new customer purchase history record, you will notice that the most current record is always displayed for editing. All prior records are displayed in the list view control and are read-only at this point.

Also notice that the list view control looks very similar to a grid control but with a couple of extra enhancements. First, the list view control provides full row select, that is the full row is highlighted, not just the first column. Second, it provides hot tracking whereby the row highlighted follows the cursor as it is moved from row to row. The columns are adjustable just like a grid control and can be adjusted as needed.

Financial data has also been added to the checklist and is required before the Add New Customer button will become enabled. You need simply to complete the fields on the Financial form, click the Add Institute button, and the checkbox for Financial Data will be checked.

Summary

This case study has taken you through the steps of modifying your database design to add enhanced functionality. We have performed the process of coding SQL statements that create new tables and modify existing tables. You have learned how to add primary and foreign keys through the use of SQL statements, and how to set permissions on our objects. You have also learned the importance of creating a script to modify the database and the logical steps that need to be taken when modifying your database structure.

We have covered some familiar territory by creating new stored procedures to support our new tables, and we have learned how to modify existing stored procedures. By now you should feel very comfortable creating complex stored procedures that use input and output parameters and that return a return value. You should also feel comfortable using logic in your stored procedures, to control the flow of processing logic and to perform data validations. You have seen at first hand how using transactions in our stored procedures helps maintain the integrity of data in our database, and should have no problems using transactions.

This case study has covered more on joins, column aliases, and correlation names, and you should feel quite comfortable using these techniques. You should know when a `LEFT OUTER JOIN` is required and when an `INNER JOIN` (`JOIN`) is required. We have used table prefixes to prefix columns in the `SELECT` list that appear in multiple tables. These techniques should be second nature to you by now, however, Chapter 9 can be used to refresh your memory when needed.

By adding a column to a table in our database we were forced to modify a stored procedure, which in turn caused us to modify a public function in our business server component. This change caused us to break binary compatibility and we therefore had to recompile a new compatibility component.

This book has covered several techniques for creating functions that return recordset data. Our component implements these techniques in functions that accept a `Recordset` object by reference and open it, and also functions that return a `Recordset` object instead of a return code.

Our UI has utilized several interesting techniques to perform data validations. The first technique, using the `Validate` event, was introduced in Chapter 13 and this case study introduced event handlers to handle the events raised by our controls. The combination of the two provides a powerful data validation technique that rivals the VB Masked Edit control. Data validation is a critical part of ensuring that the data we pass to our business server component, and ultimately to our stored procedures, is as accurate as possible and helps to ensure data integrity in our database.

Overall this case study has combined several new techniques while helping to reinforce the techniques and skills you have already learned. This case study should serve as a good example and reference point while building your own applications that implement the features covered throughout this book and the new techniques covered in this case study.

Our second case study expands and enhances the application further, and we will learn how to create reports from the data in the database.

WROX AUTO WORKS RACING

Case Study 2 – Wrox Auto Works Sales Staff Application

Wrox Auto Works Sales Staff Application – Part 1

In the last case study we examined how to modify the database using scripts that contained SQL statements. You learned how to add new tables as well as modify existing tables. You also learned how to add primary and foreign key constraints and set permissions using SQL statements. This chapter expands on those skills that you have learned by altering the structure of the database once again. You will have the opportunity to apply your existing skills and at the same time learn something new, when we create a clustered index on a new table using SQL statements in our script.

This case study also explores some new techniques in stored procedures, as we take a look at how to create and use temporary tables. We will also take a look at some SQL Server aggregate functions that allow us to perform calculations on data in the columns returned by our `SELECT` SQL statements.

To finish up this case study, we will modify the `AutoWorks` server component and the UI to implement the new stored procedures and functions that we will write. As a result of the modifications to the database and our VB programs, we will be able to design and display a report using the **Data Environment** and **Data Report Designers**. We will be using the Data Environment Designer to establish a connection to the database, and to execute a `Command` object that uses a stored procedure that accepts parameters. This `Command` object will then be used to design our report. Once our report has been designed, we will remove the Data Environment Designer from our project and manipulate the Data Report properties through code, using a `Recordset` object to supply the necessary data.

In this case study we will cover:

- SQL statements that modify the database structure
- SQL Server aggregate functions
- Creating and using temporary tables in a stored procedure
- How to use the Data Environment Designer
- How to use the Data Report Designer

Because of the size of this case study, it has been broken down into three parts. The first part concentrates on the changes required to the database and stored procedures, implementing those changes, and modifying the business component. The second part looks at modifying the UI to take advantage of those changes. The final part of this case study concentrates on the stored procedure that is used to create the report, and the actual creation of the report using the Data Environment Designer and Data Report Designer.

Database Design

The whole purpose behind this case study is to reinforce the skills that you have already learned, as well as to introduce you to new techniques that can be used with SQL Server and VB. To that end, the database design has once again been modified. This modification, while small, will provide the foundation on which we can apply several new techniques in SQL Server and VB.

The following diagram details the modifications that are required to our database. This diagram only shows a partial view of our database, and includes the *new table* and the *modification* required to the `Customer_Purchase_History_T` table:

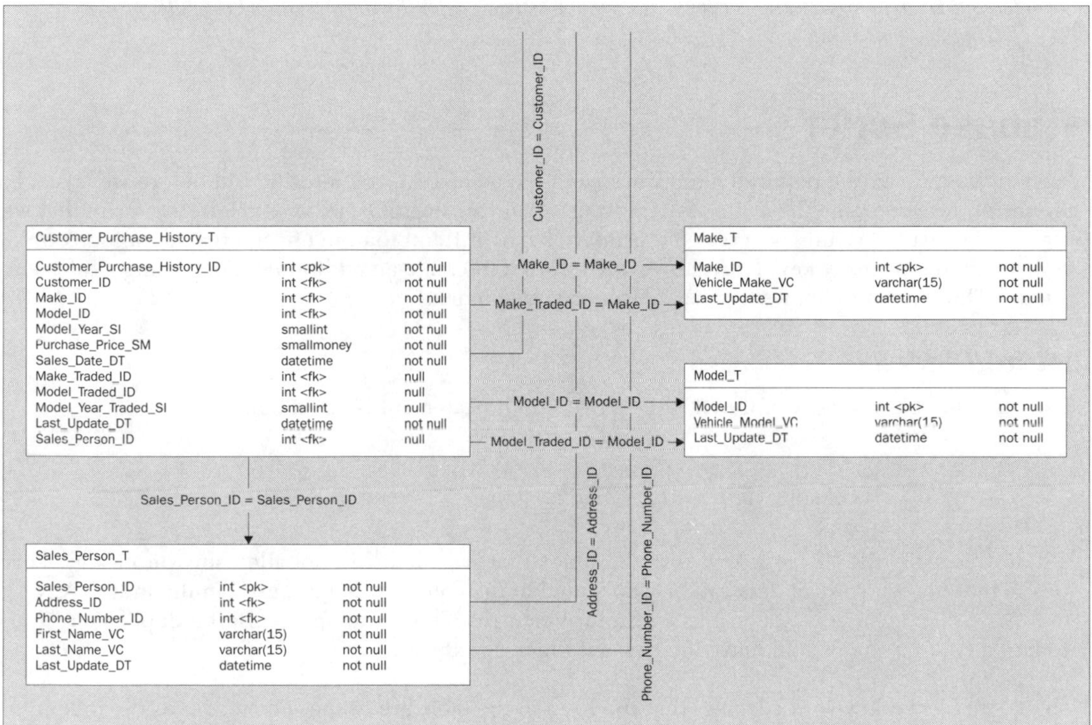

As you can see, we will be adding a new table called `Sales_Person_T`, which allows us to keep a record of every member on our **sales staff** team. This table has a design that is very similar to the `Customer_T` table. It contains the names of all of our sales staff, and contains foreign key references to the Address and Phone Number tables. Because we designed our Address and Phone Number tables generically, in other words without specifying that the tables contain *customer* addresses and phone numbers, we have seen multiple reuses of these tables, and can continue to reuse them here.

The `Customer_Purchase_History_T` table now contains a foreign key reference to the new `Sales_Person_T` table, and every purchase made from here on out will contain a reference to a **sales person**. This will allow us to determine the top sales person, calculated by the number of vehicles sold and the total dollar amount of their sales. We'll see how to report this data in Part 3 of the case study.

Notice that once again we have modified a table (Customer_Purchase_History_T) by *adding a new column*, Sales_Person_ID, and have specified that this column will allow null values. This is because this column is a foreign key reference to a table that contains a primary key. Since we already have entries in the Customer_Purchase_History_T table and none in the Sales_Person_T table, we *must* define this column to allow null values. We will, however, *require* a value for this column, and will control this through our stored procedures and VB functions.

> *If we were adding a new column to the* Customer_Purchase_History_T *table that was, for example, to be used to record the dollar amount given for a traded vehicle, we could define that column as not null. We could then assign a default value for that column of zero, which would be inserted into the column for all existing rows. However, since the column we have added contains a foreign key reference to another table, we cannot assign a default value because of the rules of the foreign key constraint.*

Database Script

We will be making the required modifications to the database using a script, but before we take a look at the script, let's examine the syntax for creating an index using SQL statements. In the script that we used in the last case study we created a primary key constraint that, in effect, created an index on the table using the primary key. Here, however, we want to create an additional index using a different syntax. The type of index we'll be using is a clustered index.

Clustered Index

To recap, the basic syntax of the CREATE INDEX SQL statement is listed below:

```
CREATE [Unique] [Clustered | NonClustered] INDEX index_name ON table_name
           (column_name, column_name)
```

When we specify the Unique keyword, the index that is created will not allow any duplicates. This means that no two rows of data can be duplicated in the columns that are used in the index. Any INSERT or UPDATE SQL statements will return an error if they attempt to insert a duplicate row or update a column that would make the row a duplicate in the index.

The Clustered keyword specifies that the rows in the table are in the same order as the index. In Chapter 1 we mentioned that a clustered index is kind of like a phone book. All rows are sorted in the table by the columns listed in the index, just as all the rows in the phone book are sorted by last name and first name. Using a clustered index to select rows of data by a column specified in a WHERE clause is highly efficient. A clustered index is actually part of the table, as the table rows are contained at the bottom level of the index.

We can use a clustered index on a table such as the Customer_T or Sales_Person_T table and efficiently select rows by the customer's or sales person's last name, since these are the columns that are used in the clustered index. Likewise, all the rows in the SELECT statement are returned based on the clustered index, unless the primary key is used in the WHERE clause of the SELECT statement. This saves the extra overhead of having to use the ORDER BY clause, because the rows are already sorted using the clustered index.

When the `NonClustered` *keyword is specified, an index is created that contains pointers to the rows of data in the table. In this case, the index and table rows are not sorted in the same order. A non-clustered index can be created on a table that already has a clustered index defined. In this case the non-clustered index will point to the entries in the clustered index to locate the rows.*

The index name assigned must be unique for each table but does not have to be unique in the database. In other words you can assign an index name of `IX_Clustered_Index_On_Last_Name` for both the `Customer_T` and `Sales_Person_T` tables. However, to cause less confusion, each index should ideally have a unique name. The index name must follow the rules for identifiers, which we have already covered in Chapter 3, and this name can be up to 128 characters in length.

The `table_name` parameter specified in the syntax above is the name of the table that the index should be created on. The `column_name` parameters specify one or more column names that are to be included in the index, and a comma separates each column name. The entire column list must be enclosed in parentheses. Columns that contain text, image, and bit data types cannot be used in the index.

Now that we have examined the syntax of the `CREATE INDEX` SQL statement, let's look at an example. The following code fragment demonstrates a unique clustered index being created on the `Make_T` table:

```
CREATE Unique Clustered INDEX IX_Make_T ON Make_T (Vehicle_Make_VC)
```

This index will not allow duplicate vehicle makes to be inserted into the `Make_T` table, and all entries would be automatically sorted by vehicle make. Therefore you could select data from this table to populate a combo box, and would not have to specify the `ORDER BY` clause in the `SELECT` statement.

Try It Out – Creating the Database Script

Given the modified database design shown earlier, we will code a database script to achieve the following:

- Create the new `Sales_Person_T` table and modify the `Customer_Purchase_History_T` table.
- A clustered index should be created on the `Sales_Person_T` table using the `Last_Name_VC` and `First_Name_VC` columns.
- Foreign key references should be made from the `Sales_Person_T` table to the Address and Phone Number tables, and also from the `Customer_Purchase_History_T` table to the `Sales_Person_T` table.
- After the new table has been created, the appropriate permissions should be set on this table for the various roles that we have defined.

The database script is listed below, and is available in the download files. Enter this code in the Query Analyzer:

```
--
*********************************************************************************
-- Create Sales_Person_T Table
--
*********************************************************************************
CREATE TABLE Sales_Person_T
   (
   Sales_Person_ID          Int         IDENTITY(1,1) NOT Null,
   Address_ID          Int         NOT Null,
   Phone_Number_ID          Int         NOT Null,
   First_Name_VC          VarChar(15) NOT Null,
   Last_Name_VC          VarChar(15) NOT Null,
   Last_Update_DT          DateTime    NOT Null
   )
GO

--
*********************************************************************************
-- Add a Clustered Index To Sales_Person_T
--
*********************************************************************************
CREATE CLUSTERED INDEX IX_Sales_Person_T ON Sales_Person_T
   (Last_Name_VC, First_Name_VC)
GO

--
*********************************************************************************
-- Add Constraints (Primary and Foreign Keys) To Sales_Person_T
--
*********************************************************************************
ALTER TABLE Sales_Person_T
   ADD
   CONSTRAINT PK_Sales_Person_T PRIMARY KEY NONCLUSTERED (Sales_Person_ID),
   CONSTRAINT FK_Sales_Person_T_Address_T FOREIGN KEY (Address_ID)
      REFERENCES Address_T (Address_ID),
   CONSTRAINT FK_Sales_Person_T_Phone_Number_T FOREIGN KEY (Phone_Number_ID)
      REFERENCES Phone_Number_T (Phone_Number_ID)
GO

--
```

```
--
*******************************************************************************
-- ALTER TABLE Customer_Purchase_History_T To Add A New Column
--
*******************************************************************************
ALTER TABLE Customer_Purchase_History_T
   ADD
   Sales_Person_ID         Int         Null
GO

--
*******************************************************************************
-- Add Constraints (Foreign Key) To Customer_Purchse_History_T
--
*******************************************************************************
ALTER TABLE Customer_Purchase_History_T
   ADD
   CONSTRAINT FK_Customer_Purchase_History_T_Sales_Person_T FOREIGN KEY
      (Sales_Person_ID)
      REFERENCES Sales_Person_T (Sales_Person_ID)
GO

--
*******************************************************************************
-- Grant Permissions On Sales_Person_T
--
*******************************************************************************
GRANT SELECT, INSERT, UPDATE, DELETE ON Sales_Person_T TO Developers
GRANT SELECT, INSERT, UPDATE ON Sales_Person_T TO [Sales Staff]
GRANT SELECT ON Sales_Person_T TO Management
GO
```

How It Works – Creating the Database Script

We learned how to create and use database scripts in Chapter 16, so you should be familiar with the concept. As we discussed in the last case study, we use the GO command to execute a batch of SQL statements. This ensures that the SQL statements are executed and the changes are applied in the database before we move on to the next set of SQL statements. This way our table is created before we try to add our constraints or indexes.

The first thing this script does is to create the new table, with the code shown below. The first column in our table is an identity column and has been specified as such with the `Identity` keyword. We have also specified the seed and increment values for the Identity column. All columns in this table must contain data, and as such we have specified the `NOT Null` keywords for each column:

```
--
*************************************************************************************
-- Create Sales_Person_T Table
--
*************************************************************************************
CREATE TABLE Sales_Person_T
   (
   Sales_Person_ID        Int           IDENTITY(1,1) NOT Null,
   Address_ID             Int           NOT Null,
   Phone_Number_ID        Int           NOT Null,
   First_Name_VC          VarChar(15) NOT Null,
   Last_Name_VC           VarChar(15) NOT Null,
   Last_Update_DT         DateTime      NOT Null
   )
GO
```

After our new table has been created in the database, we specify the SQL statements to create a *clustered index* on this table. Here we are using the `Last_Name_VC` and `First_Name_VC` columns in the index. These columns will be used to sort all rows in this table in the index. Notice that we are not using a *unique* index, as it is likely that there could be duplicate last and first names in our table.

Because we have used both first and last names in the clustered index, we do not have to specify an `ORDER BY` clause in our `SELECT` statement when we want the results ordered by name. We will see this shortly when we create our stored procedures.

```
--
*************************************************************************************
-- Add a Clustered Index To Sales_Person_T
--
*************************************************************************************
CREATE CLUSTERED INDEX IX_Sales_Person_T ON Sales_Person_T
   (Last_Name_VC, First_Name_VC)
GO
```

This next batch of SQL statements alters the new table we have just created, `Sales_Person_T`, by adding the primary and foreign key constraints to it. The primary key is defined on the `Sales_Person_ID` column, and the foreign keys are defined on the `Address_ID` and `Phone_Number_ID` columns:

```
--
**************************************************************************************
-- Add Constraints (Primary and Foreign Keys) To Sales_Person_T
--
**************************************************************************************
ALTER TABLE Sales_Person_T
   ADD
   CONSTRAINT PK_Sales_Person_T PRIMARY KEY NONCLUSTERED (Sales_Person_ID),
   CONSTRAINT FK_Sales_Person_T_Address_T FOREIGN KEY (Address_ID)
      REFERENCES Address_T (Address_ID),
   CONSTRAINT FK_Sales_Person_T_Phone_Number_T FOREIGN KEY (Phone_Number_ID)
      REFERENCES Phone_Number_T (Phone_Number_ID)
GO
```

We now need to alter the `Customer_Purchase_History_T` table, to add a new column that will reference the sales person in the `Sales_Person_T` table:

```
--
**************************************************************************************
-- ALTER TABLE Customer_Purchase_History_T To Add A New Column
--
**************************************************************************************
ALTER TABLE Customer_Purchase_History_T
   ADD
   Sales_Person_ID          Int          Null
GO
```

The `Sales_Person_T` table has had the primary key constraint added, and we have just added a new column to the `Customer_Purchase History_T` table, which will be used to reference the `Sales_Person_T` table. Now we need to define the *foreign key constraint* that will tie these two tables together.

> *This is an example of just one of the many reasons why we must specify the `Go` command after each batch of SQL statements – the new `Sales_Person_T` table must be created and the primary key defined before we can alter another table to reference it.*

```
--
**************************************************************************************
-- Add Constraints (Foreign Key) To Customer_Purchse_History_T
--
**************************************************************************************
ALTER TABLE Customer_Purchase_History_T
   ADD
   CONSTRAINT FK_Customer_Purchase_History_T_Sales_Person_T FOREIGN KEY
(Sales_Person_ID)
```

```
        REFERENCES Sales_Person_T (Sales_Person_ID)
GO
```

The last step in our database script is to grant the appropriate permissions on the new table to the various roles. Notice that the words `Sales Staff` are enclosed in square brackets; this is because there are two words separated by a space, and the brackets indicate that they should be treated as one continuous item:

```
--
*************************************************************************************
-- Grant Permissions On Sales_Person_T
--
*************************************************************************************
GRANT SELECT, INSERT, UPDATE, DELETE ON Sales_Person_T TO Developers
GRANT SELECT, INSERT, UPDATE ON Sales_Person_T TO [Sales Staff]
GRANT SELECT ON Sales_Person_T TO Management
GO
```

If you use the Enterprise Manager, you can view the modifications to the database and will be able to see the new `Sales_Person_T` table. If you open the `Customer_Purchase_History_T` table you will be able to see the additional column (`Sales_Person_ID`) that we just added.

Stored Procedures

Now that the database modifications have been completed, we need to move on to alter some of our existing stored procedures and to create some new ones, to reflect the changes we have just made to the structure of the database.

Existing Stored Procedures

Because of the additional column added to the `Customer_Purchase_History_T` table, we must modify the stored procedures that reference this table. In our discussions above we mentioned that we would control the requirement to have a sales person for each new row added to this table. We will do this in two ways. Firstly, we will modify the `up_parmins_customer_purchase` stored procedure and validate that the `Sales_Person_ID` is passed as a parameter. Secondly, we will require this parameter in the function that calls this stored procedure, which we will cover later.

The modifications that we will be making to our stored procedures are small. This is due to the fact that all management of data in the new `Sales_Person_T` table will be carried out in a separate form, which we'll be creating later. The stored procedures that insert and update data in the `Customer_Purchase_History_T` table will only accept the ID of the sales person. These stored procedures will not insert or update data in the `Sales_Person_T` table.

Try It Out – Modifying Existing Stored Procedures

The amount of code that we want to add to the existing stored procedures is not significant. Therefore we will use the Enterprise Manager to make these modifications. If you prefer, you can use the Query Analyzer. If using the Query Analyzer, you must first drop the existing stored procedures using the steps outlined in the last case study.

1. In the Enterprise Manager, expand the `Wrox_Auto_Works` database and click on Stored Procedures in the tree view pane. Then find the `up_parmins_customer_purchase` stored procedure and double click on it to bring it up in edit mode. Maximize the Stored Procedure Properties dialog so it is easier to work with.

2. Modify the beginning of this stored procedure by adding the `@Sales_Person_ID` parameter as shown in the code fragment below:

```
CREATE PROCEDURE up_parmins_customer_purchase
   (@Customer_ID Int, @Make_Purchased_ID Int,
   @Make_Purchased VarChar(15), @Model_Purchased_ID Int, @Model_Purchased
VarChar(15),
   @Model_Year_Purchased SmallInt, @Purchase_Price SmallMoney, @Sales_Date
   DateTime,
   @Make_Traded_ID Int, @Make_Traded VarChar(15), @Model_Traded_ID Int,
   @Model_Traded VarChar(15), @Model_Year_Traded SmallInt, @Sales_Person_ID Int,
   @Message VarChar(300) OUTPUT) AS
```

3. Modify the validations by adding the following code:

```
--
*********************************************************************************
-- Validate sales person ID exists
--
*********************************************************************************
IF @Sales_Person_ID IS Null OR @Sales_Person_ID = 0
   BEGIN
   SELECT @Message = 'Sales person id is required. '
   SELECT @Continue = 0
   END

--
*********************************************************************************
-- All data has been validated, either return to the caller with a bad return
-- code and messages or continue on and insert the values
--
*********************************************************************************
```

4. Modify the final INSERT statement by adding the sales person ID and parameter to the statement:

```
--
******************************************************************************
-- Finally, insert all purchase data in the customer purchase history table
--
******************************************************************************
INSERT INTO Customer_Purchase_History_T
   (Customer_ID, Make_ID, Model_ID, Model_Year_SI, Purchase_Price_SM,
      Sales_Date_DT, Make_Traded_ID, Model_Traded_ID,
      Model_Year_Traded_SI, Sales_Person_ID, Last_Update_DT)
   VALUES(@Customer_ID, @Make_Purchased_ID, @Model_Purchased_ID,
      @Model_Year_Purchased, @Purchase_Price, @Sales_Date,
      @Make_Traded_ID, @Model_Traded_ID, @Model_Year_Traded,
      @Sales_Person_ID, GetDate())
```

5. Now click on the Check Syntax button to ensure that you have not made any syntax errors. You should get the Check Syntax Successful message and you can click OK to dismiss that dialog. Next click the OK button in the Stored Procedure Dialog to save the changes to your stored procedure.

6. The next stored procedure that we want to modify is the up_parmupd_customer_purchase stored procedure. The exact same modifications are to be made to this stored procedure, and the code that needs to be added is listed in the three blocks below without any further explanations:

```
CREATE PROCEDURE up_parmupd_customer_purchase (@Customer_Purchase_History_ID Int,
   @Make_Purchased_ID Int, @Make_Purchased VarChar(15), @Model_Purchased_ID Int,
   @Model_Purchased VarChar(15), @Model_Year_Purchased SmallInt,
   @Purchase_Price SmallMoney, @Sales_Date DateTime, @Make_Traded_ID Int,
   @Make_Traded VarChar(15), @Model_Traded_ID Int, @Model_Traded VarChar(15),
   @Model_Year_Traded SmallInt, @Sales_Person_ID Int, @Message VarChar(300)
OUTPUT) AS
```

```
--
******************************************************************************
-- Validate sales person ID exists
--
******************************************************************************
IF @Sales_Person_ID IS Null OR @Sales_Person_ID = 0
   BEGIN
   SELECT @Message = 'Sales person id is required. '
   SELECT @Continue = 0
   END
--
******************************************************************************
```

```
-- All data has been validated, either return to the caller with a bad return and
-- messages or continue on and insert the values
--
**********************************************************************************


   --
*******************************************************************************
   -- Finally, update all purchase data in the customer purchase history table
   --
*******************************************************************************
   UPDATE Customer_Purchase_History_T
      SET Make_ID = @Make_Purchased_ID,
      Model_ID = @Model_Purchased_ID,
      Model_Year_SI = @Model_Year_Purchased,
      Purchase_Price_SM = @Purchase_Price,
      Sales_Date_DT = @Sales_Date,
      Make_Traded_ID = @Make_Traded_ID,
      Model_Traded_ID = @Model_Traded_ID,
      Model_Year_Traded_SI = @Model_Year_Traded,
      Sales_Person_ID = @Sales_Person_ID,
      Last_Update_DT = GetDate()
      WHERE Customer_Purchase_History_ID = @Customer_Purchase_History_ID
```

7. The last stored procedure that we want to modify is the stored procedure that selects the customer purchase history, in other words `up_parmsel_customer_purchase_history`. This stored procedure requires a bit more explanation, as we are joining the `Sales_Person_T` table in order to get the sales person's first and last name.

8. We start our modifications to this stored procedure by inserting the columns from the `Sales_Person_T` table into the `SELECT` statement, after the vehicle make and model traded, as shown in the following code fragment.

9. Notice that we have specified the table name for the `Sales_Person_ID` column, as this column exists in both the `Customer_Purchase_History_T` and `Sales_Person_T` table, and we need a method to distinguish from which table this column should be selected.

```
--
-- Select make and model traded
--
   Make_Traded.Make_ID AS Vehicle_Make_Traded_ID,
   Make_Traded.Vehicle_Make_VC AS Vehicle_Make_Traded,
   Model_Traded.Model_ID AS Vehicle_Model_Traded_ID,
   Model_Traded.Vehicle_Model_VC AS Vehicle_Model_Traded,
--
-- Select sales person
--
   Sales_Person_T.Sales_Person_ID, First_Name_VC, Last_Name_VC
--
-- From
--
   FROM Customer_Purchase_History_T
```

10. Because data already exists in the Customer_Purchase_History_T table, we must use a LEFT OUTER JOIN when joining the Sales_Person_T table. This will ensure that all existing rows from the Customer_Purchase_History_T table are returned, and the columns from the Sales_Person_T table will be returned with null values if data does not exist in the Customer_Purchase_History_T table for those columns.

11. Using a simple JOIN here would not give us the results that we need, because any rows that contained a null Sales_Person_ID would not be returned in the results.

```
--
-- Left outer join model_t to get vehicle model traded if any
--
   LEFT OUTER JOIN Model_T AS Model_Traded ON
      Customer_Purchase_History_T.Model_Traded_ID = Model_Traded.Model_ID
--
-- Left outer join sales_person_t to get sales person
--
   LEFT OUTER JOIN Sales_Person_T ON
      Customer_Purchase_History_T.Sales_Person_ID = Sales_Person_T.Sales_Person_ID
--
-- Where
--
   WHERE Customer_ID = @Customer_ID
```

This covers all of the stored procedure *modifications* that we need to make. Now we need to create the *new* stored procedures that are required to support the Sales_Person_T table.

New Stored Procedures

Since we will be managing the data in the Sales_Person_T table in a separate form in our project, we need a stored procedure to select all sales persons to display in the Sales Person form. Once a sales person is selected in the combo box, we need to select and display their address information. This requires another stored procedure, one that *selects* the sales person's address. Likewise, we need a stored procedure to *insert* a new sales person, as well as a stored procedure to *update* a sales person.

All of these stored procedures will be called from the business server component, which in turn will be called from our new form (which we'll create in Part 2 of this case study) that manages the sales staff.

Try It Out – Sales Person Stored Procedures

The stored procedure that we use to insert a *customer's* address and phone number has been designed generically and can also be used to insert a *sales person*'s address and phone number. The up_parmins_address stored procedure accepts the necessary address and phone number parameters, and returns the Address_ID and Phone_Number_ID of the entries inserted as output parameters. These parameters will then be used as input parameters to the new stored procedures that we are about to create.

1. The code for the four new stored procedures is listed below, and is also available for download. Enter these stored procedures in the Query Analyzer and execute them.

2. The first stored procedure is `up_select_sales_staff`:

```
CREATE PROCEDURE up_select_sales_staff AS

SELECT Sales_Person_ID, First_Name_VC, Last_Name_VC, Last_Update_DT
   FROM Sales_Person_T
```

3. Next we have `up_parmsel_sales_person_address` which selects the address for a specific sales person, and is almost a duplicate of the `up_parmsel_customer_address` stored procedure. In fact the `up_parmsel_customer_address` stored procedure can be used as a basis for building this stored procedure, and we simply need to replace the `Customer_ID` column and `Customer_T` table names with `Sales_Person_ID` and `Sales_Person_T` respectively:

```
CREATE PROCEDURE up_parmsel_sales_person_address (@Sales_Person_ID Int) AS

SELECT Address_T.Address_ID, Street_Address_1_VC, Street_Address_2_VC,
   Street_Address_3_VC,
   Address_T.Last_Update_DT,
   City_T.City_ID, City_Name_VC,
   State_T.State_ID, State_Name_VC,
   Zip_Code_T.Zip_Code_ID, Zip_Code_CH,
   Phone_Number_T.Phone_Number_ID, Area_Code_SI, Phone_Number_IN,
   'Phone_Number_Last_Update_DT' = Phone_Number_T.Last_Update_DT

   FROM Sales_Person_T

   JOIN Address_T ON Sales_Person_T.Address_ID = Address_T.Address_ID
   JOIN City_T ON Address_T.City_ID = City_T.City_ID
   JOIN State_T ON Address_T.State_ID = State_T.State_ID
   JOIN Zip_Code_T ON Address_T.Zip_Code_ID = Zip_Code_T.Zip_Code_ID
   JOIN Phone_Number_T ON Sales_Person_T.Phone_Number_ID =
         Phone_Number_T.Phone_Number_ID

   WHERE Sales_Person_ID = @Sales_Person_ID
```

4. Here is the code for the third new procedure, `up_parmins_sales_person`:

```
CREATE PROCEDURE up_parmins_sales_person (@Address_ID Int, @Phone_Number_Id Int,
@First_Name VarChar(15), @Last_Name VarChar(15), @Message VarChar(100) OUTPUT) AS

--
*************************************************************************************
-- Declare variables
--
*************************************************************************************
```

```
DECLARE @Continue   Bit

--
-- Turn on default value to continue
--
SELECT @Continue = 1

--
************************************************************************************
-- Validate required ID parameters are present
--
************************************************************************************
IF @Address_ID IS Null OR @Address_ID = 0
   BEGIN
   SELECT @Message = 'Address id is required. '
   SELECT @Continue = 0
   END

IF @Phone_Number_ID IS Null OR @Phone_Number_ID = 0
   BEGIN
   SELECT @Message = @Message + 'Phone number id is required. '
   SELECT @Continue = 0
   END

--
************************************************************************************
-- Validate required names are present
--
************************************************************************************
IF @First_Name IS Null OR DATALENGTH(LTRIM(@First_Name)) = 0
   BEGIN
   SELECT @Message = @Message + 'First name is required. '
   SELECT @Continue = 0
   END

IF @Last_Name IS Null OR DataLength(LTrim(@Last_Name)) = 0
   BEGIN
   SELECT @Message = @Message + 'Last name is required. '
   SELECT @Continue = 0
   END

--
************************************************************************************
-- All data has been validated, either return to the caller with a bad return and
-- messages or continue on and insert the values
--
************************************************************************************
```

```
IF @Continue = 0
   BEGIN
   --
   -- Return to the caller with a bad return code
   -- The messages are in the @message output parameter
   --
   RETURN 1
   END
ELSE
   BEGIN
   --
*******************************************************************************
   -- Insert the data into the sales person table
   --
*******************************************************************************
   INSERT INTO Sales_Person_T
      (Address_ID, Phone_Number_ID, First_Name_VC, Last_Name_VC, Last_Update_DT)
      VALUES(@Address_ID, @Phone_Number_ID, @First_Name, @Last_Name, GetDate())

   --
*******************************************************************************
   -- Return to the caller with a good return code
   --
*******************************************************************************
   RETURN 0
   END
```

5. The final stored procedure, up_parmupd_sales_person, is listed below.

```
CREATE PROCEDURE up_parmupd_sales_person (@Sales_Person_ID Int, @First_Name
   VarChar(30), @Last_Name VarChar(30)) AS

--
*******************************************************************************
-- Update the sales person's name
--
*******************************************************************************
UPDATE Sales_Person_T
   SET First_Name_VC = @First_Name,
   Last_Name_VC = @Last_Name,
   Last_Update_DT = GetDate()
   WHERE Sales_Person_ID = @Sales_Person_ID
```

6. Once all the stored procedures have been created, don't forget to set the appropriate permissions for the various roles that we have defined.

How It Works – Sales Person Stored Procedures

The first two stored procedures are really quite simple and merely select sales person data.

The up_select_sales_staff stored procedure (not listed here) selects all sales persons in the Sales_Person_T table. Notice the absence of the ORDER BY clause in this stored procedure. Since we want the results ordered by last and first names we need do nothing. The clustered index that we built on this table has taken care of this for us.

The next stored procedure, up_parmsel_sales_person_address, selects the appropriate address and phone number data. Notice that we are using a column alias for the Last_Update_DT column in the Phone_Number_T table:

```
'Phone_Number_Last_Update_DT' = Phone_Number_T.Last_Update_DT
```

The primary table that the data is coming from is the Sales_Person_T table. This table contains the foreign keys that reference the entries in the Address and Phone Number tables.

The first table that we join is the Address_T table. This table is joined on the foreign key in the Sales_Person_T table. The City_T, State_T, and Zip_Code_T tables are joined to the Address_T table using the foreign keys in the Address_T table. The Phone_Number_T table is joined using the foreign key in the Sales_Person_T table.

A simple JOIN is used to join all of the tables because all of the data is required and present. The WHERE clause limits the selection of data to the one row where the Sales_Person_ID matches the input parameter:

```
JOIN Address_T ON Sales_Person_T.Address_ID = Address_T.Address_ID
JOIN City_T ON Address_T.City_ID = City_T.City_ID
JOIN State_T ON Address_T.State_ID = State_T.State_ID
JOIN Zip_Code_T ON Address_T.Zip_Code_ID = Zip_Code_T.Zip_Code_ID
JOIN Phone_Number_T ON Sales_Person_T.Phone_Number_ID =
         Phone_Number_T.Phone_Number_ID

WHERE Sales_Person_ID = @Sales_Person_ID
```

The next stored procedure that we want to take a look at is the stored procedure to insert a new sales person – up_parmins_sales_person. This stored procedure will run after the stored procedure to insert a new address and phone number for a sales person. Therefore the only input parameters required are the address and phone number IDs of the entries inserted into the Address and Phone Number tables, along with the sales person's first and last name. Notice that once again we are using the @Message output parameter to return any data validation error messages:

```
CREATE PROCEDURE up_parmins_sales_person (@Address_ID Int, @Phone_Number_ID Int,
@First_Name VarChar(15), @Last_Name VarChar(15), @Message VarChar(100) OUTPUT) AS
```

Next we declare our variables, only one in this case, and set the default value for this variable. This is straightforward enough, so we don't need to reproduce the code.

Similarly, the validation routines are really pretty simple. We simply ensure that the @Address_ID and @Phone_Number_ID input parameters do not contain null or zero values.

The validations for the sales person's first and last name simply check that some data exists for these input parameters:

```
--
*******************************************************************************
-- Validate required names are present
--
*******************************************************************************
IF @First_Name IS Null OR DataLength(LTrim(@First_Name)) = 0
   BEGIN
   SELECT @Message = @message + 'First name is required. '
   SELECT @Continue = 0
   END

IF @Last_Name IS Null OR DataLength(LTrim(@Last_Name)) = 0
   BEGIN
   SELECT @Message = @Message + 'Last name is required. '
   SELECT @Continue = 0
   END
```

If the validations have failed, we return to the caller with a return code of 99. The error messages are in the output parameter @Message and are available for the caller to retrieve:

```
--
*******************************************************************************
-- All data has been validated, either return to the caller with a bad return and
-- messages or continue on and insert the values
--
*******************************************************************************
IF @Continue = 0
   BEGIN
   --
   -- Return to the caller with a bad return code
   -- The messages are in the @message output parameter
   --
   RETURN 1
   END
```

If all was successful, then we insert the values into the Sales_Person_T table and return to the caller with a return code of zero. Since we are modifying only one table, we have not used transactions; this insert will either work or fail.

Once an address has been assigned to a sales person, the Address_ID and Phone_Number_ID values do not change. We use the stored procedure that updates addresses to update the sales person's address. Therefore, the stored procedure to update the sales person needs only to update the sales person's first and last name.

The up_parmupd_sales_person stored procedure (not listed here) does not perform any validations whatsoever, and simply updates the Sales_Person_T table with the new first and last names that are passed as input variables.

Now that all of our new stored procedures have been created and some of our existing stored procedures modified, it's time to make the appropriate modifications and additions to our business server component. The changes that we will be making will represent a major change to our component.

AutoWorks Business Component

Because we have modified some of the stored procedures that select, insert, and update data in the Customer_Purchase_History_T table, we need to also make modifications to the classes of our component. In the case of the Vehicle class, because we are modifying the functions by adding another parameter, we are going to break binary compatibility. This change will necessitate a recompile of our binary component before we compile a new component for distribution. We will also need to recompile all programs that implement this component.

For this book, breaking binary compatibility does not cause a major problem because we have not implemented this application into a test or production environment. However, in the real world we need to be cognizant of the changes to our database structure and the impact that it can have on compiled components and programs. If we change the parameters that a stored procedure expects without changing our components, then the components will fail.

Let's get started by first looking at the necessary changes to the Vehicle class.

Try It Out – Modifying the Vehicle Class

As we mentioned above, changes have been made to the Customer_Purchase_History_T table, which caused us to modify some existing stored procedures that select, insert, and update data in this table. The Vehicle class contains two functions that need to be altered as a result of these changes.

1. The first function that we need to change is the InsertCustomerPurchase function. This function inserts a new customer purchase record, and we need to add the ID of the sales person to this function. The following code fragment shows where the lngSalesPersonID parameter should be placed in the list of input parameters to this function:

```
ByVal strModelTraded As String, _
ByVal intModelYearTraded As Integer, _
ByVal lngSalesPersonID As Long, _
ByRef strMessage() As String, _
ByRef objConn As ADODB.Connection, _
ByRef objCmd As ADODB.Command) As Long
```

2. The only other modification to this function is to add this new parameter to the `Parameters` collection, as shown in the following code fragment:

```
objCmd.Parameters.Append objCmd.CreateParameter("ModelYearTraded", adSmallInt, _
        adParamInput, , intModelYearTraded)
objCmd.Parameters.Append objCmd.CreateParameter("SalesPersonID", adInteger, _
        adParamInput, , lngSalesPersonID)
objCmd.Parameters.Append objCmd.CreateParameter("Message", adVarChar, _
        adParamOutput, 300)
```

3. The second function that needs to be modified is the `UpdateCustomerPurchase` function. The changes required here are the exact same changes that we just made to the `InsertCustomerPurchase` function. The following two code fragments show the necessary changes required to the input parameters and the `Parameters` collection:

```
    ByVal strModelTraded As String, _
    ByVal intModelYearTraded As Integer, _
    ByVal lngSalesPersonID As Long, _
    ByRef strMessage() As String, _
    ByRef objConn As ADODB.Connection, _
    ByRef objCmd As ADODB.Command) As Long
```

```
objCmd.Parameters.Append objCmd.CreateParameter("ModelYearTraded", adSmallInt, _
        adParamInput, , intModelYearTraded)
objCmd.Parameters.Append objCmd.CreateParameter("SalesPersonID", adInteger, _
        adParamInput, , lngSalesPersonID)
objCmd.Parameters.Append objCmd.CreateParameter("Message", adVarChar, _
        adParamOutput, 300)
```

That is all we need to do to the Vehicle class. The Address class also needs a minor modification. The form that manages the sales staff (which we'll be creating soon) displays the sales persons in a combo box. When we select a new sales person in the combo box, we need to execute the `GetAddress` function to retrieve the address for the sales person selected. To that end we need to modify the `GetAddress` function.

Try It Out – Modifying the Address Class

1. The modifications required are shown in the following code fragment. For this and the rest of the code in this case study you will need to change the user prefix of the stored procedures to your own user prefix:

```
If lngAddressType = Customer Then

  'Open the recordset
  objRS.Open "willist.up_parmsel_customer_address (" & _
     lngParentID & ")", objConn, adOpenForwardOnly, _
     adLockReadOnly, adCmdStoredProc
```

```
    Else

    'Open the recordset
    objRS.Open "willist.up_parmsel_sales_person_address (" & _
       lngParentID & ")", objConn, adOpenForwardOnly, _
       adLockReadOnly, adCmdStoredProc

    End If
```

Because we had a little forethought when we designed this function, we already had it set up to handle selecting the address for a sales person. All we needed to do was to add the call to the stored procedure, as we have done here.

SalesStaff Class

In order to support the form that manages the sales staff, we need to create a new class to execute the stored procedures that will be called to select, insert, and update the sales staff. This class has three functions, which we'll create one at a time, beginning with the insert function.

Try It Out – Create the Insert Function

1. Create a new class and sets its Name property to `clsSalesStaff`.

2. We need to create a public function that will execute the `up_parmins_sales_person` stored procedure to insert a new sales person into the `Sales_Person_T` table. Prior to executing this function, the caller will have executed the `InsertAddress` function in the Address class to insert the sales person's address.

3. Keeping that in mind, this function needs to accept the address and phone number IDs to be inserted, along with the first and last name of the sales person.

4. The code below (also available as a download) lists this new function. Don't forget to change the owner prefix of the stored procedure:

```
Public Function InsertSalesPerson(ByVal lngAddressID As Long, _
      ByVal lngPhoneNumberID As Long, _
      ByVal strFirstName As String, _
      ByVal strLastName As String, _
      ByRef strMessage() As String, _
      ByRef objConn As ADODB.Connection, _
      ByRef objCmd As ADODB.Command) As Long

   'Setup error handling
   On Error GoTo InsertSalesPerson_EH

   'Declare local variables
   Dim intIndex As Integer
```

```
   'Set the Command object properties
   Set objCmd.ActiveConnection = objConn
   objCmd.CommandText = "willist.up_parmins_sales_person"
   objCmd.CommandType = adCmdStoredProc

   'Append the parameters
   objCmd.Parameters.Append objCmd.CreateParameter("RC", adInteger, _
         adParamReturnValue)
   objCmd.Parameters.Append objCmd.CreateParameter("AddressID", adInteger, _
         adParamInput, , lngAddressID)
   objCmd.Parameters.Append objCmd.CreateParameter("PhoneNumberID", adInteger, _
         adParamInput, , lngPhoneNumberID)
   objCmd.Parameters.Append objCmd.CreateParameter("FirstName", adVarChar, _
         adParamInput, 15, strFirstName)
   objCmd.Parameters.Append objCmd.CreateParameter("LastName", adVarChar, _
         adParamInput, 15, strLastName)
   objCmd.Parameters.Append objCmd.CreateParameter("Message", adVarChar, _
         adParamOutput, 100)

   'Execute the Command object
   objCmd.Execute

   'If the return code is greater than zero
   If objCmd("RC") <> 0 Then
      'Add the message to the message string
      ReDim Preserve strMessage(0)
      strMessage(0) = objCmd("Message")
   End If

   'Return to the caller with the return code from the
   'stored procedure
   InsertSalesPerson = objCmd("RC")
   On Error GoTo 0
   Exit Function

InsertSalesPerson_EH:
   Dim objErr As ADODB.Error
   intIndex = -1
   'Add each ADO error to the message string
   For Each objErr In objConn.Errors
      intIndex = intIndex + 1
      ReDim Preserve strMessage(intIndex)
      strMessage(intIndex) = objErr.Description
   Next
   'Add any VB error message to the message string
   intIndex = intIndex + 1
   ReDim Preserve strMessage(intIndex)
   strMessage(intIndex) = Err.Description
   'Return to the caller
   InsertSalesPerson = 99
   On Error GoTo 0
End Function
```

How It Works – Create the Insert Function

This function works like the other insert functions that we have created in this component. We pass all of the input parameters to the stored procedure by value, and the output parameter for the stored procedure is passed by reference. The `Connection` and `Command` objects are also passed by reference, as we will be modifying these parameters:

```
Public Function InsertSalesPerson(ByVal lngAddressID As Long, _
      ByVal lngPhoneNumberID As Long, _
      ByVal strFirstName As String, _
      ByVal strLastName As String, _
      ByRef strMessage() As String, _
      ByRef objConn As ADODB.Connection, _
      ByRef objCmd As ADODB.Command) As Long
```

Next, we set up the error handling and declare our local variables:

```
   'Setup error handling
   On Error GoTo InsertSalesPerson_EH

   'Declare local variables
   Dim intIndex As Integer
```

Then we set the `Command` object properties and append the input and output parameters to the `Parameters` collection. The `up_parmins_sales_person` stored procedure will be returning a value, so we have specified the return value as the first parameter that we append to the `Parameters` collection:

```
   'Set the Command object properties
   Set objCmd.ActiveConnection = objConn
   objCmd.CommandText = "willist.up_parmins_sales_person"
   objCmd.CommandType = adCmdStoredProc

   'Append the parameters
   objCmd.Parameters.Append objCmd.CreateParameter("RC", adInteger, _
         adParamReturnValue)
   objCmd.Parameters.Append objCmd.CreateParameter("AddressID", adInteger, _
         adParamInput, , lngAddressID)
   objCmd.Parameters.Append objCmd.CreateParameter("PhoneNumberID", adInteger, _
         adParamInput, , lngPhoneNumberID)
   objCmd.Parameters.Append objCmd.CreateParameter("FirstName", adVarChar, _
         adParamInput, 15, strFirstName)
   objCmd.Parameters.Append objCmd.CreateParameter("LastName", adVarChar, _
         adParamInput, 15, strLastName)
   objCmd.Parameters.Append objCmd.CreateParameter("Message", adVarChar, _
         adParamOutput, 100)
```

We execute the `Command` object and then check the return value for a number other than zero, which indicates that an error has occurred. If an error occurred, we add the message returned from the stored procedure to the `strMessage` variable:

```
   'Execute the Command object
   objCmd.Execute

   'If the return code is greater than zero
   If objCmd("RC") <> 0 Then
      'Add the message to the message string
      ReDim Preserve strMessage(0)
      strMessage(0) = objCmd("Message")
   End If
```

Regardless of the return value from the stored procedure, we return it to the caller as the return code from this function:

```
   'Return to the caller with the return code from the
   'stored procedure
   InsertSalesPerson = objCmd("RC")
   On Error GoTo 0
   Exit Function
```

Our error handling routine is the same as in previous examples, and simply loops through the `Errors` collection, appending any errors it finds to the `strMessage` variable. If there is an associated VB error, then we also append that error to the `strMessage` variable:

```
InsertSalesPerson_EH:
   Dim objErr As ADODB.Error
   intIndex = -1
   'Add each ADO error to the message string
   For Each objErr In objConn.Errors
      intIndex = intIndex + 1
      ReDim Preserve strMessage(intIndex)
      strMessage(intIndex) = objErr.Description
   Next
   'Add any VB error message to the message string
   intIndex = intIndex + 1
   ReDim Preserve strMessage(intIndex)
   strMessage(intIndex) = Err.Description
   'Return to the caller
   InsertSalesPerson = 99
   On Error GoTo 0
End Function
```

This is all of the code required for this function. As we mentioned earlier, this function is very similar to all other insert functions in this component. The next function we need to look at is the update function.

Try It Out – Create the Update Function

The update function that we need to create will only update the sales person's first and last name. Their address is updated using the `UpdateAddress` function in the Address class. With this in mind, the function that we need to create really only requires three input parameters for the stored procedure. The rest of the input parameters to this function are required in order to execute the stored procedure.

1. The code for this function, which should be added to the SalesStaff class, is listed below. Again, don't forget to change the owner prefix.

```
Public Function UpdateSalesPerson(ByVal lngSalesPersonID As Long, _
      ByVal strFirstName As String, _
      ByVal strLastName As String, _
      ByRef objConn As ADODB.Connection, _
      ByRef objCmd As ADODB.Command) As Long

   'Setup error handling
   On Error GoTo UpdateSalesPerson_EH

   'Set the Command object properties
   Set objCmd.ActiveConnection = objConn
   objCmd.CommandText = "willist.up_parmupd_sales_person"
   objCmd.CommandType = adCmdStoredProc

   'Append the parameters
   objCmd.Parameters.Append objCmd.CreateParameter("SalesPersonID", adInteger, _
         adParamInput, , lngSalesPersonID)
   objCmd.Parameters.Append objCmd.CreateParameter("FirstName", adVarChar, _
         adParamInput, 15, strFirstName)
   objCmd.Parameters.Append objCmd.CreateParameter("LastName", adVarChar, _
         adParamInput, 15, strLastName)

   'Execute the Command object
   objCmd.Execute

   'Return with a good return code
   UpdateSalesPerson = 0
   On Error GoTo 0
   Exit Function

UpdateSalesPerson_EH:
   'Return to the caller
   UpdateSalesPerson = 99
   On Error GoTo 0
End Function
```

How It Works – Create the Update Function

The UpdateSalesPerson function accepts the ID of the sales person to update along with their first and last name, all of which are passed by value. The Connection and Command objects are passed by reference, as we will be modifying them:

```
Public Function UpdateSalesPerson(ByVal lngSalesPersonID As Long, _
      ByVal strFirstName As String, _
      ByVal strLastName As String, _
      ByRef objConn As ADODB.Connection, _
      ByRef objCmd As ADODB.Command) As Long
```

Again, we set up the error handling, set the Command object properties, and append the parameters to the Parameters collection:

```
   'Setup error handling
   On Error GoTo UpdateSalesPerson_EH

   'Set the Command object properties
   Set objCmd.ActiveConnection = objConn
   objCmd.CommandText = "willist.up_parmupd_sales_person"
   objCmd.CommandType = adCmdStoredProc

   'Append the parameters
   objCmd.Parameters.Append objCmd.CreateParameter("SalesPersonID", adInteger, _
         adParamInput, , lngSalesPersonID)
   objCmd.Parameters.Append objCmd.CreateParameter("FirstName", adVarChar, _
         adParamInput, 15, strFirstName)
   objCmd.Parameters.Append objCmd.CreateParameter("LastName", adVarChar, _
         adParamInput, 15, strLastName)
```

We execute the Command object and then return to the caller:

```
   'Execute the Command object
   objCmd.Execute

   'Return with a good return code
   UpdateSalesPerson = 0
   On Error GoTo 0
   Exit Function
```

Our error handler simply returns to the caller with a return code of 99 if an error occurred:

```
UpdateSalesPerson_EH:
   'Return to the caller
   UpdateSalesPerson = 99
   On Error GoTo 0
End Function
```

Our class currently has functions to *insert* and *update* sales staff – but we now need a function to allow sales staff data to be *selected.*

Try It Out – Create the Select Function

We need to create a function to execute the up_select_sales_staff stored procedure and return all records in a Recordset object. This function will be called to get a recordset of the sales staff, and will be used to populate the combo box on the form that manages the sales staff, as well as the Customer Purchase History form.

1. The code for this function, which again should be added to the SalesStaff class, changing the owner prefix as required, is listed below:

```
Public Function GetSalesStaff(ByRef objConn As ADODB.Connection, _
      ByRef objRS As ADODB.Recordset) As Long

   'Setup error handling
   On Error GoTo GetSalesStaff_EH

   'Set a reference to the Recordset object
   Set objRS = New ADODB.Recordset

   'Open the recordset
   objRS.Open "willist.up_select_sales_staff", objConn, _
      adOpenStatic, adLockReadOnly, adCmdStoredProc

   'Return with a good return code
   GetSalesStaff = 0

   'All was successful, exit function
   On Error GoTo 0
   Exit Function

GetSalesStaff_EH:
   GetSalesStaff = 1
   On Error GoTo 0
End Function
```

How It Works – Create the Select Function

This function accepts the Connection and Recordset objects by reference. The Recordset object will be used to return the records retrieved from the stored procedure.

```
Public Function GetSalesStaff(ByRef objConn As ADODB.Connection, _
      ByRef objRS As ADODB.Recordset) As Long
```

We set up the error handling and then set a reference to the ADO Recordset object:

```
   'Setup error handling
   On Error GoTo GetSalesStaff_EH

   'Set a reference to the Recordset object
   Set objRS = New ADODB.Recordset
```

We open the Recordset object, which in turns executes the stored procedure. We are using a static cursor in case the caller wants to navigate the recordset. If you recall our discussion of static cursors from a previous chapter, we mentioned that this type of cursor allows a user to navigate forwards and backwards in a recordset. The recordset is opened using a read only lock type because we only want to select data and not update it:

```
   'Open the recordset
   objRS.Open "willist.up_select_sales_staff", objConn, _
      adOpenStatic, adLockReadOnly, adCmdStoredProc
```

We then return to the caller with a return code of zero and exit the function. The error handler simply returns to the caller with a return code of 99:

```
   'Return with a good return code
   GetSalesStaff = 0

   'All was successful, exit function
   On Error GoTo 0
   Exit Function

GetSalesStaff_EH:
   GetSalesStaff = 1
   On Error GoTo 0
End Function
```

We have now added all of the necessary functions to our new class, and have made the required modifications to the existing class. The final step we will carry out is to recompile the component.

Try It Out – Re-compile the Modified Component

We have completed the modifications required to our component, but before we compile our component we want to change the version numbers for it. Because the changes that we have made represent a *major* change to our component, we want to increment the major version number.

1. Bring up the Project Properties dialog and on the Make tab, change the Major Version Number to 3, the Minor Version Number to 0, and the Revision Version Number to 0. On the Component tab, change the Version Compatibility option to Project Compatibility. Click OK to save your changes.

2. Now compile your component in the Compatibility folder. This will compile a new binary compatibility version of our component.

3. Open the Project Properties dialog again and change the Version Compatibility option to Binary Compatibility. Click OK to save your changes. Compile your component again, but this time compile it in your project folder. Save all changes and close the project.

That's it – we now have a modified business component to go with our amended database. The next step is to adjust the user interface elements to incorporate our changes into the application.

Wrox Auto Works Sales Staff Application – Part 2

We have now made all the amendments to the database and business component and are ready to move on to the second part of the case study – modifying the user interface to reflect the changes we have made, and to provide a means of managing the sales staff data.

Modifying the UI

There are several aspects of the UI that need to be modified. The Sales Staff form will manage the entire sales staff data independently of the rest of the application. This means that we must first add a sales person to our tables before we can use them in the Customer Purchase History form. This is because the Customer Purchase History form uses only the ID of the sales person as a parameter to the function to add and update a customer's purchase.

The changes that need to be made to the UI are to share some code from the Main form, modify the Customer Purchase History form, and create a new form to manage the sales staff.

Try It Out – Modifying the Main Form

Since the Sales Staff form will implement many of the same types of fields as the Main form, we need to share some of the code from the Main form, in particular the `LoadCityStateZip` procedure.

1. Move the `LoadCityStateZip` procedure from the Main form to the Utility module and make it a public procedure. The following code fragment shows this change.

```
Public Sub LoadCityStateZip(ByRef m_objConn As ADODB.Connection, _
      ByRef m_objRSAddress As ADODB.Recordset, _
      ByRef cboCity As ComboBox, _
      ByRef cboState As ComboBox, _
      ByRef cboZipCode As ComboBox, _
      ByRef arrCity() As Long, _
      ByRef arrState() As Long, _
      ByRef arrZipCode() As Long, _
      ByRef StatusBar1 As StatusBar)
```

2. The only modifications made to this procedure are to pass by reference all of the controls that this procedure accesses. The other modifications required are in the Main form. We need to search the code in the Main form and replace all references to call the `LoadCityStateZip` procedure with the new call. The code fragments below shows the old and new calls to the `LoadCityStateZip` procedure:

```
'Load City, State and Zip Code combo boxes
Call LoadCityStateZip
```

```
'Load City, State and Zip Code combo boxes
Call LoadCityStateZip(frmMain.m_objConn, m_objRSAddress, cboCity, _
   cboState, cboZipCode, arrCity(), arrState(), arrZipCode(), StatusBar1)
```

3. Since the Sales Staff form operates independently of the application, we will only add a menu item to be able to view the Sales Staff form. Using the Menu editor, add an entry to the View menu to view the Sales Staff form. (This was explained in Chapter 13). Set its Caption property to &Sales Staff and its Name property to mnuViewSalesStaff. It is up to you whether or not you want to add a separator between the existing entries and the new one.

4. Add the following code to the `mnuViewSalesStaff` procedure to show the Sales Staff form:

```
Private Sub mnuViewSalesStaff_Click()
   frmSalesStaff.Show vbModal
End Sub
```

Sales Staff Form

The Sales Staff form will display all sales persons that reside in the `Sales_Person_T` table. We will also be able to insert a new sales person and update an existing sales person.

Try It Out – Implement the Sales Staff Functionality

1. To begin, add a new form to your project and set the form's properties using the table below:

Property	Value
Name	`frmSalesStaff`
BorderStyle	3 – Fixed Dialog
Caption	Sales Staff
Height	5880
Icon	None
StartupPosition	1 – Center Owner
Width	6216

2. Now that the form's properties have been set, we need to add the controls to the form. Using the table and figure below, add the following controls to the form:

Control	Name	Properties
Frame	`Frame1`	Caption = Sales Person
Label	`Label1(0)`	Caption = Last Name
Label	`Label1(1)`	Caption = First Name
ComboBox	`cboLastName`	Style = 0 – Dropdown Combo
TextBox	`txtFirstName`	Text = Nothing
Frame	`Frame2`	Caption = Address
Label	`Label1(2)`	Caption = Address Line 1
Label	`Label1(3)`	Caption = Address Line 2
Label	`Label1(4)`	Caption = Address Line 3
Label	`Label1(5)`	Caption = City
Label	`Label1(6)`	Caption = State
Label	`Label1(7)`	Caption = Zip Code
Label	`Label1(8)`	Caption = Area Code
Label	`Label1(9)`	Caption = Phone Number
TextBox	`txtAddress1`	Text = Nothing
TextBox	`txtAddress2`	Text = Nothing
TextBox	`txtAddress3`	Text = Nothing
ComboBox	`cboCity`	Style = 0 – Dropdown Combo
ComboBox	`cboState`	Style = 2 – Dropdown List
ComboBox	`cboZipCode`	Style = 0 – Dropdown Combo
TextBox	`txtAreaCode`	Text = Nothing
TextBox	`txtPhoneNumber`	Text = Nothing
Frame	`Frame3`	Caption = Actions
CommandButton	`cmdAdd`	Caption = Add Sales Person
CommandButton	`cmdUpdate`	Caption = Update Sales Person
StatusBar	`StatusBar1`	Panel 1: Key = Msg, AutoSize = 1 – sbrSpring

3. Once you've finished the form it should look like this:

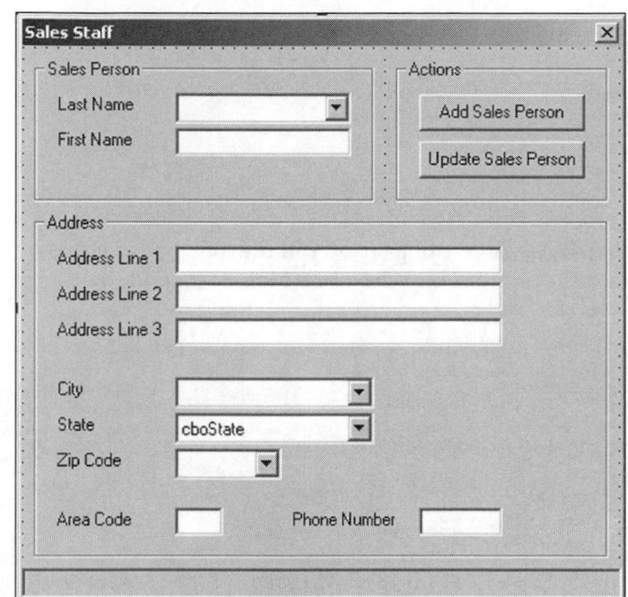

4. The Sales Staff form resembles the Main form in many ways, but mostly in the fields that are on the form. We need to implement the code behind this form to enable us to display, insert, and update a sales person. Using the Main form (`frmMain`) as a base we need to implement the changes to the code in this form (`frmSalesStaff`) as described in the *How It Works* section below.

How It Works – Implement the Sales Staff Functionality

You have already seen all of the code that is contained in this form, so we are only going to cover the highlights and the sections that need changing. First we need to mention that the Area Code and Phone Number fields on this form implement the Controls class to help in validation. We also validate the data in each of the fields, in the `Validate` events. There is only one entry point into this form and that is through the `Form_Load` event when the form is shown modally.

Displaying a Sales Person's Data

The `LoadSalesStaff` procedure gets called from the `Form_Load` event and the `Add` and `Update` procedures. Looking at the code in this procedure, we set up our error handling and declare our local variables. Then we clear any existing entries in the last name combo box:

```
Private Sub LoadSalesStaff()
   'Set up error handling
   On Error GoTo LoadSalesStaff_EH

   'Declare local variables
   Dim lngIndex As Long, lngRC As Long

   'Clear any existing entries
   cboLastName.Clear
```

If the recordset that we are using is already opened, then we close it before calling the function to populate it:

```
'If the recordset has been set and is open, then close it
If Not m_objRS Is Nothing Then
   If m_objRS.State = adStateOpen Then
      m_objRS.Close
   End If
End If
```

Next, we set a reference to our business object and call the function to populate our recordset. Notice that we are passing the `Connection` object from the Main form and the `Recordset` object from this form. We then check for errors and raise an error if something went wrong:

```
'Set a reference to the business object
Set m_objWroxSalesStaff = New AutoWorks.clsSalesStaff

'Get a list of customer names
lngRC = m_objWroxSalesStaff.GetSalesStaff(frmMain.m_objConn, m_objRS)

'If the return code is not zero, raise an error
If lngRC <> 0 Then
   Err.Raise vbObjectError + 513, "frmSalesStaff.LoadSalesStaff", _
      "Call to clsSalesStaff.GetSalesStaff failed"
End If
```

If everything was successful, we load the last name combo box and add the ID of the sales person to the `ItemData` property of the combo box:

```
'Load the combo box
lngIndex = -1
Do While Not m_objRS.EOF
   'Add the last name
   cboLastName.AddItem m_objRS!Last_Name_VC
   lngIndex = lngIndex + 1
   'Add the customer id
   cboLastName.ItemData(lngIndex) = m_objRS!Sales_Person_ID
   m_objRS.MoveNext
Loop
```

We then check for an `EOF` or `BOF` condition on the recordset, which indicates that we have no records. If neither of these conditions is true, then we set the `ListIndex` property of the combo box to the first entry, and set focus to the combo box:

```
'Set the index to the first entry and exit sub
If Not m_objRS.EOF Or Not m_objRS.BOF Then
   On Error Resume Next
   cboLastName.ListIndex = 0
   cboLastName.SetFocus
End If
On Error GoTo 0
Exit Sub
```

We have already covered the error handling routine, but basically it displays each error message in the status bar:

```
LoadSalesStaff_EH:
   'Ensure the error came from ADO
   If frmMain.m_objConn.Errors.Count > 0 Then
      For Each m_objErr In frmMain.m_objConn.Errors
         StatusBar1.Panels("Msg") = StatusBar1.Panels("Msg") & " " & _
         m_objErr.Description
      Next
   Else
      StatusBar1.Panels("Msg") = Err.Description
   End If
End Sub
```

Adding a Sales Person

The next major procedure we want to cover is the procedure to add a new sales person. We begin this procedure by setting up our error handling and declaring our local variables:

```
Private Sub cmdAdd_Click()
   'Set up error handling
   On Error GoTo cmdAdd_EH

   'Declare local variables
   Dim strMsg() As String, lngRC As Long, lngAddressID As Long, _
      lngPhoneNumberID As Long, lngCityID As Long, _
      lngZipCodeID As Long, varText As Variant
```

Then we determine if an existing city and zip code were chosen or if a new entry was entered for either one of them. We then set the local variables to hold the IDs accordingly:

```
   'Set city and zip code ids
   If cboCity.ListIndex = -1 Then
      lngCityID = 0
   Else
      lngCityID = cboCity.ItemData(cboCity.ListIndex)
   End If

   If cboZipCode.ListIndex = -1 Then
      lngZipCodeID = 0
   Else
      lngZipCodeID = cboZipCode.ItemData(cboZipCode.ListIndex)
   End If
```

We then set a reference to our business object and insert the address for this sales person. The `lngAddressID` and `lngPhoneNumberID` variables are being passed to this function by reference, and will be modified with the ID of the entry inserted if all was successful. Notice that we are calling the same function that inserts an address for a customer:

```
'Set a reference to the objects
Set m_objCmd = New ADODB.Command
Set m_objWroxAddress = New AutoWorks.clsAddress

'Insert the address
lngRC = m_objWroxAddress.InsertAddress(txtAddress1.Text, _
   txtAddress2.Text, _
   txtAddress3.Text, _
   lngCityID, _
   cboCity.Text, _
   cboState.ItemData(cboState.ListIndex), _
   lngZipCodeID, _
   cboZipCode.Text, _
   CInt(txtAreaCode.Text), _
   EditPhoneNumber(txtPhoneNumber.Text), _
   lngAddressID, _
   lngPhoneNumberID, _
   strMsg(), _
   frmMain.m_objConn, _
   m_objCmd)
```

We check for errors and then de-reference our objects:

```
'Display any error messages
If lngRC <> 0 Then
   For Each varText In strMsg
      StatusBar1.Panels("Msg").Text = StatusBar1.Panels("Msg").Text & _
         varText
   Next
   Exit Sub
End If

'De-reference objects and clear message variable
Set m_objCmd = Nothing
Set m_objWroxAddress = Nothing
ReDim strMsg(0)
```

Inserting a New Sales Person

In the function to insert a new sales person, we set a reference to the business object and call the function to insert the sales person, passing it the `lngAddressID` and `lngPhoneNumberID` parameters that were set in the last function that we called. We also pass the first and last name of the sales person using the `Text` property of the textbox and combo box:

```
   'Set a reference to the objects
   Set m_objCmd = New ADODB.Command
   Set m_objWroxSalesStaff = New AutoWorks.clsSalesStaff

   'Insert the customer information
   lngRC = m_objWroxSalesStaff.InsertSalesPerson(lngAddressID, _
      lngPhoneNumberID, _
      txtFirstName.Text, _
      cboLastName.Text, _
      strMsg(), _
      frmMain.m_objConn, _
      m_objCmd)
```

We once again check for errors and de-reference our objects:

```
   'Display any error messages
   If lngRC <> 0 Then
      For Each varText In strMsg
         StatusBar1.Panels("Msg").Text = StatusBar1.Panels("Msg").Text & _
            varText
      Next
      Exit Sub
   End If

   'De-reference objects
   Set m_objCmd = Nothing
   Set m_objWroxSalesStaff = Nothing
```

Just in case any address information was added, we reload the City, State, and Zip Code combo boxes. Then we call the function to reload the Last Name combo box, which contains all the sales persons. Next, we display a message that the sales person was added.

The error handling routine is the same as our other error handling routines and needs no further explanation:

```
   'ReLoad City, State and Zip Code combo boxes
   Call LoadCityStateZip(frmMain.m_objConn, m_objRSAddress, cboCity, _
      cboState, cboZipCode, arrCity(), arrState(), arrZipCode(), StatusBar1)

   'Reload data from new recordset
   Call LoadSalesStaff

   'Display message
   StatusBar1.Panels("Msg").Text = "Sales Person Added"
   Exit Sub

cmdAdd_EH:
   Dim objErr As ADODB.Error
   'Ensure the error came from ADO
   If frmMain.m_objConn.Errors.Count > 0 Then
      For Each objErr In frmMain.m_objConn.Errors
```

```
         StatusBar1.Panels("Msg") = StatusBar1.Panels("Msg") & " " & _
            objErr.Description
      Next
   Else
      StatusBar1.Panels("Msg") = Err.Description
   End If
End Sub
```

Updating a Sales Person

The last major procedure that we will cover in this form is the procedure to update a sales person. Again we set up our error handling and declare our local variables.

We go through the same procedure as the last function to determine if a city or zip code was selected, or if a new one is to be added:

```
Private Sub cmdUpdate_Click()
   'Set up error handling
   On Error GoTo cmdUpdate_EH

   'Declare local variables
   Dim strMsg() As String, lngRC As Long, lngCityID As Long, _
      lngZipCodeID As Long, varText As Variant

   'Set city and zip code IDs
   If cboCity.ListIndex = -1 Then
      lngCityID = 0
   Else
      lngCityID = cboCity.ItemData(cboCity.ListIndex)
   End If

   If cboZipCode.ListIndex = -1 Then
      lngZipCodeID = 0
   Else
      lngZipCodeID = cboZipCode.ItemData(cboZipCode.ListIndex)
   End If
```

We set a reference to our objects, and then call the same procedure that updates an address for a customer to update the address for the sales person in question:

```
   'Set a reference to the objects
   Set m_objCmd = New ADODB.Command
   Set m_objWroxAddress = New AutoWorks.clsAddress

   'Update the address
   lngRC = m_objWroxAddress.UpdateAddress(m_lngAddressID, _
      txtAddress1.Text, _
      txtAddress2.Text, _
      txtAddress3.Text, _
      lngCityID, _
      cboCity.Text, _
      cboState.ItemData(cboState.ListIndex), _
      lngZipCodeID, _
      cboZipCode.Text, _
```

```
    m_lngPhoneNumberID, _
    CInt(txtAreaCode.Text), _
    EditPhoneNumber(txtPhoneNumber.Text), _
    strMsg(), _
    frmMain.m_objConn, _
    m_objCmd)
```

We check for errors and then de-reference our objects:

```
'Display any error messages
If lngRC <> 0 Then
   For Each varText In strMsg
      StatusBar1.Panels("Msg").Text = StatusBar1.Panels("Msg").Text & _
         varText
   Next
   Exit Sub
End If

'De-reference objects and clear message variable
Set m_objCmd = Nothing
Set m_objWroxAddress = Nothing
ReDim strMsg(0)
```

Next, we set a reference to our objects to update the sales person, and call the `UpdateSalesPerson` procedure. Then we check for errors and de-reference our objects:

```
'Set a reference to the objects
Set m_objCmd = New ADODB.Command
Set m_objWroxSalesStaff = New AutoWorks.clsSalesStaff

'Update the customer record
lngRC = m_objWroxSalesStaff.UpdateSalesPerson(m_lngSalesPersonID, _
   txtFirstName.Text, _
   cboLastName.Text, _
   frmMain.m_objConn, _
   m_objCmd)

'Display any error messages
If lngRC <> 0 Then
   StatusBar1.Panels("Msg").Text = "Update of sales person failed"
   Exit Sub
End If

'De-reference objects
Set m_objCmd = Nothing
Set m_objWroxSalesStaff = Nothing
```

We save the record position for the current sales person and then reload all combo boxes on our form:

```
'Save the current record position
lngRecordPosition = cboLastName.ListIndex

'ReLoad City, State and Zip Code combo boxes
```

```
   Call LoadCityStateZip(frmMain.m_objConn, m_objRSAddress, cboCity, _
      cboState, cboZipCode, arrCity(), arrState(), arrZipCode(), StatusBar1)

   'Reload data from new recordset
   Call LoadSalesStaff
```

We then reposition the Last Name combo box using the `lngRecordPosition` variable and call the `cboLastName_Click` procedure to load the address and phone number for this sales person. Then we display a message that the sales person was updated.

The error handling routine needs no further explanation:

```
   'Reload from the address fields
   cboLastName.ListIndex = lngRecordPosition
   Call cboLastName_Click

   'Display message
   StatusBar1.Panels("Msg").Text = "Sales Person Updated"
   Exit Sub

cmdUpdate_EH:
   Dim objErr As ADODB.Error
   'Ensure the error came from ADO
   If frmMain.m_objConn.Errors.Count > 0 Then
      For Each objErr In frmMain.m_objConn.Errors
         StatusBar1.Panels("Msg") = StatusBar1.Panels("Msg") & " " & _
            objErr.Description
      Next
   Else
      StatusBar1.Panels("Msg") = Err.Description
   End If
End Sub
```

At this point you can run your project and add one or two sales persons. These will need to be added before we complete our modifications to the UI.

Once you've done this, you are ready to modify the Customer Purchase History form to incorporate the sales staff data.

Try It Out – Implement Sales Staff Functionality in the Customer Purchase History Form

The modifications that are needed in the Customer Purchase History form are minor, as we only need to add two controls, and add the code to support the loading of the sales staff data. We also need to slightly modify the calls to the Add and Update procedures, to include the ID of the sales person that is selected in the combo box.

1. The following diagram shows the placement of the new controls. Use it with the table below to add the controls and to set their properties:

Control	Name	Properties
Label	`Label1(8)`	Caption = Sales Person
ComboBox	`cboSalesPerson`	Style = 2 – Dropdown List

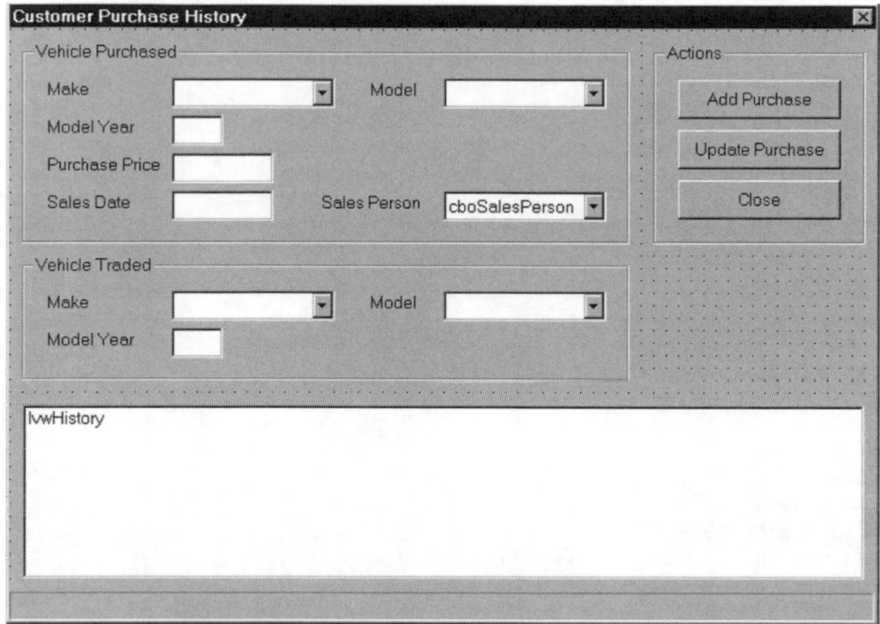

2. As we mentioned above, the code to implement the sales staff functionality to the Customer Purchase History form is minimal. We only need to validate that a sales person was selected, and we do not allow the user to add a new entry in the Sales Staff combo box. Therefore we need only to implement a procedure to load the Sales Person combo box, and modify the Add and Update procedures to pass the `SalesPersonID` of the entry selected.

3. The code listed below contains the addition and modifications required. First, add the following variable declarations to the Customer Purchase History form (`frmHistory`):

```
'Declare module level variables
Private m_blnLoaded As Boolean
Private arrMake() As Long
Private arrModel() As Long
Private arrSalesPerson() As Long
```

4. Next, add the following new procedure, `LoadSalesStaff`, to the Customer Purchase History form:

```
Private Sub LoadSalesStaff()
   'Set up error handling
   On Error GoTo LoadSalesStaff_EH

   'Declare local variables
   Dim lngIndex As Long, lngLastValue As Long, lngRC As Long

   'Clear any existing entries
   cboSalesPerson.Clear

   'Set a reference to the objects
   Dim objRS As New ADODB.Recordset
   Dim objSalesStaff As New AutoWorks.clsSalesStaff

   'Get a list of customer names
   lngRC = objSalesStaff.GetSalesStaff(frmMain.m_objConn, objRS)

   'If the return code is not zero, raise an error
   If lngRC <> 0 Then
      Err.Raise vbObjectError + 513, "frmHistory.LoadSalesStaff", _
         "Call to clsSalesStaff.GetSalesStaff failed"
   End If

   'Load the combo box
   lngIndex = -1
   lngLastValue = -1
   Do While Not objRS.EOF
      'Add the last name and first name
      cboSalesPerson.AddItem objRS!last_name_vc & ", " & objRS!first_name_vc
      lngIndex = lngIndex + 1
      'Add the customer id
      cboSalesPerson.ItemData(lngIndex) = objRS!Sales_Person_ID
      If lngLastValue < objRS!Sales_Person_ID Then
         'Redim the array
         ReDim Preserve arrSalesPerson(objRS!Sales_Person_ID)
         lngLastValue = objRS!Sales_Person_ID
      End If
      'Add the current position of the sales person to the array
      arrSalesPerson(objRS!Sales_Person_ID) = lngIndex
      objRS.MoveNext
   Loop
   objRS.Close

   'Dereference objects
   Set objRS = Nothing
   Set objSalesStaff = Nothing

   On Error GoTo 0
   Exit Sub
```

```
LoadSalesStaff_EH:
   'Ensure the error came from ADO
   Dim objErr As ADODB.Error
   If frmMain.m_objConn.Errors.Count > 0 Then
      For Each objErr In frmMain.m_objConn.Errors
         StatusBar1.Panels("Msg") = StatusBar1.Panels("Msg") & " " & _
         objErr.Description
      Next
   Else
      StatusBar1.Panels("Msg") = Err.Description
   End If
End Sub
```

5. The code to validate the selection of a sales person is listed next:

```
Private Sub cboSalesPerson_Validate(Cancel As Boolean)
   'Display an error if no entery was selected
   If cboSalesPerson.ListIndex = -1 Then
      StatusBar1.Panels("Msg").Text = "Sales Person is required"
      Label1(8).ForeColor = vbRed
      Beep
      Cancel = True
   Else
      'Validation passed
      StatusBar1.Panels("Msg").Text = Empty
      Label1(8).ForeColor = vbWindowText
      Cancel = False
   End If
End Sub
```

6. Modify the `Process` procedure as shown in the next code fragment:

```
Public Sub Process(ByRef objConn As ADODB.Connection, _
      ByVal lngCustomerID As Long, _
      ByVal frmParent As Form)

   'Set up error handling
   On Error GoTo Process_EH

   'Load vehicle make and model combo boxes
   Call LoadMakeModel(objConn)

'Load Sales Staff
Call LoadSalesStaff

   'Declare local variables
   Dim lngRC As Long, lstItem As ListItem
```

7. Modify the `cmdAdd_Click` procedure as follows:

```
'Insert the customer purchase
lngRC = objVehicle.InsertCustomerPurchase(m_lngCustomerID, _
   lngMakePurchasedID, _
   cboMakePurchased.Text, _
   lngModelPurchasedID, _
   cboModelPurchased.Text, _
   CInt(txtYearPurchased.Text), _
   CCur(txtPurchasePrice.Text), _
   txtSalesDate.Text, _
   lngMakeTradedID, _
   cboMakeTraded.Text, _
   lngModelTradedID, _
   cboModelTraded.Text, _
   intYearTraded, _
cboSalesPerson.ItemData(cboSalesPerson.ListIndex), _
   strMsg(), _
   frmMain.m_objConn, _
   objCmd)
```

8. Modify the `cmdUpdate_Click` procedure as follows:

```
'Update the customer's purchase
lngRC = objVehicle.UpdateCustomerPurchase(m_lngCustomerHistoryID, _
   lngMakePurchasedID, _
   cboMakePurchased.Text, _
   lngModelPurchasedID, _
   cboModelPurchased.Text, _
   CInt(txtYearPurchased.Text), _
   CCur(txtPurchasePrice.Text), _
   txtSalesDate.Text, _
   lngMakeTradedID, _
   cboMakeTraded.Text, _
   lngModelTradedID, _
   cboModelTraded.Text, _
   intYearTraded, _
cboSalesPerson.ItemData(cboSalesPerson.ListIndex), _
   strMsg(), _
   frmMain.m_objConn, _
   objCmd)
```

How It Works – Implement Sales Staff Functionality in the Customer Purchase History Form

As you can see, the amount of code that we had to add and modify was very minimal. Let's talk about the `LoadSalesStaff` procedure for just a moment. This is basically the same procedure that was implemented in the Sales Staff form, but has been tailored to this form, in that the combo box that gets loaded has a different name. Since the majority of the code is the same, we won't cover the details again.

The validation event for the Sales Person combo box only ensures that an entry was selected. We do not allow the user to type in their own entry, so we do not need to check the *content* of the entry. This code ensures that the `ListIndex` property is not `-1`, which indicates that an entry has not been selected. If it is, then we display a message and set the text of the label for this combo box to red. We then set the `Cancel` parameter to `True`, which prevents the user from tabbing away from this field:

```
Private Sub cboSalesPerson_Validate(Cancel As Boolean)
   'Display an error if no entery was selected
   If cboSalesPerson.ListIndex = -1 Then
      StatusBar1.Panels("Msg").Text = "Sales Person is required"
      Label1(8).ForeColor = vbRed
      Beep
      Cancel = True
```

Once the data has been validated, we clear any messages that exist in the status bar and return the text for the label back to normal:

```
   Else
      'Validation passed
      StatusBar1.Panels("Msg").Text = Empty
      Label1(8).ForeColor = vbWindowText
      Cancel = False
   End If
End Sub
```

The modification required to the `Process` procedure is simply to add a line to call the `LoadSalesStaff` procedure, which in turn loads the Sales Person combo box.

The `cmdAdd_Click` procedure has been modified in the code that calls the `InsertCustomerPurchase` procedure. We are passing the `SalesPersonID` that is contained in the `ItemData` property of the Sales Person combo box:

```
      'Insert the customer purchase
      lngRC = objVehicle.InsertCustomerPurchase(m_lngCustomerID, _
         lngMakePurchasedID, _
         cboMakePurchased.Text, _
         lngModelPurchasedID, _
         cboModelPurchased.Text, _
         CInt(txtYearPurchased.Text), _
         CCur(txtPurchasePrice.Text), _
         txtSalesDate.Text, _
         lngMakeTradedID, _
         cboMakeTraded.Text, _
         lngModelTradedID, _
         cboModelTraded.Text, _
         intYearTraded, _
      cboSalesPerson.ItemData(cboSalesPerson.ListIndex), _
         strMsg(), _
         frmMain.m_objConn, _
         objCmd)
```

The cmdUpdate_Click procedure contains the same modification that was made to the cmdAdd_Click procedure above.

This concludes the changes needed to the UI. You should have a couple of sales persons entered by now, so we can test the modifications made to the History form. You should perform a test to update an existing customer, assign them a sales person, and add a purchase record for the existing customer.

In preparation for the next part of this case study, you should enter at least four or five sales persons, and create a purchase record for different customers using all of these sales persons. Ensure you use at least one sales person two or more times. This is because the Customer History Purchase records that contain a sales person ID will be used by the stored procedure, which we'll be developing shortly, to produce the Top Sales Person report. Therefore you should have multiple sales for one or more sales persons, in order to produce an interesting report.

Wrox Auto Works Sales Staff Application – Part 3

In the first two parts of this case study you implemented the database changes required to add the `Sales_Person_T` table. You also created the necessary stored procedures to manage the sales staff and to have a sales person associated with every sale of a vehicle. You modified the user interface and entered some customer purchases, assigning a sales person to each of those purchases.

Now it's time to concentrate on creating a report that displays the top sales person. This report is created using the VB Data Environment and Data Report Designers. The **Data Environment Designer** (which we met in Chapter 5) is used to create an ADO `Connection` object that connects to the database, and a `Command` object to execute the command to retrieve the data. The **Data Report Designer** is then bound to the Data Environment Designer to retrieve the fields for the report.

We will use this setup to design and test our report. However, when our report is complete, we will remove the Data Environment Designer from our project and manipulate the Data Report Designer properties through code, and use a stored procedure as the source of our report data.

The stored procedure that we will create will accept parameters to limit the selection of data to the current month chosen. This stored procedure uses **temporary tables** and **aggregate functions** to select and display the data. So let's get started by looking at the features that we want to implement in our stored procedure.

Temporary Tables

SQL Server provides **temporary tables** that are created and managed in the `TempDB` database and are automatically deleted when no longer used. There are two types of temporary tables – local and global. **Local temporary table** names are prefixed with a single pound sign (#) and are local to the user who has created them. This means that a temporary table is created in the `TempDB` database and only that user has access to that table. Unless specifically destroyed, SQL Server will drop this type of temporary table when the current user ends their session with SQL Server.

A **global temporary table** name is prefixed with two pound signs (##) and is available to all users of the database in which it is created. When the last user who is referencing the temporary table ends their session, SQL Server will drop that temporary table. Global temporary tables have no security rights and therefore any user can access the table and modify the data contained in it.

There are several reasons for creating temporary tables. One reason might be to combine the data from two or more tables into a single table, where the data can be manipulated and then selected for display. Another reason might be to populate data into a temporary table that was created with aggregate functions, and then to select the data in a specific order. There are many reasons to use temporary tables and you are sure to find one as you use SQL Server more and more.

The temporary tables that we will be dealing with here are local temporary tables. They will be created and dropped in one session. There are two ways to create a temporary table - **implicitly** and **explicitly**. When SQL Server creates a temporary table it is created implicitly. The following figure shows a temporary table being created for us by SQL Server:

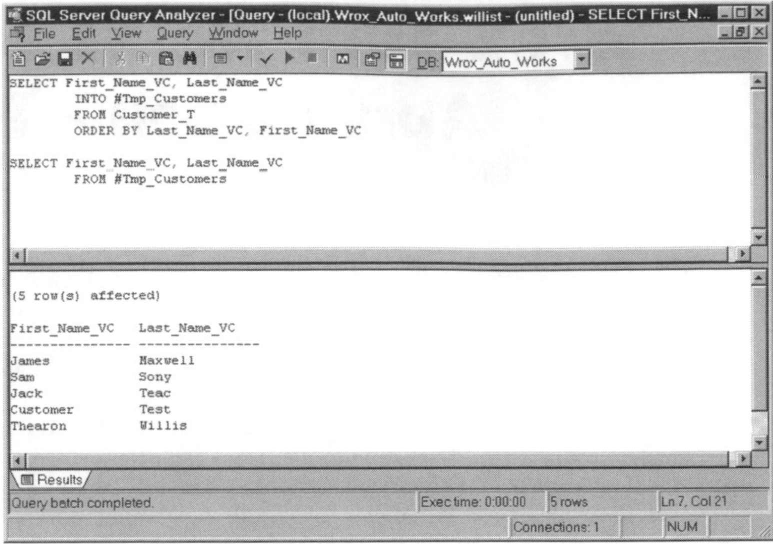

As you can see, we have specified the temporary table name in the `SELECT` statement and SQL Server took care of creating the temporary table for us. This is an implicit creation of a temporary table. We do not explicitly specify the column names or data types that are to make up the temporary table when it is created implicitly. SQL Server creates the columns in the temporary table using the column names and data types of the columns that are contained in the `SELECT` list.

A temporary table created explicitly is created using the format of the `CREATE TABLE` SQL statement. Using the explicit method we control what columns are added, as well as their data types and whether or not they can contain null values. The following figure shows a temporary table being created, populated, used, and dropped.

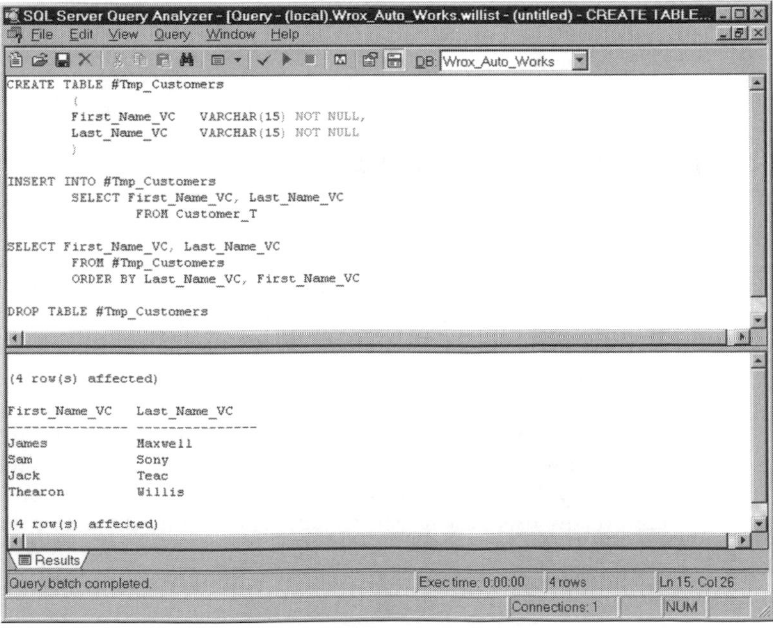

As you can see in the figure above, we create the temporary table using the same format as we used when we created the Sales_Person_T table and can specify column names and data types. Only this time we have prefixed the table name with a single pound sign, which indicates to SQL Server that this is a temporary table. We then populate the temporary table using an INSERT statement, and are selecting the data to be inserted from the Customer_T table. Next we select the data from the temporary table and order the results as we see fit. In order to save space on the TempDB database, we explicitly drop our temporary table so SQL Server does not have to clean up behind us.

When creating a temporary table explicitly, we have the option to add as many columns as we need and to populate the columns as required. The next figure shows a temporary table being created with an extra column that could be populated later, for example with an UPDATE statement:

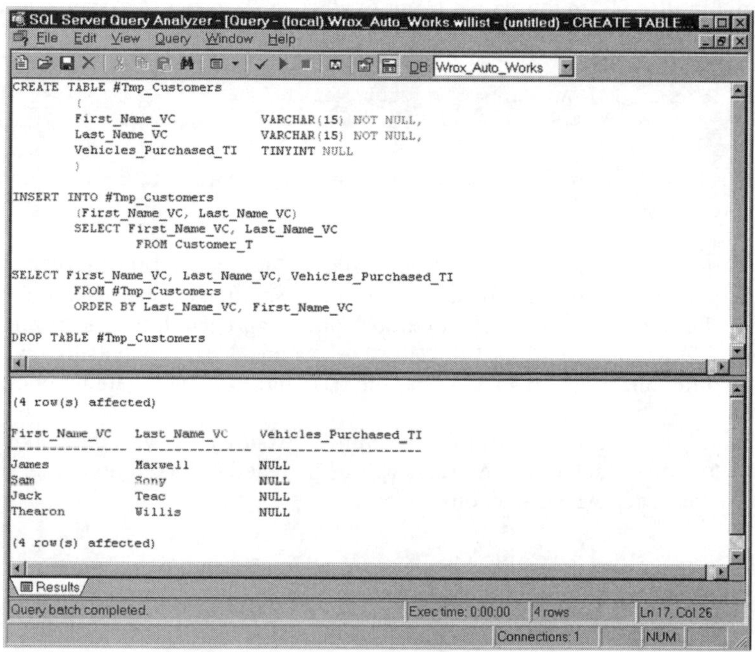

As you can see in the figure above, we have added the column Vehicles_Purchased_TI, which can be populated using an UPDATE statement using data from another table. The INSERT statement used to populate the First_Name_VC and Last_Name_VC columns must now list those columns that we want to insert data into, as shown above.

As you can see, creating a temporary table explicitly provides a lot of flexibility. The columns in the temporary table do not have to be populated from one table – you can use many tables.

Which method you use to create a temporary table depends on the type of processing that needs to be done. It also depends on whether or not you need to manipulate the data in the temporary table. Creating a temporary table *implicitly* provides a table that has been populated from one or more tables using the SELECT INTO statement. This type of temporary table provides little flexibility in populating the table. Creating a temporary table *explicitly* allows you to define the column names and data types that you need. You can then populate this table using one or more tables. This method provides more flexibility and allows you to control what data is inserted into the temporary table and when.

Aggregate Functions

SQL Server provides **aggregate functions** that perform calculations on values in a column, or columns, and return a single value. For example, the COUNT aggregate function can be used to return one single value indicating the number of rows in a table, as shown in the following code fragment:

```
SELECT COUNT(Customer_ID)
   FROM Customer_T
```

While this code would return the number of rows in the Customer_T table, it does not return a column name in the results because this is an aggregate function. Aggregate functions only return the results of summing a value for all rows, in this case a count of all rows. In order to assign a column name, we must use a column **alias,** as shown in the next code fragment:

```
SELECT COUNT(Customer_ID) AS Number_Of_Customers
   FROM Customer_T
```

This code would return the number of customers in the Customer_T table in a single column named Number_Of_Customers.

Aggregate functions can only be used in a SELECT statement and a COMPUTE or HAVING clause. The COMPUTE clause generates totals that appear as additional summary columns at the end of the results set. The HAVING clause specifies a search condition for an aggregate function. Some of the more common aggregate functions are AVG, SUM, COUNT, MIN and MAX. We have already taken a look at the COUNT aggregate function, so let's take a look at the MIN and MAX aggregate functions.

The following code fragment will return the minimum Customer_ID and the maximum Customer_ID in the Customer_T table. Each of these values will be assigned to a column name, as we have used column aliases for these aggregate functions:

```
SELECT MIN(Customer_ID) AS Lowest_Customer_ID,
   MAX(Customer_ID) AS Highest_Customer_ID
   FROM Customer_T
```

As we have shown, aggregate functions can be used to calculate values from multiple columns and return a single result. This can come in handy when you need to combine the values from multiple rows in a table into a single row in the results set.

As your stored procedure skills progress, you will without a doubt find a use for aggregate functions. Keep in mind that these functions summarize values in a column and return a single result. They are particularly useful in summarizing values in a column and returning the final result.

Top Sales Persons Stored Procedure

Our Top Sales Persons report will be derived from the data from a stored procedure. This stored procedure will select all of the sales persons who have sold a vehicle and the number of vehicles sold. The number of vehicles sold is the value that we are most interested in. However, there could be one or more sales persons who have sold the same number of vehicles, so we must also select the total sales amount for all of the vehicles that they have sold.

We want to order the results of our selection in descending order by the number of vehicles sold, and then by the total sales amount. This will give us the desired results, listing the top sales persons first.

Try It Out – Top Sales Persons Stored Procedure

Using the `Customer_Purchase_History_T` and `Sales_Person_T` tables, we will create a stored procedure that will select the sales person's first and last name, the total number of vehicles sold, and the total sales amount for all of the vehicles that they have sold. We will use a column alias of `Vehicles_Sold` for the number of vehicles that a sales person has sold, and a column alias of `Total_Sales` for the total sales amount for all vehicles sold. The results should be ordered in descending order by the `Vehicles_Sold` and then by `Total_Sales`.

When we run this stored procedure, we should be able to select data in a date range. Therefore we want to use the `Sales_Date_DT` column, to select data whose dates fall between a starting and ending date.

1. The code for this stored procedure is listed below. Enter this code in the Query Analyzer and execute it.

```
CREATE PROCEDURE up_parmsel_top_sales_persons (@Begin_Date VarChar(22),
   @End_Date VarChar(22)) AS

-- ***************************************************************************
-- Create temporary table
-- ***************************************************************************
CREATE TABLE #Tmp_Top_Sales_Persons
   (Vehicles_Sold   Int   Null,
   Total_Sales      Money Null,
   Sales_Person_Id  Int   Null)

-- ***************************************************************************
-- Populate temporary table
-- ***************************************************************************
INSERT INTO #Tmp_Top_Sales_Persons
   SELECT COUNT(Sales_Person_ID) AS Vehicles_Sold,
      SUM(Purchase_Price_SM) AS Total_Sales, Sales_Person_ID
      FROM Customer_Purchase_History_T
      WHERE Sales_Date_DT BETWEEN @Begin_Date AND @End_Date
      GROUP BY Sales_Person_ID
```

```
-- ***************************************************************************************
-- Select data from temporary table and sales_person_t
-- ***************************************************************************************
SELECT Vehicles_Sold, Total_Sales, #Tmp_Top_Sales_Persons.Sales_Person_ID,
   First_Name_VC, Last_Name_VC
   FROM #Tmp_Top_Sales_Persons
   JOIN Sales_Person_T ON
      #Tmp_Top_Sales_Persons.Sales_Person_ID = Sales_Person_T.Sales_Person_ID
   ORDER BY Vehicles_Sold DESC, Total_Sales DESC

-- ***************************************************************************************
-- Drop temporary table
-- ***************************************************************************************
DROP TABLE #Tmp_Top_Sales_Persons
```

2. After you have created this stored procedure, set the appropriate permissions on it.

How It Works – Top Sales Person Stored Procedure

While there are few comments in this stored procedure, they do help to quickly identify what each section of code is doing. The first line of our stored procedure defines it as a stored procedure that selects data and accepts parameters. The parameters accept the beginning and ending dates for the selection of data:

```
CREATE PROCEDURE up_parmsel_top_sales_persons (@Begin_Date VarChar(22),
   @End_Date VarChar(22)) AS
```

The next section of code in our stored procedure creates a local temporary table that contains three columns, all of which can contain null values. Notice that we have specified the data types for each column and have enclosed the column list in parentheses.

The single pound sign prefixing the table name indicates to SQL Server that this is a temporary table. If we do not delete it when we are through with it, SQL Server will delete it when our session ends:

```
-- ***************************************************************************************
-- Create temporary table
-- ***************************************************************************************
CREATE TABLE #Tmp_Top_Sales_Persons
   (Vehicles_Sold   Int   Null,
   Total_Sales      Money Null,
   Sales_Person_ID  Int   Null)
```

We want to populate our temporary table with data, and we use the `INSERT` statement to insert values into all of the columns in our temporary table:

```
-- ***************************************************************************************
-- Populate temporary table
-- ***************************************************************************************
INSERT INTO #Tmp_Top_Sales_Persons
```

The first line of our SELECT statement that is being used to insert values into our temporary table is using an aggregate function. Here we are selecting a count of the Sales_Person_ID and assigning the resulting value to the column alias of Vehicles_Sold. The GROUP BY clause of our SELECT statement will cause a count to be taken of each unique Sales_Person_ID in the Customer_Purchase_History_T table.

The next part of our SELECT statement returns a total sum for the Purchase_Price_SM column as one value for a given sales person. Again this is limited to each sales person by the GROUP BY clause, which groups all values for each Sales_Person_ID. The last part of our SELECT statement selects the Sales_Person_ID for each sales person.

All of this data is selected from the Customer_Purchase_History_T table, where the date contained in the Sales_Date_DT falls between the @begin_date and @end_date parameters. The BETWEEN keyword selects all data between the parameters specified, up to and including the data that matches the parameters. The Sales_Person_ID groups all of the results:

```
SELECT COUNT(Sales_Person_ID) AS Vehicles_Sold,
    SUM(Purchase_Price_SM) AS Total_Sales, Sales_Person_ID
    FROM Customer_Purchase_History_T
    WHERE Sales_Date_DT BETWEEN @Begin_Date AND @End_Date
    GROUP BY Sales_Person_ID
```

At this point our temporary table contains data created through the use of aggregate functions from the Customer_Purchase_History_T table. We now want to select that data and join the Sales_Person_T table, in order to get the names of the sales persons whose data is contained in the temporary table.

This next SELECT statement selects all of the columns from the temporary table, and two columns from the Sales_Person_T table. The Sales_Person_T table is joined to the temporary table using the Sales_Person_ID. The results of the SELECT statement are ordered in descending order by the Vehicles_Sold and Total_Sales columns:

```
-- ************************************************************************************
-- Select data from temporary table and sales_person_t
-- ************************************************************************************
SELECT Vehicles_Sold, Total_Sales, #Tmp_Top_Sales_Persons.Sales_Person_ID,
   First_Name_VC, Last_Name_VC
   FROM #Tmp_Top_Sales_Persons
   JOIN Sales_Person_T ON
      #Tmp_Top_Sales_Persons.Sales_Person_ID = Sales_Person_T.Sales_Person_ID
   ORDER BY Vehicles_Sold DESC, Total_Sales DESC
```

At this point we are through with the temporary table, and want to clean up behind ourselves by removing the temporary table. The `DROP TABLE` SQL statement deletes a table, permanent or temporary, and all of its data, indexes, and triggers.

```
-- ***************************************************************************************
-- Drop temporary table
-- ***************************************************************************************
DROP TABLE #Tmp_Top_Sales_Persons
```

Data Environment Designer

The **Data Environment Designer** provides a design-time environment for creating ADO objects. We demonstrated this in Chapter 5 when we created simple `Connection` and `Command` objects. We then used the fields from the `Command` object, dragging and dropping them onto our form. We can control the Data Environment Designer properties through code, and use this as our database connection, if we so desire.

However, our focus here is to exploit the Data Environment Designer's design-time environment to create our report. We want to create a `Connection` object and `Command` object, and have the `Command` object execute our stored procedure. We will then bind the **Data Report Designer** to the Data Environment Designer to access the fields from the `Command` object.

The `Connection` object in the Data Environment Designer provides numerous choices for OLE DB providers to connect to just about any data store that you have, including Jet, SQL Server, and Oracle. We also have the choice of using a DSN or DSN-less connection to connect to the database.

The `Command` object in the Data Environment Designer allows us to use a table, stored procedure, or view, as the source of data. We can also execute query strings if we want to select and update data. We also have the option to set what type of recordset the `Command` object returns. By default, the `Command` object returns a static, client-side recordset that is opened for read-only access.

Try It Out – Data Environment Designer

We want to add the Data Environment Designer to our UI, and connect to the database using a DSN connection. We should then add a `Command` object that will execute the `up_parmsel_top_sales_persons` stored procedure. We can accept all default names for the Data Environment Designer, `Connection` object, and `Command` object.

The following figure shows the Data Environment Designer and the objects that we will create:

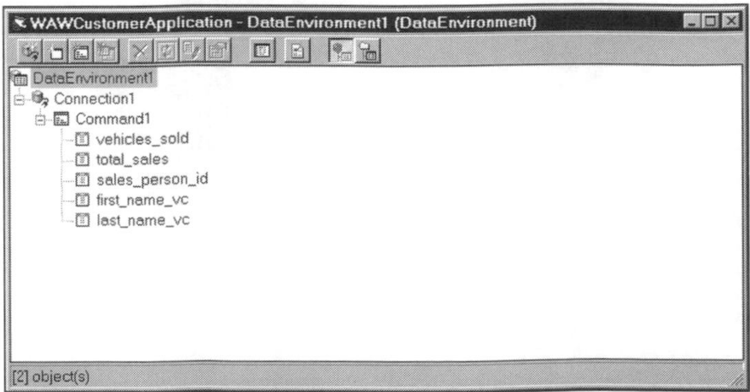

1. On the Project menu, choose Add Data Environment. If you do not see it on the Project menu, look under the Project sub menu More ActiveX Designers. A new Data Environment Designer is added with a default `Connection` object named Connection1.

2. Click on the Connection1 object, and then either click on the Properties icon on the Data Environment Designer toolbar, or right click and choose Properties from the popup menu.

3. The Data Link Properties dialog appears and has four tabs that will assist us in establishing a connection to the database. The first tab, Provider, lists all of the OLE DB providers that it found registered on your machine. You can experiment using the Microsoft OLE DB Provider for SQL Server but I have found that it won't correctly execute the stored procedures that accept parameters. Instead, we want to use the Microsoft OLE DB Provider for ODBC Drivers. Once selected, click the Next button to advance to the next tab, Connection.

4. The Connection tab is where we specify all of the information required to connect to the database. We want to use a data source name, so select the Wrox Auto Works DSN from the list.

5. Next, enter your User name and Password. If you set yourself up to use NT authentication in SQL Server, use one of the other logons that you defined that uses SQL Server authentication, because NT authentication is not supported here.

6. Check the Allow saving password checkbox. This saves your password so you are not prompted for it every time you run the project.

7. In the Enter the initial catalog to use combo box, select the Wrox_Auto_Works database if it is not already selected. Then click on the Test Connection button to test the connection.

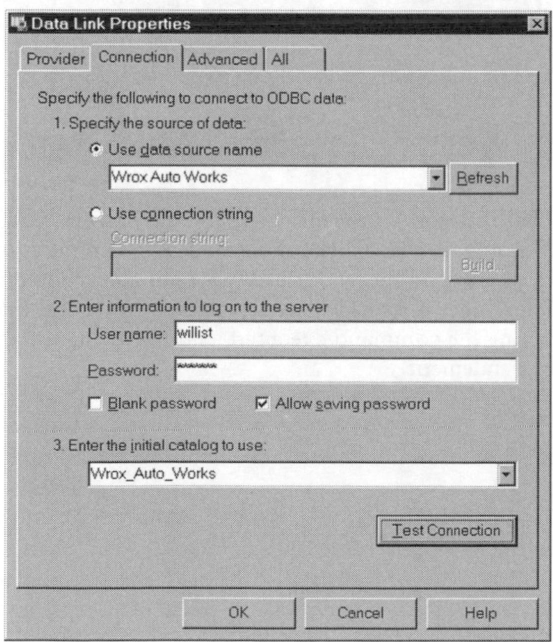

As you can see, this dialog is a lot like setting up a DSN, and you provide all of the pertinent information required to establish a connection with the database.

The Advanced tab lets you set the permissions that this connection should have. You can set the Timeout Value for the connection, and set the various Access Permissions that the connection is allowed, such as read-only access.

The All tab lists all of the information provided in the second and third tabs. You can edit these values here if you so choose.

8. Click OK to save the information and to dismiss the dialog.

9. While the Connection1 object is highlighted, click on the Add Command icon on the Data Environment Designer toolbar, or right click and choose Add Command from the popup menu. The `Command` object appears and is named Command1.

10. Stored Procedure is selected as the default Database Object and this is what we want to use. Select the `up_parmsel_top_sales_persons` stored procedure in the Object Name combo box, as shown below:

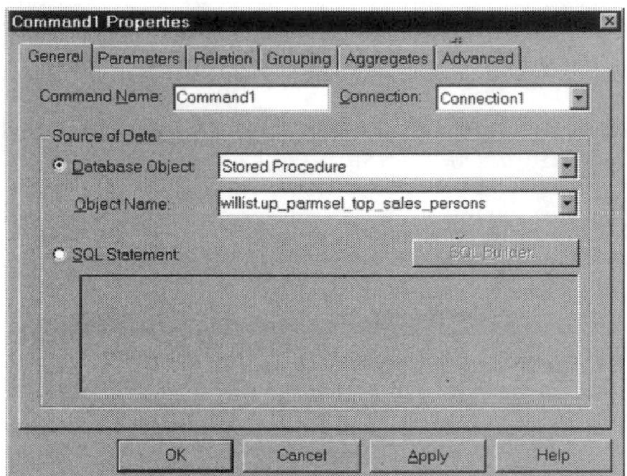

11. The parameters that this stored procedure expects have been extracted from SQL Server, and are listed in the Parameters list. Click on the `begin_date` parameter and enter a date in the Value textbox. Next, click on the `end_date` parameter and enter an end date parameter in the Value box. There does not need to be any data for the dates that you enter. All we are interested in is having the command executed, and retrieving the fields from the stored procedure `SELECT` statement.

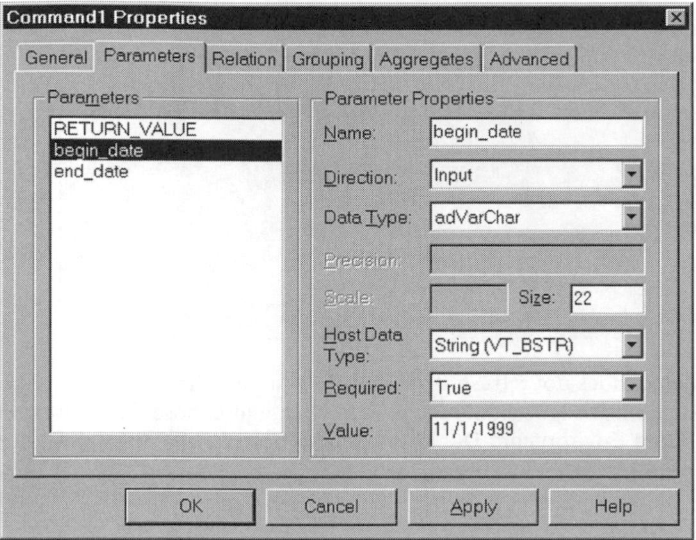

This is all of the information that we need to supply. The Relation tab is used to relate child `Command` objects with a parent `Command` object, and is used in the same way as we use a `JOIN` in SQL Server. The Grouping tab lets you group selected fields together in much the same way as we use the `GROUP BY` clause in SQL Server. The Aggregates tab lets you specify aggregate functions on certain fields, just as we used the aggregate function in SQL Server to create the stored procedure we are using now.

The last tab, Advanced, lets you change the type of `Recordset` object that is returned as a result of the execution of the `Command` object. You can change the type of recordset here and can also limit the number of records returned. If you wanted to change this report from *Top Sales Persons* to the *Top 10 Sales Persons*, you would use this tab, and limit the number of records returned to 10 in the Max Records textbox, as shown in the next figure:

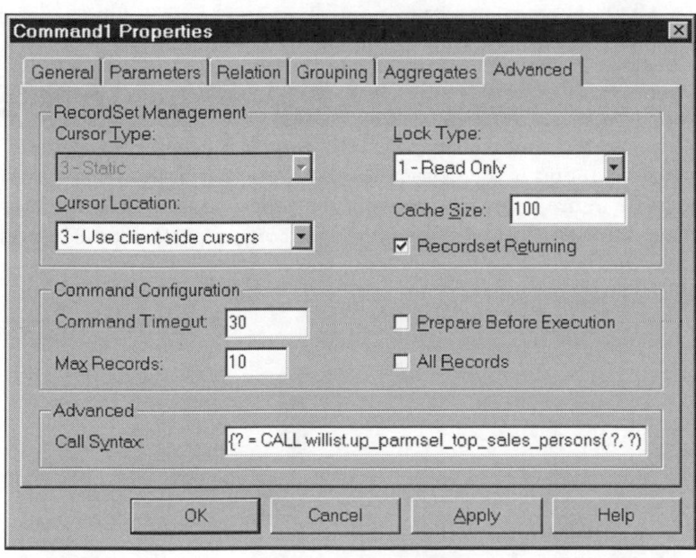

12. Click OK to save the changes to the Command object. You will receive the following warning that data may be modified in the database. Click Yes to continue.

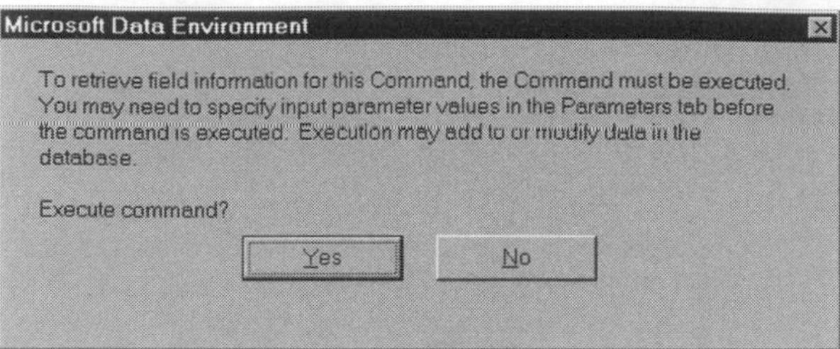

If your Command object does not refresh itself and show a plus sign next to it, click on the Refresh icon on the Data Environment Designer toolbar, or right click and choose Refresh from the popup menu. At this point, your Data Environment Designer should look like the one shown at the start of the example.

Data Report Designer

The **Data Report Designer** provides a design-time environment for creating reports using drag and drop methods. When used with the Data Environment Designer, you can drag fields from a Command object and drop them onto the Data Report Designer, thus adding the fields to your report. All of the appropriate properties for the report field are automatically set during the drag and drop operation.

The Data Report Designer can be used to preview reports, or the reports can be programmatically printed without first previewing them. A report can also be printed while in preview mode, by clicking on the Print icon in the report toolbar. You can also export the report to HTML, Unicode HTML, Text, or Unicode Text formats. This allows you to share your reports on the Web, if you so desire.

The toolbox provided in the Data Report Designer provides a limited set of tools, but does include all of the basic tools such as a Label control, Textbox control, Image control, Line control, Shape control, and a Function control. These tools function just like their VB counterparts.

Try It Out – Data Report Designer

In this example, we will create a report using the Data Report Designer that will list the top sales persons. The source for this report is the Command object created in the Data Environment Designer in the previous example. The figure below shows what the report should look like in design-time. The second label in the Page Header (For) will have its Caption property set during run-time to display the month that the report is for:

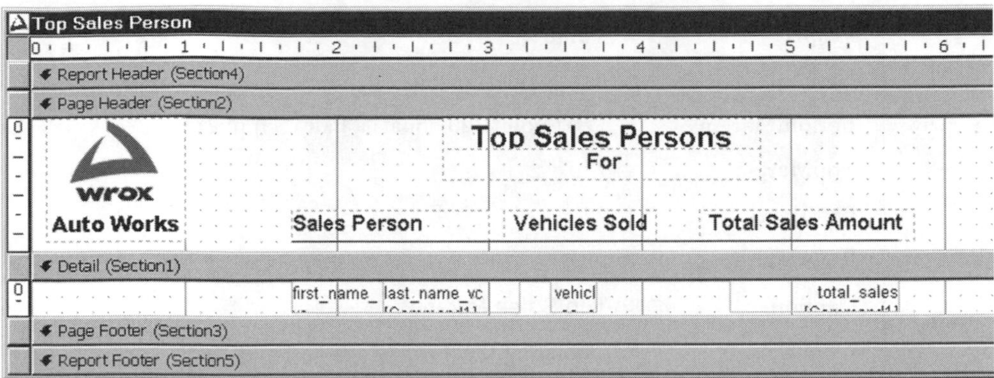

The final report is shown, in preview mode, below:

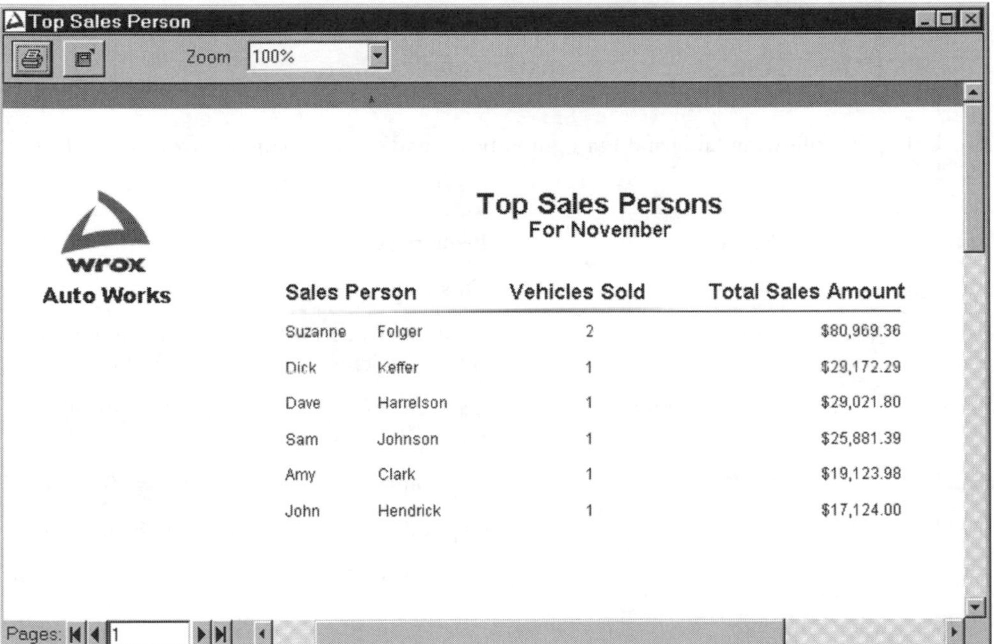

1. To add the Data Report Designer to your project, click on the Project menu and choose Add Data Report. If this option is not listed here, check the More ActiveX Designers sub-menu on the Project menu. Once the designer has been added, set the Data Report Designer properties as shown in the table:

Property	Value
Name	drTopSalesPersons
BottomMargin	720 (Note: 720 equals a half inch margin)
TopMargin	720
LeftMargin	720
RightMargin	720
Caption	Top Sales Person
Icon	Changing this property is optional
DataSource	DataEnvironment1
DataMember	Command1
ReportWidth	10800
WindowState	2 - vbMaximized

2. Using the following table and the figure above, add the following controls to the Data Report Designer:

Control	Name	Properties
RptImage	`Image1`	This control is optional
RptLabel	`Label1`	Caption = Top Sales Persons, Alignment = 2 – rptJustifyCenter, Font = 14 pt Bold
RptLabel	`lblReportPeriod`	Caption = For, Alignment = 2 – rptjustifyCenter, Font = 10 pt Bold
RptLabel	`Label2`	Caption = Sales Person, Font = 10 pt Bold
RptLabel	`Label3`	Caption = Vehicles Sold, Font = 10 pt Bold
RptLabel	`Label4`	Caption = Total Sales Amount, Font = 10 pt Bold
RptLinc	`Line1`	
RptTextBox	`Text1`	DataMember = Command1, DataField = First_Name_VC
RptTextBox	`Text2`	DataMember = Command1, DataField = Last_Name_VC
RptTextBox	`Text3`	DataMember = Command1, DataField = Vehicles_Sold, Alignment = 1 – rptJustifyRight, DataFormat = Number
RptTextBox	`Text4`	DataMember = Command1, DataField = Total_Sales, Alignment = 1 – rptjustifyRight, DataFormat = Currency

3. The easiest way to add report fields in your report is to drag them from the Data Environment Designer and drop them onto your Data Report Designer. However, using this method drops a label as well as the text field. You would then need to cut the label and paste it into the Page Header of your report. There is another drawback, the label has the same name as the data field that you drag and drop, and as this is not something you want displayed on your report, it would need to be changed. The preferred method to creating fields on your report is to click the RptTextBox control in the toolbox and then draw it on your report where you want it positioned. You can also double click the control to have it added to your report, and then reposition it. This method is just like adding a textbox to a form in VB.

4. Once all text fields have been placed on your report and assigned a `DataField` property, it's time to remove the white space in your report. All white space in the designer will be displayed in the final report. Therefore, since we have not used the Report Header section of the report, drag the Page Header up to close the gap between the Report Header and Page Header.

5. Next, drag the Detail section of the report to just below the line on the Page Header section. This will leave just a little white space between the Page Header fields and the start of the Detail section of the report.

6. Now drag the Page Footer up to just below the fields in the Detail section, leaving just a little white space to separate each detail line.

7. Since we have not used the Page Footer or Report Footer sections of the report, drag the Report Footer up to the bottom of the Page Footer and then drag the bottom of the report page up to the bottom of the Report Footer, eliminating any remaining white space:

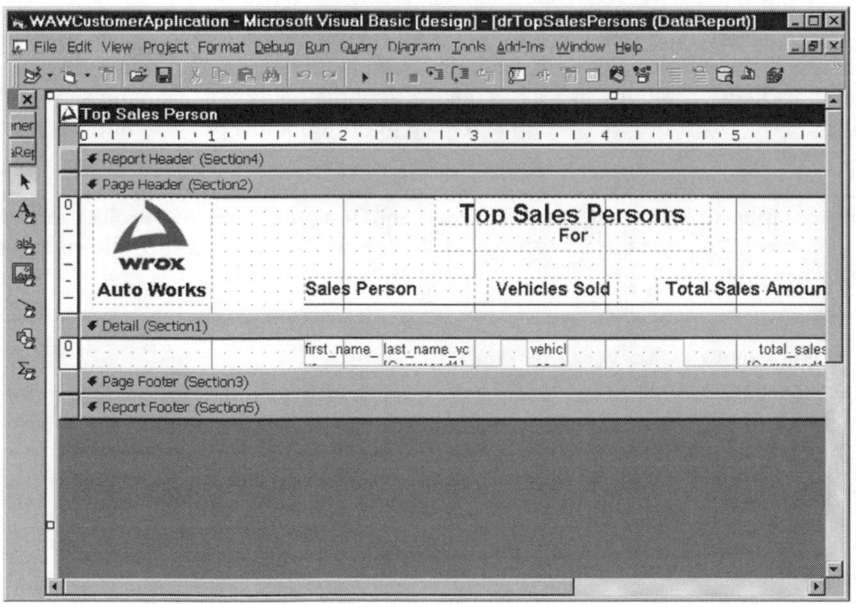

8. At this point you'll want to preview the report to verify that you don't have too little or too much white space in the Page Header or Detail sections of the report. In order to do this we need to add a new menu option to the Main form.

9. In the Menu Editor, add a new menu between View and Help, set its Caption property to &Reports and its Name property to zmnuReports. Add a menu item to this menu, and set its Caption property to Top 10 &Sales Persons and its Name property to mnuReportsSalesPerson. Refer back to Chapter 13 if you need help with this step.

10. Add the following code to the `mnuReportsSalesPerson_Click` procedure, substituting a date range that includes data in your database. The first line of this code sets the `begin_date` and `end_date` parameters of the `Command` object for the stored procedure.

    The second line of this code sets the `Caption` property of the label `lblReportPeriod`. Notice that we must specify the `Section` of the report that the control is in, and specify an `Item` in the `Controls` collection for that section. Set the caption to the month that contains data in your database.

    The last line of this code shows the report in preview mode, as shown earlier in the example:

```
Private Sub mnuReportsSalesPerson_Click()
   DataEnvironment1.Command1 "11/1/1999", "11/30/1999"
   drTopSalesPersons.Sections(2).Controls.Item("lblReportPeriod").Caption = _
            "For November"
   drTopSalesPersons.Show
End Sub
```

11. At this point save and run your project. Then run the report by clicking on the Reports menu and then Top 10 Sales Persons. You may need to adjust the white space in your report and the report fields' positions, as well as the width of the fields. After you make some adjustments, run your report again and keep performing this process until the report meets your satisfaction.

12. Once complete, remove the Data Environment Designer from your project, and replace the code in the `mnuReportsSalesPerson_Click` procedure with the following code, changing the owner prefix:

```
Private Sub mnuReportsSalesPerson_Click()
   'Declare local variables
   Dim intIndex As Integer, strSQL As String, strInput As String, _
      strYear As String, strStartDate As String, strEndDate As String, _
      blnContinue As Boolean

   'Get the month and year for the report
   strInput = InputBox ("Enter the month for the Top Sales Persons Report", _
      "WAW Customer Application", "January")
   strYear = InputBox("Enter the year for the Top Sales Persons Report", _
      "WAW Customer Application", Year(Now))
```

```
'Set the start and end dates for the stored procedure parameters
'and set the full month name for the report
blnContinue = True
Select Case StrConv(strInput, vbProperCase)
   Case "Jan", "January", "1"
      strStartDate = "Jan 1 " & strYear
      strEndDate = "Jan 31 " & strYear
      strInput = MonthName(1)

   Case "Feb", "February", "2"
      strStartDate = "Feb 1 " & strYear
      'Determine if this is a leap year
      If (Month(DateSerial(CInt(strYear), 2, 29)) = 2) Then
         'This is a leap year
         strEndDate = "Feb 29 " & strYear
      Else
         'This is not a leap year
         strEndDate = "Feb 28 " & strYear
      End If
      strInput = MonthName(2)

   Case "Mar", "March", "3"
      strStartDate = "Mar 1 " & strYear
      strEndDate = "Mar 31 " & strYear
      strInput = MonthName(3)

   Case "Apr", "April", "4"
      strStartDate = "Apr 1 " & strYear
      strEndDate = "Apr 30 " & strYear
      strInput = MonthName(4)

   Case "May", "5"
      strStartDate = "May 1 " & strYear
      strEndDate = "May 31 " & strYear
      strInput = MonthName(5)

   Case "Jun", "June", "6"
      strStartDate = "Jun 1 " & strYear
      strEndDate = "Jun 30 " & strYear
      strInput = MonthName(6)

   Case "Jul", "July", "7"
      strStartDate = "Jul 1 " & strYear
      strEndDate = "Jul 31 " & strYear
      strInput = MonthName(7)

   Case "Aug", "August", "8"
      strStartDate = "Aug 1 " & strYear
      strEndDate = "Aug 31 " & strYear
      strInput = MonthName(8)

   Case "Sep", "September", "9"
      strStartDate = "Sep 1 " & strYear
      strEndDate = "Sep 30 " & strYear
      strInput = MonthName(9)
```

```
      Case "Oct", "October", "10"
         strStartDate = "Oct 1 " & strYear
         strEndDate = "Oct 31 " & strYear
         strInput = MonthName(10)

      Case "Nov", "November", "11"
         strStartDate = "Nov 1 " & strYear
         strEndDate = "Nov 30 " & strYear
         strInput = MonthName(11)

      Case "Dec", "December", "12"
         strStartDate = "Dec 1 " & strYear
         strEndDate = "Dec 31 " & strYear
         strInput = MonthName(12)

      Case Else
         blnContinue = False
   End Select

   'If the date was correct, then continue
   If blnContinue Then

      'Open the recordset for the report
      strSQL = "willist.up_parmsel_top_sales_persons ('" & strStartDate _
         & "','" & strEndDate & "')"
      Set m_objRSAddress = New ADODB.Recordset
      m_objRSAddress.Open strSQL, m_objConn, adOpenForwardOnly, _
         adLockReadOnly, adCmdStoredProc

      'Remove references to the data enviroment designer
      Set drTopSalesPersons.DataSource = Nothing
      drTopSalesPersons.DataMember = ""
      Set drTopSalesPersons.DataSource = m_objRSAddress
      For intIndex = 1 To drTopSalesPersons.Sections(3).Controls.Count
         drTopSalesPersons.Sections(3).Controls.Item(intIndex).DataMember = ""
      Next

      'Set the report period and show the report
      drTopSalesPersons.Sections(2).Controls.Item("lblReportPeriod").Caption = _
         "For " & strInput
      drTopSalesPersons.Show vbModal

      'Close and de-reference the recordset object
      m_objRSAddress.Close
      Set m_objRSAddress = Nothing
   End If
End Sub
```

13. We are now ready to run this new code and test the report again. The first dialog prompts the user for a month name, as shown in the figure below:

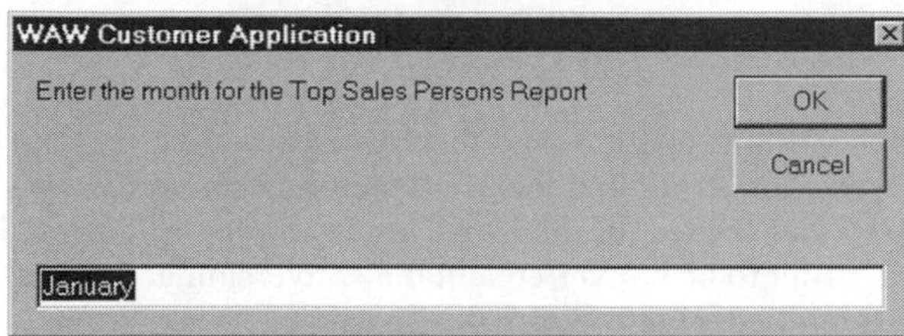

Enter a month name, month abbreviation, or the number of a month, for a month that appears in your database.

When you click OK, a dialog appears as shown in the next figure. This time we want to enter the year for a year that appears in your database:

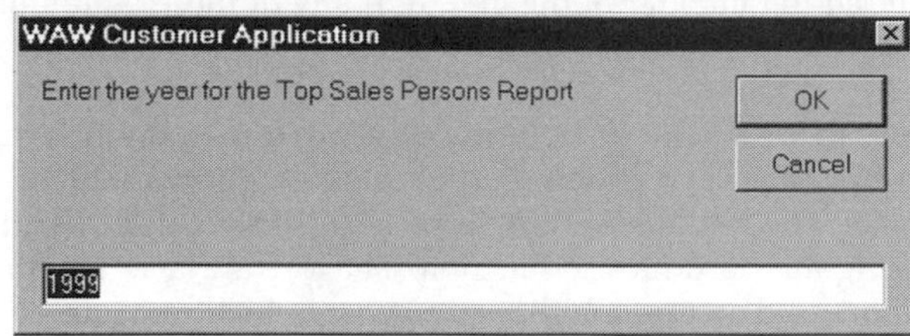

The report should be displayed and should resemble the report that you displayed earlier, before the code changes.

How It Works - Data Report Designer

We want to keep the Data Environment Designer in case we need to come back and modify the report in any way; this is why we *removed* it from the project rather than *deleting* it. The Data Environment Designer provides the design-time environment for editing and modifying the report.

In the code we added in step 12, we are replacing the Data Environment Designer with run-time objects that will supply the `Connection` and `Recordset` objects for our report. The first thing we want to do is declare the local variables for this procedure:

```
Private Sub mnuReportsSalesPerson_Click()
   'Declare local variables
   Dim intIndex As Integer, strSQL As String, strInput As String, _
      strYear As String, strStartDate As String, strEndDate As String, _
      blnContinue As Boolean
```

Regardless of whether we are using the Data Environment Designer or run-time objects, we need to prompt the user for the input parameters. The next two lines of code prompt the user for the month and year for the report using the VB `InputBox` function. The responses are assigned to our local variables, which we will use next. The choice to use the `InputBox` function versus creating another form was driven by the fact that there is little overhead, and you can add more data validation to validate the user's input. It wasn't worth creating a new form for just two fields.

```
'Get the month and year for the report
strInput = InputBox("Enter the month for the Top Sales Persons Report", _
   "WAW Customer Application", "January")
strYear = InputBox("Enter the year for the Top Sales Persons Report", _
   "WAW Customer Application", Year(Now))
```

We set the `blnContinue` variable to `True` and then perform a `Select Case` block to select the month that the user entered. The string that the user entered is converted to proper case (meaning that the first letter is capitalized and the rest of the letters are in lower case) using the `StrConv` function. This function accepts the string to be converted and the conversion argument, which is provided in a dropdown list using the **IntelliSense** feature of VB:

```
'Set the start and end dates for the stored procedure parameters
'and set the full month name for the report
blnContinue = True
Select Case StrConv(strInput, vbProperCase)
```

The `Case` statements check to see if the user entered the abbreviation for the month, or spelled the month name out, or entered the number of the month. If any of these conditions are true, a `Case` statement is executed.

Within each `Case` statement we set the `strStartDate` variable to the first day of the month and append the year chosen by the user. We then set the `strEndDate` variable to the last day of the month and again append the year. The last line of code in each `Case` statement sets the `strInput` variable to the long month name using the `MonthName` function. The `MonthName` function accepts the numeric representation of the month and an optional Boolean value, which indicates the month name to be returned as an abbreviated month name. Since we want the long name for the month we omit the second parameter:

```
   Case "Jan", "January", "1"
      strStartDate = "Jan 1 " & strYear
      strEndDate = "Jan 31 " & strYear
      strInput = MonthName(1)
```

The `Case` statement for the month of February must contain a little extra code to handle leap years. We can set the start date parameter to the first of the month. Now we must determine if this is a leap year before setting the end date parameter.

This is done with the code shown below, which returns `True` if this is a leap year. The `DateSerial` function accepts the date parameters year, month, and day, and returns a variant date. The `Month` function accepts a date (string or variant) and returns a variant value indicating the month number. If these two functions combined equal the value 2 then the date supplied to the `DateSerial` function is valid. This indicates that this is a leap year and a value of `True` is returned, otherwise a value of `False` is returned. We set the end date for the month of February to the correct day based on the leap year check:

```
      Case "Feb", "February", "2"
         strStartDate = "Feb 1 " & strYear
         'Determine if this is a leap year
         If (Month(DateSerial(CInt(strYear), 2, 29)) = 2) Then
            'This is a leap year
            strEndDate = "Feb 29 " & strYear
         Else
            'This is not a leap year
            strEndDate = "Feb 28 " & strYear
         End If
         strInput = MonthName(2)
```

The rest of the Case statements are similar to the Case statement for January and are not repeated here.

If we reach this point in the code, the user did not enter a valid month and we set our blnContinue variable to False, which indicates that we should not display the report:

```
      Case Else
         blnContinue = False
   End Select
```

If the blnContinue variable is True, then we set our SQL string to the stored procedure to execute the top sales person report, and pass it the start and end date variables:

```
   'If the date was correct, then continue
   If blnContinue Then

      'Open the recordset for the report
      strSQL = "willist.up_parmsel_top_sales_persons ('" & strStartDate _
         & "','" & strEndDate & "')"
```

Next we set a reference to the Recordset object and open our recordset using a forward-only cursor and a read-only lock. This will allow us to only navigate forward in the recordset and only read the records:

```
      Set m_objRSAddress = New ADODB.Recordset
      m_objRSAddress.Open strSQL, m_objConn, adOpenForwardOnly, _
         adLockReadOnly, adCmdStoredProc
```

The Data Report Designer still has references to the Data Environment Designer, so we must remove those before we can set the properties to our Recordset object. We set the DataSource property to nothing and set the DataMember property to a zero length string. Now we set the DataSource property to our Recordset object:

```
      'Remove references to the data enviroment designer
      Set drTopSalesPersons.DataSource = Nothing
      drTopSalesPersons.DataMember = ""
      Set drTopSalesPersons.DataSource = m_objRSAddress
```

We need to remove the reference to the Command object in the DataMember property. We loop through the Controls collection and for each control in the **Detail** section of the report, we set the DataMember property to a zero length string:

```
      For intIndex = 1 To drTopSalesPersons.Sections(3).Controls.Count
         drTopSalesPersons.Sections(3).Controls.Item(intIndex).DataMember = ""
      Next
```

We set the Caption property of the lblReportPeriod label to the current month in the strInput variable that we set above. Then we show the report modally:

```
      'Set the report period and show the report
      drTopSalesPersons.Sections(2).Controls.Item("lblReportPeriod").Caption = _
         "For " & strInput
      drTopSalesPersons.Show vbModal
```

After control has been returned from the report, we close and de-reference our database objects:

```
      'Close and de-reference the recordset object
      m_objRSAddress.Close
      Set m_objRSAddress = Nothing
   End If
End Sub
```

As you can see from this part of the case study, creating a report involves many steps. The Data Environment Designer could conceivably be used to supply all your data access needs. However, we chose to use a Connection object defined in our code for the run-time connection, and used the Data Environment Designer as a design-time connection to supply the fields for our report.

Summary

This case study has introduced several new topics in both SQL Server and Visual Basic. In SQL Server, we have introduced the creation and use of temporary tables. We now know of several ways to create and use temporary tables in our stored procedures and queries. We have seen the benefits that they provide in the selection and manipulation of data.

Along with temporary tables, we learned how to use some of the aggregate functions provided in SQL Server. We have seen first hand how they can be used in a stored procedure to count and summarize data from multiple rows into one single value.

Looking back to the beginning of the first part of this case study, we sharpened our skills by creating another database script and also learned how to create indexes in our scripts. We examined creating a clustered index that contained multiple columns. By creating this index on the Sales_Person_T table, we eliminated the need to specify the ORDER BY clause in our stored procedure that selects the sales persons.

The final part of the case study took a closer look at the Data Environment Designer, and we should have a better understanding of how to use this tool. We have now seen how we can use this tool to build a `Command` object that executes a table definition to return all columns and rows of data in a table, and how it can execute a stored procedure that accepts parameters. We set the parameters for the `Command` object in code, and should now have a better understanding of how to manipulate the Data Environment Designer through code.

In designing our report, we have gained more knowledge of the Data Report Designer. Like the Data Environment Designer, we have manipulated the Data Report Designer through code, and now understand how to use the Data Report Designer with or without the Data Environment Designer. We also know how to manipulate the various controls in the Data Report Designer through code, as we set and cleared the various properties in the `mnuReportsSalesPerson_Click` procedure.

To summarize, you should know how to:

- Create a clustered index using multiple columns
- Create, use, and drop a temporary table
- Use the most common aggregate functions
- Add and use the Data Environment Designer
- Add and use the Data Report Designer

Our final case study finishes off our application by making it easier to use for those who are not familiar with the structure of our database and stored procedures. We will be looking at setting up an English Query application to allow such users to interrogate the database using more simplistic search terms.

WROX AUTO WORKS RACING

Case Study 3 – Customer English Query Application

Probably one of the biggest complaints from upper management and regular users is that the information they need is too hard to get. It often requires detailed knowledge of the database and/or the application, and when new applications are developed the users must learn yet another system to retrieve the information that is vital to the success of the organization.

SQL Server solves this problem by providing a tool called **English Query**. English Query uses natural English sentences to retrieve information, thus allowing you to provide users with an easy means to retrieve the information they need, without them having to learn new applications or complex SQL statements. The English Query tool provides a rapid development environment in which you can build new English Query applications that use the databases that you have already built and populated.

In an English Query application the user asks a question such as "*What is James' phone number?*" The **English Query Run-time Engine** uses your compiled English Query application to translate the question into SQL statements, and then your application executes the SQL statements and returns the results. In order for this translation to work, you must define **entities** and **relationships** in your English Query application. Entities describe your tables and columns, and the relationships describe the relationship between these objects.

This case study shows you how to build an English Query application using the `Wrox_Auto_Works` database. Once the English Query application has been built, you can deploy your application in a number of ways, including using the Internet or an intranet, as well as using Visual Basic or Visual C++. Since the focus of this book is to use SQL Server with Visual Basic, we will be briefly presenting Visual Basic as the tool to deploy your English Query application.

In this case study we will:

- Install English Query
- Cover an overview of English Query and its tools
- Build the Customer English Query application
- Examine the deployment of an English Query application

English Query Installation

English Query installs like most programs in that it doesn't require a lot of complicated choices. It simply asks you in which directory you want to install, and what program options you want installed. You have the choice to install the *complete* application or choose the *components* that you want installed. If you don't already have English Query installed on your machine, follow the steps below.

Try It Out – Installing English Query

1. The install program is located on the CD that was used to install SQL Server. To begin the installation, simply insert the SQL Server installation CD. If after a few moments you do not see the following screen, execute the `AutoRun.exe` program in the root directory of the CD.

2. We want to choose the Install SQL Server 7.0 Components option so click on the hyperlink on this screen.

3. The next screen lists the SQL Server components that can be installed and we want to choose English Query. Click on this hyperlink to start the installation process.

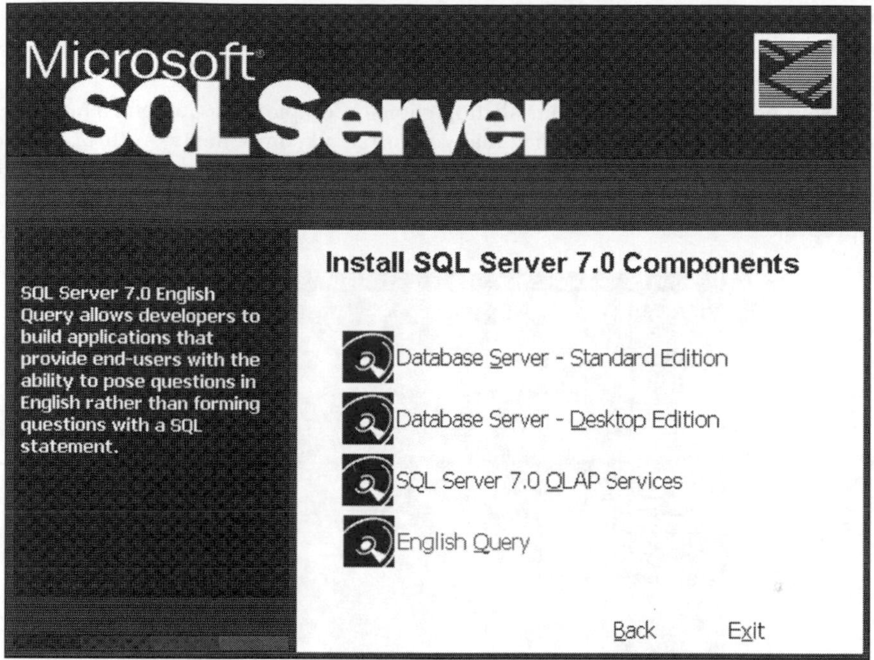

4. At this point the Microsoft Data Access Components (MDAC) version 2.1 will start to install. You have no choice but to let it install as it does not provide a cancel button. Note that it should not overwrite the latest version that you have. After MDAC has been installed, the welcome screen for English Query appears and provides general information about installation. Click the Continue button to advance to the next step of the installation.

5. This step prompts you for the location in which to install English Query. The default location can be changed to any folder on any drive that you want, by clicking the Change Folder button. Once you are satisfied with the location, click the OK button to proceed to the next step.

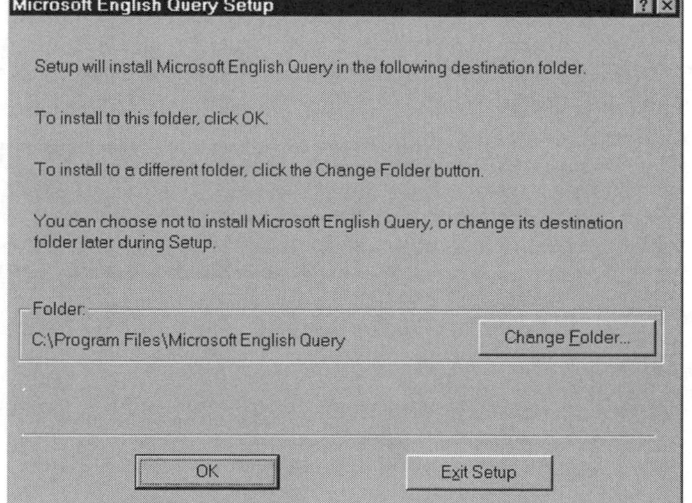

6. The next step displays the End User License Agreement. Read this license agreement and then click the I Agree button to continue the installation.

7. This step prompts you for the installation choice: Complete or Custom. The choice you make is up to you but it is recommended that you install all components. At this point you once again have the option to change the installation folder by clicking on the Change Folder button. Make your installation choice and click on either the Complete or Custom buttons as appropriate.

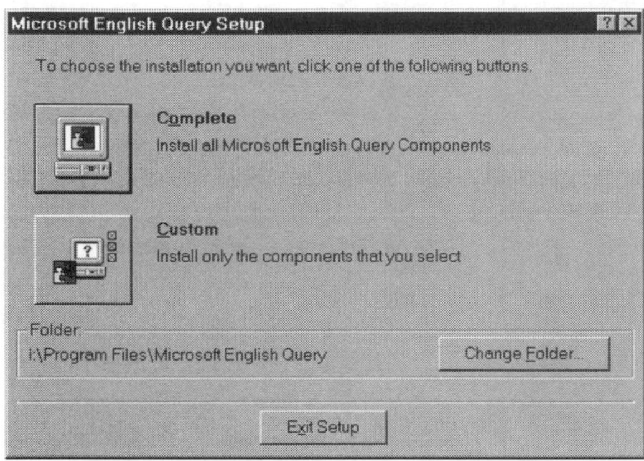

8. If you chose the Custom option in the last step you will see the screen shown in the figure below. This screen displays the components that can be installed. Again, it is recommended that you install *all* of the options. The first option contains the core components that make up English Query, and you must check this option to install English Query. The English Query Developer option installs the English Query application development tool, and the English Query Help option installs online help. The last option installs the English Query Samples, which include an English Query application for the `pubs` database and sample deployment programs written in Visual Basic, Visual C++, and Active Server Pages. We will be using the VB sample program later in this case study so we need to install this option. Click the Continue button to allow the setup program to start copying files.

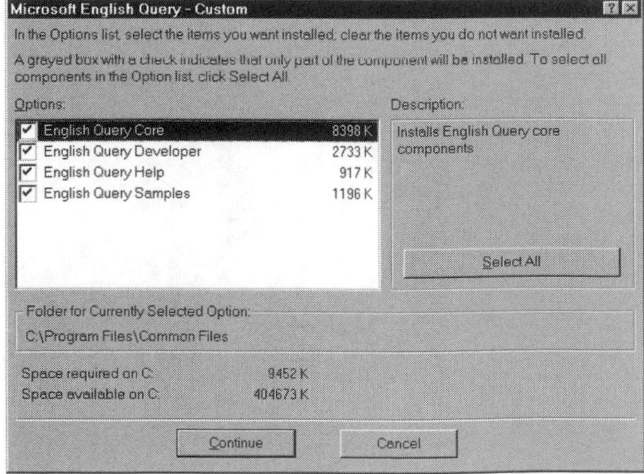

After the setup program has finished installing all of the required files, it will display a dialog indicating that setup was completed successfully. The English Query program group has been installed in the Microsoft SQL Server 7.0 program group. At this point, English Query is installed and is ready for use.

English Query Overview

As we mentioned earlier, English Query enables us to write applications that allow us to use normal English to query the database for information. The **English Query development environment** consists of two components: the **English Query Domain Editor** and the **English Query Run-time Engine**.

We create our English Query application using the **English Query Domain Editor**, which we will cover shortly. Once our application has been created and tested, we compile our English Query application, which can then be deployed using Visual Basic, Visual C++, or Active Server Pages. The following diagram shows how our final application works:

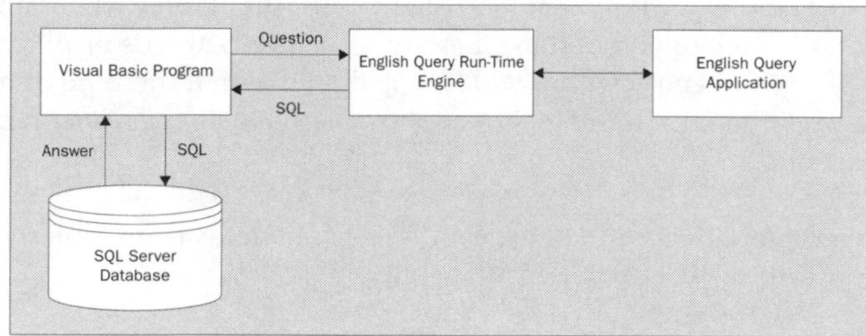

The user of the VB program asks a question in natural English terms and your VB program submits the question to the English Query Run-time Engine. The English Query Run-time Engine uses your English Query application to translate the question into SQL statements. It then passes the translated SQL statements back to your VB program, which in turn executes those SQL statements and then receives the results back from SQL Server to be displayed.

The **English Query Domain Editor** is a tool that allows you to quickly build English Query applications. This graphical tool provides three main functions. First, it allows you to build your application. Second, it provides a built-in testing component so you can test the application as or after you build it. Last, it provides the functionality to compile your English Query application for deployment.

The following figure shows the English Query Domain Editor. As you can see, this editor provides three views, as indicated by the tabs at the bottom of the window. The first view, which is shown here, is the Files tab and this gives a combined view of the contents of the Database and Semantic tabs. It displays the objects that make up the entire project.

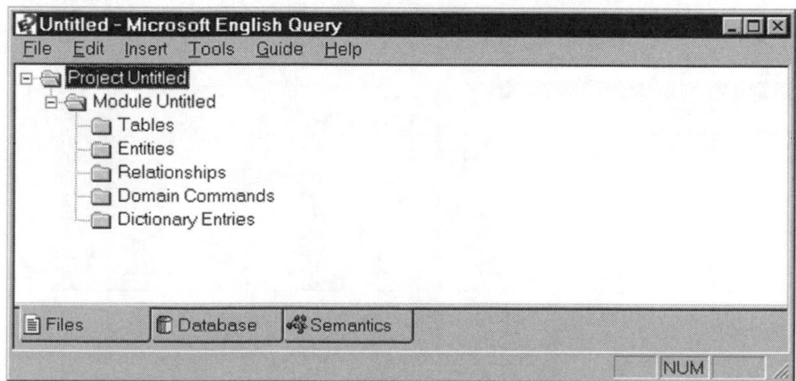

The Database tab displays the Tables in your project. The tables can be expanded to display all of the fields (known as columns in SQL Server) that make up an individual table, and also the joins (foreign keys) that are contained in a table. When you create a new project you load the structure of your database by selecting the appropriate option, which we will be covering shortly. The English Query Domain Editor will automatically read your database structure, which includes all tables, fields, keys, and joins, and will use this information to populate the screen shown above.

The Semantics tab displays the Entities, Relationships, Domain Commands, and Dictionary Entries that you have defined. We will be expanding on these next.

Semantic Objects

Semantic objects include **entities** and **relationships**. Entities define real world objects that are nouns, such as a person, place, or thing. **Major** entities usually represent tables while **minor** entities represent fields (columns) in a table. When you define an entity, you supply words or phrases that define the entity. Then you associate the entity with a table or field, and assign the type of name that the entity represents, such as a *proper* name (John Doe), *common* name (vehicle), *classifier* name (sales department), or a *model* name (Mustang).

Entities can also have **remote fields** added to them. These are fields from tables which are joined to the table you are working with in order to define the entity.

Once you have two or more entities defined, you can define the relationship between the entities. This will be demonstrated shortly in a practical exercise. **Relationships** are associations between entities that describe how the entities relate to one another. These relationships are usually described in simple English statements such as "*Customers have Phone Numbers*". In this situation you would have an entity that defines *Customers* and an entity that defines *Phone Numbers.*

When you define the relationship between two entities, you choose the **phrasing** that best describes the relationship. There are several phrasings to choose from such as Name, Trait, Preposition, Adjective, Subset, and Verb. For each one of these phrasings an example is provided so it is easy to choose the appropriate one. We will be covering this in more detail later, but the example for trait phrasing is shown below:

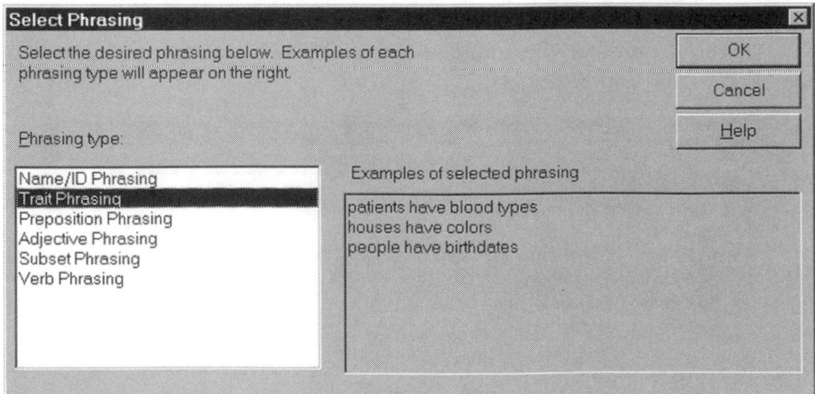

English Query interprets questions such as "*Who are the customers*" and commands such as "*Show all customers*". English Query also provides the functionality to allow you to add your own specific commands, which are called **domain commands**.

Domain commands are defined in much the same way as relationships are defined. You choose the appropriate entities and the appropriate phrasing, and assign a command to this relationship. If the command you choose is not associated with the database, the command is sent to your application for processing. Suppose you were listing all customers who had bought a vehicle in the last week. You could define a domain command such as "*Send thank you letter to all customers*" that in turn could be passed back to your application for processing. Your application could then generate the thank you letters for these customers.

Like most word processors, English Query has a **dictionary**. This dictionary is used by English Query to answer questions posed in English. However, there may come a time when you need to add special terminology to your application that English Query may not know about. You may, for example, be in the pharmaceutical business and need to define special terms that are unique to your line of business and database. English Query allows you to add entries to the English Query dictionary, and doing so allows English Query to answer the questions that use your unique terminology.

The Customer English Query Application

There are only a few steps in building an English Query application, however, some of these are very repetitive. The steps that get repeated over and over are those for defining the entities and relationships. Since these steps are key in building a successful English Query application, we need to take a look at planning the entities that we want to define and the relationships between those entities. For our application we will only be using a subset of the tables in the `Wrox_Auto_Works` database.

Let's start by defining the tables that we want to use in our English Query application. Since this is a *Customer* English Query application it stands to reason that we would want to include the `Customer_T` table. From there we can expand on the information that will be provided by this application. The following table lists the database tables and columns that will be displayed in our application:

Table	Column
`Customer_T`	`First_Name_VC`
	`Last_Name_VC`
`Phone_Number_T`	`Area_Code_SI`
	`Phone_Number_IN`
`Address_T`	`Street_Address_1_VC`
`City_T`	`City_Name_VC`
`State_T`	`State_Name_VC`
`Zip_Code_T`	`Zip_Code_CH`
`Employer_T`	`Company_Name_VC`

To keep this application simple, we are only using the first address line `Street_Address_1_VC` *from the* `Address_T` *table. You can expand on this later if you wish, and include all three address lines.*

Now that we know what data we want to display, we can use the tables and columns above to define the entities. The major and minor entities can be derived from the tables above using simple names for our database tables and columns. The next table displays the major and minor entities:

Major Entity	Minor Entity
Customer	Customer Name
Phone Number	
Address	
Employer	Employer Name

What we have done here is to take the `Customer_T` table and define a major entity called Customer. Since the Customer entity can contain multiple distinct customers we define a minor entity called Customer Name. When we define a minor entity, a relationship is automatically created between the major and minor entity. We normally only define minor entities for entities that contain proper names, such as Customer. Tables are usually represented by major entities and fields of a table are usually represented by minor entities. Thus a minor entity of Customer Name allows us to ask specific questions such as "*What is James' last name*".

Phone numbers and addresses are related to customers and we do not want to define minor entities for them because it is highly unlikely that we would ask a question such as "*Whose phone number is 123-45567*". An address consists of the `Street_Address_1_VC`, `City_Name_VC`, `State_Name_VC`, and `Zip_Code_CH` columns. The English Query Domain Editor will recognize that we have a normalized database and will automatically join the related tables to the `Address_T` table. All we have to do is select the columns that we want displayed as part of the address from the joined tables, which we'll be seeing how to do shortly.

Since employers have proper names, we want to define a minor entity for Employer called Employer Name.

Now that we know what entities need to be defined, let's look at the relationships. In order to determine what type of relationship should be added, we need to look at what types of questions could be asked. Suppose you want a list of all customers, you would ask a question such as "*List all customers*" or "*Show all customers*". In this case the only table involved in this query is the `Customer_T` table, so no relationship needs to be defined.

Now what if we rephrase this question to include addresses, such as "*List all customers and their addresses*" or "*Show all customers and their addresses*". This query needs to select data from two tables: `Customer_T` to get a list of customers and `Address_T` to get the customers' addresses. The relationship that we must define between these two tables is **trait phrasing**. Trait phrasing is when one entity is an *attribute* of another. In this case Address is a trait of Customer.

Using our list of entities that we determined above we derive the most probable questions that could be asked, and use those questions to define our relationships. The table below lists the questions and the entities and relationships needed.

Question	Entities	Relationship
Show all customers and their addresses	Customer	Customers have addresses
	Address	
What is James' last name	Customer	Customer Names are the names of customers
	Customer Name	
What is James' phone number	Customer	Customer Names are the names of customers
	Phone Number	Customers have phone numbers
What is James' address	Customer	Customer Names are the names of customers
	Address	Customers have addresses
Who is James' employer	Customer	Customer Names are the names of customers
	Employer	Customers have employers

This is a comprehensive list of questions providing all of the basic information about a customer. However, what if we were interested in what city a customer lives in or what state they live in? This information requires some additional entities to be defined. Since we may want to know what city a particular customer lives in, we may also want to know which customers live in a particular city.

Given this we will need to define two more entities. Since these entities represent proper names, we need to also define minor entities for the major entities that we define. The table below lists the two additional major and minor entities that we need to define.

Major Entity	Minor Entity
City	City Name
State	State Name

Now that we have defined additional entities, we can complete our list of questions, as shown in the table below:

Question	Entities	Relationship
What city does James live in	Customer	Customer Names are the names of customers
	City	Customers live in cities
What state does James live in	Customer	Customer Names are the names of customers
	State	Customers live in states

Question	Entities	Relationship
What customers live in Charlotte	City	City Names are the name of cities
	Customer	Customers live in cities
What customers live in North Carolina	State	State Names are the names of states
	Customer	Customers live in states

We now have enough information to actually begin creating our English Query application. The next series of examples will walk you through building our English Query application and setting up the entities and relationships that we have just defined.

Try It Out – Creating the Customer English Query Application

1. Start Microsoft English Query by selecting it from the program group where English Query was installed. The English Query Domain Editor comes up and displays the New Project dialog as shown in the next figure. We want to load the structure from the database so choose this option, as shown below, and click OK to proceed to the next step.

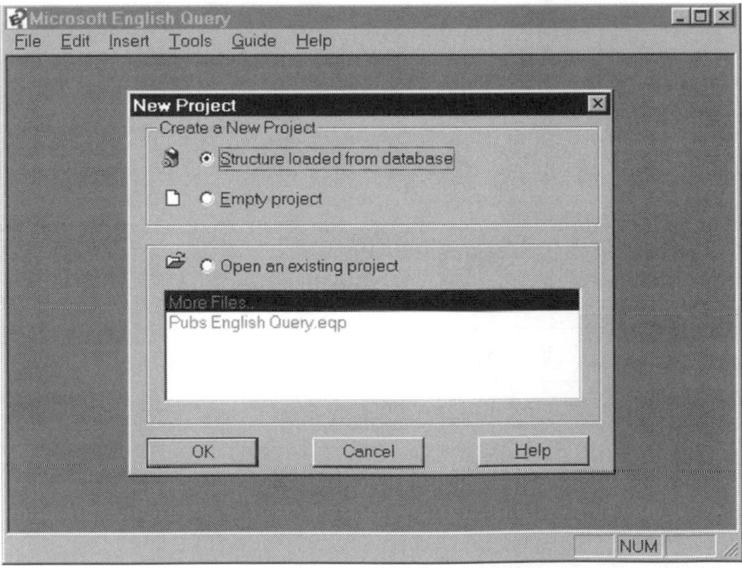

2. The Select Data Source dialog is displayed and we need to choose the Wrox Auto Works DSN under the Machine Data Source tab. This dialog tells the English Query Domain Editor how to connect to our database. After you have chosen the appropriate DSN, click OK to proceed.

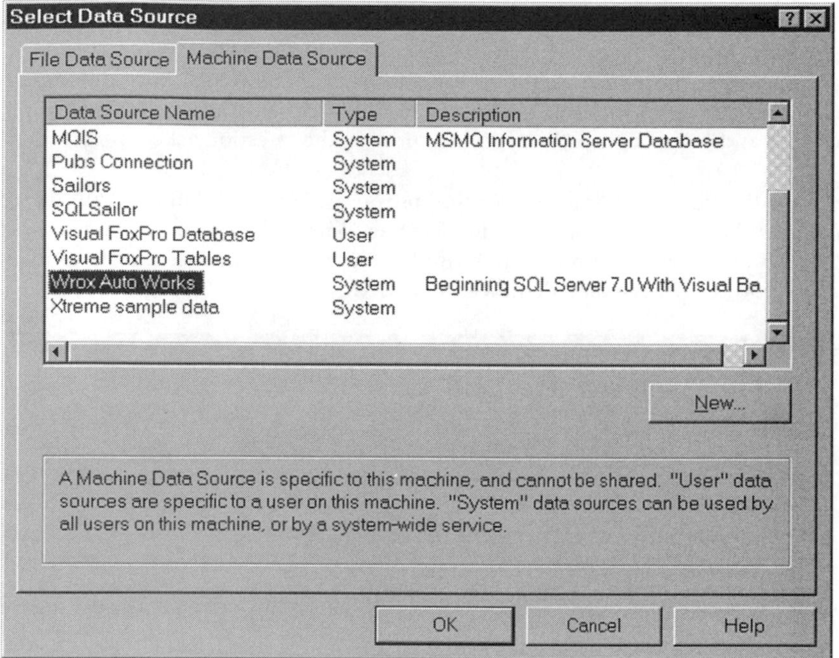

3. The next dialog that is shown is the SQL Server Login dialog. This dialog prompts you for your Login ID and Password. If you are using SQL Server authentication, supply this information. If you are using NT authentication, check the Use Trusted Connection checkbox. When you click OK on this dialog, the English Query Domain Editor will load the structure of your database.

4. At this point, you can see what has been loaded in the various tabs that we mentioned earlier. The Files tab displays the entire project view, combining the information from the Database and Semantics tabs. If you expand the Tables folder, you will see a list of all tables in the database. Expanding a table shows the Fields and Joins folders, and you can expand them to list all the fields and joins for a particular table.

5. It does not matter what tab is being displayed while we work, but it would be beneficial to have the data in the Semantics tab displayed. This allows us to view the entities and relationships as we define them, without showing the tables. If you have not done so, select the Semantics tab at the bottom of the screen.

6. The first entity that we want to define is for customers. On the Insert menu select Entity to display the New Entity dialog. In the Words/phrases identifying entity box, we enter one word or phrase that identifies this entity, in this case customer. After the identifying word or phrase, we can add **synonyms** for this word or phrase. Synonyms are words that have similar meaning and help English Query in interpreting the question asked.

7. Let's use the figure below for illustration purposes. We have defined client as a synonym for customer. We can now ask a question such as "*Show all customers*" or "*Show all clients*". Both questions posed will return the same results. It is important to define all common synonyms for the word or phrase that identifies the entity.

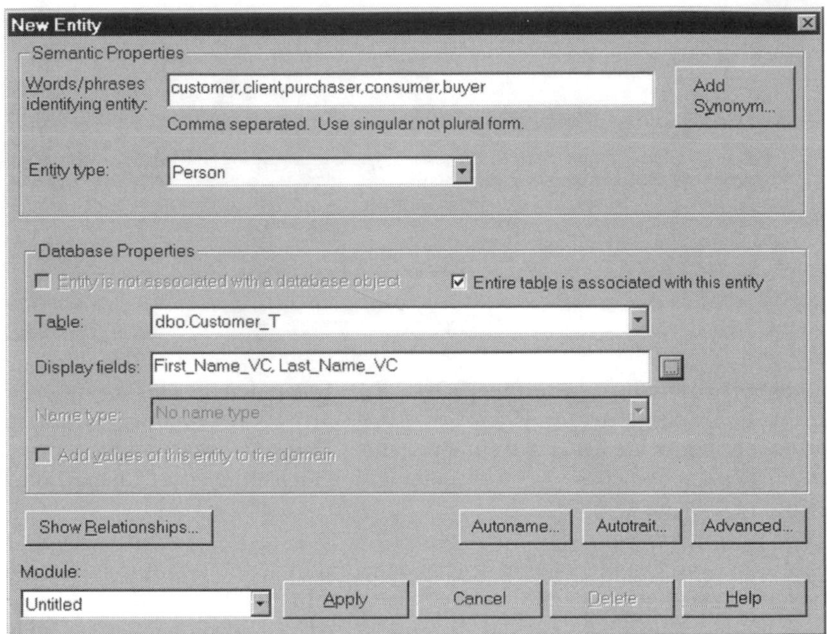

8. Entity type describes what type of entity we are defining. Since customer is a person, we choose Person in this combo box.

9. Since this entity exists in the `Customer_T` table and the entire table is associated with customers, we need to check the Entire table is associated with this entity checkbox. Then we choose the Customer_T table in the Table listbox.

10. The textbox for Display fields contains the fields from the table that will be displayed when this entity is queried. If you click the button next to this textbox, the Fields dialog is displayed, listing all the fields in the table. Select the fields you want to display, in this case the first and last name fields, and then click OK to have the fields added to the Display fields textbox.

11. Since the entity type is a person, we want to click the Autoname button to invoke the Autoname dialog. This dialog allows us to choose the name type of our entity. It is also worthy to note that using this dialog creates a minor entity for customer and also a relationship between customer and customer name. When you click this button, you will be prompted with a dialog that informs you that you need to save the form first. Click OK on this dialog to proceed. Since customer contains a proper name, we need to select the Proper name option button. We have a first and last name for a customer so we select the Multiple field person's name option and then choose the appropriate fields in the table in the First name and Last name listboxes.To complete this dialog, ensure that the Add values of this name entity to the domain checkbox is checked. Then click Accept to save these choices and to have the minor entity and the relationship between the major entity and minor entity created.

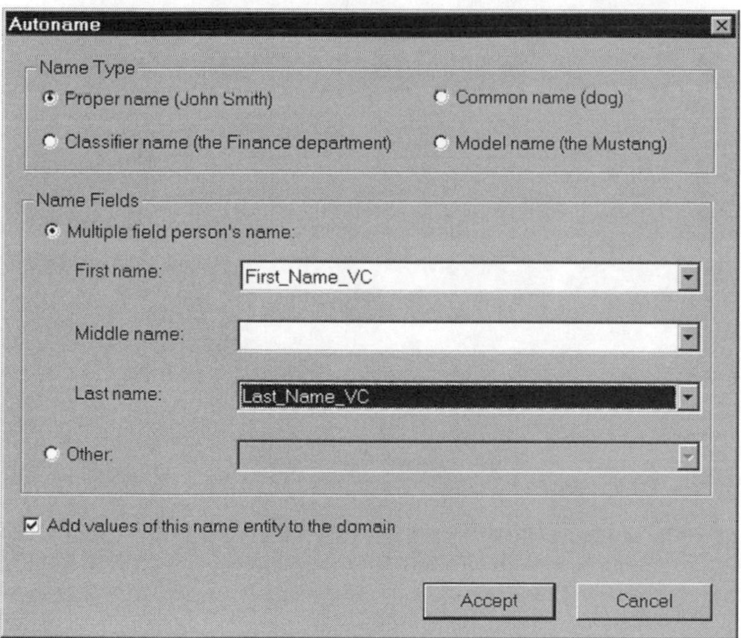

14. At this point if you expand the Entities and Relationships folder, you will be able to see one major entity and one minor entity defined, as well as the relationship that ties the minor entity to the major entity.

15. The next entity that we want to create is for phone numbers. On the Insert menu select Entity and then fill in the details for this dialog as shown below. Notice that we are using the phrase phone number to identity this entity and using the synonyms of phone and number for this entity. This allows us to ask a question such as "*What is James' number*" without having to specify the phrase *phone number*.

16. Notice that since this entity does not fit into any of the entity categories, we have chosen an Entity type of None. This entity is associated with the entire table so we have checked the Entire table is associated with this entity checkbox and have specified the Phone_Number_T table for the table name. The fields that we want displayed when this entity is shown are the area code and phone number fields, so we have chosen the appropriate fields in the Display fields textbox.

17. When you have entered all the information shown below, click the Apply button to create this entity.

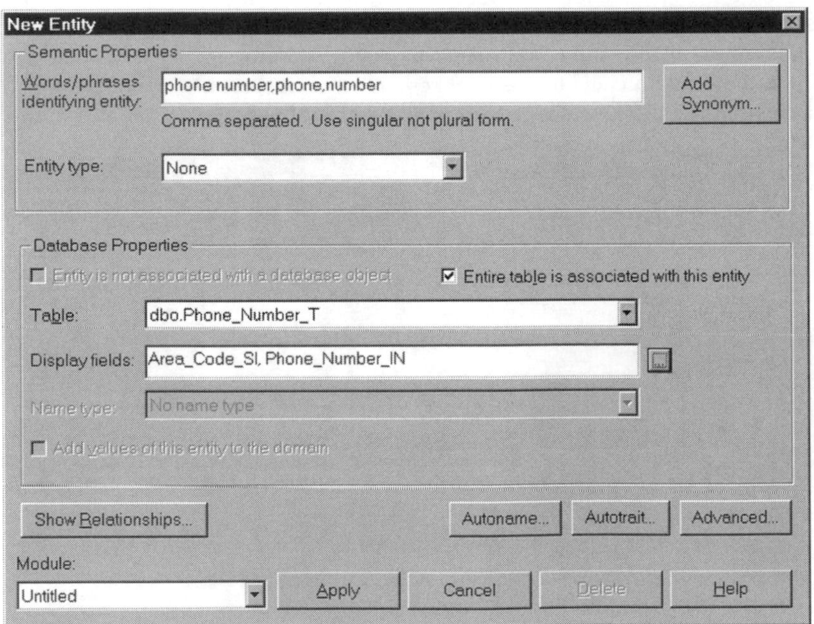

18. Now that we have two entities defined, we need to create a relationship between them to associate phone numbers with customers. On the Insert menu select Relationship to invoke the New Relationship dialog.

19. On the Entities tab, click the Add Entity button and a list of all defined entities (major and minor) will be displayed. Select the customer and phone_number entities.

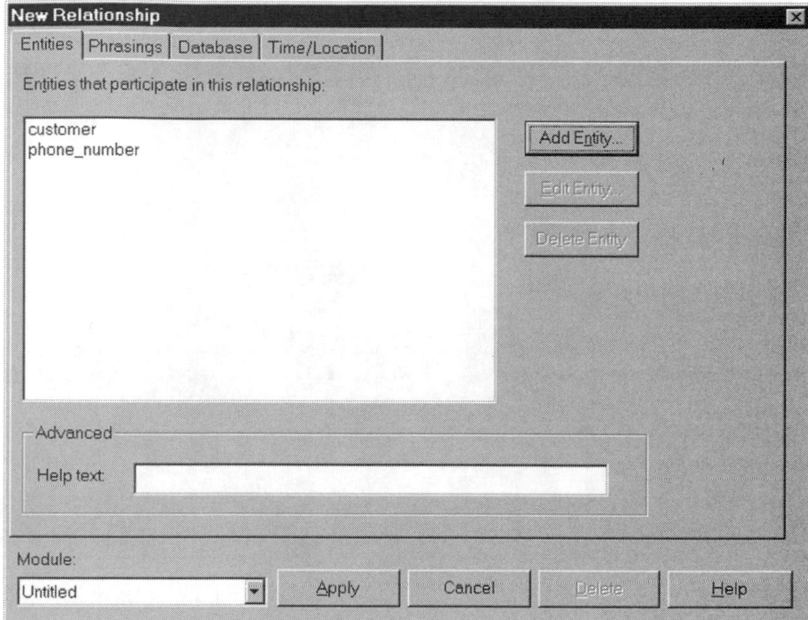

20. Now that we have selected the entities for which we want to define a relationship, we must define the phrasing of the relationship. Click on the Phrasing tab and then click on the Add button to select a phrasing to add.

21. This next dialog lists all available phrasings and gives an example of each phrasing to assist you in choosing the correct phrasing for your relationship. At this point take a moment and click on each of the phrasing types to see an example of each. When you are done, click on Trait Phrasing and then click OK.

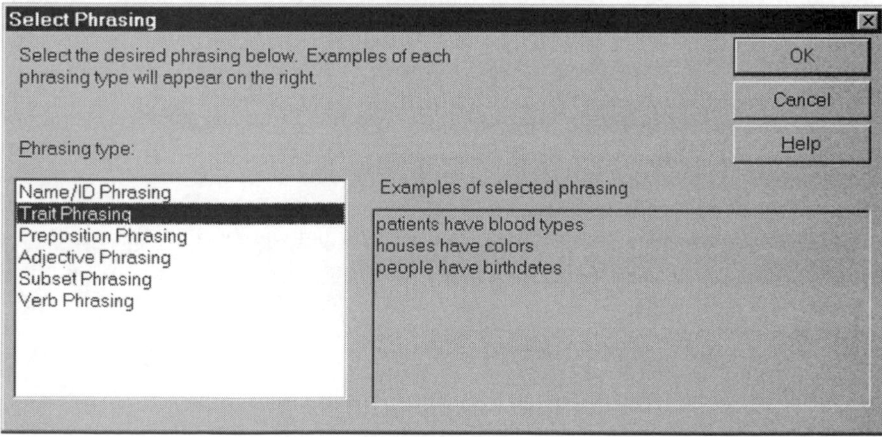

22. The relationship we want to define is "*customers have phone numbers*" so we select customers in the Subject combo box and phone_numbers in the Object listbox as shown below. Then we click the OK button on this dialog to dismiss it, and click the Apply button in the New Relationship dialog to have the new relationship added.

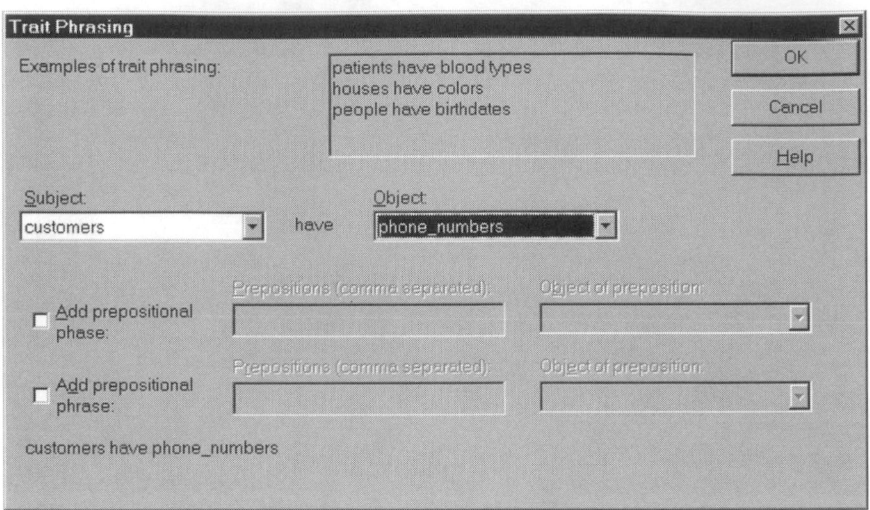

At this point we want to test the entities and relationships we have defined, using natural English questions, to ensure that we get the results expected. Once you become more experienced at building English Query applications, you can define all of your entities and relationships and then test them. For now we want to test each entity and relationship that we define as we go along, rather than leaving all the testing until the end.

Try It Out – Testing the Application

1. To test your English Query application select Test Application on the Tools menu. The Test Application dialog contains many parts. First there is the Question combo box, where you enter new questions and can select questions you have already entered. The Restatement box shows how English Query restates the question you have asked. When the Execute SQL checkbox is checked, the question is restated, transformed into SQL statements and then executed.

2. The Answer tab contains three parts. First there is the natural English phrasing of the answer to your question followed by the SQL statements that are executed to retrieve your answer. Then the actual answer is provided in a grid at the bottom of the dialog.

3. The Analysis tab lists the entities and relationships that were used to answer the question that you have asked.

4. The Submit button submits the question asked to English Query for processing and the Close button closes the dialog. The Add to Question File button adds the current question to the question file for your English Query application. The question file is used later for regression testing when you modify your English Query application. This ensures all previous questions still work the way you intended. The Help button provides help for this dialog and the Suggestion button provides suggestions to questions that English Query does not understand.

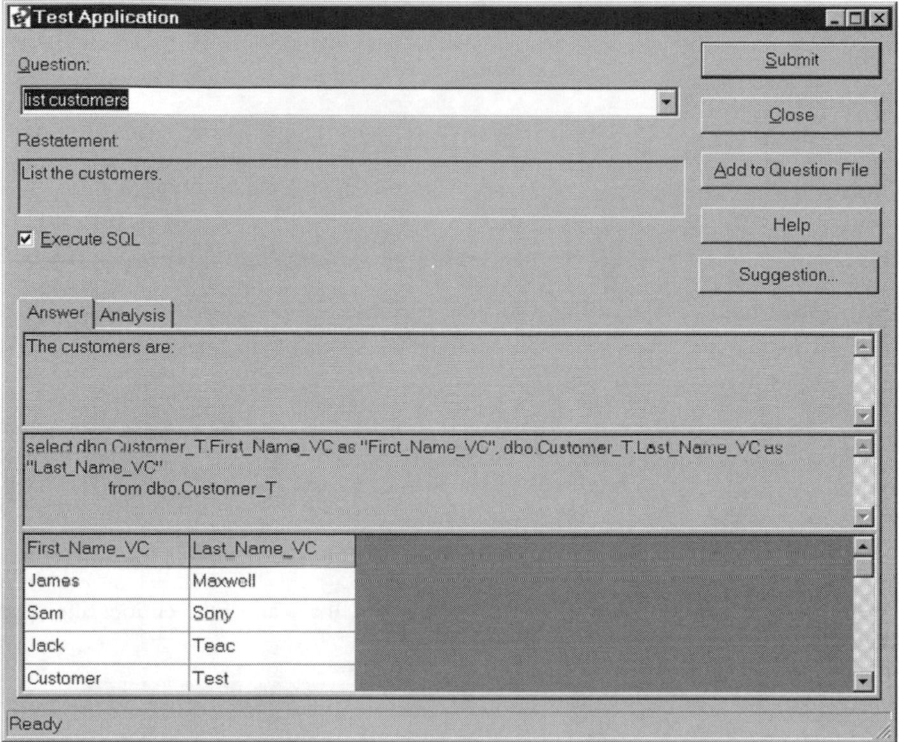

5. To start your testing, enter your question as shown in the figure above and click on the Submit button. Notice that the question has been restated and English Query has displayed the SQL that will be executed. On the Analysis tab, the entities that are used to resolve this question are listed, in this case customer.

6. To have the SQL statements executed, check the Execute SQL checkbox. The results of the executed SQL statements are listed at the bottom of the Answer tab.

7. Save each question to the Question File before moving on to the next.

8. The next question we want to test is to ask for a phone number for a specific customer. Select the first or last name of one of your customers that are listed in the Answer tab and enter the question as shown below. Substitute James with the first or last name of your customer. The results should be similar to the one listed below:

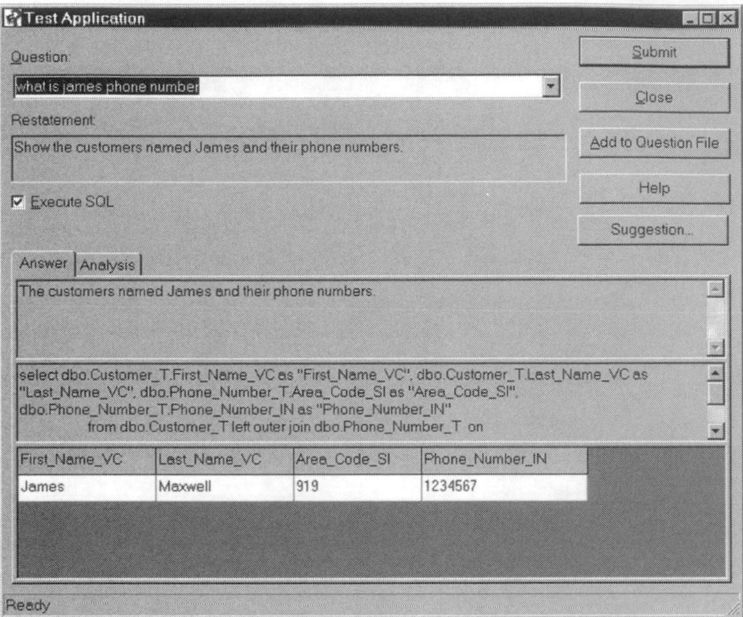

9. At this point take a look at the Analysis tab. You will see all of the entities and relationships that were used to answer this question:

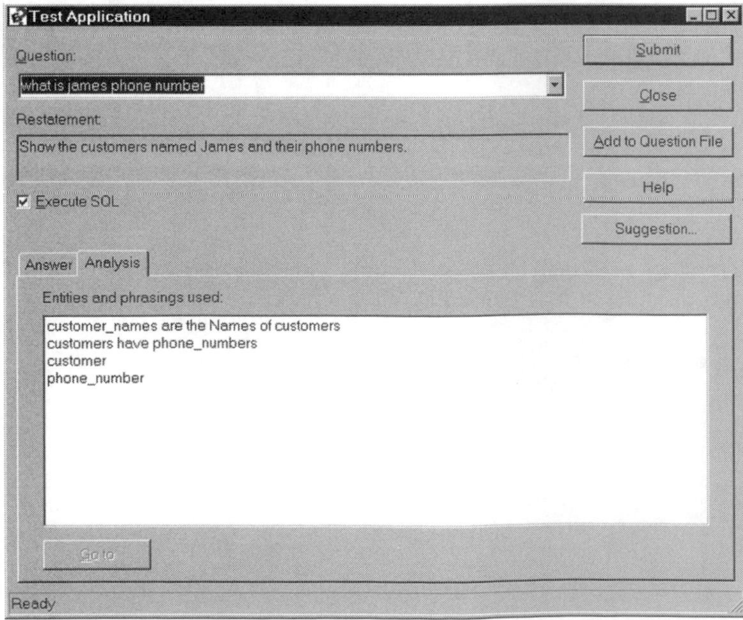

10. To continue the testing of the entities and relationships defined, ask the questions in the table below. You should see the results of each of these questions. Substitute James with the first name of a customer that you have defined. Watch your English when asking questions such as what is someone's last name. You will need to be careful to correctly use apostrophes,for example "*What is Sam's last name*" or "*What is James' last name*".

Show all customers
Show all buyers
Show all customers and their phone numbers
Show all customers and their numbers
What is James' last name
What is Maxwell's first name

As you can see, we can ask many questions for the two entities and relationships defined. Because we used synonyms for phone number and customer we can use the synonyms defined to ask the questions. After each question, take a look at the Analysis of each question to see what entities and relationships were used to answer the question.

Try It Out – Adding an Address Entity

1. Moving along, we want to define an entity for address next. On the Insert menu choose Entity and complete this dialog using the information shown in the figure below.

2. The Entity type that has been chosen this time is Geographical Location as this best describes this entity. We are only using the first address line in the `Address_T` table for demonstration purposes but you should select all three address lines in the Display fields box.

3. In order to also display the city name, state name and zip code, which are all part of the address, click on the Advanced button at the bottom of this dialog.

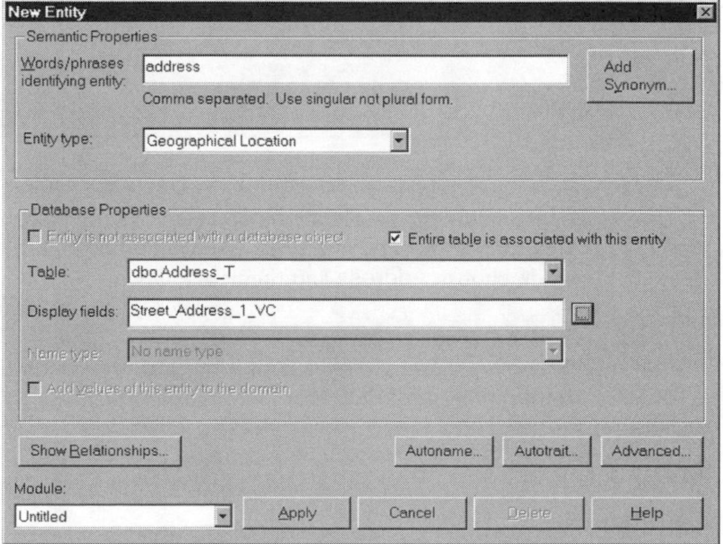

4. The Advanced Entity Properties dialog is displayed and we want to select the Display Properties tab. Next to the textbox for Remote fields is a button titled Add Fields. Click this button to invoke the Select Remote Fields dialog. This dialog allows us to select fields from the tables that are joined to the `Address_T` table. English Query was smart enough to recognize the foreign keys that we have defined in the `Address_T` table and has joined those tables and listed them in this dialog.

Before selecting the tables and fields in this dialog, be aware that the order in which you select these tables and fields are the order in which they will be displayed. There is no way to reorder the fields once selected.

5. The first table you want to select is the City_T table in the Table listbox. Then select the City_Name_VC field in the Field listbox. Once the table and field have been selected, click the Add button to add the table and field to the Selected fields listbox.

6. Repeat this process for the `State_Name_VC` field in the `State_T` table and the `Zip_Code_CH` field in the `Zip_Code_T` table. Click the OK button to close this dialog and then click the OK button to close the Advanced Entity Properties dialog. Finally click the Apply button to create this entity.

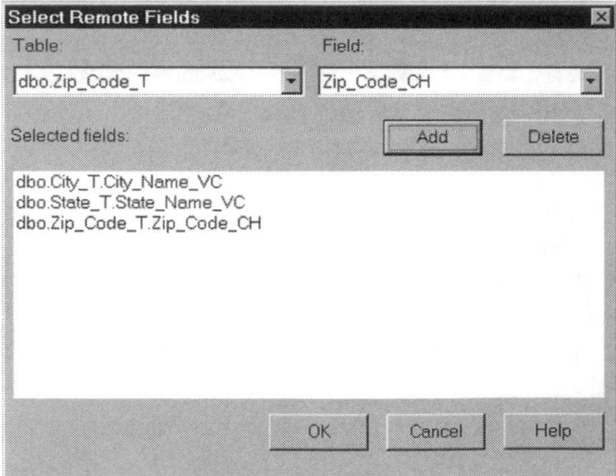

7. Now that we have defined another entity, let's define the relationship for this entity. On the Insert menu choose Relationship to invoke the New Relationship dialog. On the Entities tab, click the Add Entity button, choose Customer and then click OK. Click the Add Entity button again, choose Address and then click OK.

8. On the Phrasing tab, click the Add button to invoke the Select Phrasing dialog. We want to choose a phrasing type of Trait Phrasing so click on this entry. Notice the examples given for trait phrasing and then click the OK button.

9. Customers have addresses so we want to choose customers in the Subject listbox and choose addresses in the Object listbox. Click OK to dismiss this dialog and then click the Apply button to create this relationship.

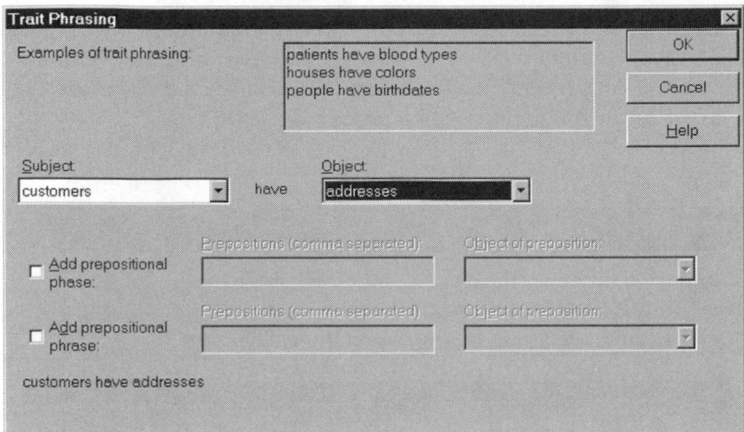

10. Again we want to test this new relationship before proceeding further, so click Test Application on the Tools menu. If you click the Question combo box, you will notice that all of the questions that you have asked are listed. These questions will remain until you end your session with the English Query Domain Editor.

11. The next question we want to ask should test the functionality of the entity and relationship that we just added. To that end enter the question "*Show customer addresses*" and you should see results similar to those listed in the figure below. You can rephrase the question as "*Show all customers and their addresses*" and still see the same results. Notice that each customer has been listed along with the fields that you defined for their address.

12. Again notice the SQL statement that was built to execute the query, and also take a look at the Analysis tab to see the entities and relationships used in this query.

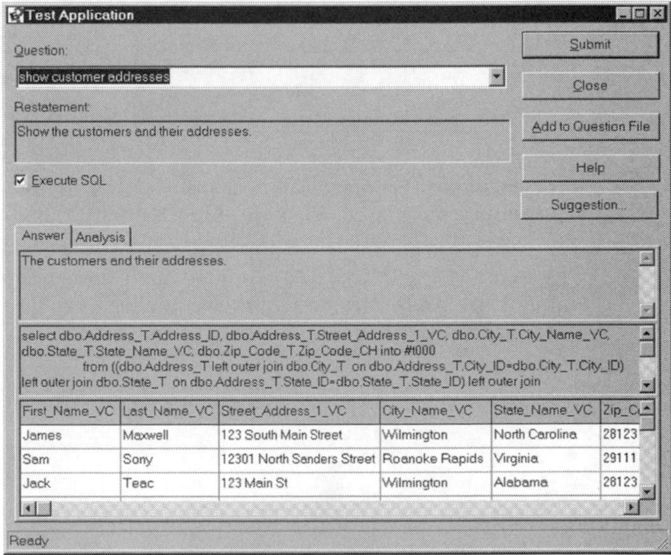

13. You should also test the relationship by querying a specific customer and asking the question "*What is James' address*". You will need to substitute James with the first name of one of your customers. The results should list the customer name and the address for that customer.

14. You can also test multiple relationships by asking the question "*What is James' address and phone number*". This will result in the customer name, address, and phone number being listed. If you take a look at the Analysis tab for this query, you will see the list of entities and relationships growing larger as the questions become more complex.

Try It Out – Adding a City Entity

1. We want to define an entity for city so choose Entity from the Insert menu. Fill in the details of the New Entity dialog as shown in the figure below. City represents a Geographical Location and as such we have chosen this as the Entity type.

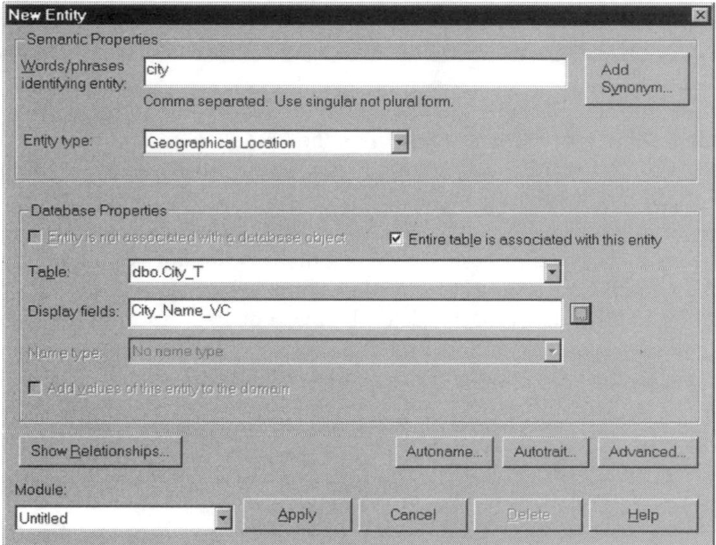

2. In order to query a specific city name we must define the field in the `City_T` table that represents a city name. Click the Autoname button to invoke the Autoname dialog.

3. City name is a Common name and as such we need to check the appropriate option for the Name Type. In the Name Fields section of this dialog, we want to choose the Other option and select the City_Name_VC field in the listbox.

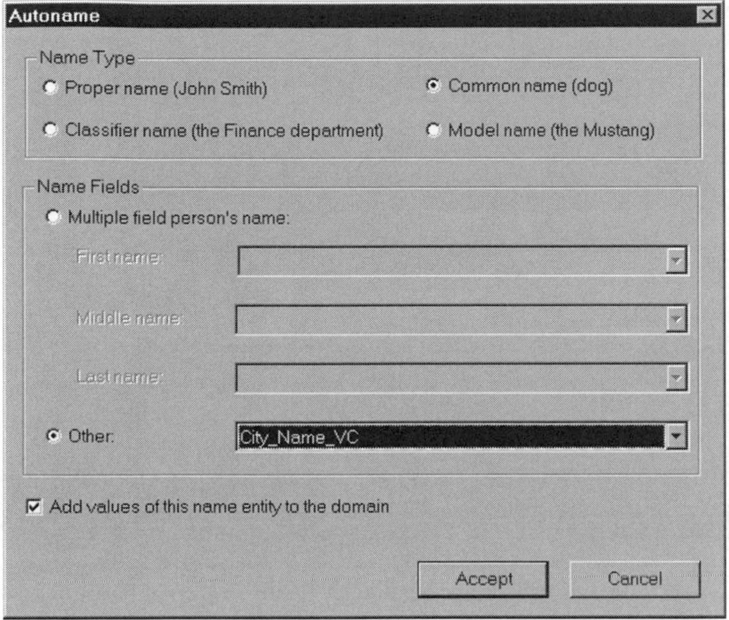

4. Click Accept to close this dialog and then click Apply to add this new entity.

5. Because we have chosen a name for the city entity, English Query has created a minor entity of city_name_vc, which is the name of the field that we chose. It has also created a relationship between the major and minor entity named city_name_vcs_are_the_names_of_cities. You can see the entity and relationship that English Query has created on the Semantics tab.

6. We also want to create a relationship of our own between customers and cities. Choose Relationship from the Insert menu to invoke the New Relationship dialog. On the Entities tab click the Add Entity button to add the customer and city entities.

7. On the Phrasing tab click the Add button, choose Verb Phrasing and then click OK.

8. The Verb Phrasing dialog shown overleaf provides many options and your college English classes will now pay off. There are all kinds of verb sentence types to choose from but we want to choose Subject Verb in the Sentence type listbox.

9. The Subject is customers and the Verb is live. This verb must be in the singular form. We want to add a prepositional phrase so we check the first Add prepositional phrase checkbox and enter the preposition of in. In the Object of preposition combo box we want to choose cities.

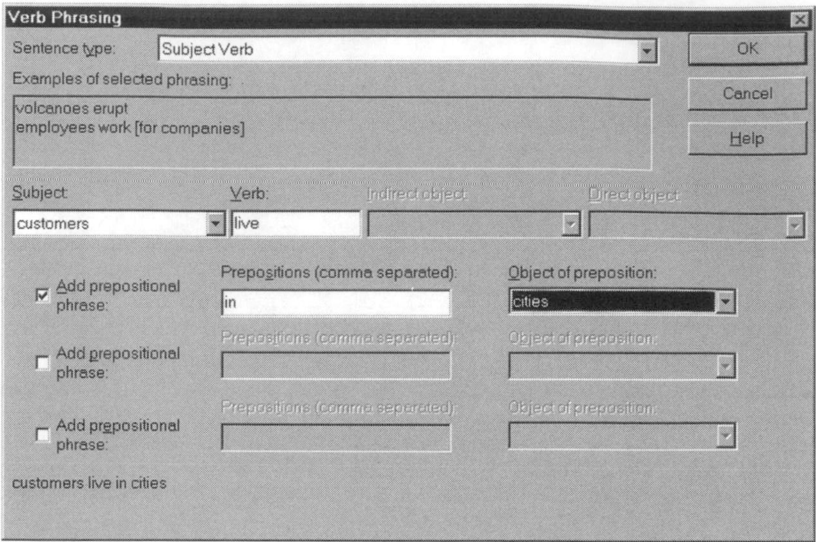

10. When you click the OK button on this dialog, English Query will display an informational message as shown below. Click OK to dismiss this dialog.

11. On the Time/Location tab check the This relationship occurs at the location specified by this entity checkbox and choose cities in the listbox.

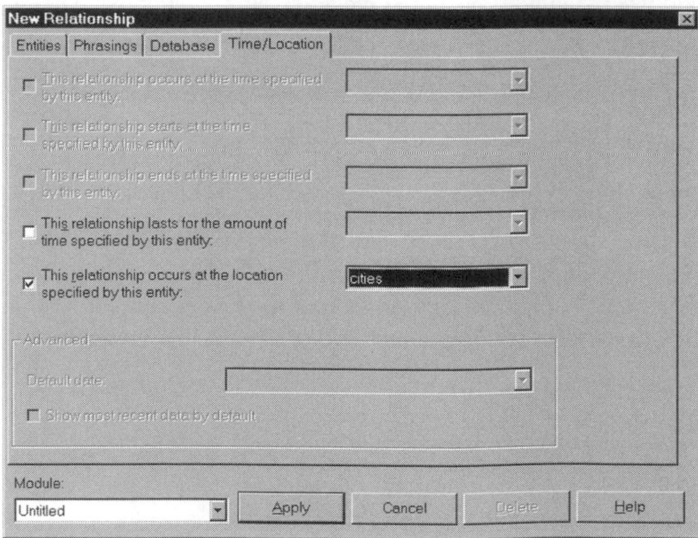

12. We want to add one additional phrasing for this entity so back on the Phrasing tab click Add. We want to choose Prepositional Phrasing in the Phrasing type listbox. Click the OK button to invoke the Prepositional Phrasing dialog.

13. Preposition phrasing allows us to ask a question such as what customer is in a specific city. In the Subject listbox we want to choose customers, specify a preposition of in and choose cities as the Object. Click OK to close this dialog and you should receive the same informational message that we received above when we added the verb phrasing.

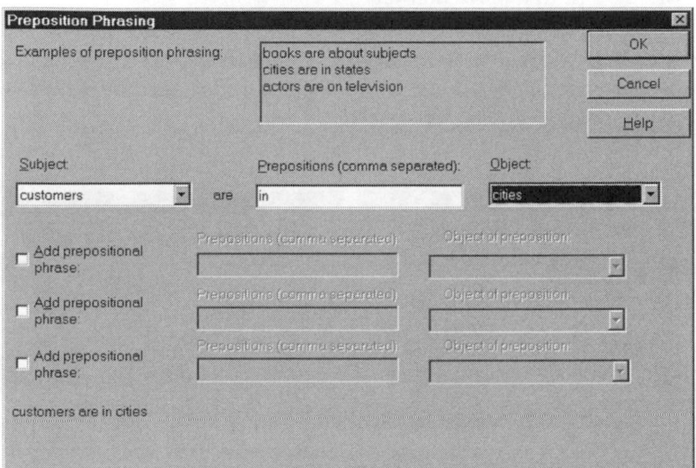

14. The New Relationship dialog should now have two phrasings listed, as shown in the next figure. Click the Apply button to create this new relationship.

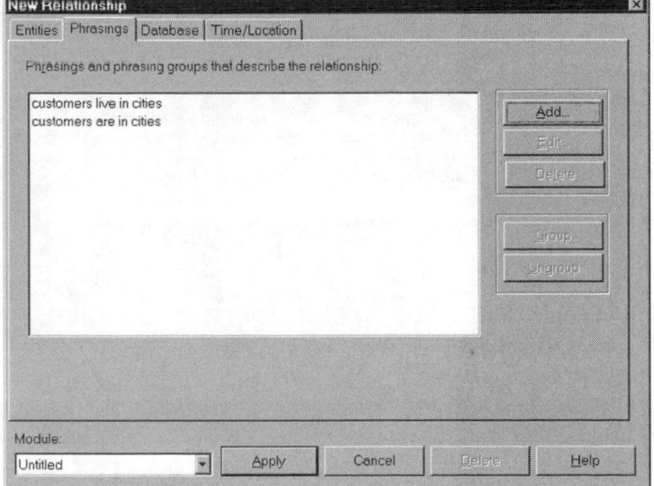

15. Once again we want to test this new entity and relationship that we have defined. Start the Test Application dialog from the Tools menu and enter the question shown in the figure below. Substitute the first name of one of your customers for James.

16. If you asked the question "*Where does James live*" you should get the same results and the same entities and relationships should be used.

17. When you ask the question "*What customers live in Charlotte*", English Query will list all customers that live in that particular city.

18. After asking each of these questions, look at the Analysis tab to see what entities and relationships were used. You should be starting to understand how these entities and relationships are used to answer the questions.

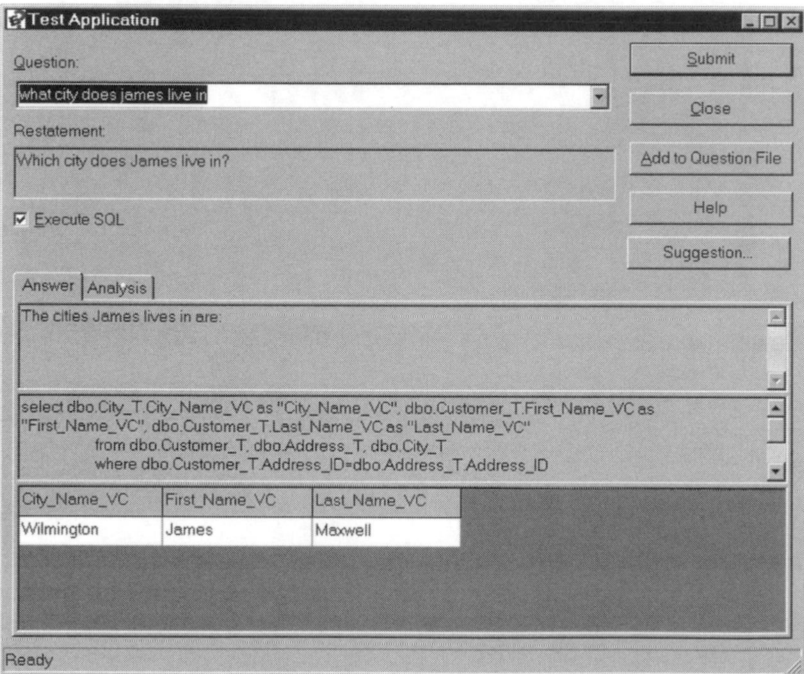

Try It Out – Adding a State Entity

1. We want to also add an entity for state. Insert a new entity and fill in the properties of the New Entity dialog as shown below. This is the same process that we just went through for city.

2. Notice that we have chosen a synonym of province for state. This allows us to ask a question using the word province instead of state.

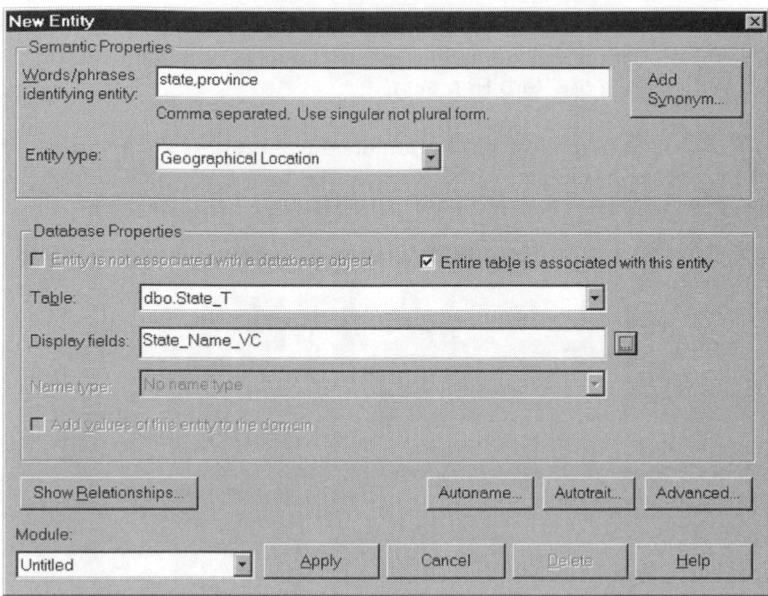

3. We want to add a minor entity for state, so click on the Autoname button. Again we choose the Common name option and specify the State_Name_VC field in the Other listbox. Click Accept to close this dialog.

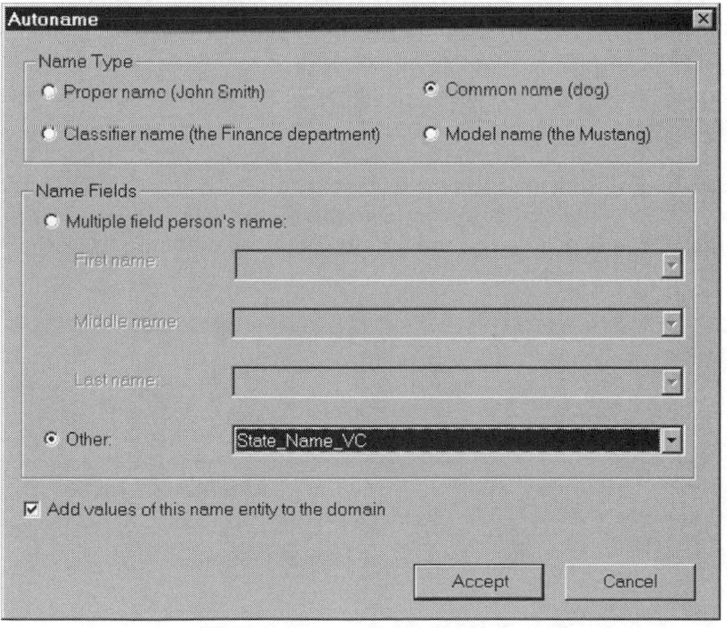

4. We now want to add a relationship between customer and state so choose Relationship from the Insert menu. On the Entities tab insert the customer and state entities. On the Phrasing tab, click Add and choose Verb Phrasing.

5. Again we choose Subject Verb in the Sentence type listbox. We specify customers in the Subject listbox and enter the word live for the Verb. The Preposition of in is specified along with states as the Object of preposition. Click OK to close this dialog.

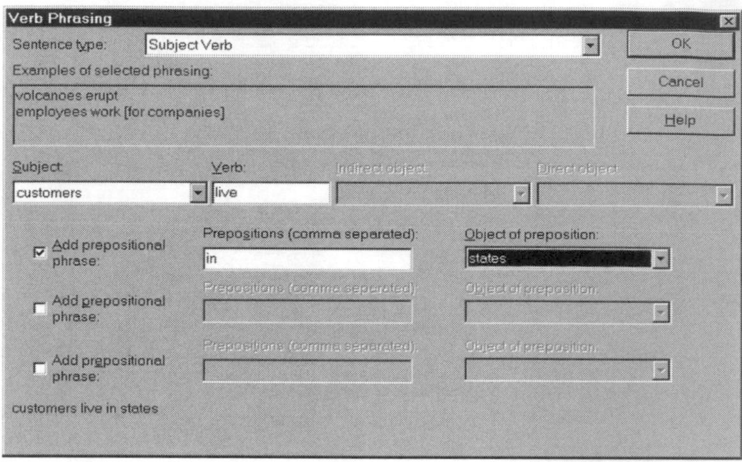

6. On the Time/Location tab, check the This relationship occurs at the location specified by this entity checkbox and choose states in the listbox.

7. Back on the Phrasing tab, we need to add one more phrasing, this time a Preposition Phrasing.

8. We want to choose customers as the Subject and specify in as the Prepositions. We also want to choose states as the Object to complete this dialog. Click OK to close this dialog and OK to dismiss the informational message about the Time/Location tab. Click the Apply button to create this new relationship.

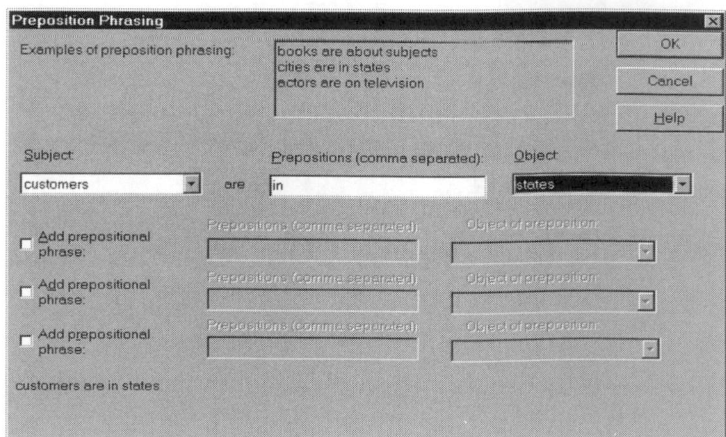

9. At this point we are ready to test the new entity and relationship we have just added. Again start the Test Application dialog from the Tools menu.

10. We can ask the question shown in the figure below, and state name and customer name will be displayed in the results. We can also ask what customers live in a particular state.

11. When you ask the question "*Where does James live*" you will receive two answers. The reason for this is that we have defined two relationships that describe where a customer lives, one for city and one for state. The two answers that are returned are listed in the next two figures.

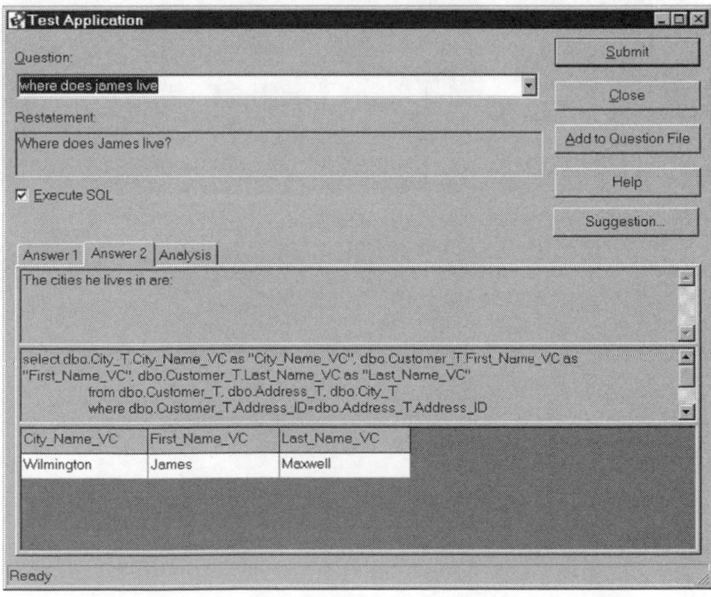

12. This is why we ask the question "*What state does James live in*" to narrow the search to the state in which James lives.

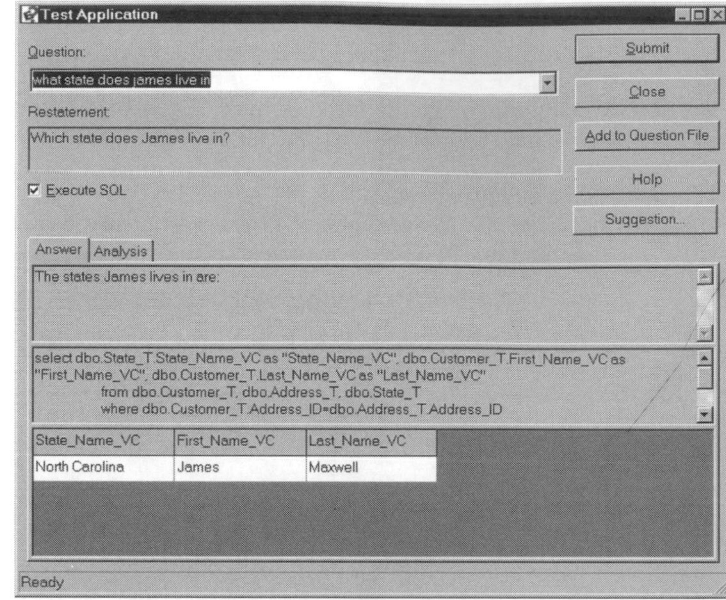

Try It Out – Adding an Employer Entity

The last entity that we want to add to our Customer English Query application is for employer.

1. In the New Entity dialog we enter employer as the name of this entity and add two synonyms for employer: company and job. This entity does not fall into any specific category so we choose an Entity type of None.

2. Again this entity is associated with the entire table so we check the appropriate checkbox and choose the Employer_T table as the Table and the Company_Name_VC field as the Display fields.

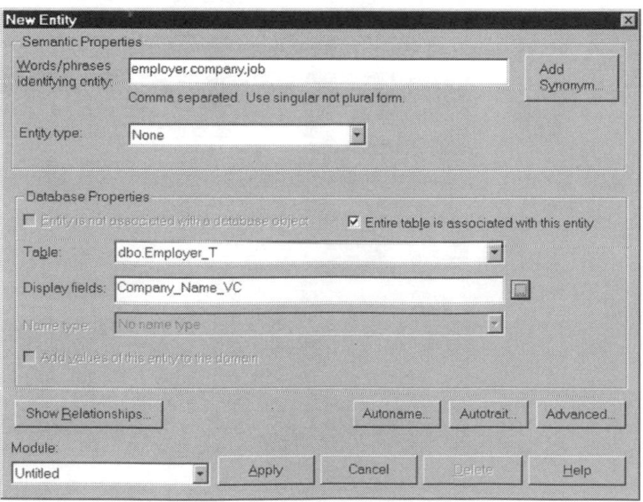

3. We want to associate a minor entity with employer so that we can query a specific employer. We do this by clicking on the Autoname button and selecting the Common name option in the Autoname dialog. We also want to choose the Company_Name_VC field in the Other listbox.

4. Click Accept to close this dialog and then click Apply to add the new entity.

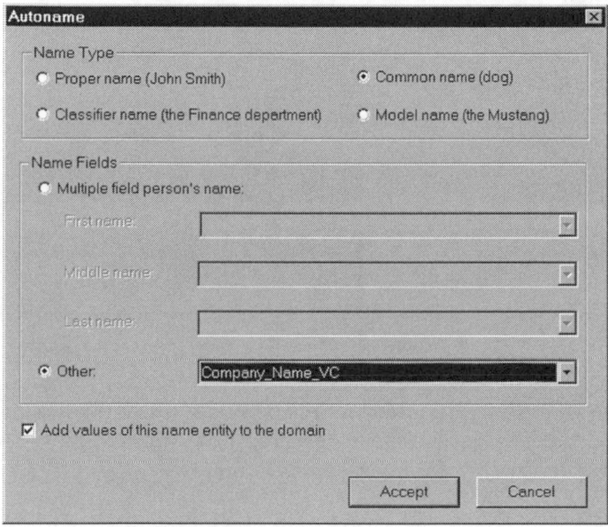

5. We need to define a relationship between customer and employer so that we can ask specific questions about customers and their employers. Select Relationship from the Insert menu and add customer and employer in the Entities tab.

6. On the Phrasings tab we want to add a Trait Phrasing. In the Trait Phrasing dialog we want to choose customers as the Subject and employers as the Object. This allows us to list the customers and their employers. Click OK to close this dialog.

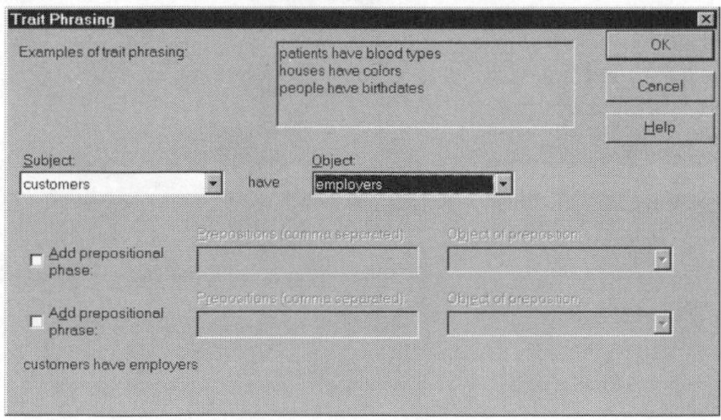

7. We also want to add a second phrasing to the Phrasing tab, so click Add and choose Verb Phrasing.

8. This Verb Phrasing will allow us to ask what customers work for a specific employer. We need to choose Subject Verb as the Sentence type and select customers as the Subject. We then specify work as the Verb and check the Add prepositional phrase checkbox. We specify at as the Prepositions and select employers as the Object of preposition.

9. Click OK to close this dialog and then Apply to add this relationship.

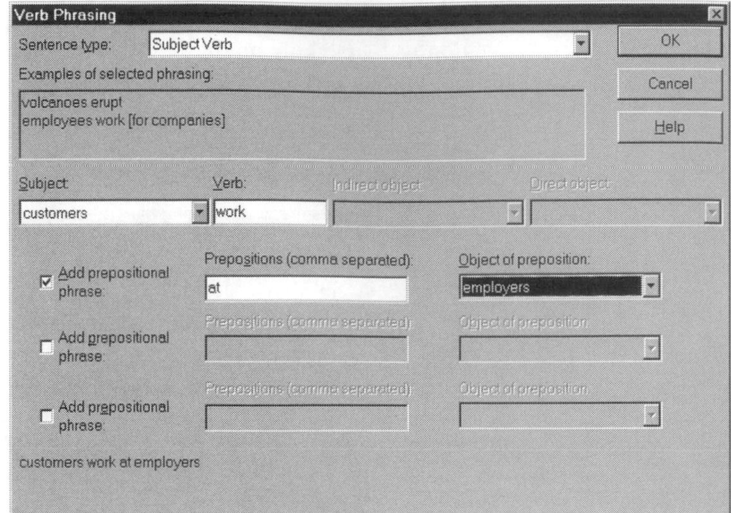

10. Once again we want to test the new entity and relationship that we have just added. Start the Test Application dialog and enter the question shown in the figure below. Again you will need to substitute the first name of one of your customers.

11. You can also ask the question in another way, such as "*Who is James' employer*", and the results are displayed differently, with the company name being listed last.

12. You can also ask the question "*Show all customers and their employers*" to get a list of all customers and their employers.

13. If you want to know who works at a specific company you can ask the question "*Who works at ATI Technologies*" to get a list of all customers who work at this company.

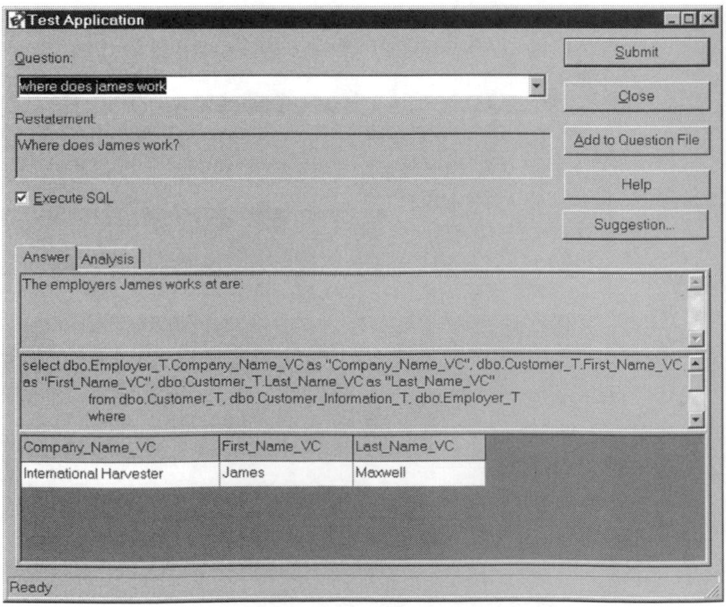

This covers all of the entities and relationships that we are going to define for this English Query application. As a result of adding the various entities and relationships your Semantics tab should look like the one shown below:

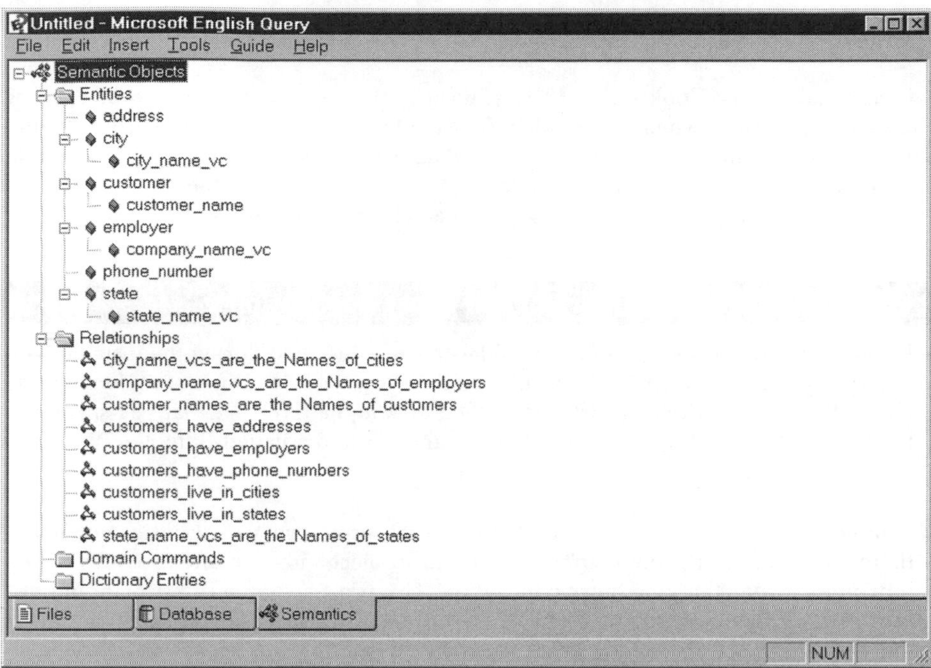

After you have thoroughly tested your English Query application using the Test Application dialog and you are satisfied with the results to the questions you have asked, you are ready to *build* your application.

Try It Out – Building the Customer English Query Application

You must build your application so that the English Query Run-time Engine can access your application to resolve questions into SQL statements. The build process creates a compiled project file (`.eqd`) that is used by the English Query Run-time Engine.

1. Before we build our application, we should save our work. On the File menu select Save Project. Select the folder you wish to save your project in and specify a name for your project, such as Wrox Customers.

2. To build your application, select Build Application from the Tools menu. You will be prompted with a dialog specifying that it may take a while to build your application. Since our application is very small this message does not apply to us so we can click OK to dismiss it and continue.

3. After your application has been successfully built, you will receive a message in a dialog to that effect. At this point, save your project one final time and close the English Query Domain Editor.

Deploying Your English Query Application

SQL Server provides many alternatives to deploying your English Query application. You can deploy your application over the Web through an intranet and/or the Internet using Active Server Pages. You can also embed your English Query application in a Visual Basic or Visual C++ program.

We are going to take a brief look at using Visual Basic as the deployment method. Because we chose to install the sample programs when we installed English Query, there are sample programs provided for each of the deployment methods that we mentioned above, and we are going to use one of those here. As competent VB developers, you should have no problems figuring out the VB code to achieve this. You have already covered the most complex part: namely, creating the English Query application itself.

Try It Out – Deploying the Customer English Query Application

1. Locate the Microsoft English Query folder that was installed during the installation of English Query. By default this folder is installed in the Program Files directory. If you chose an alternative directory during installation then look in the directory that you specified. Under the Microsoft English Query folder there is another folder called Samples. We are interested in the files in the Vbui folder under Samples.

2. Double click on the `EQVBUI.VBP` file to start this project in Visual Basic. You will see that there are quite a few forms associated with this project and each one provides a specific function for your English Query application. This project can be run straight out of the box, so to speak, without any modifications.

3. Run the project and the first dialog that comes up prompts you for the location and name of your English Query application file and question file. Replace the default location and names provided with the location and names of your files. Then click the Run button to proceed.

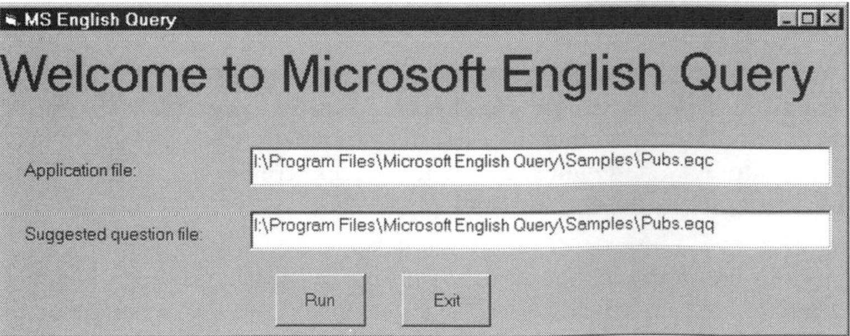

4. You are then prompted with the Select Data Source dialog. Choose the Wrox Auto Works DSN in the Machine Data Source tab. You are prompted to enter your Login and Password in the SQL Server Login dialog. If you are using a SQL Server login, enter the information and click OK. If you are using NT authentication, then check the Use Trusted Connection checkbox and then click OK.

5. The next screen that appears is the Query screen. This screen is where you enter your questions and view the restatement of your question and the answer. If you added questions to the question file during testing, you can click the History and Suggested Questions button to see a list of questions that have been added by you.

6. After you have asked a question and clicked on the Submit button the answer is shown, as in the following figure. At this point, if you want to view the SQL statements that were generated and executed, click the Show SQL button.

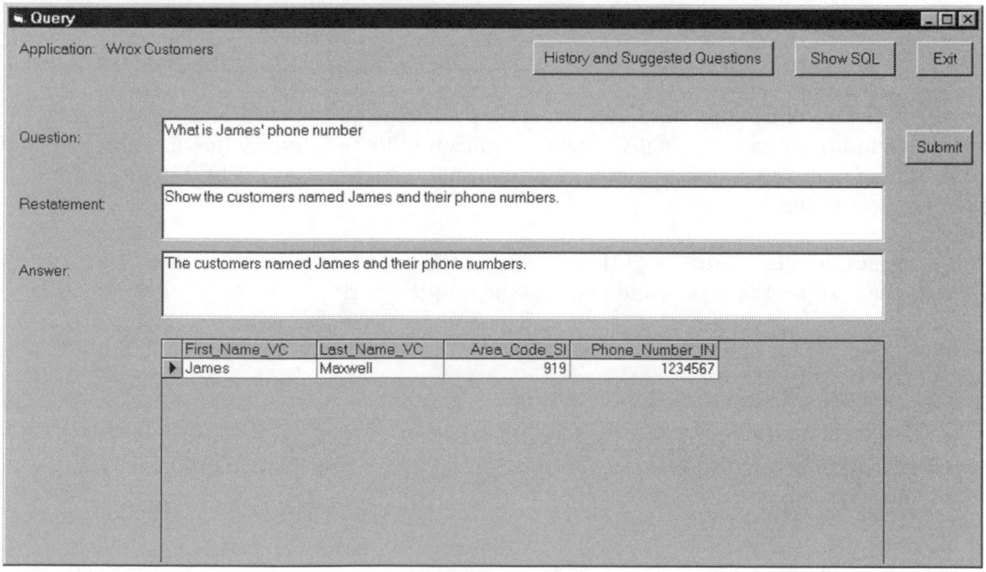

How It Works – Deploying the Customer English Query Application

So how does all of this work? Let's take another look at our diagrammatic overview of English Query.

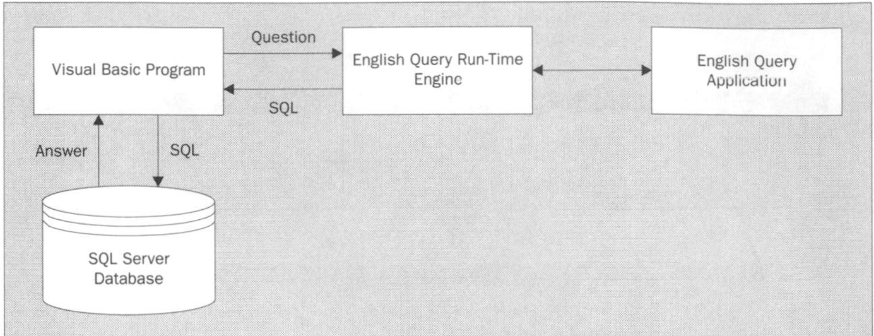

This VB program has a reference set to the English Query Run-time Engine:

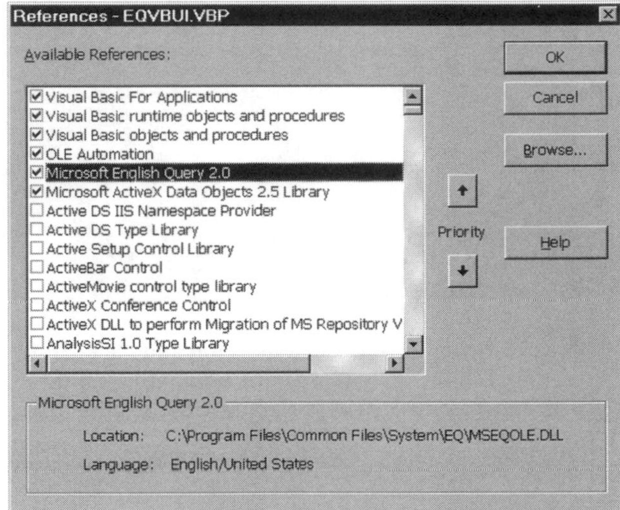

When you click on the Submit button the program passes the question to the English Query Run-time Engine which in turn uses your English Query application file to interpret the question and convert it into SQL statements. The English Query Run-time Engine then passes the SQL string back to the VB program for processing.

The VB program then executes the SQL string using the connection that it made to your SQL Server database. It then parses the results and displays them in the grid.

The English Query Run-time Engine also returns the restatement of the question and the English answer to the question.

You can use this example program as the basis for your own program. You can then build a program to deploy your Customer English Query application to upper management, or whoever needs read-only access to your application.

Summary

The installation of English Query was very straightforward and we covered the installation process. We have also briefly covered the deployment of an English Query application using a Visual Basic program. This section really shows how an English Query application works, as summarized in the figure above, and brings everything all together.

The bulk of this chapter has been about creating the English Query application, and defining the entities and relationships. From our testing, you should have come to realize the importance of these two semantic objects. During our testing we saw how creating the appropriate relationships can help to answer specific questions. We have only scratched the surface in using the various phrases available that help to define the relationships to answer questions.

The correct phrasing of a relationship between two entities is key to the successful processing of a question. We have shown that you can define more than one type of phrasing per relationship, and that there are several phrasing types that we did not have the opportunity to cover.

Hopefully you will take the opportunity to enhance this English Query application by applying the other tables of the `Wrox_Auto_Works` database as entities and defining new relationships between these entities.

To summarize we have:

- Covered the installation of English Query
- Defined what English Query is and how it works
- Explored the English Query Domain Editor
- Created and tested entites and relationships
- Covered how VB can be used for final deployment for an English Query application

We have come to the end of this book and you will hopefully walk away with a better understanding of SQL Server and the knowledge to begin coding real world applications. Keep this book handy for future reference as we have covered some important techniques and topics.

To advance your skill set to the next level, check out *Professional SQL Server 7.0 Programming* (ISBN 1-861002-31-9) by Wrox Press. This book can be ordered online at `http://www.wrox.com`.

WROX AUTO WORKS RACING

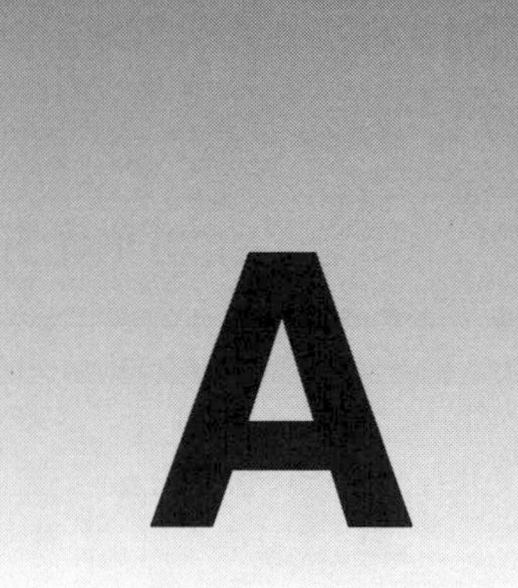

T-SQL and VB Data Types

There are some subtle differences in the SQL Server data types versus the Visual Basic data types. This table lists a side by side comparison of these data types:

SQL DataType	Range	VB DataType	Range
Bit	1 or 0	Boolean	True/False
TinyInt	0 to 255	Byte	0 to 255
Money	-922,337,203,685,477.5808 to 922,337,203,685,477.5807	Currency	-922,337,203,685,477.5808 to 922,337,203,685,477.5807
DateTime	1/1/1753 to 12/31/9999	Date	1/1/100 to 12/31/9999
Decimal	-10^38-1 to 10^38-1	Decimal	+/- 79,228,162,514,264,337,593,543,950,335 w/no decimal +/- 7.9228162514264337593543950335 w/28 places to the right of the decimal
Float	-1.79E + 308 to 1.79E + 308	Double	4.94065645841247E-324 to 1.79769313486232E308 for positive values. -1.79769313486232E308 to -4.94065645841247E-324 for negative values.
SmallInt	-32,768 to 32,767	Integer	-32,768 to 32,767

SQL DataType	Range	VB DataType	Range
Int	-2,147,483,648 to 2,147,483,647	Long	-2,147,483,648 to 2,147,483,647
Real	-3.40E + 38 to 3.40E + 38	Single	1.401298E-45 to 3.402823E38 for positive values. -3.402823E38 to -1.401298E-45 for negative values.
Char and Varchar	8,000	String	0 to 2,147,483,647
Text	2,147,483,647	String	0 to 2,147,483,647

The following table lists, by type, all Transact-SQL data types:

SQL DataType	Range
Integers	
Bit	1 or 0
Int	-2,147,483,648 to 2,147,483,647
SmallInt	-32,768 to 32,767
TinyInt	0 to 255
Decimal and Numeric	
Decimal	-10^38-1 to 10^38-1
Numeric	Synonym for decimal
Money	
Money	-922,337,203,685,477.5808 to 922,337,203,685,477.5807
SmallMoney	-214,748.3648 to 214,748.3647
Approximate Numerics	
Float	-1.79E + 308 to 1.79E + 308
Real	-3.40E + 38 to 3.40E + 38

SQL DataType	Range
Date and Time	
DateTime	January 1, 1753 to December 31, 9999
SmallDateTime	January 1, 1900 to June 6, 2079
Numerics	
Cursor	Reference to a cursor
TimeStamp	Database-wide unique number
UniqueIdentifier	Global unique identifier
Character Strings	
Char	Fixed length character up to 8,000 characters
VarChar	Variable length character up to 8,000 characters
Text	Variable length character up to 2,147,483,647 characters
Unicode Character Strings	
nChar	Fixed length data up to 4,000 characters
nVarChar	Variable length data up to 4,000 characters
nText	Variable length data up to 1,073,741,823 characters
Binary Strings	
Binary	Fixed length binary data up to 8,000 bytes
VarBinary	Variable length binary data up to 8,000 bytes
Image	Variable length binary data up to 2,147,483,647 bytes

WROX AUTO WORKS RACING

ADO 2.5 Object Model and Constants

Object Model

This lists the objects, methods, events and properties of the Microsoft ActiveX Data Objects Library version 2.5.

Objects

Name	Description
`Command`	A `Command` object is a definition of a specific command that you intend to execute against a data source.
`Connection`	A `Connection` object represents an open connection to a data source.
`Error`	An `Error` object contains details about data access errors pertaining to a single operation involving the provider.
`Errors`	Contains all the `Error` objects created in response to a single failure involving the provider.
`Field`	A `Field` object represents a column of data with a common data type.
`Fields`	Contains all the `Field` objects of a `Recordset` or `Record` object.
`Parameter`	A `Parameter` object represents a parameter or argument associated with a `Command` object based on a parameterized query or stored procedure.
`Parameters`	Contains all the `Parameter` objects of a `Command` object.
`Property`	A `Property` object represents a dynamic characteristic of an ADO object that is defined by the provider.
`Properties`	Contains all the `Property` objects for a specific instance of an object.

Name	Description
Record	The Record object represents a row in a Recordset, or a file or directory in a file system.
Recordset	A Recordset object represents the entire set of records from a base table or the results of an executed command. At any time, the Recordset object refers to only a single record within the set as the current record.
Stream	A Stream object represents a stream of binary data or text.

Command Object

A Command object is a definition of a specific command that you intend to execute against a data source.

Methods

Name	Returns	Description
Cancel		Cancels execution of a pending, asynchronous Execute or Open method call.
CreateParameter	Parameter Object	Creates a new Parameter object with the specified properties.
Execute	Recordset Object Reference	Executes the query, SQL statement, or stored procedure specified in the CommandText property.

Properties

Name	Returns	Description
ActiveConnection	Variant	Indicates to which Connection object the specified Command, Recordset, or Record object currently belongs.
CommandText	String	Contains the text of a command that you want to issue against a provider.
CommandTimeout	Long	Indicates how long to wait, in seconds, while executing a command before terminating the attempt and generating an error. Default is 30.
CommandType	CommandTypeEnum	Indicates the type of a Command object.
Name	String	Indicates the name of an object.
Parameters	Parameters	Contains all of the Parameter objects for a Command object.

Name	Returns	Description
Prepared	Boolean	Indicates whether to save a compiled version of a command before execution.
Properties	Properties	Contains all of the Property objects for a Command object.
State	ObjectStateEnum	Indicates for all applicable objects whether the State of the object is open or closed.

Connection Object

A Connection object represents an open connection to a data source.

Methods

Name	Returns	Description
BeginTrans	Integer	Manages transaction processing within a Connection object by beginning a new transaction.
CommitTrans		Manages transaction processing within a Connection object by saving any changes and ends the current transaction. It may also start a new transaction.
RollBackTrans		Manages transaction processing within a Connection object by cancelling any changes made during the current transaction and ends the transaction. It may also start a new transaction.
Cancel		Cancels execution of a pending, asynchronous Execute or Open method call.
Close		Closes an open object and any dependent objects.
Execute	Recordset Object	Executes the specified query, SQL statement, stored procedure, or provider-specific text.
Open		Opens a connection to a data source.
OpenSchema	Recordset Object	Obtains database schema information from the provider.
Save		Saves (persists) the Recordset in a file or Stream object.

Properties

Name	Returns	Description
Attributes	Long	Indicates one or more characteristics of an object. Default is 0.
CommandTimeout	Long	Indicates how long to wait, in seconds, while executing a command before terminating the attempt and generating an error. Default is 30.
ConnectionString	String	Contains the information used to establish a connection to a data source.
ConnectionTimeout	Long	Indicates how long to wait, in seconds, while establishing a connection before terminating the attempt and generating an error. Default is 15.
CursorLocation	CusorLocationEnum	Sets or returns the location of the cursor service.
DefaultDatabase	String	Indicates the default database for a Connection object.
Errors	Errors	Contains all the Error objects created in response to a single failure involving the provider.
IsolationLevel	IsolationLevelEnum	Indicates the level of isolation for a Connection object.
Mode	ConnectModeEnum	Indicates the available permissions for modifying data in a Connection, Record, or Stream object.
Properties	Properties	Contains all of the Property objects for a Connection object.
Provider	String	Indicates the name of the provider for a Connection object.
State	Long	Indicates for all applicable objects whether the state of the object is open or closed.
Version	String	Indicates the ADO version number.

Events

Name	Description
BeginTransComplete	Fired after a BeginTrans operation finishes executing.
CommitTransComplete	Fired after a CommitTrans operation finishes executing.
ConnectComplete	Fired after a connection starts.
Disconnect	Fired after a connection ends.
ExecuteComplete	Fired after a command has finished executing.
InfoMessage	Fired whenever a ConnectionEvent operation completes successfully and additional information is returned by the provider.
RollbackTransComplete	Fired after a RollbackTrans operation finished executing.
WillConnect	Fired before a connection starts.
WillExecute	Fired before a pending command executes on the connection.

Error Object

An Error object contains details about data access errors pertaining to a single operation involving the provider.

Properties

Name	Returns	Description
Description	String	Describes an Error object.
HelpContext	Integer	Indicates the Context ID in the help file and topic associated with an Error object.
HelpFile	String	Indicates the name of the help file and topic associated with an Error object.
NativeError	Long	Indicates the provider-specific error code for a given Error object.
Number	Long	Indicates the number that uniquely identifies an Error object.
Source	String	Indicates the name of the object or application that originally generated an error.
SQLState	String	Indicates the SQL state for a given Error object.

Errors Collection

Contains all the Error objects created in response to a single failure involving the provider.

Methods

Name	Returns	Description
Clear		Removes all of the objects in a collection.
Refresh		Updates the objects in a collection to reflect objects available from and specific to the provider.

Properties

Name	Returns	Description
Count	Long	Indicates the number of objects in a collection.
Item	Error	Returns a specific member of a collection by name or ordinal number.

Field Object

A Field object represents a column of data with a common data type.

Methods

Name	Returns	Description
AppendChunk		Appends data to a large text or binary data Field object.
GetChunk	Variant	Returns all, or a portion of the contents, of a large text or binary data Field object.

Properties

Name	Returns	Description
ActualSize	Long	Indicates the actual length of a field's value.
Attributes	Long	Indicates one or more characteristics of an object.
DataFormat	Variant	Identifies the format that the data should be displayed in.
DefinedSize	Long	Indicates the defined size of a Field object.
Name	String	Indicates the name of an object.

Name	Returns	Description
NumericScale	Byte	Indicates the scale of numeric values in a Parameter or Field object.
OriginalValue	Variant	Indicates the value of a Field that existed in the record before any changes were made.
Properties	Properties	Contains all of the Property objects for a Field object.
Precision	Byte	Indicates the degree of precision for numeric values in a Parameter object or for numeric Field objects.
Type	DataTypeEnum	Indicates the operational type or data type of a Field object.
UnderlyingValue	Variant	Indicates a Field object's current value in the database.
Value	Variant	Indicates the value assigned to a Field object.

Fields Collection

Contains all the Field objects of a Recordset or Record object.

Methods

Name	Returns	Description
Append		Appends an object to a collection. If the collection is Fields, a new Field object may be created before it is appended to the collection.
CancelUpdate		Cancels any changes made to the Fields collection.
Delete		Deletes an object from the Fields collection.
Refresh		Updates the objects in a collection to reflect objects available from and specific to the provider.
Resync		Resynchronizes the data in the Field object.
Update		Saves any changes you make to the Fields Collection.

Properties

Name	Returns	Description
`Count`	`Long`	Indicates the number of objects in a collection.
`Item`	Field	Returns a specific member of a collection by name or ordinal number.

Property Object

A `Property` object represents a dynamic characteristic of an ADO object that is defined by the provider.

Properties

Name	Returns	Description
`Attributes`	`Long`	Indicates one or more characteristics of an object.
`Name`	`String`	Indicates the name of an object.
`Type`	`DataTypeEnum`	Indicates the operational type or data type of a `Property` object.
`Value`	`Variant`	Indicates the value assigned to a `Property` object.

Properties Collection

Contains all the `Property` objects for a specific instance of an object.

Methods

Name	Returns	Description
`Refresh`		Updates the objects in a collection to reflect objects available from and specific to the provider.

Properties

Name	Returns	Description
`Count`	`Long`	Indicates the number of objects in a collection.
`Item`	`Property`	Returns a specific member of a collection by name or ordinal number.

Parameter

A `Parameter` object represents a parameter or argument associated with a `Command` object based on a parameterized query or stored procedure.

Methods

Name	Returns	Description
`AppendChunk`		Appends data to a large text or binary data `Parameter` object.
`Delete`		Deletes an object from the `Parameters` collection.

Properties

Name	Returns	Description
`Attributes`	`Long`	Indicates one or more characteristics of an object.
`Direction`	`ParameterDirectionEnum`	Indicates whether the `Parameter` represents an input parameter, an output parameter, or both, or if the parameter is the return value from a stored procedure.
`Name`	`String`	Indicates the name of an object.
`NumericScale`	`Byte`	Indicates the scale of numeric values in a `Parameter` object.
`Precision`	`Byte`	Indicates the degree of precision for numeric values in a `Parameter` object.
`Properties`	`Properties`	Contains all of the `Property` objects for a `Parameter` object.
`Size`	`Long`	Indicates the maximum size, in bytes or characters, of a `Parameter` object.
`Type`	`DataTypeEnum`	Indicates the operational type or data type of a `Parameter` object.
`Value`	`Variant`	Indicates the value assigned to a `Parameter` object.

Parameters Collection

Contains all the `Parameter` objects of a `Command` object.

Methods

Name	Returns	Description
Append		Appends an object to a collection.
Delete		Deletes an object from the Parameters collection.
Refresh		Updates the objects in a collection to reflect objects available from and specific to the Provider.

Properties

Name	Returns	Description
Count	Long	Indicates the number of objects in a collection.
Item	Parameter	Returns a specific member of a collection by name or ordinal number.

Record

The Record object represents a row in a Recordset, or a file or directory in a file system.

Methods

Name	Returns	Description
Cancel		Cancels execution of a pending, asynchronous Execute or Open method call.
Close		Closes an open object and any dependent objects.
CopyRecord	String	Copies a file or directory, and its contents, to another location.
DeleteRecord		Deletes a file or directory, and all its subdirectories.
GetChildren	Recordset Object	Returns a Recordset whose rows represent the files and subdirectories in the directory represented by this Record.
MoveRecord	String	Moves a file, or a directory and its contents, to another location.
Open		Opens an existing Record object, or creates a new file or directory.

Properties

Name	Returns	Description
ActiveConnection	Variant	Indicates to which Connection object the specified Command, Recordset, or Record object currently belongs.
Fields	Fields	Contains all of the Field objects for the current Recordset object.
Mode	ConnectModeEnum	Indicates the available permissions for modifying data in a Conection, Record, or Stream object.
ParentURL	String	Returns an absolute URL string pointing to the parent Record of the current Record object.
Properties	Properties	Contains all of the Property objects for the current Recordset object.
RecordType	RecordTypeEnum	Indicates the type of Record object.
Source	Variant	Indicates the entity represented by the Record object.
State	ObjectStateEnum	Indicates for all applicable objects whether the state of the object is open or closed.

Recordset

A Recordset object represents the entire set of records from a base table or the results of an executed command. At any time, the Recordset object refers to only a single record within the set as the current record.

Methods

Name	Returns	Description
AddNew		Creates a new record for an updatable Recordset object.
Cancel		Cancels execution of a pending, asynchronous Execute or Open method call.
CancelBatch		Cancels a pending batch update.
CancelUpdate		Cancels any changes made to the current record or to a new record prior to calling the Update method.

Name	Returns	Description
Clone	Recordset Object	Creates a duplicate Recordset object from an existing Recordset object. Optionally, specifies that the clone be read-only.
Close		Closes an open object and any dependent objects.
CompareBookmarks	CompareEnum	Compares two bookmarks and returns an indication of their relative values.
Delete		Deletes the current record or a group of records.
Find		Searches a Recordset for the row that satisfies the specified criteria. Optionally, the direction of the search, starting row, and offset from the starting row may be specified. If the criteria is met, the current row position is set on the found record; otherwise, the position is set at the end (or start) of the Recordset.
GetRows	Variant	Retrieves multiple records of a Recordset object into an array.
GetString	String	Returns the Recordset as a string variant.
Move		Moves the position of the current record in a Recordset object.
MoveFirst		Moves to the first record in a specified Recordset object and makes that record the current record.
MoveLast		Moves to the last record in a specified Recordset object and makes that record the current record.
MoveNext		Moves to the next record in a specified Recordset object and makes that record the current record.
MovePrevious		Moves to the previous record in a specified Recordset object and makes that record the current record.
NextRecordset	Recordset Object	Clears the current Recordset object and returns the next Recordset by advancing through a series of commands.
Open		Opens a Recordset.
Requery		Updates the data in a Recordset object by re-executing the query on which the object is based.
Resync		Refreshes the data in the current Recordset object from the underlying database.

Name	Returns	Description
Save		Saves (persists) the Recordset in a file or Stream object.
Seek		Searches the index of a Recordset to quickly locate the row that matches the specified values, and changes the current row position to that row.
Supports	Boolean	Determines whether a specified Recordset object supports a particular type of functionality.
Update		Saves any changes you make to the current record of a Recordset object.
UpdateBatch		Writes all pending batch updates to disk.

Properties

Name	Returns	Description
AbsolutePage	PositionEnum	Specifies on which page the current record resides.
AbsolutePosition	PositionEnum	Specifies the ordinal position of a Recordset object's current record.
ActiveCommand	Object	Indicates the Command object that created the associated Recordset object.
ActiveConnection	Variant	Indicates to which Connection object the specified Command, Recordset, or Record object currently belongs.
BOF	Boolean	Indicates that the current record position is before the first record in a Recordset object.
EOF	Boolean	Indicates that the current record position is after the last record in a Recordset object.
Bookmark	Variant	Returns a bookmark that uniquely identifies the current record in a Recordset object or sets the current record in a Recordset object to the record identified by a valid bookmark.
CacheSize	Long	Indicates the number of records from a Recordset object that are cached locally in memory.
CursorLocation	CursorLocationEnum	Sets or returns the location of the cursor service.

Name	Returns	Description
CursorType	CursorTypeEnum	Indicates the type of cursor used in a Recordset object.
DataMember	String	Specifies the name of the data member to retrieve from the object referenced by the DataSource property.
DataSource	Object	Specifies an object containing data to be represented as a Recordset object.
EditMode	EditModeEnum	Indicates the editing status of the current record.
Fields	Fields	Contains all the Field objects for the current Recordset object.
Filter	Variant	Specifies a filter for data in a Recordset.
Index	String	Indicates the name of the index currently in effect for a Recordset object.
LockType	LockTypeEnum	Indicates the type of locks placed on records during editing.
MarshalOptions	MarshalOptionsEnum	Indicates which records are to be marshaled back to the server.
MaxRecords	Long	Indicates the maximum number of records to return to a Recordset from a query.
PageCount	Long	Indicates how many pages of data the Recordset object contains.
PageSize	Long	Indicates how many records constitute one page in the Recordset.
Properties	Properties	Contains all of the Property objects for the current Recordset object.
RecordCount	Long	Indicates the current number of records in a Recordset object.
Sort	String	Specifies one or more field names on which the Recordset is sorted, and whether each field is sorted in ascending or descending order.
Source	String	Indicates the source for the data in a Recordset object (Command object, SQL statement, table name, or stored procedure).
State	Long	Indicates for all applicable objects whether the state of the object is open or closed.

Name	Returns	Description
`Status`	`Integer`	Indicates the status of the current record with respect to batch updates or other bulk operations.
`StayInSync`	`Boolean`	Indicates, in a hierarchical `Recordset` object, whether the reference to the underlying child records (that is, the *chapter*) changes when the parent row position changes.

Events

Name	Description
`EndOfRecordset`	Fired when there is an attempt to move to a row past the end of the Recordset.
`FetchComplete`	Fired after all the records in an asynchronous operation have been retrieved into the Recordset.
`FetchProgress`	Fired periodically during a length asynchronous operation, to report how many rows have currently been retrieved.
`FieldChangeComplete`	Fired after the value of one or more `Field` object has been changed.
`MoveComplete`	Fired after the current position in the Recordset changes.
`RecordChangeComplete`	Fired after one or more records change.
`RecordsetChangeComplete`	Fired after the Recordset has changed.
`WillChangeField`	Fired before a pending operation changes the value of one or more Field objects.
`WillChangeRecord`	Fired before one or more rows in the Recordset change.
`WillChangeRecordset`	Fired before a pending operation changes the Recordset.
`WillMove`	Fired before a pending operation changes the current position in the Recordset.

Stream

A `Stream` object represents a stream of binary data or text.

Methods

Name	Returns	Description
`Cancel`		Cancels execution of a pending, asynchronous `Execute` or `Open` method call.
`Close`		Closes an open object and any dependent objects.

Name	Returns	Description
CopyTo		Copies the specified number of characters or bytes (depending on Type) in the Stream to another Stream object.
Flush		Forces the contents of the Stream remaining in the ADO buffer to the underlying object with which the Stream is associated.
LoadFromFile		Loads the contents of an existing file into a Stream.
Open		Opens a Stream object to manipulate streams of binary or text data.
Read	Variant	Reads a specified number of bytes from a binary Stream object.
ReadText	String	Reads specified number of characters from a text Stream object.
SaveToFile		Saves the binary contents of a Stream to a file.
SetEOS		Sets the position that is the end of the Stream.
SkipLine		Skips one entire line when reading a text Stream.
Write		Writes binary data to a Stream object.
WriteText		Writes a specified text string to a Stream object.

Properties

Name	Returns	Description
Charset	String	Specifies the character set into which the contents of a text Stream should be translated.
EOS	Boolean	Identifies whether the current position is at the end of the Stream.
LineSeparator	LineSeparatorsEnum	Specifies the character to be used as the line separator in a text Stream.
Mode	ConnectModeEnum	Indicates the available permissions for modifying data in a Connection, Record, or Stream object.
Position	Long	Specifies the current position within a Stream object.
Size	Long	Indicates the total size of the Stream in number of bytes.
State	ObjectStateEnum	Indicates for all applicable objects whether the state of the object is open or closed.
Type	StreamTypeEnum	Identifies the type of data contained in the Stream (binary or text).

Constants

The following constants are predefined by ADO.

> **Constants new to ADO 2.5 are shown *italicized*. At the time of writing some of these were undocumented and so we have guessed the descriptions. For these we have added a * character to the end of the description.**

AffectEnum

Name	Value	Description
adAffectAll	3	Operation affects all records in the recordset.
adAffectAllChapters	4	Operation affects all child (chapter) records.
adAffectCurrent	1	Operation affects only the current record.
adAffectGroup	2	Operation affects records that satisfy the current `Filter` property.

BookmarkEnum

Name	Value	Description
adBookmarkCurrent	0	Default. Start at the current record.
adBookmarkFirst	1	Start at the first record.
adBookmarkLast	2	Start at the last record.

CEResyncEnum

Name	Value	Description
adResyncAll	15	Resynchronizes the data for each pending row.
adResyncAutoIncrement	1	Resynchronizes the auto-increment values for all successfully inserted rows. This is the default.
adResyncConflicts	2	Resynchronizes all rows for which an update or delete operation failed due to concurrency conflicts.
adResyncInserts	8	Resynchronizes all successfully inserted rows, including the values of their identity columns.
adResyncNone	0	No resynchronization is performed.
adResyncUpdates	4	Resynchronizes all successfully updated rows.

CommandTypeEnum

Name	Value	Description
adCmdFile	256	Indicates that the provider should evaluate `CommandText` as a previously persisted file.
adCmdStoredProc	4	Indicates that the provider should evaluate `CommandText` as a stored procedure.
adCmdTable	2	Indicates that the provider should generate a SQL query to return all rows from the table named in `CommandText`.
adCmdTableDirect	512	Indicates that the provider should return all rows from the table named in `CommandText`.
adCmdText	1	Indicates that the provider should evaluate `CommandText` as textual definition of a command, such as a SQL statement.
adCmdUnknown	8	Indicates that the type of command in `CommandText` unknown.
adCmdUnspecified	-1	The command type is unspecified.

CompareEnum

Name	Value	Description
adCompareEqual	1	The bookmarks are equal.
adCompareGreaterThan	2	The first bookmark is after the second.
adCompareLessThan	0	The first bookmark is before the second.
adCompareNotComparable	4	The bookmarks cannot be compared.
adCompareNotEqual	3	The bookmarks are not equal and not ordered.

ConnectModeEnum

Name	Value	Description
adModeRead	1	Indicates read-only permissions.
adModeReadWrite	3	Indicates read/write permissions.
adModeRecursive	32	Used in conjunction with the `ShareDeny` values to propagate sharing restrictions.
adModeShareDenyNone	16	Prevents others from opening connection with any permissions.
adModeShareDenyRead	4	Prevents others from opening connection with read permissions.

Name	*Value*	*Description*
adModeShareDenyWrite	8	Prevents others from opening connection with write permissions.
adModeShareExclusive	12	Prevents others from opening connection.
adModeUnknown	0	Default. Indicates that the permissions have not yet been set or cannot be determined.
adModeWrite	2	Indicates write-only permissions.

ConnectOptionEnum

Name	*Value*	*Description*
adAsyncConnect	16	Open the connection asynchronously.
adConnectUnspecified	-1	The connection mode is unspecified.

ConnectPromptEnum

Name	*Value*	*Description*
adPromptAlways	1	Always prompt for connection information.
adPromptComplete	2	Only prompt if not enough information was supplied.
adPromptCompleteRequired	3	Only prompt if not enough information was supplied, but disable any options not directly applicable to the connection.
adPromptNever	4	Default. Never prompt for connection information.

CopyRecordOptionsEnum

Name	*Value*	*Description*
adCopyAllowEmulation	4	If the `CopyRecord` method fails, simulate it using a file download and upload mechanism.
adCopyNonRecursive	2	Copy the current directory, but not sub-directories.
adCopyOverWrite	1	Overwrite the existing file or directory.
adCopyUnspecified	-1	No copy behavior specified.

CursorLocationEnum

Name	Value	Description
adUseClient	3	Use client-side cursors supplied by the local cursor library.
adUseClientBatch	3	Use client-side cursors supplied by the local cursor library.
adUseNone	1	No cursor services are used.
adUseServer	2	Default. Uses data provider supplied cursors.

CursorOptionEnum

Name	Value	Description
adAddNew	16778240	You can use the `AddNew` method to add new records.
adApproxPosition	16384	You can read and set the `AbsolutePosition` and `AbsolutePage` properties.
adBookmark	8192	You can use the `Bookmark` property to access specific records.
adDelete	16779264	You can use the `Delete` method to delete records.
adFind	524288	You can use the `Find` method to find records.
adHoldRecords	256	You can retrieve more records or change the next retrieve position without committing all pending changes.
adIndex	8388608	You can use the `Index` property to set the current index.
adMovePrevious	512	You can use the `ModeFirst`, `MovePrevious`, `Move` and `GetRows` methods.
adNotify	262144	The recordset supports Notifications.
adResync	131072	You can update the cursor with the data visible in the underlying database with the `Resync` method.
adSeek	4194304	You can use the `Seek` method to find records by an index.
adUpdate	16809984	You can use the `Update` method to modify existing records.
adUpdateBatch	65536	You can use the `UpdateBatch` or `CancelBatch` methods to transfer changes to the provider in groups.

CursorTypeEnum

Name	*Value*	*Description*
adOpenDynamic	2	Opens a dynamic type cursor.
adOpenForwardOnly	0	Default. Opens a forward-only type cursor.
adOpenKeyset	1	Opens a keyset type cursor.
adOpenStatic	3	Opens a static type cursor.
adOpenUnspecified	-1	Indicates as unspecified value for cursor type.

DataTypeEnum

Name	*Value*	*Description*
adBigInt	20	An 8-byte signed integer.
adBinary	128	A binary value.
adBoolean	11	A Boolean value.
adBSTR	8	A null-terminated character string.
adChapter	136	A Chapter type, indicating a child recordset.
adChar	129	A String value.
adCurrency	6	A currency value. An 8-byte signed integer scaled by 10,000, with 4 digits to the right of the decimal point.
adDate	7	A Date value. A Double where the whole part is the number of days since December 30 1899, and the fractional part is a fraction of the day.
adDBDate	133	A date value (yyyymmdd).
adDBFileTime	137	A database file time.
adDBTime	134	A time value (hhmmss).
adDBTimeStamp	135	A date-time stamp (yyyymmddhhmmss plus a fraction in billionths).
adDecimal	14	An exact numeric value with fixed precision and scale.
adDouble	5	A double-precision floating point value.
adEmpty	0	No value was specified.
adError	10	A 32-bit error code.
adFileTime	64	A DOS/Win32 file time. The number of 100 nanosecond intervals since Jan 1 1601.

Name	*Value*	*Description*
adGUID	72	A globally unique identifier.
adIDispatch	9	A pointer to an `IDispatch` interface on an OLE object.
adInteger	3	A 4-byte signed integer.
adIUnknown	13	A pointer to an `IUnknown` interface on an OLE object.
adLongVarBinary	205	A long binary value.
adLongVarChar	201	A long String value.
adLongVarWChar	203	A long null-terminated string value.
adNumeric	131	An exact numeric value with a fixed precision and scale.
adPropVariant	138	A variant that is not equivalent to an Automation variant.
adSingle	4	A single-precision floating point value.
adSmallInt	2	A 2-byte signed integer.
adTinyInt	16	A 1-byte signed integer.
adUnsignedBigInt	21	An 8-byte unsigned integer.
adUnsignedInt	19	A 4-byte unsigned integer.
adUnsignedSmallInt	18	A 2-byte unsigned integer.
adUnsignedTinyInt	17	A 1-byte unsigned integer.
adUserDefined	132	A user-defined variable.
adVarBinary	204	A binary value.
adVarChar	200	A String value.
adVariant	12	An Automation Variant.
adVarNumeric	139	A variable width exact numeric, with a signed scale value.
adVarWChar	202	A null-terminated Unicode character string.
adWChar	130	A null-terminated Unicode character string.

EditModeEnum

Name	Value	Description
adEditAdd	2	Indicates that the AddNew method has been invoked and the current record in the buffer is a new record that hasn't been saved to the database.
adEditDelete	4	Indicates that the Delete method has been invoked.
adEditInProgress	1	Indicates that data in the current record has been modified but not saved.
adEditNone	0	Indicates that no editing is in progress.

ErrorValueEnum

Name	Value	Description
adErrBoundToCommand	3707	The application cannot change the ActiveConnection property of a Recordset object with a Command object as its source.
adErrCannotComplete	3732	The action could not be completed.
adErrCantChangeConnection	3748	The connection cannot be changed. *
adErrCantChangeProvider	3220	The provider cannot be changed. *
adErrCantConvertvalue	3724	The value cannot be converted. *
adErrCantCreate	3725	The resource cannot be created. *
adErrCatalogNotSet	3747	The action could not be completed because the catalog is not set. *
adErrColumnNotOnThisRow	*3726*	The specified column doesn't exist on this row. *
adErrDataConversion	3421	The application is using a value of the wrong type for the current application.
adErrDataOverflow	3721	The data was too large for the supplied data type. *
adErrDelResOutOfScope	3738	The resource cannot be deleted because it is out of the allowed scope. *
adErrDenyNotSupported	3750	You cannot set Deny permissions because the provider does not support them. *
adErrDenyTypeNotSupported	3751	The provider does not support the type of Deny requested. *
adErrFeatureNotAvailable	3251	The provider does not support the operation requested by the application.

Name	*Value*	*Description*
adErrFieldsUpdateFailed	3749	The `Update` method of the Fields collection failed.
adErrIllegalOperation	3219	The operation requested by the application is not allowed in this context.
adErrIntegrityViolation	3719	The action failed due to a violation of data integrity.
adErrInTransaction	3246	The application cannot explicitly close a `Connection` object while in the middle of a transaction.
adErrInvalidArgument	3001	The application is using arguments that are the wrong type, are out of the acceptable range, or are in conflict with one another.
adErrInvalidConnection	3709	The application requested an operation on an object with a reference to a closed or invalid `Connection` object.
adErrInvalidParamInfo	3708	The application has improperly defined a `Parameter` object.
adErrInvalidTransaction	3714	The transaction is invalid.
adErrInvalidURL	3729	The supplied URL is invalid.
adErrItemNotFound	3265	ADO could not find the object in the collection.
adErrNoCurrentRecord	3021	Either `BOF` or `EOF` is `True`, or the current record has been deleted. The operation requested by the application requires a current record.
adErrNotExecuting	3715	The operation is not executing.
adErrNotReentrant	3710	The operation is not re-entrant.
adErrObjectClosed	3704	The operation requested by the application is not allowed if the object is closed.
adErrObjectInCollection	3367	Can't append. Object already in collection.
adErrObjectNotSet	3420	The object referenced by the application no longer points to a valid object.
adErrObjectOpen	3705	The operation requested by the application is not allowed if the object is open.
adErrOpeningFile	3002	An error occurred whilst opening the requested file.
adErrOperationCancelled	3712	The operation was cancelled.
adErrOutOfSpace	3734	The operation failed because the server could not obtain enough space to complete the operation.

Name	*Value*	*Description*
adErrPermissionDenied	3720	The action failed because you do not have sufficient permission to complete the operation.
adErrPropConflicting	3742	Setting this property caused a conflict with other properties. *
adErrPropInvalidColumn	3739	This property is invalid for the selected column. *
adErrPropInvalidOption	3740	You have supplied an invalid option for this property. *
adErrPropInvalidValue	3741	You have supplied an invalid value for this property. *
adErrPropNotAllSettable	3743	Not all properties can be set. *
adErrPropNotSet	3744	The property was not set. *
adErrPropNotSettable	3745	The property cannot be set. *
adErrPropNotSupported	3746	The property is not supported. *
adErrProviderFailed	3000	The provider failed to complete the requested action. *
adErrProviderNotFound	3706	ADO could not find the specified provider.
adErrReadFile	3003	There was an error reading from the specified file. *
adErrResourceExists	3731	The resource already exists. *
adErrResourceLocked	3730	The resource is locked. *
adErrResourceOutOfScope	3735	The resource is out of scope. *
adErrSchemaViolation	3722	The action caused a violation of the schema. *
adErrSignMismatch	3723	The expression contained mismatched signs. *
adErrStillConnecting	3713	The operation is still connecting.
adErrStillExecuting	3711	The operation is still executing.
adErrTreePermissionDenied	3728	You do not have permission to view the directory tree. *
adErrUnavailable	3736	The command is unavailable. *
adErrUnsafeOperation	3716	The operation is unsafe under these circumstances.
adErrURLDoesNotExist	3727	The URL does not exist. *
adErrURLNamedRowDoesNotExist	3737	The URL in the named row does not exists. *

Name	Value	Description
adErrVolumeNotFound	3733	The file volume was not found. *
adErrWriteFile	3004	There was an error whilst writing to the file. *
adwrnSecurityDialog	3717	The operation caused a security dialog to appear. *
adwrnSecurityDialogHeader	3718	The operation caused a security dialog header to appear. *

EventReasonEnum

Name	Value	Description
adRsnAddNew	1	A new record is to be added.
adRsnClose	9	The object is being closed.
adRsnDelete	2	The record is being deleted.
adRsnFirstChange	11	The record has been changed for the first time.
adRsnMove	10	A `Move` has been invoked and the current record pointer is being moved.
adRsnMoveFirst	12	A `MoveFirst` has been invoked and the current record pointer is being moved.
adRsnMoveLast	15	A `MoveLast` has been invoked and the current record pointer is being moved.
adRsnMoveNext	13	A `MoveNext` has been invoked and the current record pointer is being moved.
adRsnMovePrevious	14	A `MovePrevious` has been invoked and the current record pointer is being moved.
adRsnRequery	7	The recordset was requeried.
adRsnResynch	8	The recordset was resynchronized.
adRsnUndoAddNew	5	The addition of a new record has been cancelled.
adRsnUndoDelete	6	The deletion of a record has been cancelled.
adRsnUndoUpdate	4	The update of a record has been cancelled.
adRsnUpdate	3	The record is being updated.

EventStatusEnum

Name	*Value*	*Description*
adStatusCancel	4	Request cancellation of the operation that is about to occur.
adStatusCantDeny	3	A `Will` event cannot request cancellation of the operation about to occur.
adStatusErrorsOccurred	2	The operation completed unsuccessfully, or a `Will` event cancelled the operation.
adStatusOK	1	The operation completed successfully.
adStatusUnwantedEvent	5	Events for this operation are no longer required.

ExecuteOptionEnum

Name	*Value*	*Description*
adAsyncExecute	16	The operation is executed asynchronously.
adAsyncFetch	32	The records are fetched asynchronously.
adAsyncFetchNonBlocking	64	The records are fetched asynchronously without blocking subsequent operations.
adExecuteNoRecords	128	Indicates `CommandText` is a command or stored procedure that does not return rows. Always combined with `adCmdText` or `adCmdStoreProc`.

FieldAttributeEnum

Name	*Value*	*Description*
adFldCacheDeferred	4096	Indicates that the provider caches field values and that subsequent reads are done from the cache.
adFldFixed	16	Indicates that the field contains fixed-length data.
adFldIsChapter	8192	The field is a chapter field, and contains a rowset.
adFldIsCollection	262144	The field is a collection.
adFldIsDefaultStream	131072	The field is the default Stream.
adFldIsNullable	32	Indicates that the field accepts Null values.
adFldIsRowURL	65536	The field is a URL.

Name	*Value*	*Description*
adFldKeyColumn	32768	The field is part of a key column.
adFldLong	128	Indicates that the field is a long binary field, and that the `AppendChunk` and `GetChunk` methods can be used.
adFldMayBeNull	64	Indicates that you can read Null values from the field.
adFldMayDefer	2	Indicates that the field is deferred, that is, the field values are not retrieved from the data source with the whole record, but only when you access them.
adFldNegativeScale	16384	The field has a negative scale.
adFldRowID	256	Indicates that the field has some kind of record ID.
adFldRowVersion	512	Indicates that the field time or date stamp is used to track updates.
adFldUnknownUpdatable	8	Indicates that the provider cannot determine if you can write to the field.
adFldUnspecified	-1	Attributes of the field are unspecified.
adFldUpdatable	4	Indicates that you can write to the field.

FieldEnum

Name	*Value*	*Description*
adDefaultStream	-1	When used as the index into the `Fields` collection of a record, returns the default `Stream` for the `Record`.
adRecordURL	-2	When used as the index into the `Fields` collection of a record, returns the absolute URL for the `Record`.

FieldStatusEnum

Name	*Value*	*Description*
adFieldAlreadyExists	26	The field already exists. *
adFieldBadStatus	12	The field has a bad Status value. *
adFieldCannotComplete	20	The action cannot be completed. *
adFieldCannotDeleteSource	23	The field cannot delete the source of the field. *
adFieldCantConvertValue	2	The field cannot convert the value. *

Name	Value	Description
adFieldCantCreate	7	The field cannot be created. *
adFieldDataOverflow	6	The data is too long to fit in the field. *
adFieldDefault	13	The default value has been used *
adFieldDoesNotExist	16	The field does not exist. *
adFieldIgnore	15	The field has been ignored *
adFieldIntegrityViolation	10	The field update failed with a data integrity violation. *
adFieldInvalidURL	17	The field contains an invalid URL. *
adFieldIsNull	3	The field is null. *
adFieldOK	0	The field is OK. *
adFieldOutOfSpace	22	The field ran out of space for storage. *
adFieldPendingChange	262144	The field has been changed, but the provider has not yet been updated. *
adFieldPendingDelete	131072	The field has been deleted, but the provider has not yet been updated. *
adFieldPendingInsert	65536	The field has been inserted, but the provider has not yet been updated. *
adFieldPendingUnknown	524288	The field has been changed, but it is not known what sort of change it was. *
adFieldPendingUnknownDelete	1048576	The field has been changed, but the field might have been deleted. *
adFieldPermissionDenied	9	Permission to modify the field failed due to access permissions. *
adFieldReadOnly	24	The field is read only. *
adFieldResourceExists	19	The resource specified by the field already exists. *
adFieldResourceLocked	18	The resource specified by the field is locked. *
adFieldResourceOutOfScope	25	The resource specified by the field is out of scope. *
adFieldSchemaViolation	11	The field update failed due to a schema violation. *
adFieldSignMismatch	5	The field contained mismatched signs. *

Name	Value	Description
adFieldTruncated	4	The field value was truncated. *
adFieldUnavailable	8	The field is unavailable. *
adFieldVolumeNotFound	21	The volume specified by the field was not found. *

FilterGroupEnum

Name	Value	Description
adFilterAffectedRecords	2	Allows you to view only records affected by the last `Delete`, `Resync`, `UpdateBatch`, or `CancelBatch` method.
adFilterConflictingRecords	5	Allows you to view the records that failed the last batch update attempt.
adFilterFetchedRecords	3	Allows you to view records in the current cache.
adFilterNone	0	Removes the current filter and restores all records to view.
adFilterPendingRecords	1	Allows you to view only the records that have changed but have not been sent to the server. Only applicable for batch update mode.
adFilterPredicate	4	Allows you to view records that failed the last batch update attempt.

GetRowsOptionEnum

Name	Value	Description
adGetRowsRest	-1	Retrieves the remainder of the rows in the recordset.

IsolationLevelEnum

Name	Value	Description
adXactBrowse	256	Indicates that from one transaction you can view uncommitted changes in other transactions.
adXactChaos	16	Default. Indicates that you cannot overwrite pending changes from more highly isolated transactions.
adXactCursorStability	4096	Default. Indicates that from one transaction you can view changes in other transactions only after they have been committed.

Name	*Value*	*Description*
adXactIsolated	1048576	Indicates that transactions are conducted in isolation of other transactions.
adXactReadCommitted	4096	Same as `adXactCursorStability`.
adXactReadUncommitted	256	Same as `adXactBrowse`.
adXactRepeatableRead	65536	Indicates that from one transaction you cannot see changes made in other transactions, but that requerying can bring new recordsets.
adXactSerializable	1048576	Same as `adXactIsolated`.
adXactUnspecified	-1	Indicates that the provider is using a different `IsolationLevel` than specified, but that the level cannot be identified.

LineSeparatorEnum

Name	*Value*	*Description*
adCR	13	The carriage-return character.
adCRLF	-1	The carriage-return and line-feed characters.
adLF	10	The line-feed character.

LockTypeEnum

Name	*Value*	*Description*
adLockBatchOptimistic	4	Optimistic batch updates.
adLockOptimistic	3	Optimistic locking, record-by-record. The provider locks records when `Update` is called.
adLockPessimistic	2	Pessimistic locking, record-by-record. The provider locks the record immediately upon editing.
adLockReadOnly	1	Default. Read only, data cannot be modified.
adLockUnspecified	-1	The clone is created with the same lock type as the original.

MarshalOptionsEnum

Name	*Value*	*Description*
adMarshalAll	0	Default. Indicates that all rows are returned to the server.
adMarshalModifiedOnly	1	Indicates that only modified rows are returned to the server.

MoveRecordOptionsEnum

Name	*Value*	*Description*
adMoveAllowEmulation	4	If the attempt to move the record fails, allow the move to be performed using a download, upload and delete set of operations.
adMoveDontUpdateLinks	2	Do not update hyperlinks of the source Record.
adMoveOverWrite	1	Overwrite the target if it already exists.

ObjectStateEnum

Name	*Value*	*Description*
adStateClosed	0	Default. Indicates that the object is closed.
adStateConnecting	2	Indicates that the object is connecting.
adStateExecuting	4	Indicates that the object is executing a command.
adStateFetching	8	Indicates that the rows of the recordset are being fetched.
adStateOpen	1	Indicates that the object is open.

ParameterAttributesEnum

Name	*Value*	*Description*
adParamLong	128	Indicates that the parameter accepts long binary data.
adParamNullable	64	Indicates that the parameter accepts Null values.
adParamSigned	16	Default. Indicates that the parameter accepts signed values.

ParameterDirectionEnum

Name	*Value*	*Description*
adParamInput	1	Default. Indicates an input parameter.
adParamInputOutput	3	Indicates both an input and output parameter.
adParamOutput	2	Indicates an output parameter.
adParamReturnValue	4	Indicates a return value.
adParamUnknown	0	Indicates parameter direction is unknown.

PersistFormatEnum

Name	Value	Description
adPersistADTG	0	Default. Persist data in Advanced Data TableGram format.
adPersistXML	1	Persist data in XML format.

PositionEnum

Name	Value	Description
adPosBOF	-2	The current record pointer is at `BOF`.
adPosEOF	-3	The current record pointer is at `EOF`.
adPosUnknown	-1	The Recordset is empty, the current position is unknown, or the provider does not support the `AbsolutePage` property.

PropertyAttributesEnum

Name	Value	Description
adPropNotSupported	0	Indicates that the property is not supported by the provider.
adPropOptional	2	Indicates that the user does not need to specify a value for this property before the data source is initialized.
adPropRead	512	Indicates that the user can read the property.
adPropRequired	1	Indicates that the user must specify a value for this property before the data source is initialized.
adPropWrite	1024	Indicates that the user can set the property.

RecordCreateOptionsEnum

Name	Value	Description
adCreateCollection	8192	Create a new collection record (directory) at the specified URL.
adCreateNonCollection	0	Create a new record at the specified URL.
adCreateOverwrite	67108864	Overwrite any existing record at the specified URL.
adCreateStructDoc	-2147483648	Create a new structured document record at the specified URL.
adFailIfNotExists	-1	Fail if the URL does not exist.
adOpenIfExists	33554432	Open the record at the specified URL if it exists.

RecordOpenOptionsEnum

Name	Value	Description
adDelayFetchFields	32768	Delay fetching fields until they are requested.
adDelayFetchStream	16384	Delay fetching the Stream until it is requested.
adOpenAsync	4096	Open the Record asynchronously.
adOpenSource	8388608	Open the source document at the URL, rather than the executed contents.
adOpenURLBind	1024	Indicates the connection string contains a URL.

RecordStatusEnum

Name	Value	Description
adRecCanceled	256	The record was not saved because the operation was cancelled.
adRecCantRelease	1024	The new record was not saved because of existing record locks.
adRecConcurrencyViolation	2048	The record was not saved because optimistic concurrency was in use.
adRecDBDeleted	262144	The record has already been deleted from the data source.
adRecDeleted	4	The record was deleted.
adRecIntegrityViolation	4096	The record was not saved because the user violated integrity constraints.
adRecInvalid	16	The record was not saved because its bookmark is invalid.
adRecMaxChangesExceeded	8192	The record was not saved because there were too many pending changes.
adRecModified	2	The record was modified.
adRecMultipleChanges	64	The record was not saved because it would have affected multiple records.
adRecNew	1	The record is new.
adRecObjectOpen	16384	The record was not saved because of a conflict with an open storage object.
adRecOK	0	The record was successfully updated.
adRecOutOfMemory	32768	The record was not saved because the computer has run out of memory.

Name	Value	Description
adRecPendingChanges	128	The record was not saved because it refers to a pending insert.
adRecPermissionDenied	65536	The record was not saved because the user has insufficient permissions.
adRecSchemaViolation	131072	The record was not saved because it violates the structure of the underlying database.
adRecUnmodified	8	The record was not modified.

RecordTypeEnum

Name	Value	Description
adCollectionRecord	1	The record is a collection type (directory)
adSimpleRecord	0	The record is a simple file.
adStructDoc	2	The record is a structured document.

ResyncEnum

Name	Value	Description
adResyncAllValues	2	Default. Data is overwritten and pending updates are cancelled.
adResyncUnderlyingValues	1	Data is not overwritten and pending updates are not cancelled.

SaveOptionsEnum

Name	Value	Description
adSaveCreateNotExist	1	Create a new file if the file does not already exist.
adSaveCreateOverWrite	2	Overwrite any existing file if it exists.

SchemaEnum

Name	Value	Description
adSchemaAsserts	0	Request assert information.
adSchemaCatalogs	1	Request catalog information.
adSchemaCharacterSets	2	Request character set information.
adSchemaCheckConstraints	5	Request check constraint information.

Name	*Value*	*Description*
adSchemaCollations	3	Request collation information.
adSchemaColumnPrivileges	13	Request column privilege information.
adSchemaColumns	4	Request column information.
adSchemaColumnsDomainUsage	11	Request column domain usage information.
adSchemaConstraintColumnUsage	6	Request column constraint usage information.
adSchemaConstraintTableUsage	7	Request table constraint usage information.
adSchemaCubes	32	For multi-dimensional data, view the Cubes schema.
adSchemaDBInfoKeywords	30	Request the keywords from the provider.
adSchemaDBInfoLiterals	31	Request the literals from the provider.
adSchemaDimensions	33	For multi-dimensional data, view the Dimensions schema.
adSchemaForeignKeys	27	Request foreign key information.
adSchemaHierarchies	34	For multi-dimensional data, view the Hierarchies schema.
adSchemaIndexes	12	Request index information.
adSchemaKeyColumnUsage	8	Request key column usage information.
adSchemaLevels	35	For multi-dimensional data, view the Levels schema.
adSchemaMeasures	36	For multi-dimensional data, view the Measures schema.
adSchemaMembers	38	For multi-dimensional data, view the Members schema.
adSchemaPrimaryKeys	28	Request primary key information.
adSchemaProcedureColumns	29	Request stored procedure column information.
adSchemaProcedureParameters	26	Request stored procedure parameter information.
adSchemaProcedures	16	Request stored procedure information.
adSchemaProperties	37	For multi-dimensional data, view the Properties schema.
adSchemaProviderSpecific	-1	Request provider specific information.
adSchemaProviderTypes	22	Request provider type information.
adSchemaReferentialConstraints	9	Request referential constraint information.

Name	Value	Description
adSchemaSchemata	17	Request schema information.
adSchemaSQLLanguages	18	Request SQL language support information.
adSchemaStatistics	19	Request statistics information.
adSchemaTableConstraints	10	Request table constraint information.
adSchemaTablePrivileges	14	Request table privilege information.
adSchemaTables	20	Request information about the tables.
adSchemaTranslations	21	Request character set translation information.
adSchemaTrustees	39	Request trustee information.
adSchemaUsagePrivileges	15	Request user privilege information.
adSchemaViewColumnUsage	24	Request column usage in views information.
adSchemaViews	23	Request view information.
adSchemaViewTableUsage	25	Request table usage in views information.

SearchDirectionEnum

Name	Value	Description
adSearchBackward	-1	Search backward from the current record.
adSearchForward	1	Search forward from the current record.

SeekEnum

Name	Value	Description
adSeekAfter	8	Seek the key just after the match.
adSeekAfterEQ	4	Seek the key equal to or just after the match.
adSeekBefore	32	See the key just before the match.
adSeekBeforeEQ	16	Seek the key equal to or just before the match.
adSeekFirstEQ	1	Seek the first key equal to the match.
adSeekLastEQ	2	Seek the last key equal to the match.

StreamOpenOptionsEnum

Name	Value	Description
adOpenStreamAsync	1	Opens the Stream asynchronously.
adOpenStreamFromRecord	4	Opens the Stream using an existing Record as the source.
adOpenStreamFromURL	8	Opens the Stream using a URL as the source.

StreamReadEnum

Name	Value	Description
adReadAll	-1	Reads all bytes from the Stream, from the current position to the end of the stream.
adReadLine	-2	Reads the next line from the Stream. Uses the `LineSeparator` property to identify the end of the line.

StreamTypeEnum

Name	Value	Description
adTypeBinary	1	The Stream contains binary data.
adTypeText	2	The Stream contains text data.

StreamWriteEnum

Name	Value	Description
adWriteChar	0	Writes the specified string to the Stream.
adWriteLine	1	Writes the specified string and a line separator to the Stream.
stWriteChar	0	Writes the specified string to the Stream.
stWriteLine	1	Writes the specified string and a line separator to the Stream.

StringFormatEnum

Name	Value	Description
adClipString	2	Rows are delimited by user-defined values.

XactAttributeEnum

Name	*Value*	*Description*
adXactAbortRetaining	262144	The provider will automatically start a new transaction after a `RollbackTrans` method call.
adXactAsyncPhaseOne	524288	Perform an asynchronous commit.
adXactCommitRetaining	131072	The provider will automatically start a new transaction after a `CommitTrans` method call.
adXactSyncPhaseOne	1048576	Performs a synchronous commit.

WROX AUTO WORKS RACING

SQL Server Functions

The T-SQL functions available in SQL Server 7.0 fall into 10 categories:

- String Functions
- System Functions
- Date and Time Functions
- Aggregate Functions
- Cursor Functions
- Mathematical Functions
- Metadata Functions
- Rowset Functions
- Security Functions
- Text and Image Functions

This Appendix lists the functions for the first four of these categories.

String Functions

ASCII

Returns the ASCII value for the first character of a string.

```
ASCII(string_expression)
```

`string_expression` is a column name that contains character data or a character variable such as a `VarChar` data type.

The following example contains the name Michael in the `First_Name_VC` column and returns the integer value shown:

```
SELECT ASCII(First_Name_VC)
        FROM Customer_T
        WHERE Customer_ID = 16

------------------------------------------------
77
```

CHAR

Converts an integer ASCII value to a character.

```
CHAR(integer_expression)
```

`integer_expression` is any value, numeric value or numeric variable.

The following example converts the value contained in the variable and returns the results shown below:

```
DECLARE @variable INT
SELECT @variable = 77
SELECT CHAR(@variable)

------------------------------------
M
```

CHARINDEX

Finds the starting position of an expression in a string.

```
CHARINDEX(expression1, expression2, starting_position)
```

`expression1` is the string to search for.

`expression2` is the string to be searched, usually a column.

`starting_position` is an optional starting position to start the search. If not present, or anything other than a positive number, the search starts at position 1.

The following code searches the `First_Name_VC` column, which contains the name Michael, for the starting position of the string `ael`. The results are listed below:

```
SELECT CHARINDEX('ael',First_Name_VC)
        FROM Customer_T
        WHERE Customer_ID = 16

-----------------------------------------------
5
```

DIFFERENCE

Returns an integer value indicating the difference between two SOUNDEX values.

```
DIFFERENCE(string_expression1, string_expression2)
```

`string_expression1` is a `Char` or `VarChar` string.

`string_expression2` is a `Char` or `VarChar` string.

A return value of 0 through 4 is returned, with 4 indicating the highest possible match. That is, if two expressions sound identical a value of 4 will be returned; if there is no similarity a value of 0 is returned.

The following code example shows three `DIFFERENCE` functions. The first example compares the two string expressions, which are identical, and the result of 4 is returned. The second example returns a value of 3, which indicates the string expressions are very similar. The last example returns a value of 2, which indicates there is a slight match between the two strings. The two strings compared in this example contain the string Michael in the `First_Name_VC` column and the string Dell in the `Last_Name_VC` column. Notice that the last two characters in each column match:

```
SELECT DIFFERENCE('michael', 'michael')
SELECT DIFFERENCE('michael', 'mike')
SELECT DIFFERENCE(first_name_vc, last_name_vc)
        FROM Customer_T
        WHERE Customer_ID = 16

-----------------------------------------------------------------
4
-----------------------------------------------------------------
3
-----------------------------------------------------------------
2
```

LEFT

Returns the left portion of a string expression.

```
LEFT(string_expression, integer_expression)
```

`string_expression` is a variable or string expression that contains the text.

`integer_expression` is the number of characters on the left side of the string to be returned.

The following example returns the left 5 characters of the `First_Name_VC` column and the results are shown below:

```
SELECT LEFT(First_Name_VC, 5)
        FROM Customer_T
        WHERE Customer_ID = 16

---------------------------------------------
Micha
```

LEN

Returns the number of characters in a string.

```
LEN(string_expression)
```

`string_expression` is a variable or string expression that contains the text.

The following example returns the length of the string contained in the `First_Name_VC` column, which contains the name Michael:

```
SELECT LEN(First_Name_VC)
          FROM Customer_T
          WHERE Customer_ID = 16

------------------------------------------------
7
```

LOWER

Converts a string to all lower case letters.

```
LOWER(string_expression)
```

`string_expression` is a variable or string expression that contains the text.

The following example converts the name Michael that is contained in the `First_Name_VC` column to all lower case letters. The results are displayed below:

```
SELECT LOWER(First_Name_VC)
          FROM Customer_T
          WHERE Customer_ID = 16

-----------------------------------------------
michael
```

LTRIM

Returns the string expression passed, after trimming all spaces on the left side of the string.

```
LTRIM(string_expression)
```

`string_expression` is a variable or string expression that contains the text.

The following example declares a variable and assigns a string that contains spaces to it. The `LTRIM` function is then called to remove all spaces on the left side of the variable. The results are listed below:

```
DECLARE @name varchar(15)
SELECT @name = '    Michael'
SELECT LTRIM(@name)

---------------------------------------
Michael
```

NCHAR

Returns a Unicode character for the integer value passed.

```
NCHAR(integer_expression)
```

`integer_expression` is a number ranging from 0 to 65535.

The following example displays the Unicode character for the value 77:

```
SELECT NCHAR(77)

----------------------------
M
```

PATNDEX

Returns the starting position of the first occurrence of a pattern in a string, or zero if the pattern is not found.

```
PATINDEX('%pattern_expression%', string_expression)
```

`pattern_expression` is a string expression of the pattern to search for.

`string_expression` is a variable or string expression that contains the text.

The example below searches the `First_Name_VC` column for the pattern of `ha`. The results are listed below with the first occurrence of the pattern found:

```
SELECT PATINDEX('%ha%', First_Name_VC)
        FROM Customer_T
        WHERE Customer_ID = 16

------------------------------------------------------------
4
```

REPLACE

This function searches for a specific string in a string expression and replaces that string with another.

```
REPLACE(string_expression1, string_expression2, string_expression3)
```

`string_expression1` is a variable or string expression that contains the text to be searched.

`string_expression2` is a variable or string expression that contains the search string to be replaced.

`string_expression3` is a variable or string expression that contains the text that will replace `string_expression2`.

The following example searches the `First_Name_VC` column for the characters hael and replaces them with aela which changes the name from Michael to Micaela:

```
SELECT REPLACE(First_Name_VC, 'hael','aela')
        FROM Customer_T
        WHERE Customer_ID = 16

-------------------------------------------------------------
Micaela
```

QUOTENAME

Returns a Unicode string with delimiters added to make the string expression a valid SQL Server delimited identifier.

```
QUOTENAME(string_expression,quote_character)
```

`string_expression` is a variable or string expression that contains text.

`quote_character` is a single character that is to be used as the delimiter. This character can be a single quote mark (`'`), a double quote mark (`"`) or a left or right bracket (`[]`).

The following example uses a single quote mark to enclose the selected text in single quote marks.

```
SELECT QUOTENAME(First_Name_VC,"'")
        FROM Customer_T
        WHERE Customer_ID = 16

-----------------------------------------------------
'Michael'
```

REPLICATE

Repeats a string expression a specified number of times.

```
REPLICATE(string_expression,intger_expression)
```

`string_expression` is a variable or string expression that contains the text to be repeated.

`integer_expression` is a integer number.

The following example repeats the `First_Name_VC` column twice and the results are displayed below:

```
SELECT REPLICATE(First_Name_VC,2)
        FROM Customer_T
        WHERE Customer_ID = 16

---------------------------------------------------
MichaelMichael
```

REVERSE

Reverses the order of characters in a string expression.

```
REVERSE(string_expression)
```

`string_expression` is a variable or string expression that contains text.

The following example uses the `First_Name_VC` column as the string expression and returns the name in reverse order:

```
SELECT REVERSE(First_Name_VC)
        FROM Customer_T
        WHERE Customer_ID = 16

--------------------------------------------------
leahciM
```

RIGHT

Returns the specified number of characters on the right side of a string expression.

```
RIGHT(string_expression, integer_expression)
```

`string_expression` is a variable or string expression that contains text.

`integer_expression` is an integer number.

The following example returns the right most three characters from the `First_Name_VC` column:

```
SELECT RIGHT(First_Name_VC,3)
        FROM Customer_T
        WHERE Customer_ID = 16

--------------------------------------------------
ael
```

RTRIM

Remove the trailing spaces from a string expression.

```
RTRIM(string_expression)
```

`string_expression` is a variable or string expression that contains text.

The following example declares a string variable, assigns a string with spaces to it and then uses the `RTRIM` function to remove the trailing spaces:

```
DECLARE @string VARCHAR(15)
SELECT @string = 'Michael   '
SELECT RTRIM(@string)

------------------------------------------
Michael
```

SOUNDEX

Returns a four-character (`SOUNDEX`) code to evaluate the similarity of two strings.

```
SOUNDEX(string_expression)
```

`string_expression` is a variable or string expression that contains text.

The following example converts the data in the `First_Name_VC` column to a `SOUNDEX` code.

```
SELECT SOUNDEX(First_Name_VC)
          FROM Customer_T
          WHERE Customer_ID = 16

------------------------------------------------
M240
```

SPACE

Returns a string of repeated spaces.

```
SPACE(integer_expression)
```

`integer_expression` is a integer number, indicating the length of the string.

The following example selects the `First_Name_VC` and `Last_Name_VC` columns and concatenates them together with two spaces between them:

```
SELECT First_Name_VC + SPACE(2) + Last_Name_VC
          FROM Customer_T
          WHERE Customer_ID = 16

----------------------------------------------------------------------
Michael  Dell
```

STR

Returns a string expression converted from a numeric expression.

```
STR(float_expression, length, decimal)
```

`float_expression` is a numeric variable or expression that evaluates to a `Float` data type.

`length` is the total length of the expression, including the decimal point and digits to the right of the decimal that should be returned.

`decimal` is the number of digits to the right of the decimal point that should be returned.

The following example declares a `Float` data type variable and a `VarChar` data type variable. Using the `FLOAT` function, the numeric variable is converted to a string variable:

```
DECLARE @numeric FLOAT,
        @string VARCHAR(15)
SELECT @numeric = 190.5
SELECT @string = STR(@numeric,6,2)
PRINT @string

---------------------------------
190.50
```

STUFF

Deletes a specified number of characters in a string expression and replaces them with another set of characters.

```
STUFF(string_expression, start, length, character_expression)
```

`string_expression` is a variable or string expression that contains text.

`start` is an integer value indicating the starting position in the string to start deleting characters.

`length` is an integer value indicating the number of characters to be deleted.

`character_expression` is a variable or string expression that contains the characters that are to replace the deleted characters.

The following example deletes four characters starting at position four in the `First_Name_VC` column. The character expression is inserted into the deleted characters position:

```
SELECT STUFF(First_Name_VC, 4, 4, 'aela')
        FROM Customer_T
        WHERE Customer_ID = 16

-----------------------------------------------------------
Micaela
```

SUBSTRING

Returns part of a string, text, binary or image expression.

```
SUBSTRING(expression, start, length)
```

`expression` is a string, text, binary or image variable or expression.

`start` is an integer value indicating the starting position in the string to start extracting data.

`length` is an integer value indicating the number of characters to be extracted.

The following example returns the first four characters from the `First_Name_VC` column:

```
SELECT SUBSTRING(First_Name_VC, 1, 4)
        FROM Customer_T
        WHERE Customer_ID = 16

----------------------------------------------------------
Mich
```

UNICODE

Returns an integer value representing the Unicode number for the first character in an expression.

```
Unicode('ncharacter_expression')
```

`ncharacter_expression` is a `NChar` or `NVarChar` expression.

The following example declares a `NVarChar` variable and assigns a Unicode character to it. Then we execute the `UNICODE` function to return the integer value representing that character:

```
DECLARE @nstring NVARCHAR(15)
SELECT @nstring = 'A'
SELECT UNICODE(@nstring)

-------------------------------------------------
197
```

UPPER

Converts a string to all upper case letters.

```
UPPER(string_expression)
```

`string_expression` is a variable or string expression that contains the text.

The following example converts the name Michael that is contained in the `First_Name_VC` column to all upper case letters. The results are displayed below:

```
SELECT UPPER(First_Name_VC)
        FROM Customer_T
        WHERE Customer_ID = 16

-------------------------------------------------
MICHAEL
```

System Functions

APP_NAME

Returns the application name for the current session, if one has been set by the application.

```
APP_NAME()
```

The `APP_NAME()` function returns a `NVarChar`(128) data type. The following example demonstrates that the application that initiated the session is a Query Analyzer session:

```
PRINT APP_NAME()

------------------------------------------------
MS SQL Query Analyzer
```

CASE

Evaluates a list of conditions and returns one result.

```
CASE input_expression
WHEN when_expression Then result_expression
Else else_result_expression
End
```

`input_expression` is the expression to be evaluated.

`when_expression` is an expression to which the `input_expression` is compared.

`result_expression` is the expression that is returned when the `input_expression` matches the `when_expression`.

`else_result_expression` is the expression returned when no match has been found.

The following example uses the `CASE` function to display the data from the `Spouse_First_Name_VC` column if data exists, or to display No Spouse when a spouse's name does not exist. The results are listed after the query.

```
SELECT First_Name_VC, 'Customer Spouse''s Name' =
        CASE
                WHEN Spouse_First_Name_VC IS NOT NULL Then Spouse_First_Name_VC
                Else 'No Spouse'
        End
        FROM Customer_T
```

```
--------------------------------------------------------------------------------
First_Name_VC          Customer Spouse's Name
-------------- -----------------------------------------------------------------
James                  Heather
Sam                    No Spouse
Jack                   Jill
Customer               No Spouse
Thearon                Margie
```

CAST

Explicitly converts one data type to another.

```
CAST(expression AS data_type)
```

`expression` is any single variable, constant, column or function.

`data_type` is any valid SQL Server data type.

The following example uses the `CAST` function to convert the `Phone_Number_ID` to a `Char` data type and the results are listed below.

```
SELECT CAST(Phone_Number_ID as CHAR(4))
        FROM Customer_T
        WHERE Customer_ID = 3

------------------------------------------------------------
7
```

CONVERT

Explicitly converts one data type to another.

```
CONVERT(data_type[(length)], expression, [style])
```

`data_type` is any valid SQL Server data type.

`length` is an optional parameter for the `NChar`, `NVarChar`, `Char`, `VarChar`, `Binary`, or `VarBinary` data types.

`expression` is any single variable, constant, column or function.

`style` is the style of date format you want when converting `DateTime` or `SmallDateTime` data to `Character` data.

A style of 0 or 100 returns the date and time in `mon dd yyyy hh:miAM` (or `PM`) format, while a style of 9 or 109 returns the date and time in `mon dd yyyy hh:mi:ss:mmmAM` (or `PM`) format. A style of 13 or 113 returns the date and time in a `dd mon yyyy hh:mm:ss:mmm(24h)` format, and a style of 20 or 120 returns a format of `yyyy-mm-dd hh:mi:ss(24h)`. Finally a style of 21 or 121 returns the date and time in a format of `yyyy-mm-dd hh:mi:ss.mmm(24h)`.

Other styles are available to return just the date or the time in various formats. See the SQL Server Books Online for more styles.

The following example uses the `CONVERT` function to convert the `Last_Update_DT` column to a `VarChar` data type using a style of 100, the default format:

```
SELECT CONVERT(VARCHAR(22),Last_Update_DT,100)
        FROM Customer_T
        WHERE Customer_ID = 3

----------------------------------------------------------------------------
Nov 21 1999 12:33PM
```

COALESCE

Returns the first non-null argument among its expressions. If all arguments are `NULL`, the `COALESCE` function returns `NULL`.

```
COALESCE(expression [,..n])
```

`expression` is any single variable, constant, column or function.

`n` is a placeholder indicating multiple expressions can be specified.

The following example uses the `COALESCE` function to display No Spouse when a `NULL` value is encountered in the `Spouse_First_Name_VC` column:

```
SELECT First_Name_VC, 'Customer Spouse''s Name' = COALESCE(Spouse_First_Name_VC, _
            'No Spouse')
        FROM Customer_T

------------------------------------------------------------------------------------------------------
First_Name_VC                Customer Spouse's Name
-------------- ---------------------------------------------------------------------------------------
James                        Heather
Sam                          No Spouse
Jack                         Jill
Customer                     No Spouse
Thearon                      Margie
```

CURRENT_TIMESTAMP

Returns the current date and time in a `DateTime` data type, and is the equivalent to the `GetDate()` function

```
CURRENT_TIMESTAMP
```

The following example demonstrates the results returned from the CURRENT_TIMESTAMP function:

```
SELECT CURRENT_TIMESTAMP

-----------------------------------------------
1999-12-02 05:44:11.787
```

CURRENT_USER

Returns the current user who is logged on.

```
CURRENT_USER
```

The following example shows the results of the CURRENT_USER function.

```
SELECT CURRENT_USER

---------------------
willist
```

DATALENGTH

Returns the number of bytes in an expression.

```
DATALENGTH(expression)
```

`expression` is any single variable, constant, column or function.

This example shows how you can use the DATALENGTH function to determine how many bytes are in a column:

```
SELECT First_Name_VC, DATALENGTH(First_Name_VC) AS Length_Of_First_Name
        FROM Customer_T
        WHERE Customer_ID = 3

First_Name_VC                Length_Of_First_Name
-------------- ------------------------------------------------------
James                        5
```

@@ERROR

Returns the error number of the last SQL statement executed.

```
@@ERROR
```

This example shows the error number returned after a SELECT statement has been executed:

```
SELECT First_Name_VC, Last_Name_VC
          FROM Customer_T
          WHERE Customer_ID = 3
SELECT @@ERROR AS Last_Error

First_Name_VC                    Last_Name_VC
-------------- -----------------------------------------------
James                            Maxwell

(1 row(s) affected)

Last_Error
-----------------------------------------------------------------
0
```

FORMATMESSAGE

Allows you to construct a pre-defined message from the sysmessages table.

```
FORMATMESSAGE(msg_number, parameter_value[,..n])
```

msg_number is the ID of the message from the sysmessages table.

parameter_value is the value to be substituted in the parameter of the message.

n is a placeholder indicating multiple parameter values can be specified if available in the message.

The example demonstrated here uses the following message from the sysmessage table. Notice the parameter value placeholder in the message:

```
Error   Description
-----   ----------------------------------------------
14043   The parameter %s cannot be NULL.
```

This example uses the above message and substitutes a column name for the parameter value placeholder in the message:

```
DECLARE @my_message VARCHAR(100)
SELECT @my_message = formatmessage(14043,"'First_Name_VC'")
PRINT @my_message

------------------------------------------------------------------------------------------
The parameter 'First_Name_VC' cannot be NULL.
```

GETANSINULL

Returns the default nullability for the database specified.

```
GETANSINULL('database_name')
```

`database_name` is the name of the database to be queried.

The following example returns the nullability for the `Wrox_Auto_Works` database. `GETANSINULL` returns 1 if the database allows `NULL`s.

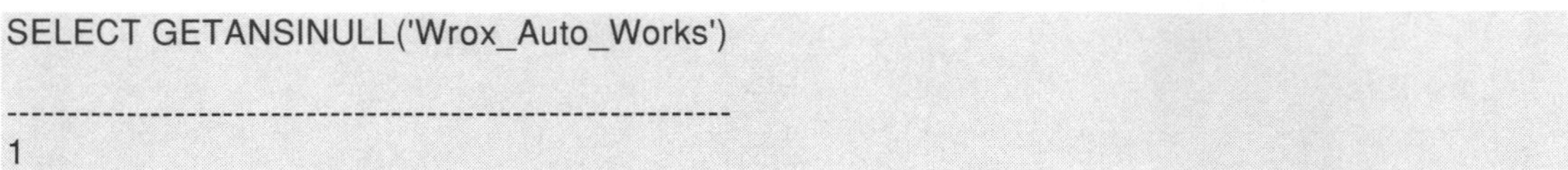

```
SELECT GETANSINULL('Wrox_Auto_Works')

-----------------------------------------------------------
1
```

HOST_ID

Returns the workstation identification number (ID).

```
HOST_ID()
```

The following example returns the workstation identification number for the workstation running the query:

```
SELECT HOST_ID()

------------------------------
345
```

HOST_NAME

Returns the workstation name.

```
HOST_NAME()
```

The following example returns the name of the workstation running the query:

```
SELECT HOST_NAME()

------------------------------------
WSDEVELOPMENT
```

IDENT_INCR

Returns the increment value for the Identity column of a table that was specified when the table was created.

```
IDENT_INCR('table_name')
```

`table_name` is the name of the table whose increment value for the Identity column should be returned.

The following example returns the identity increment value for the Identity column in the `Customer_T` table:

```
SELECT IDENT_INCR('Customer_T')

--------------------------------------------------
1
```

IDENT_SEED

Returns the seed value for the Identity column of a table that was specified when the table was created.

```
IDENT_SEED('table_name')
```

`table_name` is the name of the table whose increment value for the Identity column should be returned.

The following example returns the identity seed value for the Identity column in the `Customer_T` table:

```
SELECT IDENT_SEED('Customer_T')

--------------------------------------------------
1
```

@@IDENTITY

Returns the last inserted Identity value.

```
@@IDENTITY
```

This example inserts a new state into the `State_T` table and returns the Identity value that was inserted:

```
INSERT INTO State_T
          (State_Name_VC, State_Abbreviation_CH, Last_Update_DT)
          VALUES('Virgin Islands','VI',GetDate())
SELECT @@IDENTITY

--------------------------------------------------------------------------------------------
61
```

IDENTITY

This function is used only in a SELECT statement with an INTO table clause to insert an Identity column into a new table.

```
IDENTITY(data_type[, seed, increment]) AS column_name
```

data_type is the data type for the Identity column, and must be a numeric data type, such as Integer.

seed is the seed value for the Identity column.

increment is the increment value for the Identity column.

column_name is the name of the column that is being inserted into the new table.

The following example selects the first and last names from the Customer_T table and inserts them into a temporary table created as a result of the INTO keyword. The IDENTITY function is used to insert an Identity column into the temporary table. After the temporary table has been populated, all the rows in the temporary table are selected:

```
SELECT IDENTITY(INT,1,1) AS Customer_ID, First_Name_VC, Last_Name_VC
          INTO #Tmp_Customer
          FROM Customer_T
SELECT * FROM #Tmp_Customer

(4 row(s) affected)

Customer_ID   First_Name_VC      Last_Name_VC
----------- --------------- ------------------------------------------
1             James              Maxwell
2             Sam                Sony
3             Jack               Teac
4             Thearon            Willis
```

ISDATE

Determines if an expression is a valid date and returns 1 if it is.

```
ISDATE(expression)
```

expression is an expression to be validated as a date.

This example declares a variable and then selects a value into that variable. The ISDATE function is used to determine if the date we selected into the variable is valid:

```
DECLARE @date VARCHAR(22)
SELECT @date = '1/1/2000'
SELECT ISDATE(@date)

-------------------------------------------
1
```

ISNULL

This function replaces a NULL value with the value specified.

```
ISNULL(expression, replacement_value)
```

expression is any single variable, constant, column or function.

replacement_value is the value that should replace a null value.

This example tests whether or not the Spouse_First_Name_VC column in the Customer_T table is NULL and replaces the NULL value with No Spouse:

```
SELECT First_Name_VC, Last_Name_VC,
        ISNULL(Spouse_First_Name_vc,'No Spouse') as 'Spouse_Name'
        FROM Customer_T
        WHERE Customer_ID = 4

First_Name_VC          Last_Name_VC          Spouse_Name
--------------- --------------- ---------------------------------------------------------------------
Sam                    Sony                  No Spouse
```

ISNUMERIC

Tests whether an expression is a valid numeric data type and returns 1 if it is.

```
ISNUMERIC(expression)
```

expression is any single variable, constant, column or function.

The following example tests the Address_ID column in the Customer_T table to see if it contains a valid numeric value:

```
SELECT ISNUMERIC(Address_ID)
        FROM Customer_T
        WHERE Customer_ID = 4

-----------------------------------------------
1
```

NEWID

Creates a unique value of type uniqueidentifier.

```
NEWID()
```

This example creates a unique identifier that can be used wherever a unique identifier number is needed:

```
DECLARE @unique_ID uniqueidentifier
SET @unique_ID = NEWID()
PRINT @unique_ID

------------------------------------------------------------
2E3D1DC4-AB77-11D3-8115-00500463356C
```

NULLIF

Returns a NULL value if two expressions are equal, otherwise the first expression is returned.

```
NULLIF(expression, expression)
```

expression is any single variable, constant, column or function.

This example demonstrates both scenarios for the NULLIF function using the First_Name_VC and Last_Name_VC columns from the Customer_T table:

```
SELECT NULLIF(First_Name_VC,Last_Name_VC)
        FROM Customer_T
        WHERE Customer_ID = 4

------------------------------------------------------------------
Sam

SELECT NULLIF(First_Name_VC,First_Name_VC)
        FROM Customer_T
        WHERE Customer_ID = 4

------------------------------------------------------------------
NULL
```

PARSENAME

Returns the specified part of an object name.

```
PARSENAME('object_name',object_part)
```

object_name is a partially or fully qualified object name. If a fully qualified object name is used, this object name consists of four parts: the server name, the database name, the owner name, and the object name.

object_part is an Integer value, indicating the part of the object name to return. A value of 1 specifies that the object name is returned, and a value of 2 specifies that the owner name is returned. Values of 3 and 4 specify that the database name and server names are to be returned.

If the object name is not fully qualified and an object part is requested for a part that does not exist in the object_name, then a NULL value is returned.

The following example shows the various object parts that can be extracted from a fully qualified object name:

```
SELECT PARSENAME('WSDEVELOPMENT.Wrox_Auto_Works.dbo.Customer_T',1)

------------------------------------------------------------------------------------------------------------
Customer_T

SELECT PARSENAME('WSDEVELOPMENT.Wrox_Auto_Works.dbo.Customer_T',2)

------------------------------------------------------------------------------------------------------------
dbo

SELECT PARSENAME('WSDEVELOPMENT.Wrox_Auto_Works.dbo.Customer_T',3)

------------------------------------------------------------------------------------------------------------
Wrox_Auto_Works

SELECT PARSENAME('WSDEVELOPMENT.Wrox_Auto_Works.dbo.Customer_T',4)

------------------------------------------------------------------------------------------------------------
WSDEVELOPMENT
```

PERMISSIONS

Returns an integer value containing a bitmap that indicates the statement, object, or column permissions for the current user.

```
PERMISSIONS ([objectID [, 'column']])
```

objectID is the ID of an object. If objectID is not specified, the bitmap value contains statement permissions for the current user; otherwise, the bitmap contains object permissions on the object ID for the current user. The object specified must be in the current database. Use the OBJECT_ID function with an object name to determine the objectID value.

column is the optional name of a column for which permission information is being returned. The column must be a valid column name in the table specified by objectID.

The permissions information returned is a 32-bit bitmap.

The lower 16 bits reflect permissions granted to the security account for the current user, as well as permissions applied to Microsoft Windows NT groups or Microsoft SQL Server roles of which the current user is a member. For example, a returned value of 66 (hex value 0x42), when no objectID is specified, indicates the current user has permissions to execute the CREATE TABLE (decimal value 2) and BACKUP DATABASE (decimal value 64) statement permissions.

The upper 16 bits reflect the permissions that the current user can `GRANT` to other users. The upper 16 bits are interpreted exactly as those for the lower 16 bits described in the following tables, except they are shifted to the left by 16 bits (multiplied by 65536). For example, 0x8 (decimal value 8) is the bit indicating `INSERT` permissions when an `objectID` is specified. Whereas 0x80000 (decimal value 524288) indicates the ability to `GRANT INSERT` permissions, because 524288 = 8 x 65536. Due to membership in roles, it is possible to not have a permission to execute a statement, but still be able to grant that permission to someone else.

The table shows the bits used for statement permissions (`objectID` is not specified):

Bit (dec)	Bit (hex)	Statement permission
1	0x1	`CREATE DATABASE (master database only)`
2	0x2	`CREATE TABLE`
4	0x4	`CREATE PROCEDURE`
8	0x8	`CREATE VIEW`
16	0x10	`CREATE RULE`
32	0x20	`CREATE DEFAULT`
64	0x40	`BACKUP DATABASE`
128	0x80	`BACKUP LOG`
256	0x100	`Reserved`

The table shows the bits used for object permissions that are returned when only `objectID` is specified:

Bit (dec)	Bit (hex)	Statement permission
1	0x1	`SELECT ALL`
2	0x2	`UPDATE ALL`
4	0x4	`REFERENCES ALL`
8	0x8	`INSERT`
16	0x10	`DELETE`
32	0x20	`EXECUTE (procedures only)`
4096	0x1000	`SELECT ANY (at least one column)`
8192	0x2000	`UPDATE ANY`
16384	0x4000	`REFERENCES ANY`

The table shows the bits used for column-level object permissions that are returned when both `objectID` and `column` are specified:

Bit (dec)	Bit (hex)	Statement permission
1	0x1	SELECT
2	0x2	UPDATE
4	0x4	REFERENCES

The following example shows the permissions set on the `Customer_T` table:

```
SELECT PERMISSIONS(Object_ID('Customer_T'))

----------------------------------------------------------------
28703
```

@@ROWCOUNT

Returns the number of rows affected by the last statement.

```
@@ROWCOUNT
```

This example selects all first names from the `Customer_T` table that begin with the letter J. The `@@ROWCOUNT` function returns the number of rows affected by this `SELECT` statement.

```
SELECT First_Name_VC
        FROM Customer_T
        WHERE First_Name_VC LIKE 'j%'
SELECT @@rROWCOUNT

First_Name_VC
----------------------------------------------------------------
James
Jack

----------------------------------------------------------------
2
```

SESSION_USER

Returns the current session's username.

```
SESSION_USER
```

This example displays the current session's username:

```
PRINT 'The current user for this session is ' + session_user

-------------------------------------------------------------------------------
The current user for this session is willist
```

STATS_DATE

Returns the date that the statistics for the specified index were last updated.

```
STATS_DATE(table_id, index_id)
```

`table_id` is the ID of the table.

`index_id` is the ID of the index.

The example uses `sysobjects` and `sysindexes` to retrieve the ID of the `Customer_T` table and indexes and then uses the `STATS_DATE` function to display the indexes and the last date and time the indexes were updated:

```
SELECT ObjIndex.Name AS 'Index Name',
          STATS_DATE(ObjIndex.ID, ObjIndex.indID) as 'Statistics Date'
          FROM sysobjects ObjTable, sysindexes ObjIndex
          WHERE ObjTable.Name = 'Customer_T' and ObjTable.ID = ObjIndex.ID

Index Name                                      Statistics Date
----------------------------------------------- ---------------------------------------------------------------
IX_Customer_T                                   NULL
PK_Customer_T                                   NULL
_WA_Sys_Address_ID_1B0907CE                     1999-10-03 15:44:26.193
_WA_Sys_Phone_Number_ID_1B0907CE                1999-10-03 15:44:26.203
_WA_Sys_Customer_Information_ID_1B0907CE        1999-10-03 18:36:25.733
```

SYSTEM_USER

Returns the current system username.

```
SYSTEM_USER
```

This example displays the current system user:

```
PRINT 'The current system user is ' + system_user

---------------------------------------------------------------------
The current system user is willist
```

@@TRANCOUNT

Returns the number of active transactions for the current connection.

```
@@TRANCOUNT
```

The `BEGIN TRANSACTION` statement increments `@@TRANCOUNT` by 1. `ROLLBACK TRANSACTION` decrements `@@TRANCOUNT` to 0, except for `ROLLBACK TRANSACTION savepoint_name`, which does not affect `@@TRANCOUNT`. `COMMIT TRANSACTION` or `COMMIT WORK` decrement `@@TRANCOUNT` by 1.

This example begins a transaction, selects some data and displays the transaction count using the `@@TRANCOUNT` function before committing the transaction:

```
BEGIN TRANSACTION Demo_Tran
SELECT First_Name_VC
        FROM Customer_T
        WHERE Customer_ID = 4
SELECT @@TRANCOUNT
COMMIT TRANSACTION Demo_Tran

First_Name_VC
-----------------------------------------------------
Sam

------------------------------------------------------
1
```

USER_NAME

Returns a user database username from a given identification number.

```
USER_NAME([user_ID])
```

`user_ID` is the optional identification number of the user name to return.

The following example demonstrates two methods to return the user name. The first method specifies the ID of the user and the second method returns the name of the user who is currently logged on:

```
SELECT USER_NAME(5)

-----------------------------------
willist

SELECT USER_NAME()

------------------------------------
willist
```

Date and Time Functions

DATEADD

Returns a new DateTime value based on adding an interval to the specified date.

```
DATEADD(datepart, number, date)
```

datepart is the parameter that specifies on which part of the date to return a new value. Available date parts are Year, Quarter, Month, DayOfYear, Week, Day, Hour, Minute, Second and Millisecond.

number is the number used to increment the DatePart.

date is an expression that evaluates to a valid date.

The following example selects the date from the Last_Update_DT column in the Customer_T table and adds one year to it:

```
SELECT Last_Update_DT, DATEADD(Year,1,Last_Update_DT) as 'New_Date'
         FROM Customer_T
         WHERE Customer_ID = 4

Last_Update_DT              New_Date
--------------------------- ---------------------------------------------
1999-11-30 18:48:38.440     2000-11-30 18:48:38.440
```

DATEDIFF

Returns the difference between two dates in a specified unit of time.

```
DATEDIFF(datepart, startdate, enddate)
```

datepart is the parameter that specifies on which part of the date to return a new value. Available date parts are Year, Quarter, Month, DayOfYear, Week, Day, Hour, Minute, Second and Millisecond.

startdate is an expression that evaluates to a valid date.

enddate is an expression that evaluates to a valid date.

The example returns the number of days between the date in the Last_Update_DT column in the Customer_T table and the current date:

```
SELECT Last_Update_DT, DATEDIFF(Day,Last_Update_DT, GetDate()) AS 'Date Difference'
        FROM Customer_T
        WHERE Customer_ID = 4

Last_Update_DT                    Date Difference
-------------------------- ------------------------------------------
1999-11-30 18:48:38.440           6
```

DATENAME

Returns a character string representing the specified datepart of the specified date.

```
DATENAME(datepart, date)
```

datepart is the parameter that specifies on which part of the date to return a new value. Available date parts are Year, Quarter, Month, DayOfYear, Week, Day, Hour, Minute, Second and Millisecond.

date is an expression that evaluates to a valid date.

The following example returns the month name of the date contained in the Last_Update_DT column of the Customer_T table:

```
SELECT Last_Update_DT, DATENAME(Month,Last_Update_DT) AS 'Date Name'
        FROM Customer_T
        WHERE Customer_ID = 4

Last_Update_DT                    Date Name
-------------------------- ---------------------------------------------
1999-11-30 18:48:38.440           November
```

DATEPART

Returns an integer representing the specified datepart of the specified date.

```
DATEPART(datepart, date)
```

datepart is the parameter that specifies on which part of the date to return a new value. Available date parts are Year, Quarter, Month, DayOfYear, Week, Day, Hour, Minute, Second and Millisecond.

date is an expression that evaluates to a valid date.

This example returns the month number of the date contained in the `Last_Update_DT` column of the `Customer_T` table:

```
SELECT Last_Update_DT, DATEPART(Month,Last_Update_DT) AS 'Date Part'
          FROM Customer_T
          WHERE Customer_ID = 4

Last_Update_DT                Date Part
------------------------ ----------------------------
1999-11-30 18:48:38.440       11
```

DAY

Returns an integer representing the day `datepart` of the specified date.

```
DAY(date)
```

`date` is an expression that evaluates to a valid date.

This example returns the day of the date contained in the `Last_Update_DT` column of the `Customer_T` table:

```
SELECT Last_Update_DT, DAY(Last_Update_DT) AS 'Day'
          FROM Customer_T
          WHERE Customer_ID = 4

Last_Update_DT                Day
------------------------ ----------------------------
1999-11-30 18:48:38.440       30
```

GETDATE

Returns the current system date and time.

```
GETDATE()
```

This example returns the current date and time:

```
SELECT GETDATE() AS 'Current Date and Time'

Current Date and Time
------------------------------------
1999-12-06 10:21:54.510
```

MONTH

Returns an integer that represents the month part of a specified date.

```
MONTH(date)
```

`date` is an expression that evaluates to a valid date.

This example returns the month of the date contained in the `Last_Update_DT` column of the `Customer_T` table:

```
SELECT Last_Update_DT, MONTH(Last_Update_DT) AS 'Month'
         FROM Customer_T
         WHERE Customer_ID = 4

Last_Update_DT                Month
--------------------------- ---------------------------
1999-11-30 18:48:38.440      11
```

YEAR

Returns an integer that represents the year part of a specified date.

```
YEAR(date)
```

`date` is an expression that evaluates to a valid date.

This example returns the year of the date contained in the `Last_Update_DT` column of the `Customer_T` table:

```
SELECT Last_Update_DT, YEAR(Last_Update_DT) AS 'Year'
         FROM Customer_T
         WHERE Customer_ID = 4

Last_Update_DT                Year
--------------------------- -------------------------
1999-11-30 18:48:38.440      1999
```

Aggregate Functions

AVG

Returns the average of the values in a group.

```
AVG([ALL | DISTINCT] expression)
```

`ALL` applies the aggregate function to all values and is the default.

`DISTINCT` specifies that `AVG` be performed only on each unique instance of a value, regardless of how many times the value occurs.

`expression` is an expression of the exact numeric or approximate numeric data type category, except for the `Bit` data type.

This example selects the average purchase of a vehicle in the `Customer_Purchase_History_T` table:

```
SELECT AVG(Purchase_Price_SM) AS 'Average Purchase Price'
        FROM Customer_Purchase_History_T

Average Purchase Price
----------------------------------
28840.0200
```

COUNT

Returns the number of items in a group.

```
COUNT({[ALL | DISTINCT] expression] | *})
```

`ALL` applies the aggregate function to all values and is the default.

`DISTINCT` specifies that `COUNT` be performed only on each unique instance of a value, regardless of how many times the value occurs.

`expression` is an expression of any type except `uniqueidentifier`, `Text`, `Image`, or `NText`.

`*` specifies that all rows should be counted to return the total number of rows in a table. `COUNT(*)` takes no parameters and cannot be used with `DISTINCT`. `COUNT(*)` and does not require an `expression` parameter because, by definition, it does not use information about any particular column. `COUNT(*)` returns the number of rows in a specified table without eliminating duplicates. It counts each row separately, including rows that contain `NULL` values.

The following example selects a count of vehicles sold in the `Customer_Purchase_History_T` table:

```
SELECT COUNT(Purchase_Price_SM) AS 'Vehicles Sold'
        FROM Customer_Purchase_History_T

Vehicles Sold
---------------------
9
```

GROUPING

Is an aggregate function that causes an additional column to be output from a `SELECT` statement, with a value of 1 when the row is added by either the `CUBE` or `ROLLUP` operator, or 0 when the row is not the result of `CUBE` or `ROLLUP`.

```
GROUPING(column_name)
```

`column_name` is a column in a `GROUP BY` clause to check for `CUBE` or `ROLLUP` null values.

Grouping is allowed only in the SELECT list associated with a GROUP BY clause that contains either the CUBE or ROLLUP operator. GROUPING is used to distinguish the NULL values returned by CUBE and ROLLUP from standard NULL values. The NULL returned as the result of a CUBE or ROLLUP operation is a special use of NULL. It acts as a column placeholder in the result set and means "all."

The following example demonstrates the GROUPING function to rollup the NULL values in the Purchase_Price_SM column in the Customer_Purchase_History_T table:

```
SELECT Purchase_Price_SM, GROUPING(Purchase_Price_SM) AS 'Group'
       FROM Customer_Purchase_History_T
       GROUP BY Purchase_Price_SM WITH ROLLUP

Purchase_Price_SM          Group
---------------- ----------------------------------
17124.0000                 0
19123.9800                 0
25679.1900                 0
25881.3900                 0
25987.2700                 0
29021.8000                 0
29172.2900                 0
32588.1700                 0
54982.0900                 0
NULL                       1
```

MAX

Returns the maximum value in the expression ignoring NULL values.

```
MAX([ALL | DISTINCT] expression)
```

ALL applies the aggregate function to all values and is the default.

DISTINCT specifies that MAX should be performed only on each unique instance of a value, regardless of how many times the value occurs.

expression is a constant, column name, or function, and any combination of arithmetic, bitwise, and string operators. MAX can be used with numeric, character, and DateTime columns, but not with bit columns.

The following example uses the MAX function to return the maximum sales price listed in the Purchase_Price_SM column in the Customer_Purchase_History_T table:

```
SELECT MAX(Purchase_Price_SM) AS 'Maximum Sales Price'
       FROM Customer_Purchase_History_T

Maximum Sales Price
----------------------------------
54982.0900
```

MIN

Returns the minimum value in the expression ignoring NULL values.

```
MIN([ALL | DISTINCT] expression)
```

ALL applies the aggregate function to all values and is the default.

DISTINCT specifies that MIN be performed only on each unique instance of a value, regardless of how many times the value occurs.

expression is a constant, column name, or function, and any combination of arithmetic, bitwise, and string operators. MIN can be used with numeric, character, and datetime columns, but not with bit columns.

The following example uses the MIN function to return the minimum sales price listed in the Purchase_Price_SM column in the Customer_Purchase_History_T table:

```
SELECT MIN(Purchase_Price_SM) AS 'Minimum Sales Price'
        FROM Customer_Purchase_History_T

Minimum Sales Price
-------------------------------
17124.0000
```

SUM

Returns the sum of all the values in a numeric column ignoring NULL values.

```
SUM([ALL | DISTINCT] expression)
```

ALL applies the aggregate function to all values and is the default.

DISTINCT specifies that SUM be performed only on each unique instance of a value, regardless of how many times the value occurs.

expression is a constant, column, or function, and any combination of arithmetic, bitwise, and string operators. expression is an expression of the exact numeric or approximate numeric data type category, except for the bit data type.

The following example uses the SUM function to return the total sales listed in the Purchase_Price_SM column in the Customer_Purchase_History_T table:

```
SELECT SUM(Purchase_Price_SM) AS 'Total Sales Amount'
        FROM Customer_Purchase_History_T

Total Sales Amount
-----------------------------
259560.1800
```

STDEV

Returns the statistical standard deviation of all values in the given expression ignoring NULL values.

```
STDEV(expression)
```

expression is a numeric expression.

This example returns the standard deviation for the purchase price in the Purchase_Price_SM column in the Customer_Purchase_History_T table:

```
SELECT STDEV(Purchase_Price_SM) AS 'Standard Deviation'
        FROM Customer_Purchase_History_T

Standard Deviation
----------------------------------------------------
10932.457282554324
```

STDEVP

Returns the statistical standard deviation for the population for all values in the given expression ignoring NULL values.

```
STDEVP(expression)
```

expression is a numeric expression.

This example returns the standard deviation for the population for the purchase price in the Purchase_Price_SM column in the Customer_Purchase_History_T table:

```
SELECT STDEVP(Purchase_Price_SM) AS 'Standard Deviation for the Population'
        FROM Customer_Purchase_History_T

Standard Deviation for the Population
------------------------------------------------------------
10307.219572701892
```

VAR

Returns the statistical variance of all values in the given expression ignoring NULL values.

```
VAR(expression)
```

expression is an expression of the exact numeric or approximate numeric data type category, except for the bit data type.

This example returns the variance for the purchase price in the Purchase_Price_SM column in the Customer_Purchase_History_T table:

```
SELECT VAR(Purchase_Price_SM) AS 'Variance'
        FROM Customer_Purchase_History_T

Variance
-----------------------------------------------------
119518622.23487508
```

VARP

Returns the statistical variance for the population for all values in the given expression ignoring NULL values.

```
VARP(expression)
```

expression is an expression of the exact numeric or approximate numeric data type category, except for the bit data type.

This example returns the variance for the population for the purchase price in the Purchase_Price_SM column in the Customer_Purchase_History_T table:

```
SELECT VARP(Purchase_Price_SM) AS 'Variance for the Population'
        FROM Customer_Purchase_History_T

Variance for the Population
----------------------------------------------------------
119518622.23487508
```

WROX AUTO WORKS RACING

Support and Errata

One of the most irritating things about any programming book is when you find that bit of code you've just spent an hour typing simply doesn't work. You check it a hundred times to see if you've set it up correctly and then you notice the spelling mistake in the variable name on the book page. Of course, you can blame the authors for not taking enough care and testing the code, the editors for not doing their job properly, or the proofreaders for not being eagle-eyed enough, but this doesn't get around the fact that mistakes do happen.

We try hard to ensure no mistakes sneak out into the real world, but we can't promise that this book is 100% error free. What we can do is offer the next best thing by providing you with immediate support and feedback from experts who have worked on the book and try to ensure that future editions eliminate these gremlins. The following section will take you step by step through the process of posting errata to our web site to get that help. The sections that follow, therefore, are:

- Wrox Developers Membership
- Finding a list of existing errata on the web site
- Adding your own errata to the existing list
- What happens to your errata once you've posted it (why doesn't it appear immediately)?

There is also a section covering how to e-mail a question for technical support. This comprises:

- What your e-mail should include
- What happens to your e-mail once it has been received by us

So that you only need view information relevant to yourself, we ask that you register as a Wrox Developer Member. This is a quick and easy process, that will save you time in the long-run. If you are already a member, just update membership to include this book.

Wrox Developer's Membership

To get your FREE Wrox Developer's Membership click on Membership in the top navigation bar of our home site – `http://www.wrox.com`. This is shown in the following screenshot:

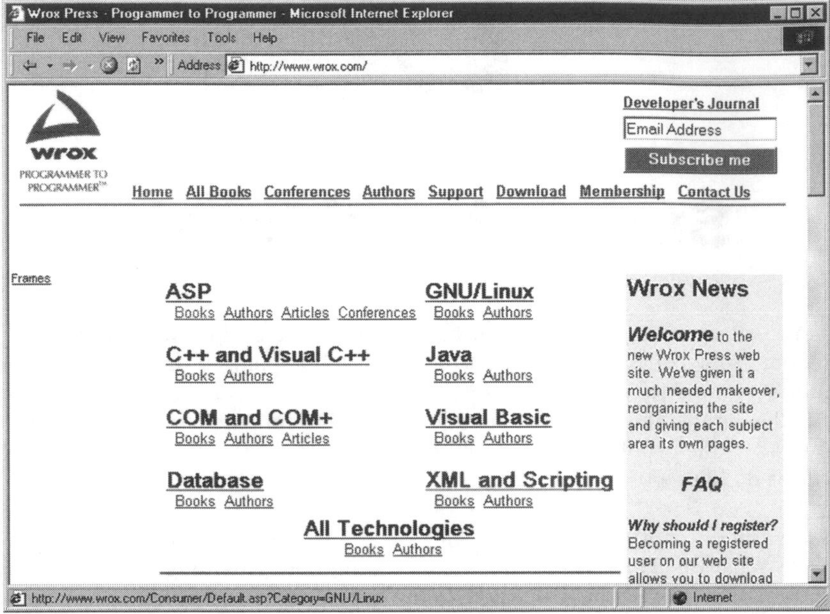

Then, on the next screen (not shown), click on New User. This will display a form. Fill in the details on the form and submit the details using the Register button at the bottom. Before you can say 'The best read books come in Wrox Red' you will get the following screen:

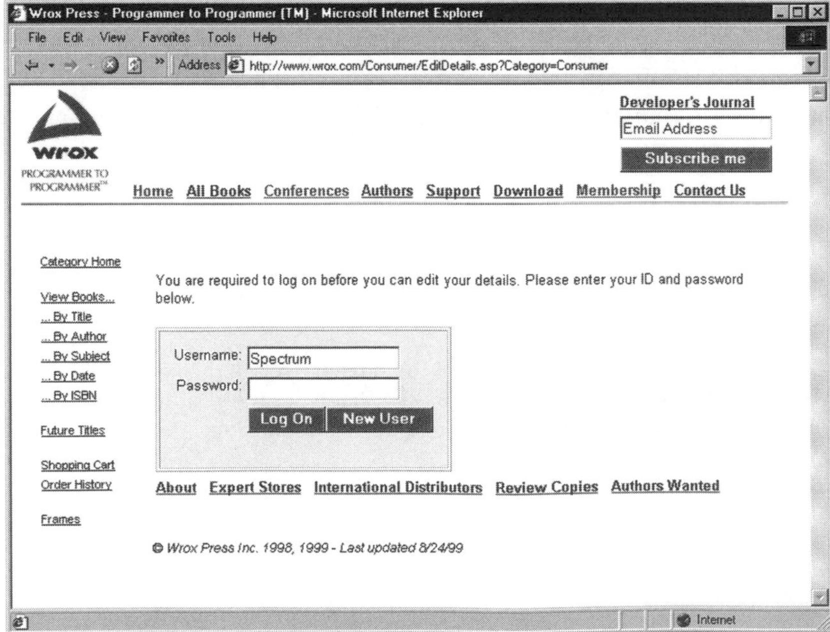

Type in your password once again and click Log On. The following page allows you to change your details if you need to, but now you're logged on, you have access to all the source code downloads and errata for the entire Wrox range of books.

Finding an Errata on the Web Site

Before you send in a query, you might be able to save time by finding the answer to your problem on our web site – `http:\\www.wrox.com`.

Each book we publish has its own page and its own errata sheet. You can get to any book's page by clicking on Support from the top navigation bar.

Halfway down the main support page is a drop down box called Title Support. Simply scroll down the list until you see Beginning Visual Basic SQL Server 7.0. Select it and then hit Errata.

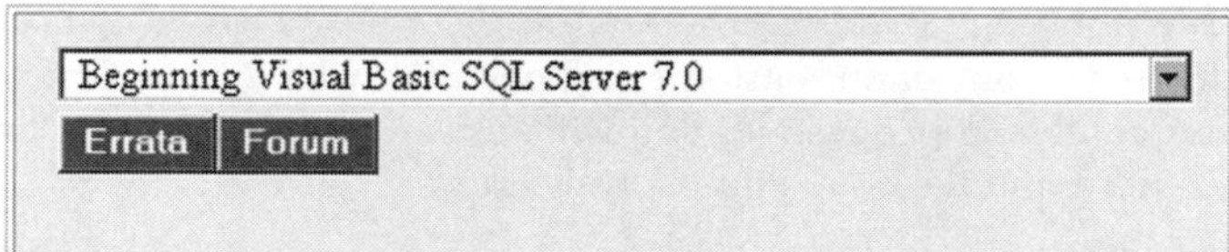

This will take you to the errata page for the book. Select the criteria by which you want to view the errata, and click the Apply criteria button. This will provide you with links to specific errata. For an initial search, you are advised to view the errata by page numbers. If you have looked for an error previously, then you may wish to limit your search using dates. We update these pages daily to ensure that you have the latest information on bugs and errors.

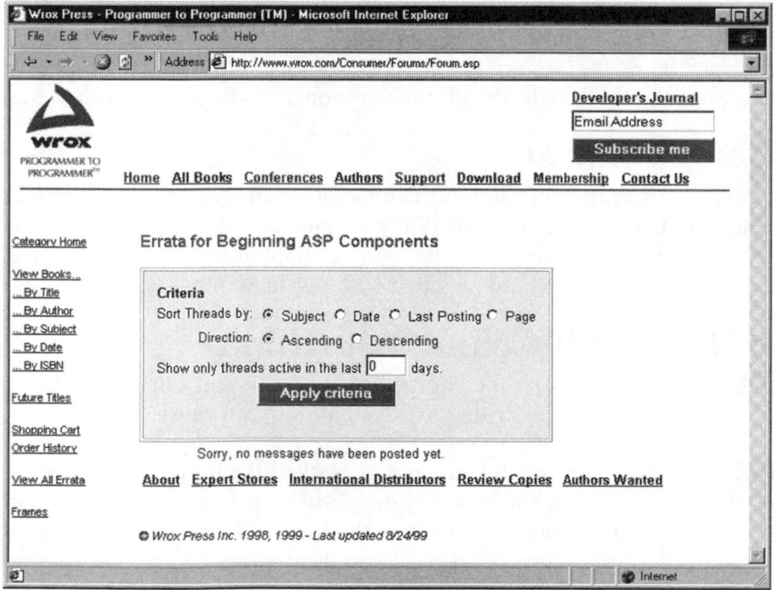

Add an Errata : E-mail Support

If you wish to point out an errata to put up on the website or directly query a problem in the book page with an expert who knows the book in detail then e-mail `support@wrox.com`, with the title of the book and the last four numbers of the ISBN in the subject field of the e-mail. A typical email should include the following things:

- The **name**, **last four digits of the ISBN** and **page number** of the problem in the Subject field.
- Your **name**, **contact info** and the **problem** in the body of the message.

We won't send you junk mail. We need the details to save your time and ours. If we need to replace a disk or CD we'll be able to get it to you straight away. When you send an e-mail it will go through the following chain of support:

Customer Support

Your message is delivered to one of our customer support staff who are the first people to read it. They have files on most frequently asked questions and will answer anything general immediately. They answer general questions about the book and the web site.

Editorial

Deeper queries are forwarded to the technical editor responsible for that book. They have experience with the programming language or particular product and are able to answer detailed technical questions on the subject. Once an issue has been resolved, the editor can post the errata to the web site.

The Authors

Finally, in the unlikely event that the editor can't answer your problem, s/he will forward the request to the author. We try to protect the author from any distractions from writing. However, we are quite happy to forward specific requests to them. All Wrox authors help with the support on their books. They'll mail the customer and the editor with their response, and again all readers should benefit.

What We Can't Answer

Obviously with an ever growing range of books and an ever-changing technology base, there is an increasing volume of data requiring support. While we endeavor to answer all questions about the book, we can't answer bugs in your own programs that you've adapted from our code. But do tell us if you're especially pleased with the routine you developed with our help.

How to Tell Us Exactly What You Think

We understand that errors can destroy the enjoyment of a book and can cause many wasted and frustrated hours, so we seek to minimize the distress that they can cause.

You might just wish to tell us how much you liked or loathed the book in question. Or you might have ideas about how this whole process could be improved. In which case you should e-mail `feedback@wrox.com`. You'll always find a sympathetic ear, no matter what the problem is. Above all you should remember that we do care about what you have to say and we will do our utmost to act upon it.

WROX AUTO WORKS RACING

Index

Symbols

A

B

C

D

E

F

G

H

J

K

L

M

N

O

P

Q

S

T

U

V

W

Y

WROX AUTO WORKS RACING